Understanding Art

Understanding Art

Eleventh Edition

Lois Fichner-Rathus

THE COLLEGE OF NEW JERSEY

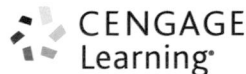

CENGAGE
Learning

Australia · Brazil · Mexico · Singapore · United Kingdom · United States

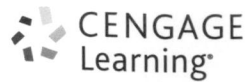

Understanding Art, Eleventh Edition
Lois Fichner-Rathus

Product Director: Monica Eckman

Product Manager: Sharon Adams Poore

Associate Content Developer: Erika Hayden

Product Assistant: Rachael Bailey

Media Developer: Chad Kirchner

Marketing Manager: Jillian Borden

Senior Content Project Manager: Lianne Ames

Senior Art Director: Cate Rickard Barr

Manufacturing Planner: Julio Esperas

IP Analyst: Christina Ciaramella

IP Project Manager: Farah Fard

Production Service: Thistle Hill Publishing Services

Compositor: Cenveo® Publisher Services

Text Designer: Cenveo® Publisher Services

Cover Designer: Wing Ngan, Ink Design, inc.

Cover Image: Sarah Sze, *Second Means of Egress*, 1998, mixed media installation view. Berlin Biennial, Akademie der Kunste, Germany, 1998–99. Collection of MORA Art Foundation, Vienna. Credit, Sze Studio.

For product information and technology assistance, contact us at
Cengage Learning Customer & Sales Support, 1-800-354-9706

For permission to use material from this text or product,
submit all requests online at **www.cengage.com/permissions**.
Further permissions questions can be emailed to
permissionrequest@cengage.com.

Library of Congress Control Number: 2015948923

Student Edition:
ISBN: 978-1-285-85929-3

Loose-leaf Edition:
ISBN: 978-1-305-87553-1

Cengage Learning
20 Channel Center Street
Boston, MA 02210
USA

Cengage Learning is a leading provider of customized learning solutions with employees residing in nearly 40 different countries and sales in more than 125 countries around the world. Find your local representative at **www.cengage.com**.

Cengage Learning products are represented in Canada by Nelson Education, Ltd.

To learn more about Cengage Learning Solutions, visit **www.cengage.com**.

Purchase any of our products at your local college store or at our preferred online store at **www.cengagebrain.com**.

Printed in the United States of America
Print Number: 01   Print Year: 2015

The eleventh edition of *Understanding Art* is dedicated to Allyn, Jordan, Taylor, and March.

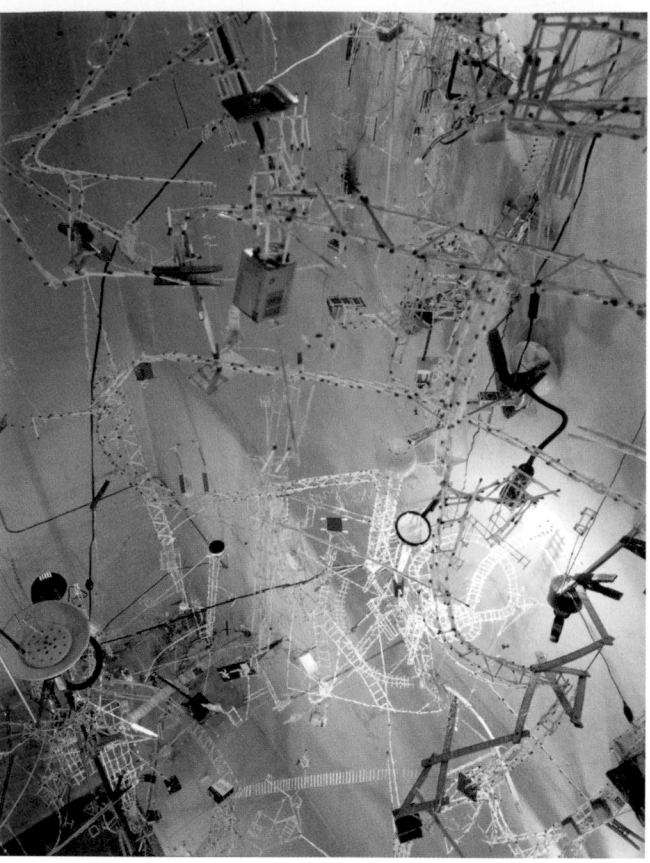

ABOUT THE COVER

Understanding Art has a track record of visually compelling covers that have encompassed, in a single, dynamic image, my concept for a particular edition, as well as the essence of my perspective as an author. My approach to art appreciation has always emphasized equally the visual elements and the history of art, provided a balance between the historical and the contemporary, and aimed to represent the world of art and culture as it truly is—one of diversity.

The eleventh edition of *Understanding Art* brings to this ongoing methodology a vital new dimension to acquiring information and engaging in critical dialogue about the arts and society. The eleventh edition is about seamless connections made possible with its accompanying MindTap® program—connections, importantly, between the text and the instructor's own indispensable materials; between the text and Cengage's exceptional digital resources; between the text and the world of electronic media.

And so it is that the eleventh edition features Sarah Sze's *Second Means of Egress* on its cover. To encounter a work by Sze is not to observe but rather to engage; to be an active participant rather than a passive spectator; to generate rather than simply to receive. Her emphasis on themes of interconnectivity and sustainability, along with what has been called a "mutable quality—as if anything could happen, or not," captures, for me, key aspects of successful learning: spontaneity, flexibility, accessibility, communicability.

CONTENTS

Preface   xv

PART I. INTRODUCTION

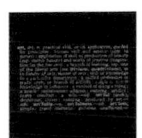 **1**

UNDERSTANDING ART   3

SUBJECT   4

CONTENT   5

FORM   7

ICONOGRAPHY   7

THEORY & PRACTICE   Giving Form to Experience: A
Visual Meditation on Cows   8

VISUAL ELEMENTS AND PRINCIPLES OF DESIGN   9

PUTTING IT ALL TOGETHER   The Visual Elements:
The Arnolfini Portrait   10

MEDIUMS AND TECHNIQUES   12

STYLE   12

PUTTING IT ALL TOGETHER   Principles of Design:
Marilyn (Vanitas)   13

COMPARE & CONTRAST   A Style by Any Other
Name . . . Appropriation and Subversion in
Contemporary Art   14

Realism   15

Expressionism   16

Abstraction   16

PART II. FOUNDATIONS OF ART AND DESIGN

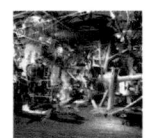 **2**

LINE AND SHAPE   19

LINE   20

The Measure of Line   20

Types and Qualities of Line   20

Actual, Implied, and Psychological Lines   22

Directionality of Line: Vertical, Horizontal, and
Diagonal   24

LINE AND SHAPE   24

Outline and Contour Line   24

Line, Value, and Shape   25

SHAPE, FORM, VOLUME, AND MASS   26

Shape   27

Form   27

Volume   27

Mass   28

TYPES OF SHAPES   28

Geometric Shapes   29

Organic Shapes   30

COMPARE & CONTRAST   The Expressive Potential
of Shape   32

Nonobjective and Abstract Shapes   33

Amorphous Shapes and Shapelessness in Art   33

POSITIVE AND NEGATIVE SHAPES, FIGURE
AND GROUND   34

SHAPE AS ICON   36

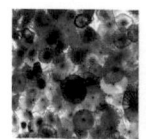

3

LIGHT AND COLOR   39

VALUE   40
Shades of Gray   40
Value Contrast   41
Value Pattern   42
Descriptive and Expressive Properties of Value   44

COLOR   45
The Science of Light   45
The Color Wheel   45
Additive and Subtractive Colors   46
Cool and Warm Colors   47
Properties of Color   47
Color Schemes   49
Local, Optical, and Arbitrary Color   51
Color and Symbolism   52

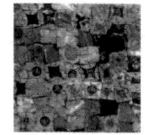

4

TEXTURE AND PATTERN   55

TEXTURE   57
Actual Texture   57
Visual Texture   58
Subversive Texture   58

PATTERN   58
COMPARE & CONTRAST   Humans versus Nature:
The Raft of the Medusa   60

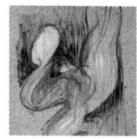

5

SPACE, TIME, AND MOTION   63

ACTUAL SPACE   64

CREATING THE ILLUSION OF SPACE   65
Relative Size   66
Overlapping   67
Location   68
Atmospheric Perspective   69

Linear Perspective   70
THEORY & PRACTICE   Creating the Illusion of Space in
Sculpture   72

COMPARE & CONTRAST   So Close and Yet So
Far: Perspective, Physical Proximity, and Emotional
Distance   74

TIME AND MOTION   76

ACTUAL MOTION   77
THEORY & PRACTICE   Chasing the Fourth Dimension:
Loïe Fuller   78

CREATING ILLUSION OF MOTION   79
Multiplication of Images and Blurred Lines   79
Optical Sensations   80

IMPLIED MOTION   80

IMPLIED TIME   81

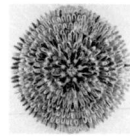

6

PRINCIPLES OF DESIGN   83

UNITY   84
The Grid   84
Proximity   84
Repetition   84
Color and Value   85
Line   87

UNITY WITH VARIETY   87
Repetition   88
Emphasis on Unity   88
Emphasis on Variety   89
Emphasis on Disunity   89
THEORY & PRACTICE   Focal Point and Emphasis   90

FOCAL POINT AND EMPHASIS   91
Directional Lines   92
Contrast   92
Placement   93

MULTIPLE FOCAL POINTS AND ABSENCE OF FOCAL
POINT   94

BALANCE AND RHYTHM   94

USING BALANCE AND IMBALANCE   95
Actual Balance   96
Visual Balance   96

Symmetrical and Asymmetrical Balance   96
Horizontal, Vertical, Diagonal, and Radial Balance   98

USING RHYTHM   99
Regular Repetition   99
Alternating Rhythm and Progressive Rhythm   100

USING SCALE   101
Relative Size   101
Hierarchical Scale   101
Distortion of Scale   102

PROPORTION   102
The Canon of Proportions   102
The Golden Mean, Golden Rectangle, and Root Five
Rectangle   103
The Spiral   104

PART III. MEDIUMS, TECHNIQUES, AND STYLE

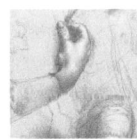

7

DRAWING   107

TYPES OF DRAWINGS   108
The Artist's Sketch   108
The Finished Drawing   108

DRAWING MATERIALS   109
Dry Mediums   109
Fluid Mediums   113
A CLOSER LOOK   Life, Death, and Dwelling in the
Deep South   114
CARTOONS   116

ALTERNATIVE APPROACHES TO DRAWING   116

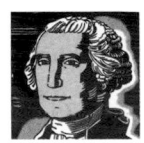

8

PAINTING   121

THE COMPONENTS OF PAINT   122

TYPES OF PAINTING   122

Fresco   123
Encaustic   123
Tempera   124
Oil   125
COMPARE & CONTRAST   Noland's *Graded Exposure*
with Davie's *Between My Eye and Heart No. 12*   126
Acrylic   127
Watercolor and Gouache   127
A CLOSER LOOK   Superheroes: East Meets
West   129
Spray Paint   130

MIXED MEDIA   130

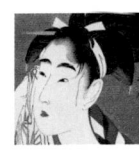

9

PRINTMAKING AND GRAPHIC DESIGN   133

METHODS OF PRINTMAKING   134
Relief   134
Intaglio   136
A CLOSER LOOK   Hung Liu: Chinese Traditions
Unbound   139
Lithography   141
Serigraphy   142
Monotype   144

GRAPHIC DESIGN   144
Typography   145
Layout   145
Logos   147

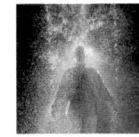

10

IMAGING: PHOTOGRAPHY, FILM, VIDEO, AND DIGITAL ARTS   149

PHOTOGRAPHY   150
Cameras   152
Film   152
Digital Photography   153
History of Photography   154
Photography as an Art Form   159

FILM   162
    Varieties of Cinematographic Techniques   163
    Varieties of Cinematographic Experience   169

VIDEO   171

DIGITAL ARTS   174
    Web Design   176

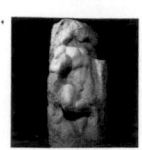

11

SCULPTURE, INSTALLATION, SITE-SPECIFIC ART, AND 3D DESIGN   179

SCULPTURE   180
    Carving   181
    Modeling   181
    Casting   181
    COMPARE & CONTRAST   (Found) Art as Idea
        as Idea   183
    Constructed Sculpture   184
    Assemblage   185
    Kinetic Sculpture   186
    Light Sculpture   186

TYPES OF MATERIALS   187
    Stone   187
    Wood   188
    Clay   189
    Metal   189
    A CLOSER LOOK   Storm King Art Center   190
    Other Materials   191

INSTALLATION   192

SITE-SPECIFIC ART   193
    Land Art   194
    A CLOSER LOOK   Christo and Jeanne-Claude:
        The Gates, Central Park, New York City,
        1979–2005   196
    Ephemeral Art   197
    Public Art   198
    A CLOSER LOOK   Barcelona's Parc Güell   199
    Monuments   200
    A CLOSER LOOK   The Vietnam Veterans Memorial—
        a Woman's Perspective   202

INDUSTRIAL DESIGN   203

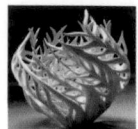

12

CRAFT ARTS   207

CERAMICS   209
    Methods of Working with Clay   209
    The Potter's Wheel   210
    Glazing   211
    Types of Ceramics   212

GLASS   214
    Techniques of Working with Glass   214
    A CLOSER LOOK   The Chandeliers of Dale
        Chihuly   216

TEXTILE ARTS   218
    Weaving   218
    Basket Weaving   220

METALWORK AND JEWELRY   221

WOOD   222

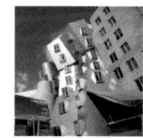

13

ARCHITECTURE AND URBAN DESIGN   225

STONE ARCHITECTURE   226
    Post-and-Lintel Construction   227
    Arches   229
    Vaults   229
    Domes   230

WOOD ARCHITECTURE   230
    Post-and-Beam Construction   231
    Trusses   232
    Balloon Framing   232

CAST-IRON ARCHITECTURE   233

STEEL-CAGE ARCHITECTURE   234

REINFORCED CONCRETE ARCHITECTURE   236

STEEL-CABLE ARCHITECTURE   238

SHELL ARCHITECTURE   239

NEW MATERIALS, NEW VISIONS   239

A CLOSER LOOK   Bringing Light to Ground Zero   240

Green Buildings   242

URBAN DESIGN   243

Washington, D.C.   244

Paris—Les Halles   244

Alexandria, Egypt   244

PART IV. ART: A CONCISE GLOBAL HISTORY

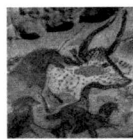

14

ART OF THE ANCIENT WORLD   247

PREHISTORIC ART   248

Paleolithic Art   248

> MAP 14.1 Prehistoric Europe   248

Neolithic Art   250

MESOPOTAMIA   251

Sumer   251

> MAP 14.2 The Ancient Near East   251

MESOPOTAMIA   251

Akkad   253

Babylonia   254

Assyria   255

Persia   255

ANCIENT EGYPTIAN ART   256

Old Kingdom   256

> MAP 14.3 Ancient Egypt   257

Middle Kingdom   260

New Kingdom   260

A CLOSER LOOK   King Tut: The Face That Launched a Thousand High-Res Images   264

> MAP 14.4 The Prehistoric Aegean   265

PREHISTORIC AEGEAN ART   265

The Cyclades   265

Crete   265

Mycenae   267

> MAP 14.5 Africa   269

THE WIDER WORLD   269

Africa   269

Asia   271

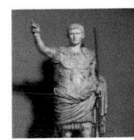

15

GREECE, ROME, AND THE EARLY JUDEO-CHRISTIAN WORLD   275

GREECE   276

> MAP 15.1 The Greek World   277

Geometric Period   277

Archaic Period   278

Early Classical Art   282

Classical Art   283

THEORY & PRACTICE   Polykleitos's Canon: The Body Beautiful   284

Late Classical Art   287

Hellenistic Art   289

THE ETRUSCANS   290

ROME   292

The Republican Period   292

> MAP 15.2 The Roman Empire in 117 CE   293

The Early Empire   295

COMPARE & CONTRAST   Stadium Designs: Thumbs-Up or Thumbs-Down?   296

The Late Empire   302

THE WIDER WORLD   306

Asia   306

The Americas   310

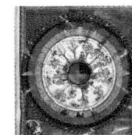

16

THE AGE OF FAITH 313

CHRISTIANITY   314

EARLY CHRISTIAN ARCHITECTURE   315

Old St. Peter's, Rome   315

BYZANTINE ART   316

San Vitale, Ravenna   317

Hagia Sophia, Constantinople   318

EARLY MEDIEVAL EUROPE   318
Christian Art in the Early Middle Ages   319
Carolingian Art   320
> MAP 16.1 The Carolingian world   320

ROMANESQUE ART   321
Architecture   322
Sculpture   324
Tapestry   325
A CLOSER LOOK   Hildegard of Bingen   326

GOTHIC ART   327
Characteristics of the Gothic Style in Architecture   327
Gothic Architecture outside France   329
Sculpture   331

ISLAM   333
> MAP 16.2 The Islamic world around 1500   334
The Umayyad Caliphate   335
The Golden Age of Islam   338

THE WIDER WORLD   340
India   340
China   342
COMPARE & CONTRAST   Ganesh, the Hindu Deity: Don't Leave Home without Him   344
Japan   346
Africa   348
The Americas   351

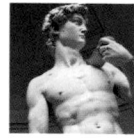

17

THE RENAISSANCE   353

> MAP 17.1 Europe in 1477   354

THE RENAISSANCE PERIOD   354

FIFTEENTH-CENTURY NORTHERN PAINTING   355
Flemish Painting: From Page to Panel   355
German Art   358

THE RENAISSANCE IN ITALY   360
Early Renaissance   360
The Renaissance Begins, and So Does the Competition   361
Renaissance Art at Midcentury and Beyond   364
High Renaissance   366

COMPARE & CONTRAST   The *Davids* of Donatello, Verrocchio, Michelangelo, and Bernini   374
High and Late Renaissance in Venice   376

HIGH AND LATE RENAISSANCE OUTSIDE ITALY   378

MANNERISM   380

THE WIDER WORLD   382
India   382
China   384
Japan   386
The Americas   387

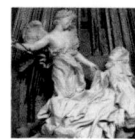

18

THE BAROQUE ERA   391

Seventeenth and Eighteenth Centuries in the West   392

THE BAROQUE PERIOD IN ITALY   392
St. Peter's   392
Gianlorenzo Bernini   392
> MAP 18.1 Europe in 1648   394
Caravaggio   395
Artemisia Gentileschi   396
COMPARE & CONTRAST   Two Views of Judith's Biblical Encounter with Holofernes   397
Baroque Ceiling Decoration   399
Francesco Borromini   399

THE BAROQUE PERIOD OUTSIDE ITALY   399
Spain   400
Flanders   401
Holland   402
France   404
England   407

THE ROCOCO   409
Jean-Honoré Fragonard   409
Élisabeth Vigée-Lebrun   409
Enlightenment, Revolution, the Scientific, and the Natural   410

THE WIDER WORLD   411
Seventeenth and Eighteenth Centuries in the East   411
India   412
China   413
Japan   414

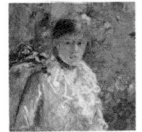

19

THE MODERN ERA   417

NEOCLASSICISM   418
   Neoclassical Painting   418
   Neoclassical Sculpture   420
   Neoclassical Architecture   421

ROMANTICISM   421
   COMPARE & CONTRAST   Ingres's *Grande Odalisque*
      with Delacroix's *Odalisque*   424
   The Academy   425

REALISM   426
   COMPARE & CONTRAST   Titian's *Venus of
      Urbino*, Manet's *Olympia*, Gauguin's *Te Arii Vahine*,
      and Valadon's *The Blue Room*   428

IMPRESSIONISM   431

POSTIMPRESSIONISM   434
   A CLOSER LOOK   Why Did van Gogh Cut Off His
      Ear?   438

EXPRESSIONISM   440

AMERICAN EXPATRIATES   442

AMERICANS IN AMERICA   443
   A CLOSER LOOK   Weaving Together Biblical and
      Personal Stories   445

THE BIRTH OF MODERN SCULPTURE   446

ART NOUVEAU   447

THE WIDER WORLD   448
   Africa   448
   India   450
   Japan   451
   Oceania   453
   > MAP 19.1 Oceania   453
   The Americas   455

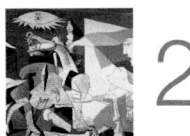

20

THE TWENTIETH CENTURY:
THE EARLY YEARS   459

   Twentieth Century: The Early Years in Europe and the
      United States   460

THE FAUVES   460

EXPRESSIONISM   462
   Die Brücke (The Bridge)   463
   Der Blaue Reiter (The Blue Rider)   463
   Neue Sachlichkeit (New Objectivity)   464

CUBISM   464
   Analytic Cubism   467
   Synthetic Cubism   468
   Cubist Sculpture   469

FUTURISM   470

EARLY-TWENTIETH-CENTURY ABSTRACTION
IN THE UNITED STATES   470
   291 Gallery   471
   The Armory Show   472

EARLY-TWENTIETH-CENTURY ABSTRACTION IN
EUROPE   473

FANTASY   475

DADA   476

SURREALISM   478

FIGURATIVE ART IN THE UNITED STATES   480

THE HARLEM RENAISSANCE   482

THE BAUHAUS   482

THE WIDER WORLD   484
   Japan   484
   China   486
   Africa   487
   Mexico   488

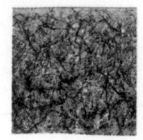

21

THE TWENTIETH CENTURY: POSTWAR TO POSTMODERN 491

THE NEW YORK SCHOOL 492

Action Painting: Focus on Gesture 492

COMPARE & CONTRAST Rothko's *Number 22* with Rothko's *Black on Grey* 496

Color-Field Painting 497

Constructed Sculpture and Assemblage 497

FIGURATION AND ABSTRACTION IN THE POSTWAR YEARS 499

Focus on the Figure 499

Abstraction 500

ART OF THE SIXTIES AND SEVENTIES 502

Pop Art 502

Realism and Photorealism 506

Minimalism 508

Performance Art 509

Conceptual Art 512

ART, IDENTITY, AND SOCIAL CONSCIOUSNESS 514

Feminist Art 514

A CLOSER LOOK Guerrilla Girls Warfare 516

Sexual Identity 517

Racial and Ethnic Identity 518

COMPARE & CONTRAST Two Views of *Napoléon Crossing the Alps* 521

ART AFTER 1980: SOME DIVERGENT TRENDS 523

New Image Painting 523

Neo-Expressionism 524

ARCHITECTURE 526

Modern Architecture 526

Postmodern Architecture 527

Deconstructivist Architecture 529

THE WIDER WORLD 531

India and Pakistan 532

China 534

Japan 535

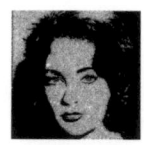

22

ART NOW: A GLOBAL PERSPECTIVE 539

GLOBALIZATION 540

Hybridity 540

Appropriation 541

Postcolonialism 541

INDIA AND PAKISTAN 542

CHINA 544

JAPAN 546

KOREA 548

THE MIDDLE EAST 548

AFRICA 552

Out of Africa: The Enduring Legacy of the Ceremonial Mask 554

THE AMERICAS 556

PART V. THEMES AND PURPOSES OF ART

VISUAL GLOSSARY 561

Glossary 579

Credits 589

Index 597

PREFACE

There are two ways of looking at things. One is simply looking at them, whereas the other involves considering them attentively. Merely to see Is nothing else than receiving into the eye the form or likeness of the object that is looked at; but to consider a thing is more like this: it is to seek with special diligence after the means of knowing this object thoroughly.

—NICOLAS POUSSIN

HERE WE ARE, together embarking on the study of art and art history between the covers of a book called *Understanding Art.* A textbook on art is unlike a textbook in other academic disciplines. Yes, there is a special vocabulary of art. Yes, this vocabulary is woven into a language that, once learned, enables us to better verbalize the visual. But the most important aspect of an art book is its images, because a student's journey toward understanding art ought to always begin with looking.

Think of this art appreciation textbook as your "*i*-book"—it begins with looking at *i*mages. Having said that, *learning to look* is equally important for art appreciation, and that's where some other "*i*-words" play an important role: *i*nformation, *i*nsight, and *i*nterpretation. We gather information about how a work of art is conceived and constructed using the visual elements of art, principles of design, composition, content, style, and symbolism. We explore the motives of artists and the historical, social, political, and personal contexts in which a work of art came into existence. These investigations lend insight into the complex factors contributing to the creation of works of art. In short, we progress beyond *looking* (using the eye passively to recognize the existence of an object) to *seeing* (using the eye actively to perceive, to contextualize, and to understand). And as we gather confidence in our knowledge and insights, we turn more comfortably to the dimension of interpretation—your dimension. It is here where the "I" really counts, for we all bring the weight of our own

Eric Protter, ed., *Painters on Painting* (New York: Dover, 2011), 69; *also* Peggy Hadden, "The Quotable Artist" (New York: Allworth Press, 2002), 204.

experience to our interpretations, our unique perceptions to our likes or dislikes of a work of art.

The artist Pablo Picasso once said, "People who try to explain pictures are usually barking up the wrong tree." The words *explain* and *understand,* though, have very different meanings. One can argue that only artists can *explain* their work, can make intelligible something that is not known or not understood. But *understanding* is defined as full awareness or knowledge that is arrived at through an intellectual or emotional process—including the ability to extract meaning or to interpret. The ability to *appreciate,* or to perceive the value or worth of something from a discriminating perspective, then, is the consummate reward of understanding.

THE APPROACH OF UNDERSTANDING ART

The eleventh edition of *Understanding Art,* as earlier editions, is intended to work for both students and professors. *Understanding Art* continues to serve as a tool to help organize and enlighten this demanding, often whirlwind course. My goal has been to write a book that would do it all: edify and inform students and, at the same time, keep them engaged, animated, and inspired—while at the same time meeting instructors' desire for comprehensive exposition. All in all, *Understanding Art* contains a fully balanced approach to appreciating art. The understanding and appreciation of art are enhanced by familiarity with three areas of art: the language of art (visual elements, principles of design, and style), the nature of the mediums used in art, and the history of art.

WHAT'S NEW IN THIS EDITION

In the spirit of the conviction that "understanding art ought always to begin with looking," the eleventh edition features hundreds of new artworks that have been chosen to touch the landmarks of Western art and the art of the wider world, and also to better illustrate the elements, mediums, and historic developments of art.

The eleventh edition of *Understanding Art*, as previous editions, discusses the visual elements of art, the mediums of art, and the history of art. However, the balance among the three areas has been enhanced in the eleventh edition.

Reorganization of Chapter Structure

The eleventh edition of *Understanding Art* expands the discussion of the visual elements of art from two chapters to five chapters:

- Ch. 2: "Line and Shape"
- Ch. 3: "Light and Color"
- Ch. 4: "Texture and Pattern"
- Ch. 5: "Space, Time, and Motion"
- Ch. 6: "Principles of Design"

Chapter-by-Chapter Changes— A Sampling

- Ch. 1, "Understanding Art," has new Putting It All Together features on the visual elements of art and on principles of design.
- Ch. 3, "Light and Color," has expanded coverage of the physical and perceptual properties of color and of the uses of color.
- Ch. 5, "Space, Time, and Motion," has new Theory and Practice features titled "Creating the Illusion of Space in Sculpture" and "Chasing the Fourth Dimension: Loïe Fuller."
- Ch. 6, "Principles of Design," has a new Theory and Practice feature titled "Focal Point and Emphasis," which explores the compositional features of Jacques-Louis David's *Oath of the Horatii.*
- Ch. 9, "Printmaking and Graphic Design," has a new section on graphic design.
- Ch. 10, "Imaging," now features sections on photography, film, video, and digital arts, including web design.
- Ch. 11 now includes sculpture, installation, site-specific art, and 3D design.
- Ch. 13 on architecture now includes urban design.
- Ch. 18, "The Baroque Era," has a Compare + Contrast feature "Two Views of Judith's Biblical Encounter with Holofernes," comparing the paintings of Caravaggio and Artemisia Gentileschi.
- Ch. 21, "The Twentieth Century: Postwar to Postmodern," has a major new section titled "Art, Identity, and Social Consciousness," which includes discussions of feminist art, sexual identity, and race and ethnic identity.

Integration of Art Outside the European Tradition into the Main Body of the Text

Understanding Art has always been the market leader in terms of numbers of works by women and artists of color and differing ethnicities. The eleventh edition goes farther. Art outside the European tradition is not sectioned off in separate chapters but is now integrated into the main body of the text. At the end of each chapter, "The Wider World" offers extensive coverage of historical and artistic developments across the globe that are contemporaneous with those occurring in Europe and the United States. For example:

- Ch. 14, "Art of the Ancient World," now includes Neolithic rock painting from Africa.
- Ch. 15, "Greece, Rome, and the Early Judeo-Christian World," now includes sections on Buddhism, Hinduism, and Pre-Columbian art.
- Ch. 16, "The Age of Faith," now includes discussion of the arts of the Tang and Song Dynasties in China, and the Buddhist and Shinto religions in Japan.
- Ch. 17, "The Renaissance," now includes discussion of the Mughal Empire in India, the Ming Dynasty in China, the Muromachi and Momoyama periods in Japan, and the Aztec civilization in the Americas.
- Ch. 18, "The Baroque Era," now discusses the British incursion into India, the Qing Dynasty in China, and the development of woodblock printing in Edo period Japan.
- Ch. 20, "The Twentieth Century: The Early Years," includes a section on the development of the militaristic Meiji period in Japan, a Connections feature that draws visual parallels between Japanese propaganda art concerning the Russo-Japanese War and Goya's Third of May, Communist Chinese propaganda art, and the post-revolution mural painters of Mexico.
- Ch. 22, "Art Now: A Global Perspective," contains more than a dozen new works from India and Pakistan, China, Japan, the Middle East, Africa, and the Americas, as well as a new Compare + Contrast feature: "Out of Africa: The Enduring Legacy of the Ceremonial Mask."

Visual Glossary

A new, unique reference focuses on the themes and purposes of art, placing essential, concise information at students' fingertips and applying it to specific images found throughout in the text. Additional visual glossaries on style and mediums are available on MindTap.

We are all aware that slides in the classroom are poor substitutes for real-life encounters with paintings and sculpture, or for the perception of form and space that comes with physically standing in a building.

This edition of *Understanding Art* includes more hybrid content than ever. It is the first that is available on MindTap®, a highly customizable multimedia teaching and learning platform. MindTap for *Understanding Art* provides an interactive digital experience for exploration, study, and development of critical-thinking skills. The MindTap ebook reader features a unique visual presentation, which provides an intuitive reading experience—one that honors the design of the printed book by positioning beautifully displayed artworks beside the accompanying

text. This MindTap reader's two-pane design allows students to view images that appear on the left side while reading about them in the scrolling text discussion on the right side. The MindTap presentation encourages more interaction with images: students can zoom and expand images; access videos, maps, and panoramas related to each image; and view cross-referenced images without having to leave the flow of the main narrative. The image integration extends to the ebook's navigation, which shows in one place all of the images within a chapter, and which reinforces the development of visual literacy.

New to this edition are interactive Art Tours, also available on MindTap. Each of the familiar Art Tours from previous edition, which highlight public art in specific cities around the world (Jerusalem, Rome, Paris, London, New York, Washington, D.C., Chicago, Dallas/Fort Worth, Florence, and Los Angeles) has been updated and is now accompanied by an interactive map, which offers students an even more hands-on experience of visiting cities and their art collections in the United States and abroad, underscoring the ubiquity of art and design in their lives. In the interactive Art Tours, students are guided from one site to another and can view related images, videos, and websites.

New architecture videos and 360-degree architectural panoramas of significant monuments and sites create the feeling of "being there" while learning more about interior and exterior details and their present-day surroundings.

FEATURES

The eleventh edition of *Understanding Art* contains unique features—many of which are new to this edition—that stimulate student interest, emphasize key points in art fundamentals and art history, highlight contemporary events in art, and reflect the ways in which professors teach.

CONNECTIONS These new features mainly illustrate how works of art from one period or one global location relate to works from another. Thumbnails are used to make these features visual in nature. Some Connections features, however, show students how they can apply the information in the text to their own lives. For example, a Connections feature in Chapter 1 asks students to list the attributes they would include in a self-portrait.

THEORY AND PRACTICE These features show how artists use principles and theories of art to arrive at their compositions. For example, the Theory and Practice feature in Chapter 1 shows how Neo-Plastic artist Theo van Doesburg "neglected the laws of nature in favor of those of artistic creation" to develop his *Study for Composition (Cow)*. A Theory and Practice feature in Chapter 5 shows how several artists sought to capture the dynamic spinning and twirling of Folies Bergère dancer Loïe Fuller's signature "Serpentine Dance" in drawings and in sculpture. The Theory and Practice feature in Chapter 15 explains how the Greek sculptor Polykleitos used his canon of proportions and *contrapposto* (the weight-shift principle) to create "The Body Beautiful," as exemplified in his statue *Doryphoros*.

PUTTING IT ALL TOGETHER These features visually summarize the ways in which artists use the visual elements of art and principles of design to render their compositions. One Putting It All Together feature in Chapter 1 uses *The Arnolfini Portrait* to show how Jan van Eyck used line, shape, value, color, and other elements of art to bring his portrait of a newly married couple to life. Another Putting It All Together feature shows how contemporary painter Audrey Flack used principles of design such as unity and variety, balance, rhythm, and symbolism to portray the iconic status of 1960s movie star Marilyn Monroe and to suggest her untimely death.

COMPARE + CONTRAST These features show two or more works of art side by side and phrase questions that help students focus on stylistic and technical similarities and differences. They parallel the time-honored pedagogical technique of presenting works in class for comparison and contrast. There are several new Compare + Contrast features in the eleventh edition. For example, Chapter 11 compares and contrasts Duchamps's *Fountain* with Sherrie Levine's *Fountains after Duchamp* in a New Compare + Contrast feature titled "(Fountains) Art as Idea as Idea." A new Compare + Contrast feature in Chapter 22, "The Undying Legacy of the African Mask," relates a traditional African mask to the fiber arts of Faith Ringgold, the paintings of Pablo Picasso, and an assemblage of women's high-heeled shoes by contemporary American artist Willie Cole.

TIMELINES The chapters on the history of art, Chapters 14–21, contain timelines for the arts of Europe and the United States, and for artistic developments in the "wider world." The timelines cover major historic events as well as artistic developments, so that the arts are placed in their historic, cultural, and social contexts.

QUOTATIONS Quotations at the top of pages by artists, critics, and others allow students to "get into the minds" of those people closest to the art world.

GLOSSARY Key terms are boldfaced in the text and defined in a glossary at the end of the textbook. Figure number references provide a visual illustration of each term.

VISUAL GLOSSARY A visual glossary focuses on themes and purposes of art—a unique reference that puts essential, concise information at students' fingertips and which cross-reference images found elsewhere in the text. Additional visual glossaries on style and mediums are available on MindTap.

THE CONTENTS OF THE ELEVENTH EDITION OF *UNDERSTANDING ART*

The book is organized into the following parts:

I. INTRODUCTION The first chapter of the text, *Understanding Art*, equips students with key content and formal terms to help them build a foundational vocabulary for discussing art—and eventually extracting meaning, understanding, and, with time, appreciation of art.

II. FOUNDATIONS OF ART AND DESIGN Chapters 2–6 provide comprehensive discussion of the visual elements of art, principles of design, and style, form, and content. The language of art is then applied throughout the remainder of the text in discussions of mediums and surveys of art through the ages and throughout the world.

III. MEDIUMS, TECHNIQUES, AND STYLE Chapters 7–10, on drawing, painting, printmaking, and imaging, explain how artists combine the visual elements of art to create two-dimensional compositions. The mediums discussed are as traditional as drawing a pencil across a sheet of paper and as innovative as spray painting color fields and clicking a mouse to access a menu of electronic techniques and design elements. Chapters 11–13 discuss the opportunities and issues provided by three-dimensional art forms, including sculpture, installation, site-specific art, industrial design, craft, and architecture.

IV. ART: A CONCISE GLOBAL HISTORY Chapters 14–18 contain a solid core of art history on the development of art from ancient times to the dawn of the modern era. Chapters 19–22 examine the great changes that have occurred in the world of art since the late eighteenth century. These chapters attempt to answer the question, "Just what is modern about modern art?" Whereas some artists have rejected the flatness of the canvas and moved art into innumerable new directions, others have maintained traditional paths. Controversy and conflict are part of the modern history of art. But movements such as Postmodern art and Deconstructivist architecture also make it possible to speak of the "modern world and beyond." The phenomenon of globalization has created a new art world in which cultures are no longer distant from one another and people and places are no longer as separate as they once were. As a result, we have trends such as hybridity, appropriation, high art and low culture, and postcolonialism in the arts. We see how these trends are expressed today within—and without—various cultural traditions around the world. Although nobody can say exactly where art is going, these chapters discuss the movements and works that appear to be vital at the current moment.

V. VISUAL GLOSSARIES The "Visual Glossary: Themes and Purposes of Art" considers the "whys" behind works of art, providing students with a useful reference that presents images found elsewhere in the text (and some that are not) in thematic categories. Additional visual glossaries on style and mediums are available on MindTap.

STUDENT RESOURCES

The MindTap learning platform guides you through the course curriculum via an innovative Learning Path Navigator where you will complete reading assignments, annotate your readings, complete homework, and engage with quizzes and assessments. This new edition features a two-pane e-reader, designed to make your online reading experience easier. Images discussed in the text appear in the left pane, while the accompanying text scrolls on the right. Highly accessible and interactive, this new reader pairs videos, Google Map links, and 360-degree panoramas with the matching figure in the text. Artworks are further brought to life through zoom capability right in the e-reader. Numerous study tools are included, such as image flashcards; downloadable Guides to Studying (a chapter outline and note taking template); the ability to synchronize your eBook notes with your personal EverNote account; Questia research library; Pathbrite e-portfolio.

New Flashcard App

The new and improved Flashcard App in MindTap gives you more flexibility and features than ever before. Study from the preexisting card decks with all the images from the text, or create your own cards with new images from your collection or those shared by your instructor. Create your own custom study deck by combining cards from separate chapters or those you've created. Once you've compiled your flashcard deck, you can save it for later use or print it for on-the-go studying.

INSTRUCTOR RESOURCES

Leverage the tools in MindTap to enhance and personalize your course. Add your own images, videos, web links, readings, projects, and more either in the course Learning Path or right in the chapter reading. Set project due dates, specify whether assignments are for practice or a grade, and control when your students see these activities in their Learning Path. MindTap can be purchased as a stand-alone product or bundled with the print text. Connect with your Learning Consultant for more details via www.cengage.com/repfinder/.

Access the Instructor Companion Website to find resources to help you teach your course and engage your students. Here you will find the Instructor's Manual; Cengage Learning Testing, powered by Cognero; and Microsoft PowerPoint slides with lecture outlines and images that can be used as offered or customized by importing personal lecture slides or other material.

Digital Image Library

Display digital images in the classroom with this powerful tool. This one-stop lecture and class presentation resource makes it easy to assemble, edit, and present customized lectures for your course. Available on Flash drive, the Digital Image Library provides high-resolution images for lecture presentations and allows you to easily add your own images to supplement those provided.

ACKNOWLEDGMENTS

Understanding Art would not be the text that it is—nor I the teacher, researcher, and author I am—were it not for the knowledge, dedication to the disciplines of art and art history, and the contagious passion of those I consider to be mentors, supporters, and friends: James S. Ackerman, Wayne V. Andersen, Stanford Anderson, Whitney Chadwick, George Heard Hamilton, Ann Sutherland Harris, Julius S. Held, Sam Hunter, Henry A. Millon, Konrad Oberhuber, John C. Overbeck, Michael Rinehart, Andrew C. Ritchie, Mark W. Roskill, Theodore Roszak, Miriam Schapiro, Bernice Steinbaum, and Jack Tworkov.

Each edition of *Understanding Art* has been undertaken to move the field of art appreciation forward—to stay current with the most recent critical inquiry, to respond thoughtfully to the needs and wants of the current generation of students, and to provide useful pedagogical materials to support instructors who dedicate themselves to imparting their knowledge about art and to creating generations of lifelong museumgoers. A book like this succeeds only to the extent that it meets the goals of instructors who use it. Thus, I wish to thank those peer reviewers whose insightful feedback informed the development of the eleventh edition: Jeanne Brody, Villanova University; Mark Damato, Averett University; Barbara England; Freed-Hardeman University; Cindy Grant, University of Mississippi; Deborah Gustlin, Gavilan College; Sherry Howard, Northwest State Community

College; Kerry Jenkins, Methodist University; Bonnie Proudfoot, Hocking College; Alice Vandergriff, Missouri State University; and Paige Wideman, Northern Kentucky University.

No revision can be undertaken, much less accomplished, without the vision, skills, and persistent dedication of a superb team of publishing professionals. First and foremost is Sharon Adams Poore, Product Manager, whose expertise and sensibilities make their mark on every project she oversees; Erika Hayden, Associate Content Developer and my newest Cengage colleague, whose knowledge of the discipline, creative mind, and well-informed pedagogical contributions contributed greatly to the profile of this edition; Lianne Ames, Senior Content Project Manager, who, as always, finds a way to concretize an author's vision for a project and to keep all of the parts moving to their grand conclusion; Chad Kirchner, Content Developer Focusing on Media, whose imagination and inventiveness have connected what is on these pages with what is out in the world, who almost never says "impossible" and almost always says "how about this?"; Cate Rickard Barr, Senior Art Director, who coordinated all of the visual aspects of the project and whose vibrant aesthetic creates the feeling that you just want to hold the book in your hands; Jillian Borden, Marketing Manager, whose dedication to discerning what is truly valuable for the instructor in art appreciation is matched only by her determination to provide it; and to all of those members of the Cengage team whose involvement in the inception and realization of the eleventh edition of *Understanding Art* enables us to present it to you, including Rachel Bailey, Senior Product Assistant; Monica Eckman, Product Director; and Lisa Mafrici, Product Development Manager. Sincerest thanks also to Jonathan Poore, Sharon Adams Poore, and Fred S. Kleiner, for providing—through considerable effort—many of the stunning photographs of monuments you will see in this text.

Last, I extend my appreciation and gratitude to the professionals at Thistle Hill Publishing for their key roles in the production process: Andrea Archer, Production Director, and Angela Urquhart, Editorial Director; to Corey Smith, Senior Permissions Project Manager with Lumina Datamatics; and to the software developers with whom we have worked to create the new MindTap reader for the eleventh edition, and to the entire team of professionals, too numerous to list fully here, who had a hand in its design, creation, and implementation.

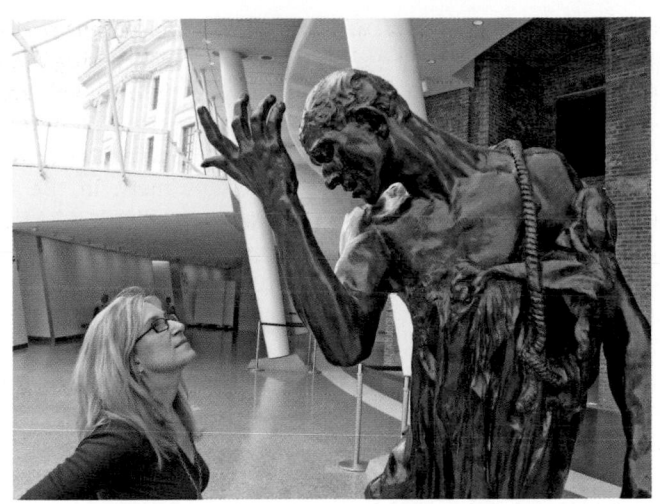

ABOUT THE AUTHOR

LOIS FICHNER-RATHUS is professor of art in the Art Department of the College of New Jersey. She holds a combined undergraduate degree in fine arts and art history, an MA from the Williams College Graduate Program in the history of art, and a PhD in the history, theory, and criticism of art from the Massachusetts Institute of Technology. Her areas of specialization include contemporary art, feminist art history and criticism, and modern art and architecture. She has contributed to books, curated exhibitions, published articles in professional journals, and exhibited her large-format photographic prints. She is also the author of *Foundations of Art and Design* and the co-author of *Culture and Values*. She resides in New York.

art, *ärt, n.* practical skill, or its application, guided by principles : human skill and agency (opp. to *nature*) : application of skill to production of beauty (esp. visible beauty) and works of creative imagination (as the *fine arts*) : a branch of learning, esp. one of the *liberal* arts (see **trivium, quadrivium**), as in *faculty of arts, master of arts :* skill or knowledge in a particular department : a skilled profession or trade, craft, or branch of activity : magic or occult knowledge or influence : a method of doing a thing : a knack : contrivance : address : cunning : artifice : crafty conduct : a wile.—*adj.* **art′ful** (*arch.*), dexterous, clever : cunning : produced by art.—*adv.* **art′fully.**—*n.* **art′fulness.**—*adj.* **art′less,** simple : (*rare*) inartistic : guileless, unaffected.—

1

ed profession or
magic or occult
of doing a thing :
nning : artifice :
art'ful (*arch.*),
uced by art.—
—*adj.* art'less,
s, unaffected.—

UNDERSTANDING ART

Everyone wants to understand art. Why not try to understand the songs of a bird? Why does one love the night, flowers, everything around one, without trying to understand them? But in the case of a painting people have to understand. If only they would realize above all that an artist works of necessity, that he himself is only a trifling bit of the world, and that no more importance should be attached to him than to plenty of other things which please us in the world, though we can't explain them. People who try to explain pictures are usually barking up the wrong tree.

— PABLO PICASSO

PABLO PICASSO lived to the age of ninety-two and was one of the most prolific artists in history. He was also an eloquent and forceful commentator on his own work, the work of others, and the ideas and philosophies of his generation of modernists. We find ourselves turning again and again to his sometimes brash but always confident insights, as in this oft-quoted passage on understanding art.

Why did Picasso find attempts to understand art so worrisome? Perhaps he was afraid we'd miss the larger point. In our attempt to comprehend the ingredients of art—the subject, the form, the symbolism—we run the risk of getting it all wrong in the end. One can argue that only artists can *explain* their work, can make intelligible something that is not known or not understood. But *understanding* is defined as full awareness or knowledge that is arrived at through an intellectual or emotional process—including the ability to extract meaning or to interpret. The ability to *appreciate*, or to perceive the value or worth of something from a discriminating perspective, then, is the consummate reward of understanding.

SUBJECT

The **subject** is the *what* of a work of art—people, places, things, themes, processes, events, ideas. For most of the history of art, the subject is recognizable or at least reflects some sort of visual experience. Categories of subjects with which artists work are often called **genres**. The word comes from French meaning "kind" or "type." Genres include religious or mythological subjects, historical subjects, portraiture, still life, landscape, nonobjective art, and so on. They also include something called *genre* subjects—images and themes from ordinary life. The modernist era, however, challenged the traditional definition of *subject*, which grew to include anything from the elements of art in their purest form, as in a painting by Wassily Kandinsky (Fig. 1.1), to the physical processes of art making, to a concept for a work of art without a tangible object fabricated by the artist.

The imagery in **abstract art** may be difficult to decipher because it no longer fully resembles the original things or scenes from which it was derived. But we cannot say that these works are without a subject. **Nonobjective art** may make no reference whatsoever to the natural world, no pretext to representing it, but even nonobjective works are not without a *subject*—at least from one

CONNECTIONS Standing in the interior of a Gothic cathedral, there is much to discuss about the floor plan, the structural elements, the design of the vaults and stained glass, the engineering, the style of the sculpture. But it is the content of the work as a whole—its role in society, the religious beliefs that gave rise to it, the symbolism of its design and its iconographic program—that leads us to better understand and appreciate the historical and sociological relevance of the work.

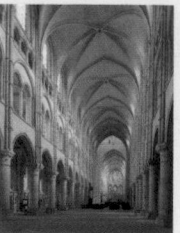

▲ Interior, Laon Cathedral (**Fig. 16.15**)

perspective. Picasso insisted, for example, that there is always a subject: "even if the painting is [nothing but] green, well then! The 'subject' is the green." Jackson Pollock also challenged the notion that a nonobjective work is necessarily a work without a subject: "There is no such thing as a good painting about nothing. We assert that the subject is critical." Even though we are accustomed to defining the subject of a work as a recognizable representation of a tangible thing, *subject* is a much more inclusive word.

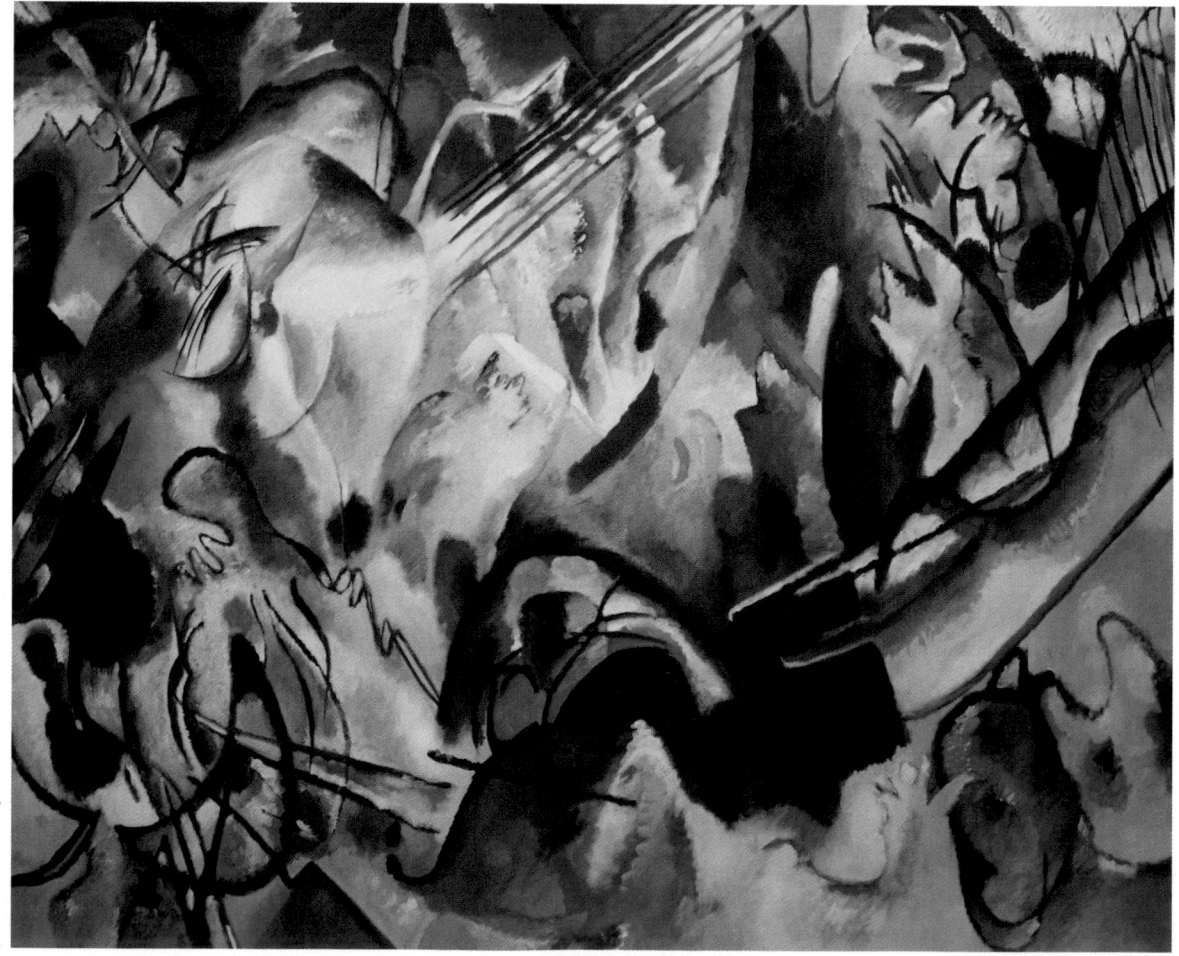

◄ **1.1 WASSILY KANDINSKY,** *Composition VI,* (1913). Oil on canvas, 76¾" × 118⅛". Hermitage Museum, St. Petersburg, Russia.

1 ft.

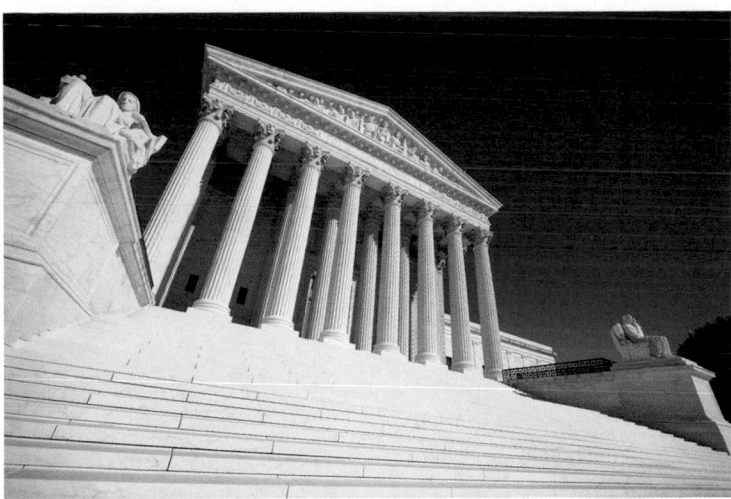

▲ 1.2 **United States Supreme Court Building,** Washington, D.C. (1935).

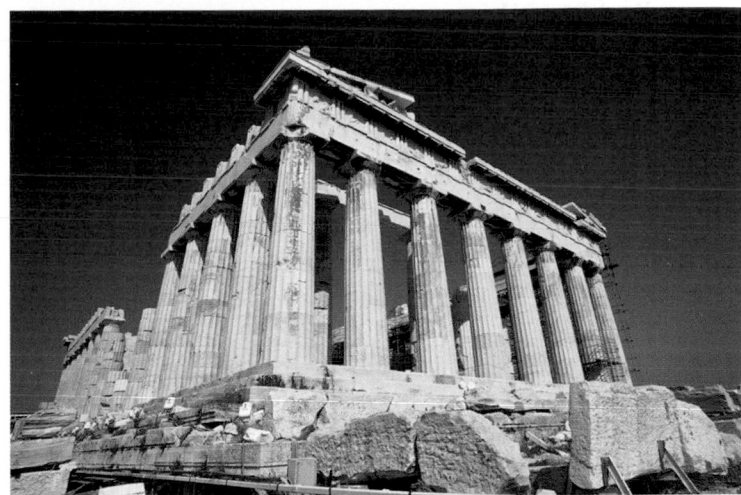

▲ 1.3 **ICTINOS AND CALLICRATES,** Parthenon, Athens, Greece (447–438 BCE).

CONTENT

A distinction is often made between subject and **content**. Whereas *subject* refers to the aspects of a work that can be described, *content* refers to a work's array of intangible aspects: the emotional, intellectual, psychological, symbolic elements. Content implies subject matter, but is a much bigger concept. Content comes close to being the *why* of a work of art in that it includes what we might consider the reasons behind its appearance: the idea, the cultural and artistic contexts, and the meaning behind the symbolism.

Symbolism is often a key component of a work's content, even if is unapparent or indecipherable to a viewer. The study of symbols is called *iconography*, literally the "writing of images." Symbols convey ideas, beliefs, messages, or the ideology underlying works of arts; investigating their significance enriches our understanding of the meaning and purpose of the work.

It may be obvious to us that paintings can be rich in content, but architecture, at first glance, may not seem the most obvious place to find content. Yet architecture informs us not only of the materials and technical means commonly used during certain periods in history; it can also embody the ideas, beliefs, and aspirations of an era. Architecture can have strong symbolic significance. It is easy to spot the influence of Greek and Roman architecture on buildings in the U.S. capital, Washington, D.C.—pristine white marble, columns, pediments, rotundas. But there is a reason why the architects responsible for designs for the United States Capitol Building and the United States Supreme Court building and others chose to emulate the architecture of ancient Greece and Rome in the capital of the New Republic (Figs. 1.2 and 1.3). It was to symbolize a connection to history's greatest contributions to civilization: democracy, the rule of law, duty to country and fellow citizen.

Contemporary architect Daniel Libeskind has said that, in the design of his buildings, he wants to

> communicate the vastness and also the legacy of things that are not completely visible. Contrary to public opinion the flesh of architecture is not cladding, insulation and structure, but the substance of the individual in society and history; a figuration of the inorganic, the body and the soul.

In other words, according to Libeskind, the "flesh of architecture" is not the form; it is the content. His extension of the Berlin Museum, dedicated to Jewish art and life and the memory of the Holocaust, is designed around the concept of a void (Fig. 1.4). A zigzag building—reminiscent in shape of a lightning bolt—was

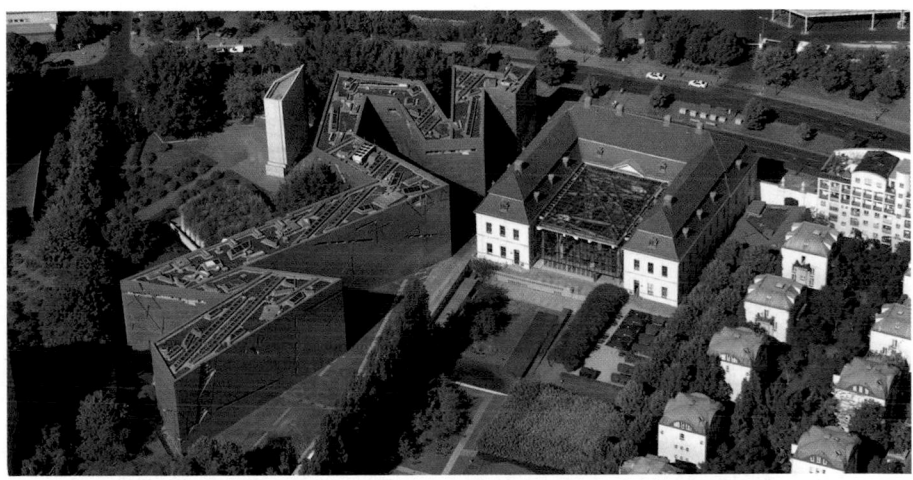

▲ 1.4 **DANIEL LIBESKIND, Extension of the Berlin Museum,** Berlin, Germany (1989–1996).

derived mathematically by plotting the home addresses of Jewish writers, artists, and composers who had lived in Berlin neighborhoods before World War II but were killed during the Nazi Holocaust. The building's jagged shape reads as a "bolt out of the blue"—a catastrophic event that could not have been anticipated. It also reads as a painful rift in the continuity of the neighborhood in which it stands; it is punctuated by voids that symbolize the absence of Jewish people and culture in Berlin. The visitor to the museum is immediately struck by the overwhelming evidence that everything at which one is looking—every structural, design, and symbolic element—has been informed by the historic circumstances that necessitated Libeskind's building. To learn more about the *whys* behind works of art, see the **Visual Glossary: Themes & Purposes of Art**.

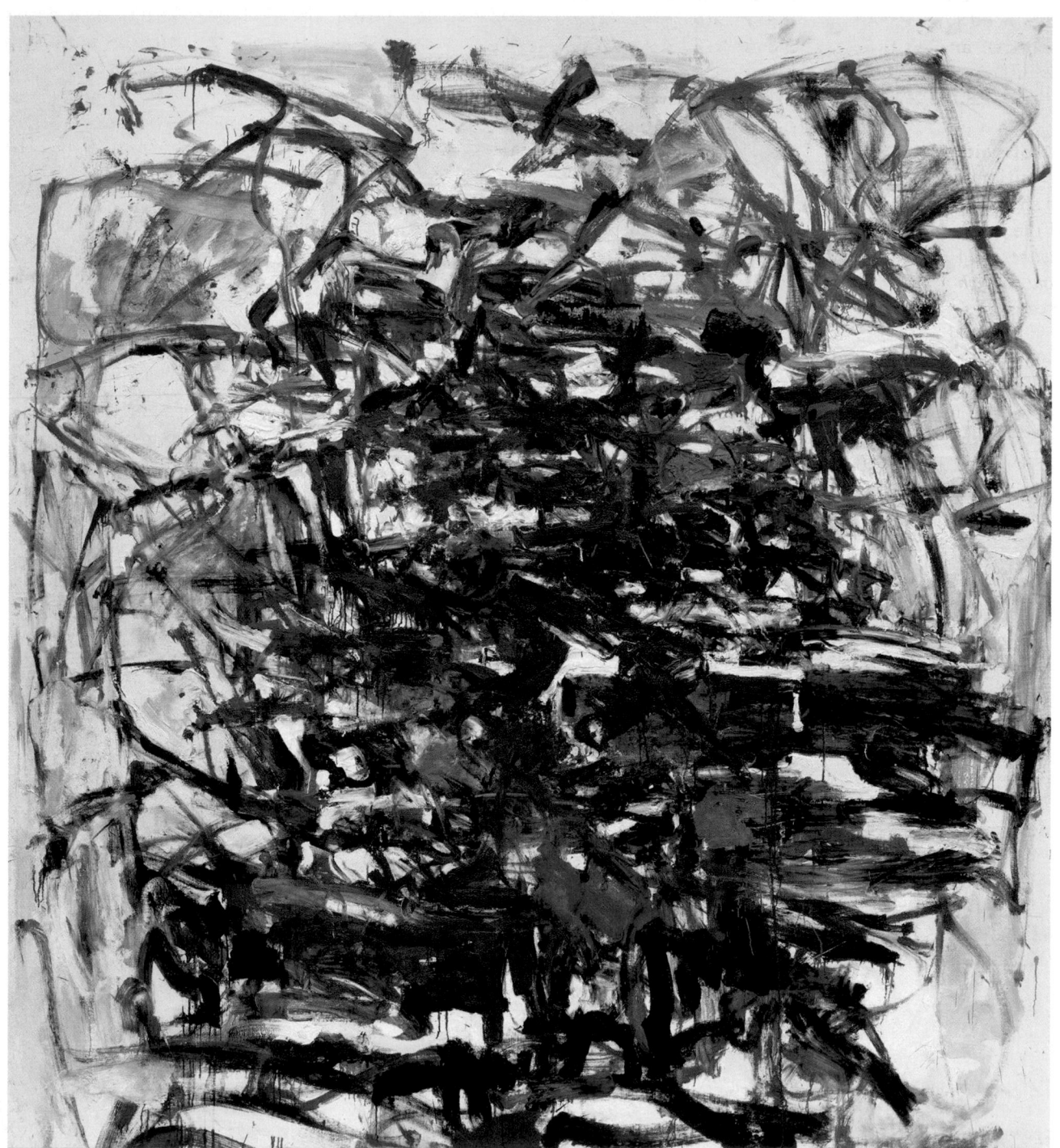

1 ft.

ᴧ 1.5 **JOAN MITCHELL**, *Cercando un Ago* (1957). Oil on canvas, 95" × 88⅛". Collection of the Joan Mitchell Foundation, New York.

FORM

In the context of art and design, the word **form** has more than one meaning. Form refers to the totality of a composition or design—the arrangement or organization of all of its visual elements. Form gives substance to a subject or an idea; think of it as the all-encompassing framework of artistic expression. It signifies the totality of technical means and materials employed by the artist, as well as all of the visual strategies and pictorial devices used to express and communicate. It is, simply, the work of art as a whole. The word *form* is also used to discuss three-dimensional shapes (spheres, cylinders, cubes, pyramids, for example) or works of art (such as sculpture or architecture). It also is used to describe areas of void space in sculptural works that serve as compositional counterpoints to solid shapes.

If the subject of a work of art is the *what,* the form is the sum total of *how* the *what* is presented. The appearance of a work of art derives from the artist's manipulation of the elements of art, principles of design, and the medium. When we consider the form of a work, we are asking ourselves how it all fits together—how color and shape are related, how the position of objects or figures reinforces the compositional structure, how brushwork is used to render meticulous detail, or perhaps how brushwork seems to exist for its own sake—free from the task of description, as in many modern and contemporary paintings.

Let's return to the beginning of this section: If subject matter is the *what* of a work of art, form is the *how*. Now let's return to Jackson Pollock. For him, as for many artists—including Joan Mitchell—producing nonobjective work, the *how* IS the *what*. That is, the materials and process may be described as the subject of the work (Fig. 1.5).

ICONOGRAPHY

Iconography, as noted, is the study of themes and symbols—figures and images that, when deciphered, reveal the underlying meaning of a work of art. Bronzino's sixteenth-century masterpiece, *An Allegory with Venus and Cupid* (Fig. 1.6) in the collection of the National Gallery in London, is a fascinating example of a work in which there must be much more than meets the eye, but whose iconographic puzzle is yet to be solved. When Bronzino conceived the painting for King Francis I of France, he clearly intended to weave an intricate allegory with many actors and many symbols.

Venus, fondled by her son, Cupid, is exposed by the gray-bearded Father Time, whose muscular arm draws back a purple drape to reveal the couple's incestuous behavior. We recognize them by their symbolic attributes, or things that they hold or have around them. Venus cups a golden apple in one hand and an arrow from the winged Cupid's quiver in the other; Time has

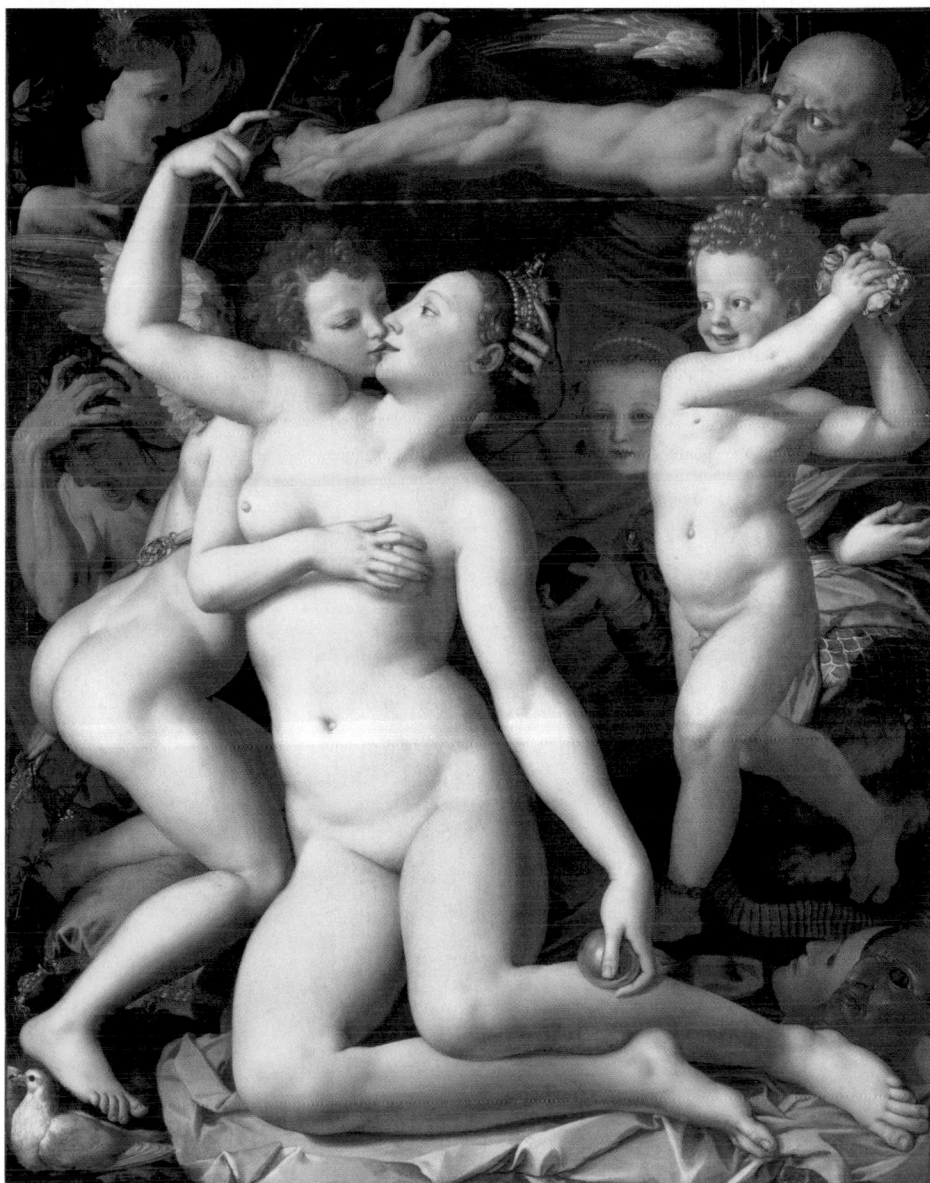

▲ 1.6 **BRONZINO,** *Venus, Cupid, Folly and Time* (c. 1546). Oil on wood, 61" × 56¾". National Gallery, London, England.

THEORY & PRACTICE

Giving Form to Experience: A Visual Meditation on Cows

DRAWN TO THE PURITY and precision of geometric shapes and committed to the synthesis of art, architecture, and design, Theo van Doesburg (1883–1931) played a principal role in the dissemination of the style and theories of the Dutch group known as De Stijl. De Stijl, meaning "the style," is also commonly referred to as Neo-Plasticism after van Doesburg's 1919 treatise on the De Stijl movement titled "Principles of Neo-Plastic Art."

Van Doesburg observed that even in works of art with subjects that seem to mimic the visible world, an artist may "neglect the laws of nature in favor of those of artistic creation" and use "natural

Drawing A is naturalistic; it represents the actual appearance of a cow.

Drawing C is characterized by the dominant contrast of black and white shapes.

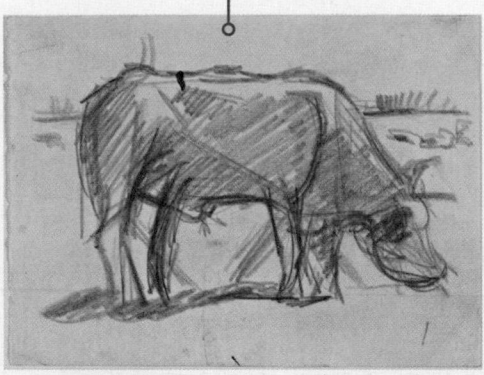

1.7A *Study for Composition VIII (The Cow)* (1917). Pencil on paper, 4⅝" × 6¼".

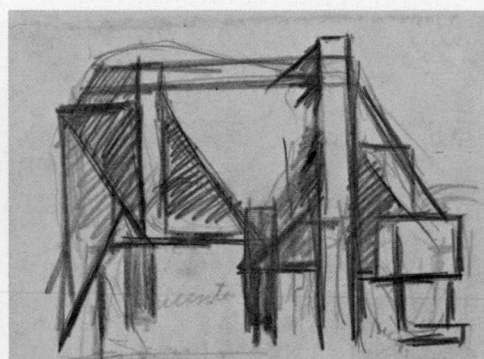

1.7B *Study for Composition VIII (The Cow)* (1917). Pencil on paper, 4⅝" × 6¼".

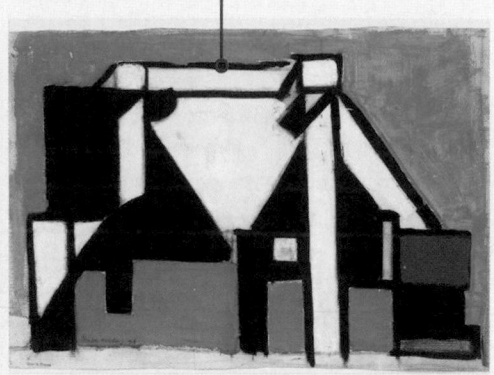

1.7C *Study for Composition VIII (The Cow)* (c. 1917). Tempera, oil, and charcoal on paper, 15⅝" × 22¾".

Drawing D depicts color and form in their purest state, creating a harmonious whole.

1 ft.

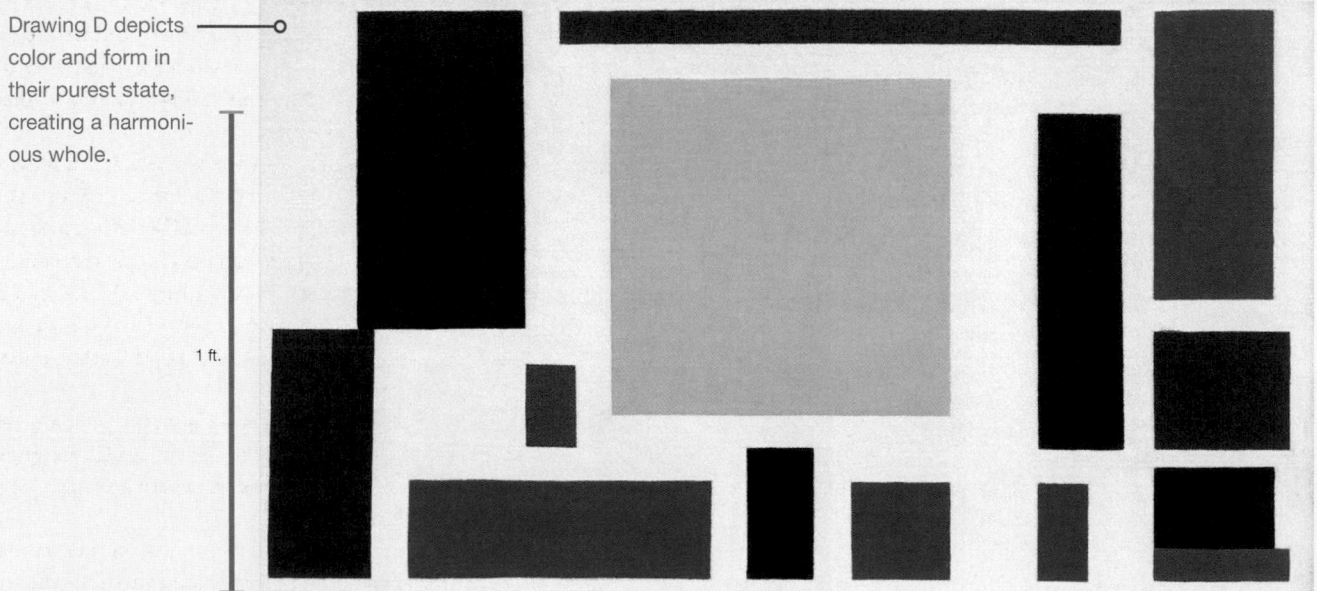

1.7D THEO VAN DOESBURG, *Composition VIII (The Cow)* (1917). Oil on canvas, 14¾" × 25". The Museum of Modern Art, New York, New York.

forms only as a means of attaining [an] artistic aim"—a harmonious whole. In other words, conventional works of art purported to be naturalistic do not truly represent the visible reality of the natural world but, rather, are constructed to correspond to the artist's idea of an aesthetic composition.

From van Doesburg's perspective, "The visual artist can leave the repetition of stories, fairy-tales, etc., to poets and writers." Artists should aim, instead, "to give form to [their] aesthetic experience of reality, or one might also say, [the] creative experience of the fundamental essence of things." How would this "fundamental essence" be given form through artistic means? Van Doesburg said,

> The only way in which visual art can be developed and deployed is by revaluing and purifying the formative means. Arms, legs, trees, and landscapes are not unequivocally painterly means. Painterly means are: colors, forms, lines, and planes.

Figure 1.7 shows the artist's series of four drawings together called *Study for Composition (The Cow)*. The style of drawing A would be described as naturalistic. That is, the artist's aim was to represent the appearance of a cow in nature. In drawing B, van Doesburg did not approach his subject "purely from the point of view of natural objective legibility." Rather, his aesthetic purpose superseded his concern for natural forms. Drawing C offers an interesting illustration of the principle that an artist should aim to "give form to his [or her] aesthetic experience of reality"—in this case, the dominant contrast of black and white shapes (aestheticized form) that signifies the breed (reality). Drawing D represents the culmination of the abstraction process and full realization of the principle of color and form in their purest state combining to create a harmonious whole.

< 1.7 THEO VAN DOESBURG, Studies for *The Cow* (1917).

Charles Harrison and Paul J. Wood, eds., *Art in Theory 1900–2000* (Malden, MA: Blackwell, 2003), p. 282.

CONNECTIONS Make a short list of attributes that you would include in a portrait of yourself. Do you think that these would more fully represent who you are than would your facial features alone? How important would it be to you that a viewer be able to interpret these symbols?

an hourglass on his shoulder. Although these figures take center stage with their prominent placement and rosy-white flesh, the painting is packed with many more objects (a dove, a cluster of rose petals, theatrical masks) and characters whose features and actions invite speculation even as they defy conclusive interpretation. Can we enjoy the painting without being able to interpret the symbolism? Of course. But attempting to unlock it may lead to a deeper understanding and appreciation of the work.

The subject, form, and content of works of art become evident through the artist's use of the elements of art, design principles, mediums, techniques, and style. These are the basic ingredients, or components, of art.

VISUAL ELEMENTS AND PRINCIPLES OF DESIGN

Line, shape, value, color, texture, space, and time and motion are the **visual elements** of art.

- *Line* is a basic—and perhaps the most essential—element of art. Line is the shortest distance between two points and is the thing created by the connection of these points. Line can also be perceived when many points are placed in proximity and adjacent to one another; it also can be implied in the space between two points even if they are not literally connected.
- *Shape*, in a two-dimensional work of art, is a flat area created when two ends of a line are connected and an area is enclosed. Shape can also describe an area of a composition that is created by other shapes surrounding it. Shapes are often made more distinguishable by adding color, pattern, or texture. In much three-dimensional art, such as sculpture or architecture, *shape* is the fundamental visual component.
- *Value* describes the relative lightness or darkness of an image. In terms of how an artist would use pigment, value refers to the broad and nuanced spectrum of grays between black and white.
- *Color* is the most complex element of art to define. Scientifically speaking, color is the thing that the human eye and brain perceive that is associated with descriptive words like *red,* or *blue,* or *yellow*. In the visual arts, *color theory* is a body of knowledge for artists that describes and categorizes color, its properties, behavior, and effects.

PUTTING IT ALL TOGETHER

The Visual Elements: *The Arnolfini Portrait*

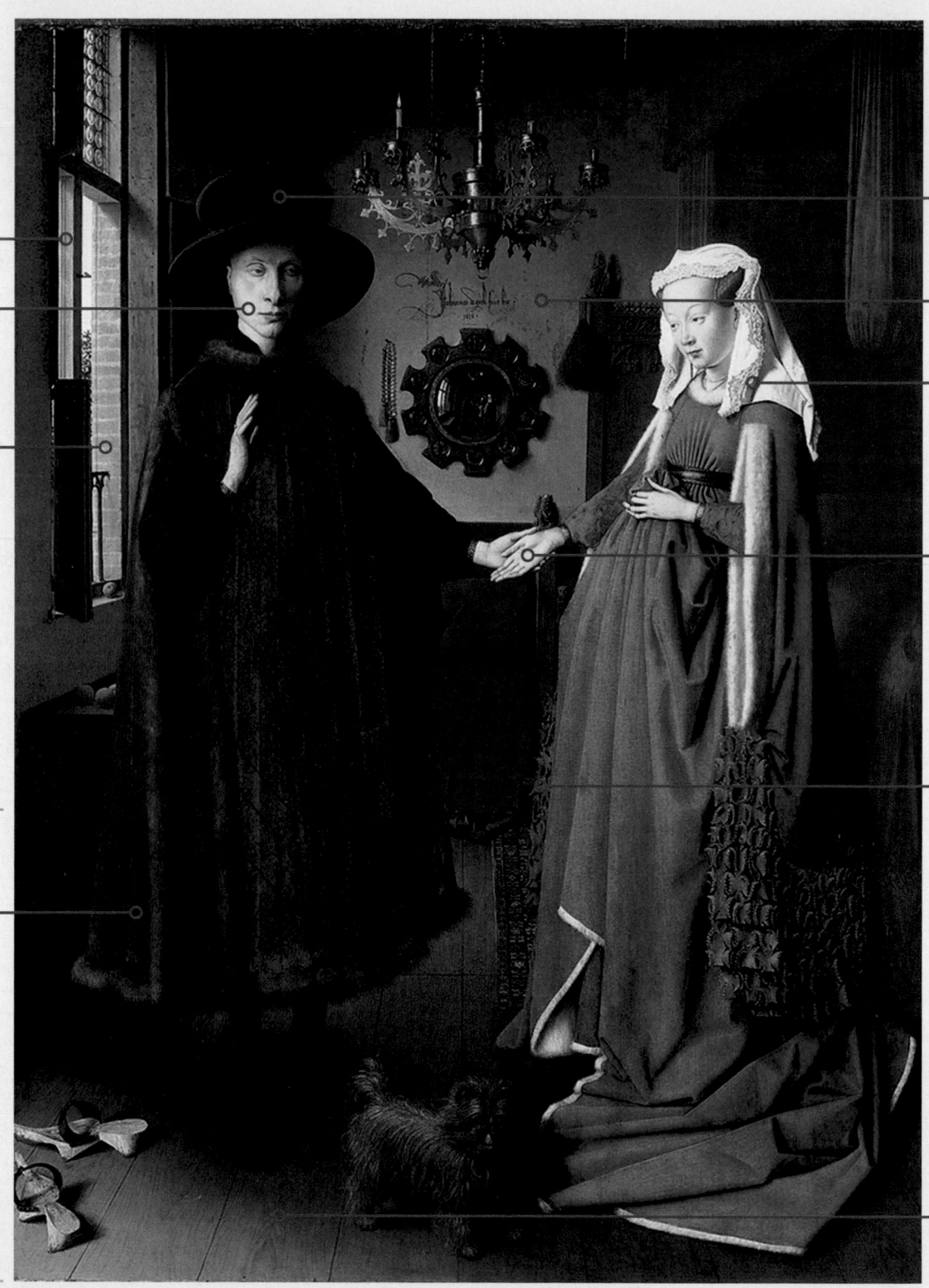

Line: Intersections of vertical and horizontal lines provide a basic structure to the composition. Juxtapositions of straight, jagged, and curving lines create visual interest.

Style: Describing objects as the eye would (theoretically) see them in reality is called *realism*.

Value: The painting shows differences in darkness and light—in value. Light coming through the window illuminates the faces of the couple but, away from direct light, Arnolfini's legs are in shadow. Van Eyck adds white to create luminosity and black to suggest areas of relative darkness.

Texture: Contrasts in texture—fur, velvet, lace—are rendered in meticulous detail. You can touch them with your eyes.

1 ft.

▲ **1.8 JAN VAN EYCK,** *The Arnolfini Portrait* (1434). Oil on wood, 32" × 23½". National Gallery, London, England.

Shape: The shape of Arnolfini's hat is distinct and memorable.

Space: The space or area of the room is so convincingly portrayed that it seems easily measurable.

Technique: Detail is rendered meticulously using very fine brushes.

Time and motion: The figures appear motionless, but time is recorded in the soft glow of evening light and in the moment when the couple join hands.

Color: The vivid contrast of red and green—complementary colors on the color wheel—keeps the eye from resting on one area of the composition for too long.

The medium is oil on wood.

- *Texture* is the surface character of materials as experienced by the senses of touch and sight. Texture can be inherent in the materials that an artist chooses or can be created through the manipulation of surfaces. It can also be implied in a work of art through the illusionistic rendering of the physical aspects of material (for example, a meticulous rendering of smooth silk fabric or the rough bark of a tree).
- *Space* describes the area around or within the components of a work of art—what Frank Lloyd Wright called "the breath of art." In the visual arts we speak of open and closed space; shallow (two-dimensional) space; the actual (three-dimensional) space in which a piece exists; and the illusion of three-dimensional space on two-dimensional surfaces.
- *Time and motion* in art are connected: motion occurs over time and distance. Motion can be actual (components of a work of art actually change position) or implied (illusory).

Principles of design refer to the visual strategies that, along with the elements of art, are used to construct a work of art. They include unity and variety, emphasis and focal point, balance and rhythm, and scale and proportion.

- *Unity* is defined as a sense of oneness or cohesiveness. It has the effect of gathering the elements of a composition into a harmonious whole.
- *Variety* can be described as contrast and diversity. It is the counterpoint of unity. Juxtaposing various or contradictory elements in a composition adds interest, spontaneity, and the element of surprise.
- *Emphasis* in a composition describes an attention-grabbing aspect that directs the viewer's eye to a particular area, giving it visual or conceptual dominance.
- *Focal point* describes the main point of interest in a work of art—one that captures and holds a viewer's attention.
- *Balance* is the distribution of weight—actual or visual—in a work of art. It results in physical stability (as in a sculpture) or a sense of equilibrium among the visual units of a composition.
- *Rhythm* in art is the equivalent of a beat in music. It describes recurrent visual motifs (like patterns) and compositional accents, movement, and flow.
- *Scale* is defined as the size of something relative to the human dimensions of a viewer.
- *Proportion* is comparative size, that is, the size of elements or images within a work of art in relation to each other or to the whole.

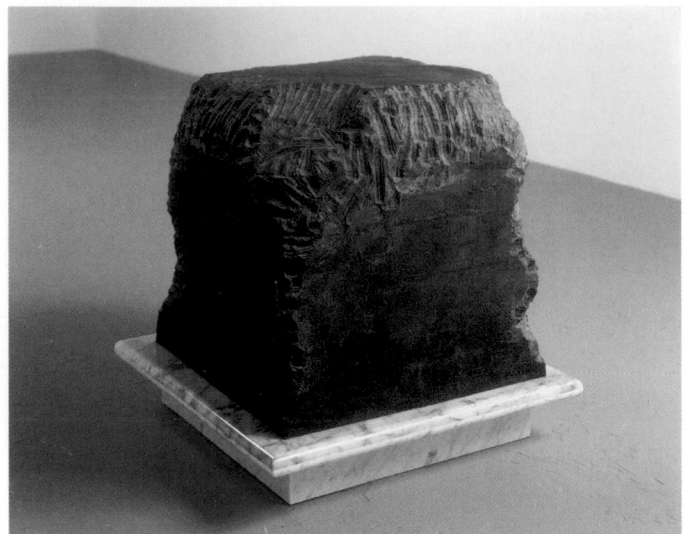

▲ 1.9 **JANINE ANTONI**, *Gnaw* (detail) (1992). Three-part art installation: 600 lb of chocolate gnawed by the artist; 600 lb of lard, gnawed by the artist; display with 130 lipsticks made with pigment, beeswax, and chewed lard removed from the lard cube, and 27 heart-shaped packages for chocolate removed from the chocolate cube. Each cube: 24" × 24" × 24"; overall dimensions variable. The Museum of Modern Art, New York, New York.

CONNECTIONS Pop artist Andy Warhol asked, "How can you say one style [of art] is better than another?" Do you think he had a point?

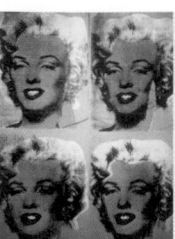

➤ Warhol's *Four Marilyns* (Fig. 9.15)

MEDIUMS AND TECHNIQUES

The materials and tools that artists use to create a work of art comprise its **medium**. Conventional mediums—or media, both plural—include oil paint on canvas, charcoal on paper, marble or bronze, and gelatin prints, to name a few. But any physical substance can be used as a medium—and often is—in modern and contemporary art; from scraps of newsprint and other found objects to human hair and body fluids, anything—including chocolate—is fair game (Fig. 1.9).

Artistic *techniques* are methods—the specific ways in which mediums are handled, controlled, and applied. Technique also implies skill or facility with tools of the trade that enable an artist to achieve a desired effect.

STYLE

Style is the distinctive mode of expression that results from the way in which an artist handles materials and the elements and principles of art and design. It is the "signature look" of an artist's work—that something that enables us to differentiate between a Rubens and a Rembrandt, a Picasso and a Pollock. Style can be consistent with some artists over the length of their careers, or it can mark one, specific direction or phase of an artist's creative output. "How can you say one style is better than another?" asked Pop artist Andy Warhol. "You ought to be able to be an Abstract-Expressionist next week, or a Pop artist, or a realist, without feeling you've given up something." Style more generally refers to distinctive characteristics of art and architecture that are common to a culture, era, or to a group of artists working at the same time or toward a common artistic goal. Pierre Auguste Renoir's paintings are recognizable, for example, by the pastel-color palette and the feathery brushstrokes that the artist typically used (Fig. 1.10) as a French Impressionist artist working in the nineteenth century.

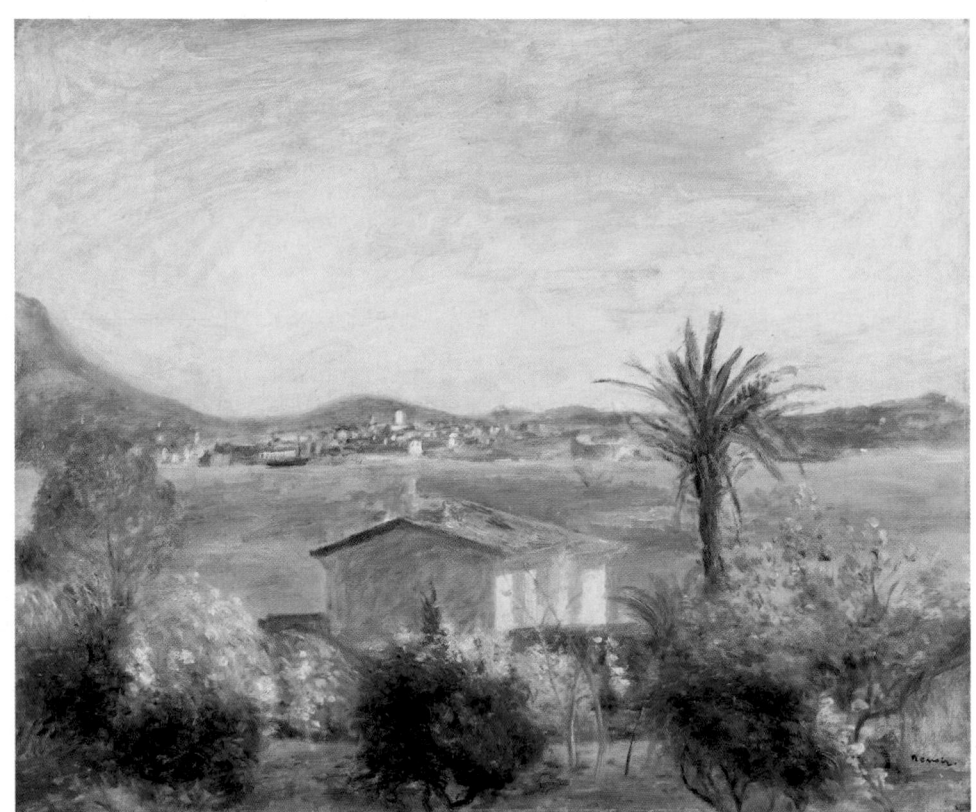

1 ft.

▲ 1.10 **PIERRE AUGUSTE RENOIR**, *Tamaris, France* (1885). Oil on canvas, 18" × 21⅝". Private collection.

PUTTING IT ALL TOGETHER

Principles of Design: *Marilyn (Vanitas)*

Rhythm: The repetitive use of similar shapes creates connections and rhythmic relationships throughout the painting.

Technique: The highly illusionistic technique is known as *trompe l'oeil*, meaning "trick the eye."

Unity and variety: Unity is achieved despite the emphasis on variety. Even though the objects are many and have different shapes, textures, and colors, they are thematically connected: they symbolize the transient nature of human existence and the meaninglessness of material objects. This theme is known as **vanitas**—related to the word *vanity*—and is one of a series of vanitas paintings by Flack.

Emphasis and focal point: Painters have conventionally placed the focal point of a composition in the center; that is where the eye naturally gravitates. Here an empty spot provides a backdrop for the only "active" image in the painting: a teardrop of red paint has just dripped off the tip of a brush that hovers like a magic wand.

Medium: The medium is oil paint over acrylic paint on canvas.

Style: Flack was a pioneer of the style called **Photorealism**.

Balance: Balance, or equilibrium, among the visual units is distributed so that the eye will move rather than fix on one object, cluster, or area. This is particularly evident in the black and white photo of Marilyn Monroe and its reflection in the oval, gilded mirror.

Symbolism: The hourglass, pocket watch, and calendar page symbolize the passage of time. Overripe and dried-out fruit pieces, a rose past its prime, and a half-burned candle signify the fleeting nature of beauty and the brevity of life.

Scale and proportion: Scale is conveyed through size relationships among the components of the still life object.

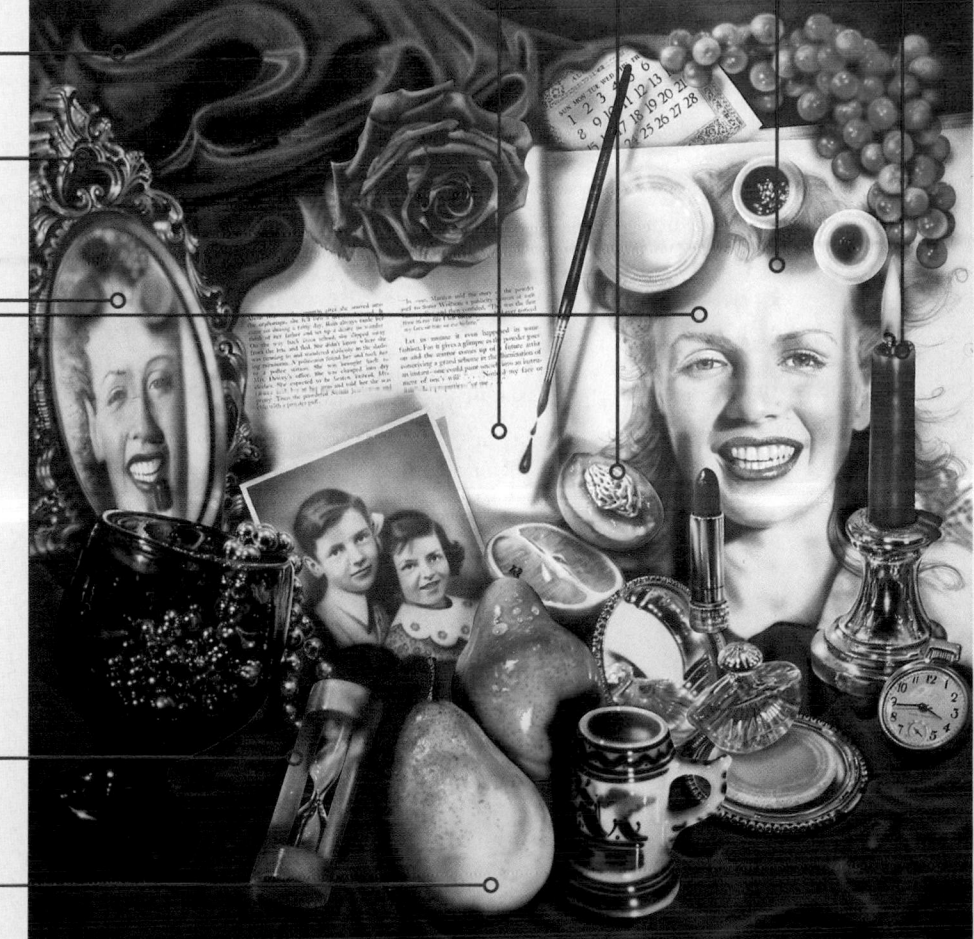

1 ft.

ʌ **1.11 AUDREY FLACK,** *Marilyn (Vanitas)* (1977). Oil over acrylic on canvas, 96" × 96". University of Arizona Museum, Tucson, Arizona.

COMPARE & CONTRAST

A Style by Any Other Name . . . Appropriation and Subversion in Contemporary Art

IN THE LATE 1940S, Jackson Pollock began painting compositions in which the "subject" consisted of the process of painting itself. Pollock rolled out a canvas on his studio floor. Spilling, dripping, flinging, and squirting enamels (Pollock sometimes used a turkey baster) onto the canvas culminated in radically different imagery that made no reference to the visible world; we call this *nonobjective* art (**Fig. 1.12**). With no single focal point, lines ebb and flow and weave in and out of the shallow pictorial space; rhythmic patterns begin to emerge as the eye traverses the expanse of canvas. To search for allusions to nature or anything else would be quite beside the point. What Pollock has given us is tangible evidence of the artist's outward gesture, carrying with it his inner self.

There is more than a first-glance resemblance between the Pollock painting, *Number 19, 1948* and *Joseph Stalin Gazing Enigmatically at the Body of VI Lenin as It Lies in State in Moscow in the Style of Jackson Pollock* (**Fig. 1.13**). Painted by Art & Language (collaborative artists Michael Baldwin and Mel Ramsden), the title of the work compels the viewer to engage in a mad search for imagery—something that would be a preposterous and pointless exercise in looking at a Pollock work. Our instinct to make sense out of things or events that seem senseless, or to try to find something recognizable in a sea of unrecognizable imagery, overtakes us. For those of us who know what Joseph Stalin looked like, the title prods us to search for his distinctive mustached face. If not, the best we can do is to try to make out a man's face somewhere amid the chaos. Oddly enough, the pressure to seek-and-find forces our eyes to follow the streaks and spills and drips in the same way that Pollock intended to have the viewer take in his nonobjective works—keeping the eye on the painted surface, what he called the optical field. (*Hint:* Stalin can be found in the upper-right quadrant of the painting, his forehead interrupted by the top of the canvas. Look for his moustache.)

After 1947, Pollock avoided giving his paintings titles that reflected or suggested something about the form or content of his work and, instead, began to simply number them. It was essential for Pollock that the viewer not be distracted from the surface of the work; for him, surface was prime. In what way is Pollock's intention subverted in the painting by Art & Language? How would you use vocabulary like *style* and *subject* and *content* to describe each of these works?

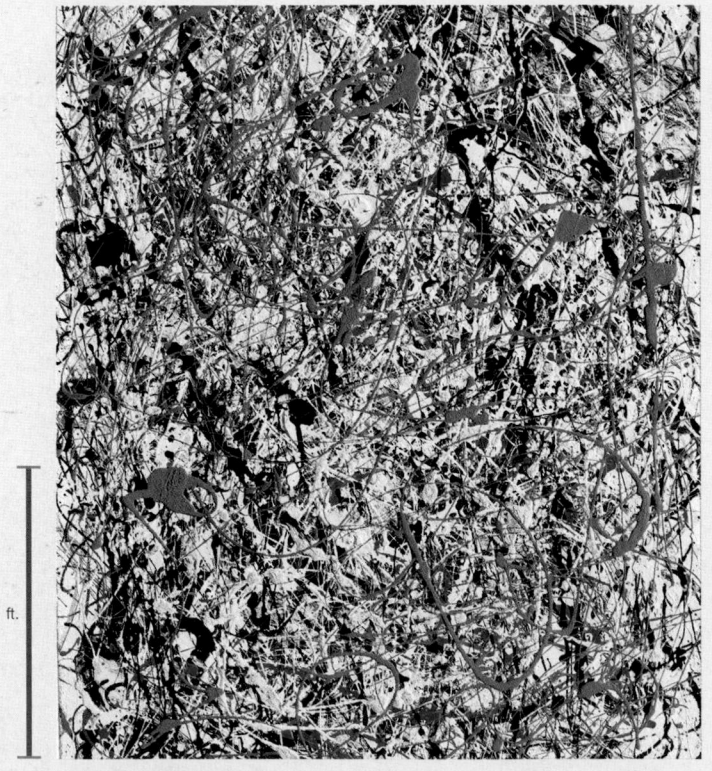

∧ **1.12 JACKSON POLLOCK,** *Number 19* (1948). Oil and enamel on paper mounted on canvas, 30¾" × 22⅝".

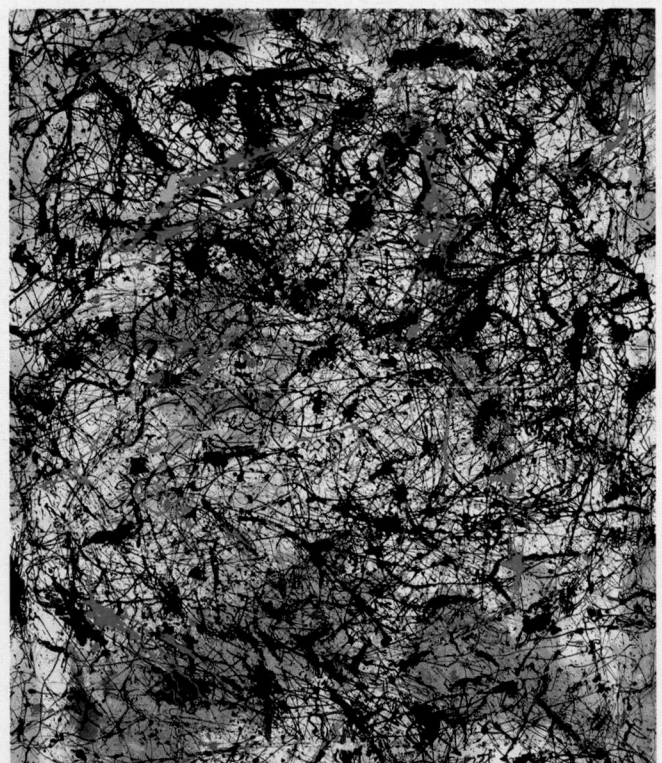

∧ **1.13 ART & LANGUAGE (MICHAEL BALDWIN AND MEL RAMSDEN),** *Joseph Stalin Gazing Enigmatically at the Body of V.I. Lenin as It Lies in State in Moscow in the Style of Jackson Pollock* (1979). Oil and enamel on board, 69¾" × 49¾". Lisson Gallery, London, England.

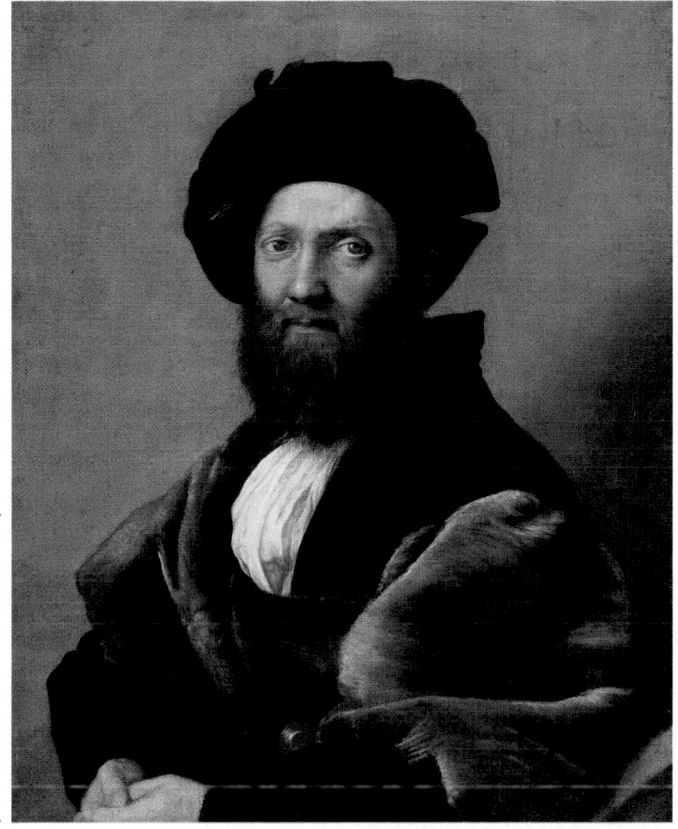

1 ft.

photography—shooting, capturing, and documenting by mechanical means—suggests impartiality, candid truth, and unadulterated reality. But, of course, photos can—and do—lie. Mediated and manipulated by the photographer, the conventional parameters of "truth" are challenged, rendering our own interpretations of what we deem to be reality invalid. Consider Andres Serrano's photographic portrait of *Johnny* (Fig. 1.15) from his *Nomads* series. As in Raphael's portrait, the sitter appears to have posed for the artist in a studio: both are placed before a neutral backdrop and are flatteringly lit in such a way as to emphasize their distinct facial features. Each wears clothing that seems to indicate something of their profession or station. Both have an air of dignity, of gravitas or solemnity.

We are likely to make assumptions about context and identity that, as it turns out, are faulty in the case of Serrano's photographic portrait. In fact, for his *Nomads* series, the artist and an assistant offered ten dollars each to homeless people in New York City—including Johnny—to pose for his camera on subway platforms in front of a portable backdrop. As critic Wendy Steiner noted, "In these photographs the physical reality of homeless people—their neglected bodies, their hunger, their displacement—is hidden behind a surface of costume."

One of the best ways to observe and articulate stylistic differences is to compare a group of works with a common genre or theme (such as those illustrated in Figs. 1.14 through 1.18). There are some basic connections among them, but there are clear differences as well: materials and techniques, implied narratives, and the diversity of artistic styles employed to represent the subject.

Realism

Realism refers to the replication—through artistic means—of people and things as they are seen by the eye or really thought to be, without idealization, without distortion. In his *Portrait of Baldassare Castiglione* (Fig. 1.14), rendered in a realist style, Raphael recreated the subtleties of human flesh along with the illusion of contrasting textures: soft fur, supple velvet, and the coarse hair of his sitter's beard.

Photographs are typically accepted as realistic representations of people and events; the very nature of

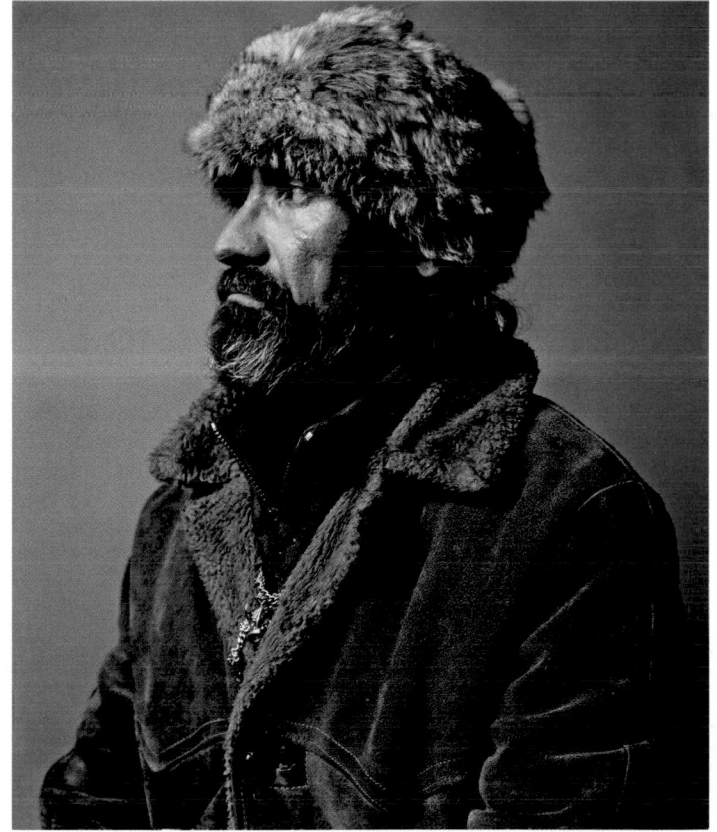

1 ft.

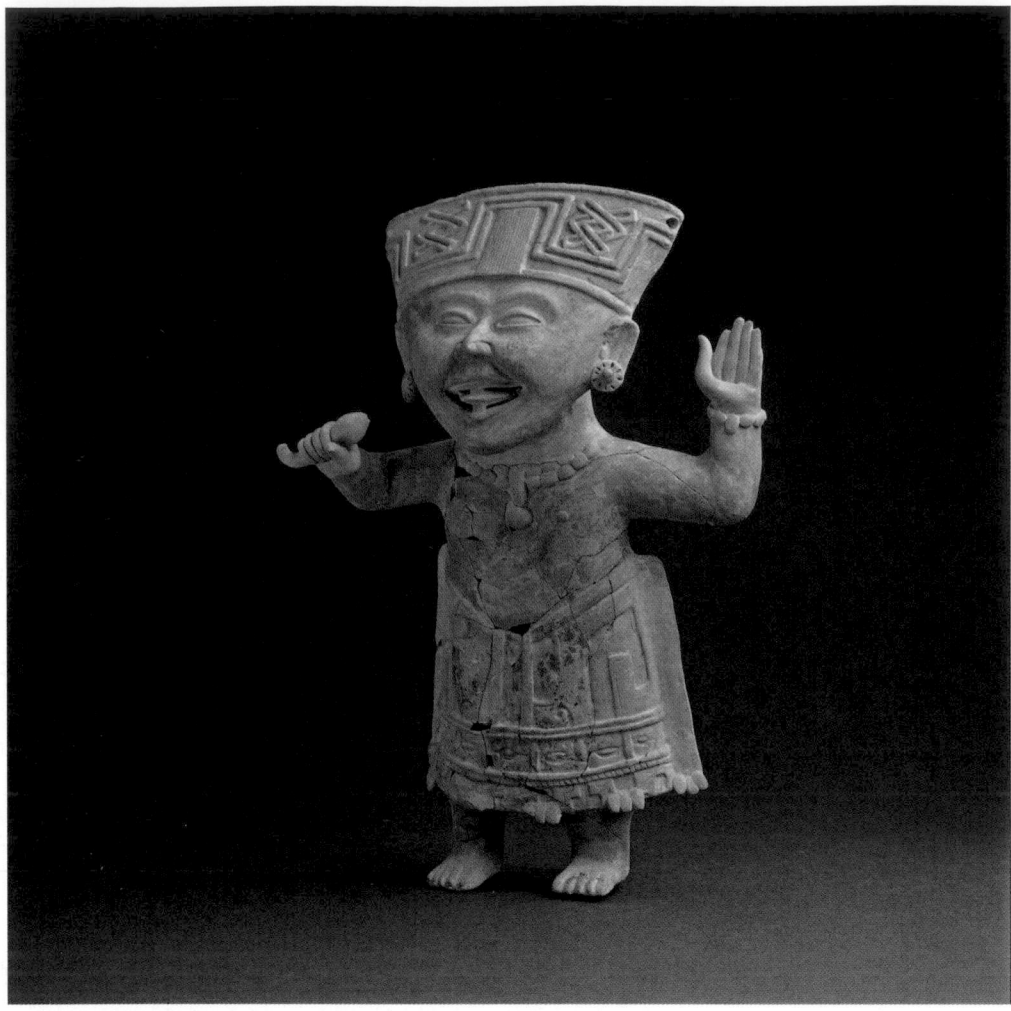

< 1.16 **Smiling figure, Mexico,** Remojadas (7th–8th century). Ceramic, 18⁷⁄₁₀" high. The Metropolitan Museum of Art, New York, New York.

REPRESENTATIONAL ART AND REALISTIC ART   We may confidently state that all art in a realist style is also representational although not vice versa. The term *representational* is used to describe forms in the natural world that most people would find recognizable even if the maker has not rendered the details with meticulous realism. The painted ceramic figure from Pre-Columbian Veracruz (Fig. 1.16) depicts a man with an elaborately decorated skirt and headdress. His features are simplified—from almond-shaped eyes and a broad, stylized smile to the almost abbreviated treatment of arms and legs. The artist's technique is not as detailed as it is, for example, in Raphael's portrait, but there is no doubt that anyone would recognize this figure as that of a man.

Expressionism

If realism can be defined as a style that is rooted in objective observation of the external world, *Expressionism* can be defined as a style that reflects a subjective, "inner world"—a style that conveys the psychological and emotional state of the artist. Distortion and exaggeration of form, color, brushwork, texture, and other elements are often used as a vehicle for expressing the sentiments of the artist and, importantly, to elicit comparable feelings or visceral responses in the viewer.

Henri Matisse's *Woman with a Hat* (Fig. 1.17) departs from reality in many ways; in other words, our eyes would not see a woman who looks like this in reality. Matisse rejected the subtle modeling of flesh—rendered through a nuanced palette and gradations of light and shade—that contribute to the realism of Raphael's portrait. He replaced them, instead, by thick, wild brushstrokes of vibrant color that do not pertain to visible reality but rather to an instinctive, spontaneous, subjective response to his subject.

Abstraction

Abstract art is usually defined as art that does not imitate or clearly represent visible reality. Abstraction is the opposite of realism, which aims to reproduce the world series abstracting of the shape of a cow by van Doesburg illustrates this process (see **Fig. 1.7**).

ABSTRACT ART AND NONOBJECTIVE ART Nonobjective art, often used a synonym for abstract art, does not begin with objects in the visible world. Rather, the artist creates compositions from the elements of art—line, shape, color, texture, and so on. The difference between abstract and nonobjective art is illustrated in the works by Kandinsky, Pollock, and Mitchell in this chapter.

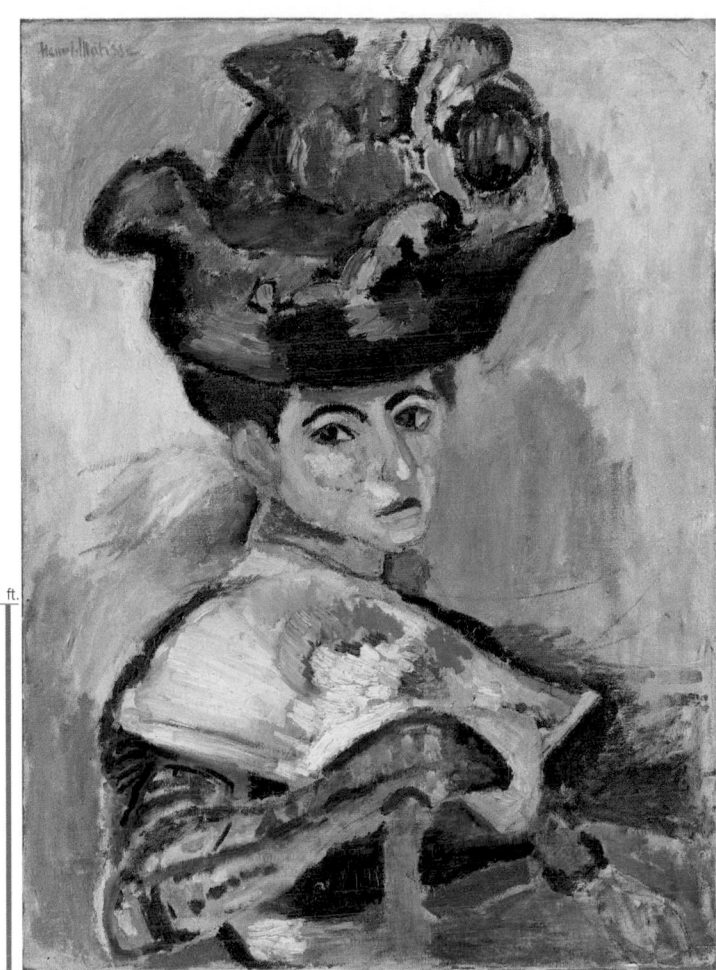

∧ 1.17 HENRI MATISSE, *Woman with a Hat* (1905). Oil on canvas, 31¼" × 23½". San Francisco Museum of Art, San Francisco, California.

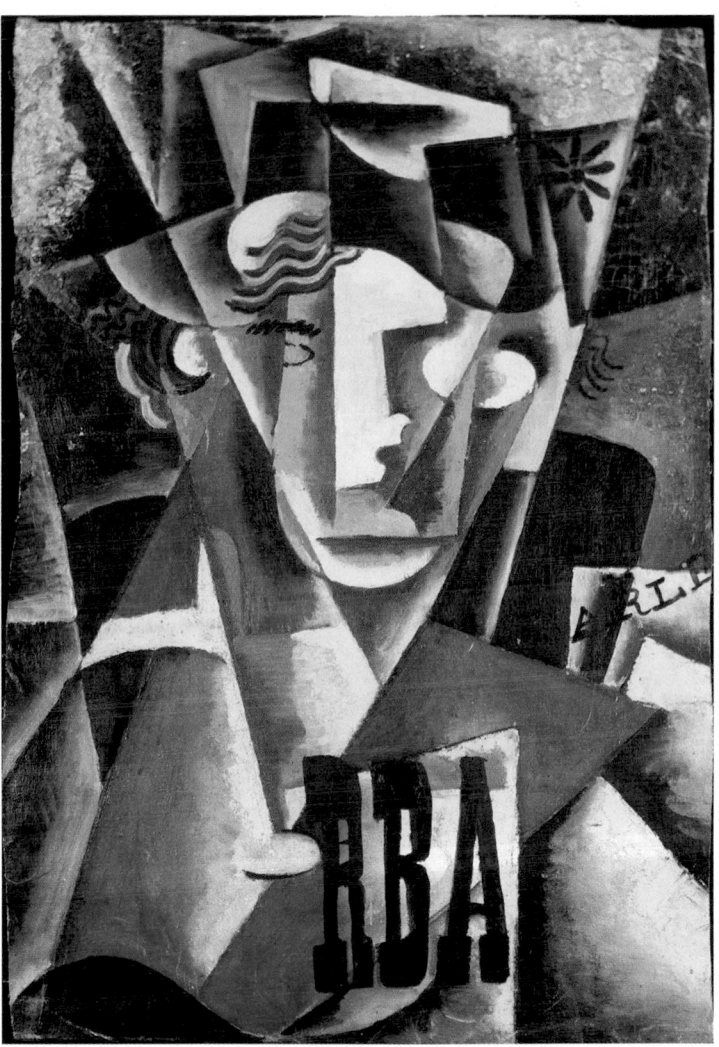

∧ 1.18 LIUBOV POPOVA, *Study for a Portrait* (1915). Private collection, Moscow, Russia.

as faithfully as possible. What abstract works of art have in common is a lack of readily distinguishable characteristics, but the level of abstraction can vary in degree. In some abstract works, the source—the object or objects that inspired them—remains visible or recognizable to some degree. This is often the way in a Cubist painting such as the *Study for a Portrait* (**Fig. 1.18**) by Liubov Popova, in which one can still make out the parts of the human figure even though they have been altered. The abstract artist often seeks to reduce objects to basic shapes and descriptive colors, focusing more on the elements and design than on the objects themselves. The

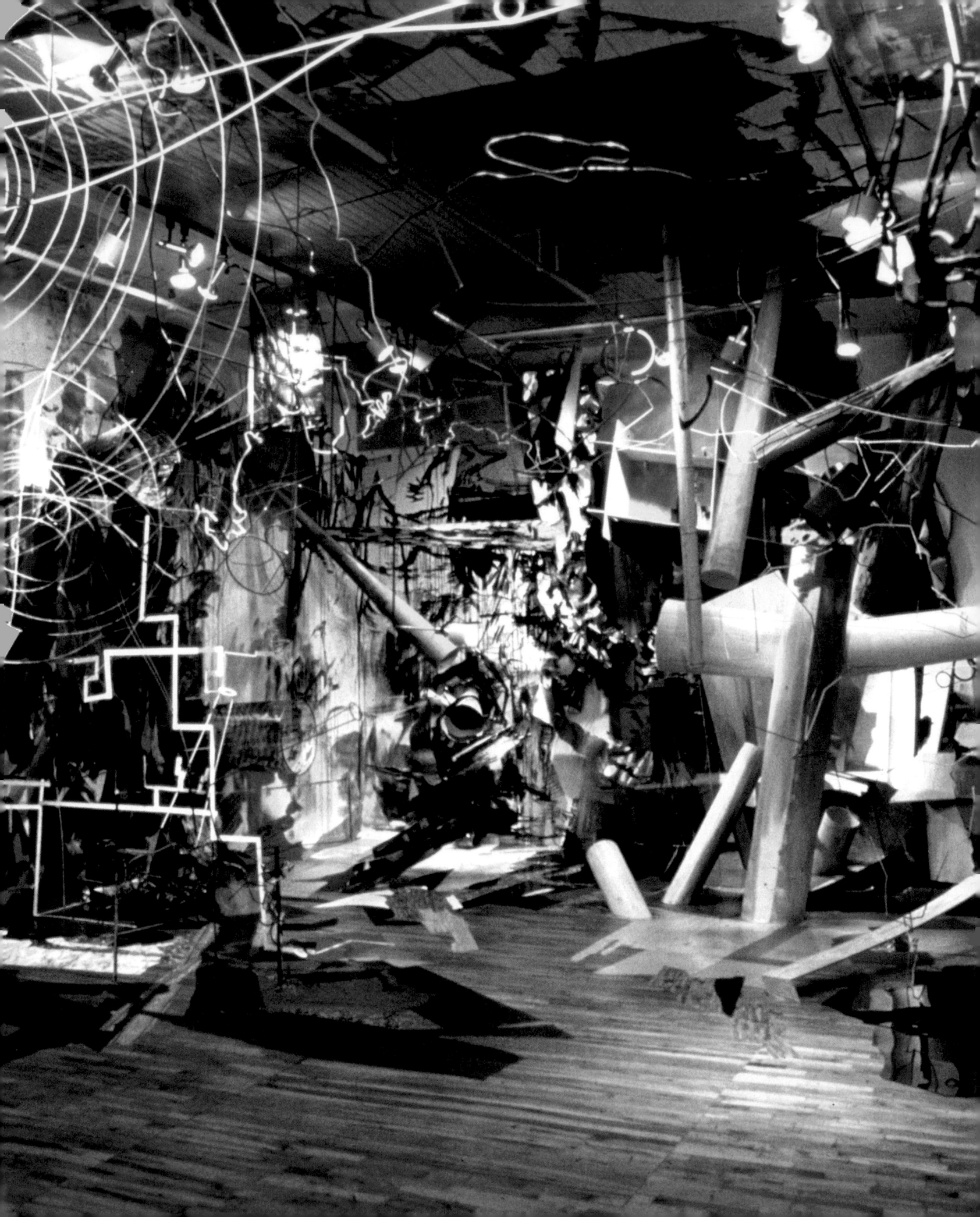

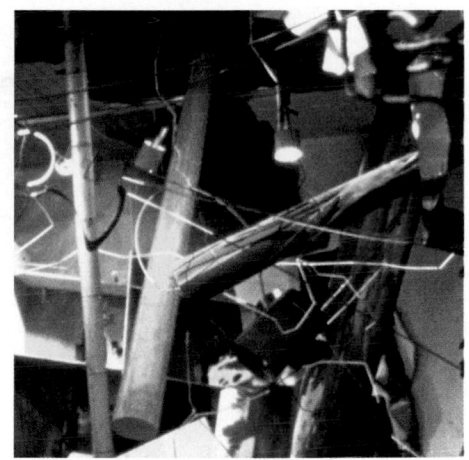

2

LINE AND SHAPE

Remember, a line cannot exist alone;
it always brings a companion along.
Do remember that one line does nothing;
it is only relation to another that it
creates a volume.

— HENRI MATISSE

CONSIDER THE pervasiveness of **line** in our lives, both literal and metaphorical. We get in line, go online, draw the line, read between the lines. We connect the dots or blur the lines between one thing and another. We can think linearly or nonlinearly. Line, by definition, is a finite concept—a mark positioned in relation to two fixed points. But the metaphorical life of a line seems endless.

The word, **shape**, is also full of associations, the source of countless idiomatic expressions. We hit the gym to stay "in shape." We feel overwhelmed by a term-paper assignment until our ideas begin to "take shape." We can get "bent out of shape" when something doesn't go according to our best-laid plans. These expressions suggest "definition," pulling or keeping something together within defined limits or boundaries that are distinct and desirable.

In its inherent simplicity and potential for complexity, line serves as the most fundamental element of art and design. It can be a means to an end or an end in itself, a tool of infinite variety and infinite suggestion. Shape is formed when line is used to demarcate and contain an area of a composition, creating boundaries that make that area (or shape) distinct from what surrounds it.

< JUDY PFAFF, *3D* (1983). Steel, perforated steel, plywood, wood veneers, Plexiglas, contact paper, tin, wire, paint.

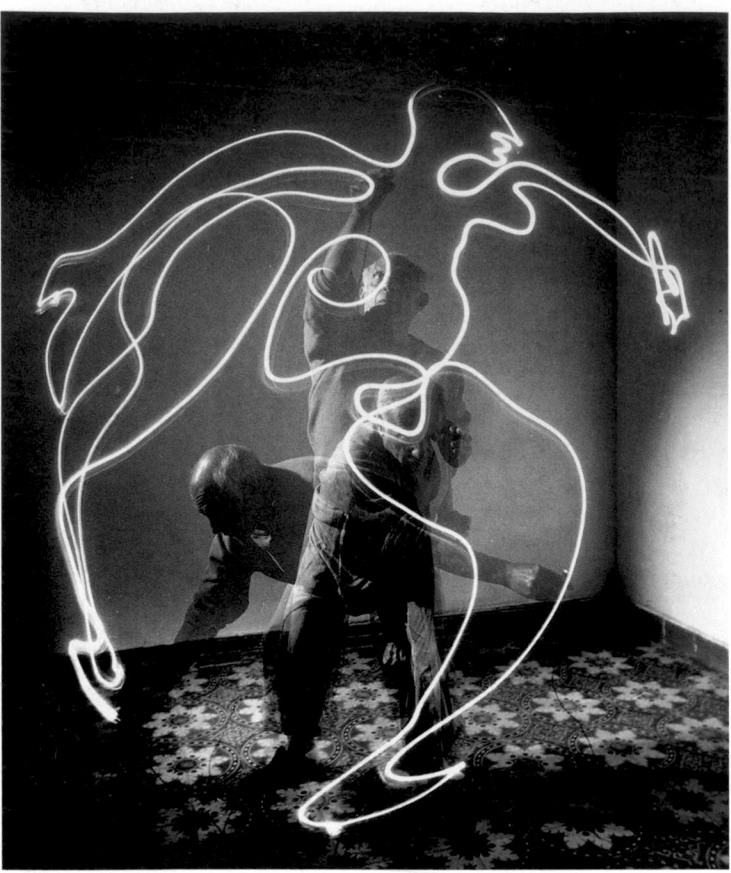

∧ 2.1 **GJON MILI**, *Picasso* (1949). Photograph.

LINE

In mathematics, a line is the path made by a moving point. Lines are created through the connection of points and are defined as the side-by-side placement of an infinite number of points. In art, a point (which has no measurable size) becomes a **dot** (which does). In an artist's theoretical vocabulary, a line is a moving dot.

Pablo Picasso turned theory into practice in what came to be known as his "light drawings" (Fig. 2.1). The photographer Gjon Mili captured the linear path of a point of light as Picasso "drew" lines in the three-dimensional space around him using a flashlight beam, delineating shapes of figures and flowers.

The Measure of Line

The measure of a line refers to its length and its width. If we conceptualize line as a moving dot, the dots that comprise it can be of any size (creating a line of lesser or greater width) and any number (creating a line of any length). Given enough width, line can play the role of shape, as in Kristin Baker's *Oculatei Der Boomen* (Fig. 2.2).

Some works of art seem to beg the exercise of measuring, such as Sylvia Plimack Mangold's *Three Exact Rules* (Fig. 2.3). Indeed the act of measuring is intrinsic to the work. By contrast, the very notion of measuring the lengths of line that comprise a Jackson Pollock painting (Fig. 1.8 in the previous chapter) or Matthew Ritchie's drawings and installations (Fig. 2.4) seems incomprehensible and beside the point.

Types and Qualities of Line

Types of line would seem to be as infinite as the number of dots that determine them. Lines can be straight or curved, vertical, horizontal, or diagonal. As a line continues, it can change direction abruptly, becoming a zigzag. Short, curved lines that form arcs can reverse direction, resulting in a wavy line. A curved line can curl around to join itself where it started and create a complete shape. Lines that move in circles and turn inward on themselves can create dizzying spirals.

The quality of line is related to its measure (for example, thick or thin) and its characteristics (smooth, jagged, continuous, broken). An artist may manipulate these characteristics to create the illusion of texture, among other things.

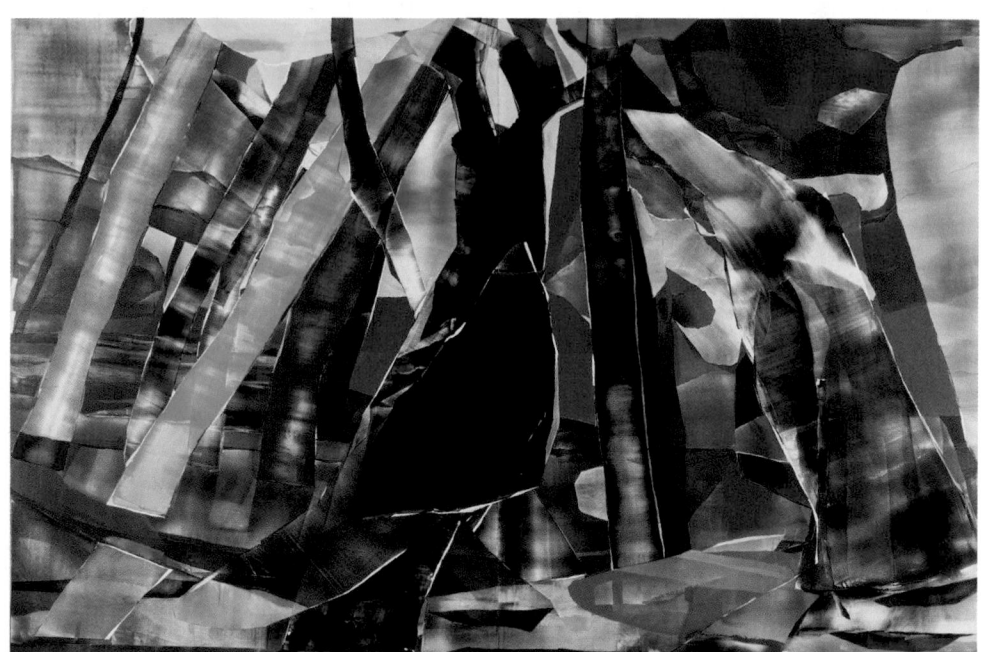

1 ft.

∧ 2.2 **KRISTIN BAKER**, *Oculatie Der Boomen* (2009). Acrylic on PVC, 2 panels, 108" × 80" (each panel).

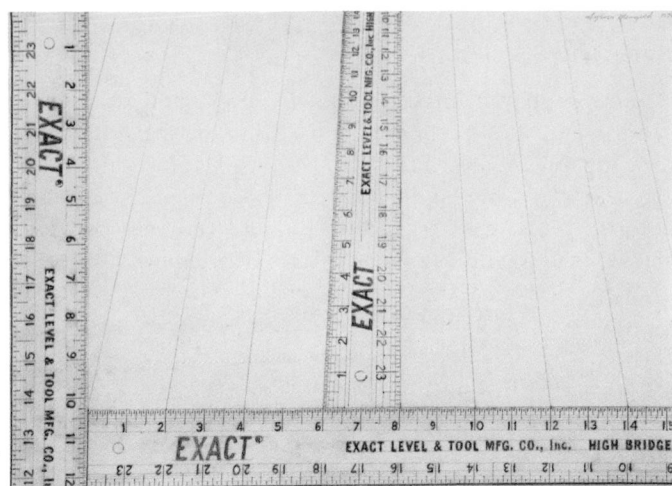

▲ 2.3 **SYLVIA PLIMACK MANGOLD,** *Three Exact Rules* (1976). Pencil on paper, 12 ½" × 17 ¼". Photo by Bill Orcutt, courtesy Alexander and Bonin Gallery, New York, New York.

1 in.

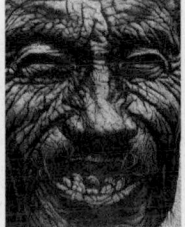

▲ Chen Xuhai's *Golden Autumn* (**Fig. 9.3**)

Even the simplest lines can suggest different moods and elicit different emotional responses. Lines may be perceived as calm or forceful, tentative or assertive, tender or brutal. The works by Mangold and Ritchie express very different things. In its mechanical, mathematical precision, Mangold's drawing conveys a certain intellectual detachment; the "human element" is deemphasized. In Ritchie's works (and Pollock's as well), the lines reflect a clear human presence—indeed a distinct energy and

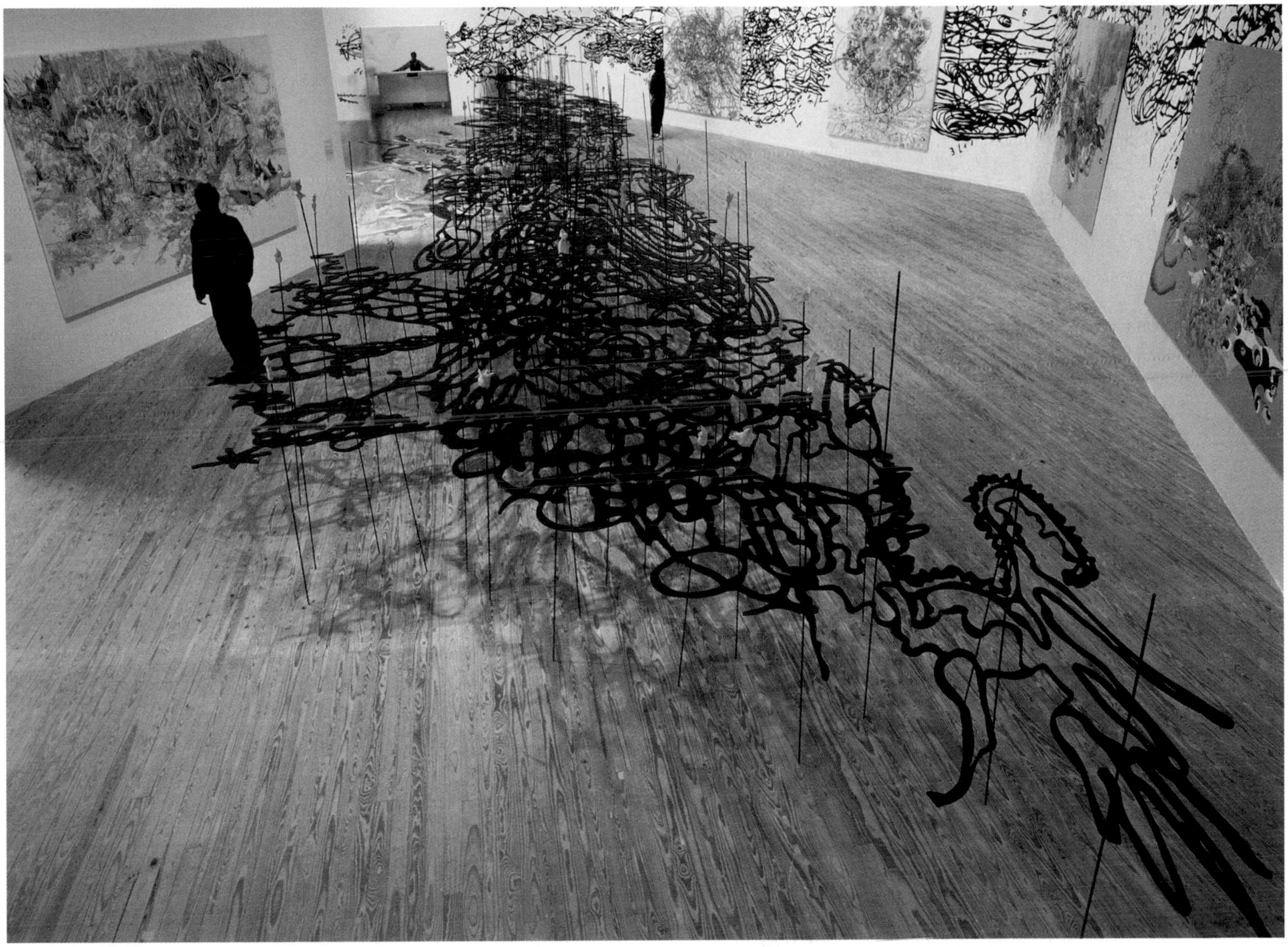

▲ 2.4 **MATTHEW RITCHIE,** *Proposition Player* (2003). Installation view. Contemporary Arts Museum, Houston, Texas, December 13, 2003–March 14, 2004. Andrea Rosen Gallery, New York, New York.

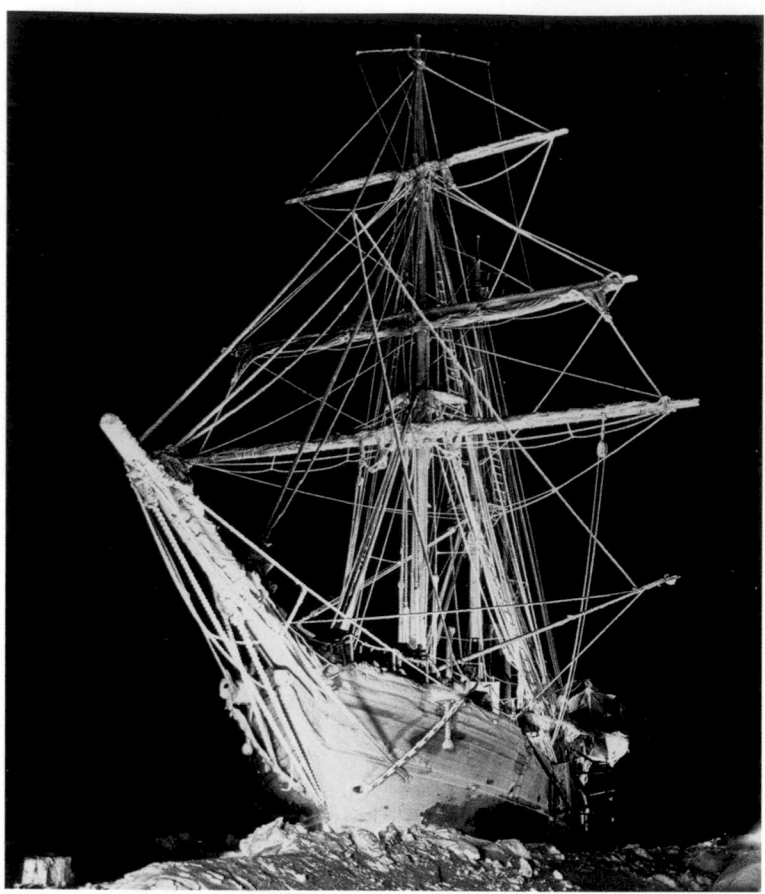

^ 2.5 FRANK HURLEY, *The* Endurance *by Night* (1915). Gelatin silver print.

personality. The dynamic movement of the linear elements brings us along on the artist's wild ride—pushing and pulling, guiding and tossing us about in an ever-changing visual arena.

Sometimes line is such a dominant aspect of an image that it carries its own symbolism. In Frank Hurley's photograph (Fig. 2.5) documenting the near-tragedy of an Antarctic exploration, a network of chalky lines—the ship's rigging—seems to ensnare the mast and fuse the vessel to its icy surroundings. The delicacy of the lines that crisscross against the unforgiving black of the sky signify the precarious position, the fragility of the *Endurance* as the ice of the sea rose up around it and stranded its crew. The character of the line evokes a certain, almost surrealistic narrative—the stuff of dreams rather than reality.

CONNECTIONS Make a short list of abstract ideas, such as peace, love, hate, loneliness, narrow-mindedness, fear, generosity, or anything else you can think of. Describe the type of line you think is most suited to the expression of each of the ideas. Compare your descriptions with those of your peers. How did your expression of ideas through line match or differ from their interpretations?

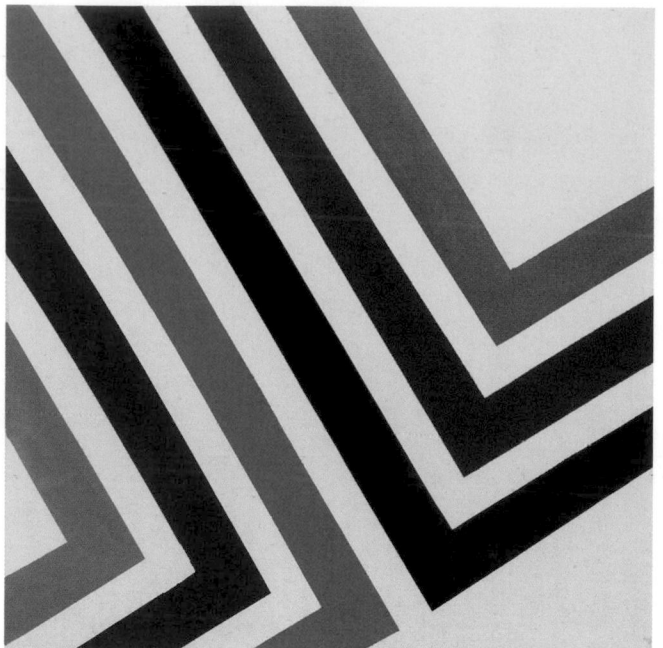

^ 2.6 SAM GILLIAM, *Swing 64* (1964). Acrylic on canvas, 35½" × 36½". David Kordansky Gallery, Los Angeles, California.

Actual, Implied, and Psychological Lines

Actual lines are those that are physically present in a work of art—as in Hurley's photograph. They are concrete. They have length, width, and other describable characteristics. **Implied line**, by contrast, refers to the "sense"

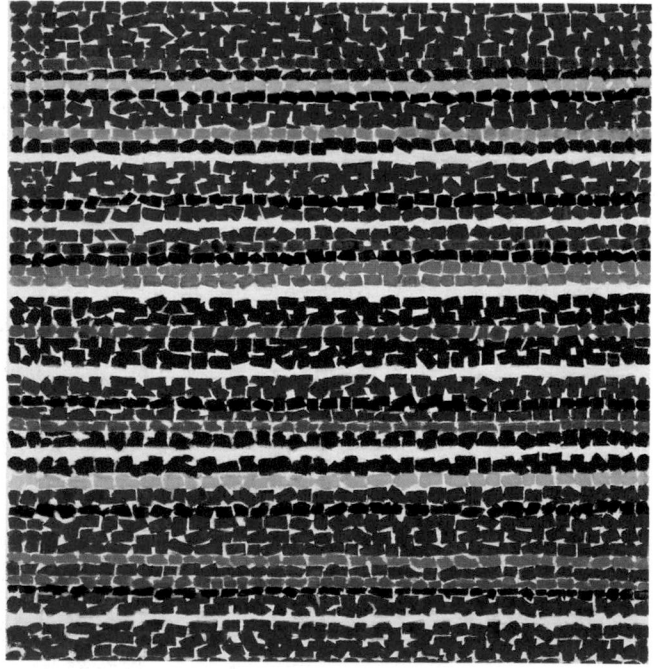

^ 2.7 ALMA WOODSEY THOMAS, *Light Blue Nursery* (1968). Acrylic on canvas, 49" × 47⅞". Smithsonian American Art Museum, Washington, D.C.

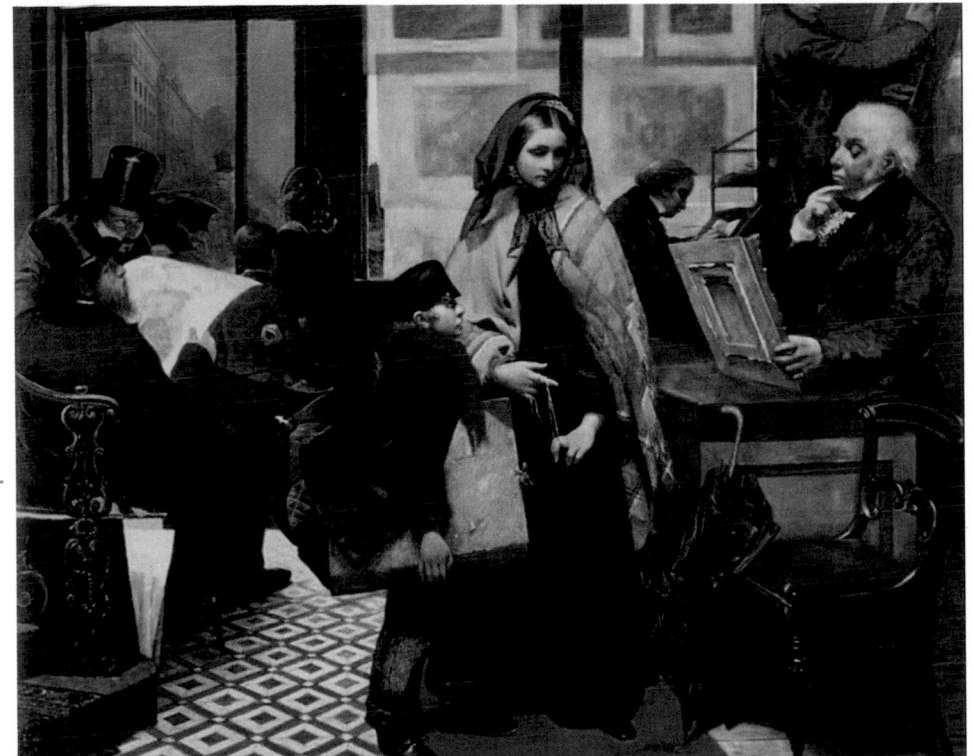

▲ 2.8 **EMILY MARY OSBORNE,** *Nameless and Friendless* (1857). Oil on canvas, 32 ½" × 40 ¾". Tate Britain, London, England.

dealer as he feigns serious consideration of a framed painting (Fig. 2.9). The boy's unflinching glance and the dealer's downcast eyes are connected by a psychological line that suggests a boldness on the part of the boy—as if with his piercing gaze he means to make the dealer accountable. A psychological line of a different sort connects the face of the young woman in the cape with a dripping wet umbrella propped up against a vacant chair. Her eyes are downcast and so, we conclude, is her mood. She fiddles with the fringe of her shawl and dares not gaze directly at the person with the power to judge her, or, for that matter, to offer her a seat. The psychological line between her eyes and the floor speaks volumes about her feelings of self worth. Yet a third psychological line can be observed in Osborne's composition, namely, one that connects the gazes of the men in top hats to the left who ogle both a drawing of a woman and the young woman herself.

of line created by the perceptual tendency to connect a series of points. **Psychological line** suggests a conceptual connection—an invisible linear path—between or among elements or characters in a composition.

In Sam Gilliam's *Swing 64* (Fig. 2.6), thick lines of color alternate with white lines, cutting across the canvas on a diagonal and then sharply shifting direction at a right angle; this composition is an illustration of the visual potency of actual line. Alma Woodsey Thomas's *Light Blue Nursery* (Fig. 2.7), in which we perceive discontinuous lines as continuous, is a good example of implied line. Tightly spaced horizontal lines are suggested by a series of short rectangular brushstrokes placed in close proximity to one another.

If a character in a painting points to an object or gazes across the pictorial space at another figure—as in Emily Mary Osborne's *Nameless and Friendless* (Fig. 2.8)—our perception of the connection between the two can be described as a psychological line. In Osborne's painting, which represents the plight of women artists, a small boy holding an artist's portfolio (perhaps her brother) stares directly at the condescending art

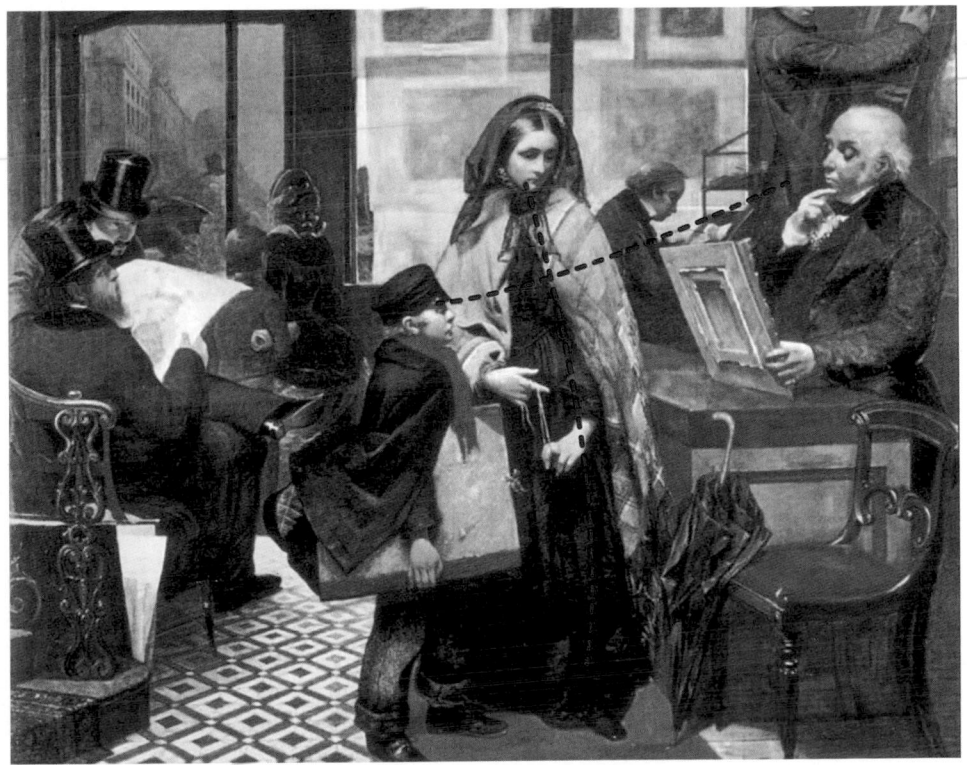

▲ 2.9 Psychological line in Emily Mary Osborne's *Nameless and Friendless.*

CONNECTIONS In *The Life of Harriet Tubman*, brightly clad children perform acrobatic leaps, their ebony and branchlike limbs forming powerful diagonals silhouetted against a mottled blue sky. So exhilarating are their movements that the horizon line that separates the earth from the sky seems to bounce along in camaraderie.

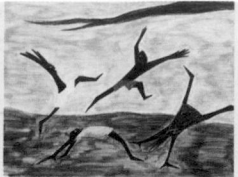

∧ Lawrence's *The Life of Harriet Tubman* (**Fig. 20.30**)

children tumbling on a hot summer day from his series titled *The Life of Harriet Tubman* (see Fig. 20.30).

LINE AND SHAPE

Artists use line to define shape. The outer edges of a shape are demarcated by line; it is line that describes objects and separates them from each other and the surrounding space in a composition.

Outline and Contour Line

When we consider the relationship or interaction between line and shape, we speak of two types of line—outline and contour line. An **outline** is an actual line—a concrete mark that defines a boundary or outer edge of an object or a figure. A **contour line** is not an actual line but an edge that is *perceived* where a three-dimensional form curves away from the viewer.

The difference between outline and contour line is illustrated in details of two famous Renaissance paintings: the *Birth of Venus* (Fig. 2.10) by Sandro Botticelli and the *Mona Lisa* (Fig. 2.11) by Leonardo da Vinci. Botticelli enunciated the contours of his figure with dark, black

Directionality of Line: Vertical, Horizontal, and Diagonal

Motion is implied in the definition of line as a moving point. When we speak of vertical, horizontal, or diagonal lines, we refer to direction of movement they imply.

Horizontal lines—like a horizon line in nature—suggest calm and stability. Vertical lines—as we see in skyscrapers—seem to defy gravity, rising from our earth-bound perspective to seemingly limitless heights. The most dynamic, restless lines, however, are diagonal; they convey energy, spontaneity, and whimsicality, as in the case of Jacob Lawrence's tempera painting of slave

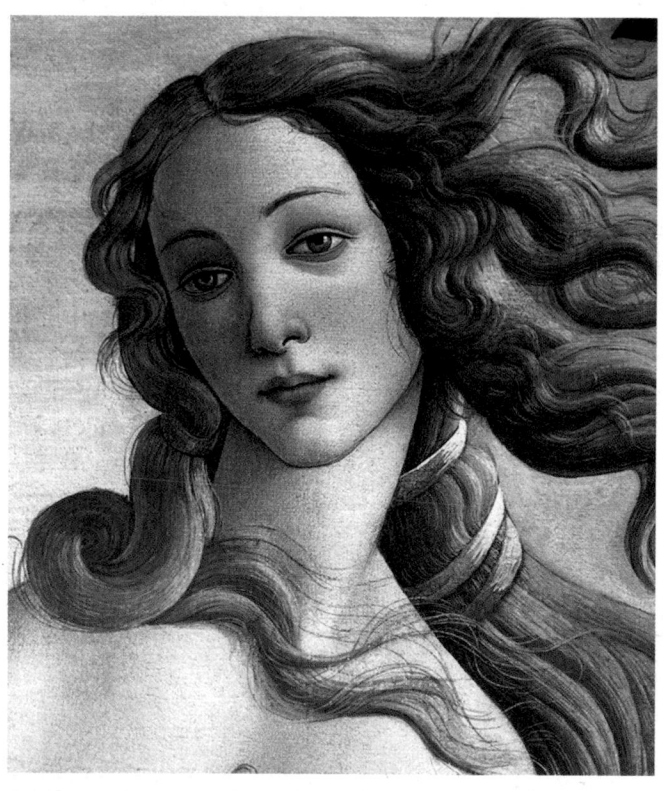

∧ **2.10 SANDRO BOTTICELLI,** *Birth of Venus* (c. 1480). Detail. Tempera on canvas, 69" × 110" (entire work). Uffizi Gallery, Florence, Italy.

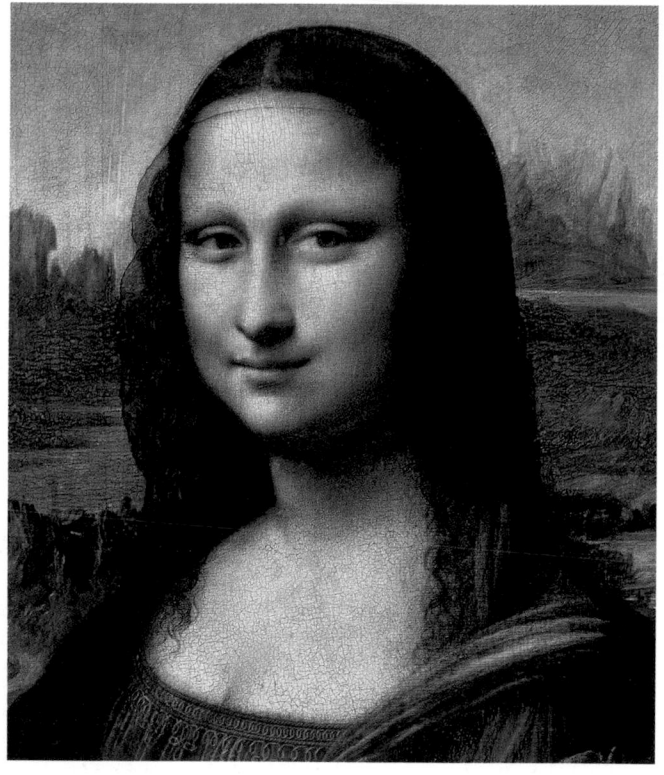

∧ **2.11 LEONARDO DA VINCI,** *Mona Lisa* (c. 1503). Detail. Oil on wood, 30¼" × 21" (entire work). Louvre, Paris, France.

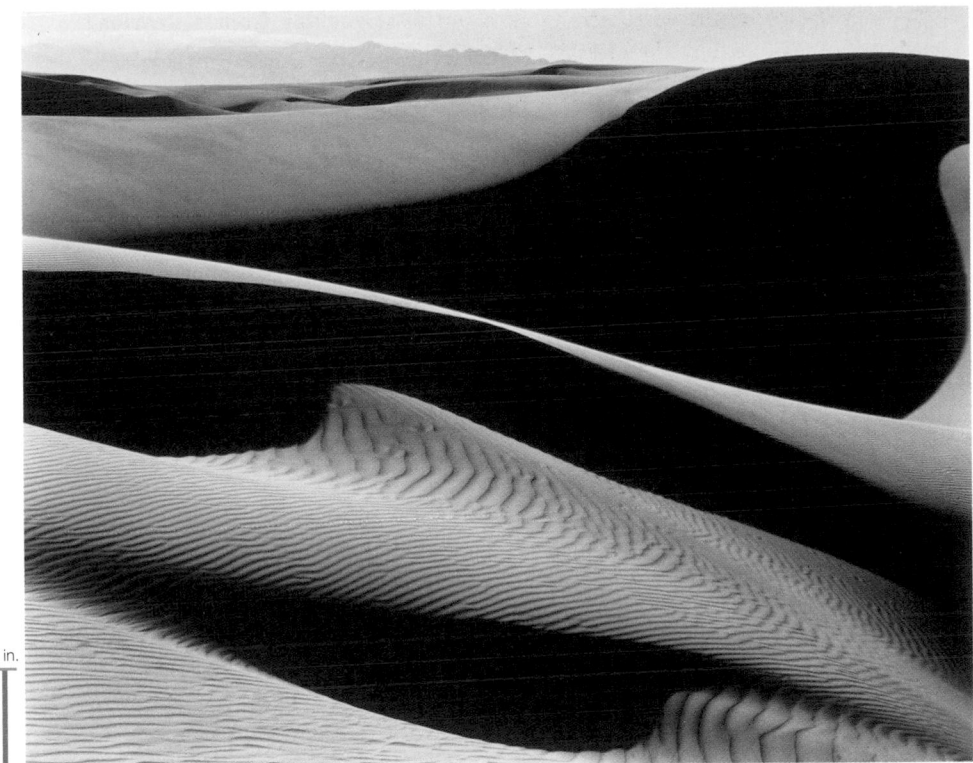

of bright light and velvety shadow create a razor-like edge where the peaks and valleys of the sand dunes meet.

Line, Value, and Shape

By altering the measure or density of lines, gradations of **value** (a progression from light to dark; see Chapter 3, page 40) can be achieved and, as in Leonardo's *Mona Lisa*, these subtle gradations can create a sense of fullness or roundness. In Angelica Kauffman's *Hebe* (Fig. 2.13), a full spectrum of values—from bright white to velvety black—is captured through the varying density of line. Dense patterns of crisscrossed lines—**crosshatching**—create a sense of volume in shapes that might otherwise appear flat. **Stippling**, a more or less dense pattern of dots, and **hatching**, closely spaced parallel

1 in.

∧ 2.12 **EDWARD WESTON**, *Dunes, Oceano* (1936). Gelatin silver photograph, 7⅝" × 9⅝". Art Gallery of New South Wales, Sydney, Australia.

lines, clearly separating the face and hair, chin and neck, fingertips and chest. This use of line has a flattening effect; our eye stops abruptly at the edge of the face, for example, and does not reconcile what the brain knows is a three-dimensional head. It is a bit like coloring with uniform pressure within the lines in a coloring book. On the other hand, if you apply more pressure or add layers of color near the black outlines, you decrease their visibility and create an illusion of roundness to the form. The head of *Mona Lisa* is handled quite differently. There are no outlines—only contour lines ("edges") softened by hazy shadow. The absence of harsh lines enables the perception of the subtle roundness of the face and head.

Neither approach is more "correct"; the artists simply had different aims. Botticelli was intrigued by the capabilities of line and entranced by the decorative potential of linear patterns. Leonardo was more interested in shape, using the contrast and gradations of light and shade—a technique called **chiaroscuro** or **modeling**—to create the illusion of three-dimensionality on the two-dimensional surface.

Edward Weston's photograph, *Dunes, Oceano, 1936* (Fig. 2.12) highlights the aesthetic possibilities of contour line and shape. The dramatic contrasts

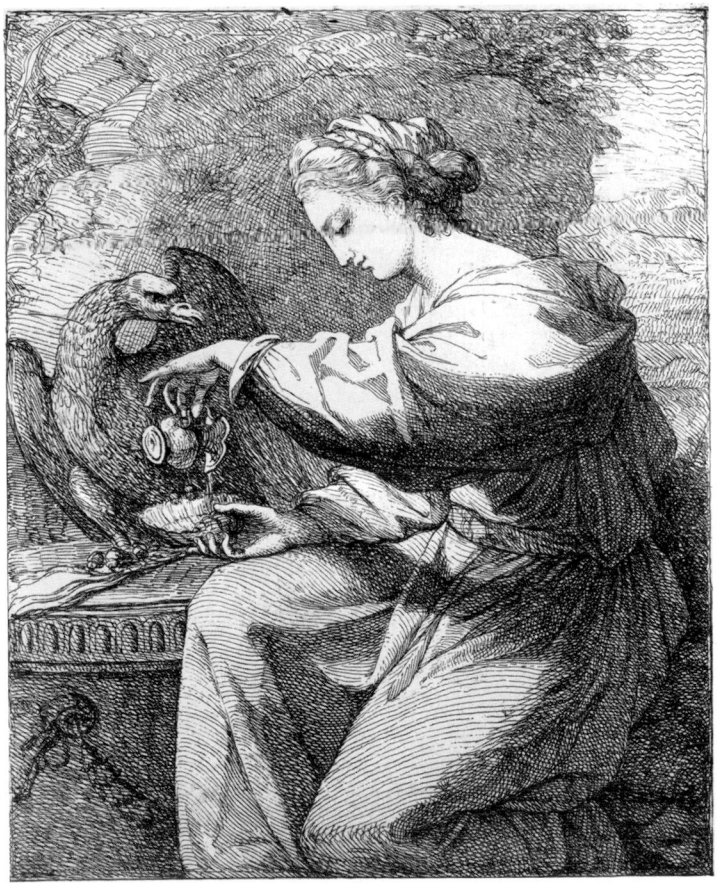

1 in.

∧ 2.13 **ANGELICA KAUFFMAN**, *Hebe* (1770). Etching, 8⅛" × 6½". Private collection.

Line and Shape | 25

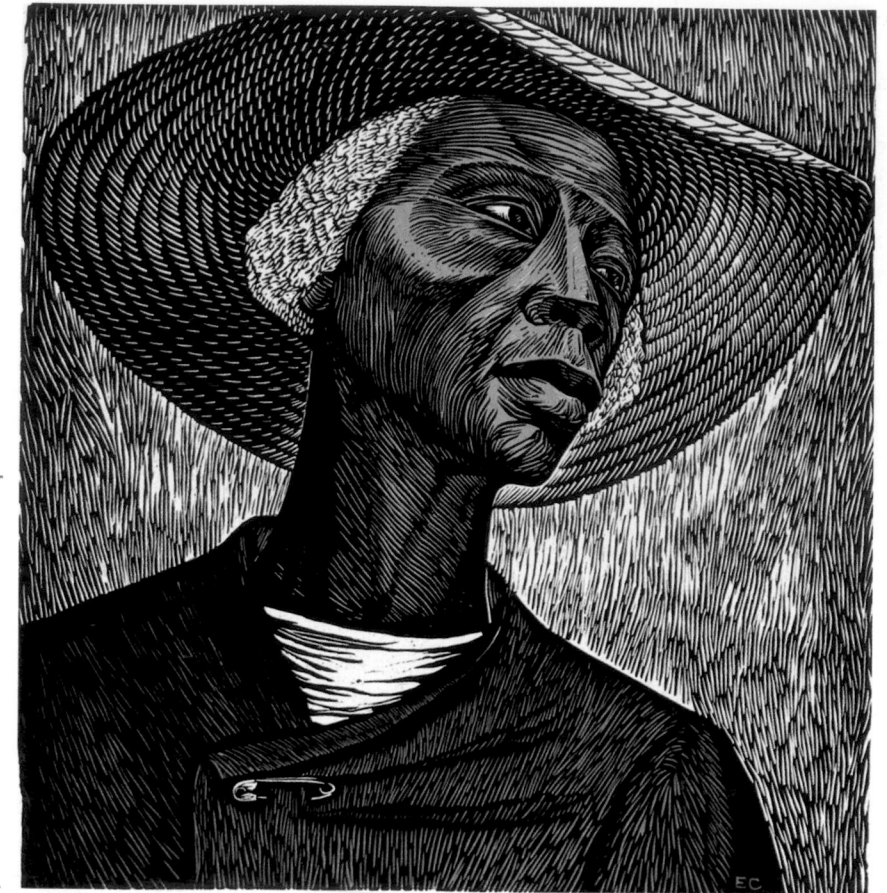

1 ft.

^ **2.14 ELIZABETH CATLETT,** *Sharecropper* (1968). Color linocut, 26" × 22". Hampton University Museum, Hampton, Virginia.

lines, achieve similar effects. Subtle contours, as in the face of Elizabeth Catlett's *Sharecropper* (Fig. 2.14), can be created with directional changes in hatched lines; they convey the gaunt and wearied countenance of a life of labor.

SHAPE, FORM, VOLUME, AND MASS

Shape, form, and *volume* are interrelated words used to define distinct areas or parts of works of art and architecture. *Shape* is generally used to describe flat, enclosed areas, like a circle or a square. **Form** is often used to describe three-dimensional shapes such as a sphere or a cube. **Volume** is the measurable space within a three-dimensional form or object—in other words, its capacity. The volume of an empty cube, for example, can be calculated

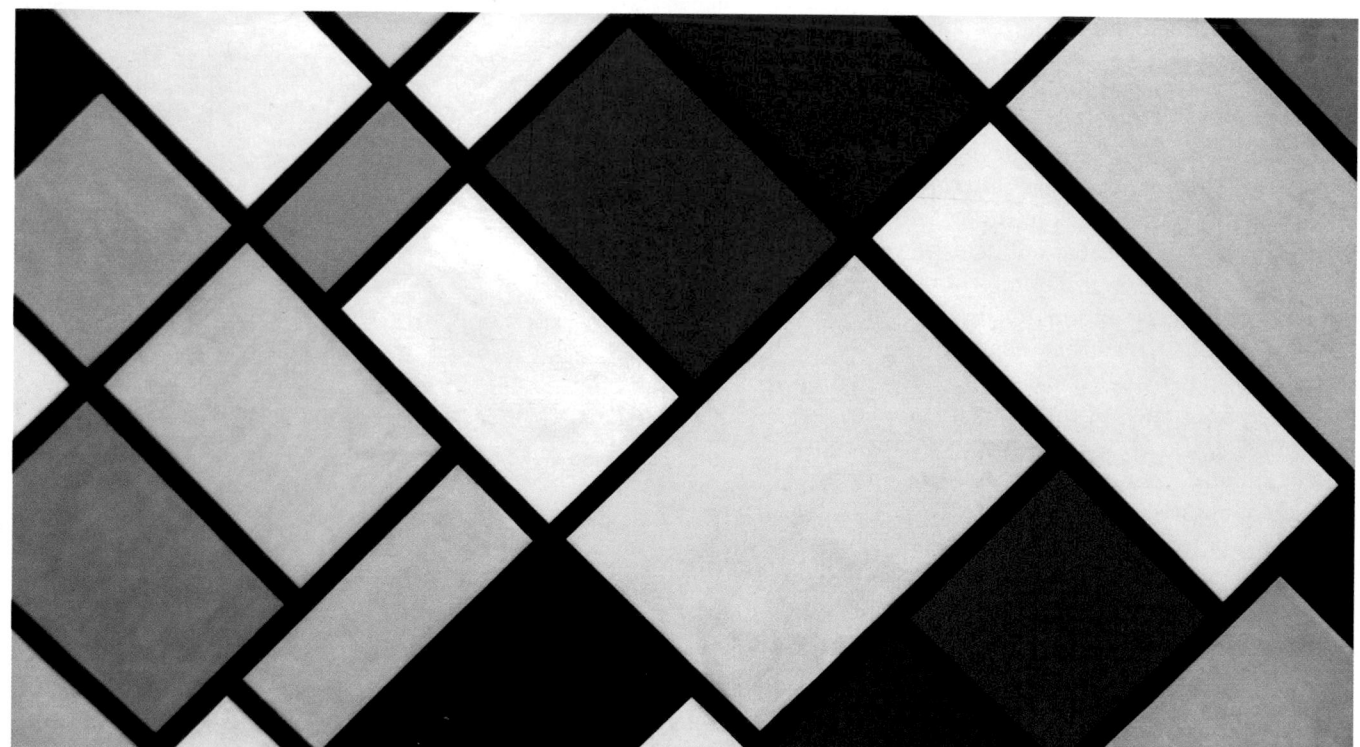

1 ft.

^ **2.15 THEO VAN DOESBURG,** *Counter-Composition of Dissonances* (1925). Oil on canvas, 70⅞" × 39⅝".

by multiplying the length and width and height of the cube. **Mass** is also measurable. In physics, mass refers to the amount of matter that something contains; in art, we use the word *mass* to describe the bulk of a solid, three-dimensional form. A solid form—such as one may find in sculpture—has *actual* mass. In a painting, by contrast, the *illusion* of a solid three-dimensional form on a two-dimensional surface has *implied* mass.

The interrelatedness of shape, form, and volume can be seen in three works of art that have similar characteristics.

Shape

Shapes are distinct areas on a two-dimensional surface that can be created in several ways: by connecting a line to itself, thereby enclosing an area; when intersecting lines enclose an area; by surrounding an area with shapes, giving that area (now read as a shape) distinct boundaries; and by using value, color, or texture to distinguish areas from that which from surrounds them. In Theo van Doesburg's *Counter-Composition of Dissonances* (Fig 2.15), black lines intersect at right angles, creating distinct squares and rectangles. The work provides a clear example of the character and meaning of shape in a two-dimensional work of art.

Form

Just as van Doesburg's painting is a study in shape, so is his *Model Maison d'Artiste* a study in form. The model for an Amsterdam residence by van Doesburg and Cornelis van Eesteren (Fig. 2.16) is almost a direct translation of van Doesburg's paintings into three dimensions; geometric shapes are replaced with geometric forms. It appears as though the familiar components of the surface configuration were separated and reassembled in a freestanding cluster.

Form also has another meaning in the context of art and design. It can describe the totality of a work of art—its elements, design principles, and composition. Form, then, is the visual expression of an idea; a work's *form* may include the colors that are used, the textures and shapes, the illusion of three dimensions, the balance, rhythm, or unity of design. **Formalism,** by extension, is an approach to art criticism that concentrates primarily on the elements and design of works of art, rather than their historical contexts or the biographies of the artists who created them.

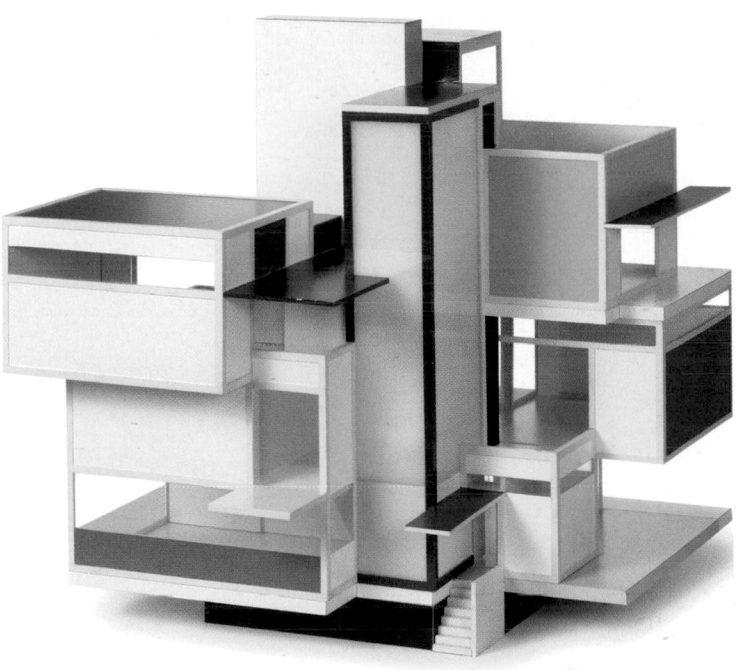

∧ 2.16 THEO VAN DOESBURG, CORNELIS VAN EESTEREN, *Model Maison d'Artiste* (1923). Reconstruction. Municipal Museum The Hague, The Netherlands.

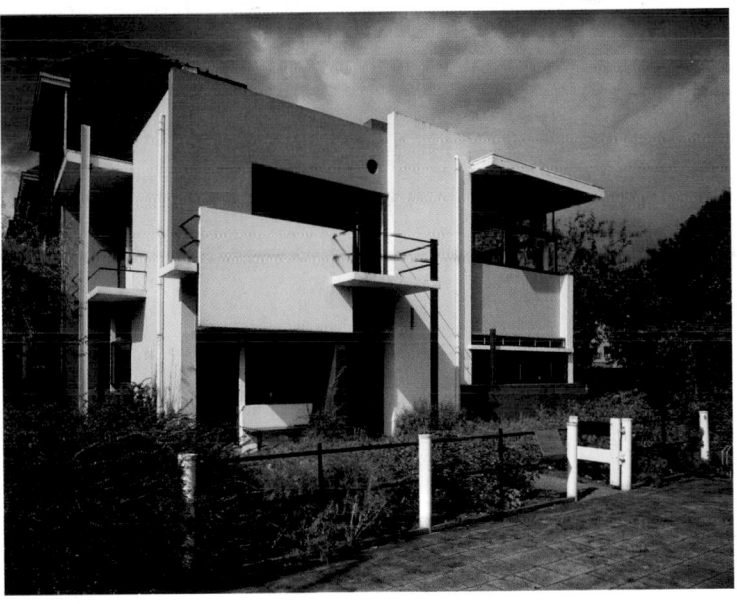

∧ 2.17 GERRIT RIETVELD, Schröder House, Utrecht, Netherlands (1924).

Volume

Volume implies containment—the amount of space in an enclosed three-dimensional area or in an empty (as opposed to solid) three-dimensional object. *Volume* is the word we would use to describe the space *within* the areas, or rooms, of Gerrit Rietveld's *Schröder House* (Fig. 2.17),

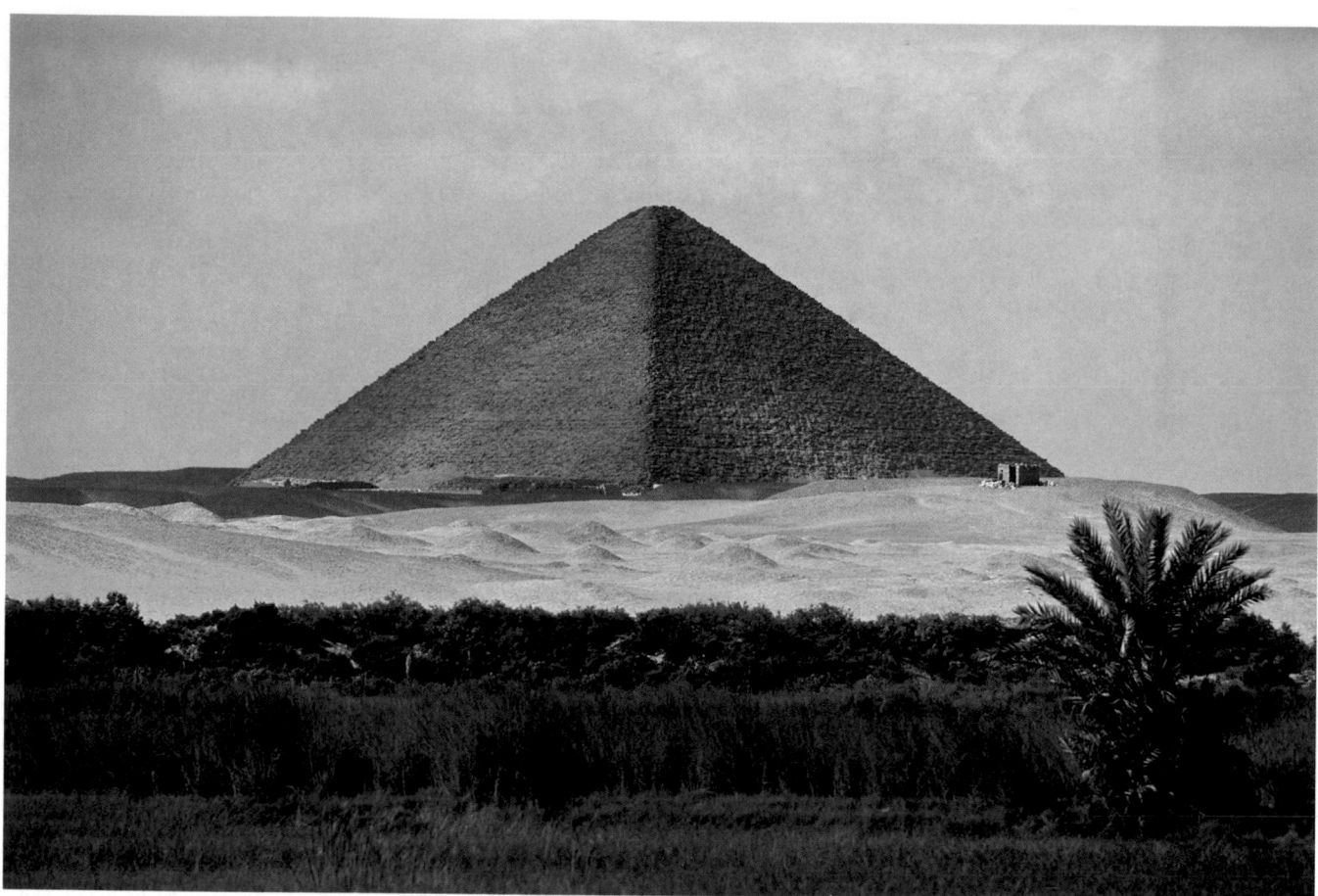

∧ 2.18 SNEFURU, Red Pyramid, Dashur, Egypt (2613–2589 BCE).

a volumetric adaptation of van Doesburg's elements and design principles.

Volume, of course, also describes the relative loudness of sound. In mediums such as film or video, volume is a quality of sound that can be manipulated for expressive purposes.

Mass

In three-dimensional art, the mass of an object refers to its bulk. We would be hard pressed to conjure a better illustration of mass than the pyramids of ancient Egypt (Fig. 2.18). By contrast, while I. M. Pei's contemporary design for the entrance to the Louvre Museum in Paris (Fig. 2.19) may evoke images of its ancient counterpart in the sands of Egypt, Pei's empty glass pyramid foregoes mass for volume.

ACTUAL MASS VERSUS IMPLIED MASS The pyramids of Egypt are three-dimensional forms that occupy three-dimensional space and have *actual mass* that is measurable. Objects depicted on a two-dimensional

surface may convey a sense of mass (Fig. 2.20) even though, obviously, they do not possess it. We say that such objects have *implied mass*. In Ger van Elk's mixed-media work, *Untitled II*, the implied mass of a dense-looking charcoal-gray pyramid is exaggerated by the lack of space and air between the sloping sides of the pyramid and the two men in suits whose bodies appear to be stuck against them.

TYPES OF SHAPES

The outer edge of a shape characterizes its type. Shapes with straight edges and angular corners are described as **rectilinear**; shapes with curving edges are described as **curvilinear**. Both rectilinear and curvilinear shapes can also be described as **geometric** in that they may be derived from mathematical formulas and are rendered with great precision. Pure geometric shapes—such as circles, spheres, and cones—are labeled **nonobjective** in that they are not derived from visible reality and make

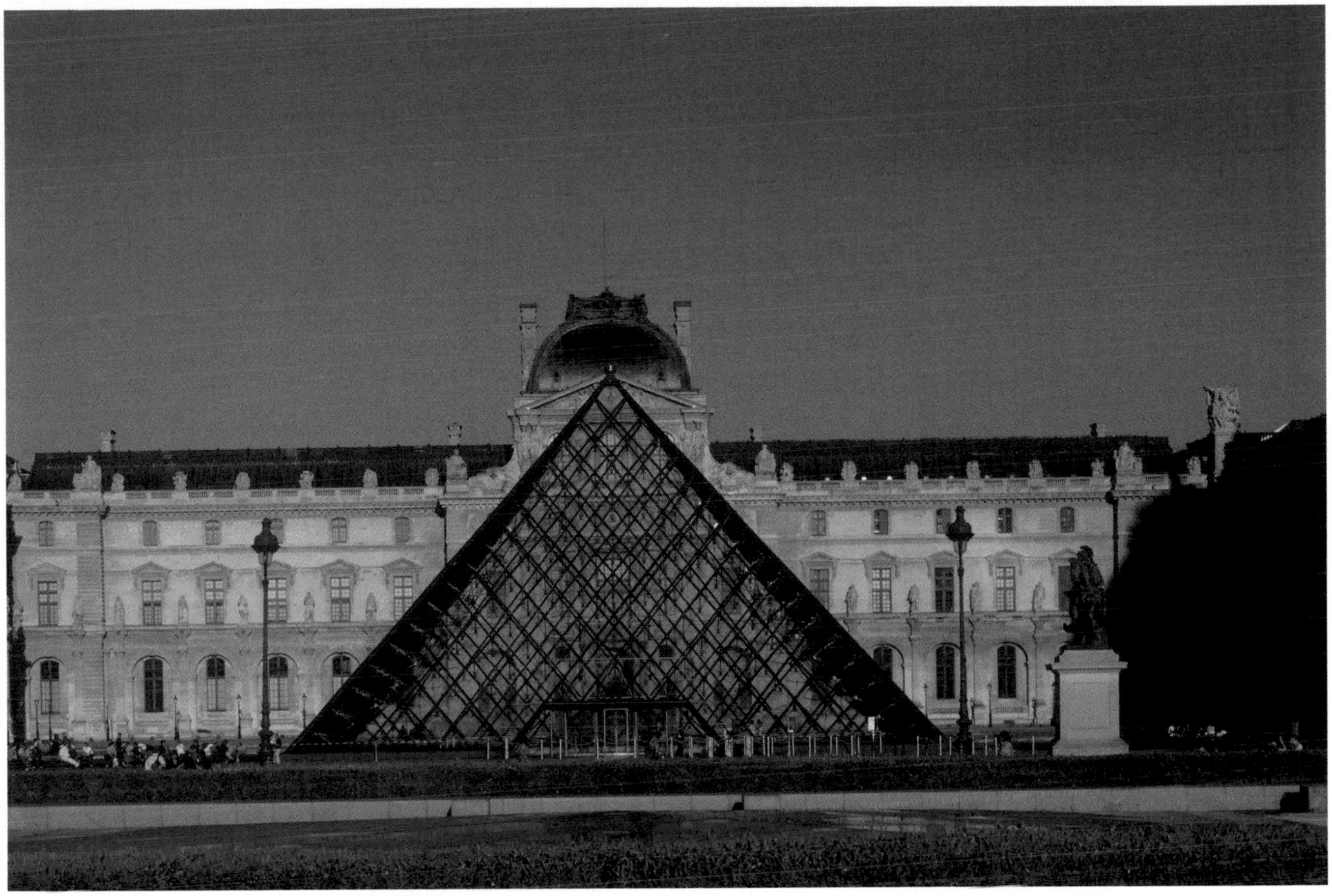

2.19 I. M. PEI, **Pyramid at the Louvre, Paris, France** (1989). Photograph with Sully façade of the museum visible behind.

no reference to it. **Abstract** shapes are radical alterations of visible reality—simplifications, exaggerations, or transmutations—that sometimes bear little resemblance to the original entities from which they were derived. **Amorphous** shapes are essentially implied shapes; they are, visually speaking, vague. The eye interprets them as shape even though they have no actual outer edges.

Geometric Shapes

Geometric shapes, as the type implies, are related to concepts in geometry—rectangles, cubes, triangles, pyramids, circles, and spheres.

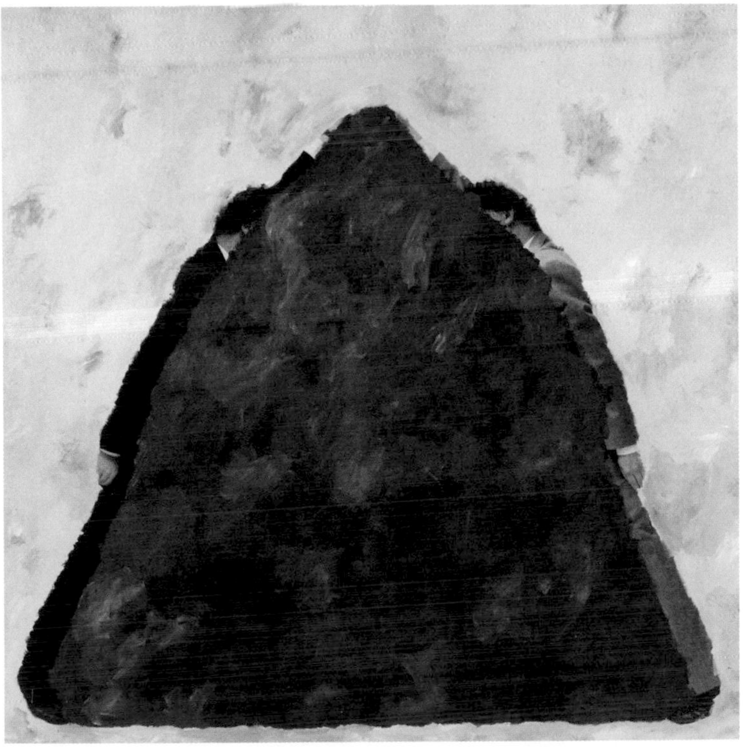

> 2.20 **GER VAN ELK,** *Untitled II* (1981). Photo laid down on canvas and acrylic paint, 110¼" × 110⅜". Grimm Gallery, Amsterdam, The Netherlands.

1 ft.

Guided by her interest in mathematics, much of Dorothea Rockburne's work can be described as a study of pure form. In *Pascal's Provincial Letters* (Fig. 2.21) she explores the interplay of precisely rendered geometric shapes using overlapping and transparency. Pascal's theorem specifically refers to the connections of points and lines in hexagons.

The geometric shapes in Rockburne's painting are rectilinear, that is, the artist uses intersecting straight lines to create them, resulting in corners that are sharp and angular. Geometric shapes can be described as curvilinear when they are formed by—and emphasize—curving lines, as in Frank Gehry's Getty Museum in Bilbao, Spain (Fig. 2.22). Gehry referred to his building as a "metallic flower"; others have found the billowing curvilinear shapes to be reminiscent of ships, linking the machine-tooled structure that is perched on the water's edge to the history of Bilbao as an international seaport. It almost appears that free-floating shapes collided on site, and that, on another day, they might have assumed a completely different configuration.

Organic Shapes

Organic shapes are derived from those found in nature—the world of living things. Whereas geometric shapes are somewhat of a rarity in nature (although crystals are a good example of an exception), organic shapes are commonly found, their curvilinear qualities implying growth and movement.

The idea of organic shapes in architecture would almost seem oxymoronic given the degree to which technology and the mathematics are embedded in the engineering of structures, but the work of the Catalan architect Antoni Gaudí gives lie to that premise. His Casa Mila, an apartment house in Barcelona, Spain, also known as La Pedrera (Fig. 2.23), subverts the geometric, steel-cage construction that forms the skeleton of the typical multistory apartment-style residence. The building façade of undulating carved stone has few straight lines or flat surfaces, the rooftop is wavelike, and the forest of chimneys resemble, in shape, the peaks of soft-serve ice-cream cones. The playful organic shapes infuse the building with warmth, spontaneity, and implied movement, and evoke an illusion of "living and breathing" stone.

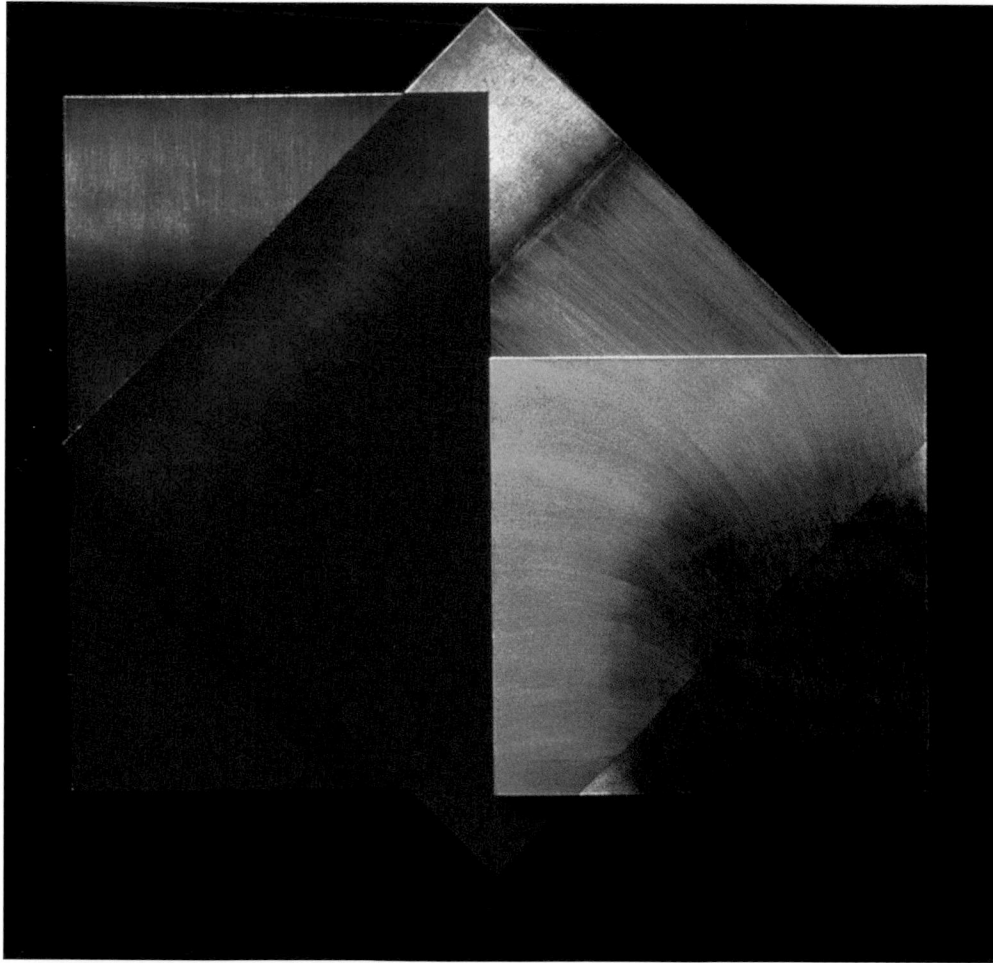

1 ft.

⌃ 2.21 **DOROTHEA ROCKBURNE,** *Pascal's Provincial Letters* (1987). Oil on linen, 67" × 67" × 8".

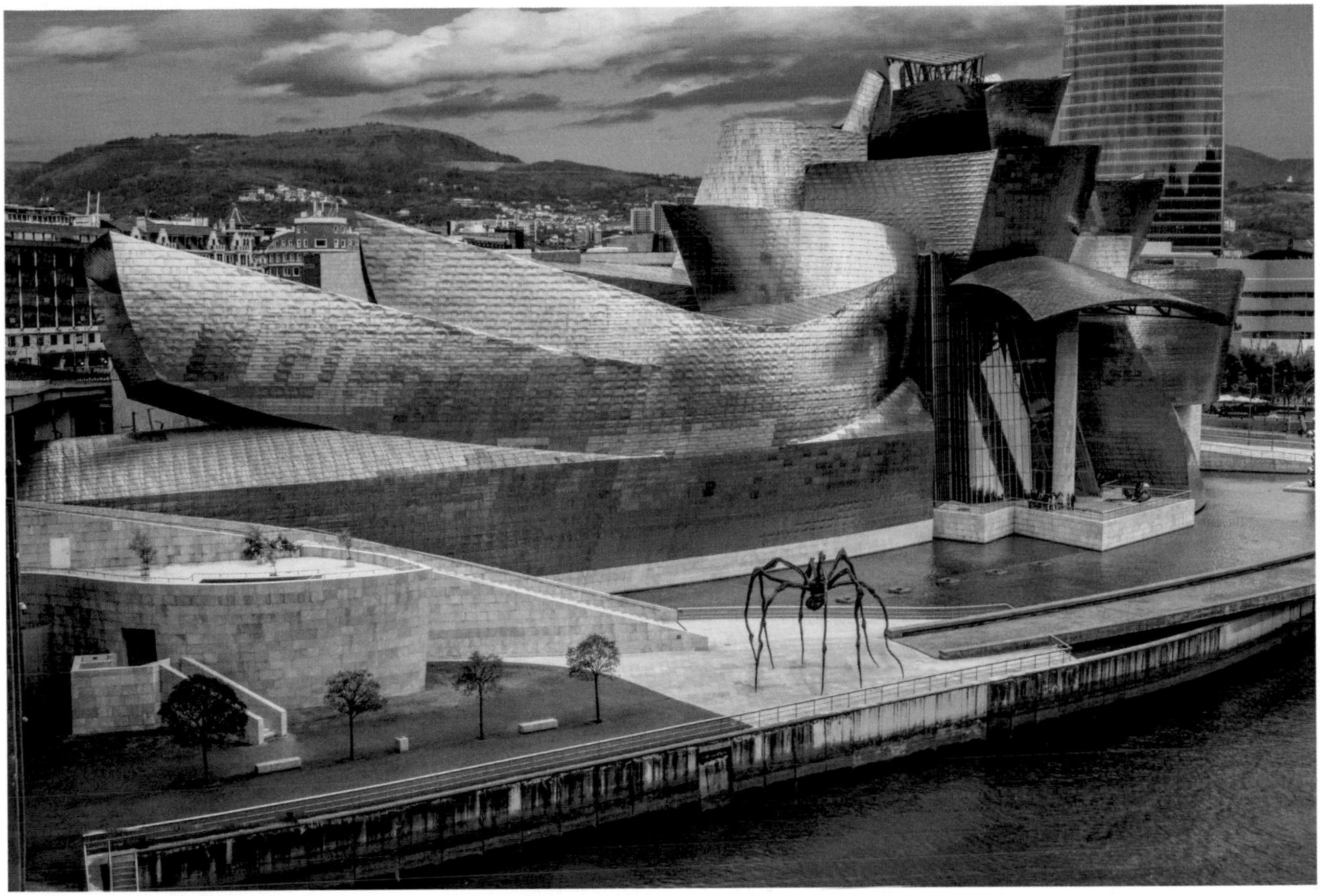

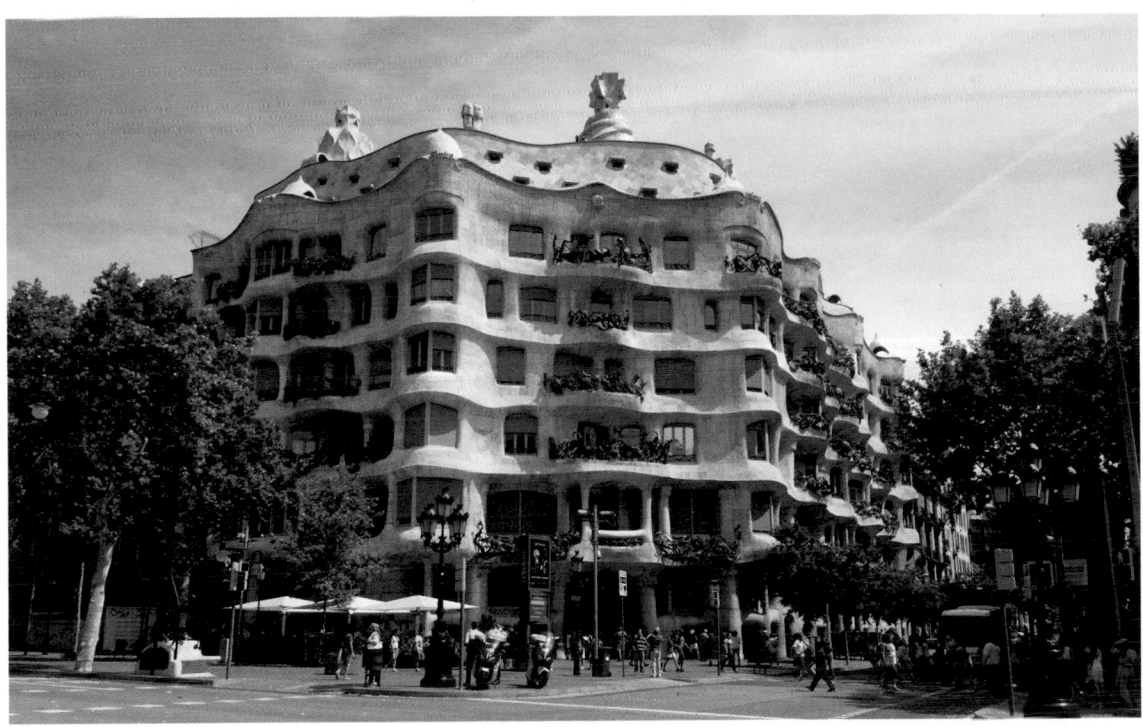

∧ 2.22 **FRANK GEHRY**, Guggenheim Museum, Bilbao, Spain (1997).

∧ 2.23 **ANTONI GAUDÍ**, Casa Mila Apartment House, Barcelona, Spain (1905–1907).

COMPARE & CONTRAST
The Expressive Potential of Shape

IN THE YEAR 1907, a young Pablo Picasso unveiled a painting that he had been secretly working on for a couple of years. A culmination of what was known as his Rose Period, this new work—*Les Demoiselles d'Avignon* (Fig. 2.24)—would turn the tide of modern painting. Picasso had studied the work of African and Iberian artists in Parisian museums and galleries. He was struck by the universality of the masks, believing that their rough-hewn, simplified and angular features crossed time and culture. *Demoiselles* was the painting that launched the movement called Cubism, which geometricizes organic forms. The contours of the body in *Demoiselles* are harsh and rectilinear, forming straighter lines than are found in nature. The women in the painting are expressionless and lack identity; some of them even have masks in lieu of faces. The intellectual exercise of transforming the human form into geometric shapes takes precedence over any interest in expressing the plight of these women who are prostitutes in the French underworld. The "figures" in the work transcend the period and culture in which the women lived and worked.

You have heard the expression "Clothing makes the man." In Robert Colescott's *Les Demoiselles d'Alabama: Vestidas* (Fig. 2.25),

it could be argued that clothing makes the woman. The women in Picasso's painting are dehumanized in part by their nudity. The subjects of Colescott's painting, executed some eighty years later, are given strong individuality by their choice of costume. Colescott's painting is one of the thousands of instances in which one artist transforms the work of another in a certain way to make a certain point. Picasso's nudes are harsh and jagged yielding an overall splintered quality to his work; the movement of the women seems to be abrupt and choppy. By contrast, Colescott's women are well rounded and fleshy—they are natural, organic, "real" counterparts to Picasso's geometry. The flowing, curvilinear lines of the women cause them to undulate across the canvas with fluid movement.

Whereas Picasso's rectilinear women are timeless (and "placeless"), the curvilinear, clothed women of Colescott are very much tied to their time and place—an American South full of life and spontaneity and emotion. Whereas Picasso seemed to relish the intellectual transformation of the prostitutes of Barcelona into timeless figures, Colescott seems to revel in the tangibility and sensuality of his subjects.

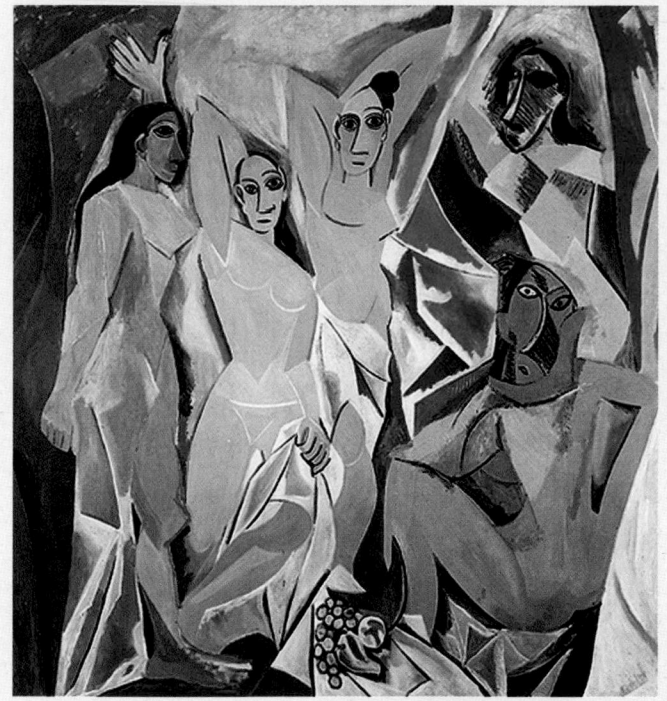

∧ **2.24 PABLO PICASSO,** *Les Demoiselles d'Avignon* (1907). Oil on canvas, 96" × 92". The Museum of Modern Art, New York, New York.

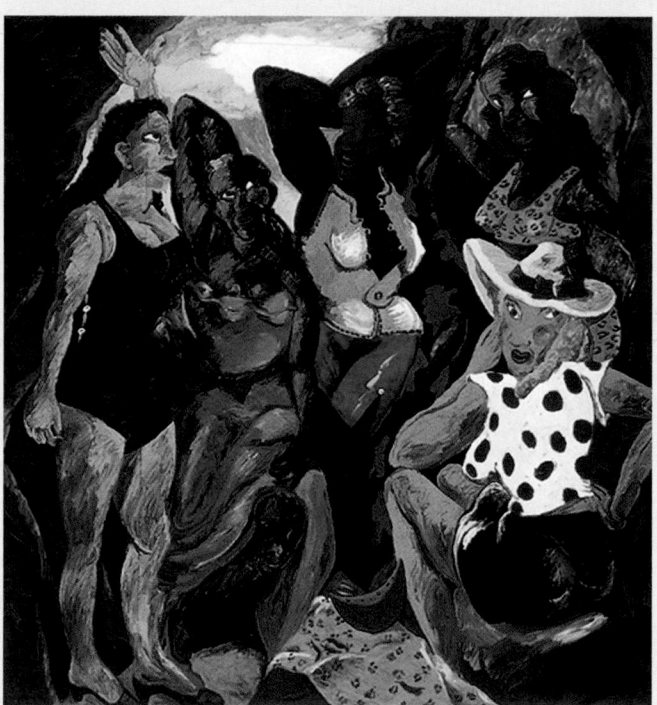

∧ **2.25 ROBERT COLESCOTT,** *Les Demoiselles d'Alabama: Vestidas* (1985). Acrylic on canvas, 96" × 92".

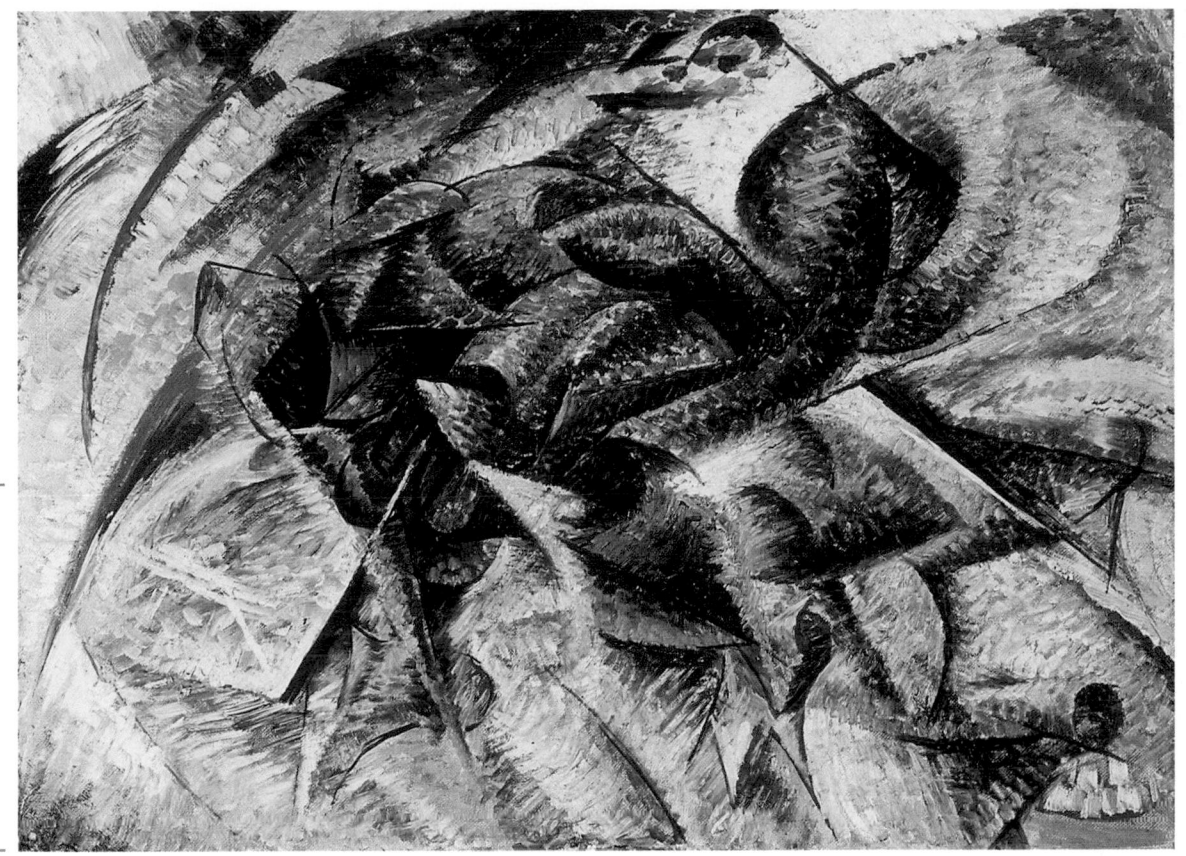

1 ft.

Nonobjective and Abstract Shapes

Nonobjective shapes, like nonobjective works of art in general, make no reference to visible reality. In their purest form, geometric forms are nonobjective; the shapes in Dorothea Rockburne's *Pascal's Provincial Letters* (Fig. 2.21) can be called nonobjective.

Abstract shapes, by contrast, are not nonobjective. They are connected to the world of visible reality even though that connection may be more or less tenuous. For example, Picasso's *Demoiselles d'Avignon* is composed of abstract shapes but the overall integrity of the figures is not really compromised. In Umberto Boccioni's *Dynamism of a Cyclist* (Fig. 2.26), the figure is almost completely camouflaged amid the collision of abstract shapes.

Amorphous Shapes and Shapelessness in Art

The imagery in Helen Frankenthaler's *Before the Caves* (Fig. 2.27) may be described as amorphous or, perhaps better, shapeless—more the result of the irregular pooling of poured paint than shape

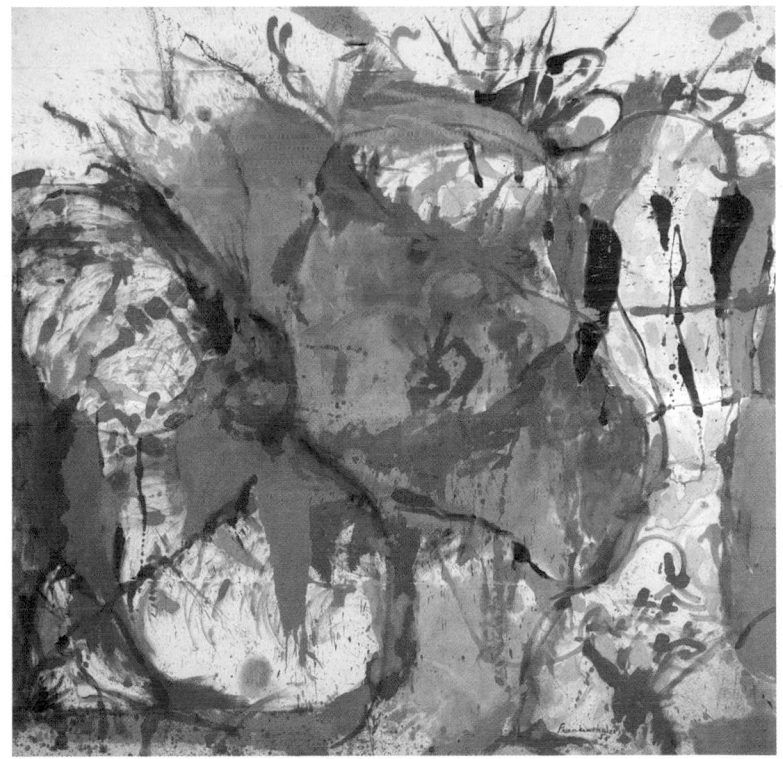

1 ft.

∧ 2.27 HELEN FRANKENTHALER, *Before the Caves* (1958). Oil on canvas, 102⅜" × 104⅜". The University of California, Berkeley.

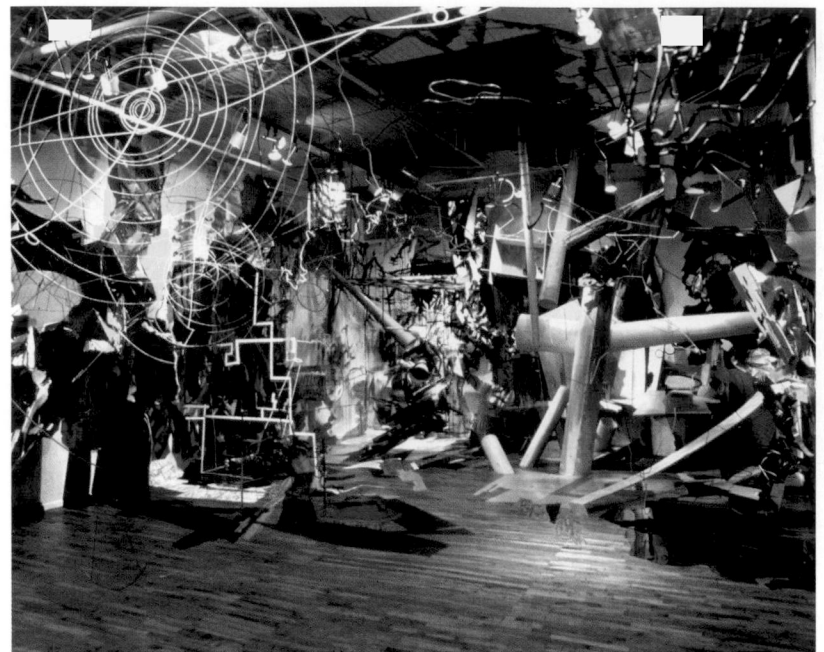

< 2.28 **JUDY PFAFF**, *3D* (1983). Steel, perforated steel, plywood, wood veneers, Plexiglas, contact paper, tin, wire, paint.

POSITIVE AND NEGATIVE SHAPES, FIGURE AND GROUND

In a two-dimensional composition, a shape is referred to as **figure** and the empty area surrounding it (or the area that it is distinct from it) is referred to as **ground**. The figure is regarded as **positive shape** in a composition and the ground is regarded as **negative shape**. In Edgar Degas's painting *The Laundresses (The Ironing)* (Fig. 2.29), the women are the figures (positive shapes) and the ochre-colored backdrop is the ground (negative shape). The relationship between figure and ground, positive and negative is clear. Not so, however, in a painting of the same subject by Paul Gauguin; in his *Laundresses at Arles* (Fig. 2.30), positive and negative shapes coexist, shifting and changing positions in an ambiguous space. The push–pull effect between the

per se. The components of Judy Pfaff's mixed-media installation, *3D* (Fig. 2.28), include an abundance of discrete shapes and forms—geometric and organic—but the design of the installation appears shapeless. From inside the space, mingling among the elements, composition seems shape-shifting, limitless, without boundaries.

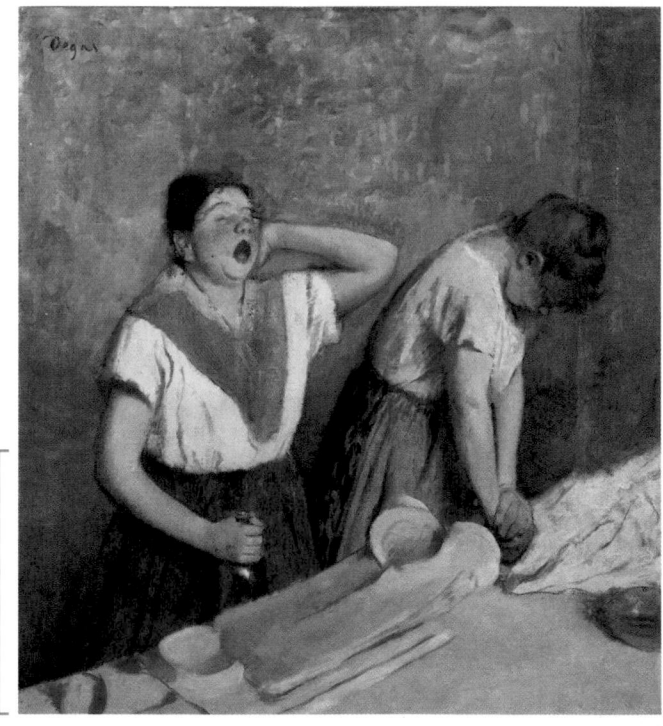

1 ft.

▲ **2.29 EDGAR DEGAS**, *The Laundresses (The Ironing)* (c. 1874–1876). Oil on canvas, 30" × 32". Private collection.

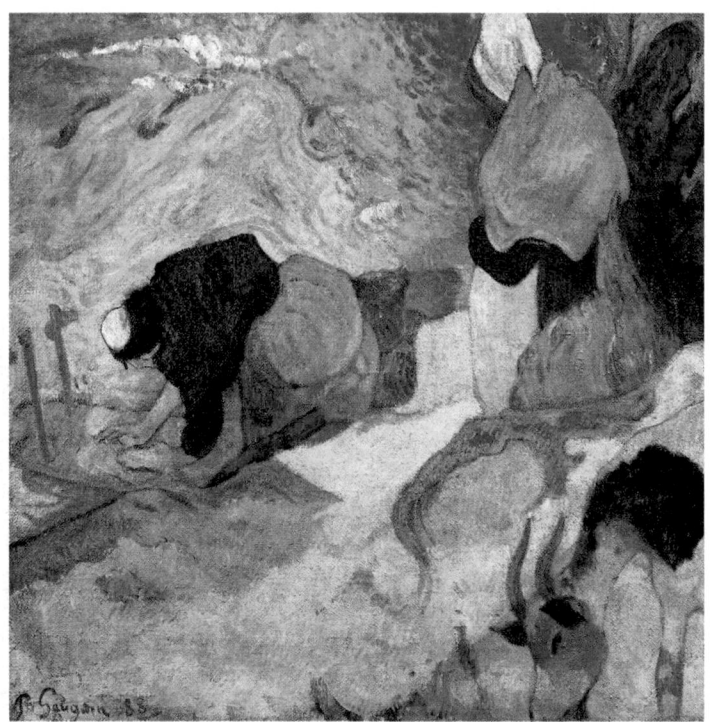

1 ft.

▲ **2.30 PAUL GAUGUIN**, *Laundresses at Arles* (1888). Oil on canvas, 29⅛" × 36¼".

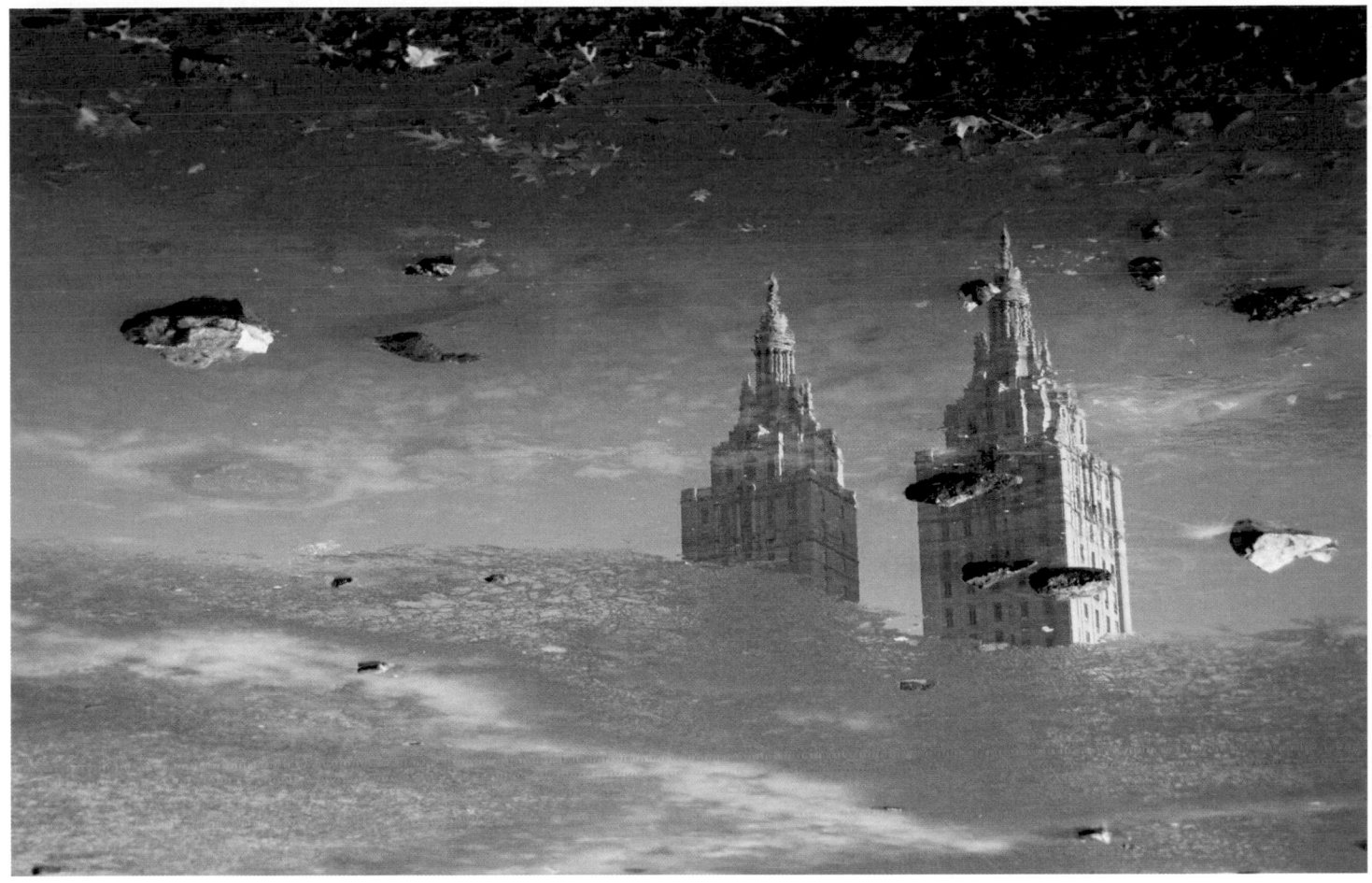

▲ 2.31 **ANDREW ADOLPHUS,** *Untitled* (2013). Photograph.

figure and ground creates a composition that is dynamic rather than static.

The fluidity of figure and ground that we see in Gauguin's painting is brought to a new level in a photograph by Andrew Adolphus, leading to what we call **figure-ground reversal** (Fig. 2.31). By shifting our focus from figure to ground and back again, the artist creates the illusion of an atmosphere in which meteor-like forms menace the towers of a New York City apartment building, set against the backdrop of an otherwise serene blue sky. In fact, what we see as floating "space junk" is a group of small rocks reflected—along with the towers—in an ordinary rain puddle.

The tendency of the eye and brain to shift focus when figure and ground are ambiguous was also noted by Gestalt psychologists who used the Rubin vase as an illustration (Fig. 2.32). When the viewer focuses on the black area—the positive shape— a pedestal vase appears; when the eye focuses on the negative space around the black shape, two facing profiles appear. Figure becomes ground and ground becomes figure, and vice versa.

▲ 2.32 **A Rubin vase.**

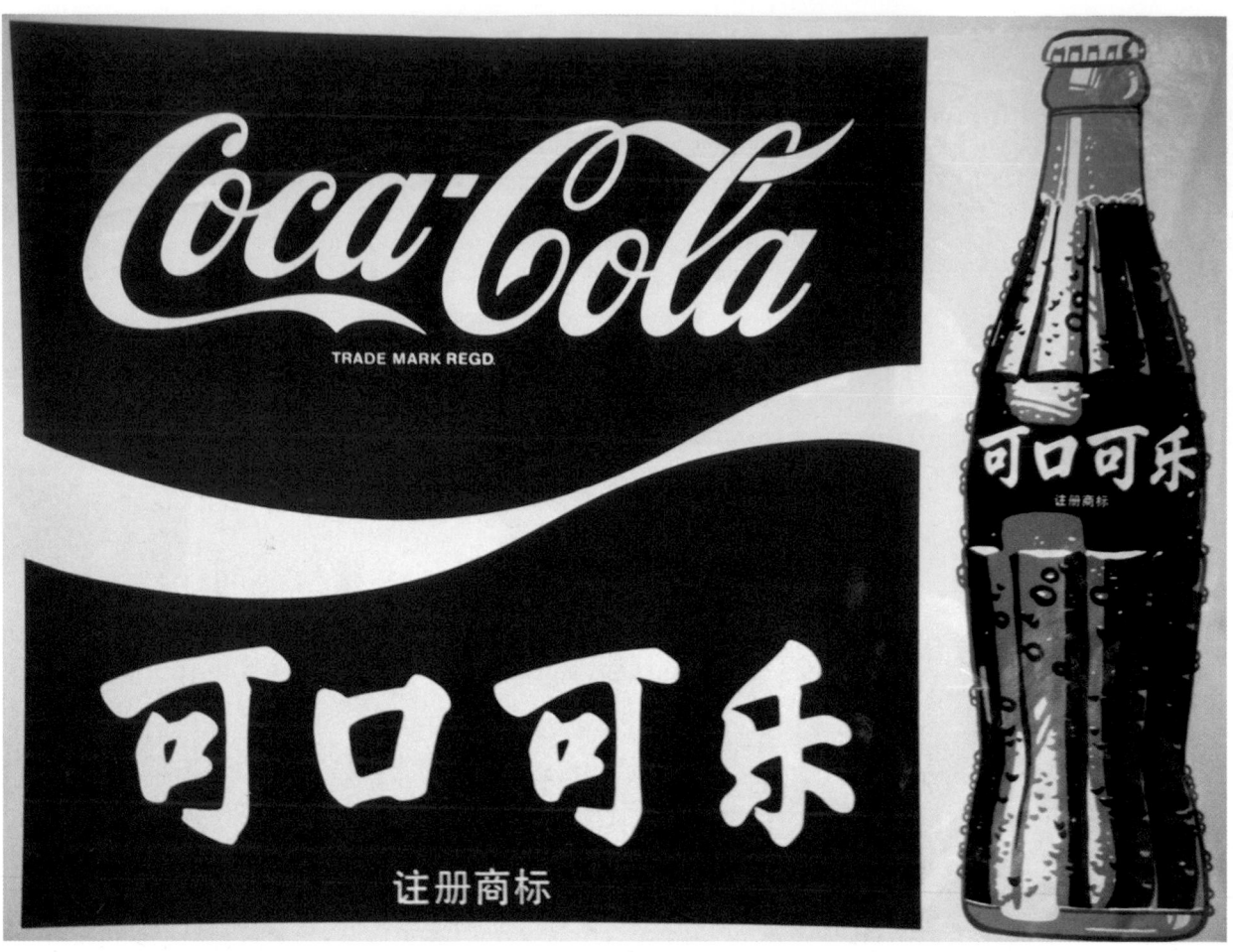

∧ 2.33 Coca-Cola in its iconic bottle is advertised on a sign in Beijing, China.

SHAPE AS ICON

Some shapes have entered our consciousness in such a way as to carry with them immediate associations. They are never mistaken for anything else. We could say that they have become cultural icons in the same way that an icon of a folder in the toolbar of a word-processing program signifies "click here to view a list of your files." Some of these shapes have symbolic resonance that raises them above their actual configuration. Consider, for example, the shape of a cross for Christians, a six-pointed Star of David for Jews, or the Chinese symbol of yin and yang.

The shape of a Coke bottle is universally familiar—and instantly recognizable—as the container for the world's most popular soft drink (Fig. 2.33). Similarly, the simple shape of an apple with a bite taken out of it has come to signify the worldwide Apple brand (Fig. 2.34).

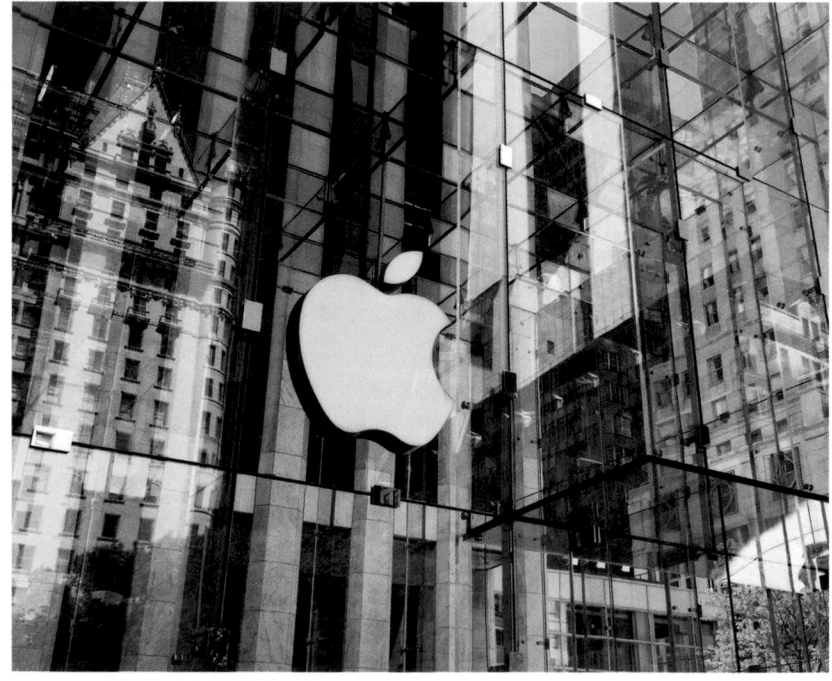

∧ 2.34 Façade of the Apple Store, 5th Avenue, New York.

Iconic shapes are not associated only with objects or products. Some celebrities—such as Che Guevara and Barack Obama—have become instantly, globally recognizable due in part to iconic shape-dominant renderings of their faces (Figs. 2.35 and 2.36). Based on what has been called the most famous photograph in the world, the stylized shape of the social activist and revolutionary, Che Guevara, has become an icon associated with class struggle, guerrilla warfare, and, in general, counterculture. Although people wear merchandise emblazoned with the bearded, beret-sporting Che, it is not necessarily because they are familiar with who he was and what he did (an Argentinian physician-turned-Marxist revolutionary who joined Fidel Castro's efforts to depose Cuba's U.S.-backed dictator). For most people, Che's is the face of rebellion against authority and ideological struggle.

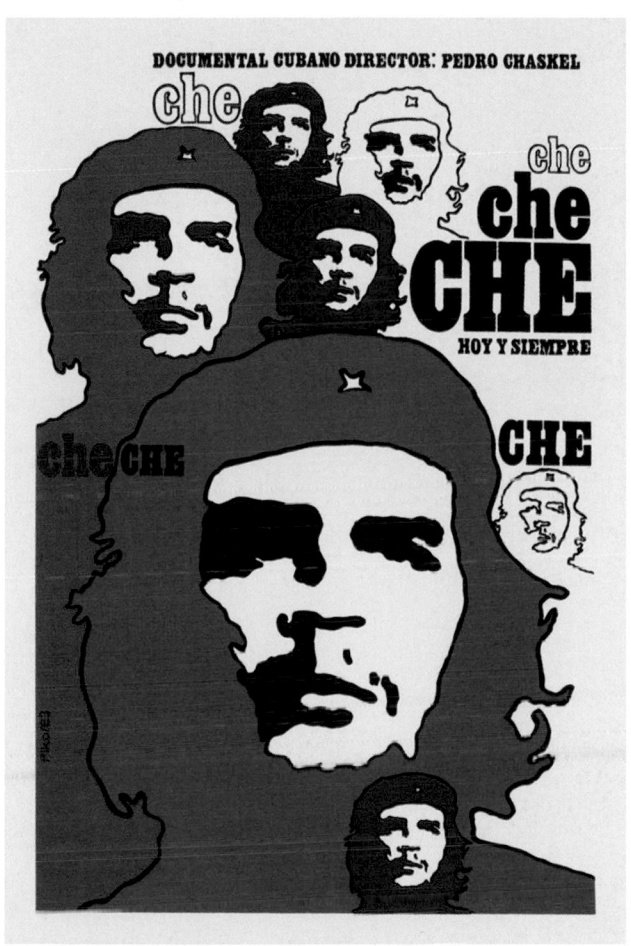

⌃ 2.35 NIKO, Movie Poster for *Che, Hoy y Siempre (Che, Now and Forever)* (1983). Print on paper.

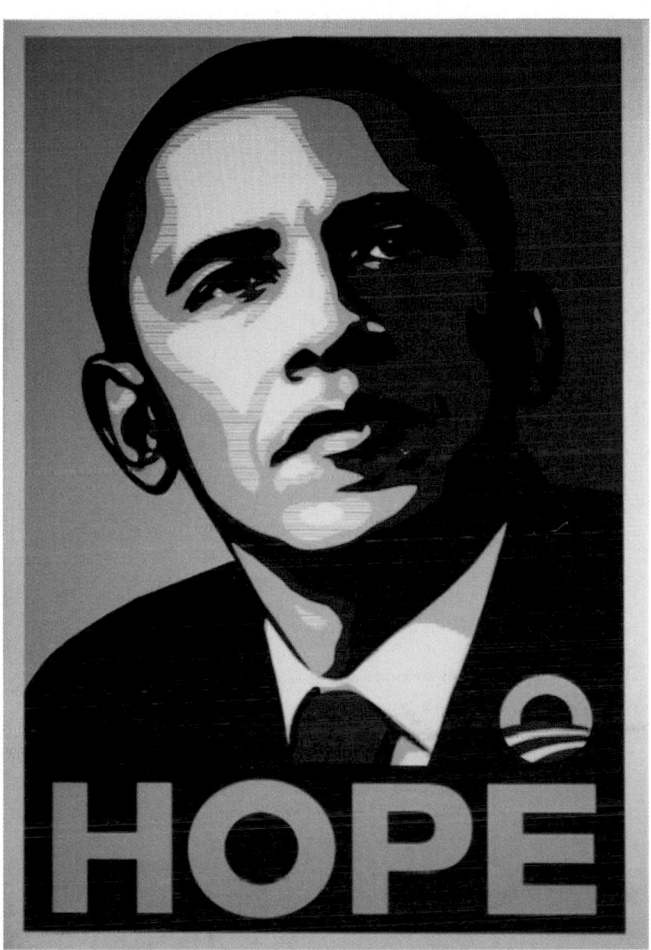

⌃ 2.36 SHEPARD FAIREY, *Barack Obama "Hope" Poster* (2008).

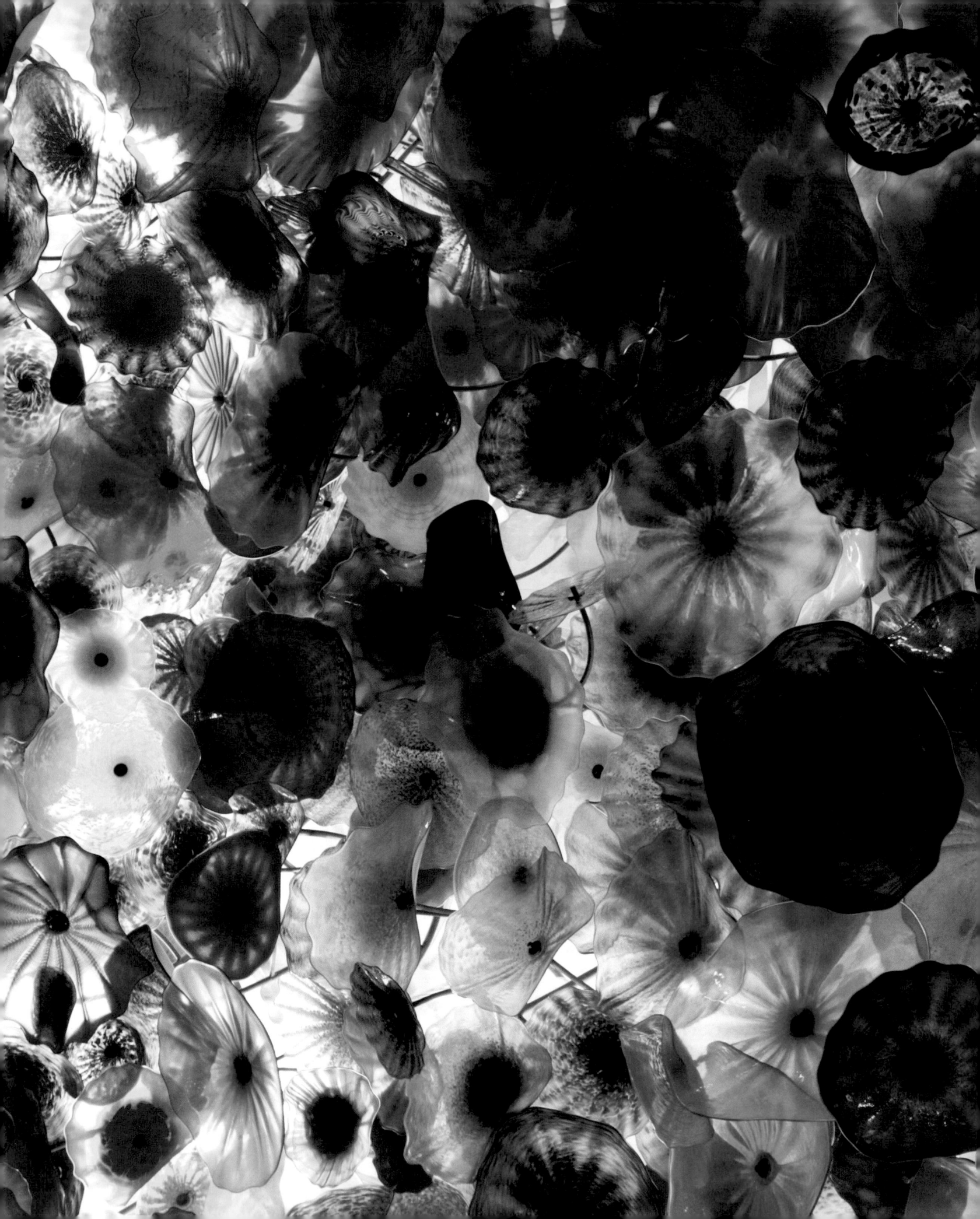

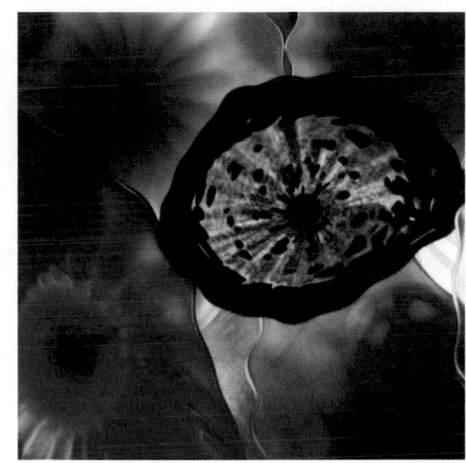

3

LIGHT AND COLOR

Harmony is the analogy of contrary and of similar elements of tone, of color, and of line, conditioned by the dominant key, and under the influence of a particular light, in gay, calm, or sad combinations.

— GEORGE SEURAT

IT WAS Sir Isaac Newton who demonstrated the relationship between light and color with the simplest of experiments, laying the crucial groundwork for the most complex investigations of color theory. He introduced a beam of sunlight into a darkened room through a small hole in a window shutter, and positioned a triangular glass prism in the room in such a way that the stream of light might pass through it. As it did, the prism—a transparent surface—bent the light waves, disbursing the white light that entered and separating it into a multicolored spectrum that was displayed on a white surface opposite the darkened window. Newton recreated the colors of the rainbow, otherwise known as the **visible spectrum** (Fig. 3.1). Without light there is no color; color is the function of light. Isolate a bit of landscape in the distance and then view it first in full sunlight and, later, at nightfall. Your perception of the colors of the plants and trees will be very different. The brighter the light, the more able you will be to distinguish among colors and nuances of color; the lower the light, the less able you will be to do so.

◄ DALE CHIHULY, Glass Flowers (1998). Bellagio Casino, Las Vegas, Nevada.

39

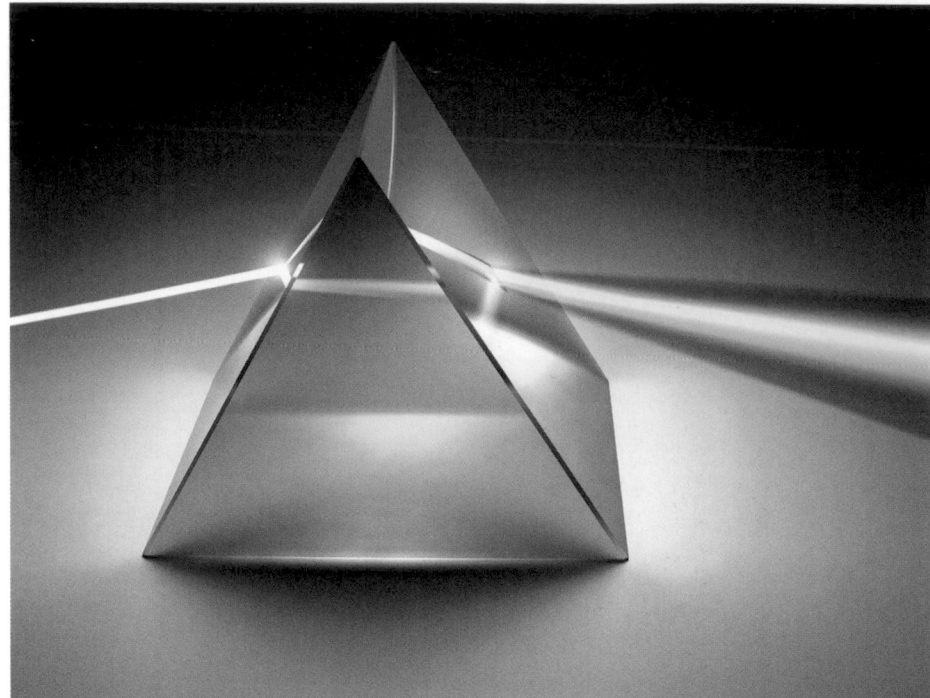

∧ 3.1 The Visible Spectrum.

VALUE

Value refers to the relative degree of lightness or darkness of a surface or a color. The value of a color is determined by the amount of light reflected by the color. It describes the blacks and whites and grays in works of art—their presence, absence, and relationship to one another.

Shades of Gray

On opposite ends of the value spectrum are white and black; in between is a vast and nuanced spectrum of grays. Figure 3.2 is a value scale with nine progressions, or shades of gray ranging from one that is almost black to one that is slightly off-white. Grays that are achieved by mixing various amounts of black and white are called **achromatic**. The Greek prefix *a-* means "without," and these grays are said to be without color. When we mix certain colors we can also obtain grays, but they will differ in tone from those found in the achromatic gray scale. Grays that contain color are referred to as grayed neutrals, or **chromatic** grays.

The spectrum of grays can be divided into two parts. The center point—like the center band in Figure 3.2—marks a "middle gray." As we move toward black, we enter

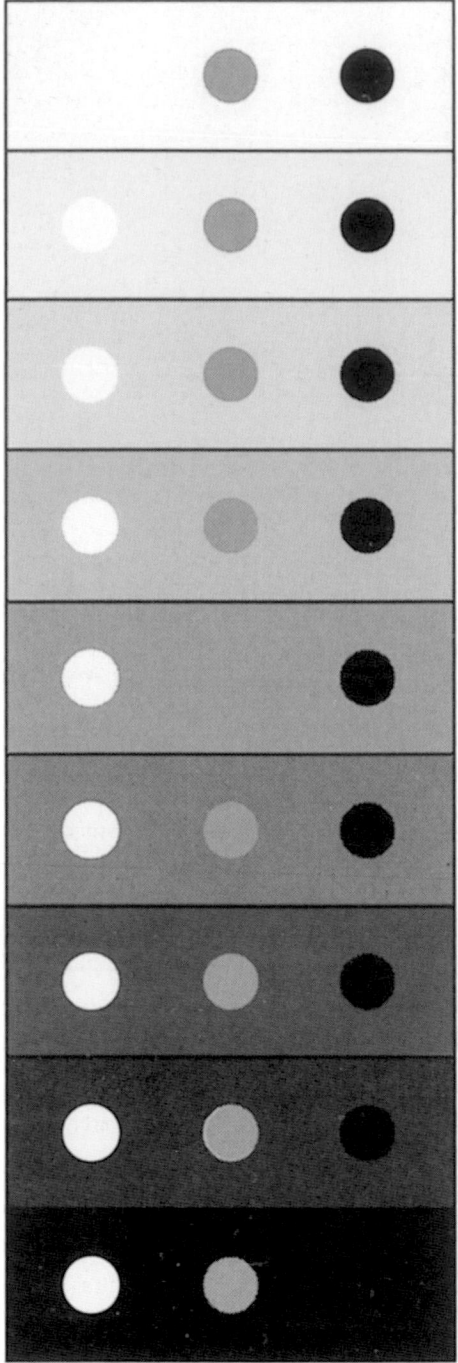

∧ 3.2 A Value Scale of Grays.

what is known as the **low-key value range**; as we move toward white, we are in the **high-key value range**. The key of a work of art can suggest a mood. Low-key works are often read as somber or relaxing; high-key works appear to be more uplifting or stimulating.

Marc Brandenburg's *Untitled* (Fig. 3.3), a pencil-on-paper drawing of Michael Jackson that emulates a photographic negative in its tonal contrasts, is an exploration

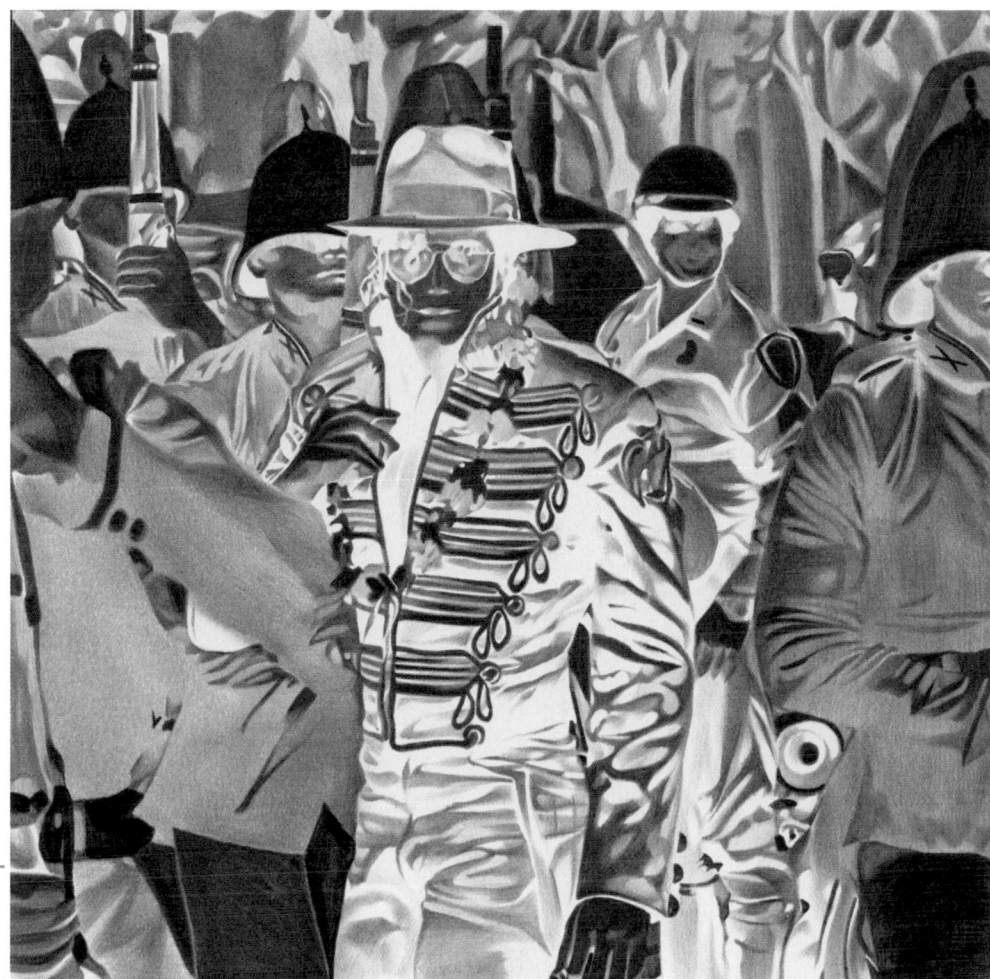

1 in.

< 3.3 MARC BRANDENBURG, *Untitled* (2004). Pencil on paper, 8 ¼" × 8 ⅜". The Museum of Modern Art, New York, New York.

of the value scale that begins with the binaries of black and white and incorporates a full spectrum of grays.

Value Contrast

When we describe the value of a color or surface we do so in relative terms. **Value contrast** refers to the degrees of difference between shades of gray. Look again at Figure 3.2; each of the white, gray, and black circles within each band of the value scale has precisely the same value. However, the value contrast of the circles within the bands of gray change as the scale progresses from light to dark. The highest value contrast can be seen in the top and bottom bands.

Imagery with high value contrast is easier to perceive than that with little or no value contrast. Figure 3.4 shows the same graphic on black, white, and gray backgrounds. High value contrast (black type on white or white type on black) provides sharpness and clarity and is easy to read. The impact of value contrast—or the lack thereof—can be seen in three distinct views of Hank Willis Thomas's

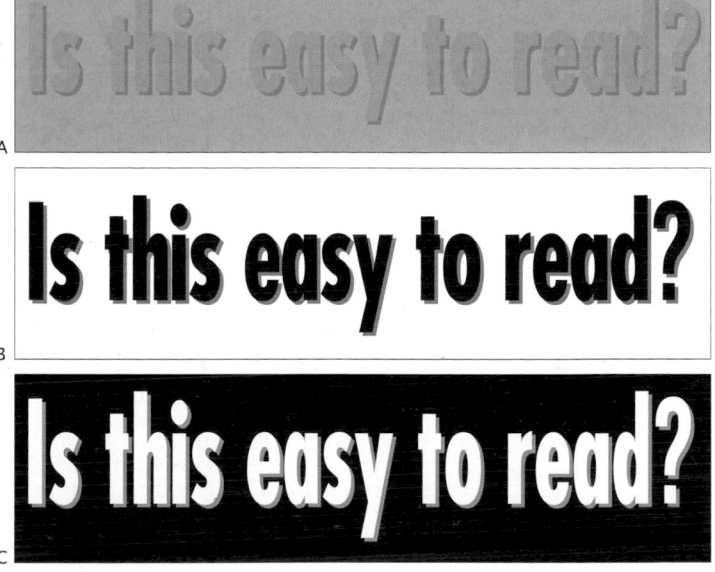

A
B
C

∧ 3.4 Value Contrast.

Value | 41

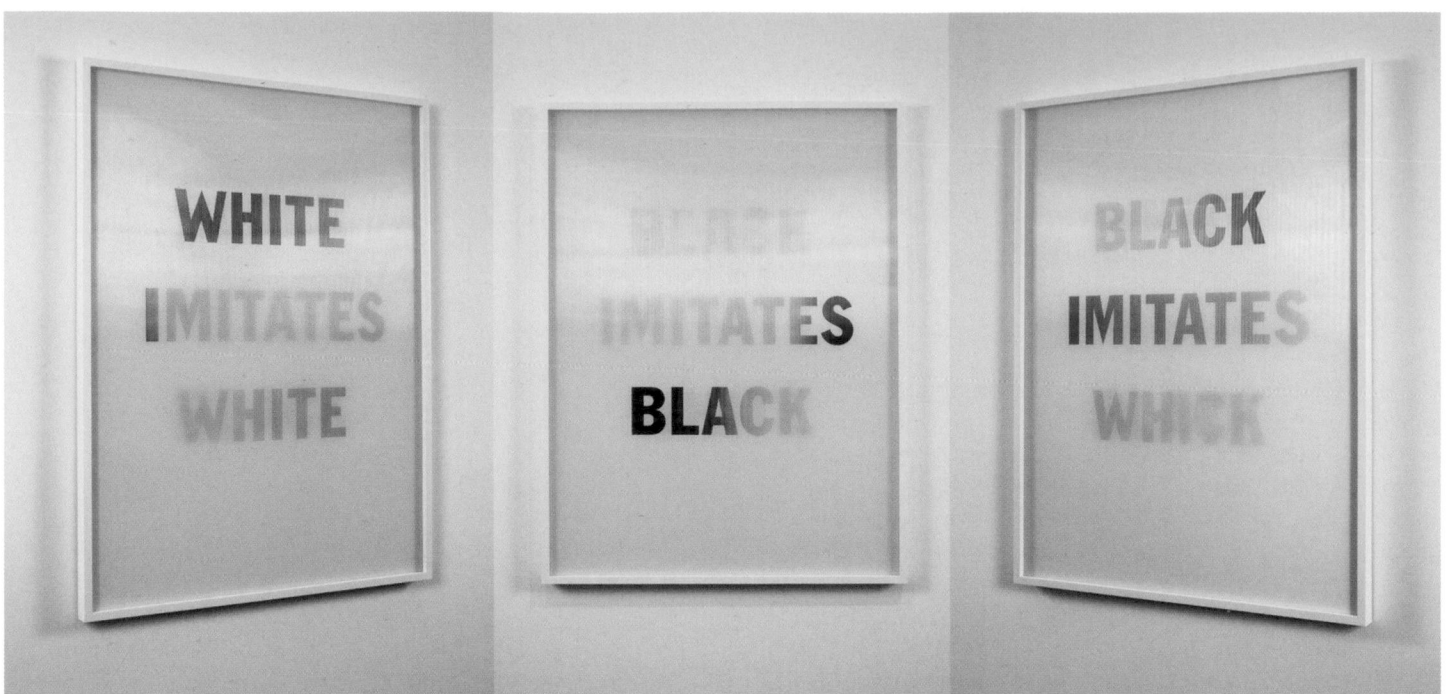

▲ 3.5 **HANK WILLIS THOMAS,** *White Imitates Black* (multiple views) (2009). Lenticular print, 40" × 30". Jack Shainman Gallery, New York, New York.

White Imitates Black (Fig. 3.5), a lenticular print in which the image changes depending on the angle from which it is viewed. (You have probably seen a version of this kind of printing on greeting cards with, for example, an eye that seems to open and close as you tilt the image in different directions.) In Thomas's print, the type changes with the viewer's perspective, a clear and compelling reference to perspectives on race.

Value Pattern

Value pattern describes the variation in light and dark within a work of art and the ways in which they are arranged within a composition. The term *value pattern* applies to full-color works as well as works in black and white. Value patterns can be low contrast or high contrast; Low-contrast value patterns can tend toward the dark or light ends of the value scale. Both types of value patterns can be seen in David Salle's *Angel* (Fig. 3.6).

CHIAROSCURO AND TENEBRISM
Artists use various methods to create the illusion of three dimensions in two-dimensional

mediums like painting, drawing, or printmaking; value pattern is one of them. *Chiaroscuro* is a value pattern defined by a gradual progression from light to dark through a successive gradation of tones across a curved surface. *Tenebrism* is a value pattern characterized by abrupt and dramatic juxtapositions of light and dark.

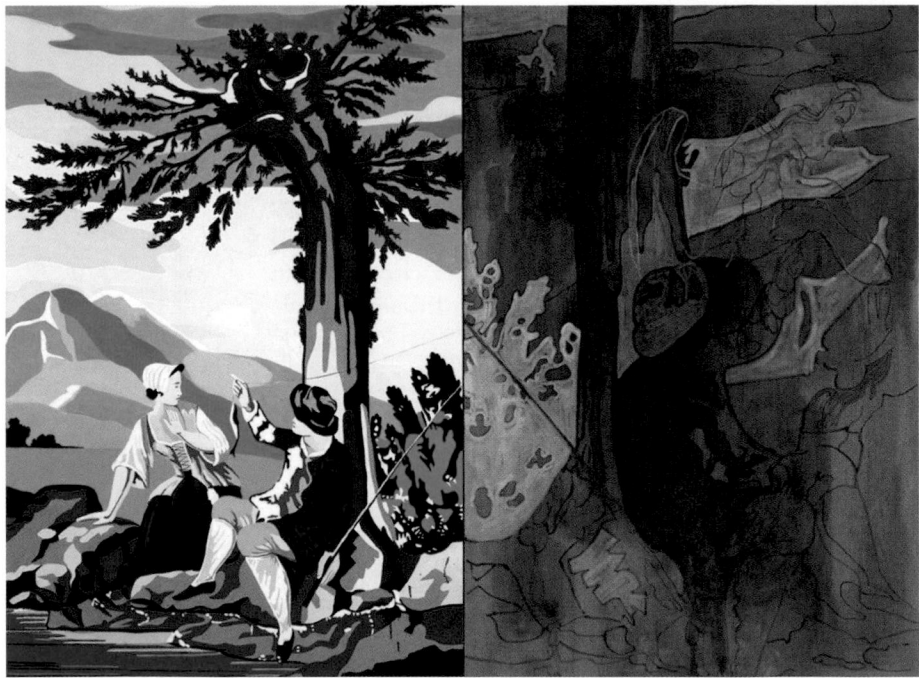

1 ft.

▲ 3.6 **DAVID SALLE,** *Angel* (2000). Oil and acrylic on canvas and linen (two panels), 72" × 96".

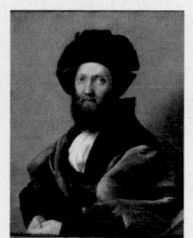
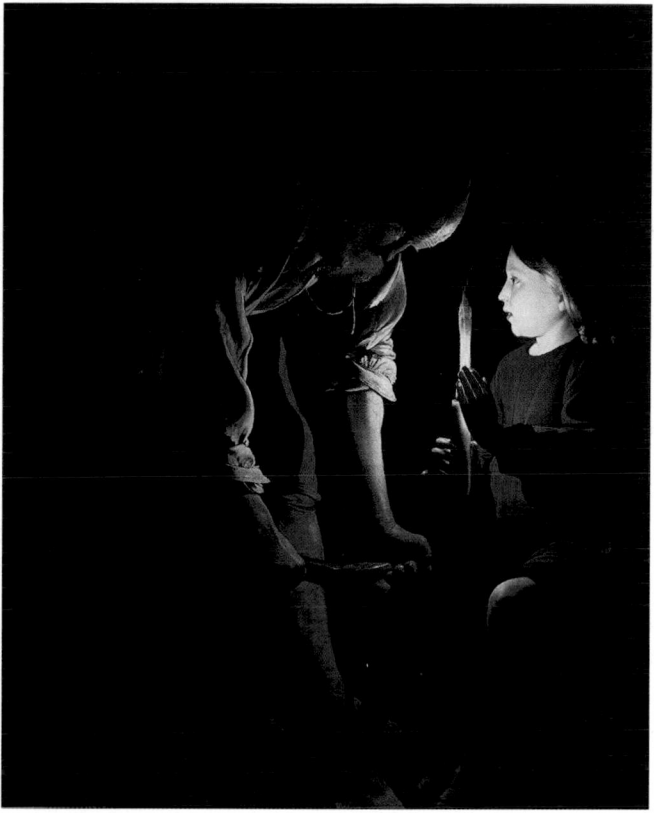

∧ 3.7 GEORGES DE LA TOUR, *Saint Joseph the Carpenter* (1642). Oil on canvas, 54" × 40". Louvre, Paris, France.

The technique of chiaroscuro reached the peak of perfection during the High Renaissance in Italy. Artists including Leonardo da Vinci, Michelangelo, and Raphael created an impression of three-dimensionality on a two-dimensional surface by modeling the figures in their paintings—that is, manipulating light and shadow to re-create what the eye sees. A prime example of Raphael's perfection of the technique is his *Portrait of Baldassare Castiglione* (see Fig. 1.14).

Whereas chiaroscuro relies on bathing subjects in more or less uniform light, tenebrism, from the Italian meaning "shadowy manner," mimics the effects of a harsh "spotlight" emanating from a single light source with clear directionality. Tenebrism was developed during the seventeenth century by artists who desired an element of theatricality in their work; it heightened the sense of drama, mystery, and intimacy.

When people and objects are sharply lit, as with the use of tenebrism, the lighted areas of these objects and their accompanying shadows can be exaggerated. The placement of patches of bright light is termed **highlighting**; when the lighting is harshest, cast shadows are most pronounced. In Georges de la Tour's *Saint Joseph the Carpenter* (Fig. 3.7), a single light source— a burning candle—draws our attention to the young Jesus's face as he speaks to the elderly Joseph. Jesus's fingertips glow as the light passes through them, the touch of bright red echoed on the crown of Joseph's balding head. As in other paintings that feature tenebrism, the contrast between areas of bright light and velvety darkness is striking. The artist heightens this contrast with the judicious placement of highlights and cast shadows.

In architecture, highlights and cast shadows can add an intriguing decorative element. Consider Antoine Predock's design for the Nelson Fine Arts Center at Arizona State University (Fig. 3.8)—a structure whose surfaces become a "stage" for a choreographed interplay of light and shadow. Solid, smooth expanses of concrete are broken up, visually,

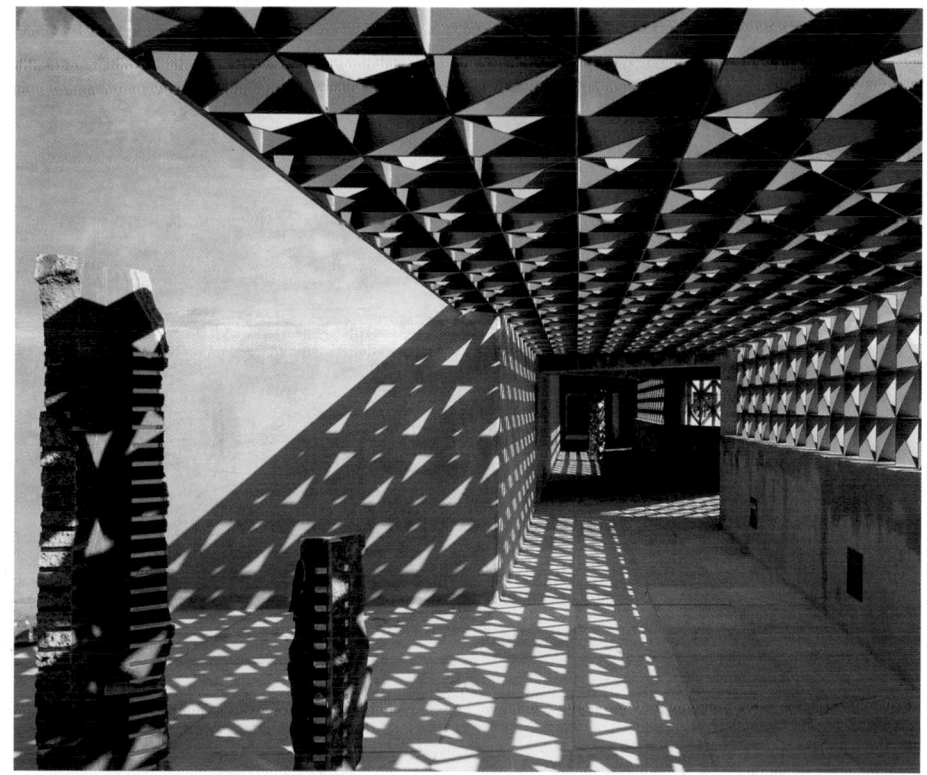

∧ 3.8 ANTOINE PREDOCK, ARCHITECT, Nelson Fine Arts Center, Arizona State University, Tempe, Arizona (1989).

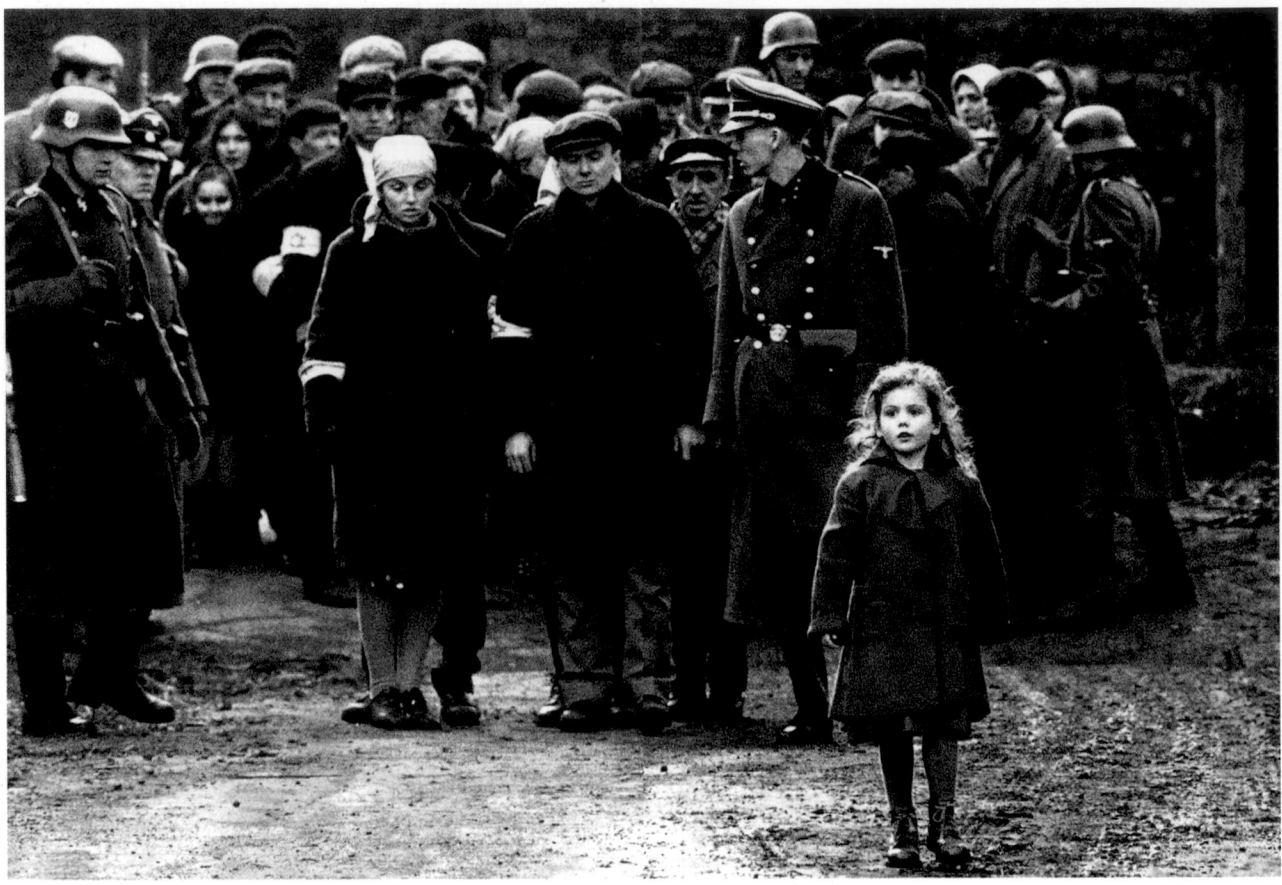

^ 3.9 STEVEN SPIELBERG, Film Still from *Schindler's List* (1993).

by intricate patterns of geometric shapes (shadows) that are formed as light streams through the open, ramada-like structure of the roof.

Descriptive and Expressive Properties of Value

Value plays a key role in design, but can be used by the artist for narrative or symbolic purposes or to evoke an emotional response in the viewer. In *Guernica* (see Fig 20.10), which ranks as one of the most powerful black-and-white paintings in the history of art, Pablo Picasso portrayed the destruction and agony of a Spanish town as it was attacked in the early 1930s by Germany in history's first example of carpet-bombing. Our eyes are drawn to the desperate drama unfolding in the interposed faces, torsos, and limbs—individuals unified by their fear and anguish. Values ranging from pale gray to velvet black evoke the darkness of night and seem to symbolize a descent into chaos and death.

Although most feature-length Hollywood motion pictures today are shot with color film, some directors purposefully use black-and-white film to reference the quality and tone of early filmmaking or for its expressive potential. Steven Spielberg's *Schindler's List*, inspired by events of the Holocaust that were described in eyewitness

testimony, was shot almost exclusively in black and white. The film is bracketed by scenes shot in color: it opens with a Jewish family celebrating the Sabbath—life as it was and ought to have remained—and closes with footage of actual Holocaust survivors visiting the grave of the man who rescued them—Oskar Schindler. In between, as events unfold, the film switches to black and white. The extensive archives of photographs and film footage of the atrocities committed by the Nazis, of course, are all black and white and Spielberg's restricted palette gives his film a documentary quality, an air of authenticity. Spielberg made one exception to his black-and-white palette: A small girl

CONNECTIONS

In *Guernica*, Picasso's manipulation of value contrast focuses the eye on every individual's fate—a wailing woman holds her dead

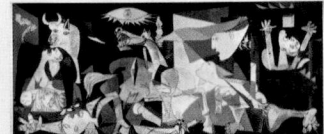

^ Picasso's *Guernica* (Fig. 20.10)

child, another screams from the torturous flames that engulf her; at the same time, the common denominator of the gray spectrum ties all of the victims together. The black, white, and gray palette also suggests photographs in newspapers resulting in a stunning balance of art and documentary.

appears in several, disconnected scenes wearing a red coat that stands out in an otherwise colorless world (Fig. 3.9).

Spielberg personalizes the fate of a single child as she periodically appears throughout the film (and through the process of the liquidation of a ghetto). Instantly and persistently recognizable for the colors of her blonde curly hair and bright red coat, we develop an emotional attachment to a victim whose particularity makes real the incomprehensible numbers of dead. Spielberg understood the expressive power of color.

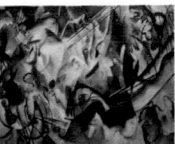
COLOR

Color matters. It is fundamental to our perception of the physical world and can convey our inner thoughts and moods. The science of color optics explains things like the physics of light, the spectral sensitivity of the human eye, and the brain's interpretation of light waves of varying lengths as distinct colors. But the power of color as an expressive tool transcends the spheres of physics or biology. We say we are blue when we are sad, see red when we are enraged, turn white with fright, and can be green with envy. The science of color and the emotional associations of color—as far apart as they may seem—together form the foundation of color theory in art.

The Science of Light

The visible spectrum (see Fig. 3.1) is composed of an array of colors that can be perceived by the naked human eye. Newton described the spectrum in order: red, orange, yellow, green, blue, indigo, and violet—memorized by students for decades with the acronym *Roy G. Biv*. Each of these colors corresponds to a specific region of wavelengths of radiant energy emitted by the sun or an artificial source of white light; the human eye is sensitive to only a narrow band of these wavelengths, measured in nanometers, or billionths of a meter. Within a region defined by a single color name—red, blue, green, for example—variations of the color appear at toward the borders of that region, so that we perceive a range of reds rather than a single red. Reds have the longest wavelength and violet has the shortest wavelength. Beyond what can be seen by the human eye—again, the visible spectrum—lie wavelengths that are invisible. These include the better-known ultraviolet and infrared waves, as well as gamma rays and x-rays, radio waves, and microwaves.

The Color Wheel

It might seem logical that the farther apart colors are along the visible spectrum, the more different they would appear. After all, their wavelengths would be the most different. But Newton noticed that the colors at the distant ends of the visible spectrum—red and violet—actually looked more similar to each other than colors closer to them in the middle of the spectrum. Newton toyed with bringing the ends of the spectrum together and thus conceived the color circle. However, he noted that although purple existed in nature, it was missing from the visible spectrum. He found that he could generate purple by overlapping red with violet at the opposite ends of the spectrum. Newton made the center of his proposed color circle white to illustrate his observation that all light, or all wavelengths that had been refracted into color regions by a prism, could be recomposed into white light when passed through another prism.

Newton's color circle served as the precedent for the twelve-point **color wheel** (Fig. 3.10) and foundation of color theory in art. The twelve-point wheel—a method of organizing color relationships—was conceived by the American physicist Herbert E. Ives, and was based on the three **primary pigment colors**—red, blue, and yellow—from which

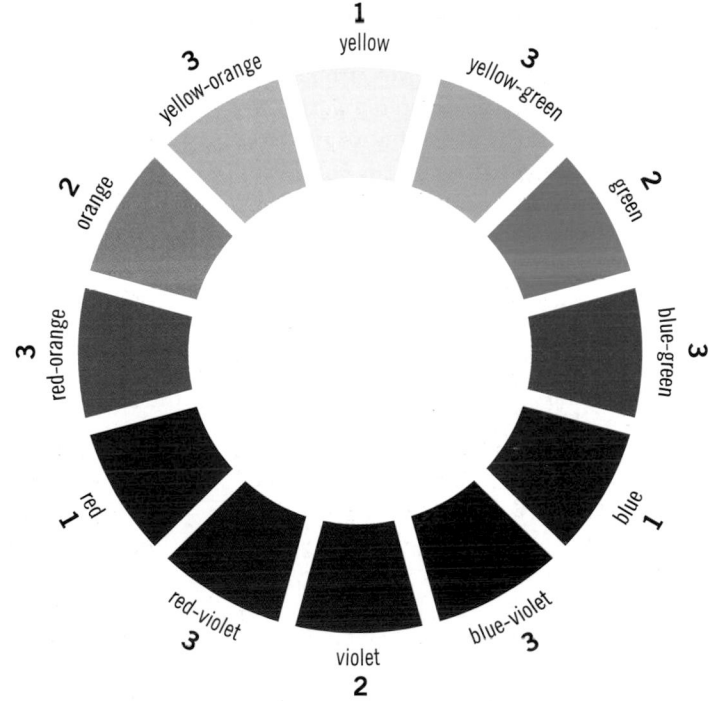
∧ 3.10 The Twelve-Point Color Wheel.

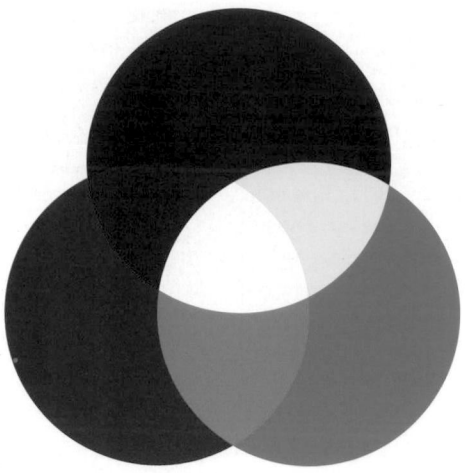

▲ 3.11 Additive Color Mixtures.

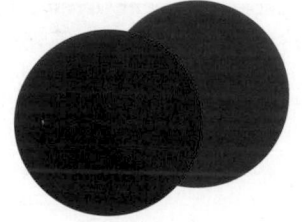 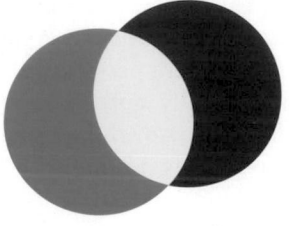

Red + Blue Light = Magenta   **Green + Red Light = Yellow**

▲ 3.12 The Overlapping of the Additive Primary Colors.

all other colors of pigment could be derived. **Secondary pigment colors** could be created through the mixing of the primary colors, resulting in green (from blue and yellow), orange (from red and yellow), and violet (from red and blue). Six so-called **tertiary colors**—yellow-orange, orange-red, red-violet, violet-blue, blue-green, and green-yellow—could be created through the mixing together of a primary and secondary color.

Additive and Subtractive Colors

When all those years as a child you were mixing finger-paints together on a glossy white sheet of paper, you probably thought you were adding colors to other colors. Sometimes, two of those colors—like red and blue—made purple; yellow and blue gave you green. But if you blended all of your colors, you likely wound up with a muddy brown. What you probably didn't know is that the colors you were *perceiving* were not the result of the *physical* additive process, but of the *physics* of the subtractive process. **Additive color** is color that is created by mixing colored light. **Subtractive color** is color that is created by mixing pigments.

Additive color refers to rays (or beams) of colored light that, when overlapped or "mixed" with other colored light, produce added (lighter) colors as well as pure, white light (Fig. 3.11). The white spotlight, for example, that you see on stage can be created by the intersection of beams of red, blue, and green light. When two of these rays of colored light are overlapped, they form lighter colors; the overlap of orange-red and green, for example, creates yellow and the overlap of blue-violet and orange-red blend to form magenta (Fig. 3.12).

Subtractive color refers to the mixing of pigments, dyes, and inks rather than light, and is therefore more relevant to the actual practice of the artist. The process of mixing pigments is called subtractive because the color that is perceived is based on the absorption, or "subtraction," of

light. What actually happens is that when you cover a surface with a specific paint color, that layer *absorbs* colors of the spectrum *other than the one that you applied*. So if your paint contains red pigment, your painted canvas reflects wavelengths within the red range and absorbs the others (Fig. 3.13). Your surface will appear "red" to the human eye if it absorbs all wavelengths except for ones between 625 and 740 nanometers. In sum, the pigment you apply to a surface results in the *subtraction* of all the other colors of the visible spectrum—that is, all of the wavelengths being reflected by the surface except for those that correspond to red. And what about the blank, white surface you began with before you were inspired to cover it with red paint? It was reflecting all wavelengths of the visible spectrum. None is being absorbed, or subtracted from the spectrum.

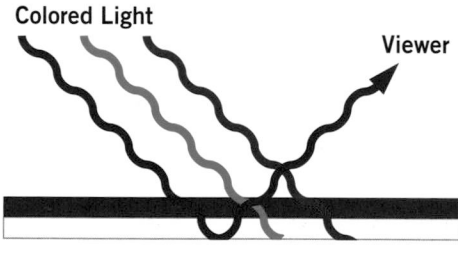

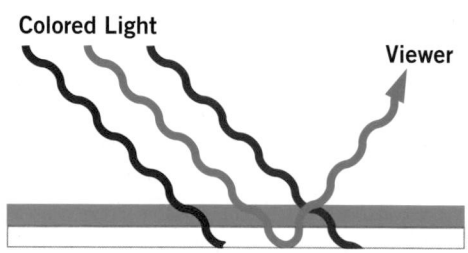

▲ 3.13 The Perception of Color Reflected from a Surface.

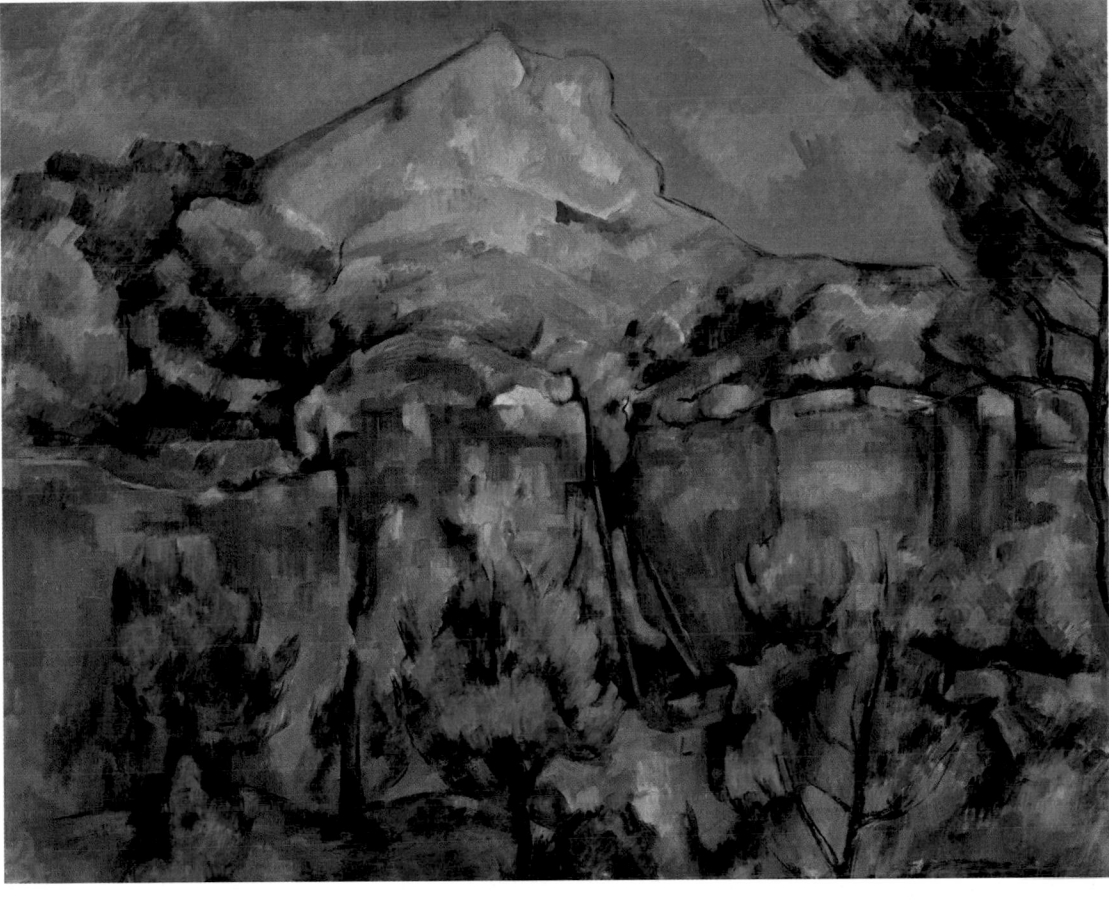

1 ft.

> **3.14 PAUL CÉZANNE,** *Mont Sainte-Victoire Seen from Bibemus Quarry* (c. 1897). Oil on canvas, 25⅛" × 31½". The Baltimore Museum of Art, Baltimore, Maryland.

Cool and Warm Colors

Cool and *warm* apply, in typical usage, to temperature and so-called cool and warm colors have that association. Just as getting close to the red-orange flames of a crackling fire creates a literal sense of warmth, compositions bathed in yellow, orange, and red convey a feeling of warmth or heat. Plunging into the blue waves after basking in the sun on the beach cools our bodies instantly and walls painted blue have been known to give office workers an unpleasant case of the chills.

When the human eye focuses on color, muscular movements in the eye force warm colors—red, orange, yellow—to advance toward the eye and cool colors—blue, green, purple—to move away from it. Color can thus be used to contribute to the visual impression of depth in a two-dimensional work like a painting. Color provides an important spatial cue in Paul Cézanne's landscape, *Mont Sainte-Victoire Seen from Bibemus Quarry* (Fig. 3.14): the warm reddish and ochre tones of the quarry stone in the lower half of the painting visually advance to the foreground and the mountain peak recedes into the background by virtue of its blue, gray, and purple hues set against a mottled blue sky.

Properties of Color

Color is discussed in terms of its physical properties and visual perceptual properties. Its physical properties—such as wavelength and light absorption and reflection—can be measured with scientific instruments. The perceptual properties of color, on the other hand, are based on the interactivity of light receptors—cone cells—in the human eye with the visible light spectrum. Stimulation of these cells leads to the perception of color.

The three key perceptual properties of color are **hue**, value, and **intensity**.

CONNECTIONS John Sloan, a painter and renowned art educator, thought it was good practice to draw everything that you draw from a model from memory as well. The next time you are walking or driving from one place to another, pay attention to the colors that you encounter along the way. At the end of the day, try to recall which colors made the greatest impression in your memory. How would you describe them in terms of hue, value, and intensity?

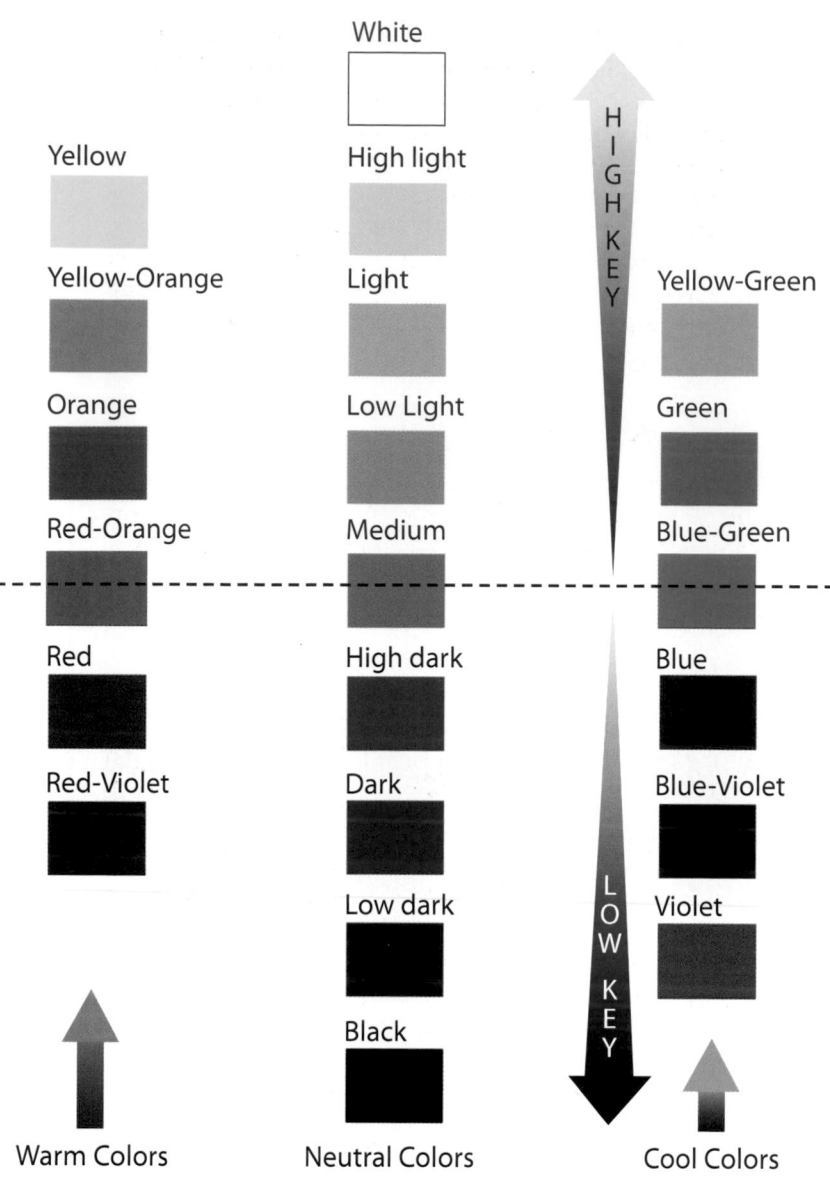

White

Yellow — High light

Yellow-Orange — Light — Yellow-Green

Orange — Low Light — Green

Red-Orange — Medium — Blue-Green

Red — High dark — Blue

Red-Violet — Dark — Blue-Violet

Low dark — Violet

Black

HIGH KEY

LOW KEY

Warm Colors — Neutral Colors — Cool Colors

∧ 3.15 Color Values Relative to the Gray Scale.

HUE Simply defined, hue is pure, unadulterated color—as it appears on the color wheel. Our perception of hue is connected to the eye's sensitivity to specific parts of the visible spectrum—red, yellow, blue, and green—sometimes referred to as "unique hues." These hues, however, can be expanded to create any number of variations and gradations of that hue. Black and white are colors, or pigments; they are not on the visible spectrum, however, and therefore are not considered hues. Black, white, and gray are considered neutral colors.

VALUE Value refers to the lightness or darkness of a hue—its degree of luminosity. The value of a hue can be altered by adding black or white to that hue. The addition of black results in **shades** of that hue; adding white produces **tints** of that hue. Mixing gray with a color can create a variety of **tones**. Maroon or burgundy are shades of red; pink is a tint of red. Whereas hues are few in number, tints and shades of hues are numerous. The human eye can perceive at least forty tints and shades of any one color.

Colors have different values because each one in the visible spectrum reflects a different quantity of light. Yellow and orange are called high-value colors because they reflect a greater amount of light than low-value colors such as blue or violet (Fig. 3.15).

The perception of the value of a color is dependent on that which surrounds it. Figure 3.16 illustrates the visual sensations of the same colors against different backgrounds. The center blue square appears more luminous and of higher value when seen against black than it does when seen against white.

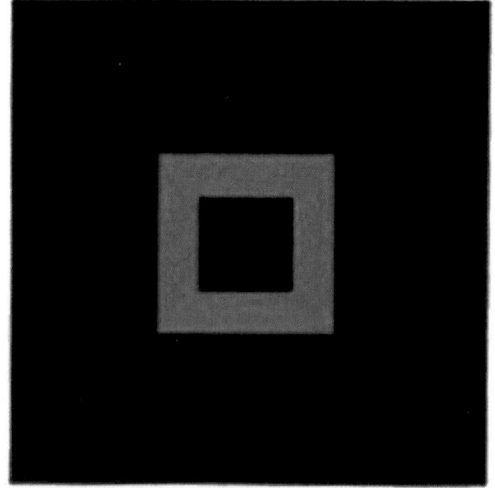
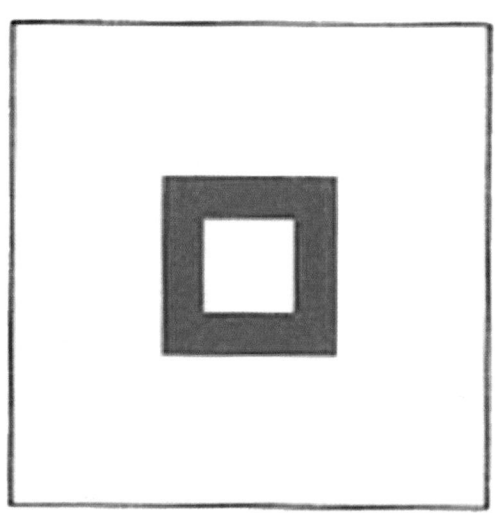

< 3.16 Color in Different Value Contrasts.

3.17 Hue, Value, and Intensity.

INTENSITY AND SATURATION Intensity and **saturation** are synonymous terms that describe the brightness or dullness of a color. A color is most intense or most saturated when it is most pure—like the color that is perceived when a beam of light is refracted through a prism, or the color of pure pigment that has not been mixed with black or white. When colors are mixed with black or white or their complement their intensity is affected, as is their value. Colors can have similar values but different intensities—different degrees of brightness (Figs. 3.17 and 3.18).

Color Schemes

Artists use color instinctively or intuitively at times but they can also be quite conscious of the science and theory of color in their arrangement of color in a composition. Planned combinations of color are referred to as **color schemes**. *Monochromatic* and *analogous* color

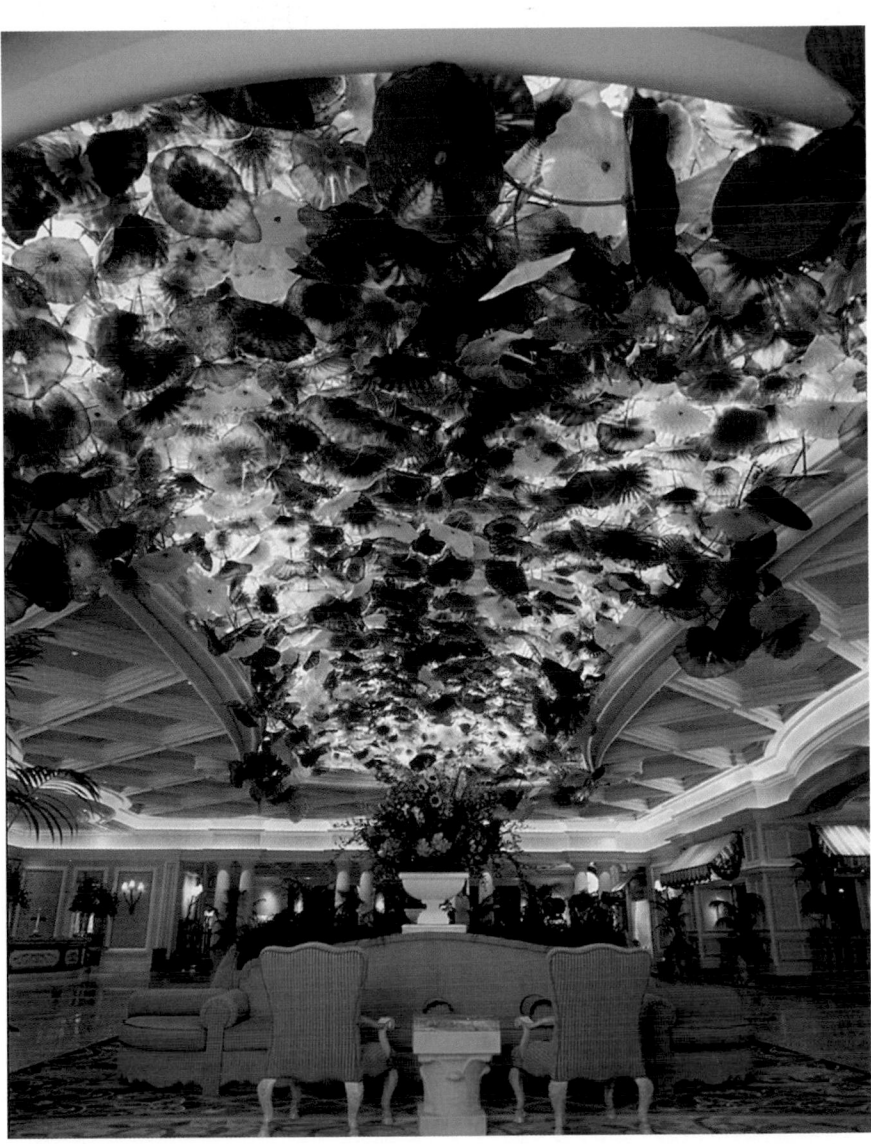

3.18 DALE CHIHULY, *Fiori di Como* (1998), 70 × 30 × 12'. Bellagio resort, Las Vegas.

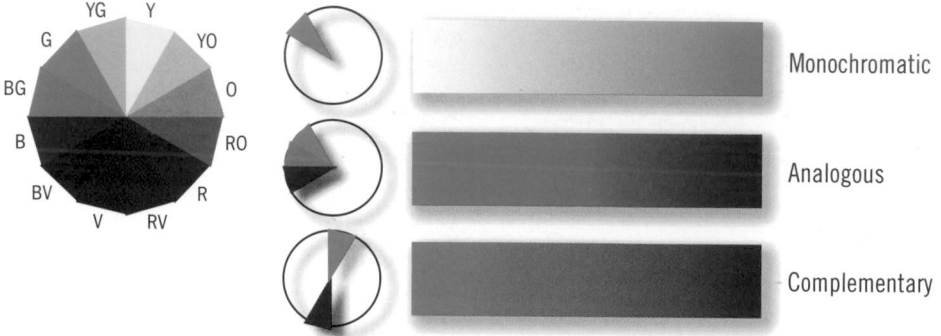

Monochromatic

Analogous

Complementary

∧ 3.19 Color Schemes.

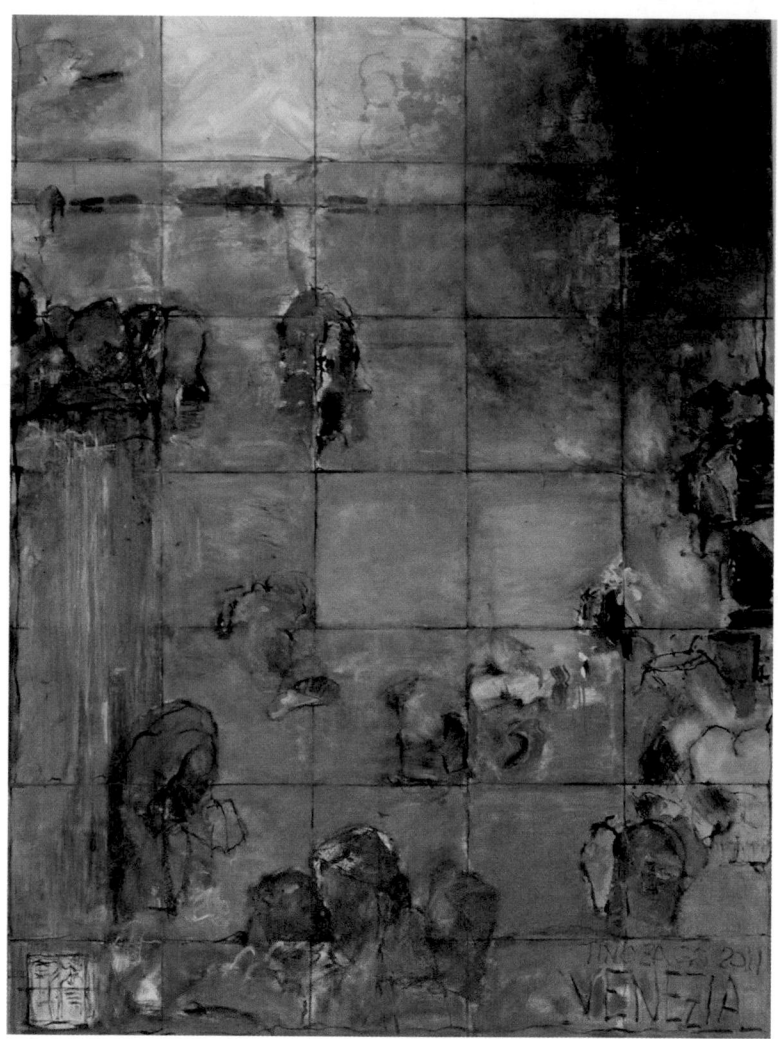

1 ft.

∧ 3.20 **TINO ZAGO,** *Venezia #27 Revisited* (2011). Oil on canvas, 72" × 54". OK Harris Gallery, New York, New York.

schemes tend to be visually harmonious. By contrast, a *complementary* color scheme will exhibit disharmony (Fig. 3.19).

A **monochromatic color scheme** features one (*mono*) dominant hue (*chroma*). To avoid monotony, monochromatic

schemes often include a range of tints and shades of a single color, as in Tino Zago's *Venezia #27 Revisited* (Fig. 3.20).

Analogous colors are adjacent on the color wheel and are more similar to each other than to colors elsewhere in the spectrum. When used together in a composition, as in Mark Messersmith's *Lost Hindsight* (Fig. 3.21), **analogous color schemes** create a feeling of harmony. A palette of shades and tints of red, pink, mauve, and peach visually unify the complicated patchwork design of flowers and colored squares. It bears mentioning that squares of highly saturated red are concentrated in a diamond-shaped area at the center of the heart-shaped canvas, creating emphasis and focal point in the otherwise frenzied field.

Because **complementary color schemes** are based on colors that are across from one another on the color wheel—colors that "tug" equally at the eye—these schemes are very dynamic and can be used to great effect. Mary Cassatt's extraordinary pastel painting, *In the Loge* (Fig. 3.22), is organized completely around the bold contrast of red and green. The emphatic, alternating bands of red and green, along with the bright red vertical strip that runs along the right edge of the composition (and defines the loge of the theater), are balanced by the dominant central shape of the green fan. The woman's clothing is accented with complementary strokes of green and red. Touches of raw red pigment seem here and there to iridescent—from her hair, her fan, her high-necked lacy blouse. This "unnatural" combination of colors recreates the rosy atmosphere of a theater bathed in artificial light.

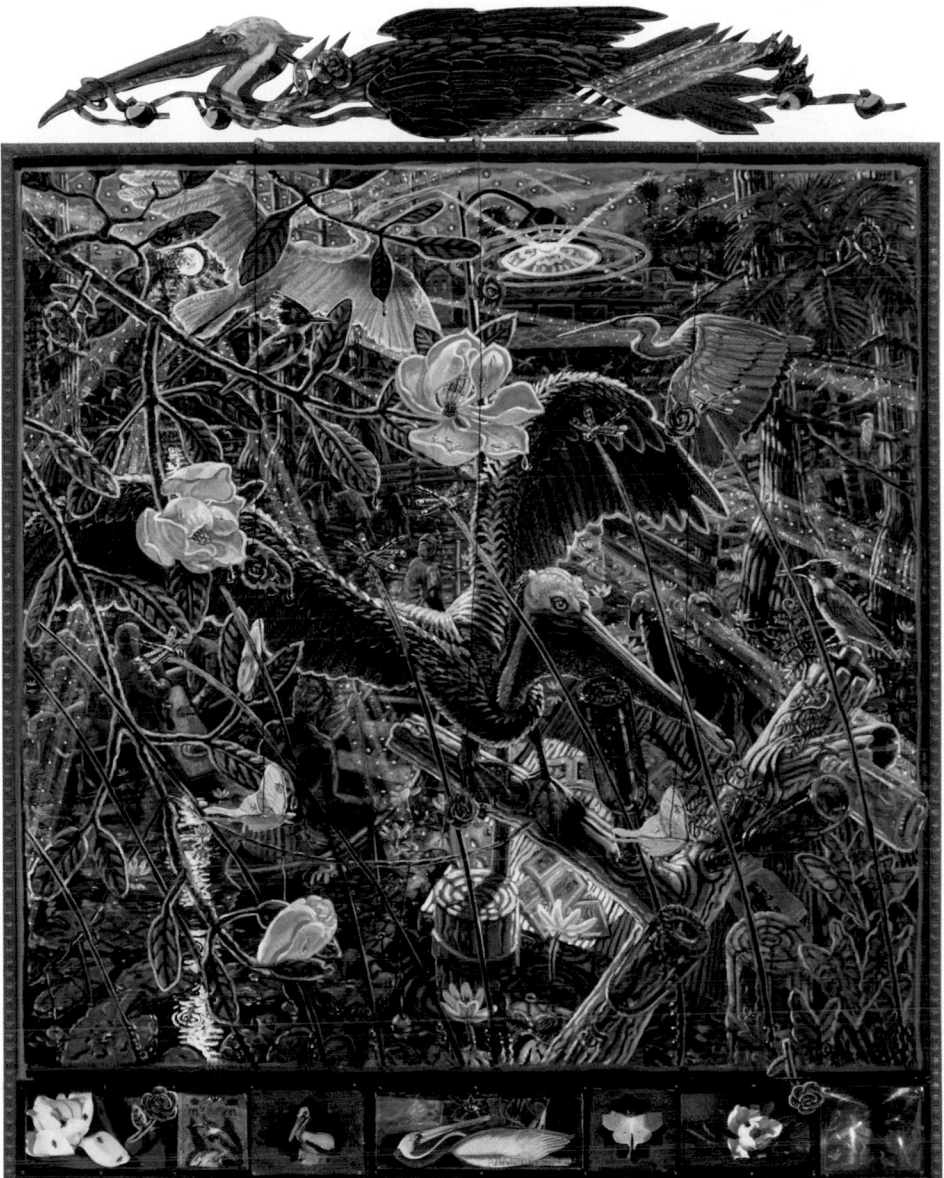

1 ft.

Local, Optical, and Arbitrary Color

Artists who aim to recreate visible reality as accurately as possible will likely use what is referred to as **local color**—the color that we typically associate with the natural appearance of things. We think of the sky as blue, the sun as yellow, and the grass as green. And because most of the world does too, local color is seen as objective. It is something that is known and seen, rather than something that exists in the mind of an individual.

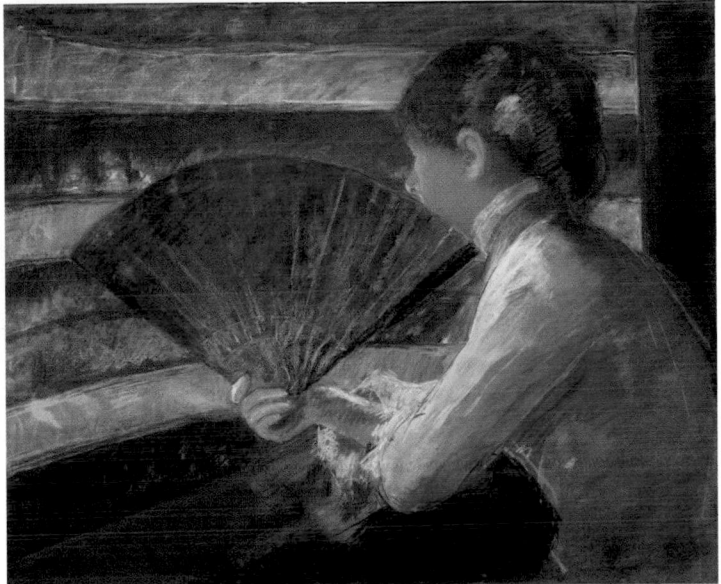

1 ft.

> 3.22 MARY CASSATT, *In the Loge* (1879). Pastel, 25⅝" × 32". The Philadelphia Museum of Art, Philadelphia, Pennsylvania.

Local color is color as it would be perceived in direct sunlight. But changes in light change our perception of color. That is because the color that is perceived by the eye is related to the quantity of light that is reflected off an object. When artists simulate the visual effects of different lighting conditions and their effect on the objects we are looking at, they are working with the principle of **optical color**. Consider Claude Monet's use of optical color in *Rouen Cathedral* (Fig. 3.23). The cold stone surfaces of the medieval church façade seem to dissolve into fine dabs of color as Monet tries to reproduce the visual effects of light and atmosphere on the tangible solids before him. These are not colors that we associate with

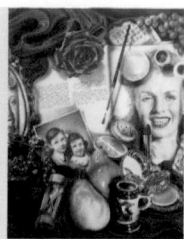

CONNECTIONS Audrey Flack's over sized Photorealist still life paintings—such as *Marilyn (Vanitas)*—take advantage of local color to underscore the familiarity of her everyday objects. An orange is orange; grapes are green. Even our "concept" of lipstick is confirmed as a pillar of creamy red. Between the objective colors and the enormous scale of the work (this painting is eight feet square), the viewer cannot escape the reality of the commonplace and the eventuality of death symbolized by objects like the hourglass, burning candle, and overripe fruit.

∧ Flack's *Marilyn (Vanitas)* (**Fig. 1.9**)

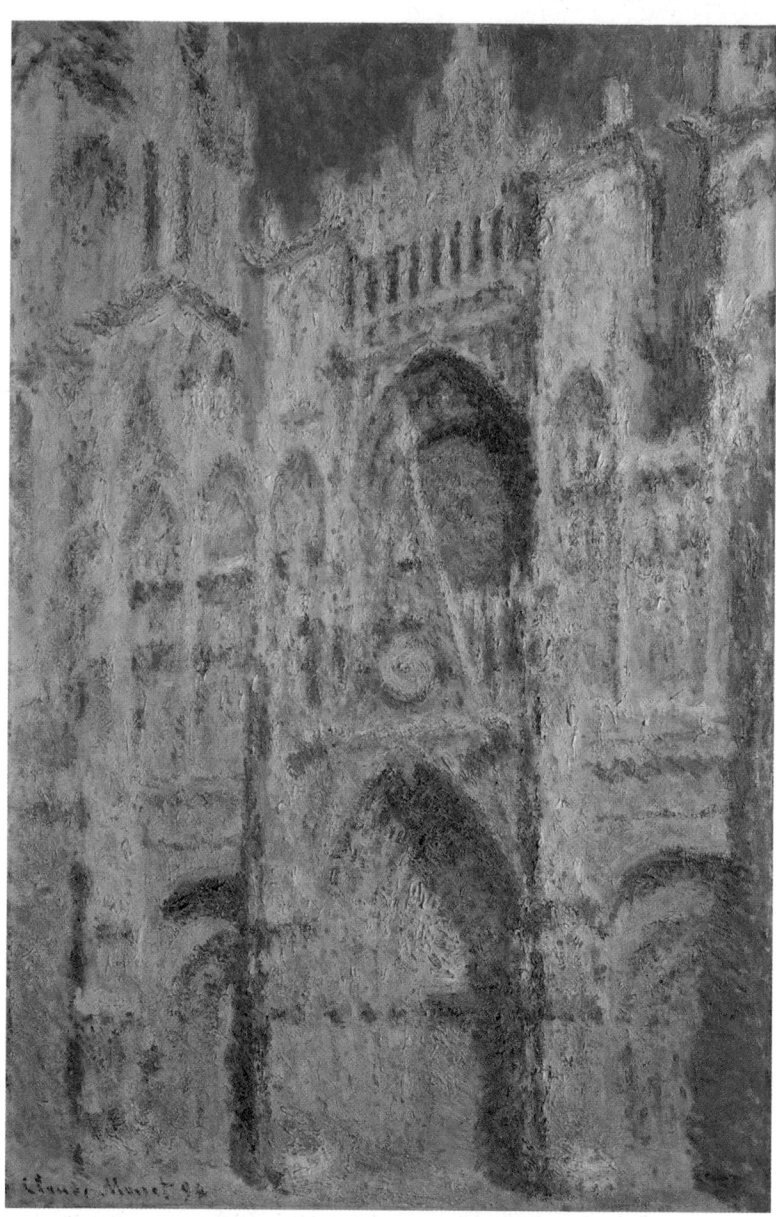

1 ft.

∧ **3.23 CLAUDE MONET,** *Rouen Cathedral: The Portal (in Sun)* (1894). Oil on canvas, 39¼" × 25⅞". The Metropolitan Museum of Art, New York, New York.

Gothic buildings in our minds. Rather, Monet would maintain that these are colors that we actually see if we look hard enough.

Both local and optical color are rooted in experience. Whether it is color that is perceived in daylight and fair weather or dusk during a storm, visual effects are being reproduced in some way. **Arbitrary (subjective) color**, by contrast, does not accurately reflect the visible reality of things (Fig. 3.24). Artists use subjective color for purposes other than realism—perhaps to convey emotion, to find the pictorial equivalent of inner feelings.

Color and Symbolism

The connectedness between emotion and color often explains an artist's palette choices. But abstract notions and ideas also have their symbolic color coordinates. For example, what does it mean if one is true to the red, white, and blue? If you are an American citizen, it means, of course, that you are loyal to your country—the United States of America—as symbolized by the red, white, and blue colors of the flag. But this would also be true if you were, say, British or French because their national flags (the Union Jack or the Tri-Color) have the same color combination, albeit with different designs.

In a subtle but chilling commentary on issues of equality, oppression, and difference, contemporary Nigerian British artist Yinka Shonibare reworked typical Victorian costume in fabrics expressing African identity, both constructed and adopted. In *Victorian Couple* (Fig. 3.25) the profiles of the coat and bustle may seem familiar, but the colorful textiles and printed designs create a cultural

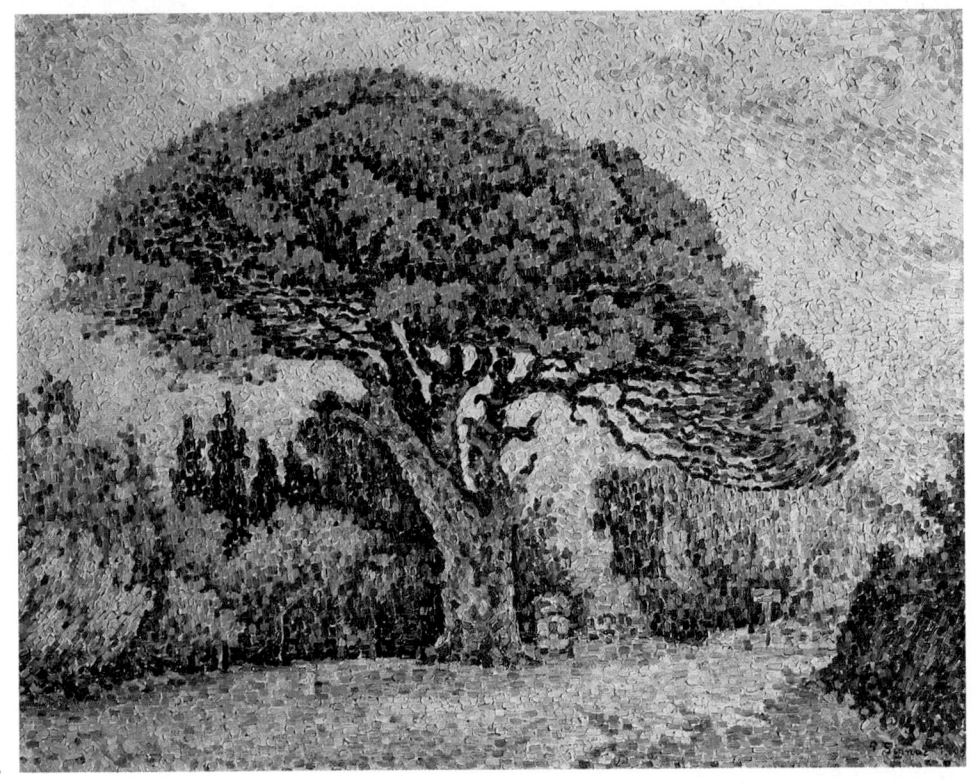

1 ft.

< 3.24 PAUL SIGNAC, *The Pine Tree at St. Tropez* (1909). Oil on canvas, 28 ¼" × 36 ¼". Pushkin Museum, Moscow, Russia.

disconnect with symbolic ramifications. Shonibare was born in London of Nigerian parents and spent most of his childhood in Nigeria. He returned to England to study at the University of London and has focused his art on issues of African identity and authenticity in which the symbolism of color play a central role. The symbolism of colors, their meanings, are culture-specific.

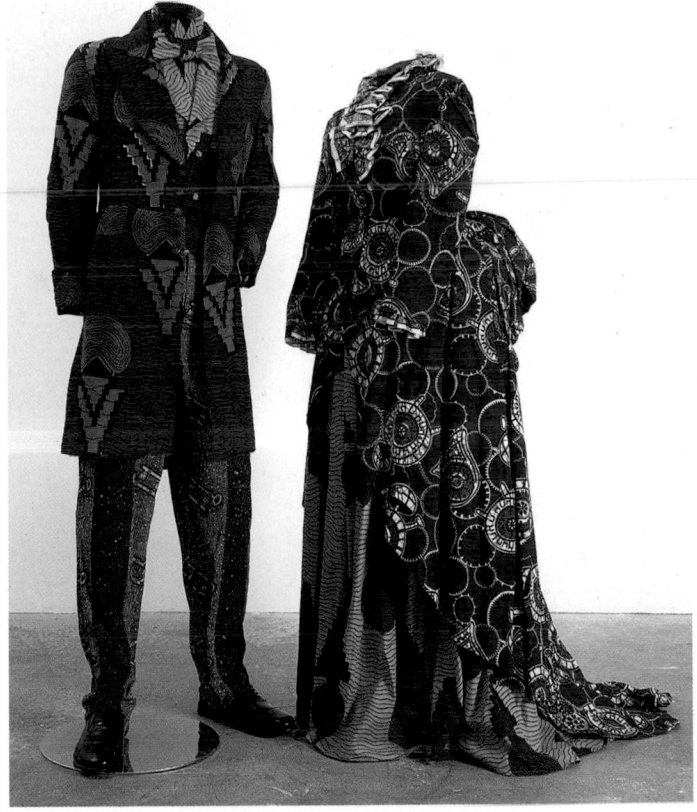

^ 3.25 YINKA SHONIBARE, *Victorian Couple* (1999). Wax printed cotton textile, approximately 60" × 36" × 36" and 60" × 24" × 24".

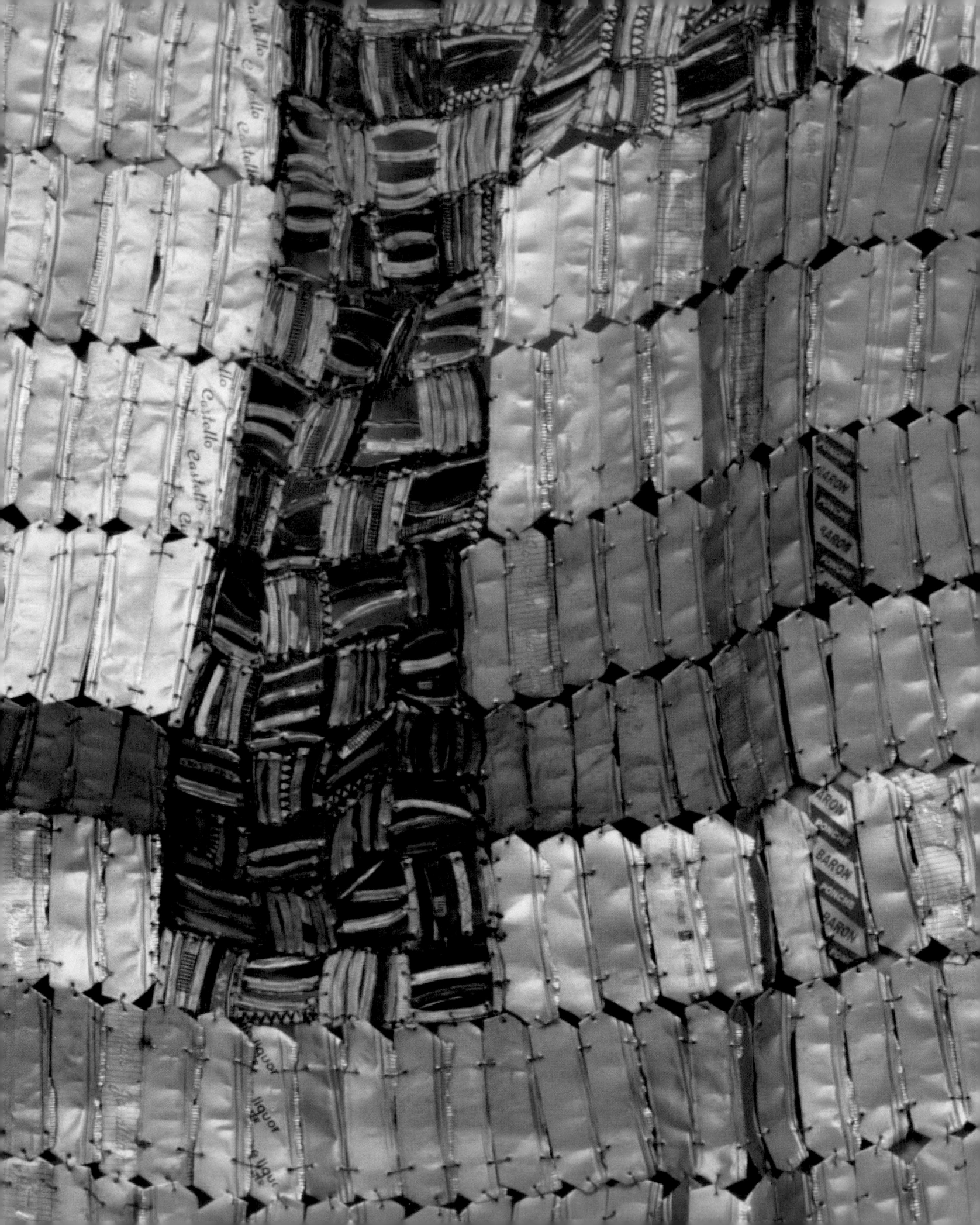

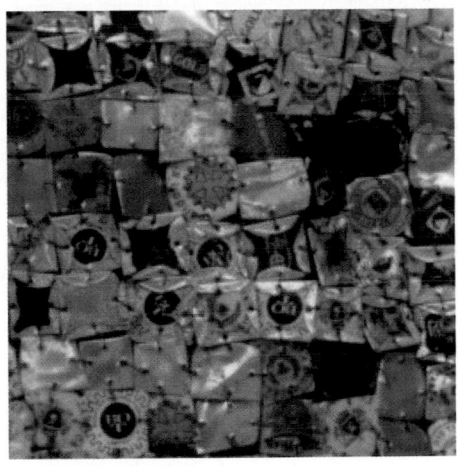

4

TEXTURE AND PATTERN

There is a better chance of getting an exciting painting from a labored study with texture than from a fine line drawing without it.

— JOHN SLOAN

EXPERIENCES ARE shaped by senses other than sight and perhaps the most basic of these is touch. The human body is covered with a sensory organ—the skin—that responds with pleasure or revulsion to textures in the environment. Animals, including people, nestle with one another for warmth. Stuffed teddy bear companions and cuddly blankets reliably provide feelings of security. But just as we are drawn to comforting textures, so too do we recoil from those that are cold, rough, sharp, or prickly. As an element of art, artists and designers may manipulate texture to evoke similar emotional responses or moods.

Consider the very different associations that emerge in two landscape paintings with the same subject by the same artist—Vincent van Gogh. The pleasant, almost fragile quality in his *Orchard in Blossom (Plum Trees)* (Fig. 4.1) can be attributed to the pastel palette and high-key values coupled with brushstrokes so delicate that the texture of the canvas can be seen around and through them. The painting evokes a sense of tranquility; it is uplifting. The effect is quite the opposite in his *Mulberry Tree* (Fig. 4.2) in which brushstrokes thick with paint create an irregular tactile surface and a sensation of turbulence. Try to imagine the sensory or emotional impact on you that each of these settings might have.

The element of texture then adds a significant dimension to our interpretation of or relation to works of art. Artists may exaggerate or even distort textures to communicate their own feelings and these textures can produce an empathetic response in the spectator.

< EL ANATSUI, *Between Earth and Heaven* (2006). Aluminum, copper wire; 91" × 126". The Metropolitan Museum of Art, New York, New York.

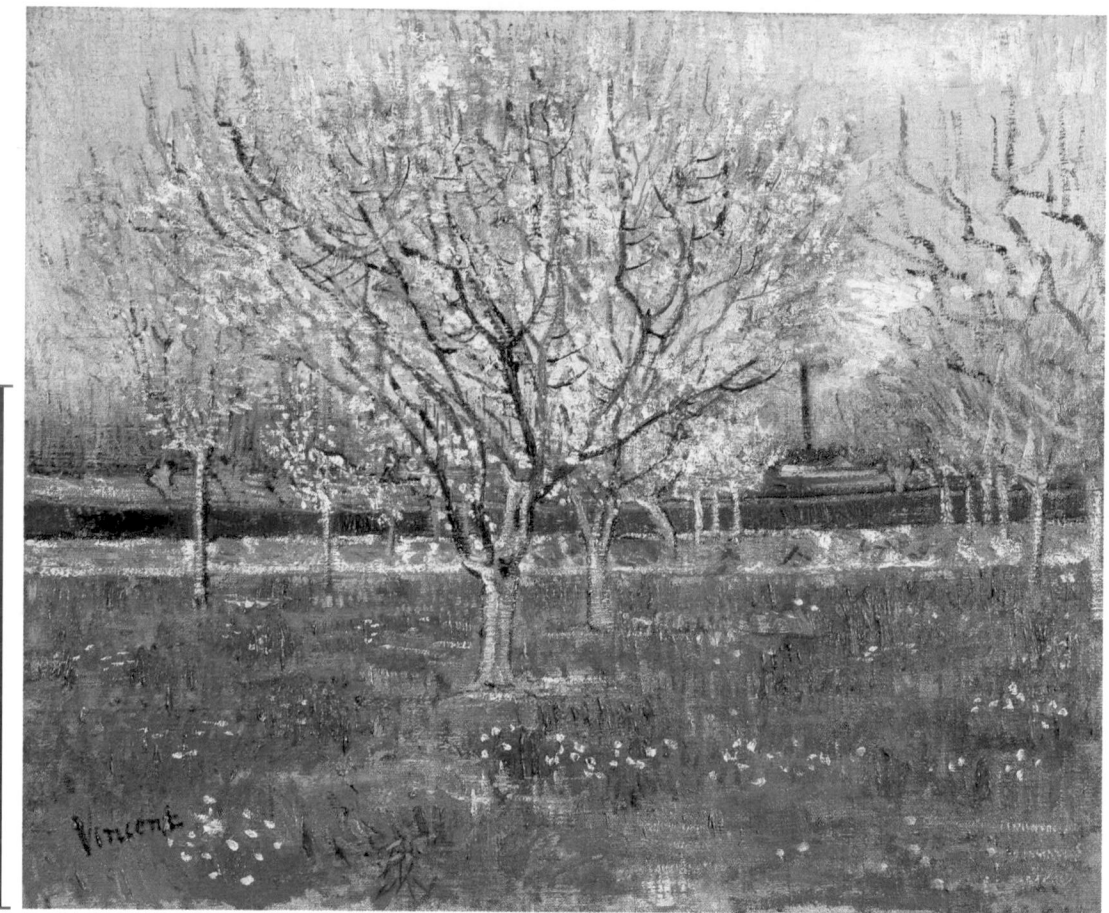

1 ft.

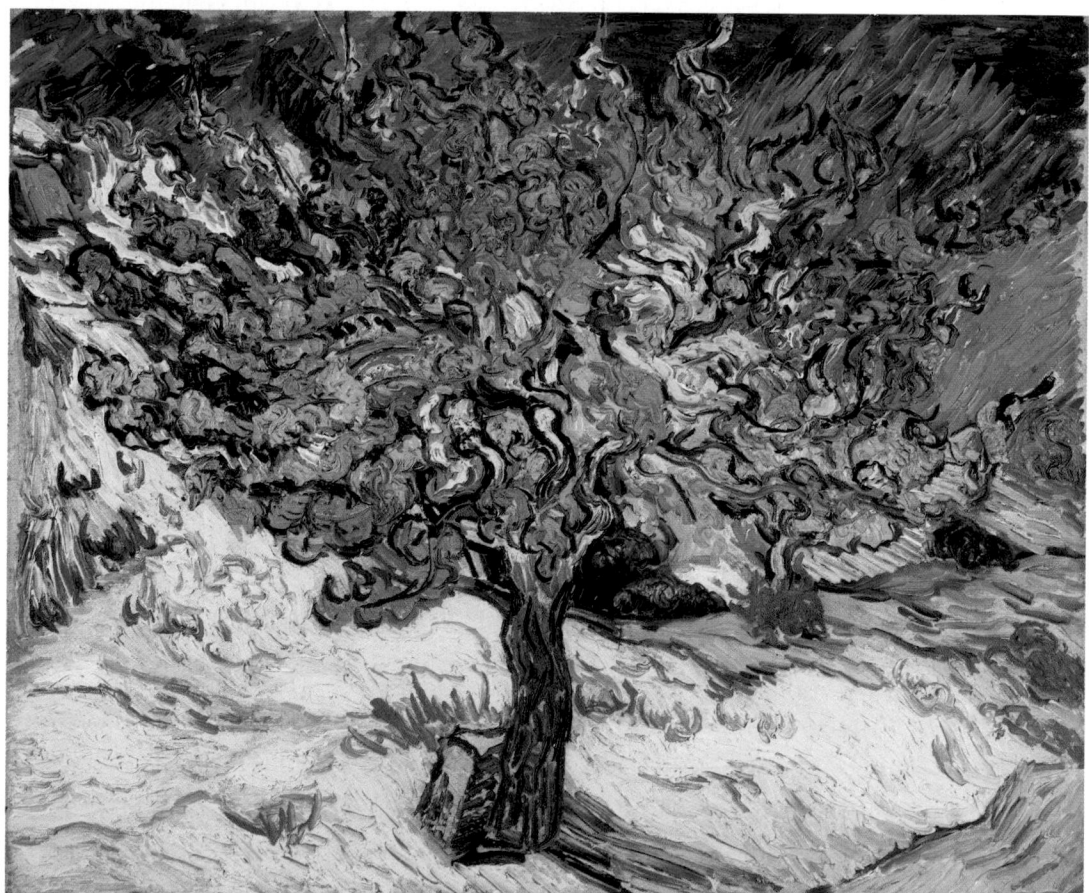

1 ft.

> 4.2 VINCENT VAN GOGH, *Mulberry Tree* (1889). Oil on canvas, 21 1/4" × 25". Norton Simon Art Foundation, Pasadena, California.

TEXTURE

The word *texture* derives from Latin for "weaving," and it is used to describe the surface character of woven fabrics and other materials as experienced primarily through the sense of touch. In sculpture, crafts like ceramics or fiber art, and architecture materials have actual surface textures. We can feel them if we run our hands over them. But artists also create the illusion of texture in two-dimensional art forms such as drawing or painting. When a subject is rendered meticulously, the artist may trick the eye into perceiving actual texture even though the surface is smooth.

For most works of art, we describe texture as *actual* or *visual*. **Actual texture** is *actually* related to the materials used to create the work. **Visual texture** is the illusion of an actual texture. Céleste Boursier-Mougenot's installation

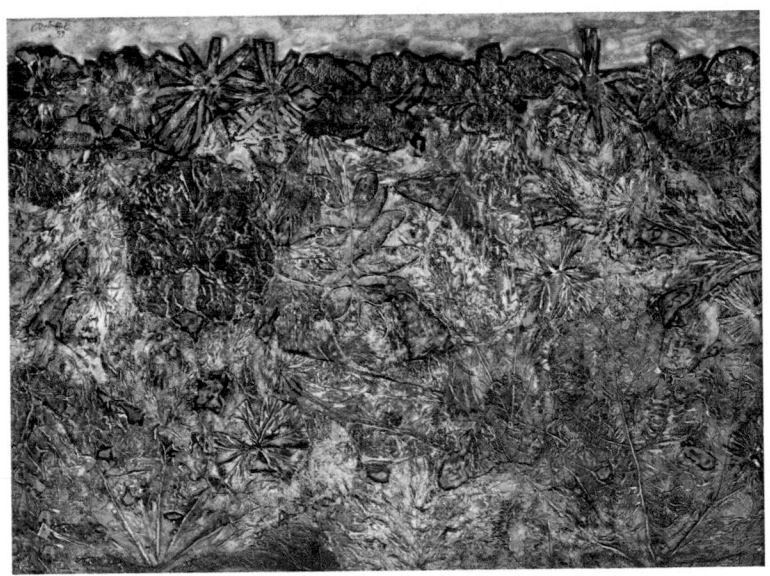

∧ 4.4 JEAN DUBUFFET, *Blossoming Earth* (1959). Oil and collage from vegetation mounted on canvas, 19⅛" × 26". On Loan to the Hamburg Kunsthalle, Hamburg, Germany.

1 ft.

(Fig. 4.3) is a contrast in *actual textures:* tufts of small, supple grasses are planted in sand that is surrounded by smooth wooden planks, and are juxtaposed with incongruous metal, human-made objects.

Actual Texture

Actual texture then is *tactile*; it is physical. When you touch an object, your fingertips register sensations—rough, smooth, sharp, hard, soft. In truth, you can say that *any* work of art has actual texture—whether it is the hard, cold surface of marble or the smooth, glasslike finish of a meticulously painted canvas. We talk about texture as an element of art, however, when the artist particularly *features it* or manipulates it in a work of art.

The most common painting technique that yields actual texture is **impasto**, a layer of thickly applied pigment. The surfaces of some of Jean Dubuffet's most experimental works began with an exaggerated use of impasto. To this tactile ground, he added a multitude of actual textured materials including everything from vegetation to butterfly wings (Fig. 4.4). The constructed surface emulates the undergrowth of a densely planted flowerbed.

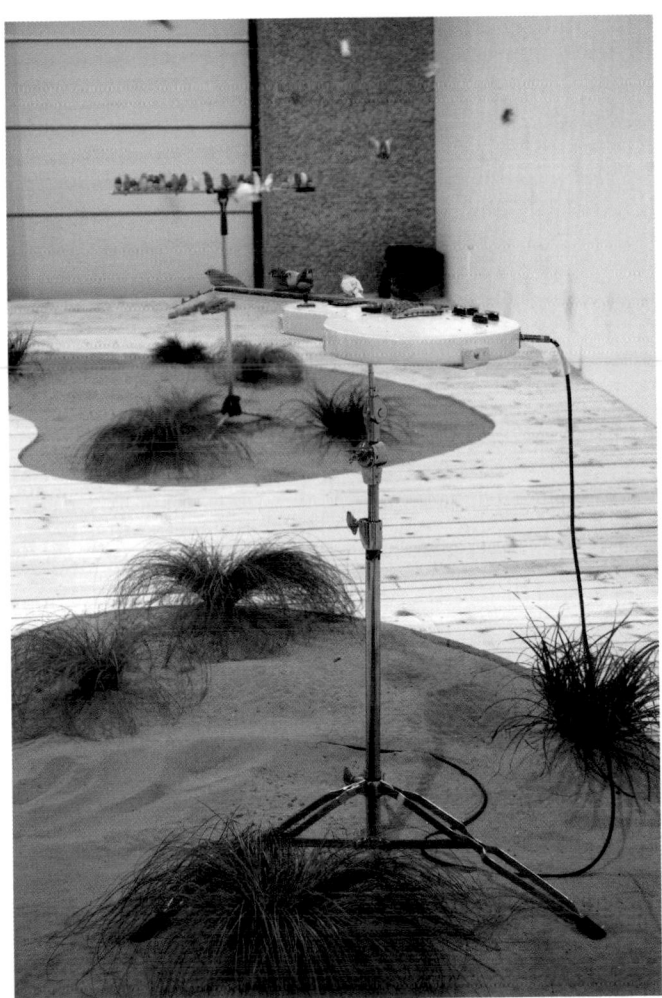

∧ 4.3 CÉLESTE BOURSIER-MOUGENOT, *From Here to Ear* (1999– ongoing). Installation view, zebra finches and electric guitars at the Barbican Art Gallery, London, England.

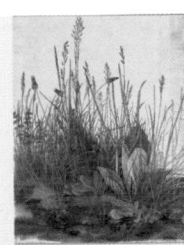

CONNECTIONS The illusion of texture—or *visual texture*—is seen in Albrecht Dürer's *Great Piece of Turf*, a meticulously rendered watercolor painting that virtually tricks the eye into perceiving actual texture.

∧ Dürer's *Great Piece of Turf* (Fig. 8.10)

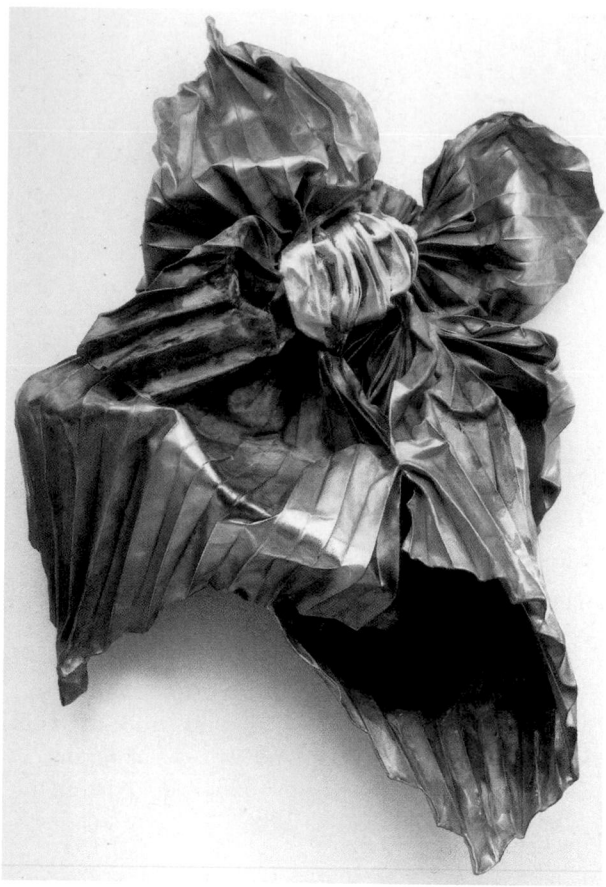

∧ 4.5 **LYNDA BENGLIS**, *Morisse* (1985–1987). Copper, nickel, chrome, and gold leaf; 48" × 43" × 14".

under a forbidding sky. As with many textures rendered with *trompe l'oeil* (trick the eye) illusionism, these seem *almost*—but not quite—familiar.

Subversive Texture

Textures may be used to subvert or undermine our expectations of the familiar and fixed notions of reality. **Subversive texture** is often both intriguing and repellent, provoking—as in Hatoum's *Doormat II* (Fig. 4.7)—an approach-avoidance conflict in the viewer. By replacing the stiff, plastic, turflike texture of a welcome mat with stainless steel and nickel-coated pins, Hatoum transmutes a familiar object into a strange one, and the comfort of the ordinary into the discomfort of the bizarre.

Visual Texture

The goal of visual texture is to simulate the look and feel of actual surfaces and textures. In *Morisse* (Fig. 4.5), sculptor Lynda Benglis creates the impression of soft, pleated, and billowing silken cloth with materials that could not be further removed from the one they suggest: copper, nickel, and chrome. Because the illusion is so convincing, it is tempting to reach out and touch the work to reconcile that which the eyes see with what the brain knows.

INVENTED TEXTURE **Invented texture** is a version of visual texture that makes no reference to visible reality. Max Ernst's surrealist canvas *L'oeil du silence (The Eye of Silence)* (Fig. 4.6) is a primordial-like landscape in which rock-hard and gelatinous formations coexist

PATTERN

Texture can be used in concert with pattern—design based on the repetition or grouping of elements such as line, shape, color, or texture. A pattern on a flat surface such as a fabric or paper may be enriched by contrasts in visual texture, as in a nineteenth-century design for a book's decorative end papers (Fig. 4.10). El Anatsui's magnificent "woven" wall hangings (Fig. 4.11), composed of scrap metal—including bottle caps and wine bottle foils—mimic the patterns of traditional cloth from his native Ghana. The piece ripples and glimmers like fine silken fabric, the rough textures of the hammered bits of aluminum sparkling with reflected light.

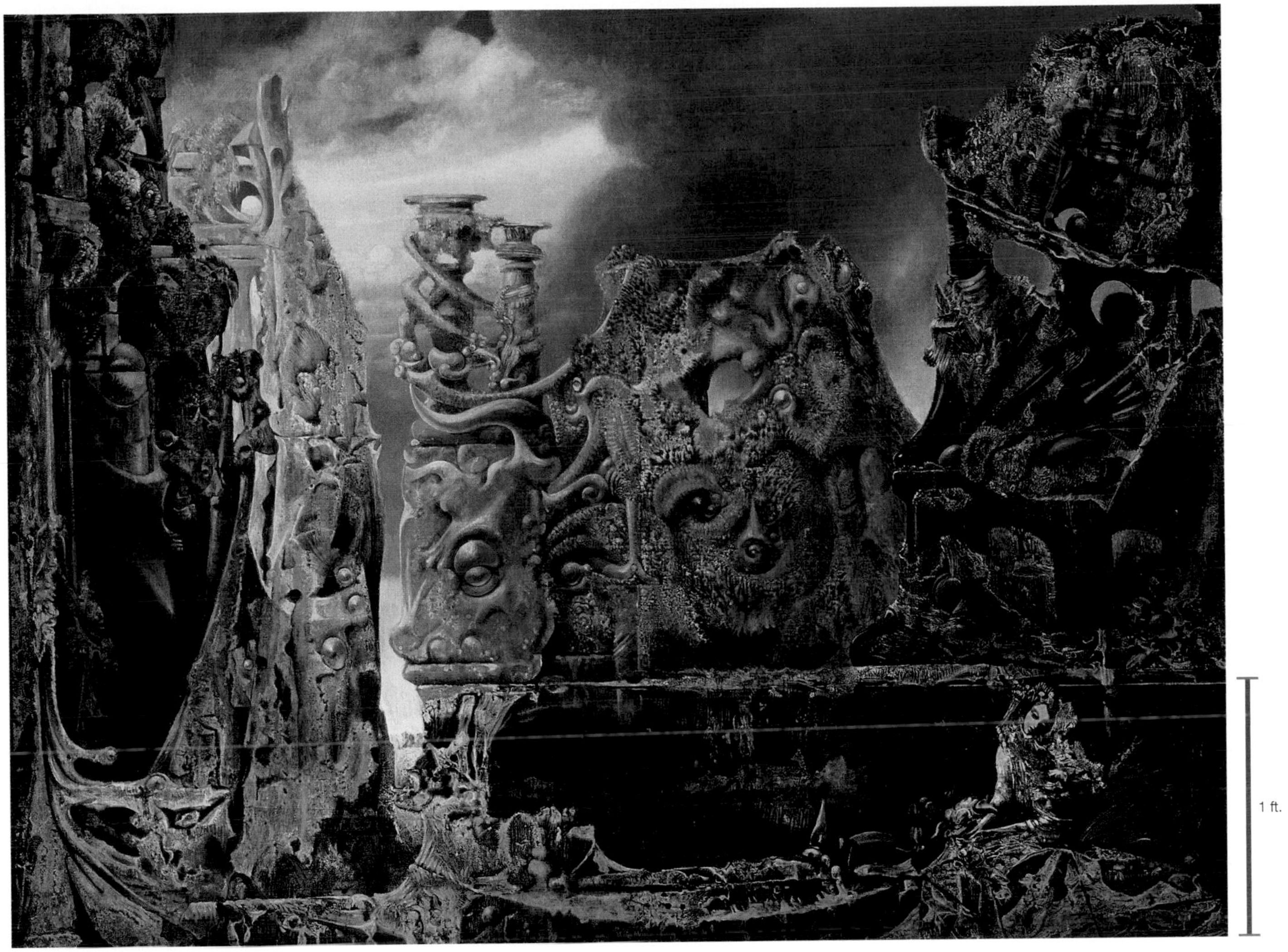

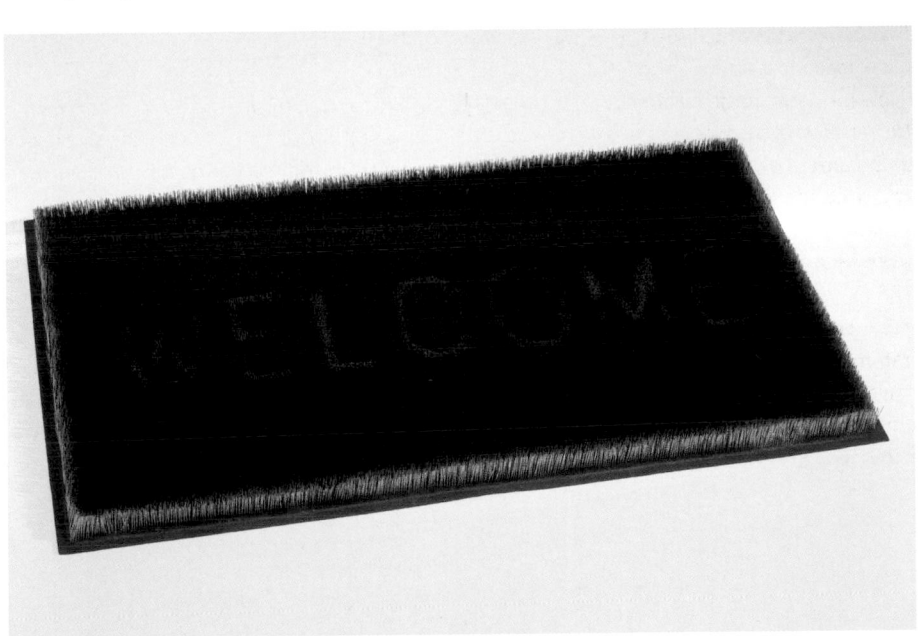

1 ft.

< 4.6 MAX ERNST, *L'oeil du silence (The Eye of Silence)* (1943–1944). Oil on canvas, 43¼" × 56¼". Mildred Lane Kemper Art Museum, St. Louis, Missouri.

∧ 4.7 MONA HATOUM, *Doormat II* (2000–2001). Stainless steel and nickel-plated pins, glue, and canvas; 1⅛" × 28½" × 16½".

COMPARE & CONTRAST

Humans versus Nature: *The Raft of the Medusa*

IN THE YEAR 1816, off the coast of West Africa, a makeshift raft overloaded with Algerian immigrants was set adrift by the captain and crew of the crippled French ship, *Medusa*. Two years later, the artist Théodore Géricault began what was to be his most controversial and political painting: *The Raft of the Medusa* (**Fig. 4.8**). Like many of his liberal contemporaries, Géricault opposed the French monarchy and used the tragedy of the *Medusa* to call attention to the mismanagement and ineffectual policies of the French government. The plight of the survivors and victims of the *Medusa* became a national scandal, and Géricault's authentic documentation—based on interviews with those rescued—was construed as a direct attack on the government. His powerful composition explores the full gamut of human emotion under extreme hardship and duress. The drama of the composition rests on the diagonal placement of the figures, from the corpse in the lower left that will soon slip into the dark abyss of the ocean, upward along a crescendo that culminates in the muscular torso of a black man waving a flag toward a rescue ship barely visible on the horizon. The fractured raft is tossed mercilessly by the winds and waves; humans battle against nature, and their own, for sheer survival.

Almost 175 years later, Frank Stella revisited the subject of the tragedy of the raft of the *Medusa* (**Fig. 4.9**) in an aluminum and steel sculpture. While Géricault's version highlights the human drama, in Stella's work the consequence of the violent forces of nature becomes the subject. The structure of the raft—parts of it turned to twisted steel by the forces of the ocean—is overrun by the coarse textures of aluminum fashioned to suggest the frothing of assaulting waves. These textures convey the uneven match between the ill-fated castaways and the unleashed power of nature.

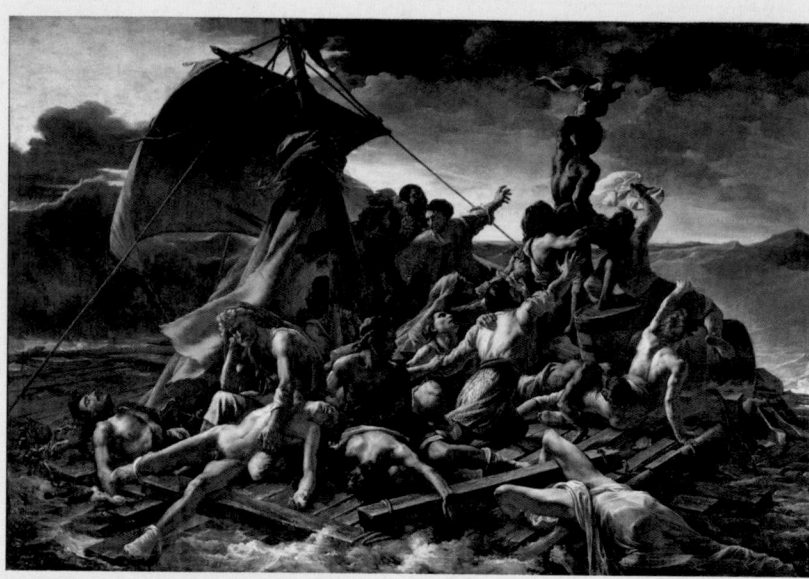

∧ **4.8 THÉODORE GÉRICAULT,** *The Raft of the Medusa* (1818–1819). Oil on canvas, 16'1" × 23'6". Louvre, Paris, France.

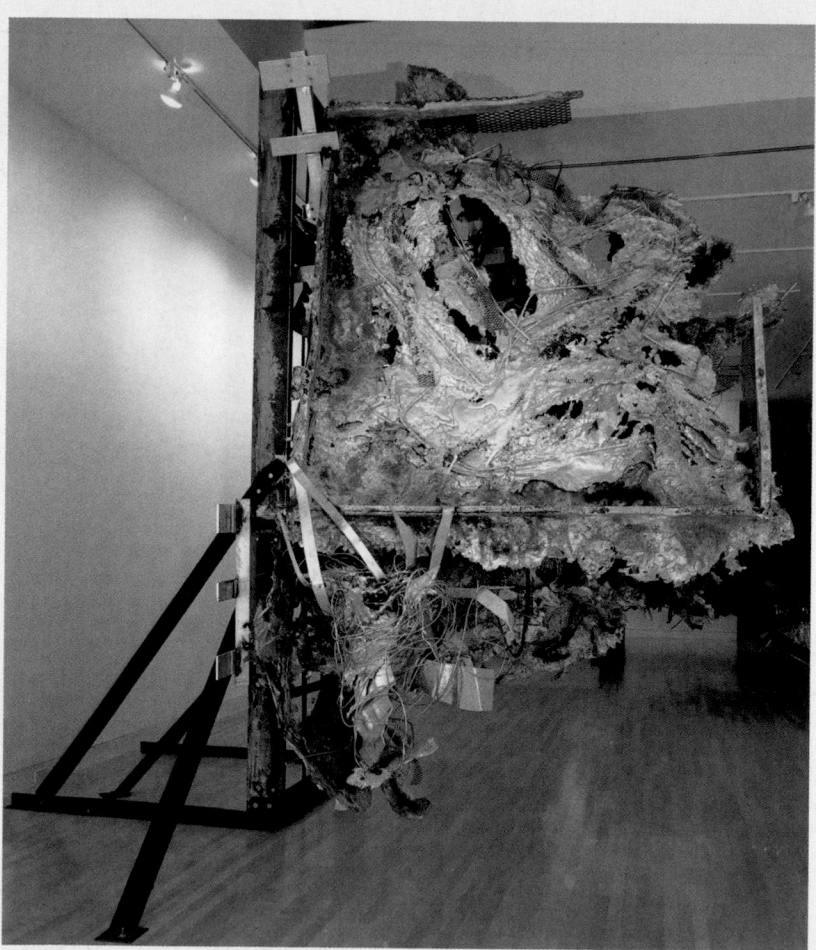

> **4.9 FRANK STELLA,** *Raft of the Medusa, Part I* (1990). Aluminum and steel, 167 ½" × 163" × 159".

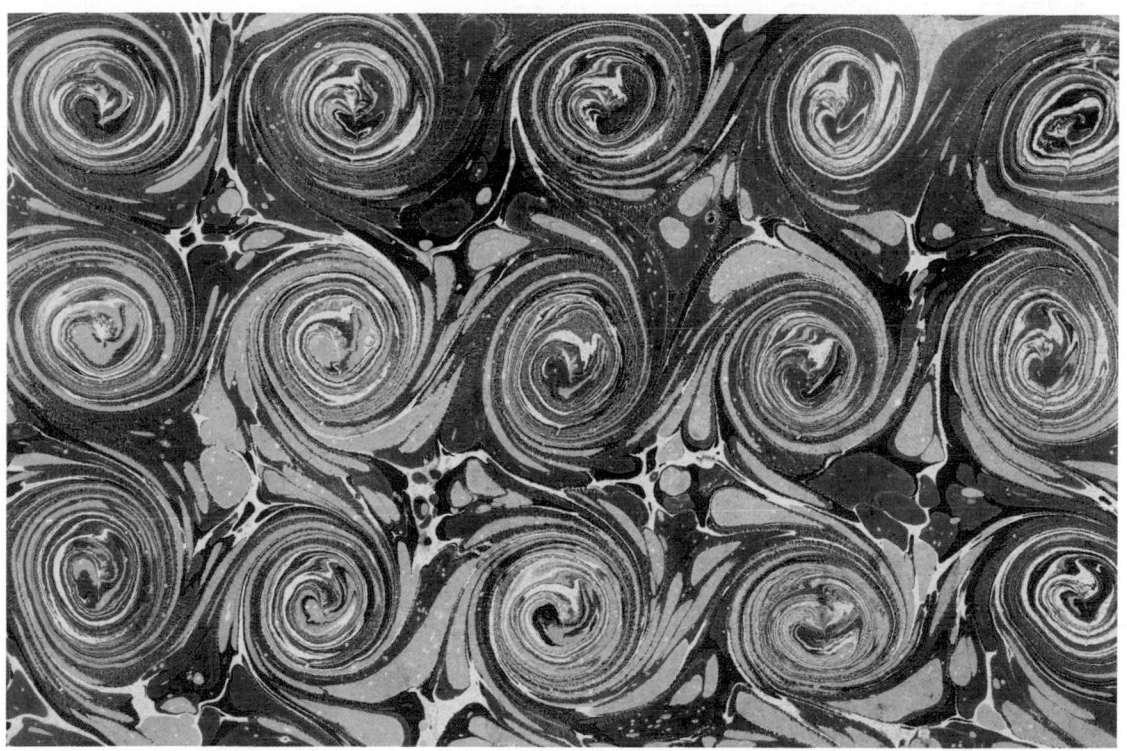

ᴧ **4.10 Decorative end paper** (19th century). Color lithograph.

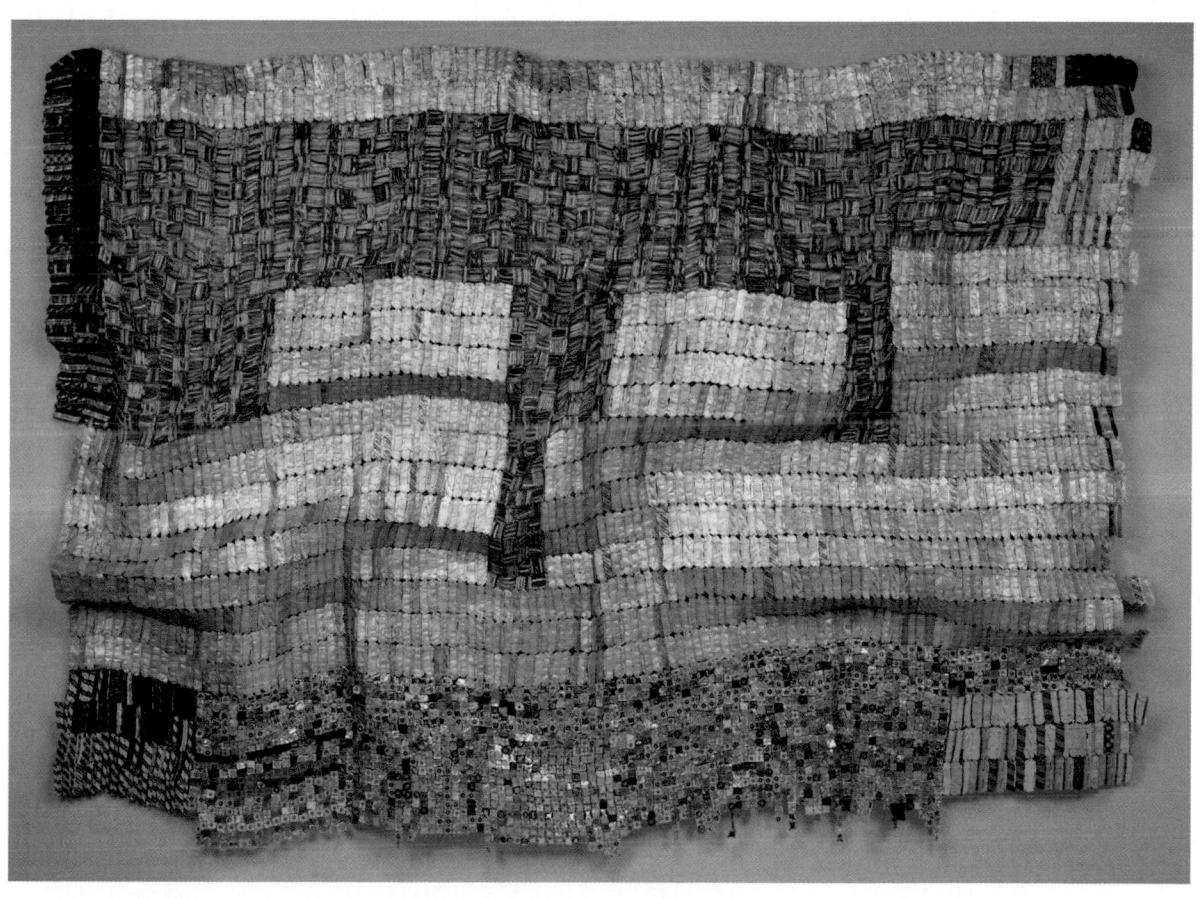

ᴧ **4.11 EL ANATSUI,** *Between Earth and Heaven* (2006). Aluminum, copper wire; 91" × 126". The Metropolitan Museum of Art, New York, New York.

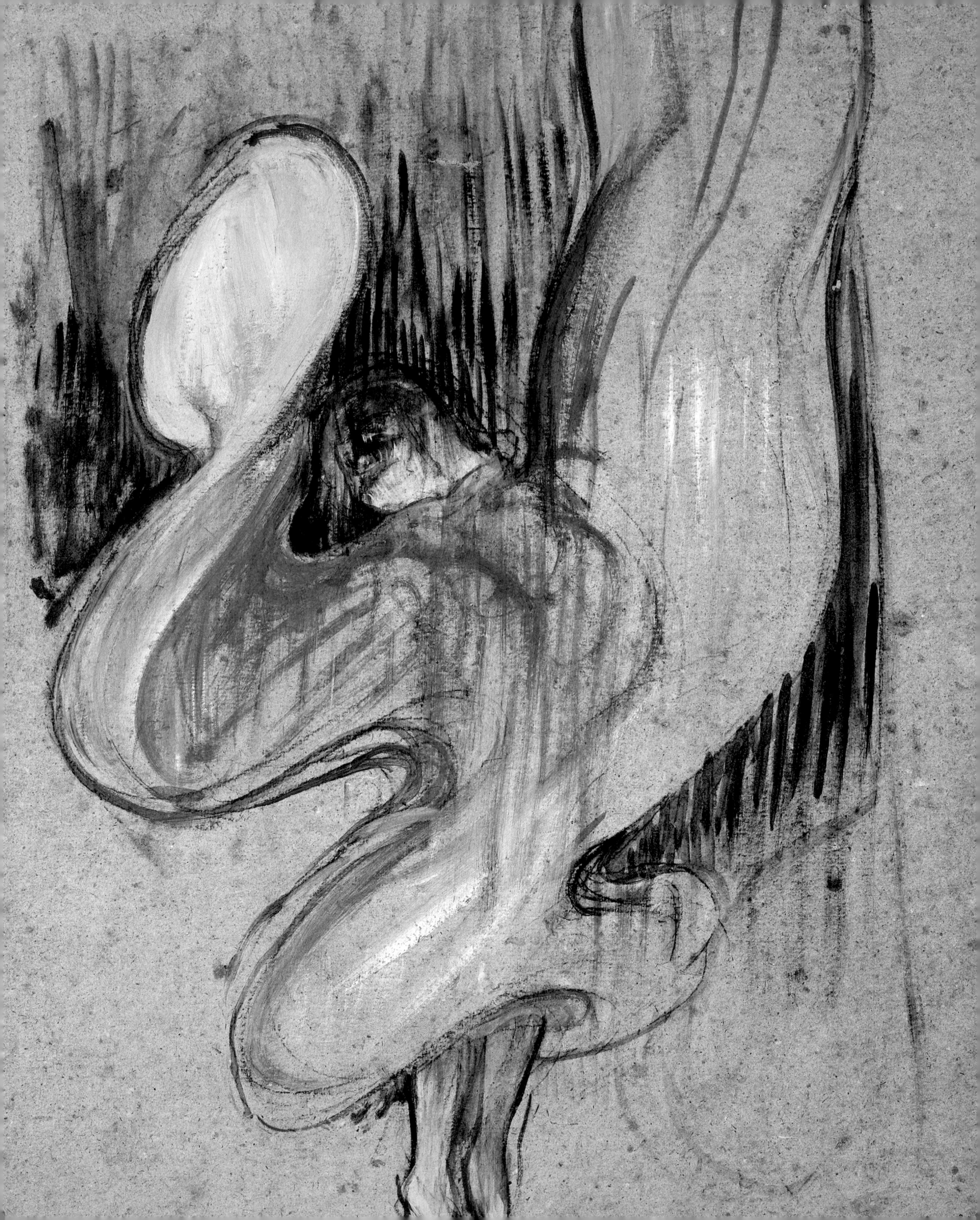

5

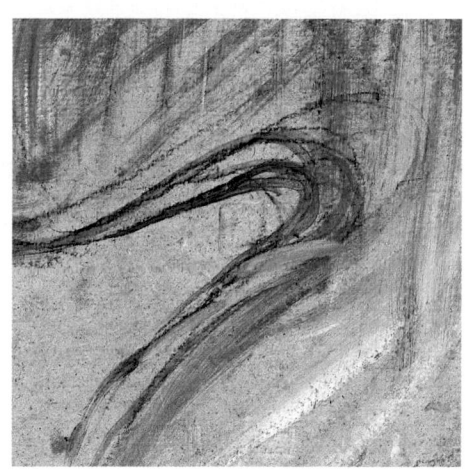

SPACE, TIME, AND MOTION

Einstein, in the special theory of relativity, proved that different observers, in different states of motion, see different realities.

— LEONARD SUSSKIND

"SPACE, THE final frontier." Every diehard Trekkie is familiar with the opening mantra of the TV and film series, *Star Trek*. But it just as well describes the "mission impossible" of millennia of artists seeking to recreate three-dimensional space on a two-dimensional surface. The space explored by the starship *Enterprise* was that beyond Earth's atmosphere—the space between celestial spheres and galaxies. Artists are less ambitious. They seek to explore ways to visually and psychologically extend the space of a finite rectangle—a canvas, let's say—into nothing less than a vast universe. From simple methods such as relative size and overlapping to complex systems of linear perspective, the goal of entire eras of artists was to transcend the space at their fingertips, to defy its limitations—to make the leap from reality to illusion.

Just as artists manipulate elements of art to create three-dimensional effects, so do they employ visual strategies to suggest motion. Life in the world around us is not static; it moves and progresses over time. We live in the fourth dimension—one that has length, width, height, and time. Time-based art mediums such as film, video, and computer-based technologies are best suited to works in which duration is a dimension.

< HENRI DE TOULOUSE-LAUTREC, *Study for Loïe Fuller at the Folies Bergère* (1893). Oil on cardboard, 24 7/8" × 17 7/8". Musee Toulouse-Lautrec, Albi, France.

63

ACTUAL SPACE

Three-dimensional works of art (sculpture, architecture, and other freestanding works) define and occupy actual—as opposed to illusory—space. In the context of these mediums, *space* is more accurately considered as an element of art.

Freestanding sculpture occupies three-dimensional space; it is sculpture that one can walk around or otherwise observe from every angle. Some freestanding sculpture is meant to be seen from a single vantage point—frontally; everything the artist wants us to know about the work is revealed in a single, fixed pose. With other freestanding sculpture, new vantage points provide new revelations. Consider two different representations of David, the heroic youth who—according to the Bible—slew the towering Philistine warrior, Goliath. Andrea del Verrocchio's earlier *David* (see Fig. 17.21) is to be viewed from a frontal perspective. David faces forward, directly engaging the viewer's eye. Even the severed head of Goliath at David's feet is propped up for the best frontal view.

In Gianlorenzo Bernini's version of the same subject (see Fig. 17.23), we catch David in the split-second before he releases the stone from his slingshot, the weapon that will fell Goliath. If we were to settle for a single view of the work, we would be missing much of the composition—and the narrative. David twists and turns, his arms braced in powerful diagonals that pull the sling taut across this body. These diagonals, echoed in the folds of drapery, seem to forcibly drag the viewer around the sculpture. The reward for not standing still is the unfolding of the action before one's eyes. As the viewer moves in actual space, David likewise appears to move.

A similar effect is achieved in Allen Jones's *Echo* (Fig. 5.1A and 5.1B). Shapes of colored metal suggest clothing, arms, and legs. Any sense of completion—of an integrated whole—depends on the viewer's movement around the piece and the synthesis of the lost and found contours of the figures. As they glide and twirl, the intertwined

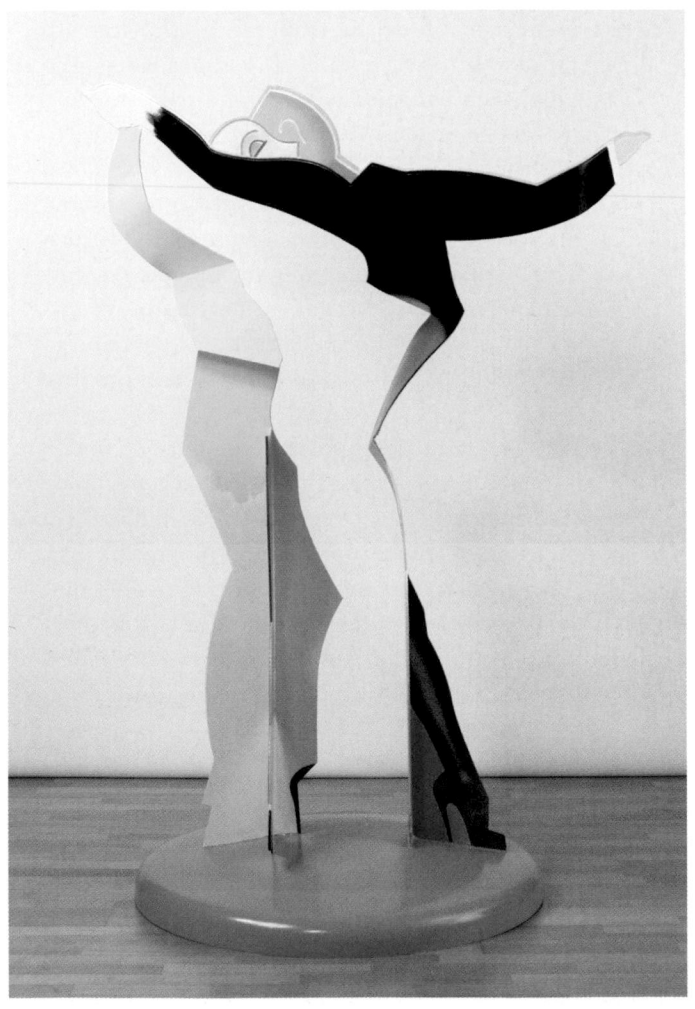
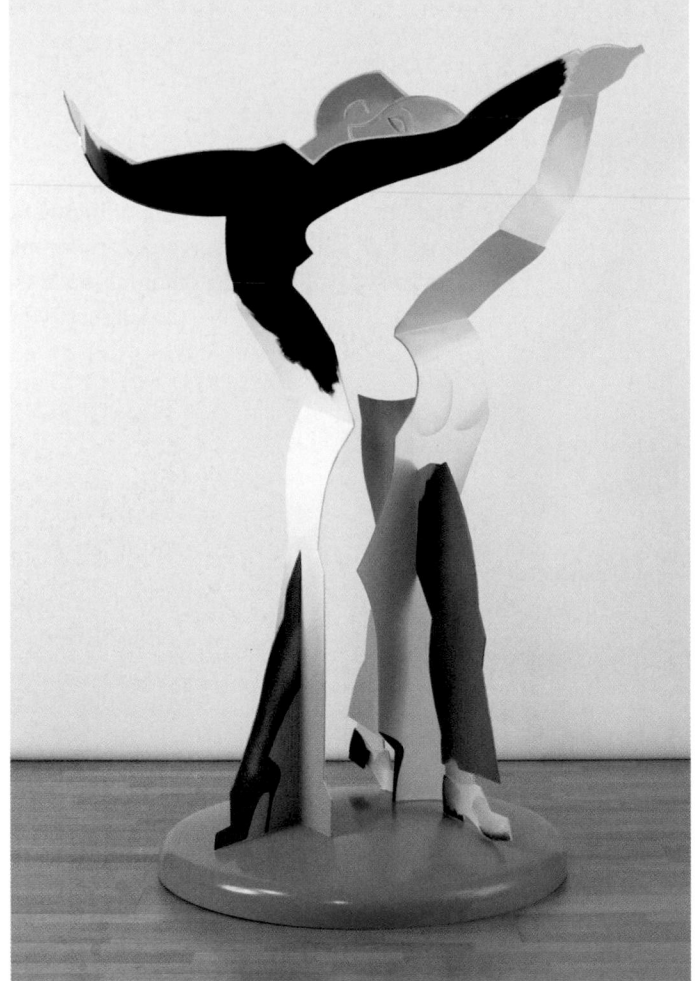

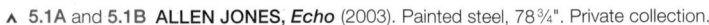

▲ **5.1A** and **5.1B** ALLEN JONES, *Echo* (2003). Painted steel, 78¾". Private collection.

cutouts are like so many glimpses we might have of the couple floating on a dance floor. The principle of closure—the eye's tendency to integrate disparate parts based on scant cues—infuses these figures with movement and renders dynamic the otherwise static strips of metal.

CREATING THE ILLUSION OF SPACE

Actual space, then, refers to the dimensions in which we live and move (Fig. 5.2). The **illusion of space** is the suggestion of three dimensions on a two-dimensional surface (Fig. 5.3). Another way of saying this is that the illusion of depth is the suggestion of distance in a picture. The illusionistic space of a two-dimensional composition is

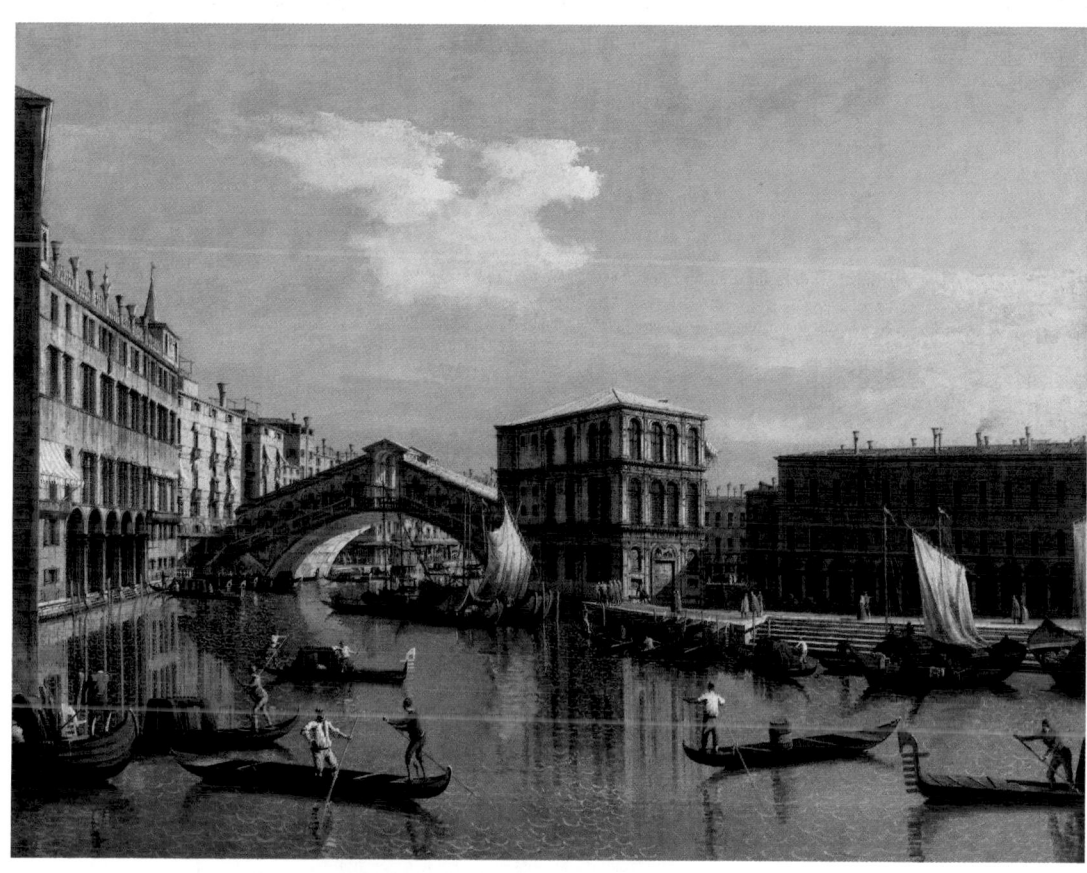

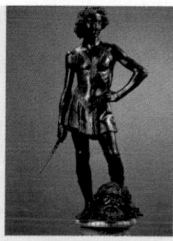

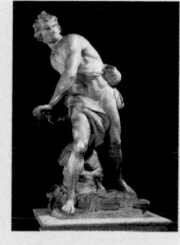

∧ 5.2 **SARAH QUILL,** *View Towards the Rialto Bridge.* Grand Canal, Venice, Italy. Photograph.

1 ft.

< 5.3 GIOVANNI ANTONIO CANALETTO, *The Rialto Bridge* (c. 1735). Oil on canvas, 46⅞" × 60¾". Louvre, Paris, France.

CONNECTIONS
Verrocchio's *David* is intended to be viewed from the front. Bernini's *David* is meant to be viewed from many different vantage points.

∧ Verrocchio's *David* (Fig. 17.22)

∧ Bernini's *David* (Fig. 17.24)

sometimes called its **implied space** or **pictorial space;** it is created by the artist using devices or techniques to approximate the way things would be seen by the human eye in actual space. They include *relative size* (based on the observation that nearby objects appear larger to the eye than do objects in the distance), *overlapping, transparency, vertical positioning, atmospheric perspective, linear perspective,* and other more complicated versions of perspective.

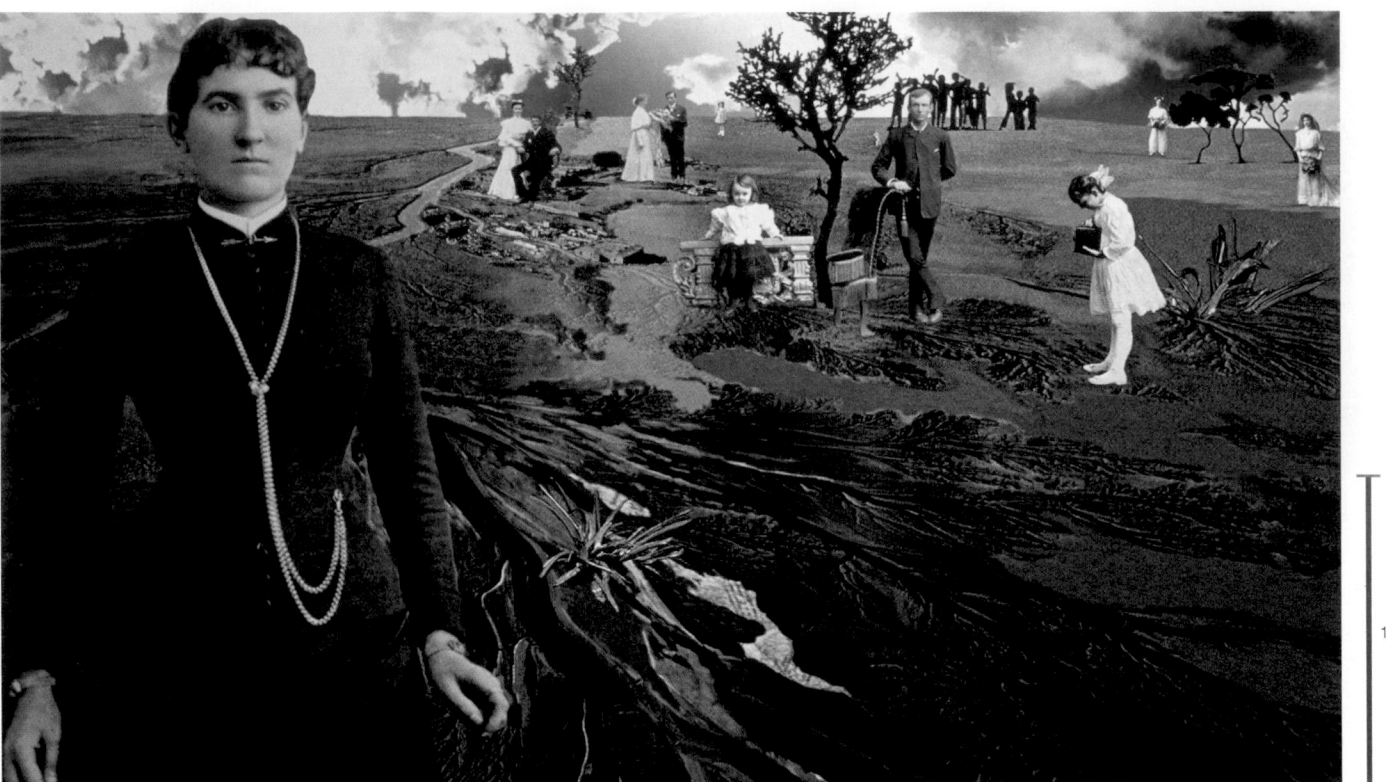

1 ft.

∧ 5.4 MARTINA LÓPEZ, *Heirs Come to Pass, 3* (1991). Silver dye bleach print made from digitally assisted montage, 30" × 50". Art Institute of Chicago, Illinois.

Relative Size

The farther objects are from us, the smaller they appear to the eye. One of the ways, then, that artists suggest space is to vary the size of the objects within it. Things that are supposed to be closer to the viewer will be sized larger than the things that are to be perceived as farther away.

Relative size accounts for spatial complexity in Martina López's *Heirs Come to Pass, 3* (Fig. 5.4). A broad, muddy-looking landscape fills most of the space of the digitally manipulated photographic print, leaving just a narrow strip at the top for a cloud-soaked sky. Figures cut out from old, black-and-white and sepia-toned photographs are digitally "patched into" the landscape. They range in size from large and looming to tiny and barely visible; it is precisely their placement and size in relation to one another that creates an illusion of depth. For López, this is a "visual terrain" that is open to receiving not only her own memories (here represented by photographs of her own family members), but one that has ample space to accommodate those of the viewer.

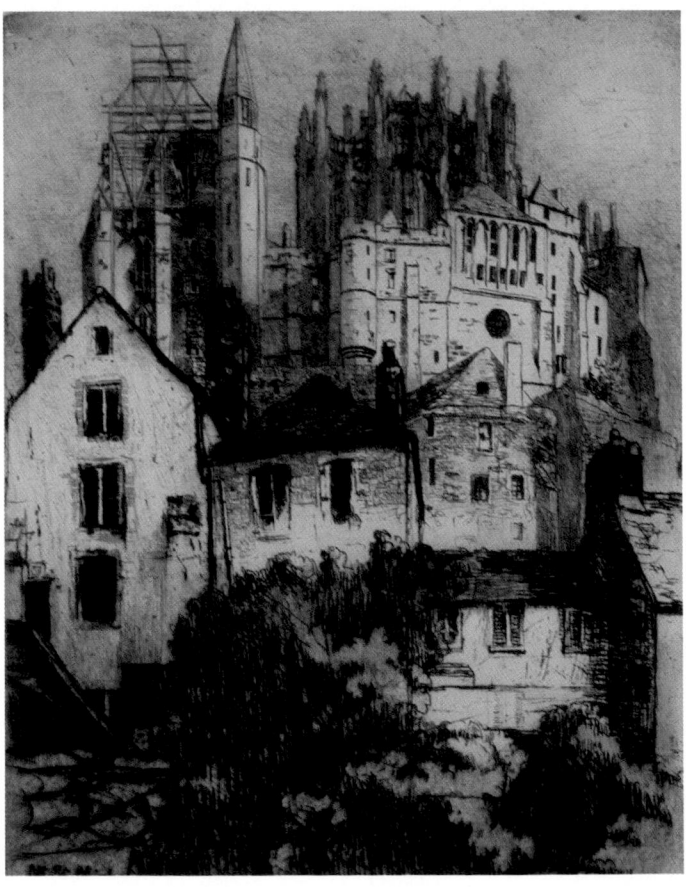

> 5.5 GABRIELLE DE VEAUX CLEMENTS, *Church and Castle, Mont Saint Michel* (1885). Etching on paper, 8½" × 6⅜". National Museum of Women in the Arts, Washington, D.C.

1 in.

Overlapping

Relative size and overlapping often work hand-in-hand to suggest space. If you look out the window of a high-rise building onto the rooftops of a cityscape, you will see that the buildings closer to you obscure parts of the buildings that are farther away. To suggest space, artists incorporate such real-world observations. Overlapping is an especially useful device if there is not much actual space between the objects or figures being portrayed. In her nineteenth-century etching *Church and Castle, Mont Saint Michel* (Fig. 5.5), Gabrielle de Veaux Clements used overlapping to convey the feeling of cramped space in an old medieval town.

Overlapping is used frequently in still life compositions in which depth is usually limited and when the artist wants to emphasize the relationships between and among the objects and spaces—as in a typical arrangement by Jean-Baptiste Simeon Chardin, one of the most well-known historical figures working in this genre (Fig. 5.6). But overlapping does not, by definition, create a sense of space. In fact, it can have quite the opposite effect—that of flatness or spatial compression. In Juan Gris's collage, *The Bottle of Banyuls* (Fig. 5.7), the overlapping shapes reinforce the work's two-dimensionality. The effect is not so much of one object in front or behind another on the table but of compressed space, flatness.

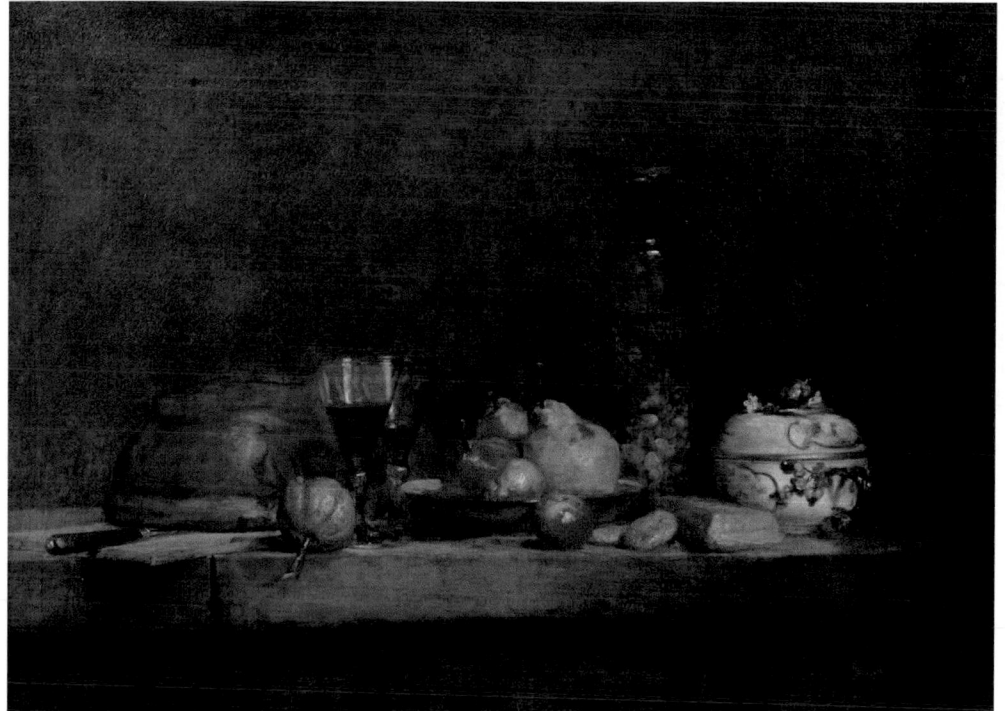

1 ft.

▲ 5.6 **JEAN-BAPTISTE SIMEON CHARDIN,** *Still Life with Bottle of Olives* (1760). Oil on canvas, 28" × 38½". Louvre, Paris, France.

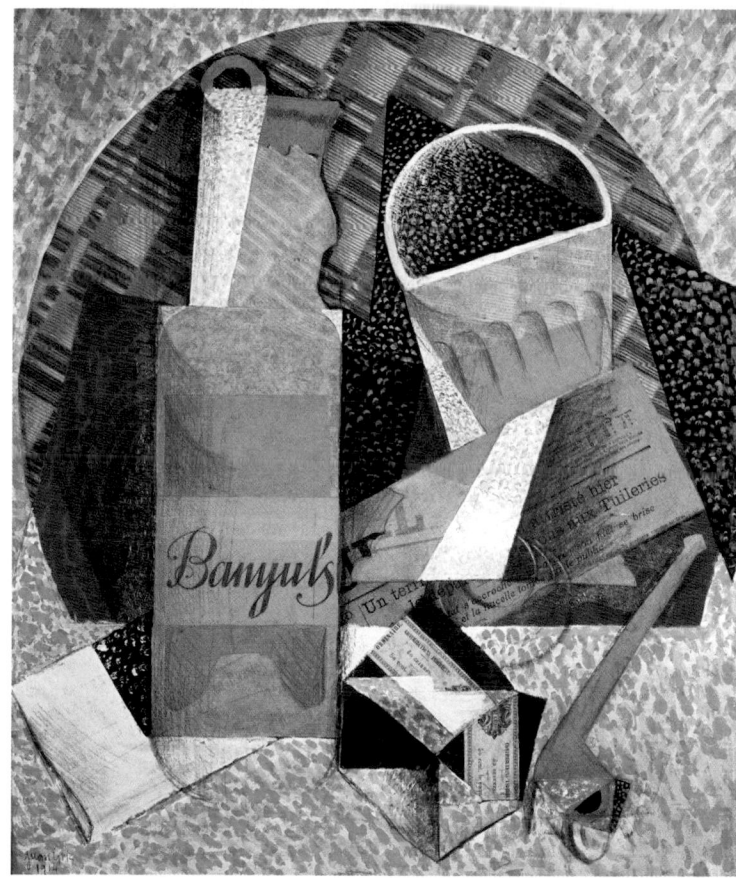

▲ 5.7 **JUAN GRIS,** *The Bottle of Banyuls* (1914). Gouache and collage. Kunstmuseum, Bern, Switzerland.

CONNECTIONS Pick a location outside in nature. Look through the viewfinder or at the LCD screen of a camera and pan the landscape until you isolate a portion of the scene that you want to shoot. Take the picture and look at it; the things that are closest to you will be at the bottom of the frame and the things that are most distant from you will be at the top. If you were to copy that photograph in a drawing or painting, the way you would signify space in the landscape is through location.

Location

Artists use location—also known as **vertical positioning**—in their compositions as a strategy to signify depth. The use of the word *signify* is purposeful because location does not really create an illusion of space in the same way that other devices do. The artist relies on the viewer's tendency to read things at the top of the composition as farther away than things at the bottom, based on the way that reality is perceived.

In the Tiffany Studios *Magnolia and Irises* (Fig. 5.8), relative size, overlapping, and location all play roles in signifying depth. The magnolia tree on the right appears to be closest to the viewer because it overlaps the irises, mountains, and, of course, the sky. Its large size reinforces its apparent closeness to the viewer. However, the irises on the left overlap the tree on the left, suggesting that they are closer to the viewer. Considering location, the irises, mountains, and sky occupy three distinct strata: The irises, the lower part of the composition, appear closest to the viewer; as the viewer's gaze rises, the indigo mountains and brilliant yellow-orange sky in the upper part of the composition seem to be farthest away. The cool hues of the hills also recede from the eye, contributing to an impression of distance. Everything seems to bask in the glow of sundown. Devices for creating the illusion of depth are often used in concert with one another.

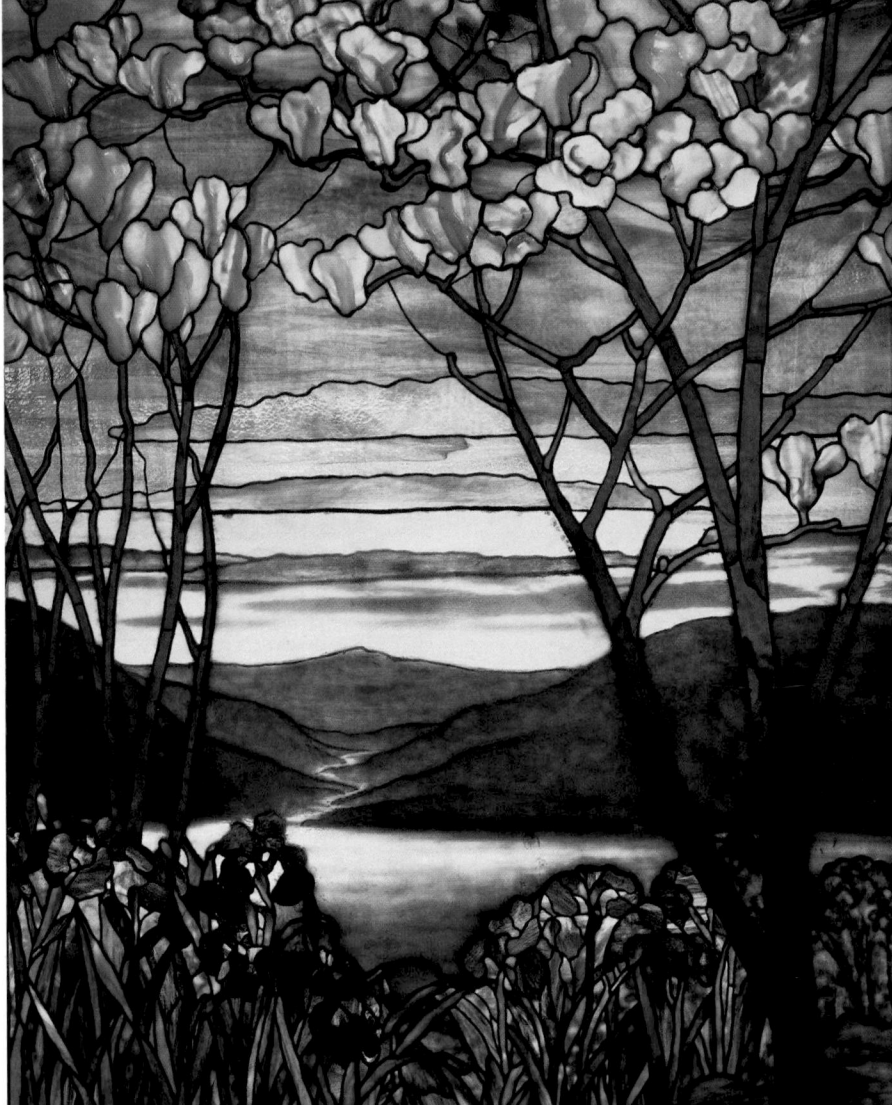

< 5.8 TIFFANY STUDIOS, *Magnolia and Irises* (c. 1908). Leaded favrile glass, 60¼" × 42". The Metropolitan Museum of Art, New York, New York.

1 ft.

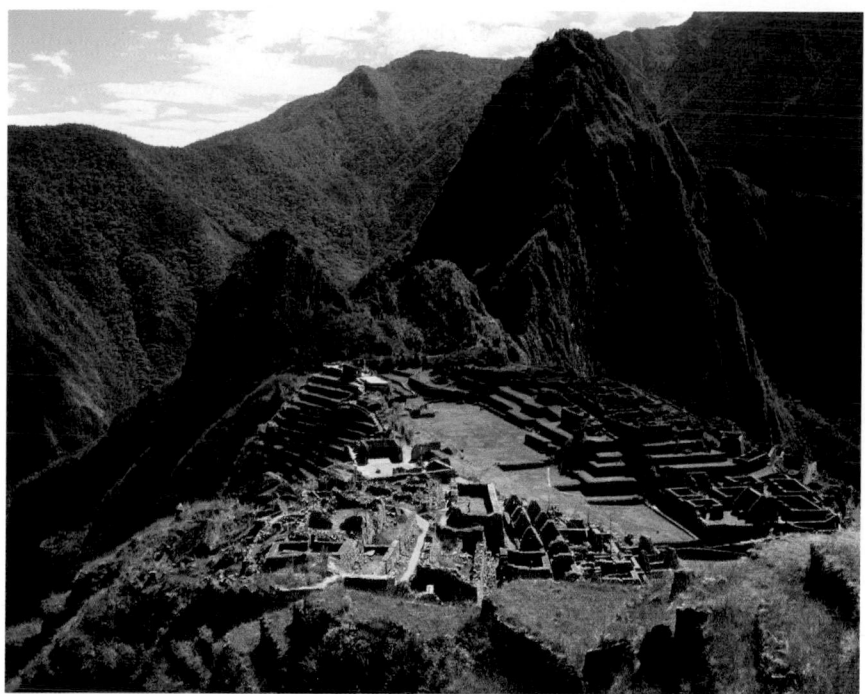

▲ 5.9 View of the Incan Citadel at Machu Picchu, Urubamba Valley, Peru (1490–1530).

Atmospheric Perspective

Atmospheric perspective, also known as *aerial perspective,* is a technique for illustrating depth that incorporates such devices as texture gradient, brightness gradient, color saturation, and the interplay of warm and cool colors. It refers to the indistinct quality of distant objects, the character of which is affected by the atmosphere that stands between them and the viewer. On a hot summer's day, a heavy haze will seem to bleach the outlines of distant buildings. And during a winter storm, the crystalline snowflakes that dust objects nearest to us will seem to merge into a white vapor that all but obscures the far-off shapes.

To the human eye, atmospheric effects alter the lines and substance of objects in gradations as distance increases. Closer objects are perceived as having more detail or texture. They are also brighter and their colors purer. To create the illusion of depth, artists will vary the texture of objects (show less detail as the objects recede from the picture plane) and lessen their brightness and color saturation. The changes will be gradual, mimicking the gradation of change in objects viewed in actual depth. The terms **texture gradient** and **brightness gradient** refer to these gradations.

The photograph of the mountain fortress of Machu Picchu (Fig. 5.9) illustrates the role of actual atmospheric effects in the perception of depth. The imposing ruin was built in the Peruvian Andes by the Incas some 500 years ago. There is great detail in the terraced hill and fortress walls in the foreground but as the viewer gazes upward, distant mountains become blurs of color. The greens of the vegetation in the foreground are more intense than those of the slopes of the mountains in the middle ground. In the distant mountains, atmospheric effects transform the blanket of green to a palette of cobalt blues.

Scenes such as these have inspired artists such as Frederic Edwin Church to replicate such effects. In his painting *The Heart of the Andes* (Fig. 5.10), Church applies the same elements of atmospheric perspective to create the illusion of space. Also set in the Andes, it provides the viewer with a window on an infinitely receding vista. The foreground of the picture contains great botanical detail, as if the painting were meant as a scientific record of the species of the region. As the vista recedes from the viewer, the plant life and the hills grow less textured, and the colors lose their saturation. The light source in the distance may be the sun, but it serves as a metaphor for heaven. Pictorially, it washes out all detail in the vast distance.

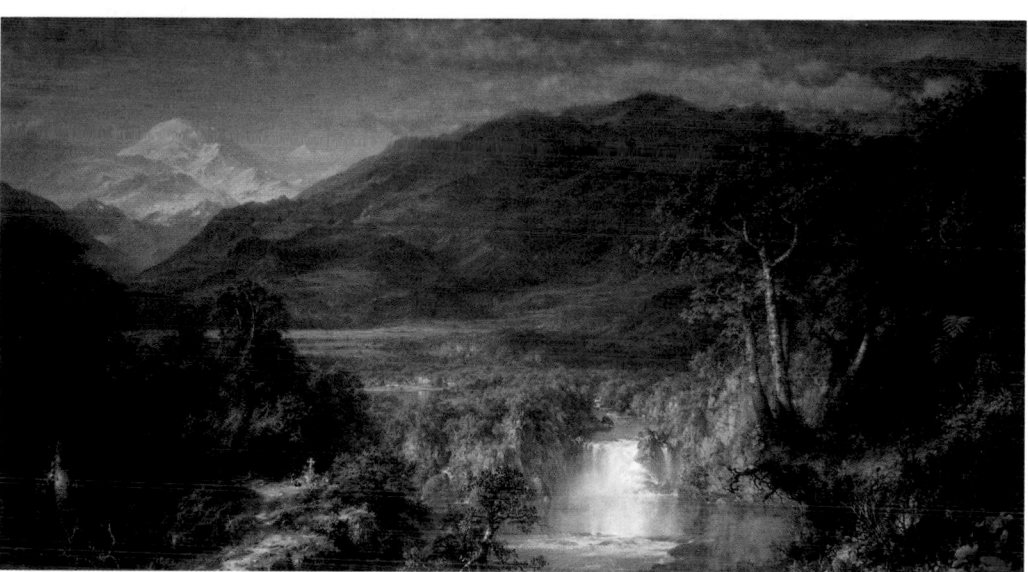

1 ft.

▲ 5.10 FREDERIC EDWIN CHURCH, *The Heart of the Andes* (1859). Oil on canvas, 66⅛" × 119¼". The Metropolitan Museum of Art, New York, New York.

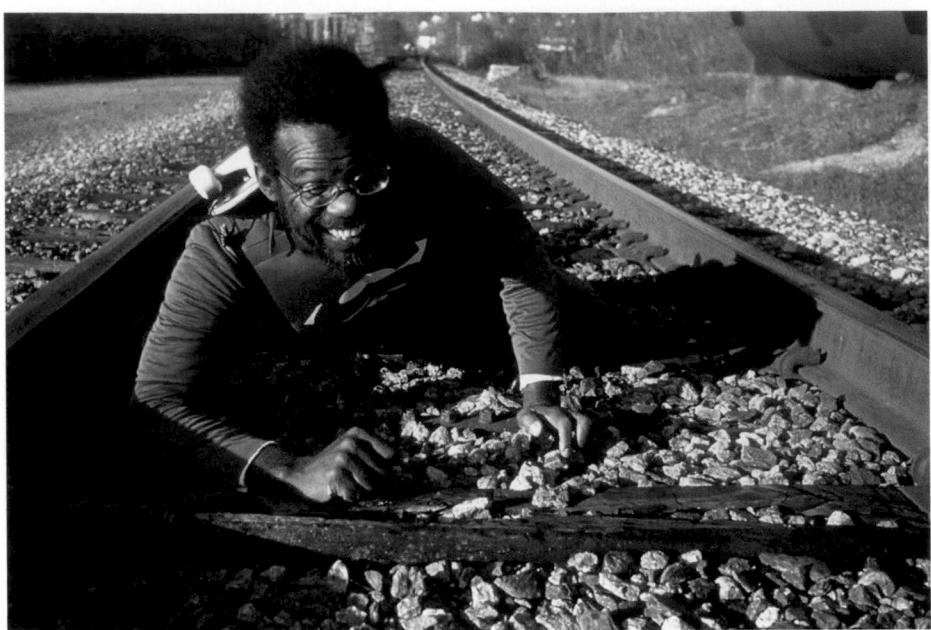

5.11 **WILLIAM POPE.L,** *Training Crawl, Lewiston, ME* (2001). Photo of street performance. Lewiston, Maine. William Pope.L trains for "The Great White Way," his marathon five-year crawl up Broadway in Manhattan.

Linear Perspective

Linear perspective refers to formal systems developed by artists to portray three-dimensional objects in two-dimensional space. The goal is to provide the viewer with the same impression of relative size, position, or distance that would be created by viewing the objects from a particular point called a **vantage point**. As objects recede from the viewer, they diminish in size and eventually become so small that they vanish. The point at which they "vanish" is called the **vanishing point**. Imagine that you are standing between the two rails of a railroad track and looking toward the **horizon** (that imaginary line perceived where the earth and the sky meet)—or as far into the distance that you possibly can. The rails will appear to converge the closer they get to the horizon until they look as if they come together. That single point at which they seem to touch is a vanishing point on the horizon line. This phenomenon is captured in a photograph of a performance piece by William Pope.L titled *Training Crawl, Lewiston, ME* (Fig. 5.11).

ONE-POINT PERSPECTIVE One-point perspective is a system that enables the artist to project the three-dimensional world onto a two-dimensional surface by accurately representing the size of objects relative to the depth of the receding space. First a horizon line (equivalent to the artist's eye level) is determined and a single point placed somewhere along it—typically in the exact center (Fig. 5.13). Diagonal lines representing depth are then drawn from the four corners—and four edges—of the composition toward the center point; these diagonals are called **orthogonals**. The lines in the diagram that are parallel to the horizon line are called **transversals**. The intersection of the orthogonals and transversals create a grid that the artist can use to determine the "visually correct" size of figures or objects or to arrange architecture within the illusionistic space so that it appears to be three-dimensional. Figure 5.12 shows how cubes

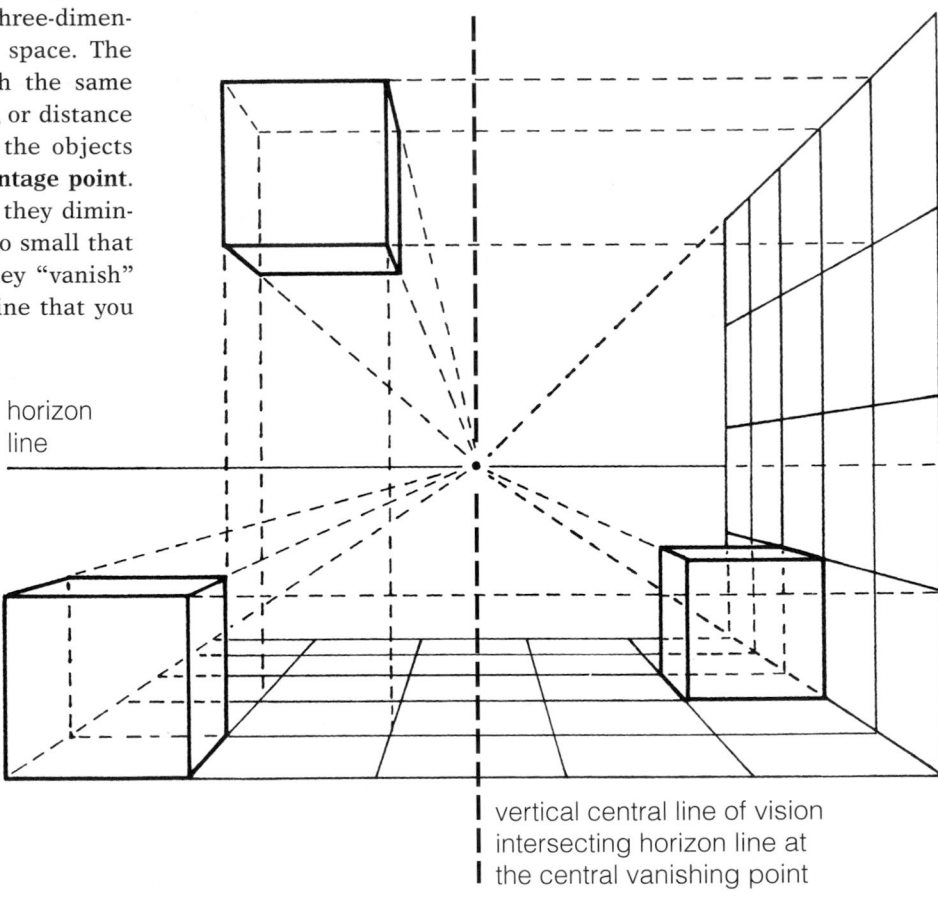

horizon line

vertical central line of vision intersecting horizon line at the central vanishing point

5.12 Diagram of one-point linear perspective.

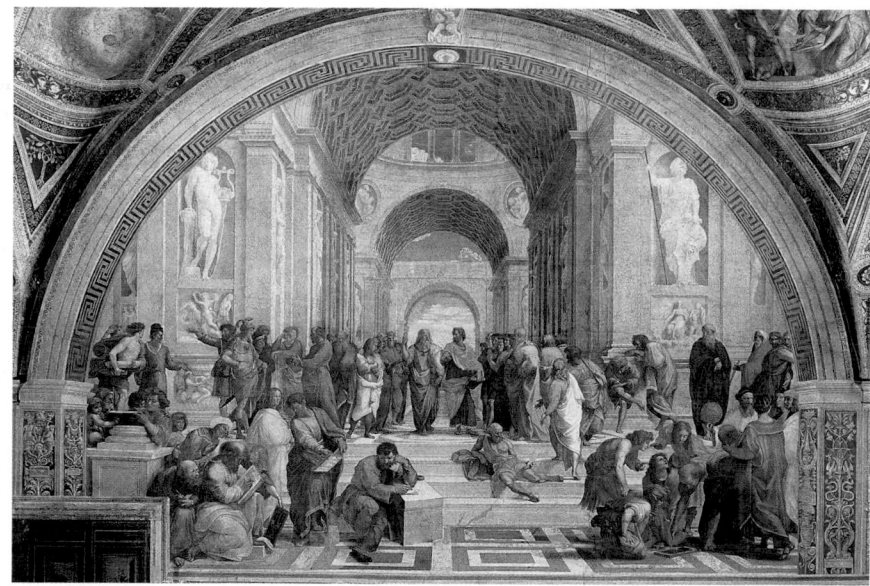

PART A. *Philosophy; or The School of Athens* (1509–1511). Fresco, approximately 26' × 18'. Musei Vaticani, Rome, Italy.

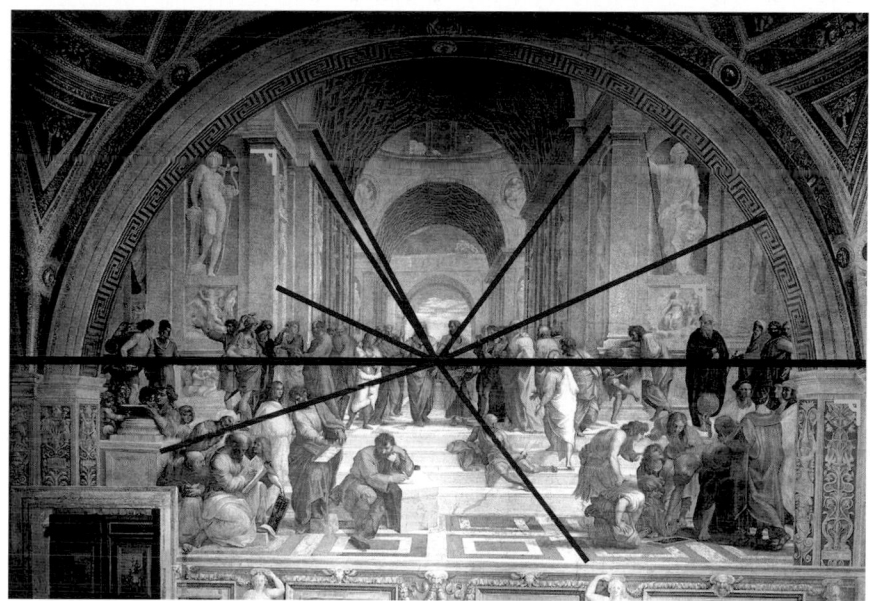

Part B. Perspective in Raphael's *The School of Athens* (1509–1511).

∧ 5.13 RAFAELLO SANZIO (CALLED RAPHAEL), *The School of Athens.*

would be drawn using one-point perspective. The cubes that straddle the horizon line are at eye level. The cubes below the horizon line are below eye level, and thus the tops of the cubes are visible. Following this pattern, the cubes that are positioned above the horizon line are above eye level; we look up to see the underside of the cubes.

Raphael's (1483–1520) fresco, *The School of Athens* (Fig. 5.13A), is a monumental example of one-point perspective. The painting is a virtual who's-who of intellectual shakers and movers from antiquity to the Renaissance. Plato (left) and Aristotle (right), representing divergent philosophical perspectives, share the spotlight in the center of the composition. The horizon line cuts through them and the vanishing point is positioned between them (Fig. 5.13B). Diagonal lines in the marble floor and the architecture converge at this point, drawing the eye into the receding space. The illusion of distance is enhanced by a series of arches that diminishes in height as they approach the horizon line.

THEORY & PRACTICE
Creating the Illusion of Space in Sculpture

DEVICES FOR CREATING AN ILLUSION of space in drawing and painting are analogous to those used in **relief sculpture**, that is, sculpture in which figures project from the two-dimensional surface (like a slab of marble, plank of wood, or piece of bronze) of which they are a part. Sometimes the figures project significantly from the surface (*high relief*) and appear almost three-dimensional; sometimes they are no higher than the surface (*low relief*). Regardless, with relief sculpture, the viewer is meant to observe the work from a frontal perspective, much as with painting or drawing.

Joseph of Egypt Sold by His Brothers (**Fig. 5.14**), one of ten reliefs from early Renaissance artist Lorenzo Ghiberti's bronze doors for the Baptistry of the Cathedral of Florence, was renowned for its spatial illusionism. It showcases several devices for creating depth

in this work that we might also find in painting: The architectural elements recede into space, their arches diminishing in height and span; the familiar use of orthogonal lines in a tile floor appear to converge at a single point in the distance; the figures diminish in size relative to their location in the pictorial space; and location is used in the top-right corner to suggest the deepest recesses of space.

Ghiberti's variation in levels of relief also dramatically heightens the illusion of space. Figures in the foreground, modeled in high relief, appear almost three-dimensional—so much so that they even cast shadows on the surface. Those in the middle ground and background, in much shallower relief, are less fully rounded, appear less distinct, and therefore are perceived as more distant from the viewer.

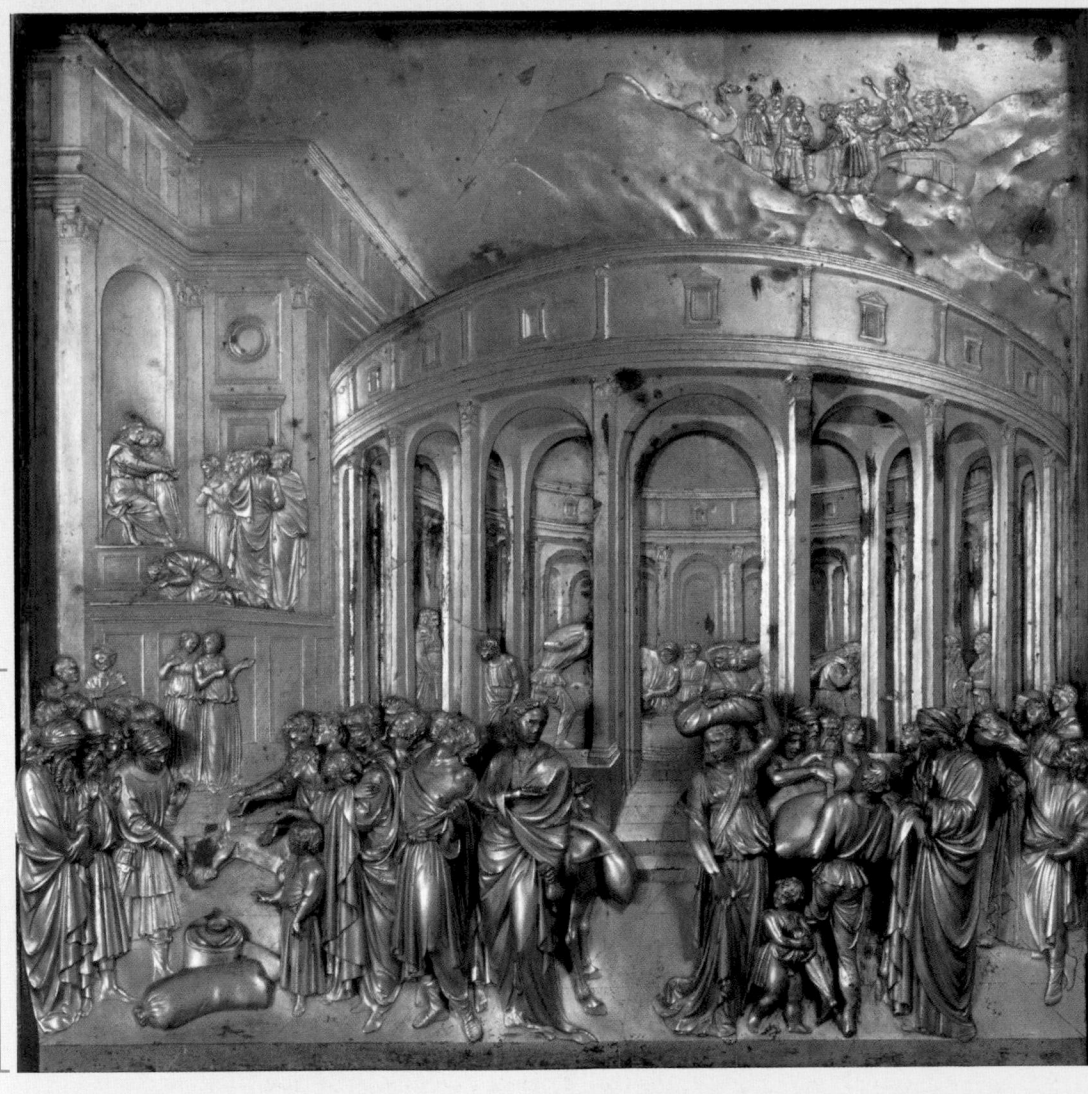

< **5.14 LORENZO GHIBERTI,** *Joseph of Egypt Sold by His Brothers* (1425–1452). Panel from *The Gates of Paradise*. Gilded bronze, 31 ½" × 31 ½". Museo Nazionale del Bargello, Florence, Italy.

1 ft.

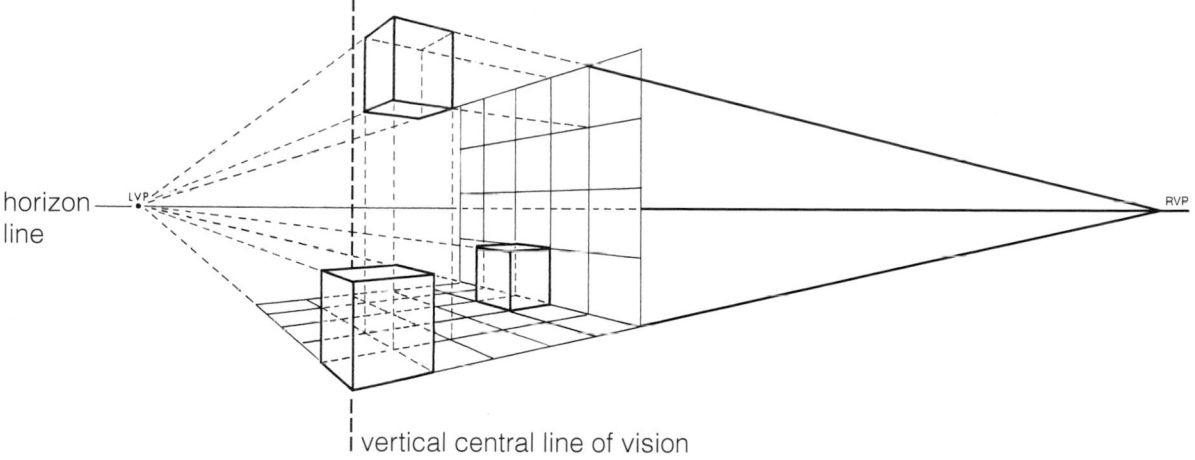

horizon line

vertical central line of vision

▲ 5.15 Diagram of two-point linear perspective.

TWO-POINT PERSPECTIVE **Two-point perspective** is used to represent the recession of objects that are seen from an angle, or obliquely. In the diagram for two-point perspective (Fig. 5.15), the imaginary sight lines that extend from the edges of the cubes converge on the horizon. Two-point perspective can be seen, in practice, in Gustave Caillebotte's *Paris Street* (Fig. 5.16A and 5.16B). The diagonal lines in the building in the left background originate at two distinct points on a horizon line that is positioned at the eye level of the couple strolling with the umbrella in the right foreground.

OPTICAL AND CONCEPTUAL REPRESENTATION The representation of figures and objects from a single vantage point is called **optical representation**. *The School of Athens* and *In a Café* are paintings that feature optical representation. **Conceptual representation**, by contrast, assembles the distinctive characteristics of figures and objects as they are viewed from different perspectives rather than a single, fixed vantage point.

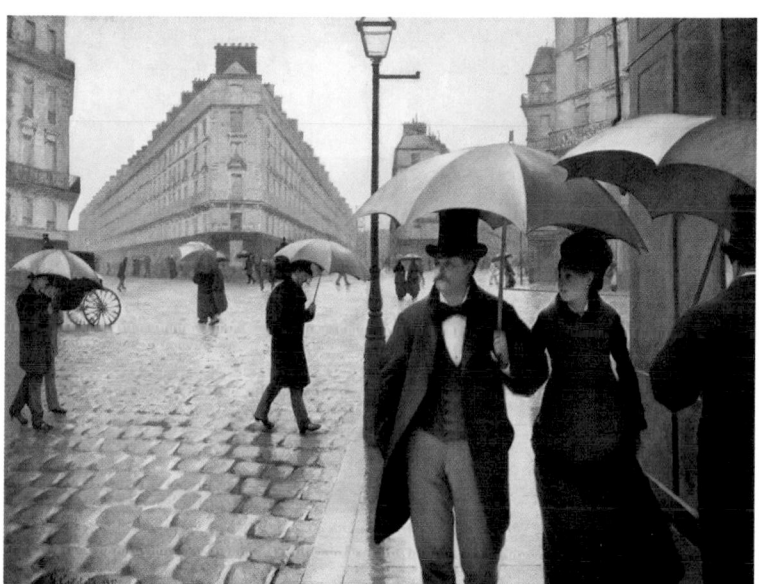

Part A. *Paris Street: Rainy Day* (1877). Oil on canvas, 83½" × 108¼". The Art Institute of Chicago, Illinois.

1 ft.

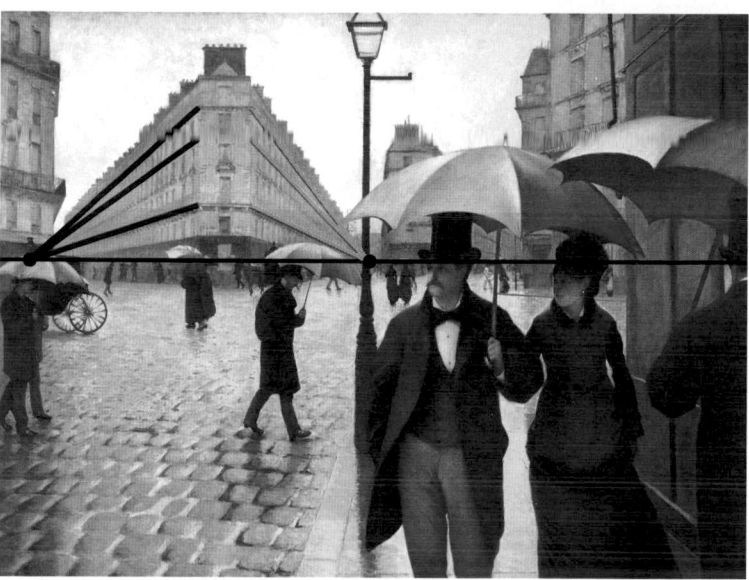

➤ 5.16 GUSTAVE CAILLEBOTTE.   Part B. Perspective in Caillebotte's *Paris Street: Rainy Day.*

COMPARE & CONTRAST

So Close and Yet So Far: Perspective, Physical Proximity, and Emotional Distance

IN BAZ LUHRMANN'S FILM *Moulin Rouge*, Toulouse-Lautrec and his motley entourage follow a green fairy into what seems like an alternate universe. Complete with a wand trailing streams of glittery green-gold, she is the absinthe-induced muse, both temptress and consoler. The lime-colored alcoholic beverage is both intoxicating and toxic and many turn-of-the-century luminaries—artists, writers, and composers among them—partook of its devastating charms.

The couple in Edgar Degas's painting *In a Café* (also called *Absinthe,* **Fig. 5.17**) seems emotionally detached but they are spatially connected—two points, so to speak, on the same diagonal that will have to continue well beyond the border of the canvas before it meets a horizon line in the far right distance. The diagonal is formed by the alignment of marble-topped tables in a banquette along a mirrored wall; the figures are squeezed into the narrow space in-between the two. Another table is positioned in the lower-left quadrant of the composition so that the diagonal line along its outer edge would, if continued, intersect with the first and meet the horizon line at another distinct point in the left distance. Degas's use of two-point perspective—with divergent sets of orthogonals

that converge at a point on the horizon line *outside the composition*—creates an impression that the scene before us is just one small part of the café setting.

Contrast Degas's café painting with William H. Johnson's *Café* **(Fig. 5.18)** in which, it would seem, the goal of the artist was to subvert the devices typically used to create the illusion of space. The lines of the floorboards do not converge at a vanishing point; if anything, they splay out subtly from the center. The juncture of the walls seems more like a meeting of color fields in a continuous plane than a corner space. Like paper cutouts, the figures are defined by flat areas of color and the grid-pattern overlay on the man's suit negates any sense of three-dimensionality. The woman's red-gloved hand overlaps the man's shoulder but it looks more like a separate shape than it does an extension of her arm.

Although the figures in the Johnson painting are comprised of flat, overlapped, and seemingly disjointed shapes, the narrative of the painting is one of connectedness rather than isolation. Johnson's partygoers are social and interactive. The figures in the Degas painting are lost in their own worlds—the worlds of loosely connected words and images conjured under the influence.

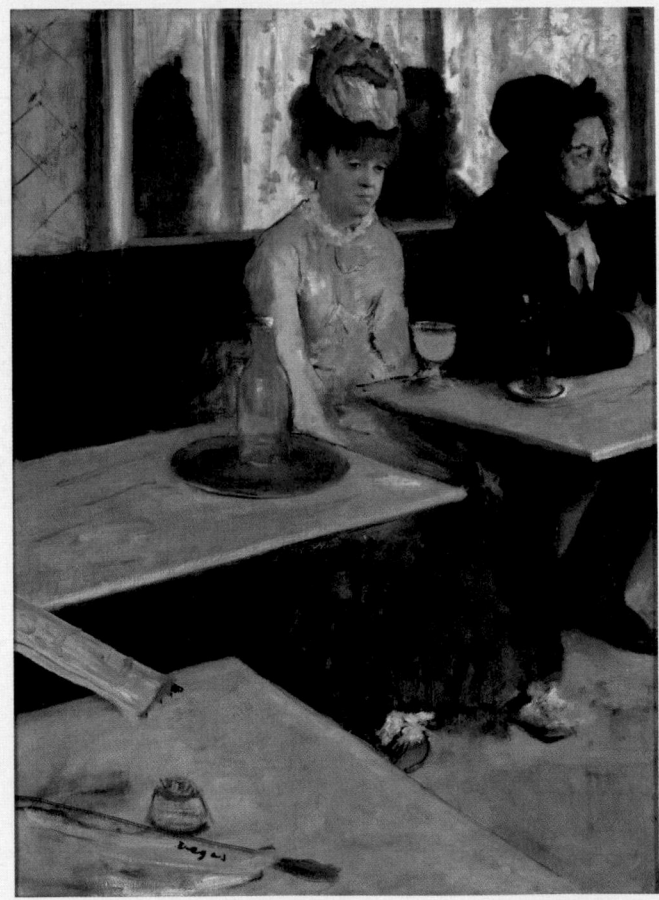

⌃ **5.17 EDGAR DEGAS,** *In a Café* (1873). Oil on canvas, 36⅛" × 26¾". Musée d'Orsay, Paris, France.

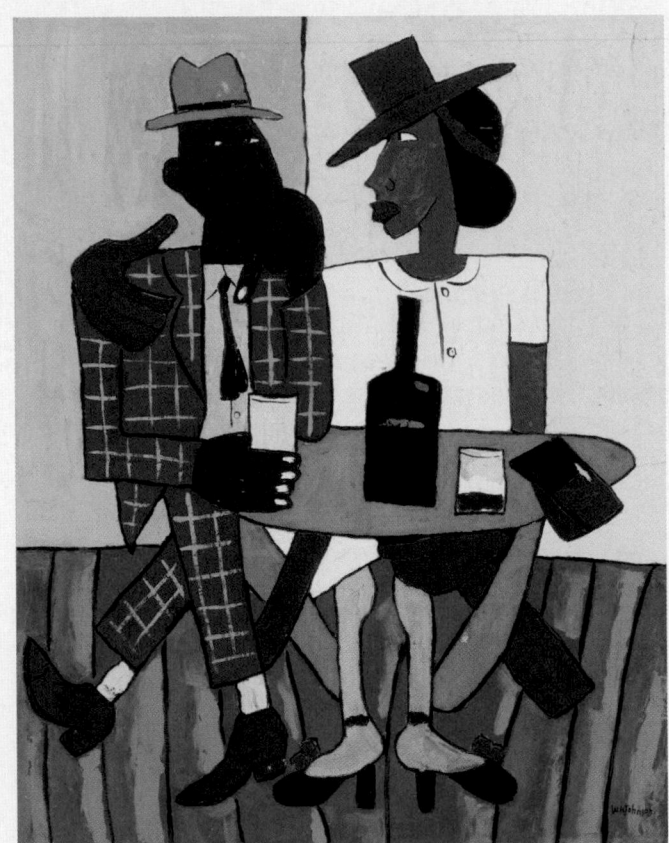

⌃ **5.18 WILLIAM H. JOHNSON,** *Café* (1939–1940). Oil on canvas, 36½" × 28⅜". Smithsonian American Art Museum, Washington, D.C.

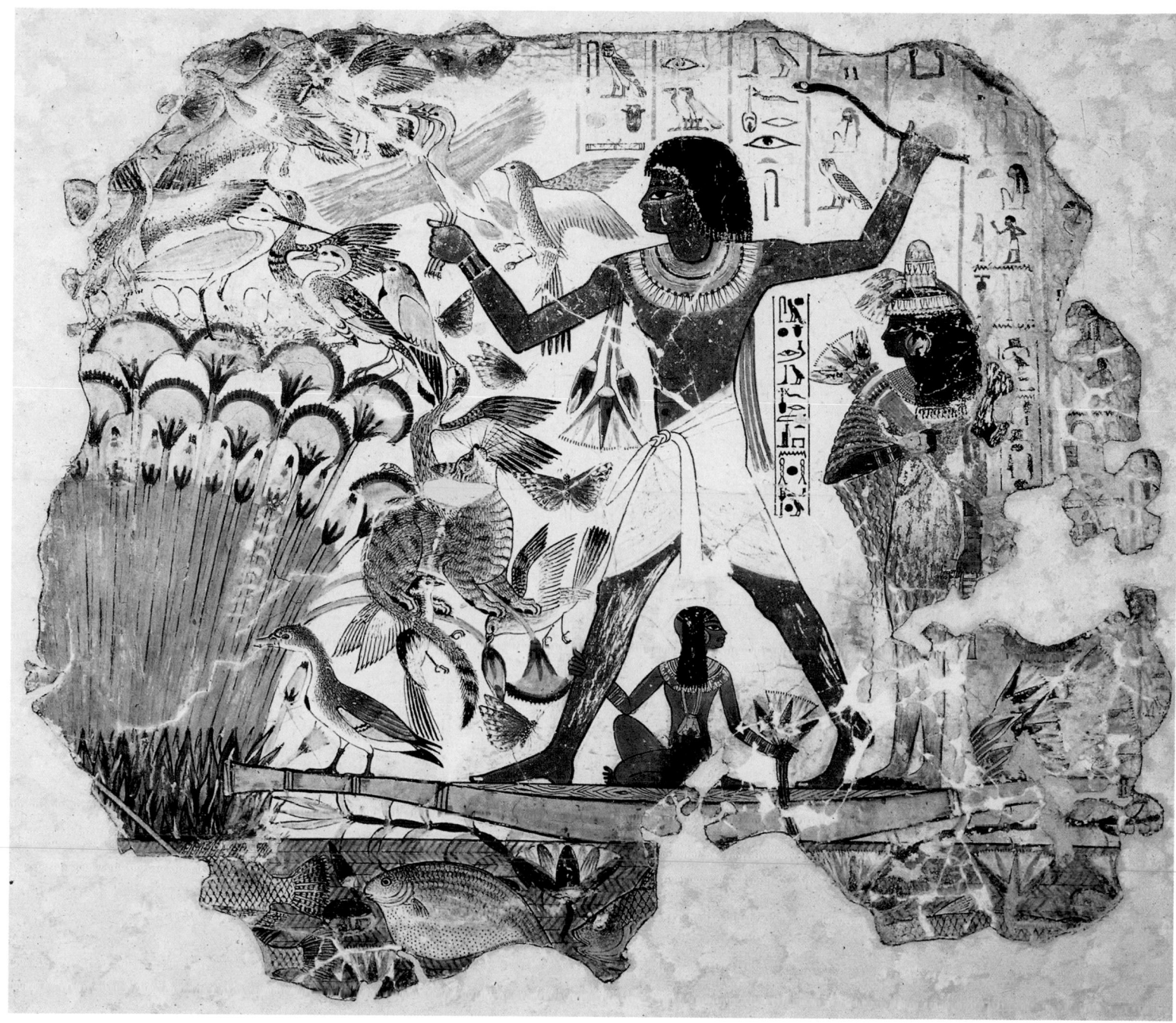

∧ 5.19 **Fowling (Bird-Hunting) Scene** from the tomb of Nebamun, Thebes, Egypt (c. 1400–1350 BCE). Fresco fragment, 36⅝" × 38⅝". British Museum, London, England.

In the Egyptian fresco from the tomb of a nobleman depicting bird hunting (Fig. 5.19), the figures are constructed of a combination of views that offer optimal visual information. The heads, arms, and legs are in profile; the eyes and torsos are shown frontally. If you think about it, the best way to illustrate legs and what they do is to show them in profile, astride. Looking at a face in profile does not offer you the same clear image of the shape of a human eye that a frontal perspective will. The same is true of the breadth of the shoulders, which would not at all be evident in a profile view. On the other hand, the "topography" of the face—the projection of the nose and the chin—is best conveyed in a profile view. This combination of different perspectives is also called a **composite view** or **twisted perspective**.

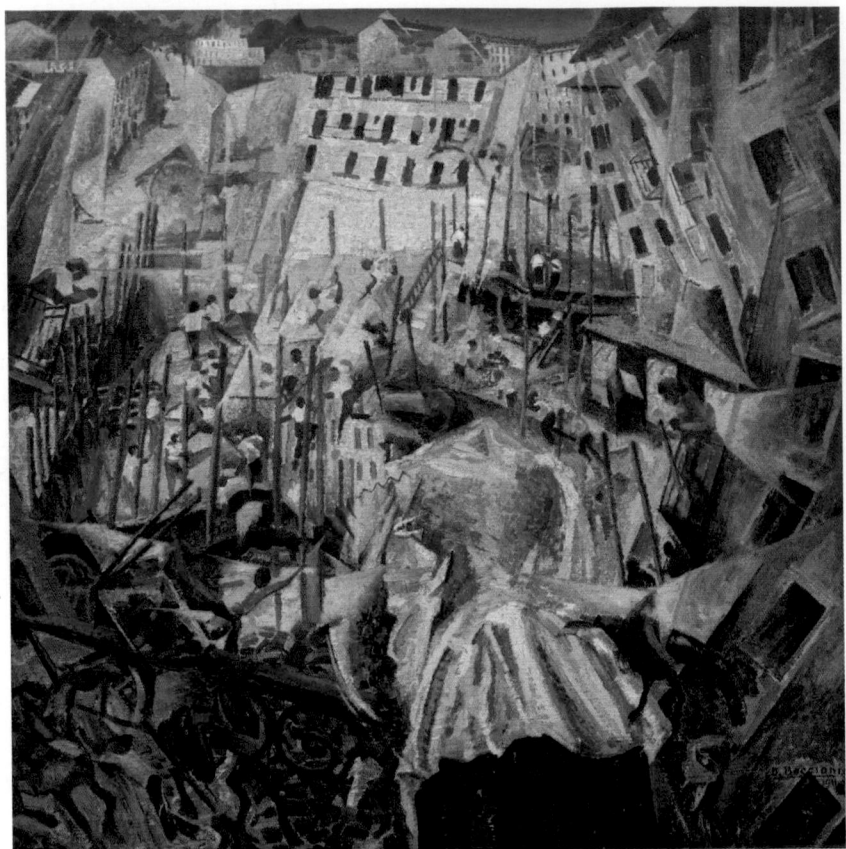

▲ 5.20 **UMBERTO BOCCIONI**, *The Street Enters the House* (1911). Oil on canvas, 39⅜" × 39⅝". Sprengel Museum, Hanover, Germany.

MULTIPLE PERSPECTIVES The use of **multiple perspectives** may provide a more complete visual and sensory impression of a pictorial whole than could be obtained from a single vantage point. It is also a way to suggest the fourth dimension—time and motion.

Umberto Boccioni and other artists of the Futurist movement (see the nearby "Connections" feature) were interested in speed, simultaneity, and the physical relationship between objects and the environment. They believed that the true experience of reality was not static or fixed but rather was one of incessant movement and continual bombardment of visual imagery. In Boccioni's *The Street Enters the House* (Fig. 5.20), this principle of

Futurism is illustrated in the use of multiple perspectives. Lines follow unpredictable paths and shapes are angled in different directions. The artist places the viewer in the middle of the action on a balcony overlooking a city square alive with swirling colors and bustling movement. Our sense of the scene is based not on a single point of view or sight line but rather on the sum total of bits and pieces that the eye observes as we survey the setting.

TIME AND MOTION

Futurist artists, like Boccioni, were seduced by the motion and speed of the instruments of the industrial age—locomotives, automobiles, airplanes, power generators, and the pistons and turbines that drive factory and machine. Their goal was to express this speed, this sensation of rapid movement—a fourth dimension—in two- and three-dimensional art. Much of Boccioni's "Technical Manifesto of Futurist Painting" was devoted to suggestions on how to see and how to replicate the "dynamic sensation" of movement and speed in pictorial art. If the Renaissance masters perfected the representation of the third dimension—depth, mass, and volume—on a two-dimensional surface, the Futurist artists brought us as close to the representation of motion in painting and sculpture as one can imagine.

The Street Enters the House is the physical manifestation of Boccioni's obsession with motion and speed. The viewer is struck by the sensation of movement long before it becomes possible to decipher the figures, the building facades. Shapes swirl around a core of energy and outward toward the edges. Patches of paint break the solids into bits of prismatic color; the viewer is visually drawn into the work by lines and shapes that appear to encircle and ensnare.

The work of the Futurists represents an exaggeration, an extreme in the depiction of movement. One must abandon oneself to the sensation, foregoing the details of representation for an abstract rendition of speed and dynamic force. But many artists have used a variety of techniques to illustrate motion and the passage of time less radically. And the introduction of mediums such as cinematography and video have made it possible to present motion and the passage of time in "real time"—or in slow or accelerated motion. In this section we consider movement and art, both actual and implied. Movement takes place within time; thus the two are intertwined.

CONNECTIONS

The Futurists suggested that the subjects of their works were less important than the "dynamic sensation" of the works.

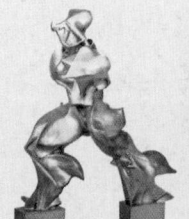

▲ Umberto Boccioni's *Unique Forms of Continuity in Space* (**Fig. 20.14**)

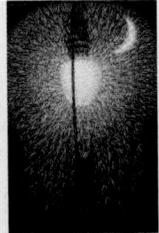

▲ Giacomo Balla's *Street Light* (**Fig. 20.15**)

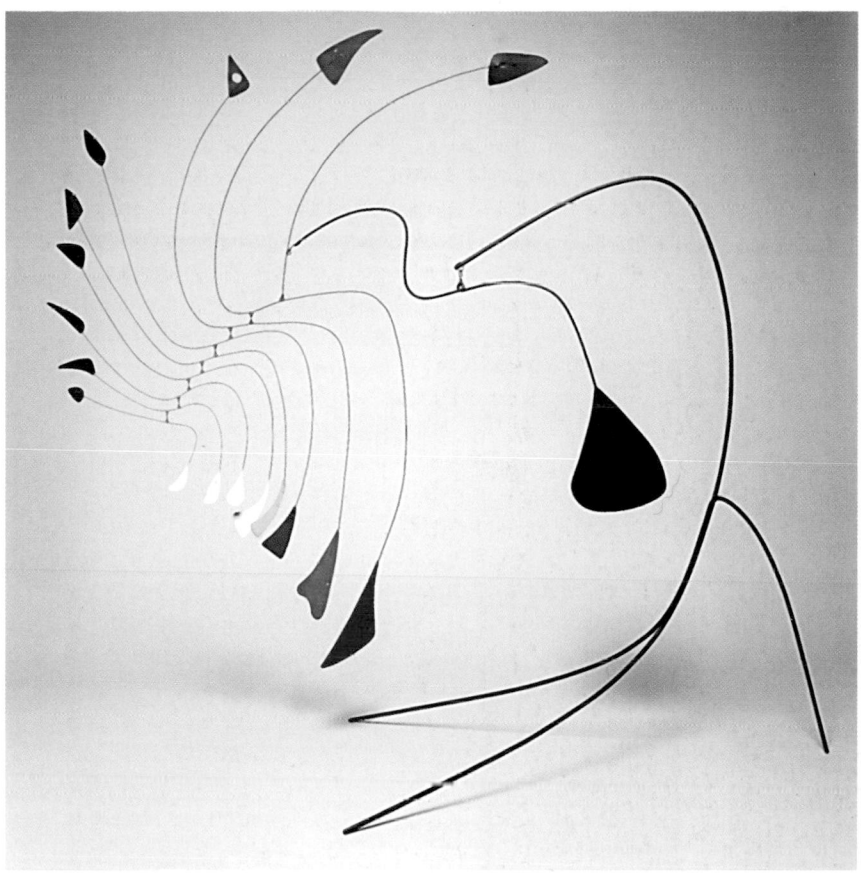

▲ 5.21 **ALEXANDER CALDER**, *Little Spider* (c. 1940). Sheet metal, wire, and paint, 43¾" × 50" × 55". The Museum of Modern Art, New York, New York.

colors that are cantilevered from metal rods in such a way that they can rotate horizontally—in orbits—in the breeze. However, the center of gravity remains stable, so that the entire sculpture is hung from a single point. The composition changes—and keeps changing—with air currents and the viewer's vantage point. The combination of movements is, essentially, infinite; the observer never sees the work in quite the same way.

Photographs of kinetic works of art do nothing to describe their actual character and thus these works cannot be experienced or appreciated unless the motion that is integral to their aesthetic is recorded—captured on film or video or in time-lapse photography.

Early experiments with photography showed the figure in motion through rapid multiple exposures on a single photographic plate. In his motion study of Jesse Godley running (Fig. 5.22), Thomas Eakins used photo sequences to capture the movement of the human body. In the wake of these experiments, a number of artists created the illusion of motion by applying the visual results of multiple-exposure photography to their paintings.

ACTUAL MOTION

Artists work with motion as they would any other element in creating a work of art. From fountains in which the movement of water is intrinsic to the design, to shape-shifting kinetic sculptures whose compositions are transformed by even the slightest breeze, artists have been intrigued by the potential of motion to convert a static image into an active one.

The mobiles of Alexander Calder are among the most popular examples of modern kinetic art. His *Little Spider* (Fig. 5.21) is composed of disks of different sizes and

▼ 5.22 **THOMAS EAKINS**, *Jesse Godley* (1884). Gelatin silver print, 3¾" × 4¾". Philadelphia Museum of Art, Philadelphia, Pennsylvania.

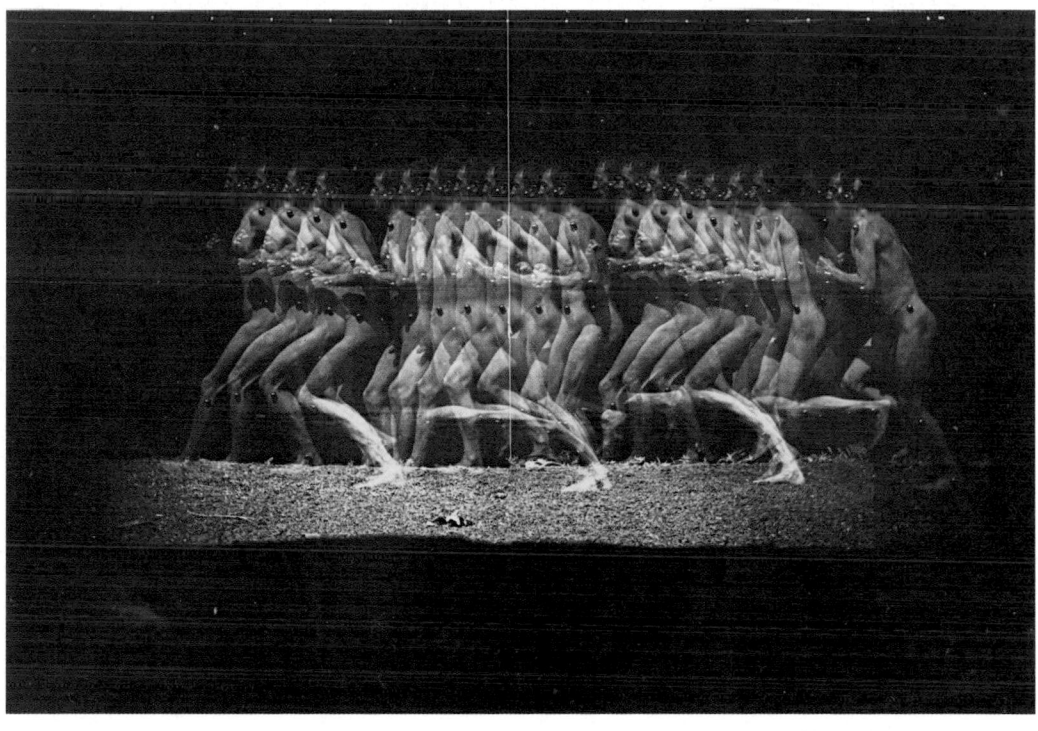

THEORY & PRACTICE

Chasing the Fourth Dimension: Loïe Fuller

AT THE TURN OF THE CENTURY in Paris, when the famous cabaret and music hall, the Folies Bergère was in its heyday, an American dancer named Loïe Fuller captivated her French audiences with her signature "Serpentine Dance." Nicknamed the "Butterfly Girl," Fuller spun in circles, dipping and twirling copious yards of silken fabric around her body as she moved her arms up, down, and around (the Toulouse-Lautrec work that opens this

chapter and **Figs. 5.23** and **5.24**). It was a multimedia spectacle, pushed to the limits with colored stage lights pointed at costumes tinted with luminescent gels (watch a video of Fuller's dance at https://archive.org/details/LoieFuller). It was all about the movement, of course, and so it is interesting to see the ways in which the artists of her day attempted to capture its essence using some of the strategies for creating the illusion of motion in this chapter.

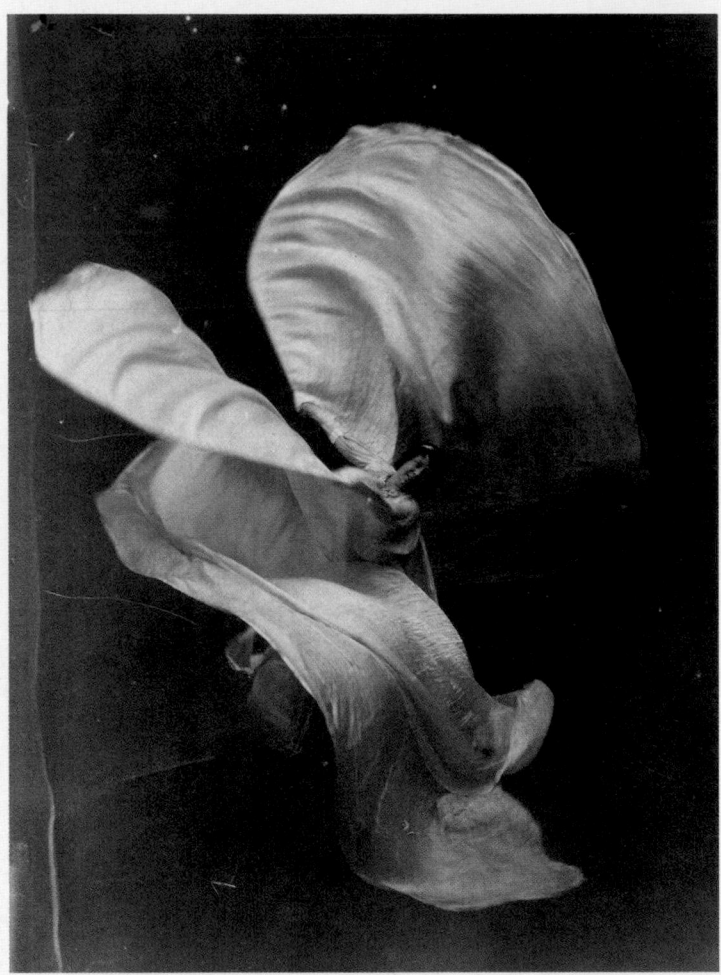

∧ 5.23 ISAIAH WEST TABER, *Loïe Fuller Dancing* (1897). Photograph, 8⅞" × 7¼".

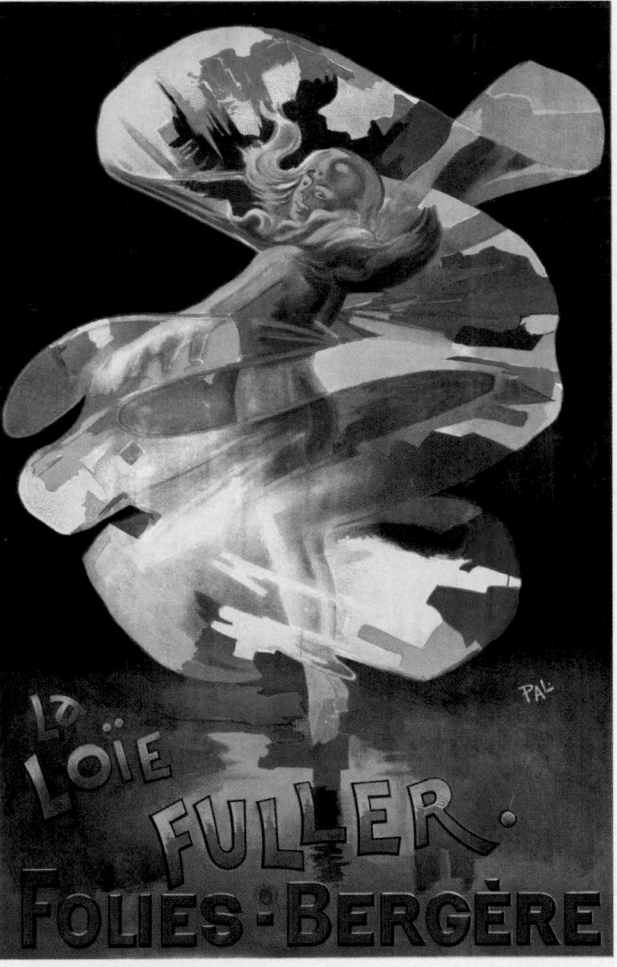

∧ 5.24 PAL (JEAN DE PALEOLOGOU), *La Loïe Fuller, Folies-Bergère* (1897). Poster, color lithograph.

CREATING ILLUSION OF MOTION

When artists use techniques successfully to suggest that motion is *in the process of occurring*, they achieve the illusion of motion. These techniques include multiplication of images or fragments, blurred lines, and optical sensations.

Multiplication of Images and Blurred Lines

With rapid movement, the discrete boundaries of figures or objects can be difficult to perceive; they can be "lost in a blur." Blurring outlines is therefore another way to create the illusion of motion. Photographers sometimes purposefully elongate exposure times to create this effect. This is how it works: Imagine throwing a baseball into the air and watching it come down. If the baseball is photographed with a very short exposure time, the camera will capture the ball at one specific hair of a moment; if the exposure time is longer, the camera will capture the ball at *several* moments in its trajectory in the same image.

Blurring and simulating the result of multiple exposures in photography will create the illusion of motion in paintings and drawings. Giacomo Balla's *Girl Running on the Balcony* (Fig. 5.25), for example, is a painting that mimics the camera technique with which Eakins

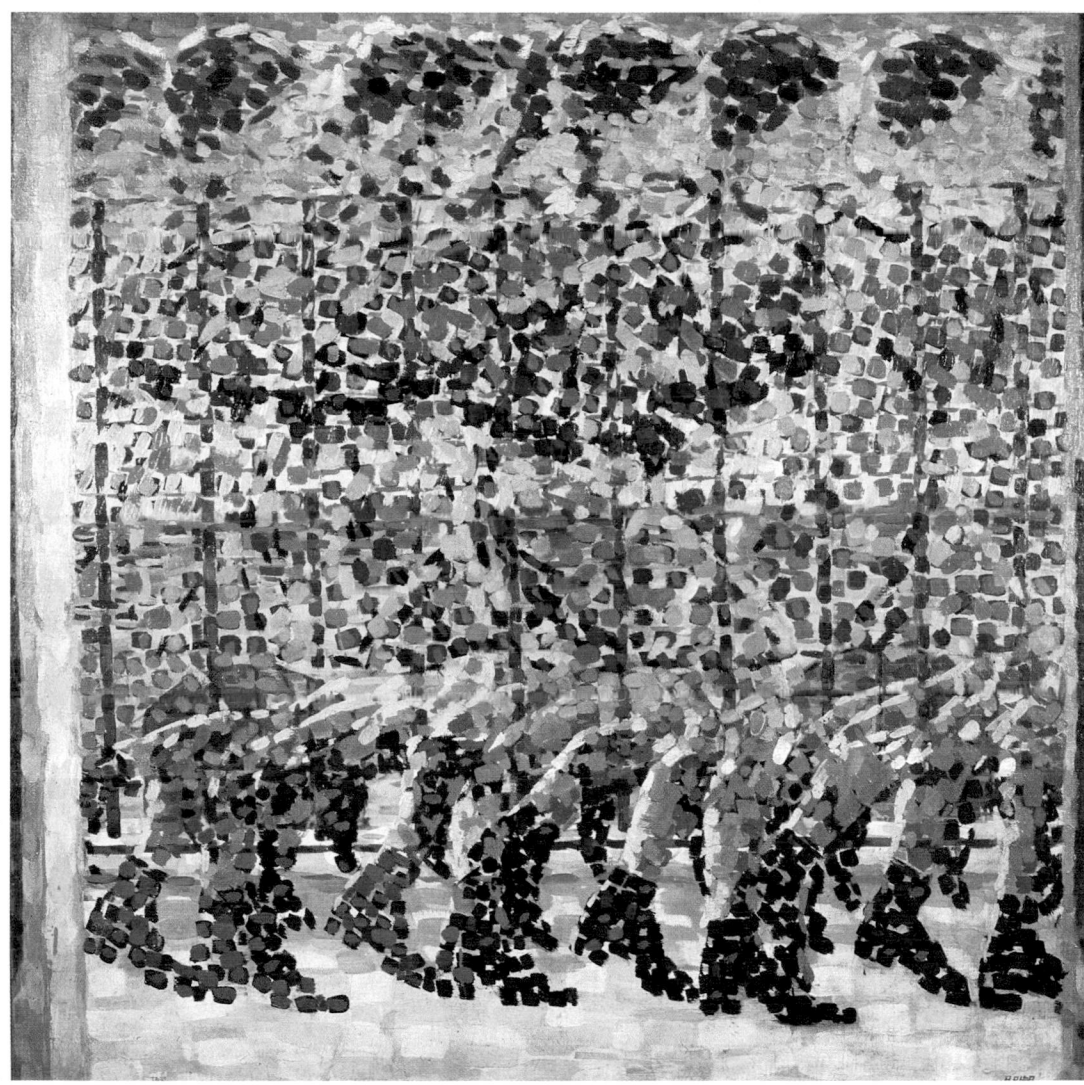

< 5.25 **GIACOMO BALLA,** *Girl Running on the Balcony* (1912). Oil on canvas, 49⅛" × 49⅛". Private collection.

1 ft.

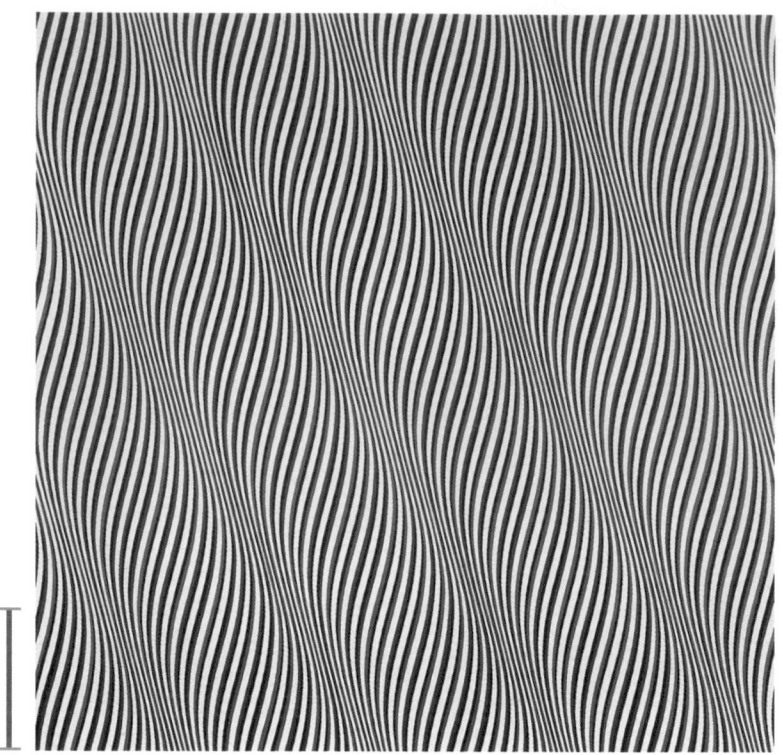

1 ft.

▲ 5.26 **BRIDGET RILEY,** *Gala* (1974). Acrylic on canvas, 5'2¾" × 5'2¾".

IMPLIED MOTION

Let's go back to baseball to explain **implied motion**. Two photographs show a baseball catcher squatting in position. The first (Fig. 5.27A) records his gesture just as the ball hits the pocket of his mitt. In the second (Fig. 5.27B), we see him poised and ready to catch the ball as it approaches. We assume that a ball will land in his mitt based on everything we know already about baseballs and catchers and odds—even though the action is not complete. The photographer has captured a specific moment in the event (what photographer Henri Cartier-Bresson termed "the decisive moment") when the viewer experiences the most anticipation and when the tension of pent-up (implied) energy and motion is even more effective than closure. In works of art, implied motion in a figure may be suggested by the tensing of muscles.

Implied motion may also suggest that a change in the position or location of elements is occurring. This effect can be achieved by using lines of movement; the diagonal lines in Bernini's *David* are an example (see Fig. 17.23). Simple multiplication of images with variations likewise can imply progressions or subtleties of movement, as in Edgar Degas's *Frieze of Dancers* (Fig. 5.28). The rhythmic placement of the dancers, slight variations on a theme, so to speak, implies a common ritual (tying the ribbons of pointe shoes) but can also be read as different views of one individual compressed into a single frame.

experimented. Repetition, overlap, and the blurring of boundaries between the loosely constructed shapes create an illusion of a figure in a blue dress and blue stockings running along an iron railing.

Optical Sensations

By creating optical sensations with the repetition of line and shape and the manipulation of high-contrast values and complementary colors, movement truly is in the eye of the beholder. Bridget Riley's *Gala* (Fig. 5.26) seems to vibrate. The painting is composed of a simple series of curved lines that change in thickness and proximity to one another, creating a powerful illusion of rippling movement. The close juxtaposition of complementary colors red and green also contributes to the illusion of vibration or pulsation.

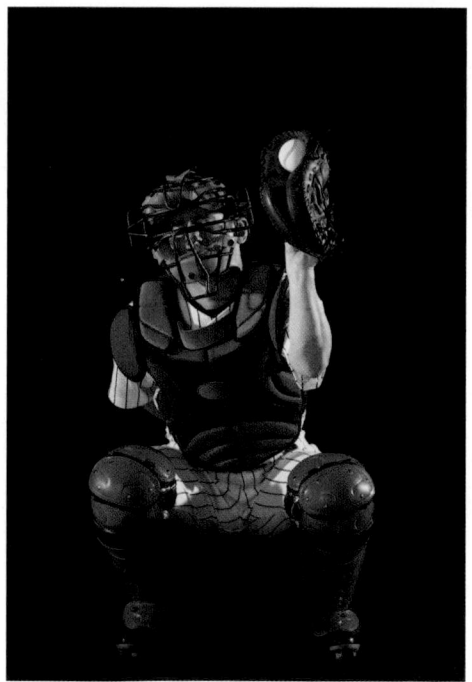

Part A. Holding the ball in the mitt.

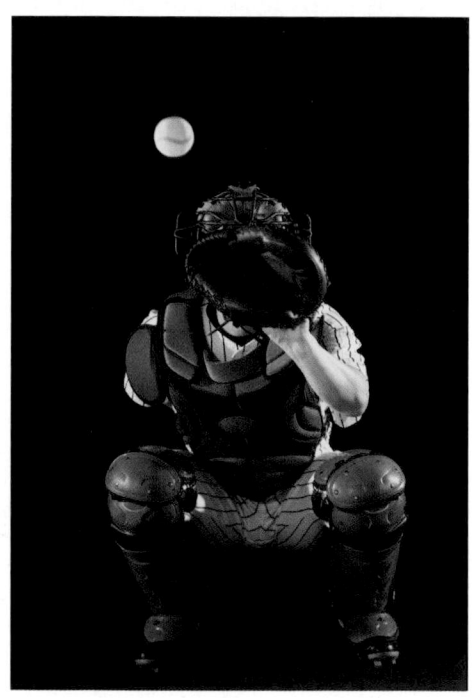

Part B. Catching the ball.

▲ 5.27 **HIDEKI YOSHIHARA,** *Baseball Catcher* (2008).

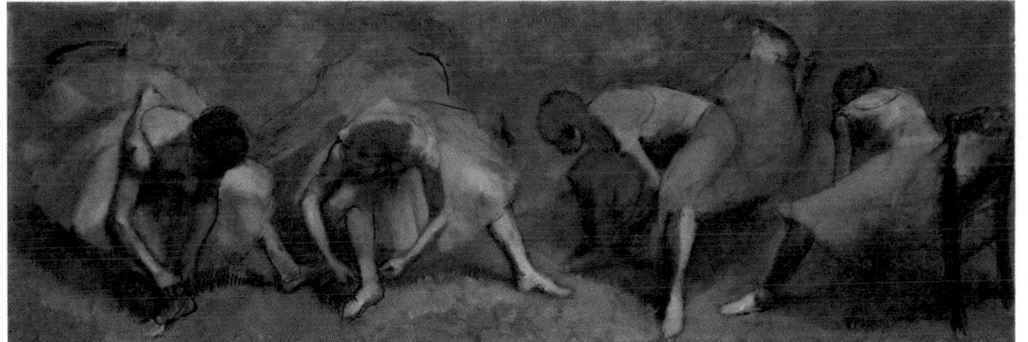

1 ft.

IMPLIED TIME

Motion occurs over time—duration—thus the two are inextricably linked. In the performing arts, works unfold in actual time at a specific location: rock concerts, ballets, or performance art pieces such as Dennis Oppenheim's *Reading Position for a Second Degree Burn* (Fig. 5.29) have a beginning, an end, and are of a certain duration. The details describing the process and the result of Oppenheim's work are in a caption that separates the "before and after" photographs of the artist.

Implied time is the portrayal or suggestion of the passage or duration of time. In an illustration from the medieval Moutier-Grandval Bible (Fig. 5.30), the story of Adam and Eve—from their creation by God through their bitter struggles after expulsion from the Garden of Eden—is told in four parallel bands using figure repetition. The details of the setting are kept to a minimum, focusing our attention on the principal characters and the progression of the narrative.

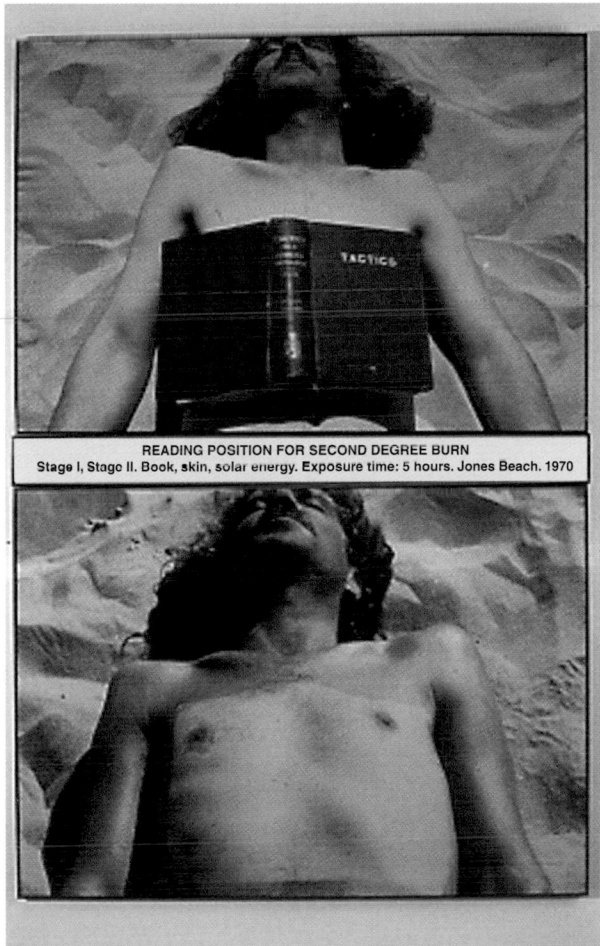

READING POSITION FOR SECOND DEGREE BURN
Stage I, Stage II. Book, skin, solar energy. Exposure time: 5 hours. Jones Beach. 1970

∧ 5.29 DENNIS OPPENHEIM, *Reading Position for a Second Degree Burn* (1970). Color photography and collage, 85" × 59⅞".

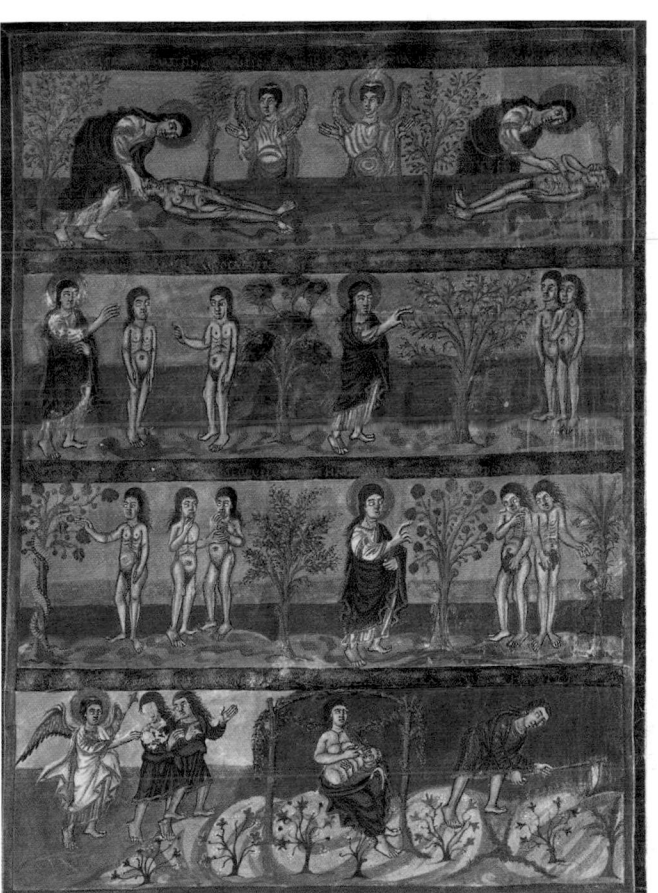

1 ft.

∧ 5.30 **Scenes from Genesis** (c. 840). Illustration in the Moutier-Grandval Bible. 20" × 14¾". The British Library, London, England.

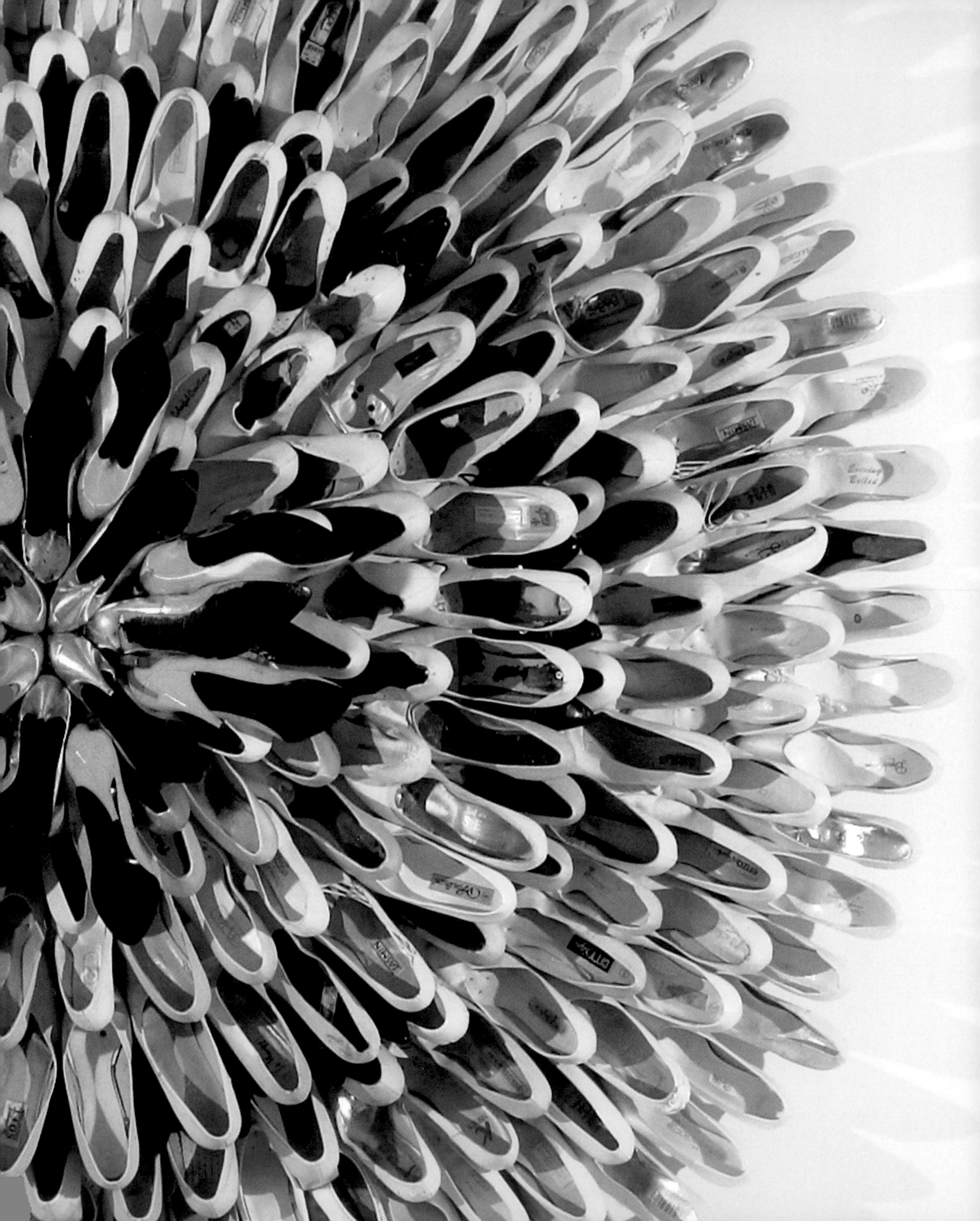

6

PRINCIPLES OF DESIGN

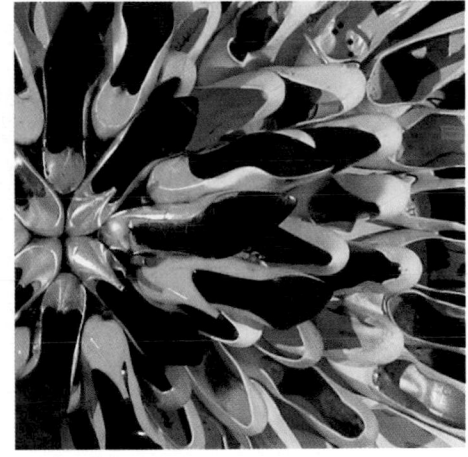

The clarification of visual forms and their organization in integrated patterns as well as the attribution of such forms to suitable objects is one of the most effective training grounds of the young mind.

— RUDOLF ARNHEIM

DESIGN OR **composition** is a process—the act of organizing the visual elements to effect a desired aesthetic in a work of art. Designs can occur at random, as exemplified by the old mathematical saw that an infinite number of monkeys pecking away at an infinite number of typewriters would eventually (though mindlessly) produce *Hamlet.* But when artists create compositions, they consciously draw upon design principles such as unity and variety, balance, emphasis and focal point, rhythm, scale, and proportion. This is not to say that all artists necessarily apply these principles, or even always recognize the extent of their presence in their work. In fact, some artists prefer to purposefully violate them. But in some fashion, and to varying extents, the elements of art and principles of design work hand-in-hand toward the goal of a unified whole that communicates the artist's intent.

◄ WILLIE COLE, *With a Heart of Gold* (2005–2006). Shoes, wood, screws, metal, and staples. 85' diameter, 16' depth. Courtesy of Alexander, and Bonin, New York.

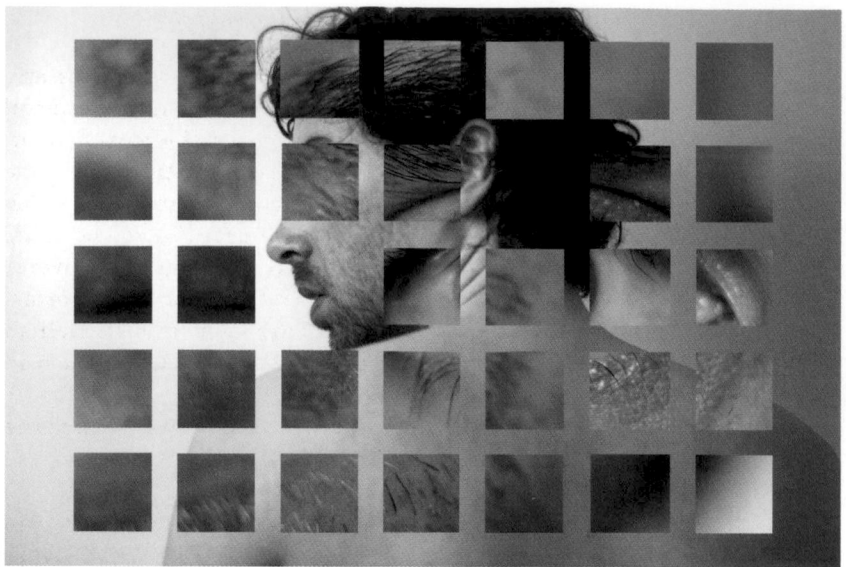

▲ 6.1 **ANDREW ADOLPHUS**, *Divergence 2* (2013). Digital photograph.

the individual components may appear inseparable and the effect of the wholeness or oneness is achieved. Delilah Montoya's *Los Jovenes (Youth)* (Fig. 6.2) is a group portrait of eight teenagers, some interacting with one another, some not; some confronting the viewer with their gaze, some not the least interested in doing so. In spite of the differences among them, they are united first and foremost by their proximity. Even though the placement of their bodies in the graffiti-covered room seems random, almost all of the figures—in the flattened space of the photograph—appear to touch. The unity of the composition as well as the cohesiveness of the group are further strengthened by the warm, blended sepia tones of the photograph and, of course, by the implied bond of friendship born from common roots and experiences.

UNITY

Unity is oneness or wholeness. A work of art exhibits unity when its parts seem necessary to the composition as a whole. Unity can be suggested with the repetition of similar elements (as in, for example, a grid), the strategic placement of figures or shapes or colors in proximity to one another, or by using line to draw connections among disparate components.

The Grid

The grid is the ultimate unifying device. If adhered to firmly, almost nothing will override its visual impact. The central image of Andrew Adolphus's *Divergence 2* (Fig. 6.1) is the artist's profile, but the dominant feature of the composition is the grid. Thirty-five squares featuring enlarged details of the face, ranging from sharp to blurred in terms of focus, alternately disassemble and assemble parts of the interrupted whole. Our eyes lock onto the squares and then travel around them, flipping our focus from foreground to background and vice versa.

Proximity

Visual unity in a composition can be achieved by placing figures or objects in close **proximity** to one another or, in some cases, physically connecting them. When proximity is reinforced with repetitive elements such as line, shape, value, or color,

Repetition

Even when a great deal is going on in a work of art, such as in Linda Mieko Allen's *Atmospherics XIX (ultraviolet)* (Fig. 6.3), the brain will perceive unity because the eye has a tendency to search for and pick out common shapes, colors, textures, lines, and just about anything else. The first impression may be one of chaos, but the more we get lost in the work, the more we find. Scattered bits of red and yellow pop and draw our eyes to their other

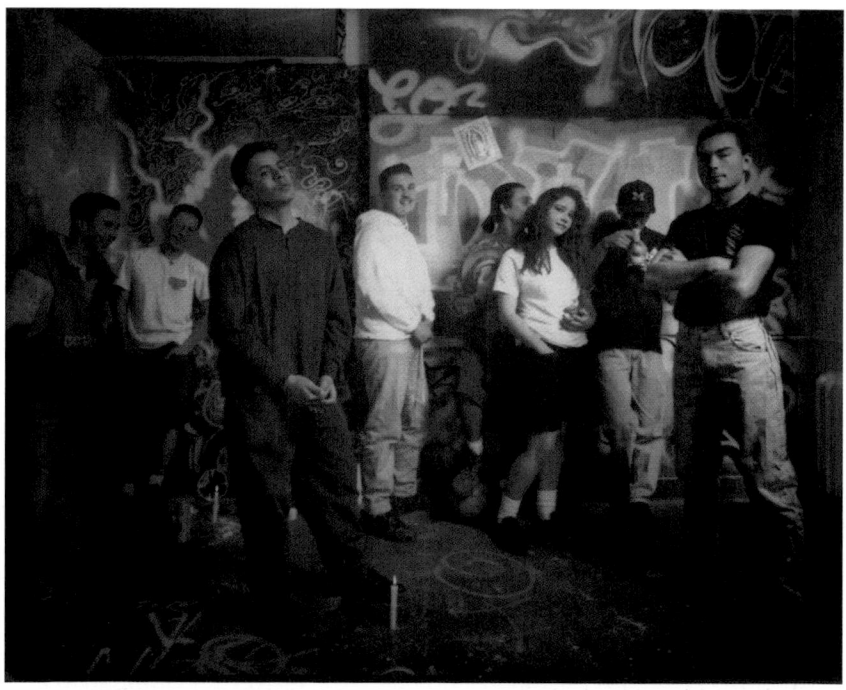

1 in.

▲ 6.2 **DELILAH MONTOYA**, *Los Jovenes (Youth)* (1993). Collotype, 9¼" × 10". Smithsonian American Art Museum, Washington, D.C.

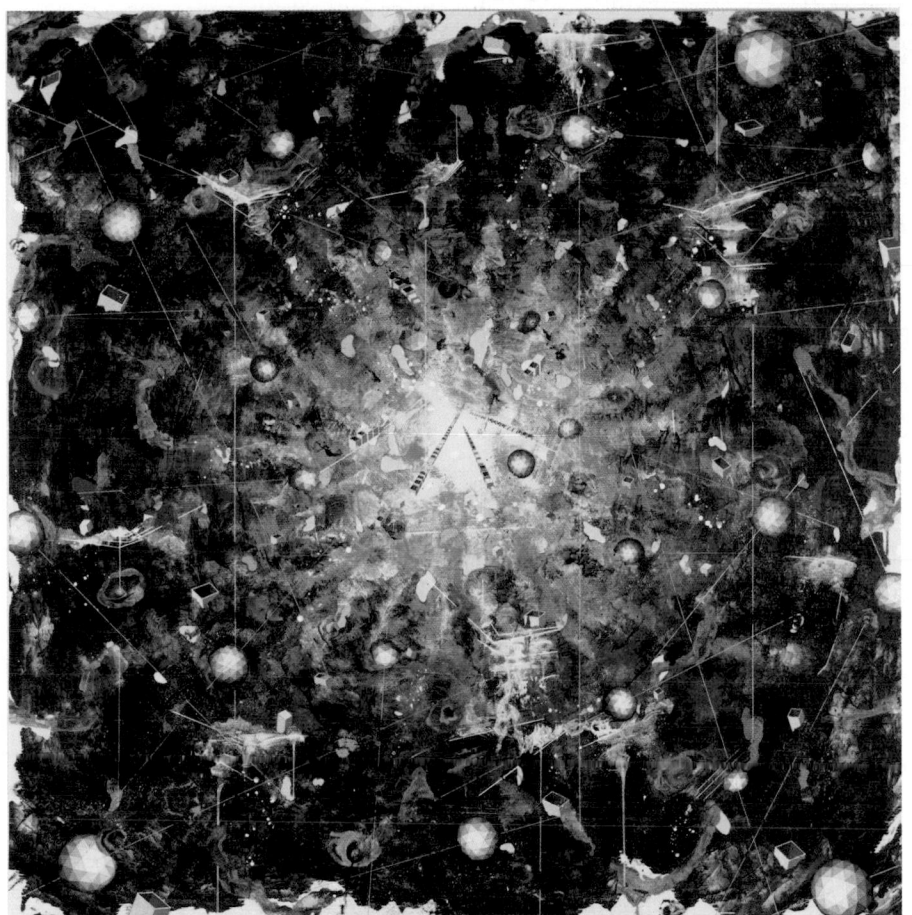

^ 6.3 **LINDA MIEKO ALLEN,** *Atmospherics XIX (ultraviolet)* (2011). Mixed media, 60" × 60".

1 ft.

Color and Value

The unifying elements of color and value are some of the most powerful to the eye. This can be most evident in compositions that have complex designs or narratives in which the repetitive use of color or value contrast can tie together diverse elements or highlight key information. We have seen this in Delilah Montoya's work. It is also evident in a monumental work like Picasso's *Guernica* (see Fig. 20.10) in which the value spectrum of grays unites the fractured, disconnected shapes.

The degree to which unity can be perceived with the aid of color is dramatically evident in Josiah McElheny's installation *Three Screens for Looking at Abstraction* (Fig. 6.4). The choreographed arrangement of projected imagery within the space—and the repetition of pattern and color—enables visual connections that create the feeling of a unified composition. Unity is enhanced as the intense hue of the projections spills beyond the screens, bathing the space in the same colored light.

far-flung "cousins." Golf-ball-like objects seem to be strategically placed, and many of the wildly assorted shapes are connected by the thinnest of white lines. The result is a surprising, overarching unity. The principle of unity through repetition can be present in even the most disorderly of compositions, functioning to bring together scattered bits of narrative or lead the eye "by the hand" to take in the entirety of a scene.

The viewer's experience of this event is something of sense of controlled confusion, brought about by the principle of unity. In this sea of confusion, the simple repetitive element of the line motif provides visual unity and controls the eye's path.

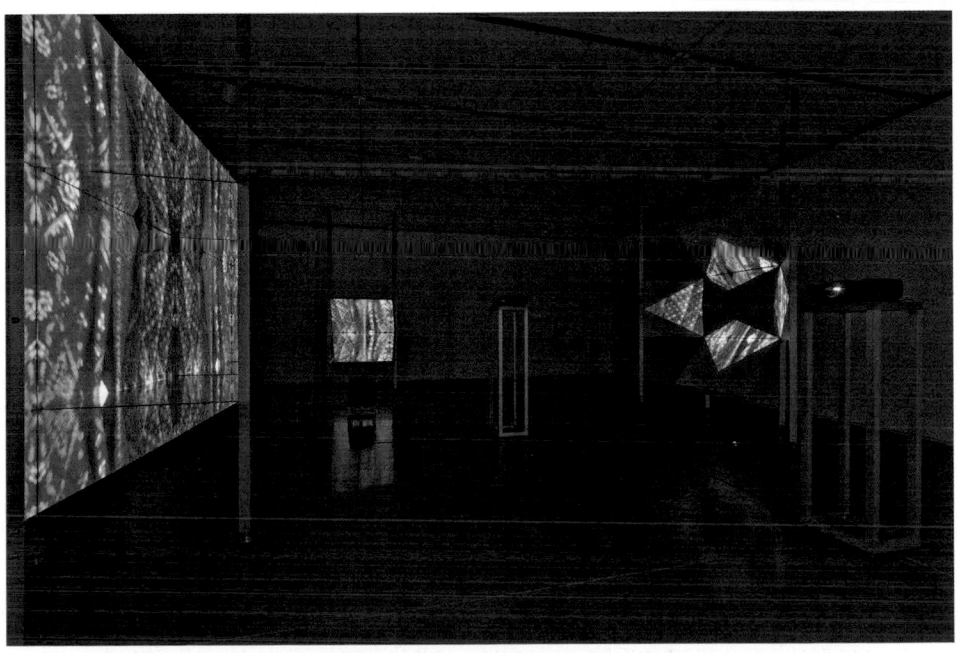

^ 6.4 **JOSIAH MCELHENY,** *Three Screens for Looking at Abstraction* (2012). Aluminum, low-iron mirror, projection cloth, film transferred to video, video projectors with stands, wood, metal hardware. Three parts, overall dimensions variable. Courtesy Andrea Rosen Gallery, New York.

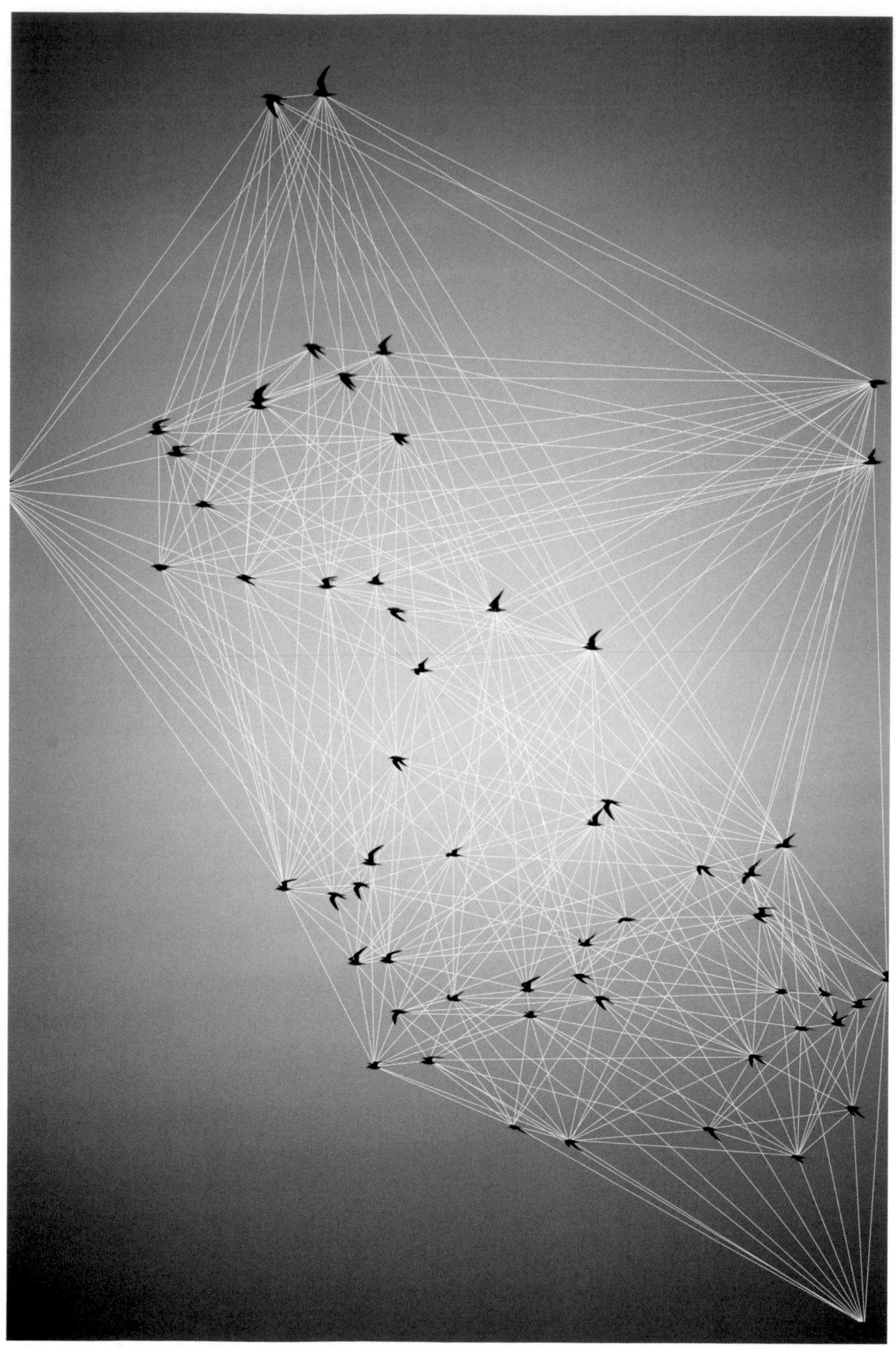

▲ 6.5 **ANDREW ADOLPHUS,** *Sight Lines (Birds)* (2013).

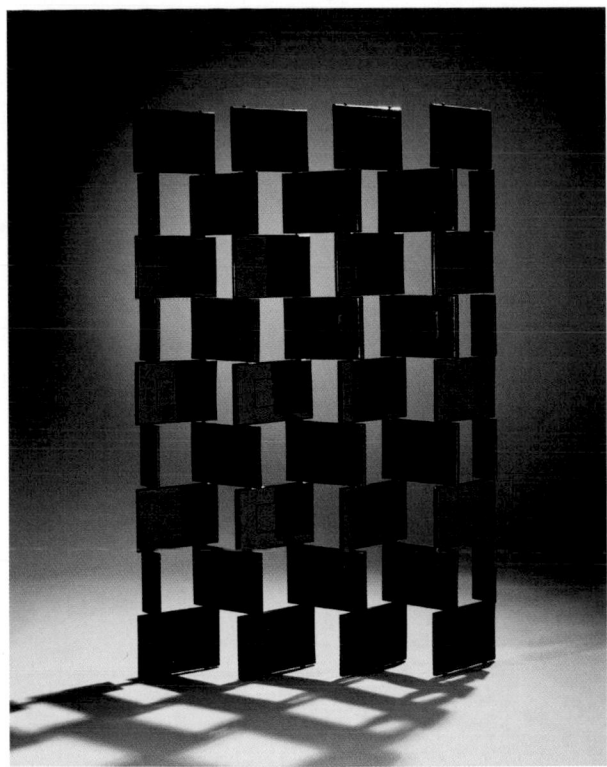

▲ 6.6 **EILEEN GRAY,** *'Brick' Screen* (1923–1925). Lacquered wood on metal rods, 74 ½" × 53 ½" × ¾".

Line

Line is a common way of unifying the components or elements of a composition or of leading the viewer's eye along some predetermined visual paths. A literal example of line in the service of unity can be seen in Andrew

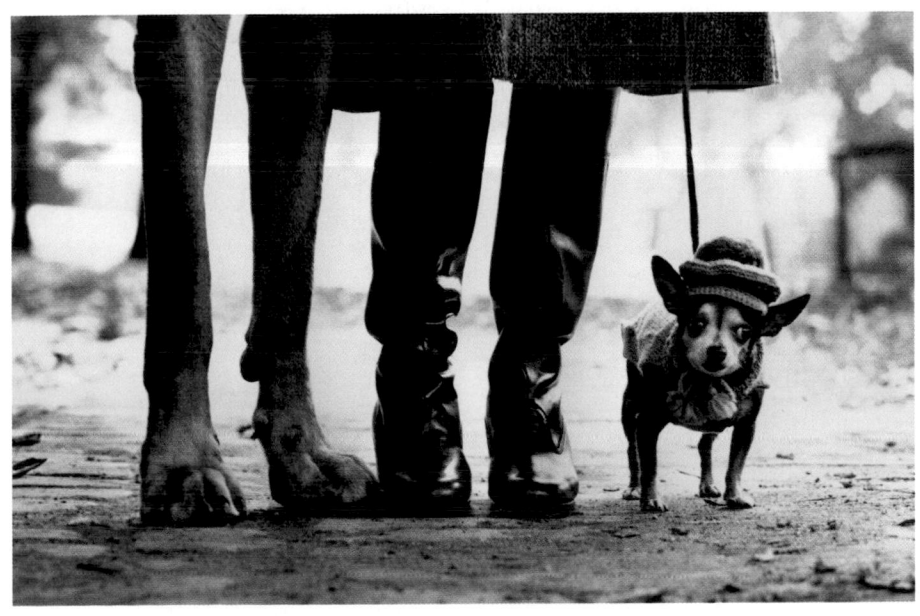

▲ 6.7 **ELLIOT ERWITT,** *Felix, Gladys, and Rover* (1974). Gelatin silver print.

CONNECTIONS

In *The Three Goddesses*, line is used to unify the triad of female torsos—a group of figures from

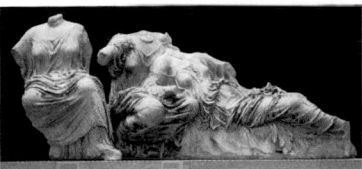

▲ *Three Goddesses* (**Fig. 15.10**)

the Parthenon (see Chapter 15). The bodies of the goddesses are substantial and weighty, but the flowing lines of the drapery ride the surface in shallowly carved folds, forming a continuous ripple over their knees and into their laps. Line defines the contours of the figures and blurs the boundaries between them, unifying the whole composition.

Adolphus's photograph of an airborne cluster of gulls in which a complex network of vector-like lines connects temporarily divergent flight paths (Fig. 6.5). In a broader sense, line can be used to unify opposing areas of a composition or diverse imagery within; linear paths or directional lines will encourage the viewer's eye to visually traverse the area within the frame or boundaries of a work.

UNITY WITH VARIETY

When a work of art has a strong sense of unity that is interrupted with some aspect or elements that diverge from the predominant compositional scheme, we say that it exhibits **variety within unity**. Artists often use variety with unity, either instinctively or in a conscious effort to stimulate interest and amplify the complexity of a work.

In her *'Brick' Screen* (Fig. 6.6), the Irish artist Eileen Gray began with several wooden panels of uniform shape and color, held together by metal rods. She injected visual interest—variety—into the grid based work by positioning the panels at various angles. So tempted are we to create our own variations on her grid theme that the panels seem to beckon us to adjust their orientation, just for the fun of it—a kind of adult busy box.

The principle of variety within unity is the premise for Elliot Erwitt's humorous photograph *Felix, Gladys, and Rover* (Fig. 6.7). In this fashion advertisement for women's boots for which the photographer brought the viewer to Chihuahua eye level, variety draws out the relationships that unify the composition.

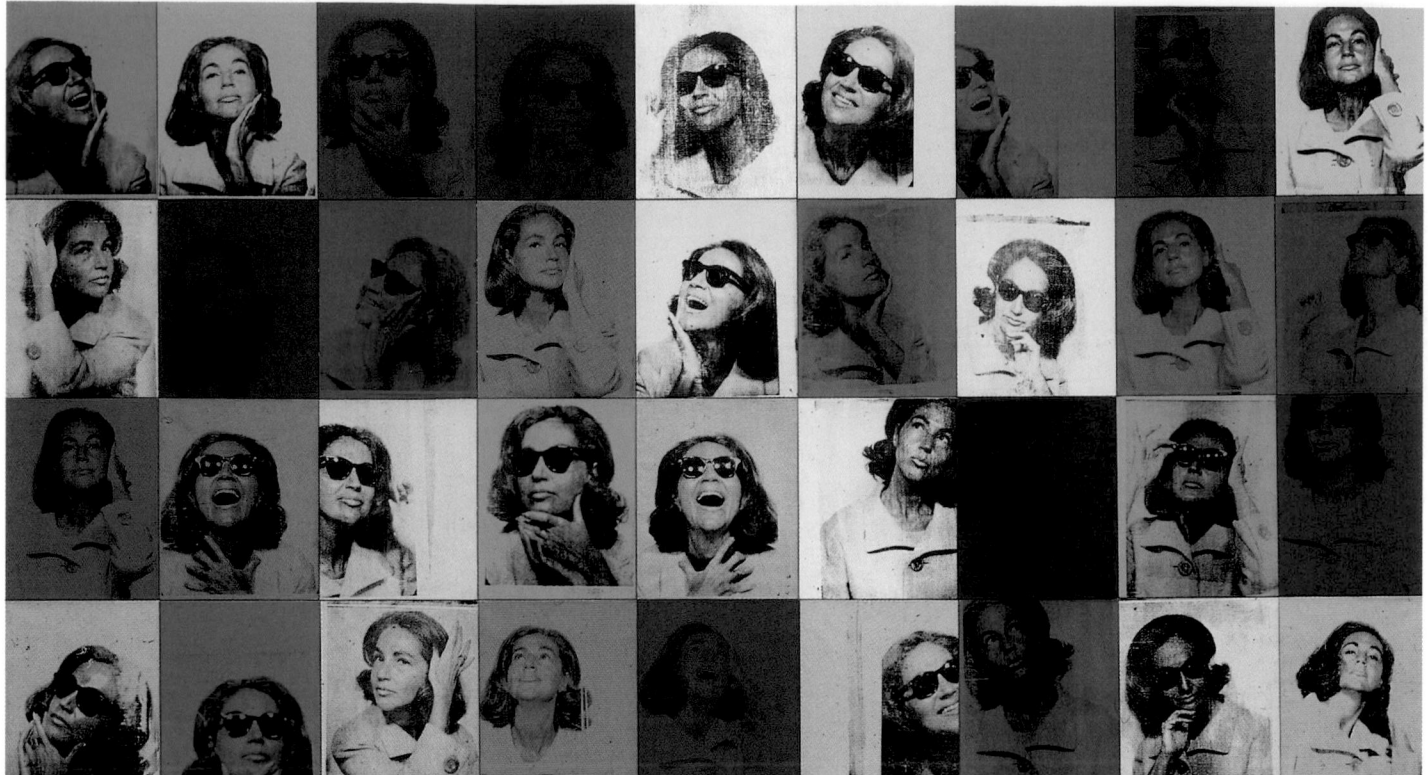

1 ft.

∧ 6.8 **ANDY WARHOL,** *Ethel Scull Thirty-Six Times,* (1963). Synthetic polymer paint silkscreened on canvas, 79¾" × 143¼". Whitney Museum of American Art, New York.

Repetition

Repetition, or the use of the same or similar elements over and over again in a composition, is a strategy for creating variety within unity. Andy Warhol built *Ethel Scull Thirty-Six Times* (Fig. 6.8) on the principle of a grid, drawing attention to the ubiquity of mass-produced consumables of any and all types, including human beings of celebrity. Reflecting his signature compositional arrangement, the work consists of the repetition of silk-screened photo-booth-type images. An overall unity abides within the nine-by-four grid and repetitive shape and color scheme, but the wide variety of expression creates a multidimensional view of Scull's appearance and personality.

Emphasis on Unity

Although unity and variety often go hand-in-hand, some works focus heavily on one or

the other. Repetition can be used by the artist to emphasize unity and, with it, order and harmony.

The emphasis on unity in Beverly Buchanan's *4 Shacks with Black-Eyed Susans* (Fig. 6.9) provides a sense of family and close-knit community. It is a by-product of the

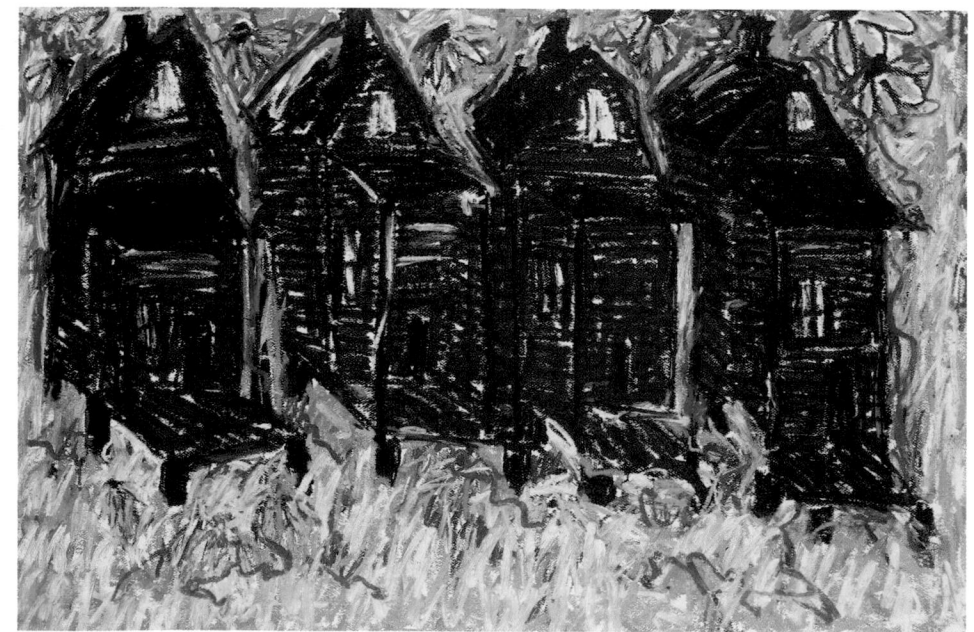

1 ft.

∧ 6.9 **BEVERLY BUCHANAN,** *4 Shacks with Black-Eyed Susans* (1995). Oil pastel on paper, 25½" × 38".

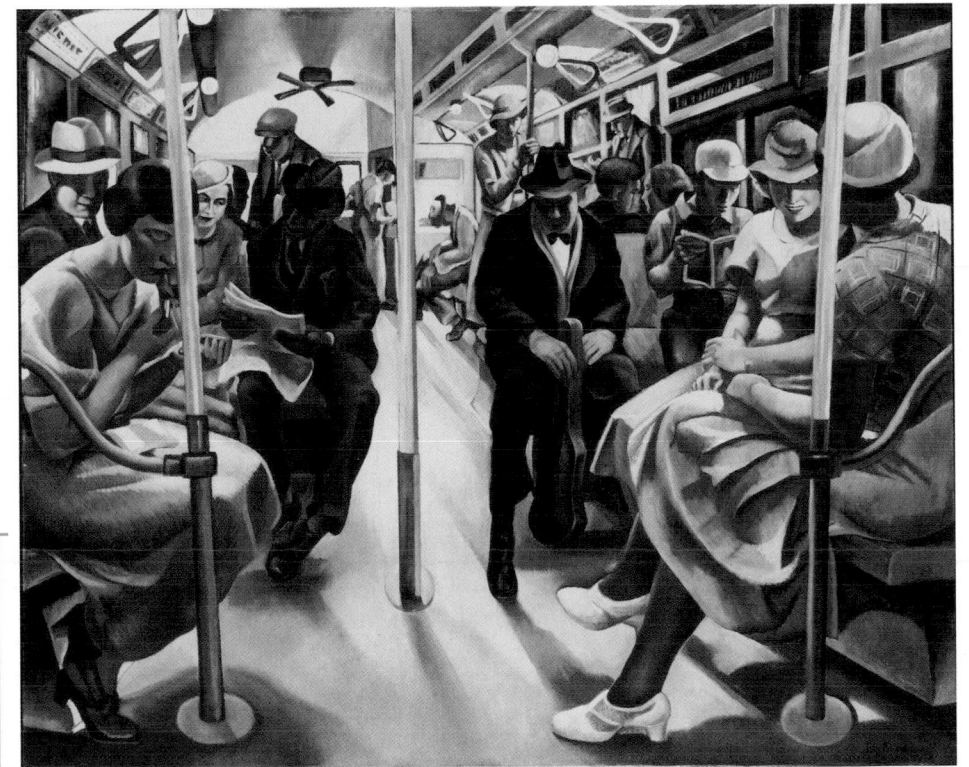

1 ft.

∧ 6.10 **LILY FUREDI**, *Subway* (c. 1934). Oil on canvas, 39" × 48¼". Smithsonian American Art Museum, Washington, D.C.

disunity, akin to sensory overload or, put another way, compositional chaos. Crazy patchwork (Fig. 6.11) is a style of quilt-making that foregoes the conventional symmetry and motif repetition more typically associated with this textile artform. The clashing patterns and shapes and colors create a deliberate disunity; the visual energy of the piece results from spontaneity and unpredictability.

ORDERED CHAOS Chaos is a part of human existence. To think of life as neatly ordered and predictable, or as consistently coherent, would not acknowledge the extremes of human behavior, for better or for worse. Chaos can be dark and devastating. It can also be light, and frivolous, and fun. These opposing emotions can be found in works of art.

repetition and emphasis on sameness that the artist adheres to in her lush oil pastel drawings. There are subtle variations to be observed, but they are subservient to the strict unity of the whole. Buchanan was born in North Carolina, where structures such as these dot the landscape, recalling the bitter days of slave communities and more bitter reality that socioeconomic conditions for the very poor in the Deep South have not, to this day, brought true liberation. Unity in a work of art, then, can serve different although complementary purposes. In Buchanan's drawing the emphasis on unity creates a certain visual effect, but it also functions symbolically.

Emphasis on Variety

When artists emphasize variety, they are usually exaggerating differences rather than similarities among their images. Lily Furedi's painting called *Subway* (Fig. 6.10) is a demographic and ethnic cross section of the strap-hanging population of 1930s New York City. Even though they are unified by the common need to move efficiently from place to place beneath the streets of the metropolis, this fact is not the main theme of the work. Rather, the artist builds his painting around the individuality and diversity of the riders.

Emphasis on Disunity

Imagine variety pumped up to the point at which it overrides any hope of unity; the result is an emphasis on

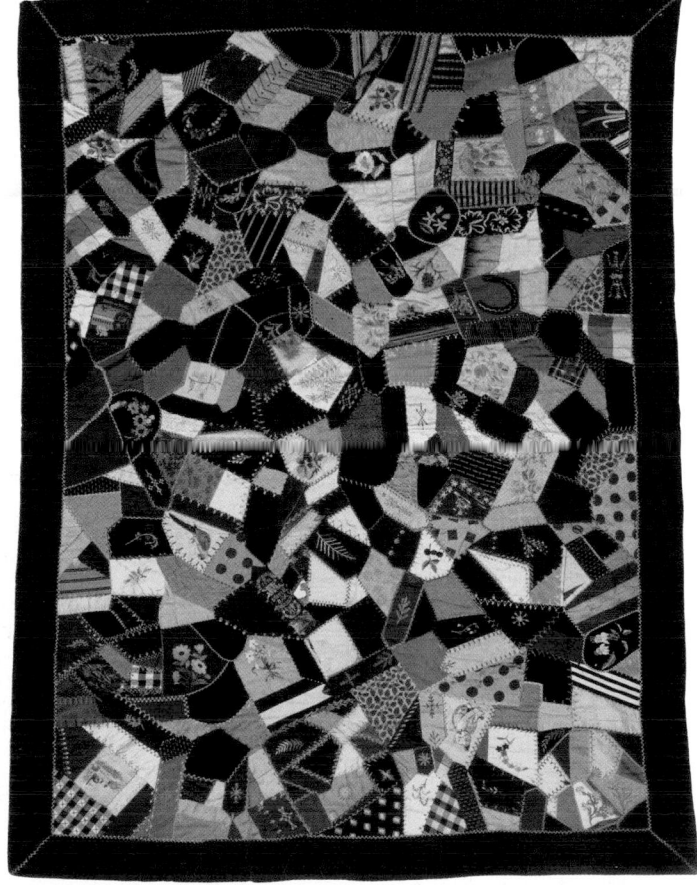

∧ 6.11 **Crazy Quilt** (1887).

THEORY & PRACTICE
Focal Point and Emphasis

ARTISTS USE FOCAL point and emphasis to draw attention to specific parts of a composition to reinforce certain themes or to create visual impact. The compositional devices, used to create three areas of emphasis in Jacques-Louis David's *The Oath of the Horatii* (Fig. 6.12), include focal point, isolation, placement, and contrasts between static and dynamic elements and between straight and curving lines. Color and directional lines are used to create a focal point.

The diagonal placement of the soldiers' arms—directional lines—draw our focus to the swords.

The subject of the painting—an oath before battle taken by three brothers and sworn on swords upheld by their father—is given prominence through the central placement of the swords and the hands. It becomes the focal point of the composition.

Color—bright red—is used to focus the viewer's eye on the central figure; the red cloak and red garment of the soldier in the left foreground create emphasis on the oath being sworn on the swords by creating a visual "bracket."

The women in the painting are isolated from the men, both physically and psychologically. They lean on one another and their shared emotion creates an area of emphasis.

Rigid, rectilinear elements characterize the physical stance of the men; soft, curving lines describe the drapery and posture of the women. These contrasts create different areas of emphasis.

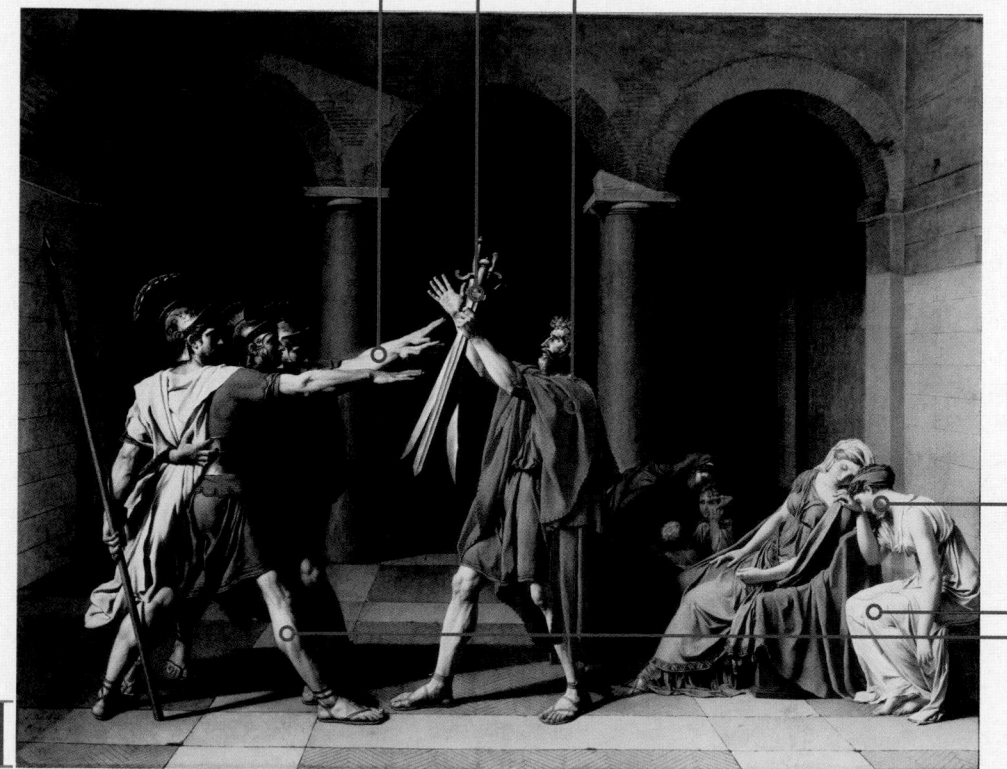

1 ft.

∧ **6.12 JACQUES-LOUIS DAVID,** *The Oath of the Horatii* (1784). Oil on canvas, 14' × 11'. Louvre, Paris, France.

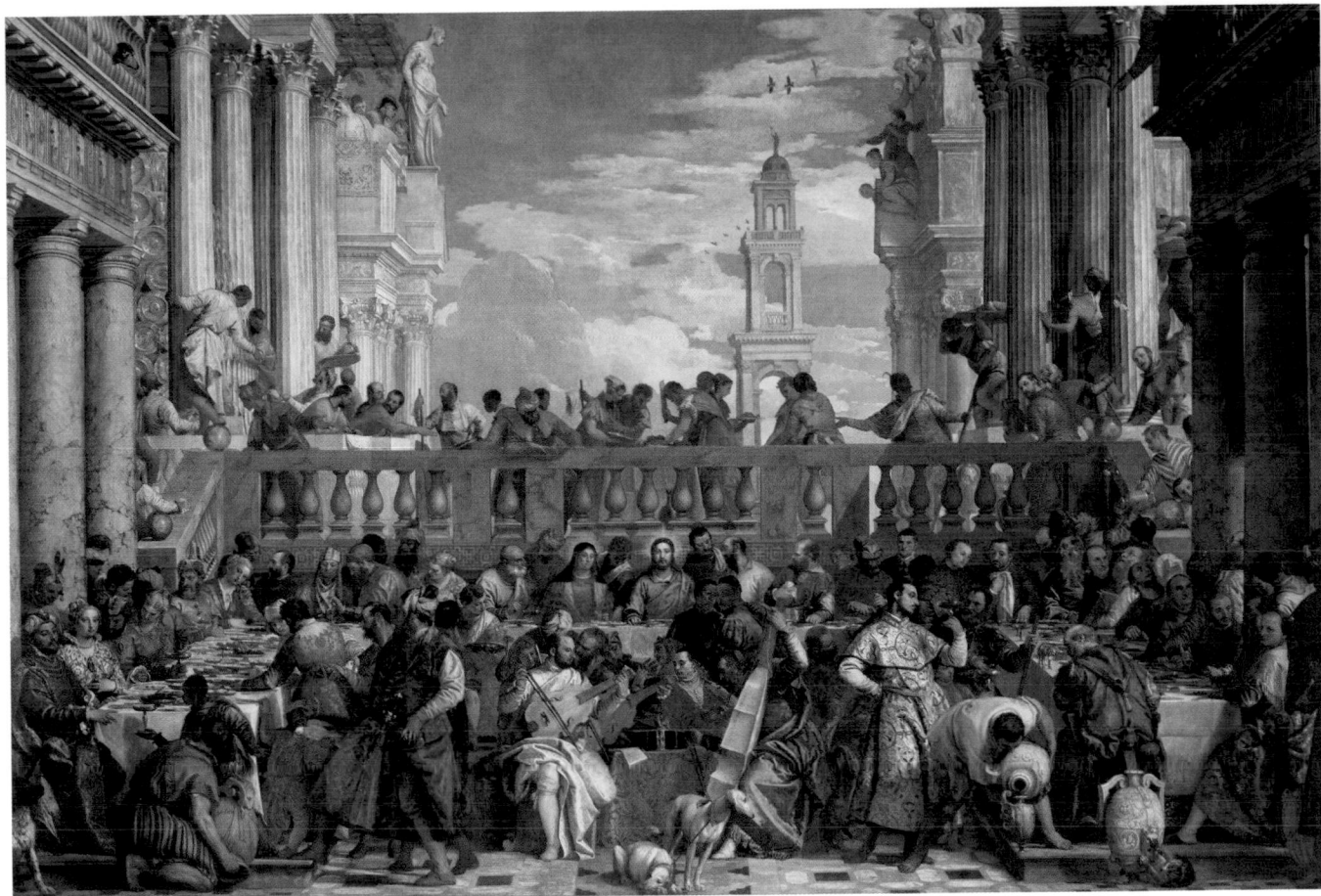

1 ft.

∧ 6.13 PAOLO VERONESE, *The Wedding Feast at Cana* (1562). Oil on canvas, 21 ⅞' × 32 ½'. Louvre, Paris, France.

While the primary text of Paolo Veronese's *The Wedding Feast at Cana* (Fig. 6.13) is a recounting of the biblical story of Jesus's first miracle (turning water into wine after the hosts ran out of it), the subtext is the human comedy of the situation—all of the pompous expressions and posturing of the celebrants. It was the artist's version of the "big fat" ethnic wedding. Why did Veronese turn his composition into such a free-for-all? Because chaos works when it fits with the theme. At a wedding celebration, people come from everywhere to eat, drink, and dance. Chaos is not just a visual device; it also advances the narrative.

But Veronese's composition is not one of pure chaos. It's more of an **ordered chaos.** The boisterous crowd is contained by the strong one-point perspective and the enframing architectural elements. And while the artist clearly wanted to humanize Jesus and Mary by surrounding them with ordinary and recognizable human types, the extraordinariness of the divine figure and his miraculous power impose a bit of order on the chaos that is part and parcel of human life. Even compositions that have a consistent emphasis on variety and that seem to verge on disunity tend to have some order, some subtle unifying aspect to keep them from dissolving into absolute disorder.

FOCAL POINT AND EMPHASIS

If you look around your room, gaze out the window, perhaps peer into a mirror, something will likely grab your attention. It might be a red sweatshirt that separates itself from the surrounding "composition" of your stuff. Maybe it's a bright orange traffic cone that's somehow found its way onto the lawn outside, or a branch that's fallen from a tree. When you look at your mirror reflection, what leaps out first? Your Ray-Bans? A piercing? A beard or moustache?

When looking at art too, our eyes tend to be drawn toward a primary point of visual interest, or **focal point**— perhaps a burst of saturated color or a strong shape or powerful directional lines. One or more focal points can be used in a composition to create areas of **emphasis** that attract and hold the viewer's attention.

In some works of art, focal point and emphasis are clearly a matter of cause and effect: a strong focal point dominates the composition, thereby emphasizing—or giving visual prominence to—the area immediately

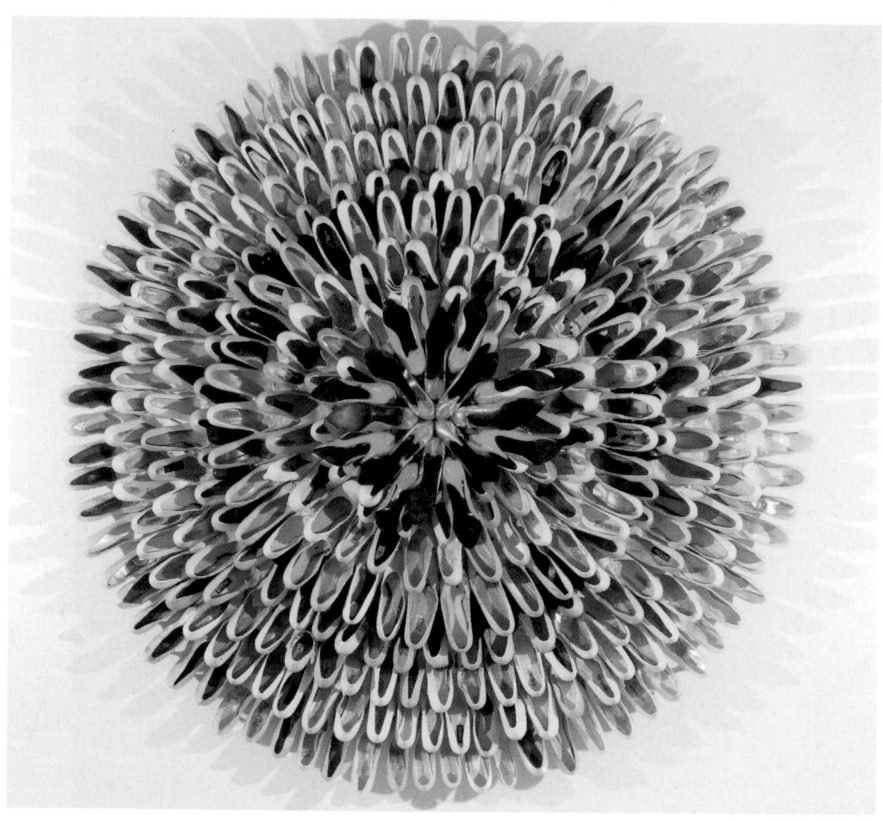

< 6.14 **WILLIE COLE**, *With a Heart of Gold* (2005–2006). Shoes, wood, screws, metal, and staples. 85' diameter, 16' depth. Courtesy of Alexander, and Bonin, New York.

diagonal lines converge at the prominent woman in the extreme left foreground. In Géricault's *Raft of the Medusa* (see Fig. 4.10), the struggling shipwreck survivors cluster along a diagonal line that draws our attention to a man waving a flag at rescuers on the horizon.

Contrast

Color and value contrast are two devices that can be manipulated to provide emphasis, as in a Gérard Fromanger's *Jean-Paul Sartre* (Fig. 6.15). This portrait of the French existentialist philosopher staring blankly over a café table littered with coffee cups and cigarettes is alive with a heated palette of reds, oranges, and yellows that bump against one another in a nondescript blend of shapes and shadows. Fromanger creates an area of emphasis with a diagonal swath of cool blues and greens, thereby

surrounding it. In Willie Cole's *With a Heart of Gold* (Fig. 6.14), assembled from women's high-heeled shoes, we are drawn to a focal point in the center of the composition around which reverberates a pattern of concentric circles that emphasize that center point. Cole, who collects found objects for his works, used a small cluster of yellow shoes in the center surrounded by hundreds of white ones positioned "toes pointed in." The bright yellow serves as a focal point, bringing emphasis to the center of the daisy-like configuration of shoes.

Emphasis in a work of art can be achieved through various means including directional lines, contrast, and placement.

Directional Lines

Focus on a specific area of a composition can be facilitated through devices such as **directional lines** that lead the eye to an area of emphasis. For example, in Willie Cole's *With a Heart of Gold*, all of the white high-heeled shoes are aimed inward toward the bright yellow focal point in the center of the composition. Similarly, the diagonal lines in several other works we have seen draw our focus to key figures within a composition: in López's *Heirs Come to Pass, 3* (see nearby "Connections" feature), multiple

> 6.15 **GÉRARD FROMANGER**, *Jean-Paul Sartre* (1976). From the series *Splendours II*. Oil on canvas, 51¼" × 38¼".

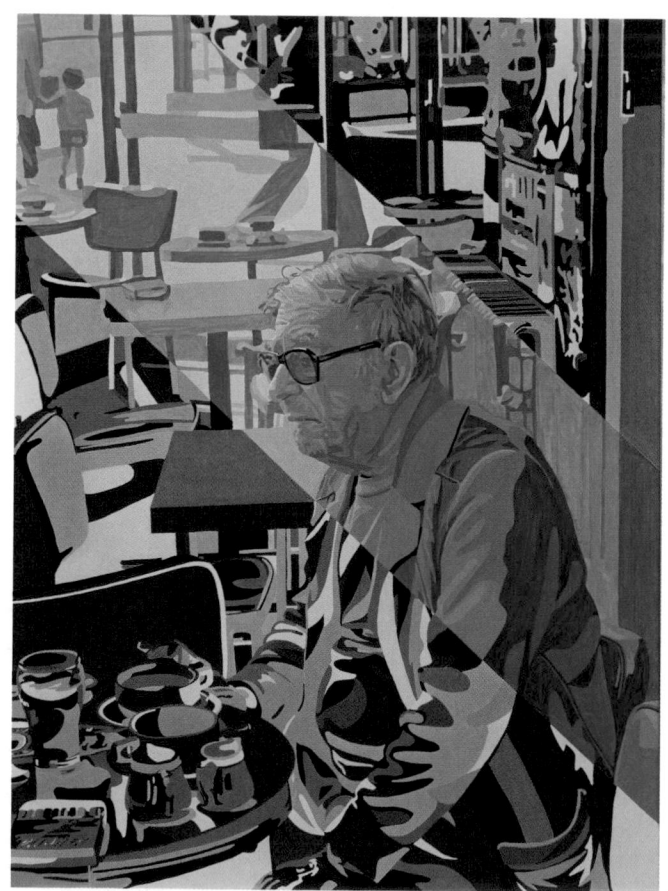

1 ft.

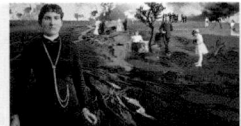

CONNECTIONS The focal point of a composition need not be in the center. Consider two works you saw in Chapter 5: Martina López's *Heirs Come to Pass, 3* and Gustave Caillebotte's *Paris Street: Rainy Day*. In both of these compositions, focal point (the figures in the extreme foreground) serves as a device used to create emphasis.

∧ López's *Heirs Come to Pass, 3* (**Fig. 5.4**)

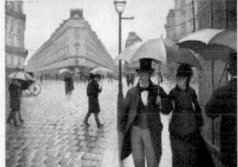

∧ Caillebotte's *Paris Street: Rainy Day* (**Fig. 5.16A**)

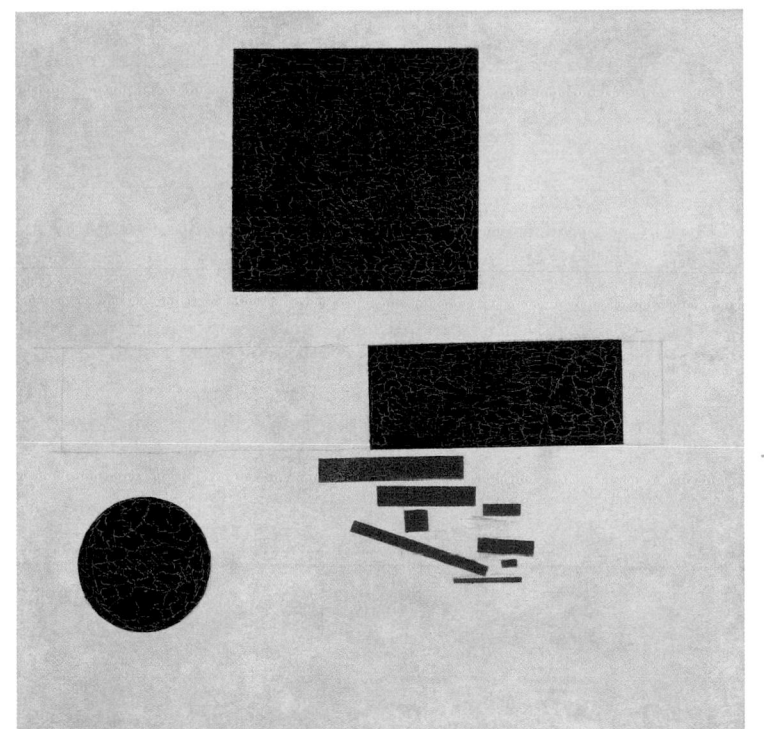

∧ 6.16 KAЗIMIR MALEVICH, *Suprematist Composition* (1916). Oil on canvas, 31¼" square.

concentrating our focus on Sartre's bespectacled profile. The artist also uses this area of emphasis for narrative purposes: The psychological associations spurred by the spectrum of blues and greens may symbolize the philosopher's rather bleak view of life.

The contrast between what appear to be stable or static elements with ones that move or are "unstable" or dynamic will also create emphasis. Kasimir Malevich's *Suprematist Composition* (Fig. 6.16) offers a perfect example. Despite the scale and density of the three black geometric shapes—a square, a circle, and a rectangle—our eyes are drawn to the area with smaller red shapes that appear to be "activated." Emphasis in this painting is achieved both through color contrast and a contrast between static and dynamic elements.

Placement

Emphasis on a particular area or image in a composition can be affected when several of its components direct the viewer's gaze toward a focal point. In Ger van Elk's *Lunch II* from his *Missing Persons* series (Fig. 6.17), one chair at the table is separated from the rest both physically and psychologically. It is the one that captures our attention—not for what is there but for what is *not* there. The men around the table do not engage with one another but, rather, fix their gaze on the empty chair, remaining attentive to someone who is invisible or nonexistent. Van Elk eradicated one of the guests, leaving a false photographic record; it is the vacant chair (and all that implies in terms of narrative) that is emphasized.

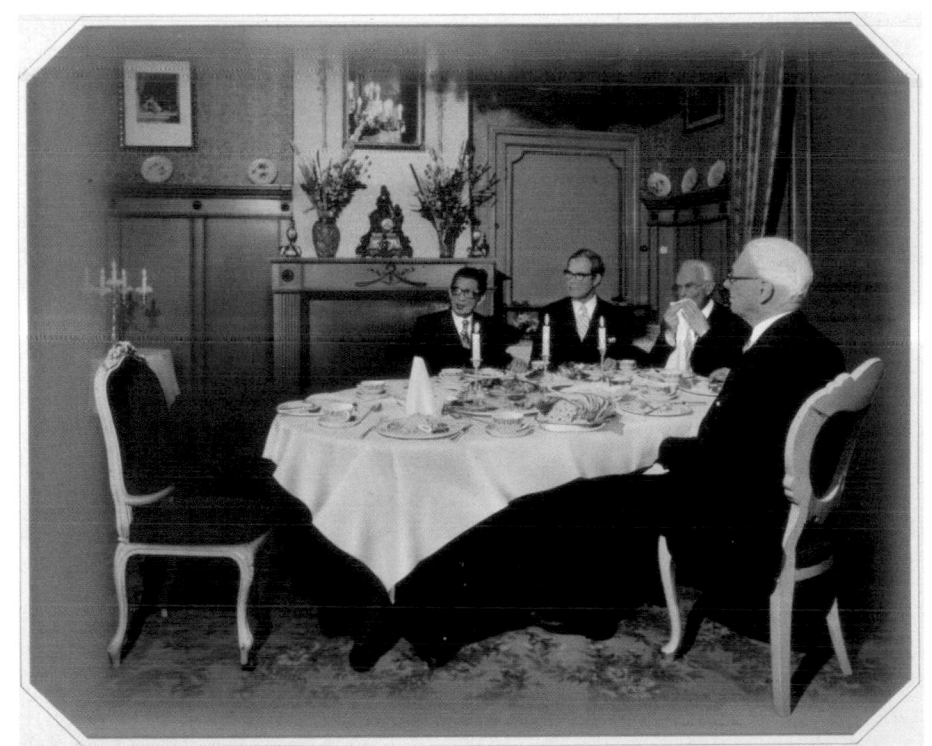

∧ 6.17 GER VAN ELK, *Lunch II* (1976). From the *Missing Persons* series. Photograph, drawing, and oil on ivory and metal; 31½" × 39⅜". Tate Modern, London, England.

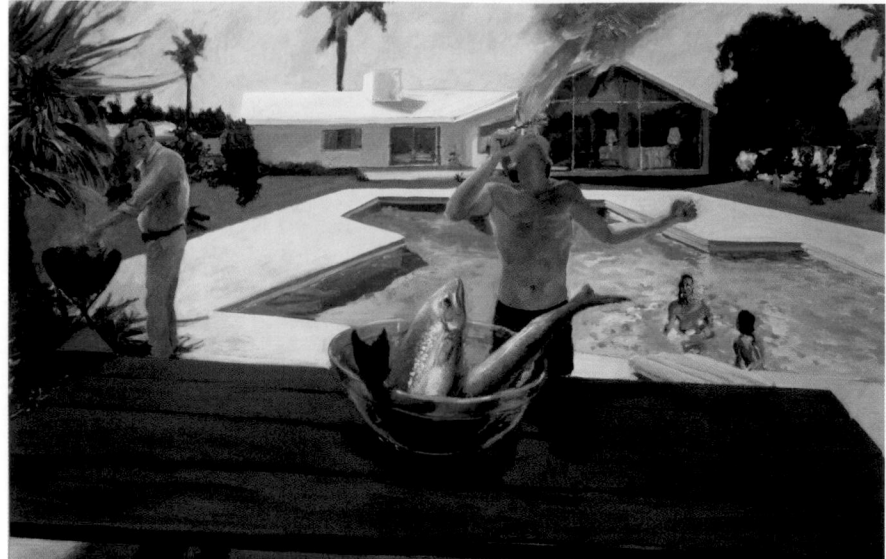

1 ft.

▲ 6.18 **ERIK FISCHL,** *Barbeque* (1982). Oil on canvas, 65" × 100".

MULTIPLE FOCAL POINTS AND ABSENCE OF FOCAL POINT

Some compositions feature multiple focal points. This strategy does two, seemingly contradictory things: It draws our attention to a number of different images or areas in a composition, giving each due importance and at the same time diminishes the significance of each, compelling the viewer to consider the whole over any one part. In Eric Fischl's *Barbeque* (Fig. 6.18), the juxtaposition of bizarre, incongruous images substantiates the notion that suburban bliss is a false construction.

The lack of a focal point or any one area of emphasis reinforces the conceptual framework of John Kessler's *The Palace at 4 A.M.* (Fig. 6.19). Kessler's mixed-media installation may be described as organized chaos, with images of destruction and symbols of unchecked authority flashing by on clusters of monitors. Between these images and the rattling and clanging sounds of infernal machinery overhead, the

lack of emphasis contributes to the feeling of confusion and sensory overload.

BALANCE AND RHYTHM

Balance and rhythm come naturally to humans. As we learn to walk or ride a bike or ski, we shift our weight in small degrees—left and right, forward and back—until we get it right. We learn to balance ourselves to stand erect against the forces of gravity, or stay mounted, or keep ourselves centered as we head down the slopes. Balance creates a sense of stability. Once we master it, rhythm takes over. We learn to put one foot in front of the other in a rhythmic pattern to walk or run. We learn to pedal our bikes in a smooth rhythm. We advance from an awkward downhill form that inspires terror to a rhythmic cadence as we weave left and right, descending in a fluid, curving, continuous line. Rhythm is the equivalent of serenity.

The French painter Henri Matisse sought "an art of balance," one that would have a "soothing, calming, influence on the mind." He also believed that in order to make pleasing works of art, artists would do well to identify with the rhythms of nature. But what if the goal is completely different? What if the artist aims for the uncomfortable, for disquietude rather than serenity? Artists may choose imbalance over balance or chaotic, disruptive rhythms in their compositions to penetrate the viewer's

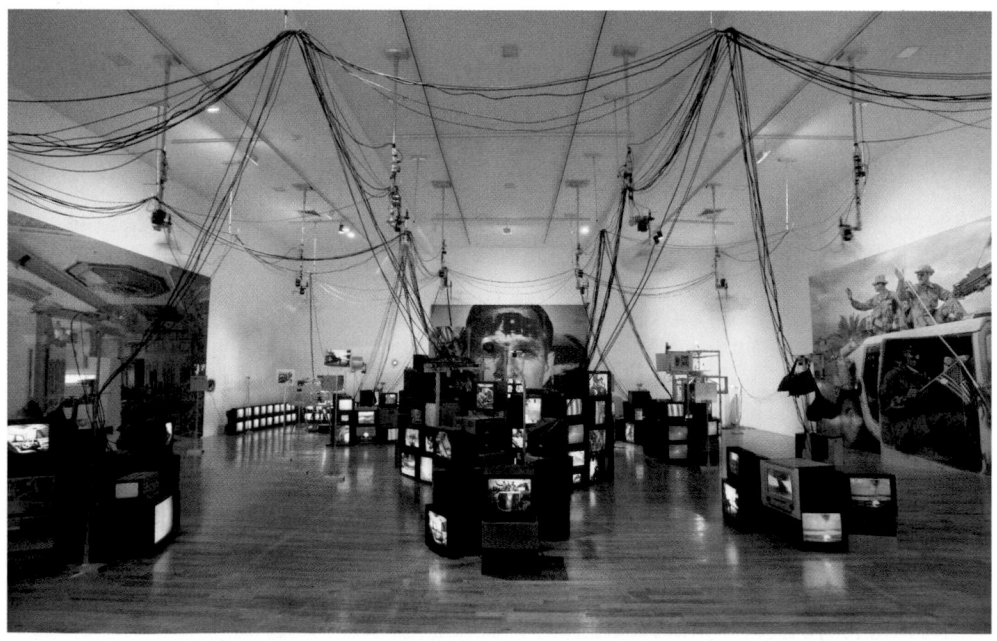

▲ 6.19 **JOHN KESSLER,** *The Palace at 4 A.M.* (2005). Mixed media with monitors, cameras, aluminum, large format inkjet prints. Dimensions variable.

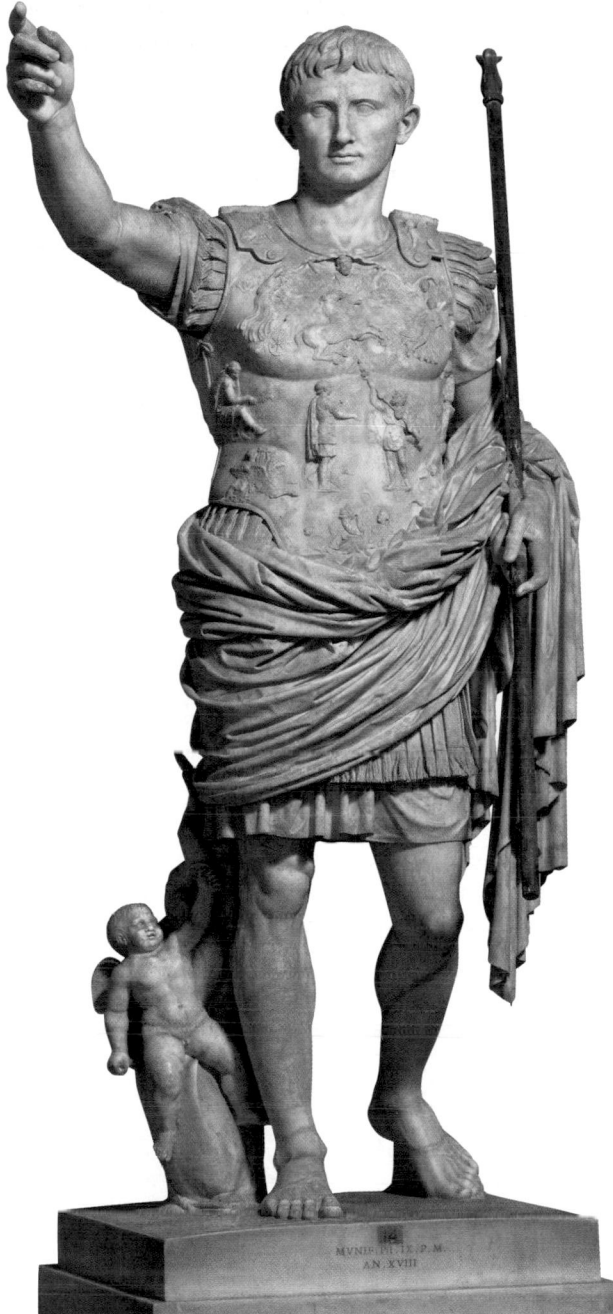

▲ 6.20 *Augustus of Primaporta.* Early first-century CE copy of a bronze original (c. 20 BCE). Marble, 80". Musei Vaticani, Rome, Italy.

comfort zone, to challenge the conventional and predictable, or to convey a certain message.

USING BALANCE AND IMBALANCE

Balance refers to the way in which our physical weight is distributed, or shifts, so that we remain in control of our movements when we walk, run, or engage in athletic activity. **Balance**, in art, also refers to the distribution of weight—actual or visual. As an athlete uses balance to control movement, so might an artist use balance to control the distribution or emphasis of elements such as line or shape or color in a composition.

Augustus of Primaporta (Fig. 6.20) is a monumental portrait of the Roman emperor Augustus as an armed general addressing his troops. The weight of the body is born on the straight leg, strengthened—and physically balanced—by a connected piece of marble carved with the figure of Cupid riding a dolphin. Visual balance is achieved in the composition by echoing the rigidity of the weight-bearing leg in the bronze staff, which is clutched by the emperor's left arm on the *opposite* part of the body. Similarly, the bent shape of the leg at rest is visually balanced *across the body* by the bent elbow of the raised right arm (see the discussion of *contrapposto* in the feature "Theory and Practice: Polykleitos's Canon: The Body Beautiful" [Fig. 15.10A and 15.10B] in Chapter 15.) The overall effect of balance in this work is that of authority, calm, and control.

How different is our impression of the god Dionysus (Roman, Bacchus) in a work by Michelangelo. Here the effect of *imbalance* speaks volumes (Fig. 6.21).

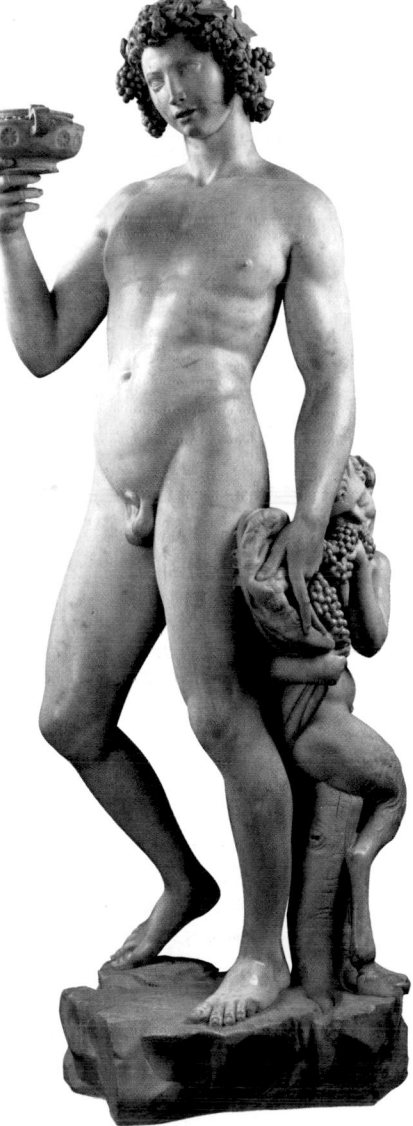

▲ 6.21 MICHELANGELO, *The Drunkenness of Bacchus* (1496–1497). Marble, 80". National Museum of Bargello, Florence, Italy.

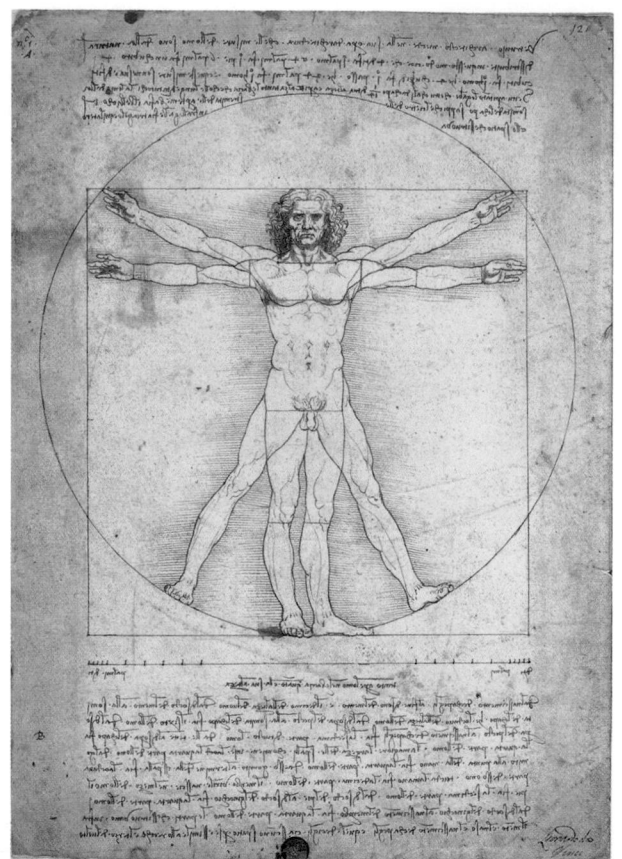

▲ 6.22 **LEONARDO DA VINCI**, *Proportions of the Human Figure* (after Vitruvius) (c. 1485–1490). Pen and ink, 13½" × 9¾". Accademia, Venice, Italy.

Dionysus, the Greek god of winemaking and wine, is barely able to stand on his own under the influence of alcohol. His hips sway and he totters from one foot onto the other; the languid S-curve of his body exaggerates his instability. Although the sculpture has actual balance (as in the portrait of Augustus, a large, carved chunk of marble shores up the weight-bearing leg), Michelangelo's remarkable representation of drunkenness is a result of rendering visual imbalance so convincingly. Just as balance communicated the stature of Augustus, so did the use of imbalance convey the weaknesses of the god Dionysus.

Actual Balance

Little Spider (see Fig. 5.21), a so-called *stabile* by Alexander Calder, is a more "stable" or anchored version of his *mobiles*,

CONNECTIONS Alexander Calder's stabiles, including *Little Spider*, share absolute precision in balance with his mobiles.

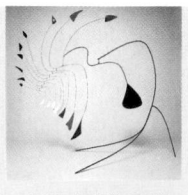

▲ Calder's *Little Spider* **(Fig. 5.21)**

which typically hang from ceilings. What stabiles and mobiles have in common, however, is absolute precision in balance. In *Little Spider*, both actual and visual balances come into play. From the viewpoint of this particular photograph of the work, thin S-shaped wires of different lengths nest together, each culminating in a distinctive colored shape cut from sheet metal. This delicate cluster of lines and shapes is connected to, and balanced by, a thicker wire and a single, large black shape. All of these are connected to a C-shaped stand from which they hang. The wires of the stand are much thicker, much weightier than the combination of the free-moving parts; this is how the artist achieves actual balance. Visual balance (also called *compositional balance* or *pictorial balance*), on the other hand, is achieved through the juxtaposition of the large, single black shape that holds its visual weight with the spirited grouping of smaller, more delicate multicolored shapes.

Visual Balance

Sculptures such as the portrait of Augustus and *Little Spider*, as different as they are, both have actual weight; thus they also have actual balance. **Visual balance** refers to the distribution of the apparent or *visual weight* of the elements in works that are basically two-dimensional, and there are many ways to achieve it.

Symmetrical and Asymmetrical Balance

If you divide the human body in half vertically, and in the ideal, as in Leonardo da Vinci's most famous drawing

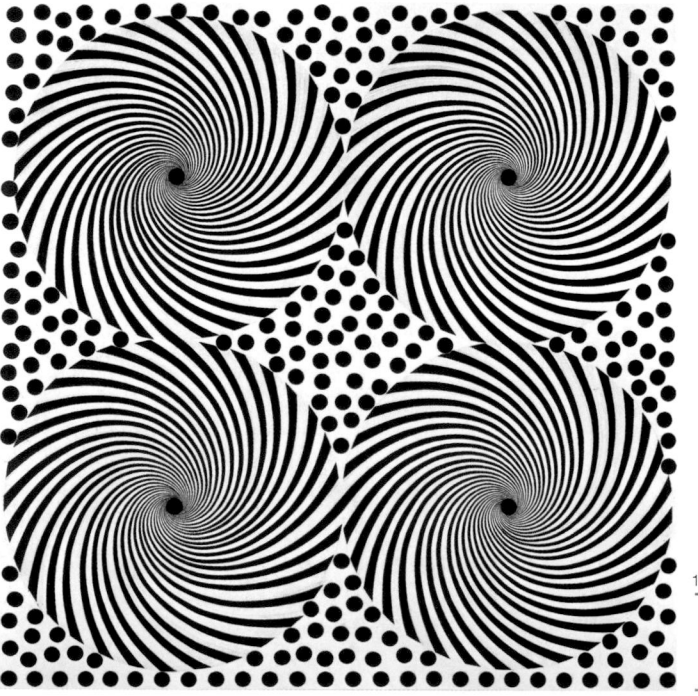

▲ 6.23 **PHILIP TAAFFE**, *Four Quad Cinema*. 84" × 82". Saatchi Gallery, London, England.

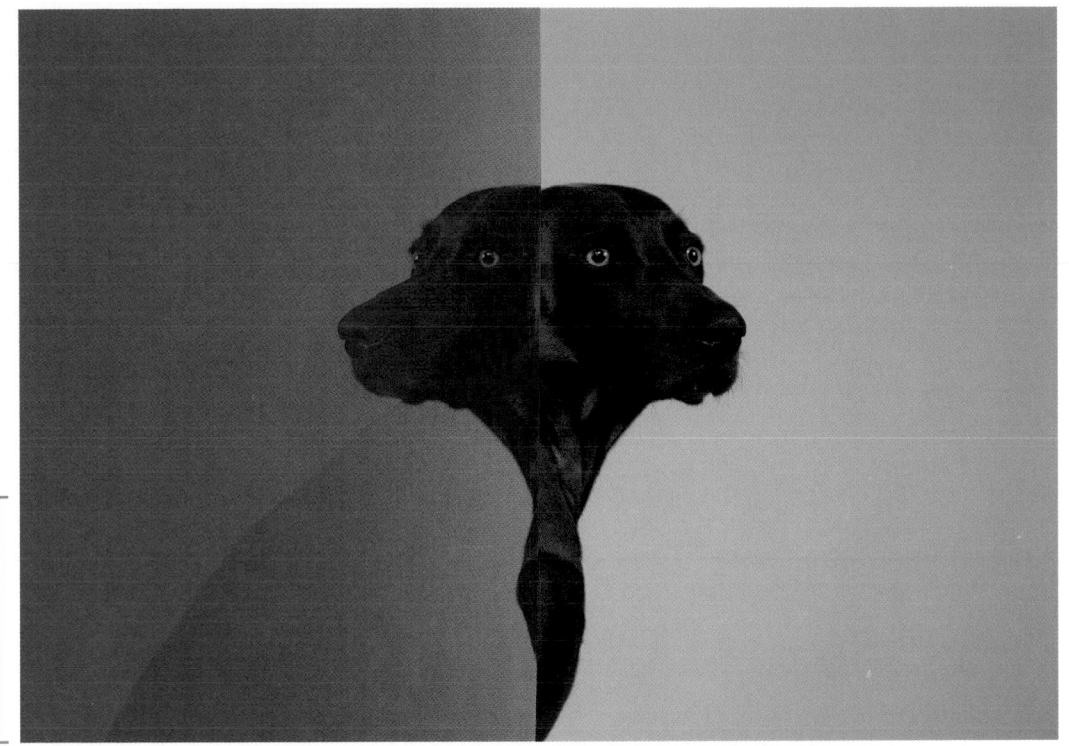

1 ft.

Proportions of the Human Figure (Fig. 6.22), there will be an exact correspondence between the left and right sides. **Symmetry** refers to similarity of form or arrangement on either side of a dividing line or plane, or to correspondence of parts in size, shape, and position. When the correspondence is exact, as in Philip Taaffe's *Four Quad Cinema* (Fig. 6.23), we refer to it as *pure* or *formal symmetry.*

Examples of pure or formal symmetry appear no more frequently in art than in nature. More typically, **symmetrical balance** is created through *approximate* symmetry, in which the whole of the work has a symmetrical feeling, but slight variations, as in William Wegman's *Ethiopia* (Fig. 6.24) provide more visual interest than would a mirror image.

When the variations to the right and left side of the composition are *more* than slight, yet there remains an overall sense of balance, there is said to be **asymmetrical balance**. Otto Steinert's photograph *Ein-Fuß-Gänger (One-Foot Walker)* (Fig. 6.25) is a clearcut example of asymmetrical balance: the left side of the composition contains virtually all of the visual weight. The iron grate encircling the trunk of a young tree in the field of concrete is

the dominant shape in the photograph, but its hold on our attention is challenged by something that is much less significant. A mere spot of black—the highly polished shoe and dark swath of a trouser leg—draws our focus and holds it beyond our expectation, largely because the suggestion of rapid movement balances the static presence of the tree trunk and grate.

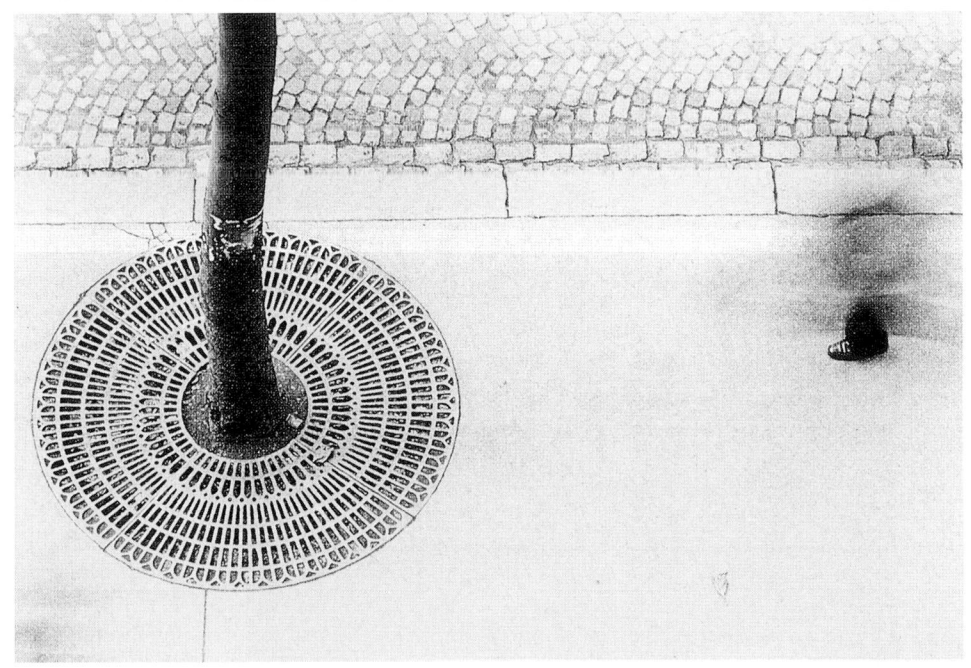

1 in.

▲ 6.25 OTTO STEINERT, *Ein-Fuß-Gänger (One-Foot Walker)* (1950). Silver bromide gelatin, time exposure; 11¼" × 15⅞". Museum Folkwang, Essen, Germany.

Horizontal, Vertical, Diagonal, and Radial Balance

In works of art displaying **horizontal balance**, such as Bruce Barnbaum's *Wall with Two Ridges, Lower Antelope Canyon* (Fig. 6.26), the elements in the left and right portions of the composition are approximately equal in number or visual emphasis. By focusing on line, shape, and value to create visual congruency, the artist draws our eye from one side of the photograph to the other. The overall impression is one of stability and serenity.

The visual appeal of horizontal balance may reflect the bilateral symmetry of the human body. Similarly, the urge toward vertical balance may reflect the relationship of the body to its environment—fighting the forces of gravity to stand. In **vertical balance**, the viewer's perceptions are organized according to a horizon line and to what is above and below that line.

In Kay Sage's *I Saw Three Cities* (Fig. 6.27), a firm horizon line separates a bleak landscape from a bleaker sky.

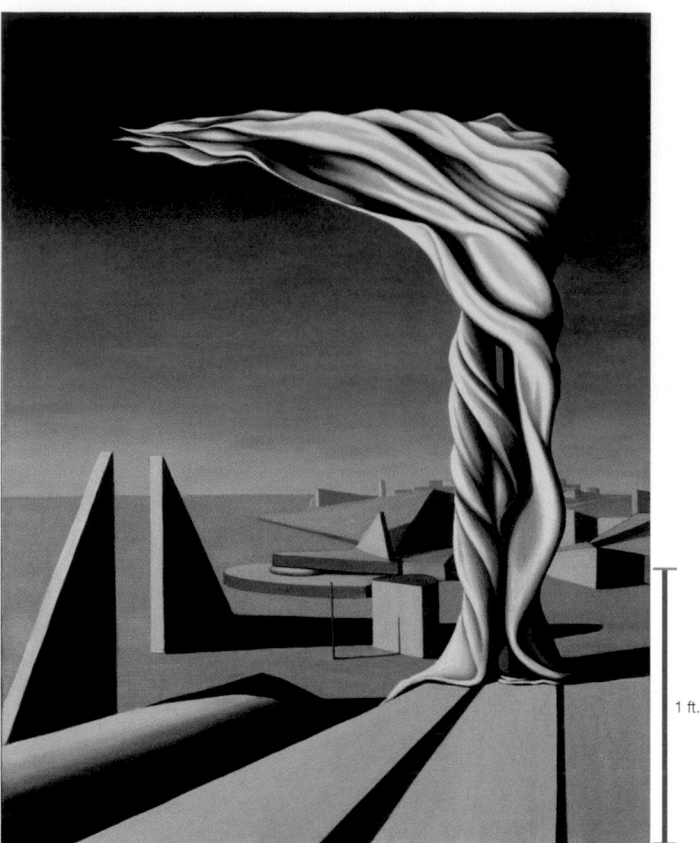

▲ 6.27 **KAY SAGE,** *I Saw Three Cities* (1944). Oil on canvas, 36¼" × 27⅞". Princeton University Art Museum, New Jersey.

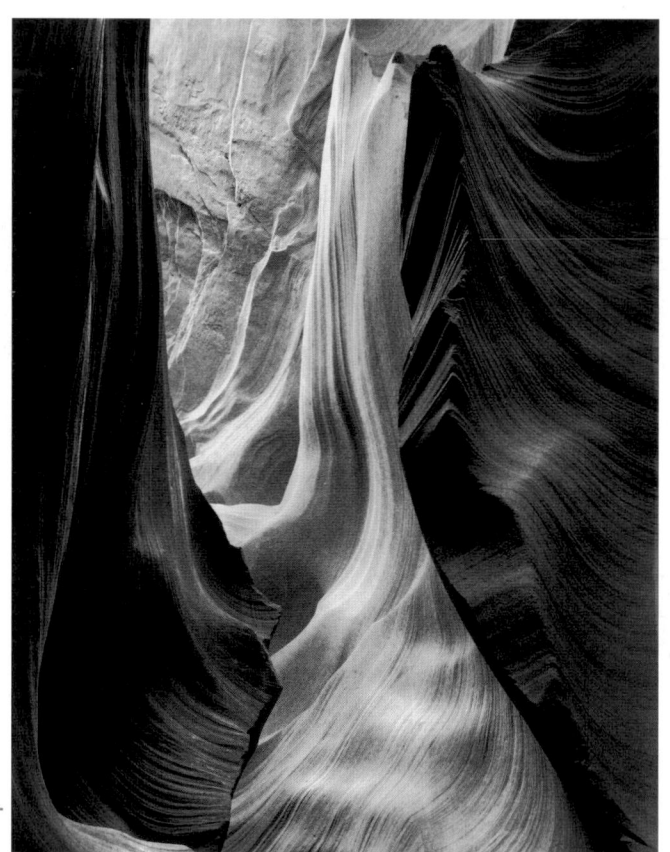

▲ 6.26 **BRUCE BARNBAUM,** *Wall with Two Ridges, Lower Antelope Canyon* (1983). Silver gelatin print, 15¼" × 19½".

Most of the visual weight in the composition occurs in the lower half, where geometric shapes casting long shadows lead your eye from the picture plane toward a kind of desolate futuristic city. The hard-edged structures that litter the landscape, however, are balanced in the upper reaches of the sky by a flowing column of drapery that billows up from the ground and across to the left, floating toward the source of the light on a strange breeze that breaks the stagnant gray air.

Pictorial balance is most often discussed in horizontal and vertical terms. However, artists also employ **diagonal balance** by establishing equal visual weight to either side of a pictorial space that is divided by a perceived diagonal. In Adil Jain's *Two Heads* (Fig. 6.28), the photographer captures the juxtaposition of evocative images and, in the process, creates a striking compositional equilibrium. The viewer's eye moves from the elderly couple on a bench to their graffiti counterparts and back again along the perceived diagonal.

Radial balance is evident in compositions in which the elements radiate from—or are organized around—a center point, as in Willie Cole's *With a Heart of Gold* (see Fig. 6.13). A decorative tabletop from nineteenth-century

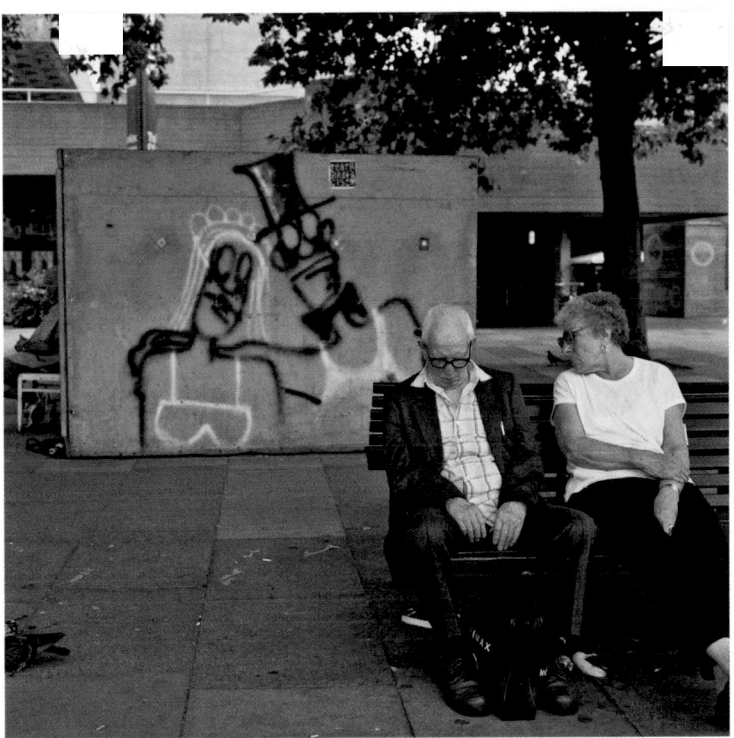

▲ 6.28 ADIL JAIN, *Two Heads* (2004). From the photographic series *London Portraits*.

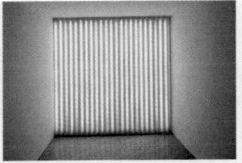
Regular Repetition

Regular repetition is the easiest and most precise way to create rhythm, as brilliantly illustrated in Dan Flavin's untitled fluorescent light sculpture. The square configurations that you see here side-by-side in the nearby Connections feature were actually placed back-to-back, with green on one side and yellow on the other. Because the sculpture, when installed, blocked passage from one side of the room to another, only a glimpse of the light filling the room on the other side could be seen through the strips of space between the walls and the piece.

Iran (Fig. 6.29) depicting scenes from the Book of Kings provides another example of radial balance. From the intricately painted tile in the center, surrounded by a decorative band of flowers and birds, lines fan outward toward the perimeter of the table like the spokes of a wheel, dividing the outer ring into trapezoidal segments. The narrow framing device around the shapes directs the gaze both outward and inward and imposes a sense of order on the busy patterns and imagery.

USING RHYTHM

Rhythm in the arts is created by repetition, and repetitive patterns convey a sense of movement. With music, the listener perceives rhythm by grouping sounds that have a specific meter or pulse. In the visual arts, the viewer perceives rhythm by groping repetitive elements such as color, line, and shape. As in music, slight variations in rhythm may add interest and major shifts in rhythm can be disconcerting.

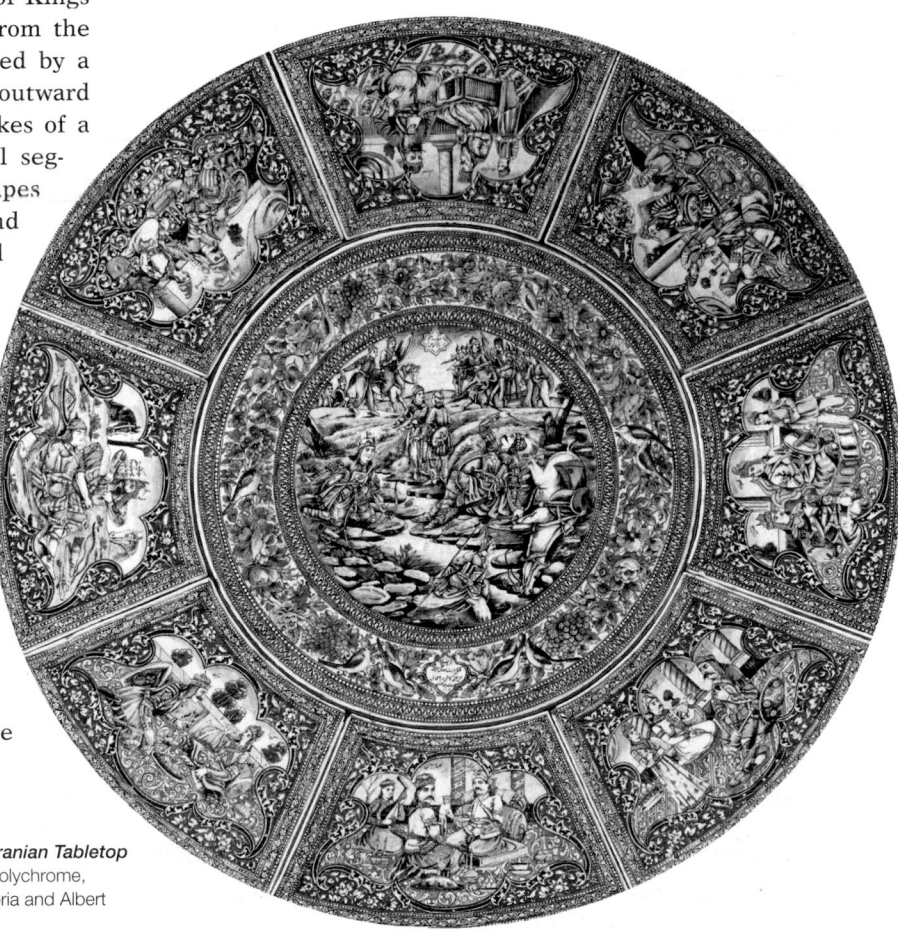

▷ 6.29 ALI MUHAMMAD ISFAHANI, *Iranian Tabletop* (1887). Fritware, underglaze painted in polychrome, nine separate tiles; 53½" diameter. Victoria and Albert Museum, London, England.

CONNECTIONS The original mosaics decorating the interior of the Dome of the Rock remain largely intact.

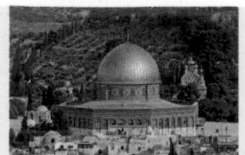

∧ Dome of the Rock
(Fig. 16.21)

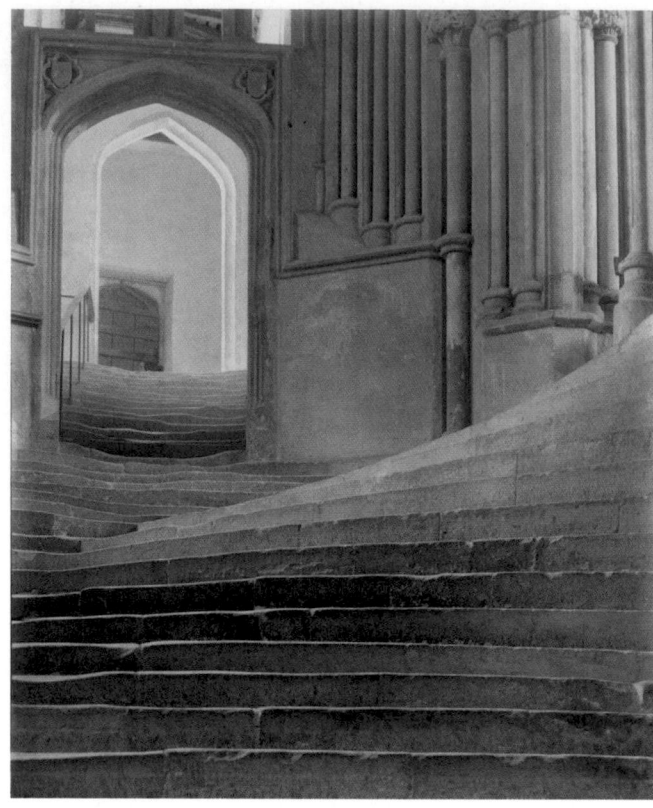

∧ **6.31** FREDERICK H. EVANS, *A Sea of Steps* (1903). Wells Cathedral, stairs to chapter house and bridge to vicar's close. Gelatin silver print, 9" × 7½". The Museum of Modern Art, New York, New York.

Alternating Rhythm and Progressive Rhythm

An **alternating rhythm** occurs when different elements in a work of art or architecture are repeated in a regular, predictable order, as in the elaborately embellished surface of the Dome of the Rock shrine on Temple Mount in Jerusalem (Fig. 6.30). The intricate façade consists of the alternate, rhythmic arrangement of shapes, colors, and patterns.

Minor variations in rhythm can add interest to a composition. Such variations are seen in **progressive rhythm**, in which the rhythm of elements of a work of art such as shape, texture, or color change slightly as they move, or progress, toward a defined point in the composition. In Frederick H. Evans's photograph *A Sea of Steps* (Fig. 6.31),

1 in.

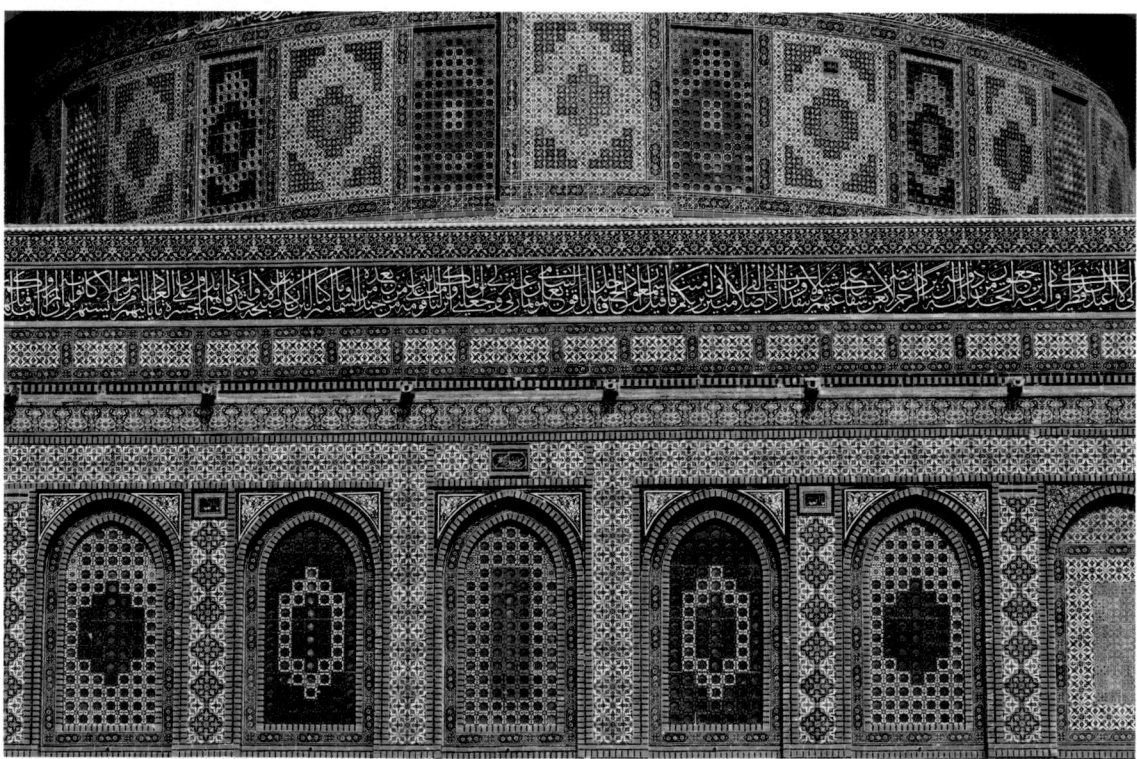

∧ 6.30 **Architectural detail of Dome of the Rock,** Temple Mount, Jerusalem, Israel.

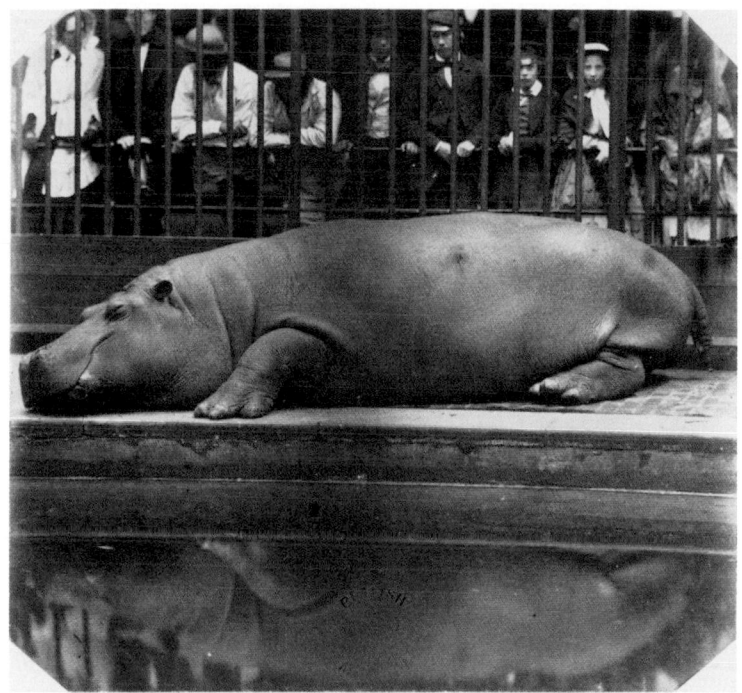

fantastic enormity of the animal. By establishing a relationship between the familiar (the visitors standing side-by-side behind an iron fence) and the unfamiliar (the exotic animal), the photographer enables us to grasp the size of something that we are not witnessing firsthand.

Hierarchical Scale

Hierarchical scale is a relative size device that an artist uses to indicate the relative importance of the objects or figures in a work of art. The use of hierarchical scale is evident in a 1942 poster urging Americans—most vividly—to support the war effort by purchasing government-issued bonds (Fig. 6.33). Uncle Sam, an allegorical figure or personification of the U.S. government, emerges triumphantly from the black clouds of war, leading American troops in battle. The size of the godlike, fearsome figure symbolizes bigger ideas of democracy, freedom, and justice.

∧ 6.32 DON JUAN CARLOS, COUNT DE MONTIZÓN, *The Hippopotamus at the Zoological Gardens, Regent's Park* (1852). Salted paper print. The British Library, London, England.

that focal point is the bright, sunlit archway at the top of a wavelike progression of stairs. As steps recede from the picture plane, the value progresses from dark through a series of grays toward white. The rippling effect of the progression of the steps creates the feeling of billowing ocean waves; in the upper-right portion of the composition, columns ascend in a complementary rhythm.

USING SCALE

Size refers to measurement, and **scale** refers to the size of a work or a form in relation to—or compared to—the average size of a human being. When we say that a drawing is 9 inches by 12 inches, or that a building is 220 feet tall, we are using specific standards of measurement to describe size. When we use the word *scale,* we are typically describing the size of objects in relation to others like them or to things around them.

Relative Size

In his photograph *The Hippopotamus at the Zoological Gardens, Regent's Park* (Fig. 6.32), Don Juan Carlos, Count de Montizón uses **relative size** to communicate the

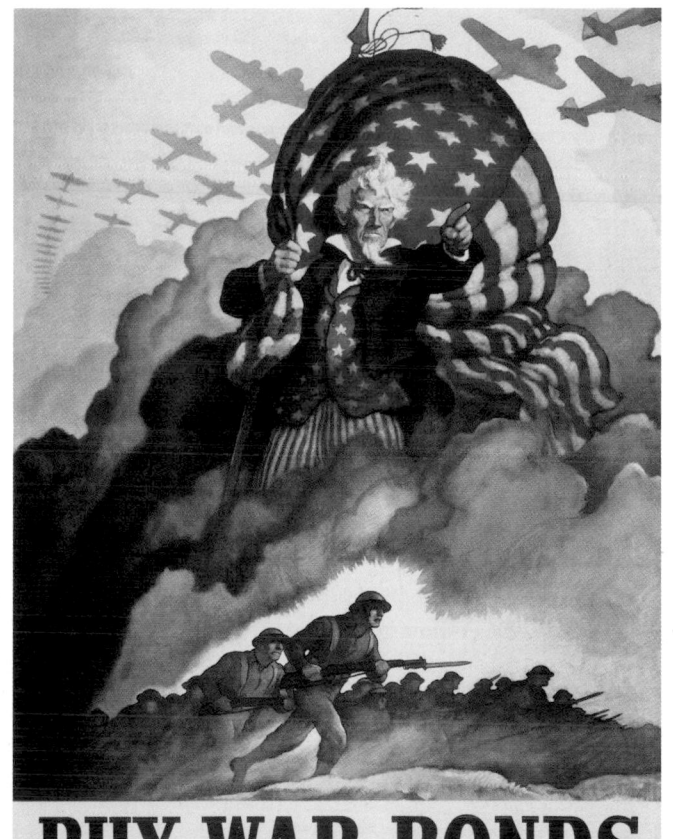

1 ft.

∧ 6.33 "Buy War Bonds" (1942). Color lithograph, 30" × 40".

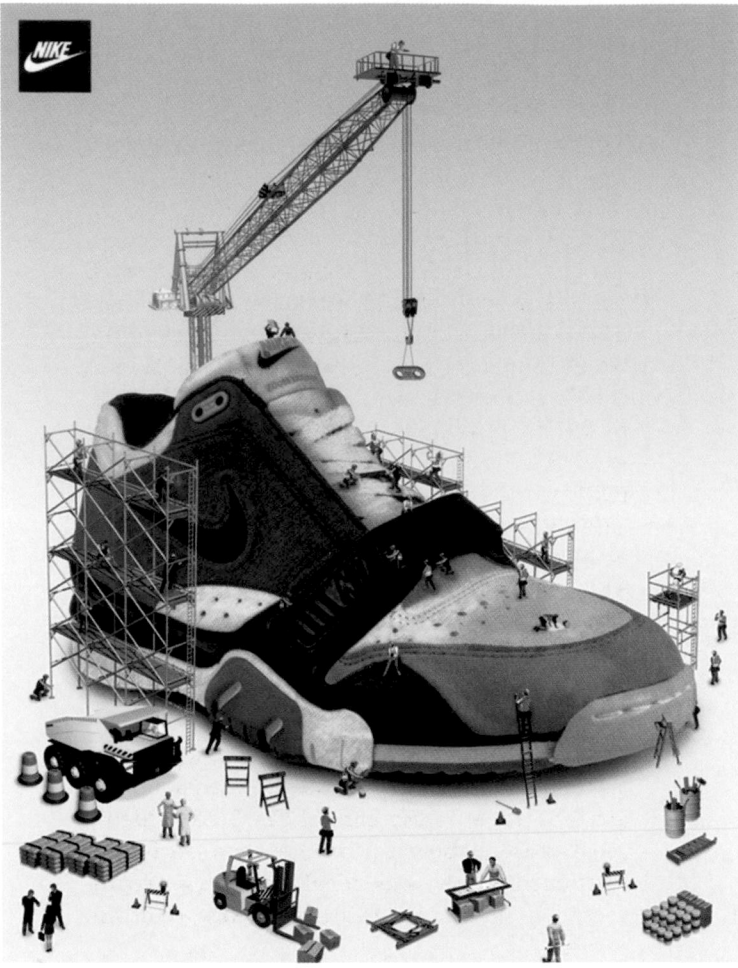

The objects depicted within works of art can also be large or small in relationship to one another (Fig. 6.35), and to the work as a whole. **Proportion**, then, is the comparative relationship, or ratio, of things to one another.

Artists have sought to determine the proper or most appealing ratios or parts of works to one another and the whole. They have used proportion to represent what they believed to be the ideal or the beautiful. They have disregarded or subverted proportion to achieve special effects—often to compel viewers to take a new look at the familiar.

The Canon of Proportions

The ancient Greeks tied their vision of ideal beauty to what they considered "proper" proportions of the human body. Polykleitos is credited with the derivation of a **canon of proportions**—a set of rules about the dimensions of body parts in relation to one another that became the standard for creating the ideal figure (see *Theory and Practice: Polykleitos's Canon: The Body Beautiful*, Fig. 15.10A and 15.10B). Every part of the body is either a specific fraction or multiple of every other part. The *Augustus of Primaporta* (see Fig. 6.20) is another example of idealized body proportions.

Distortion of Scale

Artists will distort or subvert the realistic scale of objects to challenge the viewer to look at the familiar in a new way, as in Gui Borchert's poster for Nike advertising its Restoration project (Fig. 6.34). The reference to an architectural restoration finds its humorous, captivating counterpart in a Lilliputian-like world of Nikelab designers at work on the redesign of the original cross-training shoe, Air Trainer One. The poster was only one component of the advertising program; the other was an interactive website that featured the sounds of the "workplace" and the animated versions of actual people involved in the project.

PROPORTION

"Everything is relative." That is, we tend to think of objects or of works of art as large or small according to their relationships to other things—often to ourselves.

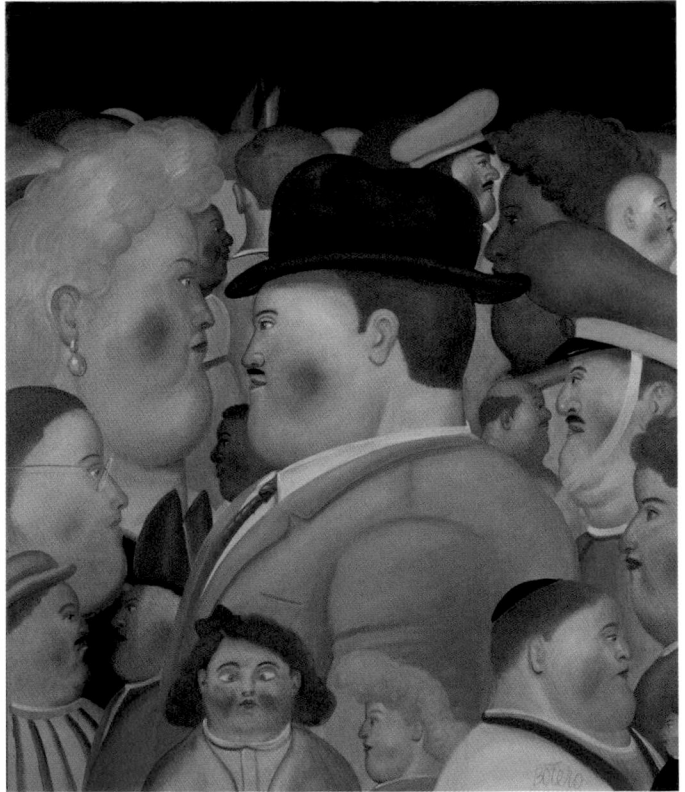

▲ 6.35 FERNANDO BOTERO, *Theatre Characters* (1977). Oil on canvas, 57" × 106¾". Marlborough Gallery, New York, New York.

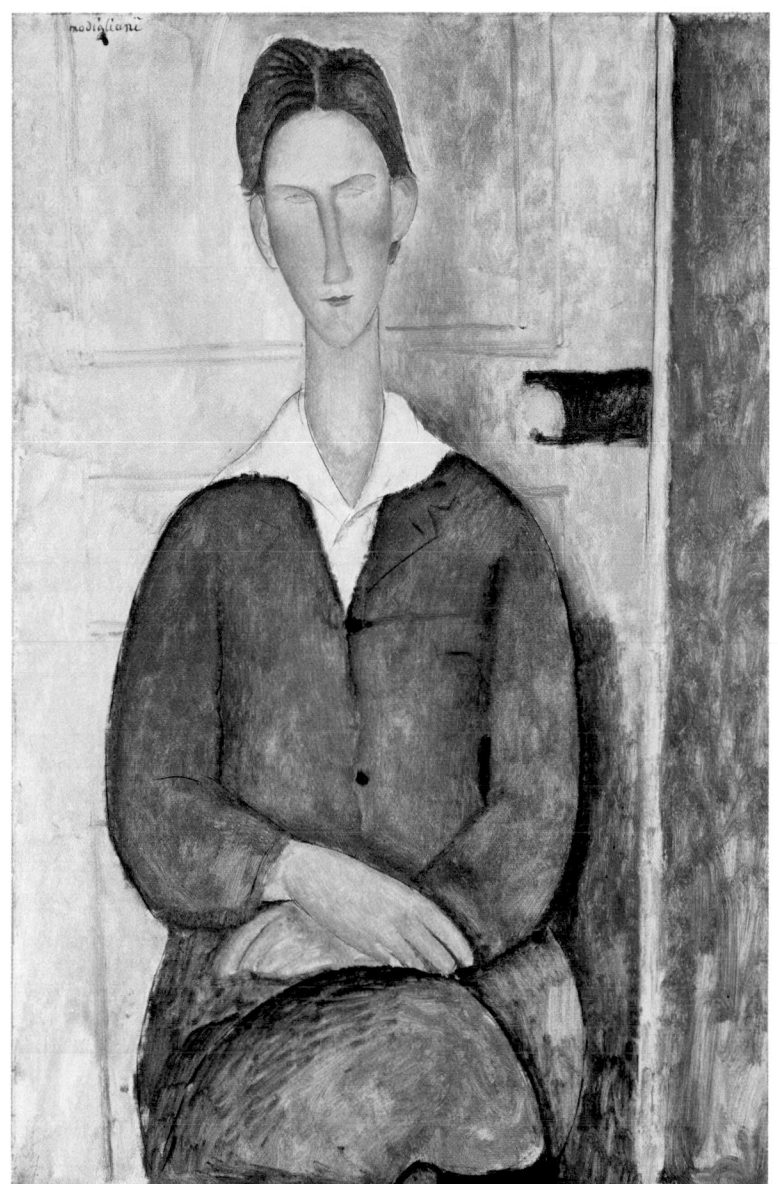

∧ 6.36 **AMEDEO MODIGLIANI,** *Young Man with Red Hair* (1919). Oil on canvas.

The Golden Mean, Golden Rectangle, and Root Five Rectangle

The **Golden Mean** (or Golden Section) in geometry was conceived by Greek philosophers and mathematicians during the Golden Age of Greece to facilitate ideal proportions in architecture. The Golden Mean requires that a small part of a work should relate to a larger part of the work, just as a larger part relates to the whole. Apply the concept of the Golden Mean to the line shown in Figure 6.37. The line is divided, or *sectioned*, at point B so that the ratio of the shorter segment (AB) is to the larger segment (BC), as the larger segment (BC) is to the whole line (AC). Or, mathematically, AB:BC = BC:AC. In order for this Golden Section to exist, segment BC must be 1.6180 times the length of AB. Segment BC is the Golden Mean: it is the line that is moderate in length between the smaller segment (AB) and the whole (AC). AB and AC are the "extremes," and BC is the mean that lies between. In mathematics, the mean is a quantity that lies between the extremes. It need not be an exact average. In the case of the Golden Mean, the Greeks believed that they had derived a relationship that was ideal because it represented for them something of the nature of the universe.

The rectangle in Figure 6.38—the so-called **Golden Rectangle**—is based on the Golden Mean: its width is 1.618 times its height. A Golden Rectangle can be created from any square mathematically—that is, by adding a rectangle whose longer side is 1.6180 times the length of the shorter side. It can also be created geometrically by rotating the diagonal of the half square.

SUBVERTING THE CANON OF PROPORTIONS Artists may manipulate or exaggerate natural or idealized proportions for expressive purposes. Amedeo Modigliani's portrait titled *Young Man with Red Hair* (Fig. 6.36) leaves the canon behind for what may be described as "unidealized form." The enlarged head, dramatically elongated neck, narrow shoulders, and voluminous thighs are a glaring departure from conventional body proportions.

A————————————B————————————————————————C

∧ 6.37 The Golden Mean.

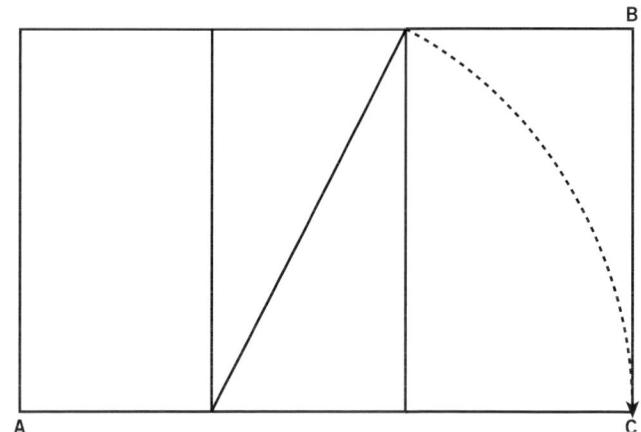

∧ 6.38 A Golden Rectangle.

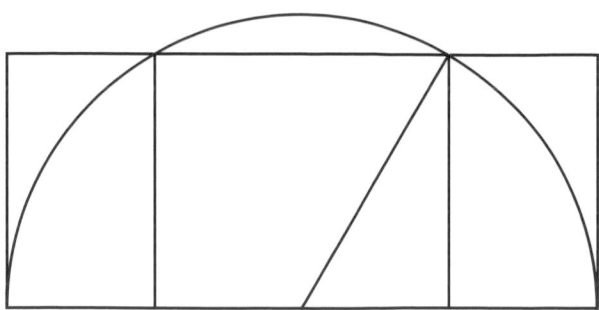

∧ 6.39 Root Five Rectangle.

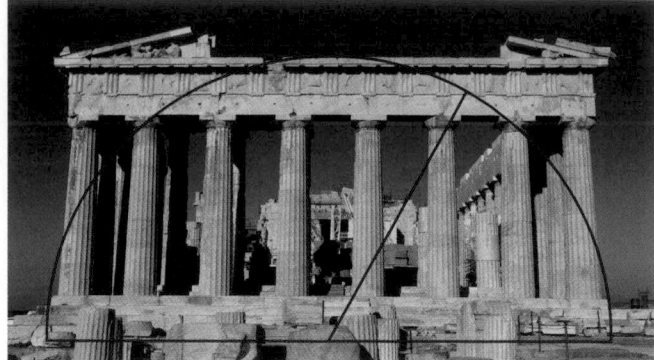

∧ 6.40 The Parthenon, West Façade, Athens.

Now let us visualize rotating the diagonal of the rectangle in Figure 6.38 in both directions, as shown in Figure 6.39. (You can think of the diagonal as a windshield wiper.) By rotating the diagonal both ways, we create a rectangle that consists of a central square and two smaller rectangles. The entire figure is called a **Root Five Rectangle** because the length of the rectangle is 2.236 (the square root of 5) times the width of the rectangle. For the Greeks, the Golden Rectangle and Root Five Rectangle represented the most pleasing dimensions and proportions of a rectangle; they became the basis for many temple designs including the west façade of the Parthenon (Fig. 6.40).

The Root Five Rectangle is the foundation of untold numbers of compositions that likewise have a harmonious and pleasing quality. Michelangelo's *The Fall of Man and the Expulsion from the Garden of Eden* (Fig. 6.41), from the Sistine ceiling, is a composition that maximizes the components of the Root Five Rectangle. The central square contains the Tree of Knowledge from the Book of Genesis, that all-important symbol of the temptation and fall of humankind. For Michelangelo, it serves as an equally important compositional device because it connects the imagery in the outer parts of the Root Five Rectangle— the repetitive figures of Adam and Eve as separated by time and the serpent. The distribution of the images is such that the rectangle to the left pulls toward the center, by virtue of the connection between the serpent and Eve, while the rectangle to the right pushes away from center—into the unwritten landscape of humankind's uncertain future—following the sword that is thrust into Adam's neck by the angel who expels them from Paradise.

The Spiral

The Greeks further related the Golden Rectangle to the **spiral**. Figure 6.42 shows that a spiral can be created by extending the Golden Rectangle in a circular manner and using a curve to connect the corners of the squares. On a microscopic level, we find that DNA, the genetic material that determines the structure of living things, takes the shape of a double spiral, or helix. On a human scale, the spiral defines the shape of the chambered nautilus (Fig. 6.43) and the pattern of the seeds in the head of a sunflower. We also find the spiral on a cosmic scale. Galaxies like our own Milky Way spin as spirals so vast that it may take light many thousands of years to travel their diameter. It's no wonder, then, that the spiral has been the source of study and inspiration.

The harmonious unwinding of the spiral is found in the evidence of creative expression among humans living in the Stone Age (Fig. 6.44) and is a motif seen across eras and cultures in architectural embellishment and all sorts of artifacts (Fig. 6.45). If you were to look downward

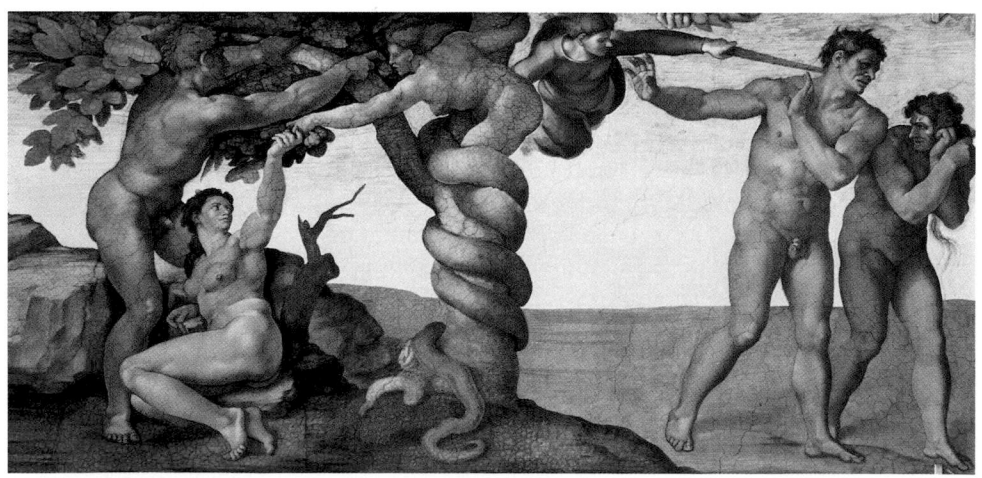

∧ 6.41 MICHELANGELO, *The Fall of Man and the Expulsion from the Garden of Eden* (1508–1512). 9' 2" × 18' 8". Section of ceiling frescoes, the Sistine Chapel, Vatican, Rome, Italy.

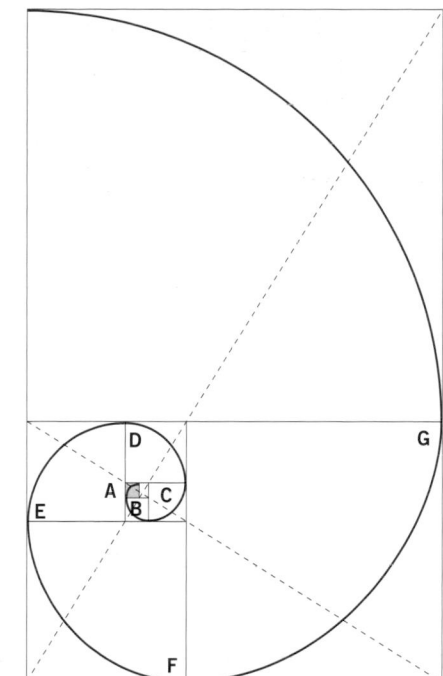

^ 6.42 A spiral.

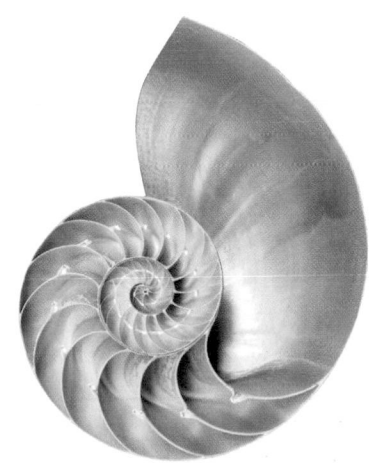

^ 6.43 The Chambered Nautilus.

on a spiral and pull it up from its center point, you would arrive at the basic form of the Great Mosque at Samarra in Iraq (see Fig. 16.26). The multitiered structure has a spiral ramp from the ground to the minaret at the very top, from which the *muezzin*, or "crier," once called Islamic worshipers to prayer.

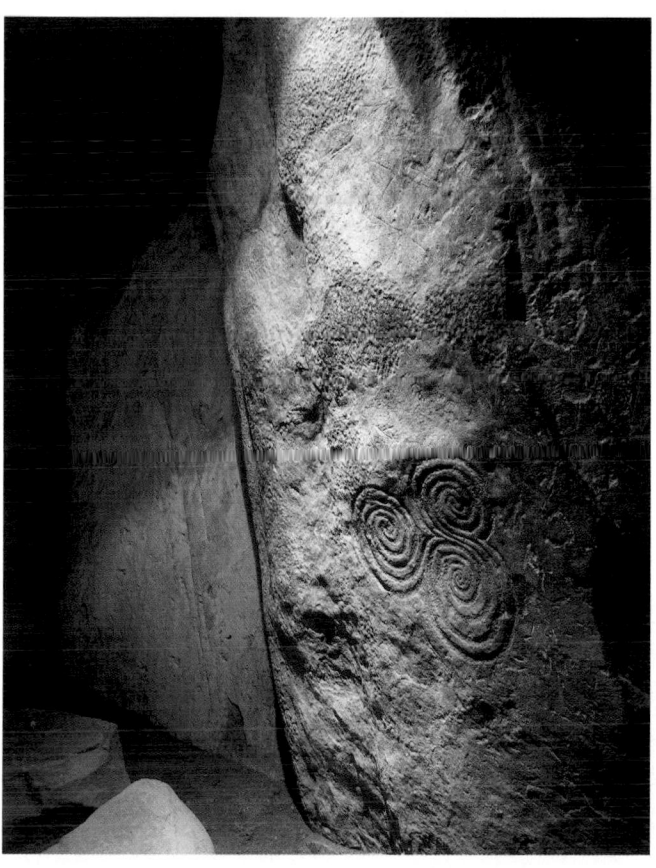

^ 6.44 **Stone with engraved spirals** (c. 3000 BCE). Megalith passage tomb, County Meath, Ireland.

CONNECTIONS The mosque at Samarra in Iraq is known for its spiraling minaret, from which followers are called to prayer.

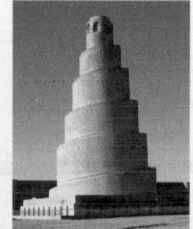

^ Mosque at Samarra (Fig. 16.26)

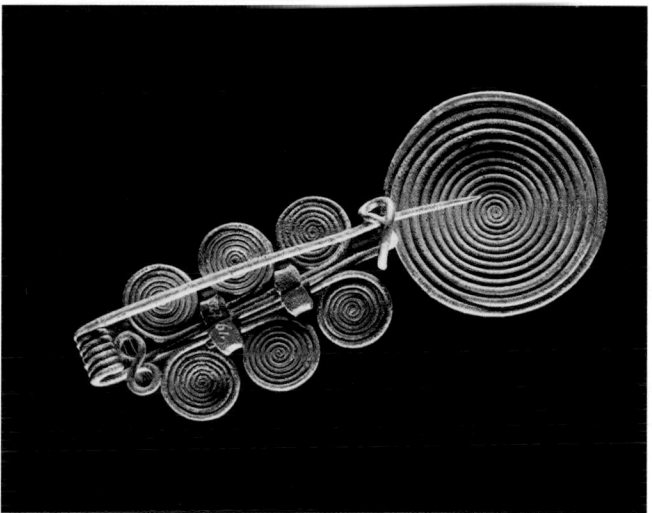

^ 6.45 **Spiral brooch** (1250–850 BCE). Feuersbrunn, Austria.

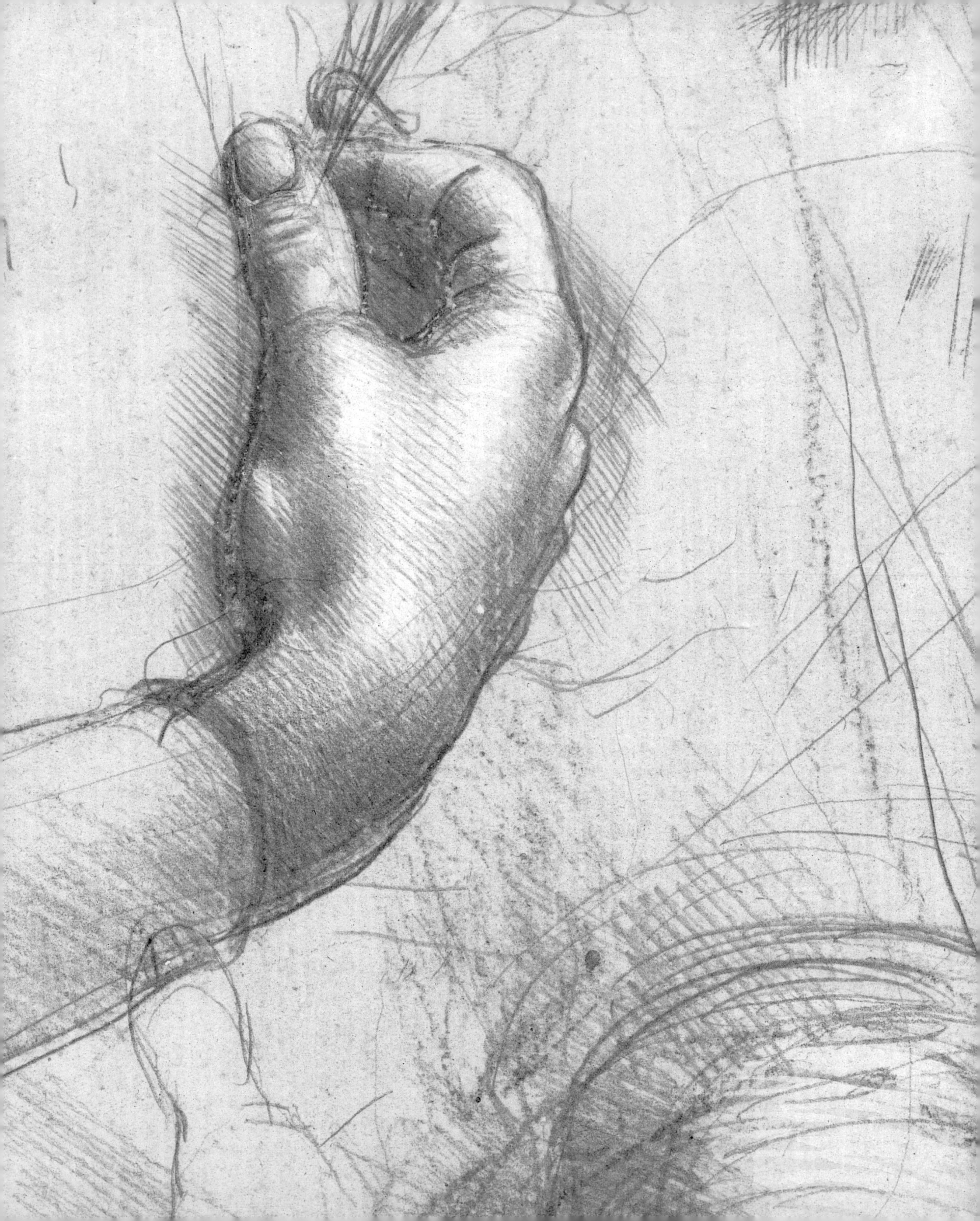

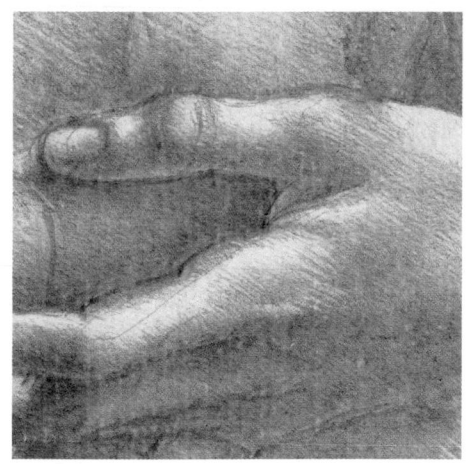

DRAWING

7

Drawing is among the most personal things you can do. It doesn't have any rhetoric or anything to tell. It's a dialogue between the art and yourself.

— SANTIAGO CALATRAVA, ARCHITECT

It is only by drawing often, drawing everything, drawing incessantly, that one fine day you discover to your surprise that you have rendered something in its true character.

— CAMILLE PISSARRO

Those who are not conversant in works of art are often surprised at the high value set by connoisseurs on drawings which appear careless, and in every respect unfinished, but they are truly valuable, and their value arises from this, that they give the idea of a whole . . .

— SIR JOSHUA REYNOLDS

IN ITS broadest definition, **drawing** is the result of running an implement over a surface and leaving some trace, some maker's mark. Most often that surface is paper, although artists will make drawings on just about anything: Stone Age humans used charcoal to outline the shapes of animals on the walls of caves, Picasso drew on paper napkins in cafés, Keith Haring used a Sharpie marker on subway walls, and Cai Guo-Qiang created burned-paper images with gunpowder he ignited by a fuse. Artists often capitalize on the idiosyncratic characteristics of their implements and surfaces to create specific effects in a drawing.

◄ LEONARDO DA VINCI, *A study of a woman's hands* (c. 1490). Metalpoint, heightening, and charcoal on paper; 8 ½" × 6". Royal Collection Trust, London, England.

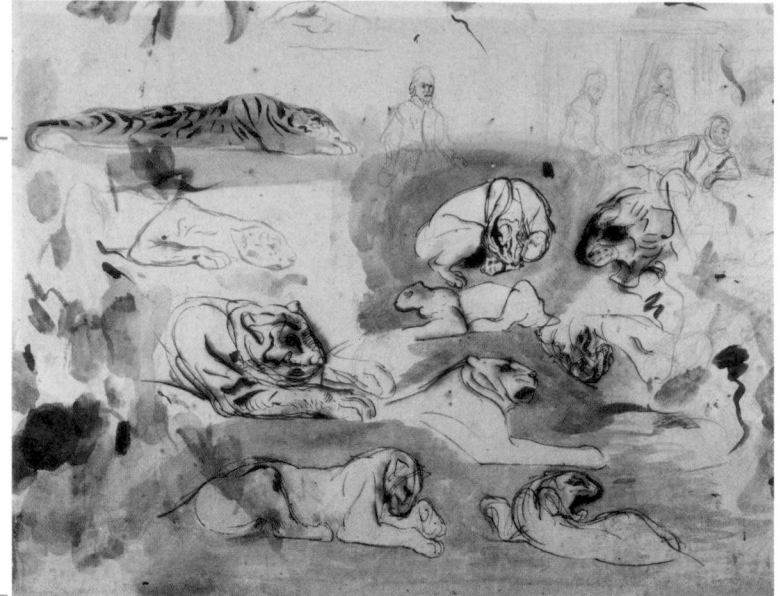

1 ft.

∧ 7.1 EUGÈNE DELACROIX, *Sketches of Tigers and Men in Sixteenth-Century Costume* (1828–1829). Watercolor, pen and iron gall ink, and graphite on ivory laid paper with blue fibers discolored to buff; 15⅝" × 20" (397 × 510 mm). Art Institute of Chicago, Chicago, Illinois.

TYPES OF DRAWINGS

Drawing is the most basic, perhaps the most instinctive, of the two-dimensional art forms. Drawings may serve as preliminary sketches for works in other mediums, as a process for articulating ideas, or can be complete works in and of themselves.

The variety of drawings (monochromatic or color, scant traces or fully executed works, thumbnail sketches or full-scale mock-ups used to transfer images to walls, ceilings, or large canvases) makes it almost impossible to categorize the medium. Add to this the variety and types of materials with which artists draw and you have what can only be described as the most unrestrained of all mediums.

The Artist's Sketch

Artists carry sketchbooks everywhere, and perhaps no one is better known for his "little book of leaves" than Leonardo da Vinci, who advised artists to note everything, and when the book was "full, [to] keep it to serve [their] future plans, and take another and carry on with it." Leonardo's notebooks may be legendary, but most practicing artists keep sketchbooks and journals, such as the one by nineteenth-century French artist Eugène Delacroix (Fig. 7.1), the pages of which can reveal a

great deal of how an artist sees the world or works out an idea.

The Finished Drawing

Drawing can be the most direct way of bringing what is in the artist's mind to the artist's surface. Many artists enjoy the sheer spontaneity of drawing, tracing a pencil or piece of chalk across a sheet of paper to capture directly their thoughts or to record the slightest movement of their hand. Yet a drawing can stand as a complete work of art. Gary Kelley's sensual and rhythmic pastel drawing (Fig. 7.2) possesses all of the detail, all of the finish of a work in a medium like painting. The zigzag positioning of the figures, and the contrast between the harsh angularity of the male singer's suit and the sinuous curves of the woman who moves to his music, convey the spirit and sultriness of the blues club atmosphere.

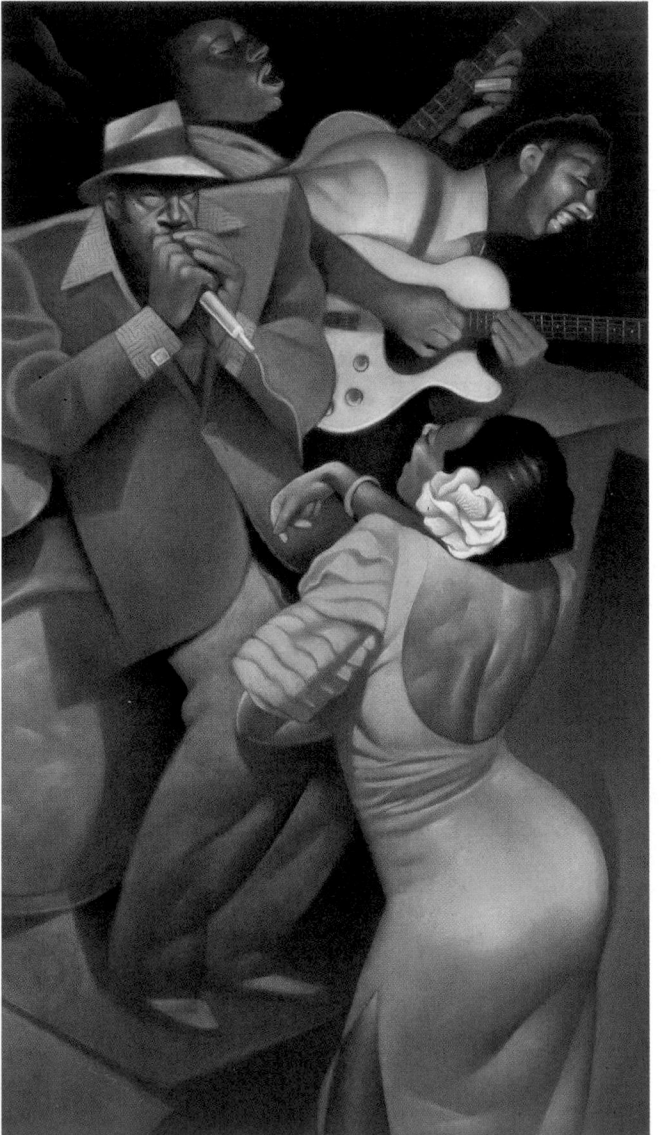

1 ft.

> 7.2 GARY KELLEY, *Promotion for the Mississippi Delta Blues Festival* (c. 1989). Pastel, 24" × 14".

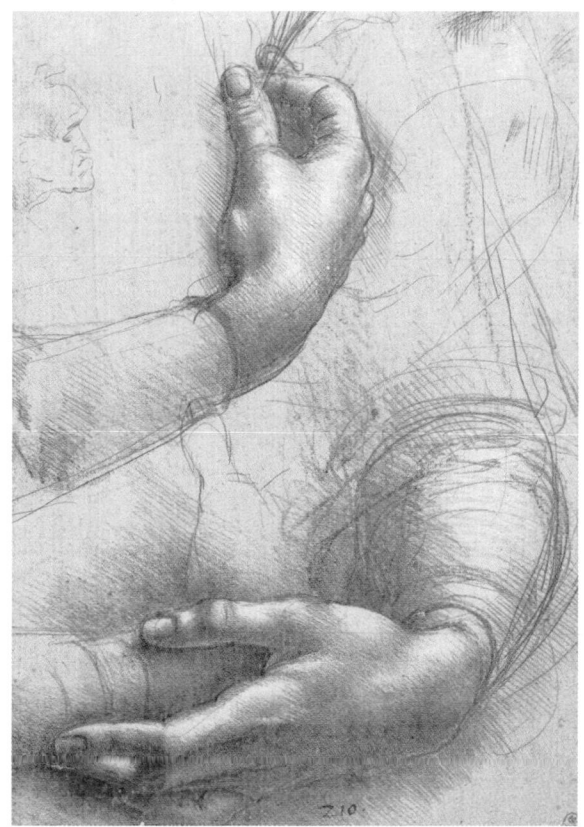

▲ 7.3 **LEONARDO DA VINCI**, *A study of a woman's hands* (c. 1490). Metalpoint, heightening, and charcoal on paper; 8½" × 6". Royal Collection Trust, London, England.

1 in.

DRAWING MATERIALS

Conventional drawing materials can be divided into two groups: dry mediums and fluid mediums. **Dry mediums** include metalpoint, pencil, charcoal, chalk, pastel, and wax crayon. The primary fluid medium used in drawing is ink, and the instruments used to carry this medium are pen and brush. But, once again, almost anything can be used to make a drawing, as we will see.

Dry Mediums

METALPOINT Metalpoint was used widely from the late Middle Ages to the early 1500s—before the discovery of graphite. A metalpoint drawing is created by dragging a silver-tipped (or other metal-tipped) implement over a surface that has been coated with a **ground**—a sort of base layer—of bone dust or chalk mixed with **gum**, water, and **pigment**. This ground is sufficiently coarse to allow small flecks of metal from the instrument to adhere to the prepared surface as it is drawn across. These bits of metal form the lines of the drawing; they are barely visible at the start but eventually oxidize, becoming tarnished or darkened. Each line, a soft gray to begin with, mellows and darkens to a grayish brown hue.

Because they lack sharp tonal contrasts, the resultant drawings are often extremely delicate in appearance. Metalpoint is challenging, allowing for little or no correction. Thus, the artist is not in a position to experiment while working but, rather, must have a fairly concrete notion of what the final product will look like. The lines must be accurate and confidently drawn.

Oftentimes, as in Leonardo's study of a woman's hands (Fig. 7.3), fuller, more rounded shapes will be created through the addition of other mediums; Leonardo used white chalk highlights and charcoal shading to amplify the form.

PENCIL Medieval monks, like the ancient Egyptians, ruled lines with metallic lead but pencils, as we know them, began to be mass-produced only in the late eighteenth century. A pencil consists of a mixture of graphite powder (a form of carbon) and clay that is baked and hardened and encased in wood or paper. The relative hardness or softness of a pencil's lead depends on the quantity of clay in the mixture; the more clay, the harder the pencil.

As a drawing medium, pencil can produce a wide range of effects. Lines drawn with hard pencil can be thin and light in tone; those rendered in soft lead can be thick and dark. The sharp point of the pencil will create a firm, fine line suitable for meticulous detail. Softer areas of tone or shading can be achieved through a buildup of parallel lines, smudging, or the dragging of the side of a lead point across a surface (Fig. 7.4).

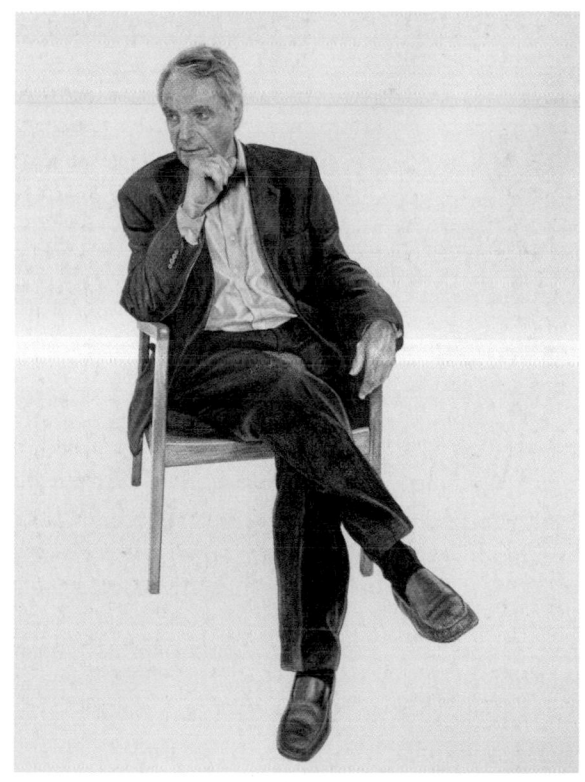

▲ 7.4 **NINA FOWLER**, *Christopher Allsopp* (2012). Pencil on paper. Collection of New College, Oxford, England.

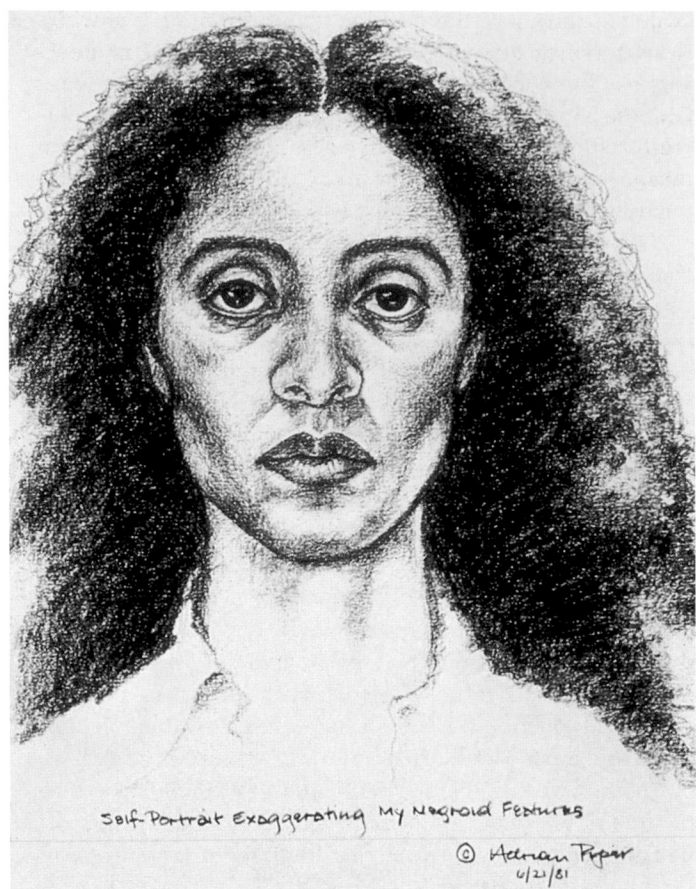

1 in.

∧ 7.5 **ADRIAN PIPER**, *Self-Portrait Exaggerating My Negroid Features* (1981). Pencil on paper, 10" × 8". Adrian Piper Research Archive, Collection Eileen and Peter Norton.

CHARCOAL   Like pencil, charcoal has a long history as a drawing implement. Used by our Stone Age ancestors to create images on the walls of the innermost recesses of caves, these initially crumbly pieces of burnt wood or bone now take the form of prepared sticks that are formed by the controlled charring of special hardwoods. Charcoal sticks are available in textures that vary from hard to soft. The sticks may be sharpened with sandpaper to form fine and clear lines or may be dragged flat across the surface to create diffuse areas of varied tone. Like pencil, charcoal may also be smudged or rubbed to create a hazy effect.

When charcoal is dragged across a surface, bits of the material adhere to that surface, just as with metalpoint and graphite pencil. But charcoal particles rub off more easily; thus the completed drawings are typically sprayed—and fixed—with a solution of thinned varnish. Also, because of the way in which the charcoal disperses, the texture of the surface is evident through each stroke. Coarsely textured paper will yield a grainy image, whereas smooth paper will provide a clear, almost pencil-like line.

The exercise of drawing from life has been integral to the art academy experience for hundreds of years, a method by which the human form might be painstakingly analyzed and recorded. Perhaps this is why, in part, Adrian Piper chose the medium of drawing to render her dramatic *Self-Portrait Exaggerating My Negroid Features* (Fig. 7.5). With it, Piper invites spectators to focus on those aspects of her physical self that reveal her mixed black and white parentage and challenges them to confront prejudice based on physical differences between races.

COLORED PENCIL   Colored pencils consist of waxlike cores mixed with pigment and other substances surrounded, as with graphite pencils, by wood or paper. Like graphite pencils, which can be sharpened to a point, colored pencils can render fine lines, as in Elizabeth Peyton's drawing *Marc (April)* (Fig. 7.6). The young man's hair is composed of myriad nesting lines that create an expressive counterpoint to the more tightly controlled, finely modeled, and realistic drawing of his face. The movement suggested in his wispy, tousled locks is echoed in the sketchy rendering of his tailored shirt.

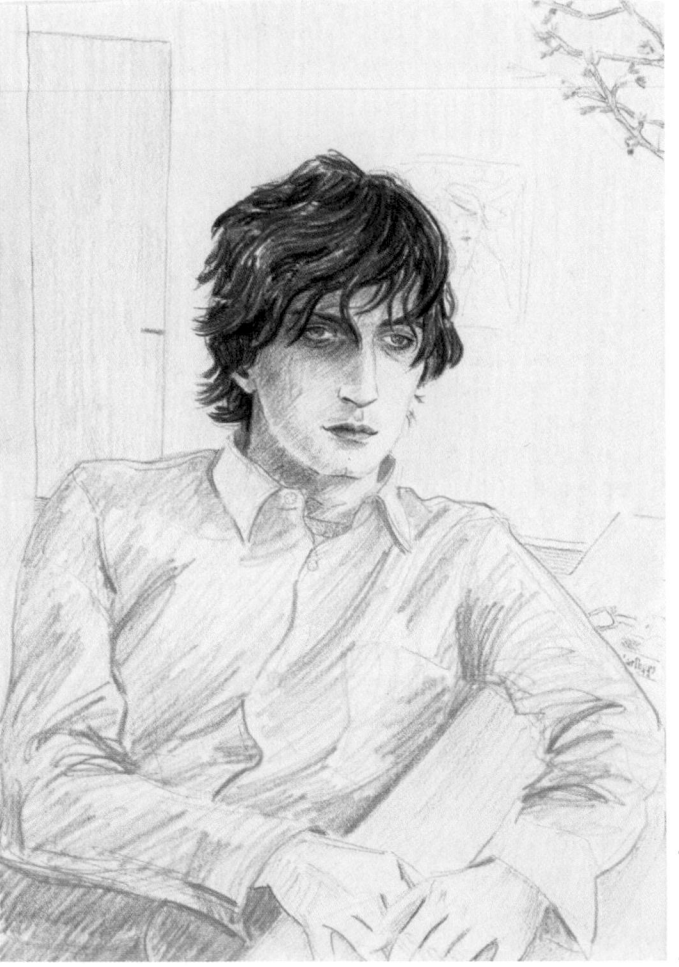

1 in.

∧ 7.6 **ELIZABETH PEYTON**, *Marc (April)* (2003). Colored pencil on paper, 8⅝" × 6". The Judith Rothschild Foundation Contemporary Drawings Collection Gift. The Museum of Modern Art, New York, New York.

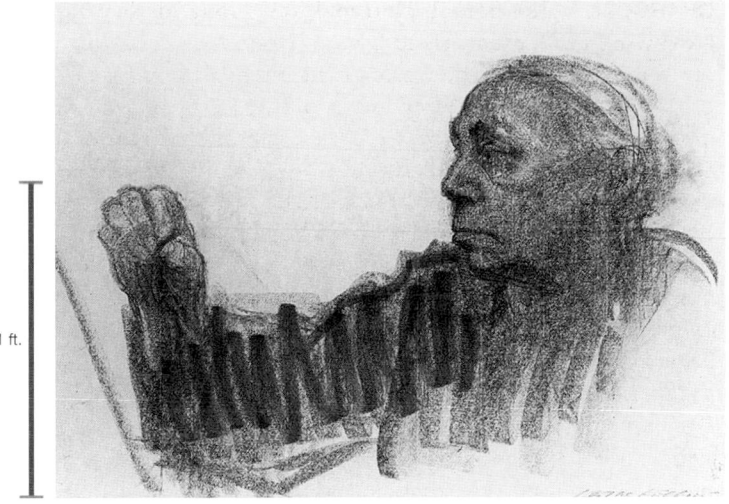

▲ 7.7 **KÄTHE KOLLWITZ,** *Self-Portrait* (1924). Charcoal, 18¾" × 25". National Gallery of Art, Washington, D.C.

A self-portrait of the German Expressionist Käthe Kollwitz (Fig. 7.7) reveals the character of the medium of charcoal. Delicate lines drawn over broader areas of subtle shading enunciate the two main points of interest: the artist's face and her hand. Between these two points, representing the connection between the conceptual and the technical, runs a surge of energy described by aggressive, jagged strokes overlaying lightly sketched contours. The

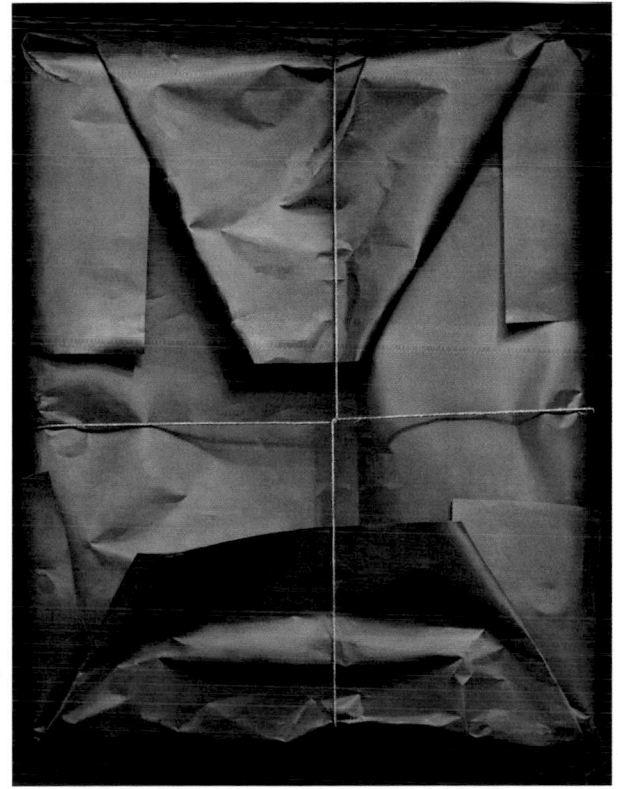

▲ 7.8 **CLAUDIO BRAVO,** *Package* (1969). Charcoal, pastel, and sanguine; 30⅞" × 22½".

value spectrum in the drawing ranges from hints of white at the artist's knuckles, cheekbone, and hair to the deepest blacks of the palm of her hand, eyes, and mouth. Finer lines seem to dance over the texture of the paper, whereas the shaded areas, particularly around the neck and chest area, reveal the faint white lines and tiny flecks of pulp that are visual remnants of the papermaking process.

Charcoal can be expressive or descriptive, depending on the way it is applied. Claudio Bravo's *Package* (Fig. 7.8) is a finely rendered, *trompe l'oeil* drawing that bears almost no trace of the artist's gesture and almost no indication of the "dusty" quality of the materials—primarily charcoal and pastel. The illusion of the smooth sheen and crinkled indentations of the wrapping paper, attributed to painstaking gradations in value, is so convincing that the illusion of texture completely overrides the actual texture of the drawing materials.

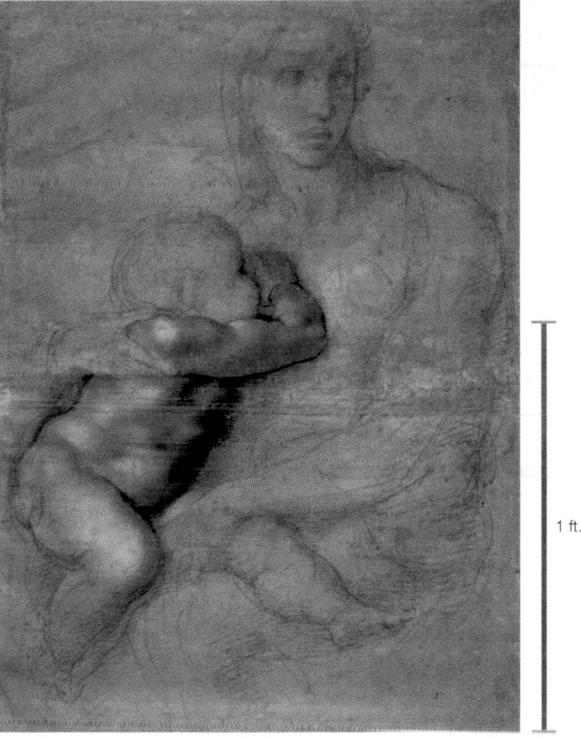

▲ 7.9 **MICHELANGELO BUONARROTI,** *Madonna and Child* (c. 1525). Pencil and red chalk on paper, 21⁵⁄₁₆" × 15⅝". Casa Buonarroti, Florence, Italy.

CHALK, PASTEL, AND CRAYON The effects of charcoal, **chalk,** and **pastel** are very similar, although the mediums differ in terms of their composition. Chalk and pastel consist of pigment and a **binder,** such as **gum arabic,** shaped into workable sticks. Chalks are available in many colors, some of which occur in nature. **Ocher,** for example, derives its dark yellow tint from iron oxide in some clay. **Umber** acquires its characteristic yellowish or reddish brown color from earth containing oxides of manganese and iron.

Michelangelo used pencil and red chalk in a sketch of the Madonna and Christ Child to work out certain aspects of the figures prior to painting (see Fig. 7.9). Quick, though confident notations describing Mary's face and torso contrast markedly with the careful rendering of the infant Jesus. The precision in the muscular detail and fully realized form of the body remind us that Michelangelo's first medium was sculpture.

Pastels consist of ground chalk mixed with powdered pigments and a binder. Whereas chalk drawings can be traced to prehistoric times, pastels did not come into wide use until the 1400s. They were introduced to France only in the 1700s, but within a century, pastels captured the imagination of many important painters. Their wide range of brilliant colors offered a painter's palette for use in the more spontaneous medium of drawing. Pastels are manipulated in countless ways to create different effects. At times, colors are left pure and intense, as in *Head #12* (Fig. 7.10) by Lucas Samaras, in which coarse splotches of vibrant color contrast with black paper to create a

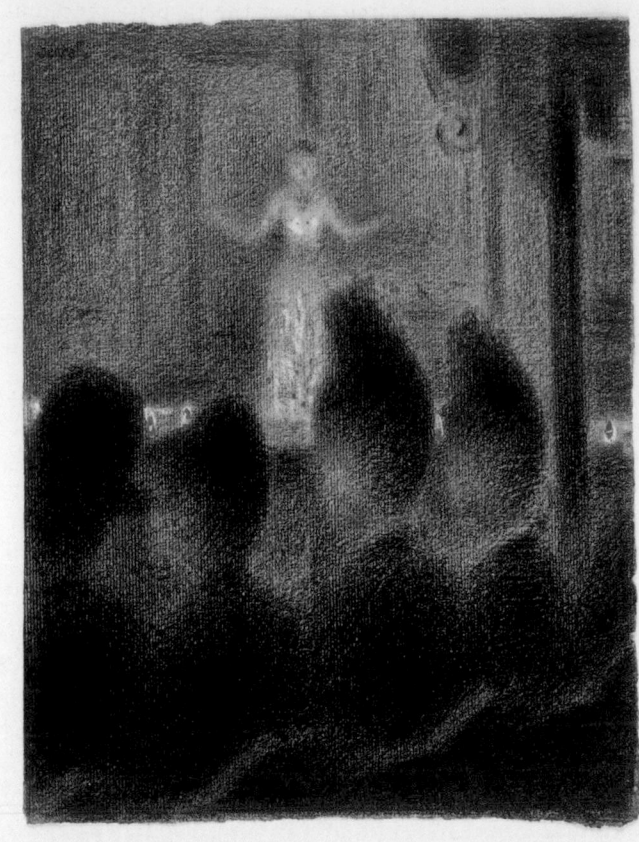

∧ **7.11 GEORGES SEURAT,** *At the Concert Européen (Au Concert Européen)* (c. 1886–1888). Conté crayon and gouache on paper, 12¼" × 9⅜". Lillie P. Bliss Collection. The Museum of Modern Art, New York, New York.

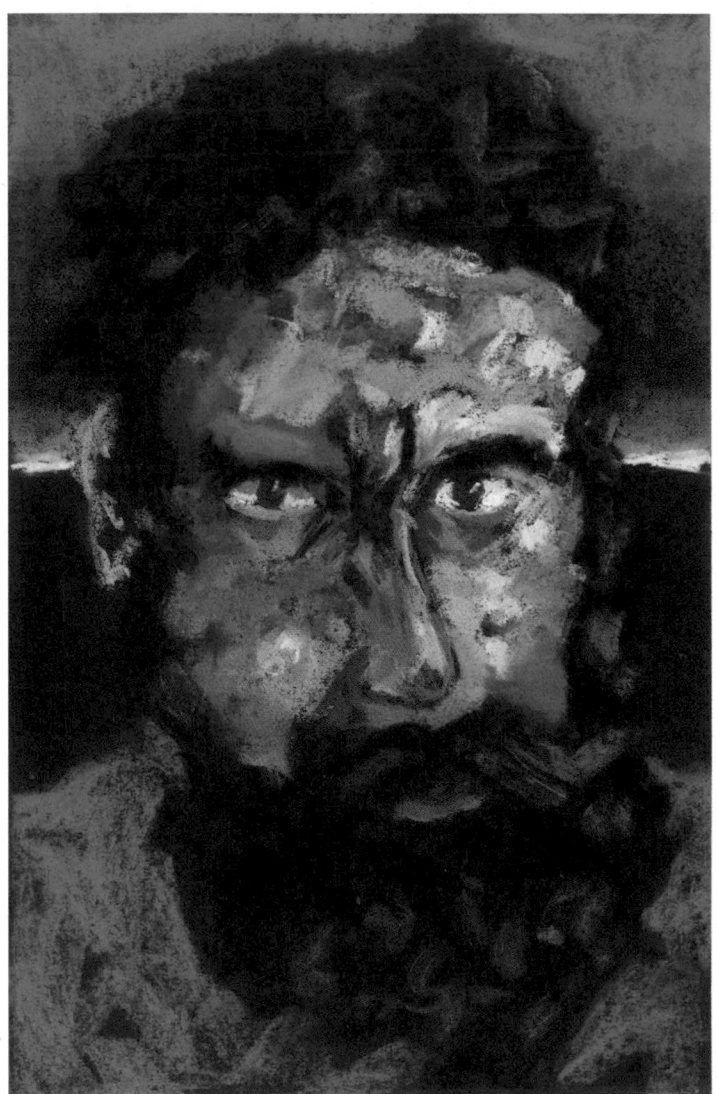

∧ **7.10 LUCAS SAMARAS,** *Head #12* (1981). Pastel on black paper, 17¾" × 11½". The Judith Rothschild Foundation Contemporary Drawings Collection Gift. The Museum of Modern Art, New York, New York.

glowing, almost iridescent effect. At other times subtle harmonies can be created through blending or smudging.

Strictly defined, the term **crayon** includes any drawing material in stick form. Thus, charcoal, chalk, and pastels are crayons, as are the familiar Crayolas you used on walls, floors, and occasionally coloring books when you were a child. Wax crayons, like pastels, combine ground pigment with a binder—in this case, wax. Wax crayon moves easily over a surface, creating lines that have a characteristic sheen. These lines are less apt to smudge than charcoal, chalk, and pastels.

One of the most popular commercially manufactured crayons for artists is the **conté crayon**, a square stick of compressed graphite or charcoal mixed with wax or clay. Like pencils, conté crayons are available in different degrees of hardness and can be manipulated to create different effects. Artists working with conté crayons often use rough paper so that bits of crayon will adhere to the surface as it is dragged across, creating an overall texture that can be a prominent feature of the drawing. The conté crayon was invented in the late eighteenth century by Nicola-Jacques Conté out of necessity: There was a shortage of graphite in France due to a blockade during the Napoleonic Wars with England. A century or so later, conté crayon became one of the favorite mediums of the French painter Georges Seurat. His *At the Concert Européen* (Fig. 7.11) is built up almost solely through contrasts of tone. Deep, velvety blacks absorb the almost invisible heads of the musicians in the orchestra pit, while a glaring strip of untouched white paper seems to illuminate the stage. The even application of crayon to coarse paper creates a diffuse light that conveys the dim atmosphere of a small café.

Fluid Mediums

The primary **fluid medium** used in drawing is ink, and while pens and brushes are the most conventional tools for applying ink to paper, there are limitless ways to do it—from sponges to sticks to fingertips (Fig. 7.12). Ink has a history that stretches back thousands of years, appearing in Egyptian **papyrus** drawings and ancient Chinese scrolls. Some ancient peoples made ink from the dyes of plants, squid, and octopus. By the second century CE, blue-black inks were being derived from galls—growths found on oak trees that are rich in resin and tannic acid. The oldest-known ink is India or China ink, composed of a solution of carbon black (tar mixed with oil) and water. It is a permanent, rich, black ink that is used in Asian **calligraphy** to this day.

As with the dry mediums, dramatically different effects can be achieved with fluid mediums through a variety of techniques. The artist may alter the composition of a fluid medium by diluting it with water to

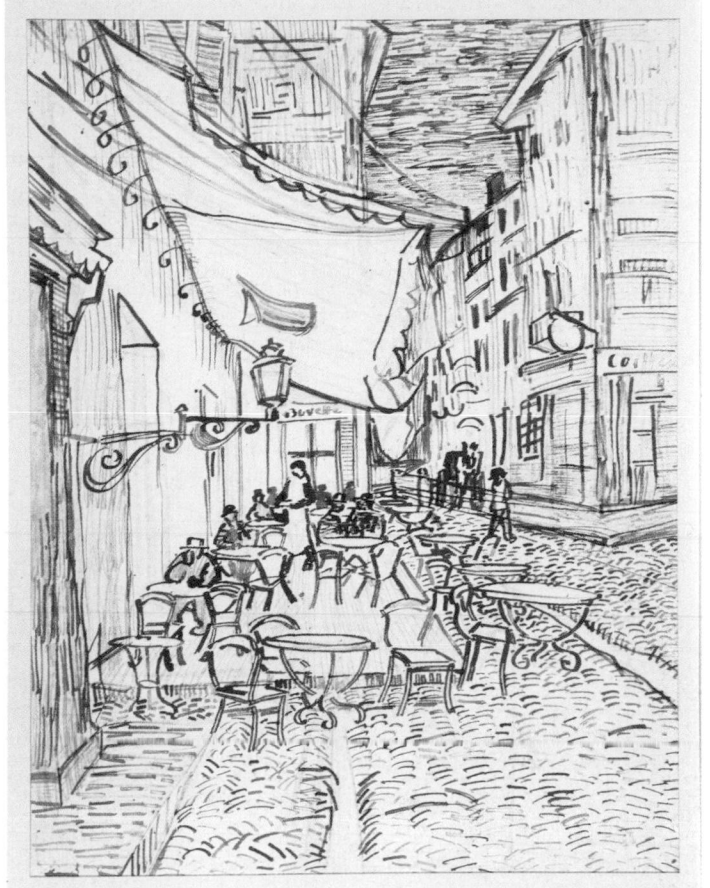

▲ **7.13** **VINCENT VAN GOGH,** *Café Terrace at Night, September 1888.* Reed pen and ink with graphite on laid paper, 34½" × 29½". Dallas Museum of Art, Dallas, Texas.

achieve lighter tones, or may vary the fullness of brushes and the width of pen nibs to achieve lines of different character.

PEN AND INK   The earliest pens were fashioned from hollow reeds, slit at the end to allow a controlled flow of ink, and quills plucked from the wings of large birds. It wasn't until the nineteenth century that the mass-produced metal **nib**, slipped into a wooden **stylus** and dipped into a well of ink, became a preferred writing instrument.

Pen and ink drawings are essentially linear, although the nature of the lines can vary considerably according to the qualities of the instrument: a fine, rigid nib will provide a clear, precise line that is uniform in thickness, whereas lines laid down with a more flexible quill tip or reed pen will vary in width according to the amount of pressure an artist exerts on the tip. Vincent van Gogh used a reed pen for a drawing of a popular café in a busy square in Arles, where he lived and worked for a year after leaving Paris for the south of France (Fig. 7.13). The reed pen is well suited to the short, brisk strokes and curvilinear flourishes characteristic of van Gogh's painterly style.

▲ **7.12** **ROSEMARIE TROCKEL,** *Untitled* (1992). Ink on paper, 13¾" × 13¾". The Museum of Modern Art, New York, New York.

A CLOSER LOOK

Life, Death, and Dwelling in the Deep South

SOME YEARS AGO, BEVERLY BUCHANAN came to know Ms. Mary Lou Furcron. They were both artists, one might say. Both the builders of structures. Both nurturing, creative, and colorful. Ever since this meeting, Buchanan's life and art have revolved around the art and life of the southern shack dweller.

This way of living is an existence unto itself, as the photographs indicate (**Fig. 7.14**). Ms. Furcron's shack reflects her life, and her life reflects the shack in which she lived. She devoted a part of each day to maintaining the structure, replacing rotted posts with new logs; using bark, lathing, and other odd materials to repair the siding. The shack stood as an organic and ever-evolving structure—an extension of Ms. Furcron herself. Because the shack required her constant attention for its survival, her move to a nursing home brought its rapid disrepair. Just one month after Ms. Furcron's departure, the shack was unrecognizable as its former self.

Buchanan's art reflects a structural approach to the creation of the shack image. As Ms. Furcron built with the recycled remnants of nature and human existence, so does Beverly Buchanan. Her oil

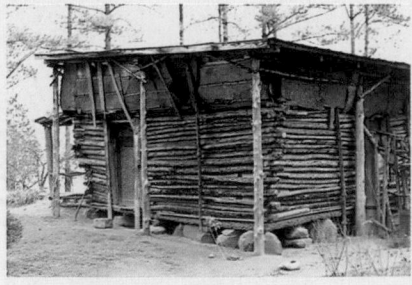 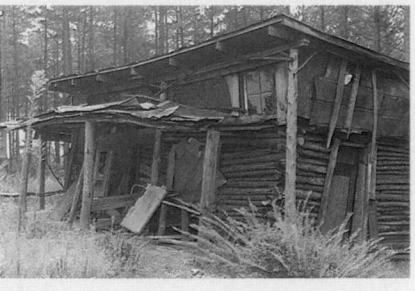

A   B

∧ **7.14 Photographs of Ms. Mary Lou Furcron's home.** Photo A shows the shack while Ms. Furcron was living in it and tending to it. Photo B shows the shack just one month after her placement in a nursing home. Courtesy of Bernice Steinbaum Gallery, Miami, Florida.

pastel drawing *Henriette's Yard* (**Fig. 7.15**) is vigorously and lovingly constructed of a myriad of vibrant strokes. These strokes at once serve as the building blocks of the shack image and the very stuff that reduces the structure to an almost indecipherable explosion of color. The precarious balance of the shacks in relation to one another and the uncertain ground on which they stand further symbolize the precious and fragile nature of the shack dwelling, and human existence.

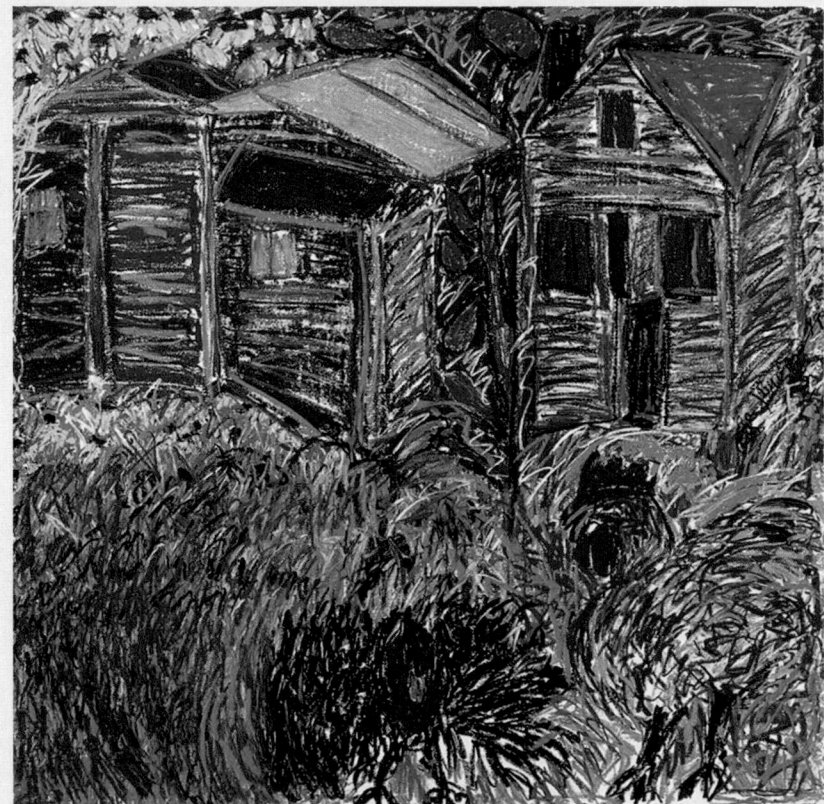

1 ft.

∧ **7.15 BEVERLY BUCHANAN,** *Henriette's Yard* (1995). Oil pastel on paper, 60" × 60".

CONNECTIONS In his oil painting of the café terrace in Arles, van Gogh preserved the brisk, short strokes of the cobblestone pavement in his drawing (see **Fig. 7.13**), but the cobalt sky in the distance—afire with stars—is a coming attraction for his famed *Starry Night* (see **Fig. 19.25**), painted a year later.

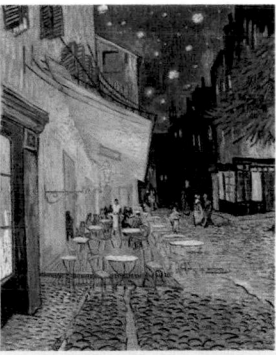

⌃ 7.16 van Gogh's *Café Terrace, Place du Forum, Arles* (1888)

BRUSH AND INK The quality of line in brush-and-ink drawing will depend on whether the brush is bristle or nylon, thin or thick, pointed or flat tipped. Likewise, characteristics of the drawing surface, such as texture or absorbency, will affect the look and feel of the completed drawing.

Japanese artists are masters of the brush-and-ink medium, employing it for centuries in everyday writing and in works of art. Their facility with the technique is evident in seemingly casual sketches, such as those done

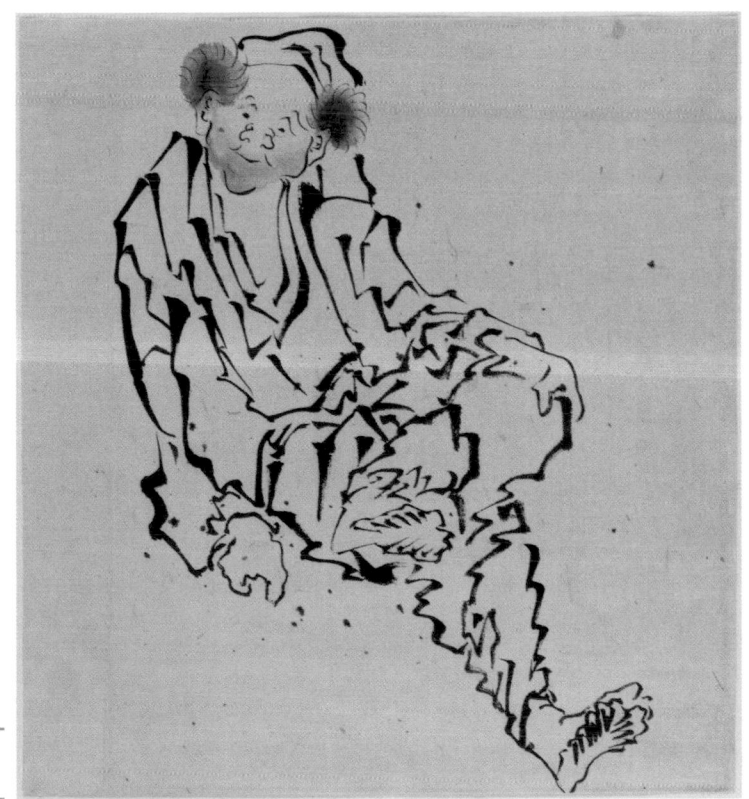

⌃ 7.17 **KATSUSHIKA HOKUSAI (1760–1849),** *Drawing of a man seated with left leg resting over right knee.* Ink on paper, 10⁹/₁₆" × 9¹¹/₁₆". Brooklyn Museum of Art, New York, New York.

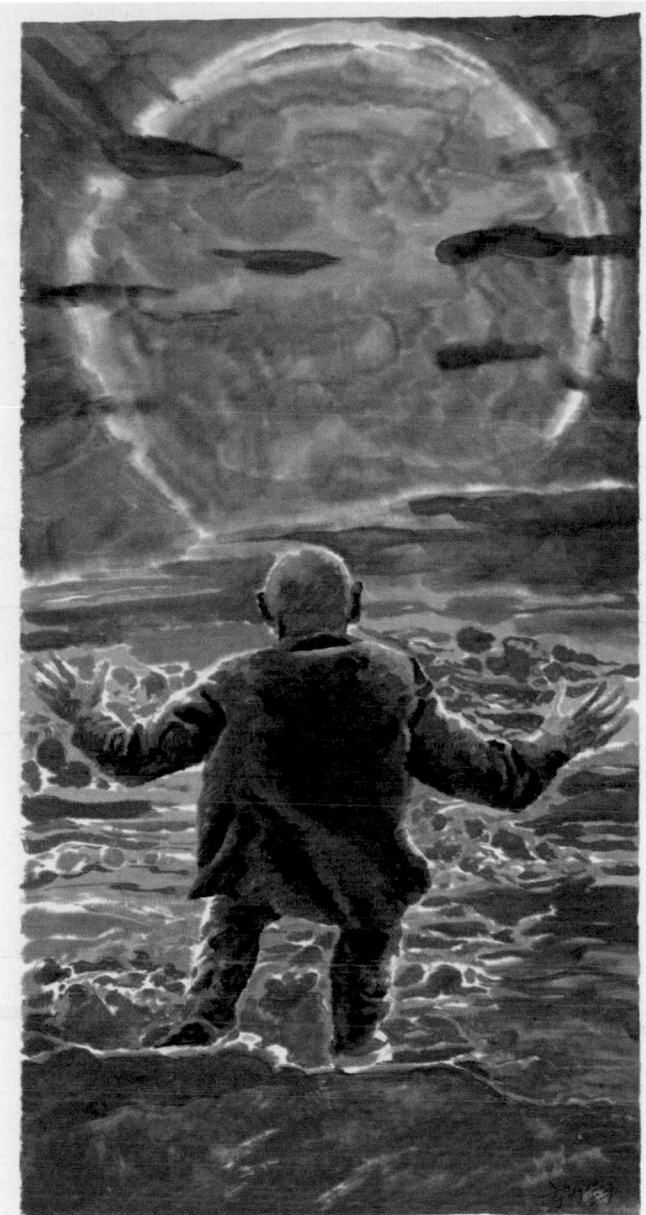

⌃ 7.18 **FANG LIJUN,** *Ink-and-Wash-Painting #3* (2004). Ink on paper, 54½" × 28½". The Museum of Modern Art, New York, New York.

in the late eighteenth and early nineteenth centuries by Katsushika Hokusai (Fig. 7.17). Longer rippling lines loosely define the contours and folds of his clothing while short, brisk strokes capture his impish smile and tufts of unruly hair. Hokusai enhanced the gestural vitality of his brush drawing with touches of **wash**—diluted, watery ink—around the hair and face, adding a bit of volume to an otherwise flat drawing.

The medium of brush and wash is versatile. It can duplicate the linearity of brush-and-ink drawings or be used to create images solely through tonal contrasts. The remarkable illusion of deep space in Fang Lijun's drawing (Fig. 7.18) is achieved through the distribution of zones of wash in spectrum of grays tones. They originate at the feet of an old man on a bluff and meander, like irregular stepping-stones, toward a large sun disk on the horizon. The glowing sphere, ringed in light (unwashed areas of paper), creates a halo effect at the edges of the man's clothing and encircles the pebble-like concentrations of wash. The detail in the drawing—from fine to fluid—is a result of the artist's control of his brush as well as the ratio of ink to water. The ink can be diluted to varying degrees to provide a wide tonal range. Different effects can be achieved either by adding water directly to the ink or by moistening the surface before drawing.

CARTOONS

The word **cartoon** derives from the Italian *cartone*, meaning "paper." Originally, cartoons were full-scale preliminary drawings done on paper for projects such as fresco

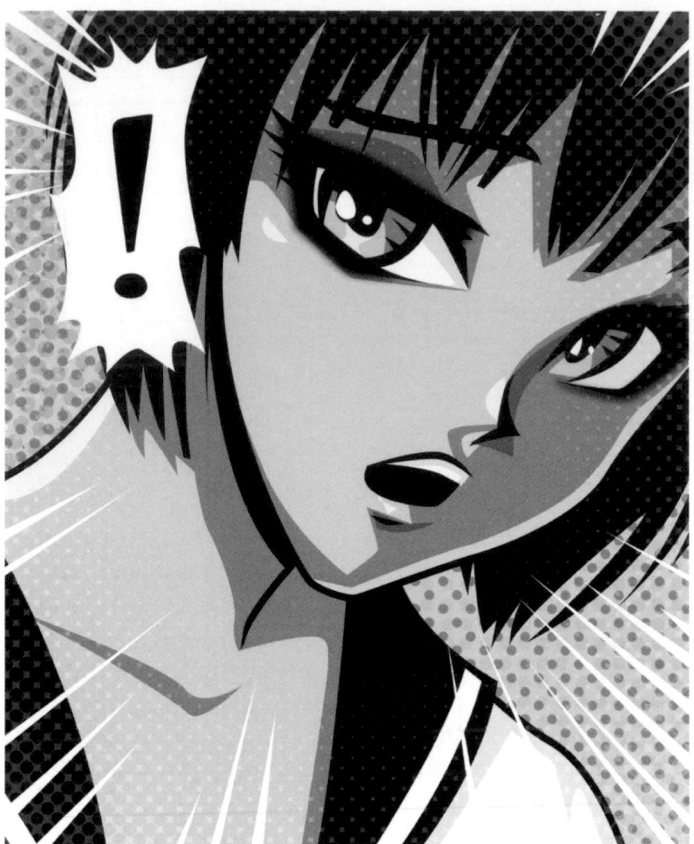

▲ 7.20 **Example of manga artwork**.

and other paintings, stained glass, tapestries, and so on. Modern cartoons rely on *caricature*, the flagrant exaggeration and distortion of natural features (Fig. 7.19) and have long been vehicles for social commentary, consciousness raising, and political activism. Cartoons created for animated films, video games, action comics, anime (Japanese animation), or manga (Fig. 7.20), as ubiquitous as they are in contemporary visual culture, have deep historical roots.

ALTERNATIVE APPROACHES TO DRAWING

Drawings display endless versatility in terms of their intended purposes, their mediums, and their techniques. It is not unusual to find drawings that are not "drawn" at all or works on paper that push the boundaries of conventional drawings. You would be right to ask, "What *is* a drawing, after all?"

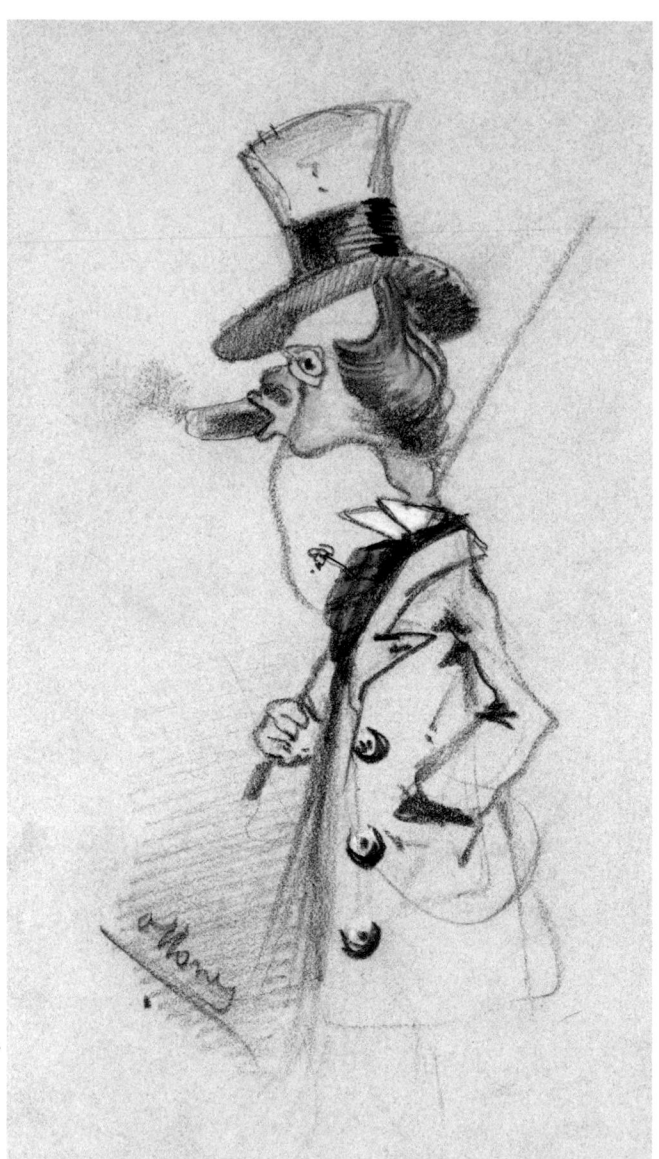

1 in.

◄ 7.19 **CLAUDE MONET**, *Dandy with a Cigar (1857)*. Pencil on paper, 9⁷⁄₁₆" × 6⁵⁄₁₆". Musée Marmottan Monet, Paris, France.

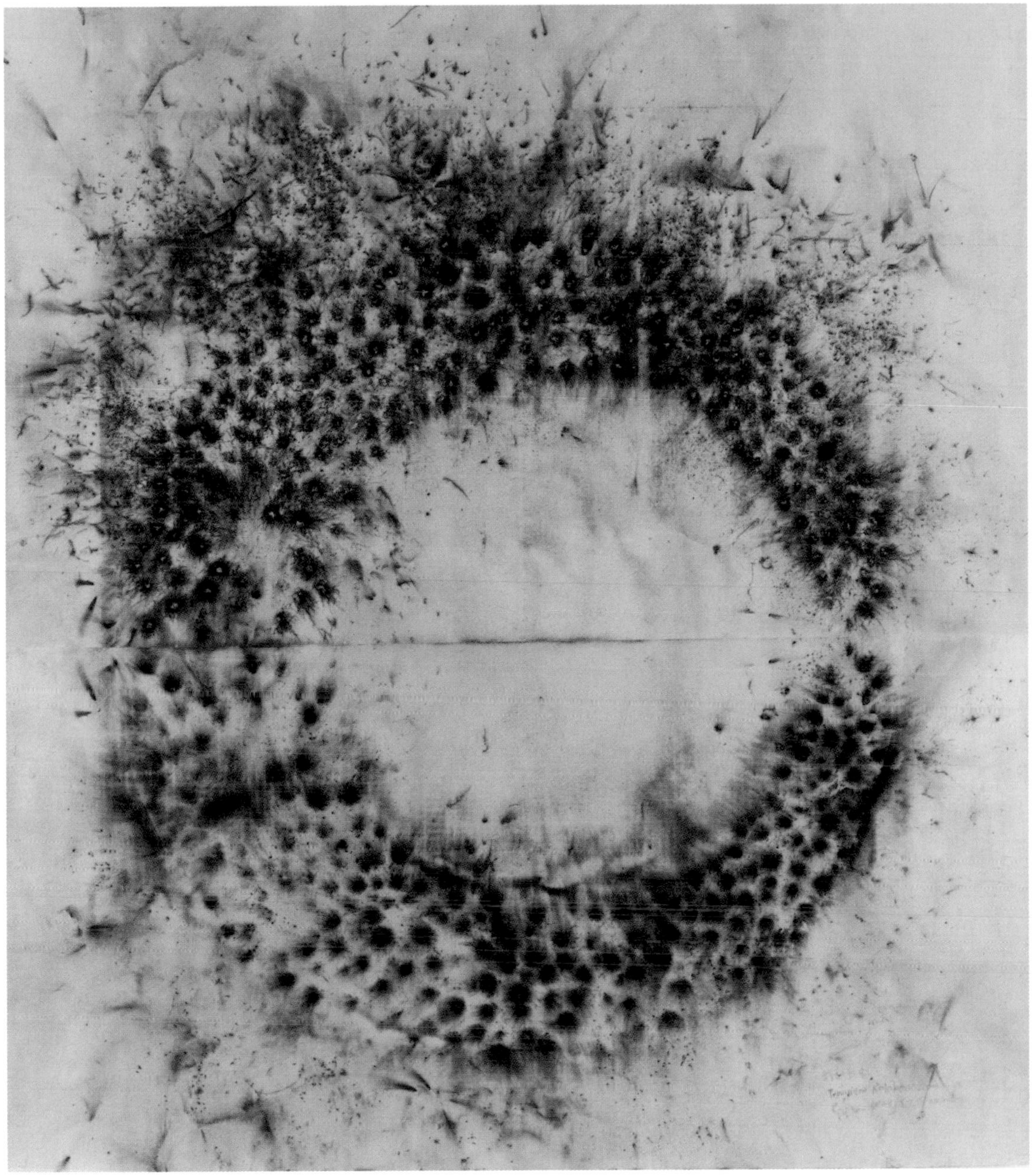

1 ft.

∧ 7.21 CAI GUO-QIANG, *Drawing for Transient Rainbow* (2003). 179" × 159½" (overall).

Cai Guo-Qiang is renowned for his works of *ephemeral art*, a contemporary genre best described as transitory and impermanent—not intended to last (except in documentation) beyond the experience of a moment. The circular image in Figure 7.21 emerges from a concentration of pinpoints of blackened paper, created through the discharge of gunpowder on two sheets of paper. As insubstantial as this work may first appear, it has more material substance—and potential longevity—than the monumental ephemeral work it inspired.

CONNECTIONS Cai Guo-Qiang's carefully calibrated fireworks displays are among his most famous pieces; this is one titled *Transient Rainbow.*

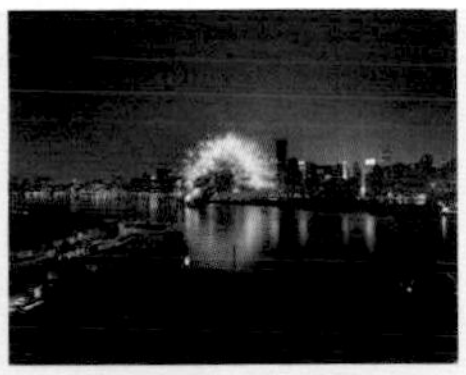

∧ Cai's *Transient Rainbow* (**Fig. 11.32**)

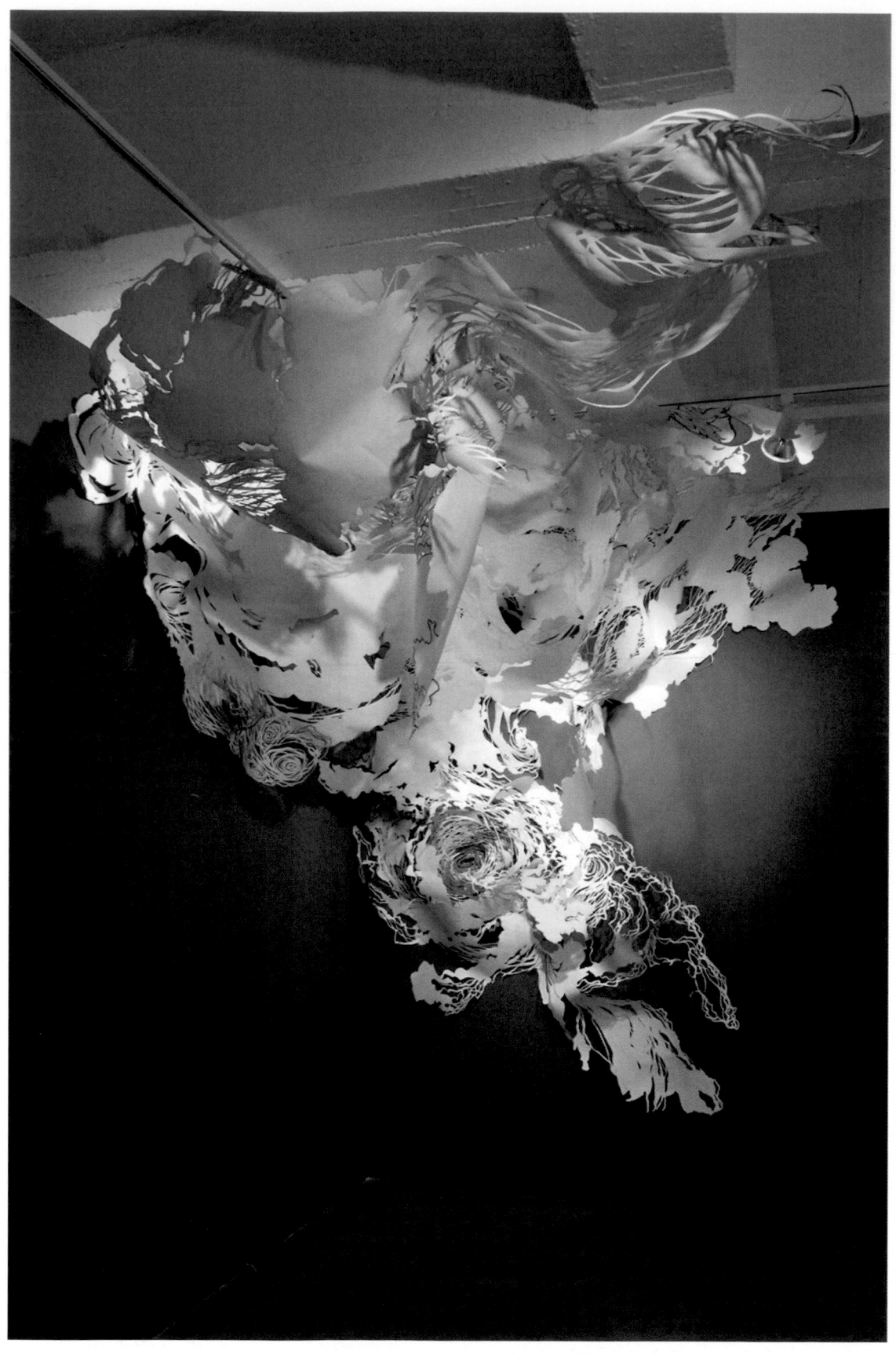

▲ 7.22 **MIA PEARLMAN,** *Eddy* (2008). Paper and India ink, 11' × 12.5' × 14'. Sears Peyton Gallery, New York, New York.

Mia Pearlman's complex, three-dimensional, cut-paper drawings (Fig. 7.22) begin with shapes rendered in India ink. Pearlman described her process in detail: "[after drawing the shapes] I cut out selected areas to create a new drawing, made of positive and negative space, on the reverse. Once they are pinned into a sculptural form, these forms create a drawing in space. And finally, their shadows produce a wholly new drawing on and around the three dimensional drawing."

In viewing Pearlman's drawings, we are ever mindful of her physical relationship to her medium and the meticulousness of her technique. It is quite the reverse in David Hockney's recent series of iPad drawings (Fig. 7.23) in which, as a critic noted, his touch is "at once present and absent." Sketched on what is now a ubiquitous device and printed in vibrant color, his method reminds us of the degree to which the process and character of drawings throughout the history of art have been driven by the technology available to the artist.

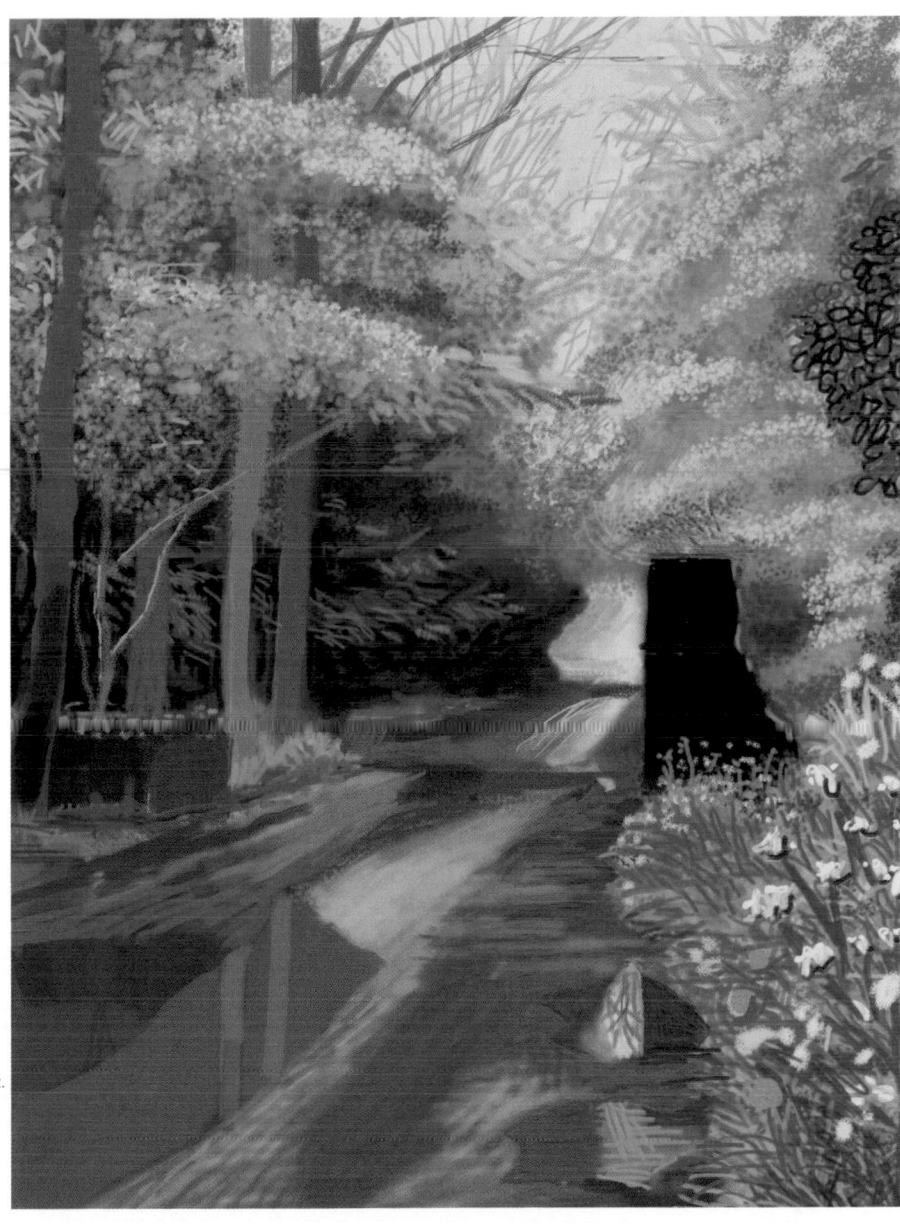

1 ft.

< 7.23 DAVID HOCKNEY, *The Arrival of Spring in Woldgate, East Yorkshire in 2011 (twenty-eleven)-11, May, 2011.* iPad drawing printed on paper, 55" × 41½".

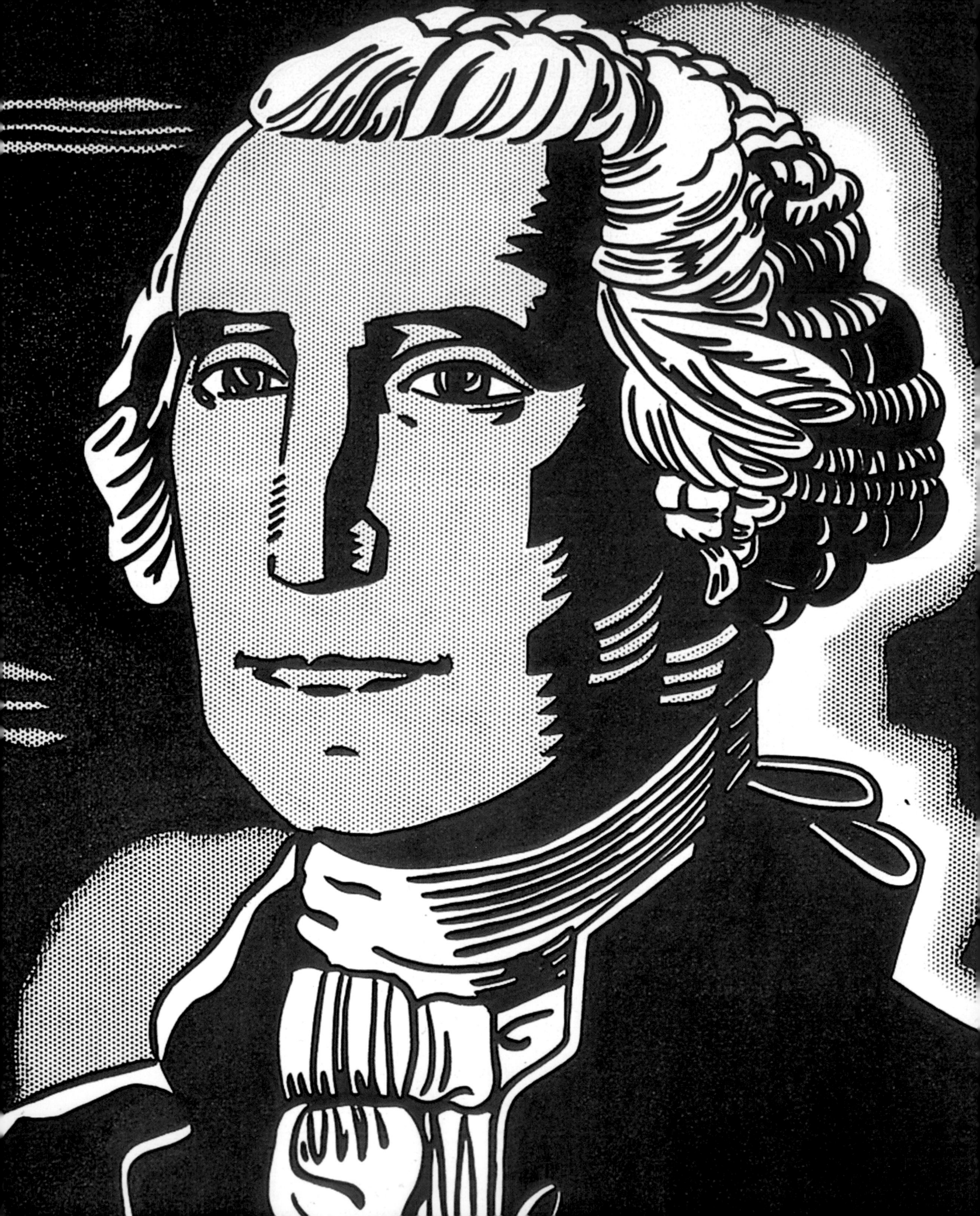

8

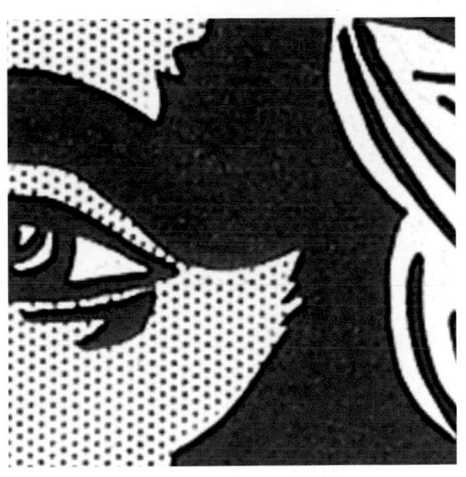

PAINTING

Suddenly I realized that each brushstroke is a decision. . . . In the end I realize that whatever meaning that picture has is the accumulated meaning of ten thousand brushstrokes, each one being decided as it was painted.

— ROBERT MOTHERWELL

Painting is concerned with all the ten attributes of sight; which are: Darkness, Light, Solidity and Colour, Form and Position, Distance and Propinquity, Motion and Rest.

— LEONARDO DA VINCI

A PAINTING is a work of art in which the primary aspect is liquid material applied to a surface with an implement. By that definition, Michelangelo's *Sistine Ceiling* and the fingerpaintings on newsprint that you once brought home to hang on the refrigerator fall into the same category, reminding us that the parameters of the medium of painting are indeed broad. Typically, that "liquid material" is pigment, the implement is a brush, and the surface is two-dimensional. As with drawing, there are almost no limits when it comes to the materials, tools, surfaces, and processes that will constitute a painting and the boundaries between the two are sometimes blurred.

‹ ROY LICHTENSTEIN, *George Washington* (1962).
Oil on canvas, 51" × 38".

> Just dash something down if you see a blank canvas staring at you. . . . You do not know how paralyzing it is, that blank staring of the canvas which says to the painter: You do not know anything.
>
> —VINCENT VAN GOGH

THE COMPONENTS OF PAINT

Paint is a liquid substance that converts to a solid film when applied to a surface. The color in paint comes from its pigment—granular solids in a wide chromatic range derived from chemicals and minerals found in plant and animal life, clay, soil, and sand. Pigment in its powdered form must be compounded with a binding agent, or **vehicle**, to adhere to a surface. The vehicle is a necessary component, but can consist of any number of substances including—but not limited to—wax, plaster, egg yolk, oil, acrylic, or water. To a large degree, characteristics of dried paint such as gloss or durability are connected to the nature of the vehicle.

The pliability or fluency of paint is a result of another component—medium. The medium is a liquid material such as water, turpentine, or other spirits used to dilute the paint for easier handling. As the paint dries, the medium evaporates and is no longer part of the solid paint film.

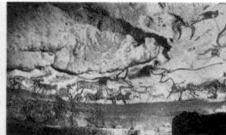

CONNECTIONS This wall painting was made in what is now France some 16,000 to 18,000 years ago.

▲ Hall of Bulls (Fig. 14.1)

surpassed their predecessors in their painting innovations. Much of what we know about Roman painting comes from the ruins of the great sites of Pompeii and Herculaneum, preserved amid the ash of the historic eruption of Mount Vesuvius. Most medieval murals were destroyed, but brilliant painted (illuminated) manuscripts survive and offer stylistic parallels to other painting of the era.

Painting, as we typically define it, came into its own during the Renaissance—the so-called Golden Age of painting. Although artists continued to paint **murals**, paintings on wood panels and on canvas exploded in

TYPES OF PAINTING

A variety of paints, surfaces, and tools have been used throughout the history of art to create paintings. In Chapter 14, you will see some of the first—Paleolithic paintings of animals on cave walls created with black pigment and red ocher that date back over 30,000 years. The ancient Egyptians painted on walls, sheets of papyrus, and linen. The Greeks were renowned for their vase painting, which gives us an idea of what their other paintings must have looked like. Although no paintings on wood panels survive from ancient Greece, we know from writings that it was a highly developed art form associated with artists who were famous for their techniques. Roman artists, who were very much influenced by the Greeks, nonetheless

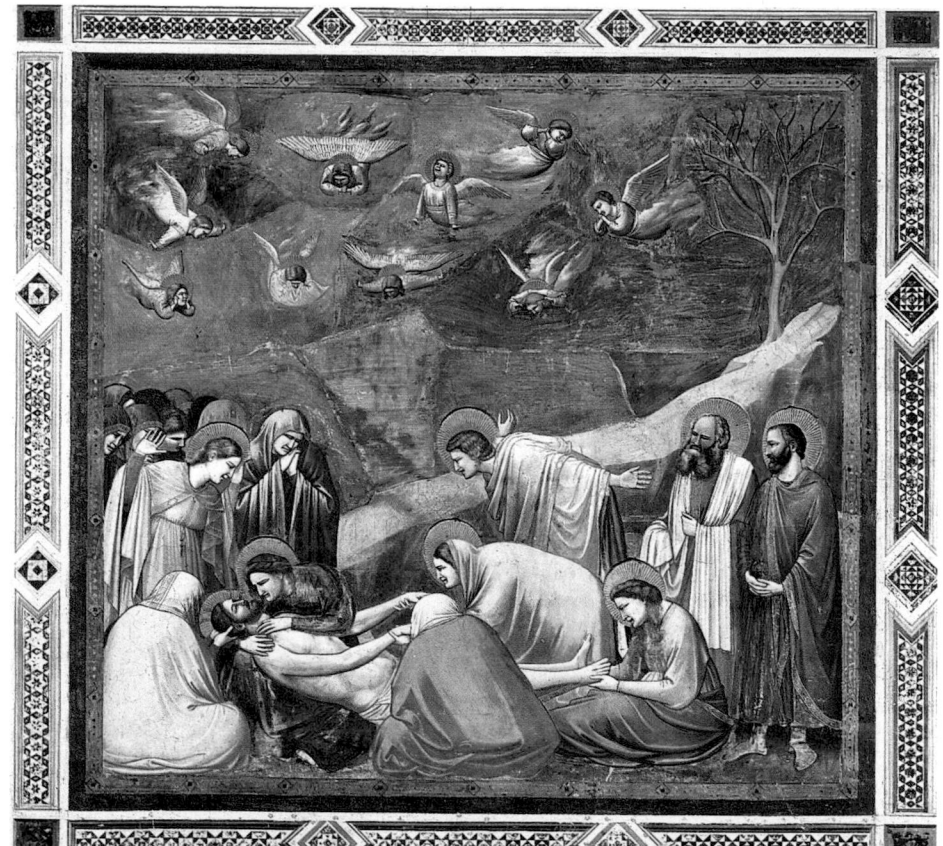

1 ft.

▲ 8.1 GIOTTO, *Lamentation* (c. 1305). Fresco, 7' 7" × 7' 9". Scrovegni Chapel, Padua, Italy.

> Remember that a picture—before being a horse, a nude, or some sort of anecdote—is essentially a flat surface covered with colors assembled in a certain order.
>
> —MAURICE DENIS

popularity, freeing the medium from its relationship to architecture. Paintings could be hung anywhere and moved anywhere, were much less expensive and time-consuming to produce, and could be bought and sold to a wide variety of patrons and clients.

Fresco

Fresco is the art of painting on plaster. **Buon fresco**, or true fresco, is executed on damp lime plaster; **fresco secco** is painting on dry plaster. In buon fresco, the pigments are mixed only with water, and the lime of the plaster wall acts as a vehicle. As the wall dries, the painted image on it becomes permanent. In fresco secco—a less permanent method—pigments are combined with a vehicle of glue that affixes the color to the dry wall.

Fresco painters encounter several challenges. Because in true fresco the paint must be applied to fresh, damp plaster, artists must work in small sections, preparing a surface that can be completed in a single day. The artist will try to arrange the sections so that the junctions will not be obvious, but sometimes it is not possible to do so. In a fourteenth-century Italian fresco painting by Giotto (Fig. 8.1), these seams—so to speak—are clearly evident, particularly in the sky, where the artist was not able to complete the vast expanse of blue all at once. In spite of this limitation, or because of it, fresco painting is often noted for its freshness and directness of expression. The sixteenth century art historian Giorgio Vasari wrote that of all the methods painters employ, fresco painting "is the most masterly and beautiful, because it consists in doing in a single day that which, in other methods, may be retouched day after day, over the work already done." Another challenge concerns chemistry. Although fresco paintings can be brilliant in color, some pigments will not form chemical bonds with lime. Thus, these pigments are

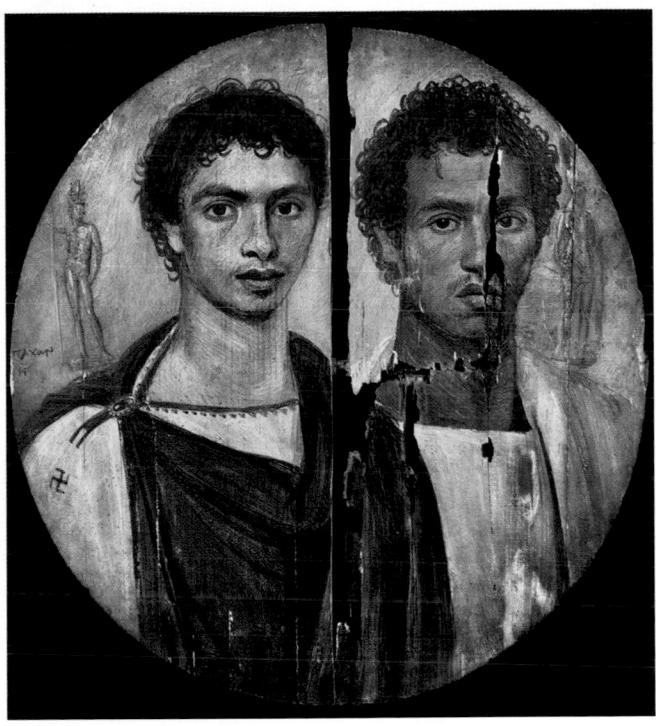

∧ 8.2 **Portrait of two brothers, from Sheikh Abada, Egyptian civilization** (Roman Empire, 2nd century). Encaustic painting on wood, 24" diameter. Egyptian Museum, Cairo, Egypt.

1 ft.

not suitable for the medium. Artists in Giotto's era, for example, encountered a great deal of difficulty with the color blue. Such lime resistance limits the artist's palette and can make tonal transitions difficult.

Despite these problems, fresco painting enjoyed immense popularity from its origins until its full flowering in the Renaissance. Although it fell out of favor for several centuries thereafter, Mexican muralists revived the art of fresco after World War I (see Diego Rivera's mural, Fig. 20.40).

Encaustic

One of the earliest painting techniques was **encaustic**, a mixture of ground pigments and a hot, molten wax vehicle applied to a prepared surface. The ancient Egyptians and Greeks tinted their sculpture and carvings with encaustic, imparting a lifelike appearance to the stone. The Romans applied encaustic to walls, using hot irons, and to wood panels covered with cloth, as in a portrait of two brothers from Sheikh Abada (Fig. 8.2) dating back to the second century CE. As evidenced by the startling realism and freshness of the piece, encaustic is an extremely durable medium whose colors remain vibrant and whose

CONNECTIONS In *The Last Supper*, the Renaissance artist and inventor Leonardo da Vinci attempted to surpass the limitations of fresco painting, only to suffer disastrous consequences. The experimental materials and methods he employed to achieve superior results were unsuccessful. He lived to see his masterpiece disintegrate beyond repair, at least until modern conservation and restoration techniques preserved what remained by his hand.

∧ Leonardo's *The Last Supper* (**Fig. 17.14**)

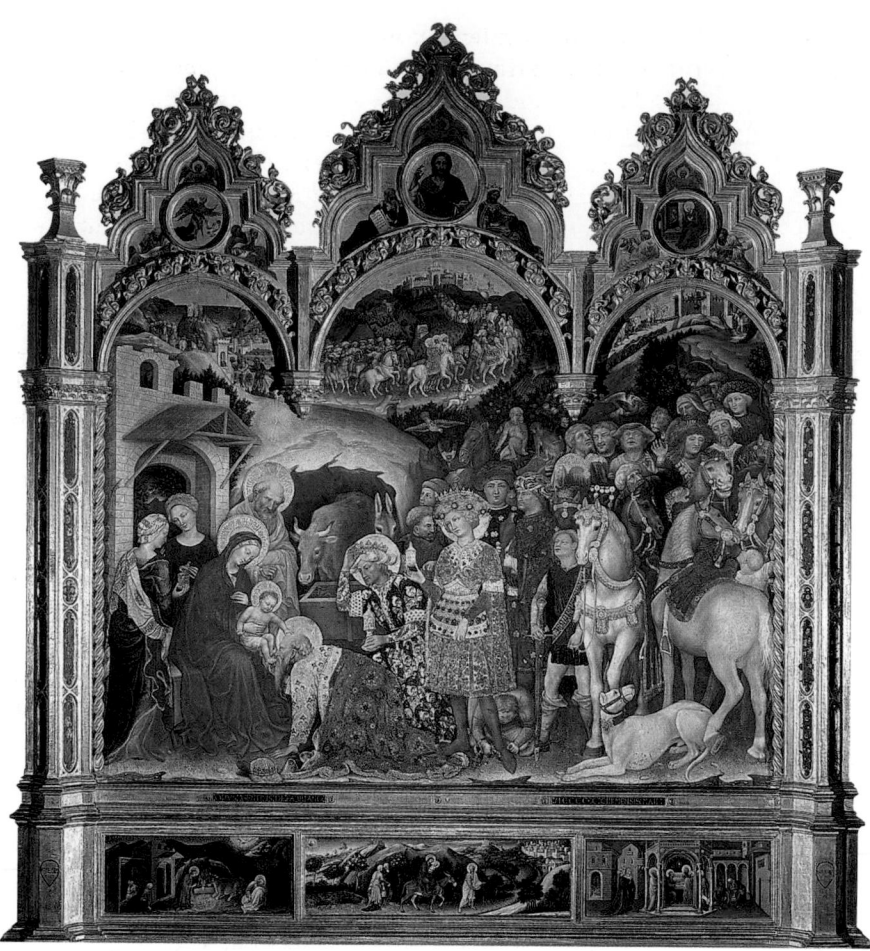

▲ 8.3 **GENTILE DA FABRIANO,** *Adoration of the Magi* (1423). Tempera on wood panel, 9' 10⅛" × 9' 3". Uffizi Gallery, Florence, Italy.

composition of tempera—ground pigments mixed with a vehicle of egg yolk or whole eggs thinned with water—is rarely used today. Tempera now describes paint in which pigment is combined with an emulsion of milk, different types of glues or gums, or the juices and saps of plants and trees.

When applied to a properly prepared surface, tempera was extremely durable. Wood panels and, later, canvas first were covered with **gesso**, a mixture of powdered chalk or plaster and animal glue that provided a smooth, white surface on which to apply the paint. Tempera has an advantage of drying quickly but, as a result, colors cannot be easily blended to provide subtle gradations of tone; the quick drying time also makes it difficult to rework passages of the painting. On the other hand, pure, brilliant colors were attainable and long lasting, and the consistency and fluidity of tempera paint allows for meticulous, precise brushwork. As can be seen in Gentile da Fabriano's *Adoration of the Magi* (Fig. 8.3), luminous reds and blues and pearly grays, along with the exquisite detail of the garments, yield an

surface maintains a hard luster. Encaustic is, however, difficult to manipulate, as the molten wax must be kept at a constant temperature. Perhaps for this reason, contemporary artists use it only rarely.

Tempera

Tempera, like encaustic, was popular for centuries. Its use dates back to the Greeks and Romans and was the exclusive technique of artists during the medieval era. Not until the development of oil painting in northern Europe in the 1300s did tempera fall out of favor. The traditional

CONNECTIONS Harlem Renaissance artist Jacob Lawrence frequently used tempera, as in *The Life of Harriet Tubman, No. 4.*

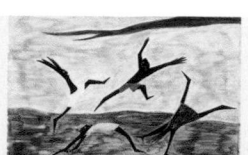

▲ Lawrence's *The Life of Harriet Tubman, No. 4* (Fig. 20.28).

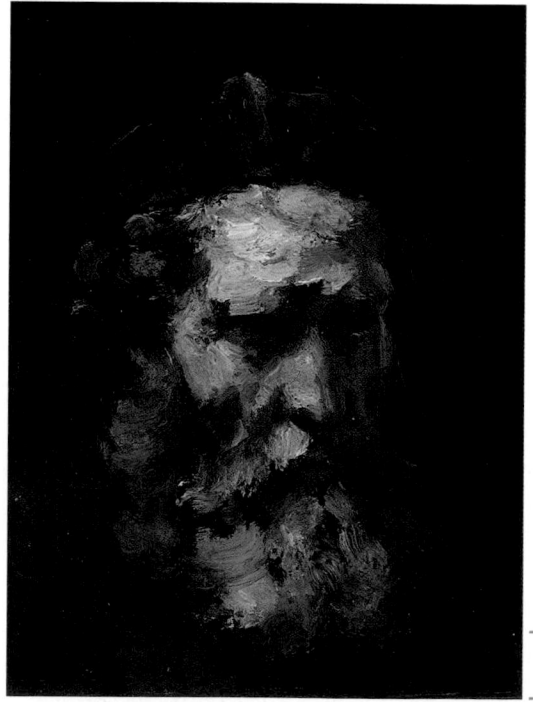

▲ 8.4 **FOLLOWER OF REMBRANDT VAN RIJN,** *Head of St. Matthew* (c. 1661). Oil on wood, 9⅞" × 7¾". National Gallery of Art, Washington, D.C.

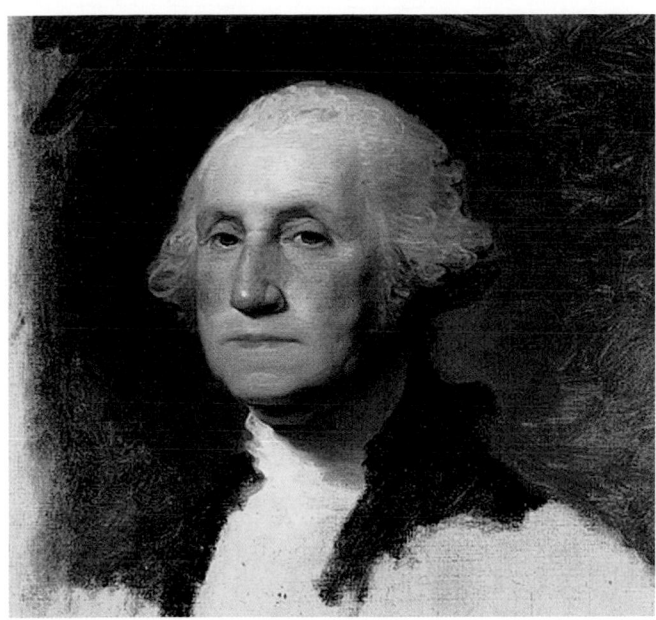

▲ 8.5 **GILBERT STUART**, *George Washington* (1796). Detail. Oil on canvas, 39⅝" × 34½" (entire work). Jointly owned by the Museum of Fine Arts, Boston, and the National Portrait Gallery, Washington D.C.

are barely evident, as in Ingres's *Grand Odalisque* (Fig. 19.7; see the nearby Connections feature). When considerably thinned and broadly brushed—or even poured—it can be used to create diaphanous fields of pulsating color, as in Helen Frankenthaler's *Before the Caves* (see Fig. 2.30). It can be applied with a palette knife or square-tipped, rough-bristled brush in thick layers or strokes (**impasto**) that assert the physical aspect of the material as well as the physical process of painting (see Fig. 8.4).

The versatility of oil paint is illustrated in portraits of George Washington by two American artists who worked centuries apart. Gilbert Stuart's iconic eighteenth-century portrait (Fig. 8.5)—the one on the U.S. dollar bill—is actually an unfinished work. Stuart created a realistic likeness through a fairly taut handling of the paint and well-placed areas of light and shadow that suggest roundness. His delicate treatment of Washington's pensive eyes and the firm outline of his determined jaw speak volumes about the personality traits of the wise and aging leader.

Roy Lichtenstein's contemporary portrait (Fig. 8.6), by contrast, is an image of glamour and success. Lichtenstein

opulent display of contrasting textures and sharp-focused realism. Although tempera is suited to painstaking detail, it is by no means used exclusively for paintings in the style of realism.

Oil

Oil paint consists of powdered pigments combined with a linseed oil vehicle and turpentine medium. Oil paint is naturally slow drying, but this property can be accelerated by the addition of various agents to the basic mixture.

The transition from tempera to oil painting was gradual. For many years following its introduction, artists used it only to apply a finishing coat—a glaze—over a tempera painting. Glazes are thin, transparent or semitransparent layers of oil tinted with color that impart a warm glow not possible with tempera alone. From the fifteenth century onward, oil painting became the standard, but artists such as Titian continued to use the glazing technique to create the illusion of subtly-modeled flesh in their paintings of the nude (see Fig. 17.24).

Oil painting's broad capability accounts for its popularity. Colors can be blended easily, offering a palette of almost limitless range. Slow drying facilitates the reworking of problem areas. It can be applied with an array of brushes or knives that will yield completely different effects. Smooth, fine bristles can capture the most intricate detail and render a smooth surface in which brushstrokes

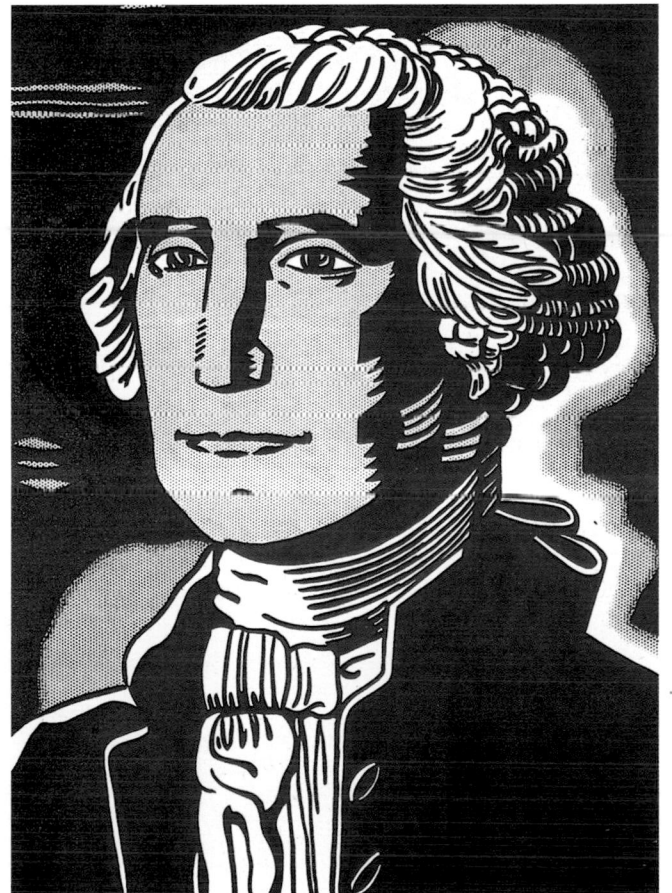

1 ft.

▲ 8.6 **ROY LICHTENSTEIN**, *George Washington* (1962). Oil on canvas, 51" × 38".

OIL AND ACRYLIC PAINTS often mimic each other in effects, but their idiosyncratic properties account for why one material may be chosen over the other for a specific painting. Why did Kenneth Noland use acrylic for his *Graded Exposure* (**Fig. 8.7**) and why did Karin Davie choose oil paint for *Between My Eye and Heart No. 12* (**Fig. 8.8**)?

Oil painting produces rich colors, but the pigment often fades and cracks over time. The drying time for oil paint is much longer than that of acrylic paint, conferring both advantages and disadvantages. A longer drying time means that artists can rework surfaces, blend colors, and apply glazes more smoothly. Also, even after oil paint is dry, it can be resuscitated with subsequent applications of turpentine mixtures. Acrylic, on the other hand, is a medium that dries quickly. The artist must work rapidly and, once the paint is dry, it cannot be resolubilized. Because of its drying time, acrylic is not conducive to color blending, but the upside is that sharply distinct zones of color can be created without the threat of colors blurring or running into each other.

Kenneth Noland was one of the pioneers of hard-edge Color Field painting in the 1960s. His *Graded Exposure* is composed of precisely delineated stripes or fields that represent abrupt transitions between variations on the color spectrum. Razor-sharp edges are achieved using tape lines and adjusting the acrylic medium so that each application dries quickly and will not leach into crevices between the tape and the canvas. The meticulous, glasslike, unbroken surface is free of gestural brushwork. The overall feeling is one of flatness, consistency, and control.

Karin Davie's oil-on-canvas painting *Between My Eye and Heart No. 12* appears to be the polar opposite of Noland's work. Lines loop around and over one another, nesting in the shallow pictorial space and pressing against the edges of the canvas. The artist's

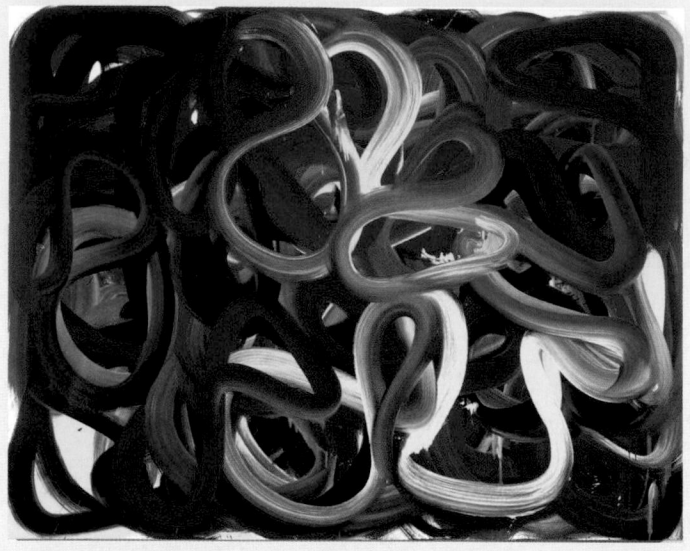

∧ **8.8 KARIN DAVIE,** *Between My Eye and Heart No. 12* (2005). Oil on canvas, 5' 6" × 7'. Margulies Warehouse Collection, Miami, Florida.

gesture is everywhere evident, though also precise in its parameters. A single brush of a specific width is used to produce all of the lines, and the palette is pretty much confined to red, yellow, and blue with some touches of white. The artist allows oil paint to do what it does best: blend. And it is the blending that adds dimension or volume to the lines. They aren't flat; they look more like tangled spaghetti. Variations in the overlapping hues also create a sense of space, with warm colors advancing and dark colors mostly receding.

Hard-edge painting can be done in oil, and color-blending certainly is seen in acrylic works. But Noland and Davie offer us excellent case studies in the specific capabilities of each medium.

∧ **8.7 KENNETH NOLAND,** *Graded Exposure* (1967). Acrylic on canvas, 7' 4¾" × 19' 1". Collection Mrs. Samuel G. Rautbord, Chicago, Illinois.

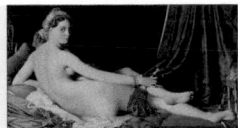
exploited oil paint's potential for clarity and precision, constructing the image with discrete lines and shapes and sharp contrasts of black and white. A younger, debonair Washington is presented as if on a campaign poster, or as a Marvel Comics hero with a classic chiseled profile. The mechanical quality of Lichtenstein's technique deprives the image of any subtlety, and deliberately so. Stylized shapes that sit flatly on the canvas replace the rich modeling that imparted a sense of roundness to Stuart's figure. Lichtenstein forsakes the psychological portrait, instead translating America's first president into a commodity.

Oil paint can be used to create the illusion of texture even as it is applied to a canvas in such a way as to create a smooth, glasslike finish. But oil paint also can be used to create actual texture—a surface that has its own tangible property and, by contrast, a dominant physical presence. In Arpita Singh's oil painting *Munna Appa's Kitchen* (Fig. 8.9), the brushstrokes are thick and brusquely applied, and the broken patches of pigment suggest movement—a departure from the "frozen moment." Singh mixes very little oil with her pigments so that the paint is thick and pasty (the technical term for this is impasto). She does not create an illusion of reality but, rather, concentrates our attention on another reality—that of the painted surface.

Acrylic

Acrylic paint is a mixture of pigment and a plastic vehicle that can be thinned with water. Unlike linseed oil, which tends to turn yellow or amber in time, the synthetic resin of the binder dries colorless and does not gradually compromise the brilliance of the colors. Also, unlike oil paint, acrylic is fast drying and can be used on a variety of surfaces that need no special preparation.

One of the few effects of oil paint that cannot be duplicated with acrylic paint is its delicate nuance of colors. Like oil, however, acrylic paint can be used thinly or thickly; it can be applied in transparent films or opaque impastos.

Watercolor and Gouache

The term **watercolor** was originally applied to any painting medium that employed water as a vehicle or medium. Thus, fresco and tempera, by definition, are watercolor processes. Ancient Egyptian artists used a form of watercolor in their paintings and it was also used extensively for manuscript illumination during the medieval period. Today watercolor refers to a specific technique called **aquarelle**, in which transparent films of paint are applied to a white, absorbent surface. Contemporary watercolors are composed of pigments and a gum arabic vehicle, diluted, of course, with a medium of water.

Transparent watercolor did not appear until the fifteenth century. It is a difficult medium to manipulate, despite its simple components. Tints are achieved by diluting the colors with various quantities of water. White, then, does not exist; white must be derived by allowing the white of the paper to "shine" through the color of the composition or by leaving areas of the paper exposed. To achieve the latter effect, all areas of whiteness must be mapped out with precision before the first stroke of color is applied.

With oil paint and acrylic, the artist is able to paint over areas of the canvas to make corrections or to blend colors. With transparent watercolors, painting over will obscure the underlying layers of color. For this reason, corrections are virtually impossible; the artist must plan ahead for the solids and void spaces that will be distributed on the paper. When used skillfully, as in Albrecht Dürer's *Great Piece of Turf* (see Fig. 8.10), watercolor can belie the difficulties of the medium and possess an unparalleled freshness and delicacy. The colors are pure and brilliant, and the range of effects surprisingly broad.

In Dürer's painting, confident strokes of color precisely define the shapes and textures of the blades

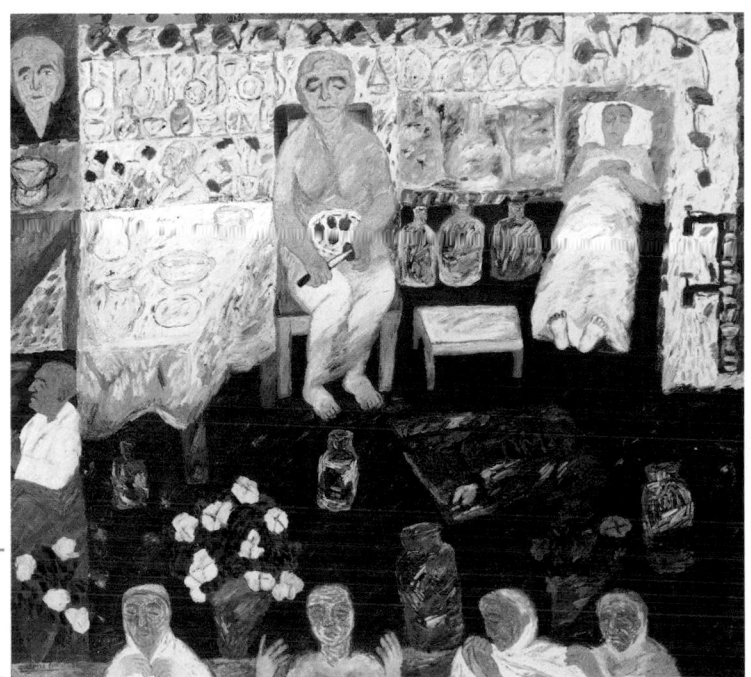

1 ft.

∧ 8.9 ARPITA SINGH. *Munna Appa's Kitchen* (1994). Oil on canvas, 60" × 66". Private collection.

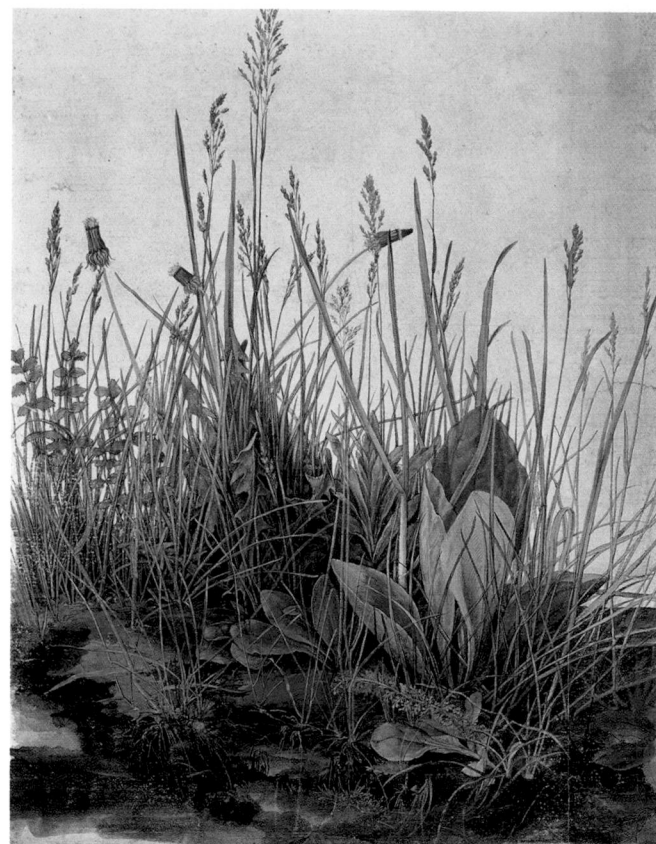

1 in.

∧ **8.10 ALBRECHT DÜRER,** *The Great Piece of Turf* (1503). Bodycolors, heightened with opaque white on vellum; 16 ¹⁄₁₆" × 12 ³⁄₈". Graphische Sammlung Albertina, Vienna, Austria.

and tufts of green and wash—transparent areas of diluted paint—are kept to a bare minimum. The broader appeal of watercolor, however, goes beyond the delicate manipulation of this unforgiving medium to thrill the eye with illusions. Paul Cézanne was enticed by the delicate fusion of colors made possible by the transparency of tinted washes (Fig. 8.11). As with the drawing medium of brush and wash, the effect is atmospheric. The edges of shapes are softened and they seem to merge with one

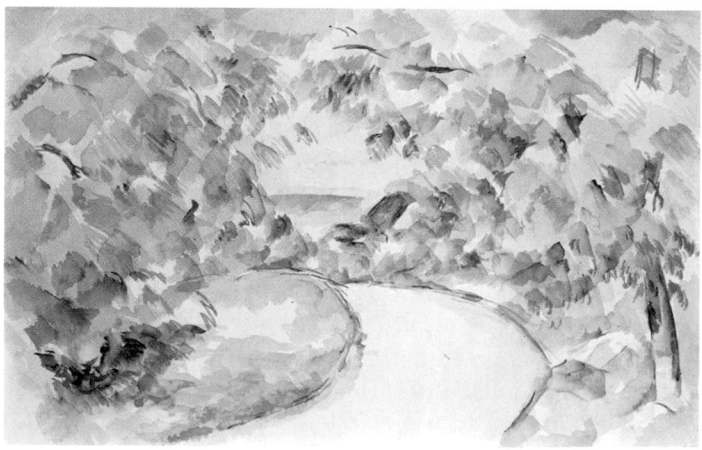

∧ **8.11 PAUL CÉZANNE,** *The Winding Road.* Watercolor on paper. Private collection.

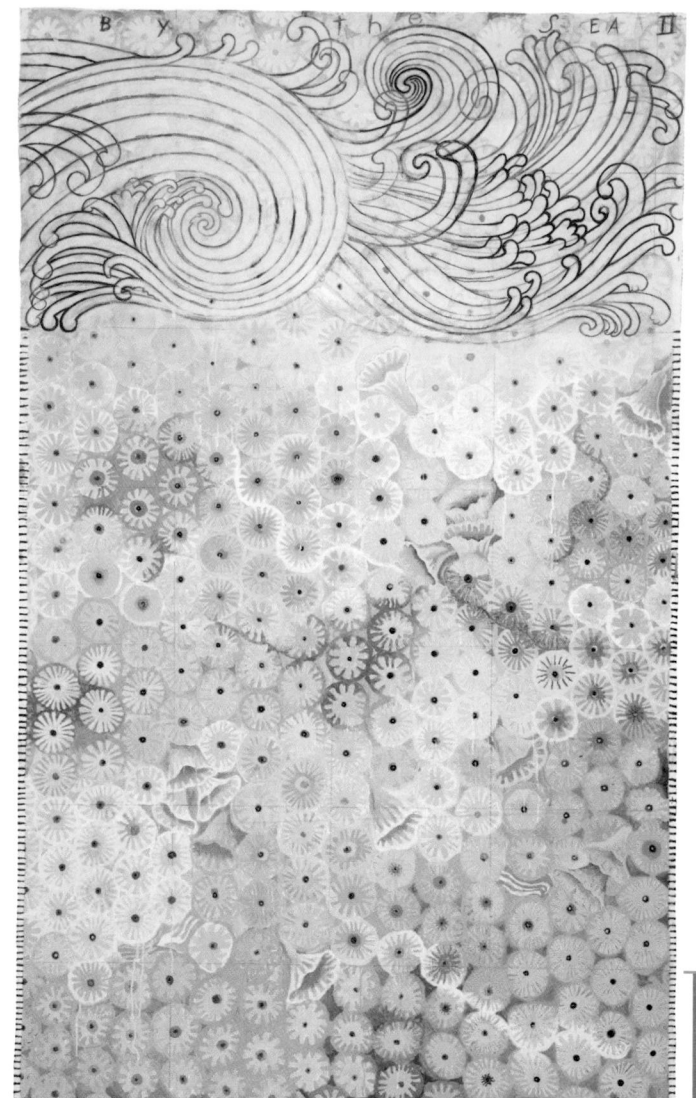

1 ft.

∧ **8.12 ROBERT ZAKANICH,** *By the Sea II* (2014). Gouache on paper, 84" × 50". Nancy Hoffmann Gallery, New York, New York.

another—and the surrounding space—imperceptibly. The composition is brightened by the white of the paper, which is brought forward to create shapes that are as visually assertive as those of color.

Gouache is watercolor mixed with a high concentration of vehicle and an opaque ingredient such as chalk and was the principal painting medium during the Byzantine and Romanesque eras of Christian art. This variation has enjoyed popularity across time and a myriad of styles and is used to great effect by many contemporary artists. Robert Zakanitch's *By the Sea II* from his *Hanging Gardens* series (Fig. 8.12) is a gouache-on-paper painting consisting of ornamental patterns of stylized blossoms and cresting waves. The delicacy of the palette and the matte finish of the gouache may have been inspired by painted porcelain objects that the artist saw while working in a ceramics factory in Sevres, France.

A CLOSER LOOK

Superheroes: East Meets West

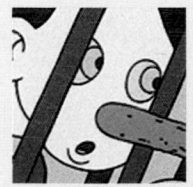

THE ACRYLIC PAINTINGS OF JAPANESE AMERICAN Roger Shimomura blend Western Pop Art with traditional Japanese imagery as found in *ukiyo-e* prints (see Kitagawa Utamaro's print, **Fig. 18.29**). As a child during World War II, Shimomura was interned with his parents and grandparents in Idaho. At the same time, ironically, his uncle served with the valiant 442nd division of Japanese Americans. Shimomura remembers statements made by white Americans about Japanese Americans during this deeply disturbing period. For example, Idaho's attorney general remarked, "We want to keep this a white man's country."

Shimomura's *Untitled* (**Fig. 8.13**) is at first glance an amusing clash of American and Japanese pop cultures. American cartoon characters such as Donald Duck, Pinocchio, Dick Tracy, and the combination Batman-Superman vie for space on the crowded canvas with Japanese samurai warriors and a contemporary Japanese portrait. The battle of East and West imagery may reflect the tensions within the artist regarding his ancestral roots and his chosen country. This is succinctly symbolized in the inclusion of Shimomura's self-portrait-as-Statue-of-Liberty in the extreme upper left. In this painting, conflicts between people and cultures are safely if not satirically played out among their stereotypes and myths.

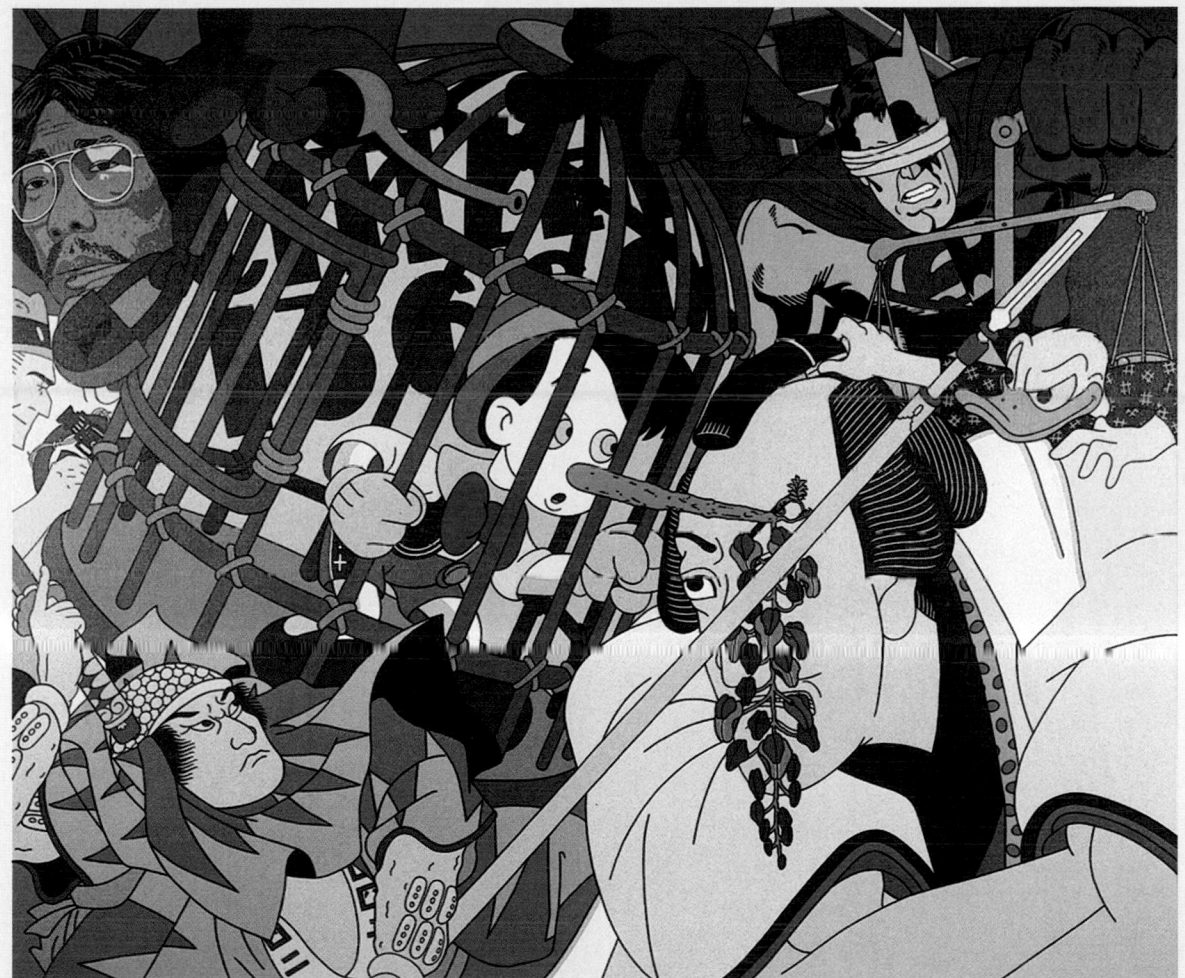

⌄ **8.13** ROGER SHIMOMURA, *Untitled* (1984). Acrylic on canvas, 60" × 72".

Spray Paint

The subtle coloration marking different species of animals on the walls of Paleolithic caves was probably achieved by blowing pigments onto a surface through hollowed-out reeds. Why are they there: decoration? ritual? history? Oddly enough, these questions can be asked of the contemporary graffiti artist and the thousands upon thousands of writings that range in definition from "tags" to "masterworks."

Everyone has seen graffiti, but the complexity of the work and the social atmosphere from which it is derived may not be common knowledge. Stylized signatures, or "tags," can be seen everywhere; it seems as though no urban surface—interior or exterior—is immune. Some are more likely to call this defacing public property than creating works of art, but how do we describe the elaborate urban "landscapes" that might cover the outside of an entire subway car, filling the space with a masterful composition of shapes, lines, textures, and colors? On the street, they are called masterworks, and their artists are indeed legendary.

Some graffiti writers have "ascended" to the art **gallery** scene, exchanging their steel "canvases" for some of fabric and their high-speed exhibition spaces for highbrow gallery walls. One such artist, Crash (or John Matos), created a parody of his own subway style in a complex canvas work called *Arcadia Revisited* (Fig. 8.14). All of the tools and techniques of his trade—commercial cans of spray paint, the Benday dots of comic-strip fame, the sharp lines of the tag writer's logos, the diffuse spray technique that adds dimensionality to an array of otherwise flat objects—are used to describe a violent clash of cultural icons that are fragmented, superimposed, and barely contained within the confines of the canvas.

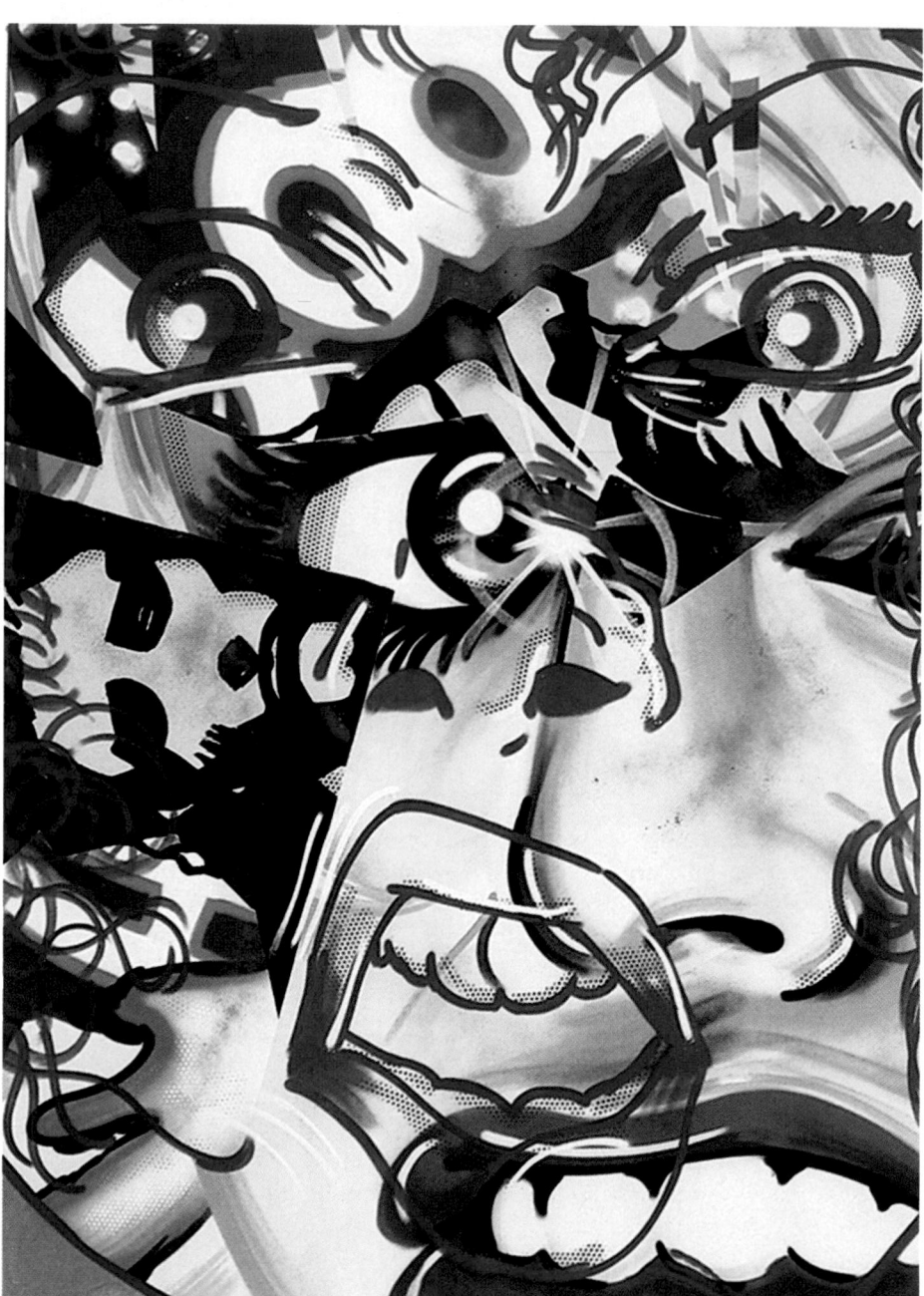

1 ft.

∧ 8.14 **CRASH (JOHN MATOS),** *Arcadia Revisited* (1988). Spray paint on canvas, 96¼" × 68".

MIXED MEDIA

Contemporary painters have in many cases combined traditional painting techniques with other materials, or they have painted on nontraditional supports, stretching the definition of what has usually been considered painting. For example, in *The Bed* (see Fig. 21.17), Pop artist Robert Rauschenberg splashed and brushed paint onto a quilt and pillow, which he then hung on a wall like a canvas work and labeled a "combine painting." The Synthetic Cubists of the early twentieth century, Picasso and Braque, were the first to incorporate pieces of newsprint, wallpaper, labels from wine bottles, and oilcloth into their paintings. These works were called *papiers collés* and have come to be called **collages**.

The base mediums for Howardena Pindell's *Autobiography: Water/Ancestors, Middle Passage/Family Ghosts* (Fig. 8.15) are tempera and acrylic, but the work,

> Painting is self-discovery. Every good artist paints what he is.
>
> —JACKSON POLLOCK

on sewn canvas, also incorporates an array of techniques and substances—markers, oil stick, paper, photo-transfer, and vinyl tape. The detail achieved is quite remarkable. The artist seems to float in a shimmering pool of shallow water, while all around her images and objects of memory seem to enter and exit her consciousness. Included among them are the prominent white shape of an African slave ship, a reference to Pindell's African ancestry, and the whitened face of the artist's portrait that may have been influenced by Michael Jackson's "Thriller" makeup. The work resembles as much a weaving as a painting, further reflecting the tapestry-like nature of human recollection.

Miriam Schapiro is best known for her paint and fabric constructions, which she has labeled "femmage," to

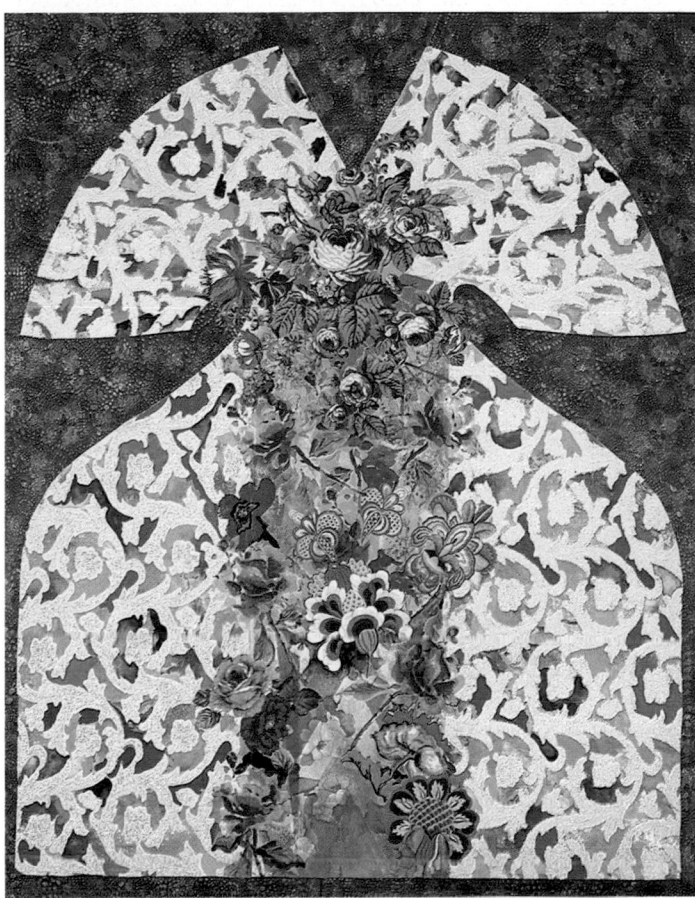

▲ 8.16 **MIRIAM SCHAPIRO**, *Maid of Honour* (1984). Acrylic and fabric on canvas, 60" × 50".

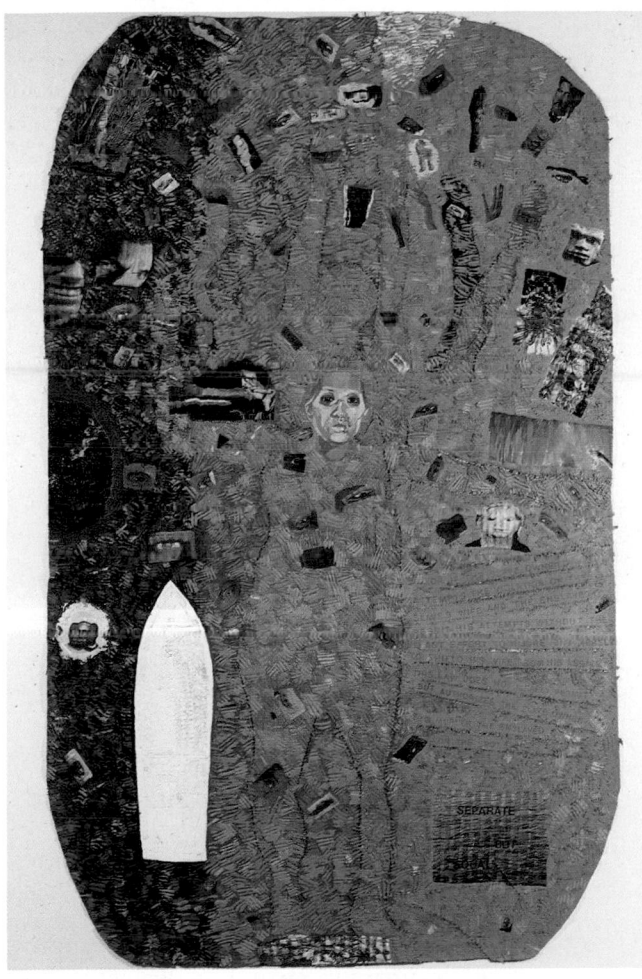

▲ 8.15 **HOWARDENA PINDELL,** *Autobiography: Water / Ancestors, Middle Passage / Family Ghosts* (1988). Acrylic, tempera, cattle markers, oil stick, paper, polymer photo-transfer, and vinyl tape on sewn canvas. 118" × 71". Wadsworth Atheneum, Hartford, Connecticut.

express what she sees as their unification of feminine imagery and materials with the medium of collage. In *Maid of Honour* (Fig. 8.16), Schapiro combines bits of intricately patterned fabric with acrylic pigments on a traditional canvas support to construct a highly decorative garment that is presented as a work of art. The painting is a celebration of women's experiences with sewing, quilting, needlework, and decoration.

The two-dimensional mediums we have discussed in Chapter 7 and in this chapter, drawing and painting, create unique works whose availability to the general public is usually limited to photographic renditions in books such as this. Even the intrepid museumgoer usually visits only a small number of collections. So let us now turn our attention to the two-dimensional medium that has allowed millions of people to own original works by masters—printmaking.

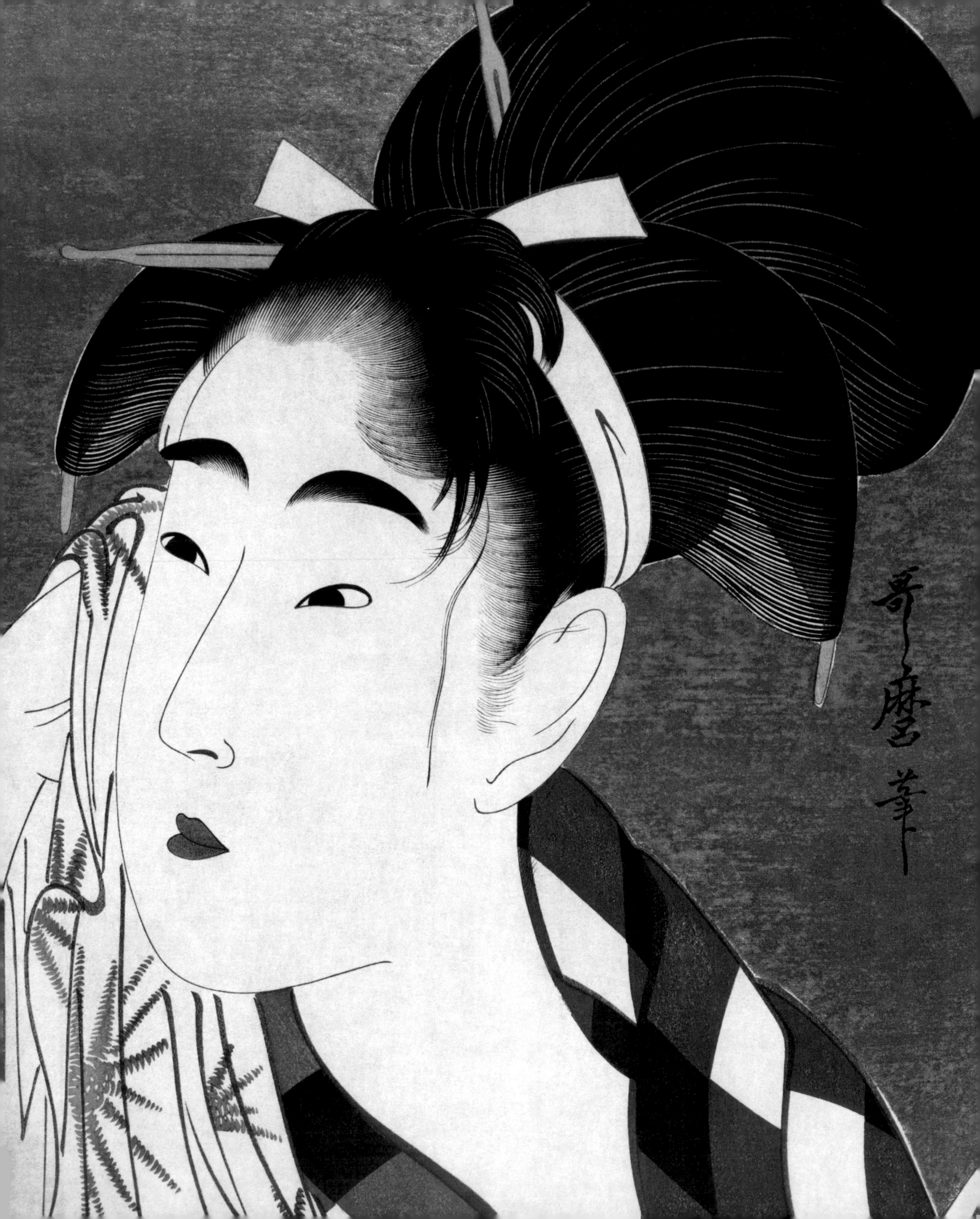

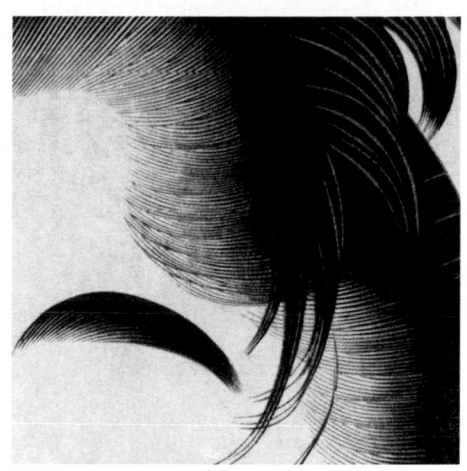

9

PRINTMAKING AND GRAPHIC DESIGN

In comparison with painting and sculpture, engraving is a cosmopolitan art, the immediate interrelation of different countries being facilitated by the portable nature of its creations.

— ARTHUR M. HIND

THE VALUE of drawings and paintings lies, in part, in their uniqueness. Hours, weeks, sometimes years are expended in the creation of these one-of-a-kind works. Printmaking permits the reproduction of these coveted works as well as the production of multiple copies of original prints. Printmaking is an important artistic medium for at least two reasons. First, it allows people to study great works of art from a distance. Second, because prints are less expensive than unique works by the same artist, they make it possible for the general public, not just the wealthy few, to own original works. With prints, art has become accessible. Like some drawings, however, prints not only serve a functional purpose but may also be considered works of art in themselves.

◄ KITAGAWA UTAMARO, *Woman Wiping Face* (1798). Ukiyo-e color woodblock print.

METHODS OF PRINTMAKING

The printmaking process begins with a design or image made in or on a surface by hitting or pressing with a tool. The image is then transferred to paper or a similar material. The transferred image is called the **print**. The working surface, or **matrix**, varies according to the printmaking technique. Matrices include wood blocks, metal plates, stone slabs, and silkscreens. There are special tools for working with each kind of matrix, but the images in printmaking are usually rendered in ink.

Printmaking processes are divided into four major categories: relief, intaglio, lithography, and serigraphy (Fig. 9.1). We will examine a variety of techniques within each of these processes. Finally, we will consider the monotype and the combining of printmaking media with other media.

Relief

In **relief printing**, the matrix is carved with knives or gouges. Areas that are not meant to be printed are cut below the surface of the matrix (Fig. 9.1A), and areas that form the image and are meant to be printed are left raised. Ink is then applied to the raised surfaces, often from a roller. The matrix is pressed against a sheet of paper, and the image is transferred. The transferred image is the print. Relief printing includes woodcut and wood engraving.

WOODCUT Woodcut is the oldest form of printmaking. The ancient Chinese stamped patterns onto textiles and paper using carved wood blocks. The Romans used woodcuts to stamp symbols or letters on surfaces for purposes of identification. During the 1400s in Europe, woodcuts provided multiple copies of religious images for worshipers. After the invention of the printing press, woodcut assumed an important role in book illustration.

Woodcuts are made by cutting along the grain of the flat surface of a wood block with a knife. As in *Family by the Lotus Pond* (Fig. 9.2), contemporary Chinese printmaker Zhao Xiaomo tightly controls the movement of his carving tools to create clean-cut

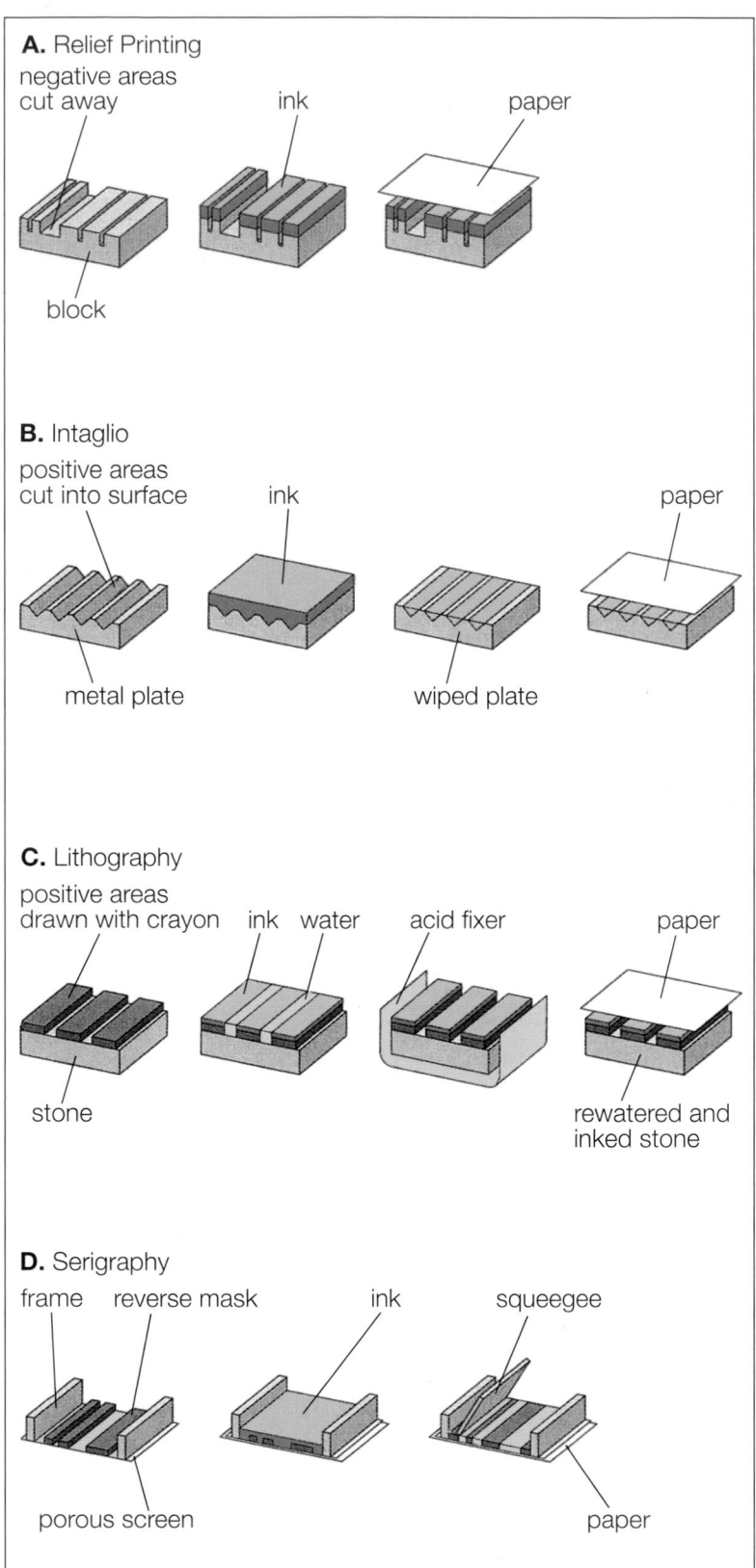

A. Relief Printing
negative areas cut away   ink   paper

block

B. Intaglio
positive areas cut into surface   ink   paper

metal plate   wiped plate

C. Lithography
positive areas drawn with crayon   ink water   acid fixer   paper

stone   rewatered and inked stone

D. Serigraphy
frame   reverse mask   ink   squeegee

porous screen   paper

▲ 9.1 **Printmaking Technologies.**

CONNECTIONS In *Sudden Shower over Shin-Ōhashi Bridge and Atake*, Ando Hiroshige, a nineteenth-century Japanese artist, used cleanly cut, uniform lines to define the steady rain and the individuals who tread huddled against the downpour across a wooden footbridge. Fine lines provide a delicate counterpoint to bold shapes and broad areas of color and create the illusion of a drawing.

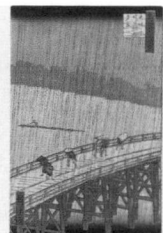

∧ Hiroshige's *Sudden Shower over Shin-Ōhashi Bridge and Atake* (Fig. 19.43)

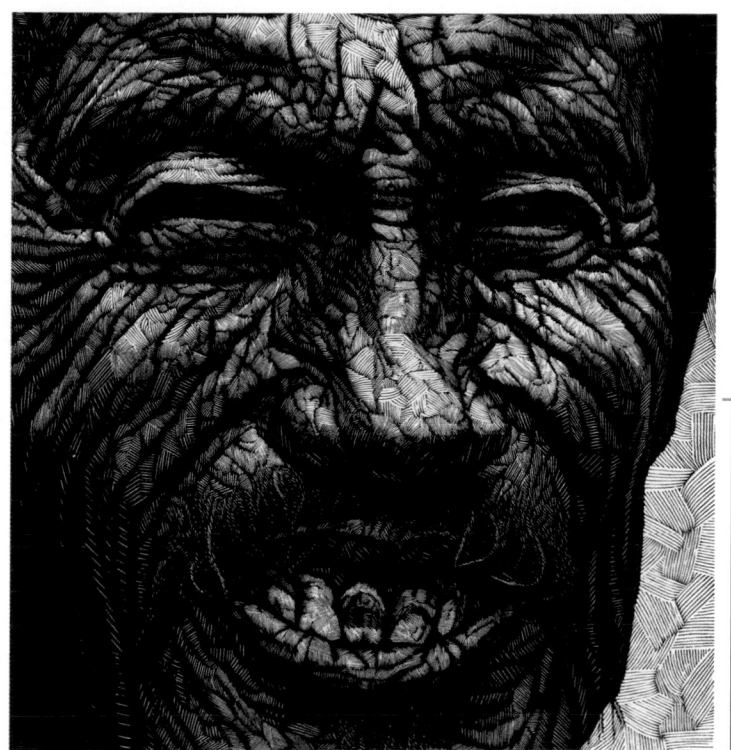

∧ **9.3 CHEN XUHAI,** *Golden Autumn* (1998). Woodcut, printed with oil-based ink; 25¼" × 24". The Art Institute of Chicago, Chicago, Illinois.

lines in close-grained wood. The result is the creation of woodblock prints with energetic compositions that often simulate oil paintings. Inspired by Chinese peasant paintings, as they are not bound by "academic rules," Xiaomo creates mosaic-like surfaces with bold, two-dimensional patterns.

Different types of wood and different gouging tools yield various effects. *Golden Autumn* (Fig. 9.3) by Chen Xuhai is a masterfully complex woodcut in which pockets of short lines of varying directions combine with long, velvet black crevices to create the signature landscape of an aging face.

WOOD ENGRAVING   The technique of **wood engraving** and its effects differ significantly from those of wood-cuts. Whereas in woodcuts the flat surface of a wood block is used, in wood engraving many thin layers of wood are **laminated**. Then the ends of these sections are planed flat, yielding a hard, nondirectional surface. In contrast to the softer matrix used for the woodcut, the matrix for the wood engraving makes it relatively easy to work lines in varying directions. These lines are **incised** or engraved with tools such as a **burin** or **graver** (Fig. 9.4), instead of being cut with knives and gouges. The lines can be extremely fine and are often used in close alignment to give the illusion of tonal gradations. This process was used to illustrate newspapers, such as *Harper's Weekly*, during the nineteenth century.

The razor-sharp tips of engraving implements and the hardness of the end-grain blocks make possible the

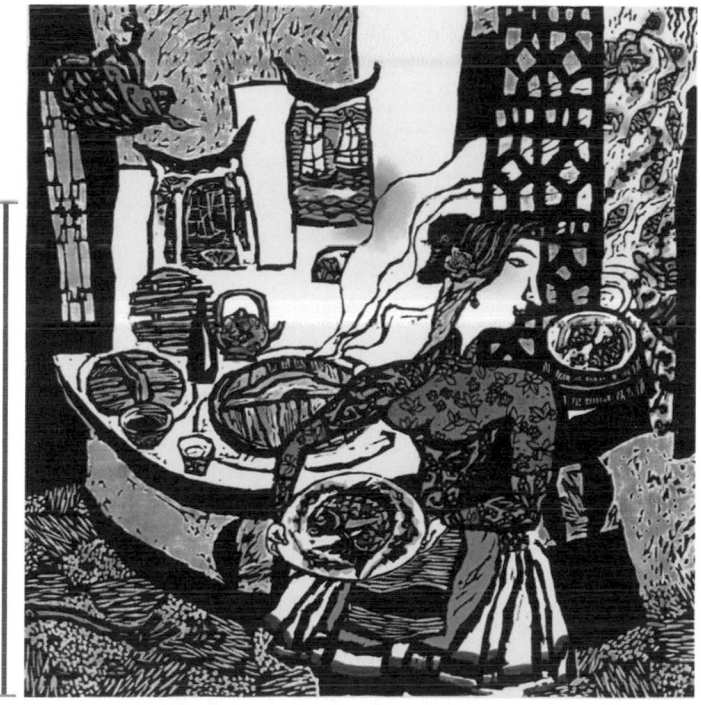

∧ **9.2 ZHAO XIAOMO,** *Family by the Lotus Pond* (1998). Multiblock woodcut printed with water-soluble ink, 16¾" × 16½". The Art Institute of Chicago, Chicago, Illinois.

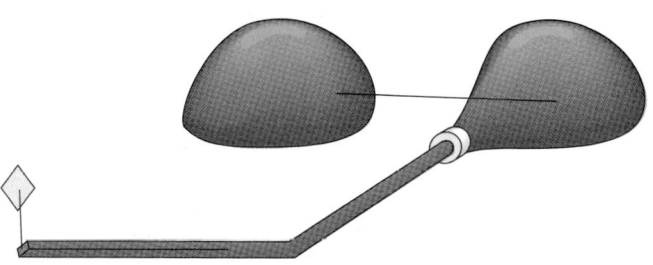

∧ **9.4 Burin.**

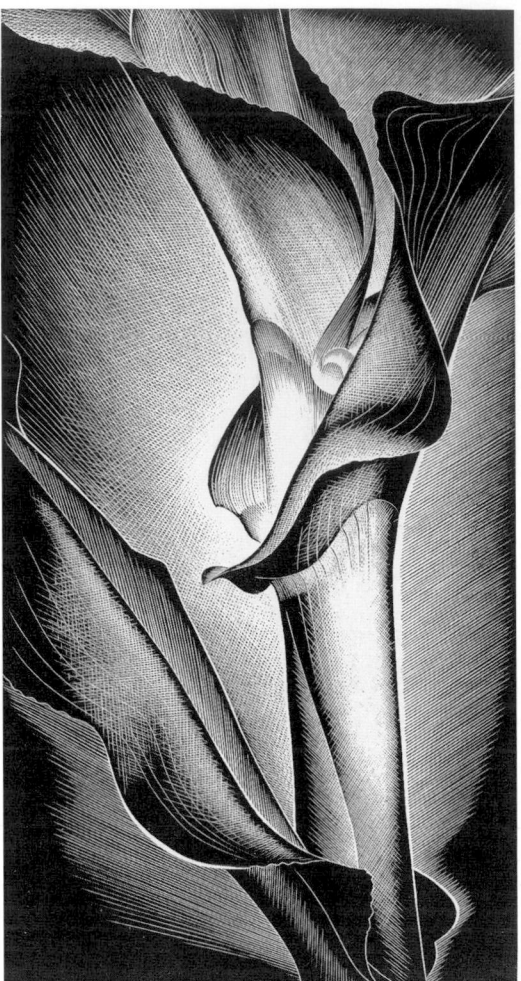

1 in.

Intaglio

The popularity of relief printing declined with the introduction of the **intaglio** process. Intaglio prints are created by using metal plates into which lines have been incised. The plates are covered with ink, which is forced into the linear depressions, and then the surface is carefully wiped. The cut depressions retain the ink, whereas the flat surfaces are clean. Paper is laid atop the plate, and then paper and plate are passed through a printing press, forcing the paper into the incised lines to pick up the ink, thereby accepting the image. In a reversal of the relief process, then, intaglio prints are derived from designs or images that lie *below* the surface of the matrix (Fig. 9.1B).

Intaglio printing encompasses many different media, the most common of which are engraving, drypoint, etching, and mezzotint and aquatint. Some artists have used these techniques recently in interesting variations or combinations and have pioneered approaches using modern equipment such as the camera and computer.

ENGRAVING   Although **engraving** has been used to decorate metal surfaces such as bronze mirrors or gold and silver drinking vessels since ancient times, the earliest engravings printed on paper did not appear until the fifteenth century. In engraving, the artist creates clean-cut lines on a plate of copper, zinc, or steel, forcing the sharpened point of a burin across the surface with the heel of the hand. Because the lines are transferred to paper under very high pressure, they not only reveal the ink from the grooves but have a ridgelike texture that can be felt by running a finger across the print.

exacting precision found in wood engravings such as that by Paul Landacre (Fig. 9.5), a well-known twentieth-century American printmaker. Tight, threadlike, parallel, and crosshatched lines compose the tonal areas that define the form. The rhythmic, flowing lines of the seedling's unfurling leaves contrast dramatically with the fine, prickly lines that emanate like rays from the young corn plant. The print is a display of technical prowess in a most demanding and painstaking medium.

▷ 9.6 ANTONIO POLLAIUOLO, *Battle of Ten Naked Men* (c. 1465–1470). Engraving, 15½" × 23³⁄₁₆". The Metropolitan Museum of Art, New York, New York.

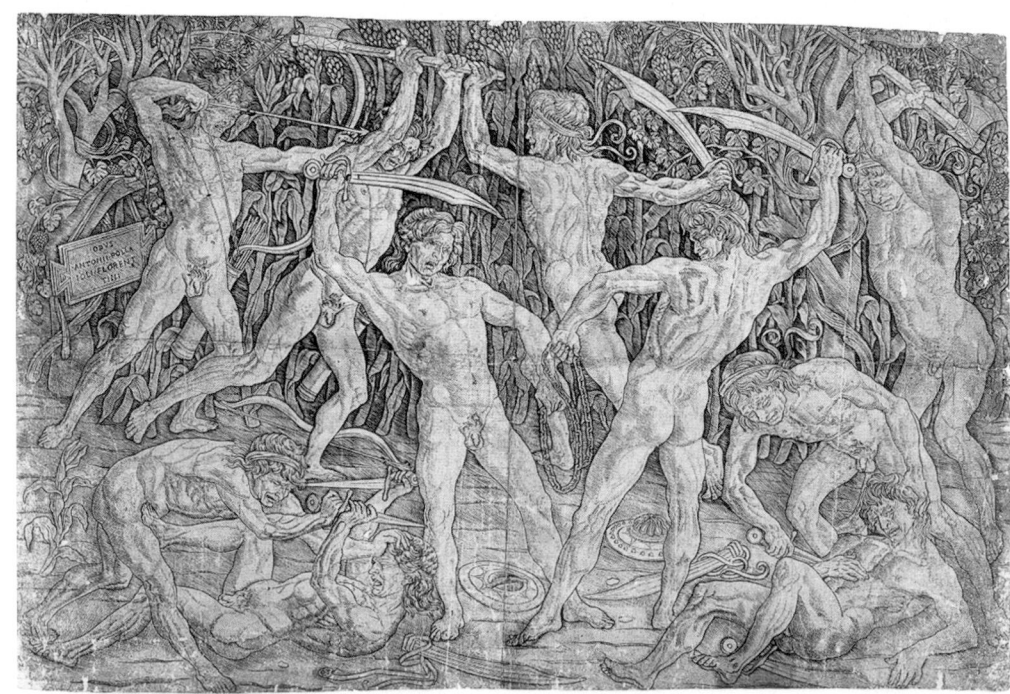

1 in.

> What I am after, above all, is expression.
>
> —HENRI MATISSE

An early, famous engraving came from the hand of the fifteenth-century Italian painter Antonio Pollaiuolo (Fig. 9.6). Deep lines that hold a greater amount of ink define the contours of the ten fighting figures. As Landacre did, Pollaiuolo used parallel groupings of thinner and thus lighter lines to render the tonal gradations that define the exaggerated musculature. The detail of the print is described with the utmost precision, revealing the artist's painstaking mastery of the burin.

DRYPOINT **Drypoint** is engraving with a simple twist. In drypoint, a needle is dragged across the surface, and a metal burr, or rough edge, is left in its wake to one side of the furrow. The burr retains particles of ink, creating a softened rather than crisp line when printed. The burr sits above the surface of the matrix and therefore is fragile. After many printings, it will break down, resulting in a line that simply looks engraved.

The characteristic velvety appearance of drypoint lines is seen in Rembrandt's *Christ Crucified between the Two Thieves* (Fig. 9.7). The more distinct lines were rendered with a burin, whereas the softer lines were created with a drypoint needle. Rembrandt used the blurriness of the drypoint line to enhance the sense of chaos attending

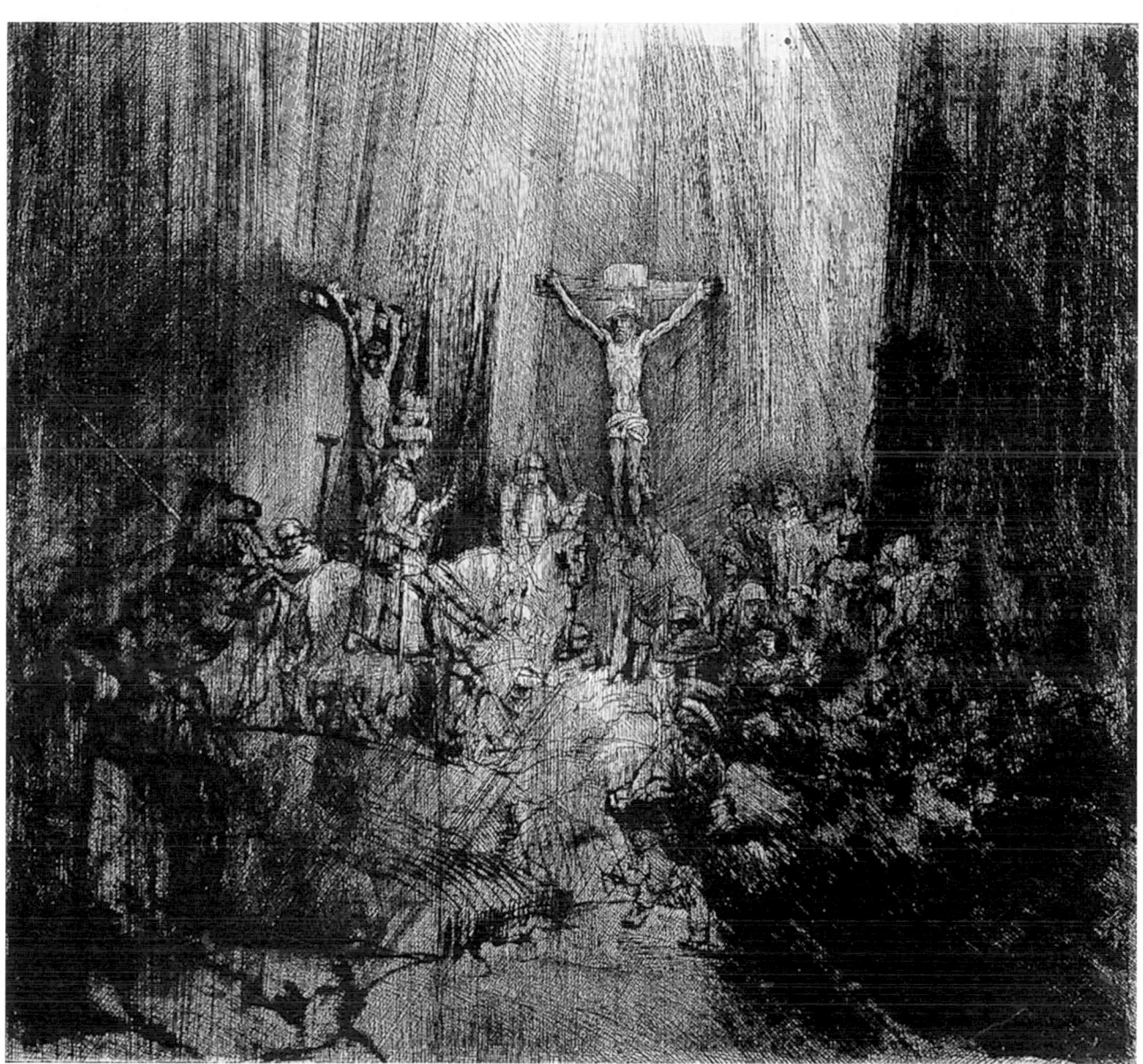

1 in.

▲ 9.7 REMBRANDT VAN RIJN, *Christ Crucified between the Two Thieves* (1653). Drypoint, 4th state; 15" × 17½". Museum of Fine Arts, Boston, Massachusetts.

the Crucifixion and the darkness of the encroaching storm. Lines fall like black curtains enshrouding the crowd, and rays of bright light illuminate the figure of Jesus and splash down onto the spectators.

ETCHING Although they are both intaglio processes, **etching** differs from engraving in the way the lines are cut into the matrix. With engraving, the depth of the line corresponds to the amount of force used to push or draw an implement over the surface. With etching, minimal pressure is exerted to determine the depth of line. A chemical process does the work. In etching, the metal plate is covered with a liquid, acid-resistant ground consisting of wax or resin. When the ground has hardened, the image is drawn upon it with a fine needle. Little pressure is exerted to expose the ground; the plate itself is not scratched. When the drawing is completed, the matrix is slipped into an acid bath, which immediately begins to eat away, or etch, the exposed areas of the plate. This etching process yields the sunken line

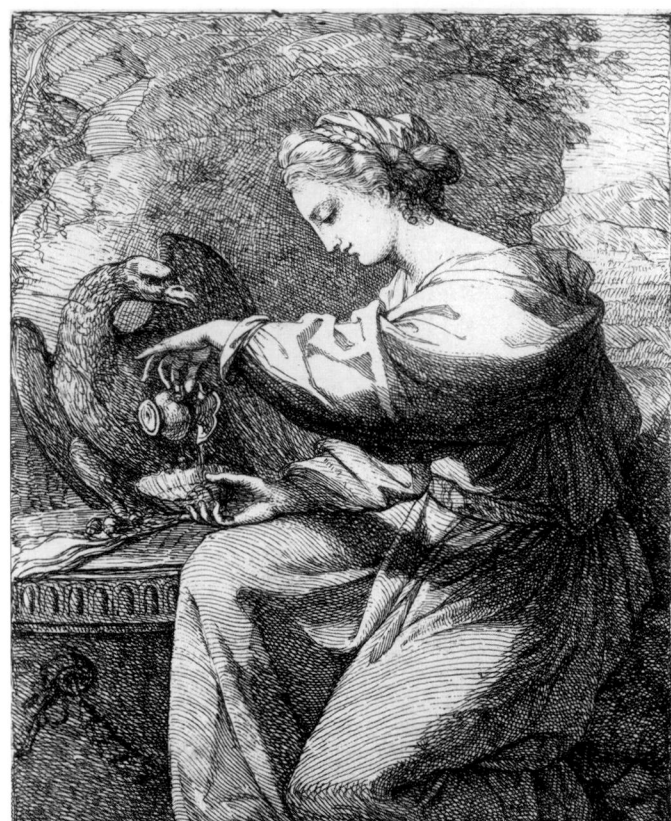

▲ 9.9 ANGELICA KAUFFMANN, *Hebe* (1770). Etching, 8⅛" × 6½".

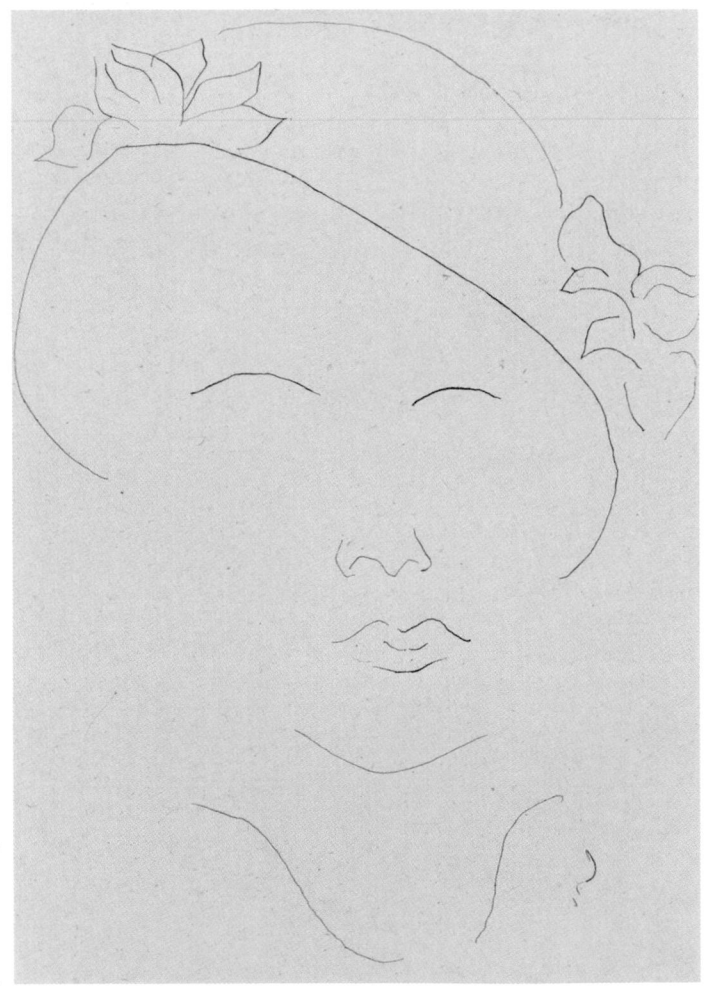

▲ 9.8 HENRI MATISSE, *Loulou Distracted* (1914). Etching, printed in black; 7⅟₁₆" × 5". Archives Matisse, Paris, France.

that holds the ink. The artist leaves the plate in the acid solution just long enough to achieve the desired depth of line. If a variety of tones is desired, the artist may pull the plate out of the acid solution after a while, cover lines of sufficient depth with the acid-resistant ground, and replace the plate in the bath for further etching of the remaining exposed lines. The longer the plate remains in the acid solution, the deeper the etching. Deeper crevices hold more ink, and for this reason they print darker lines.

Etching is a versatile medium, capable of many types of lines and effects. The modern French painter Henri Matisse used but a few dozen uniformly etched lines to describe the essential features of a woman, *Loulou Distracted* (Fig. 9.8). The extraordinarily simple, yet complete image attests to the delicacy that can be achieved with etching.

Whereas Matisse's figure takes shape through the careful placement of line, in Angelica Kauffmann's *Hebe* (Fig. 9.9), crisscross patterns of closely sketched lines—**crosshatching**—create a sense of volume in areas that might otherwise appear flat. A full spectrum of value—from bright white to velvety black—is captured through the varying density of line, differentiating hair from skin, cloth from feathers, foliage from rock, figure from ground.

A CLOSER LOOK

Hung Liu: Chinese Traditions Unbound

IN MANY WAYS, HUNG LIU (B. 1948) epitomizes the concerns and preoccupations of the Chinese artist whose life experiences during that country's Cultural Revolution have shaped their art—indeed, their very existence. In 1984, Hung Liu arrived in the United States. In her words, with her "Five-thousand-year-old culture on my back. Late-twentieth-century world in my face. . . . My Alien number is 28333359." For four years in her country of origin, she was forced to work in the fields. In her chosen country, she is now a professor at Mills College and has had one-woman shows in New York, San Francisco, Texas, and Miami. Her art focuses on what she has called "the peculiar ironies which result when ancient Chinese images are 'reprocessed' within contemporary Western materials, processes, and modes of display."

Figure 9.10 shows an untitled mixed-media print, whose main image consists of a photo-etching onto which are affixed small rectangular wooden blocks—mahjong pieces—bearing the "high-fashion" portraits of Chinese women. The inspiration for this print came from a series of photographs of Chinese prostitutes from the early 1900s that Hung Liu discovered on a recent return trip to China. When the Communist revolution took hold and all able-bodied individuals were forced into labor, these women were forced into prostitution because the tradition of oppression that led to the practice of binding their feet made them unfit for physical toil. They could barely walk.

Hung Liu feels the need to make known the pain, suffering, and degradation of generations of women before her:

> Although I do not have bound feet, the invisible spiritual burdens fall heavy on me. . . . I communicate with the characters in my paintings, prostitutes—these completely subjugated people—with reverence, sympathy, and awe. They had no real names. Probably no children. I want to make up stories for them. Who were they? Did they leave any trace in history?

In Hung Liu's work, we come to understand a piece of history. We are challenged to reflect, as she does, upon human rights and freedoms, spiritual and physical oppression, political oppression, and silenced voices.

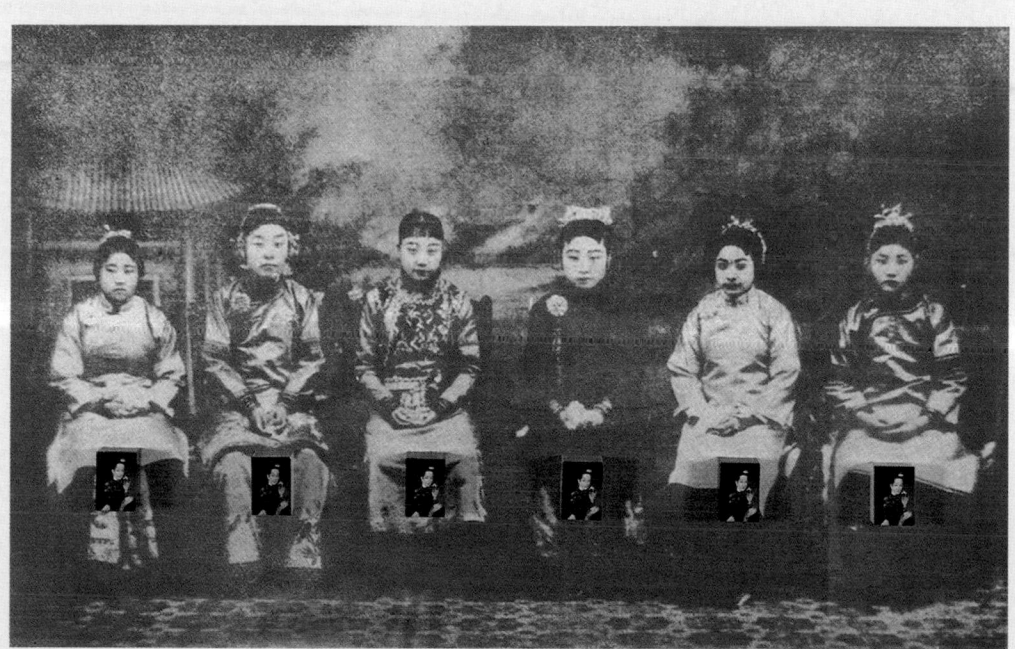

> **9.10 HUNG LIU, *Untitled*** (1992). Photo-etching, mixed media; 33" × 22½".

1 ft.

> The artist is a receptacle for the emotions that come from all over the place: from the sky, from the earth, from a scrap of paper, from a passing shape, from a spider's web.
>
> — PABLO PICASSO

MEZZOTINT AND AQUATINT Engraving, drypoint, and etching are essentially linear media. With these techniques, designs or images are created by cutting lines into a plate. The illusion of tonal gradations is achieved by altering the number and concentration of lines. Sometime in the mid-seventeenth century, the Dutchman Ludwig von Siegen developed a technique whereby broad tonal areas could be achieved by nonlinear engraving, that is, engraving that does *not* depend on line. The medium was called **mezzotint**, from the Italian word meaning "half tint."

With mezzotint engraving, the entire metal plate is worked over with a curved, multitoothed implement called a **hatcher**. The hatcher is "rocked" back and forth over the surface, producing thousands of tiny pits that will hold ink. If printed at this point, the plate would yield an allover consistent, velvety black print. But the mezzotint engraver uses this evenly pitted surface as a point of departure. The artist creates an image by gradually scraping and burnishing the areas of the plate that are meant to be lighter. These areas will hold less ink and therefore will produce lighter tones. The more persistent the scraping, the shallower the pits and the lighter the tone. A broad range of tones is achieved as the artist works from the rich black of the rocked surface to the highly polished pitless areas that will yield bright whites. Mezzotint is a rarely used, painstaking, and time-consuming procedure.

The subtle tonal gradations achieved by the mezzotint process can be duplicated with a much easier and quicker etching technique called **aquatint**. In aquatint, a metal plate is evenly covered with a fine powder of acid-resistant resin. The plate is then heated, causing the resin to melt and adhere to the surface. As in line etching, the matrix is placed in an acid bath, where its uncovered surfaces are eaten away by the solution. The depth of tone is controlled by removing the plate from the acid and covering the pits that have been sufficiently etched.

Aquatint is often used in conjunction with line etching and is frequently manipulated to resemble tones produced by wash drawings. In *The Painter and His Model* (Fig. 9.11), Pablo Picasso brought the forms out of void space by defining their limits with dynamic patches of aquatint. These tonal areas resemble swaths of ink typical of wash drawings. Descriptive details of the figures are rendered in fine or ragged lines, etched to varying depths.

OTHER ETCHING TECHNIQUES Different effects may also be achieved in etching by using grounds of different substances. **Soft-ground etching**, for example, employs a ground of softened wax and can be used to render the effects of crayon or pencil drawings. In a technique called **lift-ground etching**, the artist creates the illusion of a brush-and-ink drawing by actually brushing a solution of sugar and water onto a resin-coated plate.

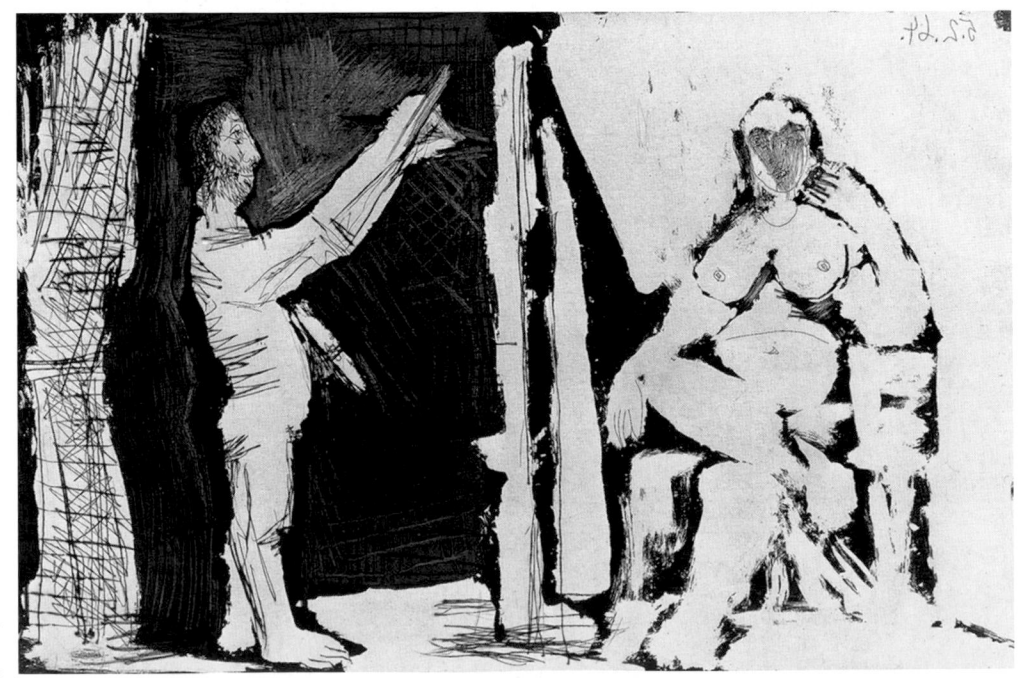

1 in.

< **9.11** PABLO PICASSO, *The Painter and His Model* (1964). Etching and aquatint, 12⅝" × 18½". Museum of Fine Arts, Boston, Massachusetts.

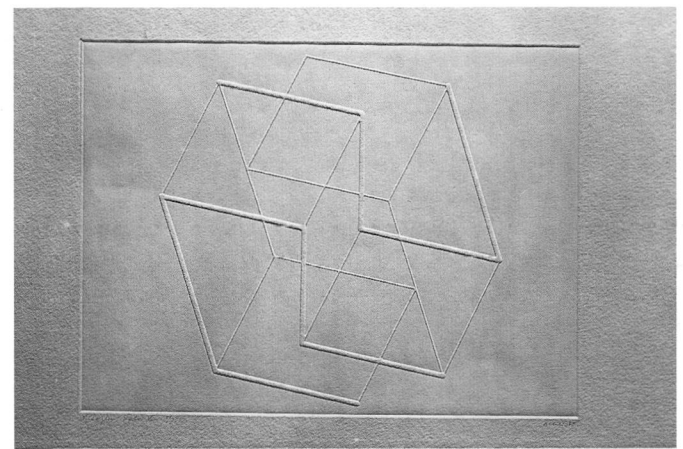

▲ 9.12 **JOSEF ALBERS**, *Solo V* (1958). Inkless intaglio, 6⅝" × 8⅝". The Brooklyn Museum, Brooklyn, New York.

When the plate is slipped into the acid bath, the sugar dissolves, lifting the brushed image off the plate to expose the metal beneath. As in all etching media, these exposed areas accept the ink.

Given that the printing process implies the use of ink to produce an image, can we have prints without ink? The answer is yes—with the medium called **gauffrage**, or inkless intaglio. Josef Albers, a twentieth-century American abstract artist, created *Solo V*, the geometric image shown in Figure 9.12, by etching the lines of his design to two different depths. Furrows in the plate appear as raised surfaces when printed. We seem to feel the image with our eyes, as light plays across the surface of the paper to enhance its legibility. Perceptual shifts occur as the viewer focuses now on the thick, now on the thin lines. In trying to puzzle out the logic of the form, the viewer soon discovers that Albers has offered a frustrating illustration of "impossible perspective."

Lithography

Lithography was invented at the dawn of the nineteenth century by the German playwright Aloys Senefelder. Unlike relief and intaglio printing, which rely on cuts in a matrix surface to produce an image, the lithography matrix is flat. Lithography is a surface or **planographic printing** process (Fig. 9.1C).

➤ 9.13 **WANG GUANGYI**, *Great Criticism: Coca-Cola* (1990–1992). Lithograph, 28¾" × 27⅛".

In lithography, the artist draws an image with a greasy crayon directly on a flat stone slab. Bavarian limestone is considered the best material for the slab. Sometimes a specially sensitized metal plate is used, but a metal surface will not produce the often-desired grainy appearance in the print. Small particles of crayon adhere to the granular texture of the stone matrix. After the design is complete, a solution of nitric acid is applied as a fixative. The entire surface of the matrix is then dampened with water. The untouched areas of the surface accept the water, but the waxy crayon marks repel it.

A roller is used to cover the stone with an oily ink. This ink adheres to the crayon drawing but repels the water. When paper is pressed to the stone surface, the ink on the crayon is transferred to the paper, revealing the image. Different lithographic methods yield different results. Black crayon on grainy stone can look quite like the crayon drawing it is. On the other hand, lithographs with large blocks of colored ink can emphasize the commercial quality of the printmaking process.

Wang Guangyi's *Great Criticism: Coca-Cola* (Fig. 9.13) reads like an anti-American propaganda poster, the kind that you could imagine seeing glued in multiples to plywood in an urban landscape. It features bold lines and a sharp definition of color and shape. The power of

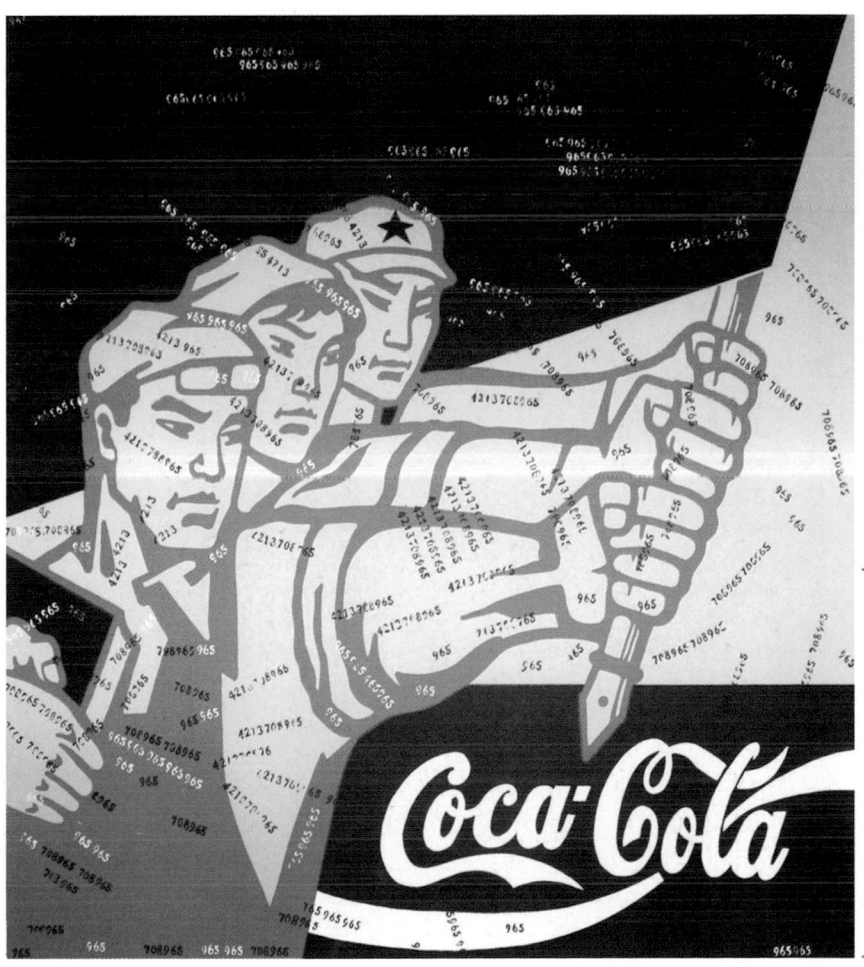

the image and its message are enhanced by the work's simplicity and directness, as well as our visual recognition of stereotypes—in this case the faces of Asian men, their standard laborer's overalls, and the Coca-Cola logo.

The impact of Käthe Kollwitz's lithograph *The Mothers* (Fig. 9.14), which highlights the plight of lower-class German mothers left alone to fend for their children after World War I, could not be further removed from that of *Great Criticism: Coca-Cola*. The high contrast of the black and white and the coarse quality of the wax crayon yield a sense of desperation suggestive of a newspaper documentary photograph. All the imagery is thrust toward the picture plane, as in high relief. The harsh contours of protective shoulders, arms, and hands contrast with the more delicately rendered faces and heads of the children—all contributing to the poignancy of the work.

Serigraphy

In **serigraphy**—also known as **silkscreen printing**—stencils are used to create the design or image. Unlike the case with other graphic processes, these images can be rendered in paint as well as ink.

One serigraphic process begins with a screen constructed of a piece of silk, nylon, or fine metal mesh stretched on a frame. A stencil with a cutout design is then affixed to the screen, and paper or canvas is placed beneath (Fig. 9.1D). The artist forces paint or ink through the open areas of the stencil with a flat, rubber-bladed implement called a **squeegee**, similar to those used in washing windows. The image on the support corresponds to the shape cut out of the stencil. Several stencils may be used to apply different colors to the same print.

Images can also be "painted" on a screen with use of a varnish-like substance that prevents paint or ink from passing through the mesh. This technique allows for more gestural images than cutout stencils would provide. Recently, a serigraphic process called **photo silkscreen** has been developed; it allows the artist to create photographic images on a screen covered with a light-sensitive gel.

Serigraphy was first developed as a commercial medium and is still used as such to create anything from posters to labels on cans of food. The American Pop artist Andy Warhol raised the commercial aspects of serigraphy to the level of fine art in many of his silkscreen prints of the 1960s, such as *Four Marilyns* (Fig. 9.15). With his numerous silkscreens of Marilyn Monroe, Warhol

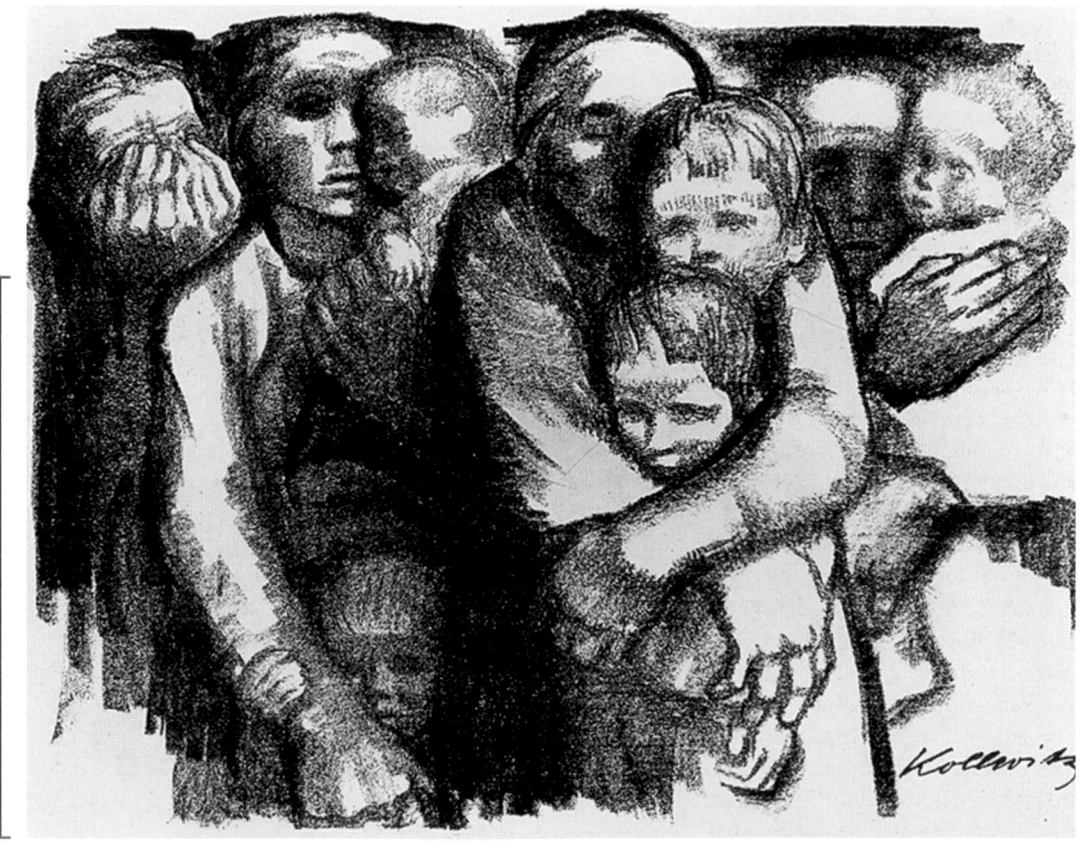

1 ft.

< 9.14 KÄTHE KOLLWITZ, *The Mothers* (1919). Lithograph, 17¾" × 23". Philadelphia Museum of Art, Philadelphia, Pennsylvania.

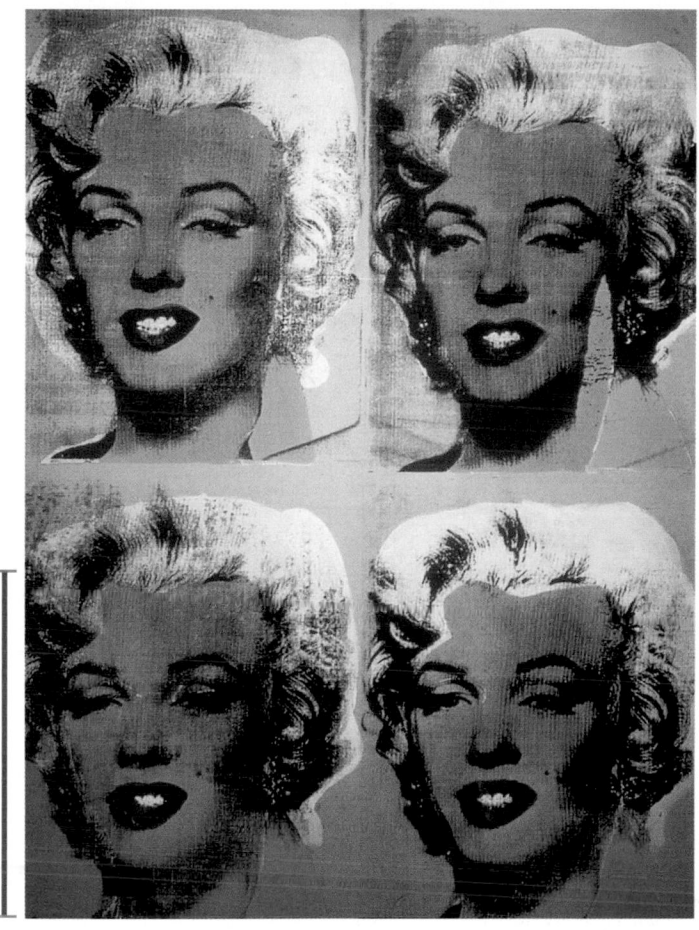

▲ **9.15 ANDY WARHOL,** *Four Marilyns* (1962). Synthetic polymer paint and silkscreen ink on canvas, 30" × 23⅞".

silkscreen *Red Coat* (Fig. 9.16) serve as a symbol of contemporary glamour. *Red Coat* looks something like a photograph transported into another medium. The individual shapes seem carved into a single plane like sawed jigsaw puzzle pieces. As in a photo, the edges of the silkscreen crop off parts of the image. The woman looks like a supermodel, with her features exaggerated as they might be in a cover girl image.

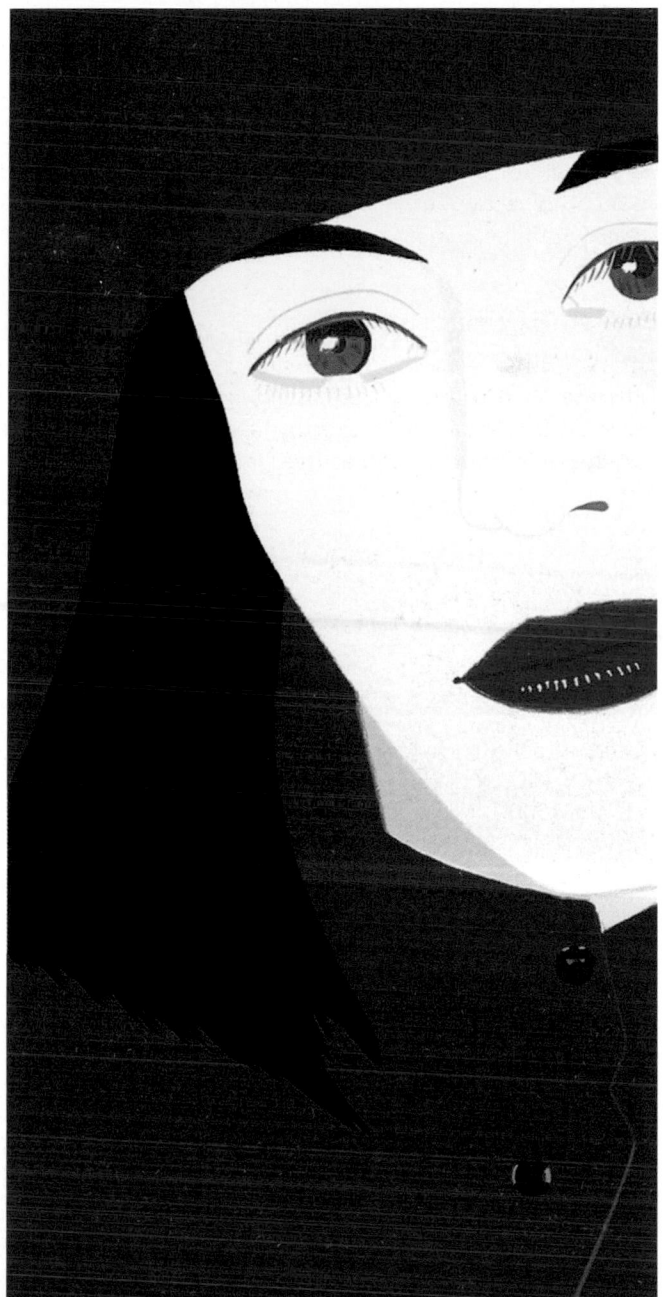

▲ **9.16 ALEX KATZ,** *Red Coat* (1983). Silkscreen, printed in color; 58" × 29". The Museum of Modern Art, New York, New York.

participated in the cultural immortalization of a film icon of the 1960s by reproducing a well-known photograph of the star on canvas. Proclaimed a "sex symbol" of the silver screen, Monroe rose rapidly to fame and shocked her fans by taking her own life at an early age. In the decades since Monroe's death, her image is still found on posters and calendars, books and songs are still written about her, and the public's appetite for information about her early years and romances remains insatiable. In other renderings, Warhol arranged multiple images of the star as if lined up on supermarket shelves, commenting, perhaps, on the ways in which contemporary flesh peddlers have packaged and sold her—in death as well as in life.

Alex Katz defines his forms with razor-sharp edges, fixing his subjects in an exact time and place by the details of their clothing and hairstyles. At the same time, he transcends their temporal and spatial limits by simplifying and transforming their figures into something akin to icons. For example, the subject's intense red lips in his

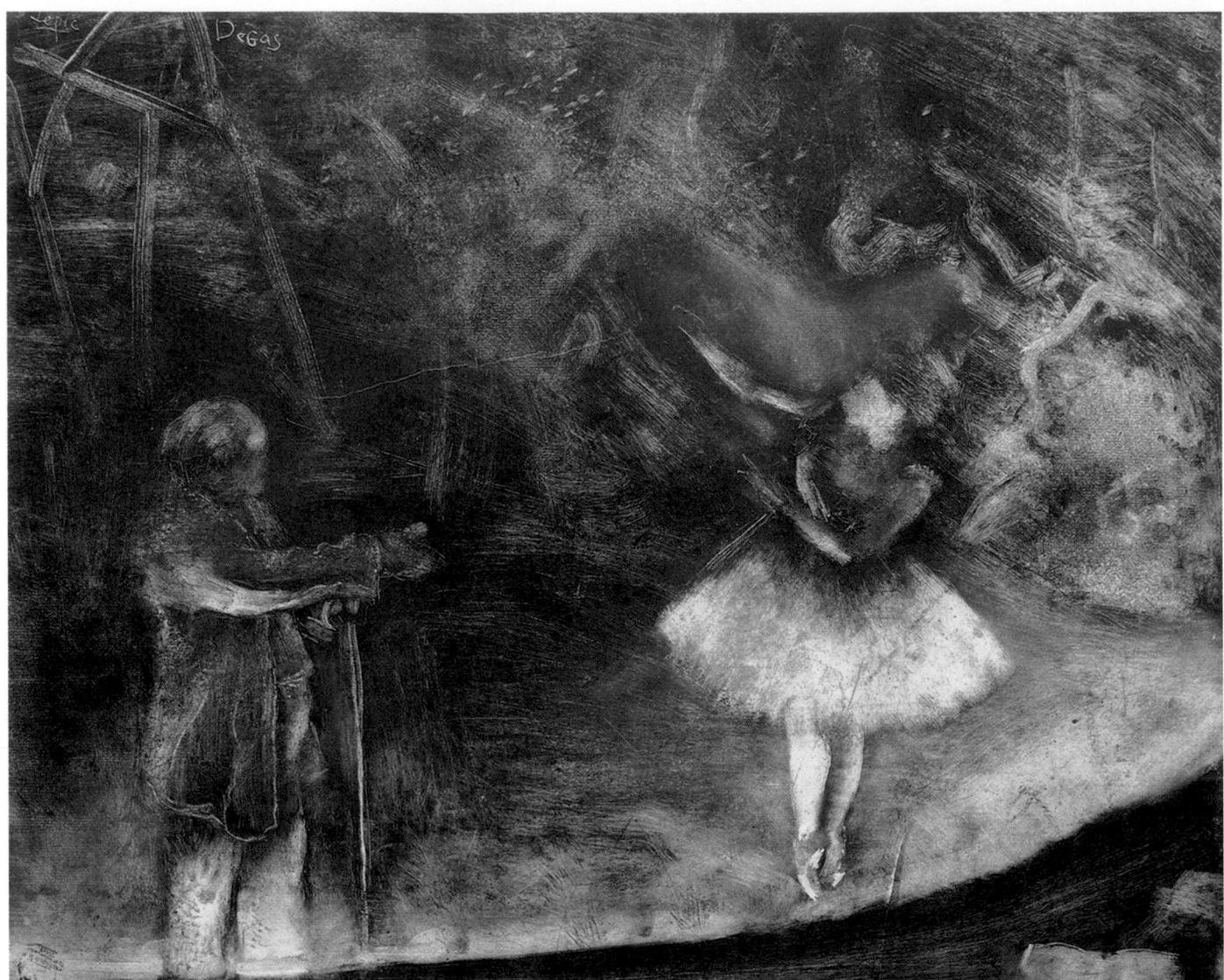

1 ft.

∧ **9.17** EDGAR DEGAS, *The Ballet Master* (c. 1874). Monotype in black ink, 22" × 27 ½". National Gallery of Art, Washington, D.C.

Monotype

Monotype is a printmaking process, but it overlaps the other two-dimensional media of drawing and painting. Like drawing and printmaking, monotype yields but a single image, and like them, therefore, it is a unique work of art.

In monotype, drawing or painting is created with oil paint or watercolor on a nonabsorbent surface of any material. Brushes are used, but sometimes fine detail is rendered by scratching paint off the plate with sharp implements. A piece of paper is then laid on the surface, and the image is transferred by hand rubbing the back of the paper or passing the matrix and paper through a press. The result, as can be seen in a monotype by Edgar Degas (Fig. 9.17), has all the spontaneity of a drawing and the lushness of a painting.

GRAPHIC DESIGN

Graphic design is an artistic process used to communicate information and ideas through writing, images, and symbols that are connected to contemporary human experience. Since the beginning of modern history, advances in technology—beginning with the printing press in the early 1400s—have enabled the global dissemination of graphic design products. Components of the graphic design include typography, page layout and book design, and corporate identity. Graphic design mediums include photography, printmaking, computer-aided design, and digital design. The history of graphic design can be traced back to marks made by humans on the walls of caves and the earliest forms of writing. In this section, we will consider contemporary examples of graphic design as it is

▲ 9.18 Signage for Women's and Men's Restrooms.

From the simplified shapes of a woman in a dress and a man in trousers, we can figure out which restroom is intended for whom, even if we find ourselves in a foreign country where we don't speak the language (Fig. 9.18). So-called barrier-free communication is also seen in the now-familiar graphic design of a red circle with a line drawn through it signifying "NO!"—whatever *no* may apply to, as in Figure 9.19.

Layout

A **layout** is a way of organizing the design elements in a printed work such as a poster, book, or magazine. Layouts typically consist of visual elements, including type and pictures, which may be drawings and photographs. The layout of children's books may also contain buttons to press, a variety of textures to feel, and speakers that make sounds.

The design of this book generally includes two columns of text that are each flush left and flush right, also known as being "fully justified." The Connections features are also flush left, but they are "ragged right" (ending in different lengths on the right side). Photographs and drawings are interspersed throughout in various locations to provide aesthetic appeal and to have works of art displayed on the same page on which they are discussed. "Running feet" display the page numbers, the chapter numbers, the names of the chapters (on the left) and the names of the sections (on the right). Major and minor heads are distinguished both by color and size. Boxed features,

the most ubiquitous of art forms, entering our consciousness and our lives in a steady stream on a daily basis.

Typography

Typography is the technical term for designing and composing letterforms. Until the digital age, printing was done with movable pieces of metal (or wood) cast or carved with letters that are raised above the surface of the piece. These pieces were put together into strings of words and lines by typesetters. Today typesetting is done on computers, as is type design. Designers can choose from hundreds of typefaces and can manipulate things like scale, color, perspective, and the overlapping of letters and other images. A designer will use type to communicate with optimal clarity—a variant of form follows function—or with expressiveness. It is an eye-opener to realize that any and all type that we come into contact with as consumers originated with a graphic designer who was skilled in typography.

The clearest, most utilitarian form of typography is probably the pictogram, which is widely used in signage.

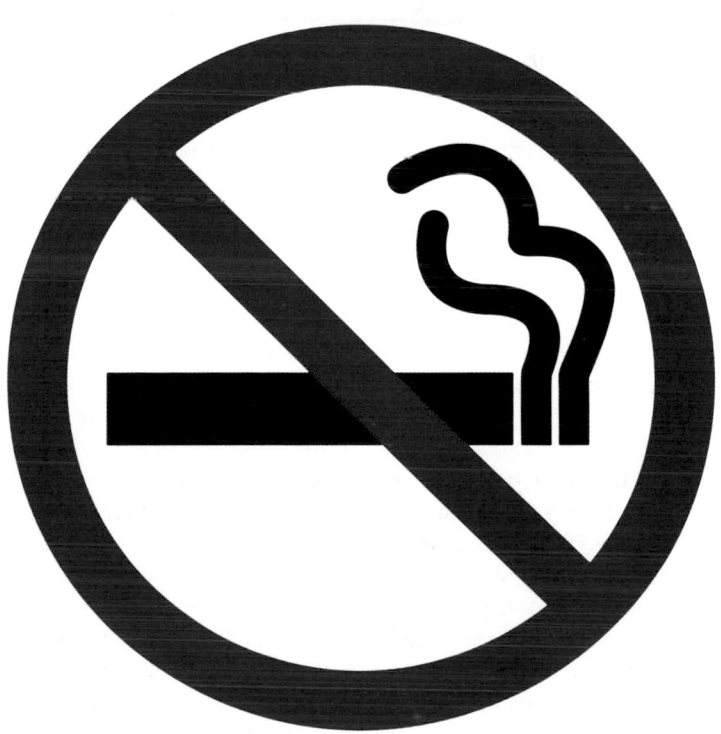

▲ 9.19 Signage for Nonsmoking Area.

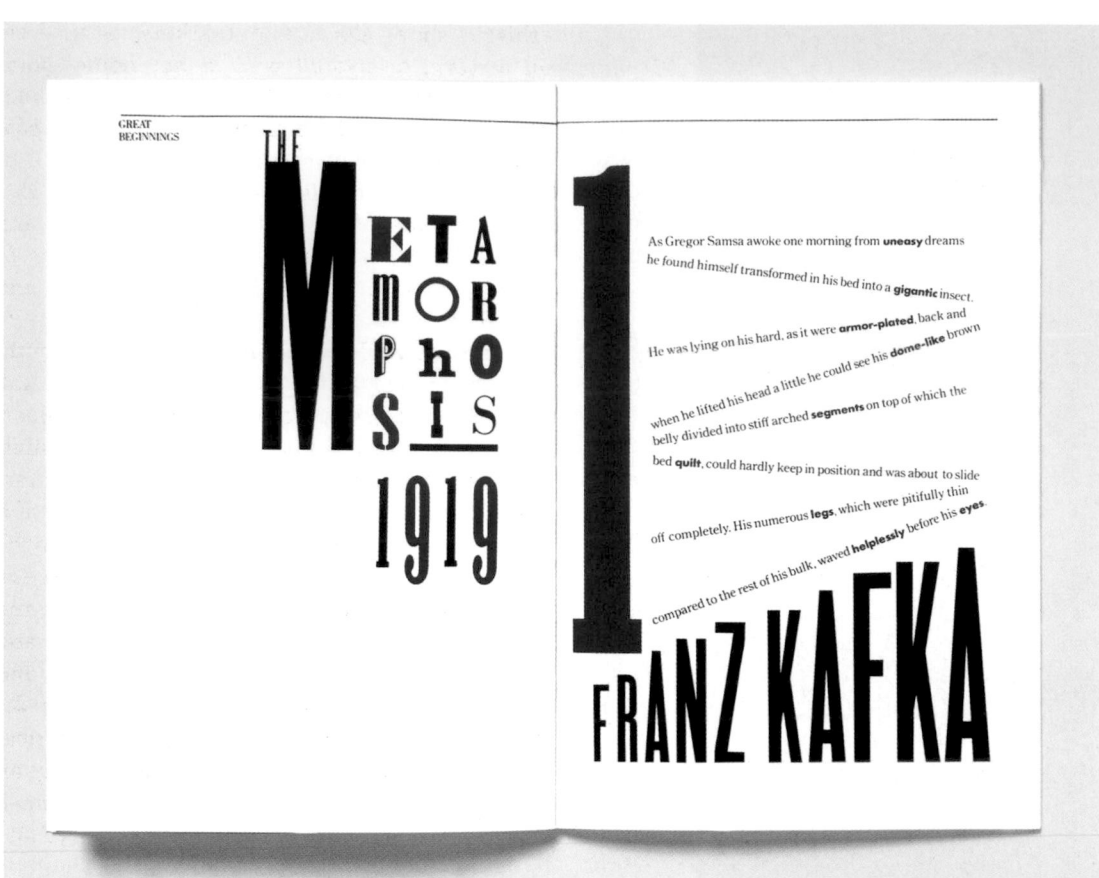

< 9.20 PAULA SCHER, "Great Beginnings" spread for Koppel & Scher promotional booklet (1984).

such as A Closer Look and Compare + Contrast, are placed on what are called *screens* or *tint panels* to help set them apart from the main text. You are not expected to be thinking about all this as you read, but the layout is intended to be stimulating yet refined, to complement the subject matter, and to assist the reader in navigating the material.

Figure 9.20 shows the layout for a spread for a promotional booklet, "Great Beginnings," by Paula Scher. Because of a tight budget, she limited her palette to three colors: black, red, and a putty color. She turned to rarely used typefaces and to features of Art Deco and Russian Constructivism (see Chapters 19 and 20) three to four generations after their passing. Put more simply, her typefaces went from thick to thin, her colors like her subject alternated, she worked her key letters and numbers like columns, and her horizontal lines of text ramped uphill then down, but always left to right, requiring dizzying backward leaps. Even the red and the black work like shocking figures against the calming putty-colored background. The layout is all "metamorphosis," or change, as is the title of the work.

Gitte Kath's poster for the Sydney Paralympics (Fig. 9.21) required her to collect materials such as the

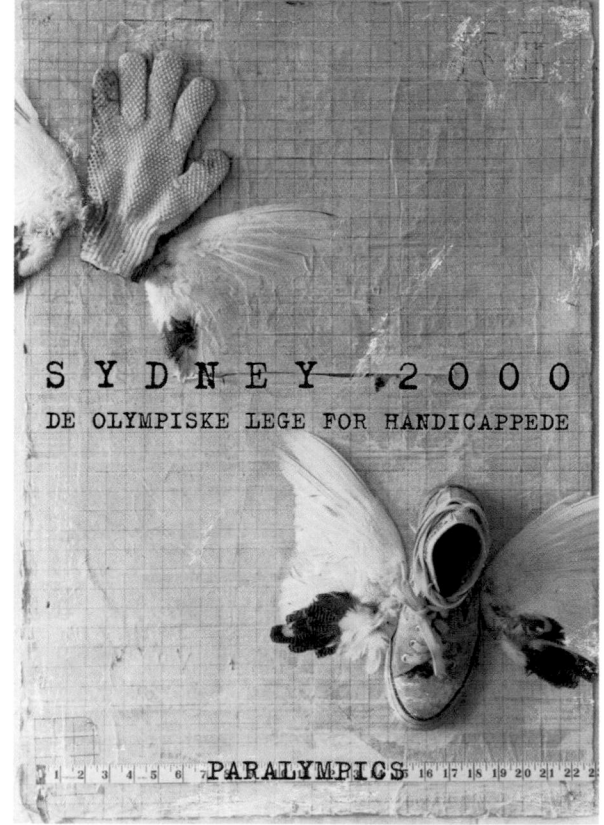

> 9.21 GITTE KATH, Poster for the Sydney 2000 Paralympics.

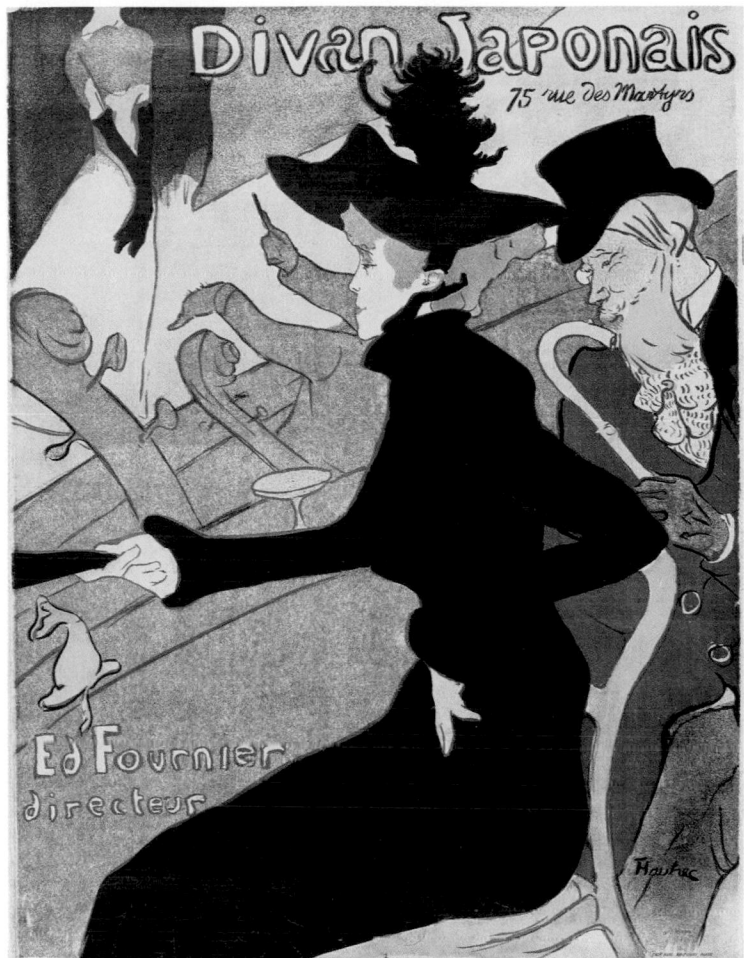

▲ 9.22 HENRI DE TOULOUSE-LAUTREC, *Le Divan Japonais* (1892). Color lithograph, 31⅝" × 23⅞". Musée Toulouse-Lautrec, Albi, France.

1 ft.

athletic shoe, glove, and feathers, post them on a worn, discolored wall in her home, paint and photograph them, then apply the graphics. The condition of the elements in the poster suggest the poignancy of the transitory nature of living things. There is nothing heroic about this poster; there is only the suggestion of loss and caring. The colors are muted, the positioning of the objects and the graphics are balanced, and the allover grid and decay provide unity.

Henri de Toulouse-Lautrec, a late-nineteenth-century French artist, is seen by some as the "father" of the color lithograph poster. Toulouse-Lautrec dwelled in nighttime Paris—its cafés, music halls, nightclubs, and brothels. The posters that he designed for concerts and other performances are among the most well known in the history of art. His designs (Fig. 9.22) are successful because they capture, in a single image, the spirit and personality of the establishment and the performer. Areas of unmodulated color and high-contrast values in the poster design evoke theater lighting and costuming. The lyrical shapes and undulating lines, coupled with an oblique perspective and bold patterns influenced by Japanese prints, combine to catch the eye and draw the patron to the party.

Logos

A **logo** is an emblematic design used to identify and advertise a company or an organization. The most successful corporate identity designs—such as Apple, Inc.'s instantly recognizable apple minus a bite (Fig. 9.23)—are inseparable from the entities they represent. The logo for the Internet search engine Google (Fig. 9.24) features broadly spaced letters of intense—mostly primary—colors. The simplicity of the design and the straightforwardness of the color scheme suggest an ease of use (even a child can do it) that the company would want to promote.

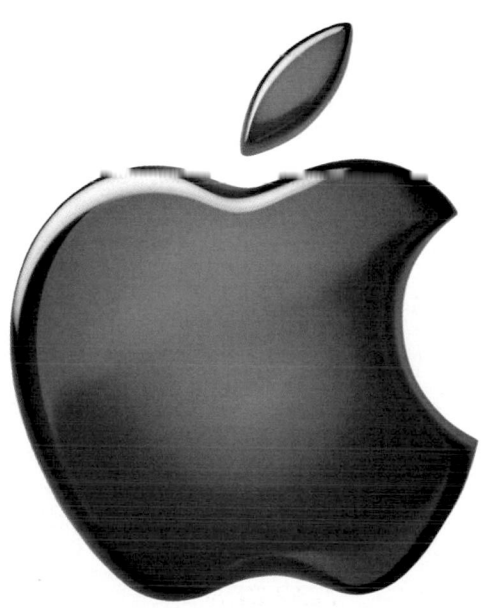

▲ 9.23 Apple Logo.

▲ 9.24 Google Logo.

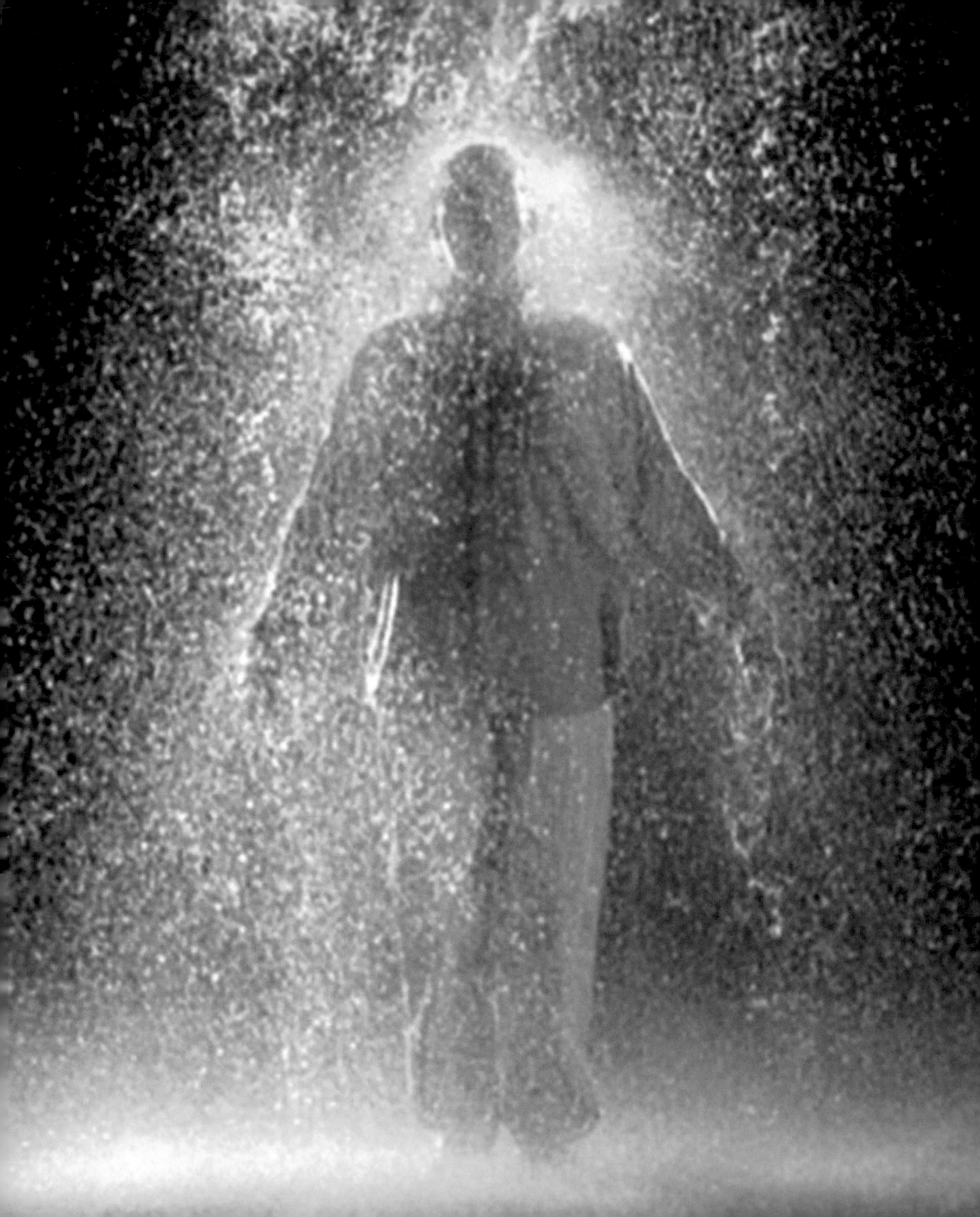

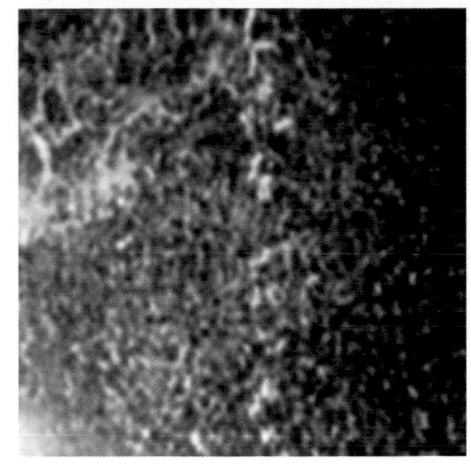

10

IMAGING: PHOTOGRAPHY, FILM, VIDEO, AND DIGITAL ARTS

Look at the things around you, the immediate world around you. If you are alive, it will mean something to you, and if you care enough about photography, and if you know how to use it, you will want to photograph that meaning.

— EDWARD WESTON

TECHNOLOGY HAS revolutionized the visual arts. For thousands of years, one of the central goals of art was to imitate nature as exactly as possible. Today, any one of us can point a camera at a person or an object and capture a realistic image. Point-and-shoot cameras no longer even require that we place the subject in proper focus or that we regulate the amount of light so as not to overexpose or underexpose the subject. Technology can do all of these things for us.

Similarly, the art of the stage was once available only to those who lived in the great urban centers. Now and then a traveling troupe of actors might come by, or local groups might put on a show of sorts, but most people had little or no idea of the ways in which drama, opera, dance, and other performing arts could affect their lives. The advent of motion pictures, or cinematography, suddenly brought a flood of new imagery into new local theaters, and a new form of communal activity was born. People from every station of life could flock to the movie theater on the weekend. Over time, cinematography evolved into an art form independent of its beginnings as a mirror of the stage.

More recently, television has brought this imagery into the home, where people can watch everything from the performing arts to sporting events in privacy and from the multiple vantage points that several cameras, rather than a single set of eyes, can provide. Fine artists have also appropriated television—or, more precisely, the technology that makes television possible—to produce **video art**. Technology has also given rise to the computer as a creative video-mediated tool. With the aid of

◄ BILL VIOLA, *The Crossing* (1996). Two-channel color video and stereo-sound installation, continuous loop; 192" × 330" × 684". Solomon R. Guggenheim Museum, New York.

artificial intelligence, we can instantly view models of objects from all sides. We can be led to feel as though we are sweeping in on our solar system from the black reaches of space, then flying down to the surface of our planet and landing where the programmer would set us down.

Millions of children spend hours playing video games, such as Tetris, which challenges them to rotate plummeting polygons to construct a solid wall, or Mario Brothers and Tomb Raider, which require them to evade or blast a host of enemies before their computer-drawn heroes and heroines plunge into an abyss. Computer technology and computer-generated images have likewise been appropriated by fine artists in the creation of **digital art**. In illustrations of blue jeans that rocket through space, snappy graphics that headline sporting events, and the web design that greets us every time we go online, computer-generated images punctuate our daily lives. DVDs, multimedia computers, and software that can blend or distort one shape or face into another are bringing a "virtual reality" into our lives that is in some ways more alluring than, well, "real reality."

In this chapter, we discuss photography, film (cinematography), video, and digital arts. These mediums have given rise to unique possibilities for artistic expression.

PHOTOGRAPHY

Photography is a science and an art. The word *photography* is derived from Greek roots meaning "to write with light." The scientific aspects of photography concern the ways in which images of objects are made on a **photosensitive** surface, such as film, by light that passes through a **lens**. Chemical changes occur in the film so that the images are recorded. This much of the process—the creation of an objective image of the light that has passed through the lens—is mechanical.

It would be grossly inaccurate, however, to think of the *art* of photography as mechanical. Photographers make artistic choices, from the most mundane to the most sophisticated. They decide which films and lenses to use, and which photographs they will retain or discard. They manipulate lighting conditions or printing processes to

achieve dazzling or dreamy effects. Always, they are in search of subjects—ordinary, extraordinary, universal, personal.

Photography is truly an art of the hand, head, and heart. Before the advent of digital photography, the photographer had to understand films and grasp skills related to developing **prints**. The photographer must also have the intellect and the passion to search for and to see what is important in things—what is beautiful, harmonious, universal, and worth recording.

Photography is a matter of selection and interpretation. Similar subjects seen through the eyes of different photographers will yield wildly different results. In Ansel Adams's *Moon and Half Dome, Yosemite National Park, California* (Fig. 10.1), majestic cliffs leap into a deep, cold sky. From our earthbound vantage point, the perfect order of the desolate, spherical moon contrasts with

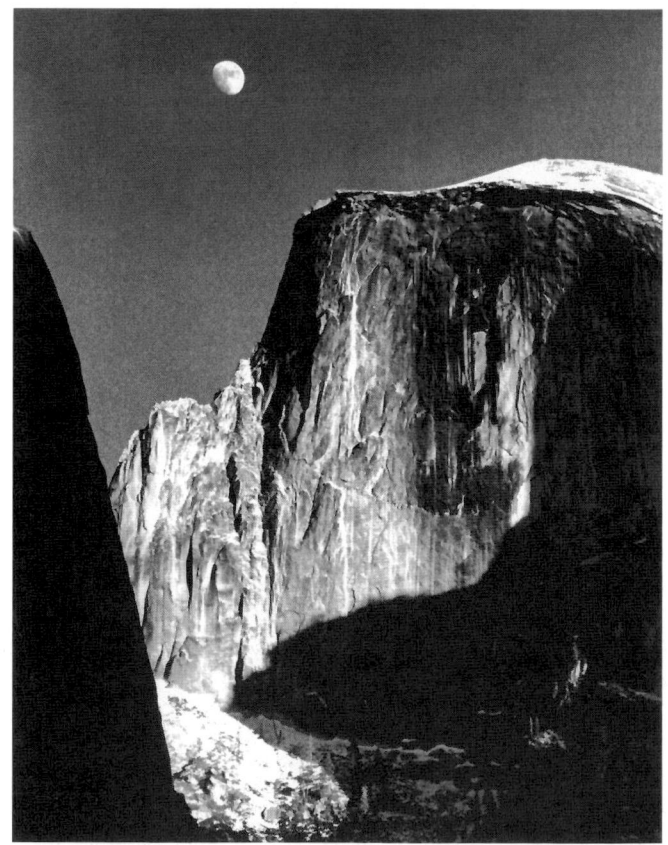

▲ 10.1 **ANSEL ADAMS**, *Moon and Half Dome, Yosemite National Park, California* (1960).

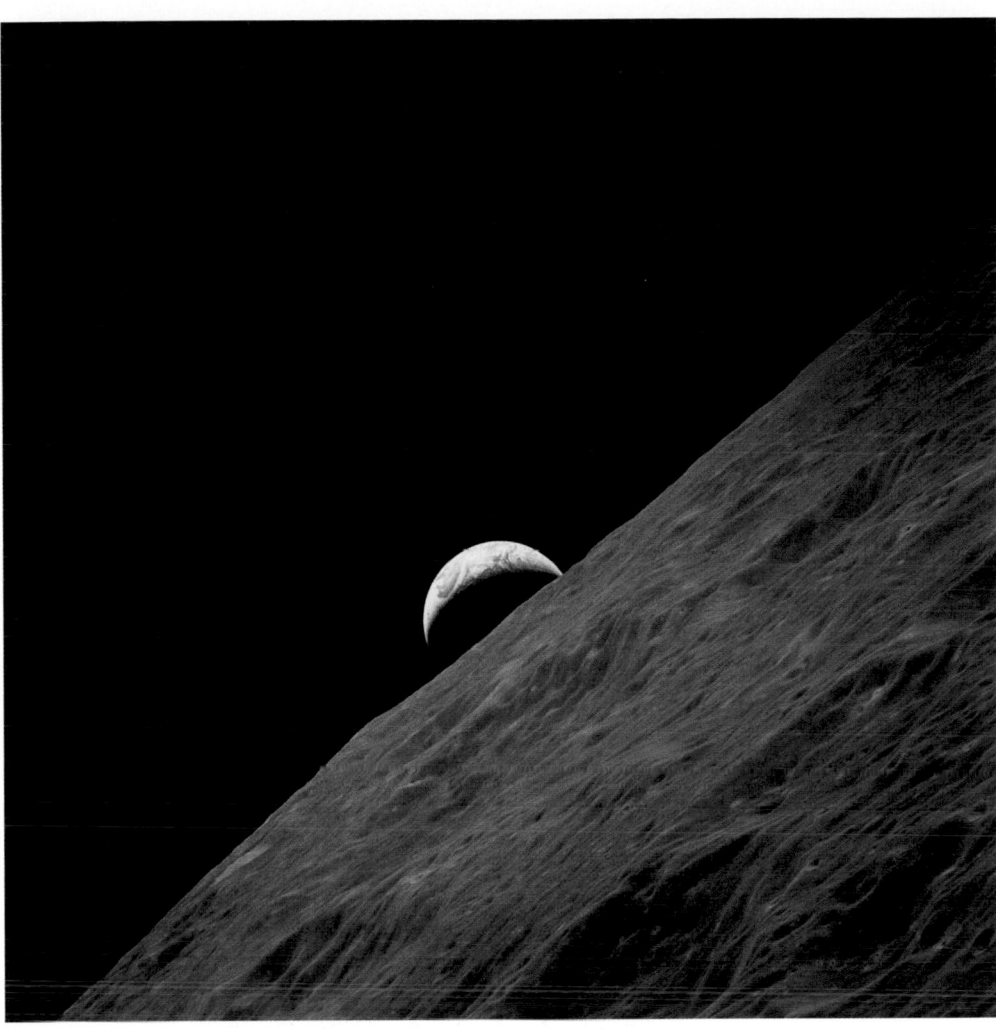

the coarseness of the living rock. Yet we know that its geometric polish is an illusion wrought by distance—the moon's surface is just as rough and chaotic. Adams's composition is as much about design elements (shape, texture, value) as it is a visual document of the California landscape. Distance and scale come sharply into focus: This is a story of humans dwarfed by nature and nature dwarfed by the stars.

In the early nineteenth century, when photography was invented, the technology that made Figure 10.2 possible would have been only fantasy. In this NASA photograph, taken during the first manned mission to the moon in July 1969, the crescent shape of sunlight blanketing a distant Earth is silhouetted against a velvet black sky. Its perfect geometry is a dramatic counterpoint to the irregular textured surface of the moon. Although only a sliver of Earth's blue color is evident at the point where light turns abruptly to shadow, it is enough to suggest a sense of life in contrast to the barren, unforgiving lunar landscape.

Both the Adams photograph and the one taken from space have artful compositions, even though the

NASA photograph was not taken by an artist. Adams chose a specific moment, when shadows were deep, the sky was clear, and the position of the sun exaggerated the textures of the rock. The black shadows and the uniform steel gray sky have such precise contours that they read as flat puzzle pieces. The NASA photograph is striking for two reasons. First, the "composition" is dramatically simple: a field bisected into two zones by the sharp diagonal created by the contour of the moon. Second, the perspective is intriguing: we sense the fluid glide of the ship through the stillness of space.

The aesthetic aspect of both photographs is not all they have in common. The history of photography is full of evidence of the artist-photographer boldly going where no one has been before or challenging the viewer to see anew the familiar and ubiquitous. The mood, stylistic inclinations, cultural biases, and technical preferences influence the nature of the creative product. As observers, we are as enriched by the diversity of this medium as much as any other in the visual arts.

> It gradually began to dawn on me that something must be wrong with the art of painting as practiced at that time. With my camera I could procure the same results as those attained by painters. . . . I could express the same moods. Artists who saw my earlier photographs began to tell me that they envied me; that they felt my photographs were superior to their paintings, but that, unfortunately, photography was not an art. . . . There and then I started my fight—or rather my conscious struggle for the recognition of photography as a new medium of expression, to be respected in its own right, on the same basis as any other art form.
>
> —ALFRED STIEGLITZ

Cameras

Cameras may look very different from one another and boast a variety of equipment, but they all possess certain basic features. Figure 10.3 shows that the camera is similar to the human eye. In both cases, light enters a narrow opening and is projected onto a photosensitive surface.

The amount of light that enters the eye is determined by the size of the *pupil*, which is an opening in the muscle called the *iris*; the size of the pupil responds automatically to the amount of light that strikes the eye. The amount of light that enters a camera is determined by the size of the opening, or **aperture**, in the **shutter**. The aperture opening can be adjusted manually or, in advanced cameras, such as "point-and-shoots," automatically. The size of the aperture, or opening, is the so-called **F-stop**. The smaller the F-stop, the larger the opening. The shutter can also be made to remain open to light for various amounts of time, ranging from a few thousandths of a second—in which case **candid** shots of fast action may be taken, stopping the action in its tracks—to a second or more.

retina (photosensitive surface)

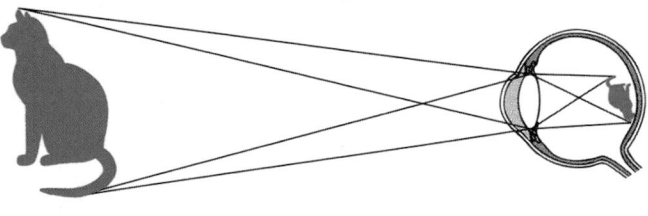

film (photosensitive surface)

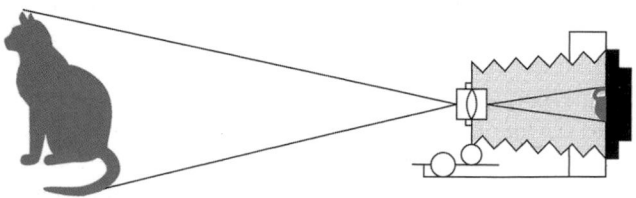

∧ 10.3 The Camera and the Human Eye Compared.

When the light enters the eye, the *lens* keeps it in focus by responding automatically to its distance from the object. The light is then projected onto the retina, which consists of cells that are sensitive to light and dark and to color. Nerves transmit visual sensations of objects from the retina to the brain.

In the same way, the camera lens focuses light onto a photosensitive surface such as **film**. A camera lens can be focused manually or automatically. Many photographers purposely take pictures that are out of focus, for their soft, blurred effects. **Telephoto lenses** magnify faraway objects and tend to collapse the spaces between distant objects that recede from us. **Wide-angle lenses** allow a broad view of objects within a confined area.

In their early days, cameras tended to be large and heavy, and were placed on mounts. Today's cameras, including those that are housed in smartphones, are usually small and handheld. Many contemporary cameras contain angled mirrors that allow the photographer to see directly through the lens and thereby to be precisely aware of the image that is being projected onto the film.

The photographer Alfred Stieglitz, who recognized the medium as a fine art as well as a tool for recording events, shot *The Steerage* (Fig. 10.4) with an early hand-held camera. He happened upon the striking composition of *The Steerage* on an Atlantic crossing aboard the *Kaiser Wilhelm II*. He rushed to his cabin for his camera, hoping that the upper and lower masses of humanity would maintain their balanced relationships to one another, to the drawbridge that divides the scene, to the stairway, the funnel, and the horizontal beam of the mast. The "steerage" of a ship was the least expensive accommodation. Here the "huddled masses" seem suspended in limbo by machinery and by symbolic as well as actual bridges. Yet the tenacious human spirit may best be symbolized by the jaunty patch of light that strikes the straw hat of one passenger on the upper deck. Stieglitz was utterly fascinated and moved by what he saw.

Film

When an image is "shot," it is captured as film or recorded on an electronic memory device. Contemporary black-and-white films are very thin, yet they contain several

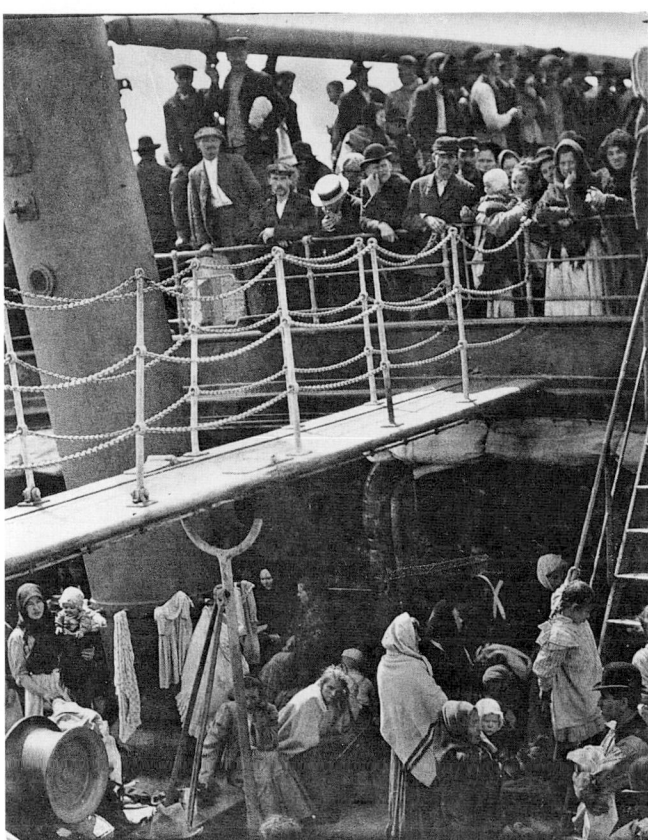

△ **10.4 ALFRED STIEGLITZ,** *The Steerage* (1907). Photograph, 12 11/16" × 10 3/16".

layers, most of which form a protective coating and backing for the photosensitive layer. The active layer contains an **emulsion** of small particles of a photosensitive silver salt (usually silver halide) suspended in gelatin.

After the film is exposed to light and treated chemically, it becomes a **negative**, in which metallic silver is formed from the crystals of silver halide. In this negative, areas of dark and light are reversed. Because the negatives are transparent, light passes through them to a print surface, which becomes the final photograph, or print. Here the areas of light and dark are reversed again, now matching the shading of the original subject. Prints are also usually made significantly larger than the negative.

Black-and-white films differ in color sensitivity (the ability to show colors such as red and green as different shades), in contrast (the tendency to show gradations of gray as well as black and white), in graininess (the textural quality, as reflective of the size of the silver halide crystals), and in speed (the amount of exposure time necessary to record an image). Photographers select films that will heighten the effects they seek to portray.

Color film is more complex than black-and-white film, but similar in principle. Color film also contains several layers, some of which are protective and provide backing. There are two basic kinds of color film: **color reversal film**

and **color negative film**. Both types of color film contain three light-sensitive layers.

Prints are made directly from *color reversal film*. Therefore, each of the photosensitive layers corresponds to one of the primary colors in additive color mixtures: blue, green, or red. When color reversal film is exposed to light and treated chemically, mixtures of the primary colors emerge, yielding a full-color image of the photographic subject.

Negatives are made from *color negative film*. Therefore, each photosensitive layer corresponds to the complement of the primary color it represents. (Additive color mixtures and primary and complementary colors are explained in Chapter 3.)

Color films, as black-and-white films, differ in color sensitivity, contrast, graininess, and speed. But color films also differ in their appropriateness for natural (daylight) or artificial (indoor) lighting conditions.

Digital Photography

Today, **digital photography** accounts for most professional photography and upward of 90 percent of amateur photography. Millions take digital photos with their smartphones—including selfies—every day. Digital cameras translate the visual images that pass through the lens into bits of digital information, which are recorded onto an electronic storage device rather than film. High-quality (translation: expensive) digital cameras take photos whose **resolution**—that is, sharpness—rivals that of film images. The stored information can either be shown on a display screen or printed, or both. Rather than have several prints made, the photographer can copy the digital information endlessly. Digital images can also be transmitted instantly over the Internet, as with Instagram and a host of other Apps. Printed images can also be scanned, converting them into digital formats, and then stored electronically or transmitted over the Internet.

Digital photography has some advantages. One is that the photographer need not deal with film—loading and unloading it and having it developed. The images can be displayed immediately on a display built into the camera or on a computer monitor. Software then permits you to manipulate the images as desired. You can also print them out as you would print out any other image or text.

The disadvantages are that (most) digital images do not have the sharpness of film images. High res images (and videos) can consume a tremendous amount of storage space, which is why so many are spending extra for more gigabytes of storage for their computers. Also, your printer may not print images that approach the quality of film images, even if you have stored enough information to do so. To get professional-quality prints, you may have to invest in professional equipment or take your camera, disk, or flash drive elsewhere, just as you have to take film to a lab or processor to be developed. But the price of this equipment is falling steadily, and with so-called retina displays, many users purchase digital equipment that rivals the resolution of more traditional photography.

History of Photography

The cameras and films described previously are rather recent inventions. Photography has a long and fascinating history. Although true photography does not appear much before the mid-nineteenth century, some of its principles can be traced back another 300 years, to the camera obscura.

THE CAMERA OBSCURA The **camera obscura**—literally, the covered-over or darkened room—was used by Renaissance artists to help them accurately portray depth, or perspective, on two-dimensional surfaces. The camera obscura could be a box, as shown in Figure 10.5, or an actual room with a small hole that admits light through one wall. The beam of light projects the outside scene upside down on a surface within the box. The artist then simply traces the scene, as shown, to achieve a proper perspective—to truly imitate nature.

DEVELOPMENT OF PHOTOSENSITIVE SURFACES The camera obscura could only temporarily focus an image on a surface while a person labored to copy it by tracing. The next developments in photography concerned the search for photosensitive surfaces that could permanently affix images. These developments came by bits and pieces.

In 1727, the German physicist Heinrich Schulze discovered that silver salts had light-sensitive qualities, but he never tried to record natural images. In 1802, Thomas Wedgwood, son of the well-known English potter, reported his discovery that paper soaked in silver nitrate

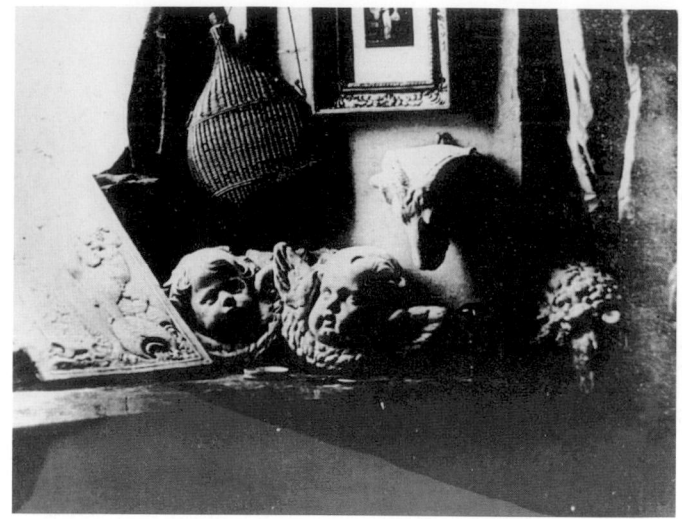

∧ 10.6 LOUIS-JACQUES-MANDÉ DAGUERRE, *The Artist's Studio* (1837).

did take on projected images as a chemical reaction to light. However, the images were not permanent.

HELIOGRAPHY In 1826, the Frenchman Joseph-Nicéphore Niepce invented **heliography**. **Bitumen**, or asphalt residue, was placed on a pewter plate to create a photosensitive surface. The bitumen was soluble in **lavender oil** if kept in the dark, but insoluble if struck by light. Niepce used a kind of camera obscura to expose the plate for several hours, and then he washed the plate in lavender oil. The pewter showed through where there had been little or no light, creating the image of the darker areas of the scene. The bitumen remained where the light had struck, however, leaving lighter values.

THE DAGUERREOTYPE The **daguerreotype** resulted from a partnership formed in 1829 between Niepce and another Frenchman, Louis-Jacques-Mandé Daguerre. The daguerreotype used a thin sheet of silver-plated copper. The plate was chemically treated, placed in a camera obscura, and exposed to a narrow beam of light. After exposure, the plate was treated chemically once more.

Figure 10.6 shows the first successful daguerreotype, taken in 1837. Remarkably clear images could be recorded by this process. In this work, called *The Artist's Studio*, Daguerre, a landscape painter, sensitively assembled deeply textured objects and sculptures. The contrasting light and dark values help create an illusion of depth.

There were drawbacks to the daguerreotype. It had to be exposed from five to forty minutes, requiring long sittings. The recorded image was reversed, left to right, and was so delicate that it had to be sealed behind glass to remain fixed. Also, the plate that was exposed to light became the actual daguerreotype. There was no negative,

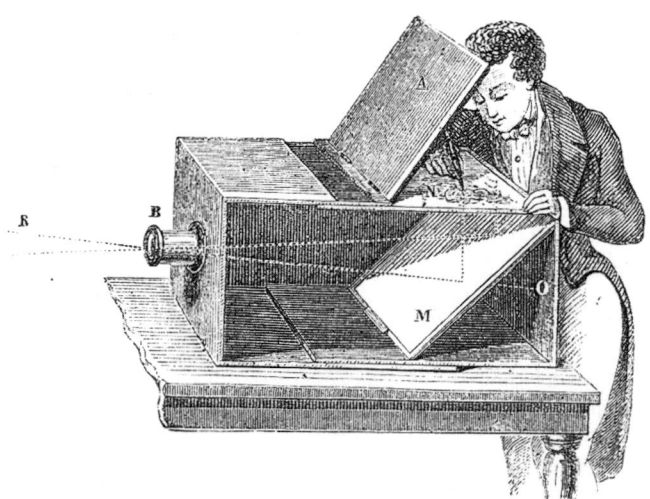

∧ 10.5 The Camera Obscura.

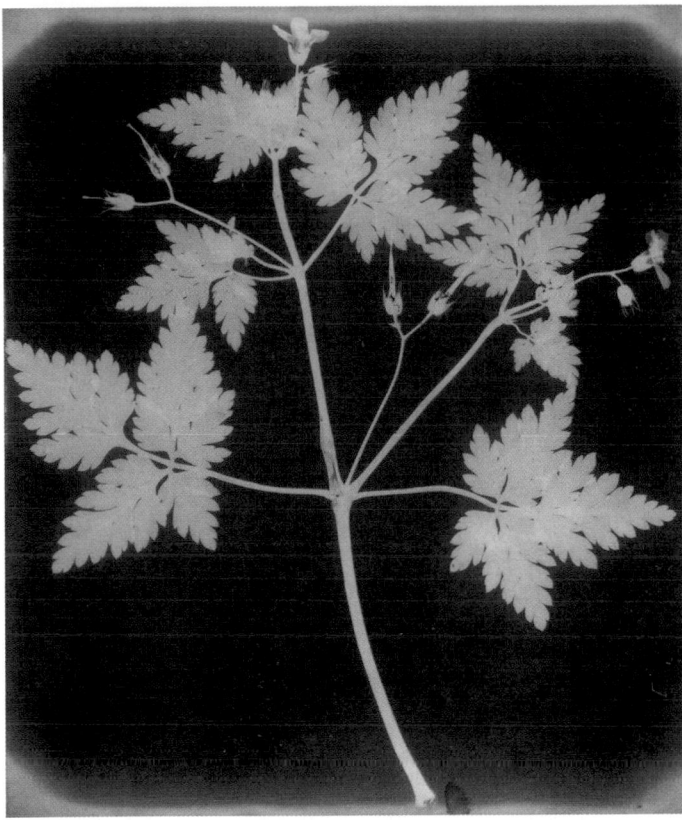

∧ 10.7 **WILLIAM HENRY FOX TALBOT,** *Botanical Specimen* (1839). Photogenic drawing.

and consequently, copies could not be made. However, some refinements of the process did come rapidly. Within ten years, the exposure time had been reduced to about thirty to sixty seconds, and the process had become so inexpensive that families could purchase two portraits for a quarter (although a quarter was actually a noticeable bit of money back then). Daguerreotype studios opened all across Europe and the United States, and families began to collect the rigid, stylized pictures that now seem to speak nostalgia and reflect days gone by.

THE NEGATIVE The negative was invented in 1839 by British scientist William Henry Fox Talbot. Talbot found that sensitized paper, coated with emulsions, could be substituted for the copper plate of the daguerreotype. He would place an object, such as a sprig of a plant, on the paper and expose the arrangement to light. The paper was darkened by the exposure in all areas except those covered by the object. Translucent areas, allowing some passage of light, resulted in a range of grays. Talbot's first so-called photogenic drawings (Fig. 10.7), created by this process, seem eerie, though lyrically beautiful. The delicacy of the image underscores the impracticality

of the process: How on earth would you "photograph" an elephant?

As with the daguerreotype, this process produced completed photographs in which the left and right of the image were reversed. In Talbot's photogenic drawings, the light and dark values of the image were also inverted. Talbot improved on his early experiments with his development of the **contact print**. He placed the negative in contact with a second sheet of sensitized paper and exposed them both to light. The resultant print was a "positive," with left and right, and light and dark, again as in the original subject. Many prints could be made from the negative. Unfortunately, the prints were not as sharp as daguerreotypes because they incorporated the texture of the paper on which they were captured. Subsequent advances led to methods in which pictures with the clarity of daguerreotypes could be printed from black-and-white as well as color negatives.

Photography improved rapidly for the next fifty or sixty years—faster emulsions, glass-plate negatives, better camera lenses—and photographs became increasingly more available to the general public. The next major step in the history of photography came with the introduction by Louis Lumière of the autochrome color process in 1907. Autochromes were glass plates coated with three layers of dyed potato starch that served as color filters. A layer of silver bromide emulsion covered the starch. When the autochrome was developed, it yielded a positive color transparency. Lumière's autochrome photographs, such as *Young Lady with an Umbrella* (Fig. 10.8), emulated late-nineteenth-century French paintings (see Chapter 19) in subject, palette, and texture. Autochrome technology was not replaced until 1932, when Kodak began to produce color film that applied the same principles to more advanced materials.

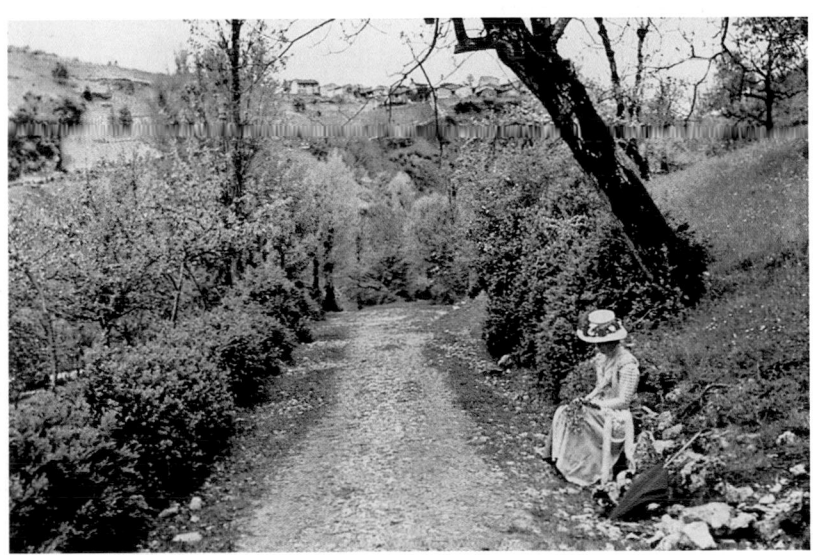

∧ 10.8 Young lady with an umbrella (circa 1910), "Autochrome Lumiere" glass plate 13 × 18 cm (5 × 7 inches)—Institut Lumiere, Lyon, France.

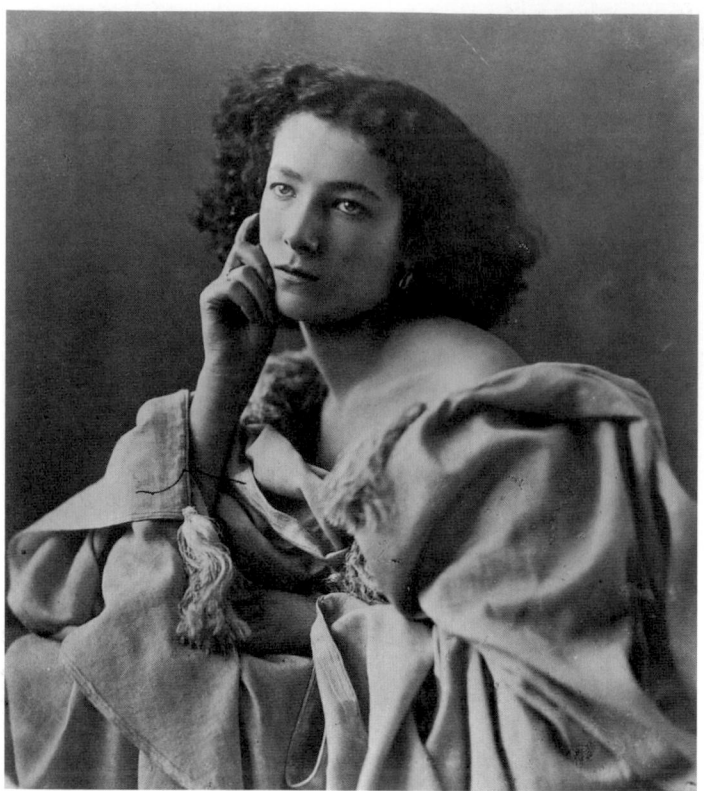

Cameron's impressive portfolio included portraits of Charles Dickens; Alfred, Lord Tennyson; and Henry Wadsworth Longfellow. Nadar's 1859 portrait of the actress Sarah Bernhardt (Fig. 10.9) was printed from a glass plate, which could be used several times to create sharp copies. Early portrait photographers such as Nadar imitated both nature and the arts, using costumes and props that recalled Romantic paintings or sculpted busts caressed by flowing drapery. The photograph is soft and smoothly textured, with middle-range values predominating; Bernhardt is sensitively portrayed as pensive, intelligent, and delicate.

The American photographer Alfred Stieglitz expressed the view that portraits ought to be taken over the course of the subject's lifetime because that was only way to reveal personality. Over a period of two decades, he photographed artist Georgia O'Keeffe (see Fig. 20.13) extensively; this body of work contains some 500 negatives. Contemporary photographer Nicholas Nixon began his documentary-portrait series *The Brown Sisters* (Fig. 10.10) in 1975 and has taken a black-and-white photograph of the group each year since. The format never changes—the sisters are always in the same position from left to right—but the locations do. More than family snapshots, although not unlike them, the series reads like a private diary of sibling relationships and the subtlety of the aging process.

PORTRAITS By the 1850s, photographic technology and the demands of a growing middle class in the wake of the American and French Revolutions came together to create a burgeoning business in portrait photography. Having a likeness of one-self was formerly reserved for the wealthy, who could afford to commission painters. Photography became the democratic equalizer. The rich, the famous, and average bourgeois citizens could now be memorialized and trumpet their existence long after their flesh had rejoined the elements from which it was composed.

Photographic studios spread like wildfire, and many photographers, such as Julia Margaret Cameron and Gaspard Felix Tournachon—called "Nadar"—vied for famous clientele.

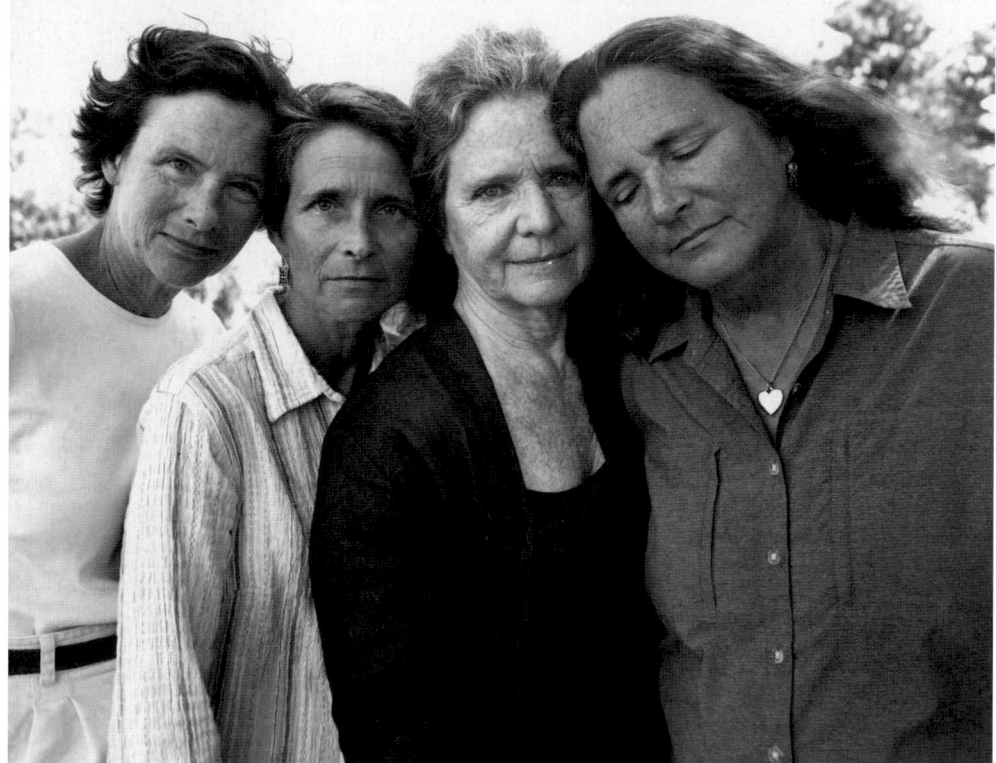

1 in.

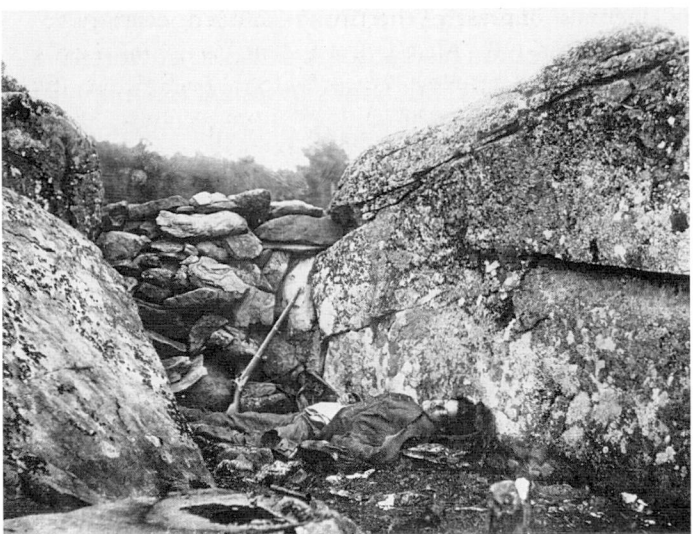

∧ 10.11 **ALEXANDER GARDNER**, *Home of a Rebel Sharpshooter, Gettysburg* (July 1863). Wet-plate photograph. Chicago History Museum, Chicago, Illinois.

PHOTOJOURNALISM Prior to the nineteenth century, there were few illustrations in newspapers and magazines. Those that did appear were usually in the form of engravings or drawings. Photography revolutionized the capacity of the news media to bring realistic representations of important events before the eyes of the public. Pioneers such as Mathew Brady and Alexander Gardner first used the camera to record major historical events such as the U.S. Civil War. The photographers and their crews trudged down the roads alongside the soldiers, horses drawing their equipment behind them in wagons referred to by the soldiers as "Whatsits."

Equipment available to Brady and Gardner did not allow them to capture candid scenes, so there is no direct record of the bloody to-and-fro of the battle lines, no photographic record of each lunge and parry. Instead, they brought home photographs of officers and of life in the camps along the lines. Although battle scenes would not hold still for Gardner's cameras, the litter of death and devastation caused by the war and pictured in Gardner's *Home of a Rebel Sharpshooter, Gettysburg* (Fig. 10.11) most certainly did. Despite their novelty and their accuracy, not many works of such graphic nature were sold. There are at least three reasons for this tempered success. First, the state of the art of photography made the photographs high priced. Second, methods for reproducing photographs on newsprint were not invented until about 1900; therefore, the works of the photojournalists were usually rendered as drawings, and the drawings translated into woodcuts before they appeared in the papers. Third, the American public might not have been ready to face the brutal realities they portrayed. In a similar vein, social commentators have suggested that the will of many Americans to persist in the Vietnam War was sapped by the incessant barrage of televised war imagery.

During the Great Depression of the 1930s, the conscience of the nation was stirred by the work of many photographers hired by the Farm Security Administration. Dorothea Lange and Walker Evans, among others, portrayed the lifestyles of migrant farmworkers and sharecroppers. Lange's *Migrant Mother, Nipomo, California* (Fig. 10.12) is a heartrending record of a 32-year-old woman who is out of work but cannot move on because the tires have been sold from the family car to purchase food for her seven children. The etching in her forehead is an eloquent expression of a mother's thoughts; the lines at the outer edges of her eyes tell the story of a woman who has aged beyond her years. Lange crops her photograph close to her subjects; they fill the print from edge to edge, forcing us to confront them rather than allowing us to seek comfort in a corner of the print not consigned to such an overt display of human misery. The migrant mother and her children, who turn away from the camera and heighten the futility of their plight, are as much constrained by the camera's viewfinder as they are by their circumstances.

During the early 1940s, photographers such as Margaret Bourke-White carried their handheld cameras into combat and captured tragic images of the butchery in Europe and in the Pacific. In 1929, Bourke-White

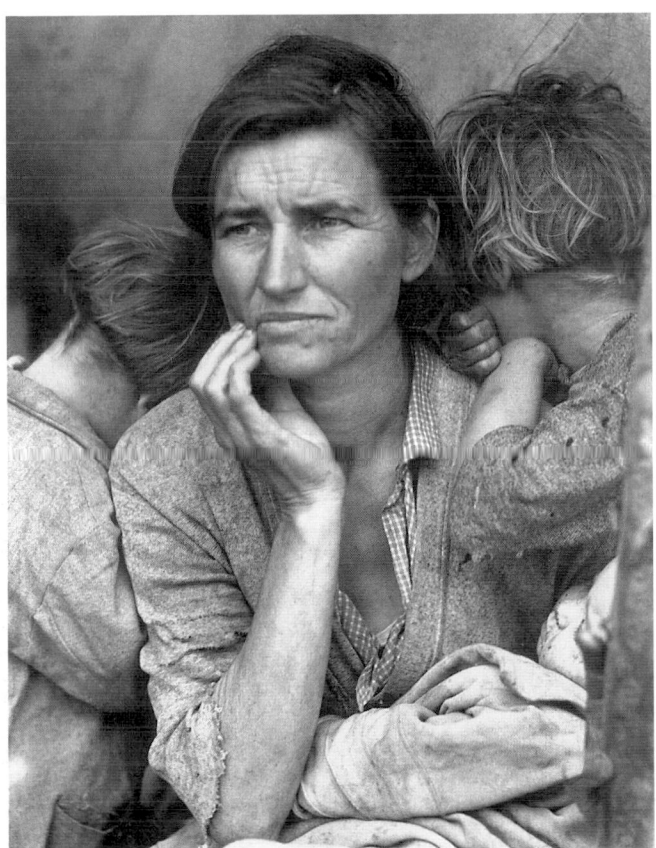

∧ 10.12 **DOROTHEA LANGE**, *Migrant Mother, Nipomo, California* (1936). Gelatin silver print, 12½" × 9⅞". The Oakland Museum of Art, Oakland, California.

> Documentary photography records the social scene of our time. It mirrors the present and documents [it] for the future. Its focus is man in his relation to mankind. It records his customs at work, at war, at play. . . . It portrays his institutions. . . . It shows not merely their facades, but seeks to reveal the manner in which they function, absorb the life, hold the loyalty, and influence the behavior of human beings.
>
> —DOROTHEA LANGE

became a staff photographer for *Fortune*, a new magazine published by Henry Luce. When Luce founded *Life* in 1936, Bourke-White became one of its original staff photographers. Like Dorothea Lange, she recorded the poverty of the Great Depression, but in the 1940s, she traveled abroad to become one of the first female war photojournalists. As World War II was drawing to an end in Europe, Bourke-White arrived at the Nazi concentration camp of Buchenwald in time for its liberation by Gen. George S. Patton. Her photograph *The Living Dead of Buchenwald, April 1945* (Fig. 10.13), published in *Life* in 1945, has become a classic image of the Holocaust, the Nazi effort to annihilate the Jewish people. The indifferent countenance of each survivor expresses, paradoxically, all that he has witnessed and endured. In her

book *Dear Fatherland, Rest Quietly*, Bourke-White put into words her own reactions to Buchenwald. In doing so, she showed how artistic creation, an intensely emotional experience, can also have the effect of objectifying the subject of creation:

> I kept telling myself that I would believe the indescribably horrible sight in the courtyard before me only when I had a chance to look at my own photographs. Using the camera was almost a relief; it interposed a slight barrier between myself and the white horror in front of me . . . it made me ashamed to be a member of the human race.[1]

---

[1] Margaret Bourke-White, *Dear Fatherland, Rest Quietly* (New York: Simon and Schuster, 1946), 73.

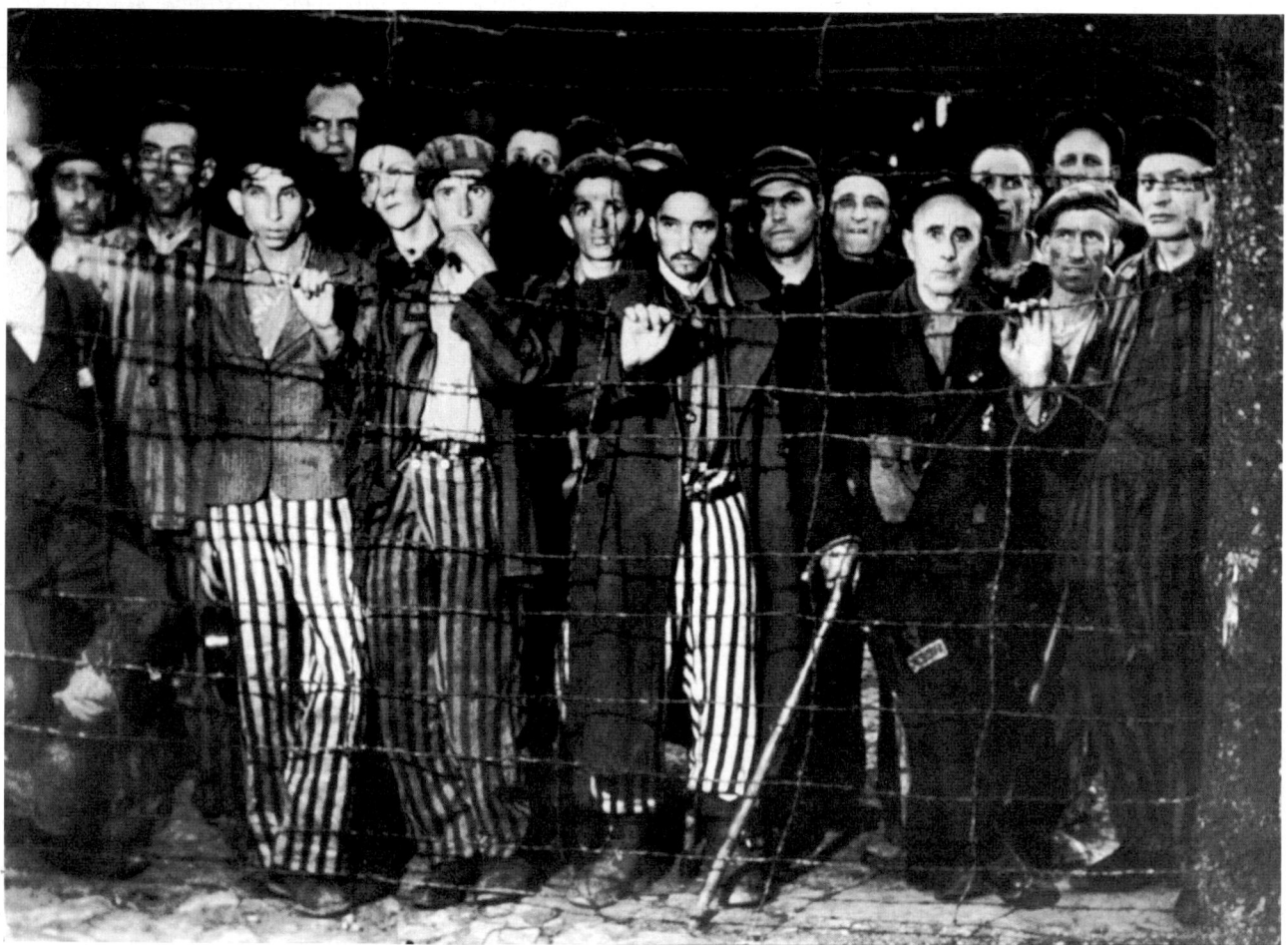

∧ 10.13 MARGARET BOURKE-WHITE, *The Living Dead of Buchenwald, April 1945* (1945).

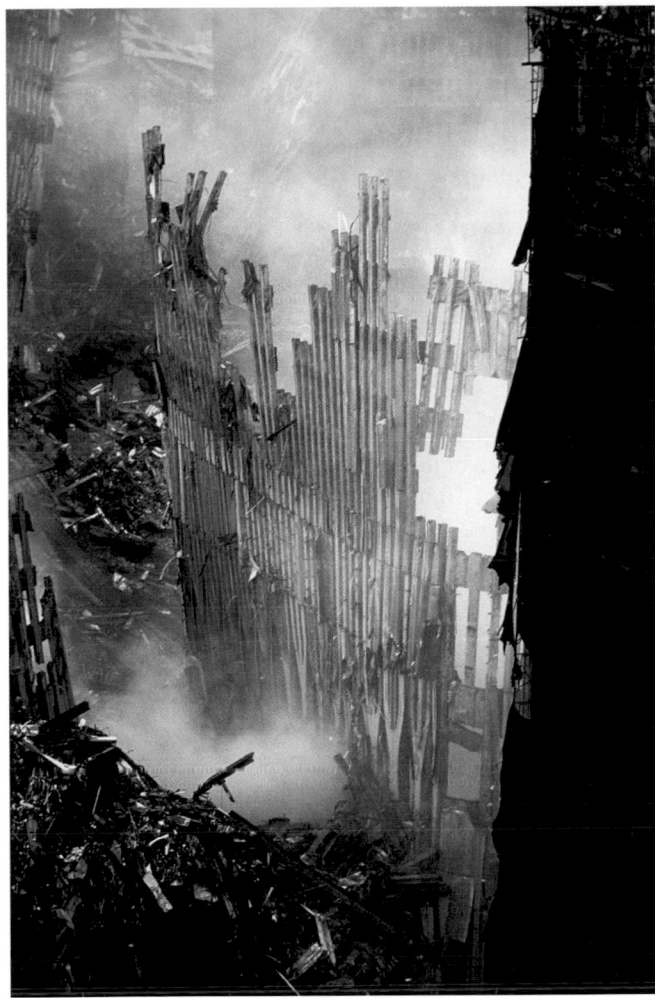

∧ 10.14 RON BERARD, *Untitled* (2001).

Dorothea Lange traveled rural America to photograph the effects of the Depression, and Margaret Bourke-White followed the U.S. troops abroad during World War II. As Bourke-White discovered, one of the keys to photojournalism is being in the presence of history in the making. On September 11, 2001, when terrorists hijacked commercial aircraft and flew them into the World Trade Center towers, photographer Ron Berard was living on an upper floor of an apartment building directly across from the devastation. His photograph (Fig. 10.14) captures the hellish and almost surreal nature of the event in which almost 3,000 people lost their lives—the shard of the curtain wall that remained, the pile of rubble, the charred facade of a still-standing neighbor. The eerie smoke that rose from the pit would continue to rise for two months.

Photography as an Art Form

Photographers became aware of the potential of their medium as an art form more than 100 years ago. Edward Weston, Paul Strand, Edward Steichen, and others argued that photographers must not attempt to imitate painting (as Lumière had) but must find modes of expression that are truer to their medium. Synergistically, painters moved toward abstraction because the obligation to faithfully record nature was now assumed by the photographer. Why, after all, do what a camera can do better? In 1902, Alfred Stieglitz founded the Photo-Secession, a group dedicated to advancing photography as a separate art form. Stieglitz enjoyed taking pictures under adverse weather conditions and at odd times of day to show the versatility of his medium and the potential for expressiveness.

Edward Steichen's *The Flatiron Building—Evening* (Fig. 10.15), photographed a century ago, is among the foremost early examples of the photograph as a work of art. It is an exquisitely sensitive nocturne of haunting shapes looming in a rain-soaked atmosphere. The branch in the foreground provides the viewer with a psychological vantage point as it cuts across the composition like a bolt of lightning or an artery pulsing with life. The values

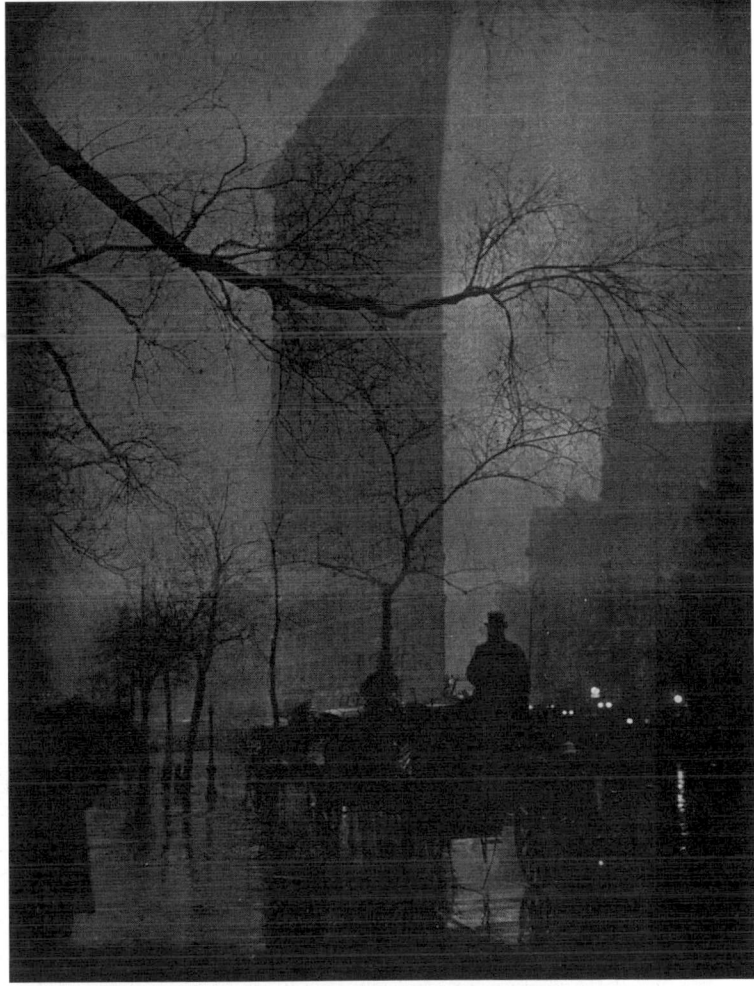

∧ 10.15 EDWARD STEICHEN, *The Flatiron Building—Evening* (1906).
Library of Congress, Prints and Photographs Division.

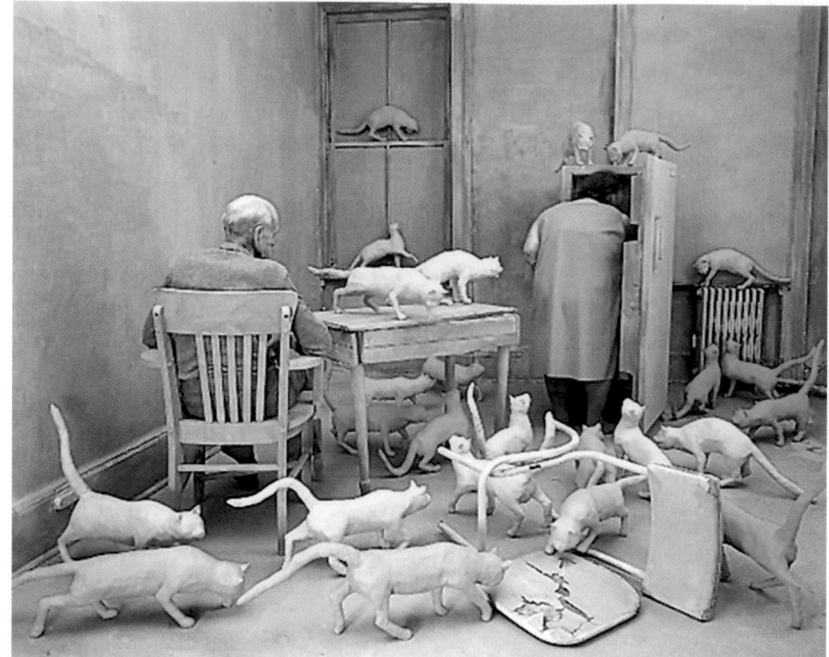

1 ft.

∧ 10.16 **SANDY SKOGLUND,** *Radioactive Cats* (1980). Cibachrome, 30" × 40".

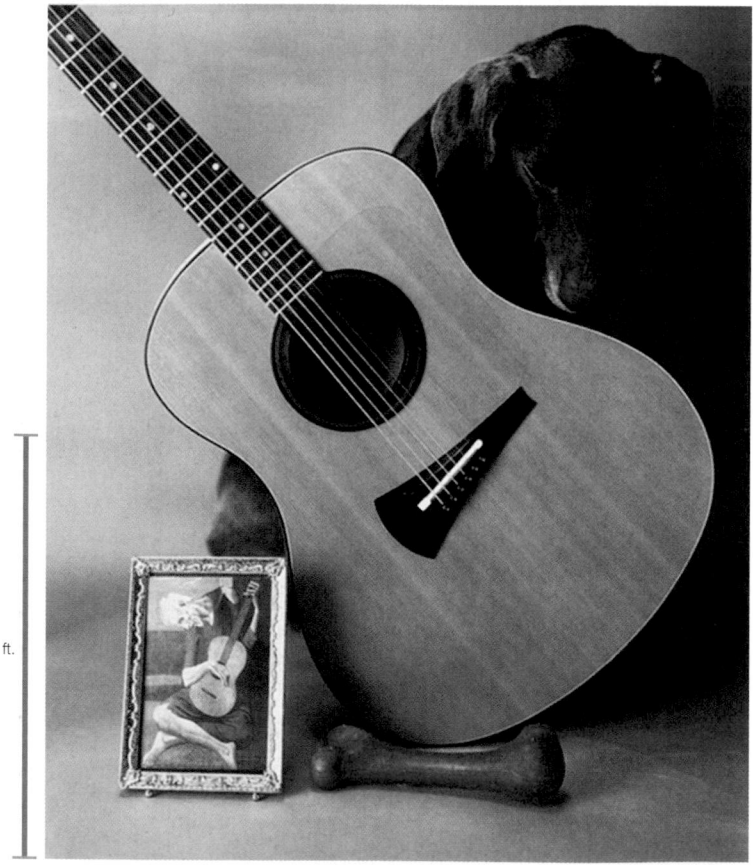

1 ft.

∧ 10.17 **WILLIAM WEGMAN,** *Blue Period* (1981). Color Polaroid photograph, 24" × 22".

are predominantly middle grays, although here and there, beaconlike, streetlamps sparkle in the distance. The infinite gradations of gray in the cast-iron skyscraper after which the picture is named, and in the surrounding structures, yield an immeasurable softness. Although much is present that we cannot readily see, there is nothing gloomy or frightening about the scene. Rather, it seems pregnant with wonderful things that will happen as the rain stops and the twentieth century progresses.

It was not long before artists began to manipulate their medium so that they, too, could venture beyond imitation. The first steps were tentative, building on the familiar and the readily acceptable. Some portrait photographers, for example, experimented with double-exposed images and tableaus—elaborate painted backdrops against which people and objects were thoughtfully and deliberately arranged. The tableau form is also seen in the works of contemporary artists.

Sandy Skoglund's *Radioactive Cats* (Fig. 10.16) portrays a phlegmatic elderly couple living out their colorless lives amid an invasion of neon green cats. Skoglund sculpted the plaster cats herself and painted the room gray, controlling every aspect of the set before she photographed the scene.

Artist-photographer William Wegman happened upon his most famous subject when his Weimaraner puppy virtually insisted on performing before his lights. Man Ray, named by Wegman after the Surrealist photographer, posed willingly in hundreds of staged sets that range from the credible to the farcical. *Blue Period* (Fig. 10.17) is a riff on Pablo Picasso's painting *The Old Guitarist* (see Fig. 20.5), enframed in a souvenir-sized reproduction in the lower-left foreground. In both works, a guitar cuts diagonally across the composition, adding the only contrasting color to the otherwise monochromatic blue background. The heads of the old man and of Man Ray hang, melancholy, over the soulful instrument. As Picasso gave the old man's flesh a bluish cast, so did Wegman tint the Weimaraner's muzzle. In Wegman's photograph, however, we find the pièce de résistance—an object laden with profound meaning for the guitarist's stand-in: a blue rubber bone.

Cindy Sherman is her own exclusive subject, adopting diverse personae for her photographs. Sherman recalls a mundane, early inspiration for her approach: "I had all this makeup. I just wanted to see how transformed I could look. It was like painting in a way."[2] Soon she set herself before elaborate backdrops, costumed in a limitless wardrobe. Dress designers began to ask her to

[2] Cindy Sherman, in Gerald Marzorati, "Imitation of Life," *Artnews* 82 (September 1983): 84–85.

> I see my work as a pictorial excursus on the topic of feminism and contemporary Islam—a discussion that puts certain myths and realities under the microscope and comes to the conclusion that these are much more complex than many of us had thought.
>
> —SHIRIN NESHAT

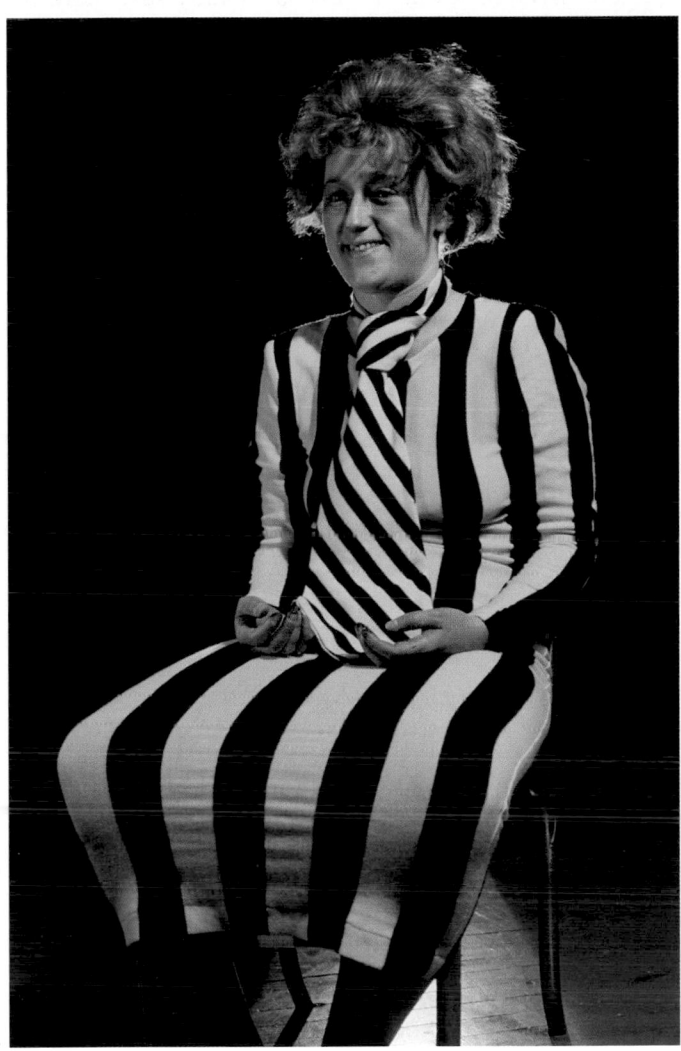

∧ 10.18 **CINDY SHERMAN,** *Untitled* (1984). Color photograph, 71" × 48½".

shadows. Light is directed from the extreme right, harshly illuminating and revealing surfaces of the body. The blacked-out areas of the setting add a somber, melancholy tone to the subject.

Iranian American photographer and video artist Shirin Neshat came to the United States as a teenager, before the shah of Iran was removed from power, and returned in 1990 to witness a nation transformed by the rule of Islamic clergy. She was particularly concerned about how life had changed for Iranian women, who now had limited

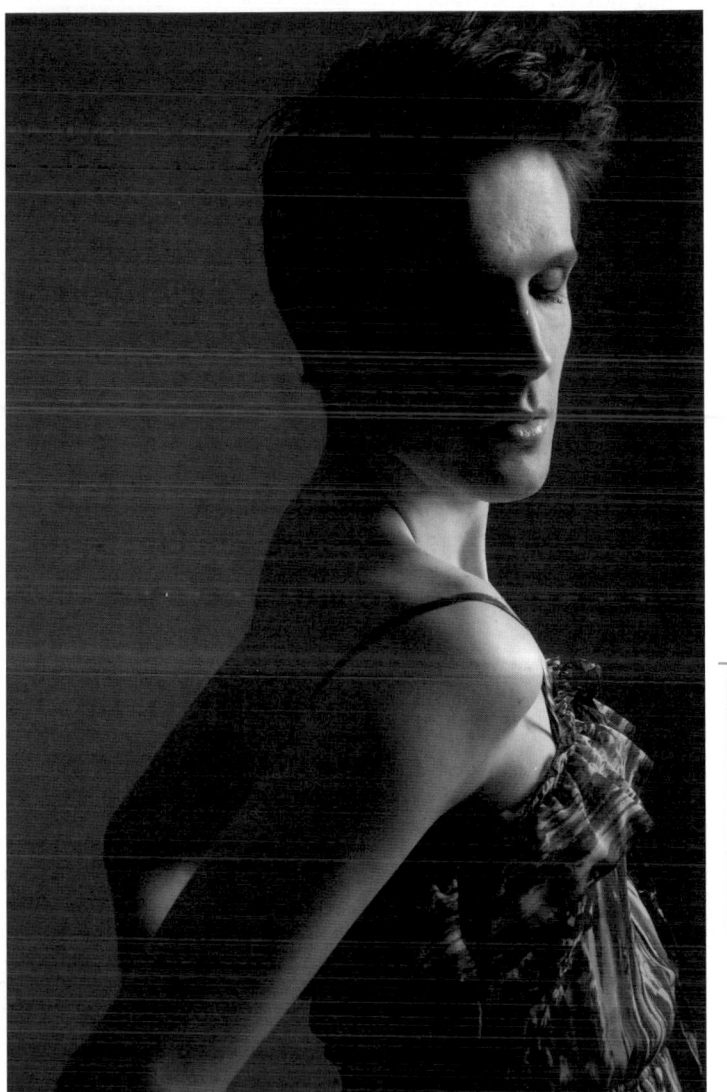

∧ 10.19 **JOHANN DERFLINGER, ASSISTED BY LIZ SWEZEY,** *Performance Gender* (2013). Digital photograph, 20" × 30".

use their haute couture in her photographs, and works such as *Untitled* (Fig. 10.18) were actually shot as part of an advertising assignment for French *Vogue*. The result is less a sales device than a harsh view of the fashion industry. Sherman appears as a disheveled model with a troubling expression. Something here is very wrong. Regimented stripes go awry as the fabric of her dress is stretched taut across her thighs and knees. Her hands rest oddly in her lap, fingertips red with what seems to be blood. And then there is the smile—an unsettling leer implying madness.

Johann Derflinger's self-portrait (Fig. 10.19) is sharply lit, exaggerating the highlighted area as well as the

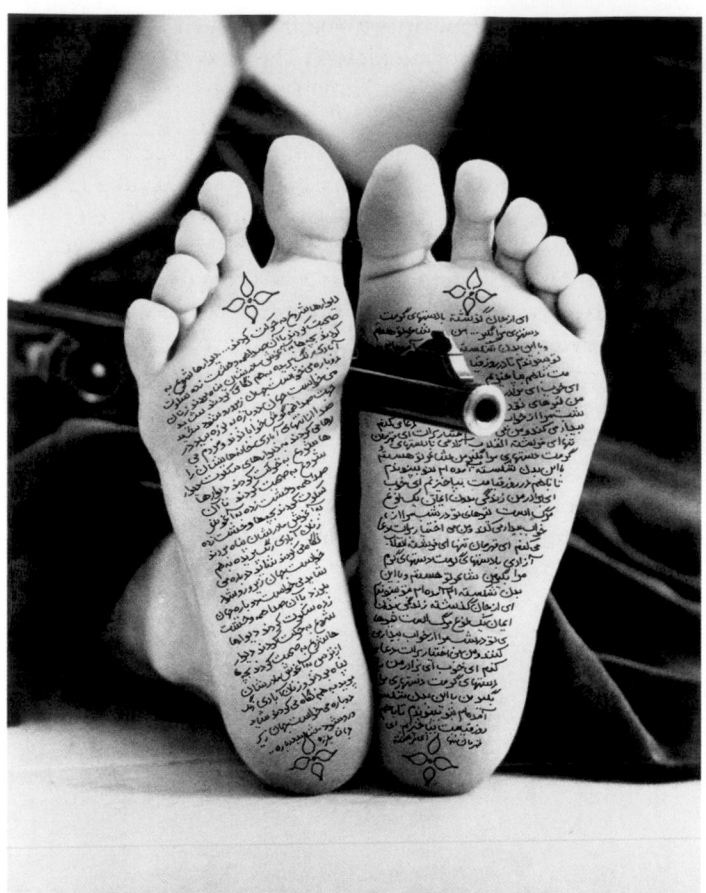

1 ft.

^ 10.20 **SHIRIN NESHAT**, *Allegiance and Wakefulness (Women of Allah)* (1994). Offset print with ink calligraphy, 3' 5¼" × 2' 9". Israel Museum, Jerusalem (anonymous gift, New York, to American Friends of the Israel Museum).

CONNECTIONS Use your smartphone, tablet computer, or digital camera to take a self-portrait—a "selfie." Use the features of your electronic equipment to crop the photo, duplicate the photo, change the colors in the photo, stretch the photo, and otherwise play with it. Which results do you prefer? Why?

the movements of objects and capture them with an open shutter at many flashes per second. Edgerton applied the technology to capture ordinary and extraordinary events—water coming out of a faucet, a simple drop of milk splashing into a pool of the liquid, bullets penetrating helium balloons, and athletes in motion.

FILM

Film and video are so-called time-based mediums in which duration, or the passage of time, is a dimension. Just as some artists manipulate elements of art to create illusions of three dimensions, others use time-based mediums to create the illusion of movement and duration.

Harold Edgerton's process (see Fig. 10.21) was the opposite of what photographer Eadweard Muybridge aimed to do in his early experiments in filmmaking. Edgerton froze each and every fraction of actual motion in a single image. Muybridge combined numerous individual photographs of a moving object into a sequence that, if viewed in rapid succession, gave the illusion of actual motion. The door to cinema was open.

opportunities outside the home and were veiled behind black *chadors*. Figure 10.20 is one of a series called *Women of Allah,* in which guns or flowers are frequently juxtaposed with vulnerable though rebellious faces, hands, and feet that emerge from beneath the veil. The exposed flesh is overwritten with sensual or political texts by Iranian women in the native tongue of Farsi. The calligraphic writing may first appear to be little more than a mélange of elegant and mysterious patterns and designs, but there is no mistaking its message of resistance. The photos are unlikely to be seen and "decoded" by the eyes of Iranians living in Iran, but the message of the artist to the world outside is clear.

Evolving technology has made it possible for photographers to achieve dazzling images such as the one in Harold Edgerton's *Milk Drop Coronet* (Fig. 10.21), featured in the Museum of Modern Art's first exhibition of photography in 1937. Edgerton, called the "father" of high-speed and stop-action photography, was an electrical engineer at MIT who pioneered the use of the stroboscope—a device that emits brief and brilliant flashes of light that seem to slow or stop the action of people or objects in motion—for photography. He would synchronize the flashes with

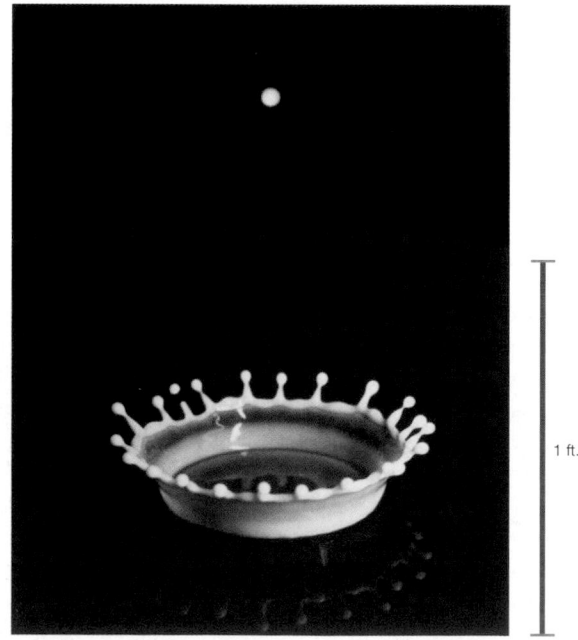

1 ft.

^ 10.21 **HAROLD EDGERTON**, *Milk Drop Coronet* (1957, printed later). Silver gelatin print, 16" × 20".

Muybridge's *Galloping Horse* (Fig. 10.22) sequence was shot in 1878 by twenty-four cameras placed alongside a racetrack and was made possible by new, fast-acting photosensitive plates. (If these plates had been developed fifteen years earlier, Brady could have bequeathed us a photographic record of Civil War battle scenes.) Muybridge had been commissioned to settle a bet as to whether racehorses ever had all four hooves off the ground at once. He found that they did, but also that they never assumed the rocking-horse position in which the front and back legs are simultaneously extended.

Muybridge is generally credited with performing the first successful experiments in making motion pictures. He fashioned a device that could photograph a rapid sequence of images, and he invented the **Zoopraxiscope**, which projected these images onto a screen. Muybridge's process was the opposite of Edgerton's, who, many decades later, froze each and every fraction of actual motion in a single image. Muybridge combined numerous individual photographs of a moving object into a sequence that, if viewed in rapid succession, gave the illusion of actual motion.

The birth of motion pictures, or cinema, was the result of specific inventions including *film* (in this usage, images printed on celluloid and cut into strips). In 1891 Thomas Alva Edison (who had met Muybridge in 1888) patented the **Kinetoscope**, a motion-picture viewing device. A sequence of images on film (something like Muybridge's galloping horse) was passed over a lamp, the light from which was broken into quick flashes by a revolving shutter placed between the film and the lamp. The light flashes illuminated each frame, and the rapidity of the progression of the frames, along with the phenomenon of persistence of vision, created the illusion of motion.

Edison's Kinetoscope was a box into which a viewer would peer to see a moving picture. The next step in the evolution of cinema was projection of the moving picture; this happened with the Cinematographe, a camera and projector in one piece of equipment, patented by the brothers August and Louis Lumière in France in 1895. Their first public motion-picture projection took place the same year, a twenty-minute program of ten short films. Among them was *The Demolition of a Wall*, a film that is known as the first to feature special effects: Lumière reversed the film to suggest that the wall was going up rather than going down. Soon after, the appearance of trick photography became the staple of Georges Melies, who used stop-motion and superimposed images to create true special effects in films that included adaptations of two novels by Jules Verne—*A Trip to the Moon* and *Twenty Thousand Leagues under the Sea*.

Within a few short years of these inventions, commercial movie houses sprang up in France and in the United States, and motion pictures were distributed for public viewing. These were silent films accompanied by live orchestral music and stage shows. The next big step in moviemaking occurred with the first feature film that incorporated sound—*The Jazz Singer* (1927). From then on, sound on film recording shaped the future of cinema.

Varieties of Cinematographic Techniques

Cinematography is the art of making motion pictures. Motion pictures begin with the creation of the illusion of movement; this illusion is created via stroboscopic motion or the presentation of a rapid progression of images of stationary objects. An audience is shown 16 to

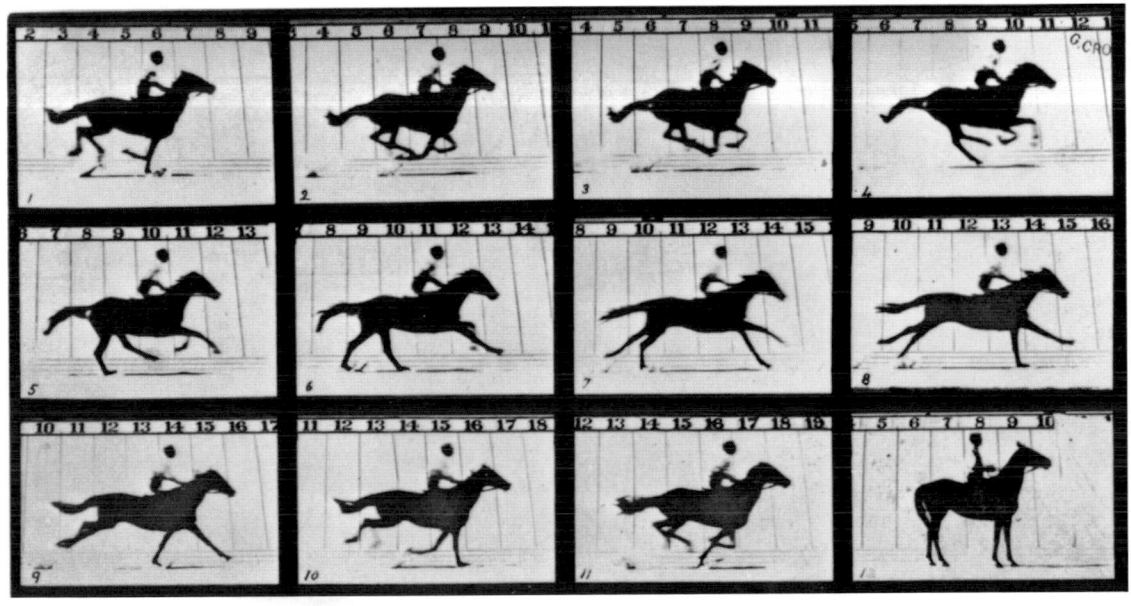

< 10.22 EADWEARD MUYBRIDGE, *Galloping Horse* (1878).

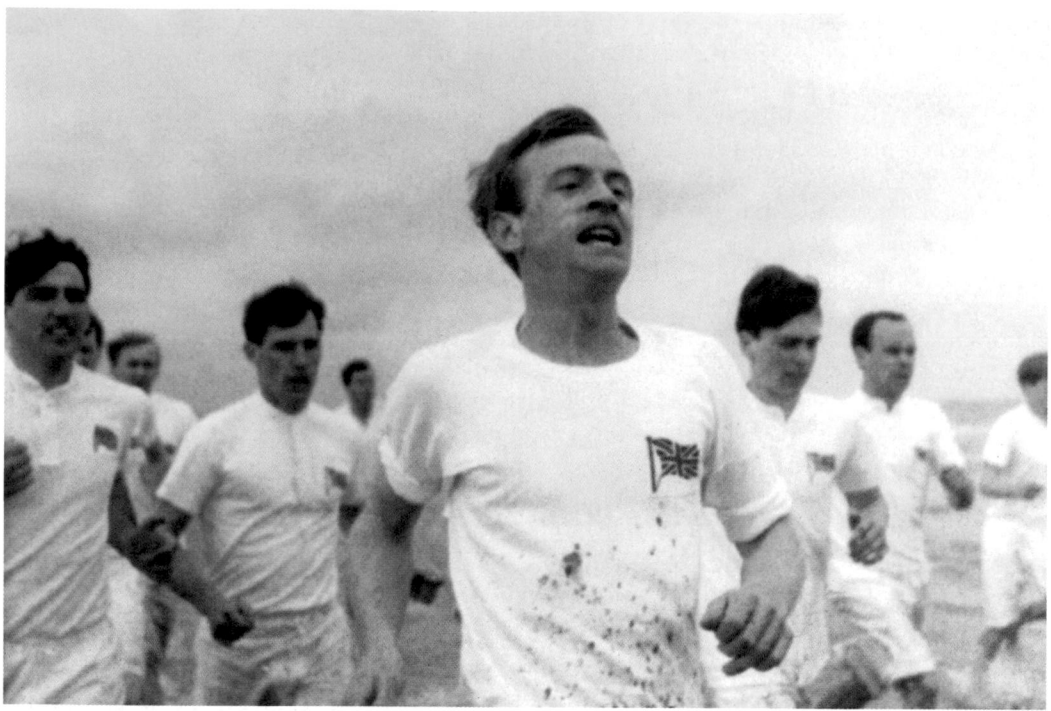

∧ 10.23 HUGH HUDSON, DIRECTOR. Film still from *Chariots of Fire* (1981).

24 pictures or frames per second (fps), and each picture or frame differs slightly from the one preceding it.

MANIPULATING TIME   At a viewing rate of 24 fps, motion in a film appears smooth, natural, and realistic. Slow motion, on the other hand, creates the appearance that time has slowed down and directs or holds our focus. It can be used to give us a strong impression of the personalities of characters, as in the famous opening scene of Hugh Hudson's *Chariots of Fire* (Fig. 10.23) or the opening credits of Quentin Tarantino's *Reservoir Dogs* (Fig. 10.24). It can also isolate specific details of actions that would otherwise be fleeting to our eyes. Achieving slow motion is not a matter of shooting fewer frames or slowing down

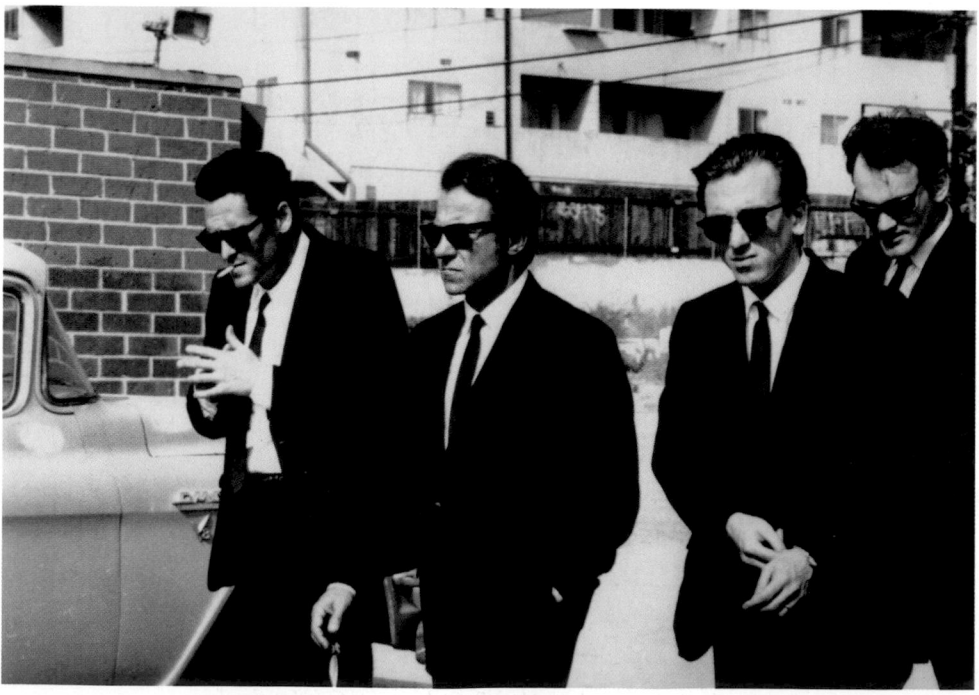

< 10.24 QUENTIN TARANTINO, DIRECTOR. Film still from *Reservoir Dogs* (1992).

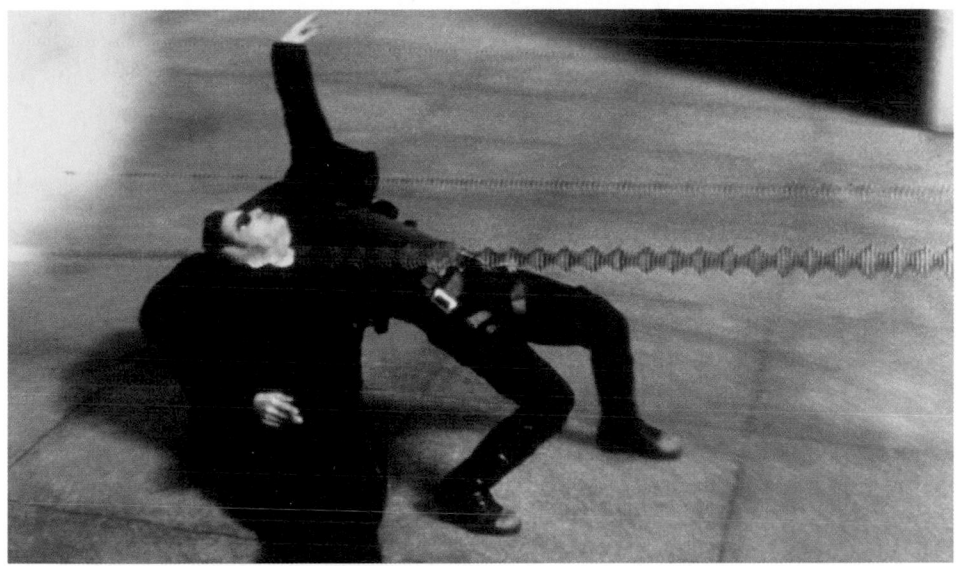

▲ 10.25 ANDY WACHOWSKI AND LANA WACHOWSKI, DIRECTORS. Film still from *The Matrix* (1999).

the number of frames per second that we see; rather, slow motion is achieved by shooting at a frame rate *faster* than 24 fps (for example, 48, 60, or 120 fps). When the films are played back at 24 fps, movement appears to be slowed down. Slow-motion—and fast-motion—clips are sometimes juxtaposed with each other and with 24-fps sequences to disrupt the predictable pace of a scene.

Andy Wachowski and Lana Wachowski's film *The Matrix* includes groundbreaking slow-motion effects known as *bullet time* in which multiple cameras, arranged at multiple angles and vantage points (above, below, alongside of, in front of, and behind the action), capture the scene in many thousands of still images. The frames are then assembled with the aid of a computer to create the illusion of frozen time or slowly moving time, as when Neo, the main character in *The Matrix*, acrobatically dodges bullets and plucks them out of the air (Fig. 10.25).

EDITING The manipulation of time begins with camerawork and comes to fruition with editing—the process of selecting, assembling, and sequencing raw shots (filmed details of the action) and effects and combining them into an aesthetic, expressive whole.

Editing techniques are used to construct cohesive and coherent narratives and heighten dramatic impact. A few commonly used examples are *cutting on action, jump cut, match cut, parallel action*, and *montage*.

Cutting on action is a "continuity editing" technique that is used within a scene to create the illusion of spatial and temporal continuity *through* an edit point (through the "cut" that joins the two shots together). Two different angles of the same action are both filmed, and the edit point (the cut) is placed midaction to connect the two shots, seemingly in *real time*.

Unlike *cutting on action*, which aims to make an edit seamless, the *jump cut* edit is intentionally jarring and can be used to condense time. Instead of using multiple shots that are taken from significantly different angles, this technique cuts from one angle to a similar angle (or even a later point within the same shot), thereby disrupting the temporal or spatial continuity of a scene. This gives the viewer a sense of jumping forward in time, which can create tension and be unsettling. The car scene in Jean-Luc Godard's *Breathless* is a classic example of the jump cut (www.youtube.com, "À bout de *souffle [Breathless]* Jean Luc Godard Car Scene" at 0:12). The character Patricia (seen in another scene in Figure 10.26) is riding in a car and is filmed from the same camera position behind her to the left. We see her with her hands in her lap when, all of a sudden, the film cuts to her looking into a small mirror. The action of raising the mirror is missing; the scene jumps from one moment in the action to the other with an obvious gap.

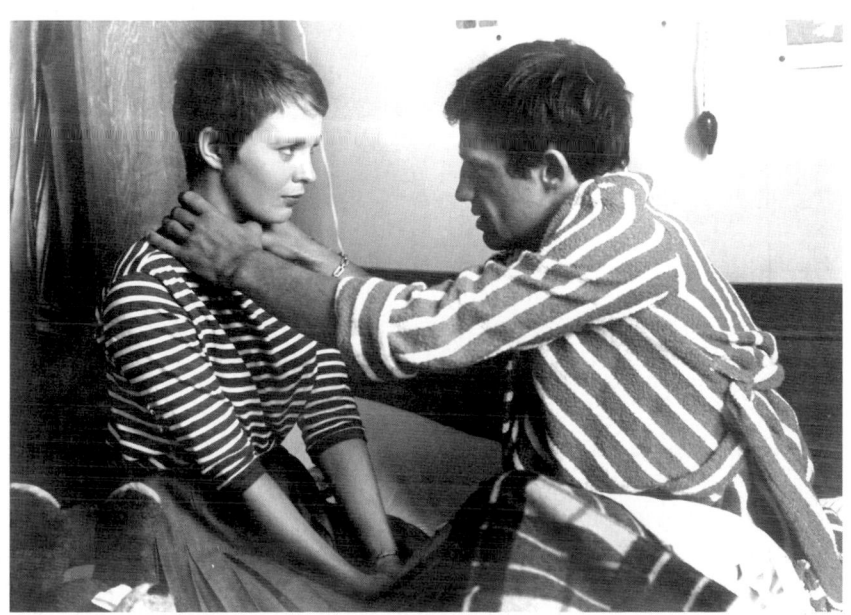

▲ 10.26 JEAN-LUC GODARD, DIRECTOR. Film still from *Breathless* (1960).

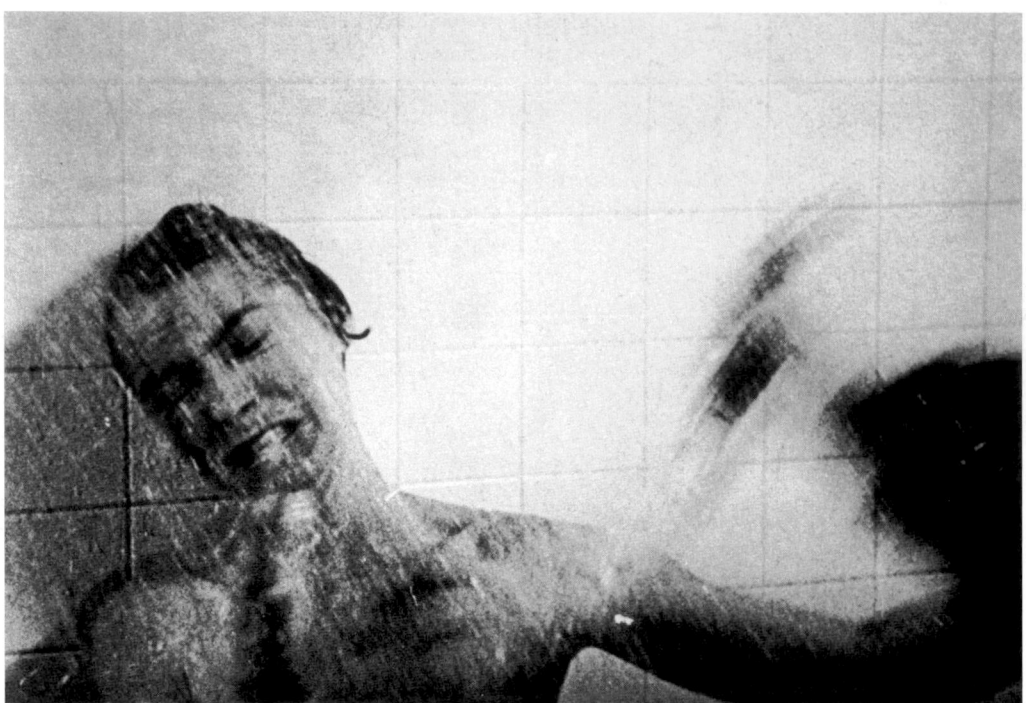

a.

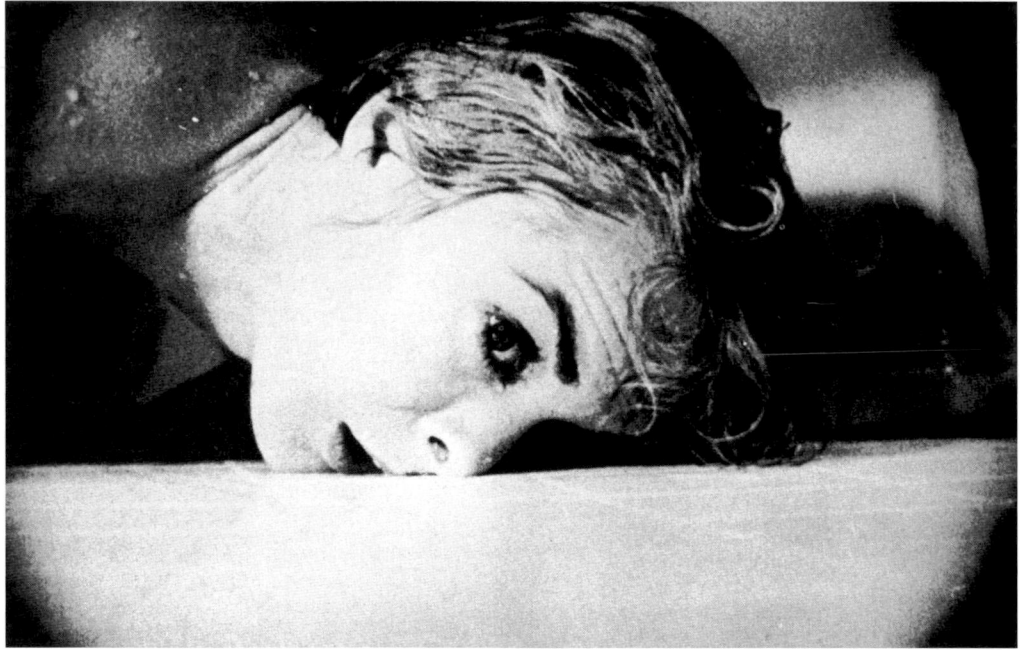

b.

⌃ 10.27 ALFRED HITCHCOCK, DIRECTOR. Film stills from *Psycho* (1960).

A *match cut*, also known as a *graphic match*, is an edit between two different objects that share similar visual qualities, such as shape. By cutting from a shot of one object to a shot of another similarly shaped object, a metaphorical connection can be made between them that wouldn't be obvious otherwise. An example of this is seen in the shower scene in Alfred Hitchcock's *Psycho* (http://movieclips.com, "*Psycho* 'The Shower' " at 2:05), in which a close-up shot of the round shower drain is juxtaposed with a close-up shot of the dying woman's round eye. Two stills from the shower scene are featured in Figure 10.27.

Parallel action editing employs the technique of *cross-cutting*, the act of cutting back and forth between two different scenes, thereby interweaving them and creating a

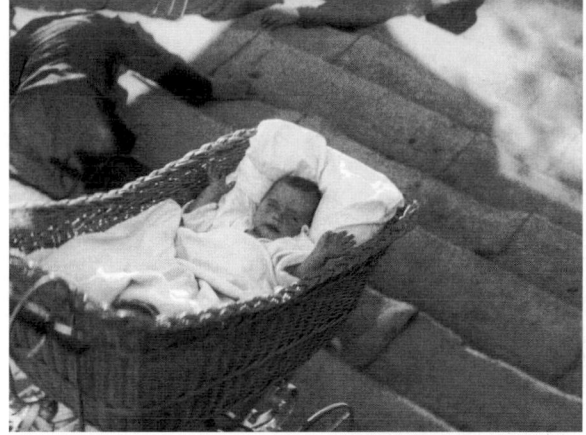

a.

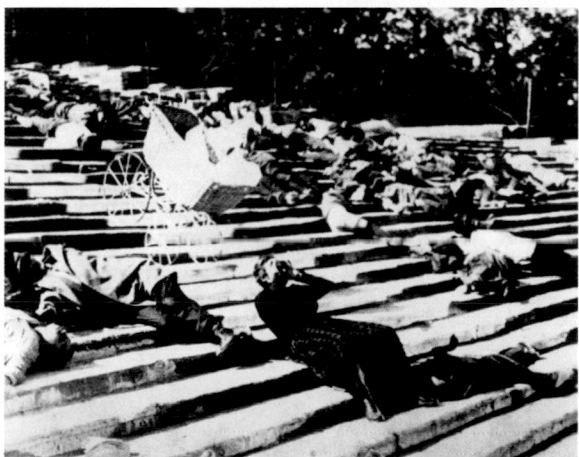

b.

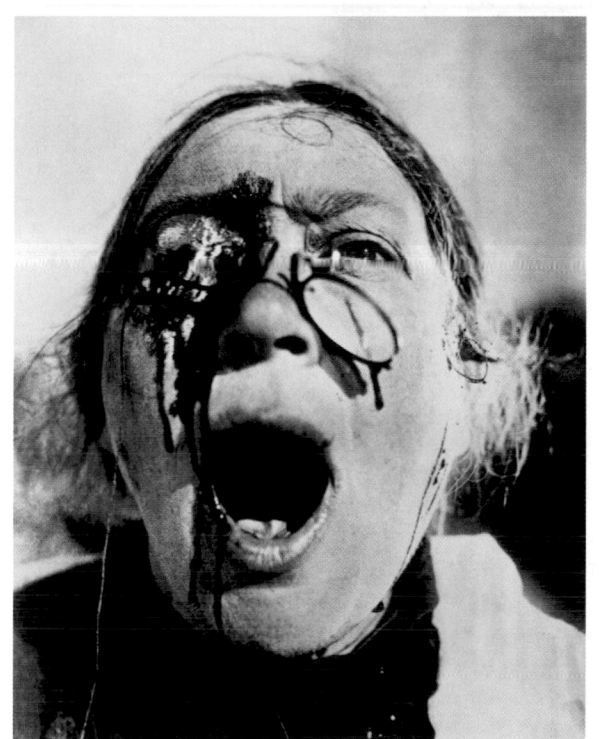

c.

meaningful connection between them. *Cross-cutting* can create the illusion that both scenes are happening simultaneously, even if they are in different locations.

The term *montage* refers to the technique of combining multiple, seemingly disparate shots into a cohesive sequence. The type of logic that is applied to montage editing exists outside the logic of temporal or spatial realism. Through *montage*, multiple spaces and time periods can be spliced together to create a new narrative connection between them. A montage sequence has a special opportunity to collapse time by jumping from moment to moment, allowing days, weeks, or years to take place within only a few seconds or minutes of screen time. Montage appeared first in Sergei Eisenstein's influential and critically acclaimed film *The Battleship Potemkin* (Fig. 10.28). The "Odessa Steps" sequence, in which Tsarist soldiers massacre Odessa civilians, is one of the most well-known scenes in the history of film.

ANIMATION **Animation** creates the illusion of movement through the manipulation and duplication of, for example, drawings, computer-generated images, or clay figures. In traditional animation, each drawing differs slightly from the one preceding it, just as with photographs in early cinematography. Today computer graphics techniques are generally used to take one image and then modify it from frame to frame to create the illusion of movement more efficiently. Images used in animation can be generated entirely by computer. Sometimes they are inserted into filmed or videotaped environments in such a way as to mix art with reality (Fig. 10.29).

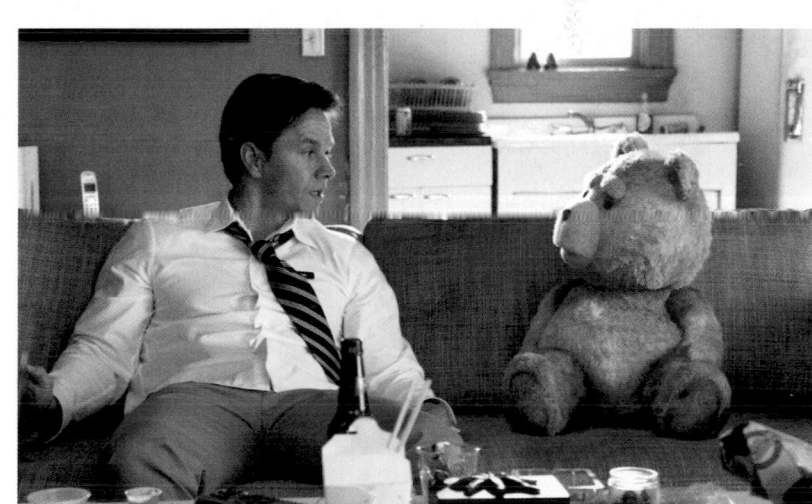

∧ 10.29 SETH MACFARLANE, DIRECTOR. Film still from *Ted* (2012).

< 10.28 SERGEI EISENSTEIN, DIRECTOR. "Odessa Steps" sequence from *The Battleship Potemkin* (1925).

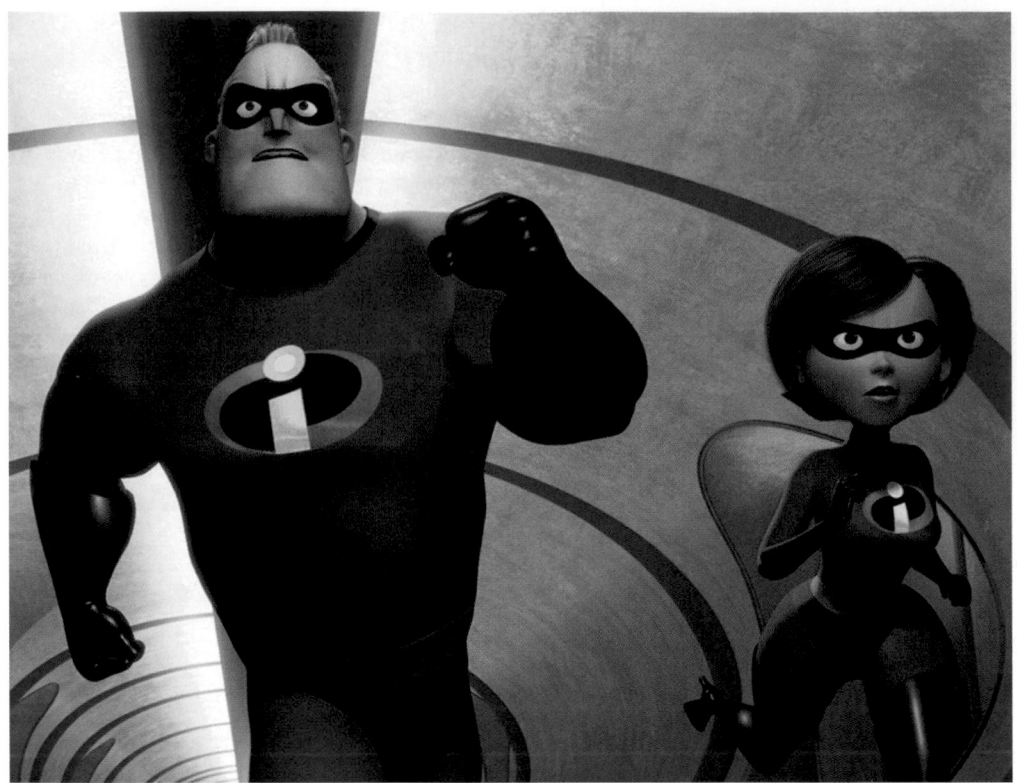

▲ 10.30 BRAD BIRD, DIRECTOR. Film still from *The Incredibles* (2004).

Many film studios use animation and computer graphics and styles vary widely, from Disney and Pixar's groundbreaking animated film *The Incredibles* (Fig. 10.30), to the more recent *Frozen* (Fig. 10.31). Tim Burton's *Corpse Bride* (Fig. 10.32) incorporated puppets constructed of stainless-steel armatures covered with foam latex or silicone. The puppets' movements were created using the tedious process of stop-motion animation. Photographs were taken with commercial digital still photography cameras and the editing was done using Apple's Final Cut Pro. According to *Corpse Bride* trivia, it took the ani-

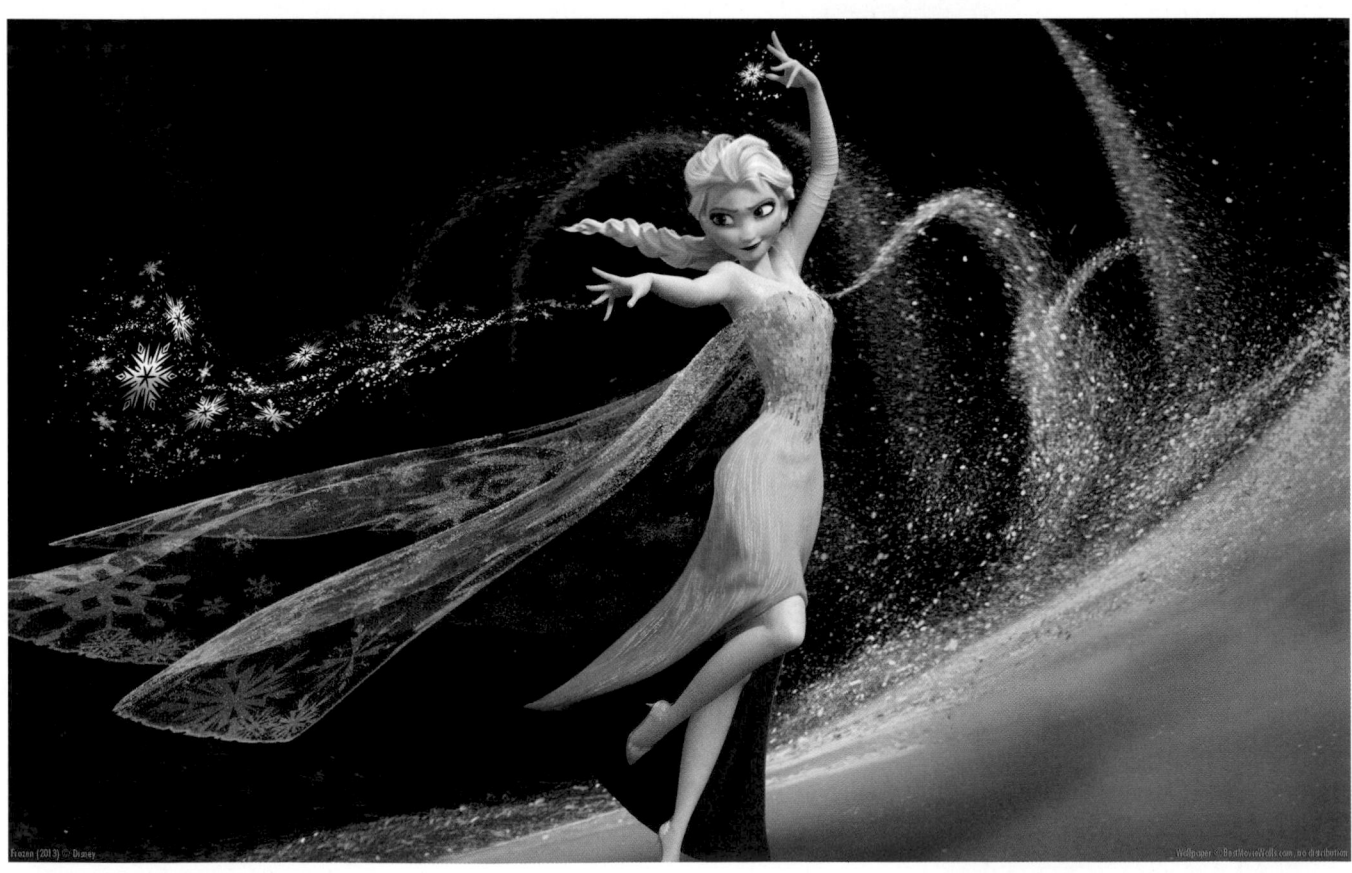

▲ 10.31 Film still from *Frozen* (2013).

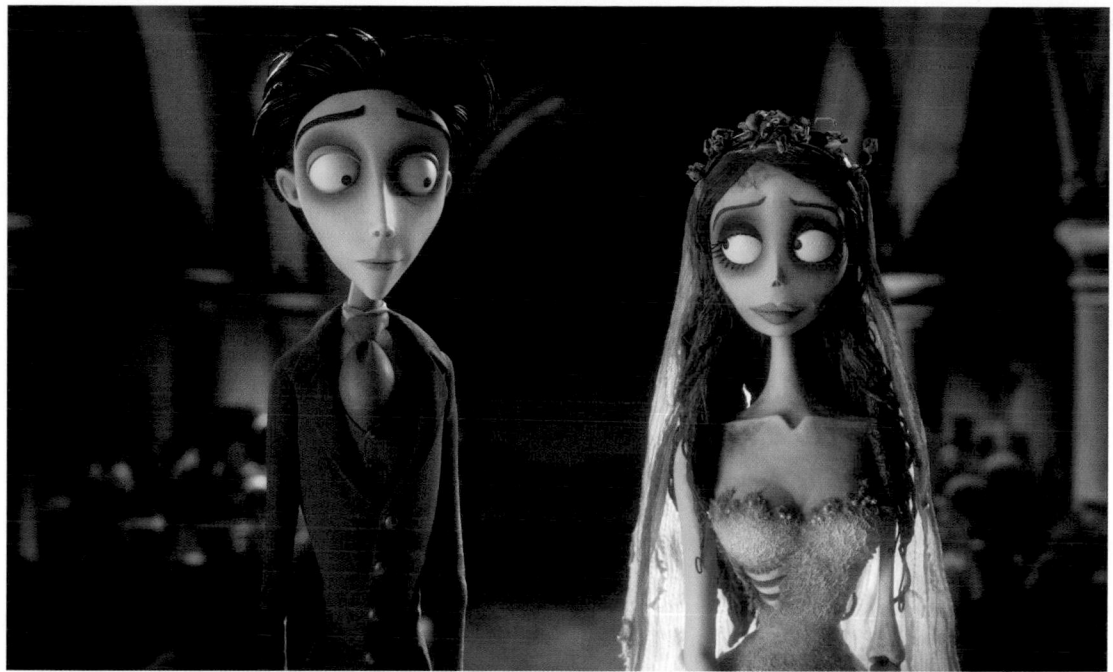

▲ 10.32 **TIM BURTON, DIRECTOR.** Film still from *The Corpse Bride* (2005).

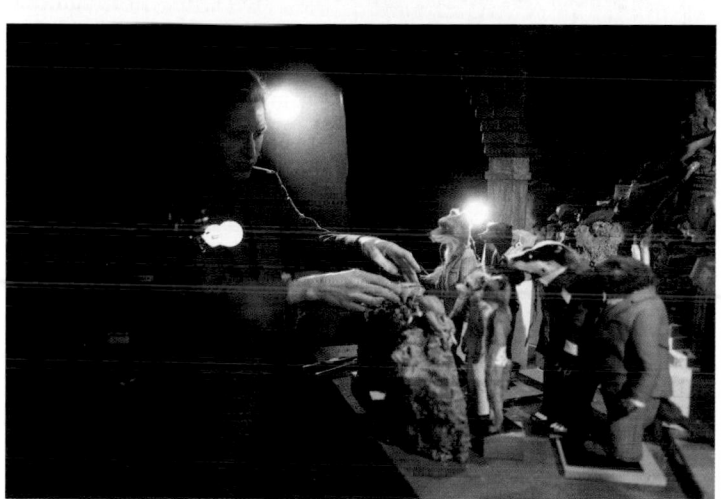

a.

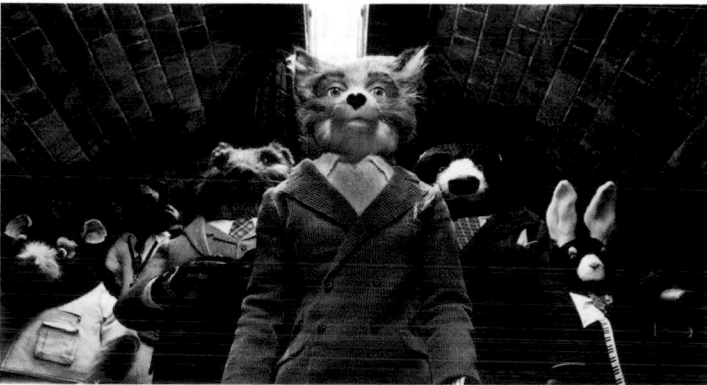

b.

▲ 10.33 **WES ANDERSON, DIRECTOR.** *Fantastic Mr. Fox* (2009). The director at work on the set (a), and film still (b).

mators twenty-eight separate shots just to make the bride blink. A very different effect was achieved using the same process of stop-motion animation in Wes Anderson's *Fantastic Mr. Fox* (Figs. 10.33A and 10.33B).

Varieties of Cinematographic Experience

No discussion of cinematography can hope to recount adequately the richness of the motion-picture experience. Broadly speaking, motion pictures are visual experiences that entertain or move us. For example, as in novels, we identify with characters and become wrapped up in plots. Like other artists, cinematographers make us laugh (consider the great films of the Marx Brothers and Laurel and Hardy); create propaganda, satire, social commentary, fantasy, and symbolism; express artistic theories; and reflect artistic styles. Let us consider some of these more closely.

PROPAGANDA Although there are some early (and choppy) film records of World War I, cinematography was ready for World War II. In fact, while many American actors were embattled in Europe and the Pacific, former president Ronald Reagan was making films for the United States that depicted the valor of the Allied soldiers and the malevolence of the enemy.

Our adversaries were active as well. Before the war, German director Leni Riefenstahl made what is considered one of the greatest (though also most

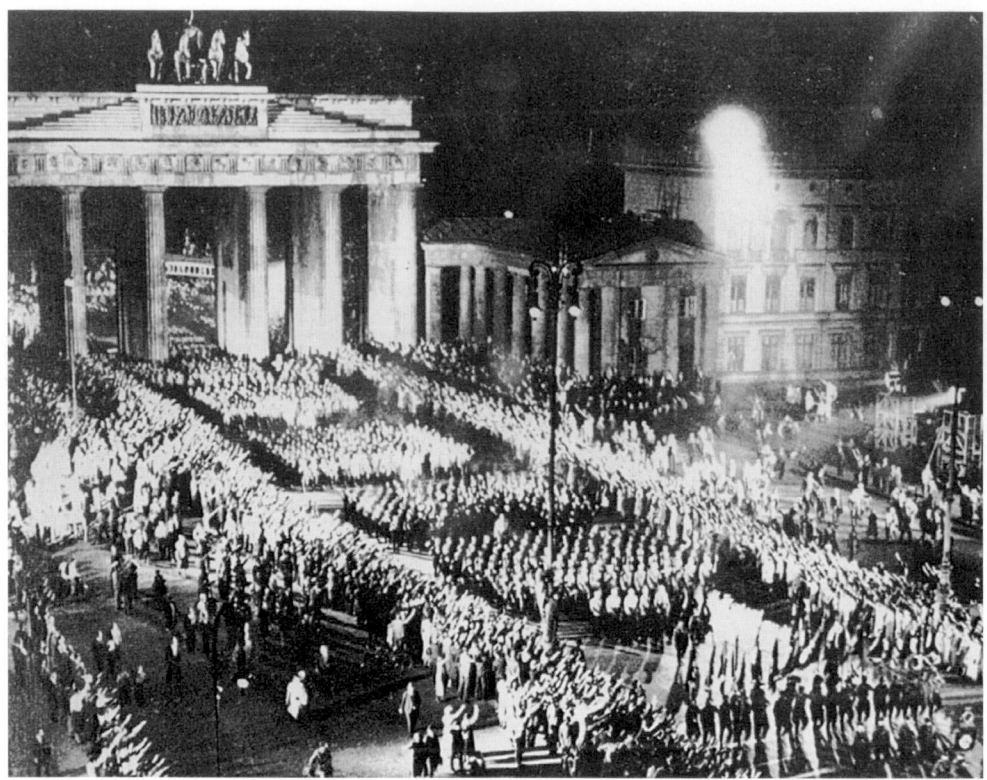

^ 10.34 **LENI RIEFENSTAHL**, Film still from *Triumph of the Will* (1936).

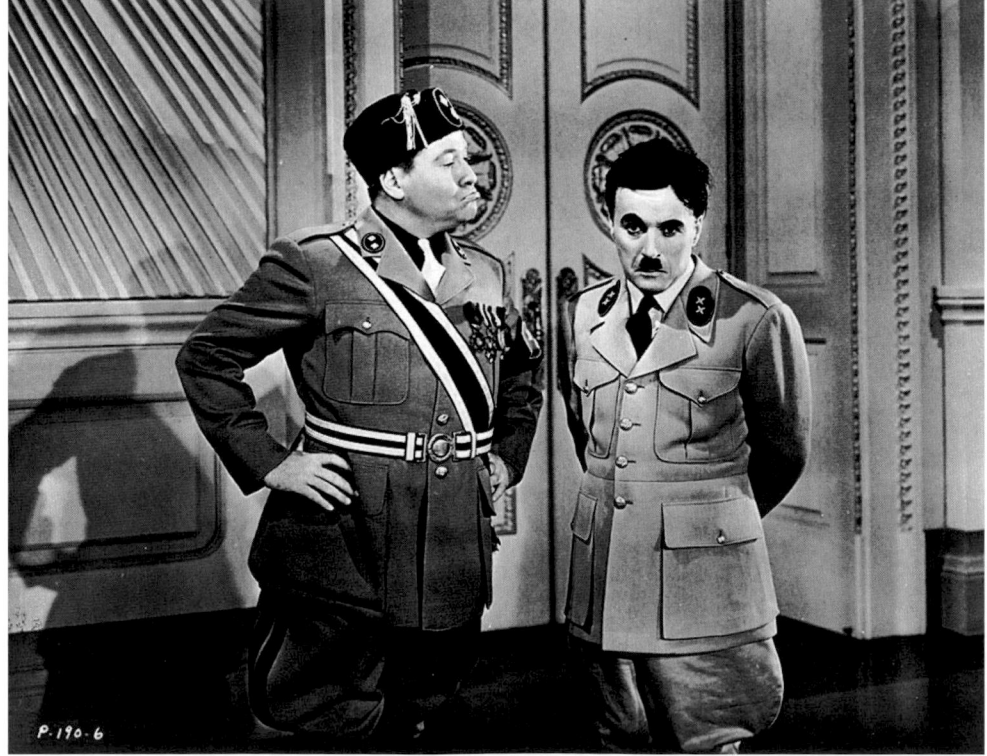

^ 10.35 **CHARLES CHAPLIN**, Film still from *The Great Dictator.*

pernicious) propaganda films of all time, *Triumph of the Will* (Fig. 10.34). Riefenstahl transformed the people and events of a historic event, the 1935 Nuremberg Congress, into abstract, symbolic patterns through the juxtaposition of longshots and close-ups, and aerial and ground-level views. Her montage of people, monuments, and flag-bedecked buildings unified flesh and stone into a hymn to Nazism. The United States, England, Canada, and some other nations paid a back-handed compliment to the power of *Triumph of the Will* by banning it.

SATIRE Satire is the flip side of propaganda. Although Riefenstahl glorified national socialism in Germany, American filmmakers derided it. In one cartoon, for example, Daffy Duck clubs a realistic-looking, speechifying Adolf Hitler over the head with a mallet. Hitler dissolves into tears and calls for his mommy. British American filmmaker Charlie Chaplin added to the derision of the Führer in *The Great Dictator* (Fig. 10.35). The film and television series *M★A★S★H* was set during the Korean War, but it satirized authoritarianism through the ages.

SOCIAL COMMENTARY Filmmakers, like documentary photographers, have made their social comments. *The Grapes of Wrath* (Fig. 10.36), based on the John Steinbeck novel, depicts one family's struggle for survival during the Great Depression, when the banks failed and the Midwest farm basket of the United States turned into

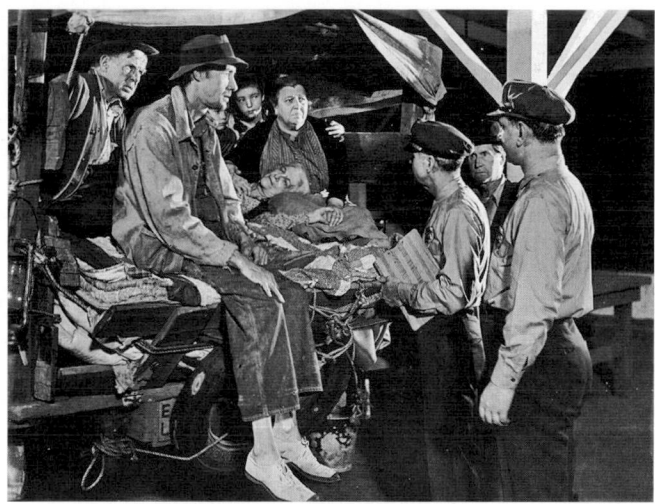

^ 10.36 JOHN FORD, Film still from *The Grapes of Wrath*.

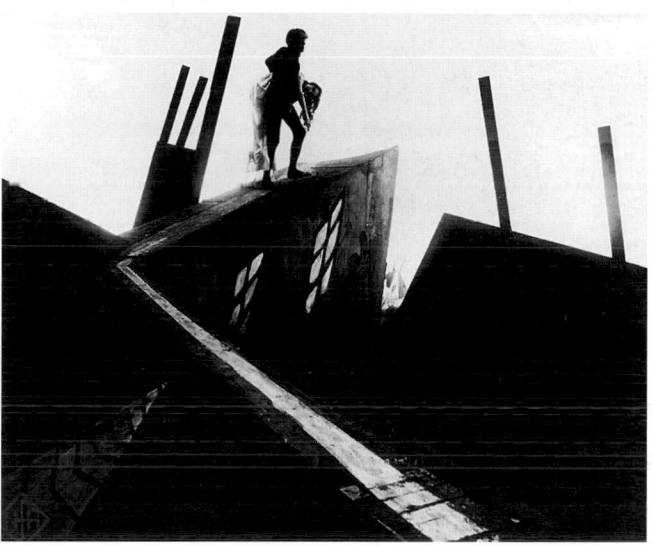

^ 10.37 ROBERT WIENE, Film still from *The Cabinet of Dr. Caligari* (1919).

the Dust Bowl. Like a Dorothea Lange photograph, the camera comes in to record hopelessness and despair. Cinematographers have commented on subjects as varied as divorce (*Divorce, American Style*); civil war in Southeast Asia (*The Killing Fields*); and the excesses of Wall Street (*Wall Street*).

FANTASY Fantasy and flights of fancy are not limited to paintings, drawings, and the written word. In the experimental films of Robert Wiene and Salvador Dalí and Luis Buñuel, events are not confined to the material world as it is; they occupy and express the innermost images of the cinematographer. The sets for Wiene's *The Cabinet of Dr. Caligari* (Fig. 10.37) were created by three painters who employed Expressionist devices such as angular, distorted planes and sheer perspectives. The hallucinatory backdrop removes the protagonist, a carnival hypnotist who causes a sleepwalker to murder

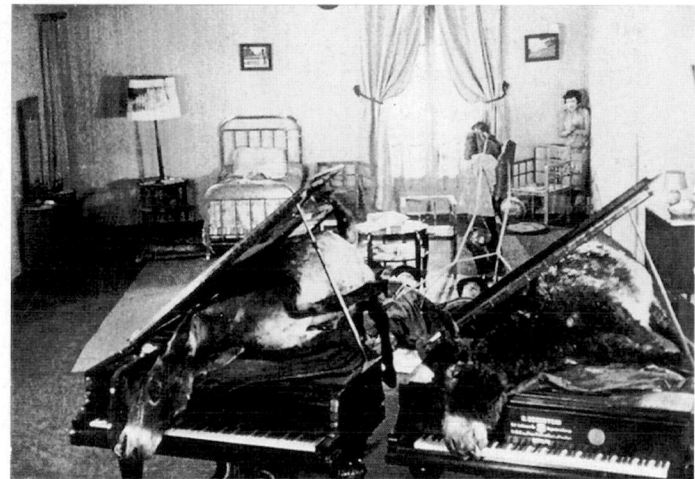

^ 10.38 SALVADOR DALÍ AND LUIS BUÑUEL, Film still from *Un Chien Andalou* (1928).

people who displease him, from the realm of reality. The muddy line between the authentic and the fantastic is further obscured by the film's ending, in which the hypnotist becomes a mental patient telling an imaginary tale. (It is akin to the ravings of the mad Salieri, who, through flashbacks, recounts his actual and fantasized interactions with Mozart in the film *Amadeus*.)

Caligari has a story, albeit an unusual one, but Dalí and Buñuel's surrealistic *Un Chien Andalou* (Fig. 10.38) has a script (if you can call it a script) without order or meaning in the traditional sense. In the shocking opening scene, normal vision is annulled by the slicing of an eyeball. The audience is then propelled through a series of disconnected, dreamlike scenes.

SYMBOLISM In writing about *Un Chien Andalou*, Buñuel claimed that his aims were to evoke instinctive reactions of attraction and repulsion in the audience, but that nothing in the film *symbolized* anything.[3] Fantastic cinematographers often portray their depths of mind literally. They create on the screen the images that dwell deep within their minds. Other cinematographers, such as Ingmar Bergman, frequently express aspects of their inner world through symbols.

VIDEO

The medium of **video** is in principle similar to that of film, but it records and plays back images differently. As with film cameras, video cameras capture and record a series of still images that are then constructed into a moving picture. With video, sights and sounds are *digitized*—that

---

[3] Luis Buñuel, "Notes on the Making of *Un Chien Andalou*," in Art in Cinema, a symposium held at the San Francisco Museum of Art (repr., New York: Arno Press, 1968).

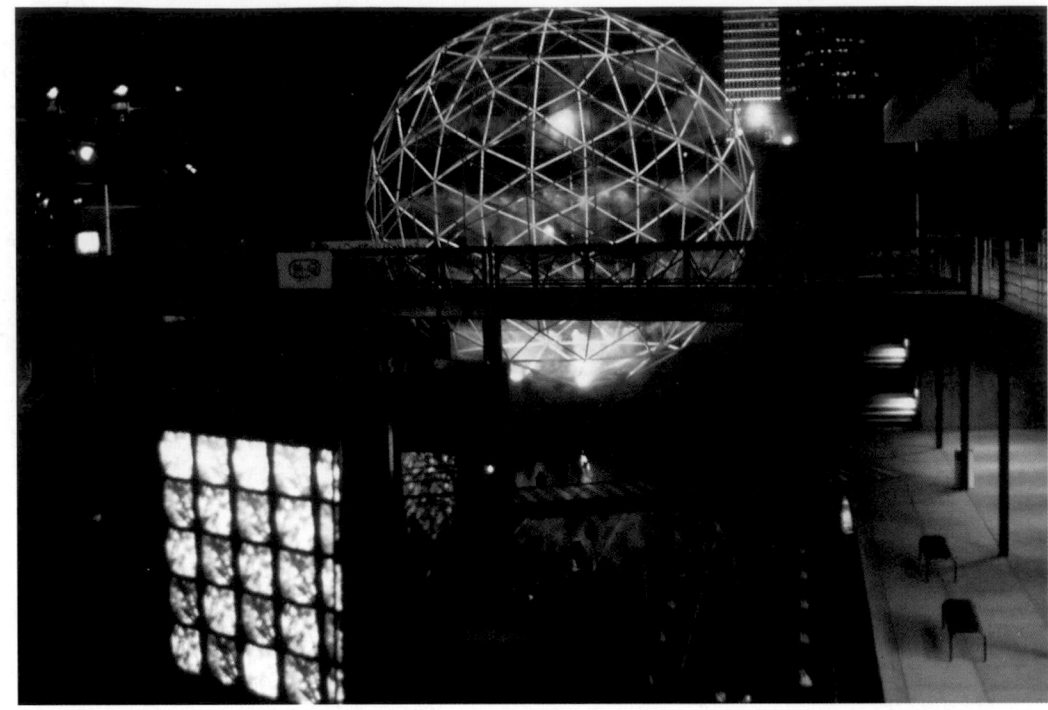

∧ **10.39 DARA BIRNBAUM,** *Rio Videowall* (1989). Installation view of videowall in the public piazza at the Rio Shopping/ Entertainment Complex, Atlanta, Georgia.

is, they are transformed into electronic messages in the form of lengthy codes (a pattern of ones and zeros). The information is stored (as on videotape or memory cards) or transmitted through the air (broadcast) or via cable. Ultimately, the digitized information is projected on a surface or received and displayed on a monitor that transforms it into visual images that consist of hundreds of lines of light and dark and color. The more lines there are, the higher the **resolution** or sharpness of the picture will be. As with film, the viewer is shown a series of still images in rapid succession—fleeting images that create the illusion of movement and the passage of time.

Video as a medium, distinguished from the commercial efforts of the television establishment, was introduced in the 1960s. Almost thirty years later, Dara Birnbaum addressed the relationship between television and video art, between the media and its mass-culture consumerism on the one hand and the discourse of contemporary art on the other. *Rio Videowall* (Fig. 10.39), an interactive public work of art commissioned by the developers of the Rio Shopping/Entertainment Complex in Atlanta, Georgia, consists of twenty-five monitors arranged in a five-by-five-foot grid, in which individual moving images are unified into a single, although shifting composition. Movement of the shoppers triggers a change of imagery on the screens that includes snippets of live news feeds juxtaposed with an almost nostalgic reflection on nature at its most pristine—the land before the onslaught of the shopping mall.

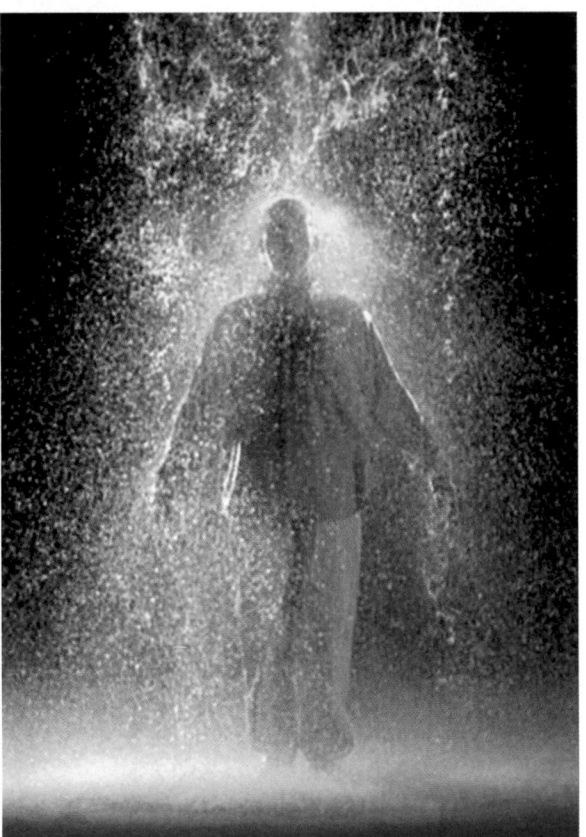

∧ **10.40 BILL VIOLA,** *The Crossing* (1996). Two-channel color video and stereo-sound installation, continuous loop 192" × 330" × 684". Solomon R. Guggenheim Museum, New York, New York.

> The role of the artist has to be different from what it was fifty or even twenty years ago. I am continually amazed at the number of artists who continue to work as if the camera were never invented, as if Andy Warhol never existed, as if airplanes, and computers, and videotape were never heard of.
>
> —KEITH HARING

Just as the Lumière brothers used film primarily as a documentary medium, artists first used video to record and document performances that were site specific and of limited duration. And just as Melies favored fantasy over reality in his early artistic films, generations of contemporary artists have appropriated video as their medium in the creation of works of art—video art.

Bill Viola's *The Crossing* (Fig. 10.40) is a video/sound installation that engulfs the senses and attempts to transport the viewer into a spiritual realm. In this piece, the artist simultaneously projects two video channels onto separate 16-foot-high screens or on the back and front of the same screen. In each video, a man enveloped in darkness appears and approaches until he fills the screen. On one channel, a fire breaks out at his feet and grows until the man is apparently consumed in flames (the content is not what we would call graphic or disturbing, however). On the other channel, the one shown here, drops of water fall onto the man's head, develop into rivulets,

and then inundate him. The sound tracks accompany the screenings with audio of torrential rain and of a raging inferno. The dual videos wash over the viewer with their contrasts of cool and hot colors and their encompassing sound. Critics speak about the spiritual nature of Viola's work, but it is also about the here-and-now reality of the sensory experiences created by his art form.

By contrast, Gillian Wearing often incorporates a documentary style in her video art. In the multiscreen *Family History* (Fig. 10.41), she juxtaposes footage from a 1974 BBC documentary series called *The Family* with a present-day interview with an original cast/family member, along with a staged narrative in which someone posing as a young Gillian Wearing is watching the old TV show. The work invites reflection on the definition of reality and the limitations of the documentary genre. It also penetrates the relationship between the private and public realms, of intimate family dynamics with spectatorship.

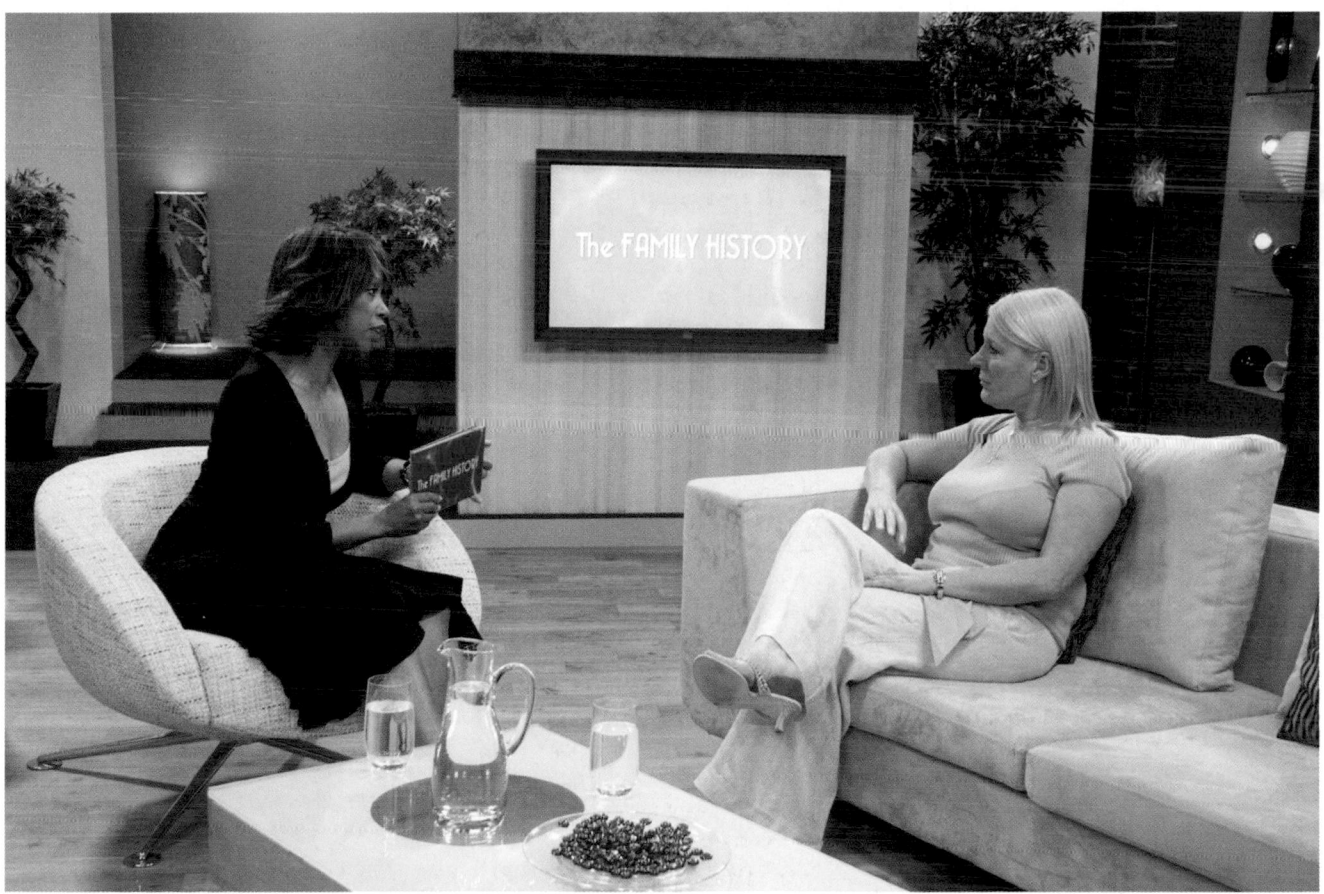

▲ 10.41 GILLIAN WEARING, *Family History* (2006). Shown at Brindley House, Newhall Street, Birmingham, England.

> Video and interactive systems became a means of following the trail of personal history. That gave me the clue to my real place in the cultural context.
>
> —LYNN HERSHMAN

DIGITAL ARTS

Most readers have toyed with applications (apps) such as Microsoft's Paint or Paintbrush or Apple's iPhoto or iMovie. Software such as this enables the user—artistic or otherwise—to create illustrations by manipulating shapes, drawing "freehand," "spray painting" color fields, or enhancing images with a variety of textural patterns—all of which are selected by directing the mouse to a menu of techniques and design elements. The

CONNECTIONS Lynn Hershman's *Digital Venus* appropriates Titian's Renaissance painting, *Venus of Urbino*.

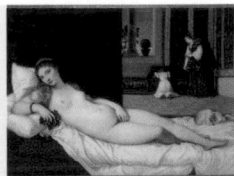

∧ Titian's *Venus of Urbino* (Fig. 17.24)

resultant shapes or drawings can be flipped and rotated or stretched in any direction. Other programs enable users to manipulate digital photographs and edit videos. One can do some photo editing even in Microsoft's *Word* program. And in today's computer-tech-savvy environment, it is no longer unusual even for teenagers to be familiar with Adobe Photoshop software. Artistic results are only a point-and-click away.

Computer graphics software programs offer palettes of millions of colors, which can be selected and produced on the monitor almost instantaneously. Compositions can be recolored in seconds. Effects of light and shade and simulated textured surfaces can be produced with the point and click of a mouse. Software programs enable artists to create three-dimensional representations with such astounding realism that they cannot be distinguished from photos or films of real objects in space. They can be viewed from any vantage point and in any perspective. Images can be saved or stored in any stage of their development, be brought back into the computer's memory at will, and modified as desired, without touching the original image. It is difficult to believe that these images are stored in computers as series of zeroes and ones, and not as pictures, but they are.

Broadly speaking, digital art is the production of images by artists with the assistance of the computer. Ruane Miller's *Blue Door* (Fig. 10.42) begins with a photograph taken by the artist that is then altered using Photoshop painterly manipulations and compositing techniques. She is "interested in creating a coherent image with a convincing reality, though, after all . . . a virtual reality." Describing her work, Miller notes "harmony, tension, complexity and counterbalance in the use of color, detail, and form are basic to the structure of [her] images."

Artists not only appropriate the technology of the day, but they also appropriate images that have special meaning within a culture. Lynn Hershman's *Digital Venus* (Fig. 10.43) starts with Titian's Renaissance painting *Venus of Urbino* (see Fig. 17.24) and substitutes digital imagery

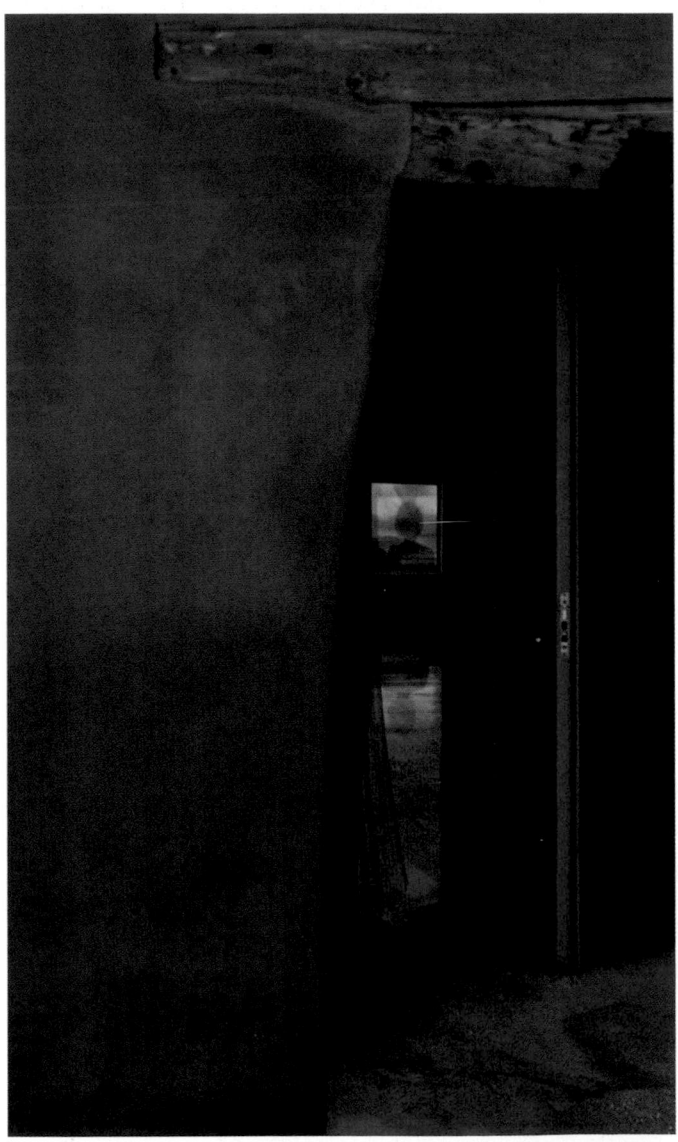

1 in.

∧ **10.42 RUANE MILLER,** *Blue Door* (2008). Archival limited edition digital print, 38" × 22¼".

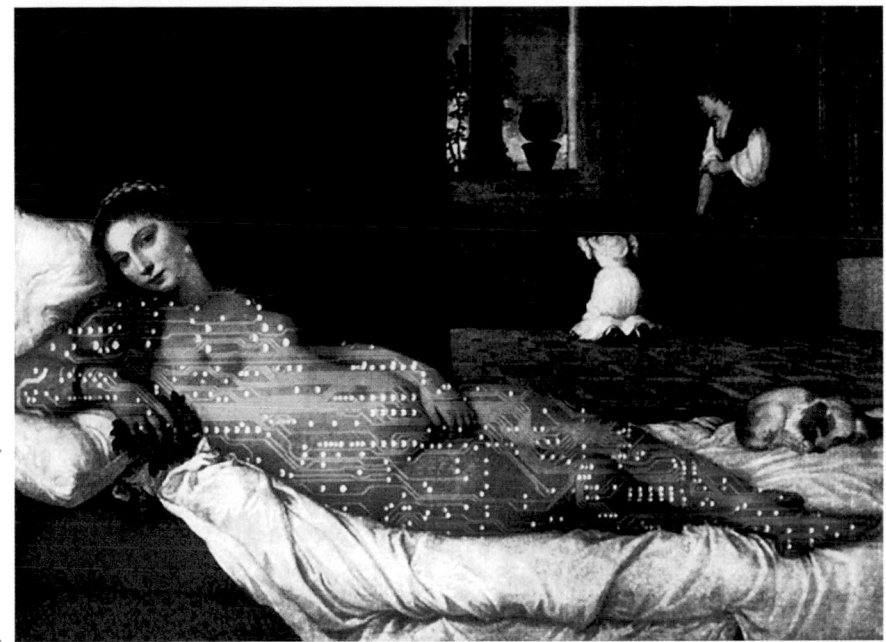

1 ft.

▲ 10.43 **LYNN HERSHMAN,** *Digital Venus* (1996). Iris print, 40⅛" × 59¾".

image into multiples in a grid that is a throwback to Andy Warhol. It is no surprise, then, that contemporary artists are creating works in mediums that narrow the gap, as it were, between them and the rest of us who are simply seeking some way of expressing ourselves. Portuguese-born artist Jorge Colombo creates his so-called fingerpaintings (Fig. 10.44) on an Apple iPad, using an App called "Brushes." Because of the responsiveness of the App to quick, loose drawing, Colombo has used his device, on location, as an electronic sketchbook and diary of his impressions of New York City. Some of these drawings, which have garnered much attention and recognition as covers for *The New Yorker* magazine, are printed with special programs that allow for high-resolution large-format images.

for the sumptuous glazes that Titian used to define the body. Many of Hershman's works comment on the voyeurism we find in the video medium, and *Digital Venus* is a way of showing how frequently the images that affect us are actually composed of pixels—microscopic bits of digital information that fool our senses into believing we are connecting with a corporeal reality. And like the work of Dara Birnbaum, *Digital Venus* addresses feminist issues pertaining to the male gaze and the exploitation of women.

Artists are now only scratching the surface of digital art as a medium. Art courses in digital arts and interactive multimedia have never been more in demand. Just as photography was once termed a "democratizer" in the visual arts—enabling anyone with a camera to capture nearly anything he or she sees—so has the ubiquitousness of the digital camera and computer opened the door to limitless experimentation by artists and amateurs alike.

The relative accessibility to nonartists of technology and software that will yield "artistic results" has spawned any number of manipulated digital photographs and videos appearing on social media websites. Apple's iPhoto, for example, allows you to take a picture of yourself and then transform it with options such as "Color Pencil," "Comic Book," or even "Pop Art"—which renders a single

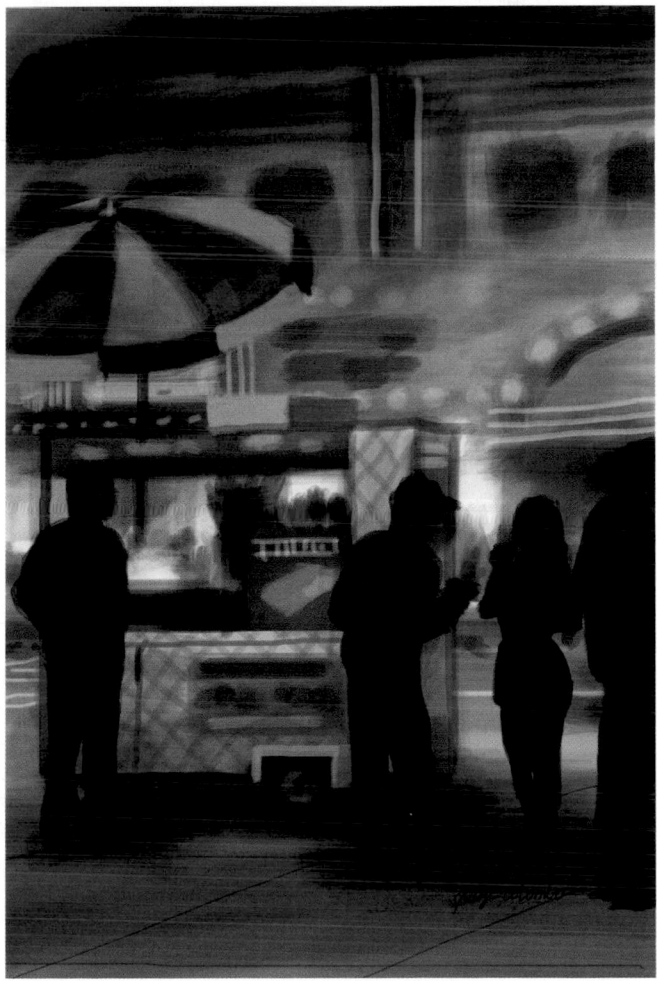

> 10.44 **JORGE COLOMBO,** *42nd Street* (2009). Finger painting (using Brushes on Apple iPad), pixel dimensions: 1,024" × 768" (7.75" × 5.82"). Originally published as the June 2009 cover image in *The New Yorker.*

1 in.

Web Design

Websites are an inextricable part of the information superhighway. Any of us cyberspace surfers can go online, access the website of a popular consumer magazine, and get the latest reviews on the new car we're drooling over. We can research without books, order books, book reservations, and bid on a special reserve wine. Part of what keeps us from surfing away from a website is the visual feedback we obtain when we click onto it. The better the website's design, the more tantalizing the product or service it offers; this is not lost on the millions of businesses, organizations, agencies, and individuals for whom the website is the electronic face perceived by the consumer, their first impression.

Web design has two key tasks. One is technical and involves programming—how users click their way around a web page, how links to other pages and sites are established, and how to insert still images or animated clips and sound. The other is aesthetic, encompassing art and design.

Art museums are among the organizations that can be accessed through websites. The home page of the website of the Metropolitan Museum of Art (Fig. 10.45) (www.metmuseum.org) includes a rotating group of appealing photographs of art or art exhibitions. The website informs you of current exhibitions, allows you to view many of the works in the collection, and includes links to pedagogical tools such as an invaluable timeline of art history. The more mundane but essential information about museum hours and current exhibits is reliably posted, but the functionality of the web design almost pales in comparison to its ability to transport virtual visitors to one of the world's great cultural centers from the comfort of their ergonomically designed computer chairs.

You can visit Google's Art Project (www.google.com/culturalinstitute/project/art-project) to view collections from various participating museums online and to create your own virtual galleries. Through Street View in Google Maps, you can enter participating museums and other cultural sites to navigate gallery spaces.

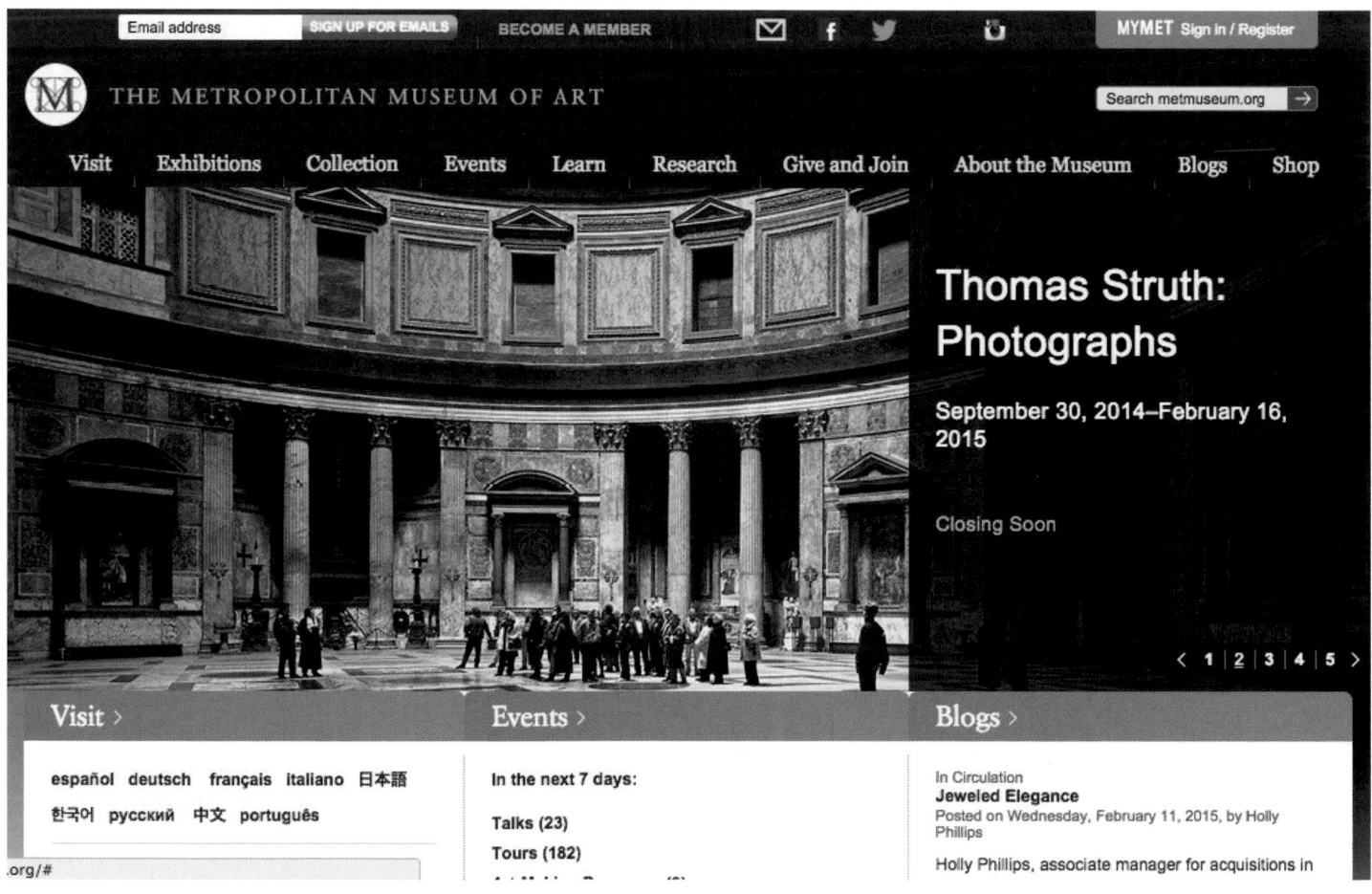

∧ 10.45 Website: Home page of the Metropolitan Museum of Art, www.metmuseum.org.

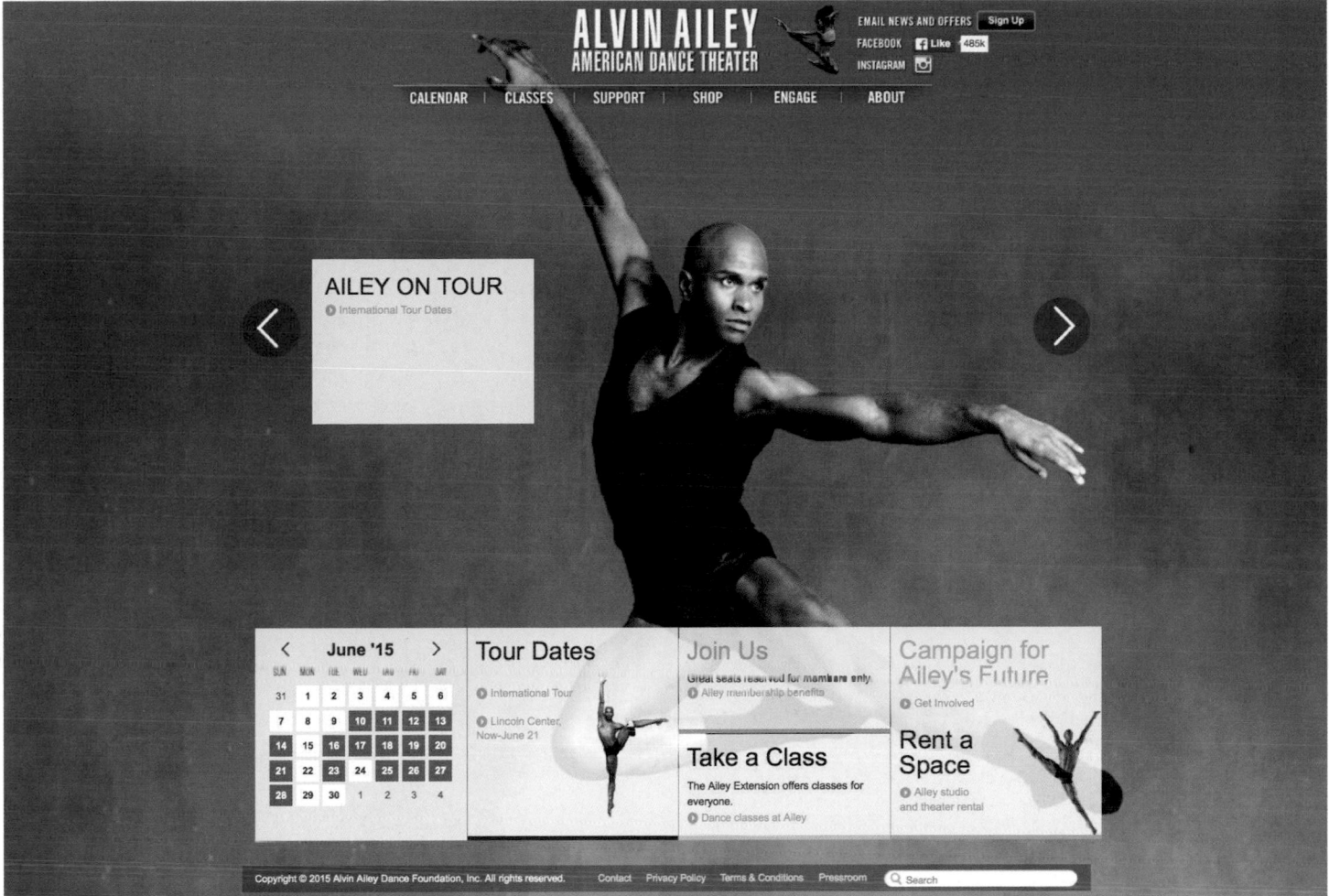

∧ 10.46 Website: Alvin Ailey American Dance Theater.

As you surf the web, you have no doubt been struck by the endless variety, quality, and quantity of web design—from sophisticated to tacky, from "high art" to "low art." I, like you, come across interesting websites almost every day, so it was hard to settle for just one or two to highlight in this chapter among the wealth of riches and rags. Some current faves include the website for the Alvin Ailey American Dance Theater in New York City (known for its brilliant, mind-and-body-stretching choreography) (Fig. 10.46). This and other websites feature hot spots that the user can click on to go to related web pages and retrieve information.

Web design is a big business, and many graphic designers set up shop in this realm. Students can now take web design in their college courses, whereas the rest of us can learn about it in how-to books such as *Web Design for Dummies*. Many individuals, like organizations, upload their photos and videos to social media. Social and business media serve as anything from electronic business cards to ways for families to keep in touch. Cyberspace collapses the distance between us and the important people in our lives; it also connects us with the great art of the world.

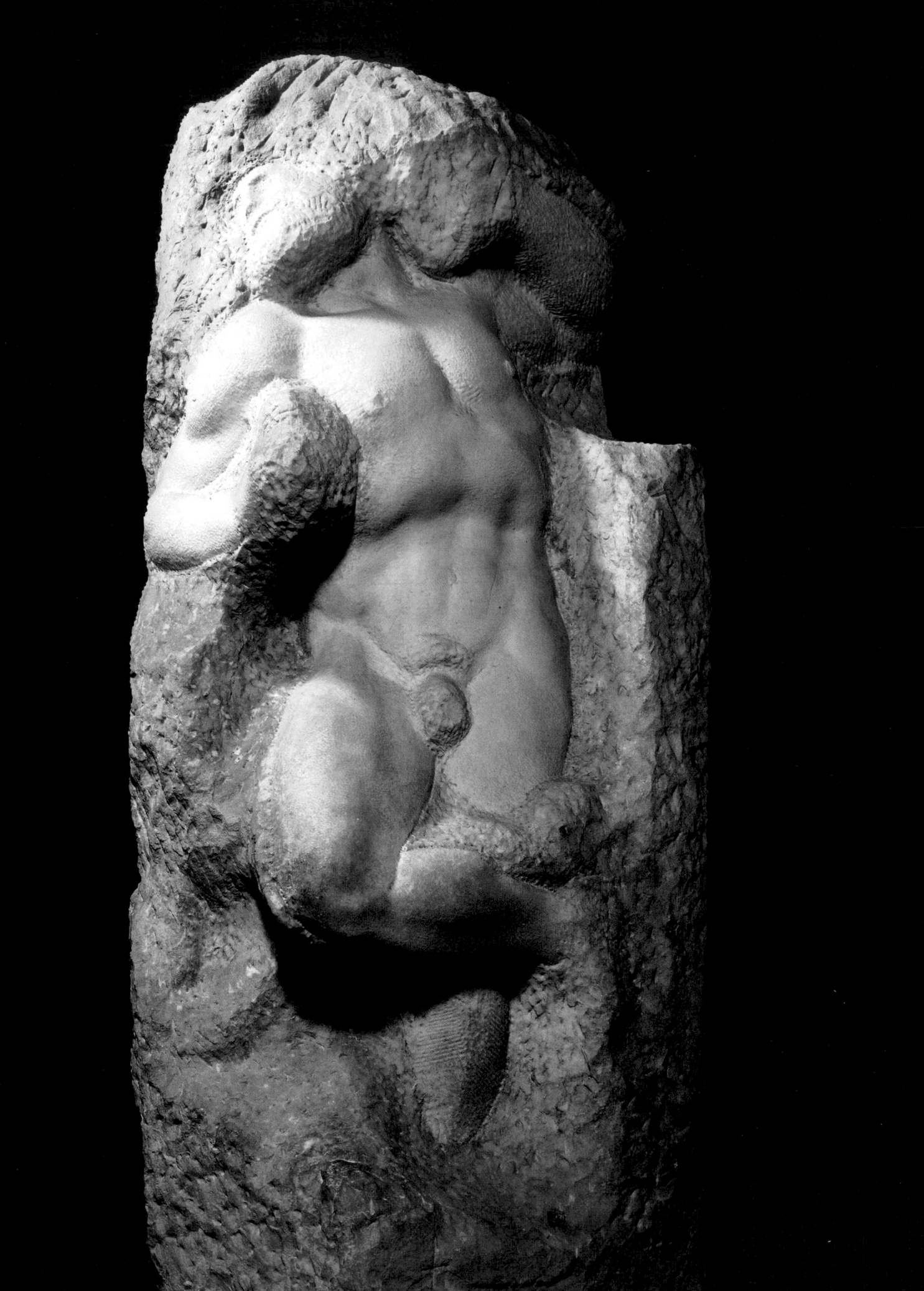

11

SCULPTURE, INSTALLATION, SITE-SPECIFIC ART, AND 3D DESIGN

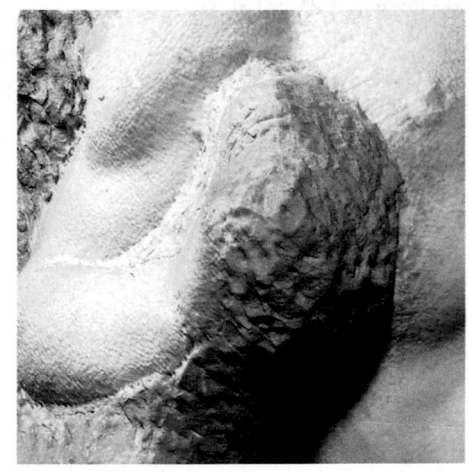

A sculptor is a person obsessed with the form and shape of things, and it's not just the shape of one thing, but the shape of anything and everything: the hard, tense strength, although delicate form of a bone; the strong, solid fleshiness of a beech tree trunk.

— HENRY MOORE

IN *METAMORPHOSIS*, Ovid's poetic narrative of the creation of the world, we meet a young Cypriot sculptor named Pygmalion. Now Pygmalion is pretty cynical about love. He vows never to marry, instead devoting his life to the perfection of his craft. Never say never. Pygmalion outdoes himself in creating a sculpture of a beautiful woman in ivory—so stunning, so lifelike, that he falls in love with his statue (**Fig. 11.1**). He makes a wish that his idol be brought to life and Venus hears his plea—the sculpture becomes flesh and Pygmalion finds his bride.

The myth of Pygmalion has been depicted in many versions and mediums, a subject that has suggested both the technical prowess of sculptors and the power to create the illusion of reality in spite of the harsh, seemingly unforgiving materials with which they work: marble, wood, bronze. Seeing Bernini's *Apollo and Daphne* (**Fig. 11.2**) in the flesh dispels any doubt that the artist's skill was nothing short of transformative. The brain can hardly register as marble that which the eye sees.

Realism, of course, is only one stylistic dimension of sculpture, and marble, wood, and bronze are only a few examples of the wealth of materials that sculptors use. This chapter considers the materials and techniques used in sculpture and the related disciplines of installation, site-specific art, and industrial design.

◄ MICHELANGELO, *The Cross-Legged Captive* (c. 1530–1534). Detail. Marble, 7' 6 ½" high (entire work). Galleria dell'Accademia, Florence, Italy.

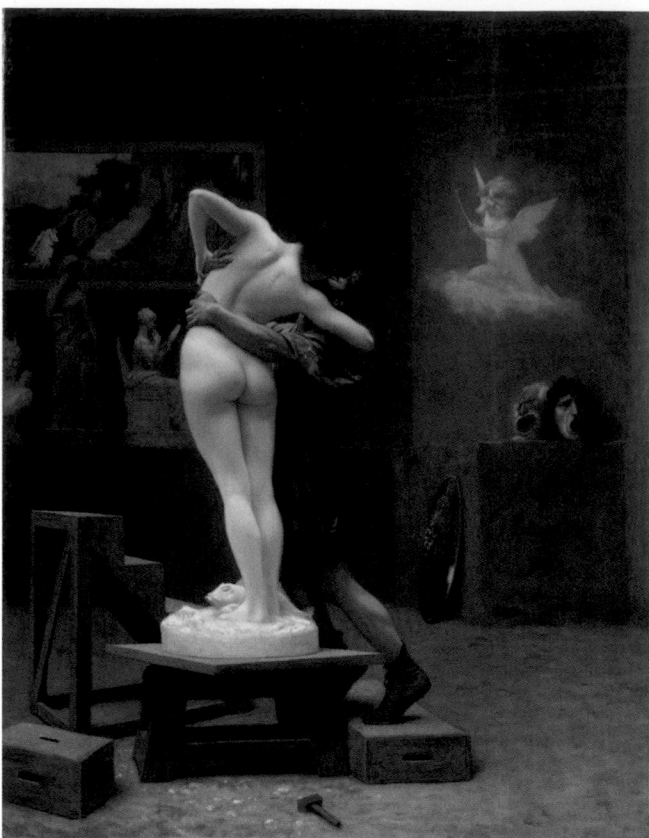

▲ 11.1 JEAN-LÉON GÉRÔME, *Pygmalion and Galatea* (c. 1890). Oil on canvas, 35" × 27". Metropolitan Museum of Art, New York, New York.

SCULPTURE

A viewer's relationship to a sculpture is often much more complex than it is to a drawing or painting. Two-dimensional works generally are viewed from a single, optimal perspective—head-on. Sculpture, on the other hand, exhibited—as it often is—in the open space of a gallery, museum, or the great outdoors beckons the viewer to participate in the revelation of its form by walking around the work and observing it from multiple viewpoints.

Not all sculpture is three-dimensional, nor is all of it intended to be viewed from more than one vantage point. Sculpture is broadly categorized into two types: **relief sculpture** and **free-standing sculpture**, or **sculpture-in-the-round**. In a relief, figures or images project to varying degrees from a two-dimensional plane (a plank of wood or a slab of marble, for example). If the imagery does not project significantly from the surface, we refer to the technique as **low relief** or **bas-relief**. In **high relief**, by contrast, figures project dramatically from the plane of the relief, so much so that they barely seem attached to the background. It is not uncommon to see a combination of high, middle, and bas-relief in a single sculpture, as in Ghiberti's *Sacrifice of Isaac* (see Fig. 17.9), and reliefs can be created in any material, including bronze.

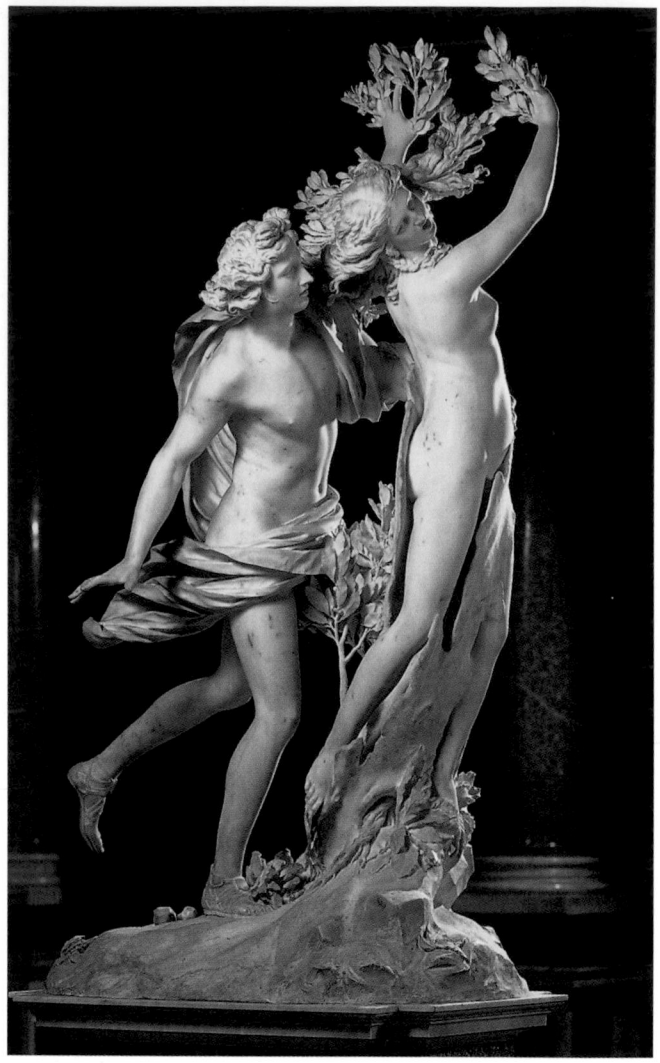

▲ 11.2 GIANLORENZO BERNINI, *Apollo and Daphne* (1622–1624). Marble, 7' 6". Galleria Borghese, Rome, Italy.

As with two-dimensional works of art, though, reliefs are intended to be viewed primarily from one perspective. It is true that some freestanding sculpture or sculpture-in-the round is meant to be seen head-on, from an optimal vantage point, or is installed in such a way that a viewer cannot walk completely around it, as in the case of Bernini's *The Ecstasy of St. Theresa* (see Fig. 18.3). But sculpture-in-the-round is not connected to a two-dimensional surface and, importantly, it is carved or cast or assembled in three dimensions.

Sculpture is also described, in the broadest of terms, by the basic process used to create it: subtractive or additive. With a **subtractive process**, such as carving, material is removed from the original, raw mass to define a figure or an image. With an **additive process**, such as modeling, material is added or built up to reach a desired form. These processes are linked to a wide variety of sculptural techniques.

> No painter ought to think less of sculpture than of painting
> and no sculptor less of painting than of sculpture.
>
> —MICHELANGELO

Carving

In **carving**, the sculptor begins with a block of material and cuts portions of it away until the desired form is created. Carving could be considered the most demanding type of sculpture because the sculptor, like the fresco painter, must have a clear conception of the final product at the outset. The material chosen—stone, wood, ivory—strongly influences the mechanics of the carving process and determines the type of creation that will emerge.

Michelangelo believed that the sculptor liberated forms that already existed within blocks of stone. *The Cross-Legged Captive* (Fig. 11.3) is one of a series of unfinished Michelangelo statues in which the figures remain partly embedded in marble. In its unfinished state, the tension and twisting in the torso almost cause us to experience the struggle of the slave to free himself fully from the marble and, symbolically, from his masters. Despite the massiveness of the musculature, the roughness of the finish imparts a curious softness and humanity to the figure, which further increase our empathy. When we view this sculpture, it's as if we await the emergence of perfection from the imperfect—from the coarse and irregular block of stone. It is Michelangelo's genius that allows the figure to transcend its humble origins.

< 11.3 MICHELANGELO, *The Cross-Legged Captive* (c. 1530–1534). Marble, 7'6½" high. Galleria dell'Accademia, Florence, Italy.

Modeling

In **modeling**, a pliable material such as clay or wax is shaped into a three-dimensional form. The artist may manipulate the material by hand and use a variety of tools. Unlike carving, in which the artist must begin with a clear concept of the result, in modeling the artist may work and rework the material until pleasing forms begin to emerge.

Casting

The transition from modeling to casting can be easily seen in Louise Bourgeois's *Portrait of Robert* (Fig. 11.4). Here the artist has expressionistically modeled a pliable material and converted the work to the more permanent bronze medium through a casting process. The white patina she has applied to finish the sculpture curiously subverts the material's typical sheen and grants the work a claylike appearance—the very material with which the artist started.

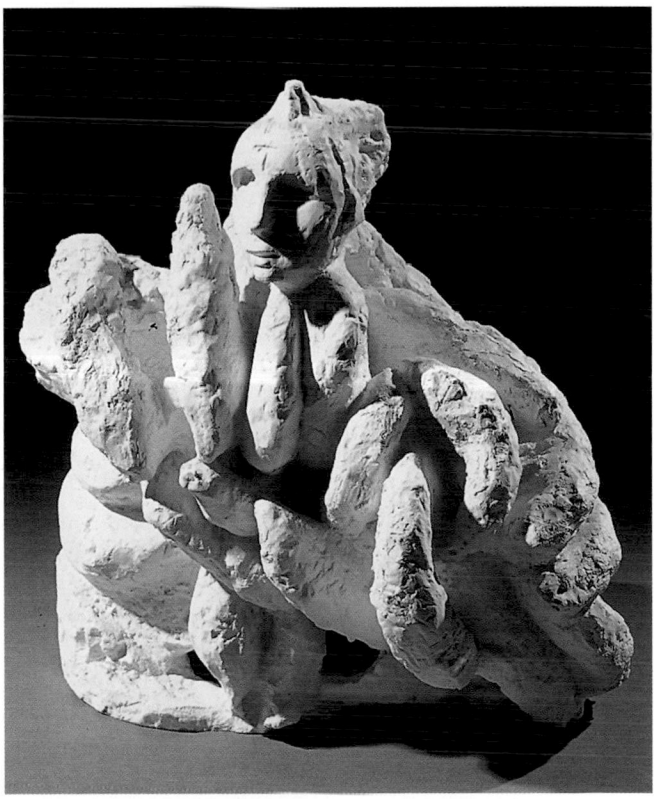

▲ 11.4 LOUISE BOURGEOIS, *Portrait of Robert* (1969). Cast bronze with white patina, 13" × 12½ × 10".

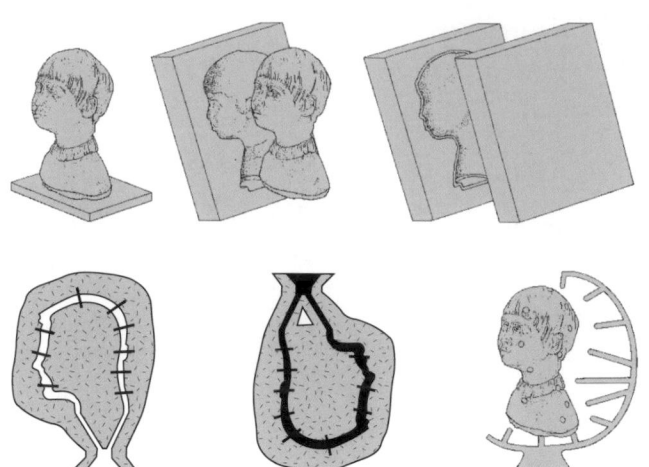

▲ 11.5 **The Lost-Wax Technique.**

In the **casting** process, a liquid material is poured into a mold. The liquid hardens into the shape of the **mold** and is then removed. In casting, an original model, made of a material such as wax, clay, or even Styrofoam, can be translated into a more durable material such as bronze. The mold is like a photographic negative, but one of form and not of color; the interior surfaces of the mold carry the reversed impressions of the model's exterior.

Any material that hardens can be used for casting. Bronze has been used most frequently because of its appealing surface and color characteristics, but concrete, plaster, liquid plastics, clay diluted with water, and other materials are also appropriate. Once the mold has been made, the casting may be duplicated.

THE LOST-WAX TECHNIQUE Bronze casting is usually accomplished by means of the **lost-wax technique** (Fig. 11.5), which has changed little over the centuries. In this technique, an original model is usually sculpted from clay, and a mold of it is made, usually from sectioned plaster or flexible gelatin. Molten wax is then brushed or poured into the mold to make a hollow wax model. If the wax has been brushed onto the inner surface of the mold, it will form a hollow shell. If the wax is to be poured, a solid core can first be placed into the mold and the liquid wax poured around the core. After the wax hardens, the mold is removed, and the

wax model stands as a hollow replica of the clay. The hollow wax model is placed upside down in a container, and wax rods called gates are connected to it. Then a sandy mixture of silica, clay, and plaster is poured into and around the wax model, filling the shell and the container. The mixture hardens into a fire-resistant mold, or **investiture**. Thus, the process uses two models and two molds: models of clay and wax, and molds of plaster or gelatin and of the silica mixture.

The silica mold, or investiture, is turned over and placed in a **kiln**. As the investiture becomes heated, the wax turns molten once more and runs out—hence the term *lost-wax technique*. The investiture is turned over again while it is still hot, and molten bronze is poured in. As the metal flows into the mold, air escapes through the gates so that no air pockets are left within. The bronze is given time to harden. Then the investiture and core are removed, leaving the bronze sculpture with strange projections where the molten metal had flowed up through the gates as it filled the mold. The projections are removed, and the surface of the bronze is **burnished** or treated chemically to take on the texture and color desired by the sculptor, as we shall see in the following bronze sculptures.

A statue by the French Impressionist Edgar Degas has an interesting history and metamorphosis from wax to bronze. As he aged, Degas developed blind spots in his eyes and found bright light painful. He turned to sculpture, in part, so that he could work out anatomical problems through the sense of touch. With one exception, his wax or clay experiments were left crumbling in his studio or discarded, although the intact figures were cast as a limited edition of bronze sculptures after his death. The exception was *Small Dancer Aged 14* (Fig. 11.6), which he showed as a wax model at the 1881 Impressionist exhibition and later cast in bronze. This diminutive painted wax figure startled the public and critics alike with its innovative sculptural realism, enhanced by human hair tied back with a satin ribbon, a canvas bodice, and a tulle skirt.

< 11.6 **EDGAR DEGAS**, *Small Dancer Aged 14* (model between 1865 and 1881). Bronze statue patinated in various colors, tulle tutu, pink satin ribbon in the hair, wooden base; 38⅜" × 13¹⁷⁄₂₀" × 9¹³⁄₂₀". Musée d'Orsay, Paris, France.

COMPARE & CONTRAST

(Found) Art as Idea as Idea

DADA ARTIST, MARCEL DUCHAMP caused an uproar in 1917 when he submitted a porcelain urinal—turned on its side and signed "R. Mutt" (**Fig. 11.7**)—to an exhibition of the Society of Independent Artists. For Duchamp, the dimension of taste, good or bad, was irrelevant. Art could be defined by an idea, and the very action of choosing an object and creating a new context for it invested it with new meaning.

Sherrie Levine's bronze *Fountains after Duchamp* (**Fig. 11.8**) are built on Duchamp's concept of the ready-made as art—"an ordinary object elevated to the dignity of a work of art by the mere choice of an artist." Levine's series of bronze urinals, turned on their backs and displayed on pedestals as if to invite serious study and contemplation, pay homage to Duchamp's infamous *Fountain*. At the heart of Levine's artistic concept and strategy: the critical appropriation of objects and images that already exist in the visual lexicon of high art and mass culture. If Duchamp invested his ready-mades with a new *idea*—the reconsideration of ordinary objects in the artist's self-defined and self-imposed context of fine art—Levine's objects and reproductions are invested with a reconsideration of issues such as authorship and originality in relation to art making.

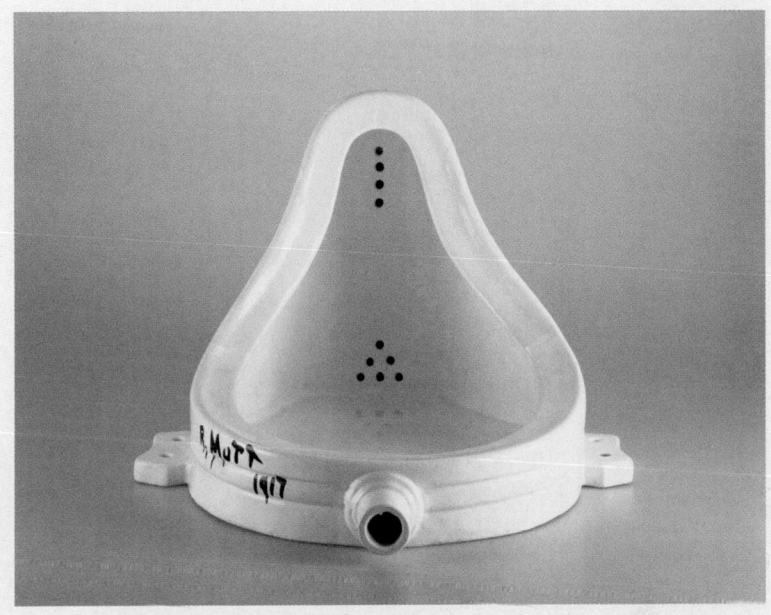

∧ **11.7 MARCEL DUCHAMP,** *Fountain* (1917/1964). 1951 version after lost original. Porcelain urinal, 24" high. San Francisco Museum of Modern Art, San Francisco, California.

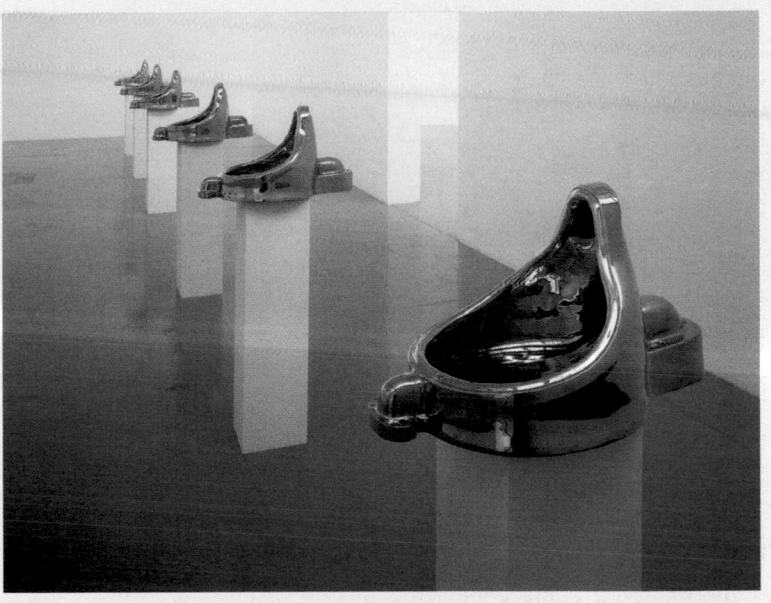

∧ **11.8 SHERRIE LEVINE,** *Fountains after Duchamp* (1991). Bronze. Installation view at Sherrie Levine Exhibition in the Zürich Kunsthalle, Zürich, Switzerland.

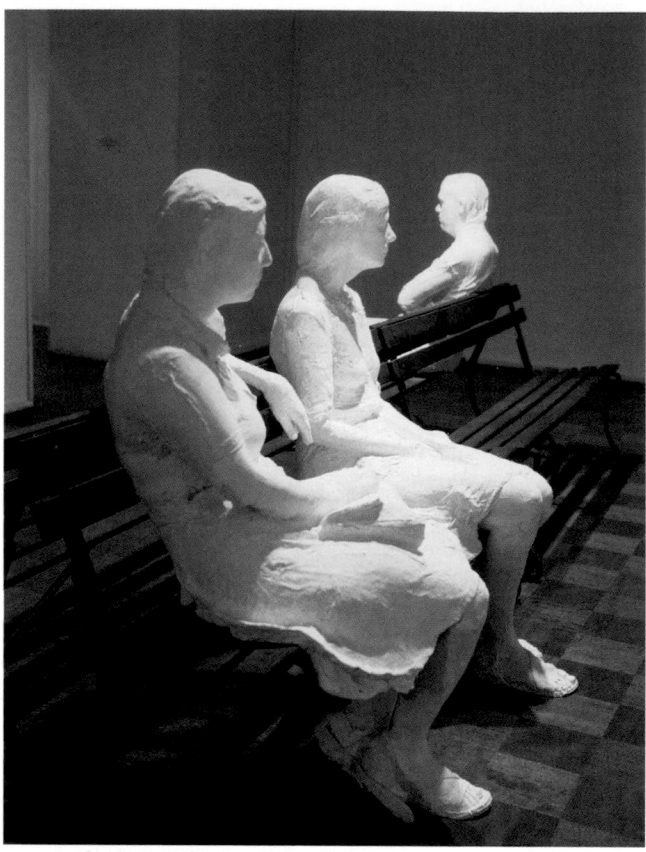

∧ 11.9 GEORGE SEGAL, *Three Figures and Four Benches* (1979). Painted bronze, 52" × 144" × 58".

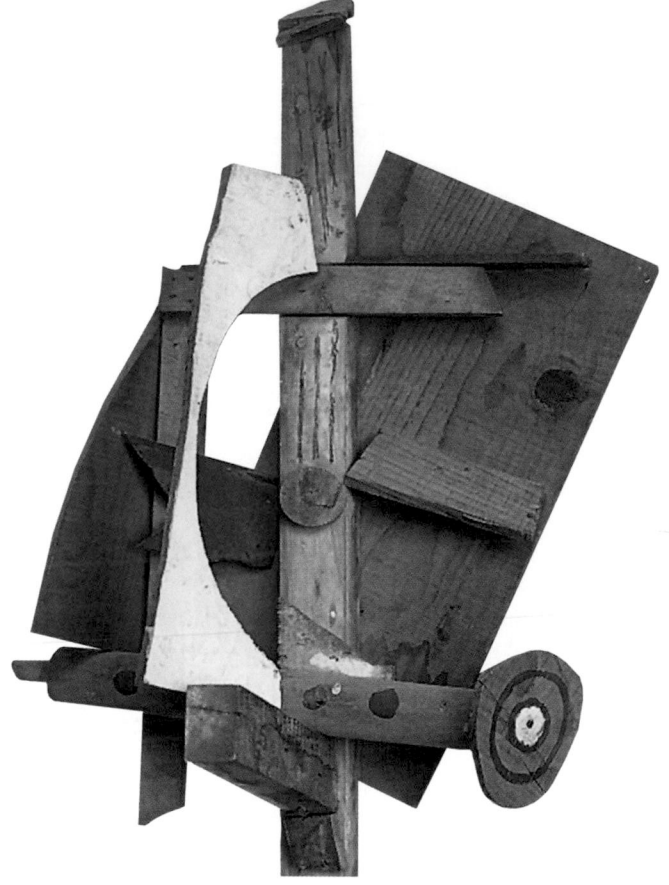

∧ 11.10 PABLO PICASSO, *Mandolin and Clarinet* (1913). Wood construction and paint, 22⅜" × 14⅛" × 9". Musée Picasso, Paris, France.

CASTING OF HUMAN MODELS *Three Figures and Four Benches* (Fig. 11.9) by George Segal features intriguing variation on the casting process. Segal produced ghost-like replicas of human beings by means of plaster casts. Live models were covered in plaster-soaked cloth, which was molded and kneaded by the artist's hands. When the plaster was dry, the cast was removed in sections and then reassembled into whole figures. *Three Figures and Four Benches* was then cast in bronze, but the white surface of the original plaster cast was retained. Segal's figures are literally and figuratively shells. In unimaginable aloneness, his apparitions occupy an urban landscape of buses, gas stations, diners, and other settings, a kind of limbo of contemporary life. Although the figures are connected by virtue of their common medium, they do not seem to speak to one another or interact in any way. They are at once connected and disconnected, sharing a place and time and yet lost in their inner worlds.

Constructed Sculpture

In constructed sculpture, the artist builds or constructs the sculpture from materials such as cardboard, celluloid, translucent plastic, sheet metal, or wire, frequently creating forms that are lighter than those made from carving stone, modeling clay, or casting metal. Picasso inspired a movement in this direction with works such as *Mandolin and Clarinet* (Fig. 11.10). As critic Robert Hughes remarked, such works were "everything that statues had not been: not monolithic, but open, not cast or carved, but assembled from flat planes."[1] In spirit and style, reliefs from this era were very close to Picasso's paintings. But

---

[1] Robert Hughes, "The Liberty of Thought Itself," *Time*, September 1, 1986, 87.

> One starts to get young at the age of sixty and then it is too late.
>
> —PABLO PICASSO

> I began using found objects. I had all this wood lying around and I began to move it around, I began to compose.
>
> —LOUISE NEVELSON

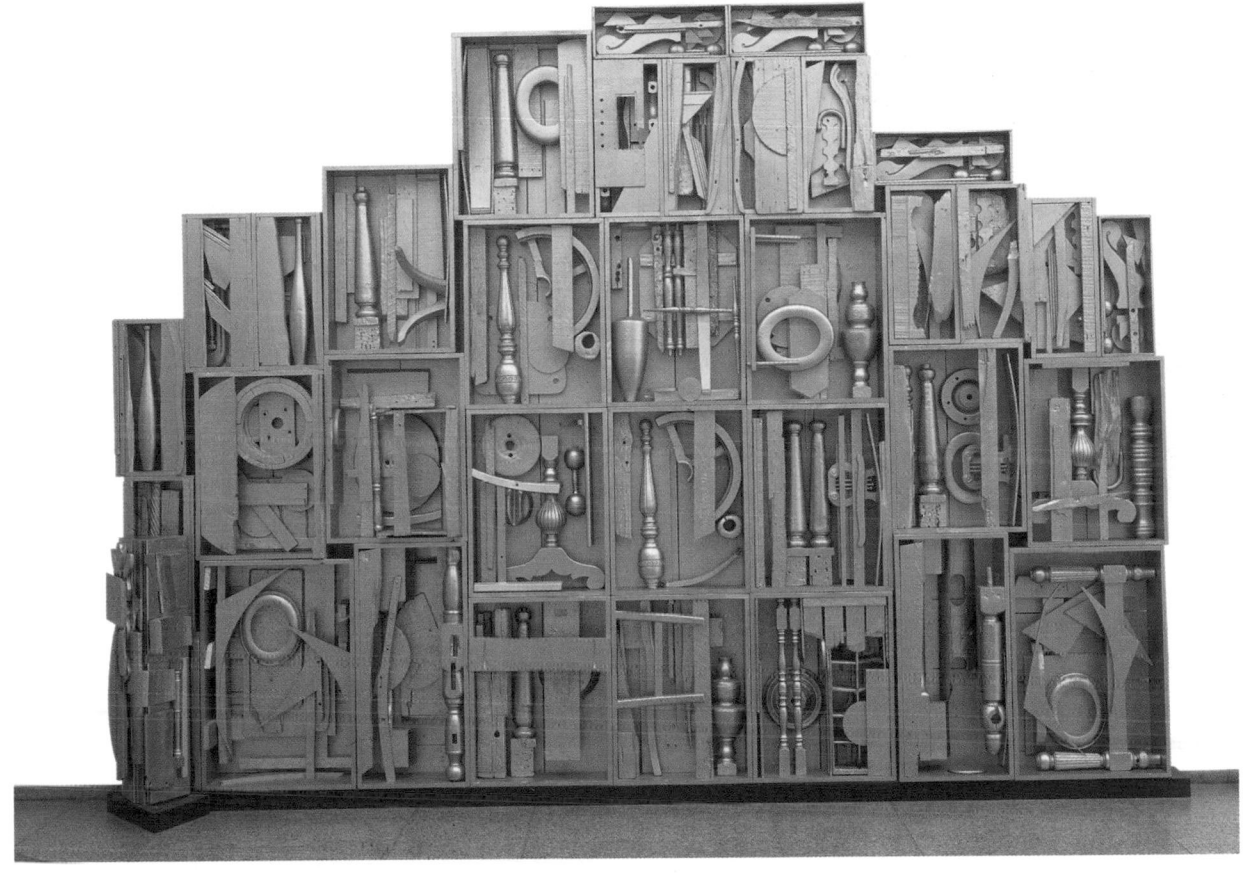

▲ **11.11 LOUISE NEVELSON,** *Royal Tide IV* (1960). Wood, with gold-spray technique; 127" × 175 ½" × 21 ½".

the unorthodox materials—wood, sheet metal, wire, found objects—challenged all traditions in art making. Sculpture would never be the same.

Assemblage

Assemblage is a form of constructed sculpture in which preexisting, or found, objects, recognizable in form, are integrated by the sculptor into novel combinations that take on a life and meaning of their own. American artist Louise Nevelson's *Royal Tide IV* (Fig. 11.11) is a compartmentalized assemblage of rough-cut geometric shapes and lathed wooden objects with previous lives, such as

finials. Similar assemblages include banal objects such as bowling pins, chair slats, and barrel staves and may be painted white or black, as well as gold.

CONNECTIONS Willie Cole's assemblages show us the degree to which discrete, familiar, found objects can lose themselves utterly in their second lives as works of art. In *Shine*, women's high-heeled shoes are stacked, squashed, and nestled into an overall shape that resembles an African ceremonial mask.

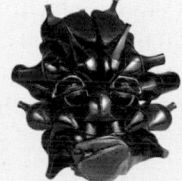

▲ Willie Cole's *Shine* (Fig. 22.26)

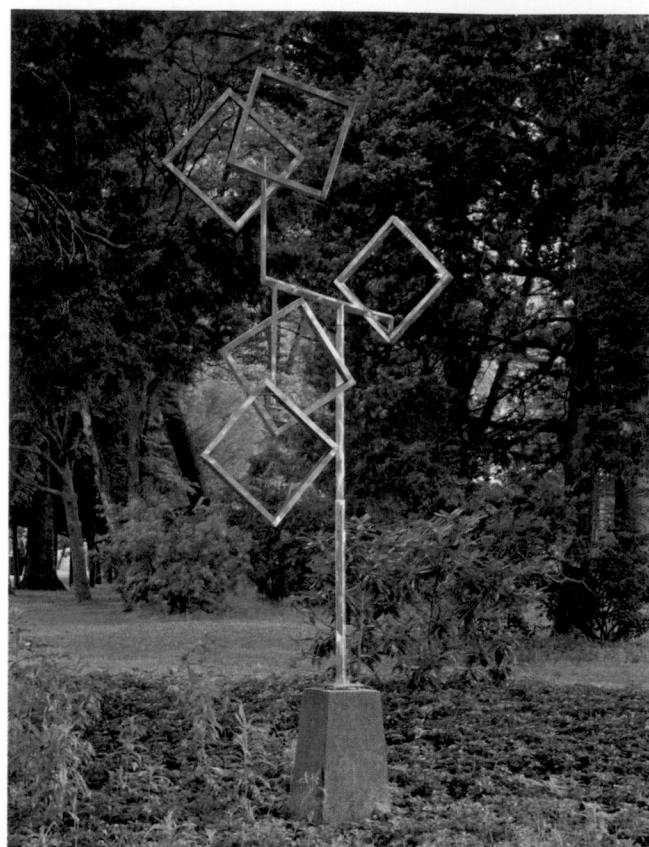

▲ 11.12 **GEORGE RICKEY,** *Five Open Squares Gyratory* (1981). Stainless steel, 9'4" × 6' × 3'6".

Why walls? Nevelson explains:

> I attribute the walls to this: I had loads . . . and loads of creative energy. . . . So I began to stack my sculptures into an environment. . . . I think there is something in the consciousness of the creative person that adds up, and the multiple image that I give, say, in an enormous wall gives me so much satisfaction.[2]

The overall effect of Nevelson's collections is one of nostalgia and mystery. They suggest the pieces of the personal and collective past, of lonely introspective journeys among the cobwebs of Victorian attics—of childhoods that never were. Perhaps they are the very symbol of consciousness, for what is the function of intellect if not to impose order on the bits and pieces of experience?

[2] Louise Nevelson, *Louise Nevelson: Atmospheres and Environments* (New York: C. N. Potter in association with the Whitney Museum of American Art, 1980), 77.

Kinetic Sculpture

Sculptors have always been concerned with the portrayal of movement, but **kinetic sculptures** actually do move. Movement may be caused by the wind, magnetic fields, jets of water, electric motors, variations in the intensity of light, or the active manipulation of the observer. During the 1930s, the American sculptor Alexander Calder was one of the early pioneers of the first form of art that made motion as basic an element as shape or color—the mobile. In Calder's mobiles (see Fig. 5.21), carefully balanced weights are suspended on wires such that the gentlest current of air sets them moving in prescribed orbits.

George Rickey's welded, stainless steel cubes bear the mark of Calder's mobile constructions. Much of the work of both artists responds to the flow of currents of air. In Rickey's *Cluster of Four Cubes* (Fig. 11.12), burnished steel "boxes" are attached by ball bearings to arms that branch from a trunklike post. The cubes are weighted and balanced to turn effortlessly in light breezes.

Light Sculpture

Natural light has always been an important element in defining sculpture, but only in the past century did sculptors begin to experiment with the use of artificial light in their compositions. Their concern has been with the physical and psychological effects of color and, at times, with the creation of visual illusions.

Dan Flavin is considered by many critics to have been the most revolutionary contemporary sculptor to have

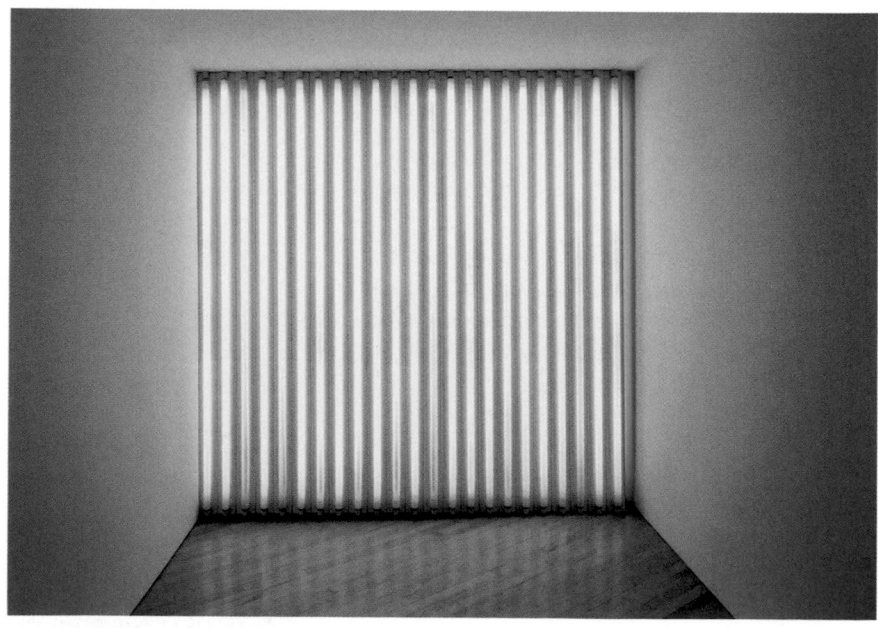

▲ 11.13 **DAN FLAVIN,** *Untitled* (to Jan and Ron Greenberg) (1972–1973). Installation view at the Dan Flavin Art Institute, Bridgehampton, New York. Fluorescent light, 96" × 96".

worked with light. Designing principally with fluorescent tubes, Flavin explored the resonance of color and its ability to define space. In his untitled piece seen in Figure 11.13, a gallery dead-ends with a screen of yellow light placed back-to-back with a matching screen of green fluorescent tubes (which you cannot see from this side). Because the sculpture, when installed, blocked passage from one side of the room to another, only a glimpse of the light filling the room on the other side could be seen through the narrow spaces on either side between the walls and the light tubes. The result was an intriguing juxtaposition of regimented tubes of yellow and the unfettered glow of green light. The opposite effect was observed in viewing the work from the other side.

TYPES OF MATERIALS

Sculptors have probably employed every known material in their works. Different materials tend to be worked in different ways, and they can also create very different effects. In this section, we will explore the varieties of ways in which sculptors have worked with the traditional materials of stone, wood, clay, and metal. In the section on modern and contemporary materials and methods, we will see how sculptors have worked with nontraditional materials, such as plastic and light.

Stone

Stone is an extremely hard, durable material that may be carved, scraped, drilled, and polished. The durability that makes stone so appropriate for monuments and statues that are meant to communicate with future generations also makes working with stone a tedious process. The granite used by ancient Egyptians was extremely resistant to detailed carving, which is one reason that Egyptian stone figures were simplified and resemble the shape of the quarried blocks. The Greeks used their abundant white marble to embody the idealized human form in action and in repose. However, they painted their marble statues, suggesting that they valued the material more for its durability than for its color or texture.

The hand tools used with stone—such as the chisel, mallet, and **rasp**—have not changed much over the centuries. But contemporary sculptors do not find working with stone to be quite so laborious because

they can use power tools for chipping away large areas of unwanted material and for polishing the finished piece.

In *Eyes* (Fig. 11.14), by Louise Bourgeois, two precisely tooled spheres are perched atop a marble cube, some of which has been chiseled to create hollows and other irregularities. The carved circular openings in the spheres suggest the penetrating pupils of eyes, a commonly used symbol among Surrealist artists (see Chapter 20). For Bourgeois, who often incorporated gender allusions in her work, the eyes may represent the female anatomy and the marble block, a house. The two strong shapes in contrast to each other may suggest a woman's relationship to her domestic role, a theme that Bourgeois revisited numerous times in her long career. Although Bourgeois's technique results in a finished work that remains close to the quarried marble block, the perfectly round eyes, the polish of the surfaces, and the carved interruptions create a striking contrast between a deliberate absence and an assertive presence of the artist's hand.

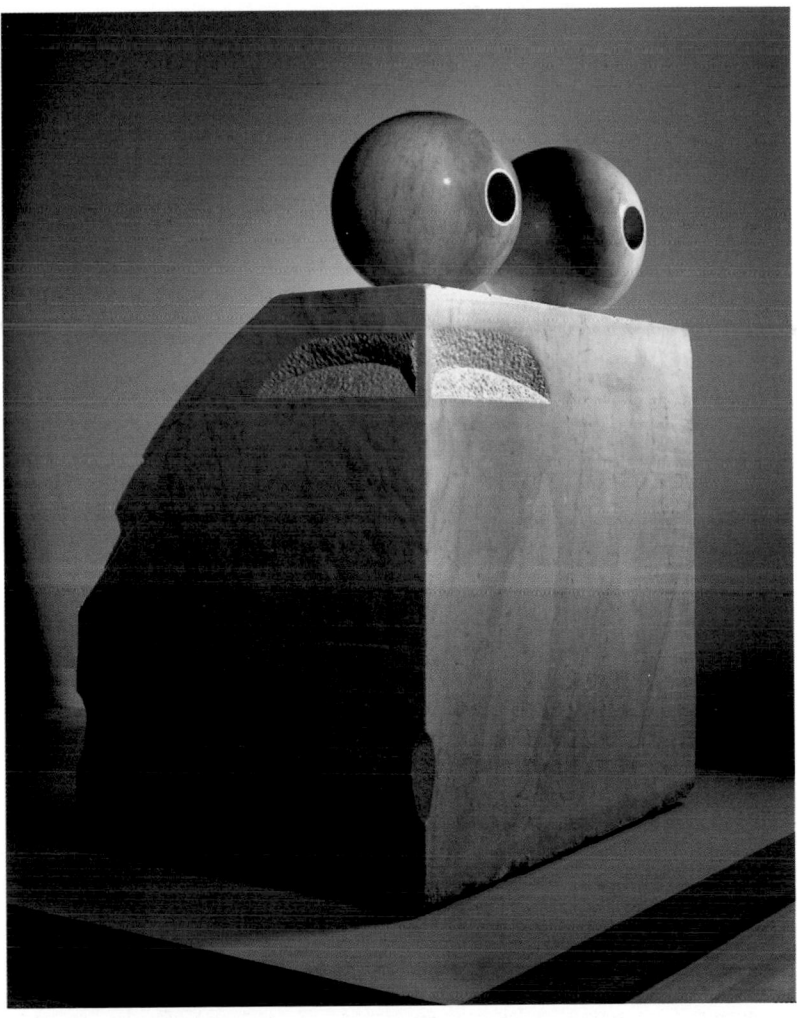

▲ 11.14 **LOUISE BOURGEOIS,** *Eyes* (1982). Marble, 74¾" × 54" × 45¾". The Metropolitan Museum of Art, New York, New York.

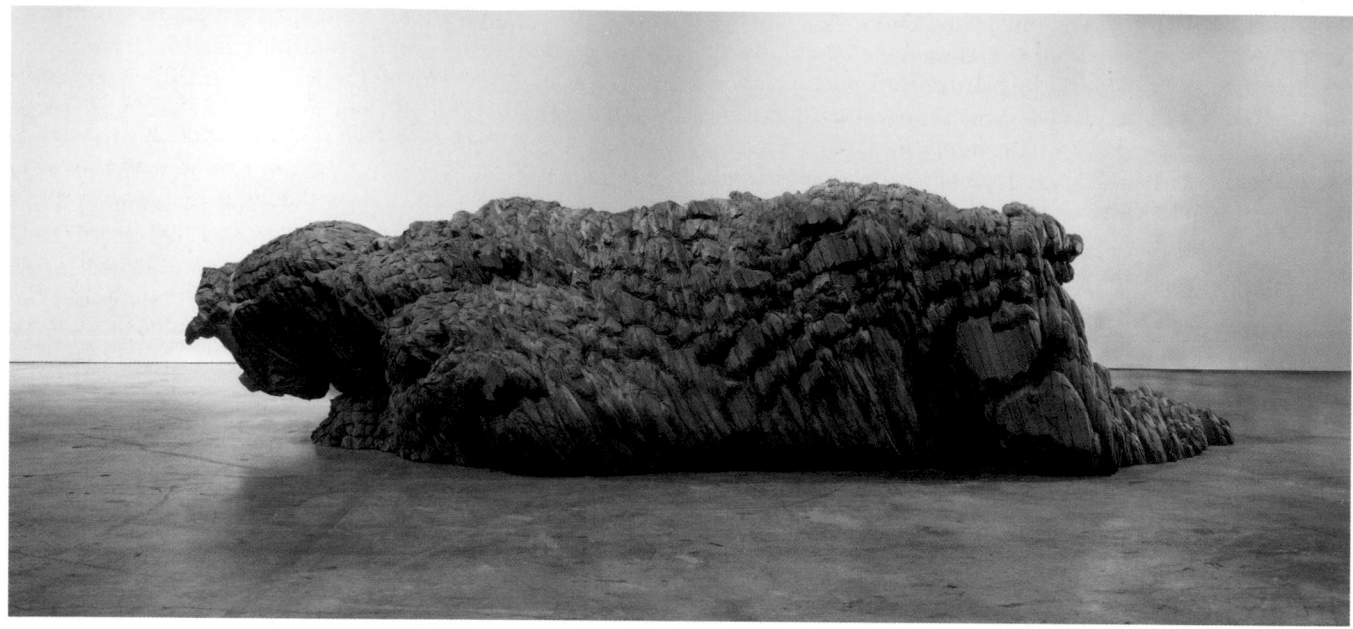

∧ 11.15 **URSULA VON RYDINGSVARD**, *Droga* (2009). Cedar and graphite, 9'6" × 18'3" × 4'6". Galerie Lelong, New York, New York.

Wood

Wood, like stone, may be carved using a variety of tools and, like stone, possesses different degrees of hardness that affect its workability and durability. Sculptors carve works from solid blocks of wood or, in the case of very large works, laminate pieces of wood together using adhesive, heat, and pressure. Wood's **tensile strength** exceeds that of stone, so parts of a wood sculpture that protrude are less likely than their stone counterparts to break off. On the other hand, stone is more impervious to disintegration over time.

Sculptors working in wood take into consideration types of wood (hard or soft), their grain patterns (straight or wavy), and their color. Tools for carving and finishing wood blocks include gouges, saws, knives, chisels, planes, mallets, sanders, and polishers. In carving wood, artists particularly study the direction of the grain, as the strength of wood is connected to its grain.

The capacity of wood to yield rough-hewn beauty is shown in the aggressively worked surface of Ursula von Rydingsvard's *Droga* (Fig. 11.15). After beginning by taking a chainsaw to commercially milled cedar beams, the artist then cut, gouged, glued, and assembled pieces into a sprawling, faceted, monumental whole (it is 10 feet high and 18 feet long). *Droga* may resemble strata of the earth's crust or a sci-fi monster taking shape from the mud and rock of a creepy underworld, but, more simply, in *Droga* the audience never loses sight of the tactile aspects of wood as a raw material.

Carving, gouging, cutting, assembling, and polishing are used to a very different effect by Po Shun Leong in his Figure 11.16. The rich mahogany surfaces have a

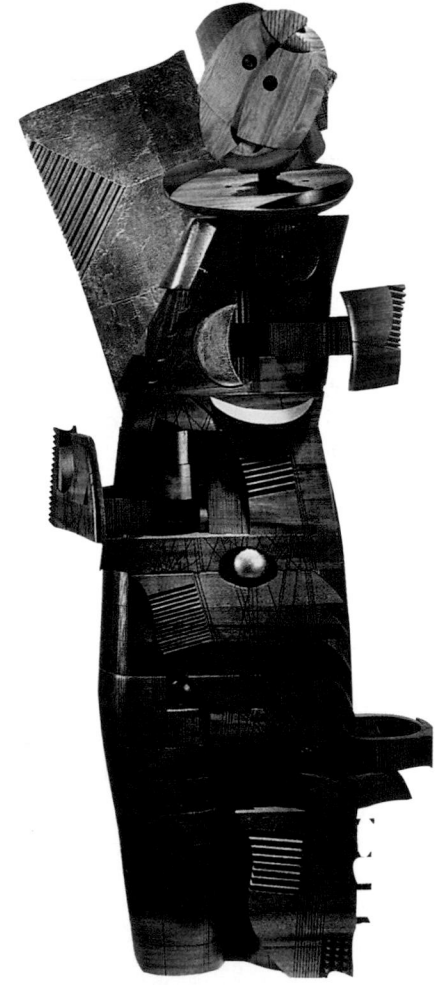

∧ 11.16 **PO SHUN LEONG**, *Figure* (1993). Mahogany with hidden drawers, 50" high.

complexity, delicacy, and intricacy. There is a restlessness to the patterns and the myriad angles at which the pieces are set in relation to one another. Coupled with the punctuation of hidden drawers that can be opened or closed, the handling of the surfaces creates a feeling of constant motion.

Clay

Clay is a naturally occurring material that is more pliable than stone or wood. Works on clay often preserve the evidence of the artist's direct handling of the medium, such as fingerprints and handprints (see Fig. 11.4). Compared to stone or wood, clay has little strength, and it is not typically considered a permanent material—unless it is exposed to heat, as in ceramics. Sculptors have always used clay to make three-dimensional sketches or models that are then cast in more durable materials, such as bronze.

Clay can be fired in a kiln at high temperatures so that it becomes hardened and nonporous, making the clay more suitable for sculpture and ceramics. Before firing, clay can also be coated with glazes that can be manipulated to create different designs and surface textures. Michael Doolan's *A Cautionary Tale Continuum (Yellow)* (Fig. 11.17) is created through a process that begins with hand-modeling and hand-building techniques to create a hollow stoneware figure. The figures are then often completed by factory professionals with expertise in surface finishes such as automotive nylon and metallic lusters. Doolan's earthenware sculptures have a *Toy Story* quality to them—familiar images of children's play objects caught in circumstances in which things seem to have gone terribly wrong.

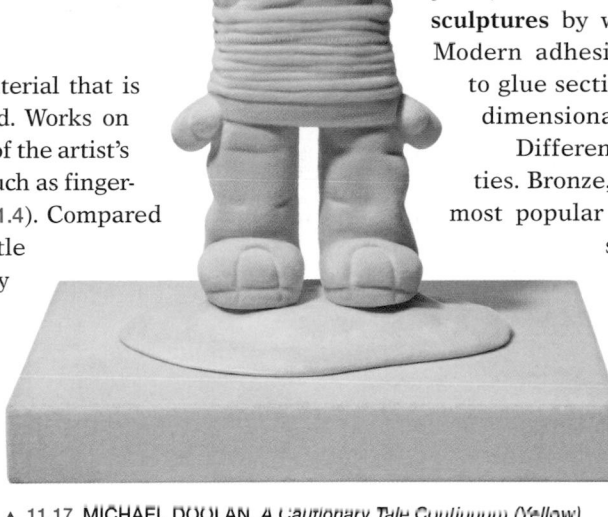

▲ 11.17 MICHAEL DOOLAN, *A Cautionary Tale Continuum (Yellow)* (2010). Hand-modeled earthenware, adhered automotive nylon; 13⅖" high.

Metal

Metal has been used by sculptors for thousands of years. Metals have been cast, **extruded**, **forged**, **stamped**, drilled, filed, and burnished. The process of producing cast bronze sculptures has changed little over the centuries. But in recent years, artists have also assembled **direct-metal sculptures** by welding, riveting, and soldering. Modern adhesives have also made it possible to glue sections of metal together into three-dimensional constructions.

Different metals have different properties. Bronze, an alloy of copper, has been the most popular casting material because of its surface and color characteristics. Bronze surfaces can be made dull or glossy. Chemical treatments can produce colors ranging from greenish blacks to golden or deep browns. Because of oxidation, bronze and copper surfaces age to form rich green or greenish blue **patinas**.

Richard Serra has worked with steel, an alloy of iron, to create minimalist sculpture that expresses the physical properties and capabilities of his material. Like the site-specific work at Storm King Mountain (Fig. 11.18), many of his works have been monumental in size and site specific. Serra's steel surfaces grow more richly textured as time and oxidation work their effects upon them, serving as an apt metaphor for the effect on the visitor's memory that the experience of the work might have.

> 11.18 RICHARD SERRA, *Schunnemunk Fork* (1990–1991). Weathering steel. Storm King Art Center, Mountainville, New York.

Part A. 96" × 589" × 2½"
Part B. 96" × 421" × 2½"
Part C. 96" × 460" × 2½"
Part D. 96" × 652" × 2½"

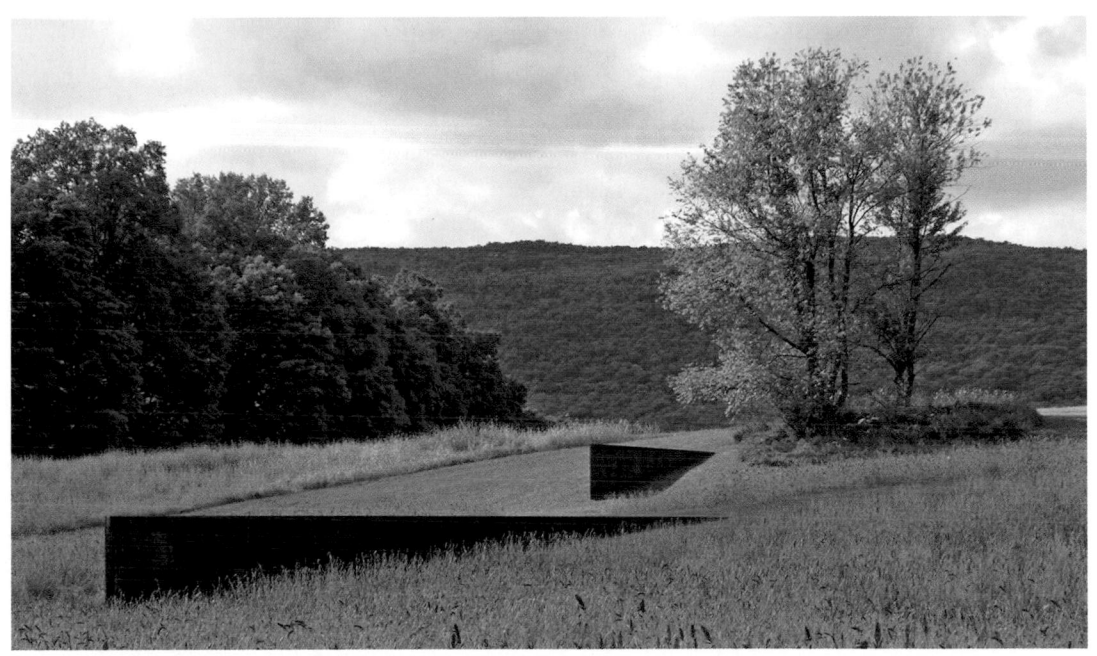

A CLOSER LOOK
Storm King Art Center

Among sculpture parks of the world, Storm King is King.

—J. CARTER BROWN

THE STORM KING ART CENTER IN MOUNTAINVILLE, New York, is a sculpture garden located about one hour north of Manhattan. But this sculpture garden consists of 500 acres of landscaped lawns and fields, hills and woodlands, including views of the mountains of the lower Hudson Valley. Since the great majority of he work is outside, the predominant materials are metal and stone. There are permanent installations of works by sculptors including Richard Serra, Isamu Noguchi, Alexander Calder (**Fig. 11.19**), Menashe Kadishman (**Fig. 11.20**), Henry Moore, Magdalena Abakanowicz, Mark di Suvero, Roy Lichtenstein, and Louise Nevelson. Works by Andy Goldsworthy and Richard Serra were commissioned for their sites. The four partially buried Serra shards of steel, *Shunnemunk Fork* (**Fig. 11.18**), named after nearby Shunnemunk Mountain, occupy ten acres.

The place is like no other: Visit once and you are ensnared. Visit twice and you are mesmerized, because no two visits are alike. The times of the day cast their own shadows, changing patterns of cloud cover dim or brighten sunlight, and the changing seasons bring a distinctive palette to grasses and leaves. What lay in shade may suddenly gush into radiance with a burst of sunlight. There is no good weather or bad weather for this art—only different weather with variable, sometimes capricious, degrees of illumination. Observe the play of the sky across the fields, as did the artists of the Hudson River School two centuries ago.

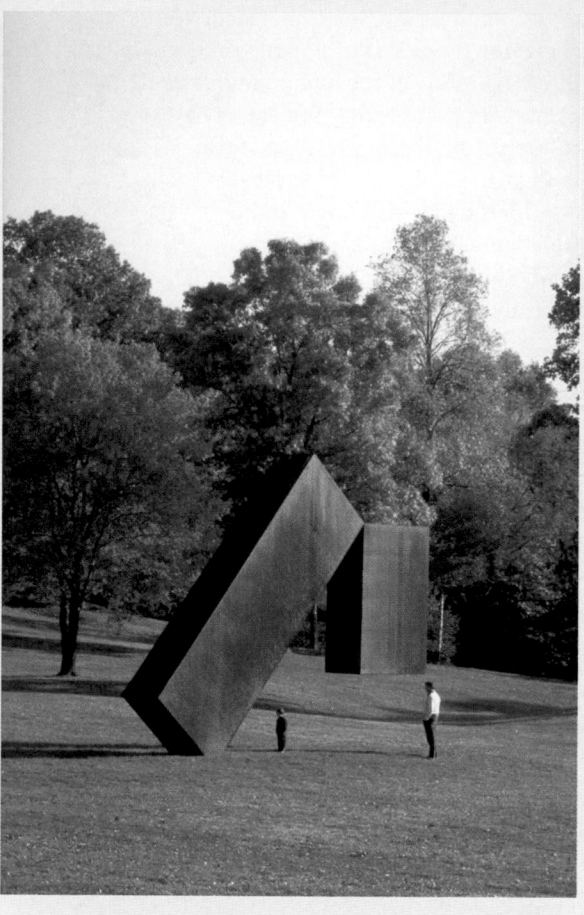

∧ **11.20 MENASHE KADISHMAN,** *Suspended* (1977). Weathering steel, 276" × 396" × 48". Storm King Art Center, Mountainville, New York.

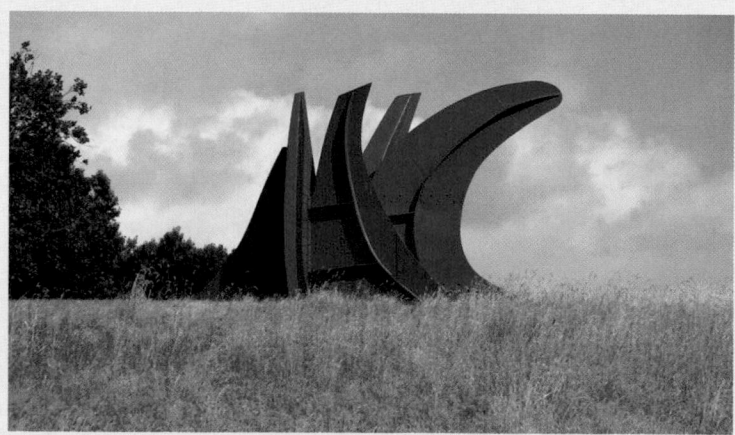

∧ **11.19 ALEXANDER CALDER,** *Five Swords* (1976). Sheet metal, bolts and paint; 213" × 264" × 348". Storm King Art Center, Mountainville, New York.

> The body is our common denominator for our pleasures and our sorrows. I want to express through it who we are, how we live and die.
>
> —KIKI SMITH

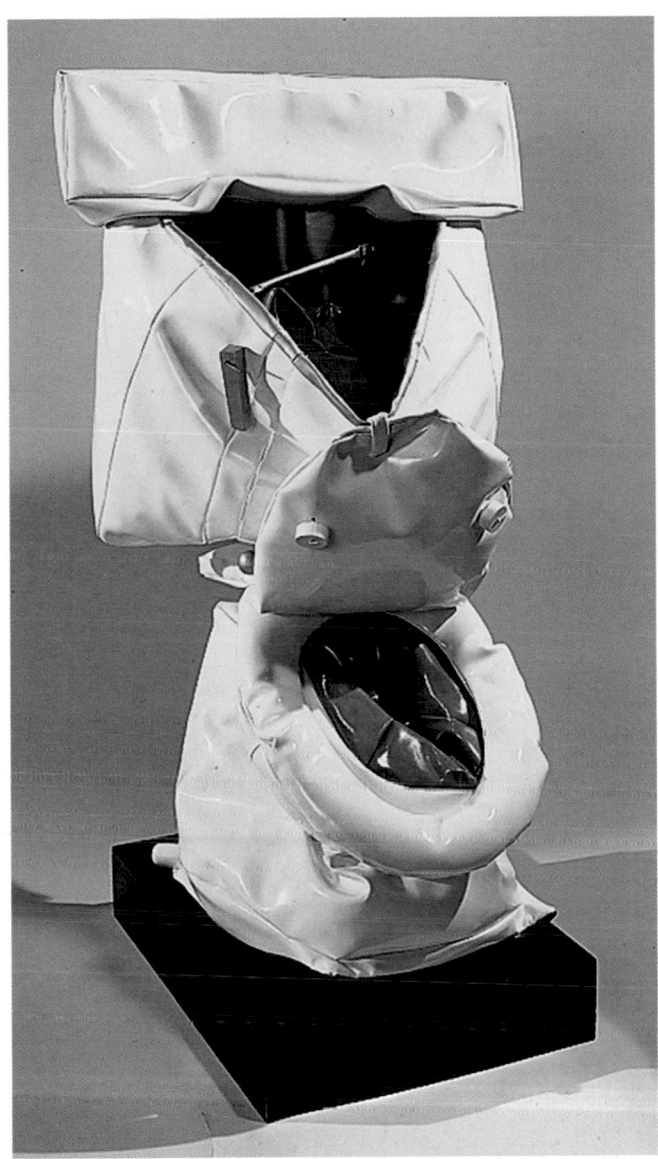

▲ 11.21 CLAES OLDENBURG, *Soft Toilet* (1966). Vinyl filled with kapok painted with Liquitex, and wood; 57 1/16" × 27 5/8" × 28 1/16". Whitney Museum of American Art, New York, New York.

Other Materials

Sculpture today is where it has always been and where it has never been before. Materials have always been traditional and innovative; they have always been enduring and transient.

Pop artist Claes Oldenburg's *Soft Toilet* (Fig. 11.21) is constructed of vinyl, kapok, cloth, and Plexiglas. Our sensibilities are challenged in a lighthearted work: A familiar object that we know to be hard, cold, and unmovable

is rendered soft, supple, and pliable—and certainly unusable.

The figures in Kiki Smith's *Untitled* (Fig. 11.22) were constructed of beeswax and microcrystalline wax. The artist's realism is, in a sense, more realistic than realism has ever been—even when compared to the Photorealism of artists such as Duane Hanson (see Fig. 21.25). The realism in Kiki Smith's couple is almost too painful to observe, too close to the realities of our own physical selves. Smith notes, "Most of the functions of the body are hidden . . . from society," and she thus has aimed to bring them out into the open. Smith has focused her eye on body parts and body by-products; one of her installations consisted of jars filled with bodily fluids from saliva to blood, reflecting her experience as an emergency medical service technician in New York City. In their state of deterioration, the effigies in Smith's untitled work have lost control over their bodily functions. The woman's figure is stained with, or drained of, milk that drips from her nipples. Semen drips down the man's leg. They are suspended in space, isolated in their loss of control, sharing the frailties of the human condition.

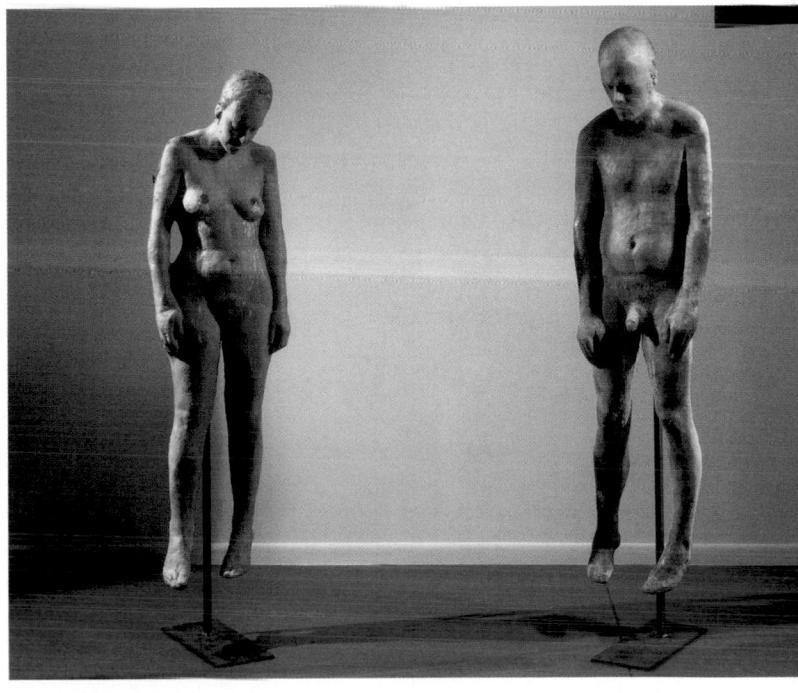

▲ 11.22 KIKI SMITH, *Untitled* (1990). Beeswax and microcrystalline wax figures on metal stands; female figure installed height 6' 1 1/2"; male figure installed height 6' 4 15/16". Whitney Museum of American Art, New York, New York.

Give me a place to light and I will invent an installation that will bring it out.

—DAN FLAVIN

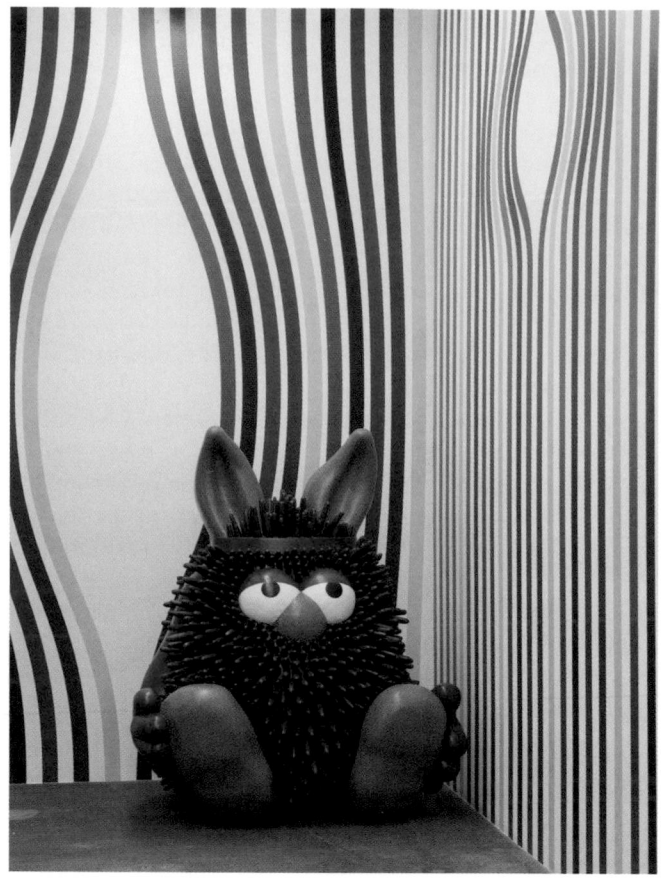

▲ 11.23 **SYLVIE FLEURY**, *Dog Toy 4 (Gnome)* (2000). Styropor, 78¾" × 74⅞" × 59¹⁄₁₆".

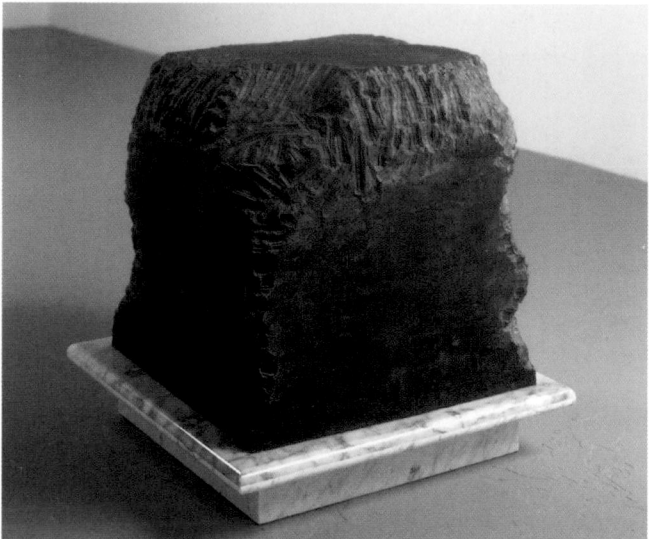

▲ 11.24 **JANINE ANTONI**, *Gnaw* (detail) (1992). Three-part art installation: 600 lb of chocolate gnawed by the artist; 600 lb of lard, gnawed by the artist; display with 130 lipsticks made with pigment, beeswax, and chewed lard removed from the lard cube, and 27 heart-shaped packages for chocolate removed from the chocolate cube. Each cube: 24" × 24" × 24"; overall dimensions variable. The Museum of Modern Art, New York, New York.

Sylvie Fleury constructed her *Dog Toy 4 (Gnome)* (Fig. 11.23) from Styropor, little balls of polystyrene that expand and stick together when heated. Styropor is commonly used for packaging and insulation because it can be shaped and molded and is virtually weightless. Chances are the last time you purchased a flat-screen TV or other electronics, they were surrounded by protective panels of the same material. Fleury's point of departure was a familiar, nonthreatening, squeaky animal toy, blown up to the same nightmarish proportions that turned the smiling marshmallow man in the film *Ghostbusters* into a menacing monster crushing everything in its wake. In the tradition of Andy Warhol and the Pop artists, who had in turn been influenced by the found objects of the Dada artists before them, Fleury elevates consumer products of a "disposable society" to the level of fine art.

Janine Antoni's *Gnaw* (Fig. 11.24) may be overall reminiscent of a minimalist cube by an artist such as Donald Judd or Tony Smith, but it holds some sensory surprises: Antoni's medium is chocolate, and her sculptural tools consist of what nature has endowed her with—a good set of teeth. The surface texture of the piece records the process, for Antoni, the most important element of art making. The companion piece to *Gnaw* was an identical chunk of lard. The artist bit off pieces and then refashioned them into small objects such as lipstick tubes and chocolate boxes, which she then arranged in a mock version of a retail shop.

INSTALLATION

Installation is an artistic medium of three-dimensional works that can be site-specific and transform the perception of the gallery, garden, or other artistic environment. Installation art can be temporary, such as Jacob Hashimoto's *Gas Giant* (Fig 11.25), which occupied the MOCA Pacific Design Center from March to June 2014. Installations can also be permanent, such as many of the site-specific works at Storm King Center (see Figs. 11.18, 11.19, and 11.20).

It took nearly a month, but *Gas Giant* required an installation crew at the MOCA Pacific Design Center to hang 30,000 thin paper sheets, or kites, from the gallery ceiling. Hashimoto (b. 1973) refers to *Gas Giant* as an all-encompassing abstract work that reflects sacred spaces,

> The more compelling artists today are concerned with "space" or "site."
> —ROBERT SMITHSON

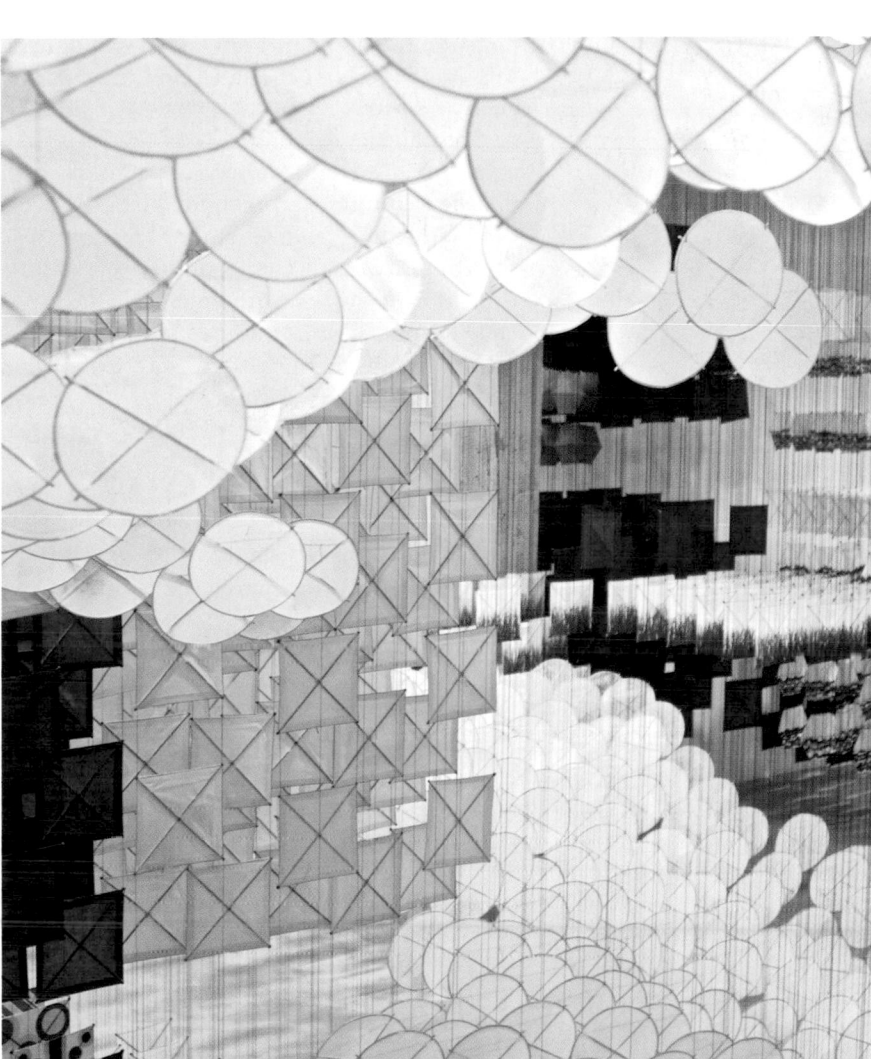

< 11.25 **JACOB HASHIMOTO**, *Gas Giant.* Installation at MOCA Pacific Design Center, Los Angeles, California, 2014.

landscape architecture, and the work of Los Angeles artists. The work combines traditional kite-making methods with collage. It alters the visual environment of the gallery in which it is exhibited, and the artist describes the installation as a "metaphor of possibility and temporality."

CONNECTIONS In Judy Pfaff's installation, *3D*, the viewer is thrust into the center of a chaotic realm of colors, shape, line, and texture—an experience that can be simultaneously stimulating, pleasurable, menacing, and overwhelming.

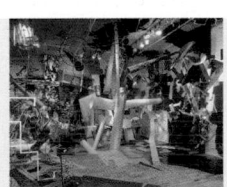

∧ Pfaff's *3D* (**Fig. 2.29**)

SITE-SPECIFIC ART

Site-specific works are distinguished from other artworks, which are typically created in a studio with no particular spatial context in mind. Site-specific art is produced in or for one location and—in theory, at least—is not to be relocated. The work is in and of its site, and often the content and meaning of the work is inextricably bound to it. By this description, the history of art is full of examples of site-specific art, ranging from the sculptural decoration on the Parthenon (see Fig. 15.10) and Michelangelo's Sistine Chapel ceiling (see Fig. 17.19) to the murals by Diego Rivera that cover the walls of the Palacio Nacional in Mexico City (see Fig. 20.40). But the term *site-specific*

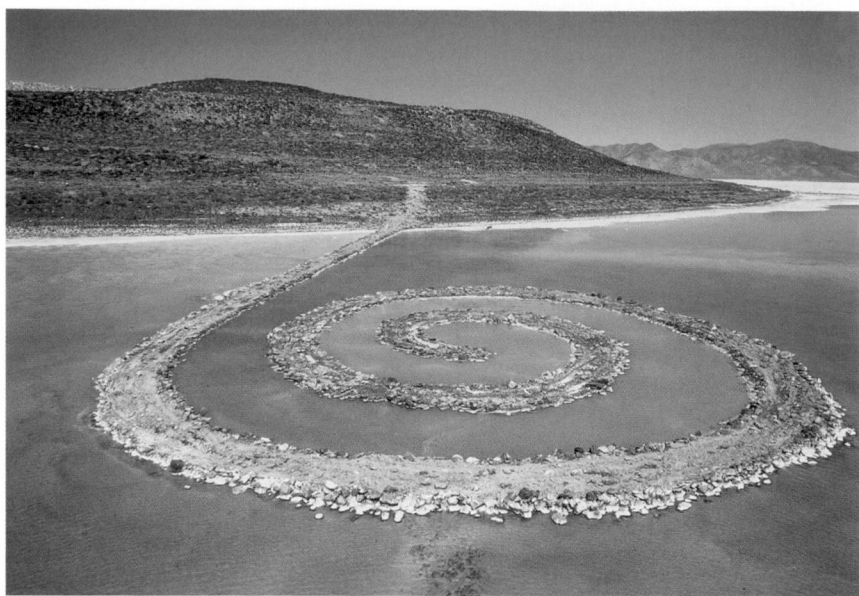

▲ 11.26 **ROBERT SMITHSON,** *Spiral Jetty,* **Great Salt Lake, Utah** (1970). Black rocks, salt, earth, water, and algae; 1,500' long, 15' wide.

came into use in the 1960s and 1970s as a blanket category for art that was created for or in a specific location. That location might be a museum or gallery, a public space, or a site in the natural landscape. Site-specific art consists of many types, goals, and styles, including land and environmental art, ephemeral art, public art, and monuments.

Land Art

Land art refers to site-specific works that are created or marked by an artist within natural surroundings. Sometimes large amounts of earth or land are shaped into sculptural forms, as in the earthworks of the 1960s and 1970s. These works could be temporary or permanent and included great trenches and drawings in the desert, bulldozed configurations of earth and rock, and delicately constructed compositions of ice, twigs, and leaves. What such works have in common is the artist's use of local materials to create pieces that are unified with or contrapuntal to the landscape.

Robert Smithson's *Spiral Jetty* (Fig. 11.26) is composed of basalt and earth bulldozed into a spiral formation in Utah's Great Salt Lake. The spiral shape of the jetty was inspired by a whirlpool, as well as the configuration of salt deposits that accumulate on rocks bordering the lake. After its creation, the jetty lay submerged underwater for many years. With a prolonged drought, the spiral

began to reemerge in 1999 and, depending on the water levels of the lake, now "comes and goes."

The delicacy of many of Andy Goldsworthy's constructions stands in marked contrast with Smithson's bulldozed mounds of earth. They communicate, from another perspective, the fragility and changeability of nature. Goldsworthy works with materials he finds on site—leaves, sticks, stones, ice fragments—manipulating them with a soft, controlled touch or even, as with *Ice Star*, his breath (Fig. 11.27). The following documentary narrative accompanied the piece:

> thick ends dipped in snow then water
> held until frozen together
> occasionally using forked sticks as
> support until stuck
> a tense moment when taking them
>   away
> breathing on the stick first to release it

Art that "makes marks" in nature is often temporary. In March 2004, Danish artist Marco Evaristti set sail in two icebreakers to find the perfect "frozen canvas" among the icebergs off the coast of Greenland. For two

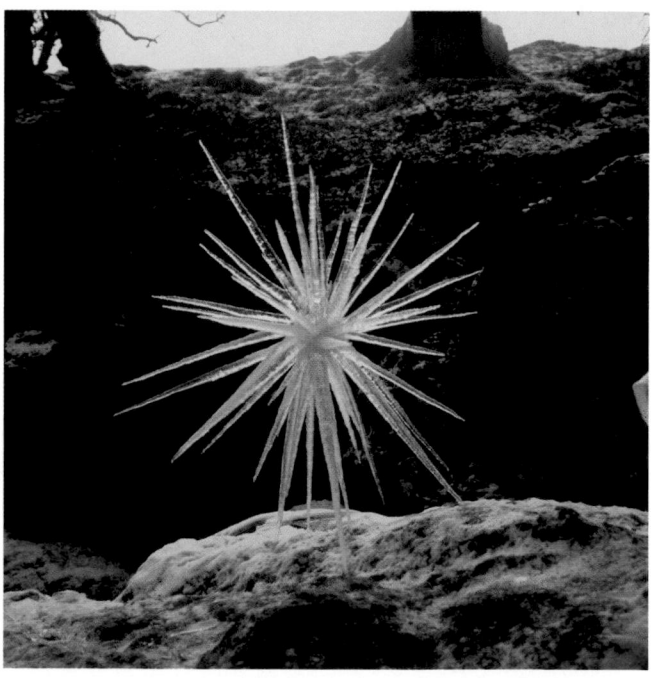

▲ 11.27 **ANDY GOLDSWORTHY,** *Ice Star* (January 12, 1987). Cibachrome photograph, 30" × 30". Scaur water, Penpoint, Dumfriesshire, Scotland.

Life is short, art endures. (Vita brevis, ars longa.)

—HIPPOCRATES (C. 460–400 BCE)

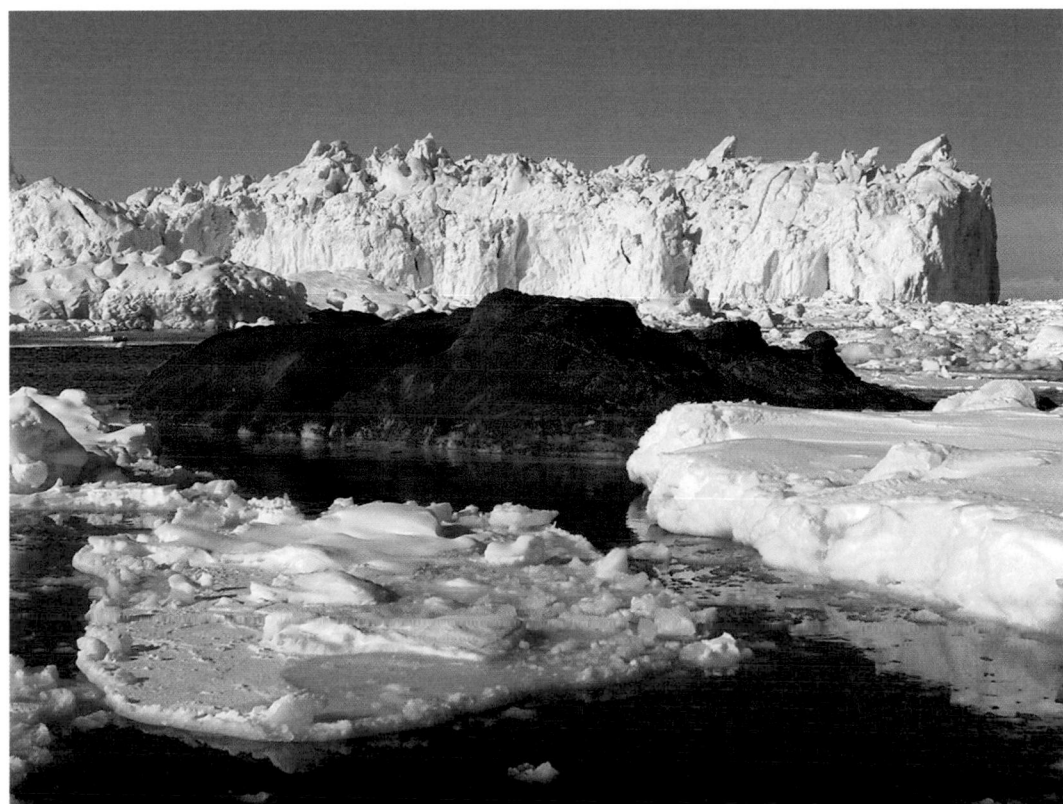

< 11.28 MARCO EVARISTTI, *The Ice Cube Project* (2004). Red dye and seawater, Greenland coast.

hours, a crew of twenty sprayed 780 gallons of red dye onto an almost 10,000-square-foot iceberg (Fig. 11.28). The dye, diluted with seawater, was the same that is used for tinting meat. Evaristti's work can be found—for the time being, at least—near Ilullissat (which means "icebergs" in the Greenlandic language), a town of 4,000 that is popular among tourists for its spectacular and *artistic* scenery.

One of the most spectacular examples of land art that combines nature and man-made materials is Walter de Maria's *The Lightning Field* (Fig. 11.29). The field is constructed of 400 stainless steel poles (lightning rods) anchored in a 1-by-62-mile plot of earth. Nature's "behavior" in the

grandest sense gives shape and meaning to the work. The enduring as well as transitory aspects of nature are woven into the varied experience of land art.

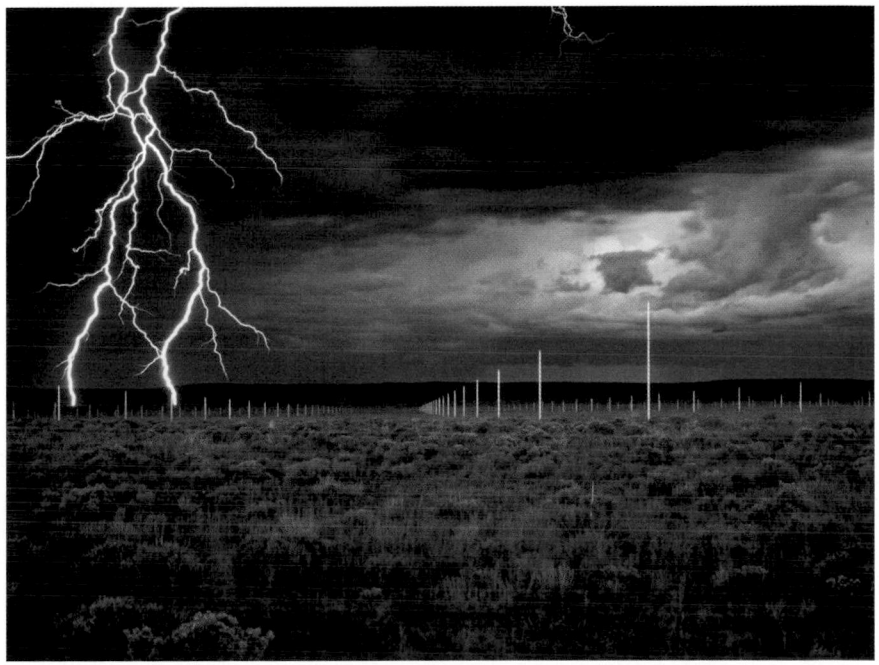

> 11.29 WALTER DE MARIA, *The Lightning Field* (1977). 400 polished stainless steel poles installed in a grid array measuring 1 mile × 1 km. The poles—2" in diameter and averaging 20' 7 1km. The poles are spaced 220' apart and have solid pointed tips that define a horizontal plane. Quemado, New Mexico.

A CLOSER LOOK

Christo and Jeanne-Claude: *The Gates, Central Park, New York City, 1979–2005*

AS IF INTENTIONALLY TIMED to shake New York City out of its winter doldrums, 7,503 sensuous saffron panels were gradually released from the tops of 16-foot-tall gates along 23 miles of footpaths throughout Central Park. It was the morning of February 12, 2005—a date that marked the end of artists Christo and Jeanne-Claude's twenty-six-year-long odyssey to bring a major project to their adopted city. For a brief sixteen days, the billowy nylon fabric fluttered and snapped and obscured and enframed our favorite park perspectives (**Fig. 11.30**). The park's majestic plan of ups and downs, of lazy loops and serpentine curves (as originally designed by Frederick Law Olmsted and Calvert Vaux), was being seen or reseen for the first time as we—the participants—wove our walks according to the patterns of the gates. The artists have said that "the temporary quality of their projects is an aesthetic decision," that it "endows the works of art with a feeling of urgency to be seen." For a brief

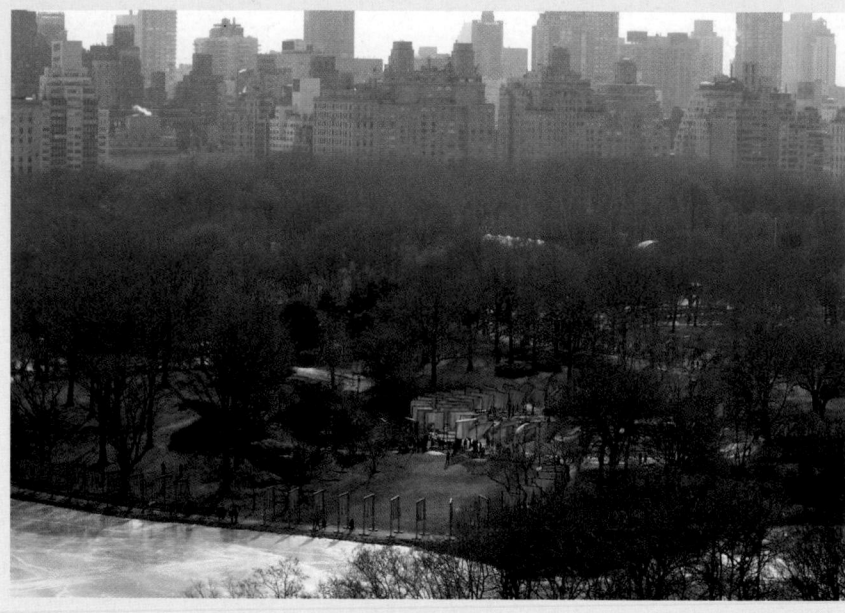

∧ **11.31** Aerial view of *The Gates* in Central Park with Manhattan skyline.

sixteen days, it was clear from the crowds in a winter park, from the constant cluster of buses at the 72nd Street entrance, and from the rubbernecking traffic on the streets and avenues bordering the park that the urgency of which Christo and Jeanne-Claude speak was very real.

As with all of Christo and Jeanne-Claude's works of environmental art, every aspect of *The Gates* project was financed and fought for by the artists. They developed the concept for *The Gates* in 1979, but their first proposal to the city in 1981 was rejected. Mayor

Michael R. Bloomberg granted permission for the 2005 version of the project on January 22, 2003. The vital statistics of *The Gates, Central Park, New York City, 1979–2005* are staggering. Placed at 12- to 15-foot intervals, 7,503 vinyl gates, 16 feet high, varying in width from 5 feet 6 inches to 18 feet, covered 23 miles of footpaths. The free-hanging, saffron-colored fabric panels dropped from the top of each rectangular vinyl gate to 7 feet above the ground—just low enough for small children on their father's shoulders to sneak a touch. The project required more than 1 million square feet of vinyl and 5,300 tons of steel. Hundreds of paid volunteers assembled, installed, maintained, and removed the work, and most of the materials were to be recycled. The estimated cost of the project—borne by the artists alone—was $20 million.

The environmental art projects of artists Christo and Jeanne-Claude have been seen by millions, who have been enticed to experience their familiar surroundings with a heightened sensibility. Like the artists, I, too, live in New York City. I walked *The Gates* many times over 16 days, each time with a group of family members and friends who made the pilgrimage (**Fig. 11.31**). When asked why it was so important to realize this work in Central Park, Christo responded, "When our son was a little boy, we used to take him to Central Park every day—he loved to climb the beautiful rocks. Central Park was a part of our life."

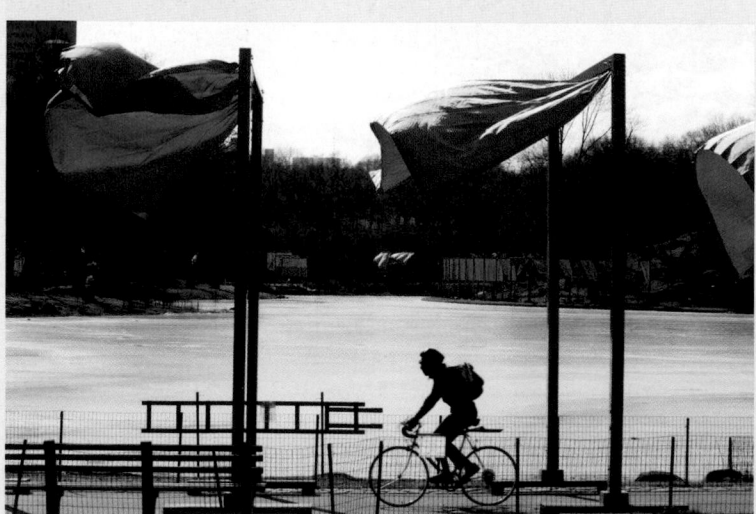

∧ **11.30** CHRISTO AND JEANNE-CLAUDE, *The Gates,* Central Park, New York City, 1979–2005.

Public art exists to thicken the plot.
—VITO ACCONCI

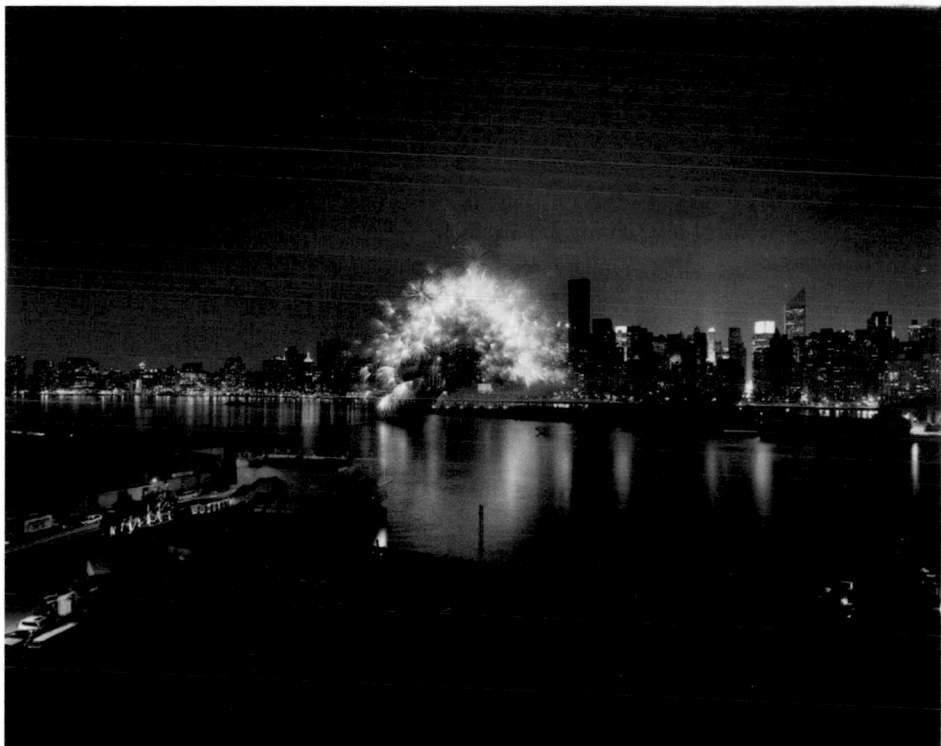

◄ 11.32 CAI GUO-QIANG, *Transient Rainbow* over East River, New York City (2002).

Ephemeral Art

Hippocrates's oft-quoted words were intended to laud the significance of art, attributable in part to its longevity and survival across generations. Is its sentiment outdated? Consider much of the work we have discussed so far in this chapter, which did not last long beyond its creation. Goldsworthy's *Ice Piece* (see Fig. 11.27) remained frozen just long enough for him to document it with his camera. Many artists work with ephemeral materials—in other words, materials that do not endure.

The term **ephemeral art** is used specifically to describe works that have a temporal immediacy or are built with the recognition that they will disintegrate. You see them one minute and the next they're gone. Most of this work is viewed only in photographs after the fact, unless one happens to be lucky enough to be present when the piece is crafted or performed. How does such work differ from land art? Sometimes it doesn't.

Cai Guo-Qiang's fireworks pieces (Fig. 11.32) are classic examples of ephemeral art. *Transient Rainbow*, commissioned by the Museum of Modern Art, was planned to coincide with the opening of a temporary gallery space in Queens—across the East River from Manhattan. As Cai wrote:

> In my hometown every significant social occasion of any kind, good or bad—weddings, funerals, the birth of a baby, a new home—is marked by the explosion of fireworks. They even use fireworks when they elect Communist party officials, or after someone delivers a speech. Fireworks are like the town crier, announcing whatever's going on in town.

The project was a masterpiece of coordination in conception, creation, and documentation. After several iterations, shaped by the concerns of the New York City Fire Department, Transit Authority, Coast Guard, and Federal Air Administration, Cai's piece came and went, in some fifteen seconds, on June 29, 2002. The fireworks display consisted of 1,000 shells that were launched in sequence from the Manhattan side of the river, ascending and descending in an arc toward Queens, on the opposite side. The brilliant color palette unfolded so that, for a moment, a transient moment, the fireworks rainbow spanned the river.

Anyone who has tried to capture a fireworks display with a camera knows that it's a tough thing to do. The vibrancy and shimmer that sends "ooooooos" through the crowd never seem to measure up in our photographic record. With a work that is literally there one minute and gone the next, its documentation becomes extremely important. Cai hired twenty photographers in all—three of whom were specialized fireworks photographers from Japan—to capture *Transient Rainbow*. The video document and still photographs have become an essential part of the work: tangible records of an ephemeral art performance.

Public Art

The history of art is also full of works created for public spaces. Michelangelo's *David* (see Fig. 17.22), even though it now has sanctuary in the Galleria dell'Accademia in Florence, was installed as a public work of art for the Piazza della Signoria, just outside the building that served as the political center of the city. A bit farther south, in Rome, one can see some of the most famous, most elaborate fountains in the world. They were created for the pleasure of the public (though often too for the glory of a pope). It is common also today for institutions (including the U.S. federal government) to allot a percentage of the overall cost of their building programs for works of art destined for the public spaces in and around buildings. You are probably familiar with works of **public art** in your own cities and towns, some dating back decades and some installed for a particular occasion or just for the season, as was Olafur Eliasson's *New York City Waterfalls* (Fig. 11.33). Constructed under the Brooklyn Bridge in the summer of 2008, it was one of four sites featuring free-standing waterfalls funded by New York's Public Art Fund.

New York's Central Park forms the geographic and spiritual heart of that city and serves as the backdrop for one of its most beloved public sculptures. *Angel of the Waters* (Fig. 11.34) (also known as Bethesda Fountain), by Emma Stebbins, towers above a circular brick plaza bordering a large lake. Warm weather brings sunbathers, break-dancers, newlyweds, and splashing dogs to this public gathering space that seems to sit protectively beneath the outspread wings of an angel.

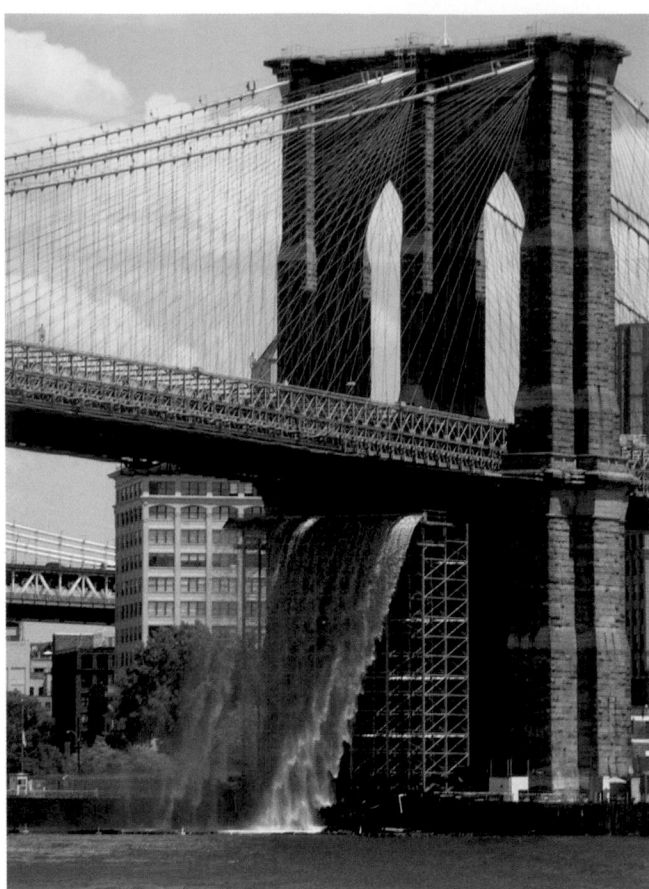

▲ 11.33 **OLAFUR ELIASSON,** *The New York City Waterfalls* (2008). Brooklyn Bridge, New York, New York.

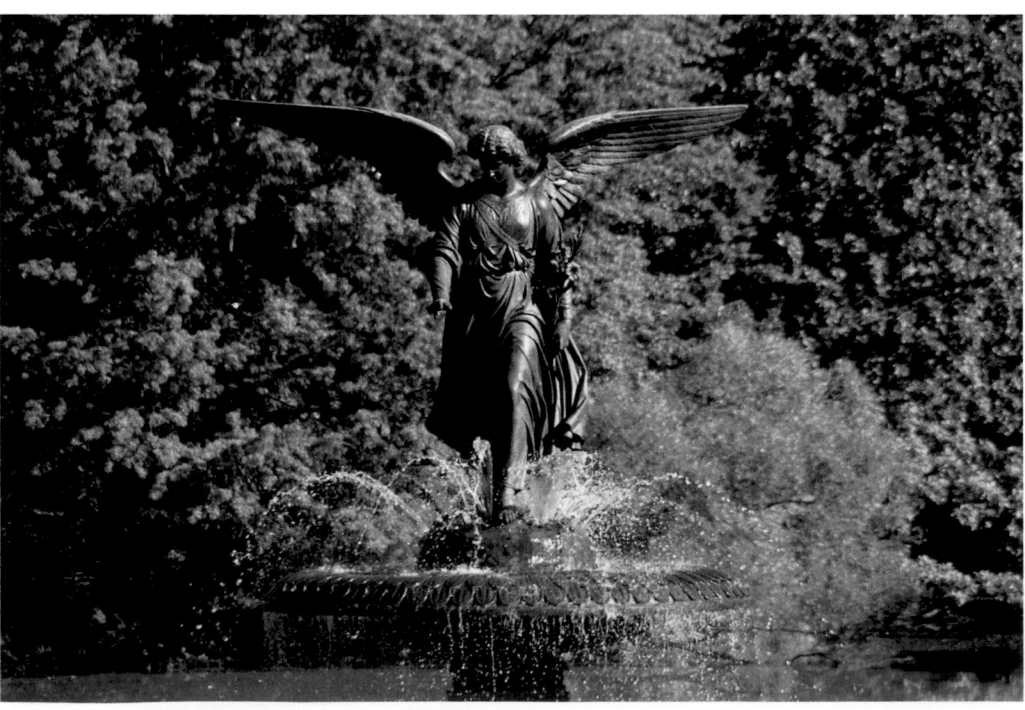

> 11.34 **EMMA STEBBINS,** *Angel of the Waters* (**Bethesda Fountain**) (1873). Central Park, New York, New York.

A CLOSER LOOK

Barcelona's *Parc Güell*

AT THE BEGINNING OF THE TWENTIETH CENTURY in Barcelona, one of its most famous native sons—Antoni Gaudí—was asked by his patron, Eusebi Güell, to create a gardenlike suburb for the very rich overlooking the city. The project was abandoned, but not before completion of what is now one of Barcelona's most treasured public sites, *Parc Güell*. A lively mosaic serpent (**Fig. 11.35**) stands at the entrance of the park and has become one of the recognizable symbols of the city. Flights of steps lead to a variation on a hypostyle hall, with a forest of columns ornamented with lavish mosaic bases. The undulating ceiling is punctuated with mosaic discs called sunbursts (**Fig. 11.36**). This space was originally intended to serve as a public market. Resting on top of the columned hall is an esplanade, the perimeter of which is lined with its serpentine, mosaic-clad stone bench (**Fig. 11.37**). Gaudí was known for his playful, organic forms (see also his *Casa Mila*, **Fig. 19.39**) that helped define the Modernista style in Catalunya (or Catalonia), Spain.

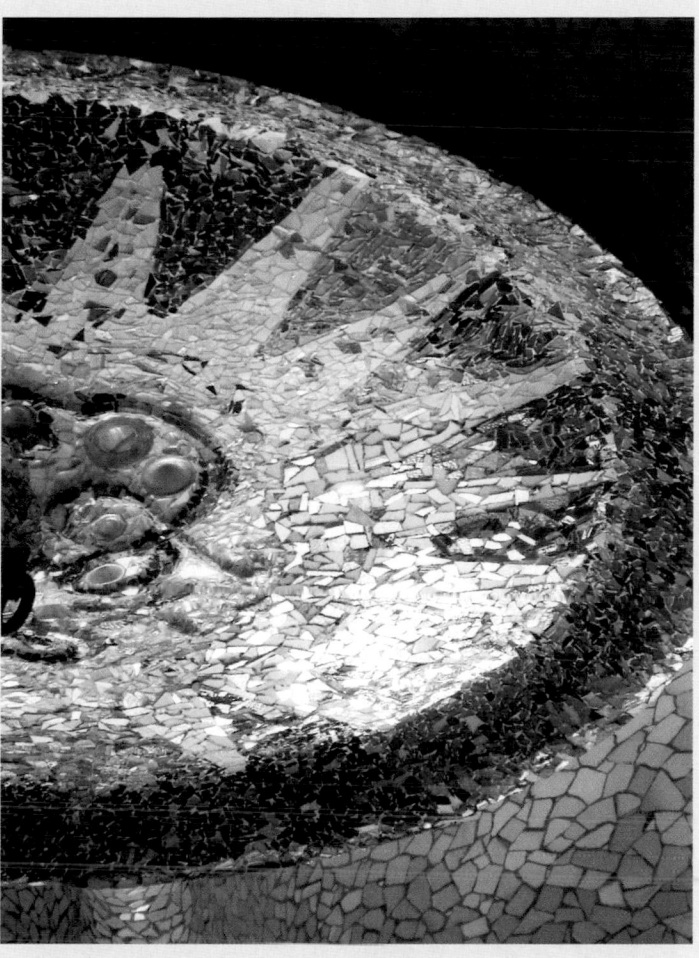

▲ 11.36 ANTONI GAUDÍ, Detail of mosaic sunburst in ceiling of hypostyle hall (1900–1914). *Parc Güell*, Barcelona, Spain

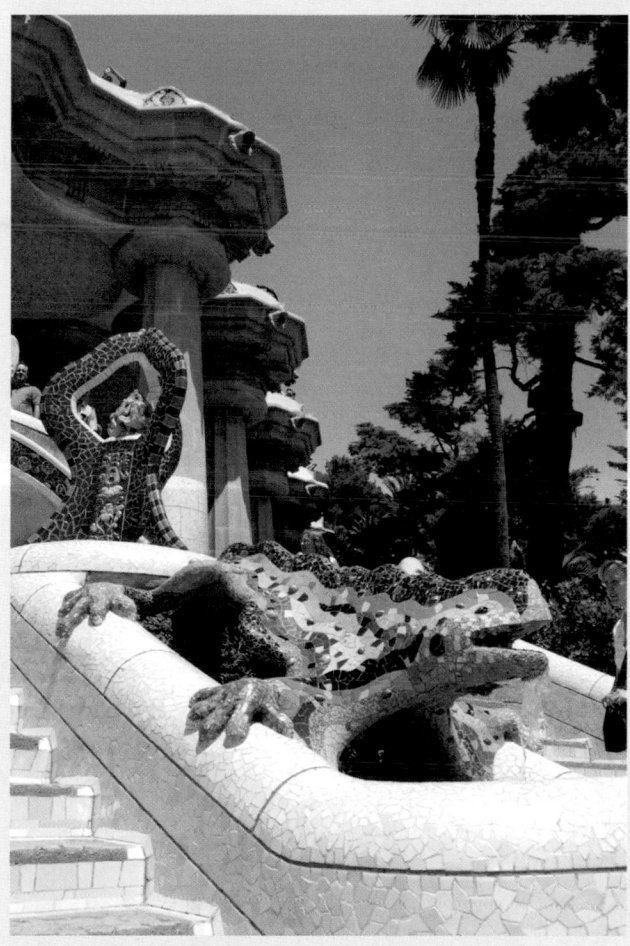

▲ 11.35 ANTONI GAUDÍ, **Serpent/Salamander** (1900–1914). *Parc Güell*, Barcelona, Spain.

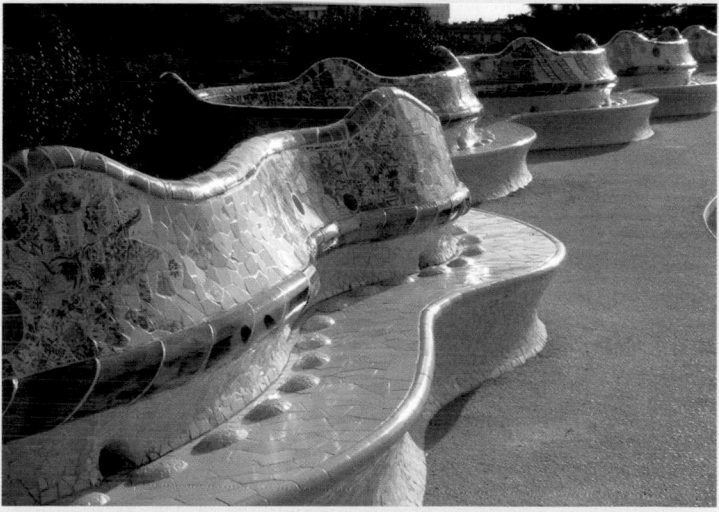

▲ 11.37 ANTONI GAUDÍ, Detail of mosaic serpentine bench, which sits in plaza above hypostyle hall (1900–1914). *Parc Güell*, Barcelona, Spain.

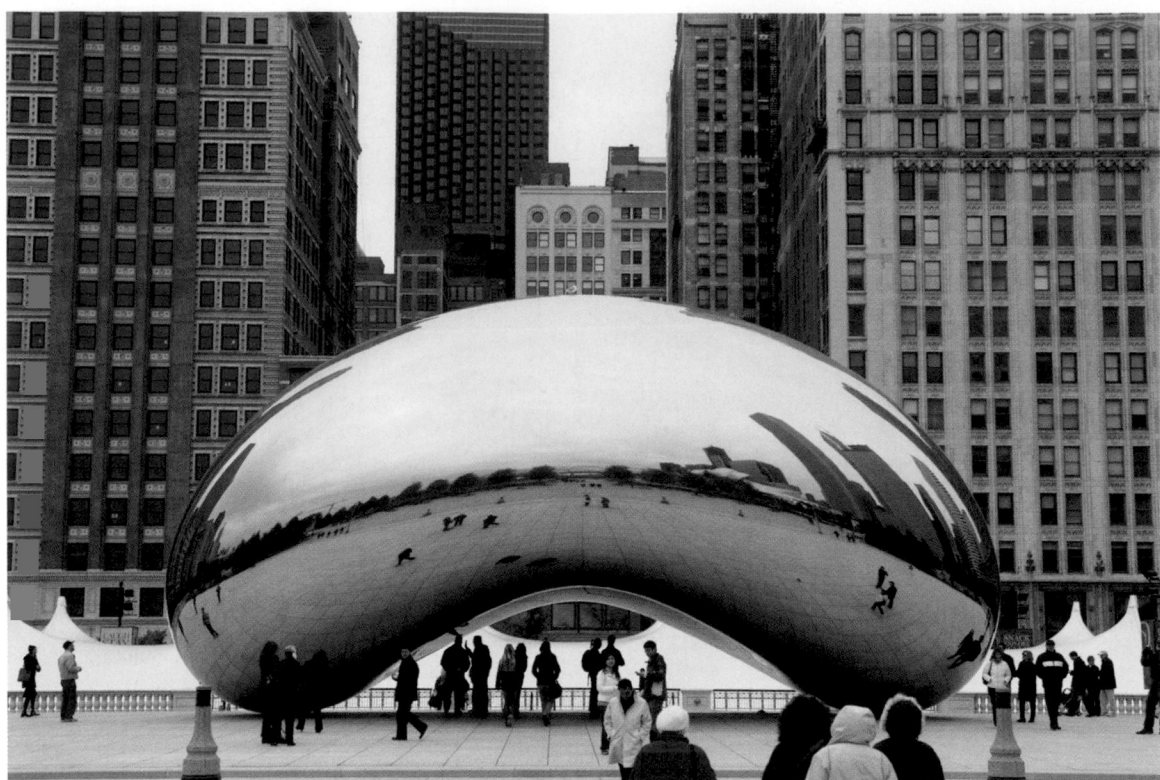

◄ **11.38 ANISH KAPOOR,**
Cloud Gate (2004–2006).
Cloud Gate's exterior
consists of 168 highly
polished stainless steel
plates. It is 33' × 66' × 42'
tall. Millennium Park,
Chicago, Illinois.

Chicago's Millennium Park has its own very popular and very new gathering space, the focal point of which is Anish Kapoor's *Cloud Gate* (Fig. 11.38). Nicknamed "the bean" because of its elliptical, beanlike shape, the work consists of highly polished, mirror-like stainless steel plates that reflect the people, places, and things surrounding it, both permanent and transient. Kapoor has called his piece "a gate to Chicago, a poetic idea about the city it reflects." The work inspired a new jazz composition (*Fanfare for Cloud Gate*) by Orbert Davis, performed in Millennium Park on the occasion of the dedication of Kapoor's sculpture.

A bit of controversy surrounding *Cloud Gate* proves interesting with regard to the nature of land and environmental art, including commissioned public works of art. Kapoor owns the rights to the piece, and therefore photographs of it cannot be reproduced commercially (as in this book) without his permission. One particular photographer learned this the hard way, when he was not permitted to photograph "the bean" without a prepaid permit. The public response to limits on publishing personal photographs of this public work of art was strong; photographs began to appear all over the Internet (you can find them on Google Images or Flickr, a photo-sharing website). If public art is public (and sometimes supported in real dollars by the public), where, in your opinion, should the artist's rights end and the public's begin?

See more *of Chicago in the online Art Tour.*

Monuments

The few examples of site-specific public art that we have looked at were designed or installed to enhance a particular open, public space. Their main purpose is or was aesthetic—to create beauty or to enhance the environment. Monuments comprise another category of site-specific public art. Their purpose is to preserve the memory of a person or an event.

The category of monuments is so broad that the few works we are able to concentrate on here represent an absurdly small percentage of what we live with in our communities. Equestrian monuments—men on horseback—seem almost ubiquitous in cities and towns, even though the identities of those memorialized are often forgotten. One of the purposes of monuments is to institutionalize memory. Monuments serve as expressions of the need or desire of a city, a country, or perhaps of a generation to "never forget."

This sense of loss and absence is central to Peter Eisenman's Holocaust Memorial in Berlin (Fig. 11.39), erected in memory of the European Jews murdered by the Nazis. Within view of the Brandenberg Gate and the Reichstag—two architectural monuments associated with Adolf Hitler and Nazism—Eisenman placed 2,711 gray, concrete **stelae** side-by-side in claustrophobic rows. The stelae are the same length and width but vary in height and are placed on slabs that are tilted in different

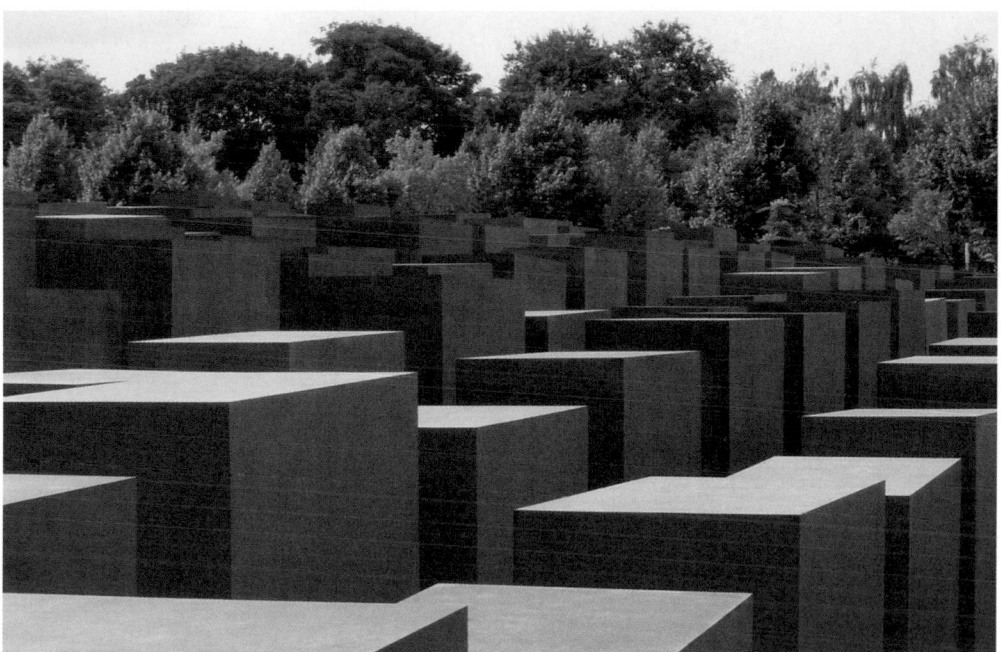

▲ 11.39 **PETER EISENMAN, Holocaust Memorial** (2004). Berlin, Germany.

the relentless grayness of the stones and the sky is somber, ashen, and funereal. The site is also home to an exhibition space, underground beneath the stelae, that is dedicated to the historical background of the Holocaust. The feeling is cryptlike, but there are no bodies, no objects that belonged to the deceased, and therein lies a point of the memorial. The Nazis planned to annihilate the Jews of Europe and any memory of them.

As the competitions ensued for the commission of Berlin's Holocaust Memorial, questions were raised about the relevance of a modern, abstract design. Would it be understood? Would it have meaning? The same questions haunted Maya Lin's proposal for the *Vietnam Veterans Memorial* in Washington, D.C., decades earlier (see A Closer Look: The Vietnam Veterans Memorial—a Woman's Perspective).

directions. The paths between the slabs slope up and then down so that the journey among these stones shifts and changes. The concentration of stelae is greatest at the center of the monument, creating a disturbing sense of confinement. In sunlight, the shadows are sharp and harsh; shady areas that ought to provide welcome respite from the sun are, instead, menacing. On an overcast day,

The National World War II Memorial (Fig. 11.40) in Washington, D.C., was dedicated in 2004, more than fifty years after the Allied victories in Europe and Japan.

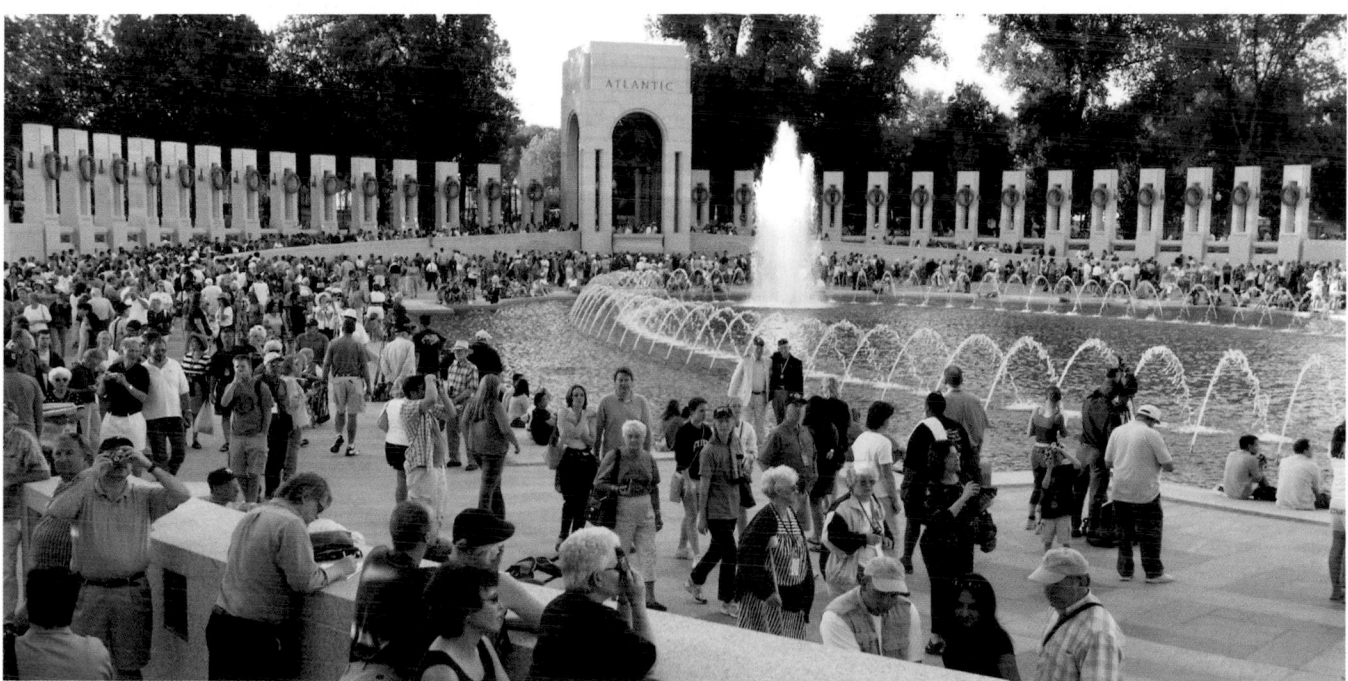

▲ 11.40 **FRIEDRICH ST. FLORIAN, National World War II Memorial** (2004). Washington, D.C.

A CLOSER LOOK

The Vietnam Veterans Memorial—a Woman's Perspective

WHEN WE VIEW THE EXPANSES of the Washington Mall, we are awed by the grand obelisk that is the Washington Monument. We are comforted by the stately columns and familiar shapes of the Lincoln and Jefferson memorials. But many of us do not know how to respond to the two 200-foot-long black granite walls that form a V as they recede into the ground. There is no label—only the names of 58,000 victims chiseled into the silent walls:

> As we descend along the path that hugs the harsh black granite, we enter the very earth that, in another place, has accepted the bodies of our sons and daughters. Each name is carved not only in the stone, but by virtue of its highly polished surface, in our own reflection, in our physical substance. We are not observers, we are participants. We touch, we write [letters to our loved ones], we leave parts of ourselves behind. This is a woman's vision—to commune, to interact, to collaborate with the piece to fulfill its expressive potential. . . .
>
> Maya Ying Lin has foregone the [format of the triumphal monument]. She has given us [the earth mother] Gaea, who, pierced by the ebony scar of suffering death, takes back her children, as she has done since the dawn of humanity.[3]

This is Maya Ying Lin's Vietnam Veterans Memorial (Fig. 11.41), completed in 1982 on a two-acre site on the Mall.

---

[3]Lois Fichner-Rathus, "A Woman's Vision of the War," *The New York Times,* August 18, 1991, p. H6.

To read the names, we must descend gradually into the earth, and then just as gradually work our way back up. This progress is perhaps symbolic of the nation's involvement in Vietnam. The eloquently simple design of the memorial also stirs controversy, as did the war it commemorates.

This dignified understatement in stone has offended many who would have preferred a more traditional memorial. One conservative magazine branded the design a conspiracy to dishonor the dead. Architecture critic Paul Gapp of the *Chicago Tribune* argued, "The so-called memorial is bizarre . . . neither a building nor sculpture." One Vietnam veteran had called for a statue of an officer offering a fallen soldier to heaven. The public expects a certain heroic quality in its monuments to commemorate those fallen in battle. Lin's work is antiheroic and antitriumphal. Whereas most war monuments speak of giving up our loved ones to a cause, her monument speaks only of giving up our loved ones.

How did the Vietnam Memorial come to be so uniquely designed? It was chosen from 1,421 entries in a national competition. The designer, Maya Ying Lin, is a Chinese American woman who was all of 22 years old at the time she submitted her entry. A native of Ohio, Lin had just graduated from Yale University, where she majored in architecture. Lin recognized that a monumental sculpture or another grand building would have been intrusive in the heart of Washington. Her design meets the competition criteria of being "neither too commanding nor too deferential" and is yet another expression of the versatility of stone.

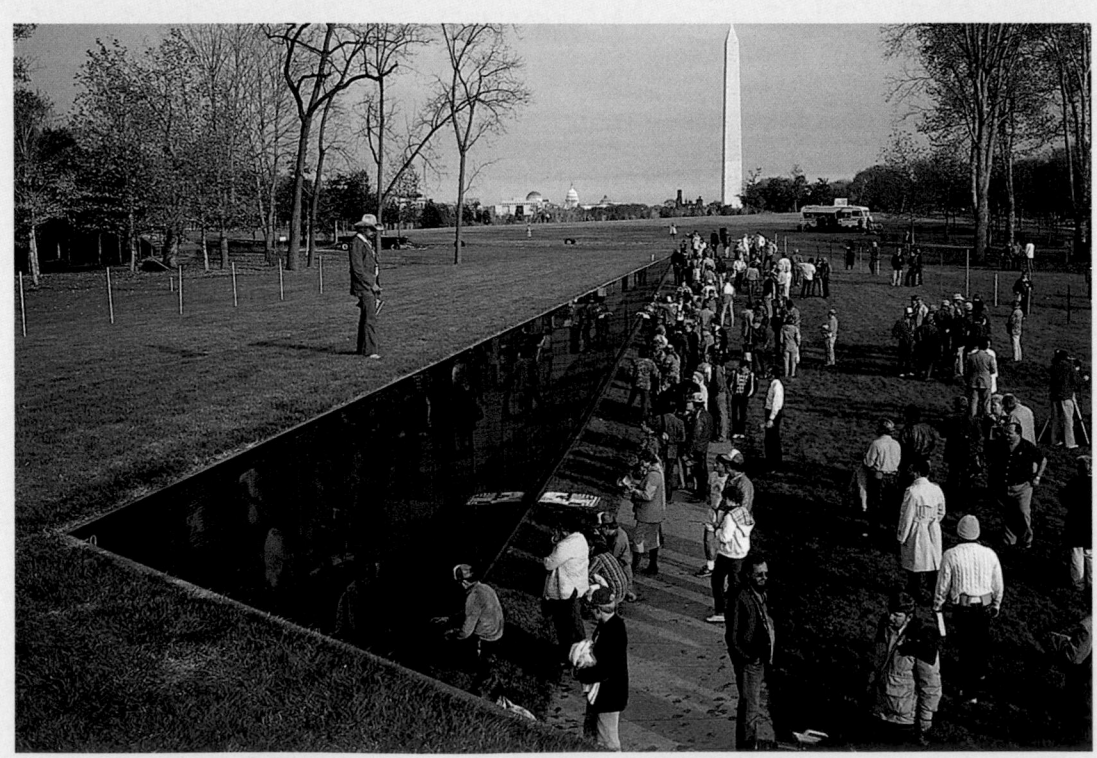

< **11.41 MAYA YING LIN,** Vietnam Veterans **Memorial** (1982). Polished black granite, 492' long. Washington, D.C.

The design for the memorial, with its pavilions and pillars, stirred a different kind of controversy in that its traditional, classical forms were reminiscent, to one journalist, of the pompous style embraced by the Fascist regimes of the 1930s, the very regimes that the Allies fought to defeat. One critic went so far as to refer to the memorial as a "monument on steroids—vainglorious, demanding of attention and full of trite imagery."[4]

The reception of the National World War II Memorial was not all negative, although the controversy raises an interesting question about the ways in which people relate to memorials and critics evaluate them. Many contemporary artists have gravitated toward designs that are interactive, educational, and reflective. Artists working in a more traditional mode emphasize the larger-than-human, the heroic. Reactions to memorials are highly personal, and the way memory is institutionalized is a very sensitive topic. Critics can find themselves in a situation in which their criticism is viewed, at best, as politically incorrect or, at worst, as unpatriotic.

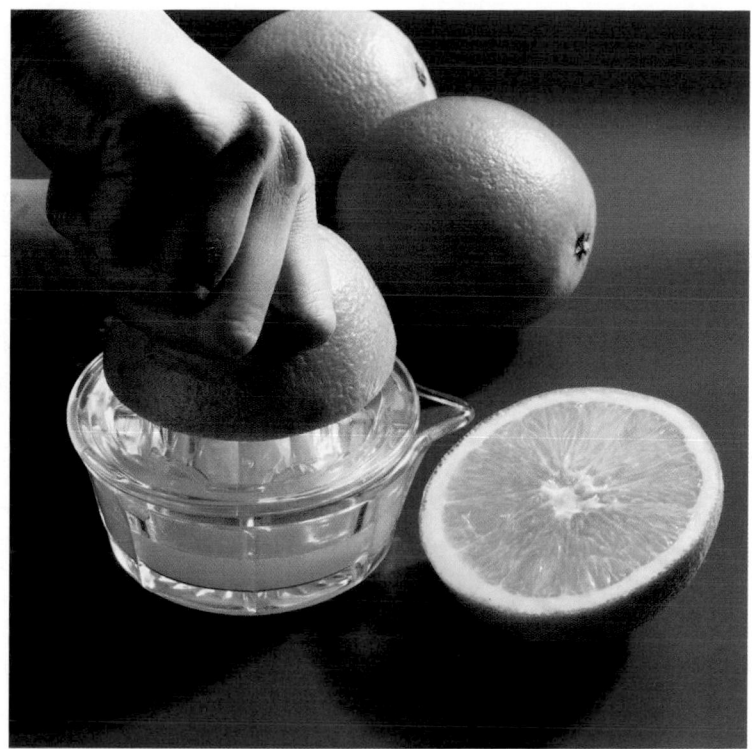

▲ 11.42 *Citrus Express.*

INDUSTRIAL DESIGN

Industrial design refers to the design of three-dimensional products intended for consumer use. Industrial designs run the gamut from utilitarian designs (form follows function) to those in which aesthetics override usability (form over function). There are good and bad designs, and then there are objects for which the question "Good or bad?" seems moot. Consider the common houseware item—the citrus juicer (Fig. 11.42). It seems to have been designed foremost with utility in mind. The user halves an orange, inverts it onto a conical glass or plastic piece with pronounced ribs or ridges, and twists it back and forth to release the juice from the orange. The juice flows down the cone into a collection bowl in a quick and tidy fashion. Now consider famed French designer Philippe Starck's citrus squeezer titled *Juicy Salif* (Fig. 11.43), purportedly conceived during a meal in which he was squeezing lemon over a squid. Is it a juicer or a sculpture? As a clear example of "form over function," Starck's juicer has become a design icon, not because it works well, but because it looks great. In fact, *Juicy Salif*'s manufacturer, Alessi, recommends it more for display than for use.

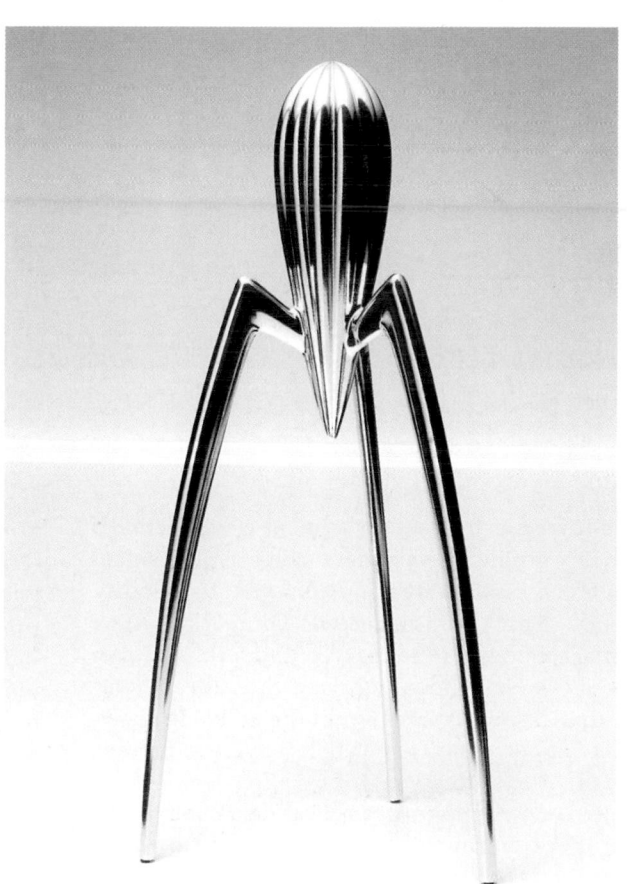

---

[4] Thomas M. Keane Jr., *The Boston Herald,* 2004.

▲ 11.43 **PHILIPPE STARCK,** *Juicy Salif.* 6" × 6" × 11".

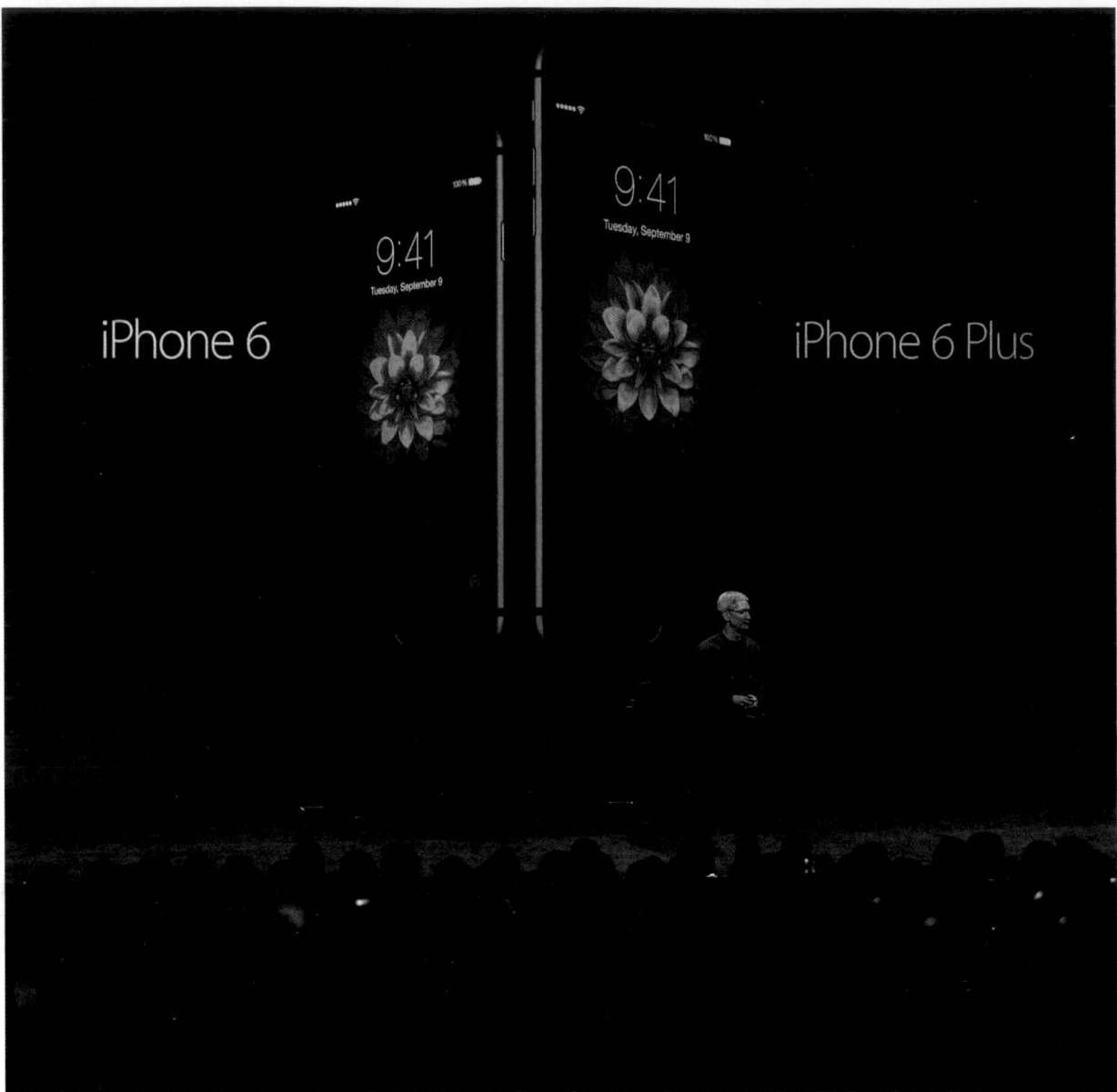

∧ 11.44 Apple CEO Tim Cook presenting the iPhone 6 Plus.

Although few of us looking for a juicer would actually opt for Starck's product, consumers often make choices based as much on product design and cache as usability. Apple's iPhone (Fig. 11.44) is a case in point. While there are many smartphones on the market, and a fair number of them are more economically priced than the iPhone, sales of the Apple product have swept the globe. In choosing an iPhone, a consumer is not only buying a product but also buying into a lifestyle.

A great deal of contemporary product design embraces the philosophy of "form follows function" put forth by the architect Louis Sullivan. Two of a multitude of examples come from the design collection of the Museum of Modern Art. Rody Graumans's *85 Lamps Lighting Fixture* (Fig. 11.45) is an unadulterated cluster of naked lightbulbs and wiring that fans out into a more classic chandelier profile as a result of the spherical shapes of the touching bulbs. The "truth in art" that Sullivan sought through his philosophy seems also to have inspired Graumans's lighting fixture design: the whole truth and nothing but the truth, in fact.

Many objects of contemporary industrial design take **ergonomics**—the applied science of equipment design intended to minimize discomfort and therefore maximize performance of the user—into account. If your shoulders, neck, elbows, or wrists hurt from the physical stress of and mesh seat and back fully adjust to accommodate bodies of any shape, height, and weight. A tilt mechanism in the chair "floats" users with support no matter which position they are sitting in, and the mesh suspension system distributes weight equally. The quirky appearance of the Aeron Chair, a by-product of its adherence to ergonomic design, has achieved a sort of cult-status among trendy office workers. One TV commercial even shows twenty-somethings playing office hockey while cruising in their Aeron Chairs.

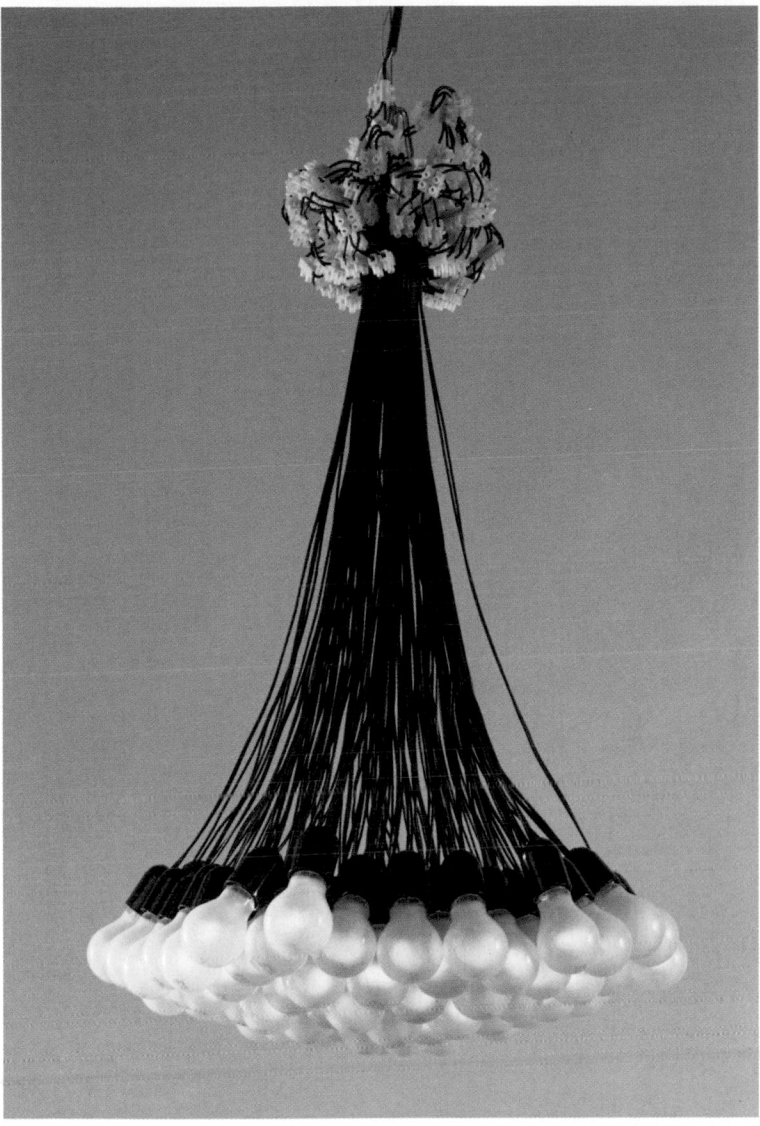

▲ 11.45 RODY GRAUMANS, *85 Lamps Lighting Fixture* (1992). Lightbulbs, cords, and sockets; 39⅜" high, 39⅜" diameter. The Museum of Modern Art, New York, New York.

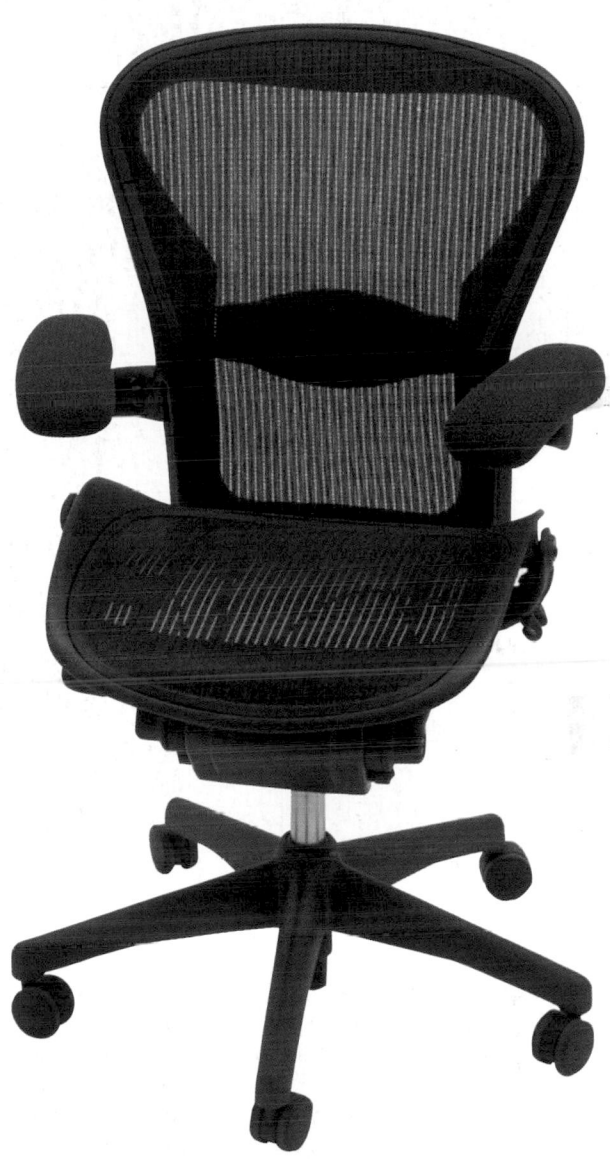

▲ 11.46 BILL STUMPF AND DON CHADWICK, Aeron Chair. The Museum of Modern Art, New York, New York.

prolonged work at your computer, you can purchase an ergonomically designed keyboard that will keep your wrists at a proper angle and a mouse that will support the weight of your arm while mousing. These designs are based on the physiognomy of the human body and typical product use.

The *Aeron Chair* (Fig. 11.46), ergonomically designed by Bill Stumpf and Don Chadwick, has emerged as the Porsche of office chairs and is also part of the design collection at the Museum of Modern Art. The metal-frame

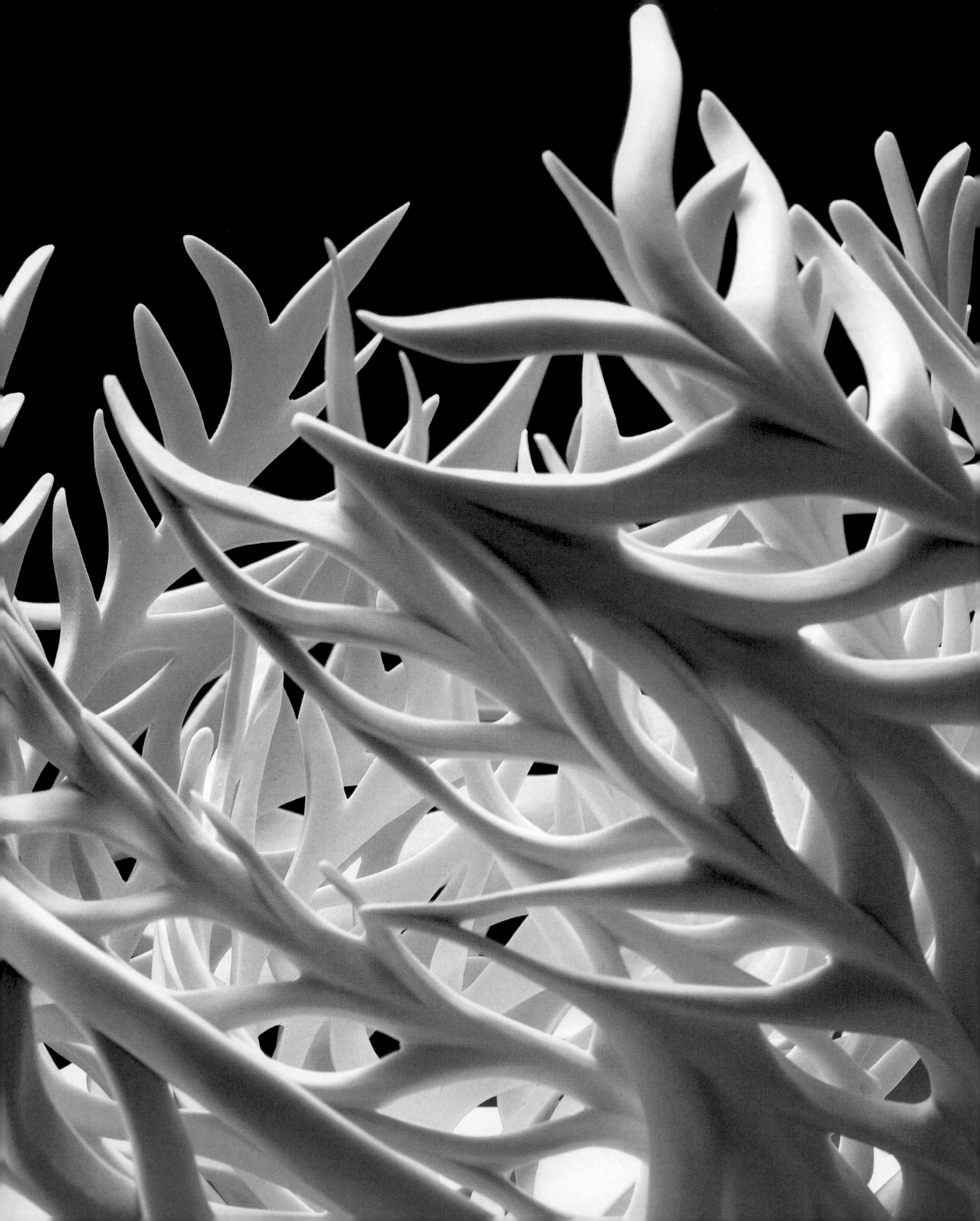

12

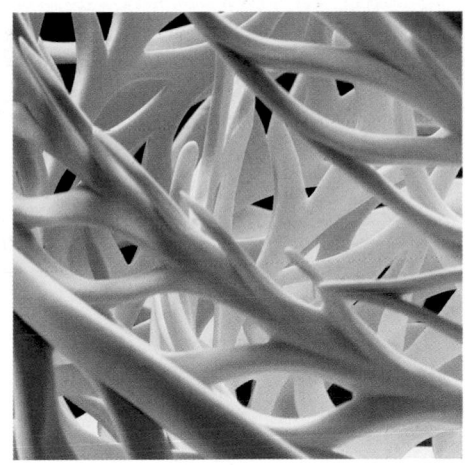

CRAFT ARTS

I think art can exist within any craft tradition. Craft is just another way of saying means. I think it's a question of conscious intention, finally, and personal gifts, or giftedness. It seems that in art there is a primacy of idea over both means or craft, and function. Idea has to transcend both. I think this is probably why it's so difficult to make art out of something functional, or in a realm where craft has been nurtured for its own sake.

— MARTIN PURYEAR

AN ATTIC vase, a Navajo rug, Tiffany glass, a Chippendale desk—which is art? Which is craft? Art critics and historians once had certain answers to these questions. Now, however, the perception of the relationship among functional objects, craft materials and techniques, and works of fine art has changed. Consider this story concerning one of the Metropolitan Museum of Art's most precious acquisitions, as retold by art critic Arthur C. Danto.[1] According to Thomas Hoving, the director of the museum at the time of the purchase, the vase in Figure 12.1 is "the single most perfect work of art I ever encountered . . . an object of total adoration." In his memoirs, Hoving further described his feelings upon his first encounter with the piece: "The first thought that came to mind was that I was gazing not at a vase, but at a painting." The director was obviously swept off his feet by this masterpiece of Greek art—a terra-cotta vessel painted with the scene of the *Dead Sarpedon Carried by Thanatos and Hypnos* and signed by both the potter and the painter. But why did Hoving diminish the significance of the potter's craft by essentially dismissing the pot as a mere support for an extraordinary painting? Danto suggests that Hoving's reaction is indicative of an art-world prejudice of sorts—one that attaches less importance to functional objects and decoration of any kind. He warns that "the painting [on the vase] is there to decorate an object of conspicuous utility" and cannot be considered without reference to the vase itself. In fact, doing so precludes any real understanding of the work in the historical and artistic context in which it was created.

---

[1] Arthur C. Danto, "Fine Art and the Functional Object," *Glass*, no. 51 (Spring 1993): 24–29.

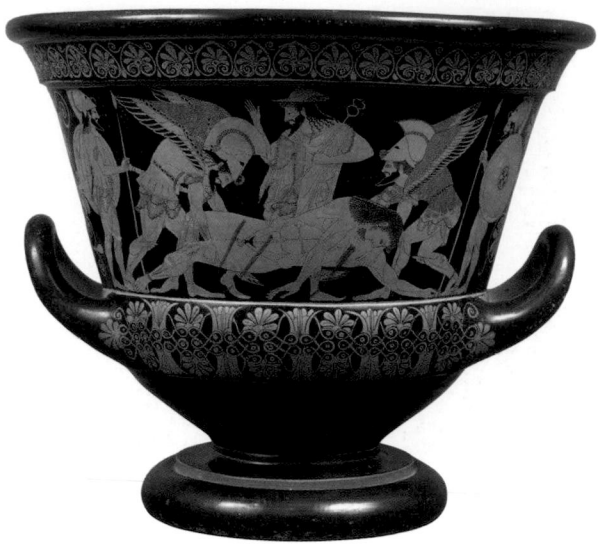

What purpose does this esoteric argument have for us who, as students, are trying to understand art? Simply this: The distinction between fine art and functional object is linked to the historical and cultural context in which a work was created. As Danto pointed out, the Greek philosophers praised craftspeople as somewhere between

artists and philosophers, but held the view that no one was lower than the artist. Danto paraphrases Plato in *The Republic*: "The carpenter knows how to fashion in real life what the painter can merely imitate; therefore . . . artists have no real knowledge at all, trafficking only in the outward appearance of things."[2] More than 2,000 years later, a French philosopher would declare, "Only what serves no purpose is truly beautiful,"[3] suggesting a sure separation between fine art and craft. The mediums of paint and bronze might be used to create works of art in which, to paraphrase Puryear, the idea transcends craft and function. But those materials closest to the artisan—clay, glass, and fiber, metal—these materials were the purview of craft art that prioritized technical skill and utility over the "idea." Today, such lines are often blurred. Miriam Schapiro's *Wonderland* (Fig. 12.2), according to this distinction, would most certainly be labeled a work of fine art. Yet the composition is a conglomeration of bits and pieces of time-honored craft techniques: quiltmaking, needlework, and crochet. The work does not have a utilitarian function, but it does cast a spotlight on some of the functional objects that provided outlets for artistic expression by women for

---

[2] Ibid.
[3] Théophile Gautier, Preface to his novel *Mademoiselle de Maupin*, 1835.

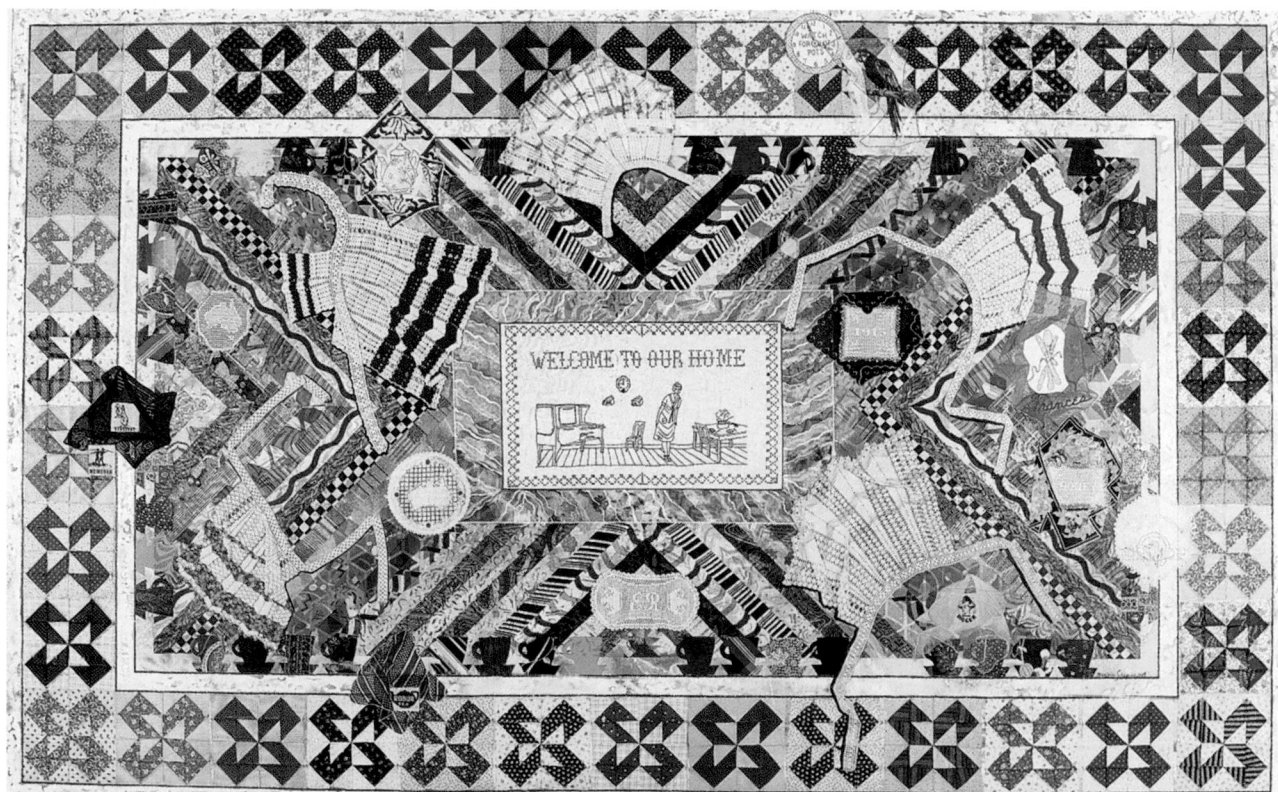

▲ 12.2 MIRIAM SCHAPIRO, *Wonderland* (1983). Acrylic, fabric, and plastic beads on canvas; 90" × 144 ½" (228.6 × 367 cm). Smithsonian American Art Museum, Washington, D.C.

whom access to the world of fine art was the equivalent of intergalactic travel. Ceramic artists are creating works of sculpture, and sculptors are finding innovative ways to manipulate clay, wood, and metal. Glassmaking has reached new heights of experimentation while employing centuries-old techniques. Some artists view the distinction between art and craft as artificial, limiting, and even denigrating. Others embrace that distinction, which has, after all, a pedigree that we can trace to Plato.

In this chapter, we discuss a variety of media and categories of artistic expression. We consider the materials traditional to craft—clay, glass, fiber, metal, and wood—using historical and contemporary works as evidence of the broad technical and stylistic ranges of the mediums. We see that the distinction between art for art's sake and art for utility's sake is sometimes blurred.

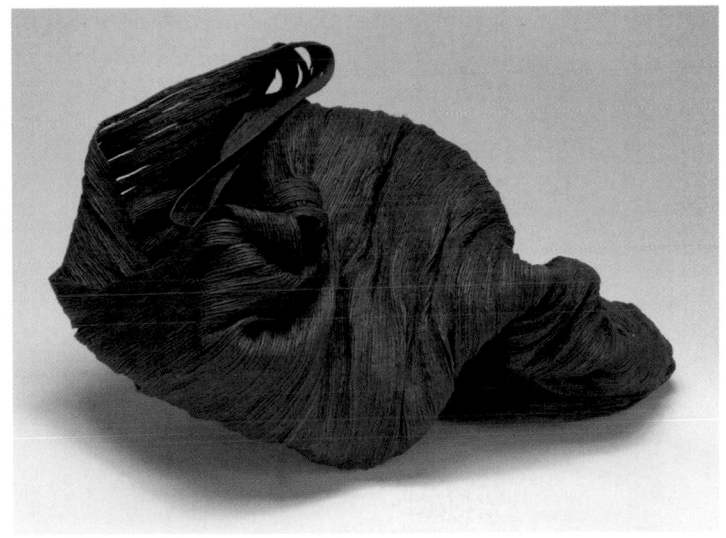

∧ 12.4 **CHERYL ANN THOMAS**, *Relic 130* (2008). Porcelain, 22" × 16" × 10".

CERAMICS

Ceramics refers to the art or process of making objects out of baked clay. Ceramics includes many objects that range from the familiar pots and bowls of **pottery**, to clay sculptures, to building bricks and the extremely hard tiles that protect the surface of the space shuttles from the intense heat of atmospheric reentry.

Methods of Working with Clay

Ceramics was a highly refined craft in the ancient Middle East and China, but its roots go back further than that. For thousands of years, people have worked wet clay with

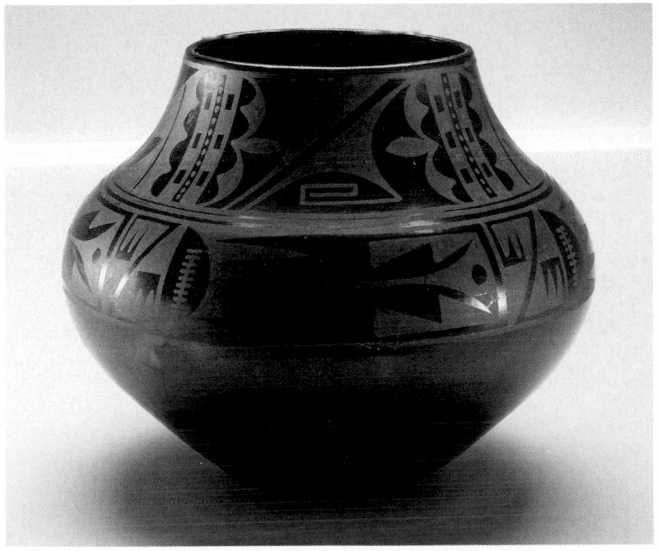

∧ 12.3 **MARIA MONTOYA MARTÍNEZ AND JULIAN MARTÍNEZ**, *Jar* (c. 1939). Blackware, 11⅛" × 1' 1". Ildefonso Pueblo, New Mexico. National Museum of Women in the Arts, Washington, D.C.

their carrying water or storing grain. Clay was patted and pinched and rolled, well before the invention of the potter's wheel, and these basic hand-built techniques continued (and still do) alongside wheel thrown pottery. Shaping clay is only part of the process. To achieve hard, durable, and waterproof vessels, clay must be exposed to heat or fire.

Ancient cultures, such as Mesopotamia and Egypt, dried or baked clay and mud bricks in the broiling desert sun. Early ceramics were also hardened by fire in stone pits covered with flammable natural materials such as dried grasses, branches, perhaps even coal. Insulated kilns, or ovens, were developed to control temperature and regulate the firing process. Facility with firing techniques—and a growing knowledge of varieties of clay composition and ways to manipulate surface coatings, or glazes —culminated in magnificent, complex objects, valued as much for their artistic as utilitarian importance.

The earliest hand-built ceramics are described by their simple techniques. Pinch pots were created by shaping a lump of clay into a small cuplike container, slab pots by seaming together five flat slabs (four for the sides, one for the bottom). Coil pots are built from ropes of clay (you probably remember making snakes in preschool in exactly the same way) that are stacked on one another or coiled like a beehive. After the ropes are stacked, tools can be used to smooth them together, inside and out, or they might be left as is to reveal the coiling process.

These different effects can be seen in two examples of coiling. The perfect contours of the black-on-black, coil-built vessel of Native American potter Maria Montoya Martínez and Julian Martínez (Fig. 12.3) were created by smoothing the ridges of the stacked coils into flat, thin walls that belie the process. The surface effect of etched glass was achieved through a complex interplay of burnishing, glazing, and firing techniques. In Cheryl Ann Thomas's work (Fig. 12.4), by contrast, individual coils

> Ceramic sculptural works are more specific than traditional sculpture with its expressive force coming from the surface of the body. The surface of the sculpture can be bare clay or clay with oxides and glazes; however, this surface tells us as much about the purpose of the sculpture as does the form itself.
>
> —TANIA DE BRUKYNER

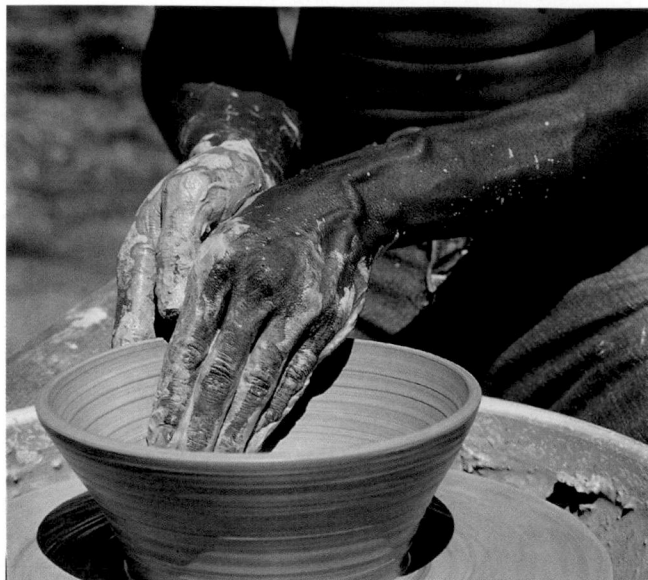

∧ 12.5 **The Hands of the Potter**. Conrad Knowles forming a tray and a bowl for his collection of artful pottery.

to a smooth finish and molded to the desired vessel shape. The walls of a wheel-thrown pot tend to be thinner and more uniform in thickness than coiled pots, and the outer and inner surfaces are smoother. This does not suggest, however, that coiled pots in the hands of some craftspeople do not approach wheel-thrown pots in their accomplishment. For example, Native Americans of the southwestern United States have never used the potter's wheel, yet their hand-built pots can be as thin walled and symmetrical as their wheel-thrown counterparts.

Anyone who has been a student in a ceramics class appreciates the difficulty of getting the rhythm of the potter's wheel. The speed of the wheel, placement of the clay, downward pressure of the hands, and force (or delicate touch) of the fingers are an extreme exercise of coordination. The goal, generally, is to achieve perfect symmetry and a smooth contour. How ironic, then, is the work of Jennifer McCurdy (Fig. 12.6), who begins by throwing on the wheel and then quickly shapes, folds, and slices into her clay with an X-Acto knife. Two firings produce rock-hard porcelain objects that, in the potter's words, "are so

retain their shape identity rather than being smoothed together. They are nestled next to one another and then folded and molded into *trompe l'oeil* objects resembling woven cloth. For Thomas, creating the delicate ropes of clay through the rhythmic movements of her hands forges an intimate connection with her material.

The Potter's Wheel

The potter's wheel (Fig. 12.5) was first used in the Middle East in about 4000 BCE and seems to have come into common use 1,000 years later. A pot can be **thrown** quite rapidly and effortlessly on a wheel once the techniques have been mastered, in contrast to the more laborious and time-consuming process of building a pot by coiling. In **coiling**, ropes of clay are fashioned, then stacked upon one another. The walls of the pot are then scraped

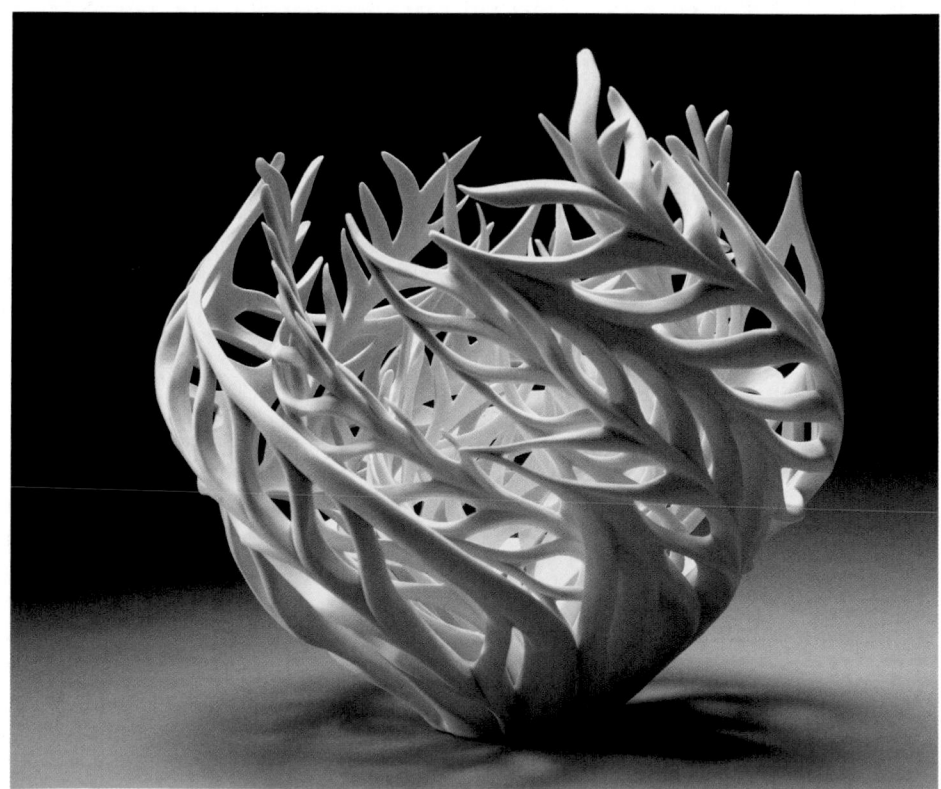

∧ 12.6 **JENNIFER MCCURDY**, *Coral Nest* (2009). Porcelain, 9" high.

CONNECTIONS Chinese vases of the Ming Dynasty are renowned for their use of painting and decorating before the glaze is applied.

> Ming vase
(Fig. 17.34)

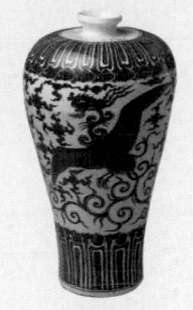

durable that they should last 10,000 years." The result subverts the wheel-thrown technique and typically utilitarian function of a clay vessel and blur the boundaries between sculpture and ceramics, fine art and craft.

Glazing

Pottery is glazed for functional and artistic reasons. Without a glaze, a clay pot would remain porous and therefore useless for carrying liquids. Even the simplest glaze—a glassy coating applied to the surface of a vessel—will make it **nonporous**—that is, impervious to water. But the variety of glazing techniques and effects devised by potters for aesthetic purposes is rich, diverse, and connected to strong cultural traditions.

Glazing appears on clay bricks that date back to a thirteenth-century BCE temple in Iran, and both the ancient Egyptian and Mesopotamian river cultures offer sophisticated examples of glazing. The earliest known glaze in Egypt—characteristically blue-green in hue—was found

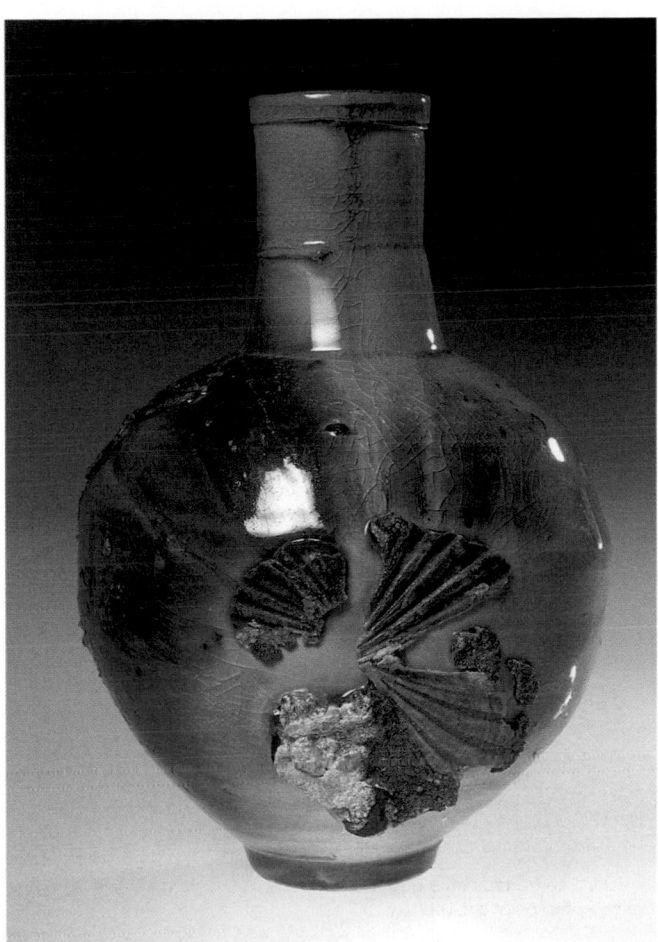

∧ 12.8 **CHESTER NEALIE,** *Bottle* (2000). Celadon glaze, 11¾" high.

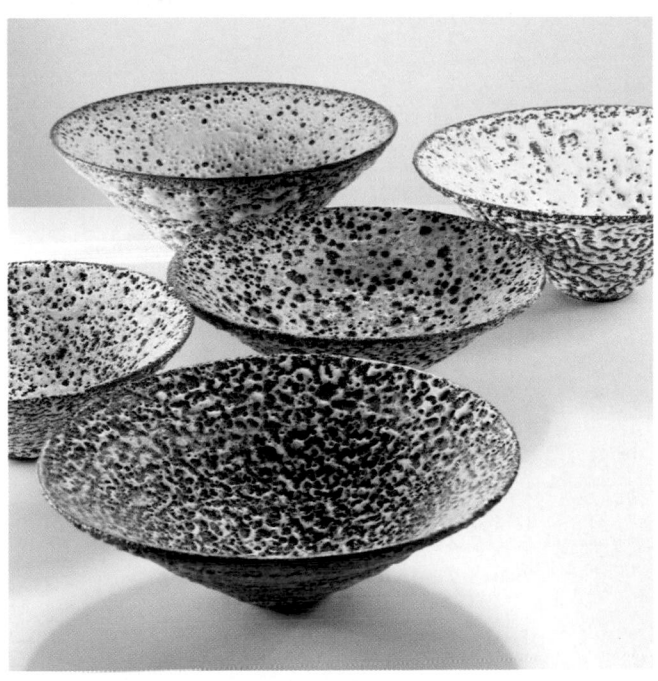

∧ 12.7 **EMMANUEL COOPER,** *Bowls.* Stoneware, thrown and turned, slip, multiple glaze; 12¼" max.

on a nonclay tile from the tomb of the Egyptian pharaoh Menes and dates from about 3000 BCE. In the sixth century BCE, ancient Babylonians constructed the Ishtar Gate from glazed bricks in a similar blue-green palette. During the early centuries of the common era, glazed ceramics became an accomplished art form across cultures from China and Japan to the Middle East, Southeast Asia, and more.

The surface characteristics of glazed pottery can be glossy or matte, smooth or textured, monochromatic or polychromatic, and simple or complex in pattern or decoration. All of these variations depend on the composition of the glaze, the temperature of the kiln, and sometimes multiple firings.

Glazes usually contain silica, found in sand or quartz, ground metals that facilitate the melting of silica into glass in the presence of heat, and other chemical compounds that produce a range of specific colors. Dry glazes can be rubbed onto clay, and liquid glazes—chemicals combined with ground minerals and liquid—can be brushed, sprayed, poured, or spattered onto the surface.

Contrast the rough textured surfaces of Emmanuel Cooper's earthenware bowls (Fig. 12.7) with the stunning glasslike finish of Chester Nealie's *Bottle* (Fig. 12.8). The glaze on Cooper's bowls is reminiscent of volcanic rock

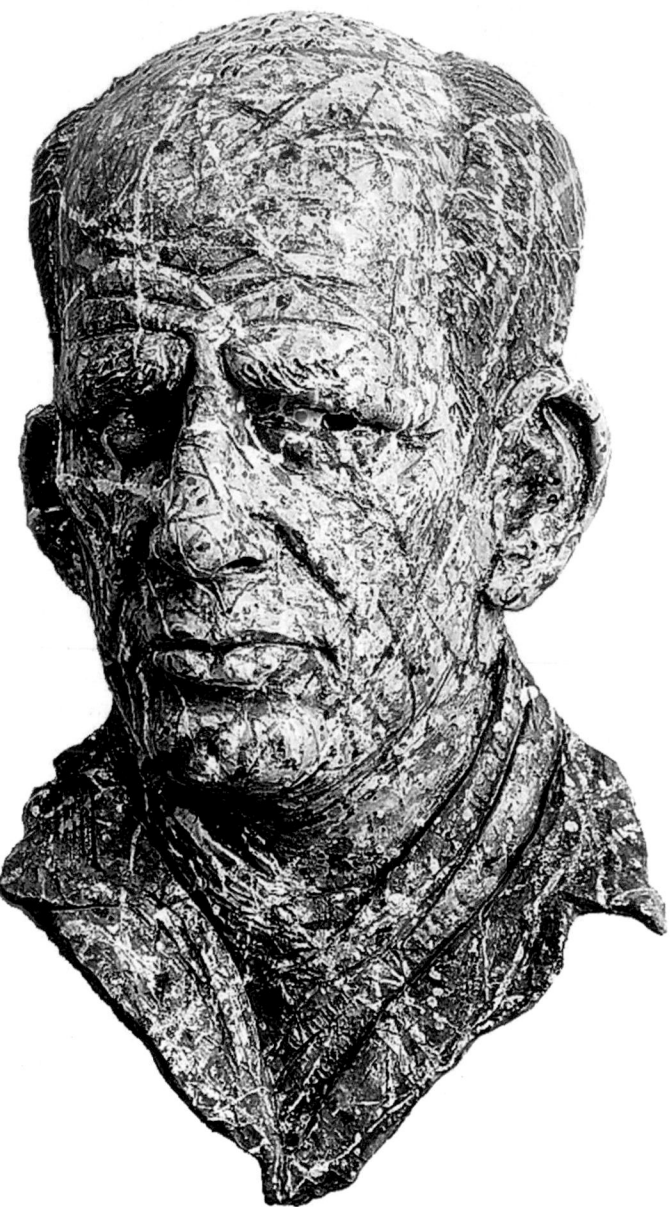

▲ 12.9 ROBERT ARNESON, *Jackson Pollock* (1983). Glazed ceramic, 23" × 13" × 7". Collection of Dr. Paul and Stacy Polydoran. Courtesy of George Adams Gallery, New York, New York.

compositions (see Chapter 21). Arneson's *Pollock* looks as if he stepped out of his Hamptons studio, his face an accidental and unsuspecting "canvas" for his signature drips, whips, and spatters. Arneson's glazed ceramics are purposefully unrefined and intentionally flawed, mirroring his view of human nature as imperfect.

Types of Ceramics

Ceramics are classified by their clay composition and by the temperature at which they are fired. **Earthenware** is pottery made from slightly porous clay that has been fired at relatively low kiln temperatures (1,000 to 2,000 degrees Fahrenheit). **Terra-cotta**, hard-baked red clay that has been fired at higher temperatures (2,070 to 2,320 degrees Fahrenheit), is used to create pottery, sculpture, building bricks, tile roofs, and architectural ornamentation with a

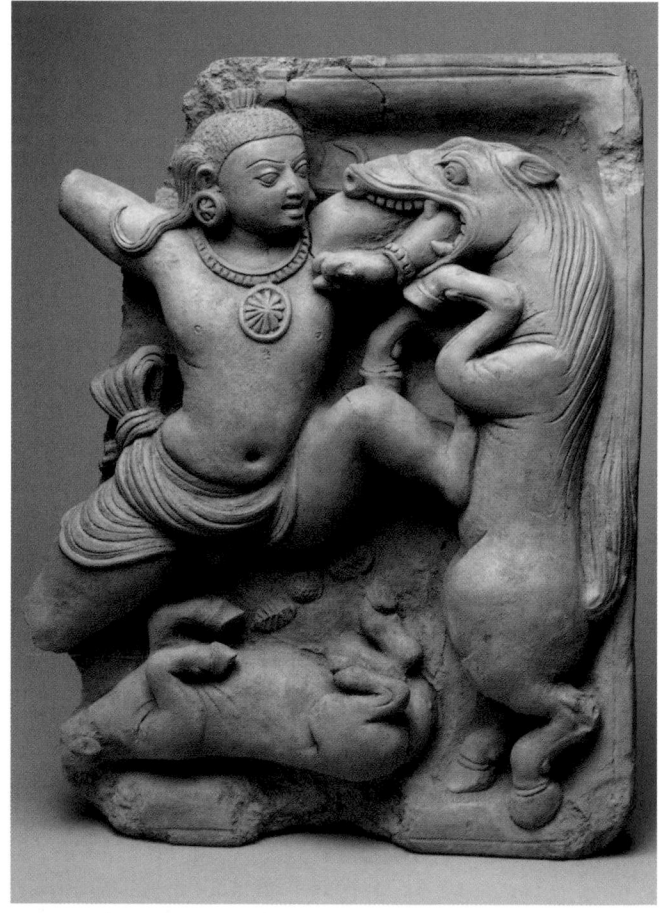

▲ 12.10 **Krishna killing the horse demon Keshi** (Gupta period, c. 321–500), 5th-century India (Uttar Pradesh). Terra-cotta, 21" high. The Metropolitan Museum of Art, New York, New York.

or the cratered surface of the moon, whereas Nealie's pearlescent glaze enhances the sensual, graceful contours of what looks like a fragile glass vessel. These represent only two examples of the degree to which glazing affects the substance and sensibility of a piece, or, as in Robert Arneson's ceramic sculpture, its very meaning. Jackson Pollock (Fig. 12.9) was an Abstract Expressionist painter who shook the art world with his large-scale drip

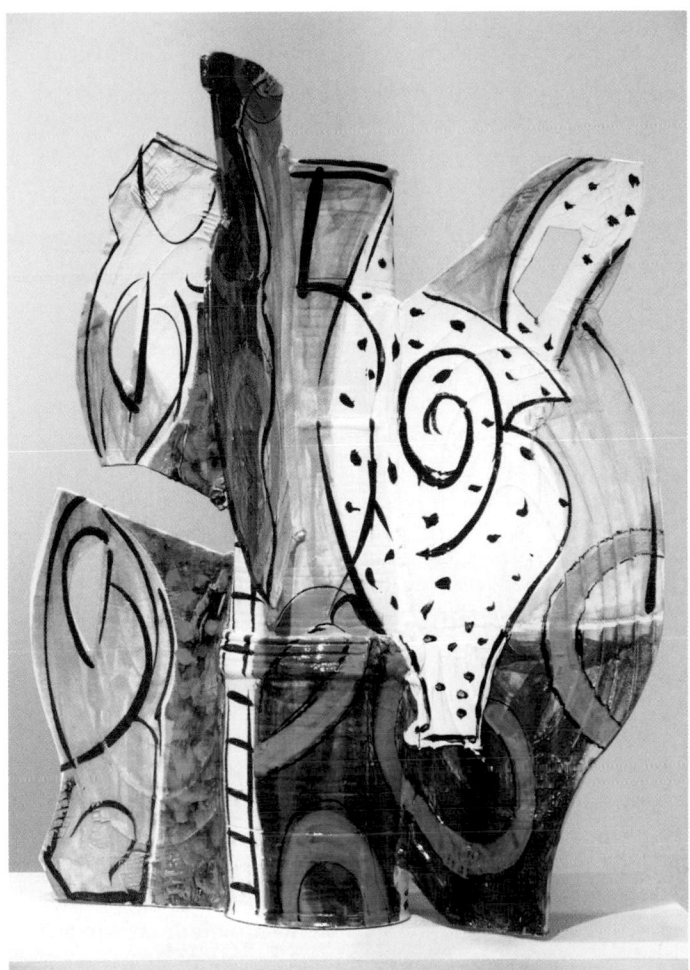

▲ 12.11 BETTY WOODMAN, *Aztec Vase #06-1* (2006). Glazed earthenware, epoxy resin, lacquer, and paint; 62" × 42" × 9".

sensibility even though they are actual vessels. Her glazes and hand-painted decoration show a wide range of artistic references gleaned from her global voyages and the history of art. Woodman freely adopts shapes and colors from styles she is most drawn to, sometimes mixing and matching them on opposite sides of a vase. Her work is marked by an eclecticism and pluralism that energize her pieces and pay homage to a host of styles.

Stoneware is usually gray or brown—owing to impurities in its clay—and vitreous or semivitreous (glasslike). It is very strong and durable and is therefore commonly used for cookware, dinnerware, and much ceramic sculpture. Claudi Casanovas's *Block #43* (Fig. 12.12) is a hollow, cubic-form, stoneware sculpture that simulates the crude textures of hardened clay found in nature. The palette of glazes—black, brown, beige, and a hint of gold—deep fissures, and irregular contours combine to create the effect of a naturally occurring rock that has been worn away by time and the elements.

Porcelain is hard, nonporous, and usually white or gray in color. It is made from minerals such as feldspar, quartz, and flint in various proportions. It is usually fired at 2,400 to 2,500 degrees Fahrenheit, and it is used for fine dinnerware. Chinese porcelain, or china, is white and fired at low temperatures. It is vitreous and nonporous, and it may be translucent. It makes a characteristic ringing sound when struck with a fingernail. Porcelain has been used by various cultures for vases and dinnerware for thousands of years, as well as for ceramic sculpture.

characteristic reddish-brown hue. Utilitarian terra-cotta vessels are common finds in ancient archaeological sites, but the material was also used for sophisticated and large-scale works. The intricately carved and graphically realistic terra-cotta relief (Fig. 12.10) from India's Gupta period illustrates Krishna, one of the avatars of the god Vishnu, battling and killing a demon in the guise of a horse. Reliefs such as this one provided sculptural ornamentation on the exterior of stone and brick temples. Other terra-cotta works in your text include a carved sarcophagus from the Etruscan civilization (see Fig. 15.17), and the renowned terra-cotta warriors from China's Han Dynasty (see Fig. 15.40).

Earthenware and terra-cotta span centuries and cultures, and contemporary potters continue to produce works from the same materials. Betty Woodman is described as one of the most important ceramic artists working today, blurring the boundaries between art and craft and conjoining cultural influences—East and West—in her painted vases. Works like *Aztec Vase #06-1* (Fig. 12.11) belie functionality in their sculptural

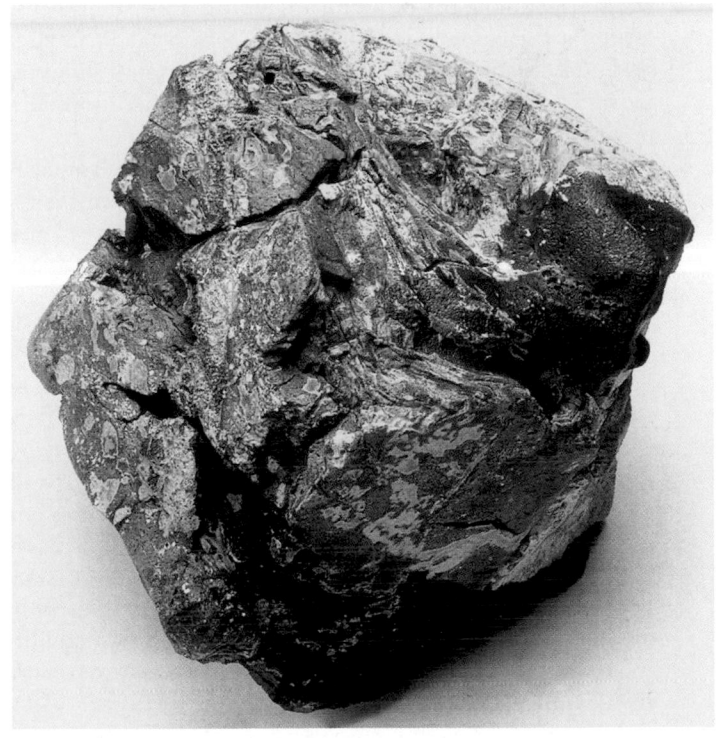

▲ 12.12 CLAUDI CASANOVAS, *Block #43* (2001). 11¾" × 11¾" × 10¼".

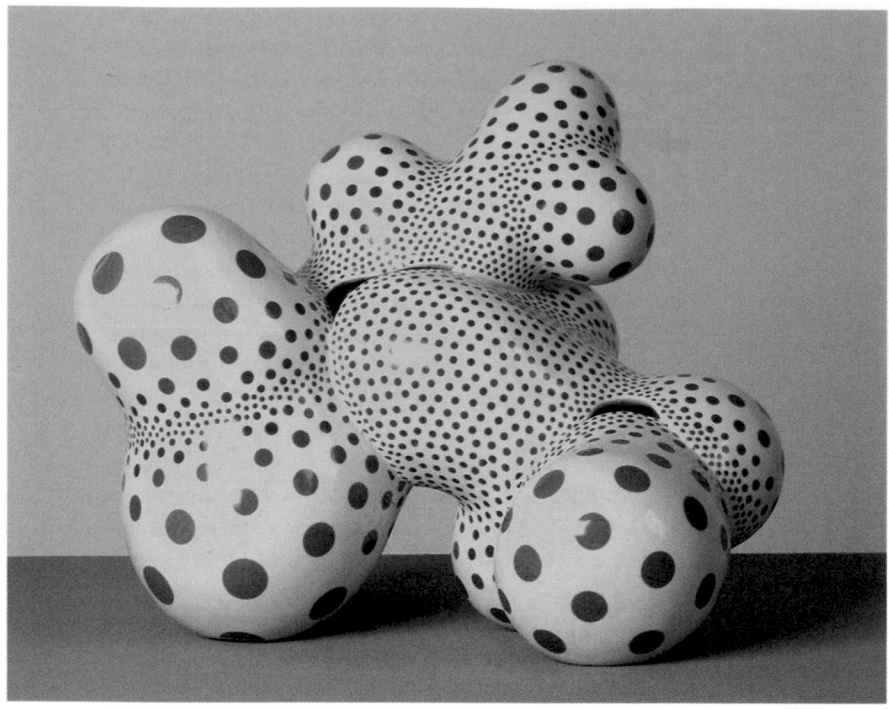

▲ 12.13 **HARUMI NAKASHIMA,** *Porcelain Form* (2001). Porcelain, inlaid decoration; 19¾" × 17¾" × 15¾". Den Bosch, Netherlands.

Harumi Nakashima's *Porcelain Form* (Fig. 12.13), with its slippery-smooth surface and meticulously rounded shapes, stands in sharp contrast to the coarse textures often given center stage in other types of ceramics. The repetition in the polka-dotted glaze complements the rhythms found in the budding, biomorphic protuberances. Whereas the colors and textures of Casanovas's *Block* suggest the essence of tactile reality, Nakashima's bulging, morphing, amoeba-like sculpture seems surreal—outside or beyond conscious experience.

One of the fascinating features of clay is its versatility. It is said that one test of the integrity of a work is its truth to its material. In the case of ceramics, however, one would be hard pressed to point to any one of the products of clay as representative of its "true" face.

GLASS

Glass, like ceramics, has a long history and has been used to create fine art and functional objects. The Roman historian Pliny the Elder traced the beginnings of glass-making (albeit accidental) to an account of Phoenician sailors preparing a meal on a beach. They set their pots on lumps of *natron* (an alkali they had on deck to embalm the dead), lit a fire, and when the hot natron mixed with the sand of the beach, molten glass flowed. In fact, glass predates the Phoenicians and the Romans (earliest examples date back to the civilizations of Mesopotamia

and Old Kingdom Egypt), and Pliny's tale is certainly anecdotal and embellished. But the truth is that the recipe for glass is quite simple. Researchers have recreated the Phoenicians' scenario and have come to this conclusion: It could happen.[4] The result may not have been that wondrous substance—transparent or translucent—that has the power to transform light into an ephemeral, jewel-like palette, but it was surely glass. Glass is generally made from molten sand, or silica, mixed with minerals such as lead, potash, soda, and lime. Rich hues in glass are achieved by adding metal oxides with distinct color properties to molten silica: copper oxide produces green, and cobalt renders a deep blue.

Techniques of Working with Glass

Glassblowing was discovered around 50 BCE, and with that the history of glassmaking was transformed. Earlier techniques included cold-working, in which room temperature lumps of glass were scratched, ground, or delicately chipped to form objects, and casting, in which molten glass was poured into heat-resistant molds. Like ceramics, glass is a versatile medium. Molten glass can be modeled, pressed, rolled into sheets as it cools, and even spun into threads, as it is for fiberglass. Fine filaments can be woven into textiles, used in woolly masses for insulation, or molded into a material that is tough enough to be used for the body of an automobile.

Historically speaking, glassblowing was the game changer. Developed by the Romans, the technique enabled the creation of glass vessels of all shapes, sizes, functions, and colors. Glassblowing begins with a hollow tube or blowpipe that is dipped into molten glass and removed. Air is blown through the tube, causing the hot glass to expand to form a spherical bubble whose contours are shaped through rolling and pulling with various tools.

The *Portland Vase* (Fig. 12.14), one of the earliest and best-known pieces of Roman glassware, was created in three steps: the body of the vessel was blown from dark blue glass; a coating of semiopaque white glass was added to the surface of the basic blue vase; and the figures and vegetation that circumscribe the vase were carved in bas-relief on the white glass in subtle gradations of depth. Where the white glass is thinnest and therefore most translucent, the blue of the vase glows through and provides shading to the images. Imagine the delicacy of the handling—glass chipped away from glass, leaving

---

[4] William S. Ellis, "Glass: Capturing the Dance of Light," *National Geographic* 184, no. 6 (December 1993): 37–69.

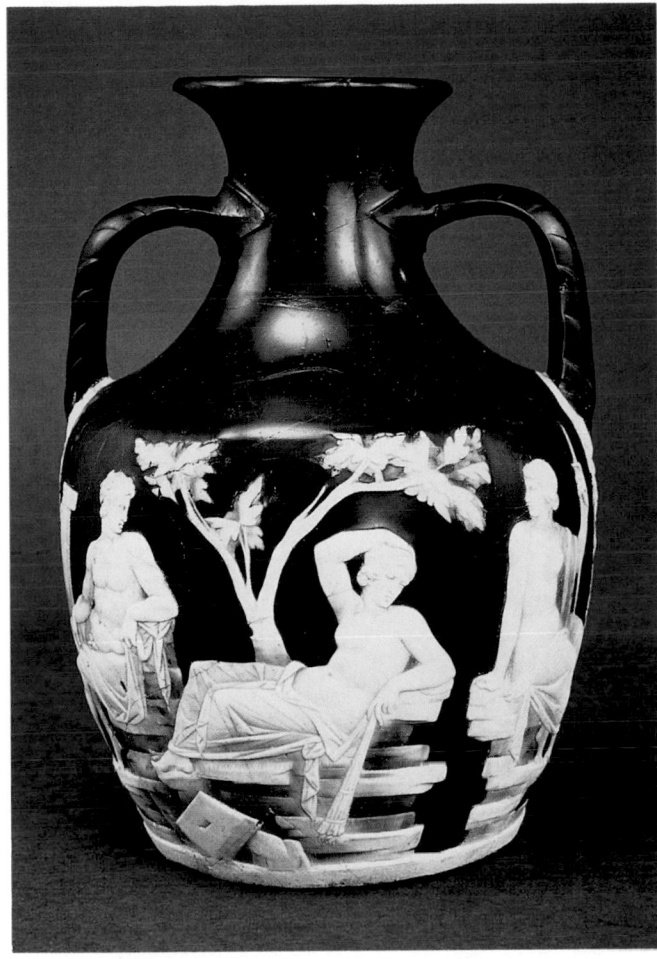

expert handling of glass as a medium. His studios produced vases whose graceful, attenuated botanical forms married simplicity and exotic refinement, but the real treasures of Tiffany's oeuvre are his stained-glass windows. Large in scale, complex in imagery, and endlessly nuanced in palette, windows such as *Magnolias and Irises* (Fig. 12.15) exhibit some of the particular material characteristics of much of Tiffany's work. Inspired by ancient glassware and the saturated colors of medieval stained glass, Tiffany sought to create recipes for glassmaking that produced rich color, yes, but also texture, opacity, and surface shimmer. In 1880, he patented Favrile glass, a technique of mixing together different colors of hot glass that yielded an iridescent finish. Tiffany described the result: "Favrile glass is distinguished by brilliant or deeply toned colors, usually iridescent like the wings of certain American butterflies, the necks of pigeons and peacocks, the wing covers of various beetles."

∧ 12.14 *Portland Vase* (Roman, 3rd century). Cameo-cut glass; 9½" high, 7" diameter. British Museum, London, England.

unscratched the brittle blue surface that serves as background for the figures. Roman glassmaking skills were renowned in the ancient world, and cultures that had contact with the Romans—such as the Hindu kingdoms of India and the Arab world—adopted their techniques.

Different world centers became renowned for glassmaking in different eras. During the Middle Ages, stained-glass windows achieved their peak of perfection in French (see Fig. 16.15) and German cathedrals, while in Venice, luxury glass was prized for its lightness and delicacy. In the eighteenth century, on the other side of the Atlantic Ocean in Pennsylvania, Stiegel glass was known for a special hardness and brilliance attributed to the use of flint (lead oxide). Flint glass was used to create lenses for optical instruments and for fine crystal. Nineteenth-century Sandwich glass—from the town of Sandwich, Massachusetts—replicated the appearance of carved glass, but its patterns were created by pressing molten glass into molds. Ornamental Sandwich glass pieces in the shapes of cats, dogs, hens, and ducks became common home decorations.

During the second half of the nineteenth century, the name of Louis Comfort Tiffany became synonymous with

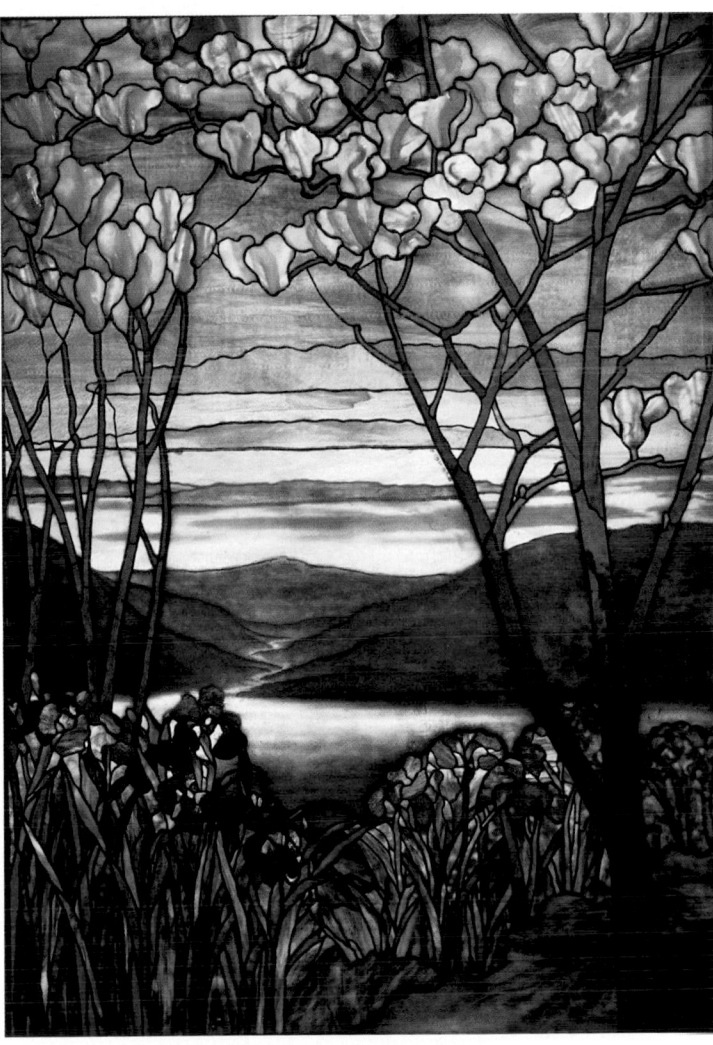

∧ 12.15 **LOUIS COMFORT TIFFANY,** *Magnolias and Irises* (c. 1908). Six pieces of glassware in Art Nouveau style made by the Tiffany Studio. Leaded Favrile glass, 60¼" × 42". The Metropolitan Museum of Art, New York, New York.

A CLOSER LOOK

The Chandeliers of Dale Chihuly

> They're going to think we're nuts over there, and of course we are a little nuts,
> but we'll get this thing built.
>
> —DALE CHIHULY, ABOUT THE ICICLE CREEK CHANDELIER

"A LITTLE BIT NUTS." Artists, and even the rest of us, may have felt this way or been characterized this way at some point or another, especially when we were seeing things in an unconventional way. Glass artist Dale Chihuly has redefined the conventional definition and function of "chandelier" by designing works he describes by this name for public spaces from Venice to Jerusalem, from the world's great museums to the wilderness of the great outdoors. Although many chandeliers, in the traditional sense, are ornamental, they are also functional objects used, with candles or electricity, to illuminate an environment. But Chihuly's chandeliers are a different species. They do not emit light of their own. Rather, they reflect and transform ambient light—batteries not included.

Chihuly's extraordinary glassworks capture, amplify, and channel light. In their unusual stylistic juxtaposition with their surroundings, his chandeliers compel passersby to take another look at the context in which they are set—whether the Byzantine architecture and canals we find in Venice (**Fig. 12.16**), the ancient ruins in Jerusalem, or in the wilderness, the literal natural state of affairs.

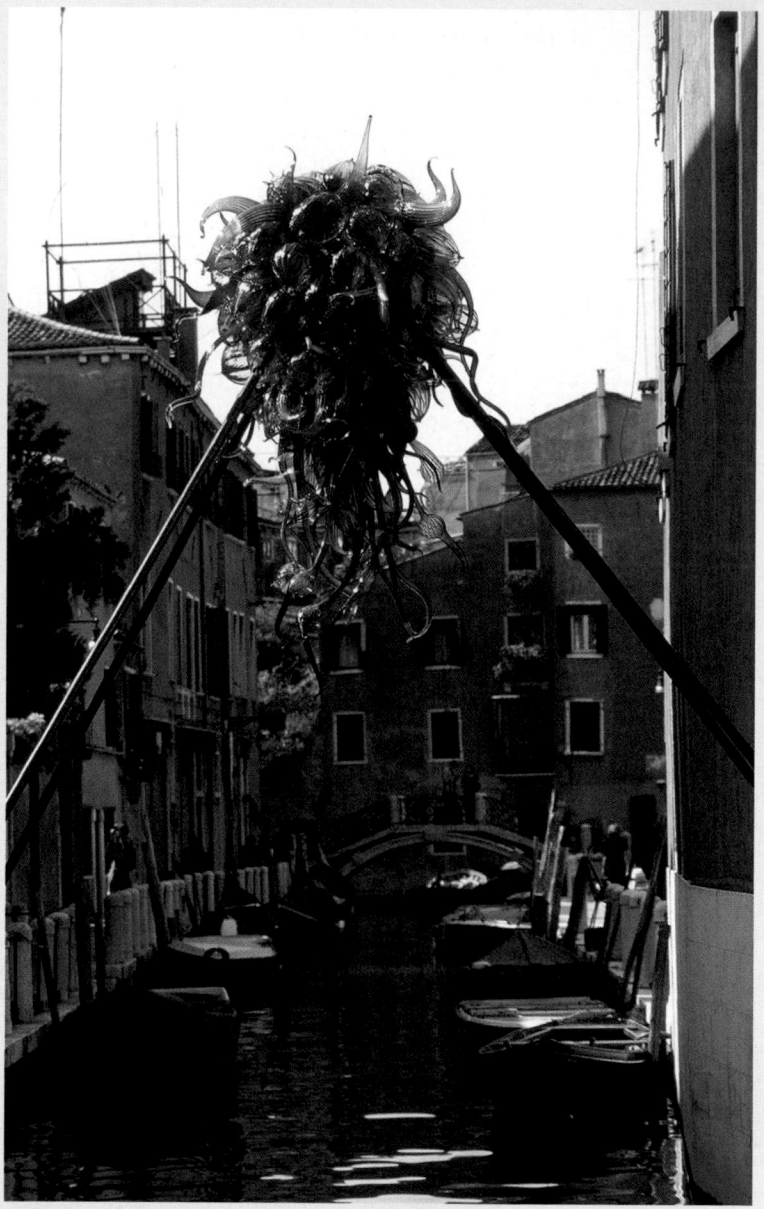

∧ **12.16** DALE CHIHULY, *Rio delle Torreselle Chandelier* (1996), 7 × 8'. A chandelier installation in the Rio delle Torreselle, part of the *Chihuly over Venice* project, Venezia Aperto Vetro. Venice, Italy.

> Chihuly is a luminist. He uses glass as a literal and metaphorical prism through which he projects both ambient and intense theatrical light to produce sublime, luminous effects. This connects him to the long history of art in which light is cherished, "otherworldly," and implies divine presence.
>
> —JACK COWART

Chihuly designed the chandelier shown in **Figure 12.17** for the Sleeping Lady mountain retreat at Icicle Creek in the state of Washington. He erected it on an ancient granite boulder among the grand pines of a primeval setting, surrounded by a river and a profusion of wildlife. The chandelier reflects and amplifies the frosted serenity of the site in winter. It enriches visitors' relationships with the area surrounding the retreat and with nature as a whole. The chandelier also adds Chihuly's—and humankind's—personal stamp to a pristine wooded site. It also says something about the vision and the passion of the artist—unique in this case to Dale Chihuly, though made visual by a team of glassblowers and technicians. Does the work have deeper symbolic meanings—meanings that connect it with the history of art and civilization, meanings that connect it with contemporary technology and modes of expression? Much of the answer to that question lies in you. Perhaps you would like to consider these lines from Wallace Stevens's poem "Anecdote of the Jar":

I placed a jar in Tennessee,
And round it was, upon a hill.
It made the slovenly wilderness
Surround that hill.
The wilderness rose up to it,
And sprawled around, no longer wild.[6]

---

[6] From *The Collected Poems of Wallace Stevens* by Wallace Stevens, © 1945 by Wallace Stevens and renewed 1982 by Holly Stevens. Used by permission of Alfred A. Knopf, a division of Random House, Inc.

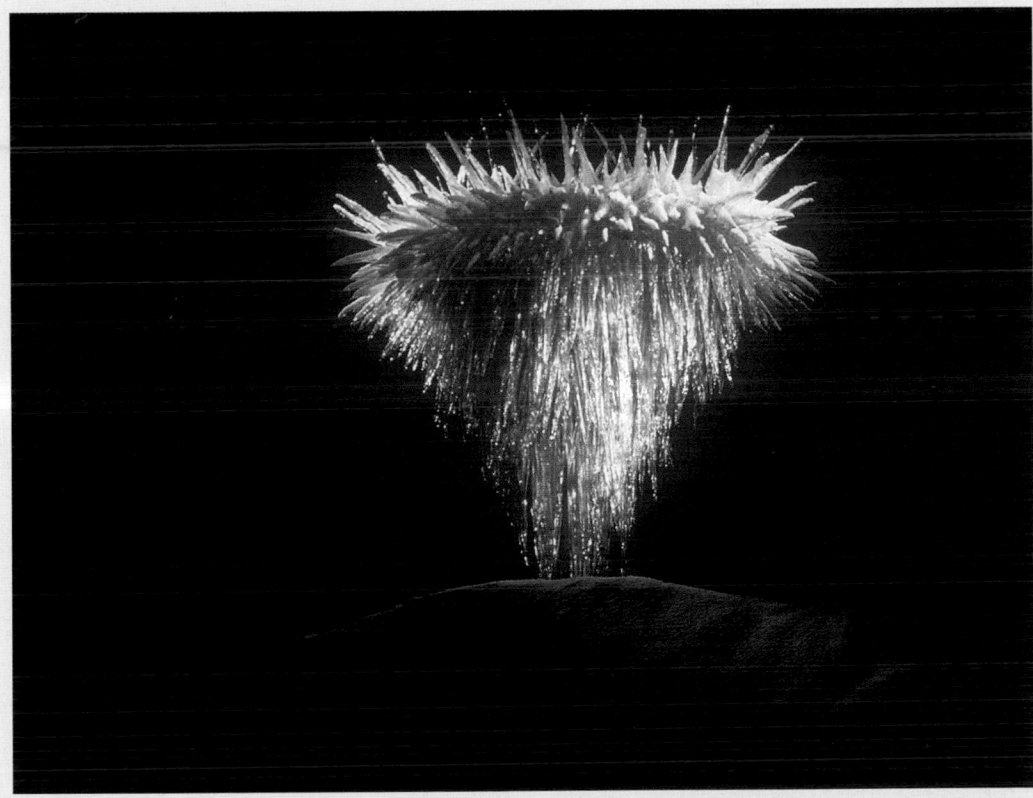

▲ 12.17 DALE CHIHULY, *Icicle Creek Chandelier* (1996), 12 × 9 × 6', Leavenworth, Washington.

TEXTILE ARTS

Textile arts are arts and crafts in which fibers are used to make functional or decorative objects or works of art. **Fibers** are slender, threadlike structures that are derived from animals (for example, wool or silk), vegetable (cotton or linen), or synthetic (rayon, nylon, or fiberglass) sources. The fiber arts refer to several disciplines in which fibers are combined to make functional or decorative objects or works of art. They include, but are not limited to, weaving, embroidery, crochet, and macramé.

Weaving

Weaving was well known to the ancient Egyptians and Mesopotamians, although some examples date back to the Stone Age. Weaving was a staple craft in ancient and traditional cultures, including Native Americans of the desert Southwest and South Americans of the Amazon region. Textile art reached a degree of unparalleled accomplishment in medieval Europe and in Islamic countries, where technological innovations contributed to the development of the craft.

The **weaving** of textiles is accomplished by interfacing horizontal and vertical threads—threads that are perpendicular to each other. The lengthwise fibers are called the **warp**, and the crosswise threads are called the **weft** or **woof**. The particular fiber and weave determine the weight and quality of the cloth. Wool, for example, makes soft, resilient cloth that is easy to dye. Nylon is strong, more durable than wool, mothproof, resistant to mildew and mold, nonallergenic, and easy to dye.

There are many types of weave structures. The **plain weave** found in burlap, muslin, and cotton broadcloth is the strongest and simplest: the woof thread passes above one warp fiber and beneath the next. In the **satin weave**, woof threads pass above and beneath several warp threads. Warp and woof form broken diagonal patterns in the **twill weave**. In **pile weaving**, which is found in carpeting and in velvet, loops or knots are tied; when the knotting is done, the ends are cut or sheared to create an even surface. In sixteenth-century Persia, where carpet weaving reached an artistic peak, pile patterns often had as many as 1,000 knots to the square inch.

The Ardabil Carpet (Fig. 12.18), completed in 1539–1540, is the oldest dated carpet in the history of art, although weaving has been an integral part of Persian culture since ancient times. Persian carpets are refined

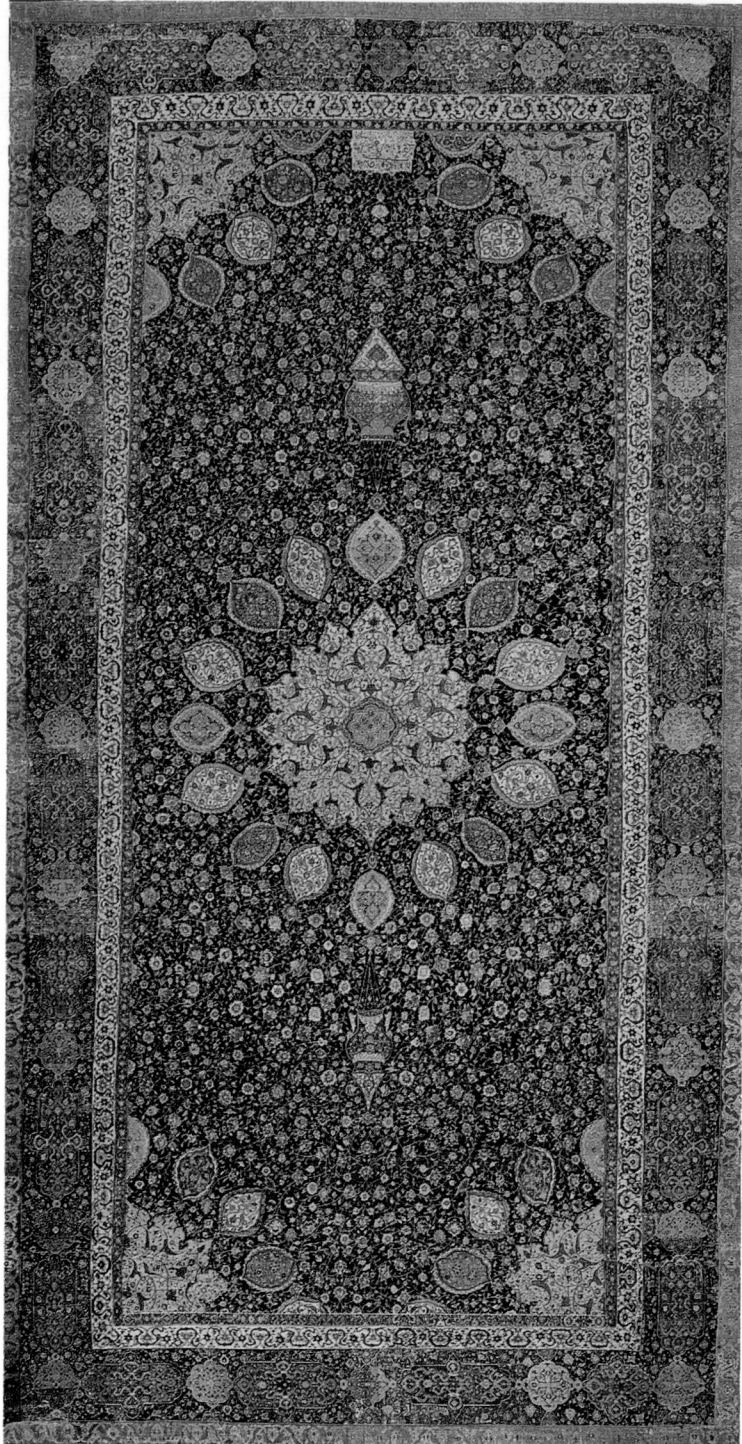

∧ **12.18 Ardabil Carpet,** probably Tabriz (1539–1540). Woolen pile, 34 ½' × 17 ½'. Victoria and Albert Museum, London, England.

in technique, ambitious in size, and dazzling in color and complexity. They are classified according to design, pattern, and motif, in traditional and innovative combinations and variations. The Ardabil Carpet was woven of short pieces of wool that were knotted onto silk warps and wefts. As each row was completed, it was packed

> My art is made in an attempt to serve the sacred in the feminine, listening and creating a relationship with my own inner nature. Because of the close connection between my hands and the material, and the time it takes to make each sculpture, the experience becomes deeply involved with a sense of devotion.
>
> —FERNE JACOBS

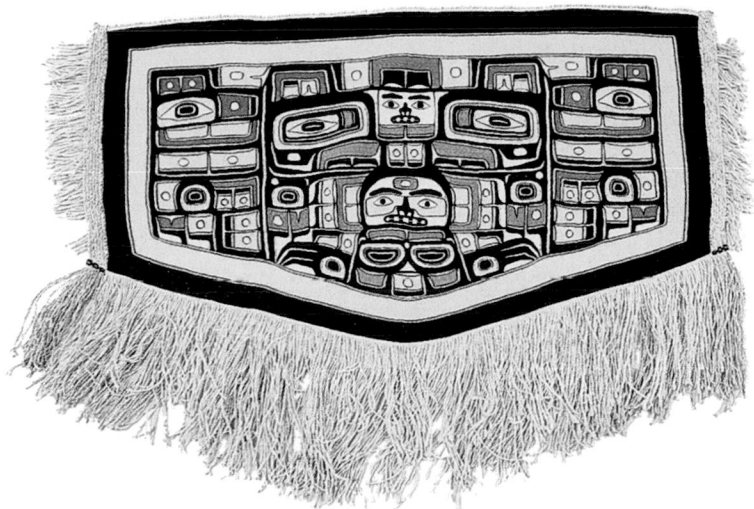

∧ 12.19 DORICA JACKSON, Chilkat robe (1976). Cedar bark warp, sheep's wool wefts; 60" wide.

by Native American weaver Dorica Jackson without a loom. Chilkat women traditionally achieved a very fine texture with a thread made from a core of a strand of cedar bark covered with the wool from a mountain goat. Clan members used robes such as these on important occasions to show off the family crest. Here a strikingly stylized, winged animal occupies the center of a field of eyes, heads, and mysterious symbols.

Ferne Jacobs creates innovative three-dimensional structures with a traditional weaving technique using a waxed linen thread that is wrapped around a coil. Jacobs began her artistic career as a painter and the turned to basketry. Her basketry evolved into the type of free-form sculpture shown in *Medusa's Collar* (Fig. 12.20). The sculpture is built about the triadic color scheme of of red, yellow, and blue. These

down and the pile trimmed to an even height after the entire rug was finished. The pattern consists of ten colors. A large field with interlacing flowers and vines provides a backdrop for a central medallion surrounded by sixteen pointed ovals. Hanging from the ovals—at 12 o'clock and 6 o'clock—are two lamps, the pointed bottoms of which face in opposite directions. The field is surrounded by four parallel bands of different widths filled with intricate patterns. The carpet, commissioned by an Iranian ruler for the shrine of an ancestor, had as many as ten weavers working on it at the same time. A curator at London's Victoria and Albert Museum, who helped raise the enormous sum of 2,000 British pounds ($10,000) to purchase the carpet, described it as "a remarkable work of art. . . . The design is of singular perfection. . . . Its size and splendour as a piece of workmanship do full justice to the beauty and intellectual qualities of the design."[6]

The Ardabil Carpet was created on a **loom**. During the Islamic Golden Age, foot pedals were introduced to operate looms, thus facilitating the weaving process. The Alaskan Chilkat robe (Fig. 12.19), however, was created

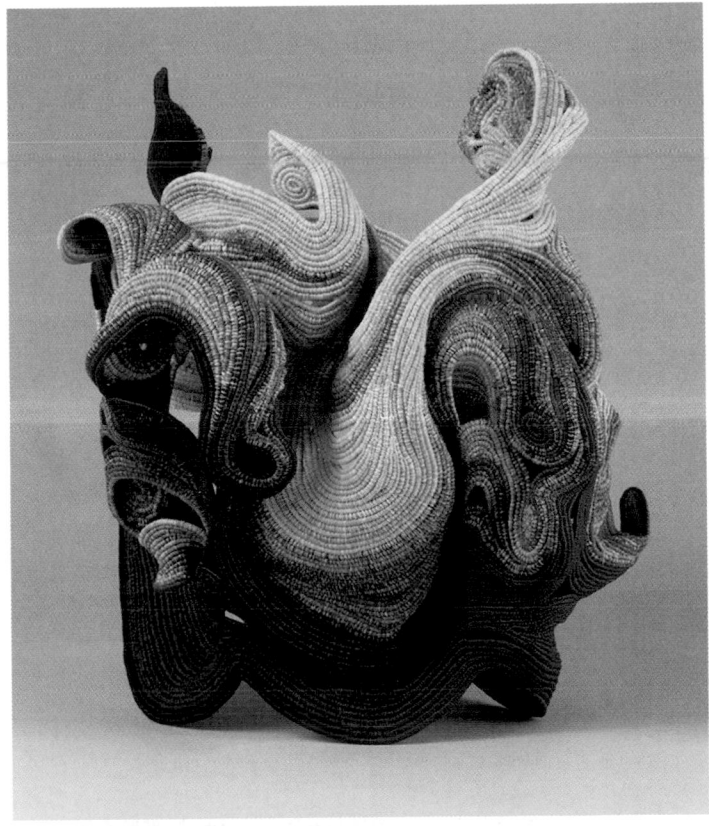

∧ 12.20 FERNE JACOBS, *Medusa's Collar* (2011). Coiled waxed linen thread, 18" × 14" × 19".

[6] William Morris, cited in Lynda Hillyer and Boris Pretzel, "The Ardabil Carpet—a New Perspective," *Conservation Journal*, no. 49 (Spring 2005).

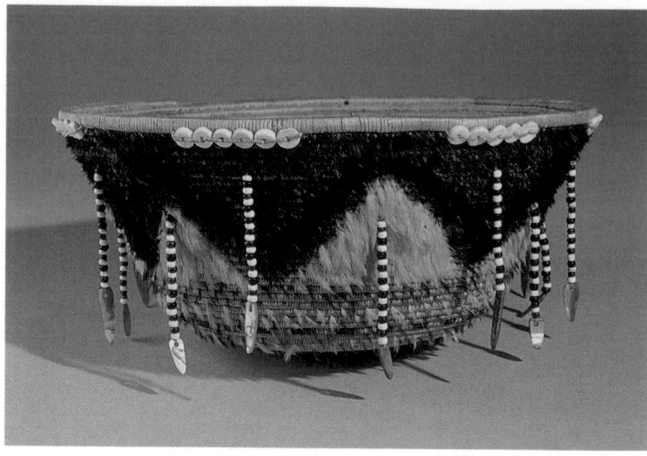

▲ 12.21 **Ceremonial feathered basket with bead and shell pendants.** (American Indian, Pomo, 1900). 3½" high. Pomo, California. Phoebe A. Hearst Museum of Anthropology, University of California, Berkeley.

place of blocks, and fabrics can be printed at astonishingly rapid rates. In **embroidery**, the design is made by needlework.

Tie-dyeing and batik both involve dyeing fabrics. In **tie-dyeing**, designs are created by sewing or tying folds in the cloth to prevent the dye from coloring certain sections of fabric, In **batik**, applications of wax prevent the dye from coloring sections of fabric that are to be kept light or white. A series of dye baths and waxings can be used to create subtly deeper colors.

Basket Weaving

In **basket weaving**, or **basketry**, animal or vegetable fibers (such as twigs, grasses, straw, and animal hair) are woven into baskets or other containers. Basket weaving is, like ceramics and textiles, an ancient craft, but because natural materials disintegrate, there is little physical evidence of such early basketry. Yet imprints of the woven patterns of baskets to decorate the surface of clay pots give us a sense of what the craft must have been. As with the other crafts we have considered, basket making crosses time and culture.

Pomo gift baskets, created by Native Americans from Northern California, are woven from materials such as grass, glass beads, shells and feathers (Fig. 12.21). The Pomo have been described as the finest basket weavers in the world. Baskets such as the one illustrated were not woven for utilitarian purposes but rather served as gifts and treasures.

primaries clash, exaggerated by the flamelike shapes that dip and swirl and curl. The tendrils formed by the coiled, waxed, linen thread evoke—albeit more benignly—the head of Medusa, the mythological Gorgon with snakes in place of hair.

The surfaces of fabrics can be enhanced by printing, embroidery, tie-dyeing, or batik. Hand printing has been known since ancient times, and Oriental traders brought the practice to Europe. A design was stamped on a fabric with a carved wooden block that had been inked. Contemporary machine printing uses inked rollers in the

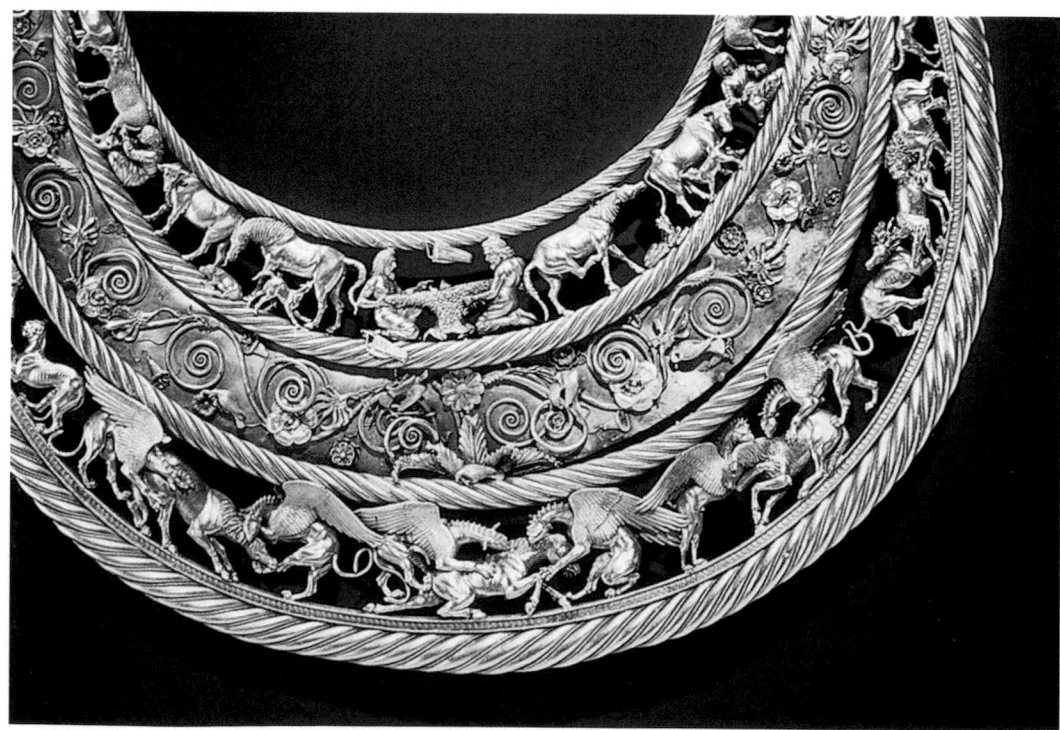

> 12.22 **Pectoral piece from Ordzhonikidze, Russia** (4th century BCE). Gold, 12" diameter. Historical Museum, Kiev.

METALWORK AND JEWELRY

The process of refining and working with metals is called **metalwork**, a word that encompasses a range of diverse objects and projects from the industrial world to the jeweler's workshop. **Iron** and its alloys were used in the Iron Age, for arrowheads, and, in the industrial age, for skyscrapers. **Stainless steel** is used in common kitchen utensils but was also used for the uncommon pinnacle of New York City's Chrysler Building and by postwar American sculptors such as David Smith (see Fig. 21.9). Lightweight **aluminum** is used in cookware and in aircraft. **Bronze** has been used for coins, weaponry, farm tools, and sculptural monuments.

Silver and gold have been prized for millennia for their rarity and their appealing colors and textures. They are used in jewelry, fine tableware, ritual vessels, and sacred objects. In jewelry, these precious metals often serve as settings for equally precious gems or polished stones, or their surfaces can be **enameled** by melting powdered glass on them. These metals even find use as currency; in times of political chaos, gold and silver are sought even as the value of paper money drops off to nothing. Threads of gold and silver find their way onto precious china and into the garments and vestments of clergy and kings. Gold leaf adorns books, paintings, and picture frames.

Metals can be hammered into shape, **embossed** with raised designs, and cast according to procedures described for bronze in Chapter 9. Each form of working metal has its own tradition and its advantages and disadvantages.

The pectoral piece shown in Figure 12.22 was meant to be worn across the breast of a nomadic chieftain from southern Russia and probably to be buried with him. People and animals are depicted with a realism that renders the fanciful griffins in the lower register as believable as the horses, dogs, and grasshoppers found elsewhere in the piece. The open work of the figures is contrasted by the refined gold-on-gold scrollwork in the central register; all are bordered by magnificent, twisted coils.

The Renaissance sculptor and goldsmith Benvenuto Cellini created a gold and enamel saltcellar (Fig. 12.23) for the French king Francis I that shows the refinement of his art. Its allegorical significance is merely an excuse for displaying the skill of Cellini's craft. Salt, drawn from the sea, is housed in a boat-shaped salt container and watched over by a figure of Neptune. The pepper, drawn from the earth, is contained in a miniature triumphal arch and guarded by a female personification of Earth. Figures on the base represent the seasons and the segments of the day—all on a pedestal only 13 inches in diameter. Unfortunately, the saltcellar is Cellini's sole major work in gold that survives.

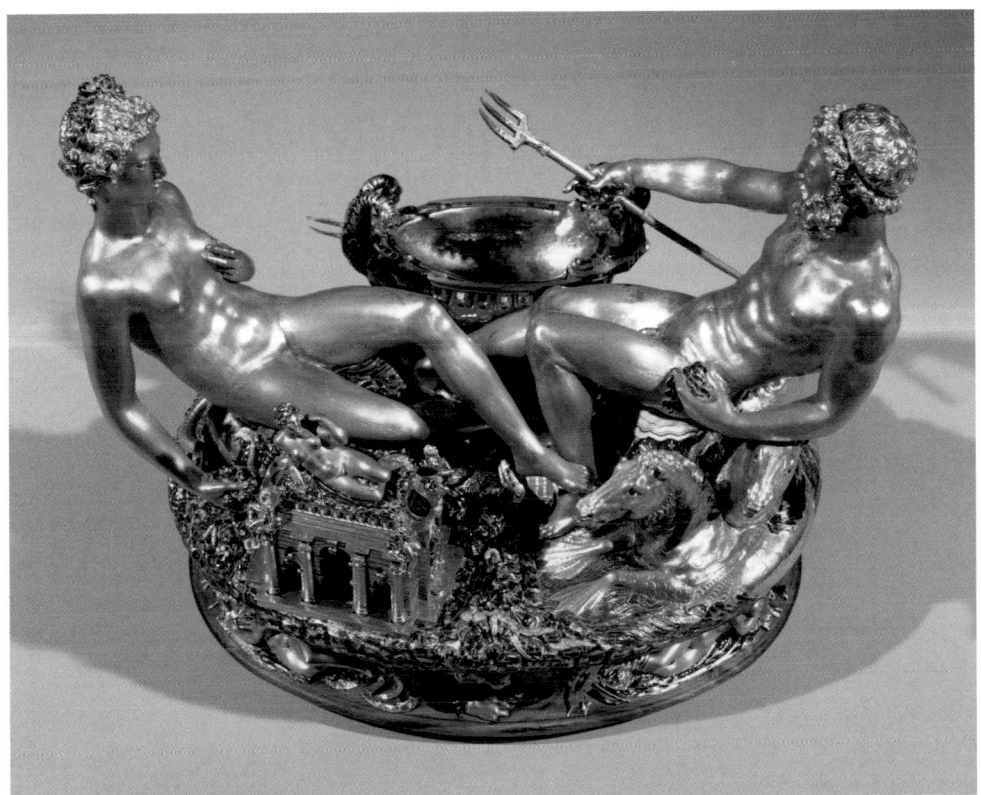

> 12.23 **BENVENUTO CELLINI,**
Saltcellar of Francis I (1539–1543). Gold and enamel; 10⅛" high, 13¹/₁₆" long. Kunsthistorisches Museum, Vienna.

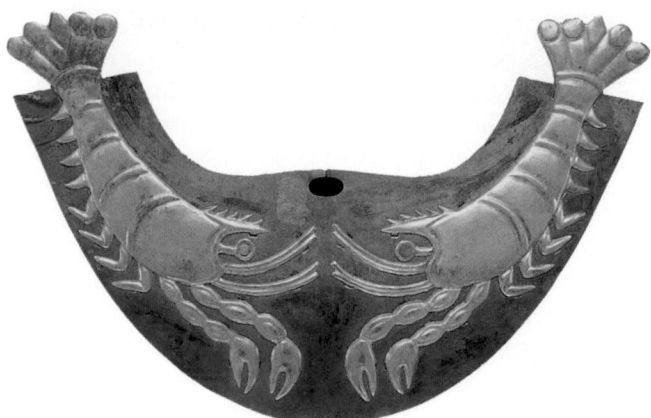

▲ **12.24 Nose ornament, crayfish, Peru** (Loma Negra, 3rd century CE). Gold, silver, turquoise inlay; 4¾" high. The Metropolitan Museum of Art, New York, New York.

Body ornament, ever growing in popularity to this day, spans history and geography. Consider the nose ornament from Peru in Figure 12.24. The piece is fashioned of gold, silver, and turquoise inlay and is a characteristic example of the ancient Peruvian facility in handling complex metal techniques. Much of the jewelry available for us to see today has been unearthed from tombs of the very wealthy among Peruvian society. The images and their symbolism remain mostly undeciphered, but archeologists have nonetheless constructed a view of these people from such artifacts.

Kiff Slemmons's *Transport* (Fig. 12.25) is a miniature sculpture that again bridges the supposed gulf between fine art and the functional object. It was constructed for the *Artworks for AIDS* exhibition that was held in Seattle in 1990. It is a miniature two-wheeled cart that refers

to the history of mass deaths. Throughout the ages, such carts have been used in cities to truck away the victims of epidemics. At the time there was no effective treatment for HIV/AIDS, and the wheels of the cart are clocks with human hands, seeming to tick away as the number of deaths due to AIDS mounts. Hospital waste and a stylized "progress" chart with an alarming indicator of the rising toll of the epidemic complete the political message.

WOOD

Some relatively sophisticated technology is required to convert glass, metal, and clay into something of use. Wood, however, has only to be cut and carved to form a functional object. Two wood vases hint at the versatility of the medium. The soft, flowing contours of Melvyn Firmager's vase (Fig. 12.26) highlight the swirling grain

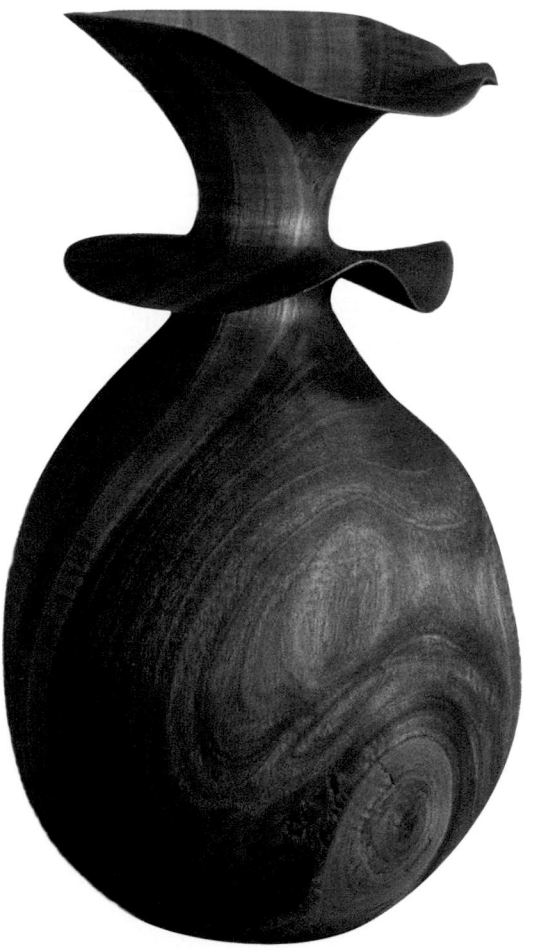

▲ **12.26 MELVYN FIRMAGER,** *Untitled* (1993). Destroyed in 1994 Los Angeles earthquake. Eucalyptus gunnii; 13½" high, 8" diameter.

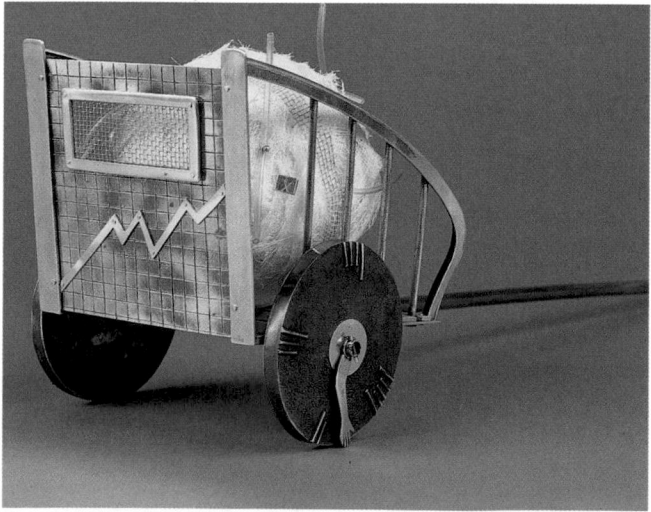

▲ **12.25 KIFF SLEMMONS,** *Transport* (1990). Sterling silver, aluminum, gauze, mesh, tape, tubing, pearls; 5" × 14" × 4½".

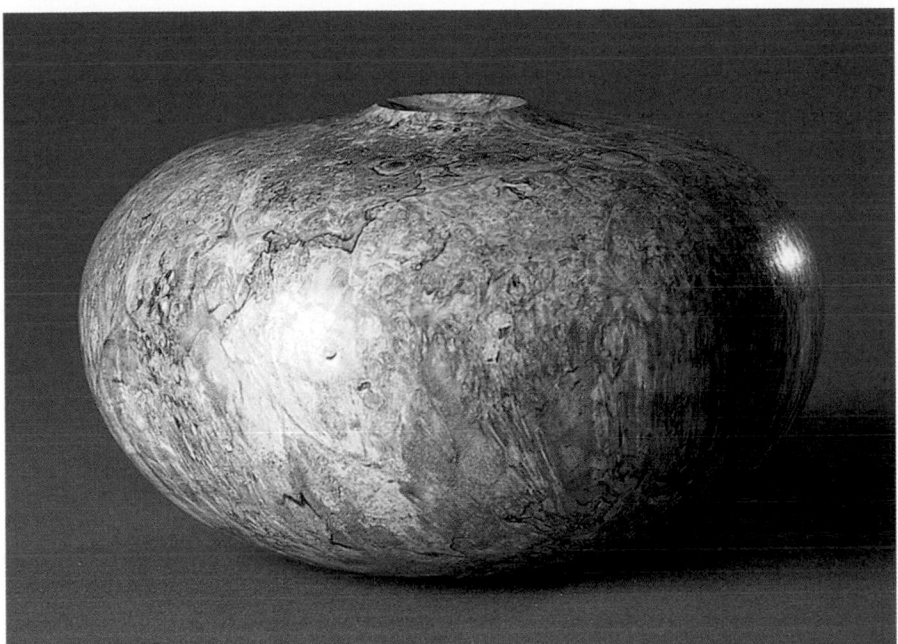

patterns of the wood, which almost take on the character of glazing on a ceramic vase. The simple roundness, highly polished surface, and inherent grain patterns in David Ellsworth's vase (Fig. 12.27) create the illusion of stone.

The roughness of the cut or split pieces of wood from which these objects were shaped has disappeared, yielding to smooth surfaces that instead emphasize the sinuous grain patterns resulting from the varying shades of the naturally-occurring growth rings. So sensuous are the contours that as we contemplate them, we can "feel" their smoothness with our eyes. A completely different sensation occurs, however, when we imagine sitting on the Campana Brothers' Favela Chair (Fig. 12.28). Rough-hewn pieces of unfinished scrapwood in all shapes and sizes are nailed and glued together in the basic shape of an armchair. The Campana Brothers were the first Brazilian designers to exhibit their work at the Museum of Modern Art.

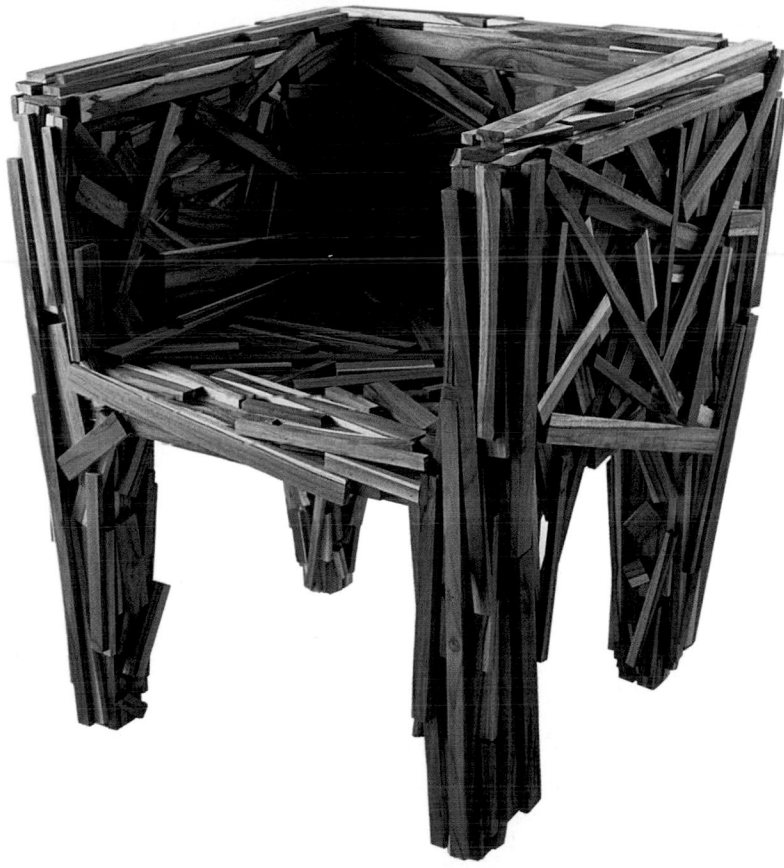

▲ 12.28 **CAMPANA BROTHERS,** *Favela Chair* (1991). Wood, nails, glue;
27¼" × 26¼" × 28¼". Metropolitan Museum of Art, New York, New York.

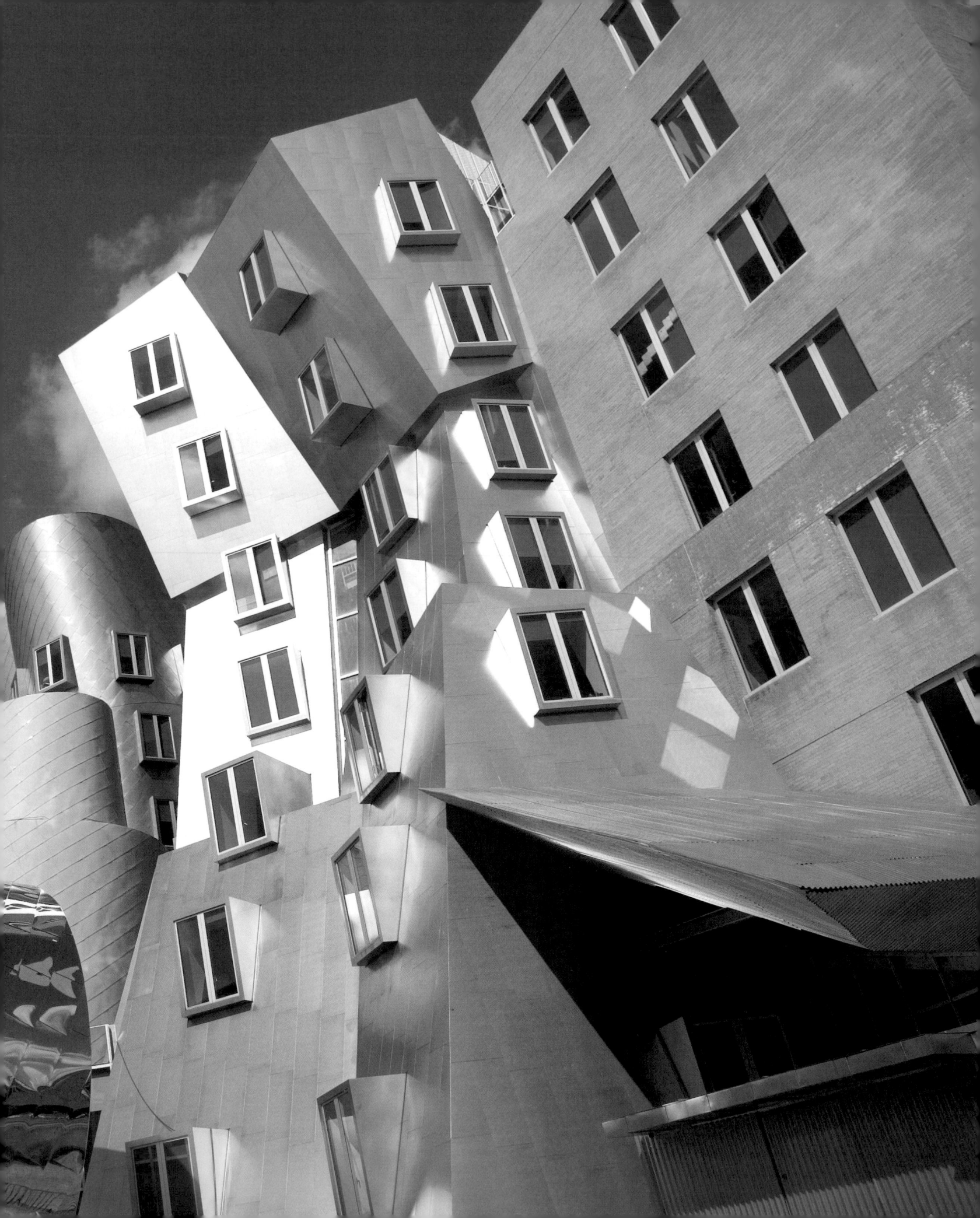

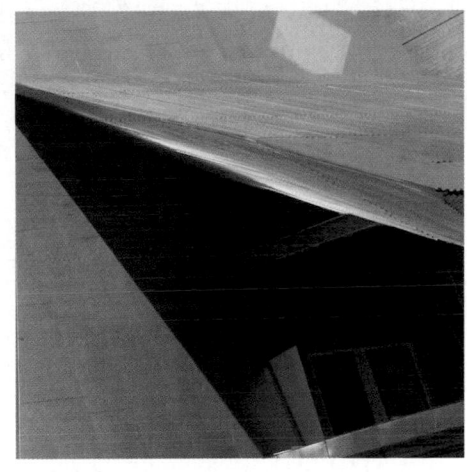

13

ARCHITECTURE AND URBAN DESIGN

The mother art is architecture. Without an architecture of our own we have no soul of our own civilization.

— FRANK LLOYD WRIGHT

EARLY HUMANS found shelter in nature's protective cocoons—the mouth of a yawning cave, the underside of a rocky ledge, the dense canopy of an overspreading tree. But the construction of dwellings goes back to the Stone Age. In the words of author Howard Bloom, "first came the mammoth, then came architecture." Before we became capable of transporting bulky materials over vast distances, we had to rely on local possibilities. During the Ice Age of about 10,000 BCE, humans dragged the skeletal pieces of wooly mammoths to a protective spot and piled them into domelike structures (**Fig. 13.1**). Native Americans carved complex communities into the sides of mesa cliffs (**Fig. 13.2**). Later they built huts from sticks and bark and conical teepees from wood poles sheathed in animal skins. African villagers wove sticks and grass into cylindrical walls, plastered them with mud, and capped them with geometrically pure cone roofs. Desert inhabitants fashioned sunbaked clay into bricks, and the Inuit stacked blocks of ice with precision to create igloos.

Architecture is the art and science of designing buildings, bridges, and other structures. Of all the arts, architecture probably has the greatest impact on our daily lives. It shapes the immediate environments in which we live, work, or entertain ourselves. And, as the history of architecture reveals, it reflects and symbolizes our concept of self and the societies in which we live, past and present.

Architects, like sculptors, work within the limits of their materials and the technology of the day. Although architects are visionaries and designers with artistic skills, they also possess the technical knowledge necessary to determine how materials may be used to span and enclose vast spaces

◄ FRANK GEHRY, Ray and Maria Stata Center for Computer, Information, and Intelligence Sciences at MIT, Cambridge, Massachusetts (2005).

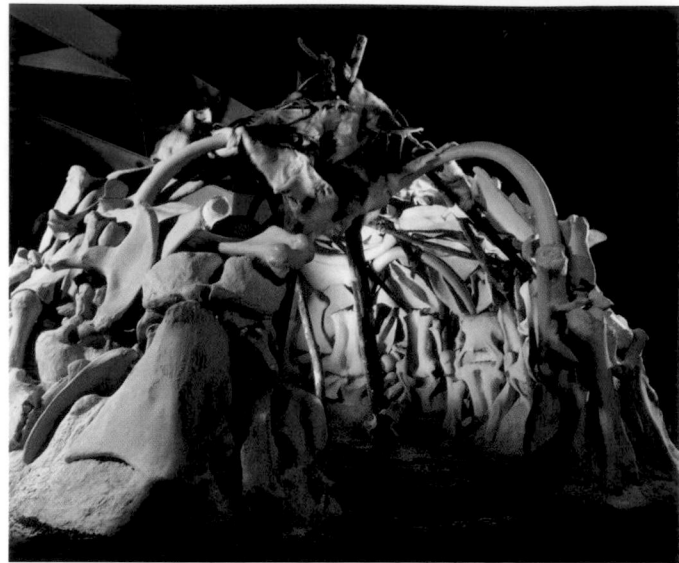

▲ **13.1** This house was built of hundreds of mammoth bones by hunters on windswept, treeless plains in what is now Ukraine, about 15,000 years ago. Working as a team, hut builders needed only a few days to haul together hundreds of massive mammoth bones, then stack them into a snug home.

the erection of 20-story-high, 20-foot-wide "sliver sky-scraper" on an expensive, narrow urban site, but at what aesthetic impact on a neighborhood? Since the 1930s, architects in New York City have had to comply with the so-called setback law and step back or contour their high-rises from the street to let the sun shine in on an environment that seemed in danger of devolving into a maze of blackened canyons. For an architect, negotiation is part of the job description. Climate, site specifics, materials, building codes, service systems, funding, and human personalities are just some of the variables that the architect encounters in an attempt to create a functional and aesthetically pleasing structure.

Architecture is also a vehicle for artistic expression in three dimensions. More than any other art form, architecture is experienced from within as well as without, and at length.

In this section, we will explore ways in which architects have come to terms with these variables. We will survey the use of building materials and methods including stone, wood, cast iron, steel, concrete, and new technologies.

efficiently and safely. Architects are collaborators. They work with other professionals—engineers, contractors and builders, tradespeople, and interior designers.

Architects are also compromisers. The architect mediates between a client and civic planning boards and building departments, historic preservation committees, and, of course, the properties and aesthetic possibilities of the site itself. Today's technology may make possible

STONE ARCHITECTURE

As a building material, stone is massive and virtually indestructible. Contemporary wood-frame homes frequently sport stone fireplaces, perhaps as a symbol of permanence and strength as well as of warmth. The

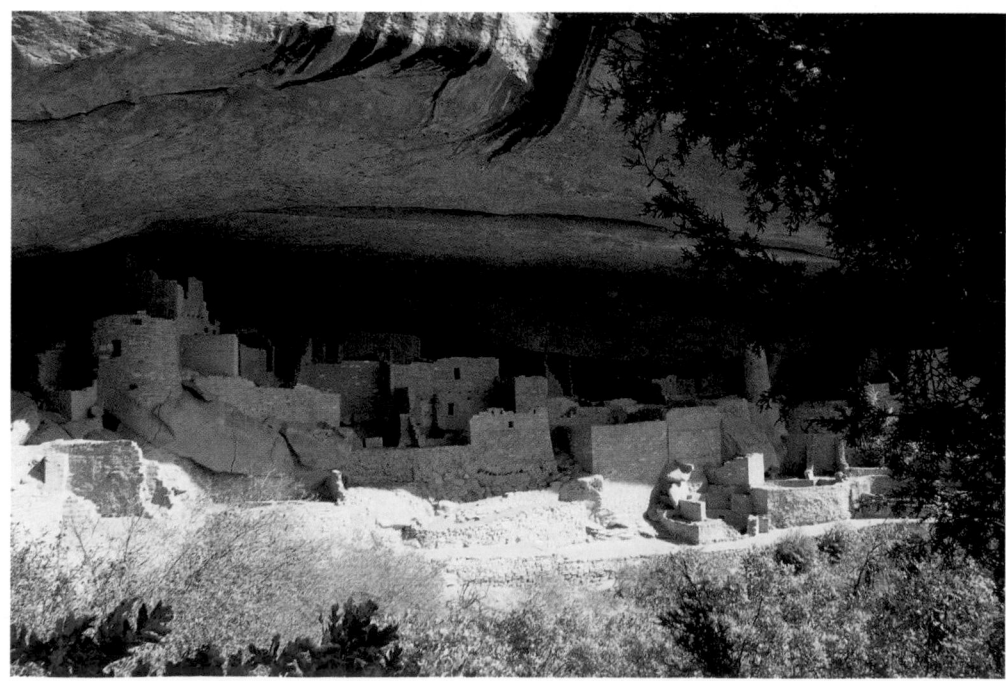

▷ 13.2 **Cliff Dwellings, Mesa Verde, Colorado,** Native American, Pre-Columbian.

Architecture completes nature.

—GIORGIO DE CHIRICO

Native American cliff dwellings at Mesa Verde, Colorado (Fig. 13.2), could be considered something of an "earthwork high relief." The cliff itself becomes the back wall or "support" of more than 100 rectangular apartments. Circular, underground **kivas** served as community centers. Construction with stone, **adobe**, and timber creates a mixed-media functional fantasy. Early humans also assembled stone temples and memorials.

Post-and-Lintel Construction

The Neolithic monument Stonehenge (see Fig. 14.3) is an example of **post-and-lintel construction** (Fig. 13.3A). Enormous stones (megaliths) were set upright first as vertical supports—the posts—on top of which equally large stones were placed in a horizontal position—the lintels. It probably served religious or astronomical purposes. Its

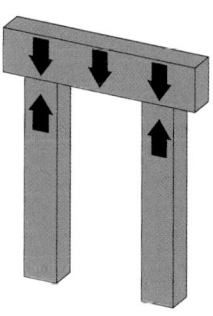

13.3A Post-and-lintel construction.

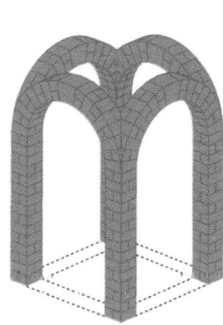

13.3B Rounded arches enclosing square bay.

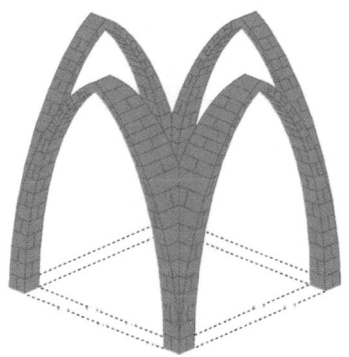

13.3C Pointed arches enclosing rectangular bay.

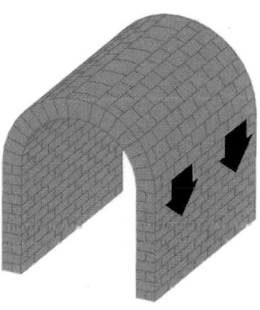

13.3D Tunnel or barrel vault.

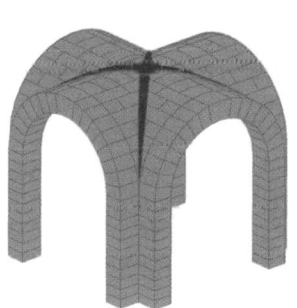

13.3E Groin vault.

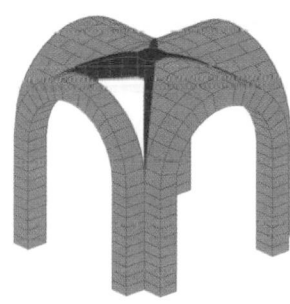

13.3F Groin vault showing ribs that carry greatest loads.

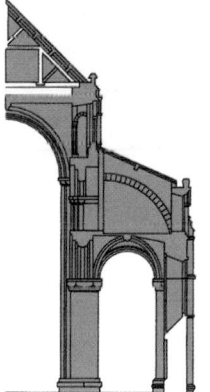

13.3G Flying buttress.

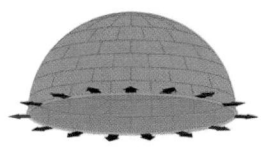

13.3H Dome.

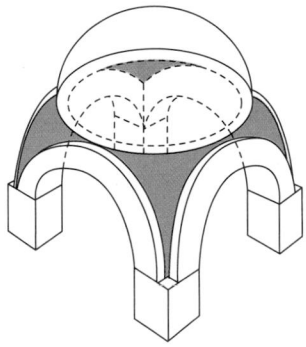

13.3I Pendentives.

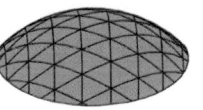

13.3J Geodesic dome.

▲ 13.3 **Structures for Spanning and Enclosing Space.**

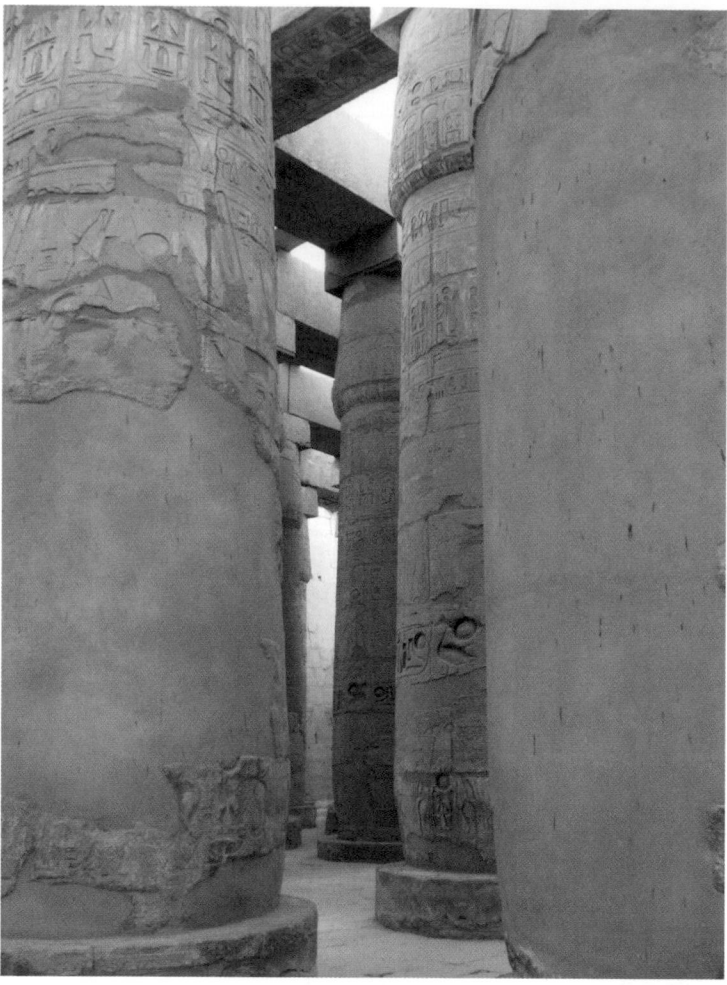

▲ 13.4 **Hypostyle Hall, Temple of Amen-Re, Karnak, Egypt** (XVIII Dynasty, 1570–1342 BCE).

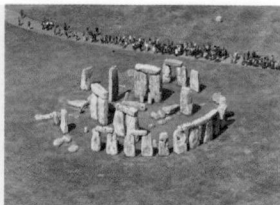

CONNECTIONS Some of the megaliths that comprise Stonehenge weigh several tons.

> Stonehenge (Fig. 14.3)

Temple of Amen-Re at Karnak (Figs. 13.4 and 13.5) and the Parthenon (see Fig. 15.9) of the Classical period of Greece begin to speak of the elegance as well as the massiveness that can be fashioned from stone. The Temple of Amen-Re is of post-and-lintel construction, but the paintings, relief sculptures, and overall smoothness of the columns belie their function as bearers of stress. The virtual forest of columns was a structural necessity because of the weight of the massive stone lintels. The Parthenon is also of post-and-lintel construction. Consistent with the Greeks' emphasis on the functional purpose of columns, the surfaces of the marble shafts are free from ornamentation. The Parthenon, which may be the most studied and surveyed building in the world, is discussed at length in Chapter 15.

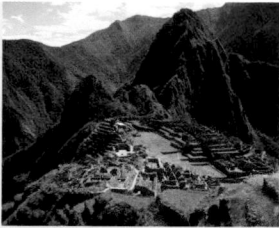

CONNECTIONS The Inkan fortress of Machu Picchu is a testament to humans' relationship to and control over nature.

> Machu Picchu (Figs. 5.9 and 17.43)

orientation toward the sun and its layout in concentric circles are suggestive of the amphitheaters and temples to follow.

Early stone structures were erected without benefit of mortar. Their dry **masonry** relied on masterly carving of blocks, strategic placement, and sheer weight for durability. Consider the imposing ruin of the fortress of Machu Picchu, perched high above the Urubamba River in the Peruvian Andes (see Fig. 5.9). Its beautiful granite walls, constructed by the Inka, are pieced together so precisely that not even a knife blade can pass between the blocks. The faces of the Great Pyramids of Egypt (see Fig. 14.11) are assembled as miraculously, perhaps even more so considering the greater mass of the blocks.

Stone became the favored material for the public buildings of the Egyptians and the Greeks. The Egyptian

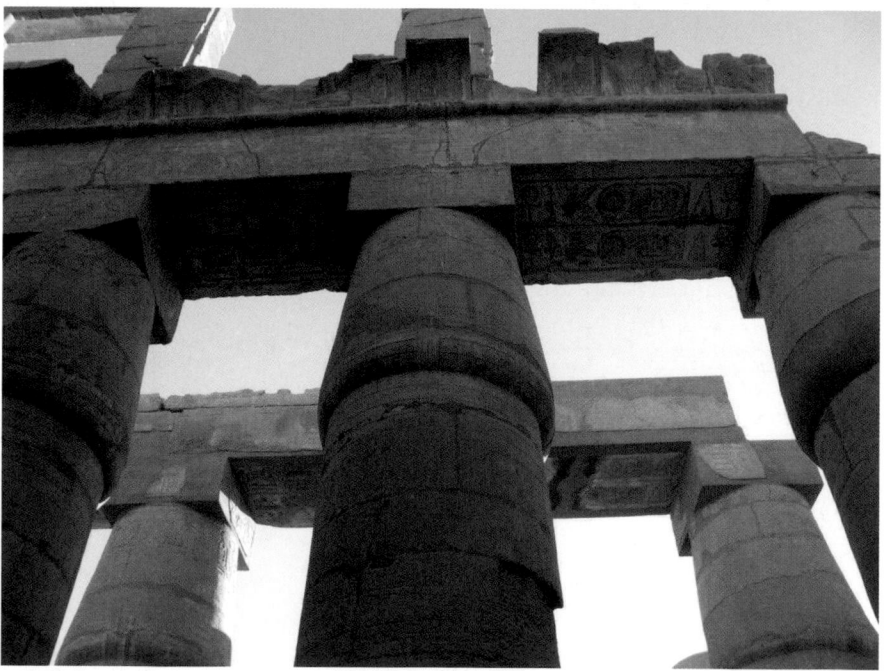

▲ 13.5 **Post-and-lintel construction, as used in the Temple of Amen-Re, Karnak, Egypt** (XVIII Dynasty, 1570–1342 BCE).

> An arch is two curves trying to fall.
>
> —ANDY ROONEY

Arches

Architects of stone also use **arches** to span distances (Figs. 13.3B and 13.3C). Arches have many functions, including supporting other structures, such as roofs, and serving as actual and symbolic gateways. An Arch of Triumph, as in the city of Paris, provides a visual focus for the return of the conquering hero. Eero Saarinen's Gateway Arch (Fig. 13.6), built in St. Louis at the edge of the Mississippi River, stands 630 feet tall at the center and commemorates the westward push of the United States after the Louisiana Purchase of 1803.

In most arches, wedge-shaped blocks of stone, called **voussoirs**, are gradually placed in position ascending a wooden scaffold called a **centering**. When the center, or **keystone**, is set in place, the weight of the blocks is all at once transmitted in an arc laterally and downward, and the centering can be removed. The pull of gravity on each block serves as "cement"; that is, the blocks fall into one another so that the very weight that had made their erection a marvel now prevents them from budging. The **compressive strength** of stone allows the builder to place additional weight above the arch. The Roman aqueduct, the Pont du Gard, consists of three **tiers** of arches, 161 feet high.

Vaults

An extended arch is called a **vault**. A tunnel or **barrel vault** (Fig. 13.3D) simply places arches behind one another until a desired depth is reached. In this way, impressive spaces may be roofed, and tunnels may be constructed. Unfortunately, the spaces enclosed by barrel vaults are dark, because piercing them to let in natural light would compromise their strength. The communication of stresses from one arch to another also requires that the centering for each arch be kept in place until the entire vault is completed.

Roman engineers are credited with the creation of the **groin vault**, which overcame limitations of the barrel vault, as early as the third century CE. Groin vaults are constructed by placing barrel vaults at right angles to cover a square space (Fig. 13.3E). In this way the load of the intersecting vaults is transmitted to the corners, necessitating **buttressing**

CONNECTIONS Snap some interesting photos of structures used for spanning and enclosing space on your campus or in your city, town, or neighborhood. What is their material? What is their function?

CONNECTIONS

The Pont du Gard near Nîmes, France, employs the arch in a bridge that is part

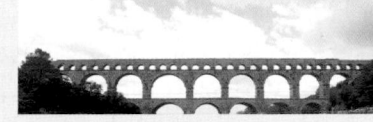

∧ Pont du Gard (Fig. 15.20)

of an aqueduct system built across many parts of Europe by the ancient Romans. Each limestone block of the Pont du Gard weighs up to two tons, and they were assembled without mortar. The bridge stands today, two millennia after its creation.

at these points but allowing the sides of the square to be open. The square space enclosed by the groin vault is called a **bay**. Architects could now construct huge

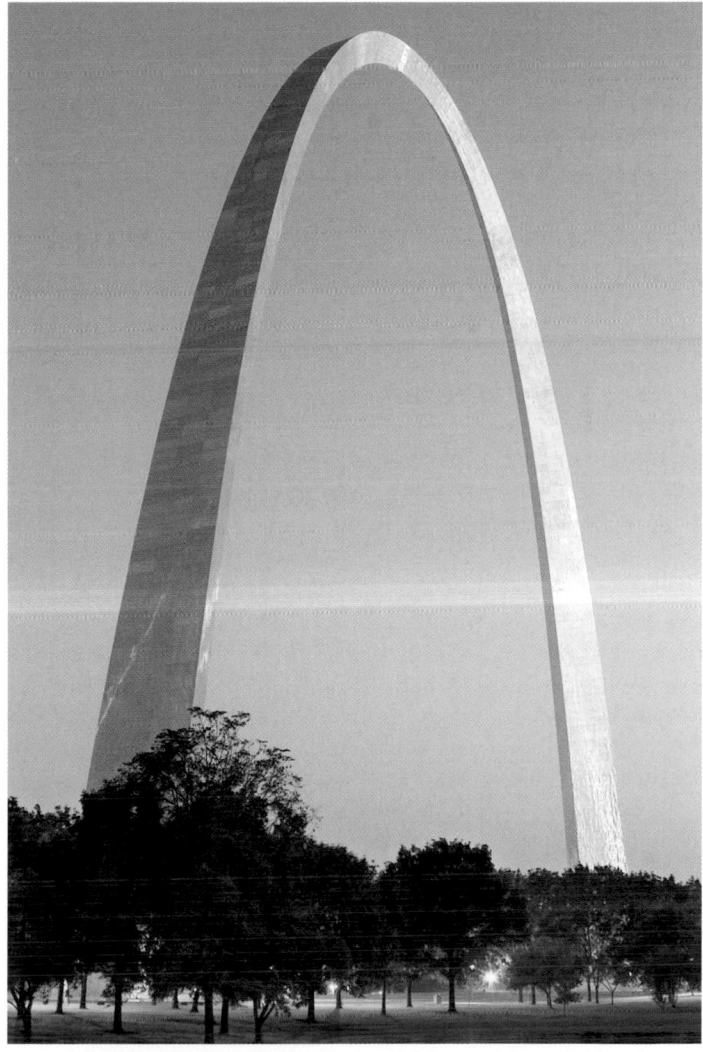

∧ 13.6 **EERO SAARINEN**, Jefferson National Expansion Memorial, Gateway Arch, St. Louis, Missouri (1966).

buildings by assembling any number of bays. Because the stresses from one groin vault are not transmitted to a large degree to its neighbors, the centering used for one vault can be removed and reused while the building is under construction.

The greatest loads in the groin vault are thrust onto the four arches that compose the sides and the two arches that run diagonally across them. If the capacity of these diagonals is increased to carry a load, by means of **ribs** added to the vault (Fig. 13.3F), then the remainder of the roof can be fashioned from stone **webbing** or other materials much lighter in weight. A true stone skeleton is created.

Note in Figure 13.3B that rounded arches can enclose only square bays. One could not use rounded arches in rectangular bays because the longer walls would have higher arches. Architects over the centuries solved the rectangular bay problem in several ingenious ways. The most important of these is found in **Gothic** architecture, discussed in Chapter 15, which uses ribbed vaults and **pointed arches**. Pointed arches can be constructed to uniform heights even when the sides of the enclosed space are unequal (Fig. 13.3C). Gothic architecture also employed the so-called flying buttress (Fig. 13.3G), a masonry strut that transmits part of the load of a vault to a buttress positioned outside a building.

Most of the great cathedrals of Europe achieve their vast, open interiors through the use of vaults. Massive stone rests benignly above the heads of worshippers and tourists alike, transmitting its brute load laterally and downward. The **Romanesque** St. Sernin (see Figs. 16.9A through 16.9C), built in France between about 1080 and 1120, uses round arches and square bays. The walls are heavy and blunt, with the main masses subdivided by buttresses. St. Étienne (see Figs. 16.10A and 16.10B), completed between 1115 and 1120, has high, rising vaults—some of the earliest to show true ribs—that permit light to enter through a **clerestory**. Stone became a fully elegant structural skeleton in the great Gothic cathedrals, such as those at Laon (see Figs. 16.15 and 16.16) and Chartres (see Fig. 16.17A). Lacy buttressing and ample **fenestration** lend these massive buildings an airy lightness that seems consonant with their mission of directing upward the focus of human awareness.

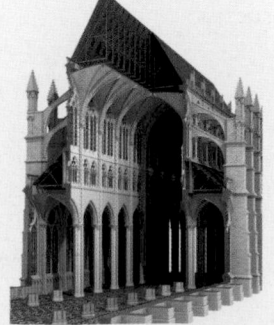

CONNECTIONS The typical Gothic cathedral was built with pointed arches and flying buttresses. The external buttressing permitted greater use of fenestration (windows), allowing entry of more light.

> Cutaway view of a typical Gothic cathedral (Fig. 16.14)

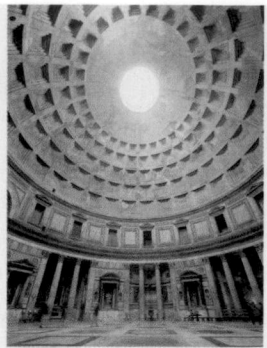

CONNECTIONS The dome of the Pantheon consists of a concrete shell that is thicker and heavier at the base and which becomes progressively thinner and lighter toward the top.

> The Pantheon, Rome (Fig. 15.27)

Domes

Domes are hemispherical forms that are rounded when viewed from beneath (see Figs. 13.3H and 13.3J). Like vaults, domes are extensions of the principle of the arch and are capable of enclosing vast reaches of space. (Buckminster Fuller, who designed the United States Pavilion [see Fig. 13.24] for the 1967 World's Fair in Montreal, proposed that the center of Manhattan should be enclosed in a weather-controlled transparent dome two miles in diameter.) Stresses from the top of the dome are transmitted in all directions to the points at which the circular base meets the foundation, walls, or other structures beneath.

The dome of the Buddhist temple or **Stupa** of Sanchi, India, completed in the first century CE, rises 50 feet above the ground and causes the worshiper to contemplate the dwelling place of the gods (see Fig. 15.36). It was constructed from stones placed in gradually diminishing concentric circles. Visitors find the domed interior of the Pantheon of Rome (see Figs. 15.26 and 15.27), completed during the second century CE, breathtaking. The rounded inner surface of the Pantheon, 144 feet in diameter, symbolizes the heavens.

Today, stone is rarely used as a structural material. It is expensive to quarry and transport, and is too massive to handle readily at the site. Metals are lighter and have greater tensile strength, so they are suitable as the skeletons or reinforcers for most of today's larger structures. Still, buildings with steel skeletons are frequently dressed with thin facades, or **veneers**, of costly marble, limestone, and other types of stone. Many tract homes are granted decorative patches of stone across the front facade, and slabs of slate are frequently used to provide minimum-care surfaces for entry halls or patios in private homes.

WOOD ARCHITECTURE

Wood is as beautiful and versatile a material for building as it is for sculpture. It is an abundant and, as many advertisements have proclaimed, renewable resource. It is relatively light in weight and is capable of being worked on

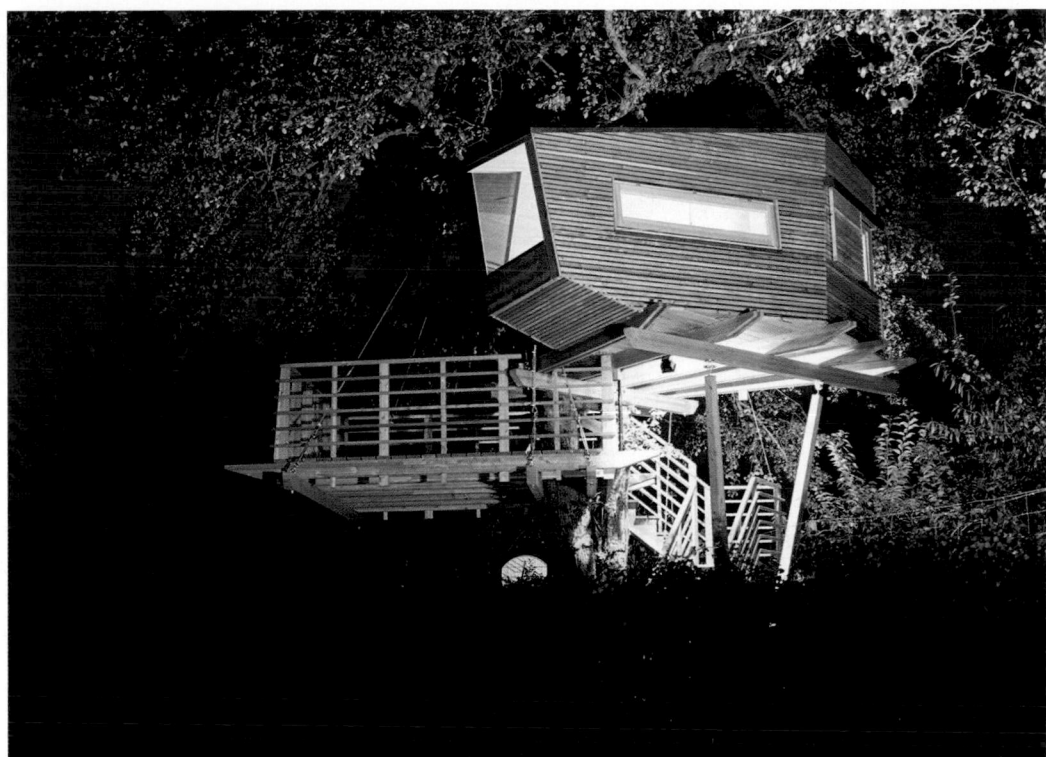

at the site with readily portable hand tools. Its variety of colors and grains, as well as its capacity to accept paint or to weather charmingly when left in its natural state, make wood a ubiquitous material. Wood, like stone, can be used as a structural element or as a facade. In many structures, it is used as both.

Wood also has its drawbacks. It warps and cracks. It rots. It is also highly flammable and stirs the appetite of termites and other devouring insects. However, modern technology has enhanced the stability and strength of wood as a building material. Chemical treatments decrease wood's vulnerability to rotting from moisture. **Plywood**, which is built up from sheets of wood glued together, is unlikely to warp and is frequently used as an under layer in the exterior walls of small buildings and homes. Laminated wood beams possess great strength and are also unlikely to become distorted in shape from exposure to changing temperatures and levels of humidity.

Architects, like artists and designers, use contrasting materials to create visual diversity and surface interest. They often reference textures found in nature to integrate a building with its site, or to create a dramatic counterpoint to it. The treehouses (Fig. 13.7) designed by the German architects studio, baumraum, are extreme and playful examples of both. The designers refer to their endeavors as a blend of architecture, landscape design, and "arboriculture," aiming to integrate the structures into their forest surrounds and, at the same time, preserve the integrity of the host trees. In designing its lofty wood dwellings, *baumraum*—which literally means "tree space" in German—also takes into consideration factors such as the species of a tree, its distance off the ground, and the amount of clear building space available in order to successfully suspend the structures. The result is a study in contrast and connection between humans and their natural surroundings.

Post-and-Beam Construction

Post-and-beam construction (Fig. 13.8A) is similar to post-and-lintel construction. Vertical and horizontal timbers are cut and pieced together with wooden pegs. The beams span openings for windows, doors, and interior spaces, and they can also support posts for another story or roof trusses.

CONNECTIONS Beijing's imposing Forbidden City, built during the Ming Dynasty (1368–1644), is made of wood. The columns consist of tree trunks.

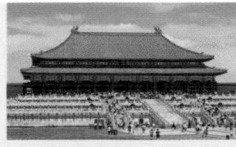

∧ Forbidden City
(Fig. 17.35)

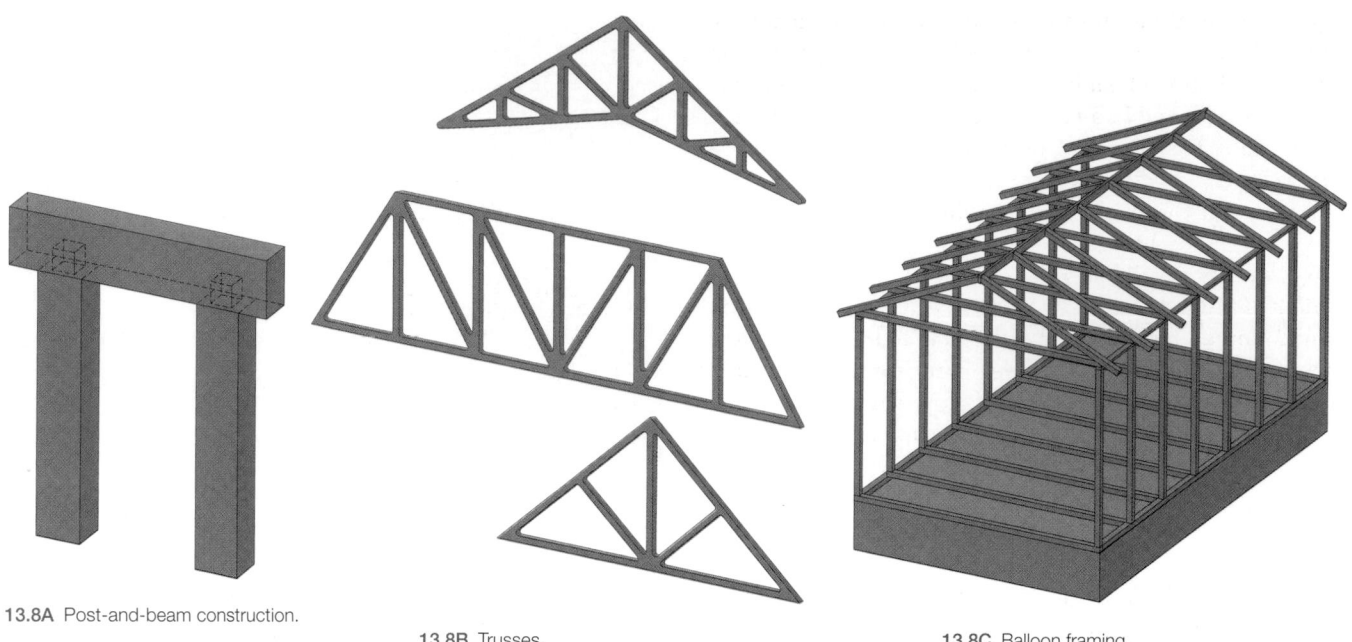

13.8A Post-and-beam construction.

13.8B Trusses.

13.8C Balloon framing.

⋀ 13.8 **Wood Architecture Construction.**

Trusses

Trusses are lengths of wood, iron, or steel pieced together in triangular shapes of the sort shown in Figure 13.8B to expand the abilities of these materials to span distances. Trusses acquire their strength from the fact that the sides of a triangle, once joined, cannot be forced out of shape. In many buildings, roof trusses are exposed and become elements of the design.

Balloon Framing

Balloon framing (Fig. 13.8C), a product of the industrial revolution, dates back to the beginning of the twentieth century. In balloon framing, factory-cut studs, including the familiar two-by-four, are mass-produced and assembled at the site with factory-produced metal nails. Light, easily handled pieces of wood replace the heavy timber of post-and-beam construction. Entire walls are framed

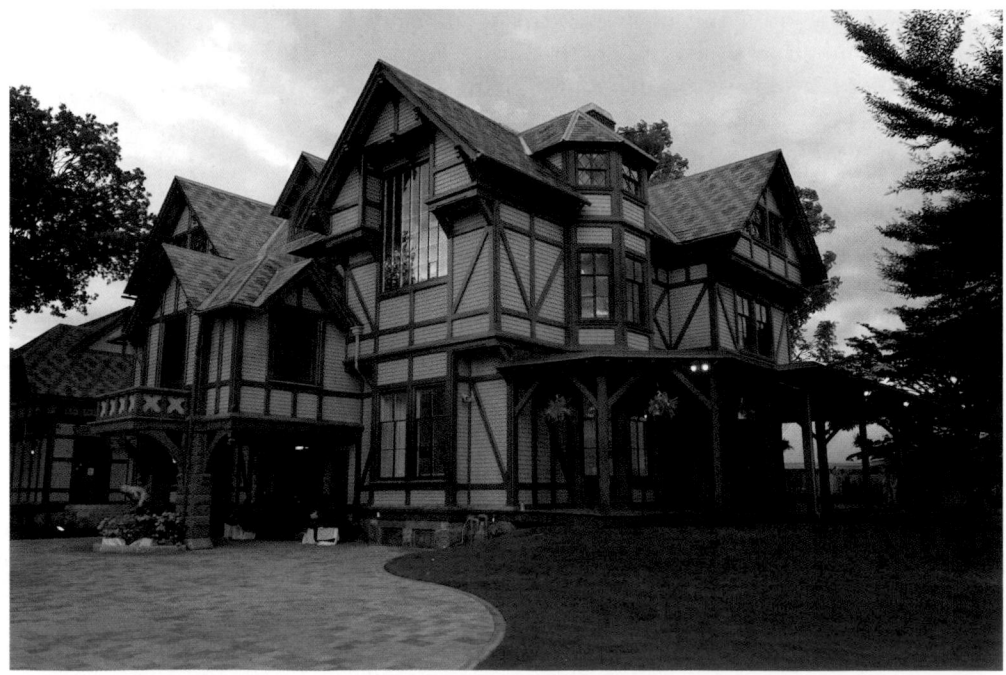

> 13.9 **RICHARD M. HUNT,**
J. N. A. Griswold House, Newport,
Rhode Island (1862–1863).

in place or on their sides and then raised into place by a crew of carpenters. The multiple pieces and geometric patterns of balloon framing give it a sturdiness that rivals that of the post and beam, permitting the support of slate or tile roofs. However, the term *balloon* was originally a derisive term: inveterate users of post and beam were skeptical that the frail-looking wooden pieces could provide a rugged building.

Balloon framing has now been used on millions of smaller buildings, not only homes. Sidings for balloon-framed homes have ranged from **clapboard** to asbestos shingle, brick and stone veneer, and aluminum. Roofs have ranged from asphalt or cedar shingle to tile and slate. These materials vary in cost, and each has certain aesthetic possibilities and practical advantages. Aluminum, for example, is lightweight, durable, and maintenance-free. However, when aluminum siding is shaped like clapboard and given a bogus grain, the intended *trompe l'oeil* effect usually fails and can create something of an aesthetic embarrassment.

Two other faces of wood are observable in American architect Richard M. Hunt's J. N. A. Griswold House (Fig. 13.9), built at Newport, Rhode Island, in 1862–1863 in the *Stick style,* and in the Cape Cod–style homes in Levittown, Long Island, a suburb of New York City (Fig. 13.10). The Griswold House shows the fanciful possibilities in wood. The Stick style sports a skeletal treatment of exteriors that remind one of an assemblage of matchsticks; open interiors; and a curious interplay of voids and solids, and horizontal and vertical lines. Turrets and gables and dormers poke the roof in every direction. Trellised porches reinforce a certain wooden laciness. One cannot imagine the Griswold House constructed in any material but wood.

The houses at Levittown are more than homes; they are a socioaesthetic comment on the need for mass suburban housing that impacted so many metropolitan regions

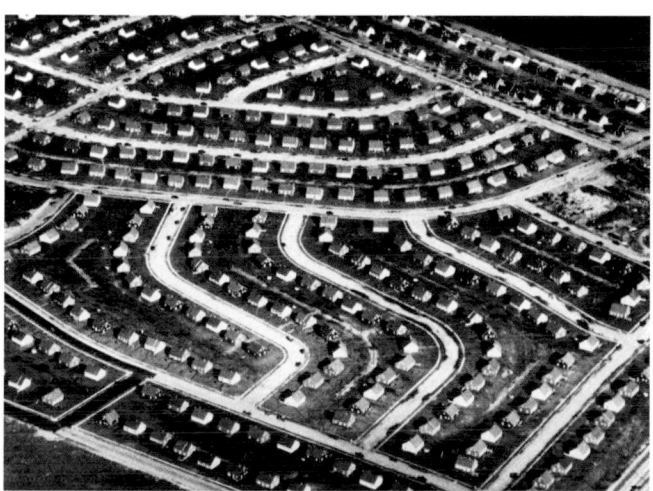

▲ **13.10 Cape Cod–style houses built by Levitt & Sons, Levittown, New York** (c. 1947–1951).

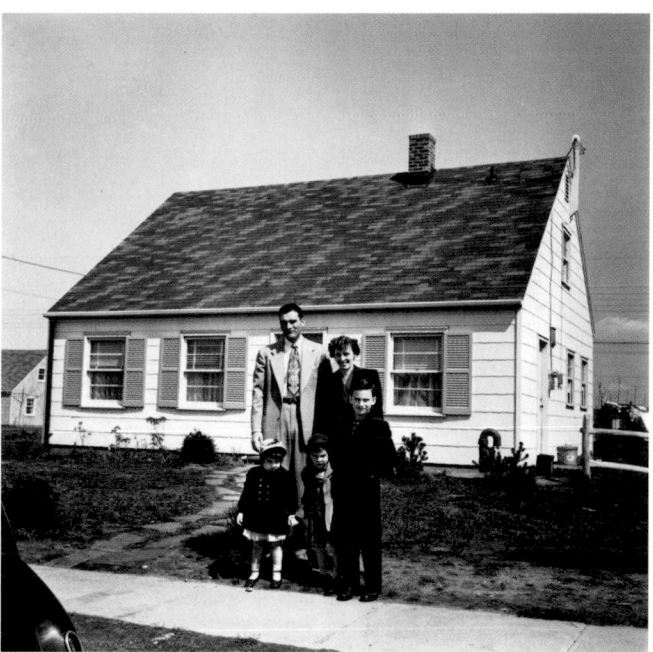

▲ **13.11** A proud family posing in front of their brand-new Levitt home (1950).

during the marriage and baby boom that followed World War II. This house (Fig. 13.11) and 17,000 others almost exactly like it were built, with few exceptions, on 60-by-100-foot lots that had been carved out from potato fields. In what was to become neighborhood after neighborhood, bulldozers smoothed already flat terrain and concrete slabs were poured. Balloon frames were erected, sided, and roofed. Trees were planted; grass was sown. The houses had an eat-in kitchen, living room, two tiny bedrooms, one bath on the first floor, and an expansion attic. Despite the tedium of the repetition, the original Levittown house achieved a sort of architectural integrity, providing living space, the pride of ownership, and an inoffensive façade for a modest price. Driving through Levittown today, it seems that every occupant thrust random additions in random directions as the family grew, despite the limitations of the lots. The trees only partly obscure the results.

CAST-IRON ARCHITECTURE

Nineteenth-century industrialization also introduced **cast iron** as a building material. It was one of several structural materials that would change the face of architecture. Cast iron was a welcome alternative to stone and wood. Like stone, iron has great strength, is heavy, and has a certain brittleness, yet it was the first material to allow the erection of tall buildings with relatively slender walls. Slender iron beams and bolted trusses are also capable of spanning vast interior spaces, freeing them from the forests of columns that are required in stone.

> No person who is not a great sculptor or painter can be an architect. . . . He can only be a builder.
>
> —JOHN RUSKIN

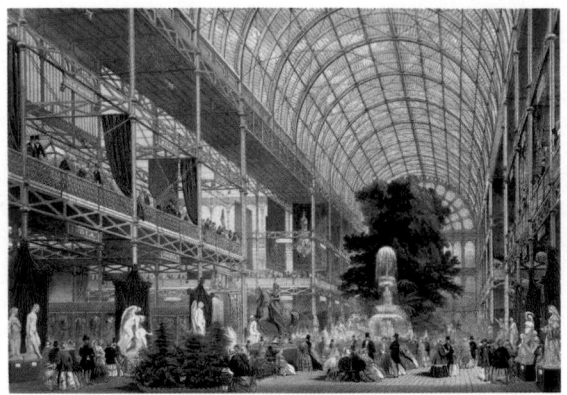

▲ 13.12 Engraving of Sir Joseph Paxton's Crystal Palace, London, England (1851).

STEEL-CAGE ARCHITECTURE

Steel is a strong metal of iron alloyed with small amounts of carbon and a variety of other metals. Steel is harder than iron, and more rust and fire resistant. It is more expensive than most other structural materials, but its great strength permits it to be used in relatively small quantities. Light, narrow, prefabricated I-beams have great tensile strength. They resist bending in any direction and are riveted or welded together into skeletal forms called **steel cages** at the site (Fig. 13.14). Facades and inner walls are hung from the skeleton and frequently contribute more mass to the building than does the skeleton itself.

At the mid-nineteenth-century Great Exhibition held in Hyde Park, London, Sir Joseph Paxton's Crystal Palace (Fig. 13.12) covered 17 acres. Like subsequent iron buildings, the Crystal Palace was **prefabricated**. Iron parts were cast at the factory, not the site. The new railroads facilitated their transportation, and it was a simple matter to bolt them together at the exhibition. It was also relatively simple to dismantle the structure and reconstruct it at another site. The iron skeleton, with its myriad arches and trusses, was an integral part of the design. The huge plate-glass paneled walls bore no weight. Paxton asserted that "nature" had been his "engineer," explaining that he merely copied the system of longitudinal and transverse supports that one finds in a leaf. Earlier architects were also familiar with the structure of the leaf, but they did not have the structural materials at hand that would permit them to build, much less conceptualize, such an expression of natural design.

The Crystal Palace was moved after the exhibition, and until heavily damaged by fire, it served as a museum and concert hall. It was demolished in 1941 during World War II, after it was discovered that it was being used as a landmark by German pilots on bombing runs.

The Eiffel Tower (Fig. 13.13) was built in Paris in 1889 for another industrial exhibition. At the time, Gustave Eiffel was castigated by critics for building an open structure lacking the standard masonry façade. Today the Parisian symbol is so familiar that one cannot visualize Paris without the tower's magnificent exposed iron trusses. The pieces of the 1,000-foot-tall tower were prefabricated, and the tower was assembled at the site in seventeen months by only 150 workers.

Structures such as these encouraged **steel-cage construction** and the development of the skyscraper.

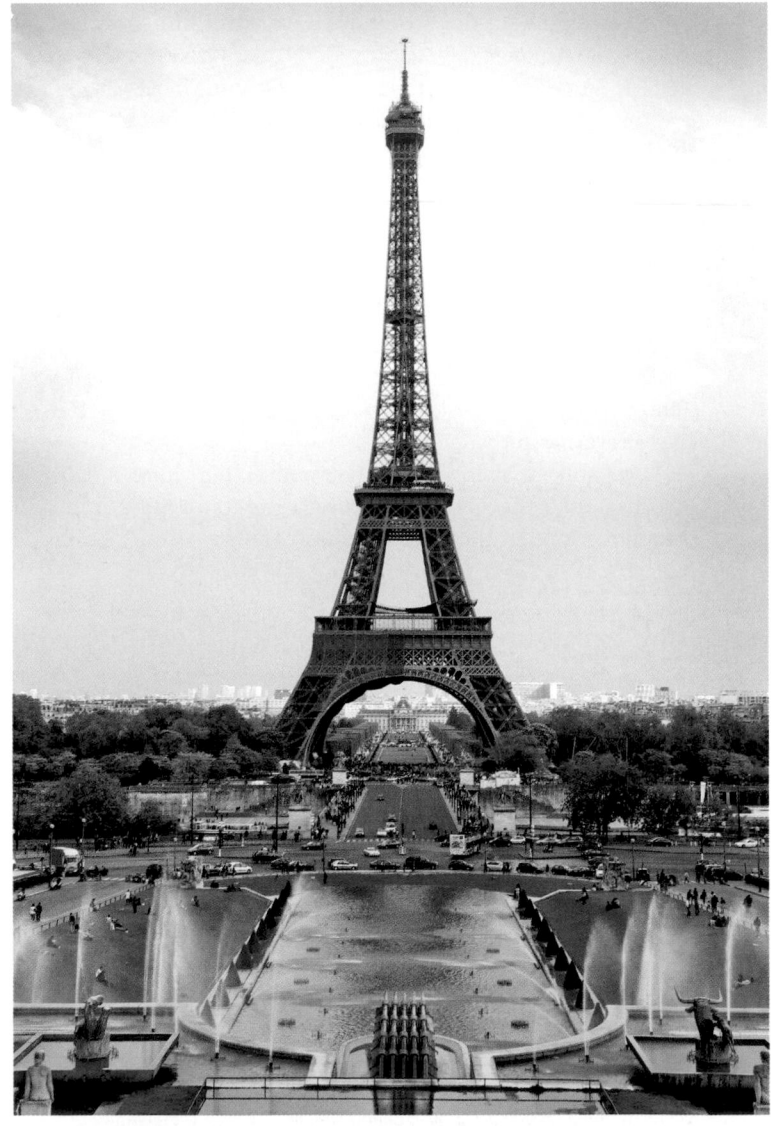

▲ 13.13 GUSTAVE EIFFEL, Eiffel Tower, Paris, France (1889). Iron, 1,050' high.

Less is more.

—MIËS VAN DER ROHE

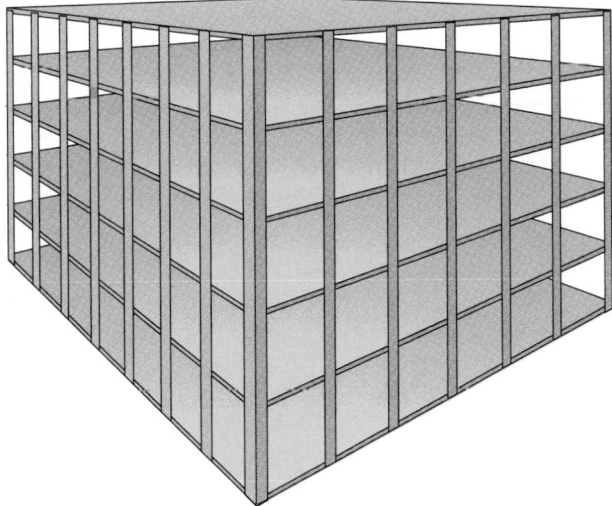

▲ 13.14 Steel-Cage Construction.

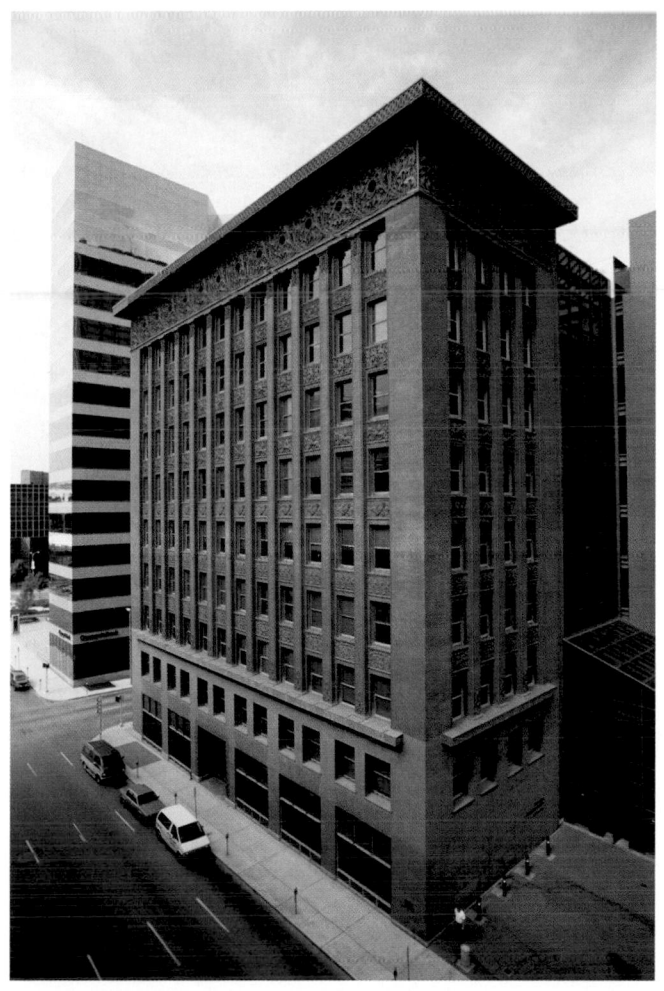

▲ 13.15 LOUIS SULLIVAN, Wainwright Building, St. Louis, Missouri (1890–1891).

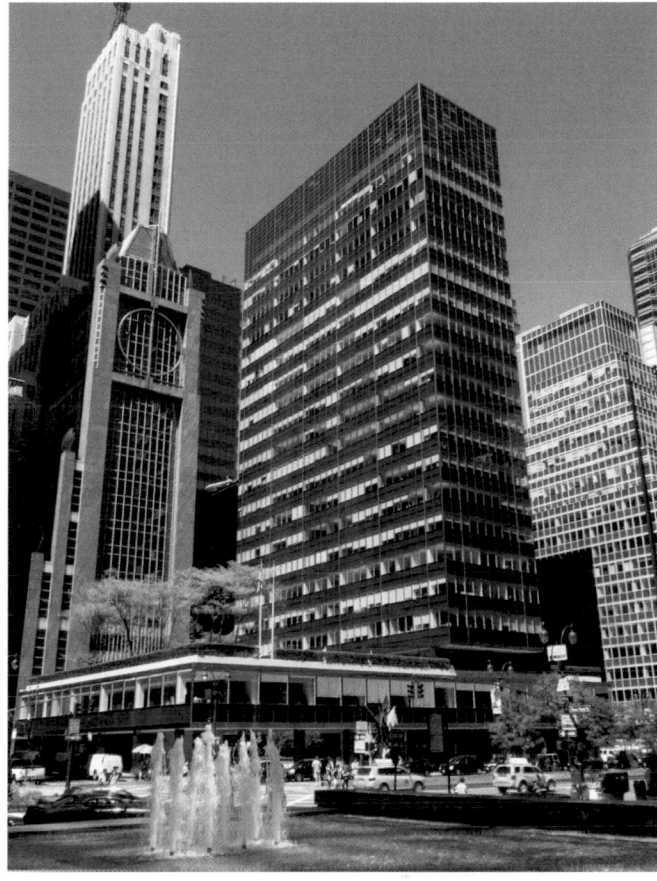

▲ 13.16 GORDON BUNSHAFT, Lever House, Park Avenue, New York, New York (1951–1952).

The Wainwright Building (Fig. 13.15), erected in the 1890s, is an early example of steel-cage construction. Architect Louis Sullivan, one of the "fathers" of modern American architecture, emphasized the verticality of the structure by running **pilasters** between the windows through the upper stories. Many skyscrapers run pilasters up their entire facades. Sullivan also emphasized the horizontal features of the Wainwright Building. Ornamented horizontal bands separate most of the windows, and a severe decorated **cornice** crowns the structure. Sullivan's motto was "form follows function,"[1] and the rigid horizontal and vertical processions of the elements of the facade suggest the regularity of the rectangular spaces within. Sullivan's early "skyscraper"— in function, in structure, and in simplified form—was a precursor of the twentieth-century behemoths to follow.

One of these behemoths is New York City's Modernist Lever House (Fig. 13.16). Lever House was designed by

---

[1] The actual quotation is "Form ever follows function," but the word "ever" is usually omitted when referring to Sullivan's motto.

> Architecture is the first manifestation of man creating his own universe.
>
> —LE CORBUSIER
>
> Well, now that he's finished one building, he'll go write four books about it.
>
> —FRANK LLOYD WRIGHT ON LE CORBUSIER

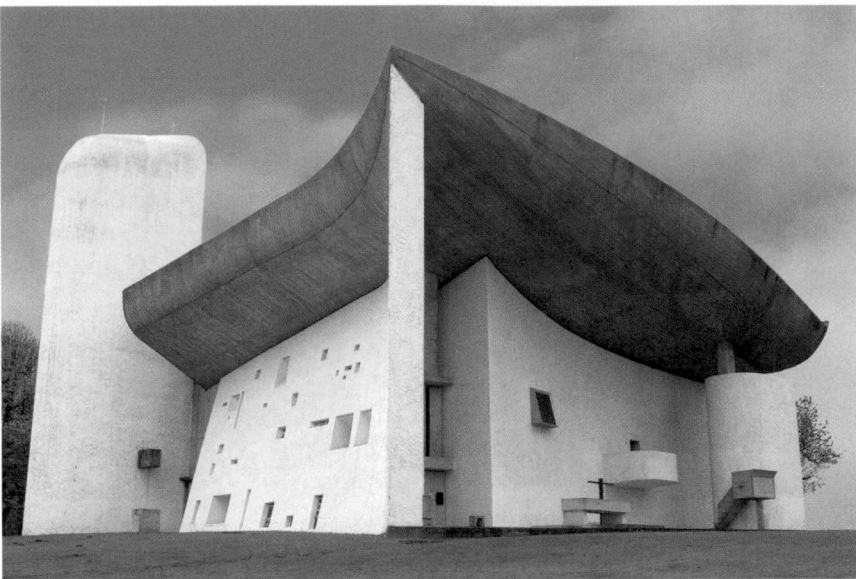

< 13.17 LE CORBUSIER, Chapel of Notre-Dame-du-Haut, Ronchamp, France (1950–1954). Concrete and stone structure.

Gordon Bunshaft of Skidmore, Owings, and Merrill, a firm that quickly became known for its "minimalist" rectangular solids with their "curtain walls" of glass. The nation was excited about the clean, austere look of Lever House and about its donation of open plaza space to the city. The plaza prevents the shaft from overwhelming its site. The evening light angles down across the plaza and illuminates the avenue beneath.

REINFORCED CONCRETE ARCHITECTURE

The use of **reinforced concrete** is said to have begun with a French gardener, Jacques Monier, who proposed strengthening concrete flower pots with a wire mesh in the 1860s. In reinforced concrete, or **ferroconcrete**, steel rods and/or steel mesh are inserted at the points of greatest stress into concrete slabs before they harden. In the resultant slab, stresses are shared by the materials.

Ferroconcrete has many of the advantages of stone and steel, without some of the disadvantages. The steel rods increase the tensile strength of concrete, making it less susceptible to tearing or pulling apart at stress points. The concrete, in turn, prevents the steel from rusting. Reinforced concrete can span greater distances than stone, and it supports more weight than steel. Perhaps

the most dramatic advantage of reinforced concrete is its capacity to take on natural curved shapes that would be unthinkable in steel or concrete alone. Curved slabs take on the forms of eggshells, bubbles, seashells, and other organic shapes that are naturally engineered for the even spreading of stress throughout their surfaces and are, hence, enduring.

Reinforced concrete, more than other materials, has allowed the architect to think freely and sculpturally. There are limits to what ferroconcrete can do, however; initial spatial concepts are frequently somewhat refined by computer-aided calculations of marginally more efficient shapes for distributing stress. Still, it would not be far from the mark to say that buildings of almost any shape and reasonable size are possible today, if one is willing to pay for them. The architects of ferroconcrete have achieved buildings that would have astounded the ancient stone builders—and perhaps Joseph Paxton as well.

Le Corbusier's chapel of Notre-Dame-du-Haut (Fig. 13.17) is an example of what has been referred to as the "new brutalism," deriving from the French *brut*, meaning "rough, uncut, or raw." The steel web is spun, and the concrete is cast in place, leaving the marks of the wooden forms on its surface. The white walls, dark roof, and white towers are decorated only by the texture of the curving reinforced concrete slabs. In places, the walls are incredibly thick. Windows of various shapes and sizes expand from small slits and rectangles to form mysterious light tunnels; they draw the

> A doctor can bury his mistakes, but an architect can only advise his clients to plant vines.
>
> —FRANK LLOYD WRIGHT
>
> We may live without architecture, and worship without her, but we cannot remember without her.
>
> —JOHN RUSKIN

observer outward more than they actually light the interior. The massive voids of the window apertures recall the huge stone blocks of prehistoric religious structures.

Frank Lloyd Wright's Kaufmann House (Fig. 13.18), which has also become known as "Fallingwater," shows a very different application of reinforced concrete. Here

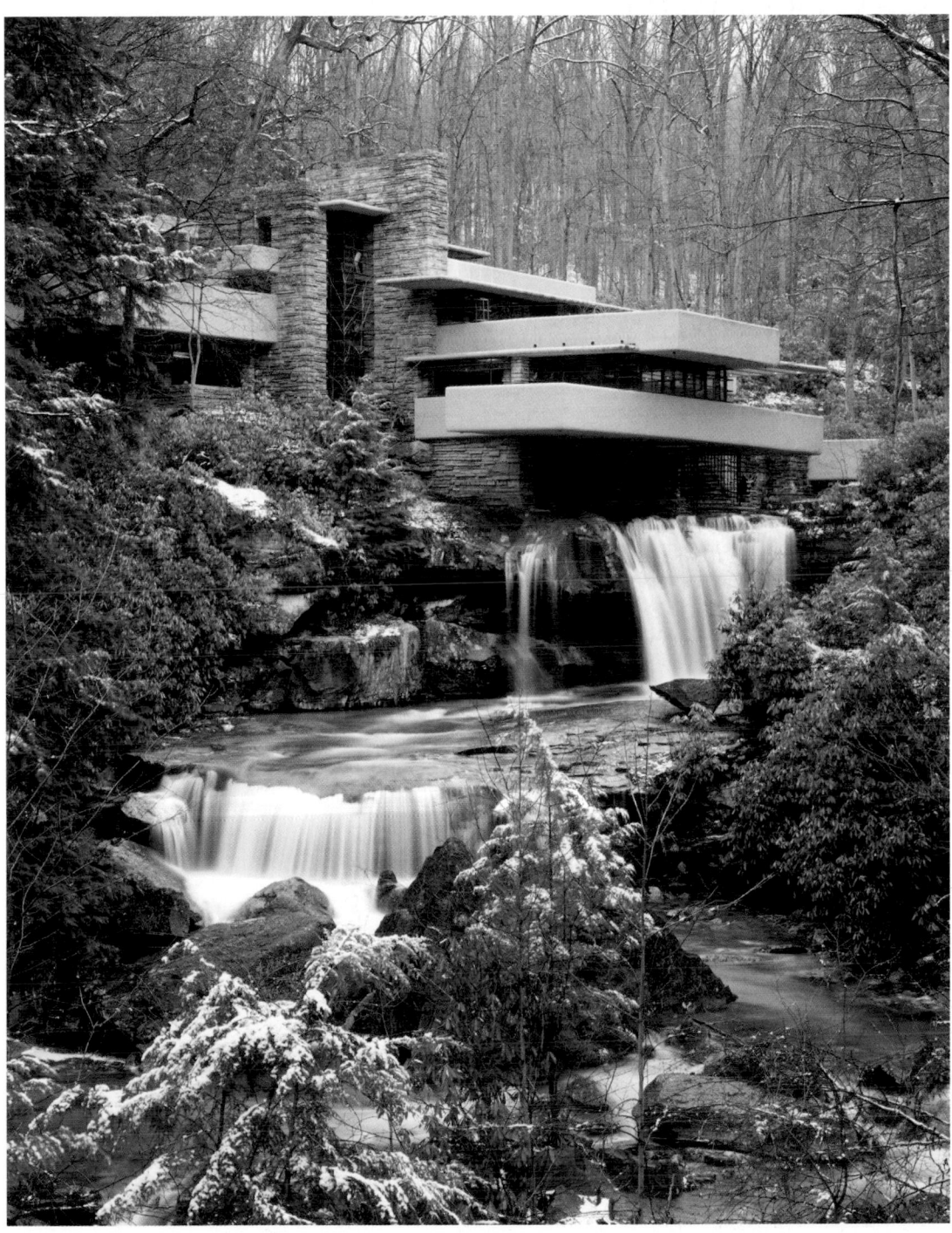

< 13.18 FRANK LLOYD WRIGHT, Kaufmann House ("Fallingwater"), Bear Run, Pennsylvania (1936).

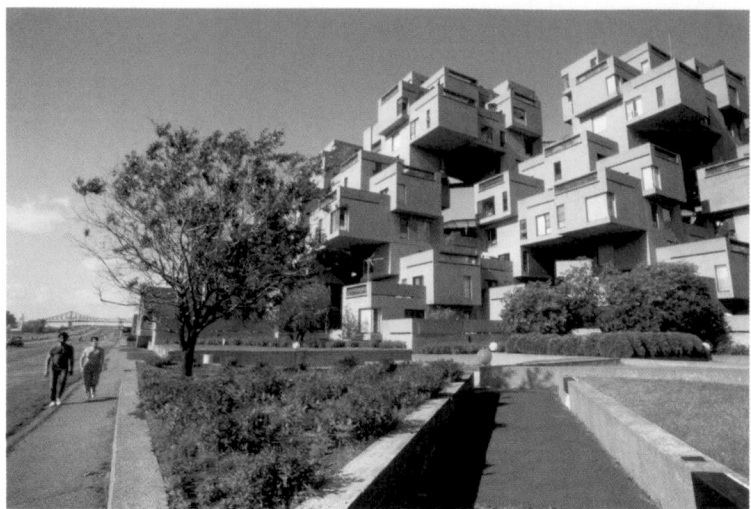

▲ 13.19 MOSHE SAFDIE, Habitat, Expo 67, Montreal, Quebec, Canada (1967).

Israeli architect Moshe Safdie's Habitat (Fig. 13.19) is another expression of the versatility of concrete. Habitat was erected for Expo 67 in Montreal as one solution to the housing problems of the future. Rugged, prefabricated units were stacked at the site like blocks about a common utility core, so that the roof of one unit would provide a private deck for another. Only a couple of Safdie-style "apartment houses" have been erected since, one in Israel and one in Puerto Rico, so today Safdie's beautiful sculptural assemblage evokes more nostalgia than hope for the future. Its unique brand of rugged, blocky excitement is rarely found in mass housing, and this is our loss.

cantilevered decks of reinforced concrete rush outward into the surrounding landscape from the building's central core, intersecting in strata that lie parallel to the natural rock formations. Wright's **naturalistic style** integrates his building with its site. In the Kaufmann House, reinforced concrete and stone walls complement the sturdy rock of the Pennsylvania countryside.

For Wright, modern materials did not warrant austerity; geometry did not preclude organic integration with the site. A small waterfall seems mysteriously to originate beneath the broad white planes of a deck. The irregularity of the structural components—concrete, cut stone, natural stone, and machine-planed surfaces—complements the irregularity of the wooded site.

STEEL-CABLE ARCHITECTURE

The notion of suspending bridges from cables is not new. Wood-and-rope suspension bridges have been built in Asia for thousands of years. Iron suspension bridges, such as the Menai Strait Bridge in Wales and the Clifton Bridge near Bristol, England, were erected during the early part of the nineteenth century. But in the Brooklyn Bridge (Fig. 13.20), completed in 1883, John A. Roebling exploited the great tensile strength of steel to span New York's East River with **steel cable**. In such a cable, many parallel wires share the stress. Steel cable is also flexible, allowing the roadway beneath to sway, within limits, in response to changing weather and traffic conditions.

Roebling used massive vaulted piers of stone masonry to support parabolic webs of steel, which are rendered lacy by the juxtaposition. In many more recent suspension

> 13.20 **JOHN A. ROEBLING, Brooklyn Bridge, New York, New York** (1869–1883). There is another stirring aspect to the photograph of the Brooklyn Bridge. In the background you can see the twin towers of the World Trade Center, which collapsed in the terrorist attack of September 11, 2001.

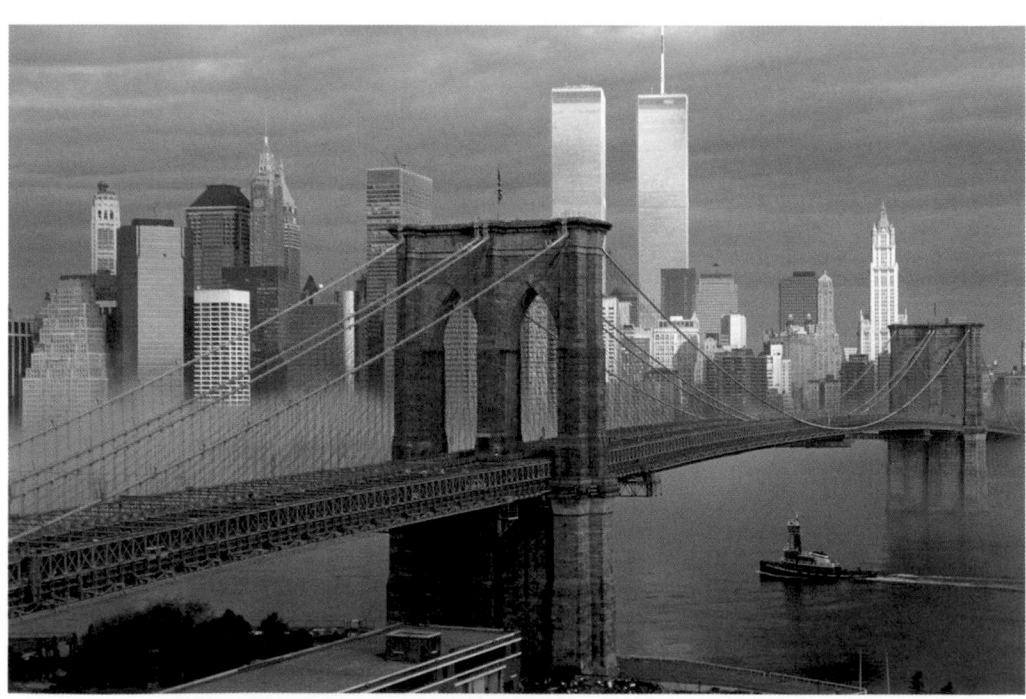

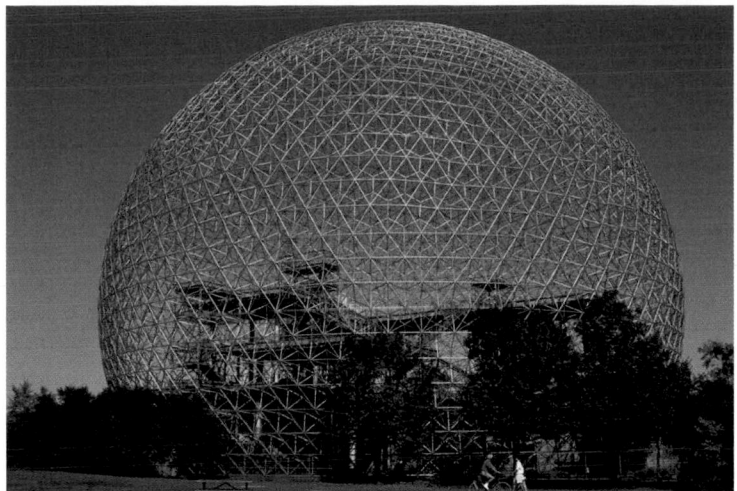

▲ 13.21 BUCKMINSTER FULLER, United States Pavilion, Expo 67, Montreal, Quebec, Canada (1967).

CONNECTIONS Frank Gehry's 1997 Guggenheim Museum in Bilbao, Spain, set a new artistic course for Gehry in terms of his own style and also nurtured the adaptation of high-tech metals such as titanium by architects worldwide.

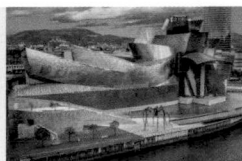

Gehry's Bilbao museum (Fig. 2.22)

compose six-sided units that give the organic impression of a honeycomb. Light floods the climate-controlled enclosure, creating an environment for any variety of human activity—and any form of additional construction—within. Such domes can be covered with many sorts of weatherproofing, from lightweight metals and fabric to translucent and transparent plastics and glass. Here the engineering requirements clearly create the architectural design.

bridges, steel cable spans more than a mile, and in bridges such as the Golden Gate, the George Washington, and the Verrazzano Narrows, the effect is aesthetically stirring.

SHELL ARCHITECTURE

Modern materials and methods of engineering have made it possible to enclose spaces with relatively inexpensive shell structures. Masonry domes have been replaced by lightweight shells, which are frequently flatter and certainly capable of spanning greater spaces. Shells have been constructed from reinforced concrete, wood, steel, aluminum, and even plastics and paper. The concept of shell architecture is as old as the canvas tent and as new as the geodesic dome (Fig. 13.21), designed by Buckminster Fuller for the United States Pavilion at Expo 67 in Montreal. In many sports arenas, fabric roofs are held up by keeping the air pressure inside the building slightly greater than that outside. Like balloons, these roof structures are literally inflated.

Fuller's shell is an assemblage of lightweight metal trusses into a three-quarter sphere that is 250 feet in diameter. Looking more closely, one sees that the trusses

NEW MATERIALS, NEW VISIONS

In architecture studios and schools, the saying goes, "Convention gets built; innovation gets published." But this adage is systematically being proven wrong as scientists and engineers have combined forces to turn architects' dreams into reality: "If you can think it, we can build it."

Frank Gehry has transformed architectural design with the use of titanium in the same way that reinforced concrete altered the look of the exterior "skin" of buildings in the 1950s and 1960s. Gehry's Ray and Maria Stata Center (Fig. 13.22), which opened in 2005 on the

> 13.22 FRANK GEHRY, Ray and Maria Stata Center for Computer, Information, and Intelligence Sciences at MIT, Cambridge, Massachusetts (2005).

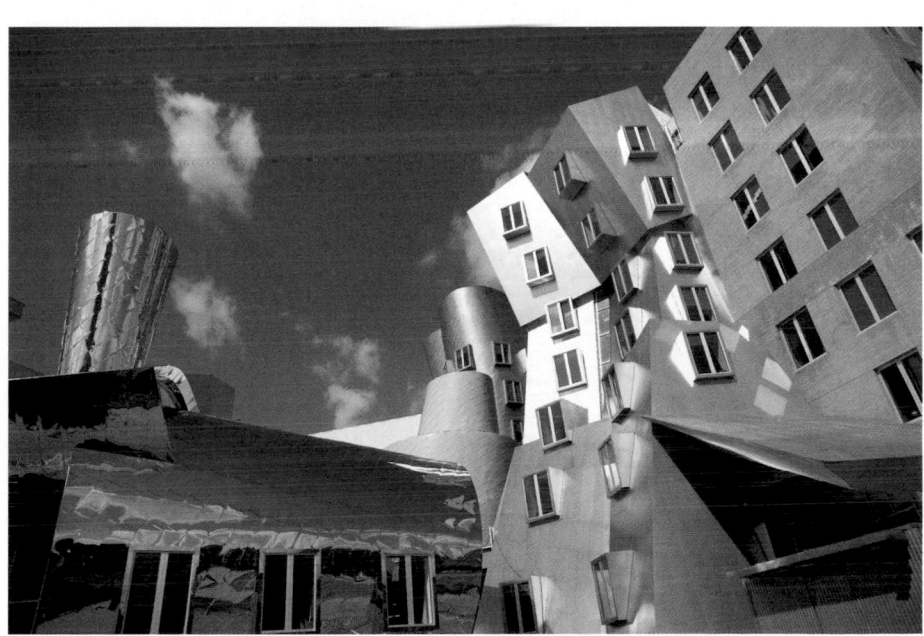

A CLOSER LOOK

Bringing Light to Ground Zero

EVERY EVENING, FOR A MONTH IN the spring of 2002, twin towers of light at Ground Zero (**Fig. 13.23**) served as an architectural memorial to the twin towers of glass and steel that had been felled, even if the medium could not be clutched by the hands. It was called *Tribute in Light*, and architectural critic Herbert Muschamp wrote about it in the *New York Times:*[2]

> "Tribute in Light" was a moving piece of urban spectacle. The project's impact surpassed even the dramatic digital renderings. In the renderings, the twin light towers appeared to be saying something. As realized, they seemed to be looking for something. More a

question than a statement, the project set a rhetorical tone worthy of emulation by those who will be shaping the future of Lower Manhattan in days to come. . . .

But where have our two towers gone? "For the moment I can only cry out that I have lost my splendid mirage," F. Scott Fitzgerald wrote in 1945. "Come back, come back, O glittering and white!"

The twin towers have now re-emerged as a single, larger tower (**Fig. 13.24**). Within months following September 11, dozens of architects and planners submitted concepts to New York City for "Ground Zero," which included a memorial to those who had been killed in the attack and new buildings that might recapture the upward spirit of the city. At one point the commission was awarded to Daniel Libeskind,

[2] Herbert Muschamp, March 12, 2002. Copyright © 2002 by The New York Times Company.

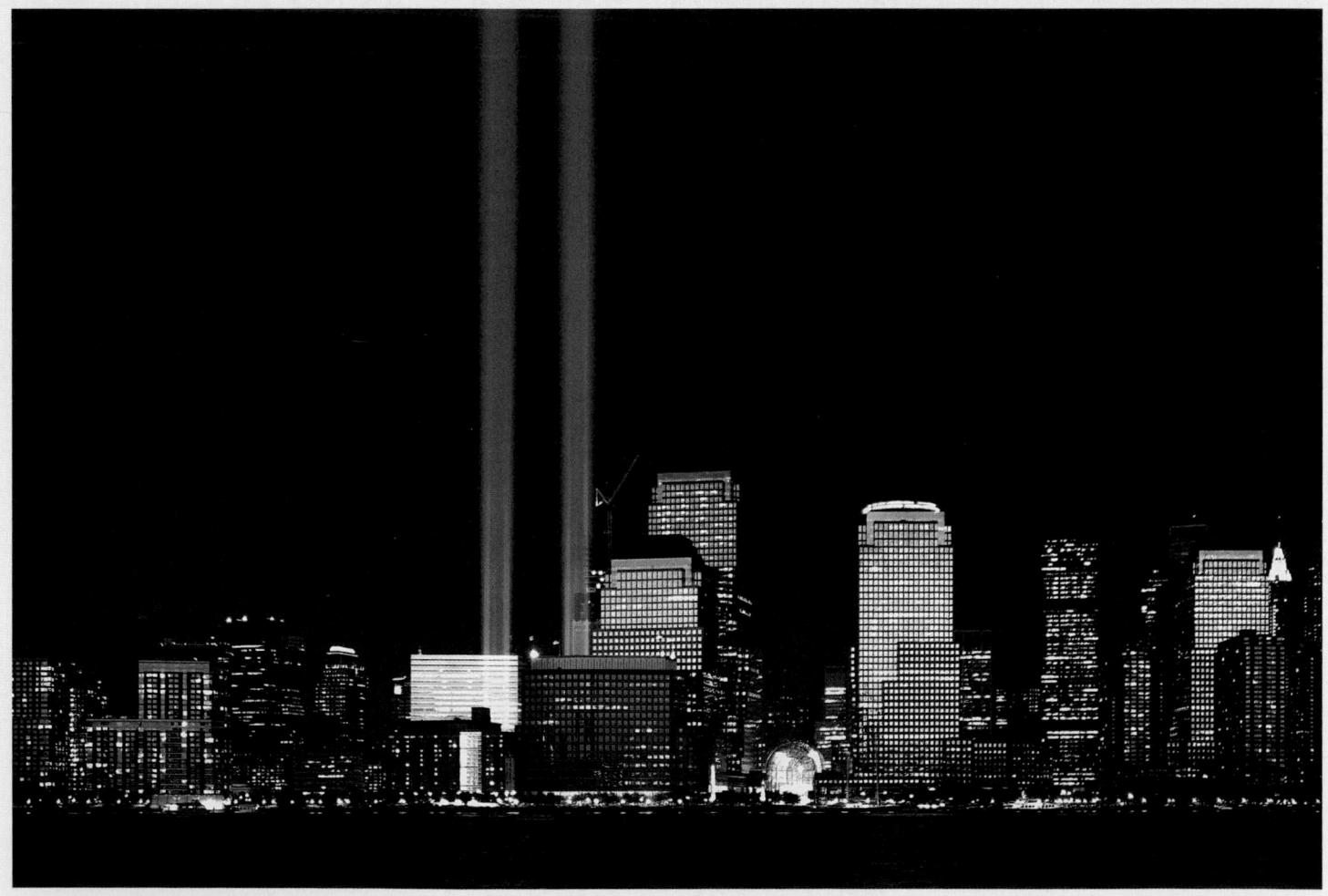

∧ **13.23 Tribute in Light** (March–April 2002).

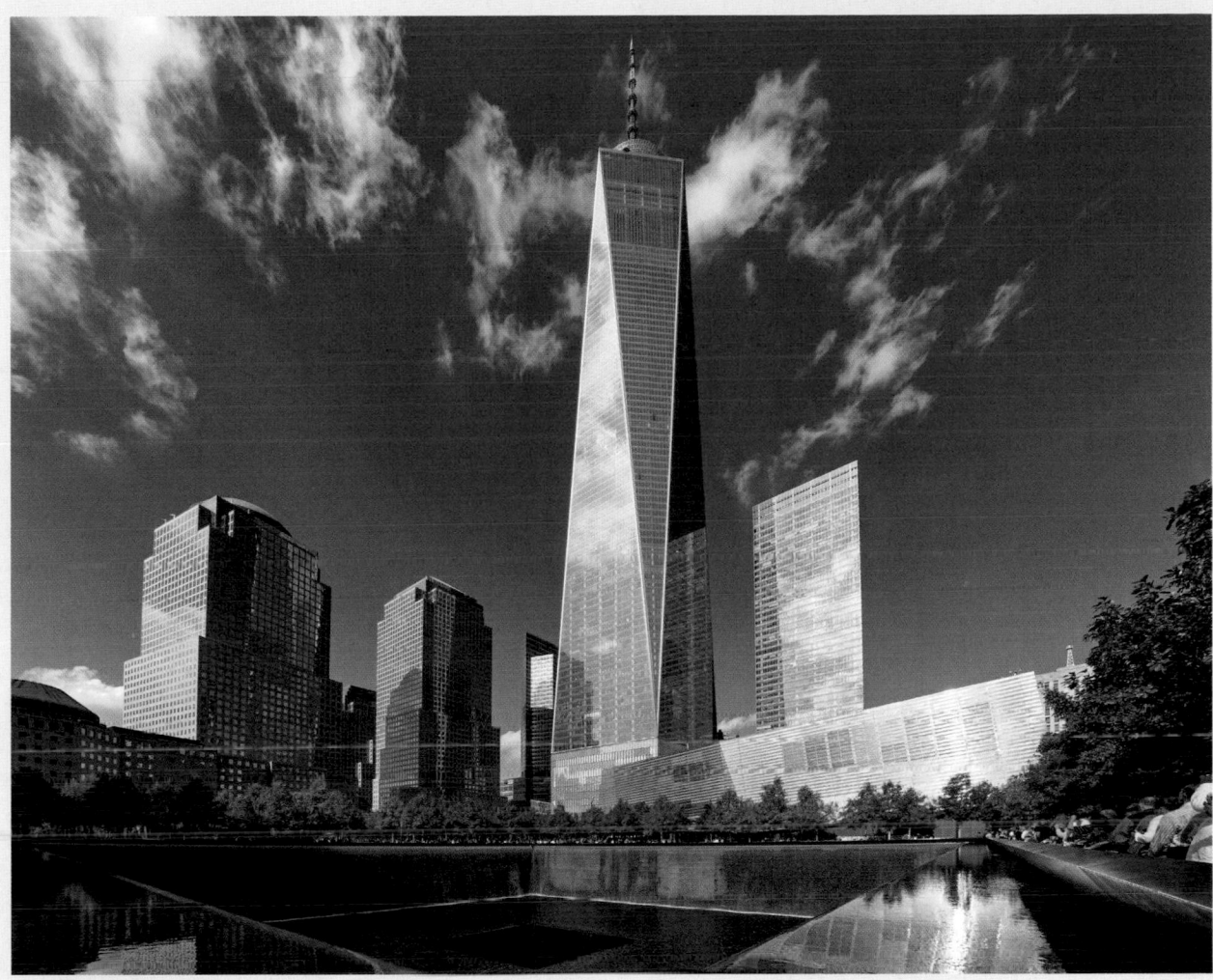

∧ **13.24** The new One World Trade Center, with the National September 11 Memorial in the foreground, sited on the footprint of the towers that were destroyed.

who designed a light and airy steel and glass tower to replace the fallen towers. Even so, his design was to be significantly stronger than the original, taking into account the sobering realities of luring tenants into a super high-rise skyscraper in a post-9/11 world and the desire of most Americans to build high and build proud.

The final design of One World Trade Center, however, is by the renowned architectural group of Skidmore, Owings, and Merrill, which pioneered mid-twentieth-century skyscraper architecture in buildings such as Lever House. According to the firm, "the design solution is an innovative mix of architecture, structure, urban design, safety, and sustainability." The tower, which is adjacent to the World Trade Center Memorial, rises a symbolic 1,776 feet from a cubic base, supporting a structure with a prismatic glass curtain wall that captures refracted light in myriad ways, depending on the time of day and atmospheric conditions. The first 186 feet of the tower have no windows and are built of a 70-ton steel base and reinforced concrete, so that the building would be impervious to nearly any vehicle explosion.

One World Trade Center not only "recaptures" the lower Manhattan skyline, but also provides communal space that integrates the office tower with a bustling plaza that contains the 9/11 Memorial Museum. There is a restaurant, zones for relaxation, and additional spaces for memory and reflection. In addition to its fortress-like base, the building overall meets or exceeds construction standards for safety and security. Even so, the overall impression is one of openness and accessibility—a careful balance that will facilitate the revival of urban life in a location that has extraordinary meaning.

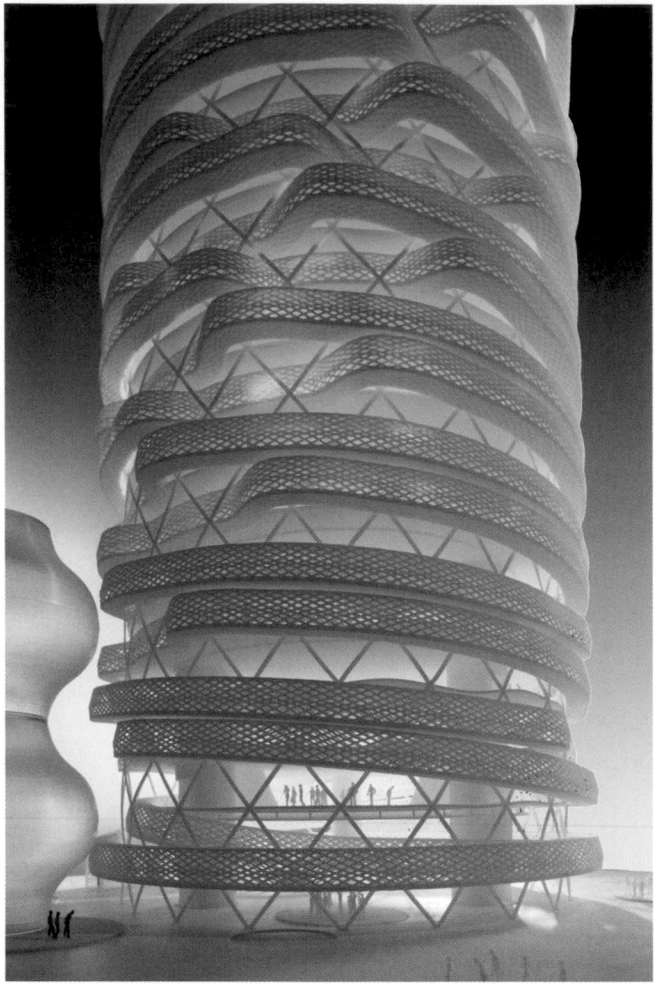

▲ 13.25 PETER TESTA AND DEVYN WEISER, TESTA ARCHITECTURE AND DESIGN, Carbon Tower.

stronger than the traditional steel. The "woven building" would have an interior that is completely open (except for elevator shafts) and void of structural support.

Green Buildings

Green is the color associated with energy efficiency and environmental awareness. The clients of many architects seek the design of "green buildings" today to save money, to protect the environment, or, sometimes, to boost a corporate image. Green buildings are efficient in terms of energy, water, and materials. They are constructed with products that do not emit harmful gases, thereby contributing to the quality of the air indoors as well as exhausting few heat-trapping gases into the environment. Sometimes the siting of a building makes it greener. For example, if it is built near efficient public transportation, residents and tenants are less likely to drive home or to work and emit greenhouse gases.

There are simple measures, such as using well-sealed and insulated glass windows. Light-colored roofs reflect heat from the sun in warm climates; dark-covered roofs trap heat from the sun in cold climates. A house can be built with pine trees on the north side to protect against icy winds, and deciduous trees (for example, oaks and

Massachusetts Institute of Technology campus, stands as a visual summation of his designs, materials, and theories of spatial relationships. The 730,000-square-foot complex is a hub for research in the fields of computer science, linguistics, and philosophy. The assertive clashing of shapes signifies the disparate disciplines that are housed in the structure, while communal lounges and shared interior spaces encourage interaction, collaboration, and the cross-fertilization of ideas. Gehry said of the Stata Center: "It reflects the different groups, the collision of ideas, the energy of people and ideas.... That's what will lead to the breakthroughs and the positive results."

Architect Peter Testa's view is that there is a "need to rethink how we assemble buildings" and that it is time to design in collaboration with materials manufacturers and to explore the potential of nascent technologies. Testa and his partner, Devyn Weiser, have designed a high-rise tower out of composite materials (Fig. 13.25). Their skyscraper would be held erect by a cross-hatched lattice made of carbon fiber—a material several times

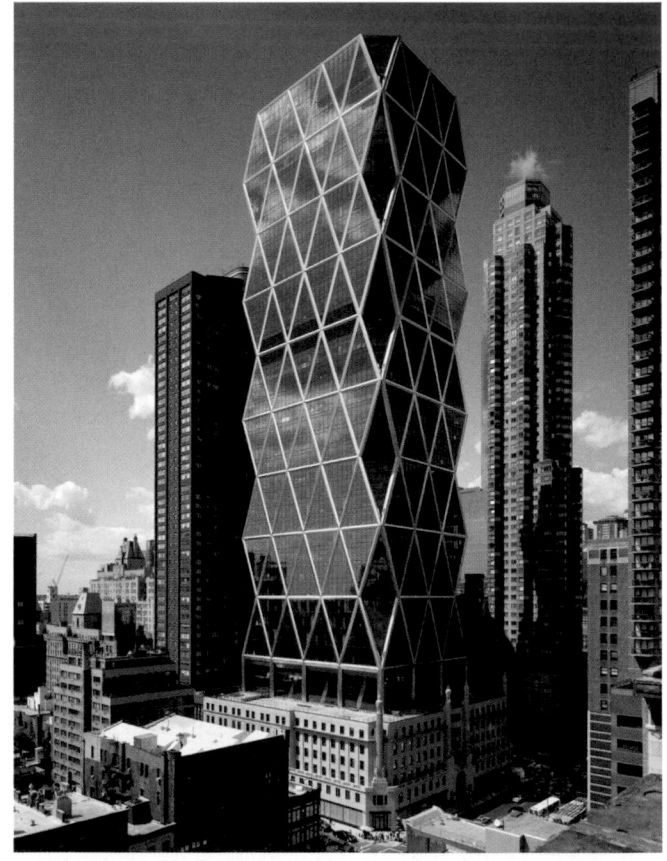

▲ 13.26 SIR NORMAN FOSTER, Hearst Tower, New York, New York (2004).

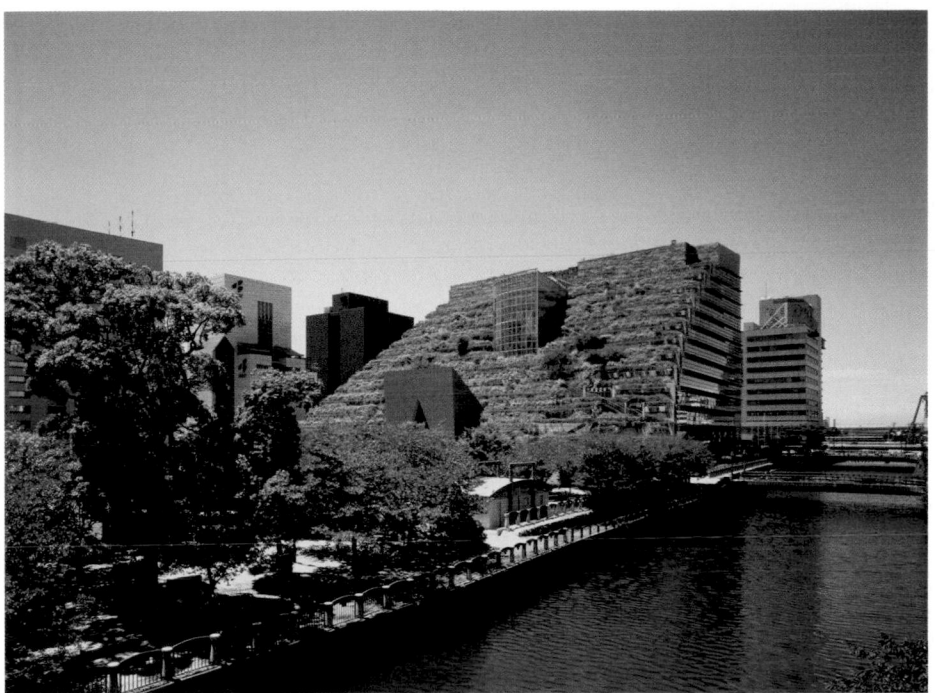

△ 13.27 EMILIO AMBASZ & ASSOCIATES, Fukuoka Prefectural International Hall, Fukuoka, Japan (1994).

in the city center of Fukuoka, so the architects, Emilio Ambrasz & Associates, managed to conserve the green space even as they added an office building with an exhibition hall, a museum, a theater that seats 2,000 people, conferences facilities, 600,000 square feet of private and government offices, along with retail shops and underground parking. One side has the appearance of a conventional steel and glass office tower, but the other side consists of a huge terraced roof that descends to a park. The terracing contains some 35,000 plants. The green roof reduces the building's energy consumption by insulating it from the elements outside. The green roof captures rainwater, as does the roof of the Hearst Tower, and in this case supports birds as well as plant life.

maples) to the south. The trees that are heavy with leaves in summer shade the house but let light through in winter when the branches are bare. Digging a well to water the lawn or fill the swimming pool saves city or town water, even though one might not want to drink it. Using Energy Star appliances decreases the fossil fuels required to make them run. Solar panels on the roof are costly initially, but they save on electrical costs year after year.

Green buildings are not necessarily the color green. The Hearst Tower (Fig. 13.26), designed by Sir Norman Foster, began by conserving the façade of the 1928 stone structure upon which it was built. It is credited with being Manhattan's first green office skyscraper. Walls are coated with vapor-free paint. Floors are made of wood from sustainable forests. About 85 percent of the steel in the building was recycled. Rain is collected on the roof and stored in a basement tank, used in the building's cooling system and to water plants in the ten-story atrium. The glass is treated to emit low amounts of radiation (in the form of heat). Although the tower is sealed, it draws in air, weather permitting, to boost the efficiency of the heating and cooling system. Sensors determine the amount of natural light entering the building and adjust the lighting fixtures accordingly. The building uses 26 percent less energy than the amount deemed desirable by the city and was certified by the LEED (leadership in environmental energy design) program of the U.S. Green Building Council.

Some green buildings are actually green, as is the Fukuoka Prefectural International Hall (Fig. 13.27). The building was constructed on the last green space

URBAN DESIGN

Perhaps it is in urban design that our desire for order and harmony achieves its most majestic expression. Throughout history, most towns and cities have more or less sprung up. They have pushed back the countryside in all directions, as necessary, with little evidence of an overall guiding concept. As a result, the masses of great buildings sometimes press against other masses of great buildings, and transportation becomes a worrisome afterthought. The Rome of the early Republic, for example, was an impoverished seat of empire, little more than a disordered assemblage of seven villages on seven hills. Later, the downtown area was a jumble of narrow streets winding through mud-brick buildings. Not until the first century BCE were the major building programs undertaken by Sulla and then the Caesars.

The new towns of the Roman Empire were laid out largely on a rectangular grid. This pattern was common among centrist states, where bits of land were parceled out to the subjects of mighty rulers. The gridiron was also found to be a useful basis for design throughout history—from the ancient Greeks to the colonial Americans. Many cities of the Near and Middle East, such as Baghdad, have a circular tradition in urban design, which may reflect the belief that they were the hubs of the universe. The throne room of the palace in eighth-century Baghdad was at the center of the circle. The palace—including attendant buildings, a game preserve, and pavilions set in perfumed gardens—was more than a mile in diameter, and the remainder of the population occupied a relatively narrow ring around the palace.

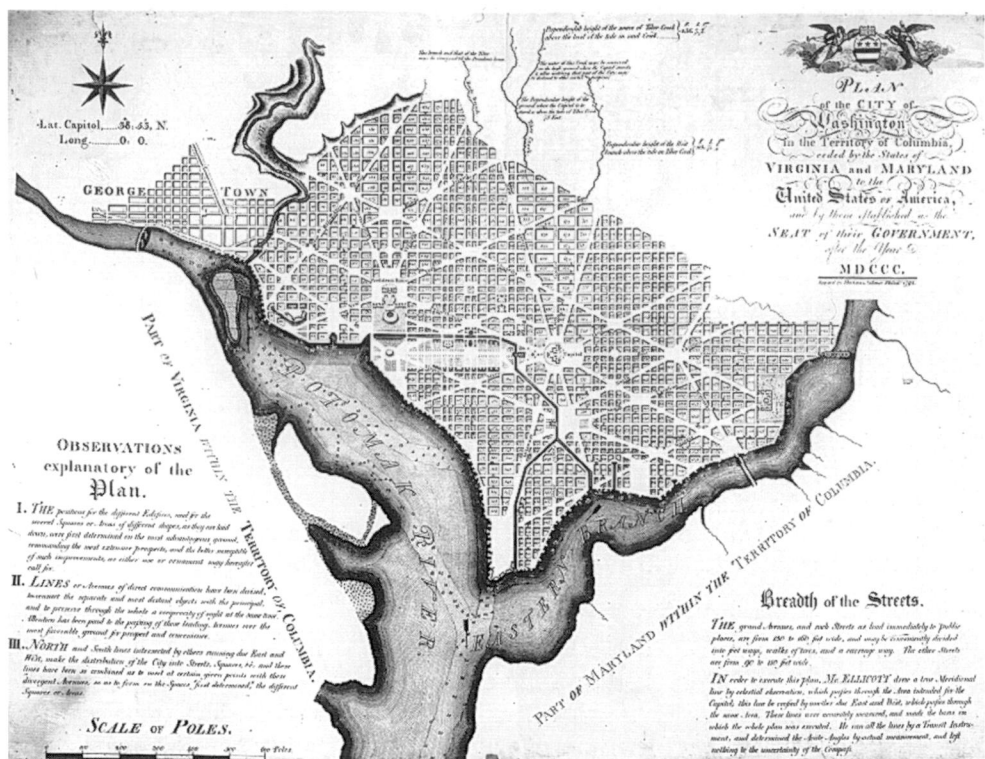

Washington, D.C.

Few urban designs are as simple and rich as Pierre Charles L'Enfant's plan for Washington, D.C. (Fig. 13.28). The city is cradled between two branches of the Potomac River, yielding an uneven, overall diamond shape. Within the diamond, a rectangular grid of streets that run east-west and north-south was laid down. Near the center of the diamond, with its west edge at the river, an enormous Mall or green space was set aside. At the east end of the Mall is the Capitol Building. To the north, at its west end, is the president's house (which is now the White House). Broad boulevards radiate from the Capitol and from the White House, cutting across the gridiron. One radiating boulevard runs directly between the Capitol and the White House, and other boulevards parallel it.

The design is a composition in which the masses of the Capitol Building and White House balance one another, and the rhythms of the gridiron pattern and intersecting diagonal boulevards create contrast and unity. The Mall provides an open central gathering place that is as much a part of American culture as it is respite from the congestion of the city.

See more of Washington, D.C., in the online Art Tour.

Paris—Les Halles

L'Enfant's plan for Washington, D.C., was inspired by the art and architecture of Neoclassical France. Today, a visitor to both cities will note that avenues and grand boulevards culminate in monuments that punctuate the end of a long vista. Paris is often called the most beautiful city in the world, a title achieved after massive renovations to the city plan by Raoul Haussmann in the nineteenth century. Then, as now, Paris was not without its pockets of urban problems requiring creative and politically sensitive solutions. The Parisian area of Les Halles has long been home to park and commercial spaces as well as a major transit hub. Architect Rem Koolhaas and his firm, OMA, submitted a design to bring together and make transparent to the surrounding neighborhood all the disparate parts of Les Halles (Fig. 13.29). Shape and color dominate the plan, with circular gardens and luminous towers rising above the city's infrastructure. With this design, the dark, discontinuous, and chaotic environs of the old Les Halles would have been transformed through an innovative and practical urban design, into a signature city monument as innovative as the new glass pyramid in the courtyard of the Louvre. Unfortunately, Koolhaas's design is apparently destined to remain within the imagination of the architect.

Alexandria, Egypt

Alexandria, the ancient center of the Western cultural world, is now a city of 4 million. It was founded around 331 BCE by Alexander the Great. Its lighthouse, a hallowed beacon on the Mediterranean Sea, now gone, was one of the Seven Wonders of the Ancient World. Its library, built by the Greeks and accidentally burned down by Julius Caesar in 48 BCE, was the largest in the world.

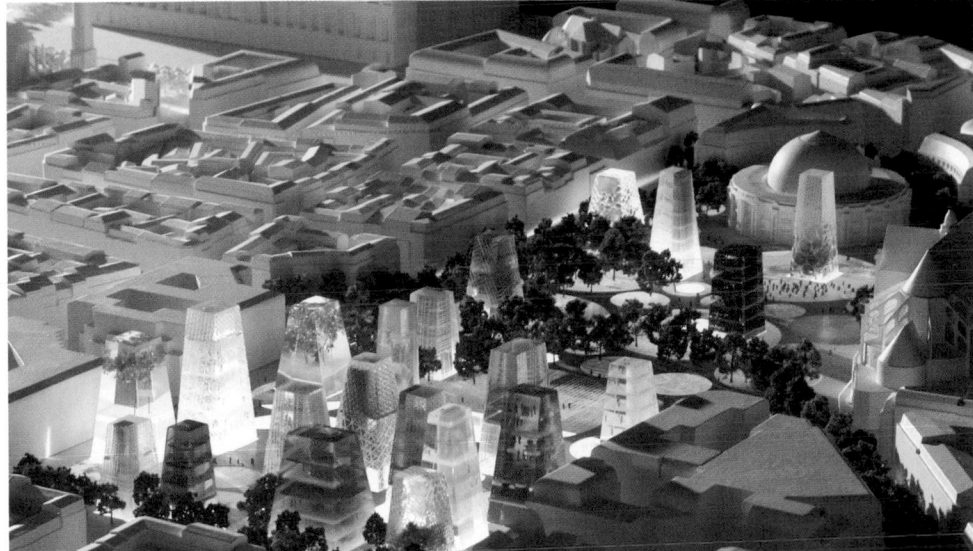

Alexandria was also a major center of shipping because of its overland proximity to the Red Sea, but with the building of the Suez Canal, completed in 1869, the city's importance as a transportation hub was diminished. The historic library has been replaced with the Bibliotheca Alexandrina, completed in 2002 at a cost of $220 million, but the once-beautiful harbor itself has remained underused and somewhat in decay.

The Master Plan by Skidmore, Owings, and Merrill (Fig. 13.30) is intended to bring new life to the Eastern Harbor and to help reestablish the city as a leading cultural center. New museums, cultural facilities, and hotels are intended to serve as magnets for the tourism industry. The design connects the harbor to various city districts via new rail lines and green pedestrian walk ways, while sidewalks and tunnels lead to underwater archeological sites. In the plan, beaches are expanded and passenger boat terminals will be constructed. One of the design's most striking elements—a new breakwater— will improve the quality of the water in the city. What time and history have torn away, urban design can perhaps create anew.

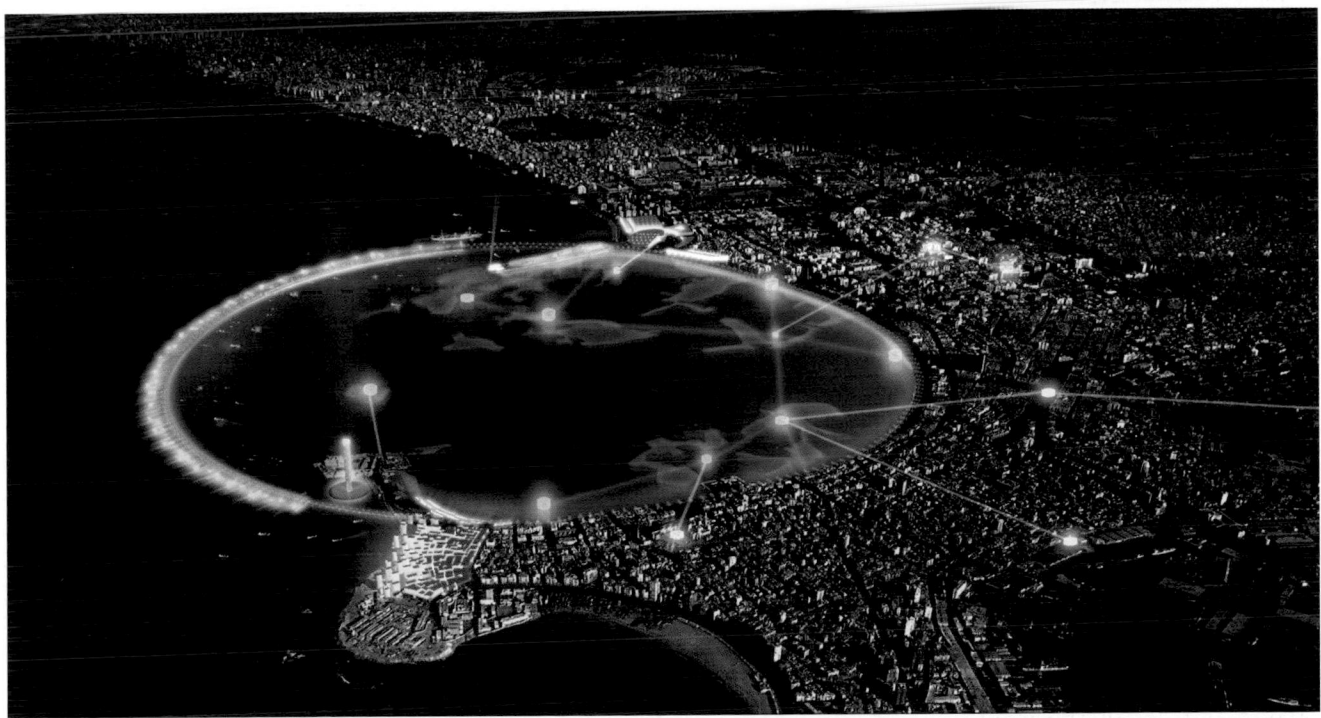

∧ 13.30 Rendering of the framework plan for Alexandria, Egypt, to complete the historic Eastern Harbor.

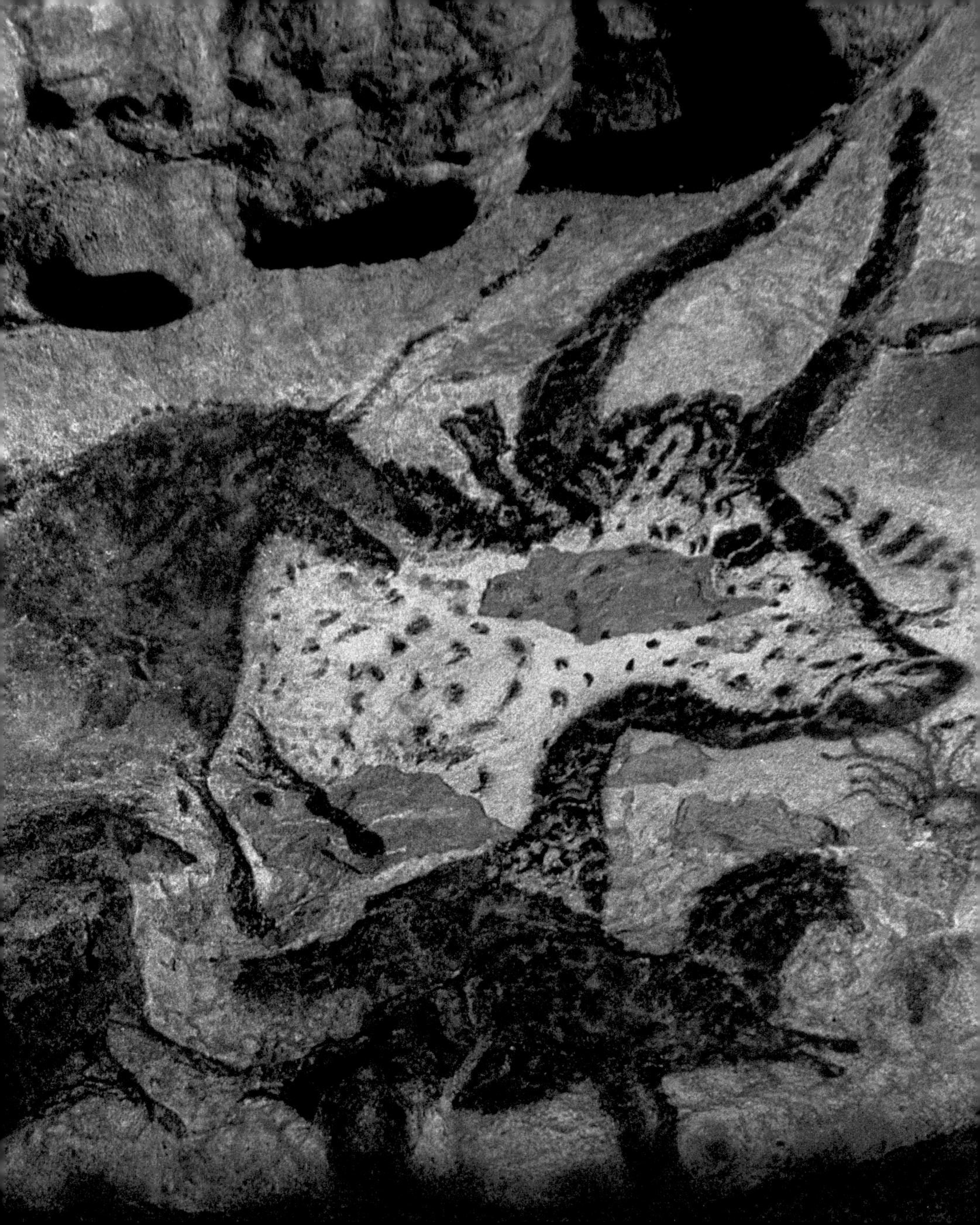

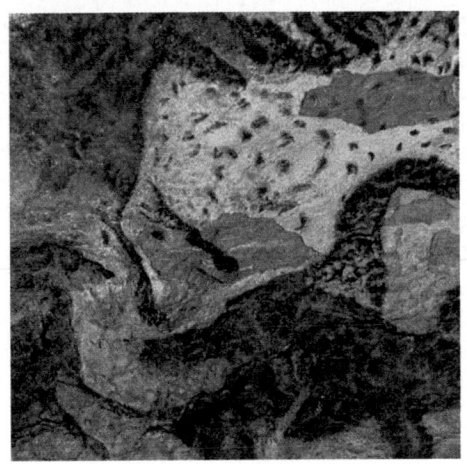

14

ART OF THE ANCIENT WORLD

Art is exalted above religion and race. Not a single solitary soul these days believes in the religion of the Assyrians, the Egyptians, or the Greeks. . . . Only their art, whenever it was beautiful, stands proud and exalted, rising above all time.

— EMIL NOLDE

THE TERM *Stone Age* often conjures an image of men and women dressed in skins, huddling before a fire in a cave, while the world around them—the elements and the animals—threatens their survival. We do not generally envision prehistoric humankind as intelligent and reflective; as having needs beyond food, shelter, and reproduction; as performing religious rituals; or as creating art objects. Yet these aspects of life were perhaps as essential to their survival as warmth, nourishment, and progeny.

As the Stone Age progressed from the Paleolithic to the Neolithic periods, humans began to lead more stable lives. They settled in villages and shifted from hunting wild animals and gathering food to herding domesticated animals and farming. They also fashioned tools of stone and bone and created pottery and woven textiles. Most important for our purposes, they became image makers, capturing forms and figures on cave walls with the use of primitive artistic implements.

Archaeological exploration of Stone Age sites in France and Spain reveals the existence of shelters, tools, and an impressive array of sculptures and paintings in which humans and animals are represented. The sheer quantity of these art objects, although they are not works of art by the usual definition, would suggest a principal role for images and symbols in the struggle for human survival. As with much ancient art, we cannot know for certain what the reasons were for creating these works. But evidence suggests that Stone Age people forged links between religion and life, life and art, and art and religion. They faced intimidating and unknown forces in their confrontation with nature. Perhaps their "art" was an attempt to record and to control.

◄ Hall of Bulls in the cave at Lascaux, France (c. 16,000–14,000 BCE).

PREHISTORIC ART

Prehistoric art is divided into three phases that correspond to the periods of Stone Age culture: **Paleolithic** (the late years of the Old Stone Age), **Mesolithic** (Middle Stone Age), and **Neolithic** (New Stone Age). These periods span roughly the years 30,000 BCE to 2000 BCE.

Works of art from the Stone Age include cave paintings, reliefs, and sculpture of stone, ivory, and bone. The subjects consist mainly of animals, although some abstract human figures have been found. There is no surviving architecture as such. Many Stone Age dwellings consisted of caves and rock shelters. Some impressive monuments such as Stonehenge exist, but their functions remain a mystery.

Paleolithic Art

Paleolithic art is the art of the last Ice Age, during which time glaciers covered large areas of northern Europe and North America. As the climate got colder, people retreated into the protective warmth of caves, and it is here that we find their first attempts at artistic creation.

The great cave paintings of the Stone Age were discovered by accident in northern Spain and southwestern France. At Lascaux, France (Map 14.1), two boys whose dog chased a ball into a hole followed the animal and discovered beautiful paintings of bison, horses, and cattle that are estimated to be more than 15,000 years old. At first, because of the crispness and realistic detail of the paintings, they were thought to be forgeries. But in time, geological methods proved their authenticity.

One of the most splendid examples of Stone Age painting, the so-called Hall of Bulls (Fig. 14.1), is found in a cave at Lascaux. Here, superimposed upon one another, are realistic images of horses, bulls, and reindeer that appear to be stampeding in all directions. With one glance, we can understand the early skepticism concerning their authenticity. So fresh, lively, and purely sketched are the forms that they seem to have been rendered yesterday.

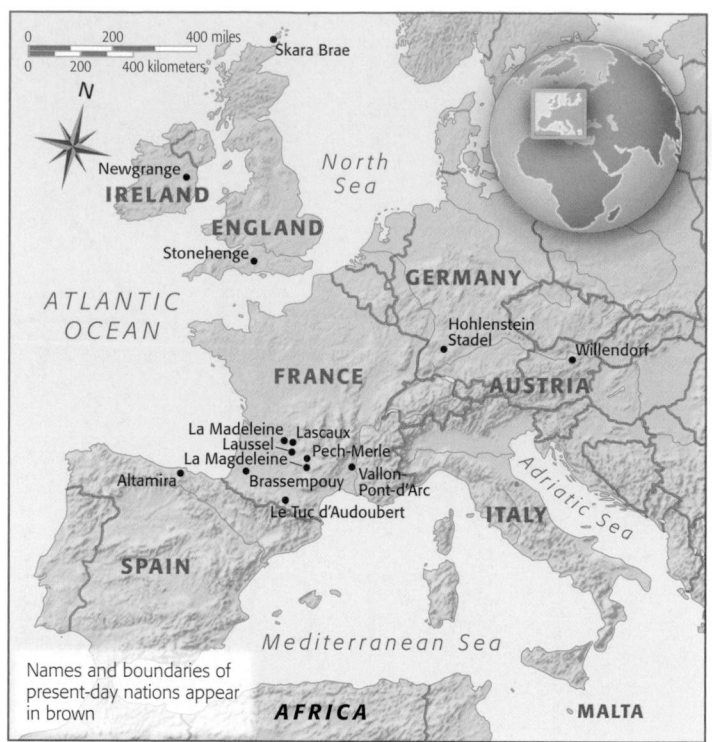

▲ **MAP 14.1** Prehistoric Europe.

In their attempt at **naturalism**, the artists captured the images of the beasts by first confidently outlining the contours of their bodies. They then filled in these dark outlines with details and colored them with shades of ocher and red. The artists seem to have used a variety of techniques ranging from drawing with chunks of raw pigment to applying pigment with fingers and sticks. They also seem to have used an early "spray painting" technique in which dried, ground pigments were blown through a hollowed-out bone or reed. Although the tools were primitive, the techniques and results were not. They used **foreshortening** and contrasts of light and shadow to create the illusion of three-dimensional forms. They strove to achieve a most convincing likeness of the animal.

BEFORE HISTORY

30,000 BCE	8000 BCE	2000 BCE
PALEOLITHIC PERIOD (OLD STONE AGE)	**NEOLITHIC PERIOD (NEW STONE AGE)**	
Humans create paintings and reliefs on cave walls and carve small figurines	Settled communities formed	
Hunting provides the main food source	Agriculture begins; animals domesticated	
Tools and weapons made of stone	Pottery made and used by farmers	
	Stonehenge erected about 4000 BCE	
	Metal tools and weaponry created	
	Written language created	

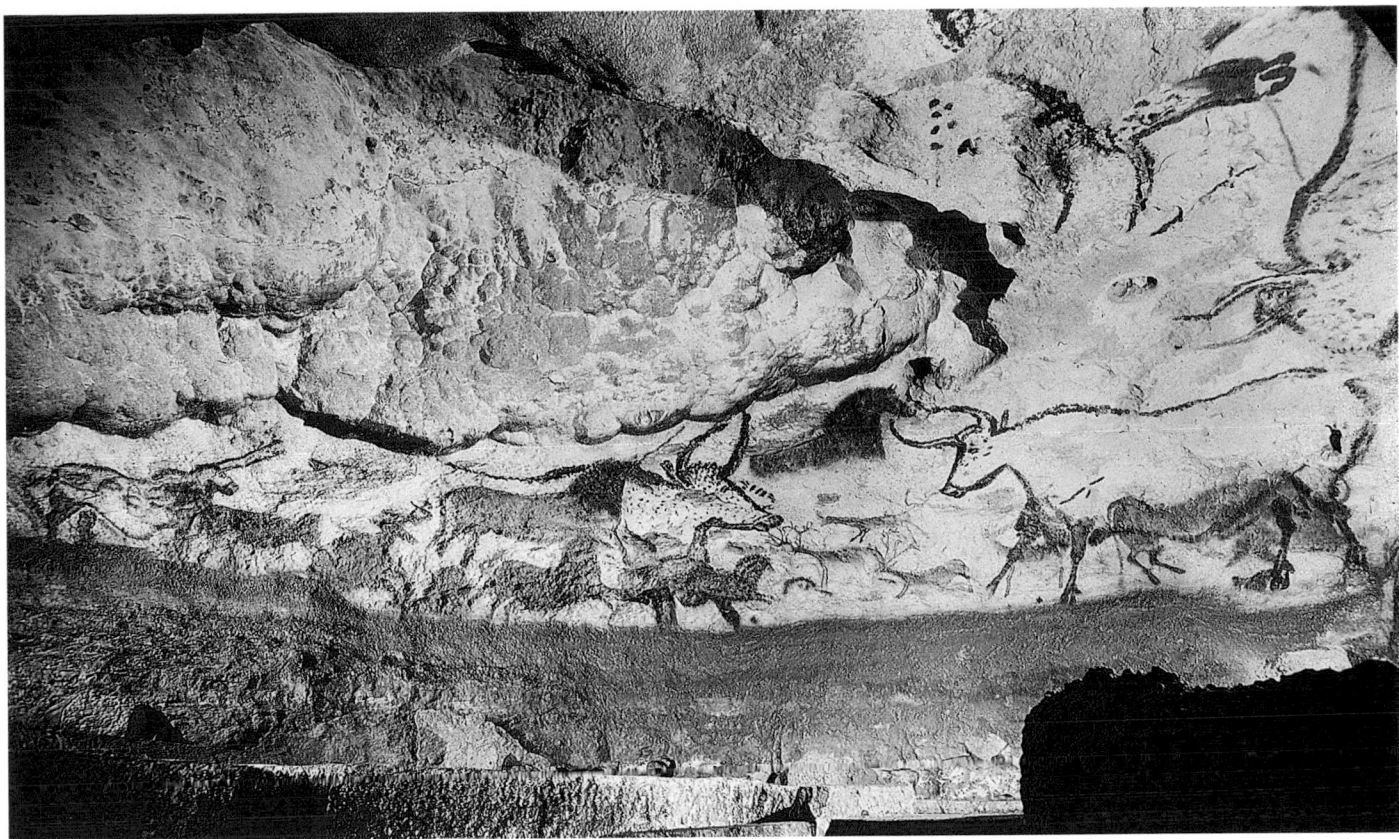

∧ 14.1 **Hall of Bulls in the cave at Lascaux, France** (c. 16,000–14,000 BCE).

Why did prehistoric people sketch these forms? Did they create these murals out of a desire to delight the eye, or did they have other reasons? We cannot know for certain. However, it is unlikely that the paintings were merely ornamental, because they were confined to the deepest recesses of the cave, far from the areas that were inhabited, and were not easily reached. Also, new figures were painted over earlier ones with no apparent regard for composition. It is believed that successive artists added to the drawings, respecting the sacredness of the figures that already existed. It is further believed that the paintings covered the walls and ceilings of a kind of inner sanctuary where religious rituals concerning the capture of prey were performed. Some have suggested that by "capturing" these animals in art, Stone Age hunters believed that they would be guaranteed success in capturing them in life. This theory, as others, is unproven.

Prehistoric artists also created sculptures called **Venuses** by the archeologists who discovered them. The most famous is the Venus of Willendorf (Fig. 14.2), named after the site at which it was unearthed. The tiny figurine

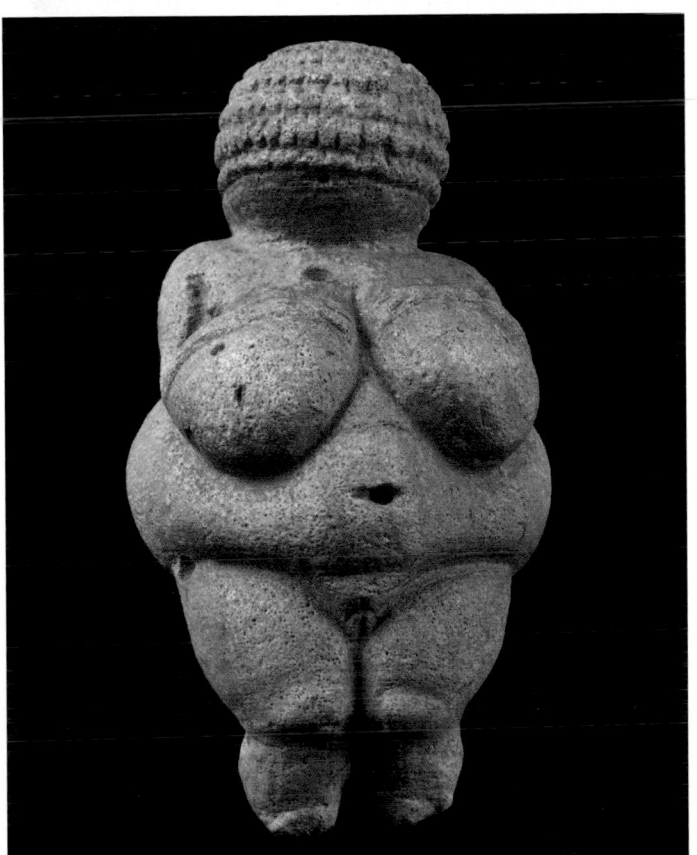

> 14.2 *Nude woman (Venus of Willendorf)* (c. 28,000–25000 BCE). Stone, 4⅜" high. Naturhistorisches Museum, Vienna, Austria.

1 in.

is carved of stone and is just over 4 inches high. As with all sculptures of this type, the female form is highly abstracted, and the emphasis is placed on the anatomical parts associated with fertility: the oversized breasts, round abdomen, and enlarged hips. Other parts of the body, like the thin arms resting on the breasts, are subordinated to those involved in reproduction. Does this difference in scale suggest a concern for survival of the species? Or was this figure of a fertile woman created and carried around as a talisman for fertility of the earth itself—abundance in the food supply? In either or any other case, people created their images, and perhaps their religion, as a way of coping with these concerns.

Neolithic Art

During the New Stone Age, life became more stable and predictable. People domesticated plants and animals, and food production supplanted food gathering. Toward the end of the Neolithic period in some areas, crops such as maize, squash, and beans were cultivated, metal implements were fashioned, and writing appeared. About 4000 BCE, significant architectural monuments were erected.

The most famous of these monuments is Stonehenge (Fig. 14.3) in southern England. It consists of two concentric rings of stones surrounding others placed in a horseshoe shape. Some of these **megaliths** (from the

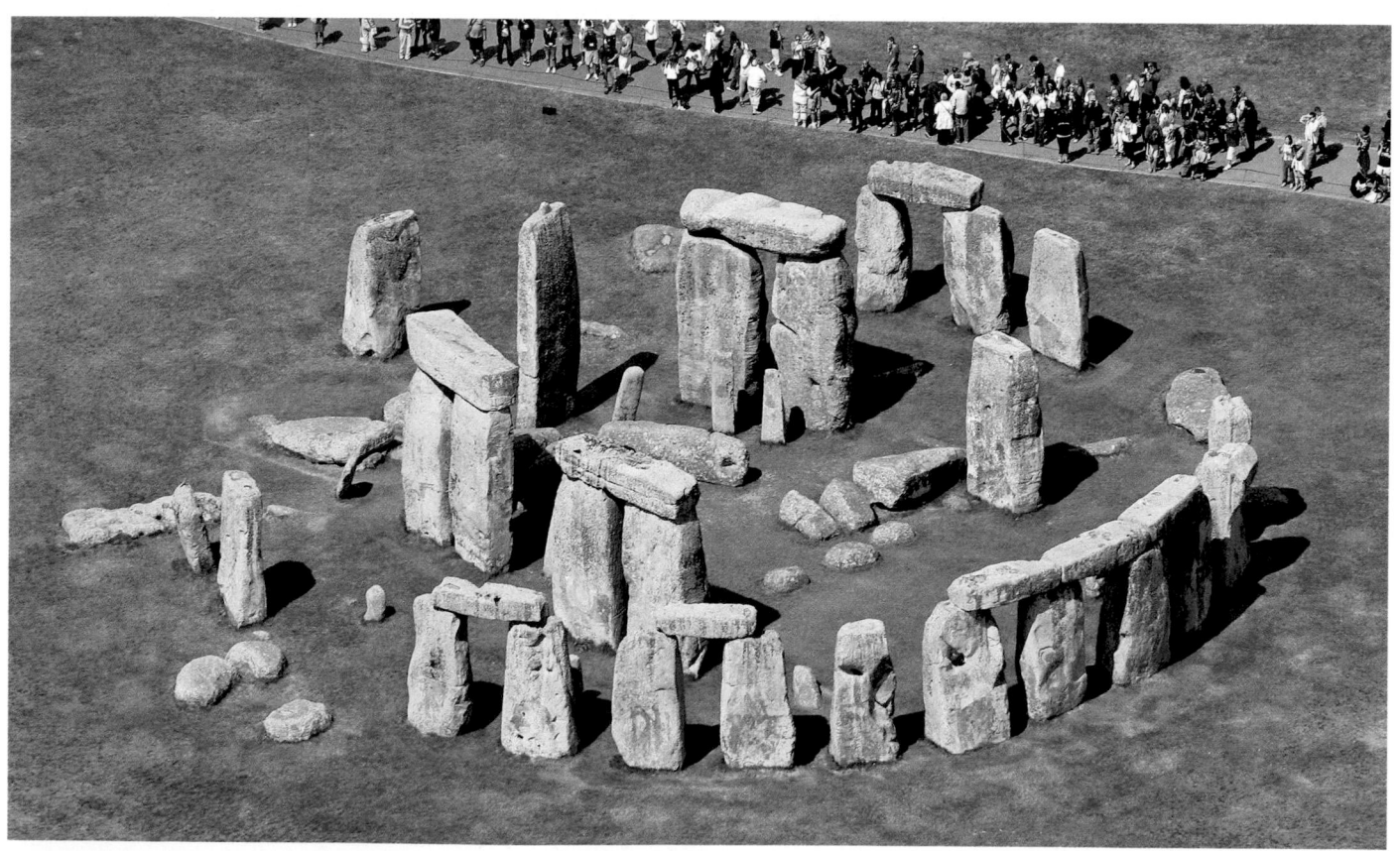

∧ **14.3 Stonehenge, Salisbury Plain, Wiltshire, England** (c. 2550–1600 BCE). Diameter of circle: 97'. Height of stones aboveground: approximately 24'.

Greek, meaning "large stones") weigh several tons. The purpose of Stonehenge remains a mystery. At one time it was believed to have been a druid temple, or the work of Merlin, King Arthur's magician. Lately, some astronomers have suggested that the monument served as a complex calendar that charted the movements of the sun and moon, as well as eclipses. Whatever the meaning or function, the fact that it was undertaken at all is perhaps its most fascinating aspect.

The Neolithic period began about 8000 BCE and spread throughout the world's major river valleys between 6000 and 2000 BCE—the Nile in Egypt, the Tigris and Euphrates in Mesopotamia, the Indus in India, and the Yellow in China. In the next section, we examine the birth of the great Mesopotamian civilizations.

MESOPOTAMIA

Historic (as opposed to prehistoric) societies are marked by a written language, advanced social organization, and developments in the areas of government, science, and art. They are also often linked with the development of agriculture. Historic civilizations began toward the end of the Neolithic period. In this section, we will discuss the art of the Mesopotamian civilizations of Sumer, Akkad, Babylonia, Assyria, and Persia. We will begin with Sumer, which flourished in the river valley of the Tigris and Euphrates about 3000 BCE.

Sumer

The Tigris and Euphrates Rivers flow through what is now Syria and Iraq, join in their southernmost section, and empty into the Persian Gulf (Map 14.2). The major civilizations of ancient Mesopotamia lay along one or the other of these rivers, and the first to rise to prominence was Sumer.

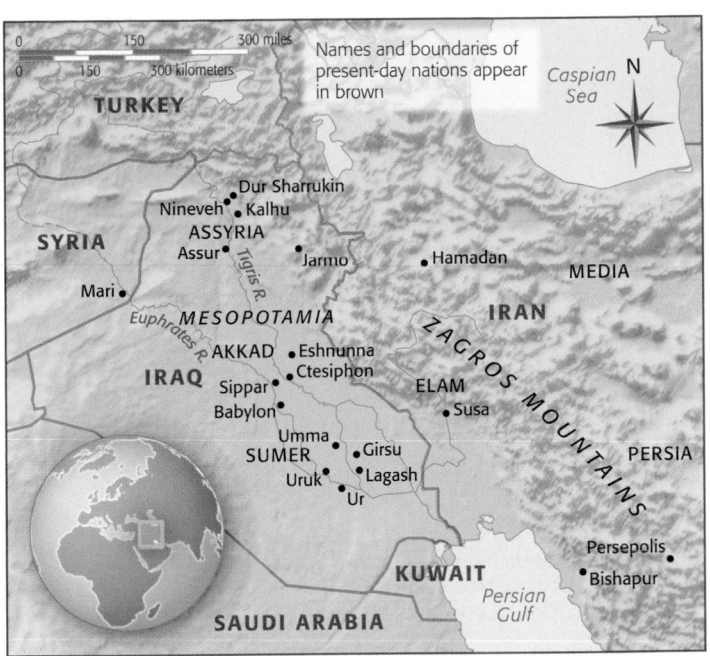

▲ MAP 14.2 The Ancient Near East.

Sumer was located in the Euphrates River Valley in southern Mesopotamia. The origin of its people is unknown, although they may have come from Iran or India. The earliest Sumerian villages date to prehistoric times. By about 3000 BCE, however, there was a thriving agricultural civilization in Sumer. The Sumerians constructed sophisticated irrigation systems, controlled river flooding, and worked with metals such as copper, silver, and gold. They had a government based on independently ruled city-states, and they developed a system of writing called **cuneiform**, from the Latin *cuneus*, meaning "wedge"; the characters in cuneiform writing are wedge shaped.

Excavations at major Sumerian cities have revealed sculpture, craft art, and monumental architecture that seems to have been created for worship. Thus, the

MESOPOTAMIA

3500 BCE	2332 BCE	2150 BCE	900 BCE	600 BCE	330 BCE
SUMER	**AKKAD**	**BABYLON**	**ASSYRIA**	**PERSIA**	
Cuneiform writing developed	Sargon unifies Mesopotamia	Akkadian empire collapses	Assyrians conquer Babylon and control Mesopotamia from about 900 to 600 BCE	Reign of Cyrus the Great and expansion of Persian Empire	
Society religion-based	Akkadian is spoken throughout the region	Mesopotamia is reunited by Hammurabi	Assyrian kings build fortified and lavishly decorated palaces	Greeks defeat Persians at Salamis in 480 BCE	
First ziggurats and shrines constructed	Akkadian art commemorates rulers and warriors	Code of law inscribed on Stele of Hammurabi		Egypt falls to Persia	

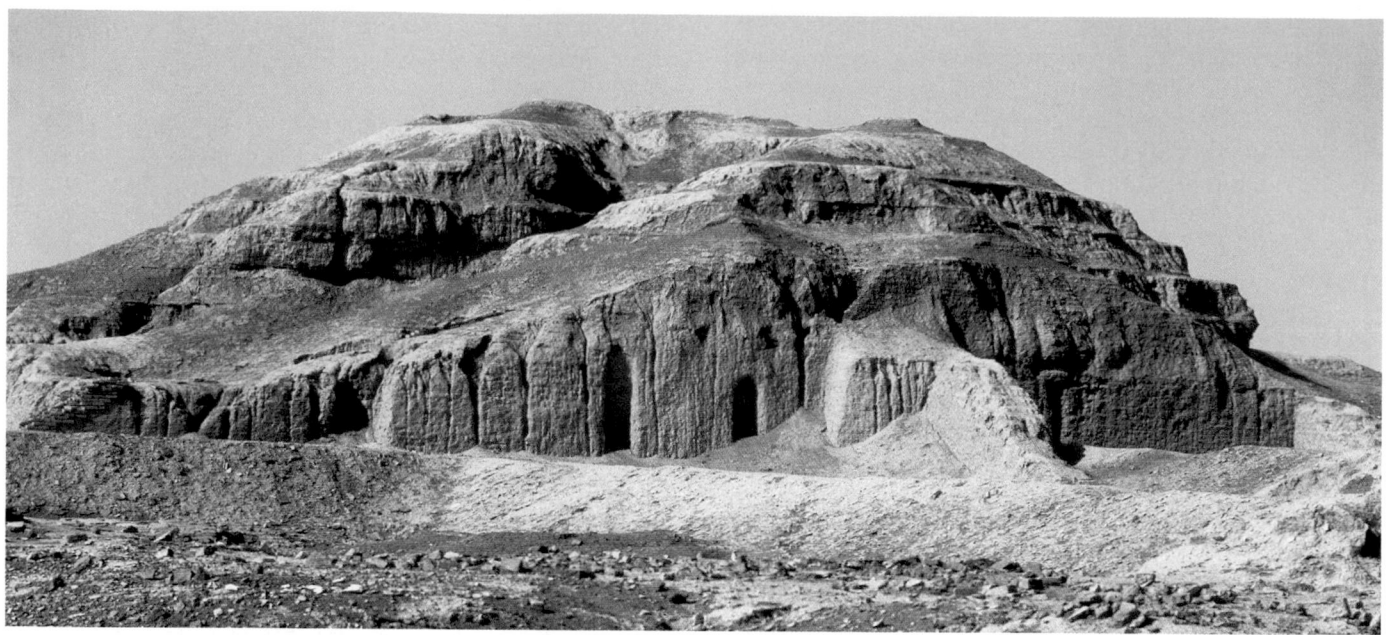

∧ 14.4A **White Temple at Uruk, Iraq** (c. 3200–3000 BCE). Sun-dried brick.

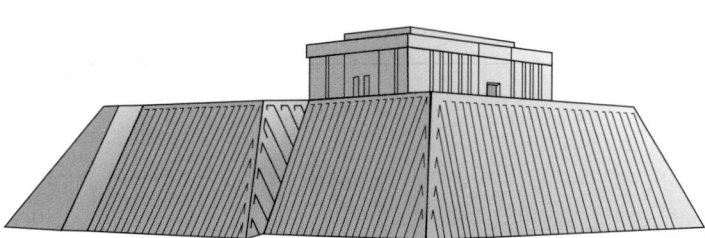

∧ 14.4B Reconstruction View of the White Temple at Uruk, Iraq.

Sumerian people may have been among the first to establish a formal religion.

One of the most impressive testimonies to the Sumerians' religion-based society is the **ziggurat**, a monumental platform for a temple also seen in the Babylonian and Assyrian civilizations of later years. The ziggurat was the focal point of the Sumerian city, towering high above the fields and dwellings. Typically, the ziggurat was a multilevel structure consisting of a core of sunbaked mud bricks faced with fired brick, sometimes bright in color. Access to the **temple**, on the uppermost level of the ziggurat, was gained by stairs or a series of ramps leading from one level to the next, or in some cases, by a spiral ramp that rose continuously from ground to summit.

The White Temple at Uruk (Fig. 14.4A and 14.4B) and ziggurat, so called because of its white-washed walls, are among the earliest and best preserved in the region. The ziggurat, the corners of which are oriented toward the compass points, is some 40 feet high but pales in comparison to the scale of later ziggurats. The ziggurat known

to the Hebrews as the Tower of Babel, a symbol of mortal pride, was some 270 feet high.

The Sumerian gods were primarily deifications of nature. Anu was the god of the sky, Nannu the god of the moon, and Abu the god of vegetation. Votive sculptures found beneath the floor of a temple to Abu in Tell Asmar (Fig. 14.5) reinforce the essential role of religion in Sumerian society. These works functioned as stand-ins, as it were, for donor-worshipers who, in their absence, wished to continue to offer prayers to a specific deity. They range in height from less than 12 inches to more than 30 inches and are carved from gypsum with alert inlaid eyes of shell and black limestone. The figures are cylindrical, and all stand erect with hands clasped at their chests around now-missing flasks. Distinctions are made between males and females. The men have long, stylized beards and hair and wear knee-length skirts decorated with incised lines describing a fringe at the hem. The women wear dresses with one shoulder bared and the other draped with a shawl. These sculptures are gypsum, a soft mineral found in rock. The Sumerians, however, worked primarily in clay because of its abundance. They were expert ceramists and, as we have seen, were capable of building monumental structures with brick, while their Egyptian contemporaries were using stone. It is believed that the Sumerians traded crops for metal, wood, and stone and used these materials to enlarge their repertory of art objects.

The Sumerian repertory of subjects included fantastic creatures such as music-making animals, bearded bulls, and composite man-beasts with bull heads or scorpion bodies. These were depicted in lavishly decorated objects of hammered gold inlaid with **lapis lazuli**. Found among present, they are coupled with a naturalism that was absent from Sumerian art.

Of the little extant Akkadian art, the *Victory Stele of Naram Sin* (Fig. 14.6) shines as one of the most significant works. This relief sculpture commemorates the military exploits of Sargon's grandson and successor, Naram Sin. The king, represented considerably larger in scale than the other figures, ascends a mountain, trampling his enemies underfoot. He is accompanied by a group of marching soldiers, spears erect, whose positions contrast strongly with those of the fallen enemy. One wrestles to pull a spear out of his neck, another pleads for mercy, and another falls headfirst off the mountain. The chaos on the right side of the composition is opposed by the rigid advancement on the left. All takes place under the watchful celestial bodies of Ishtar and Shamash, the gods of fertility and justice.

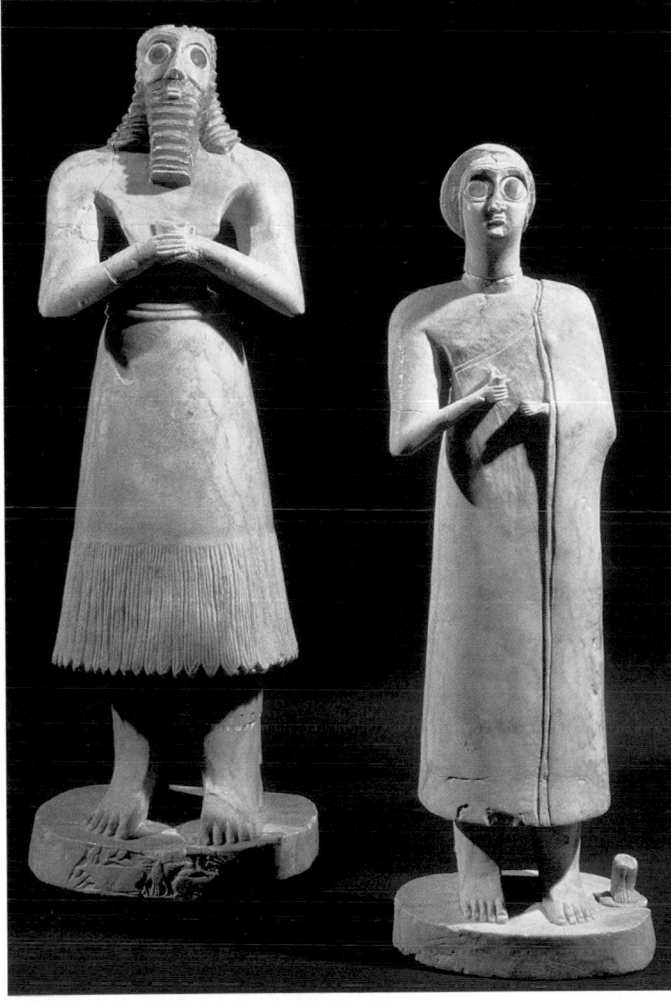

∧ 14.5 **Statues from Abu Temple, Tell Asmar, Iraq** (c. 2700 BCE). Gypsum with shell and black limestone inlay. Height of tallest figures: 30".

the remains of Sumerian royal tombs, they are believed by some scholars to have been linked to funerary rituals.

For a long time, the Sumerians were the principal force in Mesopotamia, but they were not alone. Semitic peoples to the north became increasingly strong, and eventually they established an empire that ruled all of Mesopotamia and assimilated the Sumerian culture.

Akkad

Akkad, located north of Sumer, centered around the valley of the Tigris River. Its government, too, was based on independent city-states, which, along with those of Sumer, eventually came under the influence of the Akkadian ruler Sargon. Under Sargon and his successors, the civilization of Akkad flourished.

Akkadian art exhibits distinct differences from that of Sumer. It commemorates rulers and warriors instead of offering homage to the gods. It is an art of violence instead of prayer. Also, although artistic conventions are

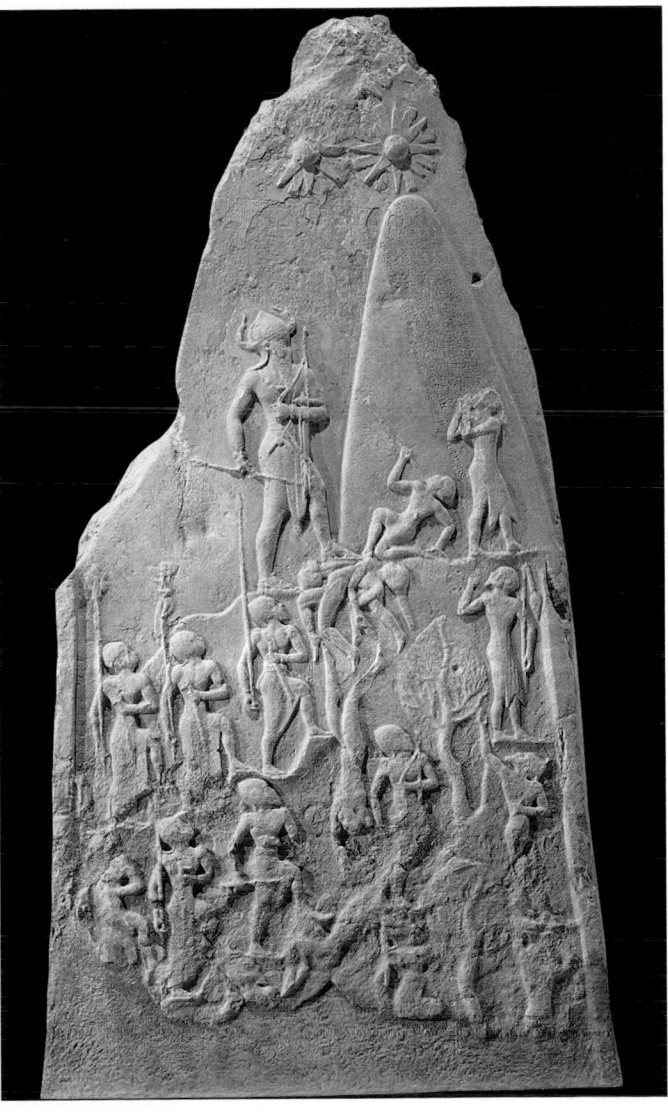

∧ 14.6 *Victory Stele of Naram Sin* (c. 2254–2218 BCE). Stone, 6'6" high. Louvre Museum, Paris, France.

When Anu the Sublime, King of the Anunaki, and Bel, the lord of Heaven and earth, who decreed the fate of the land, assigned to Marduk, the over-ruling son of Ea, God of righteousness, dominion over earthly man, and made him great among the Igigi, they called Babylon by his illustrious name, made it great on earth, and founded an everlasting kingdom in it, whose foundations are laid so solidly as those of heaven and earth; then Anu and Bel called by name me, Hammurabi, the exalted prince, who feared God, to bring about the rule of righteousness in the land, to destroy the wicked and the evil-doers; so that the strong should not harm the weak; so that I should rule . . . and enlighten the land, to further the well-being of mankind.

—PREAMBLE TO HAMMURABI'S CODE OF LAWS, TRANSLATED BY L. W. KING

The king and his men are represented in a conceptual manner. That is, the artist rendered the human body in all of its parts as they are known to be, not as they appear at any given moment to the human eye. This method resulted in figures that are a combination of frontal and profile views. Naturalism was reserved for the enemy, whose figures fall in a variety of contorted positions. It may be that the convention of conceptual representation was maintained as a sign of respect. On the other hand, the conceptual manner complements the upright positions of the victorious, whereas the naturalism echoes the disintegration of the enemy camp.

The Akkadian Empire eventually declined, for reasons that are not clear. Historians have traditionally attributed its collapse to invading tribes. However, recent archeological research has led to the theory that it was not human violence that put an end to Akkadian supremacy but rather an unrelenting drought that gripped the region for 300 years. With the end of the drought, the Sumerians regained power for a while with a Neo-Sumerian state ruled by the kings of Ur, but they, too, were eventually overtaken by fierce warring tribes. Mesopotamia remained in a state of chaos until the rise of Babylon under the great lawmaker and ruler, Hammurabi.

Babylonia

During the eighteenth century BCE, the Babylonian Empire, under Hammurabi, rose to power and dominated Mesopotamia. Hammurabi's major contribution to civilization was

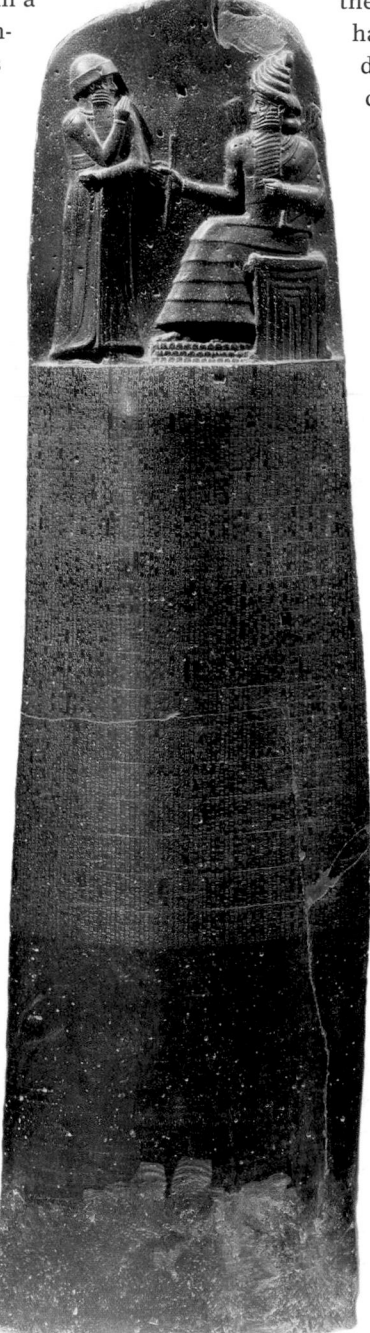

the codification of Mesopotamian laws. Laws had become cloudy and conflicting after the division of Mesopotamia into independent cities.

This code of law was inscribed on the Stele of Hammurabi (Fig. 14.7), a relief sculpture of **basalt** over 7 feet high. The lower portion of the stele is inscribed with the code itself, written in the Akkadian language with cuneiform characters. Above the code is a relief depicting Hammurabi and the sun god Shamash. Hammurabi gestures in respect and Shamash reciprocates by handing him a rod and ring, symbols of authority. The observer is led to believe, through this interaction, that Hammurabi's authority is god-given and thus not to be challenged. The sculptor of the stele engaged in some conventions for representation, combining frontal and profile views as we saw in the Stele of Naram Sin. However, in the Hammurabi stele, there are some new attempts at naturalism. The artist has turned the figure of Shamash toward the viewer a bit and has rendered the lines in his beard as diagonals (rather than strict horizontals, as in the Sumerian votive figures), suggesting an experiment in foreshortening.

After the death of Hammurabi, Mesopotamia was torn apart by invasions. It eventually came under the influence of the Assyrians, a warring people to the north who had had their eyes on the region for hundreds of years.

< **14.7 Stele inscribed with the Law Code of Hammurabi, from Susa** (c. 1780 BCE). Diorite, 7'4" high. Louvre Museum, Paris, France.

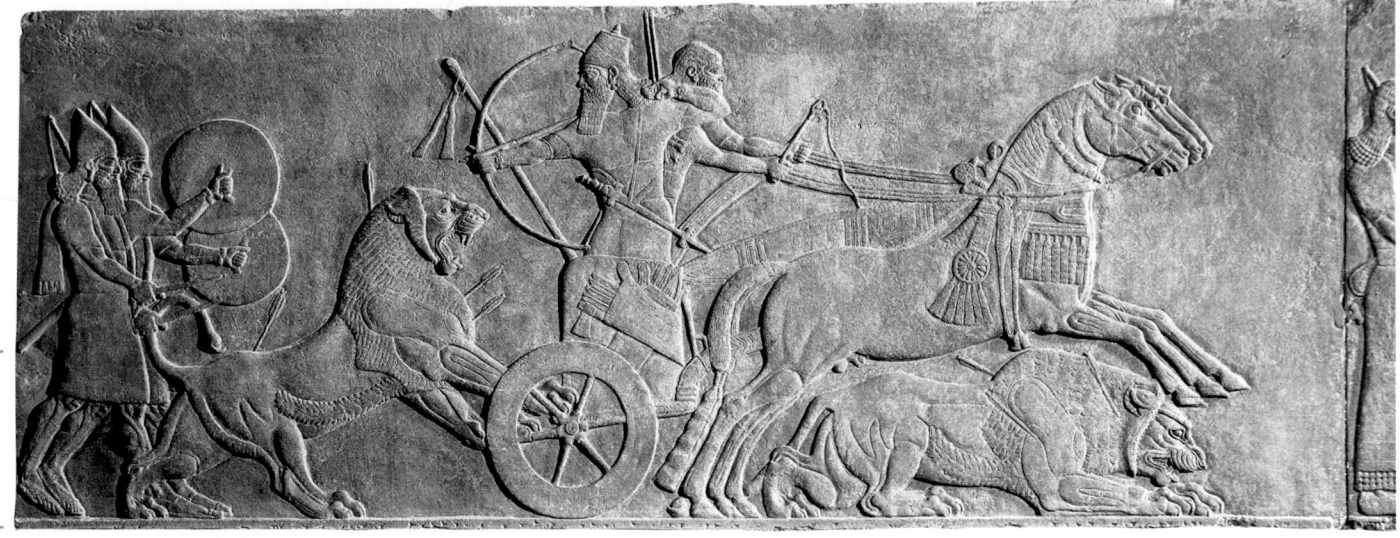

1 ft.

^ 14.8 **Ashurnasirpal II hunting lions** (645–640 BCE). Palace of Ashurnasirpal II, Nimrud, Iraq. Panel 19, alabaster relief; 88" × 35". British Museum, London, United Kingdom.

Assyria

The ancient empire of Assyria developed along the upper Tigris River. For centuries, the Assyrians fought with their neighbors, earning a deserved reputation as a fierce, bloodthirsty people. They eventually overtook the Babylonians, and from about 900 to 600 BCE, they controlled all of Mesopotamia.

The Assyrians were influenced by Babylonian art, culture, and religion. But unlike Babylonia, Assyria was an empire built on military conquests and campaigns. The Assyrians' obsession with war eventually depleted their resources, overtook their economy, and undermined their social structure. The Assyrian rulers ignored agricultural development, forcing the society to import most of its food. Their preoccupation with violence and power rather than stability and production eventually led to their demise.

Assyrian architecture consists of sprawling palaces and fortified citadels, and its extensive sculptural decoration—rendered in relief—reflects the power and might of the kings. The two most common subjects of these relief sculptures are the king's military exploits and brutal hunts that were staged and tightly controlled to safely showcase the strength of the ruler. A magnificent fortified palace complex was constructed during the reign of Ashurnasirpal II (883–859 BCE) in the Assyrian capital of Nimrud on the Tigris River. The alabaster walls of the palace interiors were decorated lavishly with carved reliefs that featured assorted scenes of violence—battles, hunts, dying soldiers, and suffering animals. The reliefs expand upon the stylistic vocabulary of earlier Mesopotamian art. In a fragment depicting the king Ashurnasirpal II hunting lions (Fig. 14.8),

the figures have vigor and move freely, their actions convincingly portrayed. The artist attempts to illustrate depth within the very shallow space by placing one figure in front of another, as in the soldiers with shields on the left and the horses rearing in unison on the right. Unlike the figures in the Victory Stele of Naram Sin, which were rendered using conceptual representation, these soldiers appear more the way the eye would actually see them—pretty much in full profile. The representation of objects and people from a fixed vantage point is called **optical representation**. Worth noting also is the repetition of imagery that tells two parts of the story simultaneously. We see the king in the center, facing backward on his chariot, shooting a lion with his bow and arrow. To the right of the relief, we see that same lion dead and trampled under the horses' hooves.

Assyria waged almost constant warfare to protect its sovereignty in the area. Ashurnasirpal's successors eventually lost control of the empire to Neo-Babylonian kings, the most famous of whom was the biblical King Nebuchadnezzar. They remained in power until the conquest of the Persians.

Persia

As Persia, led by King Cyrus, marched toward empire, Babylon was but one of a growing list of casualties. By the sixth century BCE, the Persians had conquered Egypt and, less than a century later, were poised to subsume Greece within their far-reaching realm. The Persian Empire stretched from southern Asia to northeastern Europe and would have included southeastern Europe had the Greeks not been victorious over the Persians in a decisive battle at Salamis in 480 BCE. Cyrus's successors expanded

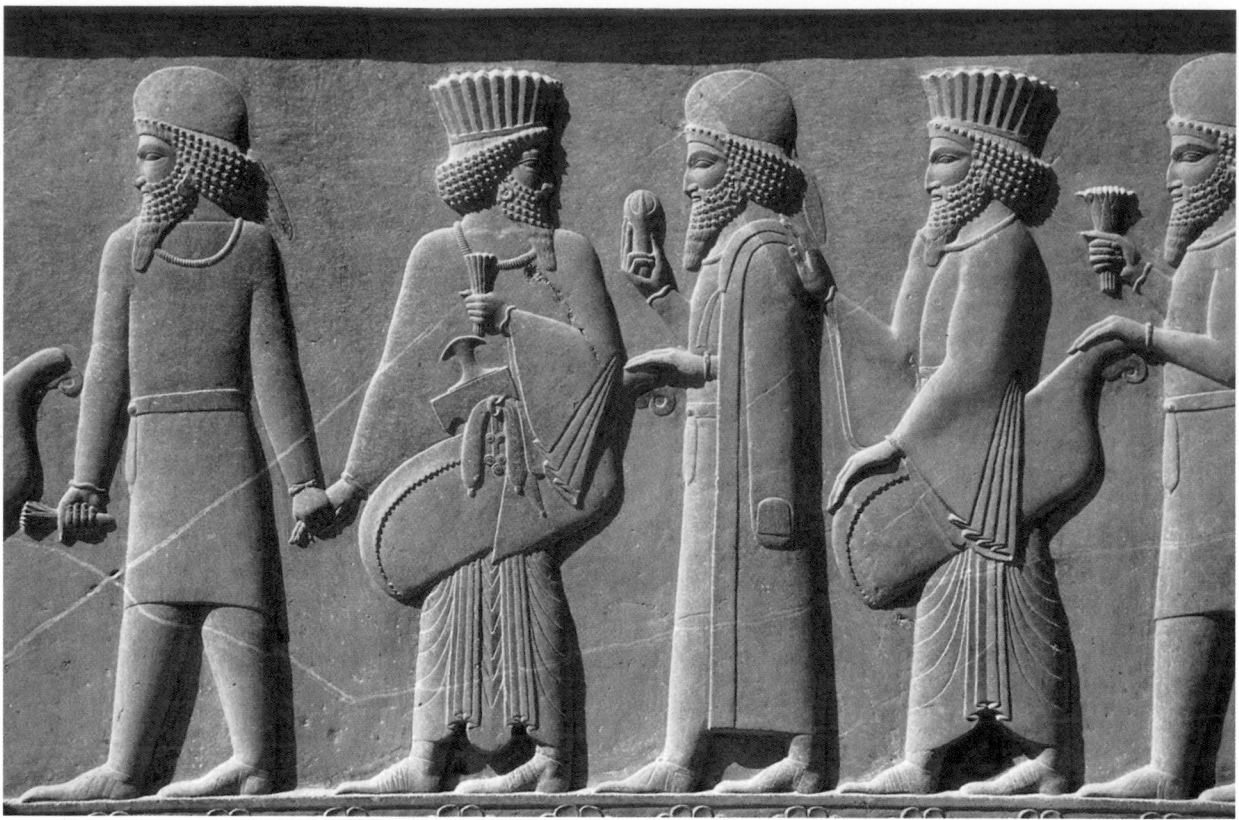

∧ 14.9 **Processional frieze (detail) from the royal audience hall, Persepolis, Iran** (c. 521–465 BCE). Limestone, 8' 4" high.

the empire until the defeat of Darius II by Alexander the Great in 330 BCE.

The citadel at Persepolis, the capital of the ancient Persian Empire, was a sprawling complex of palatial dwellings, government buildings, grand stairways, and columned halls whose architectural surfaces were richly adorned with relief sculpture. A processional frieze from the royal audience hall (Fig. 14.9) shows deeply carved, fleshy, well-rounded figures. The artist has paid particular attention to detail, distinguishing the costumes of the participants, who include Persian nobles and guards, and visiting dignitaries from nations under Persian rule. Although the procession is regimented, some figures twist and turn in space, alleviating the visual monotony.

In 343 BCE, Persia conquered the kingdom of Egypt, but civilization in Egypt had begun some 3,000 years earlier.

ANCIENT EGYPTIAN ART

The lush land that lay between the Tigris and Euphrates Rivers, providing sustenance for the Mesopotamian civilizations, is called the **Fertile Crescent**. Its counterpart in Egypt, called the **Fertile Ribbon**, hugs the banks of the Nile River, which flows north from Africa and empties into the Mediterranean Sea (Map 14.3). Like the rivers of the Fertile Crescent, the Nile was an indispensable part of Egyptian life. Without it, Egyptian life would not have existed. For this reason, it also had spiritual significance; the Nile was perceived as a god.

Like Sumerian art, Egyptian art was religious. There are three aspects of Egyptian art and life that stand as unique: their link to religion, their link to death, and their ongoing use of strict conventionalism in the arts that affords a sense of permanence.

The art and culture of Egypt are divided into three periods: The Old Kingdom dates from 2680 to 2258 BCE, the Middle Kingdom from 2000 to 1786 BCE, and the New Kingdom from 1570 to 1342 BCE. Art styles proceed from the Old to the New Kingdom with very few variations.

A break in this pattern occurred between 1372 and 1350 BCE, during the Amarna Revolution, under the unorthodox leadership of the pharaoh Akhenaton. After his death, Egypt regressed to the old order.

Old Kingdom

Egyptian religion was bound closely to the afterlife. Happiness in the afterlife was believed to be ensured through the continuation of certain aspects of earthly life. Thus, tombs were decorated with everyday objects and scenes depicting common earthly activities. Sculptures of

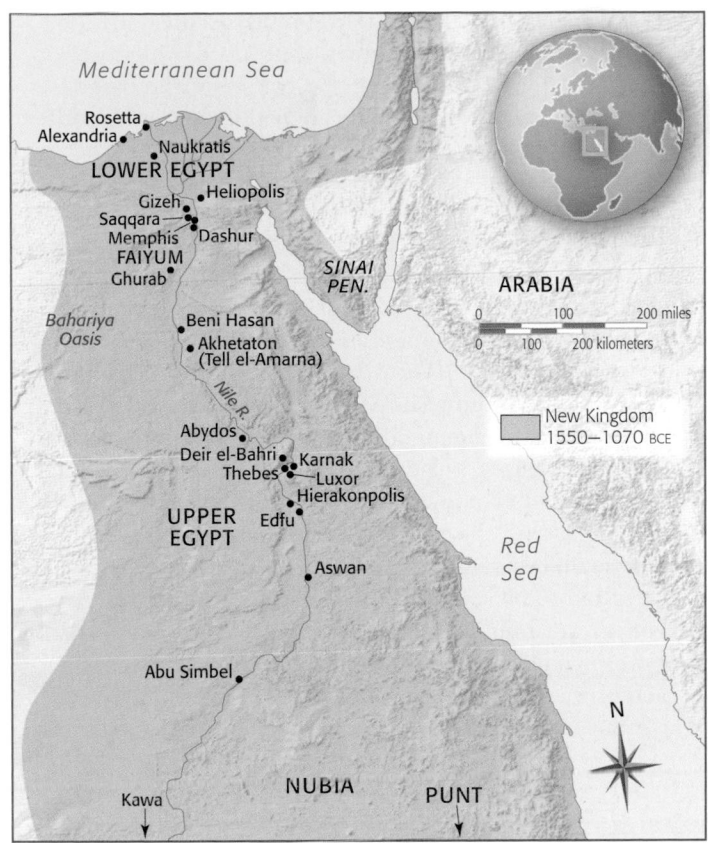

▲ MAP 14.3 Ancient Egypt.

the deceased were placed in the tombs, along with likenesses of the people who surrounded them in life.

In the years prior to the dawn of the Old Kingdom, art consisted of funerary offerings of one type or another, including small, sculpted figures, ivory carvings, pottery, and slate palettes used to mix eye makeup. Toward the end of this period, called the Predynastic period,

Egyptian stonecutters began to create the large limestone works for which Egypt became famous.

SCULPTURE Old Kingdom artists initiated a manner of representation that lasted thousands of years, a conceptual approach to the rendering of the human figure that we also encountered in Mesopotamian relief sculpture. In Egyptian reliefs, the head, pelvis, and legs are presented in profile, whereas the upper torso and eye are shown from the front. The figures tend to be flat, and they are situated in a shallow space with no use of foreshortening. No attempt was made to give the illusion of forms existing in three-dimensional space. Wall decoration was carved in very low relief with a great deal of **incised** detail. Sculpture in the round closely adhered to the block form. Color was applied at times but was not used widely because of the relative impermanence of the materials used to produce it. These basic characteristics were duplicated, with few exceptions, by artists during all periods of Egyptian art. There are instances in which a certain naturalism was sought, but the artist rarely strayed from the inherited stylistic conventions.

Art historian Erwin Panofsky stated that this Egyptian method of working clearly reflected their artistic intention, "directed not toward the variable, but toward the constant, not toward the symbolization of the vital present, but toward the realization of a timeless eternity." One of the most important sculptures from the Old Kingdom period, the Narmer Palette (Fig. 14.10), illustrates these conventions. The Narmer Palette is an example of a type of **cosmetic palette** found in Egypt (Egyptians applied dark colors around their eyes to deflect the sun's glare as football players do today), but its symbolism supersedes its function. The Narmer Palette commemorates the unification of Upper Egypt and Lower Egypt, an event that Egyptians marked as the beginning of their civilization. Upper Egypt lay to the South, and Lower Egypt

ANCIENT EGYPT

3500 BCE	2040 BCE	1550 BCE	1070 BCE
OLD KINGDOM	**MIDDLE KINGDOM**	**NEW KINGDOM**	
Hieroglyphic writing invented	Thebes becomes capital of unified Egypt	Mortuary temples built into rocky hillsides	
Religion bound to afterlife		Female pharaoh Hatshepsut builds her funerary temple	
Body portrayed conceptually		Akhenaton establishes monotheism	
Narmer Palette created		Tutankhamen ("King Tut") returns Egypt to polytheism	
Tomb sculpture includes large-scale figures			
Great Pyramids constructed			

extended to the North, where the delta of the Nile enters the Mediterranean Sea.

The back of the palette (Fig. 14.10A depicts King Narmer in the crown of Upper Egypt (a bowling pin shape) slaying an enemy. Beneath his feet, on the lowest part of the palette, lie two more dead enemy warriors. To the right, a falcon—the god Horus—is perched on a cluster of papyrus stalks that sprout from an object with a man's head. The papyrus is a symbol for Lower Egypt, and Horus's placement would appear to sanction Narmer's takeover of that territory. The top of the palette is sculpted on both sides with two bull-shaped heads with human features. They represent the goddess Hathor, who traditionally symbolized love and joy.

The king is rendered in the typical conventional manner. He is larger than the people surrounding him, symbolizing his royal status. His head, hips, and legs are carved in low relief and in profile, and his eye and upper torso are shown in full frontal view. The musculature is defined with incised lines that appear more as stylized patterns than realistic details. The artist has chosen convention over naturalism and, in the process, created a timeless image, at least as far as Egyptian history is concerned.

The front of the palette (Fig. 14.10B) is divided into horizontal segments, or **registers**, that are crowded with figures. A hollowed-out well in the center of the palette held eye paint, and it is emphasized by the long, entwined necks of lionlike figures tamed by two men with leashes. The top register depicts King Narmer once again, reviewing the captured and deceased enemy. He is now shown wearing the crown of Lower Egypt and holding instruments that symbolize his power. To his right are stacks of decapitated bodies. This is not the first time that we have seen such a monument to a royal conquest, complete with gory details. We witnessed it in the Akkadian Victory Stele of Naram Sin (Fig. 14.6). In both works, the kings are shown in commanding positions, larger than the surrounding figures, but in the Narmer Palette, the king is also depicted as a god. Viewing the ruler of Egypt as divine, along with the strict conventions of his representation, would last some 3,000 years.

Egyptian tomb sculpture included large-scale figures carved in the round, usually from very hard materials that were likely to endure. Permanence was essential, as sculptures like Khafre (Fig. 14.11) were created to house the *ka*, or soul, if the mummified remains of the

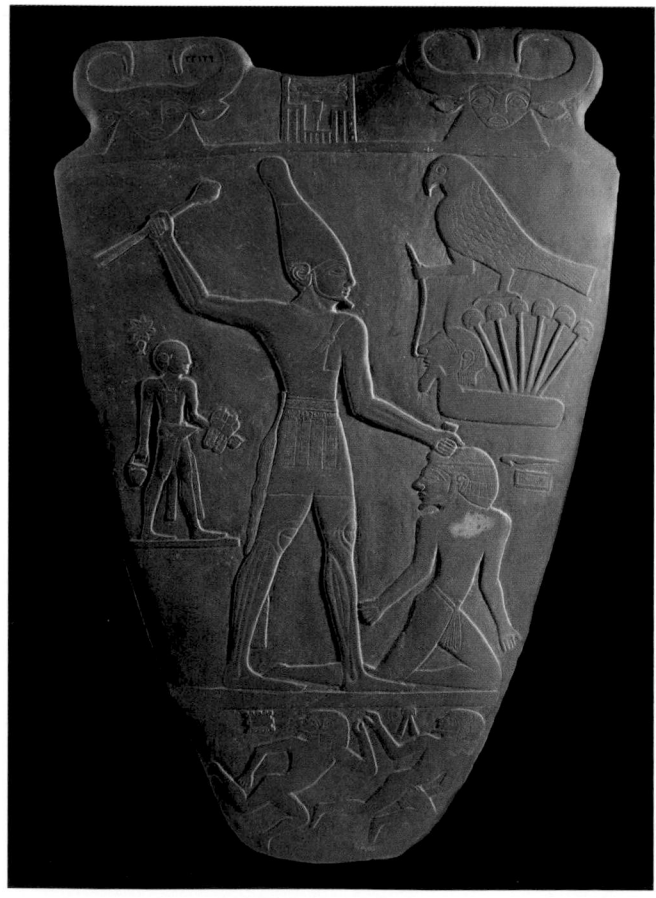

14.10A. Back of the palette.

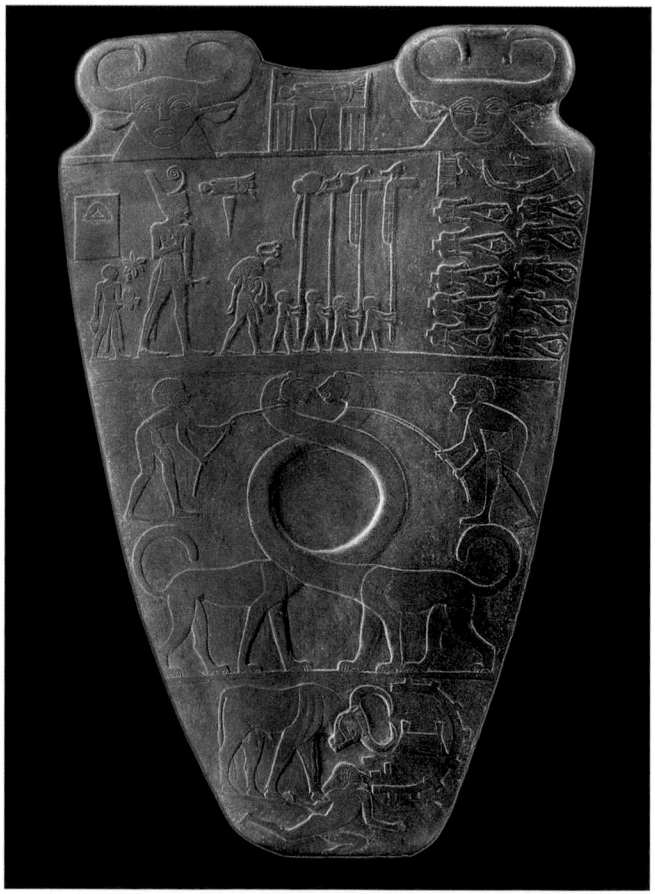

14.10B. Front of the palette.

∧ **14.10** *Narmer Palette* (c. 3000–2920 BCE). Slate, 25" high. Egyptian Museum, Cairo, Egypt.

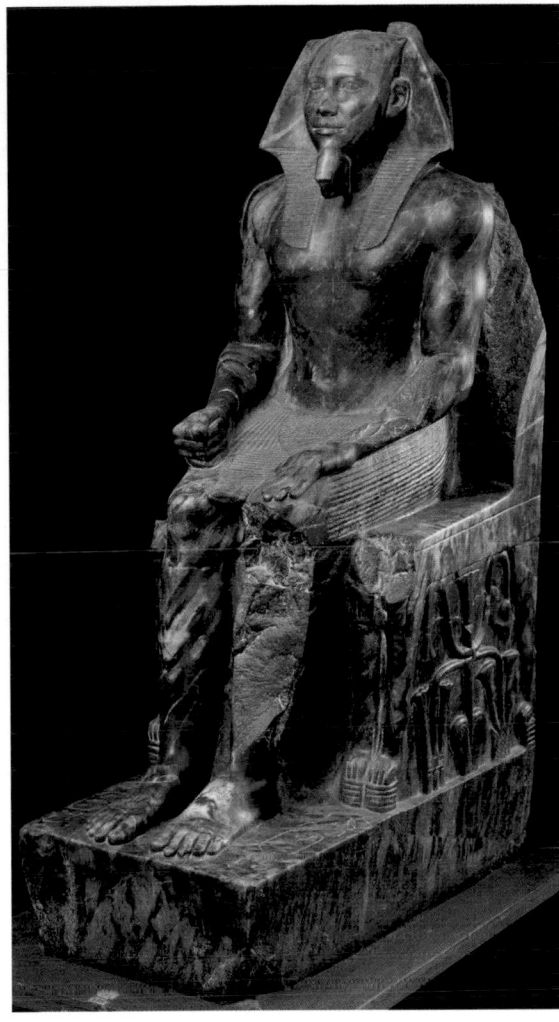

∧ **14.11 Statue of Khafre, from Gizeh** (c. 2520–2494 BCE). Diorite, 66" high. Egyptian Museum, Cairo, Egypt.

deceased disintegrated. *Ka* sculptures were not portraits. The artists used stylistic conventions, including idealism. Regardless of the age of the deceased, the *ka* figure emblemized the individual in the prime of life. The statue of Khafre, an Old Kingdom pharaoh, is typical. Carved in diorite, a gray green rock, it shows the pharaoh seated on a throne ornamented with the lotus blossoms and papyrus that symbolize Upper Egypt and Lower Egypt. He sits rigidly, and his frontal gaze is reminiscent of the staring eyes of the Mesopotamian votive figures. Khafre is shown with the conventional attributes of the pharaoh: a finely pleated kilt, a linen headdress gracing the shoulders, and a long, thin beard (present on the carved faces of both male and female pharaohs), part of which has broken off.

The sun god **Horus**, represented again as a falcon, sits behind the pharaoh's head and spreads his wings protectively around it. The artist confined his figure to the block of stone from which it was carved instead of allowing it to stand freely in space. The legs and torso appear molded to the throne, and the arms and fists are attached to the

body. The sense of the solidity of the uncarved block is maintained and, with that, a certain confidence that the sculpture would remain intact. Few, if any, pieces were likely to break off. Khafre was rendered according to a specific **canon of proportions** relating different anatomical parts to one another. That is, the forms rely on predetermined rules and not on optical fact. Naturalism was intermittent in Egyptian art, and more evident in the Middle Kingdom and the Amarna period.

ARCHITECTURE   The most spectacular remains of Old Kingdom Egypt, and the most famous, are the Great Pyramids at Gizeh (Fig. 14.12). Constructed as tombs, they provided a resting place for the pharaoh, underscored his status as a deity, and lived after him as a

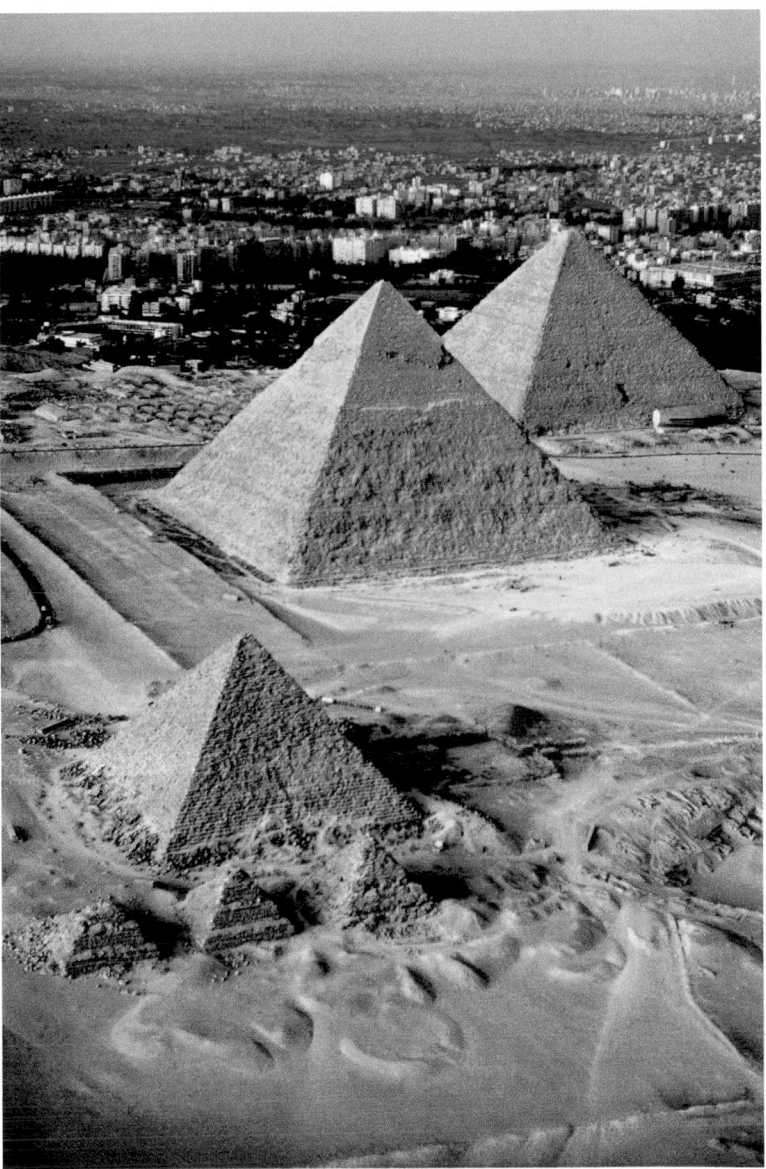

∧ **14.12 An aerial view of the Great Pyramids at Gizeh, Egypt.** From bottom: pyramid of Menkaure, pyramid of Khafre, and the Great Pyramid of Khufu. (c. 2490–2472 BCE).

Ancient Egyptian Art | 259

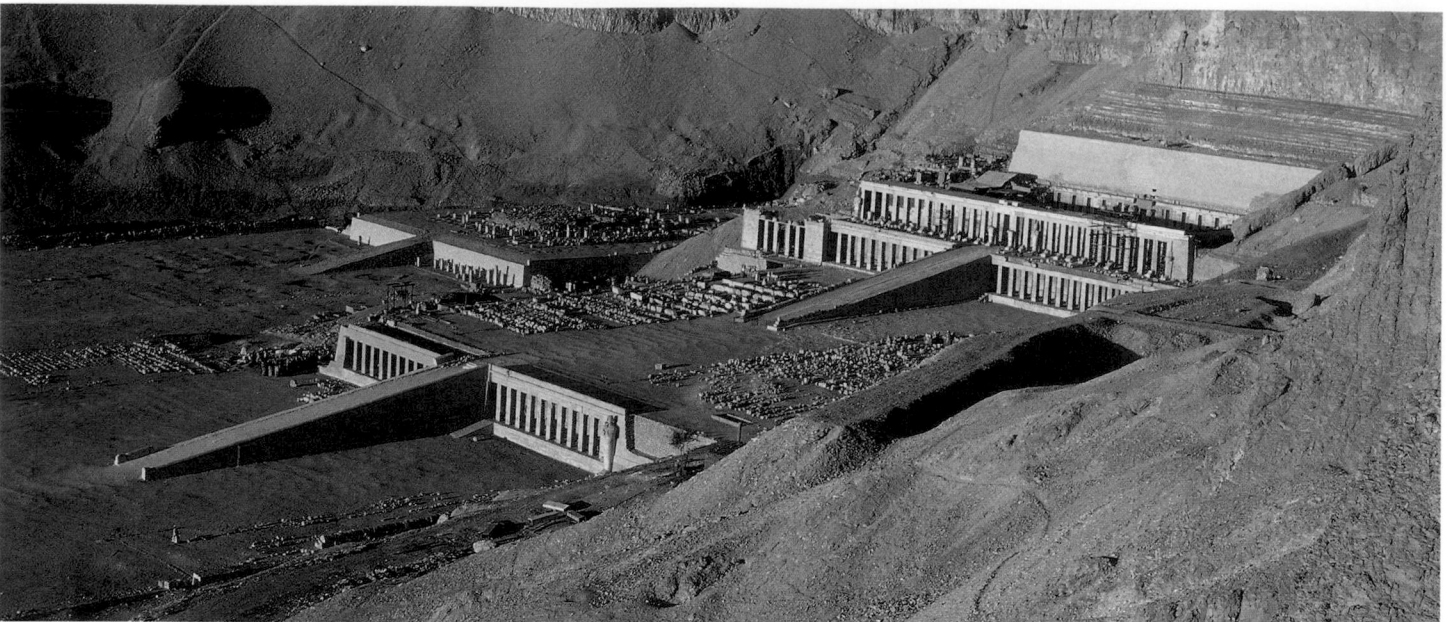

∧ 14.13 Mortuary Temple of Queen Hatshepsut, Thebes, Egypt (c. 1473–1456 BCE).

monument to his accomplishments. They stand today as haunting images of a civilization long gone, isolated as coarse jewels in an arid wasteland.

The pyramids are massive. The largest has a base that is about 775 feet on a side and is 450 feet high. It is constructed of 2,300,000 limestone blocks that weigh about 2½ tons each. The stone for the pyramids was quarried from a nearby plateau and moved by workers to the site using wooden rollers and sledlike apparatuses. Stonecutters on the site carved the blocks more finely, after which they were stacked on top of one another in rows, using systems of ropes and pulleys. Artisans finished the surfaces of the pyramid with fine limestone, creating a flawless, smooth, and gleaming sheath.

The interiors of the pyramids consist of a network of chambers, galleries, and air shafts. Ostentatious and conspicuous as the pyramids were, thieves wasted no time in plundering them. During the Middle Kingdom, Egyptians designed less easily penetrated dwelling places for their spirits.

Middle Kingdom

The Middle Kingdom witnessed a change in the political hierarchy of Egypt, as the power of the pharaohs was threatened by powerful landowners. During the early years of the Middle Kingdom, the development of art was stunted by internal strife. Egypt was finally brought back on track, reorganized, and reunited under King Mentuhotep, and art flourished once again.

Middle Kingdom art carried the Old Kingdom style forward, although there was some experimentation

outside the mainstream of strict conventionalism. We find this experimentation in sensitive portrait sculptures and freely drawn fresco paintings.

New Kingdom

The Middle Kingdom also collapsed, and Egypt fell under the rule of an Asiatic tribe called the Hyskos. They introduced Bronze Age weapons to Egypt, as well as the horse. Eventually, the Egyptians overthrew them, and the New Kingdom was launched. It proved to be one of the most vital periods in Egyptian history, marked by expansion, increased wealth, and economic and political stability.

The art of the New Kingdom combined characteristics of the Old and Middle Kingdom periods. The monumental forms of the earliest centuries were coupled with the freedom of expression of the Middle Kingdom years. A certain vitality appeared in two-dimensional works such as painting and relief sculpture, although sculpture in the round retained its concentration on solidity and permanence with few stylistic changes.

Egyptian society embraced a death cult, and some of its most significant monuments continued to be linked with death or worship of the dead. During the New Kingdom period, a new architectural form was created— the **mortuary temple**. Mortuary temples were carved out of the *living rock*—rock that remained part of the earth— as were the rock-cut tombs of the Middle Kingdom, but their function was quite different. They did not house the mummified remains of the pharaohs, but rather served as their place for worship during life, and a place at which they could be worshiped after death.

One of the most impressive mortuary temples of the New Kingdom is that of a female pharaoh, Queen Hatshepsut (Fig. 14.13). The temple backs into imposing cliffs and is divided into three terraces, which are approached by long ramps that rise from the floor of the valley to the top of pillared **colonnades**. Although the terraces are now as barren as the surrounding country, during Hatshepsut's time they were covered with exotic vegetation. The interior of the temple was just as lavishly decorated, with some 200 large sculptures as well as painted relief carvings. Sculptures of Hatshepsut are to some extent stylized according to typical conventions, although her face is recognizable from one work to another. In many portraits, her body is masculinized. She wears the same pleated kilt, royal headdress, and false beard that the male pharaohs do. In others she is represented as a woman with slender proportions, breasts, and a delicate, distinctive angular face. After the death of her husband, Hatshepsut ascended to the throne of Egypt as the regent for her son, who was still too young to succeed his father. However, in time she seized the title of pharaoh for herself and ruled Egypt for two decades.

As the civilization of Egypt became more advanced and powerful, there was a tendency to build and sculpt on a monumental scale. Statues and temples reached gigantic proportions. The delicacy and refinement of earlier Egyptian art fell by the wayside in favor of works that reflected the inflated Egyptian ego. Throughout the New Kingdom period, conventionalism was, for the most part, maintained. During the reign of Akhenaton, however, Egypt was offered a brief respite from stylistic rigidity.

THE AMARNA REVOLUTION: THE REIGN OF AKHENATON AND NEFERTITI During the fourteenth century BCE, a king by the name of Amenhotep IV rose to power. His reign marked a revolution in both religion and the arts. Amenhotep IV, named for the god Amen, changed his name to Akhenaton in honor of the sun god, Aton, and he declared that Aton was the only god. In his monotheistic fury, Akhenaton spent his life tearing down monuments to the old gods and erecting new ones to Aton.

The art of Akhenaton's reign, or that of the Amarna period (so named because the pharaoh moved the capital of Egypt to Tell el-Amarna), was as revolutionary as his approach to religion. The wedge-shaped stylizations that stood as a rigid canon for the representations of the human body were replaced by curving lines and full-bodied forms.

One of the most striking works of the Amarna period is the bust of Akhenaton's wife, Queen Nefertiti (Fig. 14.14). In profile, the arc formed by her heavy crown, sinuous neck, and delicate upper back is simply elegant. Nefertiti's refined features, enhanced by vividly painted details, give us some idea of what must have been an arresting beauty (her name means "the beautiful one is come").

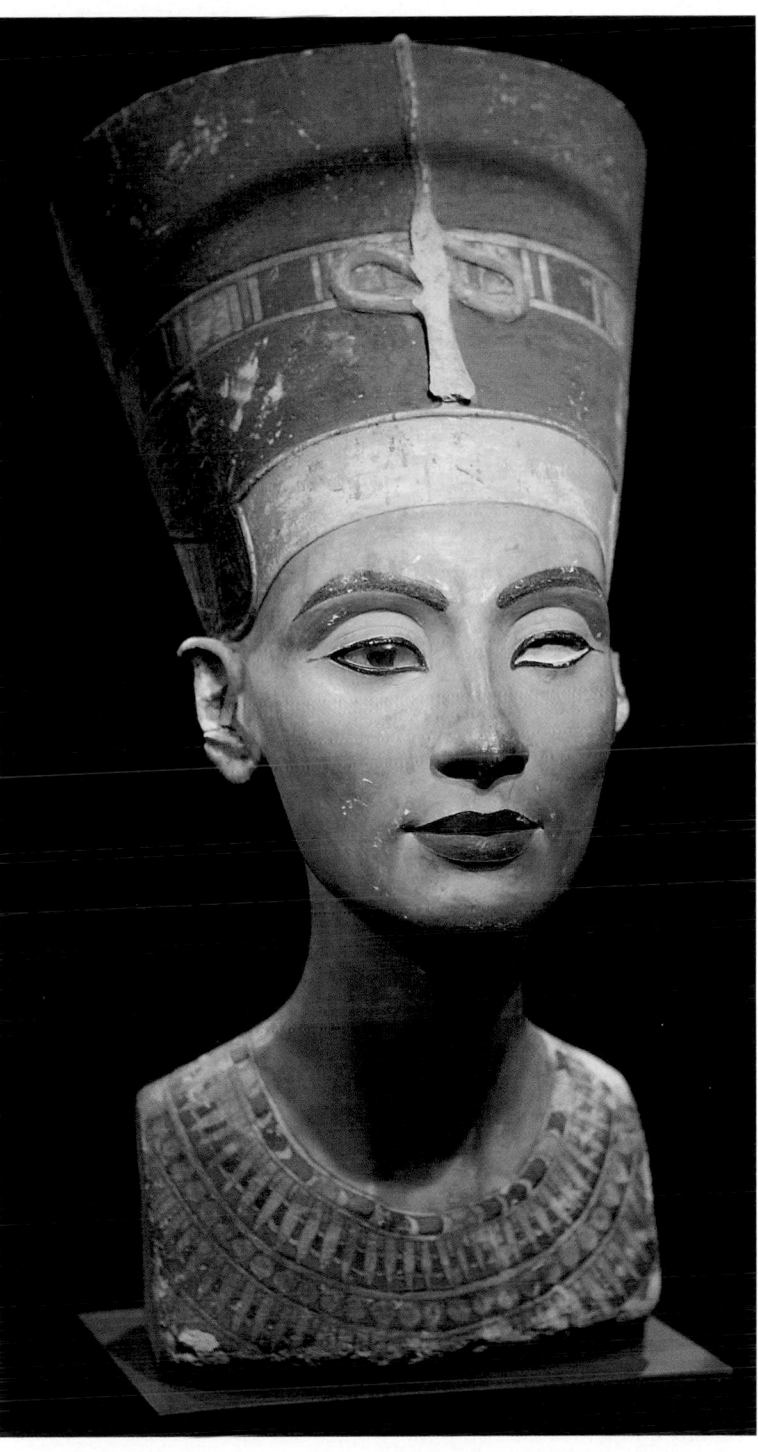

∧ **14.14 Bust of Queen Nefertiti** (c. 1353–1335 BCE). Limestone, approximately 20" high. Ägyptisches Museum, Berlin, Germany.

A eulogy of Queen Nefertiti:

And the Heiress, Great in the Palace, Fair of Face, Adorned with the Double Plumes, Mistress of Happiness, Endowed with Favours, at hearing whose voice the King rejoices, the Chief Wife of the King, his beloved, the Lady of the Two Lands, Neferneferuaten-Nefertiti, May she live for Ever and Always.

—CYRIL ALDRED, IN *AKHENATON, KING OF EGYPT*

"The beautiful one is come."

—TRANSLATION OF THE NAME NEFERTITI

The portraits of these royals take an endearing turn in a small sunken relief of Akhenaton, Nefertiti, and their three daughters (Fig. 14.15). Such intimacy had never before been seen in images of the pharaoh. Despite the looming presence of the sun disk Aton, whose rays shine on the couple and their family and sanctify the scene, Akhenaton more than anything else comes across as a dad. He holds one of his daughters gently in his arms and kisses her. Nefertiti has one of the children on her lap and another perched on her shoulder. The latter is clearly the youngest and

is playing with an object dangling from her mother's crown, as any child would.

The naturalism of the works of the Amarna period was short-lived. Subsequent pharaohs returned to the more rigid styles of the earlier dynasties. Just as Akhenaton destroyed the images and shrines of gods favored by earlier pharaohs, so did his successors destroy his temples to Aton. With Akhenaton's death came the death of monotheism—for the time being. Some have suggested that Akhenaton's loyalty to a single god may have set a monotheistic example for other religions.

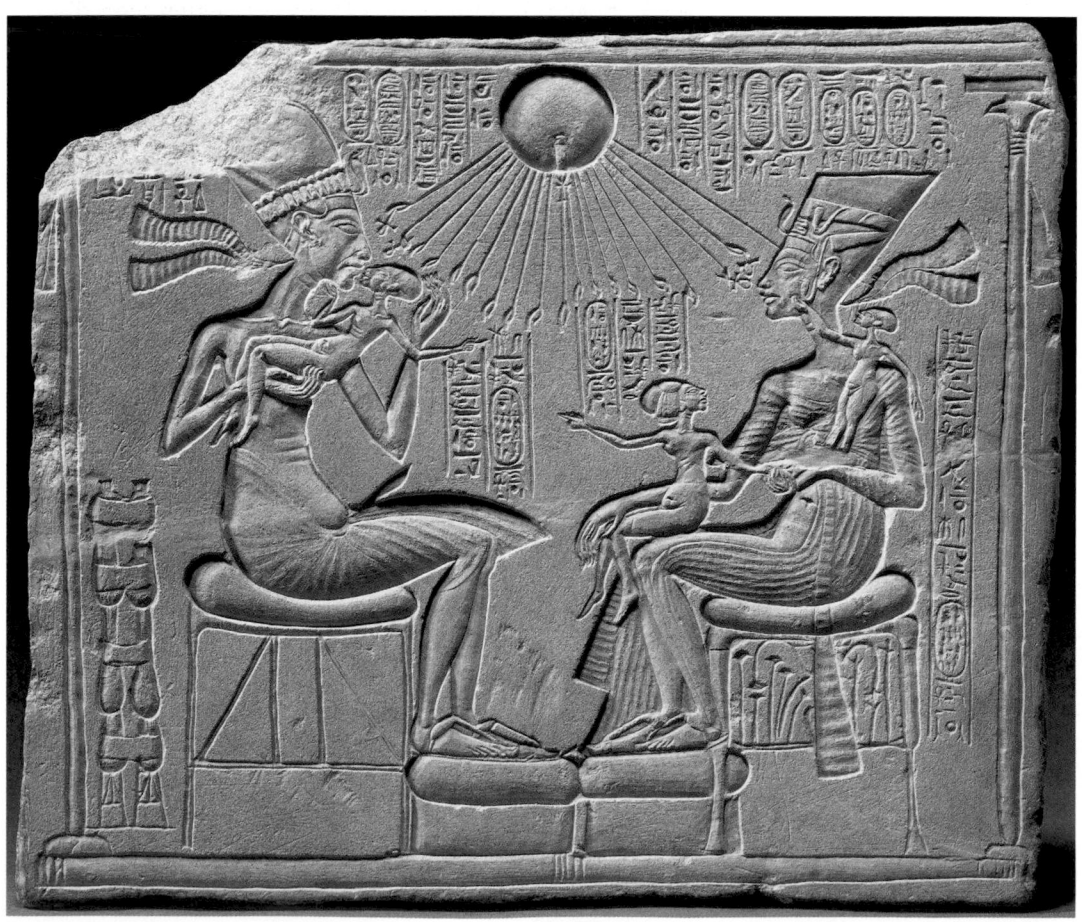

< 14.15 **Akhenaton, Nefertiti, and three of their children, Amarna, Egypt** (c. 1353–1335). Limestone relief, 13" × 15¼". Ägyptisches Museum, Berlin, Germany.

Akhenaton's immediate successor was Tutankhamen—the famed King Tut. Called "the boy king," Tut died at about age 18. His tomb was not discovered until 1922, when British archeologists led by Howard Carter unearthed a treasure trove of gold artworks, many inlaid with semiprecious stones. By far, the most spectacular find was the young pharaoh's coffin (Fig. 14.16), made of solid gold and weighing almost 250 pounds. Within this, the last of three nesting coffins, lay the body of the king, wrapped in linen, his face covered with an astounding gold mask. The lid of the coffin was fashioned out of sheet gold, with eyes of aragonite (a semihard mineral) and obsidian (black volcanic glass) and eyebrows inlaid with lapis lazuli. The hands of Tut's effigy cross over the chest and clutch the royal symbols of the crook and the flail, encrusted in deep blue faience—a signature Egyptian opaque glazed earthenware.

Carter, upon viewing the revelation of the coffin, described the sense of marvel at the sight: "And as the last was removed a gasp of wonderment escaped our lips, so gorgeous was the sight that met our eye: a golden effigy of the young boy king, of most magnificent workmanship, filled the whole of the interior of the sarcophagus." Although Tut's coffin and mask are characteristically stylized, Carter observed an element of realism in the fashioning of the face. In fact, some residual stylistic effects of the Amarna period are evident in several works from Tut's reign—curvilinear forms not unlike those seen in the statue of Akhenaton, a certain naturalism and tenderness in representations of the boy and his queen.

After Akhenaton's death, Egypt returned to "normal." That is, the worship of Amen was resumed and art reverted to the rigid stylization of the earlier stages. The divergence that had taken place with Akhenaton and been carried forward briefly by his successor soon disappeared. Instead, the permanence that was so valued by this people endured for another 1,000 years virtually unchanged despite the kingdom's gradual decline.

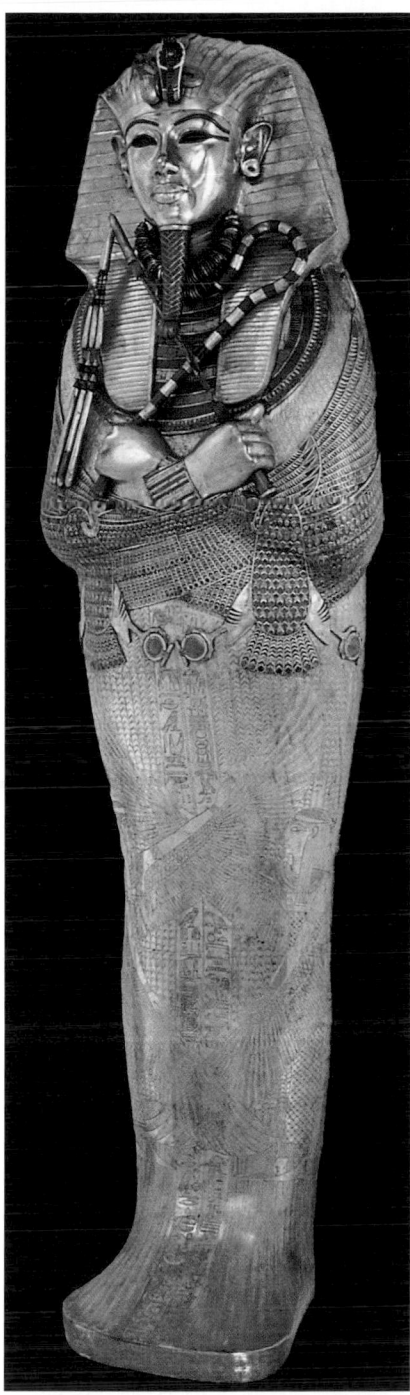

▲ 14.16 The innermost coffin of the king, from the tomb of Tutankhamen (c. 1323 BCE). Gold inlaid with semiprecious stones, 73¾" high. Egyptian Museum, Cairo, Egypt.

CONNECTIONS The discovery of King Tut's tomb in 1922 was one of the most sensational feats in archaeological history. But it was the re-discovery of the Rosetta Stone (Fig. 14.17), which had been unearthed and used in building a medieval Ottoman fort) in 1799 by a soldier in Napoleon's French army that unlocked the secret of decoding hieroglyphic text and made it possible for scholars to translate the previously untranslatable Ancient Egyptian language. The text on the stone is a decree issued by King Ptolemy V in 196 BCE that is inscribed in three scripts: Ancient Egyptian, Demotic (a script developed in Lower Egypt and typically used for documents), and Ancient Greek (a readable language that was the starting point for deciphering the Egyptian hieroglyphics).

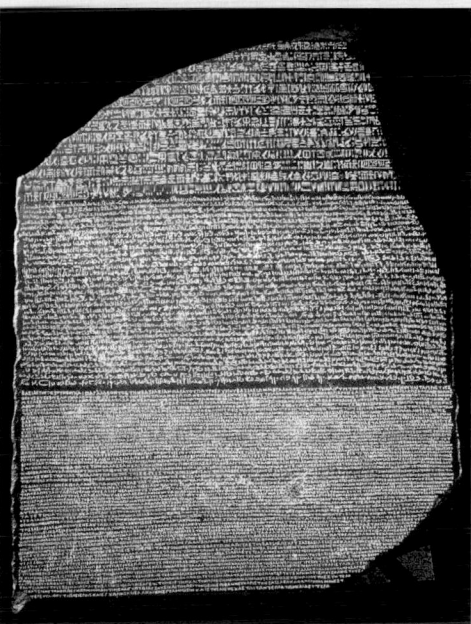

▲ 14.17 Rosetta Stone: Basalt slab inscribed with decree of pharaoh Ptolemy Epiphanes (205–180 BCE). In three languages—Greek, Hieroglyphic, and Demotic script.

A CLOSER LOOK

King Tut: The Face That Launched a Thousand High-Res Images

THE VALLEY OF THE KINGS, LUXOR, Egypt; January 5, 2005. Nearly 3,300 years after his death, the leathery mummy of the legendary "boy king" was ever so delicately removed from its tomb and guided into a portable CT—computed tomography, or what we call "cat"—scanner. It was not the first time that modern technology was employed to feed the curiosity of scientists, archeologists, and museum officials over the mysteries surrounding the reign and death of Tut. More than three decades earlier, the mummy was X-rayed twice, in part to try to solve the mystery of the young pharaoh's death; Tutankhamen was crowned at age eight and died only 10 years later. These early X-rays revealed a hole at the base of Tut's cranium, leading to the suspicion that he was murdered. This time around, the focus—and the conclusions—changed. Dr. Zahi Hawass, secretary general of the Supreme Council of Antiquities in Cairo, said, "No one hit Tut on the back of the head." Scientists instead concluded that the damage noted in earlier X-rays was probably due to the rough removal of the golden burial mask by the tomb's discoverers. But they found something else: a puncture in Tut's skin over a severe break in the youth's left thigh. As it is known that this accident took place just days before his death, some experts on the scanning team conjectured that this break, and the puncture caused by it, may have led to a serious infection and Tut's consequent death. Otherwise, the young pharaoh was the picture of health—no signs of malnutrition or disease, with strong bones and teeth, and probably five and a half feet tall.

In all, scientists (including experts in anatomy, pathology, and radiology) spent two months analyzing more than 1,700 three-dimensional, high-resolution images taken with CT scans. Then artists and scholars took a turn. Three independent teams, one each from Egypt, France, and the United States, came up with their own versions of what Tut might very well have looked like in life: a bit of an elongated skull (normal, they say), large lips, a receding chin, and a pronounced overbite that seems to have run in the family (**Fig. 14.18**). It was the first time—but certainly not the last—that CT scans would be used to reconstruct the faces of the Egyptian celebrity dead.

Although the price tag on this endeavor was most certainly steep, the Egyptian government stood to gain financially from the images. Their release was timed to coincide with the launch of the world-traveling exhibition "Tutankhamen and the Golden Age of the Pharaohs." Along with the scans and reconstruction images, the exhibit would feature King Tut's diamond crown and gold coffin, along with a total of almost 200 objects from his and various other noteworthy tombs. If history were any predictor of the insatiable thirst for things Egyptian, this, like the original exhibition of treasures from Tut's tomb, would attract millions of visitors. This time, however, it was hoped that the $10 million rental fee for each museum venue would bring in desperately needed funding for a museum being planned beside the pyramids in Gizeh. As in many parts of the world, antiquities are crumbling. "There are no free meals anymore," Hawass said. "We have a task. These monuments will be gone in 100 years if we don't raise the money to restore them."

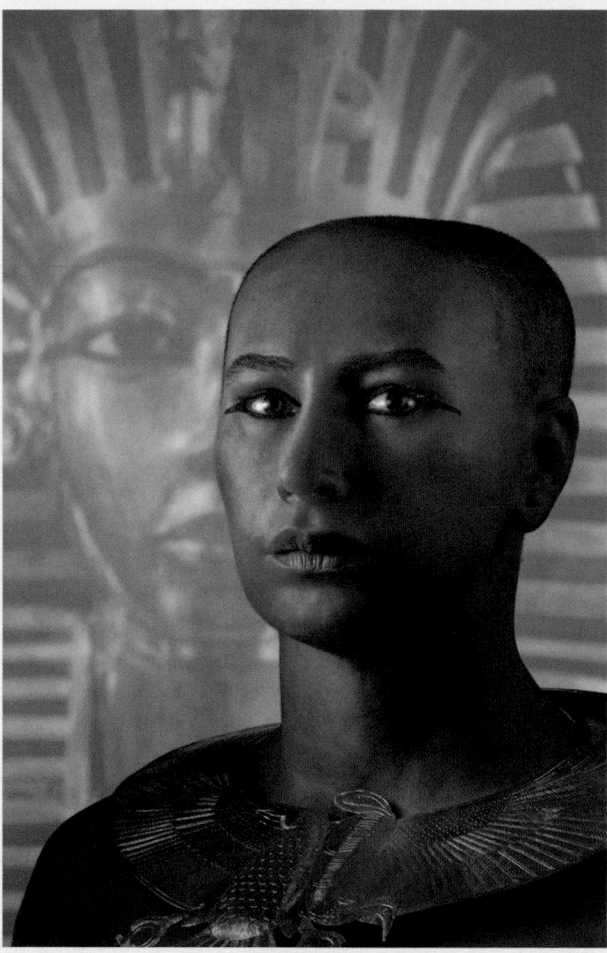

⋀ **14.18** Reconstruction of Face of King Tut.

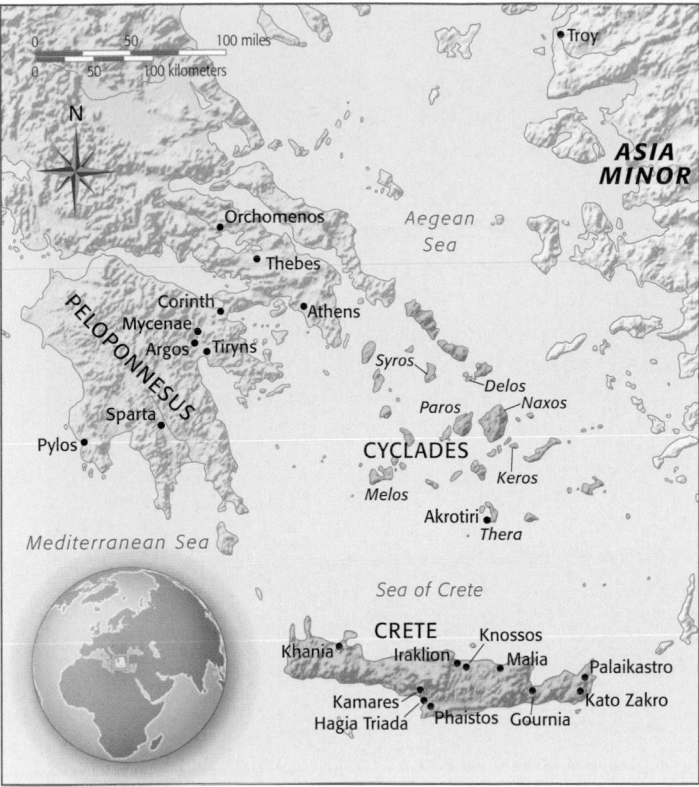

MAP 14.4 The Prehistoric Aegean.

PREHISTORIC AEGEAN ART

The Tigris and Euphrates Valleys and the Nile River banks provided the climate and conditions for the survival of Mesopotamia and Egypt. Other ancient civilizations also flourished because of their geography. Those of the Aegean—Crete in particular—developed and thrived because of their island location. As maritime powers, they maintained contact with distant cultures with whom they traded, including those of Egypt and Asia Minor.

Until about 1870 CE, the Aegean civilizations that were sung by Greece's epic poet, Homer, in the *Iliad* and the *Odyssey* were viewed as fancy rather than fact. But during the last decades of the nineteenth century, the German archeologist Heinrich Schliemann followed the very words of Homer and unearthed some of the ancient sites, including Mycenae, on the Greek mainland (Map 14.4). Following in Schliemann's footsteps, Sir Arthur Evans excavated on the island of Crete and uncovered remains of the Minoan civilization also cited by Homer. The Bronze Age civilizations of **pre-Hellenic** Greece comprised these cultures and that of the Cyclades Islands.

The Cyclades

The Cyclades Islands are part of an archipelago in the Aegean Sea off the southeastern coast of mainland Greece. They are six in number and include Melos, the site where the famed Venus de Milo (see Fig. 15.15) was found; and Paros, one of the chief quarries for marble used in ancient Greece. The Cycladic culture flourished on these six islands during the Early Bronze Age, from roughly 3000 to 2000 BCE.

The art that survives has been culled mostly from tombs and includes pottery and small marble figurines of women (Fig. 14.19) and male musicians. It is not clear what purpose the small female figures served. Some say they represent goddesses, whereas others argue for a link to fertility. They are, in a way, pared-down, geometric versions of the Venus of Willendorf (see Fig. 14.2); that is, the breasts, abdomen, and pubic area are more defined than the limbs and head. Because they were found in tombs, it would seem likely that they served a funerary function.

The figures range in height from a few inches to well over a foot, although some are life-sized. They are essentially flat, with oval or wedge-shaped heads, squared torsos, and attenuated limbs. The smooth planes of the faces generally bear only one feature—a nose. Some traces of paint have been found. Male figures are typically seated and are playing stylized musical instruments. They were also found in tombs, and their function and identity are open to speculation as well.

Crete

The civilization that developed on the island of Crete was one of the most remarkable in the ancient world, rich in painting, sculpture, and elaborate architecture. It also brought us names like King Minos (Crete's culture is known as Minoan, after the king) and creatures like the Minotaur. Homer spoke of youths sent to a Cretan labyrinth for sacrifice to the notorious man-beast, and of the hero Theseus, who slayed the Minotaur. Assuming that myths have some basis in fact, we might conclude that the extensive labyrinth that was part of the sprawling palace at Knossos—home to King Minos—inspired Homer's poetic narrative. Homeric descriptions of this island civilization were viewed as literary rather than historical. But as with Schliemann and Troy, the archeologist Sir Arthur Evan's excavations revealed Crete to have been an advanced and bustling civilization.

Evans divided the history of Minoan civilization into three parts: the Early Minoan period, known as the pre-Palace period, from which survive some small sculptures and pottery; the Middle Minoan period, or the period of the Old Palaces, which began around 2000 BCE and ended three centuries later, apparently due to a devastating earthquake; and the Late Minoan period, when these palaces were reconstructed, which began during the sixteenth century BCE and ended probably in about 1400 BCE. At that time, the stronghold of Western civilization shifted from the Aegean to the Greek mainland.

During the Middle Minoan period, the great palaces, including the most famous one at Knossos, were constructed. A form of writing based on **pictographs**, called Linear A, was developed. Refined articles of ivory, metal, and pottery were also produced.

Unlike those of Mesopotamia and Egypt, Minoan architectural projects did not consist of tombs, mortuary temples, or shrines. Instead, the Minoans constructed lavish palaces for their kings and the royal entourage. Not much is known of the old palaces, except for those that were subsequently built on their ruins. Toward the end of the Middle Minoan period, the palace at Knossos was reduced to rubble either by an earthquake or by invaders. About a century after its destruction, however, it was rebuilt on a grander scale. Also during the Late Minoan period, a type of writing called Linear B was developed. This system, finally deciphered in 1953, turned out to be an early form of Greek. The script, found on clay tablets, perhaps indicates the presence of a Greek-speaking people—the Mycenaeans—on Crete during this period.

The most spectacular of the restored palaces on Crete is that at Knossos. It was so sprawling that one can easily understand how the myth of the Minotaur arose. The adjective *labyrinthine* certainly describes it. A variety of rooms were set off major corridors and arranged about a spacious central court. The rooms included the king's and queen's bedrooms, a throne room, reception rooms, servants' quarters, and many other spaces, including rows of **magazines**, or storage areas, where large vessels of grain and wine were embedded in the earth for safekeeping and natural cooling. The palace was three stories high, and the upper floors were reached by well-lit staircases. Beneath the palace were the makings of an impressive water-supply system of terra-cotta pipes that would have provided running water for bathrooms.

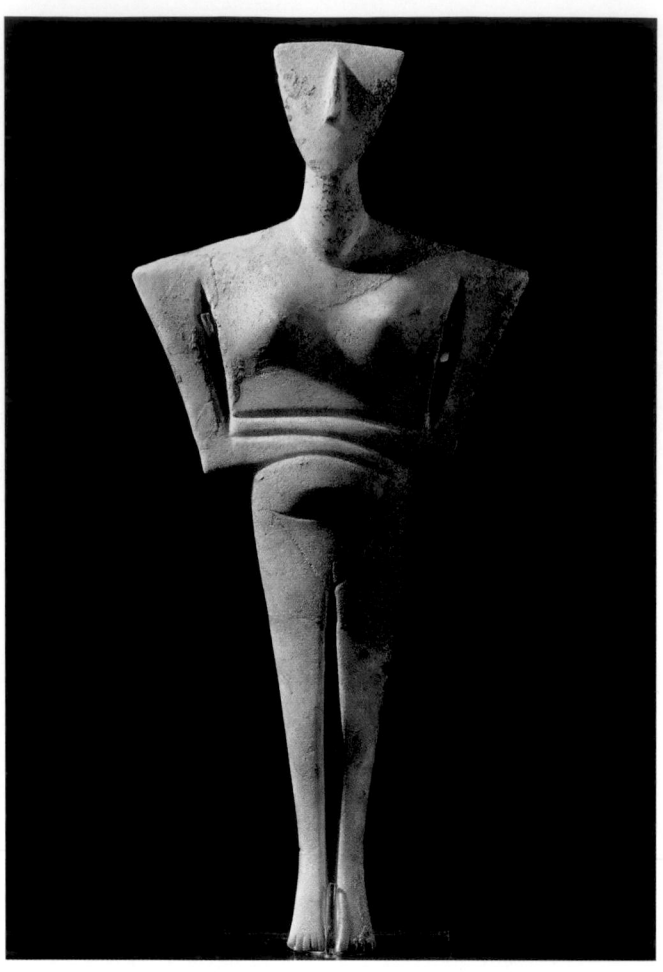

▲ 14.19 **Figurine of a woman from Syros (Cyclades), Greece** (c. 2600–2300 BCE). Marble, 1' 6" high. National Archaeological Museum, Athens, Greece.

The rough stonework of the thick palace walls was hidden behind plaster painted with vibrant, colorful landscapes like the *Spring Fresco* found on Thera. Many of the paintings depict subjects that reflect the palace's

THE PREHISTORIC AEGEAN

3000 BCE	2000 BCE	1600 BCE	1200 BCE
THE CYCLADES	**CRETE**	**MYCENAE**	
Settlements and burial sites on Cyclades and Crete indicate thriving cultures and economies	Minoans construct palace complexes on Crete that are destroyed by fire	Mycenaean civilization flourishes on mainland Greece	
Cycladic sculptors carve figurines for graves to accompany the deceased into the afterlife	Palace at Knossos on Crete is rebuilt—the legendary home of King Minos and the labyrinth of the Minotaur	Mycenaeans contrast fortified palace citadels	
		Mycenean war against Troy c. 1250 BCE	
		Gold masks and other objects are placed in graves of the elite	
		Destruction of palaces c. 1200 BCE	

island setting—fish, sea mammals, coastal plants—but others, such as the bull-leaping fresco (Fig. 14.20), clearly illustrate some sort of ceremony or ritual. As a bull leaps through space, front and hind legs splayed, a trio of youths performs daring feats. One takes the bull by the horns, a second vaults over its back, and a third lands safely with the flourish of a gymnast scoring a perfect ten. Although the body types and flowing black locks all look the same, the light-skinned youths are female and the one with dark skin is a male. This distinction between the sexes is common in ancient art: the males look suntanned because they spend more time outdoors. What are they doing and why? Bull leaping may have been a ritual or a rite of passage; we know that bulls were slain by the Minoans as a blood sacrifice. And doesn't this maneuver look exceptionally dangerous? Can one help but wonder if visitors to Crete saw such bull-leaping ceremonies—some of which must have resulted in death—and sowed the seeds of the legend of the Minotaur in the retelling of what they had witnessed?

The palace at Knossos and all of the other palaces on Crete were again destroyed some time in the fifteenth century BCE. At this point, the Mycenaeans of the Greek mainland may have moved in and occupied the island. However, their stay was short-lived. Knossos, and the Minoan civilization, had been finally destroyed by the year 1200 BCE.

Mycenae

Although the origins of the Mycenaean people are uncertain, we know that they came to the Greek mainland as early as 2000 BCE. They were a Greek-speaking people, sophisticated in forging bronze weaponry as well as versatile in the arts of ceramics, metalwork, and architecture. The Minoans clearly influenced their art and culture, even though by about 1600 BCE Mycenae was by far the more powerful of the two civilizations. Mycenaeans occupied Crete after the palaces were destroyed. The peak of Mycenaean supremacy lasted about two centuries, from 1400 to 1200 BCE. At the end of that period, invaders from the north—the fierce and undaunted Dorians—gained control of mainland Greece. They intermingled with the Mycenaeans to form the beginnings of the peoples of ancient Greece.

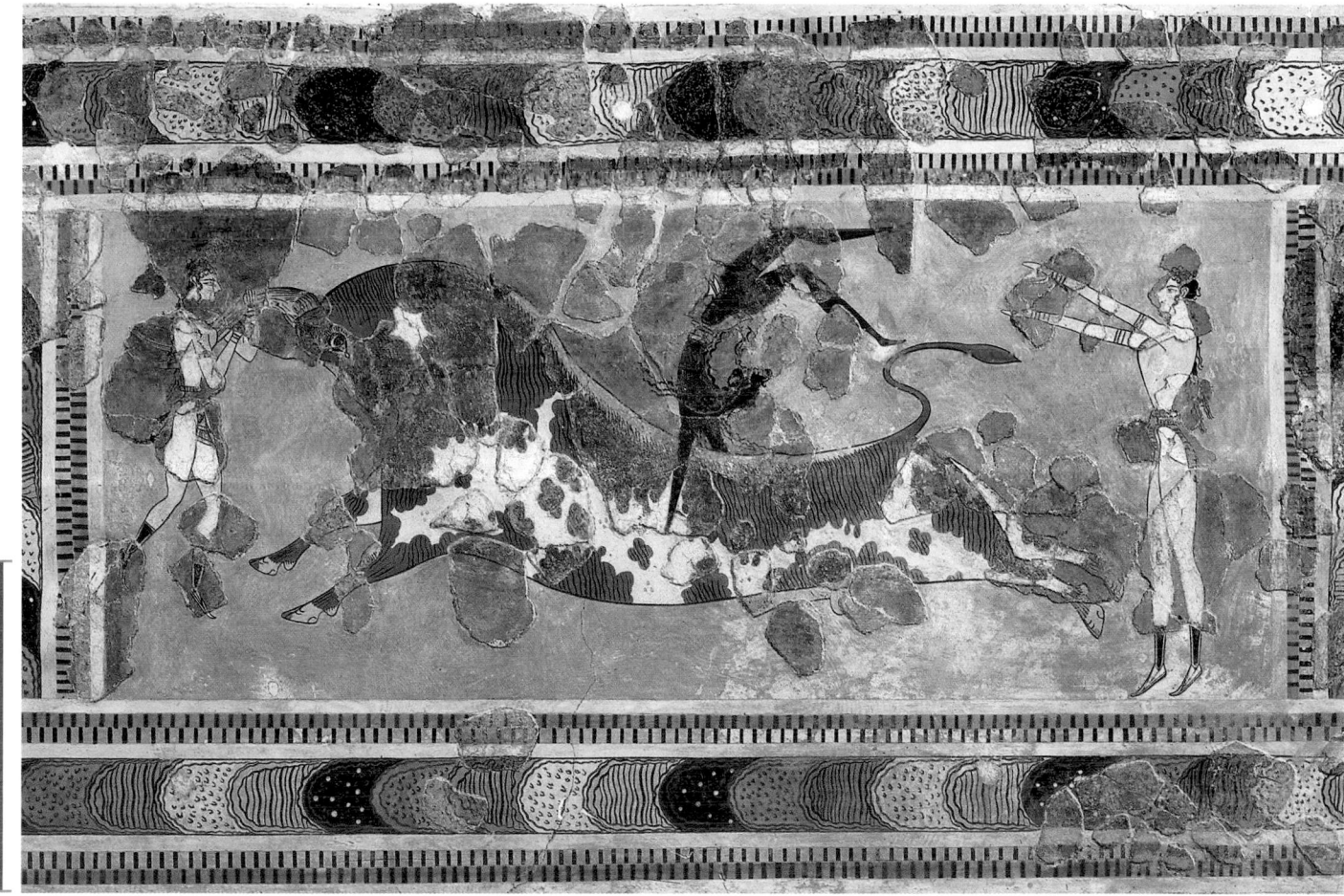

1 ft.

ʌ **14.20 Bull-leaping fresco** (c. 1500 BCE). Palace, Knossos (Crete), Greece. Fresco; 32" high, including border. Archaeological Museum, Herakleion, Greece.

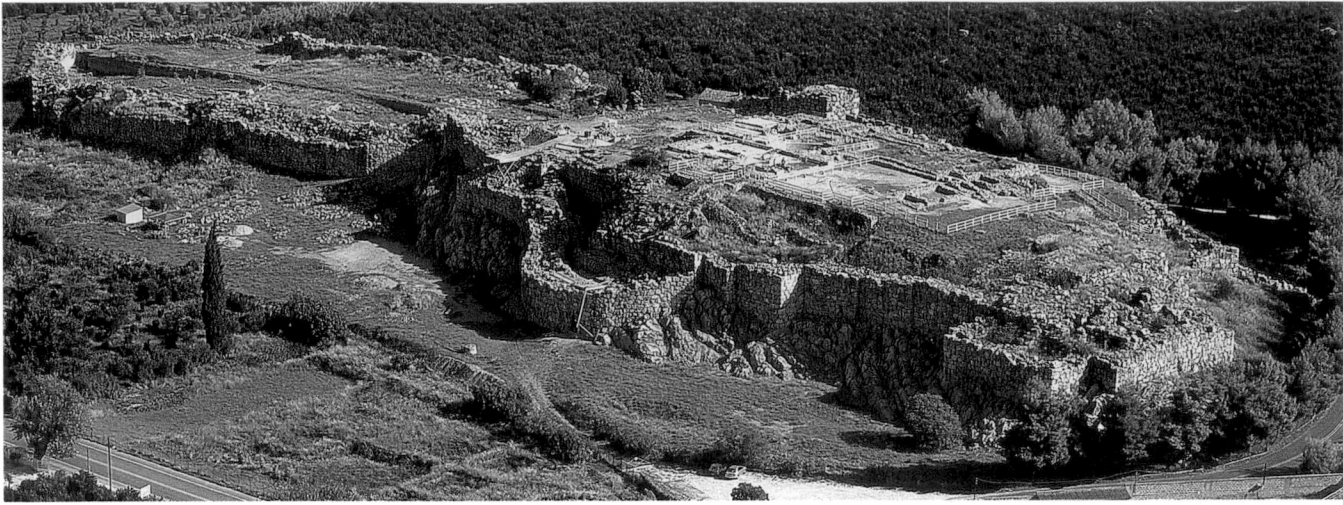

▲ 14.21 **Remains of the citadel of Mycenae, Mycenae, Greece** (c. 1400–1200 BCE).

Lacking the natural defense of a surrounding sea that was to Crete's advantage, the Mycenaeans were continually threatened by land invaders. They met these threats with strong fortifications, such as the citadels in the major cities of Tiryns (Homer, author of the *Iliad* and the *Odyssey*, referred to it as "Tiryns of the great walls") and Mycenae. Much of the architecture and art of the Mycenaean civilization reflects the preoccupation with defense. At 20 feet in thickness, the sheer scale of the defensive walls of the citadel at Mycenae (Fig. 14.21) makes the collapse of Mycenae incomprehensible. The stones laid were so enormous that Greeks later attributed the erection of the walls to a race of one-eyed giants—the **Cyclopes**. (A Cyclopes was one of the challenges faced by Odysseus in the *Odyssey*.) Art historians refer to the materials and construction techniques used in the citadels as **Cyclopean masonry**.

GOLD WORK Homer's epithet for Mycenae was "rich in gold." Archeologists came to uphold that description with the discovery of extraordinary quantities of finely wrought gold objects in graves throughout Mycenae, although the tombs, like the pyramids before them in Egypt, were plundered well before the modern excavations. Thieves found their way into the Treasury of Atreus, as they did other tombs, soon after its construction. Nevertheless, Schliemann unearthed a wealth of treasures buried in more inconspicuous graves. Archeologists refer to the mound as Grave Circle A. The most impressive find was a gold mask, which Schliemann believed was that of Agamemnon himself—the king who, in the *Iliad*, led the Mycenaeans in the assault upon Troy (Fig. 14.22). Masks such as these were created from thin, hammered sheets of gold and placed over the faces of the deceased. Some aspects of the masks were stylized, such as the ears, eyebrows, and coffee-bean-shaped eyes, but the artists did endeavor to rec-

reate specific characteristics that distinguished one portrait from another. Schliemann found other elaborate objects, including gold cups, bronze vessels, and daggers inlaid with silver and gold.

The Cyclopean walls of the Mycenaean citadels did not ward off enemies for long. After roughly 1200 BCE, the Mycenaean civilization collapsed from internal warfare, the onslaught of the better-equipped Dorian warriors, or both. The period following the Dorian invasions produced

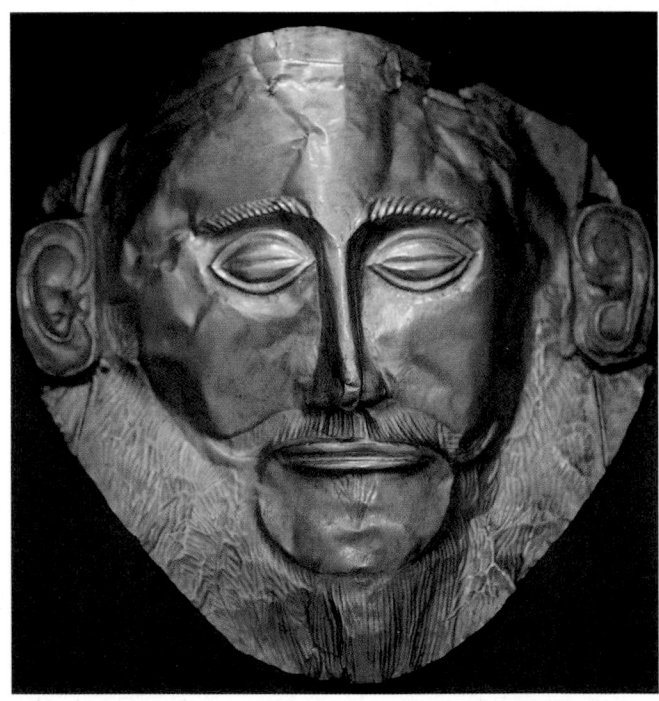

▲ 14.22 **Funerary mask, from Grave Circle A, Mycenae, Greece** (c. 1600–1500 BCE). Beaten gold, 12" high. National Archaeological Museum, Athens, Greece.

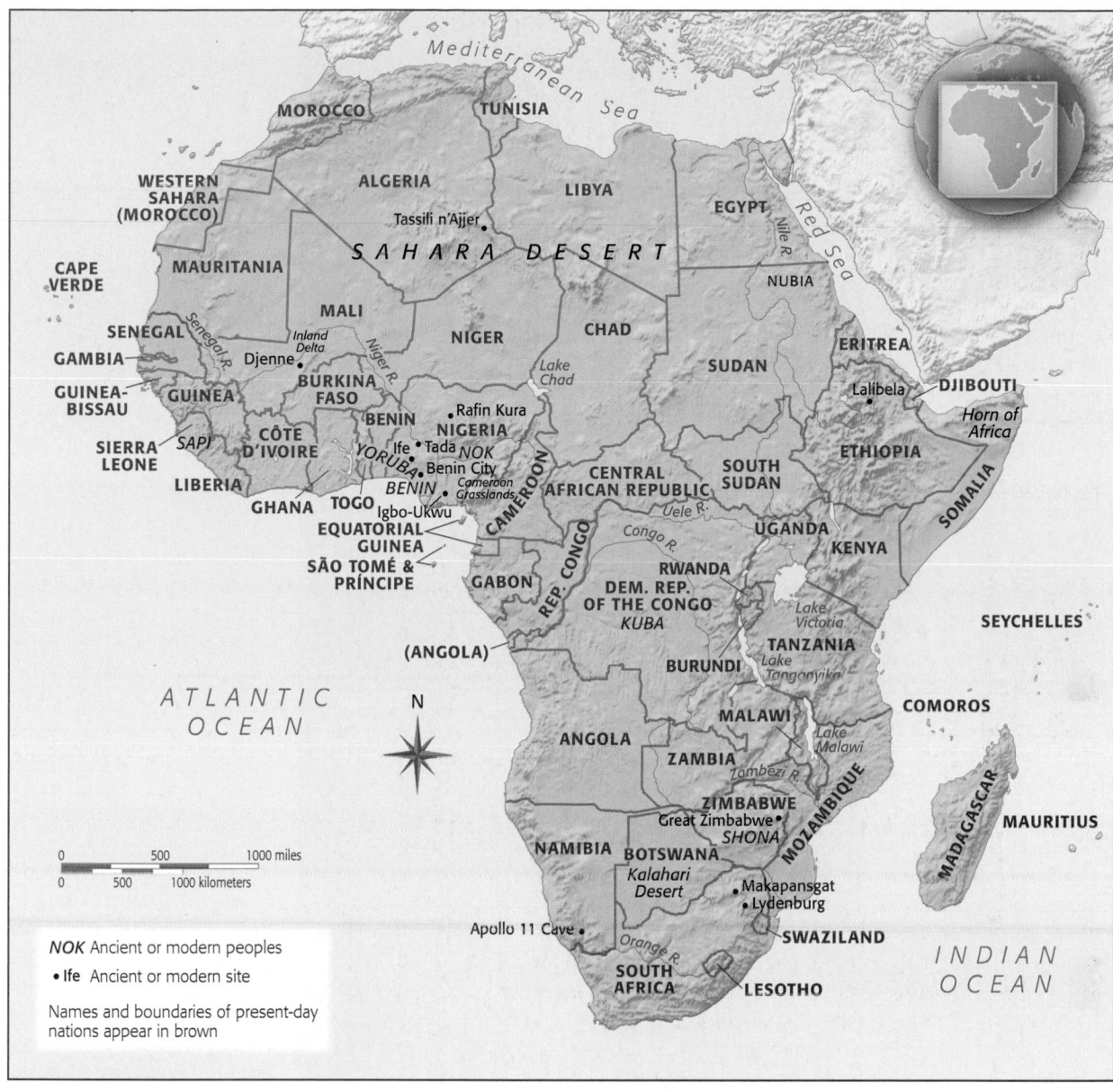

∧ MAP 14.5 Africa.

no significant art, architecture, or writing. But the people who emerged from this "Dark Age" would sow the seeds of one of the world's most influential civilizations and enduring artistic legacies—that of ancient Greece.

THE WIDER WORLD

Africa

Everything we are began in Africa. The first human species—hominids—trod the African plains and scaled African trees several million years ago. Our species emerged there some 150,000 to 200,000 years ago, and the earliest bones we know of have been unearthed in Africa. From that cradle, we began to spread to the four corners of the earth. We moved northeast into what is now the Arabian Peninsula, still farther north into Europe, eastward into Asia, down into Oceania and Australia, and across a natural land bridge—now submerged—from present-day Siberia to the Americas. Human migrations over thousands of miles go back more than 50 millennia.

Africa is vast. Its land area is more than three times that of the continental United States. Its climate and landforms are wildly diverse—from moderate Mediterranean conditions to humid rain forests, from grasslands to desert—and the cultures of African peoples that developed in these distinct zones were equally diverse.

The continent of Africa has been described in terms of two broad regions: North Africa (the territories along the Mediterranean Sea that are now part of the Arab world and Islamic) and sub-Saharan Africa (Map 14.5). One of

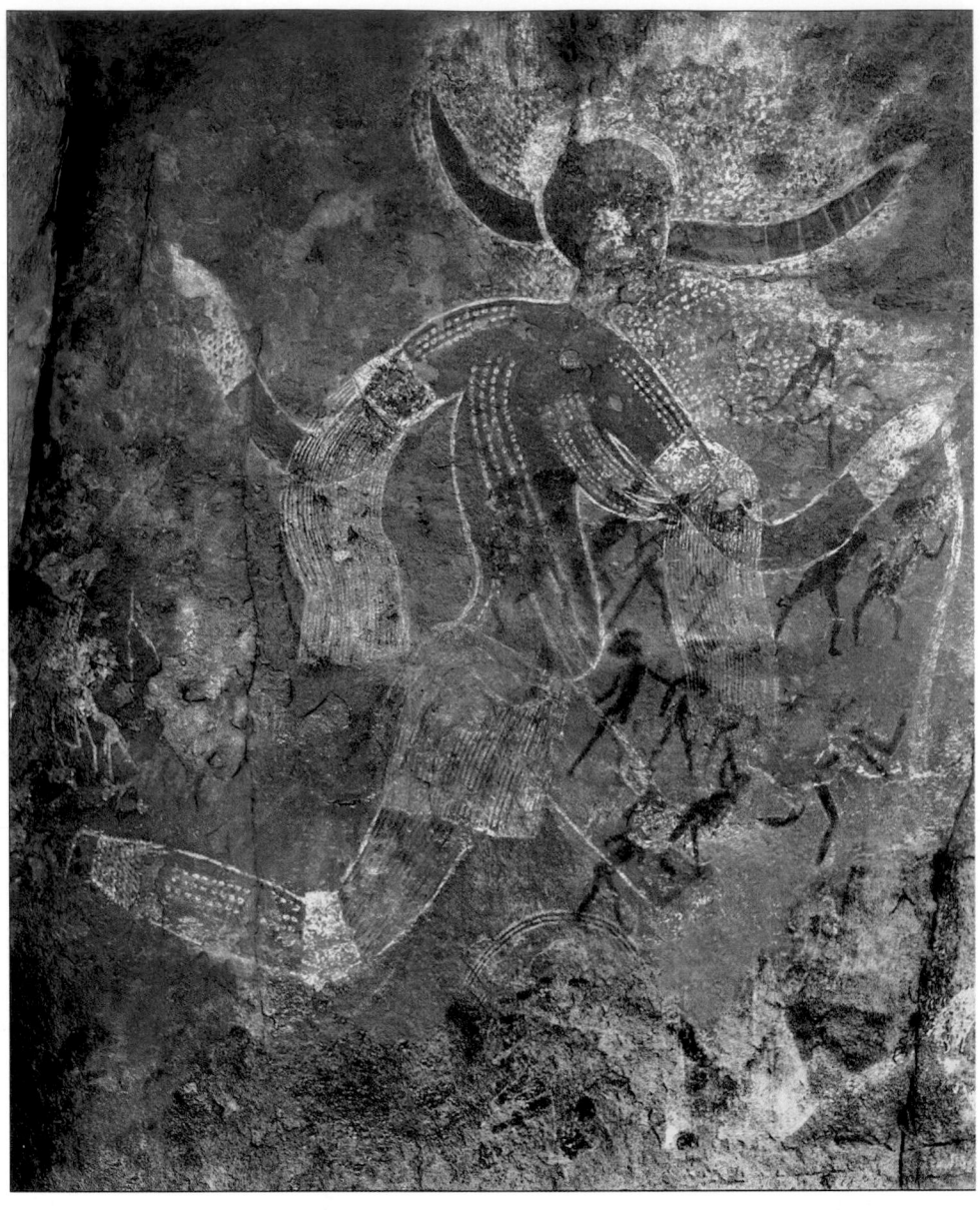

< **14.23 Running woman, rock painting, Tassili n'Ajjer, Algeria** (c. 6000–4000 BCE).

AFRICA AND ASIA

6000 BCE	1500 BCE	200 CE

Africans make Neolithic rock paintings c. 6000–4000 BCE

The earliest South Asian cities developed in the Sindh region of the Indus River Valley (modern-day Pakistan) in about 3000 BCE

Mohenjo-daro has a grid plan of streets, a central marketplace, a public bath, and a sewage system

The Aryan people settle in the Indus Valley by around 1500 BCE, bringing a caste system

In the late Neolithic period, the Longshan culture establishes cities along the Yellow River in China

The Chinese Shang Dynasty (c. 1520–1027 BCE) is a Bronze Age urban civilization that develops trade and commerce

The Zhou Dynasty (c. 1100–221 BCE) replaces the Shang Dynasty and coordinates separate kingdoms

The Qin Dynasty, from which China derives its name, is founded in 221 BCE; the emperor imposes a single writing system and standard weights and measures

The Han Dynasty is established in 202 BCE and rules China until 220 CE

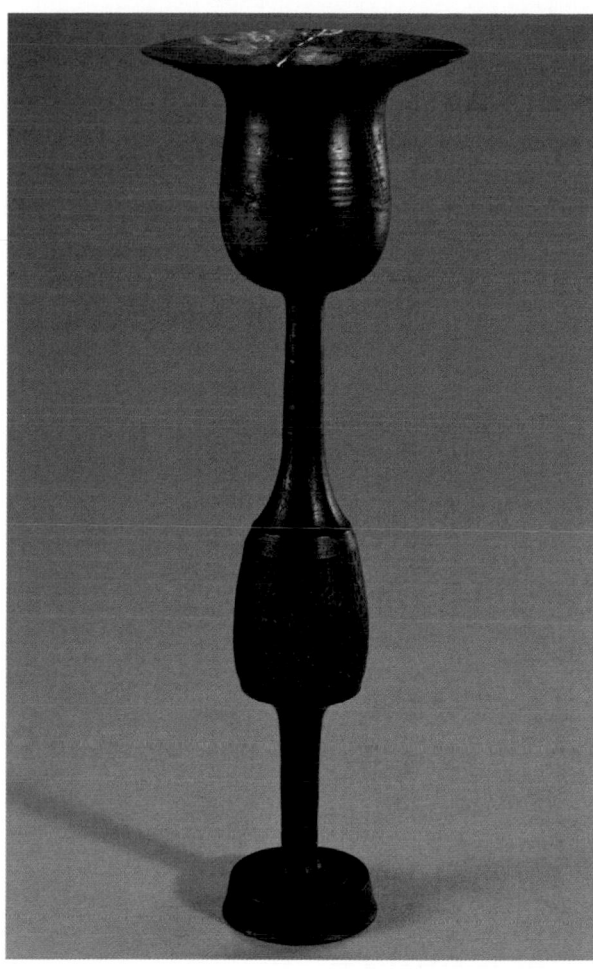

▲ 14.24 Black eggshell pottery, Longshan culture (c. 3000–2000 BCE).

scholars have tied to early written language. In the late Neolithic period, the Longshan culture developed along the Yellow River, overlapping chronologically with both the Egyptian Old Kingdom and the Sumerian civilization of Mesopotamia. As with other river civilizations we have discussed, the Longshan is marked by the establishment of cities. Of particular interest are examples of finely wrought pottery, some of which was wheel-thrown. The distinctive black pottery was thin walled (thus also called eggshell pottery), highly polished, and often decorated with elaborate patterns of incised line (Fig. 14.24).

During the years that the Shang Dynasty (c. 1520–1027 BCE) ruled China, Tutankhamen became pharaoh, the Mycenaeans lived in their fortified cities, and the Minoans decorated their elaborate palaces with brilliant frescos. The Shang Dynasty, too, was a Bronze Age urban civilization ruled by kings who, as in Egypt, inherited their positions and who, like the pharaohs, claimed their authority from the divine. The Shang culture is known for its accomplished metalwork, including bronze weaponry, fittings for chariots, and sophisticated ceremonial vessels such as the one in Figure 14.25, which was discovered in a royal tomb. The two-headed fantastic animal is embellished with elaborate, stylized, linear detail that

the oldest works discovered in Africa is a Neolithic rock painting of a woman in a horned headdress running or, perhaps, dancing (Fig. 14.23). Her body is adorned with painted patterns and she wears a skirt made of fiber from a palm tree that grew in what is now the Sahara Desert. The position of her arms and legs, shown in profile, and the sinuous lines of her fringed arm-cuffs contribute to an impressive representation of movement. Although the purpose of this painting is not known, given the elaborate costume and body art, it is likely connected with ritual.

A glance at global history—and prehistory—also reveals the simultaneity of civilizations that developed around the world's great rivers: Mesopotamia in the Tigris and Euphrates Valley, Egypt on the Nile, South Asian cities in the Indus Valley, and China along the Yellow River.

Asia

Excavations in China have revealed numerous Neolithic settlements along with pictographic carvings that some

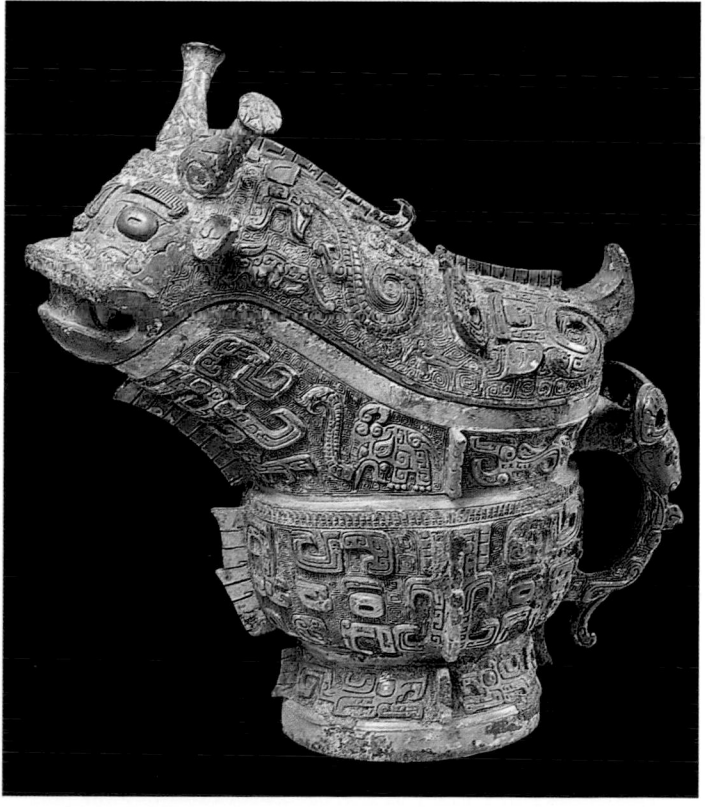

▲ 14.25 Ceremonial vessel (Guang), probably from a royal tomb at **Anyang, Henan** (Shang Dynasty, 12th or 11th century BCE). Bronze, 6½" high. Asian Art Museum of San Francisco (Avery Brundage Collection), California.

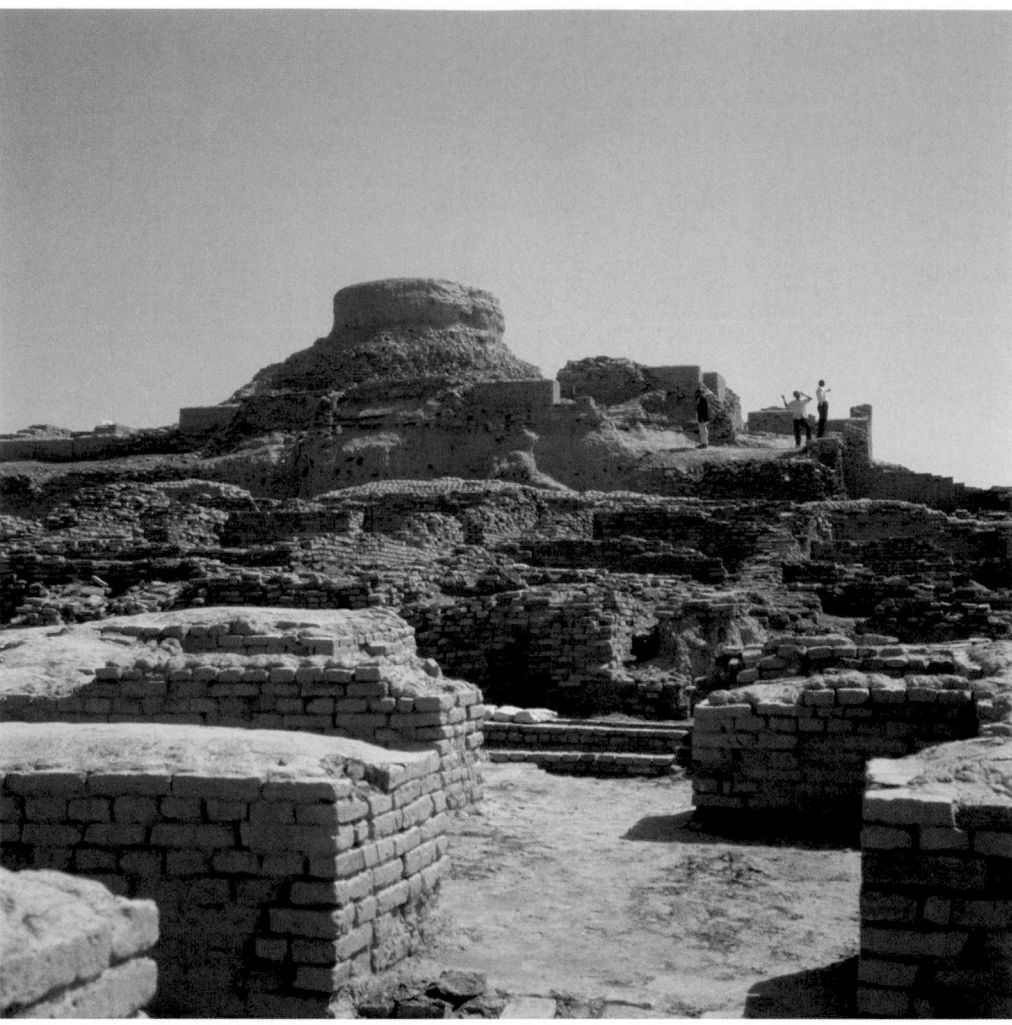

∧ **14.26 Citadel ruins at Mohenjo-Daro, in modern-day Pakistan** (c. 2600–1900 BCE). The ruins of the residential quarter lead to the citadel, which houses ritual baths and is thought to be the site of other religious rituals. Mohenjo-Daro, meaning "mounds of the dead," was once the largest city of the Indus civilization and probably the capital.

complements the curving shapes of vessel. The casting technique perfected by the Shang artisans consisted of pouring molten bronze into piece molds and, after casting, assembling the individual parts into a cohesively designed whole. The Shang royal tombs, as in Egypt and Mesopotamia, were filled with precious objects such as these.

The earliest South Asian cities developed in the Sindh region of the Indus River Valley, near the Arabian Sea in what is now Pakistan. Mohenjo-Daro was the largest and oldest of these urban centers, coinciding chronologically with the civilizations of Egypt, Mesopotamia, and Crete. The urban planning and engineering finesse of Mohenjo-Daro are impressive: a grid plan of streets with fire-brick rectilinear buildings, a central marketplace with a public well, a public bath waterproofed with bitumen, and a sewage system, to name but some of its features. The size of the city (at its peak it housed 35,000 inhabitants), its fortifications, and its variety of structures indicate that it was a city of great importance, perhaps the civilization's administrative center. Excavation of Mohenjo-Daro began in the 1920s, and today the ruins are designated as a UNESCO World Heritage Site (Fig. 14.26).

The Sindh area of the Indus Valley gave birth to the words *India* and *Hindu*, and Mohenjo-Daro is considered one of India's earliest civilizations (India was partitioned in 1947, after which Pakistan and India became self-governing states). The Indus Valley civilization produced a written pictographic language and artisans who

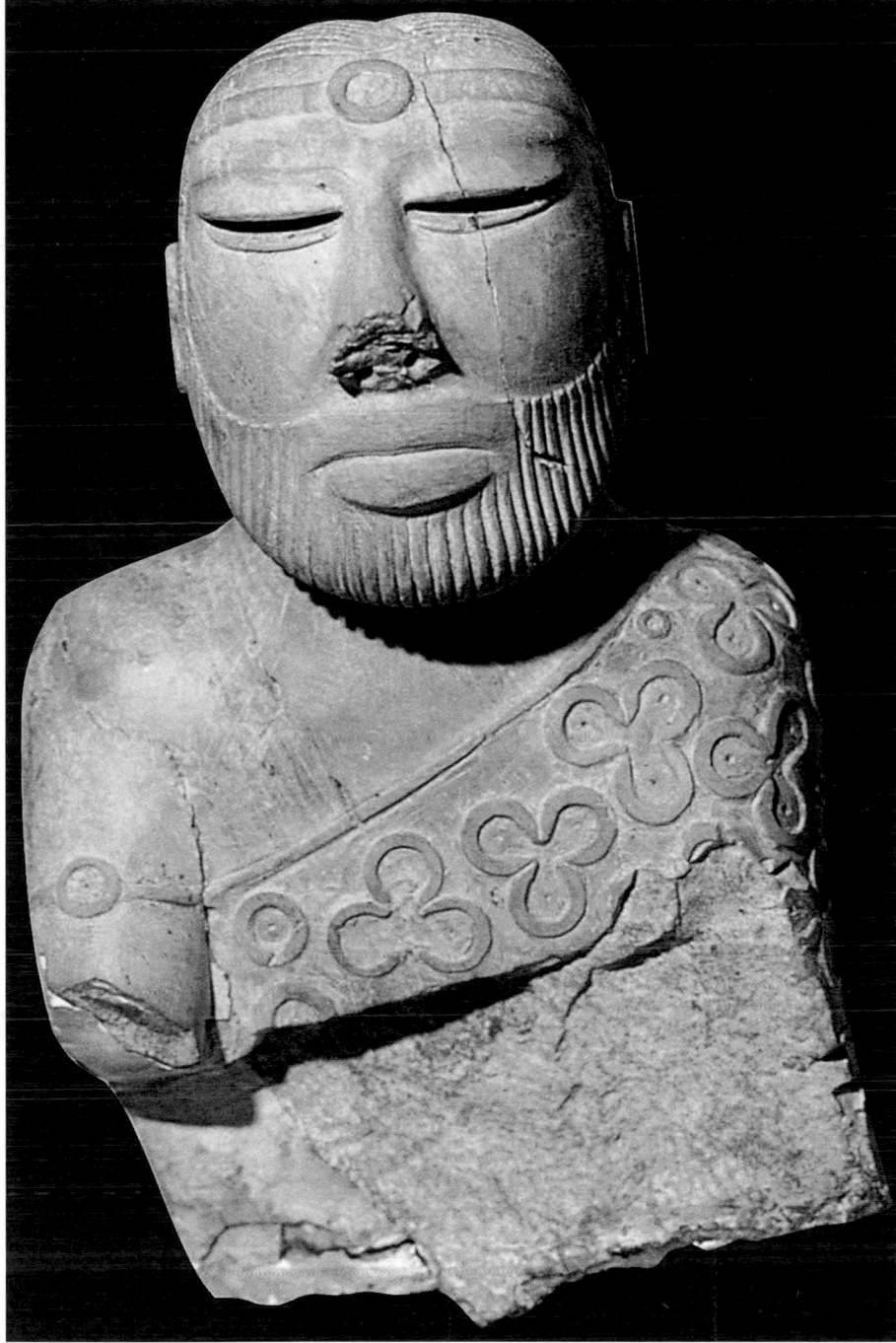

< 14.27 **Robed male figure, Mohenjo-Daro (modern Pakistan)** (c. 2000–1900 BCE). Steatite, 6⅞" high. National Museum of Pakistan, Karachi.

were highly skilled in bronze and stone sculpture. The *Bearded Man* (Fig. 14.27) from Mohenjo-Daro is carved from limestone with carefully crafted detail that seems to indicate the man's high status. His robe, draped over one shoulder, is delicately carved with a cloverleaf pattern, and he wears what appears to be jewelry around his exposed arm and head. The serene expression, enhanced by his placid lips and only slightly opened eyelids, perhaps indicates that he is a ruler or member of a priestly hierarchy.

Around the time of the New Kingdom in Egypt, Aryans invaded the Indus Valley, conquered the Sindh, and took them as slaves. The Aryans were light-skinned, semino-madic tribes who introduced the Sanskrit language and instituted the **caste system** that would persist in India until the modern era.

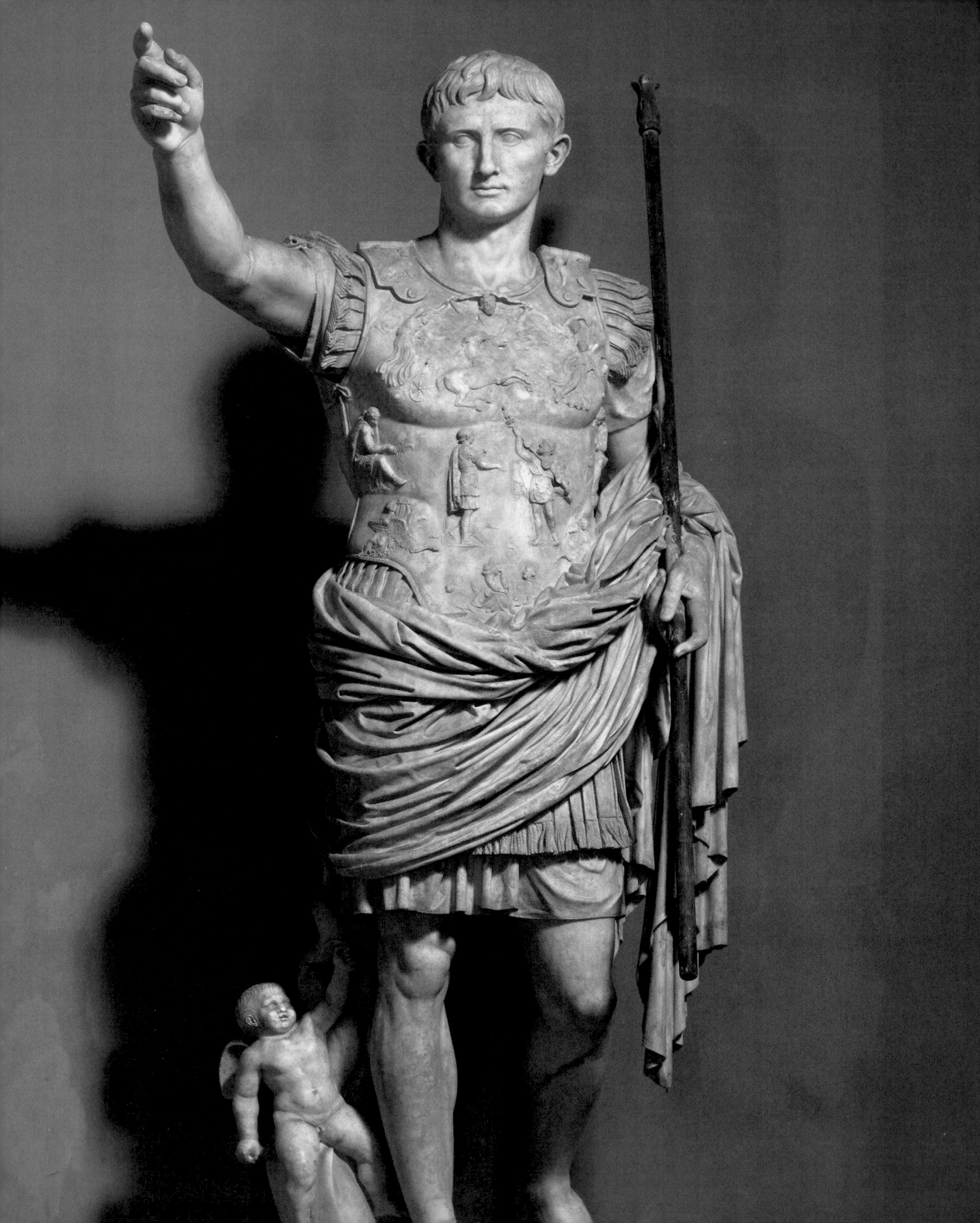

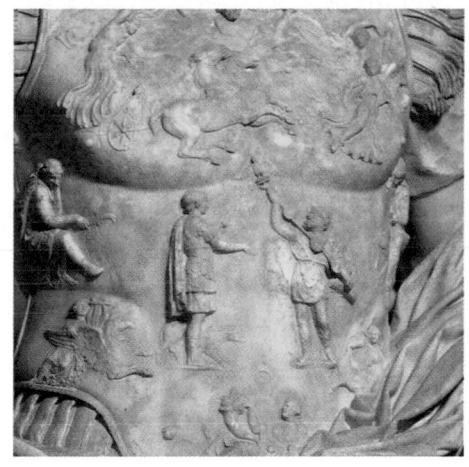

15

GREECE, ROME, AND THE EARLY JUDEO-CHRISTIAN WORLD

. . . the glory that was Greece
And the grandeur that was Rome.

—EDGAR ALLAN POE

NO OTHER culture has had as far-reaching or lasting an influence on Western art and civilization as that of ancient Greece. It has been said that "nothing moves in the world which is not Greek in origin." To this day, the Greek influence can be felt in science, mathematics, law, politics, and art. Unlike some cultures that flourished, declined, and left barely an imprint on the pages of history, that of Greece has asserted itself time and again over the 3,000 years since its birth. During the fifteenth century, there was a revival of Greek art and culture called the Renaissance, and on the eve of the French Revolution of 1789, artists of the Neoclassical period again turned to the style and subjects of ancient Greece. Our founders looked to Greek architectural styles for the buildings of our nation's capital, and nearly every small town in America has a bank, post office, or library constructed in the Greek Revival style.

Greece was conquered and absorbed by Rome— one of history's strongest and largest empires. Although its political power waned, Greece's influence as a culture did not. It was assimilated by the admiring Romans. The spirit of **Hellenism** lived on in the glorious days of the Roman Empire.

In contrast to the Greeks' intellectual and creative achievements, Rome's cultural contributions lay in the areas of building, city planning, government, and law. Although sometimes thought of as uncultured and crude, the Romans civilized much of the ancient world following military campaigns that are still studied in military academies.

◄ *Augustus of Primaporta* (c. 20 BCE). Marble, 6'8" high. Musei Vaticani, Rome, Italy.

> To claim that we can get along without study of the antique and the classics is either madness or laziness.
>
> —JEAN-AUGUSTE-DOMINIQUE INGRES

Despite its awesome might, the Roman Empire also fell. It was replaced by a force whose ideals differed greatly and whose kingdom was not of this world—Christianity. In this chapter, we will examine the artistic legacy of Greece and Rome. This legacy—called **Classical art**—has influenced almost all of Western art, from Early Christian mosaics to contemporary Manhattan skyscrapers.

Throughout the centuries that Greek and Roman tastes and arts reined over the West, there were also fascinating developments in the visual arts in Asia and the Americas. We will also consider the rise of Buddhism in India, the Qin and Han Dynasties in China, and the native arts in the Americas that gave rise to colossal statuary and great cities.

GREECE

Humanity, reason, and nature were central preoccupations of the Greek mind, together formulating their attitude toward life. The Greeks considered human beings the center of the universe—the "measure of all things." This concept is called **humanism**. The value the Greeks placed on the individual led to the development of democracy as a system of government among independent city-states throughout Greece and defined the character of Greek art, literature, and philosophy. To reach one's full potential, to be both physically and mentally fit, was an individual imperative. Perfection for the Greeks was the balance between elements: mind and body, emotion and intellect. Their love of reason and admiration for intellectual pursuits led to the development of **rationalism**, a philosophy in which knowledge is assumed to come from reason alone, without input from the senses.

The Greeks also had a passion and respect for nature and viewed human beings as a reflection of its perfect order. **Naturalism**, or truth to reality based on a keen observation of nature, guided the representation of the human figure. When what nature dispensed fell short of the Greek concept of perfection, **idealism** (the representation of forms according to an accepted standard of beauty) held sway. Humanism, rationalism, naturalism, idealism—these are the elements of Greek art and architecture.

From ancient Greece (see Map 15.1) come the names of the dramatists Aeschylus, Aristophanes, and Sophocles; the poets Homer and Hesiod; the philosophers Aristotle, Socrates, and Plato; scientists like Archimedes and

GREECE

900 BCE	660 BCE	480 BCE	450 BCE	404 BCE	323 BCE	140 BCE
GEOMETRIC PERIOD	**ARCHAIC PERIOD**	**EARLY CLASSICAL ART**	**CLASSICAL ART**	**LATE CLASSICAL ART**	**HELLENISTIC ART**	
Geometric shapes and patterns predominate in art, as seen in the Dipylon Vase	Flowing forms and fantastic animals appear in Greek pottery Black-figure painting develops, followed by the red-figure technique The format for temple architecture develops Sculptors create kouros figures	The Greeks defeat the Persians at Salamis in 480 BCE Early Classical art is marked by power and austerity Implied movement is introduced into figural sculpture, as seen in Myron's *Diskobolos*	The Parthenon is constructed Phidias oversees the sculptural program for the Parthenon Polykleitos sculpts *Doryphoros* (*Spear-Bearer*), which embodies the weight-shift principle	Late Classical sculpture is more naturalistic and emphasizes the expression of emotion Lysippos introduces a canon of proportions and becomes the court sculptor of Alexander the Great	Hellenistic art is characterized by excessive emotion, as seen in *The Laocoön* Greece becomes a province of Rome	

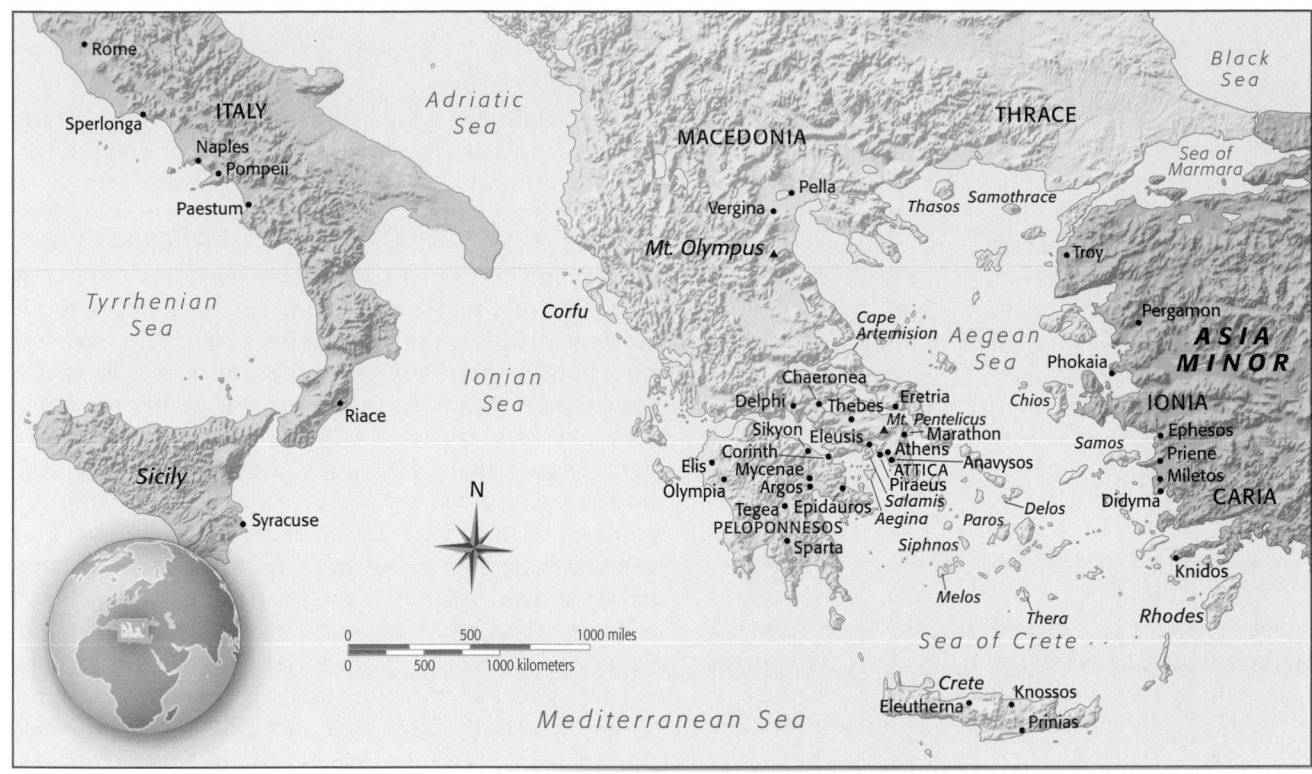

▲ MAP 15.1 The Greek World.

mathematicians like Euclid; and the historian Herodotus. It has given us gods like Zeus and Apollo, Athena and Aphrodite, and heroic figures named Achilles and Odysseus and Penelope. Even more astonishing, although Greek culture spans almost 1,000 years, its Golden Age, or period of greatest achievement, lasted no more than 80 years. As with many civilizations, the development of Greece occurred over a cycle of birth, maturation, perfection, and decline. These points in the cycle correspond to the four periods of Greek art that we will examine in this chapter: Geometric, Archaic, Classical, and Hellenistic.

Geometric Period

The **Geometric period** spanned approximately two centuries, from about 900 to 700 BCE. The period before is sometimes called the Dark Age of Greece because of a virtual collapse of civilization. Greece was gripped by chaos and poverty, the arts were lost, and its society was cut off from the outside world. During the eighth century, trade resumed, the economic situation improved, and with these, first steps were taken to regenerate the arts. The Geometric period is so called because of the predominance of geometric shapes and patterns in works of art. As in Egyptian art, the representation of the human figure was conceptual rather than optical, and usually reduced to a combination of geometric forms such as circles and triangles.

The Dipylon Vase (Fig. 15.1), a large **krater** used as a grave marker and found in the Dipylon cemetery in Athens, is an early example of the Geometric style. Except for its base, most of the vessel is decorated with

◄ 15.1 Dipylon Vase with funerary scene, Athens, Greece (c. 740 BCE). Terra-cotta, 42⅝" high. Metropolitan Museum of Art, New York.

geometric motifs, some of which may have been inspired by the patterns of woven baskets. Two thicker bands around the body of the vase feature a funeral procession composed of stylized, geometric figures. Distinctions are made between males and females, but overall, they march along with the same rigidity of the geometric patterns. The figures are a familiar combination of frontal, wedge-shaped torsos, profile legs and arms, and a profile head with a frontal eye. In the center of one of the bands, the deceased rests on a bier. Below, figures of warriors with apple core–shaped shields and teams of chariots are in attendance. The deceased was likely a Greek soldier. These geometric elements can also be seen in small bronze sculptures of the period, but the stylistic development is most evident in the art of vase painting.

Archaic Period

The **Archaic period** spanned roughly the years from 660 to 480 BCE, but the change from the Geometric style to the Archaic style in art was gradual. As Greece expanded its trade with Eastern countries, it was influenced by their art. Flowing forms and fantastic animals inspired by Mesopotamian art appeared on Greek pottery. There was a growing emphasis on the human figure, which replaced Geometric motifs.

SCULPTURE   In the Archaic period, sculpture emerged as a principal art form. In addition to sculptural decoration for buildings, freestanding, life-sized, and larger-than-life-sized statues were created. Such monumental sculpture was probably inspired by Egyptian figures that Greek travelers would have seen during the early Archaic period.

In Greek temples, the nonstructural members of the building were often ornamented with sculpture. These included the frieze and pediment. Because early Archaic sculptors were forced to work within relatively tight spaces, the figures from this period are often cramped and cumbersome.

The history of Archaic Greek sculpture, however, began more than a century earlier, about 600 BCE, with large, freestanding figures. Some of the earliest of these are called **kouros figures**, devotional or funerary statues of young men. Figure 15.2 is typical of these figures. As in Egyptian sculptures, the arms lie close to the body, the fists are clenched, and one leg advances slightly. But the kouroi (plural) are different in a principal way: the stone was carved away from the body, releasing it from the block. These male figures are also depicted in the nude. The musculature is full and thick, and emphasized by harsh, patterned lines. The kneecaps, groin muscles, rib cage, and pectoral muscles are all flexed unrealistically. The head has also been treated according to the artistic conventions of the day. The hair is stylized and intricate in pattern. The eyes are thick-lidded and stare directly forward.

The youth has very high cheekbones and clearly defined lips that appear to curl upward in a smile. This facial expression, which we also saw on the warriors of the Temple of Aphaia, seems to have been an Archaic convention and thus is called an "Archaic smile." Kouroi were found in cemeteries, where they replaced large vases as grave markers. They were also used as votive sculptures (recall the votive figures of Tell Asmar, see Fig. 14.5). In their stately repose and grand presence, these figures might impress us as gods rather than mortals. One is reminded of the oft-repeated statement, "The Greeks made their gods into men and their men into gods."

Kroisos (Fig. 15.3), a kouros figure that served as a marker on the grave of a fallen soldier by that name in Anavyssos, Greece, is later than Figure 15.2 by about seventy years, and it shows significant progress toward naturalism over that period of time. The shape and proportions of the body are more realistic, as are the flesh of the face and the flow of the hair down the back. The patterned lines describing muscle groups in the earlier kouros give way to a much more accurate portrayal of the chest, groin, kneecaps, and ankles. Some of the conventions remain the same, but the statue has a sense of vigor. Kroisos's slightly smiling lips, a feature that would become standard in Archaic sculpture, infuse the sculpture with a life-like feeling.

ARCHITECTURE   Some of the greatest accomplishments of the Greeks are witnessed in their architecture. Although their personal dwellings were simple, the temples for their gods were fantastic monuments. During the Archaic period, an architectural format was developed that provided the basis for temple architecture throughout the history and territories of ancient Greece. It consisted of a central room (derived in shape from the Mycenaean megaron) surrounded by a single or double row of columns. This room, called the cella, usually housed the cult statue of the god or goddess to whom the temple was dedicated. The overall shape of the temple was rectangular, and it had a pitched roof.

There were three styles, or orders, in Greek architecture: the **Doric, Ionic**, and **Corinthian**. The Doric order, which originated on the Greek mainland, was the earliest, simplest, and most commonly used. The more ornate Ionic order was introduced by architects from Asia Minor and was generally reserved for smaller temples. The Corinthian order, differentiated from the Ionic by its intricate column capital, was not used widely in Greece but became a favorite design of Roman architects, who adopted it in the second

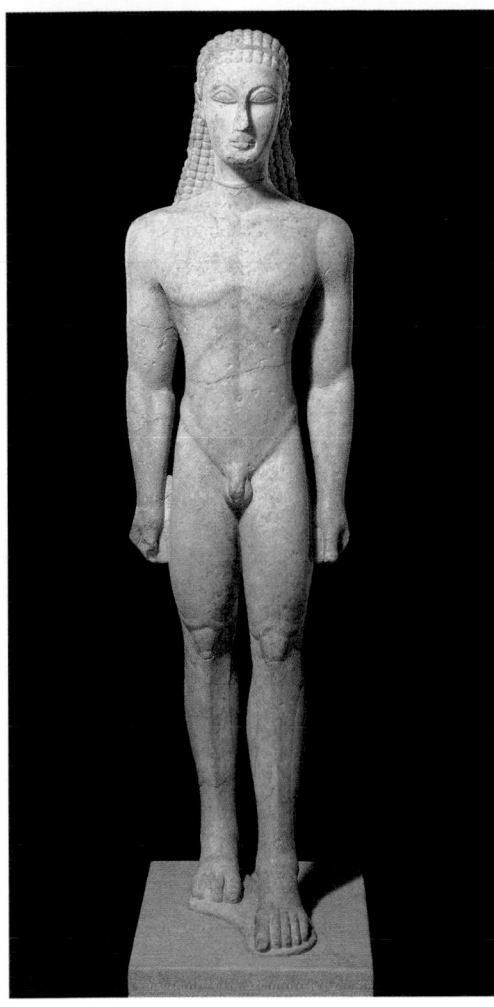

∧ **15.2** *Kouros* (c. 600 BCE). Marble, 6'4" high. Metropolitan Museum of Art, New York.

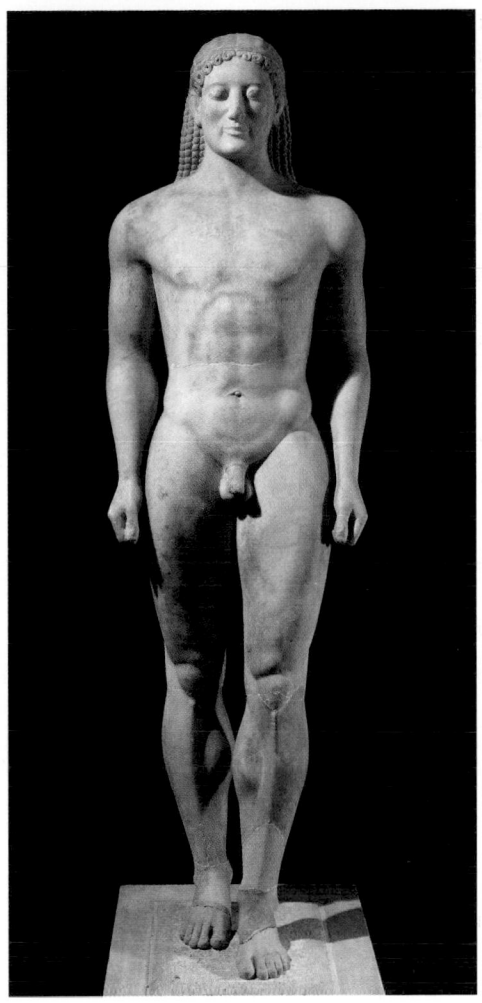

∧ **15.3** *Kroisos* (c. 530 BCE). Marble, 6'4" high. National Archaeological Museum, Athens, Greece.

century BCE. Figure 15.4 compares the Doric, Ionic, and Corinthian orders and illustrates the basic parts of the temple facade.

The major weight-bearing elements of the temple are cylindrical columns composed of drums stacked on top of one another and fitted with dowels. They sit on either a platform (**stylobate**) or a base and helped support the roof. The main vertical body, or shaft, of the column is crowned by a **capital** that marks a transition from the shaft to a horizontal member (the **entablature**) that directly bears the weight of the roof. In the Doric order, the capital is simple and cushion-like. In the Ionic order, it consists of a scroll or volute similar to those seen on the François Vase (Fig. 15.5). The Corinthian capital is by far the most elaborate, consisting of an all-around carving of overlapping acanthus leaves. The columns directly support the entablature, which is divided into three parts: the **architrave**, **frieze**, and **cornice**. The architrave of the Doric

order is a solid, undecorated horizontal band, whereas those of the Ionic and Corinthian orders are subdivided into three narrower horizontal bands. The frieze, which sits directly above the architrave, is typically carved with relief sculpture.

The Doric frieze is divided into sections called **triglyphs** and **metopes**. The triglyphs are carved panels consisting of three vertical elements. These alternate with panels that were filled with figurative sculpture carved in relief. The Ionic and Corinthian friezes, by contrast, were carved with a continuous band of figures or—particularly in the Corinthian order—repetitive, stylized motifs.

The Ionic order liberated sculptors from the constraints of the square spaces that defined the Doric frieze, allowing the figures and the narrative to flow more freely. The topmost element of the entablature is called a cornice and, together with the diagonals of the **raking cornice**, it forms a frame for the **pediment**. The triangular

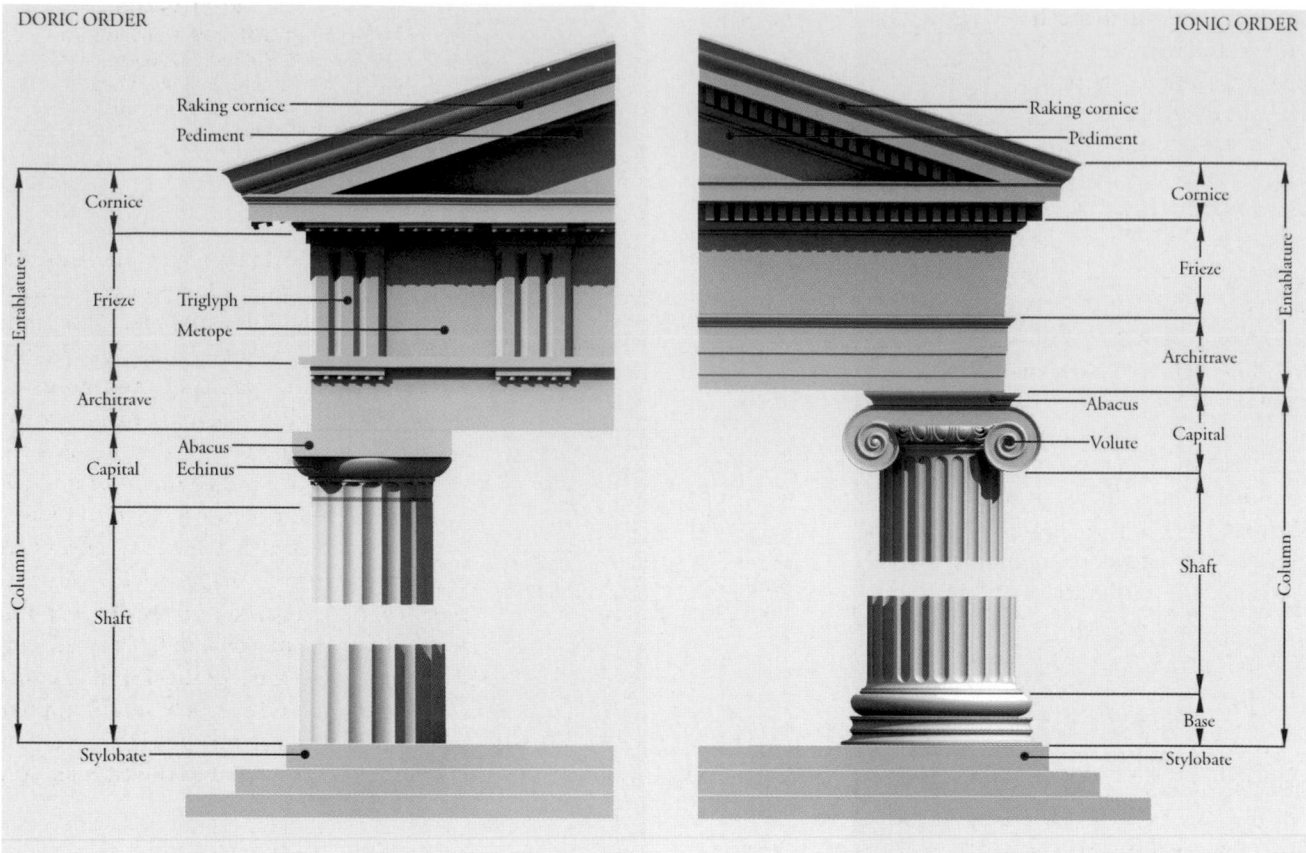

ʌ 15.4 Elevations of Doric and Ionic Orders. The Doric and Ionic orders are two of the three styles associated with Greek architecture. The third, the Corinthian order, was infrequently used, although it became a favorite among Roman architects. The distinction among the orders is mainly found in the capitals and the frieze. Artwork by John Burge.

spaces of the pediments, formed by the slope of the roof lines at the short ends of the temple, was also decorated with figurative sculpture.

The Doric order originated in the Archaic period, but it attained perfection in the buildings of the Classical period. In some buildings, like the Parthenon, the Doric and Ionic orders are combined. The Corinthian order, although developed by the Greeks, was used more universally by the Romans.

VASE PAINTING During the Archaic period, Eastern patterns and forms gradually disappeared. During the Geometric period, the human figure was subordinated to decorative motifs, but in the Archaic period, it became the preferred subject. In the François Vase (Fig. 15.5), for example, geometric patterns are restricted to a few areas. The entire body of the vessel, a volute krater, is divided into six wide bands, or registers, featuring the exploits of Greek heroes and legends, including Achilles and Theseus. Even though the drawing is somewhat stilted, the figures of men and animals have substance, and an attempt at

naturalistic gestures has been made. Unlike the figures of the Dipylon Vase, those of the François Vase are not static. In fact, the movement of the battling humans and the prancing horses is quite lively. This energetic mood is echoed in the curling shapes of the volute handles.

The François Vase is a masterpiece of Archaic vase painting. No doubt, the potter and painter were proud of their work, because the vessel is signed twice by each of them. The François Vase, named after the archeologist who found it, is an example of **black-figure painting.** The combination of black figures on a reddish background was achieved through a three-stage kiln-firing process. The figures were painted on a clay pot using a brush and a **slip,** a liquid of sifted clay, and then introduced to the kiln. The first stage of the firing process was called the **oxidizing phase,** because oxygen was allowed into the kiln. Firing under these conditions turned both the pot and the painted slip decoration red.

In the second phase of firing, called the **reducing phase,** oxygen was eliminated from the kiln, and the vase and the slip both turned black. In the third and final phase, called the **reoxidizing phase**, oxygen was again introduced into the kiln. The coarser material of the pot turned red, and the fine clay of the slip remained black. The result was a vase with black figures silhouetted against a red ground. The finer details of the figures were incised with sharp instruments that scraped away portions of the black to expose the red clay underneath or highlighted with touches of red and purple pigment. Although this technique was fairly versatile, the black figures were ultimately too visually heavy for Greek artists. Around 530 BCE, a reversal of the black-figure process was developed, enabling painters to create lighter, more realistic red figures on a black ground. By the mid sixth century BCE, there were significant innovations in vase painting. The genuine breakthrough in black-figure painting came with Exekias, whose command of the art form was unparalleled in his day. His draftsmanship and power of expression can be seen in yet another vase painting whose subject comes from the *Iliad*—Ajax the Greater playing a game of dice with his cousin Achilles (Fig. 15.6). Unlike the figures in the François Vase, which still reflect old conventions in their conceptual representation, Exekias's protagonists are rendered in almost-full profile. The almond-shaped eyes, drawn in profile, are the only feature out of sync in an otherwise optical approach. Both men hunch over a small table, their spears resting on their shoulders. Achilles is on the left, helmet on; their shields are resting behind them as if propped against a wall. It is a moment of calm between the cousins, and yet the game of chance that they play is prophetic: Ajax will carry Achilles's dead body off the battlefield.

Exekias was both the potter and the painter of this work, and the fluid relationship between the shape of the vessel and the scene reveal that fact. The imagery is placed on the broadest part of the vase and the curving lines of the men's backs are echoed in the soft tapering of the vase toward the handles and neck. Similarly, the V shape created by the intersecting spears corresponds to the taper of the vase toward its base.

However accomplished Exekias was in rendering figures, their blackness ultimately thwarted their potential for naturalism. But around 530 BCE, the **red-figure**

technique was developed, and with that, vase painting reached its apogee. The same firing process was used, but instead of painting the figures on the pot with the slip (which, remember, created black figures against the reddish background), the artist outlined the contours of the figures and then painted everything *but* the figures (the entire background, that is) with the slip. This reversal resulted in reddish figures against a black background. The red clay of the figures offered a neutral-colored expanse that could then be fleshed out with much detail, applied with a fine brush rather than incised. A glimpse at the work of Euphronios (the painter) and Euxitheos (the

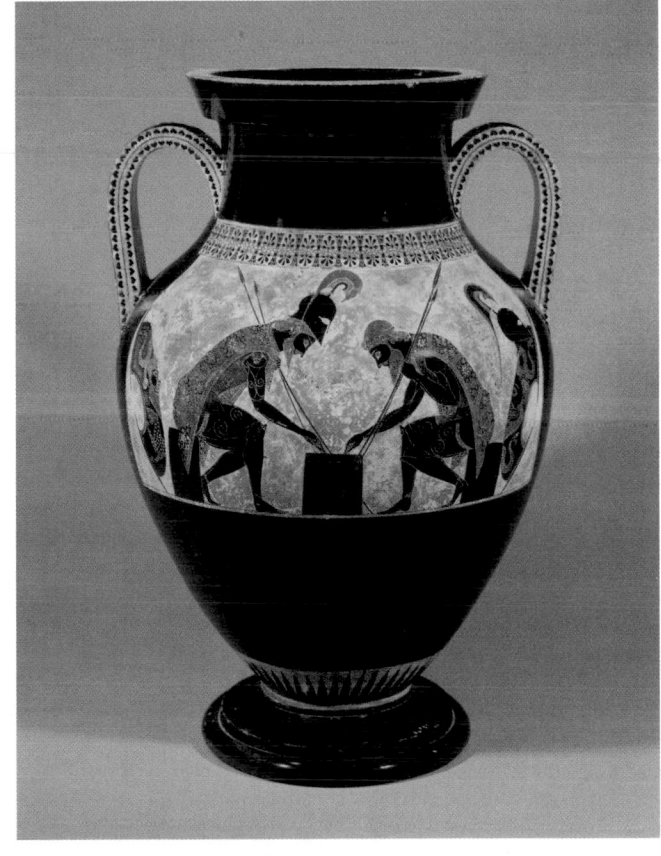

∧ 15.6 EXEKIAS, *Achilles and Ajax Playing Dice* (c. 540–530 BCE). Amphora, 2' high. Musei Vaticani, Rome, Italy.

> 15.7 EUPHRONIOS (THE PAINTER) AND EUXITHEOS (THE POTTER), *Death of Sarpedon* (c. 515 BCE). Museo Nazionale di Villa Giulia, Rome, Italy.

potter) (Fig. 15.7) will immediately show the advantages of red-figure technique over black-figure. The subject here is the death of Sarpedon, a Trojan warrior killed by Achilles's best friend, Patroclus. In the description of the moment that Sarpedon was felled by Patroclus's hand, Homer uses simile to juxtapose the graphic violence of the world of war with a mental picture of nature and ordinary life—the normalcy of familiar things longed for and taken for granted.

Euphronios depicts Sarpedon, now dead, being carried to the underworld by two winged figures, Hypnos (Sleep; the word *hypnotic* is related) and Thanatos (Death). Hermes, the messenger god, watches over the group; in his hand is the attribute that helps us identify him—a magical rod called a *caduceus*. The characters are rendered in naturalistic poses: the winged helpers are shown in profile, and Sarpedon is mostly a frontal view (although his legs and arms twist realistically). The artist has described the musculature, the wings, the armor, and the clothing in great detail—all in delicate, linear brushwork. Colorful painted accents are used on Sarpedon's flowing hair and the blood that is streaming from several wounds. The static quality that pervades Exekias's vase has disappeared. The relationship of the scene to the shape of the pot is again noteworthy—as is the symmetrical composition.

Although some artists continued to produce black-figure works (there are even a few painted in black-figure on one side and red-figure on the other), by the end of the Archaic period, almost all had turned to the new style. The last Archaic vase painters were among the greatest red-figure artists. Works such as the Euphronios Vase have a solidity and monumentality that altogether transcend the usual limitations of the medium.

The late Archaic period produced significant works of art and architecture against the backdrop of brutal war with the Persians. By the late fifth century BCE, it appeared as if that empire would consume all of Greece. After horrible, violent losses, the Greeks defeated the Persians in a decisive battle on the plain of Marathon and captured a naval victory at Salamis. Greek pride surged and a Western identity was formed—one that stood in self-conscious opposition to the perceived barbarism of the Persians and their Asian civilization.

Early Classical Art

The change from the Archaic to the Classical period coincided with the Greek victory over the Persians at Salamis in 480 BCE. The Greek mood was elevated after this feat, and a new sense of unity among the city-states prevailed, propelling the country into its "Golden Age." Athens, which was sacked by the Persians, became the center for all important postwar activity and the revival of the arts. The style of Early Classical art is marked by a power and austerity that reflected what were seen as Greek traits responsible for the defeat of the Persians. Although Early Classical sculpture developed beyond Archaic stylizations, some of the rigidity of the earlier period remains. The Early Classical style is therefore sometimes referred to as the Severe style.

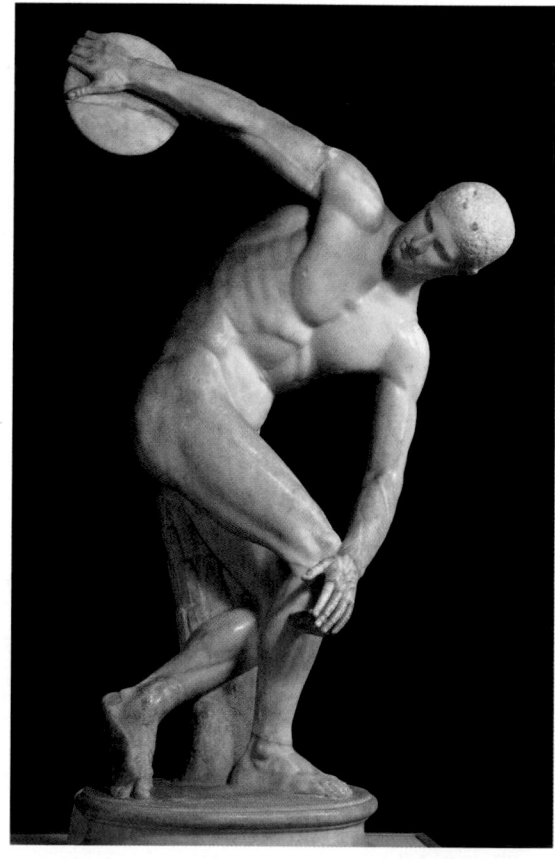

▲ 15.8 MYRON, *Diskobolos (Discus Thrower)* (c. 450 BCE). Roman marble copy after bronze original, 5'1" high. Palazzo Massimo alle Terme, Museo Nazionale Romano, Rome, Italy.

> Raphael is a great master. Velázquez is a great master. El Greco is a great master, but the secret of plastic beauty is located at a greater distance: in the Greeks at the time of Pericles.
>
> — PABLO PICASSO

SCULPTURE The most significant development in Early Classical art was the introduction of implied movement in figurative sculpture. This went hand-in-hand with the artist's keener observation of nature. One of the most widely copied works of this period, which encompasses these new elements, is the *Diskobolos* (Fig. 15.8), or Discus Thrower, by Myron. Like most Greek monumental sculpture, it survives only in a marble Roman copy after the bronze original. The life-sized statue depicts an event from the Olympic Games—the discus throw. The athlete, a young man in his prime, is caught by the artist at the moment when the arm stops its swing backward and prepares to sling forward to release the discus. His muscles are tensed as he reaches for the strength to release the object. His torso intersects the arc of his extended arms, resembling an arrow pulled taut on a bow. It is an image of pent-up energy at the moment before release. As in most of Greek Classical art, there is a balance between motion and stability, between emotion and restraint.

Classical Art

Greek sculpture and architecture reached their height of perfection during the Classical period. Greece embarked upon a period of peace—albeit short-lived—and turned its attention to rebuilding its monuments and advancing art, drama, and music. The dominating force behind these accomplishments in Athens was the dynamic statesman Pericles. His reputation was recounted centuries after his death by the Greek historian Plutarch. On the one hand, Plutarch described the anger of the Greek city-states at Pericles's use of funds that had been set aside for mutual protection to pay for his ambitious Athenian building program. On the other hand, Plutarch wrote glowingly about postwar Athens: "in its beauty, each work was, even at that time, ancient, and yet, in its perfection, each looks even at the present time as if it were fresh and newly built. . . . It is as if some ever-flowering life and unaging spirit had been infused into the creation of these works."

ARCHITECTURE After the Persians destroyed the Acropolis, the Athenians refused to rebuild their shrines with the fallen stones that the enemy had desecrated. What followed was a massive building campaign under the direction of Pericles. Work began first on the temple that was sacred to the goddess Athena, protector of Athens. This temple, the Parthenon (Fig. 15.9), became one of the most influential buildings in the history of architecture.

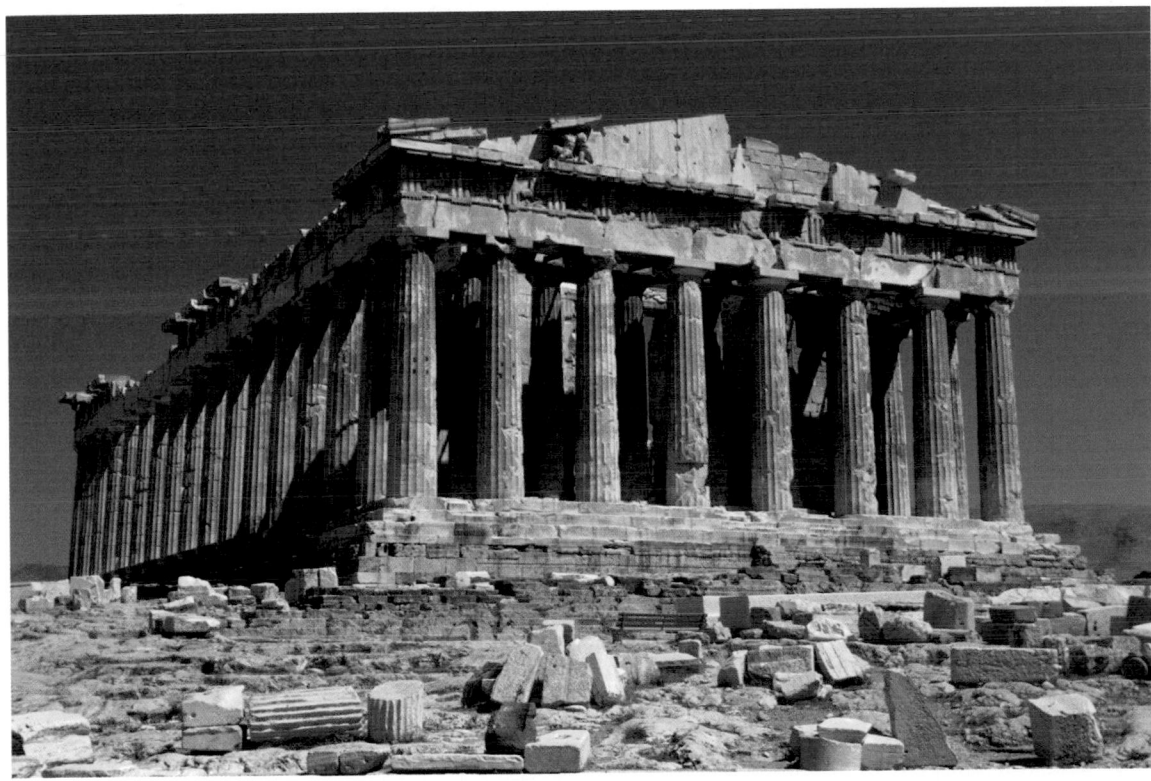

< 15.9 ICTINOS AND CALLICRATES, The Parthenon on the Acropolis, Athens, Greece (448–432 BCE).

THEORY & PRACTICE

Polykleitos's Canon: The Body Beautiful

THE ANCIENT GREEK IDEAL of beauty resides in their abstract notions of order, harmony, and perfection—in the dynamic balance between action and restraint, motion and rest. Influential philosophers such as Pythagoras, who lived in the late sixth century BCE (and whose name may be familiar to you from your geometry studies for what is known as his Pythagorean theorem), sought to explain beauty in terms of harmonic proportions observable in nature. These harmonious relationships, Pythagoras believed, could be expressed mathematically. The essence of this ideal pertained as much to a cosmos well designed and a life well lived as it did to a work of art well made.

The renowned fifth-century BCE sculptor Polykleitos built on Pythagoras's notions of harmonic proportions (and his mathematical formulae for harmonic chords in music) and codified them into a precise mathematical formula for representing the ideal human form. The idea behind his **canon** (or set of rules) was that ideal beauty (perfection) in a sculpture of the human form could be achieved through exacting application of principles regarding the ratio and proportion of body parts in relation to one another. Polykleitos's theory is lost, but it had been referred to by several important writers, including the historian Pliny the Elder and the physician-philosopher Galen of Pergamum. Galen wrote,

> [Beauty in art results from] the commensurability of the parts, such as that of finger to finger, and of all the fingers to the palm and the wrist, and of these to the forearm, and of the forearm to the upper arm and, in fact, of everything to everything else, just as it is written in the *Canon of Polykleitos*. . . . Polykleitos supported his treatise [by creating] a statue according to the tenets of his treatise, and called the statue, like the work, the Canon.

The physical manifestation of Polykleitos's canon is his *Doryphoros* (Fig. 15.10A). The work is a statue of an athlete that was not copied from life but rather designed with his principles of harmonious relationships in mind. It represents the artist's notion of ideal human form: every part of the body is either a specific fraction or multiple of every other part.

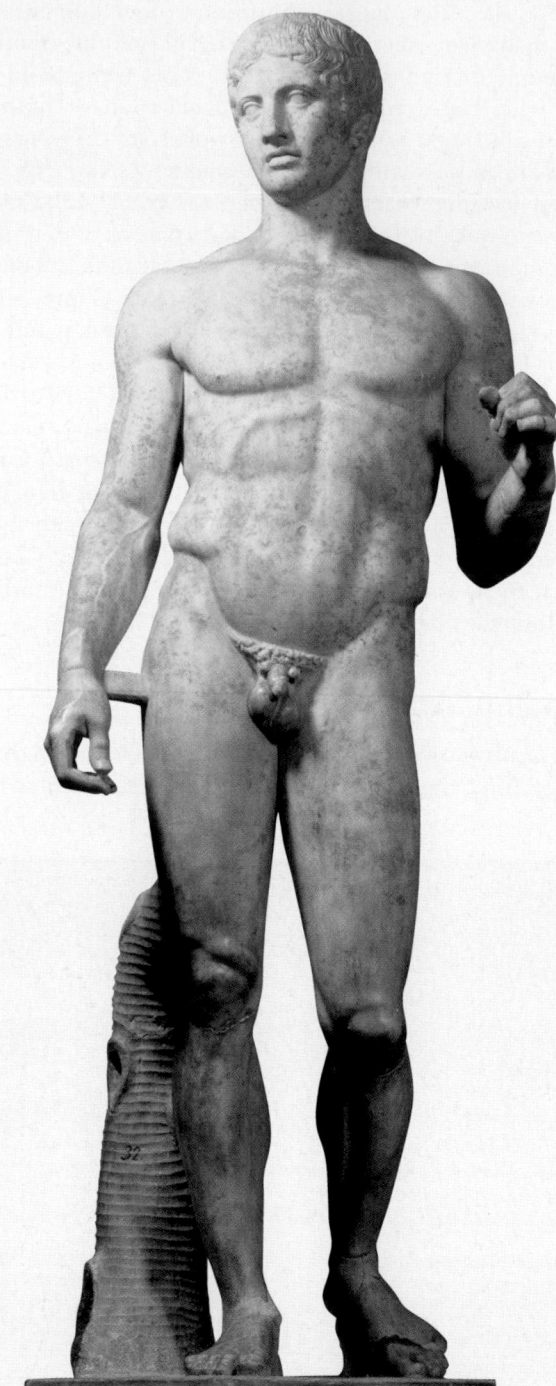

∧ **15.10A POLYKLEITOS,** *Doryphoros (Spear-Bearer)* (c. 450–440 BCE). Marble, Roman copy after Greek original; 6'11" high. Museo Archeologico Nazionale, Naples, Italy.

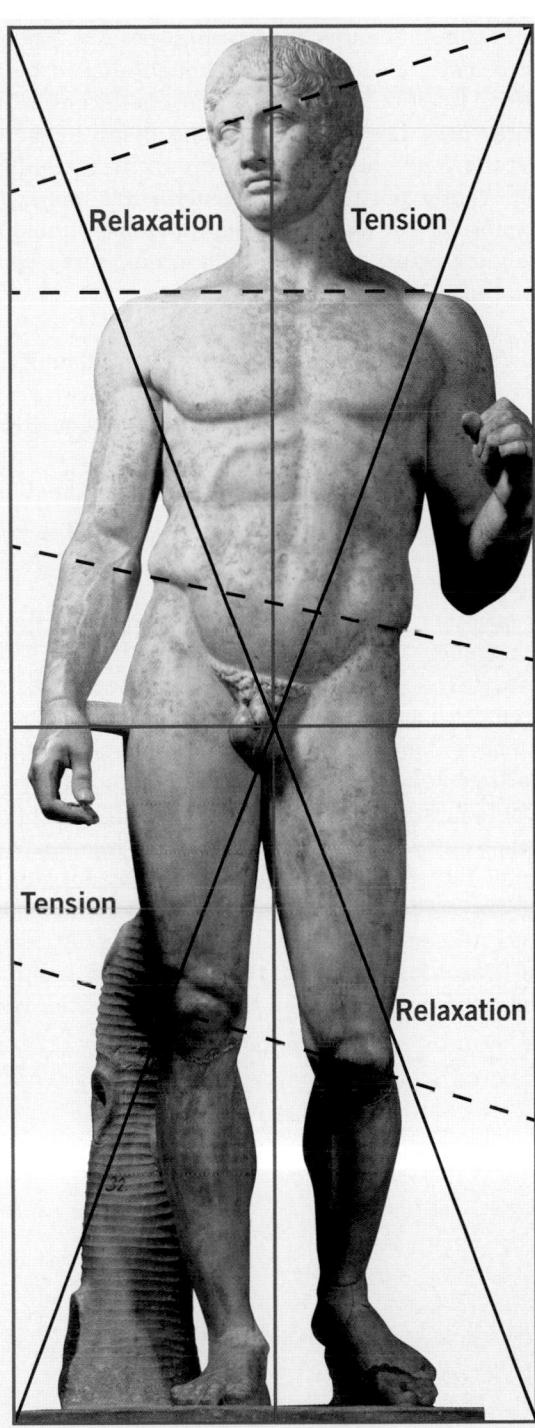

Relaxation

Tension

Tension

Relaxation

∧ **15.10B** Polykleitos's *Doryphoros (Spear-Bearer)* showing the sculptor's creation of a "harmony of opposites," as in the contrast of tension and relaxation.

Polykleitos's sense of order and harmony went beyond physical proportions. Using what can be labeled a "harmony of opposites," he imposed this sense of order on the movement implied in his statues as well. In the *Doryphoros,* the opposite sides of the body feature different actions and different lines. The right, tensed leg (on the left side of the statue, as we look at it head on) supports the weight of the figure and forms a strong vertical line. The right arm hangs down in relaxed position; the vertical line of this arm echoes the line of the leg below it. These straight lines are in opposition to a relaxed left leg bent at the knee and a tensed arm bent at the elbow. The contrast of tension and relaxation in the body is organized with a system of "cross-balance." Tension and relaxation are connected diagonally across the body; the relaxed arm *opposes* the relaxed leg, and the tensed arm *opposes* the tensed, weight-bearing leg. The positioning of the body in this manner, known as **contrapposto**, creates a slight shift in the alignment of the hips, which turn to the left; Polykleitos balances that shift by turning the head somewhat to the right. The result is a harmonious balance of opposing parts—of vertical lines of stability and diagonal lines of movement (**Fig. 15.10B**)—that creates ease and naturalism belying the rigor of the formulaic quality of the design.

To a large extent, Polykleitos's canon forms the pedagogical foundation of classes in figure drawing. Students are taught to relate one part of the body to another and to be mindful of proportions that are harmonious and accurate relative to the whole. But these proportions do not necessarily correspond to the classroom model, much less the body types of the general population. They are strictly guideposts for framing the human figure in a representational style. If the artistic goal, on the other hand, is to evoke a specific emotional response or to dramatize the subject or to emphasize parts of a composition for narrative purposes, ideal proportions can be manipulated or distorted.

Constructed by the architects Ictinos and Callicrates, the Parthenon stands as the most accomplished representative of the Doric order, although it does include some Ionic elements. A single row of Doric columns, now gracefully proportioned, surrounds a two-roomed cella that housed a treasury and a 40-foot-high statue of Athena made of ivory and gold. At first glance, the architecture appears austere, with its rigid progression of vertical elements crowned by the strong horizontal of its entablature. Yet few of the building's lines are strictly vertical or horizontal. For example, the stylobate, or top step of the platform from which the columns rise, is not straight across, but curves downward toward the ends. This convex shape is echoed in the entablature. The columns are not exactly vertical, but rather tilt inward. They are not evenly spaced; the intervals between the corner columns are narrower. The shafts of the columns also differ from one another. The corner columns have a wider diameter, for example. In addition, the shaft of each column swells in diameter as it rises from the base, narrowing once again before reaching the capital. This swelling is called **entasis**.

The reasons for these variations are not known for certain, although there have been several hypotheses. Some art historians have suggested that the change from straight to curved lines is functional. A convex stylobate, for example, might make drainage easier. Others have suggested that the variations are meant to compensate for perceptual distortions on the part of the viewer that would make straight lines look curved from a distance. Regardless of the actual motive, we can assume that the designers of the Parthenon sought an integrated and organic appearance to their building. The wide base and relatively narrower roof give the appearance of a structure that is anchored firmly to the ground yet growing dramatically from it. Although it has a grandeur based

on a kind of austerity, it also has a lively plasticity. It appears as if the Greeks conceived their architecture as large, freestanding sculpture.

The subsequent history of the Parthenon is interesting and shocking. It was used as a Byzantine church, a Roman Catholic church, and a mosque. The Parthenon survived more or less intact, although altered by these successive functions, until the seventeenth century, when the Turks used it as an ammunition dump in their war against the Venetians. Venetian rockets hit the bull's-eye, and the center portion of the temple was blown out in the explosion. The cella still lies in ruins, although fortunately the exterior columns and entablatures were not beyond repair.

SCULPTURE The sculptor Phidias was commissioned by Pericles to oversee the entire sculptural program of the Parthenon. Although he concentrated his own efforts on creating the ivory and gold statue of Athena, his assistants followed his style closely. The Phidian style is characterized by a lightness of touch, attention to realistic detail, contrast of textures, and fluidity and spontaneity of line and movement.

As on other Doric temples, the sculpted surfaces of the Parthenon were confined to the friezes and the pediments. The subjects of the Doric frieze were battles between the Lapiths and the Centaurs, the Greeks and the Amazons, and the gods and the giants. In addition, the Parthenon had a continuous, inner Ionic frieze. This was carved with scenes from the Panathenaic procession, an event that took place every four years when the **peplos** of the statue of Athena was changed. The pediments depicted the birth of Athena and the contest between Athena and Poseidon for the city of Athens.

The Three Goddesses (Fig. 15.11), a figural group from the corner of the east pediment, is typical of the Phidian

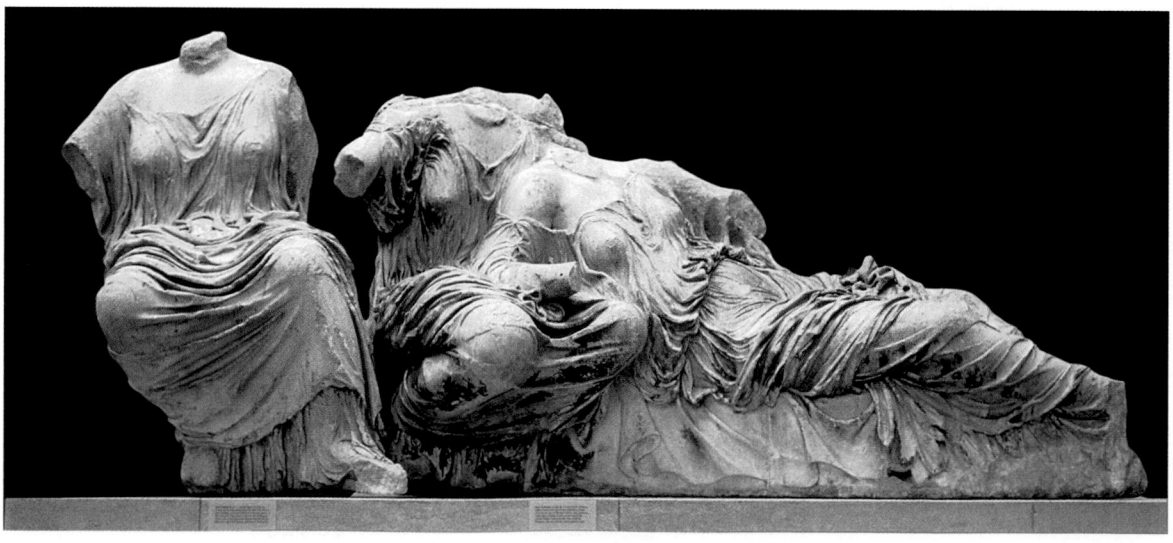

< 15.11 *The Three Goddesses* (c. 438–432 BCE). From the Parthenon, east pediment. Marble, center figure: 4"7" high. British Museum, London, England.

style. The bodies of the goddesses are weighty and well articulated, and their poses and gestures are naturalistic. The drapery falls over the bodies in realistic folds, and there is a marvelous contrast of textures between the heavier cloth that wraps around the legs and the more diaphanous fabric covering the upper torsos. The thinner drapery clings to the body as if wet, following the contours of the flesh. The intricate play of the linear folds renders a tactile quality not seen in art before this time. The lines both gently envelop the individual figures and integrate them in a dynamically flowing composition.

As mentioned previously, Greece had at one time come under Turkish rule. Some of the Parthenon sculptures were taken down by Lord Elgin between 1801 and 1803 while he was British ambassador to Constantinople. He sold them to the British government, who put them on display at the British Museum. Although there has been prolonged controversy concerning their return to Greece, there is no doubt that Lord Elgin saved the marbles from utter destruction.

Some of the greatest freestanding sculpture of the Classical period was created by a rival of Phidias named Polykleitos. His favorite medium was bronze, and his preferred subject was athletes. As with most Greek sculpture, we know his work primarily from marble Roman copies of the bronze originals. Polykleitos's work differed markedly from that of Phidias. Whereas the Parthenon sculptor emphasized the reality of appearances and aimed to delight the senses through textural contrasts, Polykleitos's statues were based on reason and intellect. Rather than mimic nature, he tried to perfect nature by developing a canon of proportions from which he would derive his "ideal" figures.

Polykleitos's most famous sculpture is the *Doryphoros* (see Fig. 15.11A and 15.11B in the nearby Theory and Practice feature), or *Spear-Bearer*. The artist has "idealized" the athletic figure—that is, made it more perfect and more beautiful—by imposing on it a set of laws relating part to part (for example, the entire body is equal in height to eight heads). Although some of Phidias's spontaneity is lost, the result is an almost godlike image of grandeur and strength. One of the most significant elements of Polykleitos's style is the **weight-shift principle**. The athlete rests his weight on the right leg, which is planted firmly on the ground. It forms a strong vertical that is echoed in the vertical of the relaxed arm. These are counterbalanced by a relaxed left leg bent at the knee and a tensed left arm bent at the elbow. Tension and relaxation of the limbs are balanced across the body *diagonally*. The relaxed arm opposes the relaxed leg, and the tensed arm is opposite the tensed, weight-bearing leg. The weight-shift principle lends naturalism to the figure. Rather than face forward in a rigid pose, as do the kouroi, the *Doryphoros* stands comfortably at rest. The ease and naturalism, however, were derived from a compulsive balancing of opposing parts.

Late Classical Art

SCULPTURE   The Late Classical period brought a more humanistic and naturalistic style, with emphasis on the expression of emotion. The stocky muscularity of the Polykleitan ideal was replaced by a more languid sensuality and graceful proportions. One of the major proponents of this new style was Praxiteles. His works show a lively spirit that was lacking in some of the more austere sculptures of the Classical period.

The *Hermes and Dionysos* of Praxiteles (Fig. 15.12), interestingly, is the only undisputed original work we have by the Greek masters of the Classical era. Unlike most other sculptors who favored bronze, Praxiteles excelled in carving. His ability to translate harsh stone surfaces into subtly modeled flesh was unsurpassed. We need only compare his figural group with the *Doryphoros* to witness the changes that had taken place since the Classical period. Hermes is delicately carved, and his musculature

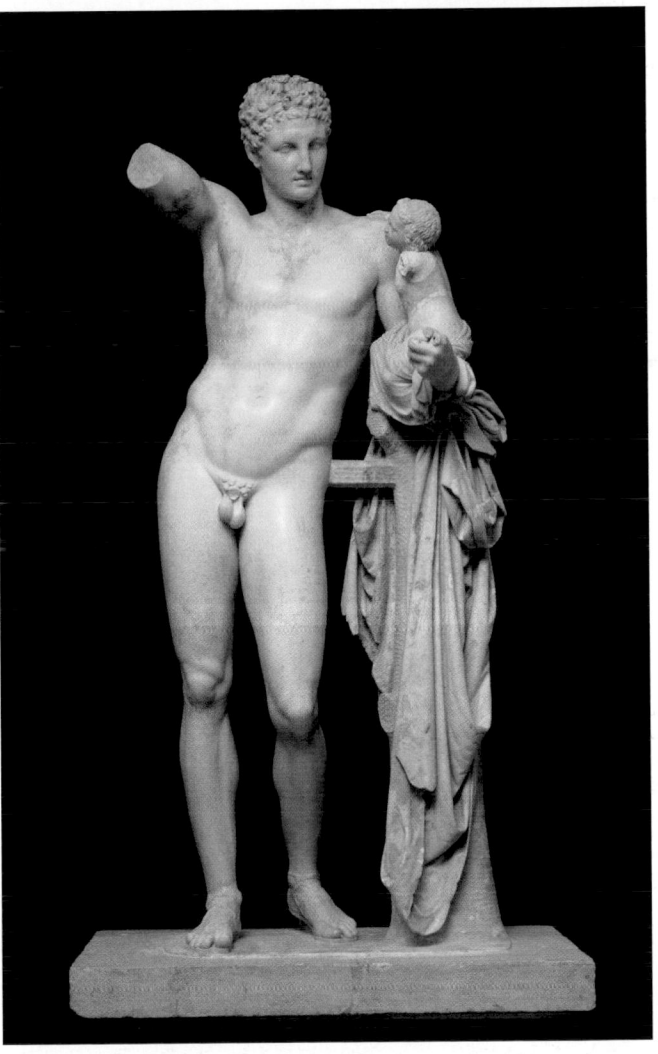

∧ 15.12 **PRAXITELES**, *Hermes and Dionysos* (c. 330–320 BCE). Marble, 7'1" high. Archaeological Museum, Olympia, Greece.

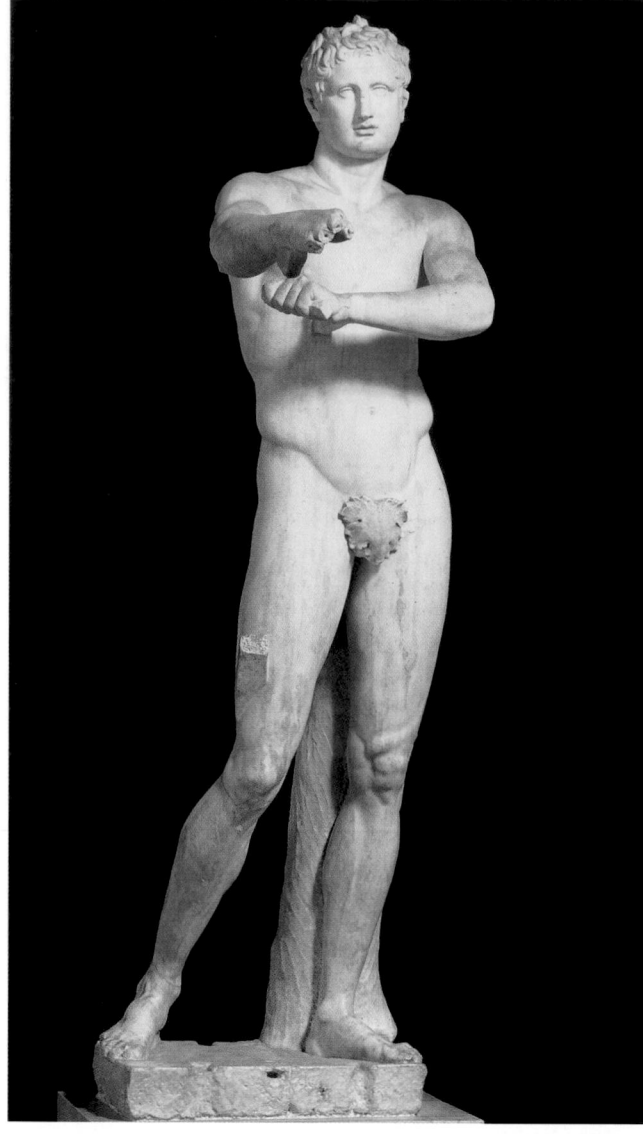

▲ 15.13 **LYSIPPOS,** *Apoxyomenos* (c. 330 BCE). Roman marble copy after a bronze original, 6'6¾" high. Musei Vaticani, Rome, Italy.

called an **S curve**, because the contours of the body form an S shape around an imaginary vertical axis.

Perhaps most remarkable is the emotional content of the sculpture. The aloof quality of Classical statuary is replaced with a touching scene between the two gods. Hermes's facial expression as he teases the child is one of pride and amusement. Dionysos, on the other hand, exhibits typical infant behavior—he is all hands and reaching impatiently for something to eat. There remains a certain restraint to the movement and to the expressiveness, but it is definitely on the wane. In the Hellenistic period, that classical balance will no longer pertain, and the emotion present in Praxiteles's sculpture will reach new peaks.

The most important and innovative sculptor to follow Praxiteles was Lysippos. He introduced a new canon of proportions that resulted in more slender and graceful figures, departing from the stockiness of Polykleitos and assuming the fluidity of Praxiteles. Most important, however, was his new concept of the motion of figure in space. All of the sculptures that we have seen so far have had a two-dimensional perspective. That is, the whole of the work can be viewed from a single point of view, standing in front of the sculpture. This is not the case in works such as the *Apoxyomenos* (Fig. 15.13) by Lysippos. The figure's arms envelop the surrounding space. The athlete is scraping oil and grime from his body with a dull knife-like implement. This stance forces the viewer to walk around the sculpture to appreciate its details. Rather than adhere to a single plane, as even the S-curve figure of *Hermes* does, the *Apoxyomenos* seems to spiral around a vertical axis.

Lysippos's reputation was almost unsurpassed. In fact, his work was so widely admired that Alexander the Great, the Macedonian king who spread Greek culture throughout the Near East, chose him as his court sculptor. It is said that Lysippos was the only sculptor permitted to execute portraits of Alexander. Years after the *Apoxyomenos* was created, it was still seen as a magnificent work of art. Pliny, a Roman writer on the arts, recounted an amusing story about the sculpture:

> Lysippos made more statues than any other artist, being, as we said, very prolific in the art; among them was a youth scraping himself with a strigil, which Marcus Agrippa dedicated in front of his baths and which the Emperor Tiberius was astonishingly fond of. Tiberius was, in fact, unable to restrain himself in this case and had it moved to his own bedroom, substituting another statue in its place. When, however, the indignation of the Roman people was so great that it demanded, by an uproar, that the Apoxyomenos be replaced, the emperor, although he had fallen in love with it, put it back.[1]

is realistically depicted, suggesting the preference of nature as a model over adherence to a rigid, predefined canon. The messenger-god holds the infant Dionysos, the god of wine, in his left arm, which is propped up by a tree trunk covered with a drape. His right arm is broken above the elbow but reaches out in front of him. It has been suggested that Hermes once held a bunch of grapes toward which the infant was reaching.

Praxiteles's skill in depicting variations in texture was extraordinary. Note, for example, the differences between the solid, toned muscles of the man and the soft, cuddly flesh of the child; or rough, curly hair against the flawless, ivory skin; or the deeply carved, billowing drapery alongside the subtly modeled flesh. The easy grace of the sculpture comes from applying a double weight-shift principle. Hermes shifts his weight from the right leg to the left arm, resting it on the tree. This position causes a sway which is

[1]J. J. Pollitt, *The Art of Greece 1400–31 BCE: Sources and Documents* (Englewood Cliffs, NJ: Prentice Hall, 1965), 144.

Hellenistic Art

Greece entered the Hellenistic period under the reign of Alexander the Great. His father had conquered the democratic city-states, and Alexander had been raised amid the art and culture of Greece. When he ascended the throne, he conquered Persia, Egypt, and the entire Near East, bringing with him his beloved Greek culture, or Hellenism. With the vastness of Alexander's empire, the significance of the city of Athens as an artistic and cultural center waned.

Hellenistic art is characterized by excessive, almost theatrical emotion and the use of illusionistic effects to heighten realism. In three-dimensional art, the space surrounding the figures is treated as an extension of the viewer's space, at times narrowing the fine line between art and reality.

SCULPTURE The Laocoön (Fig. 15.14) illustrates the Hellenistic artist's preoccupation with high drama and unleashed passion. This famous work shows the Trojan priest Laocoön, punished by the gods for his attempt to warn his people against bringing into their city the wooden horse left by the Greeks. To silence the priest, Apollo sends two sea serpents to strangle him and his

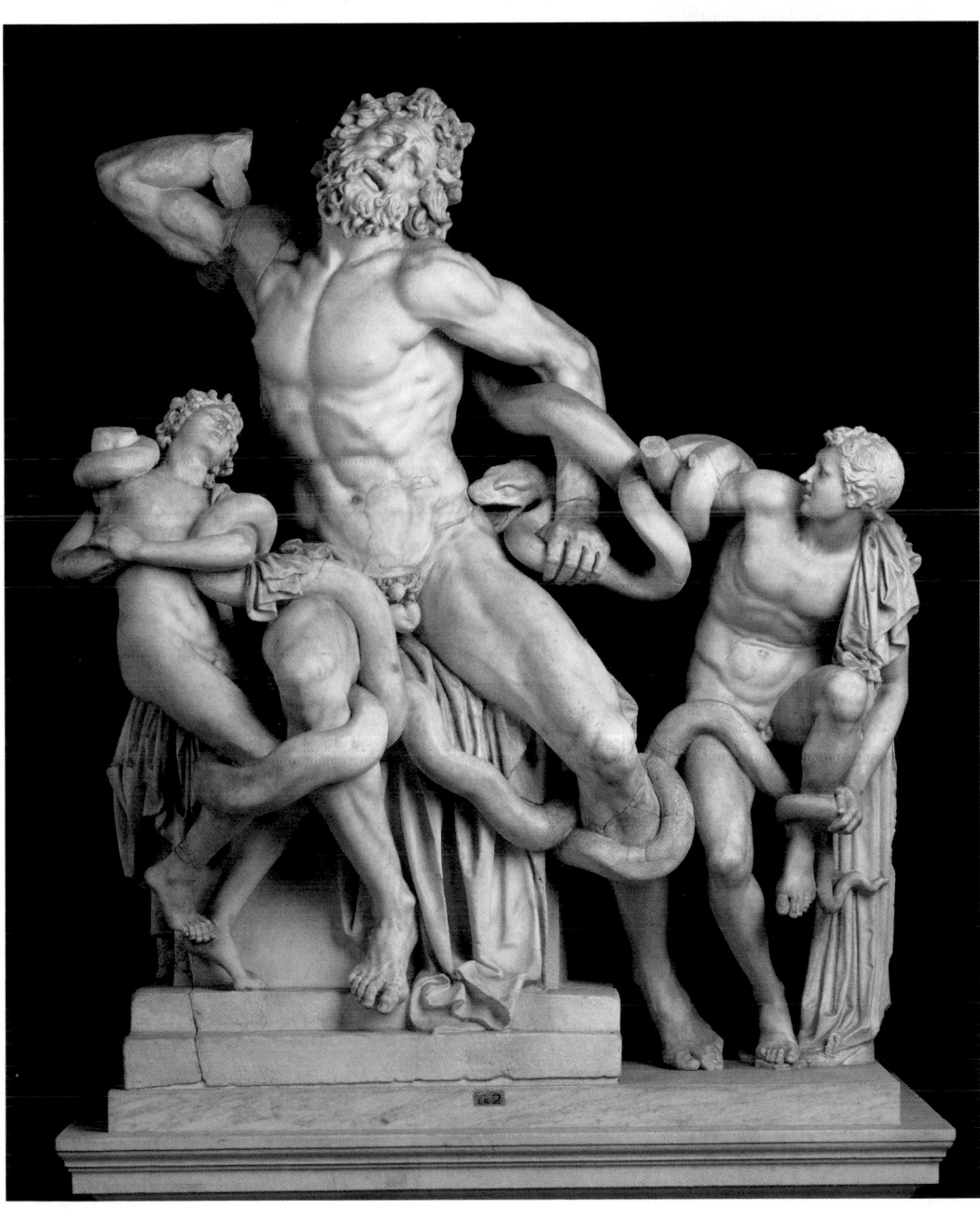

‹ 15.14 ATHENADORUS, AGESANDER, AND POLYDORUS OF RHODES, *Laocoön and His Sons* (early 1st century CE). Roman copy. Marble, 82¾" high. Musei Vaticani, Rome, Italy.

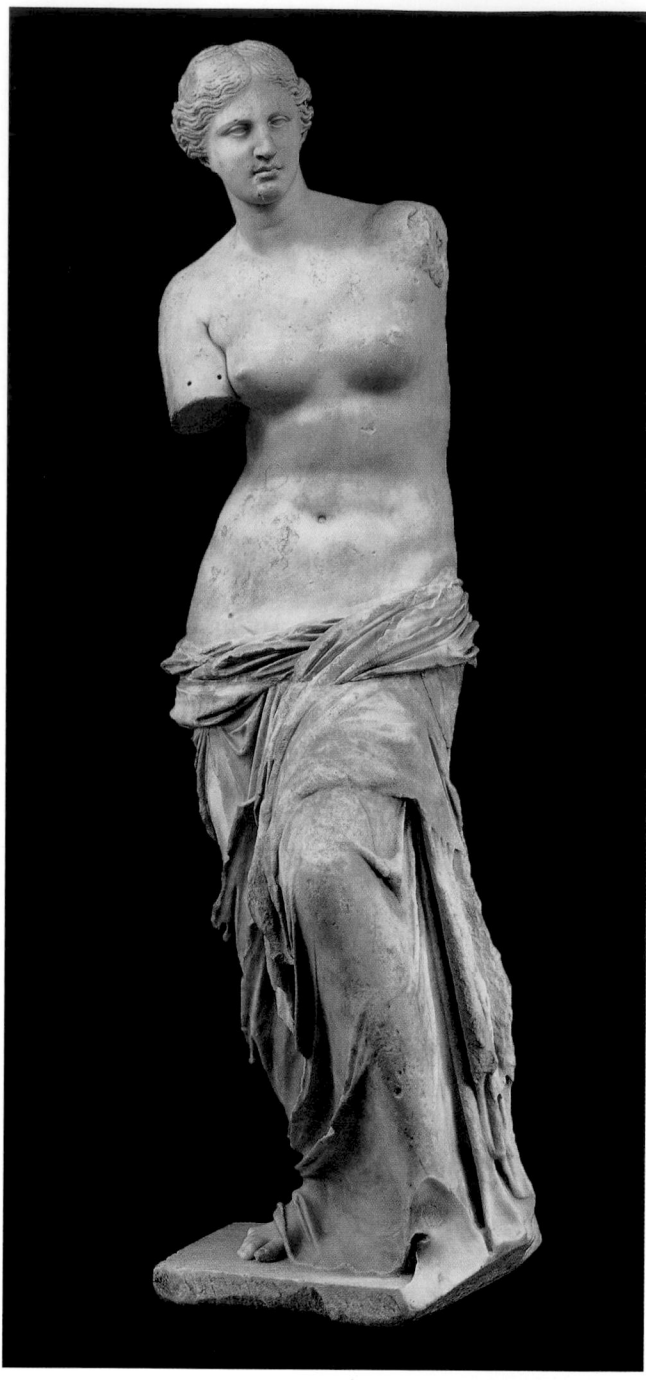

▲ 15.15 **ALEXANDROS OF ANTIOCH-ON-THE-MEANDER,** *Aphrodite (Venus de Milo)* (c. 150–125 BCE). Melos, Greece. Marble, height 6'7". Louvre, Paris, France.

of the Classical period. The harsh realism and passionate emotion of the Hellenistic artist could not be further in spirit from the serene and idealized form of the *Aphrodite* (Fig. 15.15), often called the *Venus de Milo*. This contradictory style owes much to the artistic legacy of Praxiteles.

In 146 BCE, the Romans sacked Corinth, a Greek city on the Peloponnesus, after which Greek power waned. Both the territory and the culture of Greece were assimilated by the powerful and growing Roman state. It has been said that "all roads lead to Rome," and so will this chapter. First, however, let us examine the art of the Etruscans, a civilization on the Italian peninsula that predated that of the Romans.

THE ETRUSCANS

The center of power of the Roman state was the peninsula of Italy, but the Romans did not gain supremacy over this area until the fourth century BCE, when they began to conquer the Etruscans. The Italian peninsula was inhabited by many peoples, but the Etruscan civilization was the most significant one before that of ancient Rome. The Etruscans had a long and interesting history, dating back to around 700 BCE, the period of transition from the Geometric to the Archaic period in Greece. They were not an indigenous peoples but are believed to have come from Asia Minor. This link may explain some similarities between Etruscan art and culture and that of Eastern countries.

Etruria and Greece had some things in common: Both were great sea powers, and both were divided into independent city-states. The Etruscans even borrowed motifs and styles from the art of Greece. There is one more similarity between the two civilizations: Etruria also fell prey to the Romans. They were no match for Roman organization, especially because neighboring city-states never came to one another's aid in a time of crisis. By 88 BCE, the Romans had vanquished the last of the Etruscans.

ARCHITECTURE Although the Etruscans constructed temples, none survive beyond their foundations because they were constructed of impermanent materials such as wood and mud brick (Fig. 15.16). Yet in what almost seems a throwback to ancient Egypt, underground tombs, carved out of bedrock, suggest the lives and habits of the Etruscan people. The interiors were constructed to resemble those of domestic dwellings. The walls were covered with hundreds of everyday items carved in low relief, including such things as kitchen utensils and weapons. Like the Egyptians, and unlike the Greeks, the Etruscans apparently wanted to duplicate their earthly environments in their funerary monuments.

sons. The large piece is superbly composed, with the three figures bound together by the sinuous curves of the serpents; they pull away from one another under the agony of the creatures' coils.

Hellenistic artists were often drawn to dramatic subjects. They did not focus on a balance between emotion and restraint but portrayed human excess. In the midst of this theatricality, however, another trend in Hellenistic art reflected the simplicity and idealism

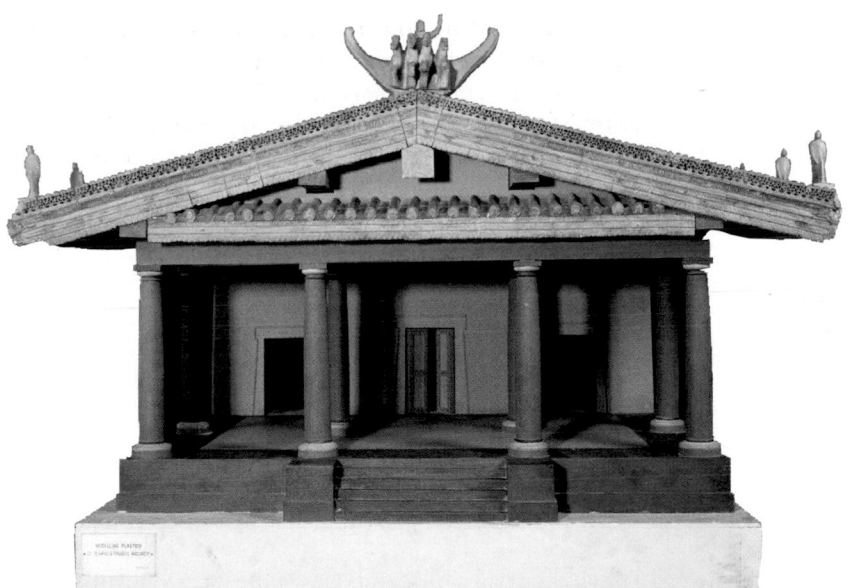

< 15.16 **Model of a typical Etruscan temple of the 6th century BCE, as described by Vitruvius.** Plastic. Instituto di Etruscologia e di Antichità Italiche, Università di Roma, Rome, Italy.

SCULPTURE Much sculpture of bronze and clay has survived from these Etruscan tombs, and we have learned a great deal about the Etruscan people from these finds. For example, even though no architecture survives, we know what the exterior of domestic dwellings looked like from the clay models of homes that served as **cinerary urns**. We have also been able to gain insight into the personalities of the Etruscan people through their figurative sculpture, particularly that found on the lids of their **sarcophagi**.

The Sarcophagus from Cerveteri (Fig. 15.17) is a translation into terra-cotta of the banquet scenes of which the Etruscans were so fond. A man and wife are represented reclining on a lounge and appear to be enjoying the dinner entertainment. Their gestures are animated and naturalistic, even though their facial features and hair are rigidly stylized. These stylizations, especially the thick-lidded eyes, resemble Greek sculpture of the Archaic period and were most likely influenced by it. However, the serenity and severity of Archaic Greek art are absent.

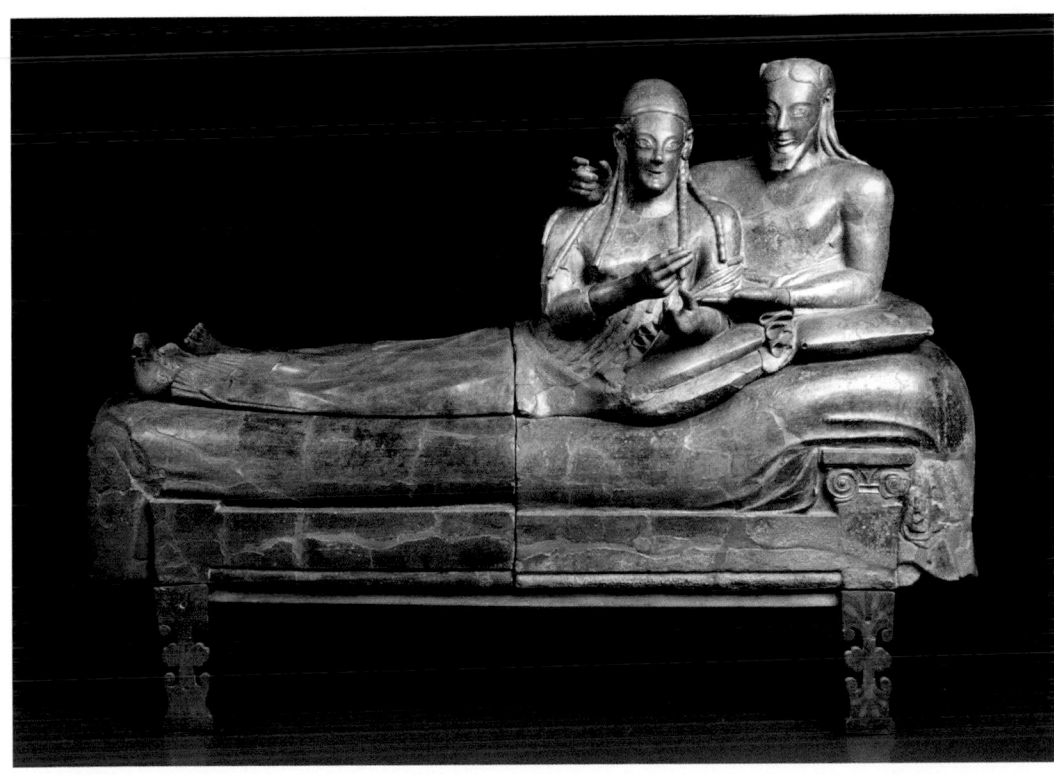

< 15.17 **Sarcophagus from Cerveteri** (c. 520 BCE). Painted terra-cotta, 6'7" long. Museo Nazionale di Villa Giulia, Rome, Italy.

Ancient art was the tyrant of Egypt, the mistress of Greece, and the servant of Rome.

— HENRY FUSELI

The Etruscans appear to be as relaxed, happy, and fun loving in death as they were in life.

ROME

In about 500 BCE, the Roman Republic was established, and it would last some four centuries. The Roman arm of strength reached into northern Italy, conquering the Etruscans, and eventually stretched in all directions, gaining supremacy over Greece, western Europe, northern Africa, and parts of the Near East (Map 15.2). No longer was this the republican city of Rome flexing its muscles—this was the Roman Empire.

Roman art combined native talent, needs, and styles with other artistic sources, particularly those of Greece. The art that followed the absorption of Greece into the Roman Empire is thus often called Greco-Roman. It was fashionable for Romans to own—or at the very least, have copies of—Greek works of art. This tendency gave the Romans a reputation as mere imitators of Greek art,

a simplistic view laid waste by scholars of Roman art history. A marvelous, unabashed eclecticism pervaded much of Roman art, resulting in vigorous and sometimes unpredictable combinations of motifs. The Romans were also fond of a harsh, almost *trompe l'oeil*, realism in their portrait sculpture, which had not been seen before their time. They were master builders (the inventors of concrete!), who created some of the grandest monuments in the history of architecture. Because of the vast expanse of the empire, these structures, or their remains, can be seen today almost everywhere.

The Republican Period

The ancient city of Rome was built on seven hills to the east of the Tiber River and served as the central Italian base from which the Romans would come to control most of the known world in the West. Their illustrious beginnings are traced to the **Republican period**, which followed upon the heels of their final victories over the Etruscans and lasted until the death of Julius Caesar in 44 BCE. The Roman system of government during this time was

ROME

700 BCE	509 BCE	27 BCE	337 CE
THE ETRUSCANS	**REPUBLICAN ROME**	**IMPERIAL ROME**	
The Etruscans, a people who occupied central Italy, emerge as a culture distinct from the rest of the Italian peninsula, Greece, and the Near East; their kings rule the region until the Roman Republic is established in 509 BCE	A myth based on the legend of Romulus and Remus places the founding date of Rome at 753 BCE	The Imperial period begins in 27 BCE when the Roman Senate bestows on Octavian the title of Augustus, acceding to him the powers of emperor; the *Augustus of Primaporta* is sculpted in c. 20 BCE	
Etruscan temple interiors are constructed to resemble domestic dwellings	The establishment of the Roman Republic in 509 BCE brings the beginning of a constitutional government—a senate of upper-class patricians and an assembly of lower-class plebeians	Aqueducts are constructed throughout the empire	
Sculptures on Etruscan sarcophagi show people as animated and naturalistic	The republic collapses after a civil war that begins with the assassination of Julius Caesar in 44 BCE and lasts until Octavian defeats the combined forces of Mark Antony and Egypt's Queen Cleopatra; Egypt becomes a Roman province	The Colosseum is dedicated in 80 CE, one year after Mount Vesuvius erupts and blankets the cities of Pompeii and Herculaneum in volcanic ash	
	Roman portrait sculpture is made highly realistic	The Pantheon with its 144-foot dome is constructed in 117 to 125 CE	
	Roman wall painters attempt to use perspective	Wall paintings with Old Testament themes are created in a synagogue in Damascus c. 245–256 CE	
		Constantine moves the center of the empire from Rome to Constantinople; the colossal sculpture of Constantine is placed in the Basilica Nova, which serves as a precedent for Christian church architecture	

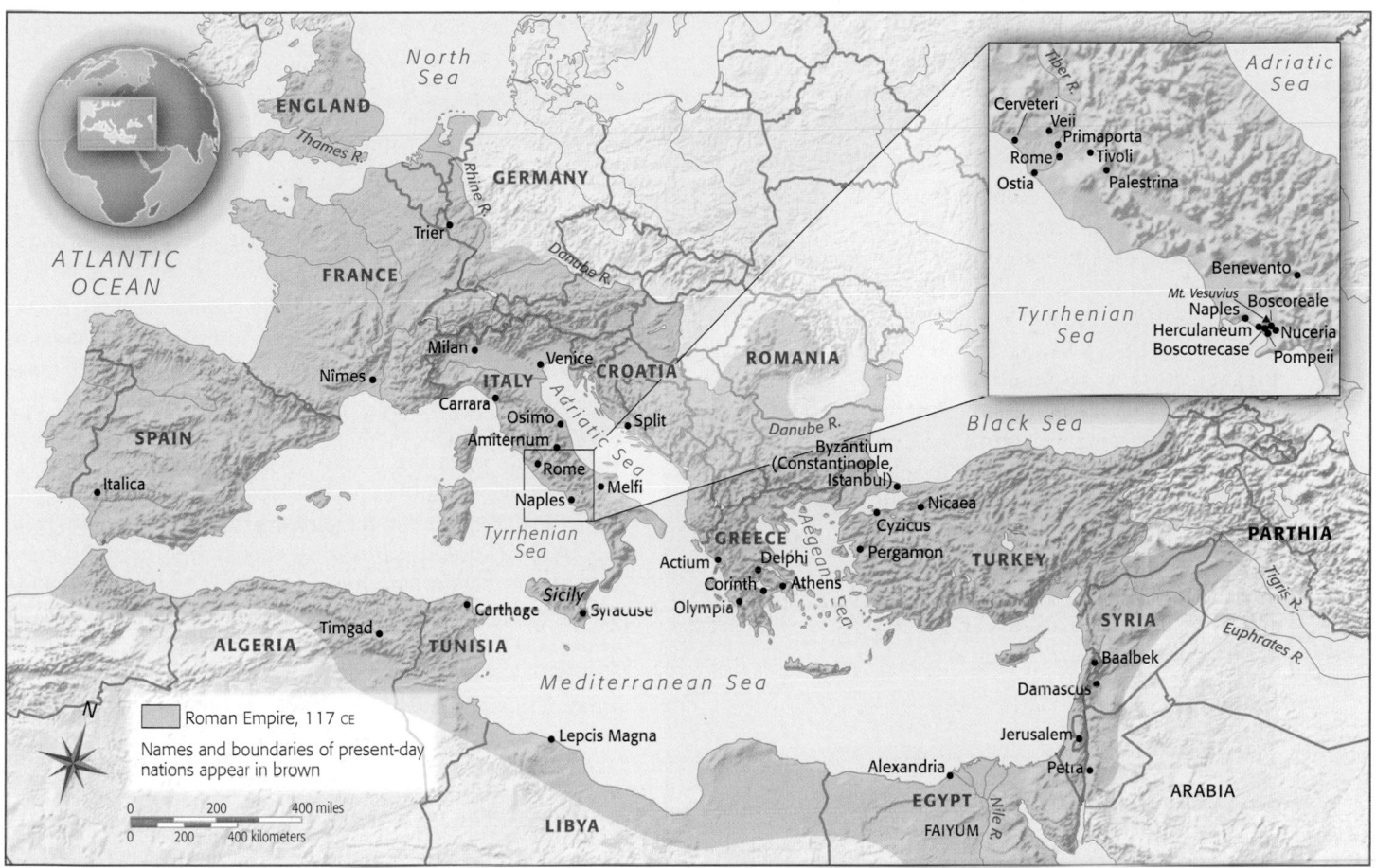

▲ MAP 15.2 The Roman Empire in 117 CE.

based on two parties, although the distribution of power was not equitable. The **patricians** ruled the country and could be likened to an aristocratic class. They came from important Roman families and later were characterized as nobility. The majority of the Roman population, however, belonged to the **plebeian class**. Members of this class were common folk and had less say in running the government. They were, however, permitted to elect their patrician representatives. During the Republican period, the famed Roman senate became the governing body of Rome. The rulings of the senate were responsible for the numerous Roman conquests that would expand its borders into a seemingly boundless empire.

By virtue of its construction, however, the republic was doomed to crumble. It was never a true democracy. The patricians became richer and more powerful as a result of the plundering of vanquished nations. The lower classes, on the other hand, demanded more and more privileges and resented the wealth and influence of the aristocracy.

After a series of successful military campaigns and the quelling of internal strife in the republic, Julius Caesar emerged as dictator of the Roman Empire. Under Caesar, important territories were accumulated, and Roman culture reached a peak of refinement. The language of Greece, its literature, and its religion were adopted along with its artistic styles.

On March 15 (the ides of March) in 44 BCE, Julius Caesar was assassinated by members of the senate. With his death came the absolute end of the Roman Republic and the beginnings of the Roman Empire under his successor, Augustus.

SCULPTURE   Although much Roman art is derived in style from that of Greece, its portrait sculpture originated in a tradition that was wholly Italian. In this sculpture, we witness Rome's unique contribution to the arts—that of realism.

It was customary for Romans to make wax death masks of their loved ones and to keep them around the

> With the Greeks there's always an aesthetic element. I prefer the virile realism of Rome,
> which doesn't embellish. The truthfulness of Roman art—it's like their buildings,
> but all the more beautiful in their genuine simplicity.
>
> —PABLO PICASSO

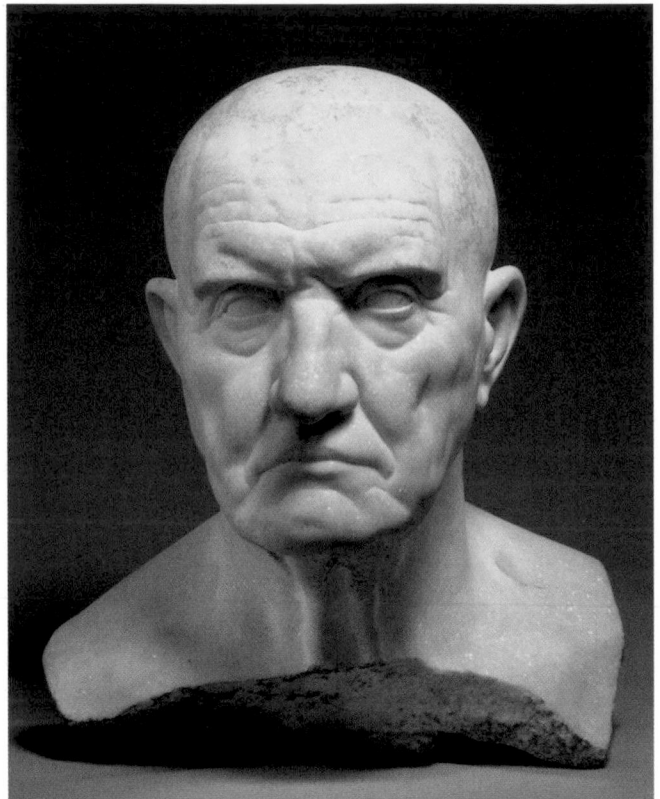

‹ **15.18** *Head of a Roman* (1st century BCE). Marble, 14⅜" high. Metropolitan Museum of Art, New York, New York..

house, as we do photographs. At times, the wax masks were translated into a more permanent medium, such as bronze or terra-cotta. The process of making a death mask produced intricately detailed images that recorded every ripple and crevice of the face. Because these sculptures were made from the actual faces and heads of the subjects, their realism is unsurpassed. The *Head of a Roman* (Fig. 15.18) records the facial features of an old man, from his bald head and protruding ears to his furrowed brow and almost cavernous cheeks. No attempt has been made by the artist to idealize the figure. Nor does one get the sense, on the other hand, that the artist emphasized the hideousness of the character. Rather, it serves more as an unimpassioned and uninvolved record of the existence of one man.

PAINTING The walls of Roman domestic dwellings were profusely decorated with frescoes and mosaics, some of which have survived the ravages of time. One

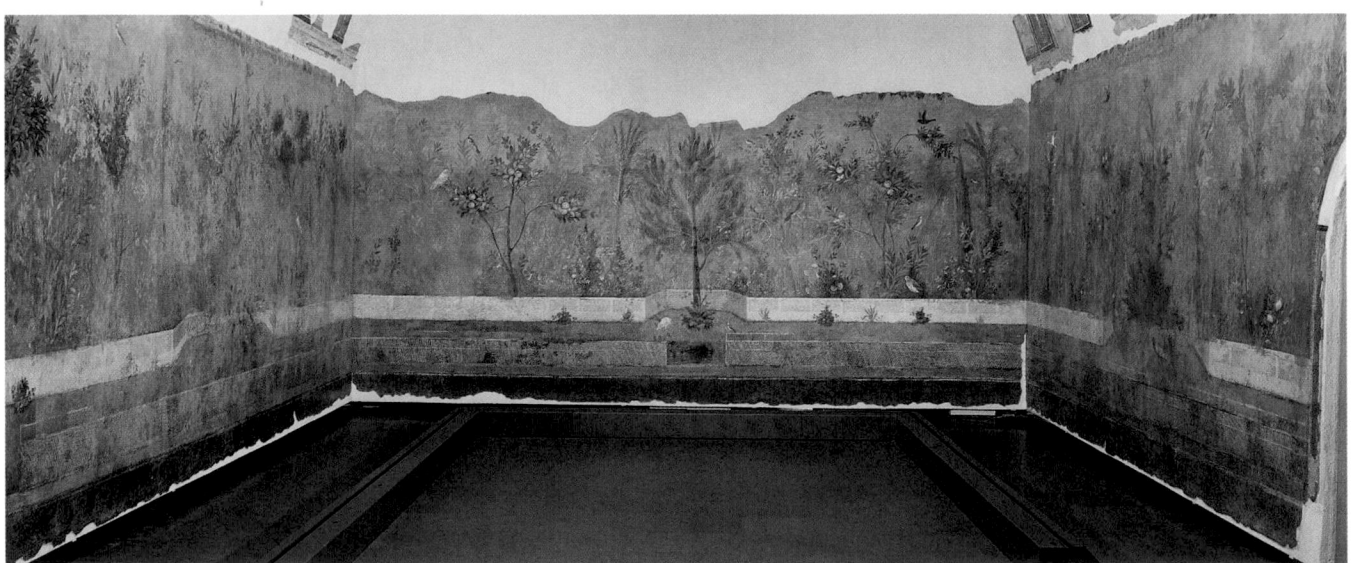

⌃ **15.19A Gardenscape, Villa of Livia, Primaporta, Italy** (c. 30–20 BCE). Second style. Fresco. Overall size: 8'11" high × 38'5" long. Museo Nazionale Romano (Palazzo Massimo alle Terme), Rome, Italy.

The series of triumphal arches in Rome is a prototype of the billboard. . . . The triumphal arches in the Roman Forum were spatial markers channeling processional paths within a complex urban landscape. On Route 66 . . . the billboards perform a similar formal-spatial function.

—ROBERT VENTURI

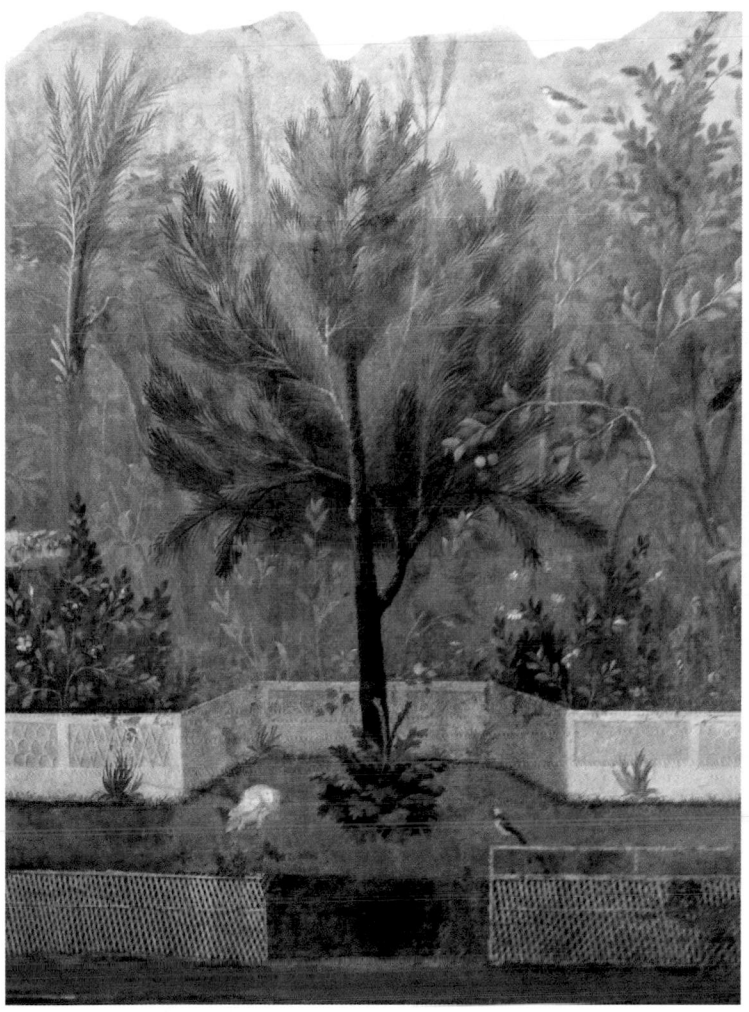

∧ 15.19B Detail of Gardenscape.

of the most stunningly beautiful frescoes of ancient Rome is a gardenscape from a villa that belonged to Livia, the wife of the Emperor Augustus (Fig. 15.19). The walls of the setting must have seemed to melt away under the spell of masterful illusion—a crisp blue sky alive with the songs of birds, the feel of lush foliage underfoot, and the sweet scent of flowering trees. The garden fresco represents one of four styles of Roman wall painting created between the second century BCE and 79 CE; many of the best—and best-preserved—examples were found among the ruins of Pompeii. Roman wall painting passed through several phases, beginning in about 200 BCE and ending with the destruction of Pompeii by the eruption of Mount Vesuvius in 79 CE.

The phases have been divided into four overlapping styles. The gardenscape is an example of the second, or **architectural style**, in which the illusion of retreating space is achieved through various pictorial devices. The painter suggests depth by attempting linear perspective in the fence surrounding the tree in the center, and by using atmospheric perspective—intentionally blurring the more distant objects.

With the death of Julius Caesar, a dictator, Rome entered its **Empire period** under the rule of Octavian Caesar—later called Augustus. This period marks the beginning of the Roman Empire, Roman rule by emperor, and the Pax Romana, a 200-year period of peace.

The Early Empire

With the birth of the empire, there emerged a desire to glorify the power of Rome by erecting splendid buildings and civic monuments. It was believed that art should be created in the service of the state. Although Roman expansionism left a wake of death and destruction, it was responsible for the construction of cities and the provision of basic human services in the conquered areas.

To their subject peoples, the Roman conquerors brought the benefits of urban planning, including apartment buildings, roads, and bridges. They also provided police and fire protection, water systems, sanitation, and food. They even built recreation facilities for the inhabitants, including gymnasiums, public baths, and theaters. Thus, even in defeat, many peoples reaped benefits because of the Roman desire to glorify the empire through visible contributions.

ARCHITECTURE Although the Romans adopted structural systems and certain motifs from Greek architecture, they introduced several innovations in building design. The most significant of these was the arch, and after the second century, the use of concrete to replace cut stone. The combination of these two elements resulted in domed and vaulted structures that were not part of the Greek repertory.

THE SPORTS STADIUM HAS BECOME an inextricable part of our global landscape and our global culture. Just as diehard U.S. fans root for their football teams in the Louisiana Superdome, Olympic spectators half a world away cheer their country's athletes on to victory under a *super* dome likely erected just for the occasion. A city's bid for host of the Olympic Games can hinge entirely on the stadium it has to offer. These megastructures are not only functional—housing anticipated thousands—but they tend to become symbols of the cities, the teams, or now, the corporations that fund them. There's something about a space like this. The passion of friends and strangers and "fors and againsts" alike creates an odd sense of uniformity regardless of diversity. This observation has led some of history's political leaders to use—and abuse—the phenomenon of the stadium for their own propagandistic purposes.

The Colosseum (**Fig. 15.20**) represented Rome at its best, but it also stood for Rome at its worst. A major feat of architectural engineering coupled with practical design, this vast stadium accommodated as many as 55,000 spectators who—thanks to 80 numbered entrances and stairways—could get from the street to their designated seats within 10 minutes. In rain or under blazing sun conditions, a gargantuan canvas could be hoisted from the arena up over the top of the stadium.

Although the Colosseum was built for entertainment and festivals, its most notorious events ranged from sadistic contests between animals and men and grueling battles to the death between pairs of gladiators. If one combatant emerged alive but badly wounded, survival might depend on whether the emperor (or the crowd) gave the "thumbs-up" or the "thumbs-down."

As in much architecture, form can follow function and reflect and create meaning. In 1936, Adolf Hitler commissioned Germany's Olympic Stadium in Berlin (**Fig. 15.21**). Intended to showcase Aryan superiority (even though Jesse Owens, an African American, took four gold medals in track and field as Hitler watched), designer Werner March's stadium is the physical embodiment of Nazi ideals: order, authority, and the no-nonsense power of the state.

How different the message, noted critic Nicolai Ourussoff, when an architect uses design to cast off the shackles of "nationalist pretensions" and "notions of social conformity" in an effort to imbue the structure—and the country—with a sense of the future. Created in

▲ **15.20 Colosseum, Rome, Italy** (80 CE). Concrete (originally faced with marble). 1,609' high, 620' and 513' in diameter.

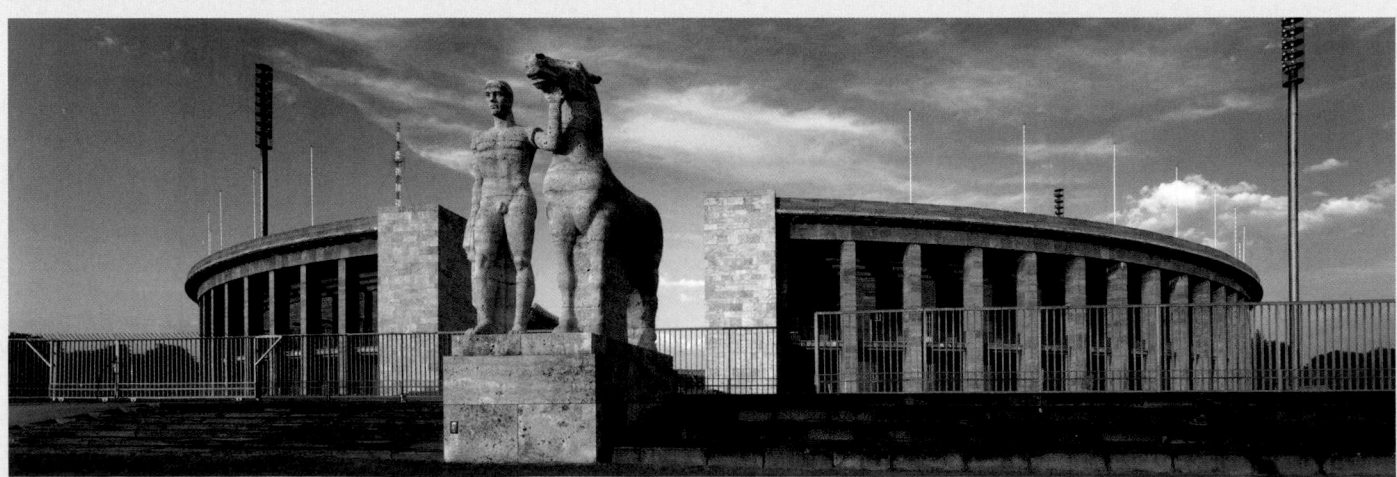

▲ 15.21 **WERNER MARCH**, Olympic Stadium, Berlin, Germany (1936).

1960 by Pier Luigi Nervi, the Palazzo dello Sport (**Fig. 15.22**) in Rome symbolized an emerging internationalism in the wake of World War II. The unadorned and unforgiving pillars of March's Berlin stadium seem of a distant and rejected past. Nervi's innovative, interlacing concrete roof beams define delicacy and seem to defy gravity.

In 2008, China hosted the Olympic Games in the city of Beijing. A doughnut-shaped shell crisscrossed with lines of steel as if it were a precious package wrapped in string, the stadium (**Fig. 15.23**) housed 100,000 spectators and came with a price tag in excess of $500 million. But beyond these staggering numbers, and like the Colosseum and the Berlin Stadium, it stands to symbolize the transformation of its city—and its country—into a major political and cultural force of its time.

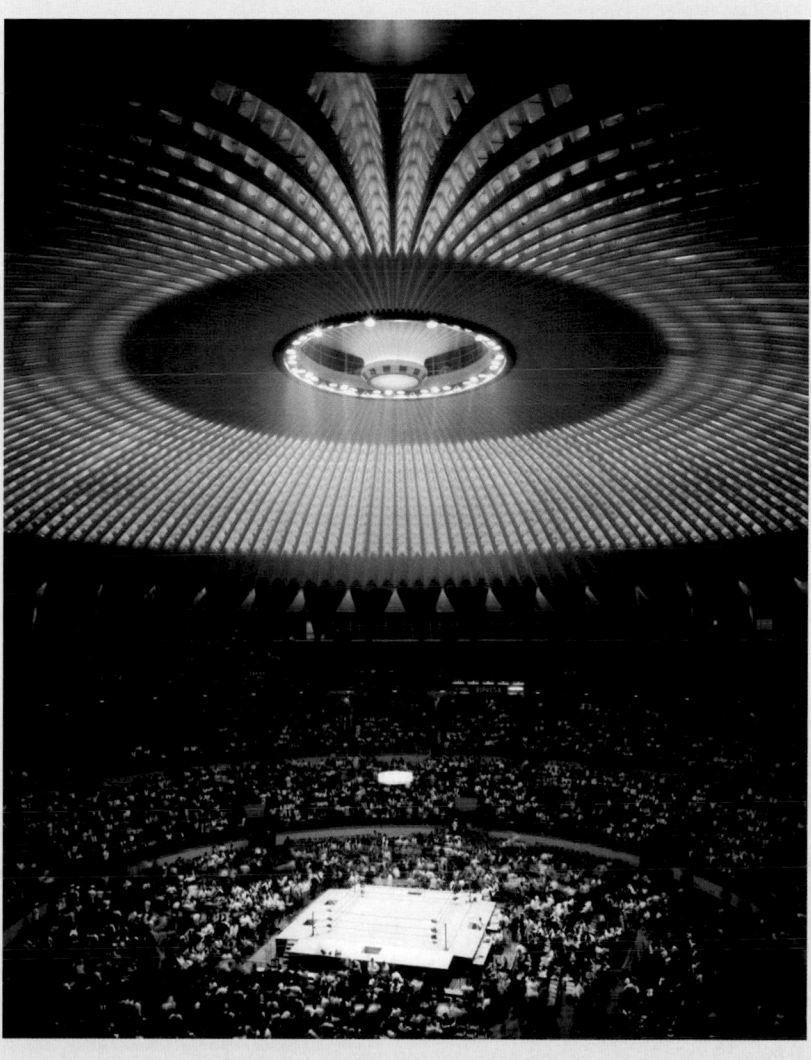

> 15.22 **PIER LUIGI NERVI, Palazzo dello Sport, Rome, Italy** (1960).

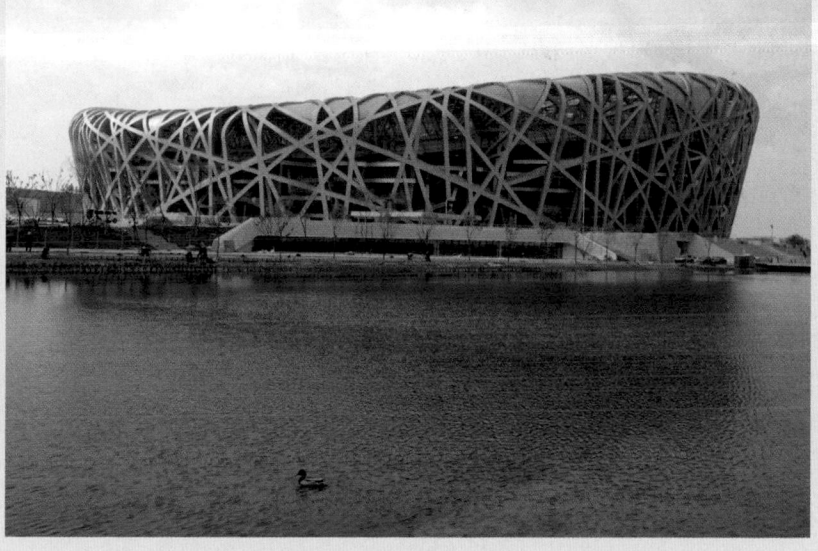

> 15.23 **HERZOG AND DE MEURON, Beijing Stadium for the 2008 Olympic Games, Beijing, China** (2005).

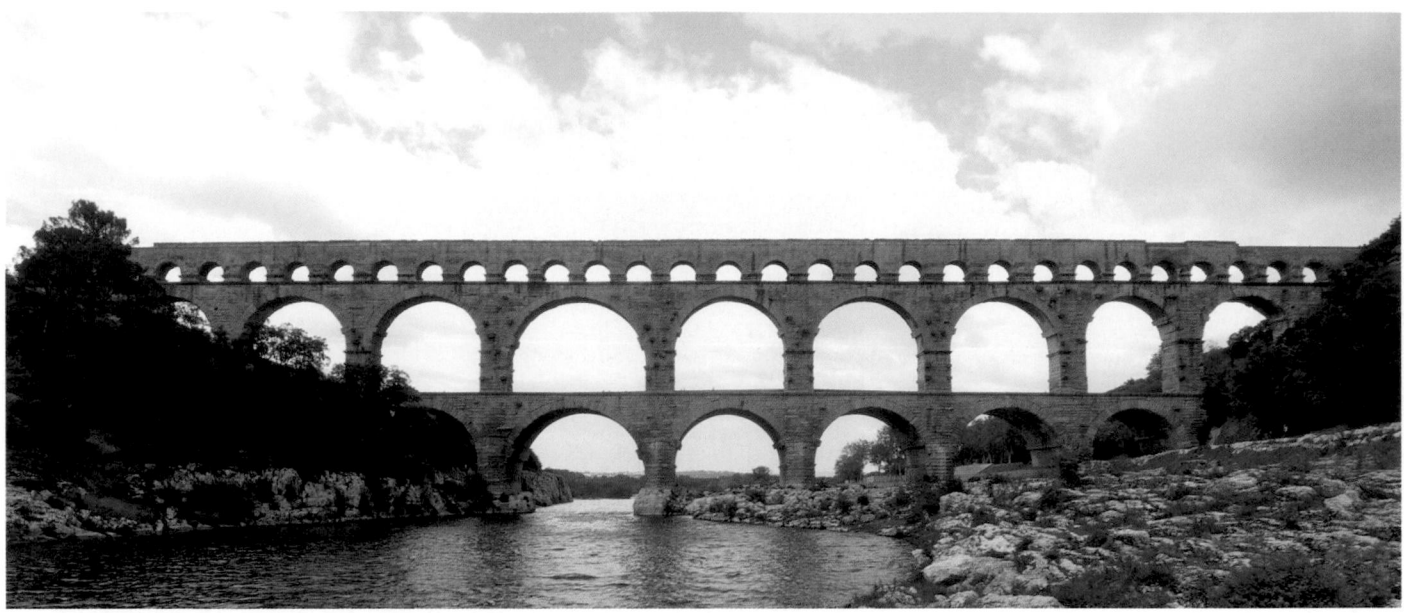

▲ 15.24 **Pont du Gard, Nîmes, France** (c. 14 CE). 900' long, 160' high.

One of the most outstanding Roman civic projects is the **aqueduct**, which carried water over long distances. The Pont du Gard (Fig. 15.24) in southern France carried water more than 30 miles and furnished each recipient with some 100 gallons of water per day. Constructed of three levels of arches, the largest of which spans about 82 feet, the aqueduct is some 900 feet long and 160 feet high. It had to slope down gradually over the long distance in order for gravity to carry the flow of water from the source.

Although the aqueduct's reason for existence is purely functional, the Roman architect did not neglect design. The Pont du Gard has long been admired for both its simplicity and its grandeur. The two lower tiers of wide arches, for example, anchor the weighty structure to the earth, whereas the quickened pace of the smaller arches complements the rush of water along the top level. In works such as the Pont du Gard, form *follows* function.

One of the most impressive and famous monuments of ancient Rome is the Colosseum (see Fig. 15.20 in the Compare + Contrast feature). Dedicated in 80 CE, the structure consists of two back-to-back **amphitheaters** forming an oval arena, around which are tiers of marble bleachers.

Even in its present condition, having suffered years of pillaging and several earthquakes, the Colosseum is a spectacular sight. The structure is composed of three tiers of arches separated by engaged columns. (This combination of arch and column can also be seen in another type of Roman architectural monument—the triumphal arch (Fig. 15.25). The Colosseum's lowest level, whose arches provided easy access and exit for the spectators, is punctuated by Doric columns. This order is the weightiest in appearance of the three architectural styles and thus visually anchors the structure to the ground. The second level features the Ionic order, and the third level the Corinthian. This

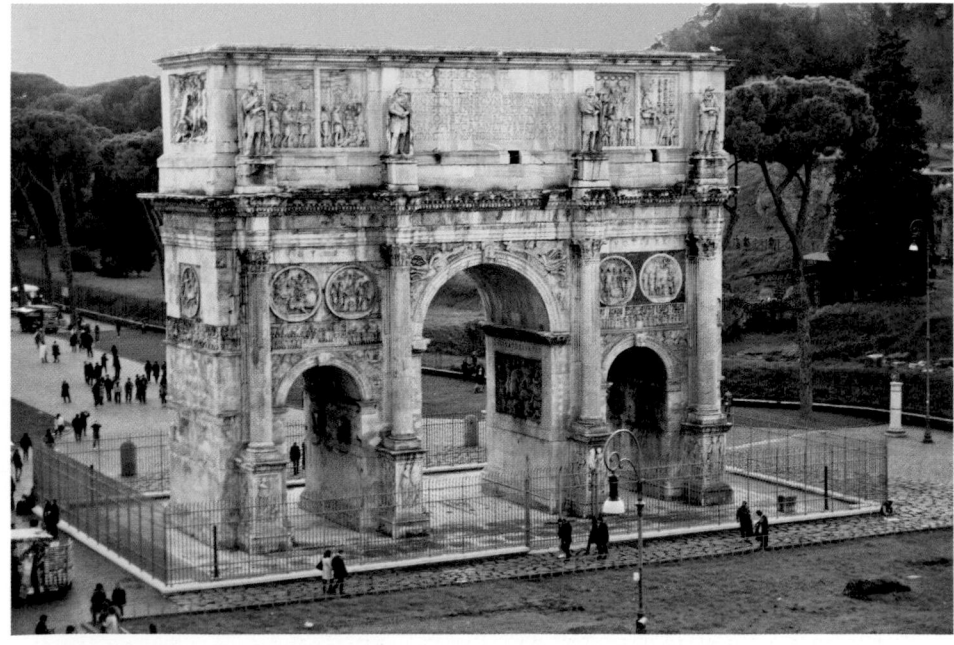

▲ 15.25 **Arch of Constantine, Rome, Italy** (312–315 CE).

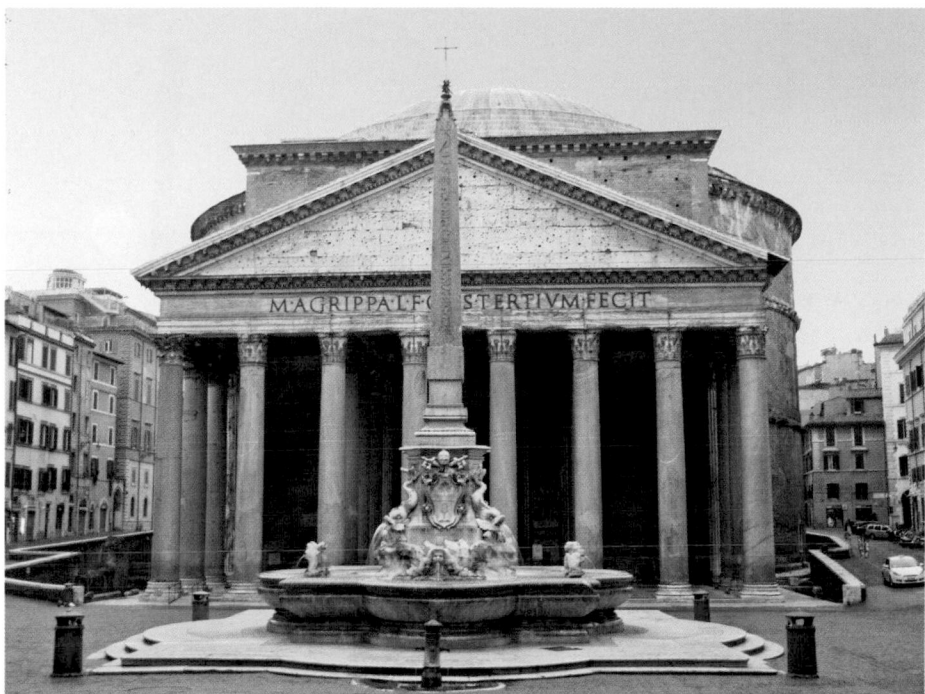

combination produces a sense of lightness as one's eye moves from the bottom to the top tier. Thick entablatures rest on top of the rings of columns, firmly delineating the stories. The uppermost level is almost all solid masonry, except for a few regularly spaced rectangular openings. It is ornamented with Corinthian pilasters and crowned by a heavy cornice.

The exterior of the Colosseum was composed of masonry blocks held in place by metal dowels. These dowels were removed over the years when metal became scarce, thus gravity keeps the structure intact.

Roman engineering genius can be seen most clearly in the Pantheon (Figs. 15.26 and 15.27), a brick and concrete structure originally erected to house sculptures of the Roman gods. Although the building no longer contains these statues, its function remains religious. Since the year 609 CE, it has been a Christian church.

The Pantheon's design combines the simple geometric elements of a circle and a rectangle. The entrance consists of a rectangular **portico,** complete with Corinthian columns and pediment. The main body of the building, to which the portico is attached, is circular. It is 144 feet in diameter and spanned by a dome equal in height to the diameter. Supporting the massive dome are 20-foot-thick walls pierced with deep niches, which in turn are vaulted to accept the downward thrust of the dome and distribute its weight to the solid wall. These deep niches alternate with shallow niches in which sculptures were placed.

The dome consists of a rather thin concrete shell that thickens toward the base. The interior of the dome is **coffered,** or carved with recessed squares that physically and visually lighten the structure. The ceiling was once

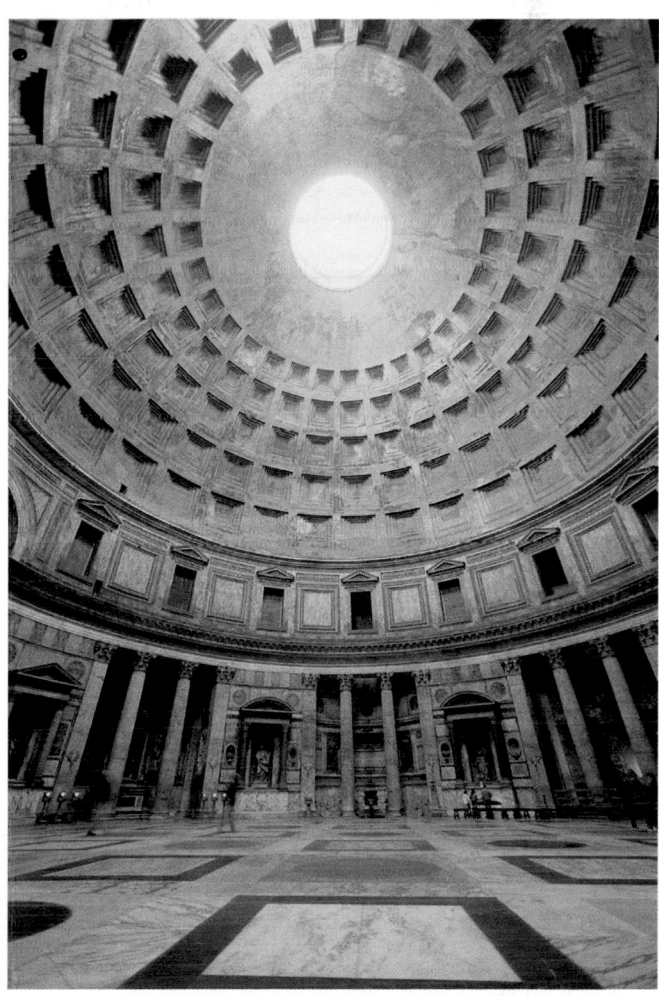

∧ 15.27 **The Pantheon, interior view, Rome, Italy** (118–125 CE).

painted blue, with a bronze rosette in the center of each square. The sole source of light in the Pantheon is the **oculus**, a circular opening in the top of the dome, 30 feet in diameter. The interior was lavishly decorated with marble slabs and granite columns that glistened in the spotlight of the sun as it filtered through the opening, moving its focus at different times of the day.

It has been said that Roman architecture differs from other ancient architecture in that it emphasizes space rather than form. In other words, rather than constructing buildings from the point of view of solid shapes, the Romans conceptualized a certain space and then proceeded to enframe it. Their methods of harnessing this space were unique in the ancient world and served as a vital precedent for future architecture.

SCULPTURE   During the Empire period, Roman sculpture took on a different flavor. The pure realism of the Republican period portrait busts was joined to Greek idealism. The result, evident in *Augustus of Primaporta* (Fig. 15.28), was often a curious juxtaposition of individualized heads with idealized, anatomically perfect bodies in Classical poses. The head of Augustus is somewhat idealized and serene, but his unique facial features are recognizable as those that appeared on empire coins. Augustus adopts an authoritative pose not unlike that of Polykleitos's *Doryphoros* (see Fig. 15.10A). Attired in military parade armor, he proclaims a diplomatic victory to the masses. His officer's cloak is draped about his hips, and his ceremonial armor is embellished with reliefs that portray both historic events and allegorical figures.

As the first emperor, Augustus was determined to construct monuments reflecting the glory, power, and influence of Rome on the Western world. One of the most famous of these monuments is the Ara Pacis, or Altar of Peace, created to celebrate the empire-wide peace that Augustus was able to achieve. The Ara Pacis is composed of four walls surrounding a sacrificial altar. These walls are adorned with relief sculptures of figures and delicately carved floral motifs.

Panels such as The Imperial Procession (Fig. 15.29) exhibit a blend of Greek and Roman devices. The right-to-left procession of individuals, unified by the flowing lines of their drapery, clearly refers to the frieze sculptures of the Parthenon. Yet the sculpture differs from its Greek prototype in several respects: (1) the individuals are rendered in portrait likenesses; (2) the relief commemorates a specific event with specific people present; and (3) these figures are set within a shallow, though very convincing, three-dimensional space. By

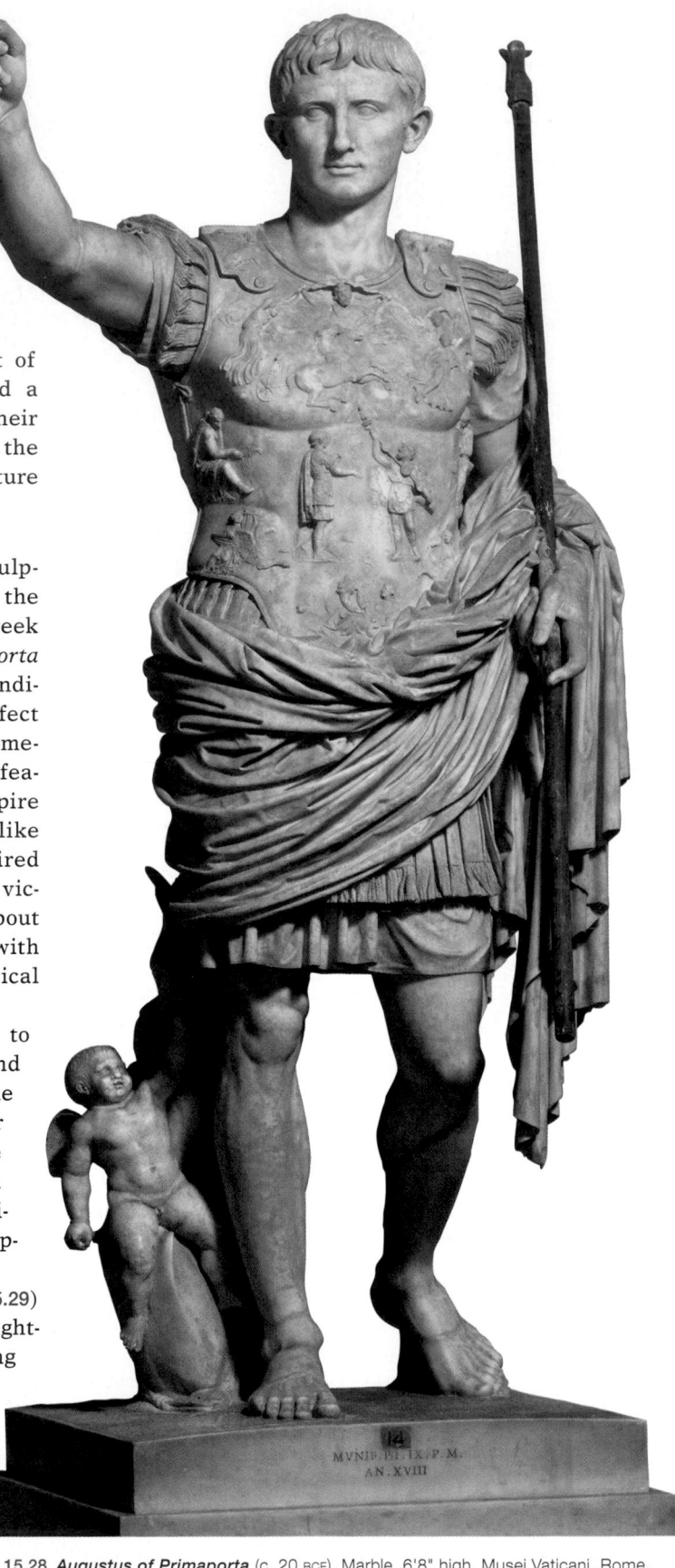

⌃ 15.28 *Augustus of Primaporta* (c. 20 BCE). Marble, 6'8" high. Musei Vaticani, Rome, Italy.

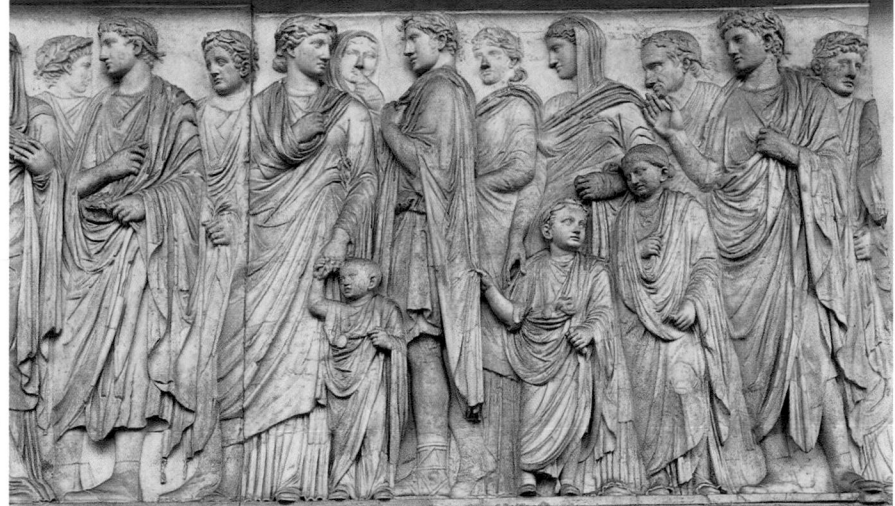

working in high and low relief, the artist creates the sense of a crowd; fully three rows of people are compressed into this space. They actively turn, gesture, and seem to converse. Despite a noble grandness that gives the panel an idealistic cast, the participants in the procession look and act like real people.

As time went on, the Roman desire to accurately record a person's features gave way to a more introspective portrayal of the personality of the sitter. Although portrait busts remained a favorite genre for Roman sculptors, their repertory also included relief sculpture, full-length statuary, and a new design—the **equestrian portrait**.

The bronze sculpture of Marcus Aurelius (Fig. 15.30) depicts the emperor on a sprightly horse, as if caught in the action of gesturing to his troops or recognizing the applause of his people. The sculpture combines the Roman love of realism with the later concern for

CONNECTIONS The
Ara Pacis, or Altar of Peace, celebrated the empire-wide peace that Augustus achieved. Many of its reliefs emphasize the importance of the family unit to the prosperity and stability of Rome. Panels such as *The Imperial*

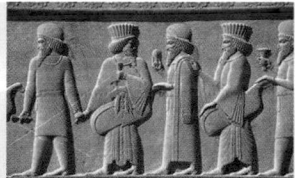

Processional frieze (detail) from the royal audience hall (c. 521–465 BCE). Persepolis, Iran. (**Fig. 14.9**)

Procession feature a combination of low and high relief with characters placed in different positions and seen from different perspectives. They gesture and converse, creating a sense of tight unity among the individuals in the group—including children. The differences between this processional relief and the one from Persepolis are considerable. How would you describe them?

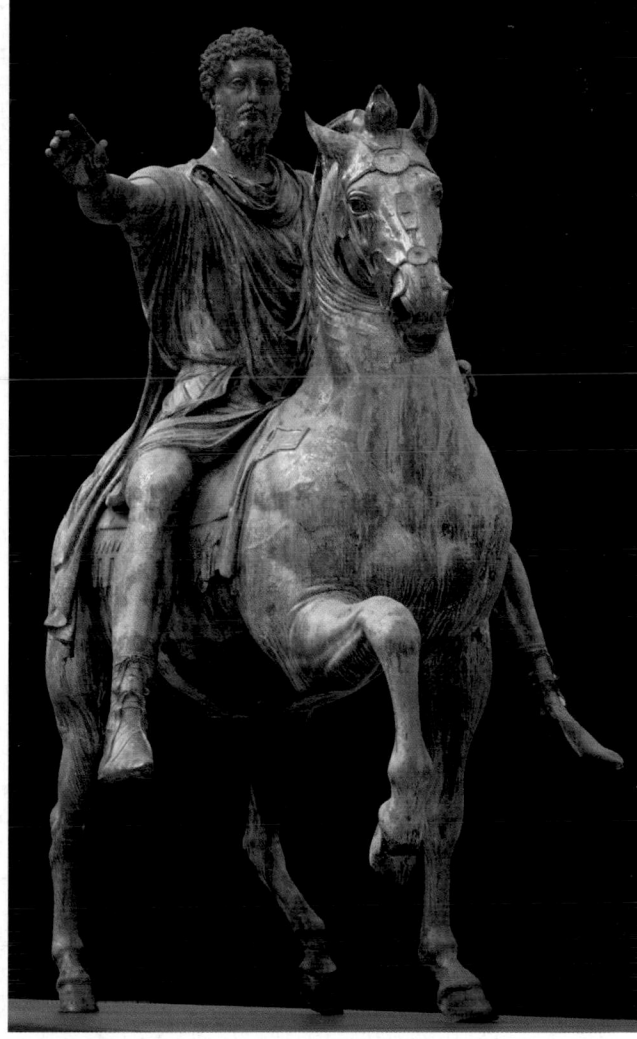

∧ 15.30 *Marcus Aurelius on Horseback* (c. 165 CE). Bronze, 11'6" high. Capitoline Hill, Rome, Italy.

psychologically penetrating portraits. The commanding presence of the horse is rendered through pronounced musculature, a confident and lively stride, and a vivacious head with snarling mouth, flared nostrils, and protruding veins. In contrast to this image of brute strength is a rather serene image of imperial authority. Marcus Aurelius, clothed in flowing robes, sits erectly on his horse and gestures rather passively. His facial expression is calm and reserved, reflecting his adherence to Stoic philosophy. **Stoicism** advocated an indifference to emotion and things of this world, maintaining that virtue was the most important goal in life.

The equestrian portrait of Marcus Aurelius survives because of a case of mistaken identity. During the Middle Ages, objects of all kinds were melted down because of a severe shortage of metals, and ancient sculptures that portrayed pagan idols were not spared. This statue of Marcus Aurelius was saved because it was mistakenly believed to be a portrait of Constantine, the first Roman emperor to recognize Christianity. The death of Marcus Aurelius brings us to the last years of the Empire period, which were riddled with internal strife. The days of the great Roman Empire were numbered.

The Late Empire

During its late years, the Roman Empire was torn from within. A series of emperors seized the reins of power only to meet violent deaths, some at the hands of their own soldiers. By the end of the third century, the situation was so unwieldy that the territory was divided into eastern and western empires, with separate rulers for each. When Constantine ascended the throne, he returned to the single-emperor model, but the damage had already been done—the empire had become divided against itself. Constantine then dealt the empire its final blow by dividing its territory among his sons and moving the capital to Constantinople (present-day Istanbul).

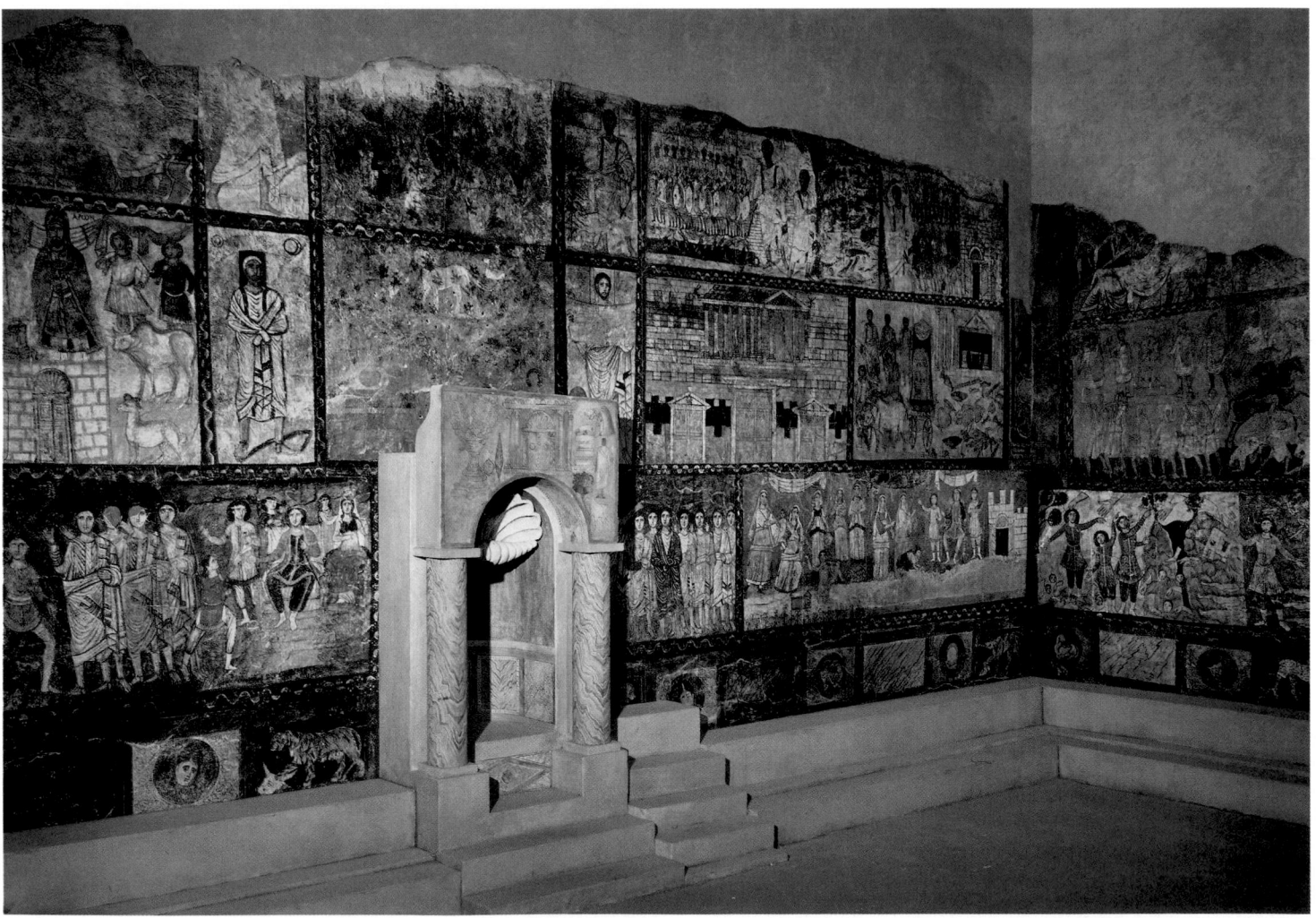

∧ 15.31 Interior of the synagogue, with wall paintings of Old Testament themes, Dura-Europos, Syria (c. 245–256 CE). Tempera on plaster. Reconstruction in National Museum, Damascus, Syria.

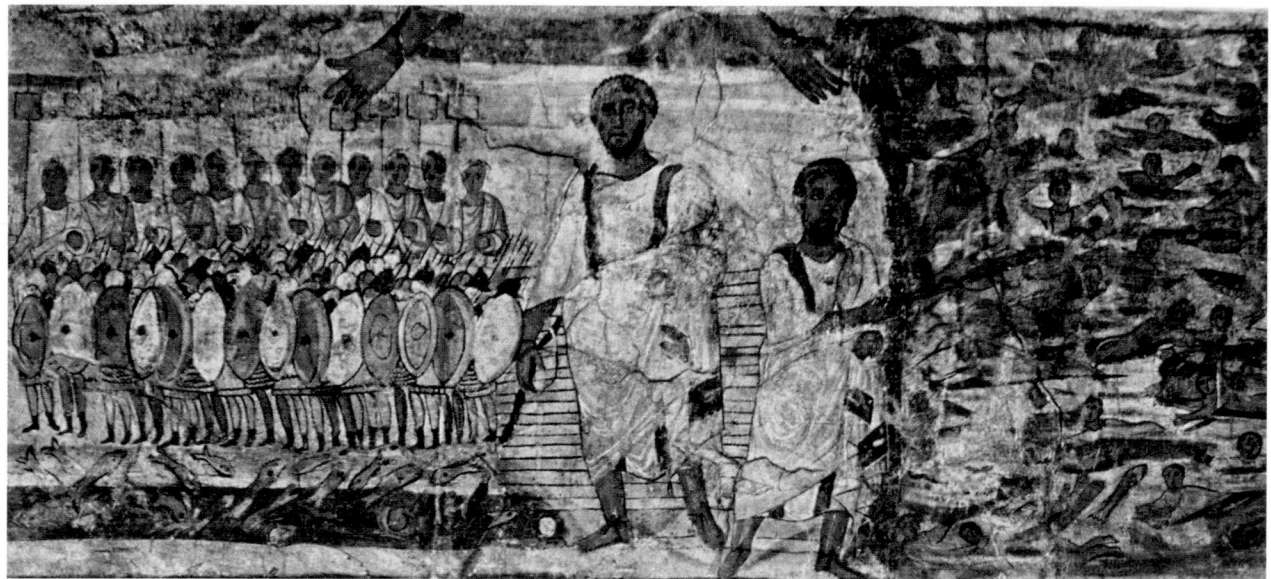

∧ 15.32 Fresco of Moses and the Exodus, Dura-Europos synagogue, Damascus, Syria.

Thus, imperial power was shifted to the eastern empire, leaving Rome and the western empire vulnerable. These were decisions from which the empire would never recover.

Some 300 years before Constantine's reign, however, a new force began to gnaw at the frayed edges of the Roman Empire—Christianity. The followers of Jesus of Nazareth were persecuted by the Romans for centuries until the emperor Constantine proclaimed tolerance for the faith in his Edict of Milan of 313, and accepted the mantle of Christianity himself.

ART AND RELIGION   In the Late Empire period, Rome continued to produce ambitious architectural monuments that glorified the empire, but sculpted portraits conveyed either an agitation in the sitter that reflected the upheaval of the times, or a curious lack of expression—as in the equestrian portrait of Marcus Aurelius—that seemed to suggest detachment. The beginning of the fourth century CE witnessed the emperor Constantine's prohibition of persecution of Christians, and his own stoic portrait, as we shall see, is a stylistic harbinger of the art of the Middle Ages. Yet it took some time for the Roman influence on art and architecture to dissipate. We should remember that Christians, Jews, and people of other beliefs and ethnicities lived under the aegis of the Roman Empire and it was Roman art that they looked to for inspiration.

The diversity and coexistence of religions in the Roman Empire of the third and fourth centuries are perhaps nowhere more apparent than in the Syrian town of Dura-Europos. From the perspectives of archeology and art history, it is a wonder that buildings from this era and this place survived at all, much less in such a well-preserved state. After an erratic history of shifting control of the town, the population of Dura-Europos left once and for all in 256 CE. It is as if they just closed the doors behind them and walked away. Among the collection of buildings: pagan temples and homes, one of which had been converted into an early Christian meeting house, and a synagogue replete with glorious frescoes.

The Synagogue in Dura-Europos (Fig. 15.31) belies the assumption that Jews, following the proscriptions of the Ten Commandments, did not create images associated with the worship of their God. The walls of the synagogue, divided into picturelike spaces, are covered with scenes from biblical stories and Jewish history. Stone benches line the walls of the meeting space, and, on one wall, there is a niche with a projecting arch and two columns that housed the Torah scroll.

In one fresco, the figure of Moses dominates a scene depicting the parting of the Red Sea and the Exodus from Egypt under the protective, outstretched arms of the Hebrew God (Fig. 15.32). Although God's face is never represented in the frescos, a guiding hand along the upper edge of a painting sometimes suggests his presence. In terms of style, Moses might look familiar to you. The frescoes of Dura-Europos owe much to Roman prototypes, both in terms the overall historical narrative and stylistic details. The emotionless expression on the face of Moses, for example, recalls the stoicism of Marcus Aurelius.

We also see reconciliation between Roman style and non-Roman beliefs in Early Christian art, that is, art created during the third and fourth centuries. Consider a

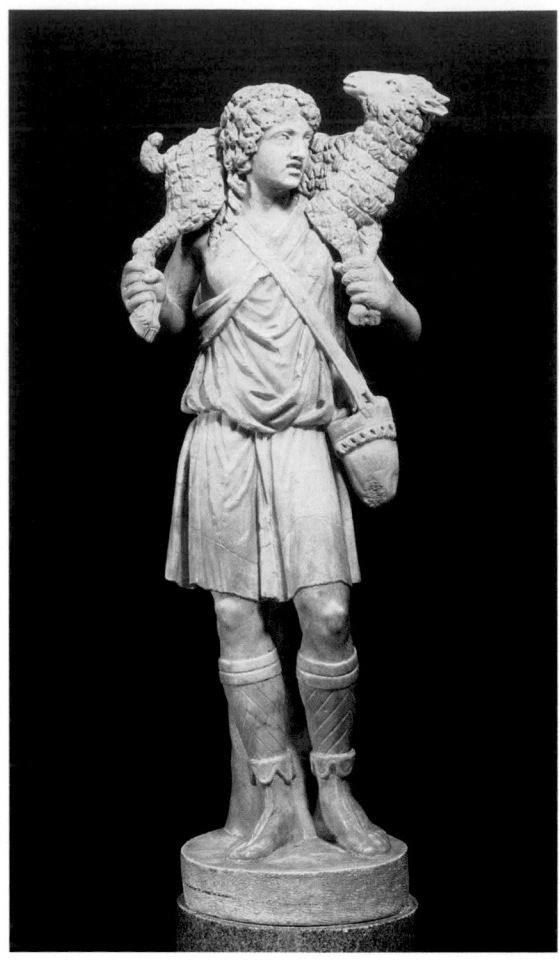

▲ **15.33** *Christ as the Good Shepherd* (c. 300–350). Marble, 3' ¼" high. Musei Vaticani, Rome, Italy.

For Christians, the image of the shepherd and his flock symbolized Jesus and his followers, his loyalty and sacrifice. The symbolism of Jonah provided an important connection between the Christian (New Testament) and Hebrew (Old Testament) Bibles: Early Christians saw the miracle of Jonah's deliverance, after three days, from the belly of the monster that swallowed him as a prefiguration of Christ's resurrection, three days after his crucifixion. And although the good shepherd image proved to be one of the most enduring in Christian iconography, it likely did not originate among Jesus's followers. It may be possible to draw a connection between sacrificial animals in Greek ritual and biblical references to a "Lamb of God" (the Messiah) who would be sacrificed to save humanity. In addition, the style of the figures in The Good Shepherd fresco is more generally reminiscent of that found in vase and wall paintings from Greece and Rome. The poses and proportions are realistic and the drapery falls over the body in naturalistic folds. Early Christians shared the art and culture of Rome, even if not its religion. There were bound to be similarities in style.

ARCHITECTURE AND SCULPTURE   Although the empire was crumbling around him, Constantine continued to erect monuments to glorify it. In 312, he completed a basilica begun by his predecessor Maxentius (Fig. 15.34), after Constantine defeated him in battle. In ancient Rome, basilicas were large public meeting halls that were usually built, like this one, in or around the

fresco depicting Christ as the Good Shepherd (Fig. 15.33) found in the Catacomb of Saints Pietro and Marcellino outside Rome. Most Christian art from this period was found in **catacombs**—underground cemeteries carved out of bedrock and designed as an extensive network of galleries, burial chambers, and mortuary chapels in which secret worship took place. In the center of the painting, Christ stands within a perfect circle, represented as a young shepherd who carries one of his rescued sheep over his shoulders. Four "arms" in the shape of a cross extend outward from the circle, culminating in semicircular frames containing scenes from the Hebrew Bible story of Jonah and the whale. The meaning and style of the fresco illustrate a convergence of three traditions: Christian, Judaic, and Roman. The reference to Christ as a shepherd is traced to his own words, according to the Evangelist, John:

> I am the good shepherd; I know my sheep and my sheep know me—just as the Father knows me and I know the Father—and I lay down my life for the sheep. I have other sheep that are not of this sheep pen. I must bring them also. They too will listen to my voice, and there shall be one flock and one shepherd. (John 10:11–18).

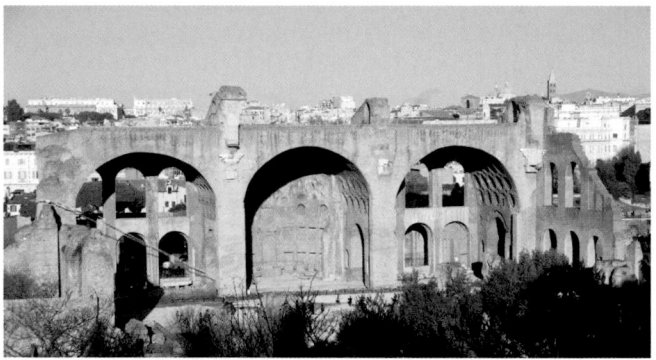

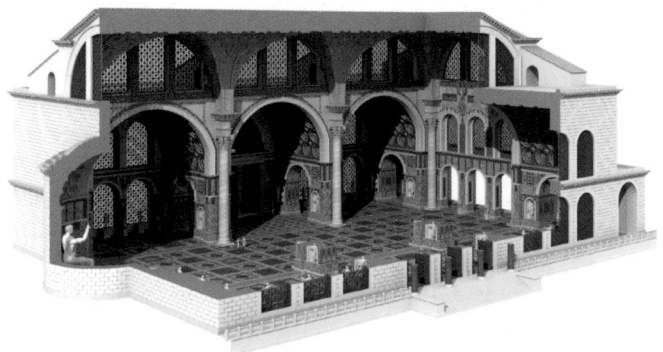

▲ **15.34 Basilica Nova, Rome, Italy.** Top, looking north-east; bottom, restored cutaway view by John Burge (c. 306–312 CE). 300' x 215'.

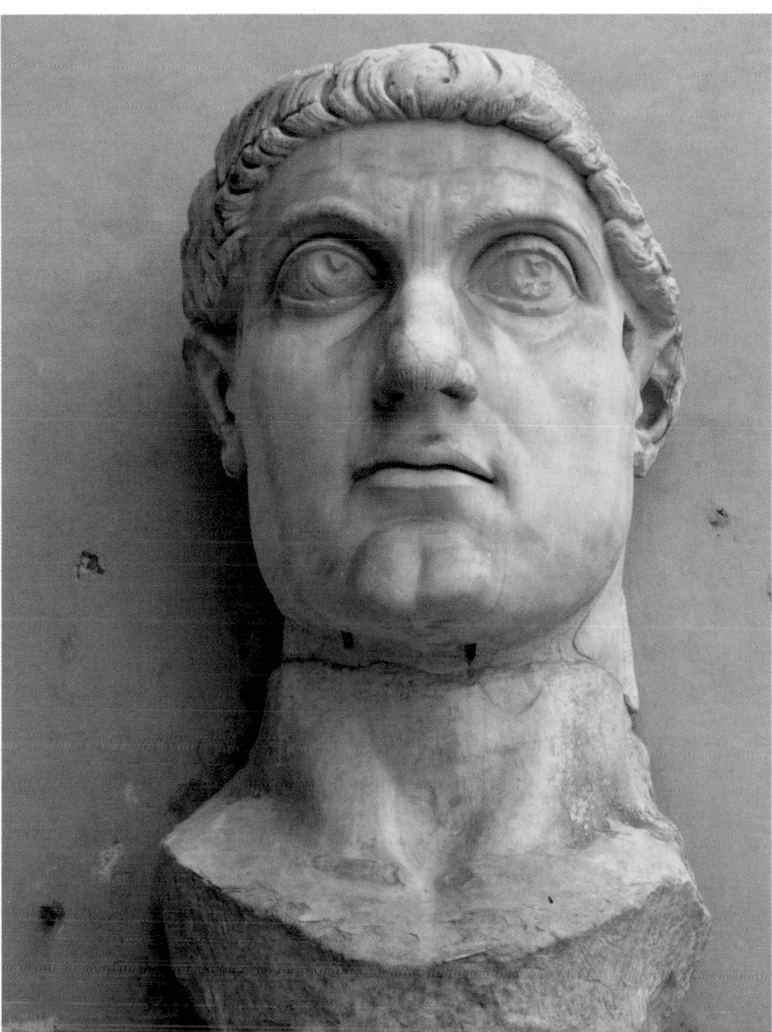

◄ 15.35 **Head of Constantine, Basilica Nova, Rome, Italy** (c. 315–330 CE). Marble, 102" high. Musei Capitolini—Palazzo dei Conservatori, Rome, Italy.

forums. The Basilica of Maxentius and Constantine, also known as the Basilica Nova, was an enormous structure, measuring some 300 by 215 feet (as a point of reference, a football field measures 360 by 160 feet). The interior space was divided into a nave (or central aisle), flanked by two side aisles. The nave ceiling consisted of a coffered groin vault reaching a height of 114 feet and the interior was richly embellished with marble. Little remains of the basilica today, but it survived long enough to set a precedent for Christian church architecture. It would serve as the basic plan for basilicas and cathedrals for centuries to come.

The grandeur of the Basilica Nova seems to belie events in the empire at the time of its construction, more reflective of a Rome that was than the one that it had become. By contrast, the Head of Constantine (Fig. 15.35)—part of a colossal sculpture of the seated emperor that was placed in the Basilica Nova—departs from the literalness and materialism of Roman art and life and gives way to a new spirituality and otherworldliness. The sculpture

consisted of a wooden torso covered with bronze and a head and limbs of marble. The head is more than 8 feet high and weighs more than 8 tons. The realism and idealism that we witnessed in Roman sculpture were replaced by an almost archaic rendition of the emperor, complete with an austere expression and thick-lidded, wide-staring eyes. The artist elaborated the pensive, passive rigidity of form that we sensed in the portrait of Marcus Aurelius. Constantine's face seems both resigned to the fall of his empire and reflective of the Christian emphasis on a kingdom that is not of this world.

Christianity spread among the ruins of the Roman Empire, even if it did not cause it to collapse. Over many centuries, Christianity also had its internal and external problems, but unlike the Roman Empire, it survived. In fact, the concept of survival is central to the understanding of Christianity and its art during the first centuries after the death of Jesus. To be a Christian before Constantine proclaimed religious tolerance, one had to endure persecution. Under the emperors Nero, Trajan, Domitian, and Diocletian, Christians were slain for their beliefs. Under Constantine, all that would change.

See more of Rome in the online Art Tour.

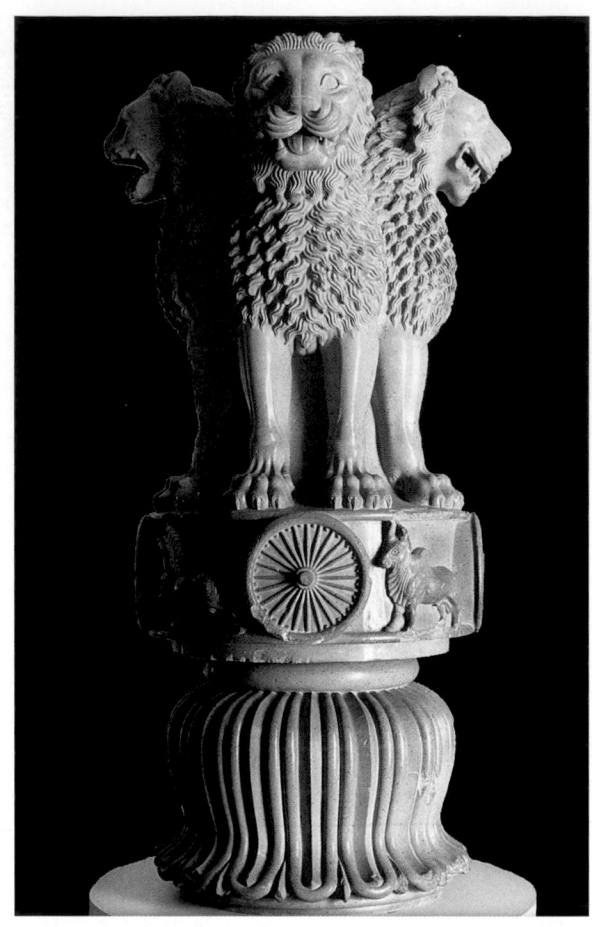

> 15.36 **Lion capital, from a column erected by Ashoka** (242–232 BCE). Polished sandstone, 84" high. Sarnath Museum, Uttar Pradesh, India.

THE WIDER WORLD

Asia

The end of the Indus Civilization brought with it a lull in the arts that lasted almost a millennium. At the same time, the roots of several religions were established in the area that would yield temples, statuary, and mural art including relief sculpture and painting. The territory of India once encompassed present-day Pakistan, Bangladesh, and the buffer states between modern India and China. Several religious traditions have clashed and, sometimes peacefully, coexisted in India, among them Hinduism, Buddhism, and Islam. Today Islam is the dominant religion of Pakistan, and Hinduism predominates in India. Indian art, like Islamic art, is found in many parts of Asia where Indian cultural influence was once strong—as in Indochina.

Buddhism and Hinduism, unlike Islam (or Judaism and Christianity) are polytheistic religions; followers believe in the existence of many deities, and that the pathways

ASIA AND THE AMERICAS

1046 BCE	272 BCE	100 BCE	600 CE
In China, the Zhou Dynasty (c. 1046–221 BCE) coordinates separate kingdoms	The Indian emperor Ashoka reins from 272 to 231 BCE, converts to Buddhism, and helps spread the religion	The city of Teotihuacán, Mexico, is constructed from c. 100 BCE to 600 CE; at its height, its population may reach 200,000	
Colossal Olmec head is sculpted at La Venta, Mexico, between 900 and 400 BCE	Ashoka erects the Lion capital between 242 and 232 BCE	From about 200 CE the Indian Gupta Empire establishes religious tolerance and economic stability, and builds universities that advance and teach medicine and mathematics	
Buddha is born c. 563 BCE	According to legend, Buddha's body parts are distributed among stupas throughout India		
Confucius is born 551 BCE	The Qin Dynasty, from which China derives its name, is founded in 221 BCE by the emperor Shi Huangdi, who connects preexisting walls to create the Great Wall of China and who places 8,000 life-sized terra-cotta warriors in his tomb		
	The Han Dynasty reigns in China from 106 BCE to 9 CE, and from 25 CE to 220 CE		

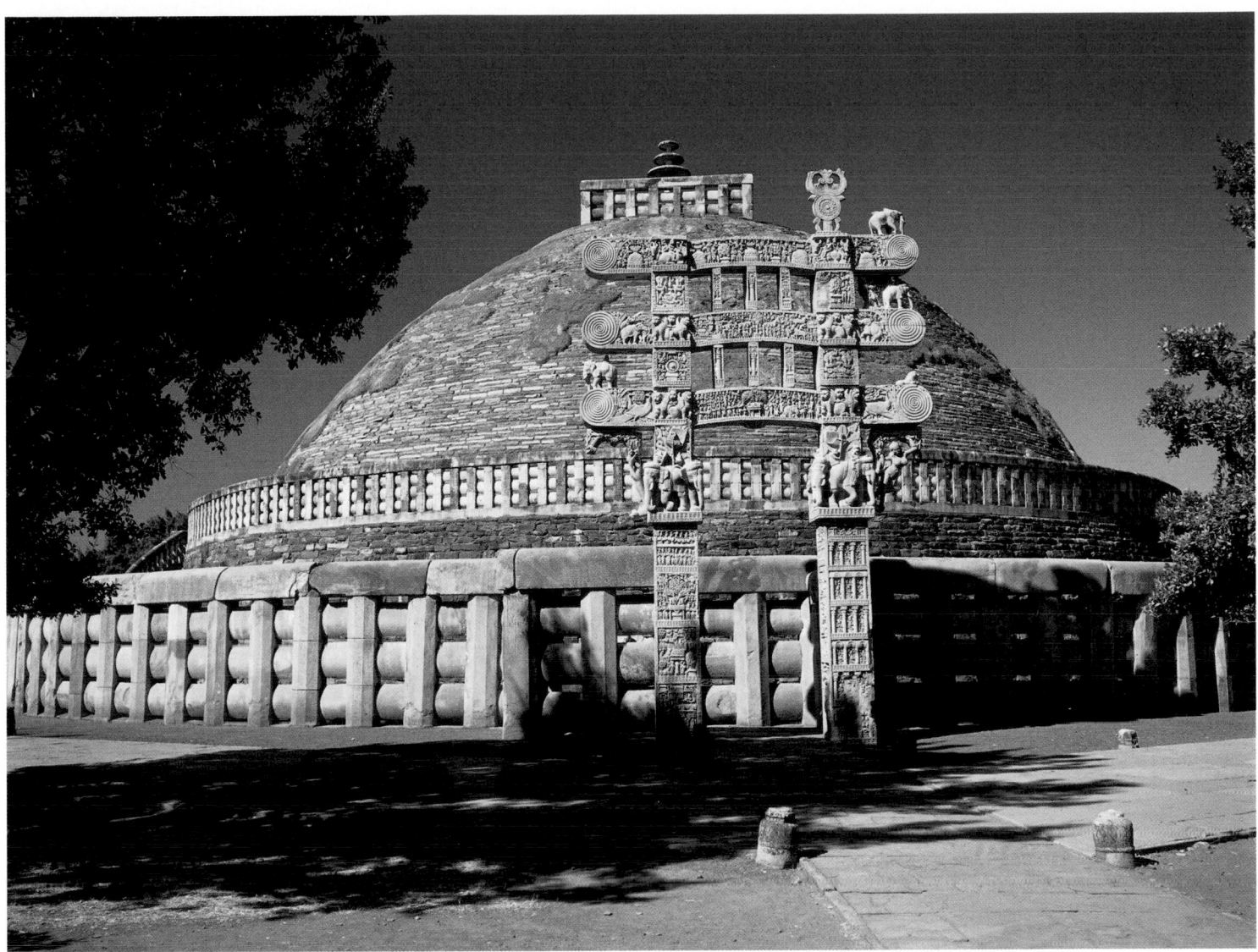

∧ 15.37 **The Great Stupa, Sanchi, India** (3rd century BCE–early 1st century CE). 65' high.

to spiritual fulfillment are likewise many, and diverse. Buddhists and Hindus also believe in reincarnation—a cycle of birth, death, and rebirth that can be broken when individuals free themselves of desire.

Buddhism flowered from earlier Indian religious traditions in the sixth century BCE. Its founder, Prince Siddhartha Gautauma—the Buddha, or Enlightened One—renounced his birthright and earthly luxuries, choosing, instead, a life of discipline, self-denial, and meditation that would lead to **nirvana**: total comprehension of the universe. The lion capital shown in Figure 15.36 is the crowning piece of a pillar erected by the Emperor Ashoka—a convert to Buddhism—to commemorate the place where Buddha is believed to have preached his first important sermon. The circular pedestal on which the lions stand represents the Wheel of the Law, set into

motion by the Buddha; the four small animals around the wheel represent the "four corners" of the Earth.

It is believed that after his death, the Buddha's cremated remains were placed in **stupas** in eight different locations in India. These sites became places of worship and devotion for his followers. The Great Stupa at Sanchi (Fig. 15.37) was completed in the first century CE. The stupa is crowned by a large dome that symbolizes the sky. The dome is visually separated from the base of the structure by a stone railing or fence—known as the vedika—echoing the separation of the heavenly and earthly spheres. Pilgrims circumnavigate the mound in a clockwise direction, as if tracing the path of the sun across the sky. The worshipers' relationship to the monument concentrates on the exterior rather than the interior as, for example, in the case of the Christian church.

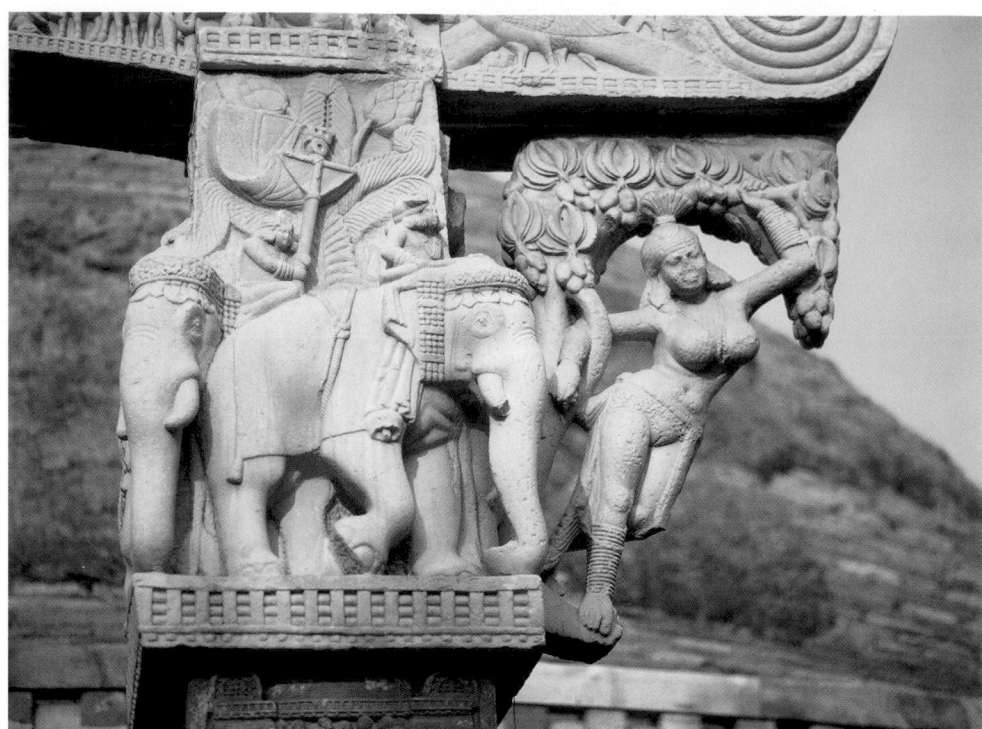

The bracket figure (Fig. 15.38) on a gateway to the Great Stupa is a yakshi, a pre-Buddhist goddess who was believed to embody the generative forces of nature. She appears to be nude, but a hemline reveals that she wears a diaphanous garment. Her ample breasts and sex organs symbolize the forces of nature and stand in contrast to the often ascetic figures we find in Western religious art.

For many hundreds of years, there were no images of the Buddha, but sculptures and other representations began to appear in the second century CE. Some sculpted Buddhas show a Western influence that can be traced to the conquest of northwestern India by Alexander the Great in 327 BCE. The Buddha shown here (Fig. 15.39) appears to be wearing an ancient Greek-style himation. Other Buddhas have a sensuous, rounded look that recalls the ancient seals and is decidedly Indian. The faces of many Buddhas exhibit a pleasant cast that is as inscrutable as the expression of La Gioconda in Leonardo's *Mona Lisa* (see Fig. 2.13).

At the same time that the Roman Republic ruled in the West, the Qin Dynasty of China—under the First Emperor of Qin, Shi Huangdi—emerged as a dominant power in the East. The word *China* is derived from *Qin,* the state of which Shi Huangdi was emperor.

Architecture and sculpture of the Qin Dynasty is associated with two renowned and ambitious works: the Great Wall (Fig. 15.40) and the terra-cotta Army of Shi Huangdi, which "stood guard" in pits next to the emperor's burial ground (Fig. 15.41). The Great Wall of China, so massive and long that it can be seen from the moon, is comprised of a series of fortification walls connected to form a continuous defense boundary along China's

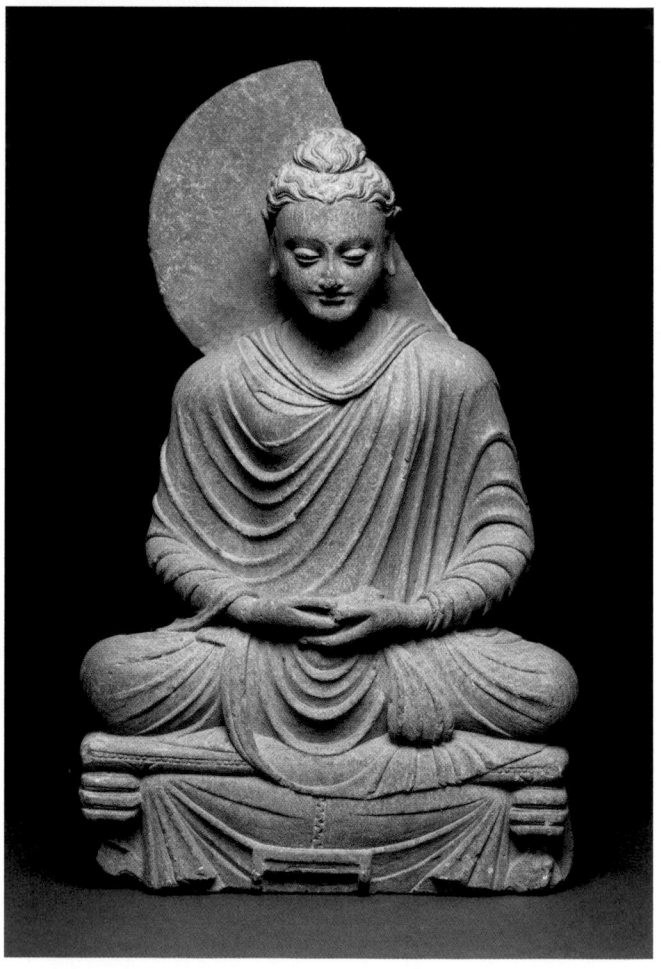

▲ 15.39 **Seated Buddha, Gandhara, Pakistan (India)** (1st–3rd century CE). Schist. Fitzwilliam Museum, Cambridge University, UK.

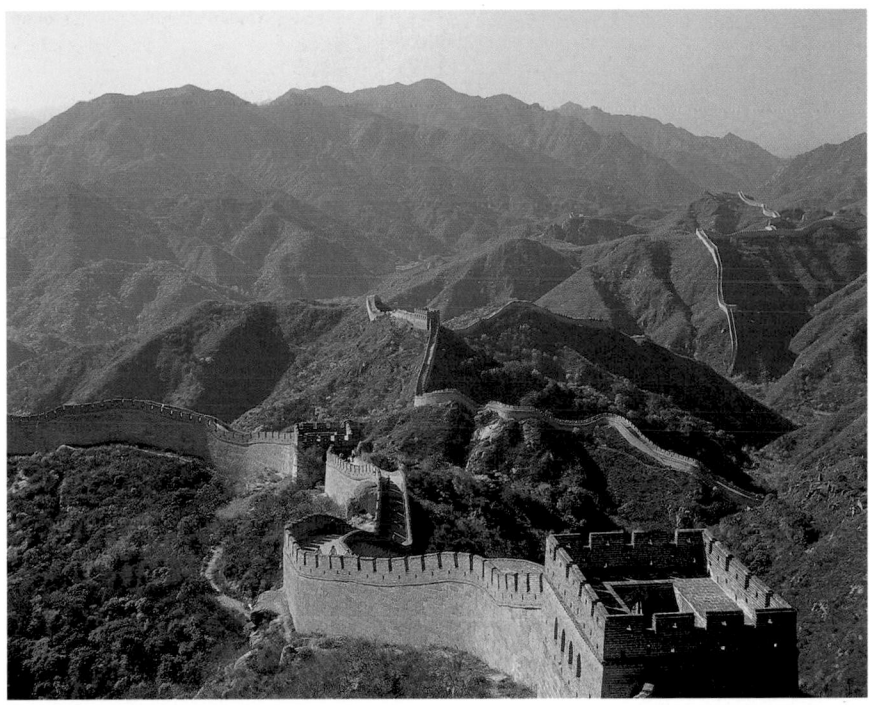

▲ 15.40 **The Great Wall of China** (Qin Dynasty). Roughly 5,500 miles long, averaging 16–20' wide × 16–26' high, plus 13' at the watchtowers.

northern border. The ancient wall was approximately 5,500 miles in length. Shi Huangdi's wall was constructed to protect the people of his empire from invaders, but his other grand project was intended to glorify himself: an imposing tomb that would befit a most powerful ruler. Rediscovered in 1974, the burial mound itself has not yet been excavated, but pits surrounding it have yielded life-sized terra-cotta warriors and bronze horses and chariots numbering in the thousands. Although the warriors are regimented in stance and precise in formation, the variation among them is remarkable. Molds were obviously used to create such a large number of figures, but their individuality indicates that body parts and specific gestures were assembled in a variety of combinations.

Shi Huangdi's reign was monumental in reforms though marked by brutality, harsh laws, and strict penal codes. It was also brief. After the First Emperor's death, the Chinese people revolted, ousting and assassinating his son.

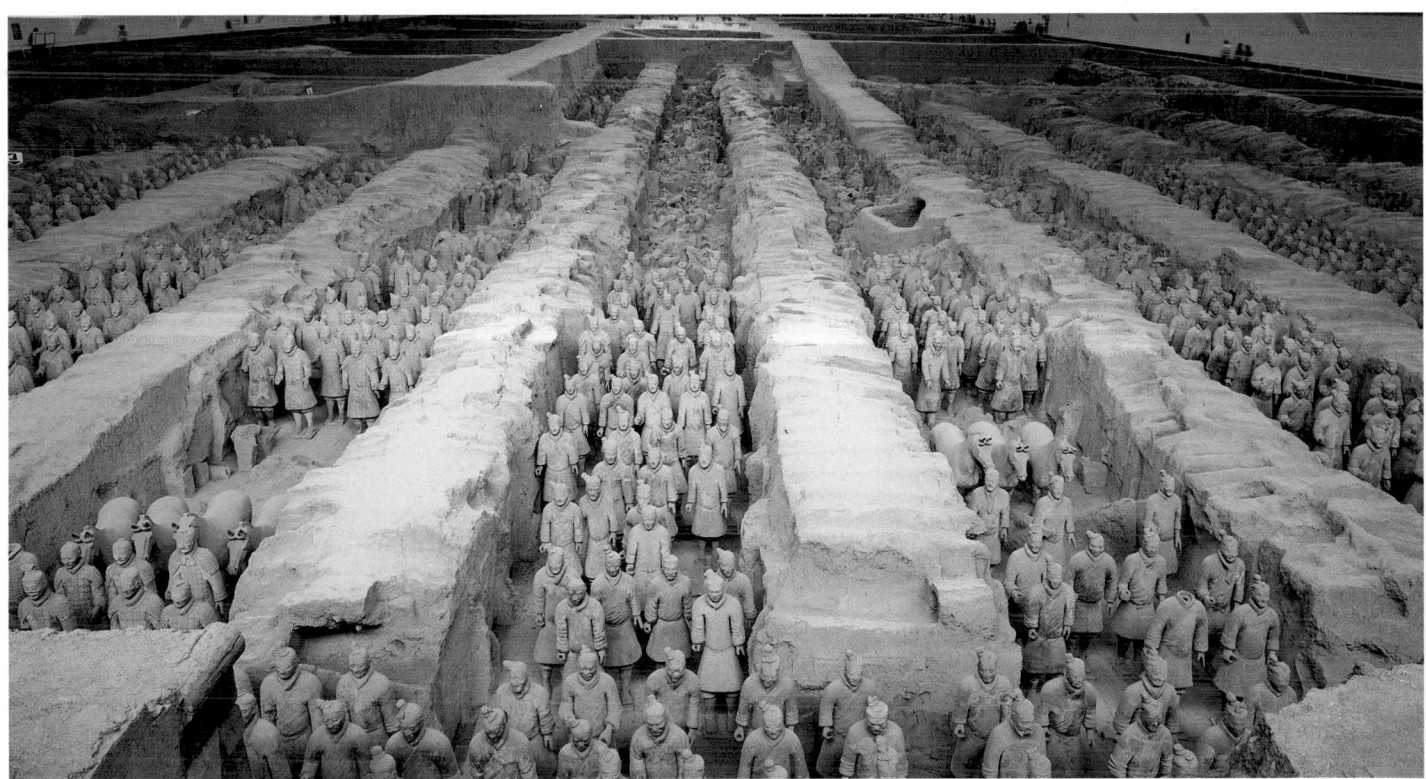

▲ 15.41 **Army of Shi Huangdi (First Emperor) in pits next to his burial mound** (c. 210 BCE , Qin dynasty). Painted terra-cotta. Average figure 71" high. Lintong, China.

Four years later, after a civil war, the Han Dynasty succeeded the Qin and governed China for some four centuries—the Western Han from 206 BCE to 9 CE, and the Eastern Han from 25 CE to 220 CE. During the reign of the Han Dynasty, Julius Caesar was assassinated in Rome, Mark Antony and Cleopatra committed suicide after their forces were defeated by Octavian, Jesus was born and died in the Middle East, Rome built aqueducts and stadiums throughout the Empire, and the Pantheon was erected. Chang'an, the Western Han capital, and Rome were the two largest cities of their day.

The Han emperor Wudi (141–86 BCE) was a great patron of the arts, philosophy, and literature. Whereas the Qin Dynasty had sought to bury dissonant thought by the burning of philosophical texts in 213 BCE and the murder of 460 Confucian scholars three years later, the Han emperor Wudi installed Confucianism as the foundation of educational practices and official conduct in China. Confucianism, named after the philosopher Confucius (551–479 BCE), is more of an ethical system than a religion, although Confucius's thinking, as propounded in the *I Ching* (*Book of Changes*), speaks of the cosmos as influenced by the metaphysical opposition of the energies of *yin* and *yang*. Confucius also believed in the value of religious rituals as a means to generating benevolence and the good life. Thus Wudi, following the teachings of Confucius, created a government defined by concern and sympathy for one's fellow beings. Ethnic Chinese still speak of themselves as being Han Chinese.

Han Dynasty art and architecture featured bronze and ceramic figurines, jade carvings, paintings on walls, screens, scrolls, and silk, and multistoried towers. The cast bronze flying horse from the tomb of the Governor-General Zhang (Fig. 15.42) is one of many horses, soldiers, and chariots unearthed in 1969. This 13 1/2-inch-long figure does not have the majesty of the life-sized soldiers and other figures in Shi Huangdi's tomb, but apparently the concept of being buried with some sort of military guard had become fashionable as a symbol of power. Native Chinese horses had been small and relatively slow. The bronze depicts the type of horse that Han emperors sought to import from

Central Asia as war-horses. Other horse figures in the tomb stand still or prance. This particular animal has fancifully taken flight, with one leg supported by the body and wings of a swallow.

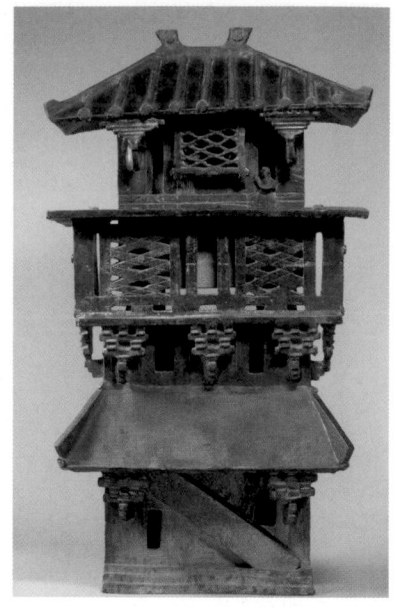

Han Dynasty architecture included palaces, city walls, and gateways with towers, as shown in the glazed, ceramic model (Fig. 15.43). The four-story building has supportive piers at the corners. There is a wide overhanging tile roof and an exterior staircase. Latticework screens shield the third story from view.

The Americas

Some 10,000 to 20,000 years ago, people of largely Asian descent crossed a now-submerged land bridge between present-day Russian Siberia and Alaska, moving southward and spreading throughout North and South America.

In what is now Mexico and Central America, the Pre-Columbian Olmec civilization—Mesoamerica's earliest—thrived from about 1500 to 400 BCE, spanning roughly the years between the Mycenaean era in the West through the Golden Age of Greece. Some of the earliest, and certainly the most massive art of the Americas was produced by the Olmec peoples in what is now southern Mexico. More than a dozen gigantic heads (Fig. 15.44) up to 12 feet in height have been found at Olmec ceremonial centers, some 100 miles from the area where the materials for these sculptures—volcanic (basalt) rock, stone, and jadeite—were obtained. The overall shape of the heads conforms to shape of the blocks from which they were carved, and all share similar characteristics: tight-fitting helmets, broad noses, full lips, and wide, flat cheeks. Whether these colossal heads represent gods or earthly rulers is unknown, but there can be no doubting the power they project. The Olmec civilization declined around 400 BCE, but aspects of its religion, ritual, and culture, lived on in the later Mayan and Aztec civilizations.

The Olmecs inhabited swampy, tropical lowlands within access of natural resources that could be exploited

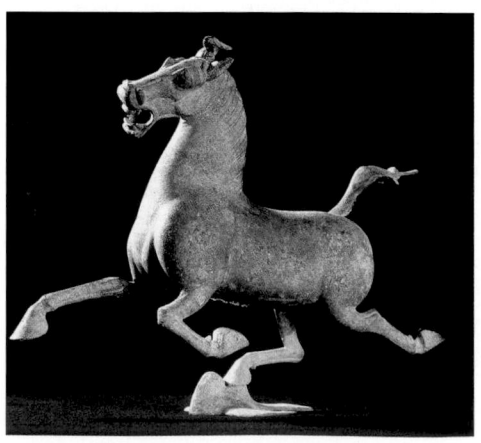

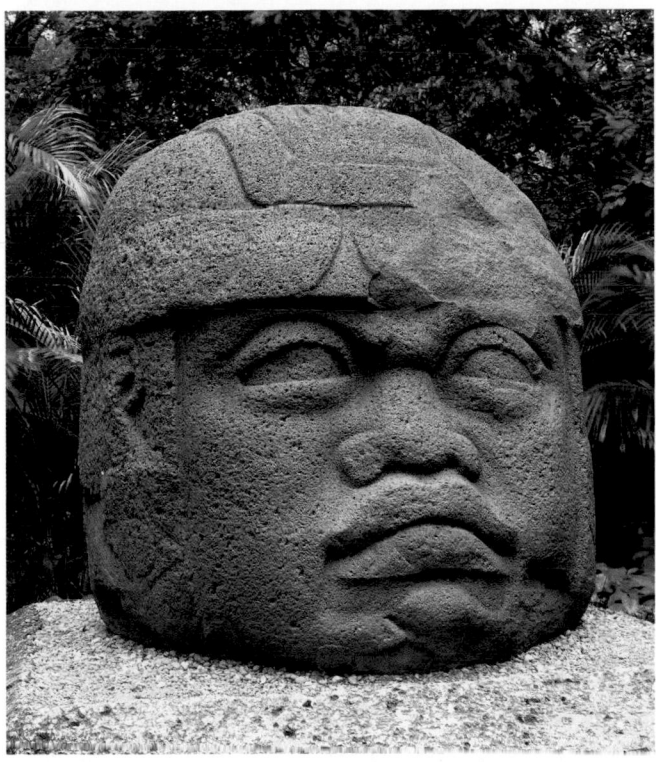

∧ 15.44 **Colossal head, La Venta, Mexico, Olmec** (c. 900–400 BCE). Basalt, 9'4" high. Museo-Parque La Venta, Villahermosa, Mexico.

for sustenance, trade, and the construction of buildings and monuments. This topography differs markedly from that of the Valley of Mexico, a highlands plateau in central Mexico that was the setting for the major urban complex of Teotihuacán established around 100 BCE.

The remains of the city we call Teotihuacán lie about 30 miles northeast of what is now Mexico City (Fig. 15.45). At its peak, in about 600 CE, as many as 200,000 people lived and worked in Teotihuacán, making it one of the largest cities in the world. The city was designed on a grid plan bisected by the broad Avenue of the Dead. It features a variety of structures including two colossal pyramids, smaller ceremonial platforms, and a shrine known as the Temple of the Feathered Serpent that was dedicated to the deity Quetzalcoatl. While the overall shape of the Pyramid of the Sun and Pyramid of the Moon—as well as the temple—are reminiscent of early Egyptian step-pyramids (see Fig. 14.12, foreground, lower left), they possess a unique feature: dramatically steep stairways that led to temples of wood and other materials that have not survived. In addition to architecture and sculptural reliefs, elaborate mural paintings have been excavated in residential areas of the city. Archaeological evidence suggests that the temples of Teotihuacán complex were destroyed by fire around 600 CE.

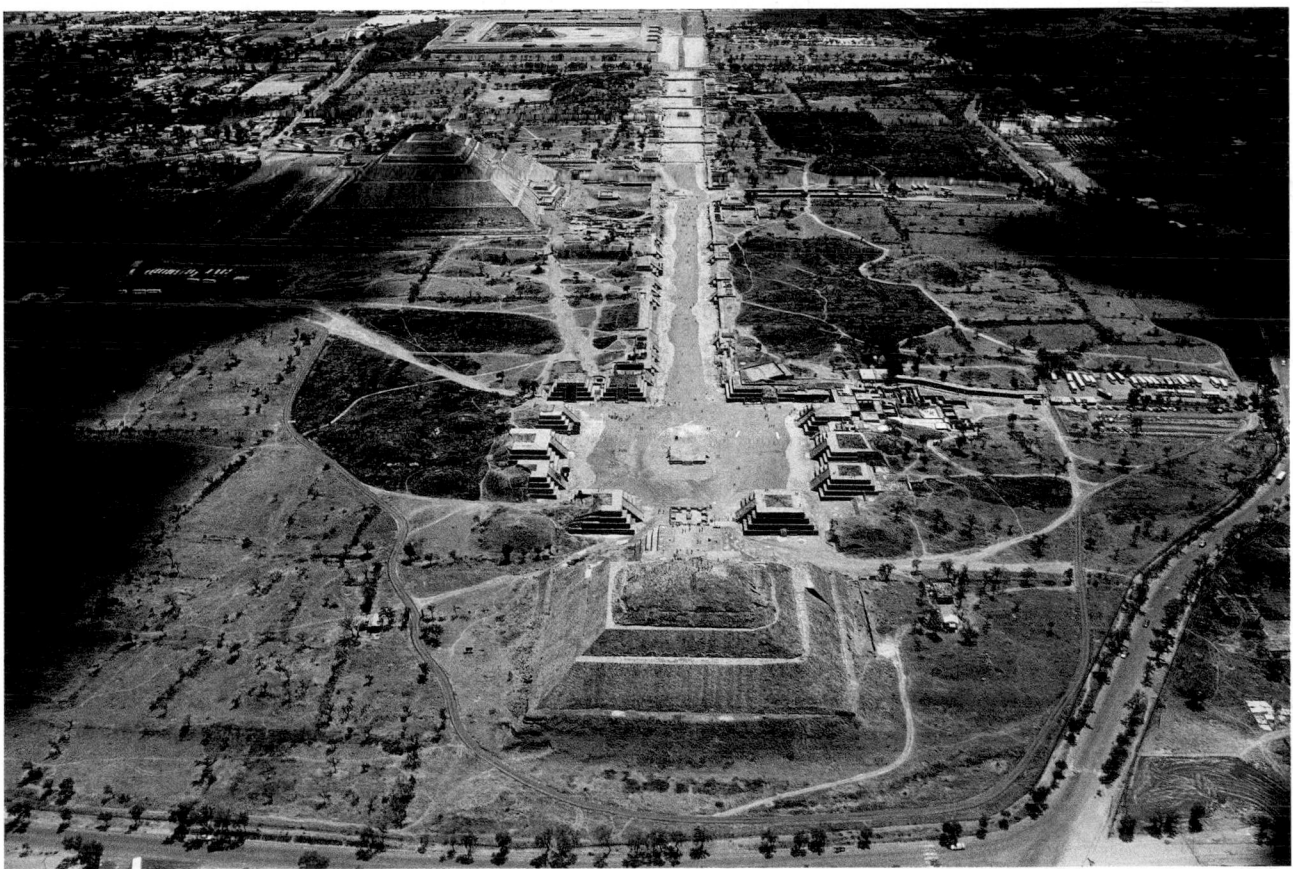

∧ 15.45 *Aerial view of Teotihuacán, Mexico* (c. 100 BCE–600 CE). The Pyramid of the Moon is shown in the foreground. The Pyramid of the Sun is in the upper left. The city has a gridlike pattern and is connected by the Avenue of the Dead, which is two miles long.

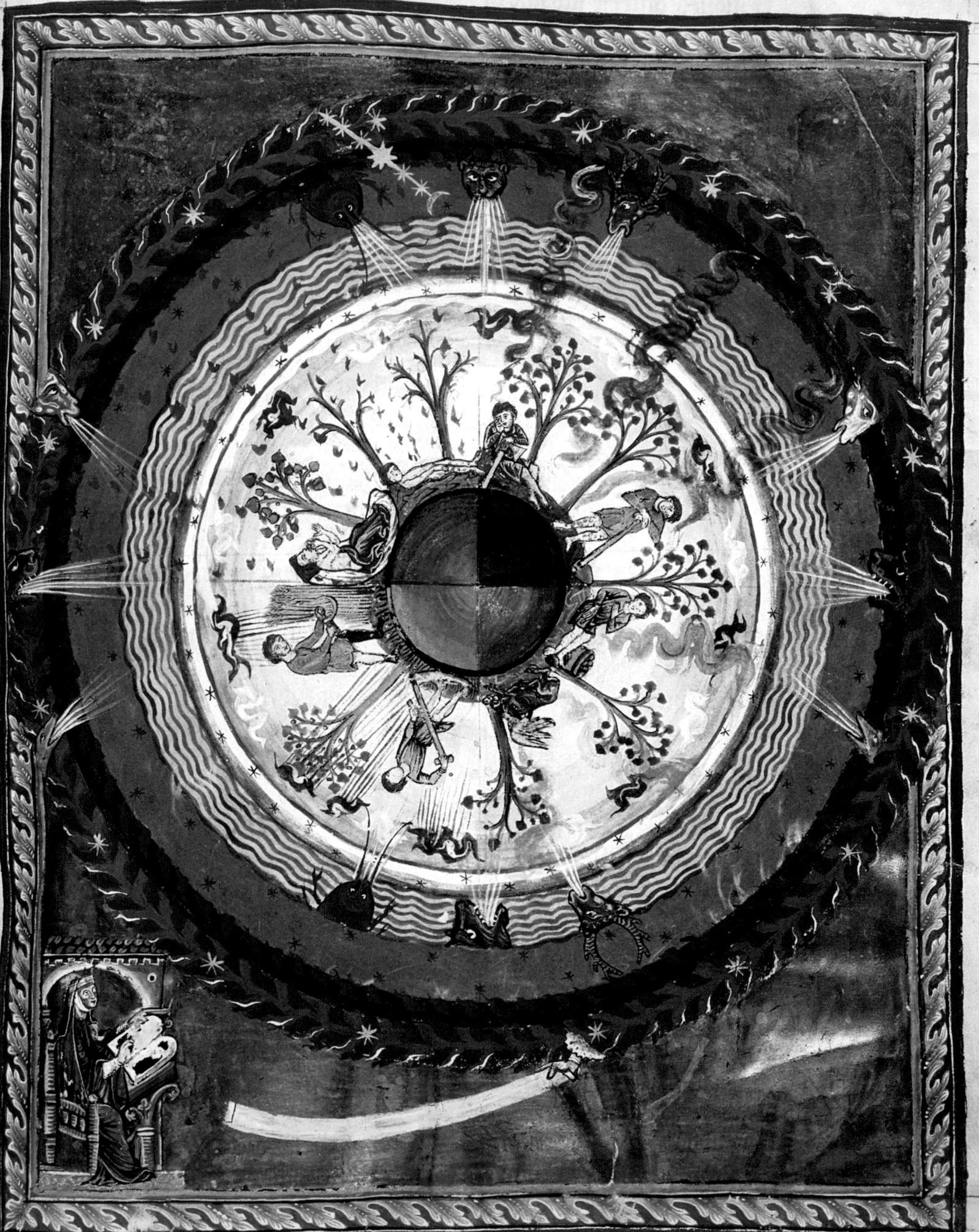

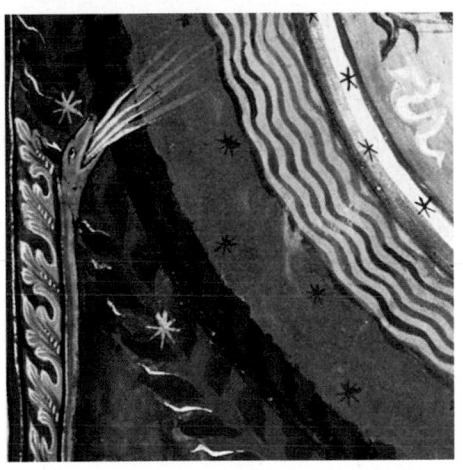

16

THE AGE OF FAITH

The lamps are different, but the Light is
the same: it comes from Beyond.

—FROM JALAL AL-DIN RUMI,

"THE ONE TRUE LIGHT"

WHEN THE Sufi mystic and poet Rumi was writing in the 1200s, Islam was in its Golden Age, Christianity was in the High Middle Ages, and it had been over two millennia since the Hebrews drafted the tenets of their faith after, according to their belief, Moses received the Ten Commandments at Mount Sinai. Judaism, Christianity, and Islam—three "lamps" representing three of the world's most influential religions—have things in common: their "light" comes from a single God, and all are built on the belief in divine revelation from "beyond." Jews believe that God, whom the ancient Hebrews called Yahweh, spoke directly to Abraham and to Moses, establishing a covenant with their generations as his "chosen people." Christians believe that the same God spoke to Jesus at his baptism, calling him his "beloved son." And Muslims believe that the same God, whom they call Allah, revealed their holy book—the Qur'an—to the Prophet Muhammad. Rumi referred to a single God as "the kernel of Existence" but acknowledged the perspectives of many religions.

In the previous chapter, we discussed the pluralism of religious belief and practice in the waning years of the Roman Empire, exploring Jewish and early Christian sites of worship in the far-flung garrison town of Dura-Europos, as well as other secret gathering spaces for ritual during the Christian period of persecution. This chapter begins with the emperor Constantine's commitment to Christianity and his construction of a grand basilica for worship in the city of Rome—the western capital of the Roman Empire. The first St. Peter's, begun in 319 CE, followed Constantine's own revelation or—more accurately—vision that led to his own conversion to

< HILDEGARD OF BINGEN, "Vision of God's Plan for the Seasons," folio 38 recto from *De operatione Dei* ("On God's Actvity") (also known as *Liber divinorum operum* "Book of Divine Works") (c. 1163–1174). Illuminated miniature on vellum in mandala form. Biblioteca Statale, Lucca, Italy.

Christianity: Before he went into the Battle of the Milvian Bridge over the Tiber River against the emperor Maxentius in 312 CE, he said he saw a cross of light in the sky, along with the words "by this, win." He ordered his soldiers to mark their shields with a Christian symbol and, indeed, the enemy was vanquished. Constantine believed he owed this victory to the Christian God. His gratitude would be expressed in riches and grandeur bestowed on the early church.

In this chapter we also discuss contemporary artistic developments in India, China, Africa, and the Americas. Hinduism ("the religion of the people of the Indus Valley") is as old as Judaism, originating perhaps one and a half millennia before the birth of Christ. China was ruled by the Song Dynasty during the West's Middle Ages, and invented printing presses and gunpowder. The native religions of Africans still find expression, even though migrations from Europe and from the Near and Middle East brought with them Christian and Islamic beliefs. The Americas, as yet undiscovered by European explorers, developed their own civilizations and artistic traditions.

CHRISTIANITY

Christianity (from the Greek *chrīstos,* meaning "messiah") is an Abrahamic religion as are Judaism and Islam. Christianity is monotheistic and based on the teachings of Jesus, as written in the New Testament, or Christian Bible. Christians believe that Jesus is the Son of God and the messiah who was prophesied in the Old Testament, or Hebrew Bible. At first a Jewish sect, Christianity flourished over its early centuries and became the dominant religion in the Roman Empire by the fourth century. Today there are some two billion Christians, almost one-third of the population of the world.

Christianity teaches that Jesus led a virtuous life, taught followers how to lead virtuous lives, and saved humankind from the consequences of original sin by his own suffering and death. Christians believe that Jesus was resurrected after his death and ascended into heaven. Most Christians believe that Jesus will return one day—on *Judgment Day*—to judge the dead and the living, and grant everlasting life to the deserving.

Theological councils in the fourth century affirmed the divinity of Jesus, putting him on an equal plane with God the Father. They also glorified the Holy Spirit. According to the gospels of Luke and Matthew, Jesus had been conceived by the Holy Spirit and was born by the Virgin Mary. These three divine "persons"—the Father, the Son, and the Holy Spirit—unified, are sometimes referred to as the Godhead. In the mid-fifth century, Jesus Christ was proclaimed to have both divine and human natures, to have had a human side subject to physical suffering, as have mortals. This duality would impact the ways in which Jesus was depicted in art, as would details of the New Testament and Gospels describing his life from birth in a simple manger, through the performance of miracles and calling of his apostles, to his crucifixion and resurrection.

CHRISTIANITY

6 BCE	381 CE	565 CE	1096 CE	1453 CE
Birth of Jesus c. 6–4 BCE	Capital of Western Empire moved from Milan to Ravenna 402	Muhammad born in Mecca 570	Gothic style begins	
Reign of Constantine 307–327		Palatine Chapel built 792–805	Oxford University founded	
Edict of Milan 313	Reign of Justinian 527–565	Charlemagne crowned emperor of Holy Roman Empire 800	Chartres Cathedral begun 1134, rebuilt after 1194	
Founding of Constantinople	Church of San Vitale constructed c. 530–548	St. Michael built c. 1001–1031	St. Denis built c. 1140	
Christianity declared state religion		*Bayeux Tapestry* c. 1070–1080	Cathedral of Notre-Dame built 1163–1250	
		St. Sernin constructed c. 1070–1120	Laon Cathedral begun c. 1190	
			Dante writes *Divine Comedy* c. 1308–1321	
			The Black Death 1348	
			Constantinople falls to Ottoman Turks 1453	

EARLY CHRISTIAN ARCHITECTURE

In Dura-Europos, Early Christians secretly worshiped in private community houses that had been renovated and adapted to accommodate their rituals and ceremonies. Persecution of Christians was officially forbidden by the Edict of Milan of 313 CE, which held "that it was proper that the Christians and all others should have liberty to follow that mode of religion which to each of them appeared best."[1] No longer compelled to hide their beliefs and practices—in catacombs or safe houses—Christians

---
[1] Lactantius, *De Mortibus Persecutorum*.

began to build churches, many of which were erected on the land on top of the catacombs where the martyrs for their faith had been buried. In terms of design, it is not surprising that they turned to what they already knew—Roman architecture. What may be surprising, on the other hand, is that the Roman Emperor Constantine was one of their most generous supporters in this effort.

Old St. Peter's, Rome

Among the many churches Constantine helped create in Rome and in Constantinople, the most significant was Old St. Peter's (Fig. 16.1). Built on the site where St. Peter was believed to have been buried, the expansive

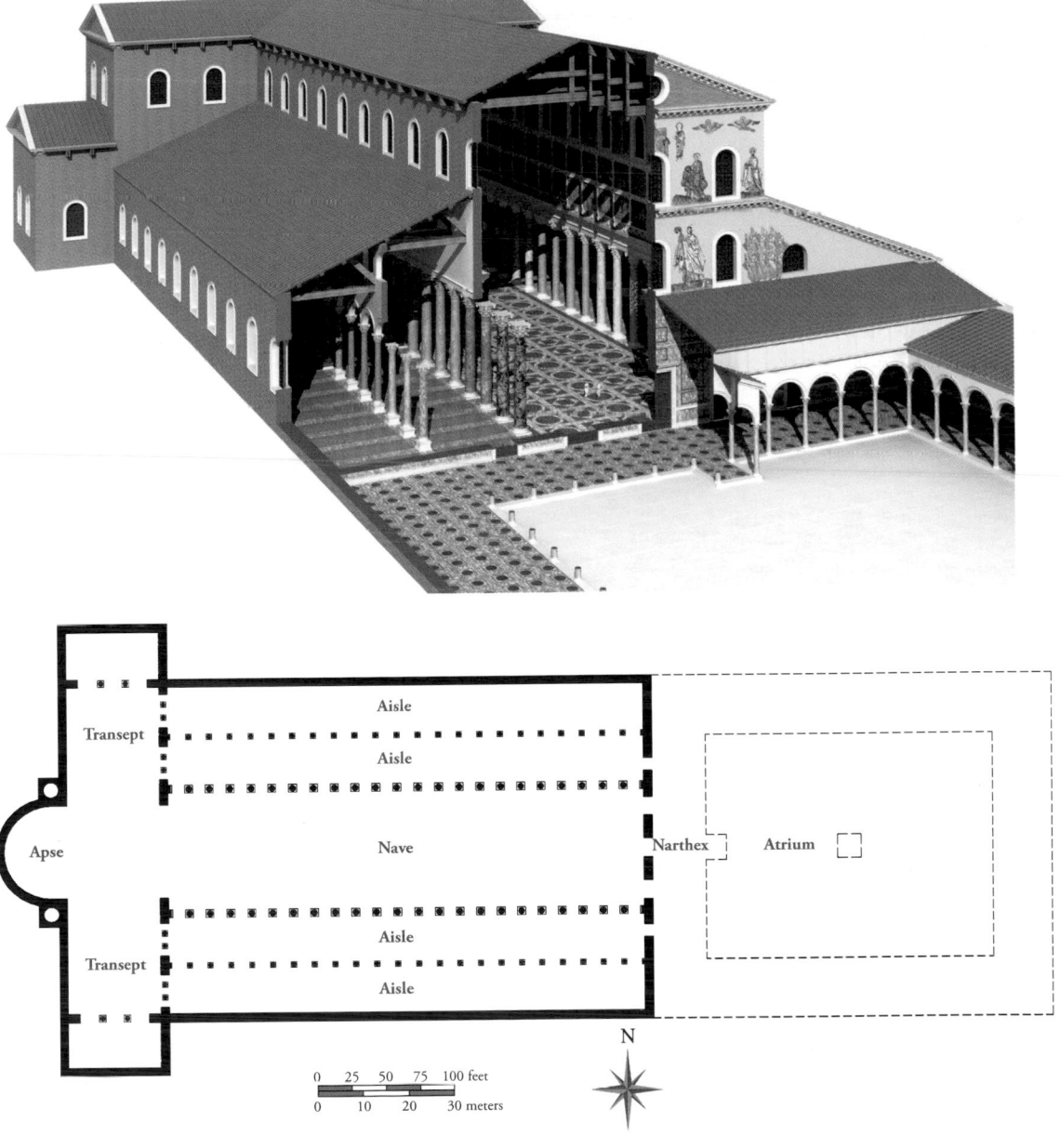

∧ 16.1 Restored cutaway view (top) and plan (bottom) of Old St. Peter's, Rome, Italy by John Burge (begun c. 319).

basilican-plan church no longer exists. What stands in its place—at the heart of Vatican City in Rome—is the present-day St. Peter's Basilica (see Fig. 18.2), constructed during the Renaissance and Baroque periods.

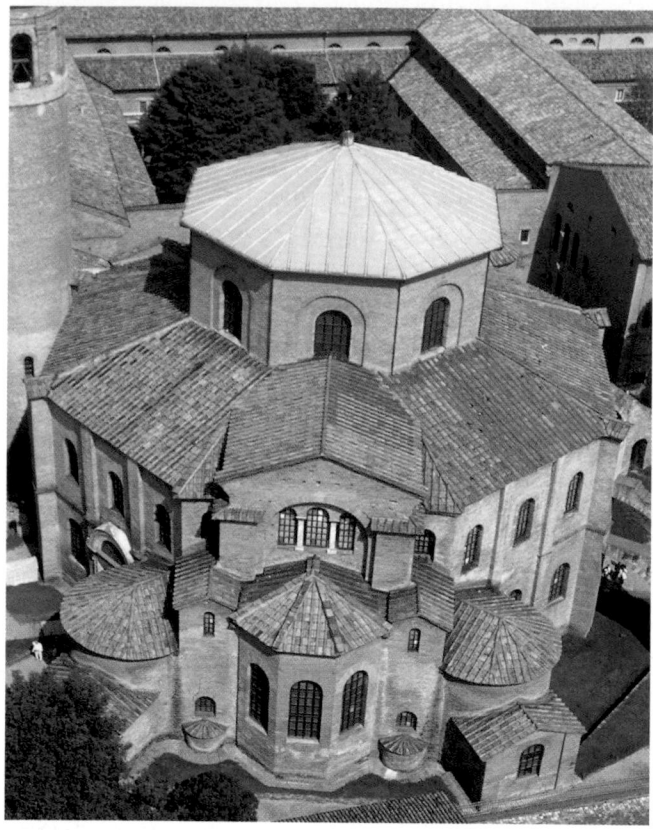

Part A. Exterior view.

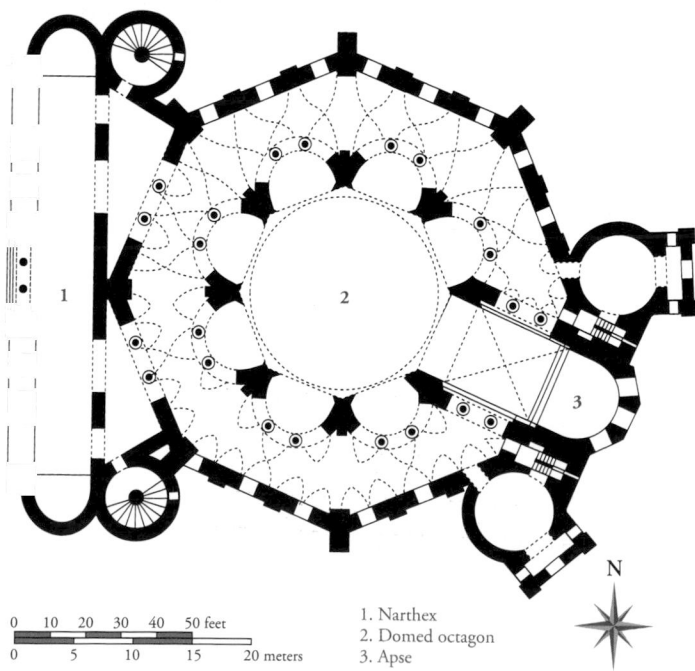

0 10 20 30 40 50 feet
0   5   10   15   20 meters

1. Narthex
2. Domed octagon
3. Apse

N

Part B. Plan.

∧ **16.2 Church of San Vitale, Ravenna, Italy** (Byzantine, 526–547).

The plan of Old St. Peter's looks to the past and to the future. The scale of the building, including many of its parts, reflects those of Roman basilicas. Both have wide, long, central **naves** flanked by two narrower **side aisles** forming the main congregational space. Unlike many Roman basilicas, however, Old St. Peter's was entered from one of the short sides, through a kind of gateway into the large open courtyard or **atrium** called the **propylaeum**. Both the propylaeum and atrium appeared in subsequent cathedral designs, but not with any regularity. All of the other parts of the plan, however, became regular features. The worshiper gained access to the heart of the basilica through a series of portals, passing first through a vestibule called the **narthex**. On the opposite end of the 300-foot-long structure was the **transept**, an aisle that crossed over and was perpendicular to the nave and side aisles, and that separated the congregational space from the altar. The transept often extended beyond the boundaries of the side aisles, resembling the arms of a cross. The altar, the focus of ritual and ceremony, was placed in a semicircular space called the **apse**, another holdover from Roman basilicas. This plan is called a **Latin Cross plan** or, because of the length of the nave and the orientation of the plan along a single dominant axis, a **longitudinal plan**. The Latin Cross plan was most prominent in western Europe, although smaller and more symmetrical plans—**central plans**—were more typical in eastern empire cities like Ravenna on the eastern coast of Italy. The central plan is characterized by a central (rather than longitudinal) focus.

Old St. Peter's was decorated lavishly with inlaid marble and mosaics, none of which survive. In fact, only one Early Christian church escaped destruction by fire, in large part because their ceilings were constructed of wood. The art of mosaic, much of it classical in style, was adopted from the Romans and comprised most of the ornamentation in Early Christian churches.

BYZANTINE ART

The term **Byzantine** comes from the town of ancient Byzantium, the site of Constantine's capital, Constantinople. The art called "Byzantine" was produced after the Early Christian era in Byzantium, but also in Ravenna, Venice, Sicily, Greece, Russia, and other Eastern countries. We may describe the difference between Early Christian and Byzantine art as a transfer from an earthbound realism to a more spiritual, otherworldly style. Byzantine figures appear to be weightless; they are placed in an undefined space. Byzantine art features a great deal of symbolism and is far more decorative in detail than Early Christian art.

San Vitale, Ravenna

The city of Ravenna, on the Adriatic coast of Italy, was initially settled by the ruler of the western Roman Empire who was trying to escape invaders by moving his capital out of Rome. As it turned out, the move was timely; only eight years later, that city was sacked. The early history of Ravenna was riddled with strife; its leadership changed hands often. It was not until the age of Emperor Justinian that Ravenna attained some stability and that the arts truly flourished.

During Justinian's reign, the church of San Vitale (Fig. 16.2), one of the most elaborate buildings decorated in the Byzantine style, was erected. San Vitale was designed as a central plan church, with an octagonal perimeter and a narthex set off axis to the apse. When you look at the plan, you can see that it is dominated by a central circle. This circle indicates a dome, which from the exterior appears as another octagon stacked wedding-cake fashion on the first. This circle is surrounded by eight massive piers, between which are semicircular niches that extend into a surrounding aisle, or **ambulatory**, like petals of a flower. The "stem" of this flower is a sanctuary that intersects the ambulatory and culminates in a multisided, or polygonal, apse. Unlike the rigid axial alignment of the Latin Cross churches that follow a basilican plan, San Vitale has an organic quality. Soft, curving forms press into the spaces of the church and are juxtaposed by geometric shapes that seem to complement their fluidity rather than restrain it. The space flows freely, and the disparate forms are unified. This vital, organic quality can also be seen in the details of the church interior. Columns are crowned by capitals carved with complex, interlacing designs. Decorative mosaic borders, inspired by plant life, comprise repetitive stylized patterns.

This stylized treatment of forms can also be seen in the representation of human figures in San Vitale's mosaics. *Justinian and Attendants* (Fig. 16.3), an apse mosaic, represents the Byzantine style at its peak of perfection in this medium. The mosaic commemorates Justinian's victory over the Goths and proclaims him ruler of Ravenna and the western half of the Roman Empire. His authority is symbolized by the military and clerical representatives in his entourage. The figures form a strong, friezelike horizontal band that communicates unity. Although they are placed in groups, some slightly in front of others, the heads present as points in a single line. Thickly lidded eyes stare outward. The heavily draped bodies have no evident substance, as if garments hang on invisible frames, and the physical gestures of the men are unnatural. Space is tentatively suggested by a grassy ground line, but the placement of the figures on this line and within this space is uncertain. Notice how the feet seem to hover rather than to support, like Colorforms stuck to a tableau background. These characteristics contrast strongly with the Classicism of Early Christian art and point the way toward a manner of representation in which the corporeality of the body is less significant than the soul.

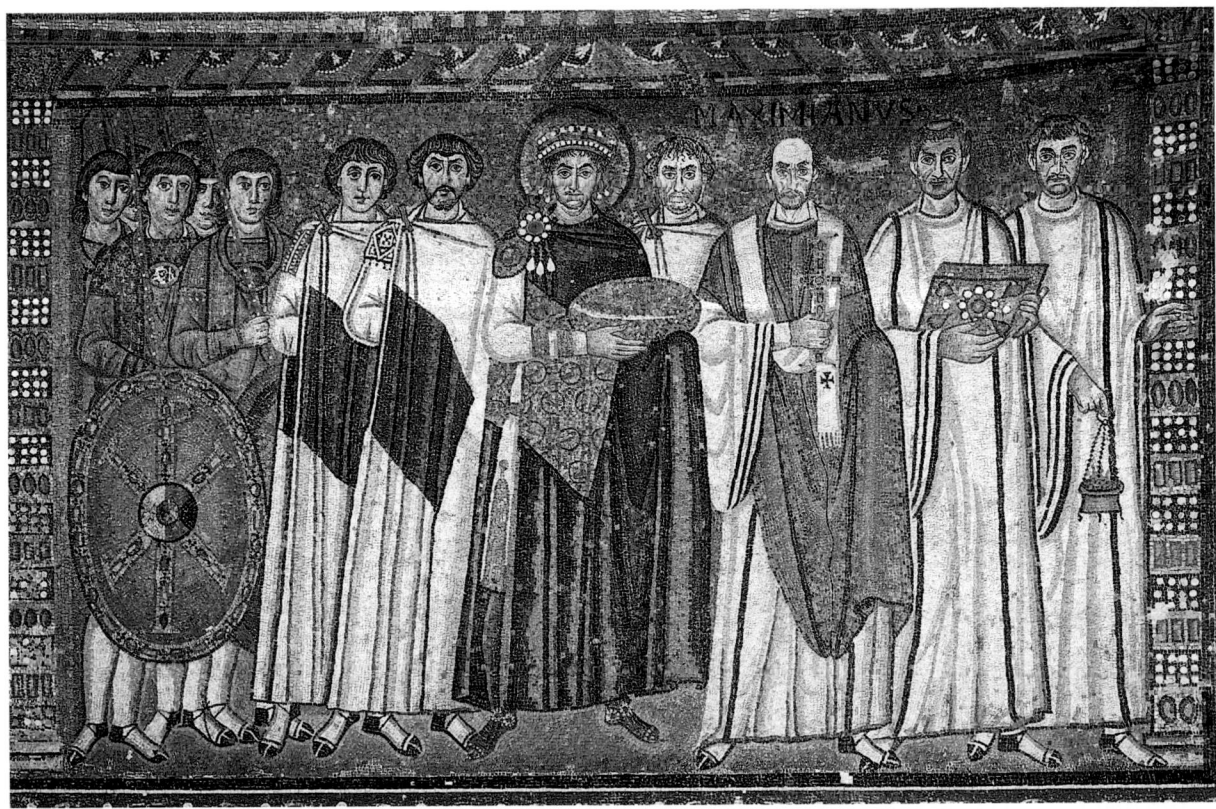

◄ 16.3 *Justinian and Attendants* (c. 547). Mosaic, north wall of the apse, Church of San Vitale, Ravenna, Italy.

Hagia Sophia, Constantinople

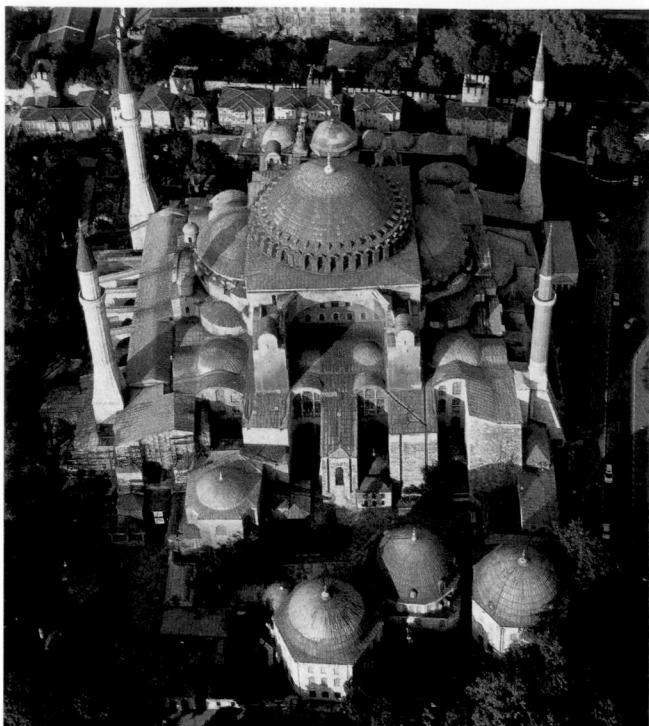

Part A. Exterior view.

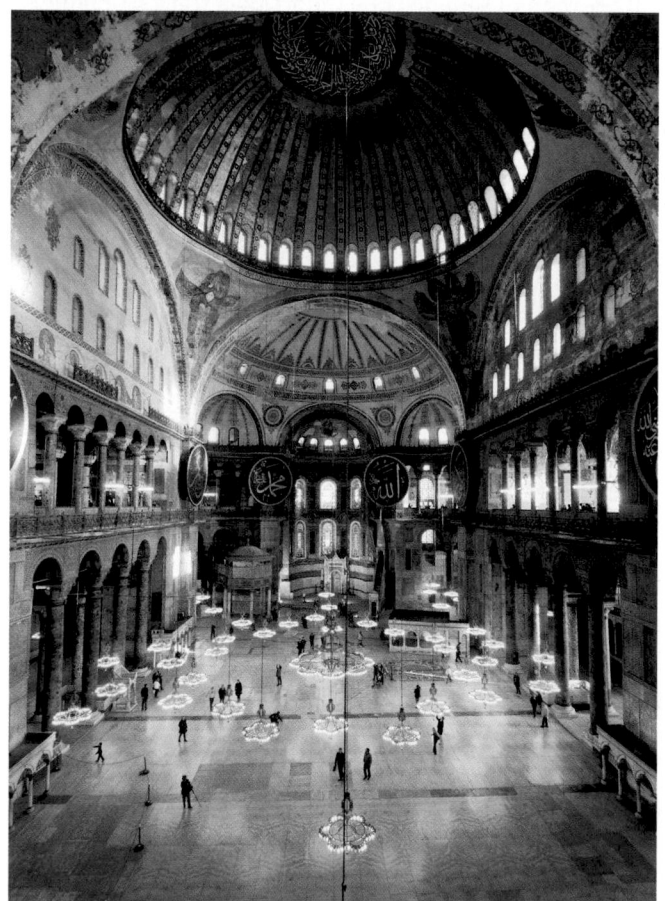

Part B. Interior view.

∧ 16.4 ANTHEMIUS OF TRALLES AND ISIDORUS OF MILETUS, Hagia Sophia, Constantinople (modern day Istanbul), Turkey (532–537).

Even though Ravenna was the capital of the western empire, Justinian's most important public building was erected in Constantinople. Centuries earlier, Constantine had moved the capital of the Roman Empire to the ancient city of Byzantium and renamed it after himself. After his death, the empire was divided into eastern and western halves, and the eastern part remained in Constantinople. It is in this Turkish city—present-day Istanbul—that Justinian built his Church of the Holy Wisdom, or Hagia Sophia (Fig. 16.4A). It is a fantastic structure that has served at one time or other in its history as an **Eastern Orthodox** church, an Islamic mosque, and a museum. The most striking aspects of Hagia Sophia are its overall dimensions and the size of its dome. Its floor plan is approximately 240 by 270 feet (Constantine's basilica in Rome was 300 by 215 feet). The dome is about 108 feet across and rises almost 180 feet above the church floor (the dome of the Pantheon, by contrast, is 144 feet high).

The grand proportions of Hagia Sophia put it on par with the great architectural monuments of Roman times. Its architects, Anthemius of Tralles and Isidorus of Miletus, used four triangular surfaces called **pendentives** to support the dome on a square base. Pendentives transfer the load from the base of the dome to the piers at the corners of the square beneath. Although massive, the dome appears light and graceful due to the placement of a ring of arched windows at its base (Fig. 16.4B). The light filtering through these windows can create the impression that the dome is hovering above a ring of light, further emphasizing the building's spaciousness. Like most Byzantine churches, the relatively plain exterior of Hagia Sophia contrasts strongly with the interior wall surfaces, which are decorated lavishly with inlaid marble and mosaic.

EARLY MEDIEVAL EUROPE

As the power of the Roman Empire declined, non-Roman peoples (including the Huns, Vandals, Franks, Goths, and others once collectively called "barbarian tribes") gained control of parts of Europe. Over the centuries of tribal migrations across Eurasia, populations coalesced in what eventually would become the familiar countries of Europe—France, Italy, Scandinavia, Great Britain, and others.

Not much in the way of art and architecture remains of these migratory tribes, although finely wrought ornaments of gold, inlaid stones, and enamelware give us some indication of their artistic capabilities as well as the wealth and importance of their leaders. Two cemeteries excavated in Sutton Hoo, England, yielded a large number of ornaments and portable artifacts as well as an

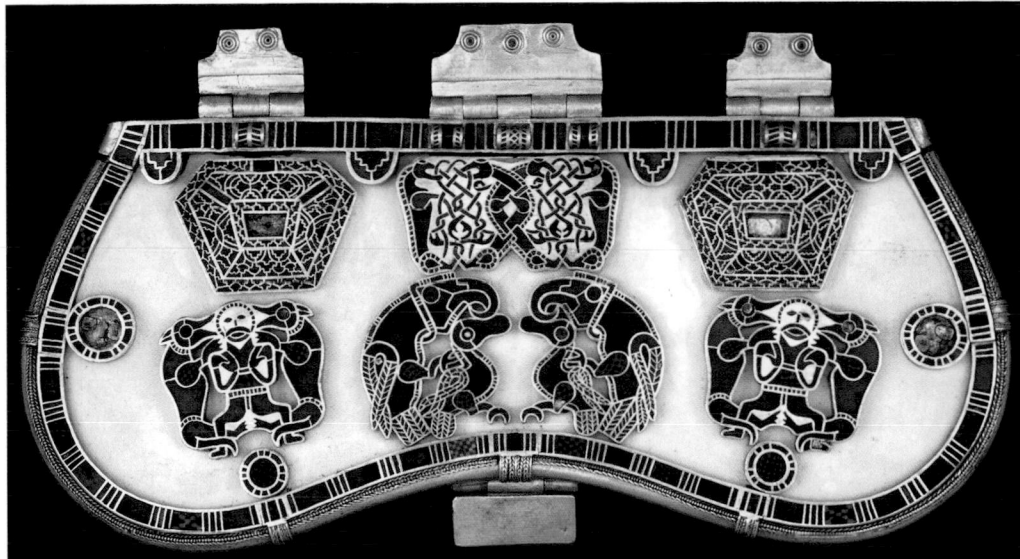

1 in.

< **16.5 Purse cover** (c. 625). Sutton Hoo ship burial, Suffolk, United Kingdom. Gold frame with three gold hinges along a straight top and central projecting gold buckle on the curved lower edge, body of whale-bone ivory (since decayed) set with seven gold-rimmed garnet cloisonné and millefiori glass designs; 7½" × 3¼" (excluding hinges). British Museum, London.

entire ship burial dating to the early seventh century. One such ornament, found in the ship, is a golden buckle intricately carved with intertwined serpents' and eagles' heads (Fig. 16.5). Every last bit of the surface of the buckle is covered with interlaced decoration, a common stylistic characteristic that suggests the tangled world of mythic monsters in epics such as *Beowulf*.

Christian Art in the Early Middle Ages

Many works of Christian art from the Early Middle Ages combine characteristics of the small carvings and metalwork of these warrior tribes with symbols of the Christian faith. A **carpet page** from the *Lindisfarne Gospels*, so called for its resemblance to intricately patterned textiles (Fig. 16.6), features a stylized cross inscribed with layers of intertwined, multicolored scrolls. The framed space surrounding the cross is similarly filled

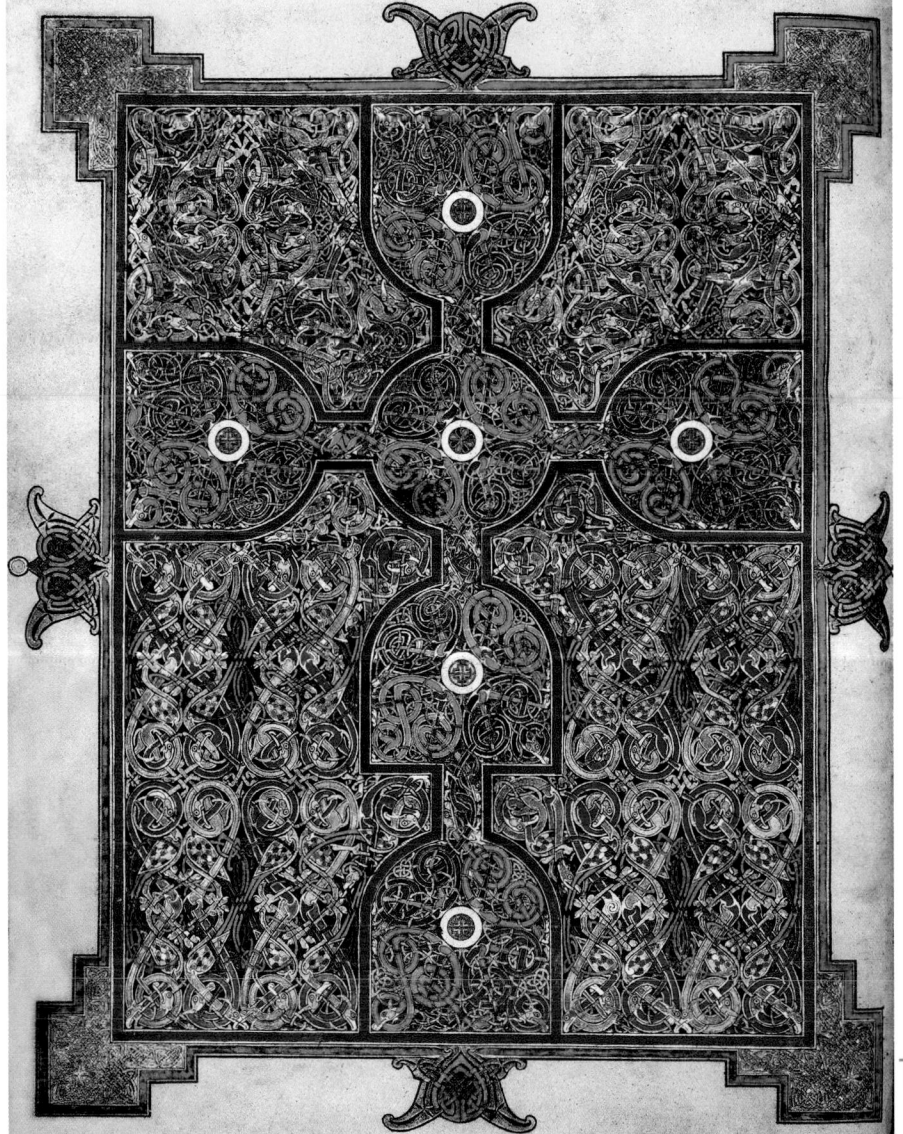

> **16.6 Cross-inscribed carpet page from the** *Lindisfarne Gospels* (c. 698–721). Illuminated manuscript, 13½" × 9¼".

1 in.

> Fine craftsmanship is all about you, but you might not notice it. Look more keenly at it and you . . . will make out intricacies, so delicate and subtle, so exact and compact, so full of knots and links, with colors so fresh and vivid, that you might say that all this was the work of an angel, and not of a man.
>
> —GIRALDUS CAMBRENSIS, C. 1185

with repetitive linear patterns that can be decoded as snakes devouring themselves—an animal-interlace motif adapted from the decorative arts of non-Roman peoples.

Carolingian Art

The most important name linked to medieval art and culture during the period immediately following the migrations is that of Charlemagne (Charles the Great). This powerful ruler tried to unify the warring factions of Europe under the aegis of Christianity, and modeling his campaign on those of Roman emperors, he succeeded in doing so. In the year 800 CE, Charlemagne was crowned Holy Roman Emperor by the pope, thus establishing a bond among the countries of western Europe that lasted more than a millennium (see Map 16.1).

The period of Charlemagne's supremacy is called the **Carolingian** period. He established his court at Aachen, a western German city on the border of present-day Belgium, and imported the most significant intellectuals and artists of Europe and the Eastern countries.

THE PALATINE CHAPEL OF CHARLEMAGNE   Charlemagne constructed his **Palatine Chapel** (palace chapel) with two architectural styles in mind (Fig. 16.7A). He sought to emulate Roman architecture but was probably also influenced by the central plan church of San Vitale, erected under Emperor Justinian. Like San Vitale, the Palatine Chapel is a central plan with an ambulatory and an octagonal dome (Fig. 16.7B). However, this is where the similarity ends. The perimeter of Charlemagne's chapel is polygonal, with almost sixteen facets instead of San Vitale's eight. There is also greater axial symmetry in the Palatine Chapel due to the more logical placement of the narthex.

The interior is also different from San Vitale. The semicircular niches that alternated with columns and pressed into the space of the Ravenna ambulatory have been eliminated at Aachen. There is more definition in the ambulatory between the central domed area and the building's perimeter. This clear articulation of parts is a hallmark of Roman design and stands in contrast to the fluid, organic character of some Byzantine architecture. The walls of the Palatine Chapel are divided into three distinct levels, and each level is divided by classically inspired archways or series of arches. Structural elements, architectural motifs, and a general blockiness of form point both backward and forward: to Roman architecture of the classical past and to the development of Romanesque architecture during the eleventh century.

MANUSCRIPT ILLUMINATION   Charlemagne's court was an intellectual and artistic hub, and his love of knowledge and pursuit of truth helped keep the flame of scholarship flickering during the Early Middle Ages. His best-known project was the decipherment of the true biblical text, which, over decades, had suffered countless errors at the hands of careless scribes.

The style of Charlemagne's own gospel book, called the Coronation Gospels (Fig. 16.8), reflects his love of Classical art. Matthew, an evangelist who was thought to have written the first gospel, is represented as an educated

∧ MAP 16.1 The Carolingian world.

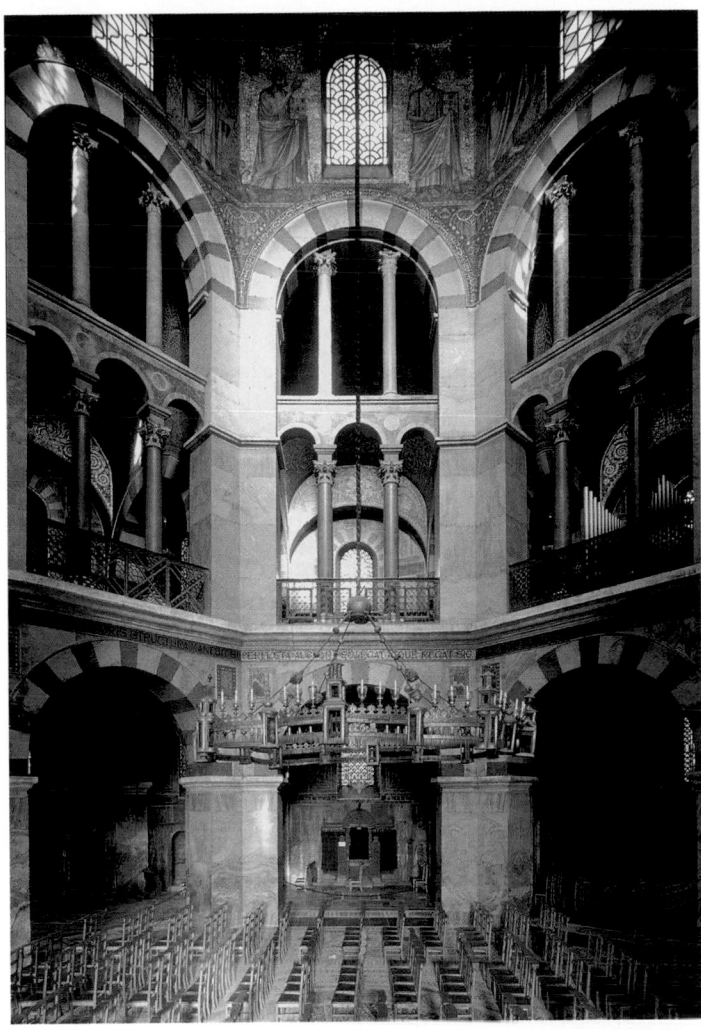

Part A. Interior view.

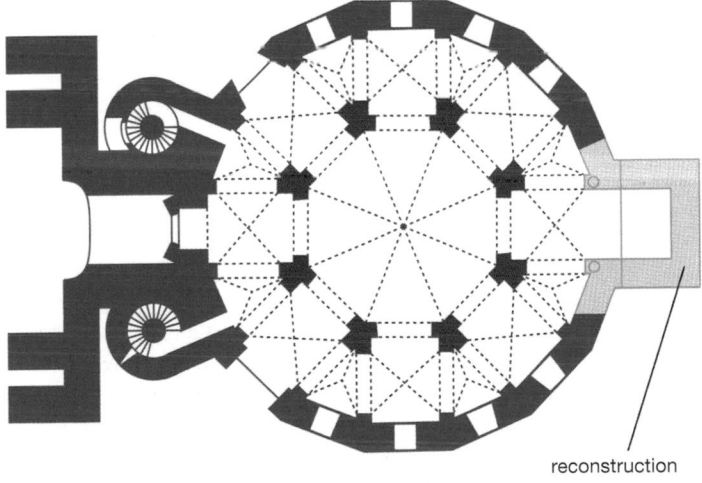

reconstruction

feet

0   20   40

Part B. Plan.

⌃ 16.7 Palatine Chapel of Charlemagne at Aachen, Germany (Carolingian, 792–805).

Roman writer diligently at work. Only the halo around his head reveals his sacred identity. He does not appear as an otherworldly weightless figure awaiting a bolt of divine inspiration. His attitude is calm, pensive, and deliberate. His body has substance; it is seated firmly, and the drapery of his toga falls naturally over his limbs. The artist uses painterly strokes and contrast of light and shade to define his forms much in the same way that the wall painters of ancient Rome had done (see Fig. 15.19).

ROMANESQUE ART

The Romanesque style appeared in the closing decades of the eleventh century among dramatic changes in all aspects of European life. Dynasties, such as those of the Carolingian and Ottonian periods, no longer existed. Individual monarchies ruled areas of Europe, rivaling one another for land and power. After the non-Roman peoples stopped invading and started settling, feudalism began to structure Europe, with monarchies at the head.

Feudalism was not the only force in medieval life of the Romanesque period. Monasticism also gained in importance. Monasteries during this time were structured communities that emphasized work and study, including manual labor (tending gardens, running bakeries,

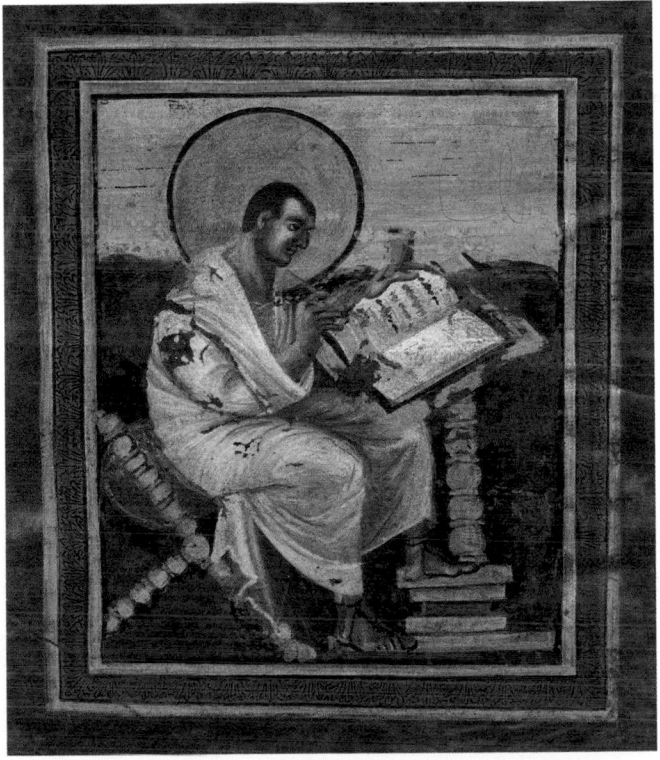

1 in.

⌃ 16.8 St. Matthew, folio 15 recto of the *Coronation Gospels (Gospel Book of Charlemagne)*, from Aachen, Germany (c. 800–810). Ink and tempera on vellum, 1'¾" × 10". Schatzkammer, Kunsthistorisches Museum, Vienna.

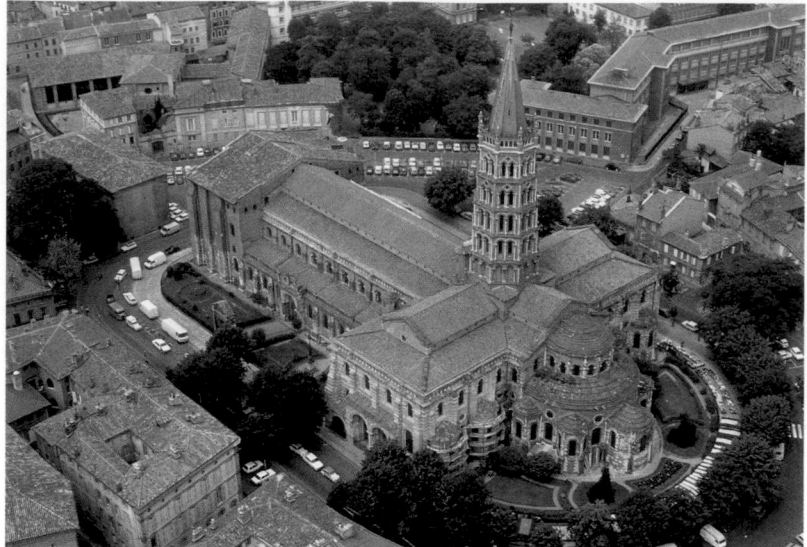

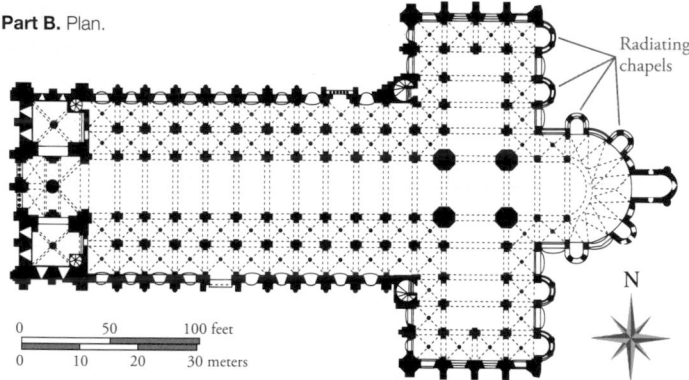

Radiating chapels

0   50   100 feet

0   10   20   30 meters

N

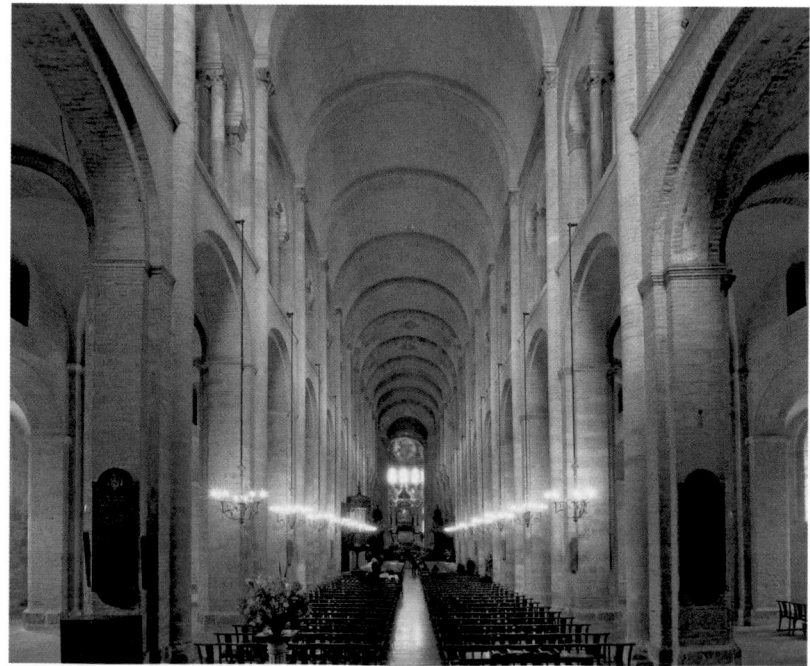

⌃ 16.9 **Church of St. Sernin, Toulouse, France** (Romanesque, c. 1070–1120).

clearing tracts of wilderness, even building roads in some cases), reading and copying of sacred texts, and memorizing music for chanting. Monasteries paved the way in education as monks became teachers. Salvation in the afterlife was a great preoccupation of the Middle Ages and served as the common denominator among classes. Nobility, clergy, and peasantry all directed their spiritual efforts toward this goal. Two phenomena reflect this obsession: the Crusades and the great pilgrimages.

The Crusades were holy wars waged in the name of recovering the Holy Land from the Muslims, who had taken it over in the seventh century. The pilgrimages were lengthy personal journeys undertaken to worship at sacred shrines or the tombs of saints. Participating in the Crusades and making pilgrimages were seen as holy acts that would help tip the scale in one's favor on Judgment Day. The pilgrims' need of a grand place to worship at journey's end gave impetus to church construction during the Romanesque period.

Architecture

In the Romanesque cathedral, there is a clear articulation of parts, with the exterior forms reflecting the interior spaces. The interiors consist of five major areas, with variations on this basic plan evident in different regions of Europe. We can add two Romanesque criteria to this basic format: spaciousness and fireproofing. The large crowds drawn by the pilgrimage fever required larger structures with interior spaces that would not restrict the flow of movement. After hostile invasions left churches in flames, it was also deemed necessary to fireproof the buildings by eliminating wooden roofs and covering the structures with cut stone.

ST. SERNIN The church of St. Sernin (Fig. 16.9A) in Toulouse, France, met all of the requirements for a Romanesque cathedral. An aerial view of the exterior shows the blocky forms that outline a nave, side aisles, narthex to the west, a prominent transept crowned by a multilevel spire above the crossing square, and an apse at the eastern end from whose ambulatory extend five **radiating chapels**. In the plan of St. Sernin (Fig. 16.9B), the outermost side aisle continues around the outer borders of the transept arm and runs into the ambulatory around the apse. Along the eastern face of the transept, and around the ambulatory, a series of chapels radiate, or extend, from the aisle. These spaces provided extra room for the crowds of pilgrims and offered free movement around the church, preventing interference with worship in the nave or the celebration of Mass in the apse. Square schematism has been employed in this plan; each rectangular bay measures one-half of the crossing square, and the dimensions of each square in the side aisles measures one-fourth of the main module.

In St. Sernin, a shift was made from the flat wooden ceiling characteristic of the Roman basilica to a stone vault that was less vulnerable to fire. The ceiling structure, called a **barrel vault**, resembles a semicircular barrel punctuated by arches that spring from engaged (attached) columns in the nave to define each bay (Fig. 16.9C). The massive weight of the vault is partially supported by the nave walls and partially by the side aisles that accept a share of the downward thrust. This is somewhat alleviated by the **tribune gallery**, which, in effect, reduces the drop-off from the barrel vault to the lower side aisles. The tribune gallery also provided extra space for worshipers.

Because the barrel vault rests directly on top of the tribune gallery, and because fenestration would weaken the structure of the vault, there is little light in the interior of the cathedral. Lack of light was considered a major problem, and solving it would be the primary concern of future Romanesque architects. The history of Romanesque architecture can be written as the history of vaulting techniques, and the need for light provided the incentive for their development.

ST. ÉTIENNE The builders of the cathedral of St. Étienne in Normandy contributed significantly to the future of Romanesque and Gothic architecture in their design of its ceiling vault (Fig. 16.10A). Instead of using a barrel vault that tunnels its way from narthex to apse, they divided the nave of St. Étienne into four distinct modules that reflect the shape of the crossing square. Each of these modules in turn is divided into six parts by ribs that spring from engaged columns and **compound piers** in the nave walls. Some of these ribs connect the midpoints of opposing sides of the squares; they are called **transverse ribs** (Fig 16.10B). Other ribs intersect the space of the module diagonally, as seen in

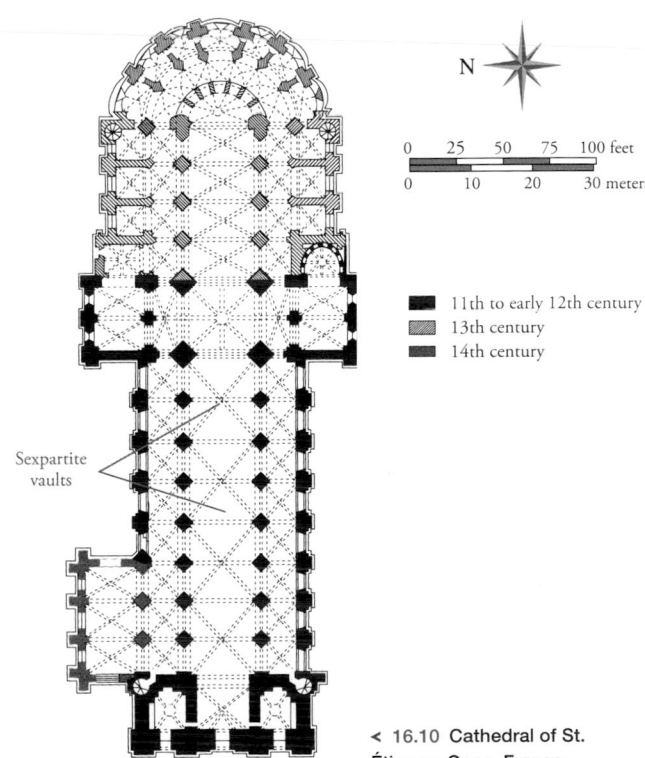

Sexpartite vaults

0   25   50   75   100 feet
0   10   20   30 meters

■ 11th to early 12th century
▨ 13th century
■ 14th century

< 16.10 Cathedral of St. Étienne, Caen, France (Romanesque, begun 1067).

Part A. West façade.

Part B. Plan.

Cathedrals are an unassailable witness to human passion. Using what demented calculation could an animal build such places? I think we know. An animal with a gorgeous genius for hope.

—LIONEL TIGER

[After the] year of the millennium, which is now about three years past, there occurred throughout the world, especially in Italy and Gaul, a rebuilding of church basilicas. . . . [Each] Christian people strove against the others to erect nobler ones. It was as if the whole earth, having cast off the old by shaking itself, were clothing itself everywhere in the white robe of the church.

—RAOUL GLABER, C. 1003

the plan; these are called **diagonal ribs**. An **alternate a-b-a-b support system** is used, with every other engaged column sending up a supporting rib that crosses the vault as a transverse arch. These engaged columns are distinguished from other nonsupporting members by their attachment to pilasters. The vault of St. Étienne is one of the first true rib vaults in that the combination of diagonal and transverse ribs functions as a skeleton that bears some of the weight of the ceiling. In later buildings, the role of ribs as support elements will be increased, and reliance on the massiveness of nave walls will be somewhat decreased.

Even though the nave walls of St. Étienne are still quite thick when compared with those of later Romanesque churches, the interior has a sense of lightness that does not exist in St. Sernin. The development of the rib vault made it possible to pierce the walls directly above the tribune gallery with windows. This series of windows that appears cut into the slightly domed modules of the ceiling is called a **clerestory**. The clerestory became a standard element of the Gothic cathedral plan.

Sculpture

Although we occasionally find freestanding sculpture from the Romanesque and Gothic periods, it was far more common for sculpture to be restricted to architectural decoration around the portals. Some of the most important and elaborate sculptural decoration is found in the **tympanum**—a semicircular space above the doors to a cathedral—such as that of the cathedral at Autun in Burgundy, France (Fig. 16.11). The carved portals of

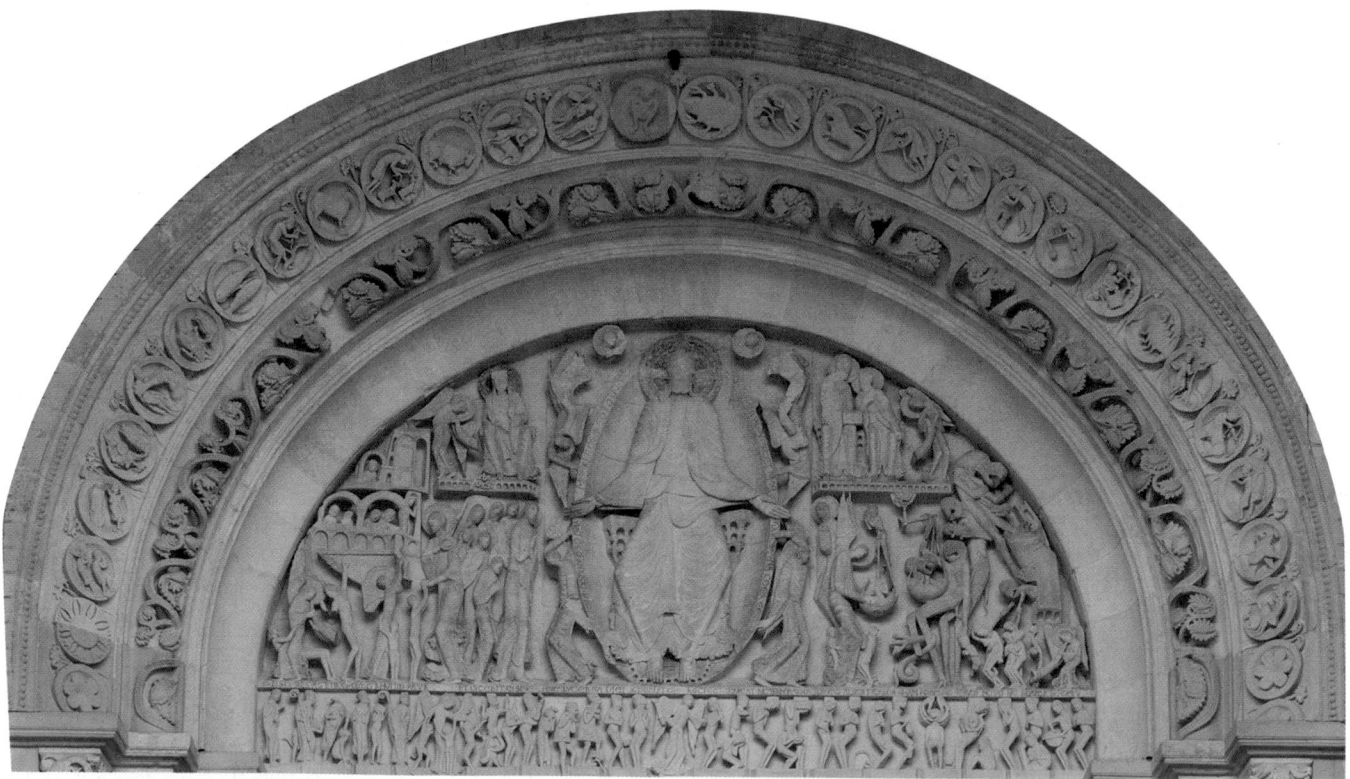

∧ 16.11 Cathedral of St. Lazare, west portal, detail of Last Judgment tympanum, *Weighing of Souls*, Autun, France (c. 1120–1135).

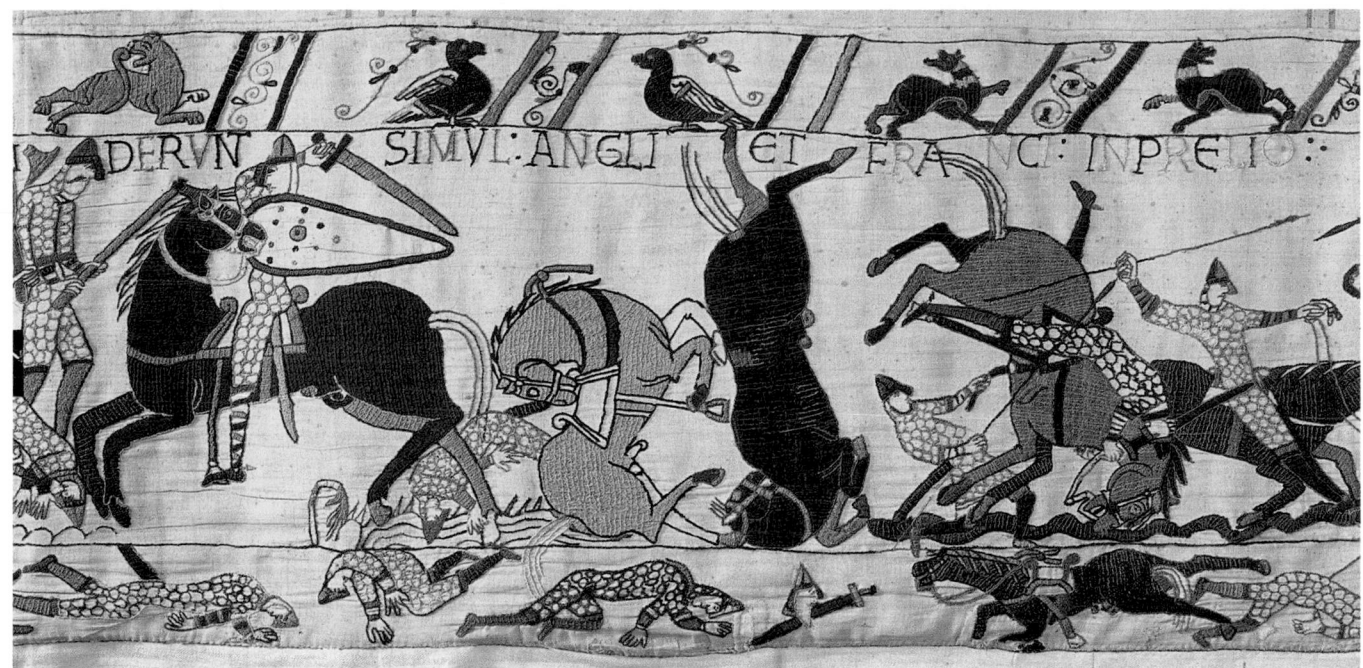

ᴧ 16.12 **Battle of Hastings, detail of the *Bayeux Tapestry,* from Bayeux Cathedral, Bayeux, France** (Romanesque, c. 1070–1080). Wool embroidery on linen; 1'8" high, 222'8" long. Centre Guillaume le Conquérant, Bayeux, France.

cathedrals bore scenes and symbols that acted as harsh reminders of fate in the afterlife. They were intended to communicate pictorially a profound message, if not direct warning, to the potential, primarily illiterate sinner that repentance through prayer and action was necessary for salvation.

At Autun, the scene depicted is that of the Last Judgment. The tympanum rests on a lintel carved with small figures representing the dead. The archangel Michael stands in the center, dividing the horizontal band of figures into two groups. The naked dead on the left gaze upward, hopeful of achieving eternal reward in heaven, while those to the right look downward in despair. Above the lintel, Jesus is depicted as an evenhanded judge. To his left, tall, thin figures representing the apostles observe the scene, while some angels lift bodies into heaven. To Jesus's right, by contrast, is a gruesome event. The dead are snatched up from their graves, and their souls are being weighed on a scale by an angel on the left and a devil-serpent on the right. The devil cheats by adding a little weight, and some of his companions stand ready to grab the souls and fling them into hell. As in the bronze doors of St. Michael's, humankind is shown as a pitiful, defenseless race, no match for the wiles of Satan. The figures crouch in terror of their surroundings, in strong contrast to the serenity of their impartial judge.

The Romanesque sculptor sought stylistic inspiration in Roman works, the small carvings of the pre-Romanesque era, and especially manuscript illumination. In the early phase of Romanesque art, naturalism was not a concern. Artists turned to art rather than to nature for models, and thus their figures are at least twice, and perhaps 100 times, removed from the original source. It is no wonder, then, that they appear as dolls or marionettes. The figure of Jesus is squashed within a large oval, and his limbs bend in sharp angles to fit the frame. Although his drapery seems to correspond broadly to the body beneath, the folds are reduced to stylized patterns of concentric arcs that play across a relatively flat surface. Realism is not the goal. The sculptor is focused on conveying his frightful message with the details and emotions that will have the most dramatic impact on the worshiper or penitent sinner.

Tapestry

Although the tasks of copying sacred texts and embellishing them with manuscript illuminations were sometimes assumed by women, the art form remained primarily a male preserve. Not so with the medium of tapestry. In the Middle Ages, weaving and embroidery were taught to women of all social classes and walks of life. Noblewomen and nuns would weave and decorate elaborate tapestries, clothing, and liturgical vestments using the finest linens, wools, gold and silver thread, pearls, and other gems.

One of the most famous surviving tapestries, the *Bayeux Tapestry* (Fig. 16.12), was almost certainly created by a team of women at the commission of Odo, the bishop of Bayeux. The tapestry describes the invasion of England by William the Conqueror in a continuous narrative. Although the tapestry is less than 2 feet in height, it originally measured in excess of 230 running feet and

A CLOSER LOOK

Hildegard of Bingen

DURING THE MIDDLE AGES, THE PRODUCTION and illustration of sacred books took place, for the most part, in the monastery and the abbey, with the greatest percentage of scribes and painters being men. Yet some upper-class women looking for an alternative to marriage and eager to follow these and other intellectual and aesthetic pursuits entered the contemplative life of the nunnery.

One such woman was the German abbess Hildegard of Bingen (1098 CE–1179 CE). Hildegard was a mystic whose visions of otherworldly phenomena began during childhood and led to a life of scholarship elucidating her extraordinary experiences. She wrote books on medicine and history, composed music, debated political and religious issues, and designed illustrations to accompany written records of her visions. Hildegard also devised a secret language. One of her most valuable works is the *Liber Scivias*, a text built around images of light and darkness that include the sun, moon, stars, and flaming orbs struggling against dragons, demons, and other denizens of evil. Another volume, *The Book of Divine Works,* describes God's plan in creation of the universe and His redemption of humankind through the gift of Christ as Savior. In her "Vision of God's Plan for the Seasons," **(Fig. 16.13)**, Hildegard visualizes, in mandala form, the cycle of life and work that progresses in concentric rings from the micro (a farmer on his land) to the macro (the cosmos).

The intensity—and specificity—of Hildegard's visions is captured in an excerpt of *Liber Scivias* in which she recounts how God, enthroned, presented Himself to her:

> I saw a great mountain the color of iron, and enthroned on it One of such great glory that it blinded my sight. . . . And behold, He Who was enthroned upon that mountain cried out in a strong, loud voice saying, "O human, who are fragile dust of the earth and ashes of ashes! Cry out and speak of the origin of pure salvation until those people are instructed, who, though they see the inmost contents of the Scriptures, do not wish to tell them or preach them, because they are lukewarm and sluggish in serving God's justice. Unlock for them the enclosure of mysteries that they, timid as they are, conceal in a hidden and fruitless field. Burst forth into a fountain of abundance and overflow with mysterious knowledge, until they who now think you contemptible because of Eve's transgression are stirred up by the flood of your irrigation. For you have received your profound insight not from humans, but from the lofty and tremendous judge on high, where this calmness will shine strongly with glorious light among the shining ones.

"Arise therefore, cry out and tell what is shown to you by the strong power of God's help, for He Who rules every creature in might and kindness floods those who fear Him and serve Him in sweet love and humility with the glory of heavenly enlightenment and leads those who persevere in the way of justice to the joys of the Eternal Vision."[2]

---

[2] From *Hildegard of Bingen*: Scivias, translated by Mother Columbia Hart and Jane Bishop, from The Classics of Western Spirituality.

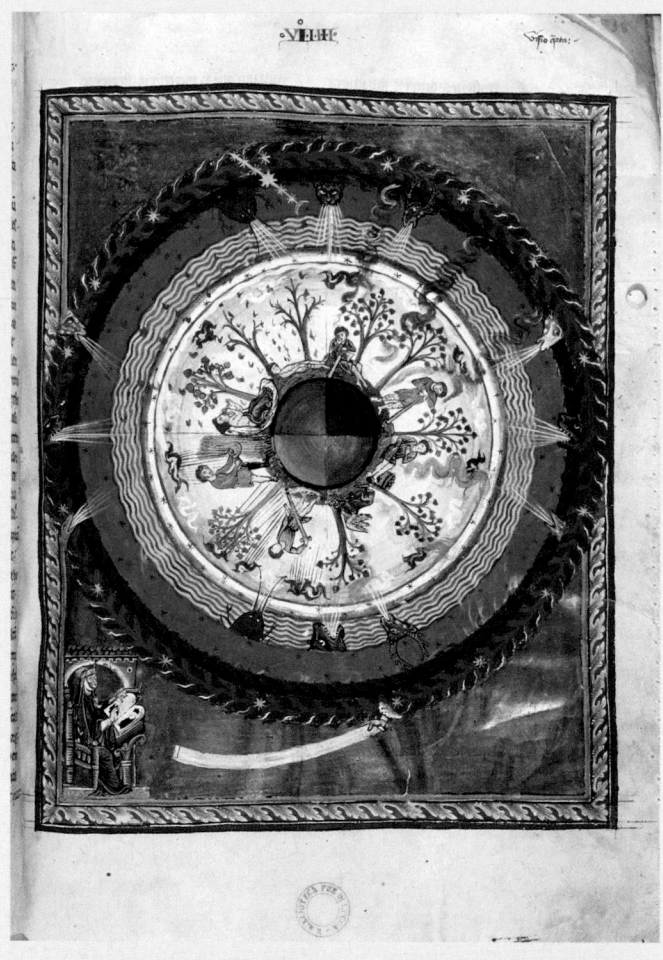

▲ 16.13 HILDEGARD OF BINGEN, "Vision of God's Plan for the Seasons," folio 38 recto from *De operatione Dei* ("On God's Activity") (also known as *Liber divinorum operum* **"Book of Divine Works"**) (c. 1163–1174). Illuminated miniature on vellum in mandala form. Biblioteca Statale, Lucca, Italy.

was meant to run clockwise around the entire nave of the Cathedral of Bayeux. In this way, the narrative functioned much in the same way as the continuous narrative of the Ionic frieze of the Parthenon.

GOTHIC ART

Art and architecture of the twelfth and thirteenth centuries is called Gothic. The term *Gothic* originated among historians who believed that the Goths were responsible for the style of this period. Because critics believed that the Gothic style only further buried the light of Classicism, and because the Goths were "barbarians," the term *Gothic* was used disparagingly. For many years, the most positive criticism of Gothic art was that it was a step forward from the Romanesque. Gothic is no longer a term of derision, and the Romanesque and Gothic styles are seen as distinct and as responsive to the unique tempers of their times.

Characteristics of the Gothic Style in Architecture

In their desire for verticality, Gothic cathedrals sought to soar to the heavens. The Gothic style is characterized by pointed arches, pinnacles and columns, and dauntingly high walls supported at least in part from exterior flying buttresses. Figure 16.14 reveals the structure of a French

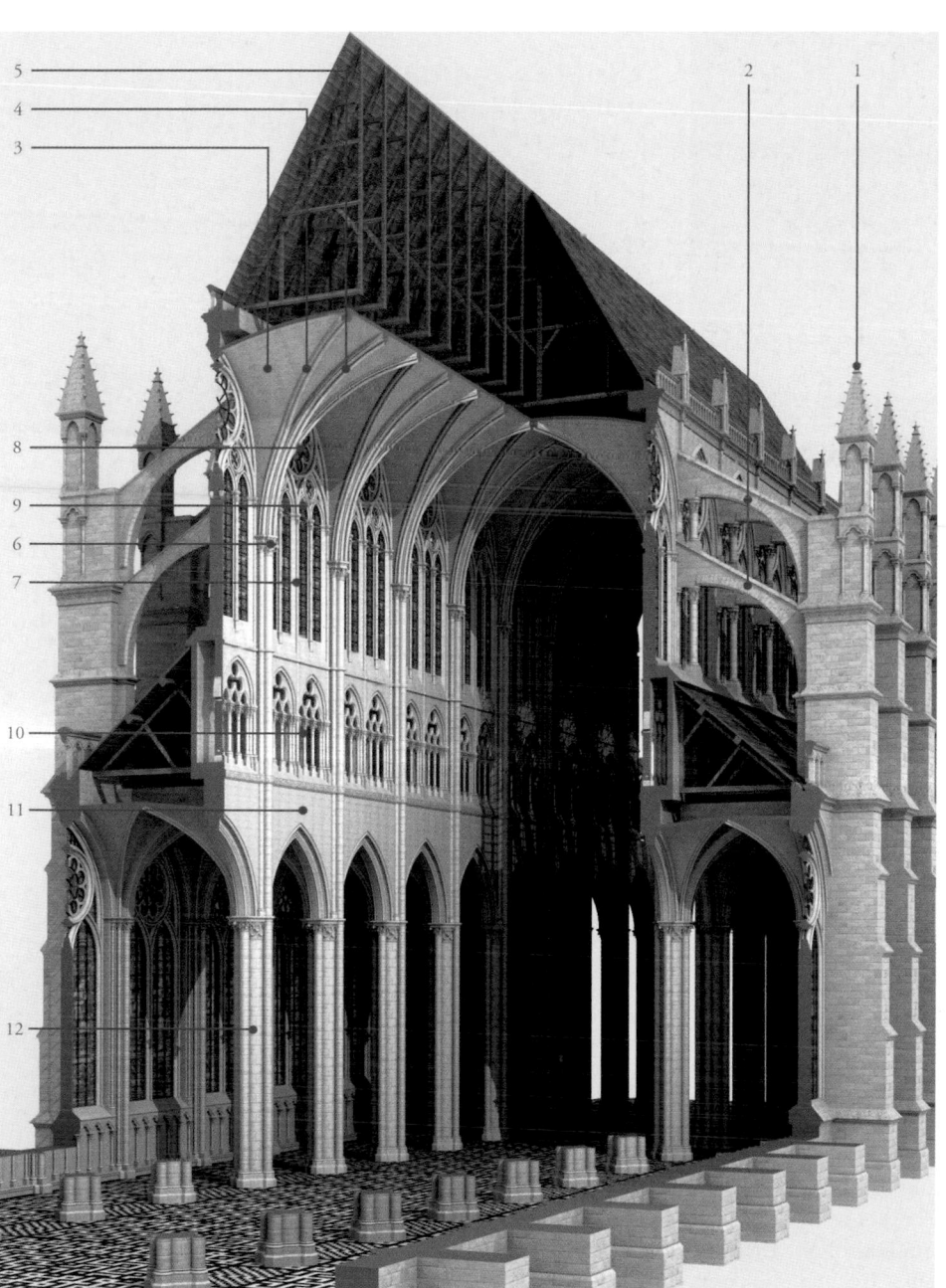

1. *Pinnacle* A sharply pointed ornament capping the piers or flying buttresses; also used on cathedral façades.

2. *Flying buttresses* Masonry struts that transfer the thrust of the nave vaults across the roofs of the side aisles and ambulatory to a tall pier rising above the church's exterior wall.

3. *Vaulting web* The masonry blocks filling the area between the ribs of a groin vault.

4. *Diagonal rib* In a plan, one of the ribs forming the X of a groin vault.

5. *Transverse rib* A rib crossing the nave or aisle at a 90-degree angle.

6. *Springing* The lowest stone of an arch; in Gothic vaulting, the lowest stone of a diagonal or transverse rib.

7. *Clerestory* The windows below the vaults in the nave elevation's uppermost level. By using flying buttresses and rib vaults on pointed arches, Gothic architects could build huge clerestory windows and fill them with stained glass held in place by ornamental stonework called tracery.

8. *Oculus* A small, round window.

9. *Lancet* A tall, narrow window crowned by a pointed arch.

10. *Triforium* The story in the nave elevation consisting of arcades, usually blind arcades but occasionally filled with stained glass.

11. *Nave arcade* The series of arches supported by piers separating the nave from the side aisles.

12. *Compound pier (cluster pier) with shafts (responds)* A pier with a group, or cluster, of attached shafts, or responds, extending to the springing of the vaults.

< 16.14 Cutaway view of a typical Gothic cathedral.

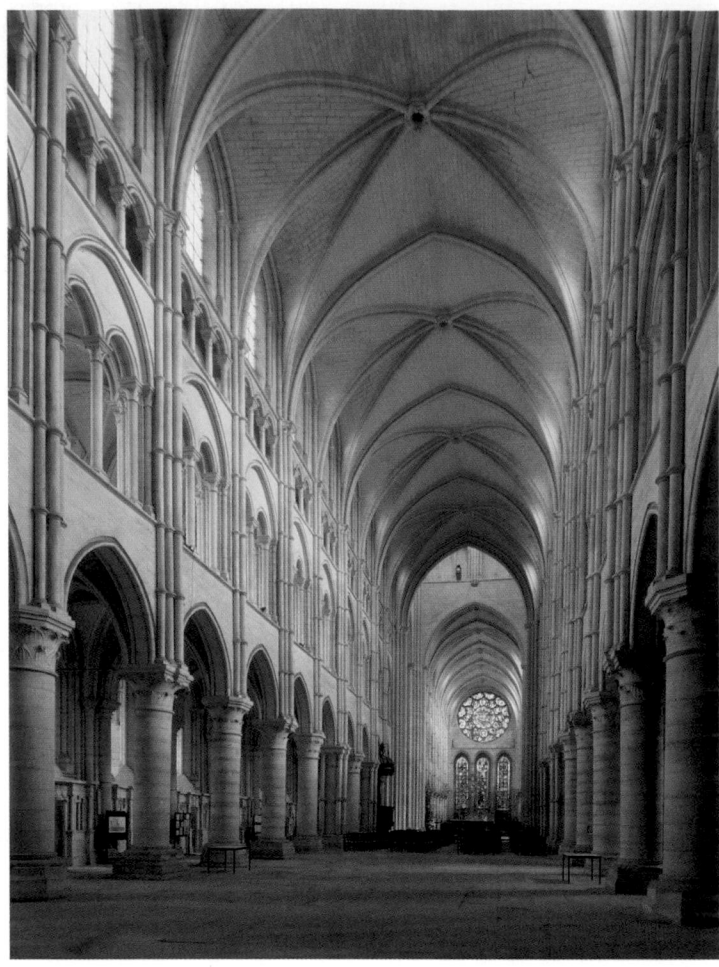

▲ 16.15 **Laon Cathedral, interior view (facing northeast), Laon, France** (begun c. 1190).

fortress-like appearance to one that seems lighter and more organic. The façade of Laon Cathedral is divided into three levels, although there is less distinction between them than in a Romanesque façade. The portals jut forward from the plane of the façade, creating a tunnel-like entrance. The stone is pierced by arched windows, arcades, and a large **rose window** in the center, and the twin bell towers seem to be constructed of voids rather than solids.

As the Gothic period progressed, all efforts were directed toward the dissolution of stone surfaces. The walls were penetrated by greater expanses of glass, nave elevations rose to new heights, and carved details became more complex and delicate. There was a mystical quality to these buildings in the way they seemed exempt from the laws of gravity.

CHARTRES CATHEDRAL   Chartres Cathedral is generally considered to be the first High Gothic church.

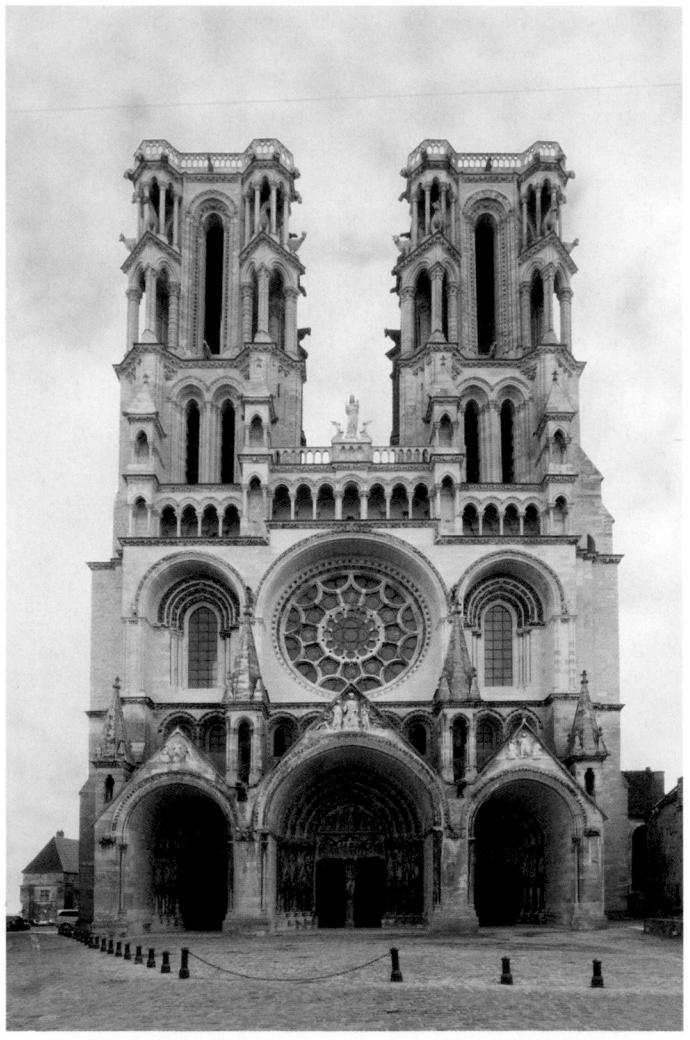

▲ 16.16 **Laon Cathedral, exterior view of west façade, Laon, France** (begun c. 1190).

Gothic cathedral. The flying buttresses direct the loads of the roof and walls sideways and then downward. Because the walls need not bear the weight of the roof, they can be punctuated with windows, allowing light to stream through stained-glass windows with such intensity that they may seem to be on fire. Pointed arches distributed weight more effectively than rounded arches, lessening the need for massive columns.

LAON CATHEDRAL   Although Laon Cathedral is considered an Early Gothic building, its plan resembles those of Romanesque churches. For example, the ceiling is a sexpartite rib vault supported by groups of columns in an alternate a-b-a-b rhythm (Fig. 16.15). Yet there were important innovations at Laon. The interior displays a change in wall elevation from three to four levels. A series of arches, or **triforium**, was added above the tribune gallery to pierce further the solid surfaces of the nave walls. The obsession with reducing the appearance of heaviness in the walls can also be seen on the exterior (Fig. 16.16). If we compare the façade of St. Étienne with that of Laon, we see a change from a massive,

Chartres was planned from the beginning to have a three-level wall elevation and flying buttresses. The three-part wall elevation allowed for larger windows in the clerestory, admitting more light into the interior (Fig. 16.17A).

In the High Gothic period, there is a change from square schematism to a **rectangular bay system** (Fig. 16.17B). In the latter, each rectangular bay has its own cross rib vault, and only one side aisle square flanks each rectangular bay. Thus, the need for an alternate support system is eliminated. The interior of a High Gothic cathedral presents several dramatic vistas. There is a continuous sweep of space from the narthex to the apse along a nave that is uninterrupted by alternating supports. There is also a strong vertical thrust from floor to vaults that is enhanced by the elimination of the triforium and the increased heights of the arches in the nave arcade and clerestory windows. The solid wall surfaces are further dissolved by quantities of stained glass that flood the interior with spectacular patterns of soft colored light. The architects directed all of their efforts toward creating a spiritual escape to another world. They did so by effectively defying the properties of matter: creating the illusion of weightlessness in stone and dissolving solid surfaces with mesmerizing streams of colored light.

Gothic Architecture outside France

The cathedrals that we have examined thus far were built in France, where the Gothic style flourished. Variations on the French Gothic style can also be seen elsewhere in northern Europe, although in some English and German cathedrals the general "blockiness" of Romanesque architecture persisted. In Italy, on the other hand, the French style was not strictly adhered to, as is seen in the

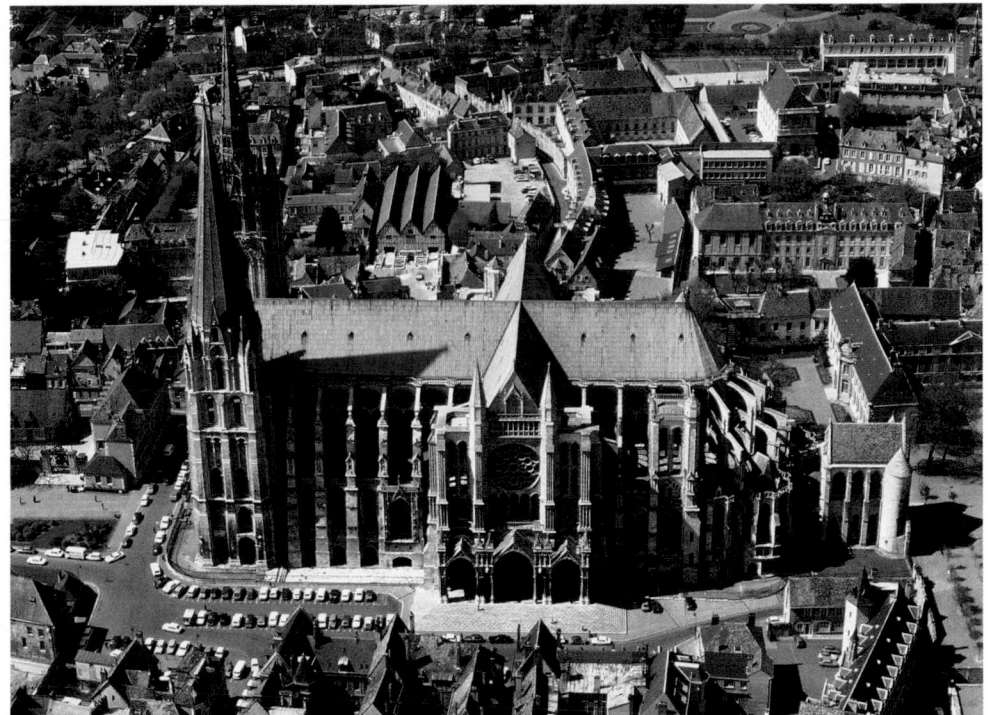

Part A. Aerial view.

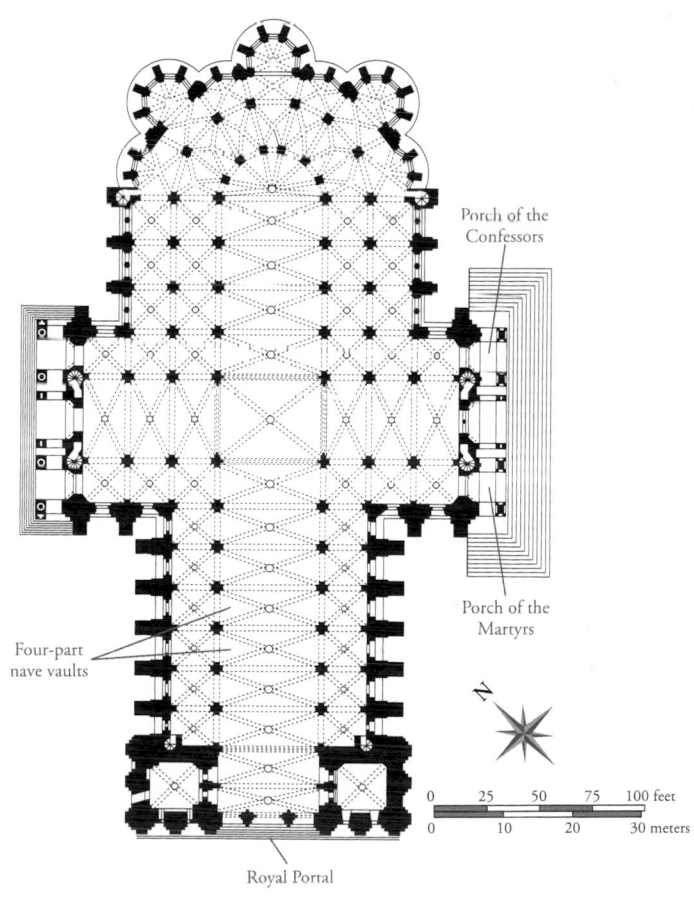

Porch of the Confessors

Four-part nave vaults

Porch of the Martyrs

Royal Portal

0   25   50   75   100 feet
0   10   20   30 meters

Part B. Plan.

∧ 16.17 **Chartres Cathedral (looking north), Chartres, France** (begun 1134, as rebuilt after 1194).

> [Florence was] the daughter and creature of Rome.
> —GIOVANNI VILLANI, C. 1270–1348

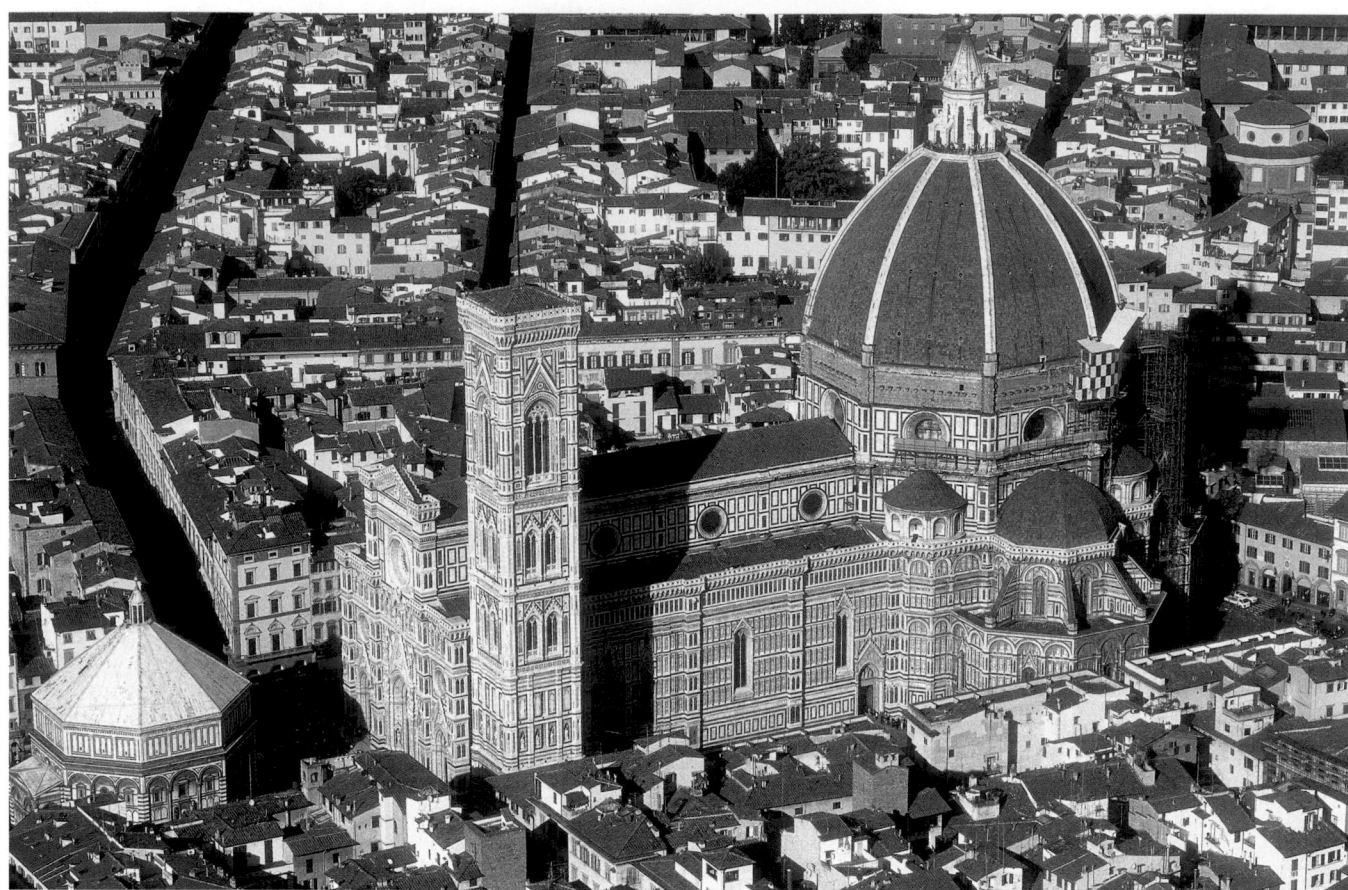

Part A. Aerial view.

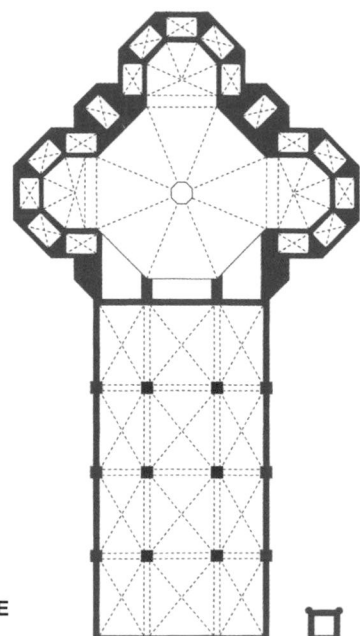

E

Part B. Plan.

∧ **16.18 Florence Cathedral** (Gothic, begun 1368).

Florence Cathedral (Fig. 16.18A). The most striking features of its exterior are the sharp, geometric patterns of green and white marble and the horizontality, or earthbound quality, of its profile.

These contrast with the vertical lines of the French Gothic cathedral that seem to reach for heaven. The French were obsessed with the visual disintegration of massive stone walls. The Italians, on the other hand, preserved the mural quality of the structure. In the cathedral of Florence, there are no flying buttresses. The wall elevation has been reduced to two levels, with a minimum of fenestration.

The Florence Cathedral is also different in plan (Fig. 16.18B) from French cathedrals. A huge octagonal dome overrides the structure. The nave consists of four large and clearly defined modules, flanked by rectangular bays in the side aisles. There is only one bell tower in the Italian cathedral, and it is detached from the façade.

Why would this Italian Gothic cathedral differ so markedly from those of the French? Given its strong roots in Classical Rome, it may be that Italy never succumbed wholeheartedly to Gothicism. Perhaps for this reason,

Italy would be the birthplace of the revival of Classicism during the Renaissance. We will discuss the Florence Cathedral further in the following chapter, because the designer of its dome was one of the principal architects of the Renaissance.

Sculpture

Sculpture during the Gothic period reveals a change in mood from that of the Romanesque. The iconography is one of redemption rather than damnation. The horrible scenes of Judgment Day that threatened the worshiper upon entering the cathedral were replaced by scenes from the life of Jesus or visions of the **apocalypse**. The

Virgin Mary also assumed a primary role. Carved tympanums, whole sculptural programs, even cathedrals themselves (for example, Notre-Dame, which means "Our Lady") were dedicated to her.

Gothic sculpture was still pretty much confined to decoration of cathedral portals. Every square inch of the tympanums, lintels, and **archivolts** of most Gothic cathedrals was carved with a dazzling array of figures and ornamental motifs. However, some of the most advanced full-scale sculpture is to be found adorning the **jambs**, such as those flanking the portals of Chartres Cathedral (Fig. 16.19). The figures are rigid in their poses, confined by the columns to which they are attached. The drapery falls in predictable stylized folds reminiscent of those seen

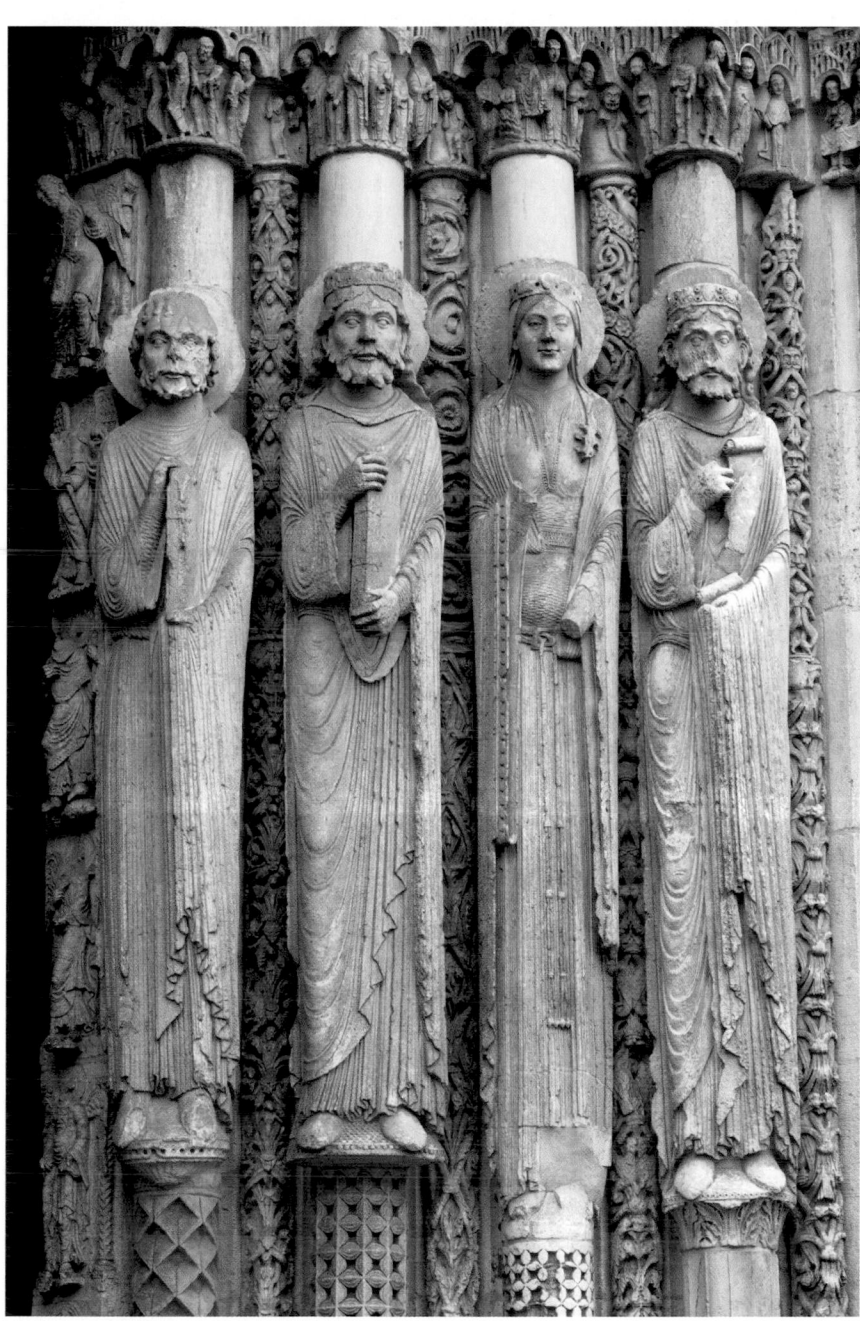

◄ 16.19 Old Testament kings and queen, jamb figures on the right side of the central doorway of the Royal Portal, west portals, Chartres Cathedral, Chartres, France (c. 1145–1155).

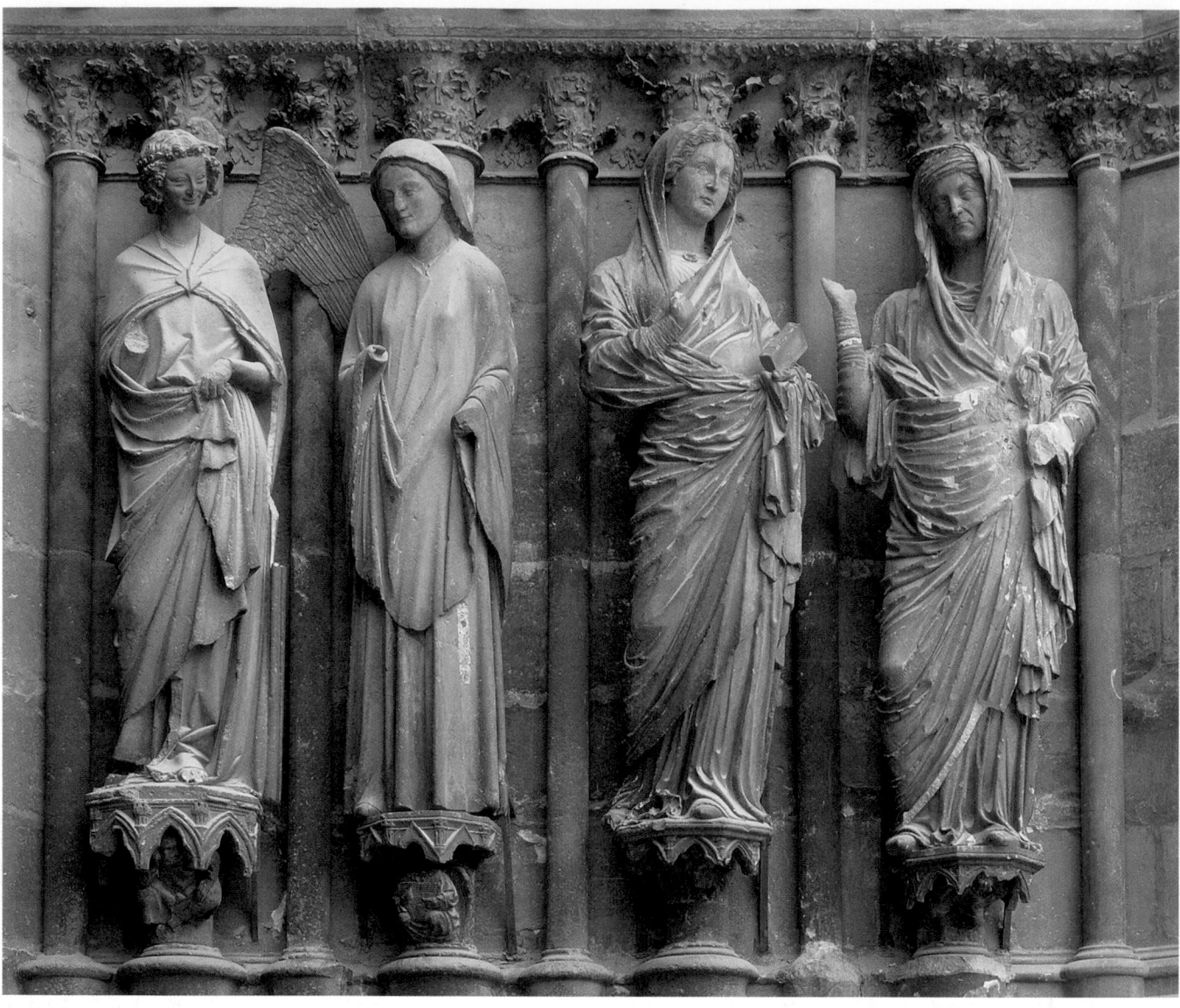

∧ 16.20 *Annunciation and Visitation,* jamb figures on the right side of the central doorway of the west façade, Reims Cathedral, Reims, France (c. 1230–1255).

in manuscript illumination. Yet there is a certain weight to the bodies, and the "hinged" treatment of the limbs is eliminated, heralding change from the Romanesque. During the High Gothic period, these simple elements led to a naturalism that had not been witnessed since Classical times.

The jamb figures of Reims Cathedral (Fig. 16.20) illustrate an interesting combination of styles. No doubt the individual figures were carved by different artists. The detail of the central portal of the façade illustrates two groups of figures. To the left is an **Annunciation** scene with the angel Gabriel and the Virgin Mary, and to the right is a **Visitation** scene depicting the Virgin Mary and St. Elizabeth. All of the figures are detached from columns and instead occupy the spaces between them.

Although they have been carved for these specific niches and are perched on small pedestals, they suggest a freedom of movement that is not found in the jamb figures at Chartres.

The Virgin Mary of the Annunciation group is the least advanced in technique of the four figures. Her stance is the most rigid, and her gestures and facial expression are the most stylized. Yet her body has substance, and anatomical details are revealed beneath a drapery that responds realistically to the movement of her limbs. The figure of Gabriel contrasts strongly in style with that of the Virgin Mary. He seems relatively tall and lanky. His head is small and delicate, and his facial features are refined. His body has a subtle sway that is accented by the flowing lines of his drapery. Stateliness and sweetness characterize this courtly style; it will be carried forward into the Early Renaissance period in the **International Gothic style.**

Yet Classicism will be the major style of the Renaissance, and in the Visitation group of the Reims portals, we have a fascinating introduction to it. The weighty figures of Mary and Elizabeth are placed in a contrapposto stance. The folds of drapery articulate the movement of the bodies beneath with a realism that we have not seen since Classical times. Even the facial features and hairstyles are reminiscent of Greek and Roman sculpture. Although we have linked the reappearance of naturalism to the Gothic artist's increased awareness of nature, we must speculate that the sculptor of the Visitation group was looking directly to Classical statues for inspiration. The similarities are too strong to be coincidental. With his small and isolated attempt to revive Classicism, this unknown artist stands as a transitional figure between the spiritualism of the medieval world and the rationalism and humanism of the Renaissance.

ISLAM

Islam, like Judaism and Christianity, is a monotheistic religion in the Abrahamic tradition. It was founded by Muhammad, who was a native of Mecca in what is now Saudi Arabia. Muhammad was born at about 570 CE, and is seen by Muslims as the final prophet in the Abrahamic tradition. Muslims see Abraham, Moses, and Jesus as revelation prophets, but they view the revelations Muhammad received from God as corrections of previous distortions or misintepretations of his divine message.

Muhammad's monotheism was rejected by the polytheistic majority in Mecca, forcing him and his followers to flee to a desert oasis—now called Medina ("City of the Prophet")—in 622 CE. This date marks the beginning of Islam. Muhammad and his soldiers returned to Mecca in 630 CE, eight years later, with several thousand soldiers. He defeated the polytheists, converted the population to Islam, removed the idols of Arabian tribal gods housed in a small cubical building—called the *Kaaba* for "cube" in Arabic—and rededicated it as an Islamic house of worship. On pilgrimages to Mecca today, Muslims circle the Kaaba, which is the spiritual center of their world. From this beginning, Islam has grown to be the world's second largest religion, after Christianity, with nearly one and a half billion adherents. Islam today stretches from communities in Europe throughout North Africa, the Middle East, much of South Central Asia, and Indonesia. It once swept into and took control of the Iberian Peninsula, but was eventually pushed back by Christians. In the Middle Ages, Christians also fought Muslims to reclaim the "Holy Land," which is now Israel and the Palestinian Territories.

The word *Islam* means to submit—to surrender the self to the will of Allah. A follower of Islam is called a Muslim, which is the past participle of *Islam*, meaning "one who has submitted to Allah." The holy book of Muslims is called the *Koran* or the *Qur'an*, and Muslims believe that it was revealed to Muhammad by the angel

ISLAM

570 CE	632 CE	1099 CE	1258 CE	1492 CE
Muhammad born in Mecca 570	Muslims capture Jerusalem 638	Christian Crusaders capture Jerusalem 1099	Mongols sack Baghdad in 1258, ending Abbasid Caliphate	
Spread of Islam to Arabia, Egypt, Iraq, northern Africa, and southern Spain	The Umayyad Caliphate r. 661–750	Saladin, the Sultan of Egypt, retakes Jerusalem 1187	Ottoman Empire founded in 1281	
Muhammad flees to Medina in 622—an event called "the Hejira"; 622 becomes Year 1 in the Islamic calendar	Dome of the Rock completed 691	Third Crusade pits Richard the Lionhearted against Saladin 1189	The Alhambra, Granada c. 1391	
	Great Mosque of Damascus 706–715	Richard and Saladin agree to a truce 1192	Constantinople falls to the Ottoman Turks in 1453, ending the Byzantine Empire	
Muhammad captures Mecca 630	Charles Martel stems Muslim expansion at Tours, France, 732		Muslims are driven from Spain in the "Reconquista" 1492	
Muhammad dies 632	The Abbasid Caliphate begins 750			
	Great Mosque of Córdoba 8th–10th century			

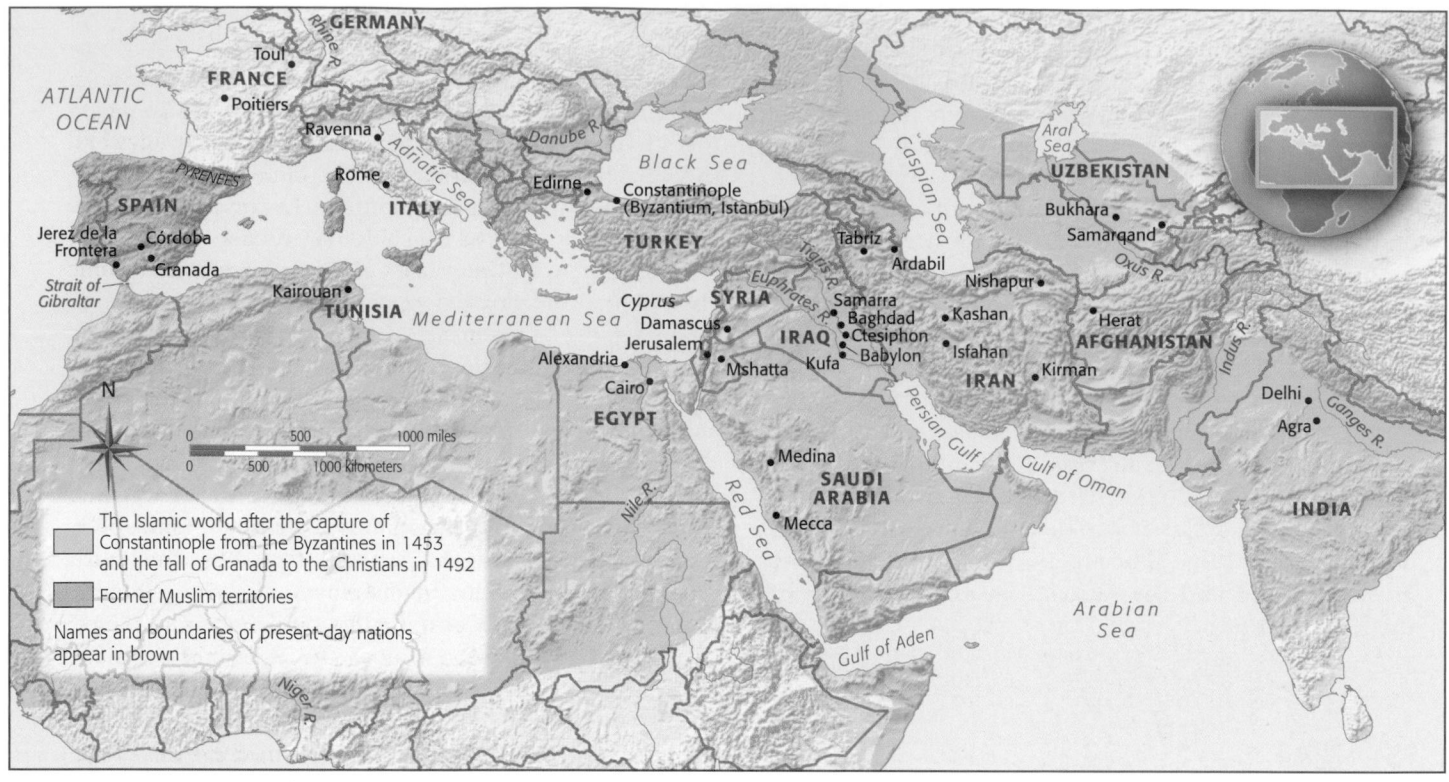

▲ MAP 16.2 The Islamic world around 1500.

Gabriel. The Qur'an and Muhammad's own words and deeds—the *Sunnah*—comprise the basic texts of Islam. Muslims worship God directly, without any hierarchy of rabbis, priests, pastors, or saints. In Islam, there is unity of church and state. The state is to be ruled by Islamic Law, or *Shariah*, as revealed in the basic texts. The proper ruler is both a religious and secular leader, a successor to Muhammad known as a *caliph*.

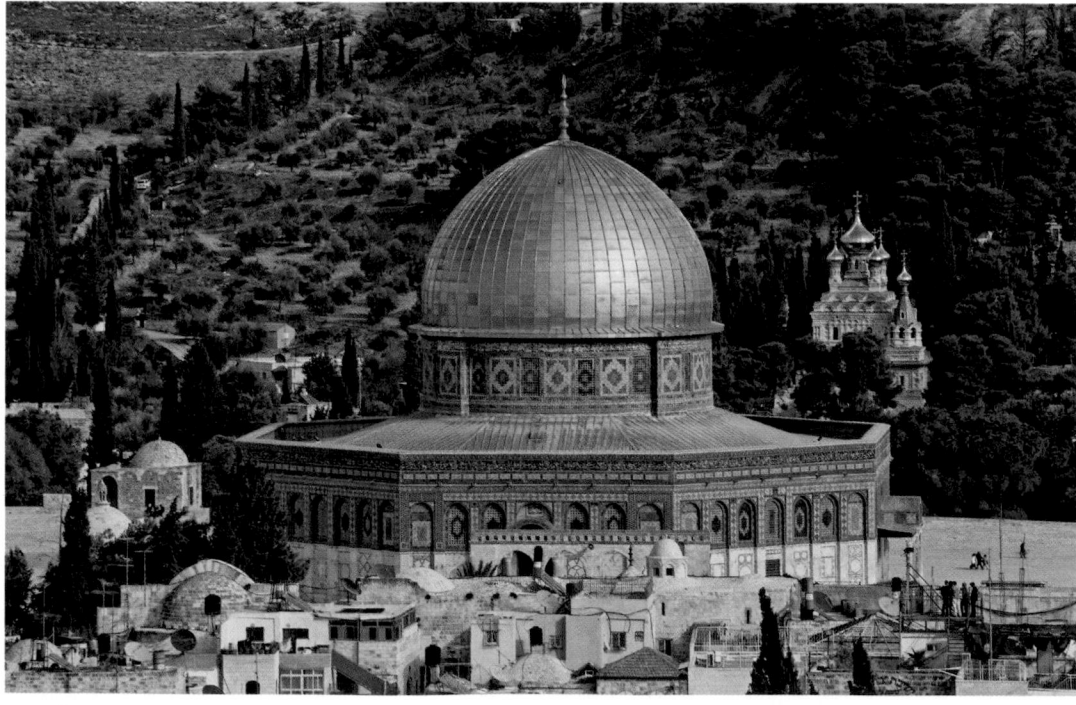

◄ 16.21 Dome of the Rock, exterior view (looking east), Jerusalem, Israel (687–692).

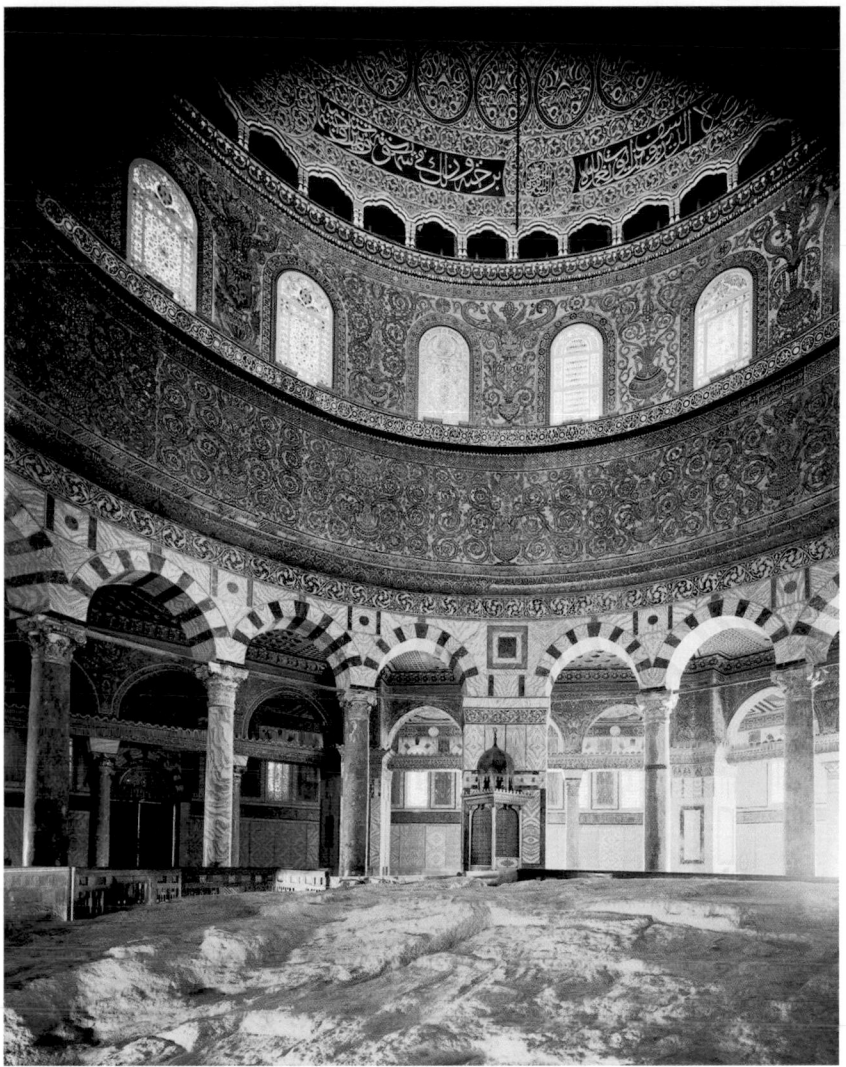

∧ 16.22 Dome of the Rock, interior view, Jerusalem, Israel (687–692).

The Umayyad Caliphate

Following the death of Muhammad in 632 CE, disputes arose over who would succeed him. A series of civil wars and assassinations eventually led to the founding of the Umayyad Caliphate (661 CE–750 CE). At its largest, the Umayyad Caliphate extended Islamic rule north into Persia, east into south central Asia (modern-day Afghanistan, Pakistan, and adjacent regions), west across the north of Africa (to present-day Morocco), and from there across what is now the Strait of Gibralter to the Iberian peninsula (now Portugal and Spain) and the south of present-day France (see Map 16.2). The Umayyads were overthrown by the Abbasid Caliphate and moved into what is now Spain, where they founded the Caliphate of Córdoba, which they ruled until 1031.

The Dome of the Rock in Jerusalem is the earliest and one of the most spectacular achievements of Islamic architecture (Fig. 16.21), built toward the end of the seventh century by Caliph Abd al-Malik of Damascus on al-Haram al-Sharif ("the Noble Sanctuary"), known by Jews as the Temple Mount, in Jerusalem. It is an elevated space that was once the site of the second Jewish temple, which was destroyed in 70 CE. The Dome of the Rock is an octagonal building capped by a golden dome, which sits on a heavy drum supported by four immense piers and twelve columns. The interior is decorated lavishly with mosaics, as was the outside of the building until, in the late Middle Ages, the mosaics were replaced by tiles. The building owes a clear debt to Roman and Byzantine architecture, but the Qur'anic verses on its inside make it clear that it was intended to serve an Islamic function.

The original mosaics decorating the interior of the Dome of the Rock remain largely intact (Fig. 16.22). The interior contains a still-visible rock outcropping that is of great significance in the Abrahamic tradition. It is believed by many to be the site of Adam's grave. Many Jews, Christians, and Muslims alike also believe that this is the rock upon which Abraham was prepared to sacrifice his son, Isaac, although at the last minute an angel stayed his sword.

See more of Jerusalem in the online Art Tour.

Another architectural achievement of the Umayyad Caliphate is the Umayyad Mosque (or Great Mosque

There are five duties or "Five Pillars" of Islam. These begin with the Shahadah, the basic tenet of submission: "I bear witness that there is none worthy of worship except Allah, the One, without any partner. And I bear witness that Muhammad is His servant and His Messenger." The Shahadah not only requires belief in Allah but also belief that Muhammad is the sole source of interpretation of the revelations of Allah. *Salat* is the requirement to pray five times a day, facing Mecca. *Zakah* is the giving of alms to the poor. *Sawin* is fasting during the holy month of Ramadan. During Ramadan, Muslims abstain from food, drink, and sex—from dawn to dusk. Children, old people, sick people, and women who are pregnant or breast-feeding may not fast. Muslims are also obliged to make the *Hajj*—the pilgrimage to Mecca—at least once if they have the means to do so. They circle the Kaaba, which, according to the Qur'an, was built by Abraham, and is believed to be directly beneath the Gate of Heaven.

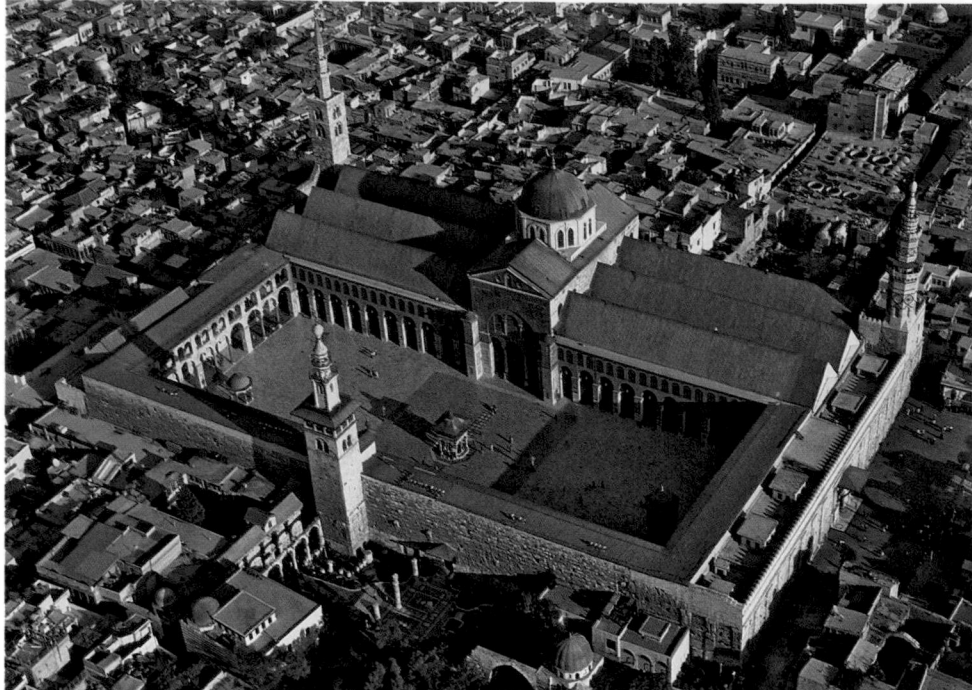

Part A. Aerial view (looking southeast).

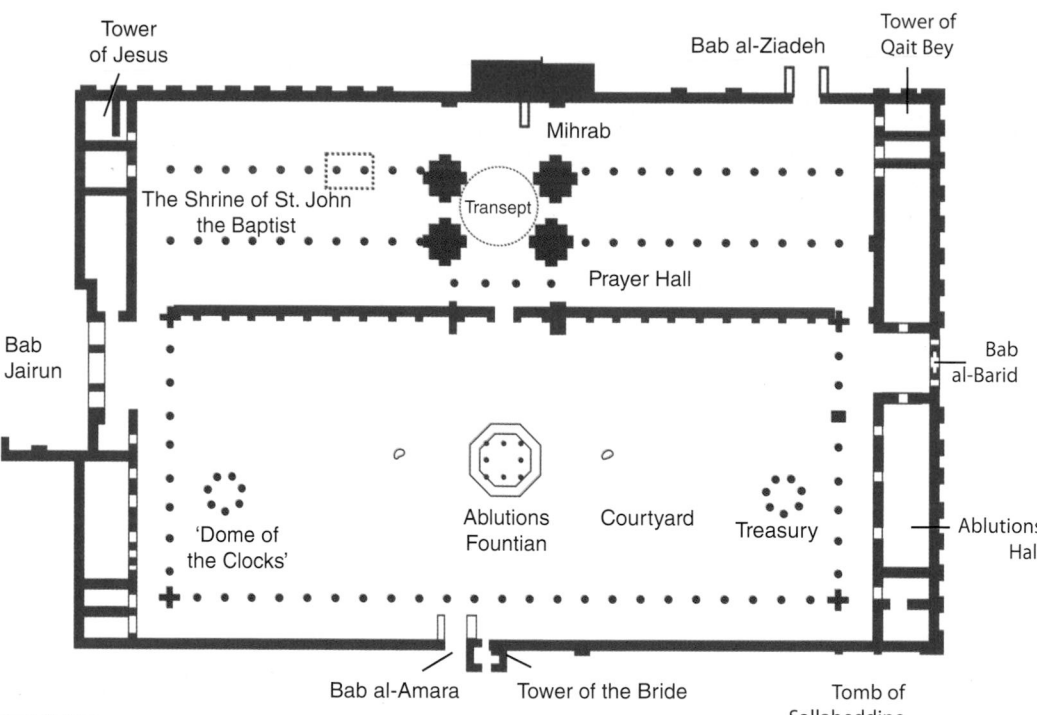

Tower
of Jesus

Bab al-Ziadeh

Tower of
Qait Bey

Mihrab

The Shrine of St. John
the Baptist

Transept

Prayer Hall

Bab
Jairun

Bab
al-Barid

Ablutions
Fountian

Courtyard

Treasury

Ablutions
Hall

'Dome of
the Clocks'

Bab al-Amara

Tower of the Bride

Tomb of
Sallaheddine

Part B. Plan.

ᴧ **16.23 The Great Mosque, Damascus, Syria** (706–715).

of Damascus, **Fig. 16.23A** and **16.23B**), which was built in what is modern-day Syria and completed in 715 CE. Using stone, marble, tile, and mosaics, it was erected on the site of a Christian basilica dedicated to John the Baptist that had existed since the rule of the Roman emperor Constantine. Both Christians and Muslims honor John as

a prophet, and there is a shrine of John the Baptist in the prayer hall of the mosque.

The most highly regarded architectural legacy of the Umayyad Caliphate is the Mezquita-Catedral (mosque-cathedral) in what is now the city of Córdoba in south central Spain. The building originated as a church in about 600 CE. After the Islamic conquest of the region, the church was divided between Christians and Muslims. The Umayyad Prince Abd ar-Rahman I purchased the Christian half and began the development in 784 CE of what would become the Great Mosque of Córdoba upon completion in 987 CE. The interior of the mosque at Córdoba, Spain (Fig. 16.24), shows the system of arches that spans the distances between columns in the hypostyle system. The hypostyle system enables expansion in any direction as a congregation grew. By bowing toward Mecca in the same yard, worshipers were granted equal psychological access to Allah. A series of vaults, supported by heavier piers, overspreads the arches. There is no grand open space as in the Western cathedral; rather, air and light flow as through a forest of high-crowned trees. The interiors of mosques and other Islamic structures have traditionally been decorated with finely detailed mosaics, as seen in the mihrab from the Madrasa Imami, from Isfahan, Iran (Fig. 16.25). A **mihbrab** is a niche in the wall facing Mecca that provides a focus of worship. There is no clerical hierarchy in Islam that is found in many Christian religions. The leader of gatherings for worship, called the **imam**, stands on a pulpit in the mosque, near the wall that faces Mecca, the spiritual capital of Islam.

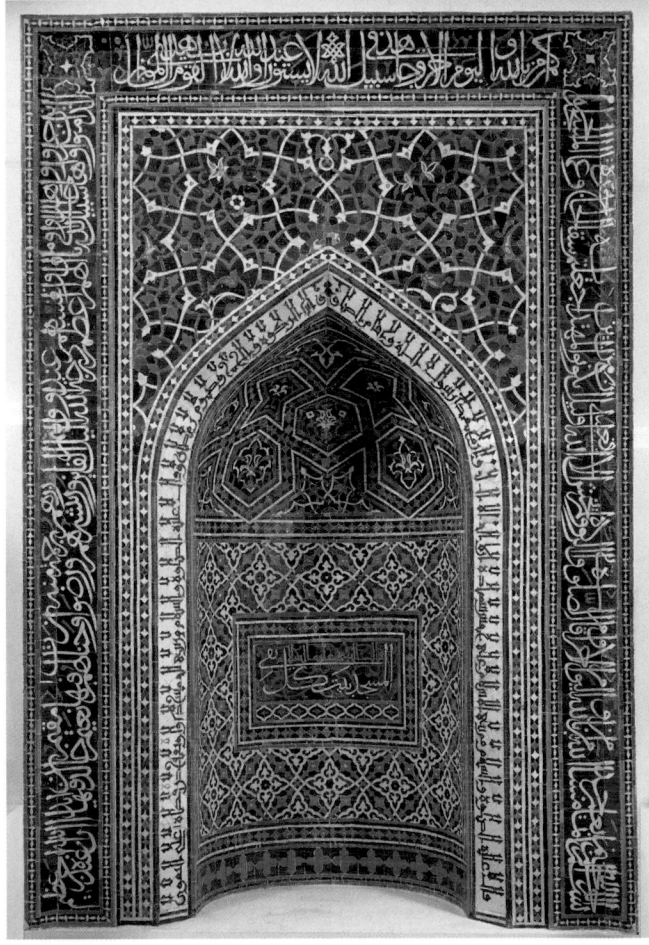

> 16.25 **Mihrab from the Madrasa Imami, Isfahan, Iran** (c. 1354). Mosaic of monochrome-glaze tiles on composite body set on plaster to create floral and geometric patterns and inscriptions, 11'3" × 7'6". Metropolitan Museum of Art, New York. Harris Brisbane Dick Fund, 1939.

1 ft.

The Golden Age of Islam

The Abbasid Caliphate, which succeeded the Umayyads, has been called the Golden Age of Islam. It spanned five centuries, from 750 CE to 1258 CE (the time of the Mongol invasion and the sacking of Baghdad). During the Golden Age, citrus fruits were imported from China, and rice, cotton, and sugarcane were brought in from India, and trained to grow in Muslim lands. A precursor of capitalism and free markets was established. The scientific method was instituted, in which hypotheses are tested through experimentation. Muslim astronomers considered the possibility that the sun was the center of the solar system and that the Earth spun on an axis. Algebra and trigonometry were invented. The concepts of *inertia* and *momentum,* later adopted by Newton, were discovered. The Mezquita was begun in Córdoba.

During the early part of the Golden Age, the Abbasid caliph Al-Mutawakkil commissioned the Great Mosque of Samarra in present-day Iraq in 848 CE and completed it in 851 CE. When built it was the largest mosque in the world. From the vast spiraling structure for which the mosque is known—the Malwiya Minaret (Fig. 16.26)—a crier known as a muezzin called followers to prayer at certain hours. *Malwiya* is Arabic for "snail shell." The photograph was taken before the top of the **minaret** was damaged by insurgents during the Iraqi war in 2006.

Mosques avoid symbols, and early mosques in particular do not show ornamentation. The mosque at Samarra was a simple building, 800 feet long and 520 feet wide,

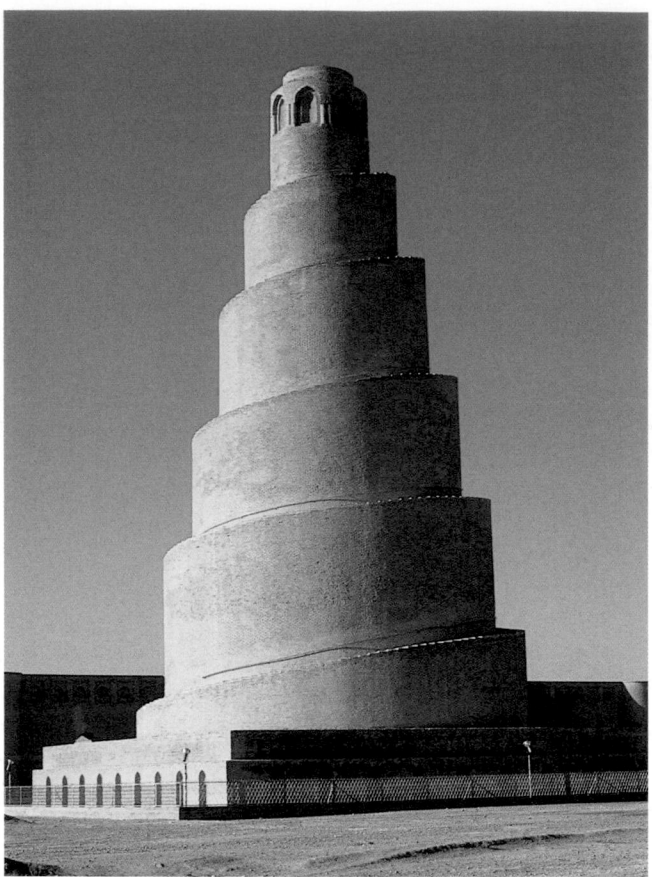

∧ 16.26 Malwiya Minaret (looking southwest), Great Mosque at Samarra, Iraq (848–852).

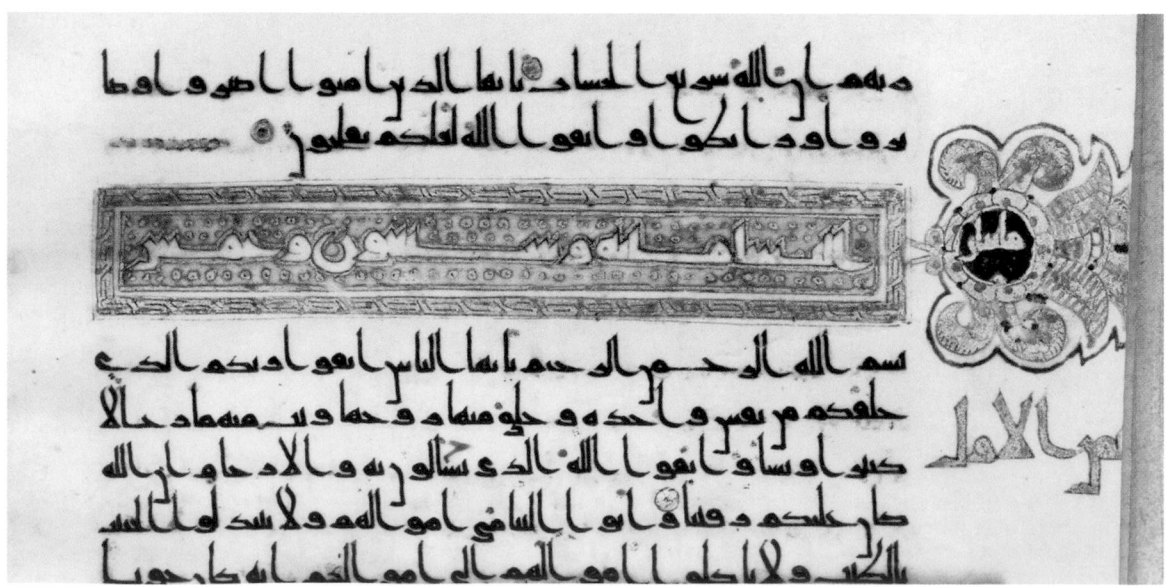

> 16.27 Qur'an page (early 10th century, North Africa or Near East). Pen and ink on vellum. Private collection.

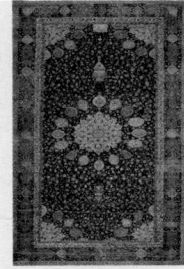
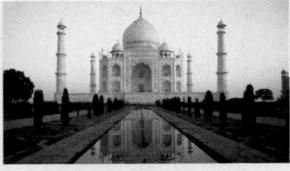
covered in part by a wooden roof, with a great open courtyard. The roof was supported by the hypostyle system of multiple rows of columns. Hundreds of years ago, the interior walls were paneled with resplendent dark blue glass mosaics.

The stylized Arabic from a leaf of the Qur'an (Fig. 16.27) was drawn in about the middle of the Golden Age. Rounded letters serve as counterpoint to the angular script. The colored marks are aids that help the reader pronounce the script, but for those of us who are not readers of Arabic, the whole has something of a mysterious pictographic quality created by strong, measured strokes.

Golden Age potters were turning out simple, elegantly glazed works often decorated with calligraphy. A dish from eleventh- or twelfth-century Iran (Fig. 16.28) shows stylized Arabic text around the rim that achieves an abstract painterly quality. Elongated letters are extended to embrace the full width of the rim. The Arabic is translated into English as follows: "Science has first a bitter taste, but at the end it tastes sweeter than honey. Good health [to the owner]."

The Golden Age was brought to an end by the Mongol invasion, but the Mongols who remained in Islamic lands converted to Islam over the following century, as did Turks, who had also come in from the East. The Ottoman Empire emerged in the thirteenth and fourteenth centuries, and was centered in present day Turkey. The Hagia Sophia (see Fig. 16.4A and 16.4B) was the cathedral of Constantinople—renamed as Istanbul—from its dedication in 360 CE to the conquest by the Ottoman Turks in 1453, who had the building converted into a mosque. The cathedrals bells, altar, and religious figures were removed; a mihrab and the four minarets we see outside the structure today were installed. The Ottoman Empire was among the losers of World War I, and in 1918; seventeen years later, in 1935, the Republic of Turkey made the Hagia Sophia into a museum—ending the Christian–Muslim conflict over the building.

The Alhambra (from the Arabic *Al-Hamra,* "the red one"), a fortress and palace, was built by Islamic Moorish rulers in Granada during the fourteenth century. It sits atop a hill on the edge of the city, in modern-day Spain. The Moors were expelled from Spain at about the same time as Columbus set sail on his western voyage, and today the Alhambra exhibits a combination of characteristic Islamic architectural elements as well as a courtyard and fountain that seems

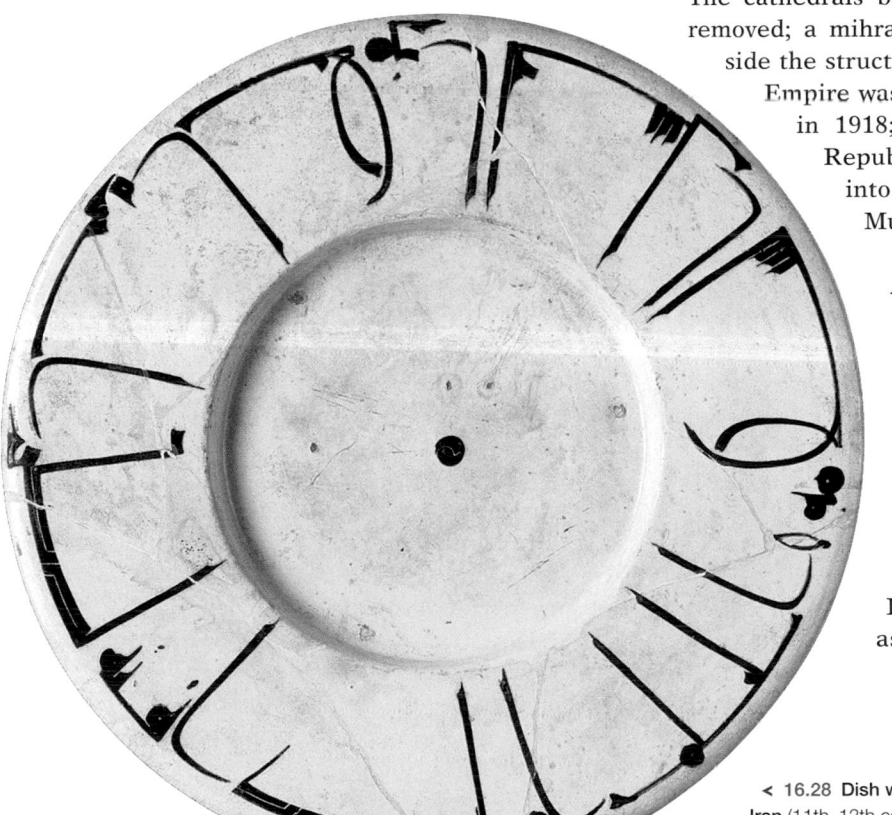

◄ **16.28 Dish with epigraphic decoration, Khurasan, Iran** (11th–12th century). Terra-cotta, white slip ground, and slip underglaze decoration; 14¾" diameter. Musée du Louvre, Paris.

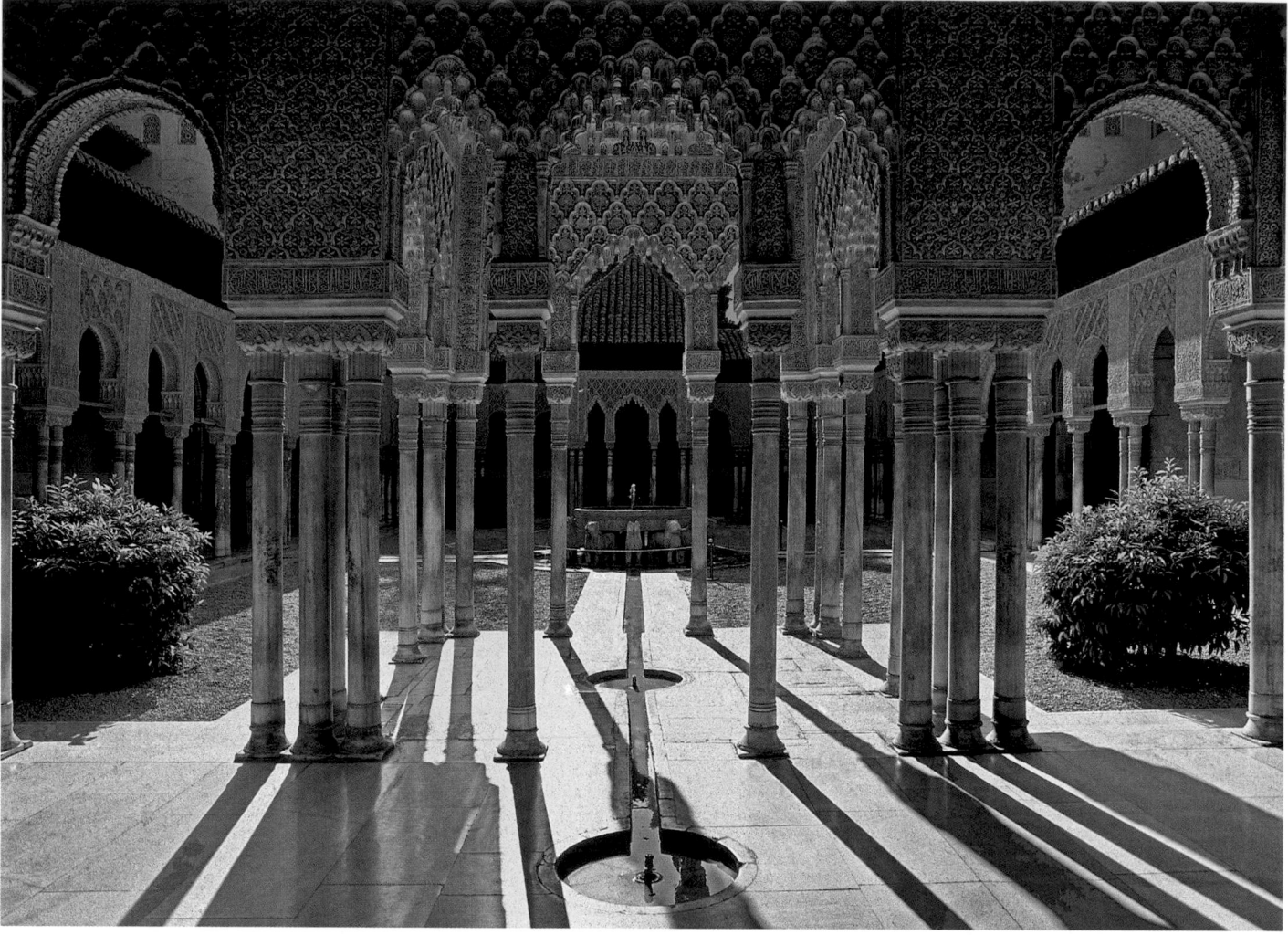

∧ **16.29** **The Court of the Lions (looking east), Palace of the Lions, Alhambra, Granada, Spain** (1354–1391). The fountain and water course.

reminiscent of those found in ancient Roman villas. Figure 16.29 shows a view of the Court of the Lions from a room of the palace. The mild Spanish winters make possible the full integration of the palace with its environment through a stately progression of intricately carved arched openings.

THE WIDER WORLD

India

While Christianity flowered in the West and Islam spread west and east from Arabia, Buddhism continued to spread eastward from India. Hinduism, which is derived from an Arabic word meaning "those who live in the Indus Valley," blossomed in the Asian subcontinent and certain parts of Southeast Asia. Unlike Judaism, Christianity, Islam, and Buddhism, the Hindu religion has no founder, no prophet.

Hinduism has been referred to as the world's oldest religion because of the ancient dating of Hindu beliefs and sacred texts called Vedas, although Hindu works of art tend to have been created at about the same time as the "Age of Faith" in the West.

Hinduism combines ritualized worship of multiple gods with an intellectual tradition that tries to comprehend the meaning of people and the cosmos. The three most important deities are Vishnu, Shiva, and Brahma. Vishnu is regarded as the preserver of the universe, and Shiva is known as the Lord of Lords and the god of creation and destruction, which in Hindu philosophy are one and the same (Fig. 16.30). Brahma, the god of creation, is also portrayed as the goddess Devi or Deva, whose name means "shining one." Sometimes referred to as "Mother of the Universe," Devi was seen as gentle and approachable.

Hindu temples are considered to be the dwelling places of the gods, not houses of worship and, indeed, the multiple "peaks" of the Vishvanatha Temple at Khajuraho

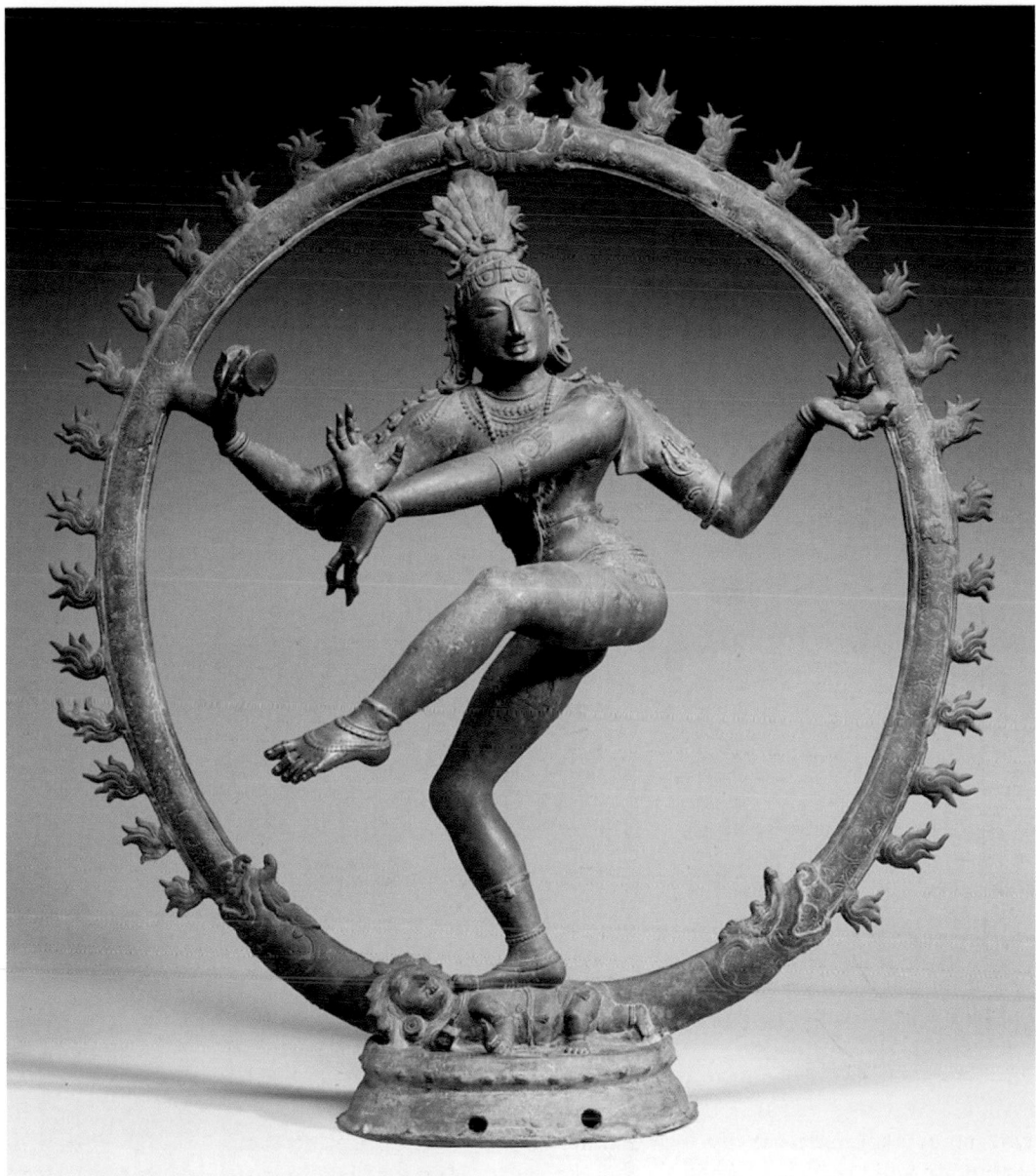

< 16.30 Shiva as Nataraja, the King of Dance, from South India, Tamil Nadu (900–13th century). Bronze, 43¼" high. The Cleveland Museum of Art, Cleveland, Ohio.

ASIA, AFRICA, AND THE AMERICAS

250 CE	960 CE	1600 CE
Classic Mayan civilization in the Americas 250–1500	Construction of Angkor Wat c. 800–1200	
Vedas committed to writing	Song Dynasty in China 960–1279	
Earliest preserved Hindu stone sculptures and temples	Construction of Vishvanatha Temple c. 1000	
Buddhism spreads from China to Japan	Phoenix Hall completed in 1053	
Tang Dynasty in China 616–906	Feudal period in Japan 1185–c. 1600	
Heian (Kyoto) period in Japan 794–1185	Europeans settle in coastal regions of Africa in the 16th century, importing Christianity	
Muslim missionaries bring Islam to Ghana in 8th century	Slave trade by Europeans begins in the 16th century	
Arabs begin slave trade in Africa c. 10th century		

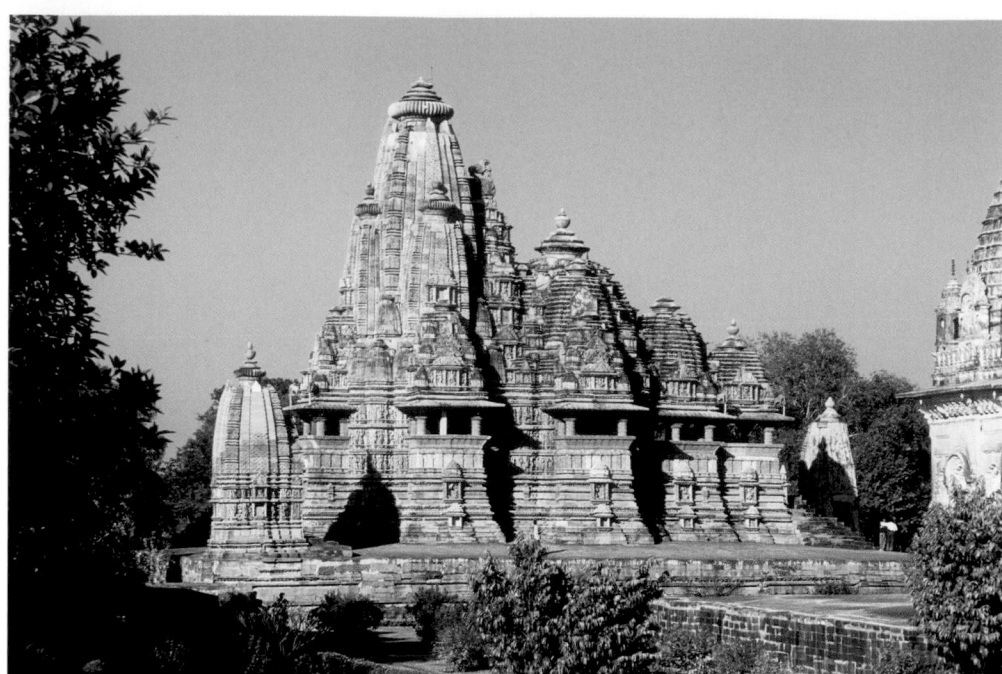

(Fig. 16.31) symbolize the rock formations of Shiva's home in the mountains. The steep, organic shapes of the multiple towers, balanced by horizontal registers and sweeping cornices, resemble physical hurdles one might encounter in the natural landscape and represent spiritual hurdles humans meet on the paths to oneness with the universe. The registers of the lower part of the temple are carved in high relief and feature representations of deities, allegorical scenes, and idealized men and women engaged in erotic activity (Fig. 16.32).

The immense temple complex in present-day Cambodia referred to as Angkor Wat (Fig. 16.33) is the largest of many built over some four centuries by a succession of Khmer kings who believed that, upon death, they would be reabsorbed by their personal gods (Angkor Wat was constructed by Suryavarman II and Vishnu was his personal god). Set within a grid, Angkor Wat features perimeter and inner walls—both comprised of towers and galleries—surrounding a tall tower and four somewhat shorter ones that anchor the four corners of the central block. The five towers represent the peaks of the sacred Mount Meru—the center of the physical and spiritual universes. Many consider Angkor Wat to be the most magnificent architectural feat on planet Earth.

China

After the fall of the Han Dynasty, civil wars wracked China for nearly four centuries until the Tang emperors (618–906 CE) unified the nation once again. Political stability facilitated travel, trade, and economic expansion,

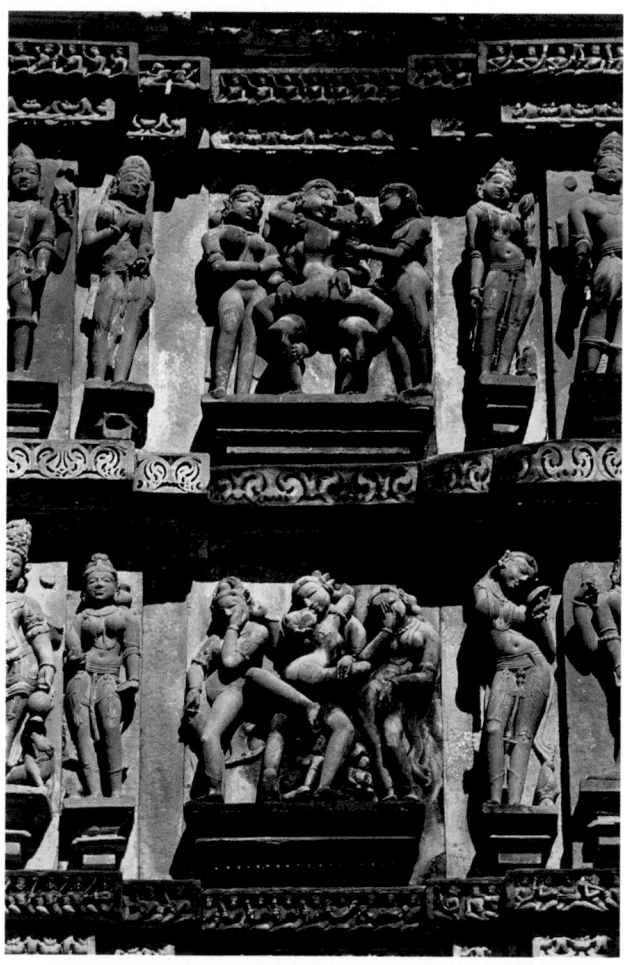

▲ 16.32 Mithuna reliefs, detail of the north side of the Vishvanatha Temple, Khajuraho, India (c. 1000).

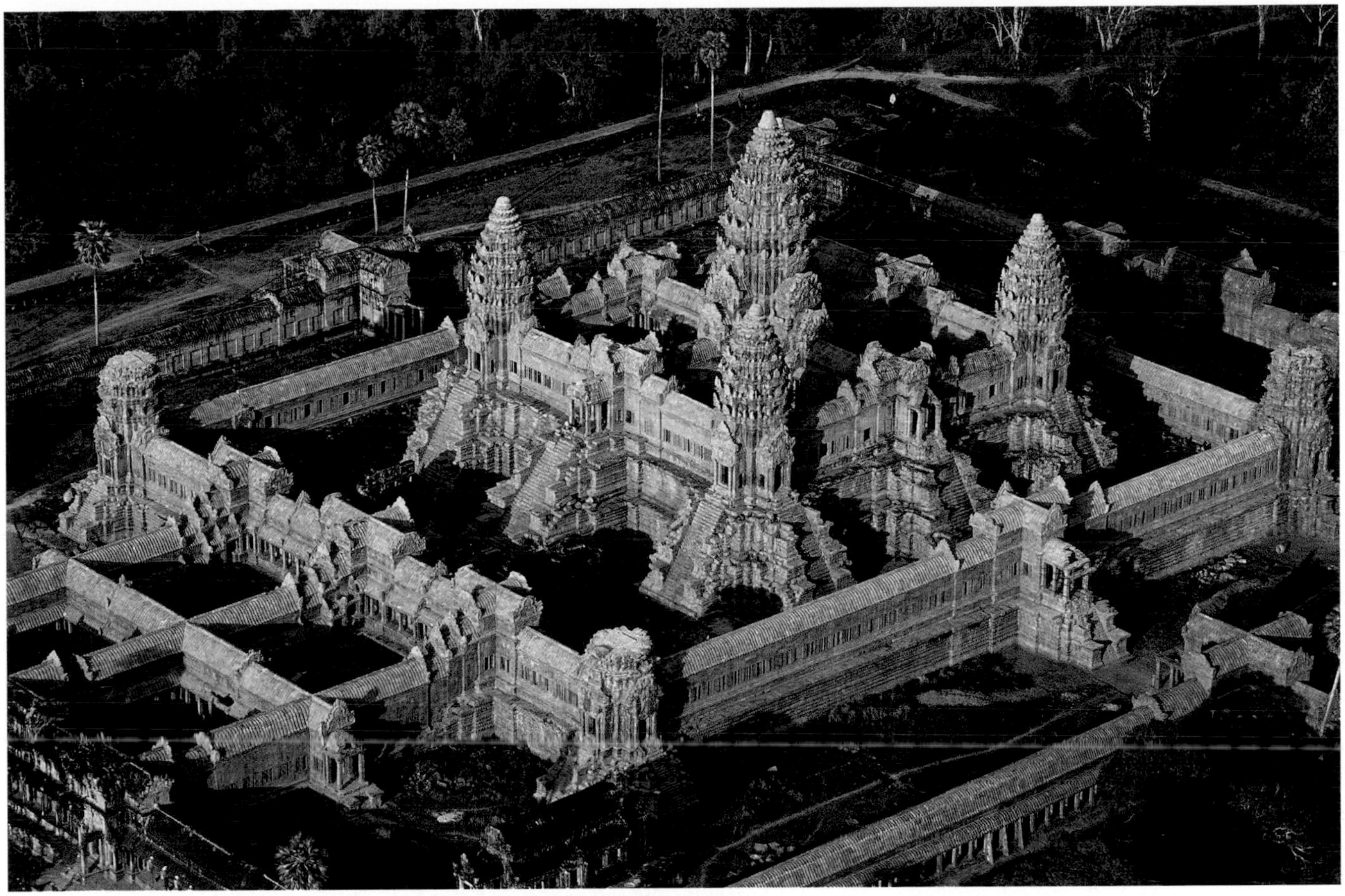

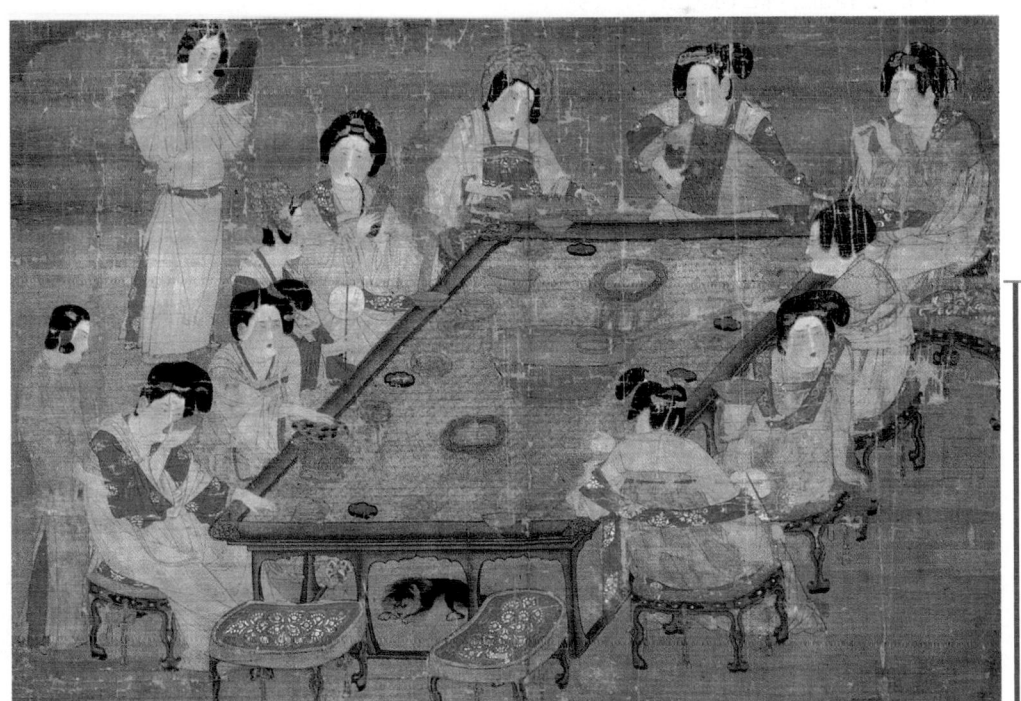

∧ 16.33 **Aerial view of Angkor Wat, Angkor, Cambodia** (9th–11th centuries). Rectangular: sides approximately 5,000" × 4,000".

and art and architecture flourished. Much like Paris in the nineteenth century or Berlin in the 1920s, the capital city of the Tang Dynasty—Chang'an—became a magnet for wealth and for foreign visitors seeking cultural enrichment and the free exchange of ideas.

A silk scroll painting from the tenth century (Fig. 16.34) shows elegant ladies of the Tang imperial court listening to music while drinking, smoking, and mingling. The setting is only loosely described but the furniture and garments, by contrast, are quite detailed. The ease of the social atmosphere is conveyed through the varying poses and gestures of the women as well as the charming touch of the tiny sleeping dog beneath the table.

1 ft.

∧ 16.34 **A palace concert** (10th century). Hanging scroll, ink and colors on silk; 19¼" × 27⅜". Collection of the National Palace Museum, Taipei, Taiwan, Republic of China.

COMPARE & CONTRAST

Ganesh, the Hindu Deity: Don't Leave Home without Him

IN HINDUISM'S VAST PANTHEON OF gods, one of the more familiar and beloved is the elephant-headed Ganesh. Also known as Ganesha or Ganapati, he is the son of Shiva, the most powerful of the Hindu deities, and Parvati, the goddess of power who gives energy to all beings. Ganesh is the Lord of Success—and the destroyer of evils and obstacles. He is also worshiped as the god of knowledge, wisdom, and wealth. Hindus interpret dreams of elephants as messages of transformation and divine power—the emergence of one's highest self from the collective unconscious mind.

The distinctive form of Ganesh is seen in temple carvings, sculptures, miniature paintings, and any number and variety of small statuettes purchased by Hindus as votives. Ganesh is always visualized as a man with a pot belly, an elephant head with one tusk (the other is broken), and multiple arms (typically four) holding attributes that vary from one representation to another including a goad (a pointed instrument) used to prod humans toward proper goals, his broken tusk, prayer beads, an ax, a mace, a noose, a lotus flower, a seashell, a small water vessel, and more. He is also shown in many incarnations, as in an eleventh-century stone sculpture (**Fig. 16.35**) in which he is dancing on a mouse, a tiny creature seen frequently in Ganesh iconography.

The clash of age-old traditions with the perils and strains of contemporary life is evoked in a painting (**Fig. 16.36**) by Prajakta Palav Aher. Aher's is not an iconic representation of the deity such as might be found in a temple or shrine. Rather, Ganesh rides a well-worn commuter train—like anyone else shuttling to the city for a day's work—accompanying those who petition him for success and good fortune. In what may be interpreted as an allusion to the "rat race" to economic success in today's world, Ganesh has an air of exhaustion, as if he has just plopped down in his seat with all of the tools of his trade at the end of a long, long day. In a true manifestation of globalization, the Destroyer of Obstacles may be returning from the realm of outsourced troubleshooters managing worldwide software glitches and catching his breath before moving on to the next.

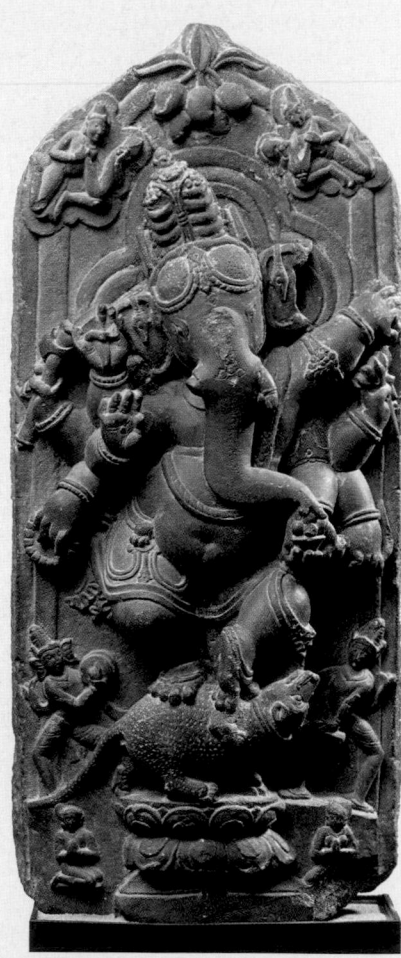

∧ **16.35** Dancing Ganesh (Ganesha), North Bengal, India (11th century). Slate, 22⅛" × 9⅞". Museum für Asiatische Kunst, Berlin, Germany.

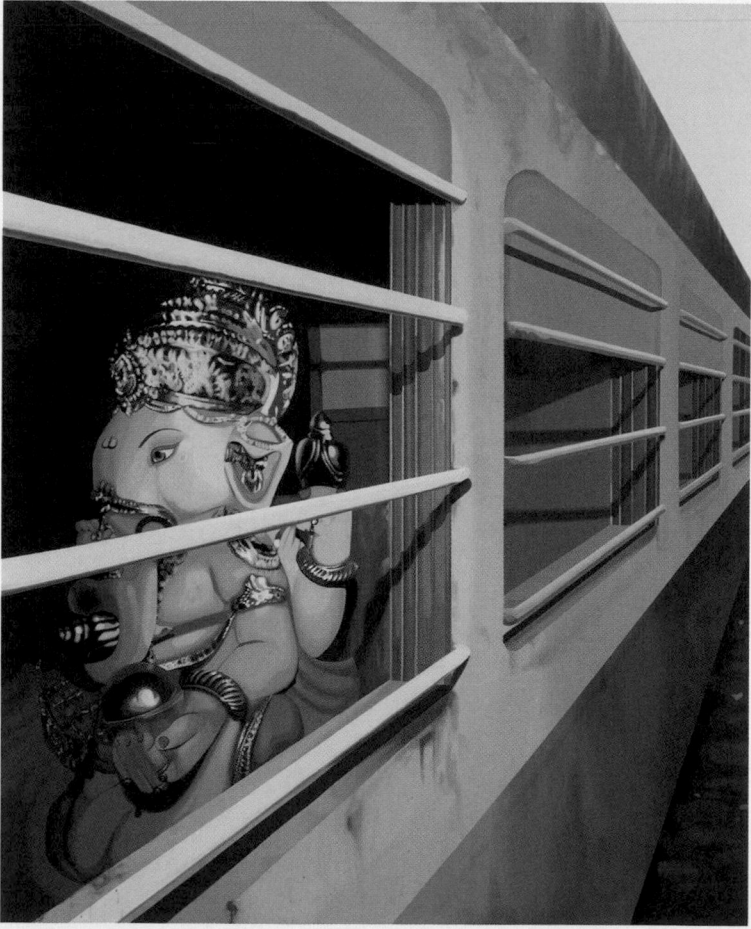

∧ **16.36** PRAJAKTA PALAV AHER, *Untitled I* from the Ganpati Series (2007). Acrylic on canvas, 96" × 72".

Artists of the Song Dynasty (960–1279) achieved what some consider the height of landscape painting, transporting viewers to unfamiliar, magical realms. But this period in Chinese history is also known for an abundance of societal changes and technological discoveries, including the movable-type printing press (centuries before Gutenberg accomplished the same feat in Germany) and gunpowder.

Fan K'uan's imaginary landscape *Travelers among Mountains and Streams* (Fig. 16.37) is a brush and ink painting on a silk scroll measuring nearly 7 feet in length. In contrast to the perspective typical of Western landscapes, there is no single vanishing point or set of vanishing points. Rather, the perspective shifts, offering the viewer a freer journey back and forth across the many paths and bridges nestled among the trees and rocks. Sharp brushstrokes clearly delineate conifers, deciduous trees, and small temples on a cliff in the lower third of the composition, silhouetted against a strip of brightness. Gently rounded mountain peaks composed of wispy, textural strokes rise in orderly, rhythmic fashion in the top half of the painting, pierced by the balanced verticals of a waterfall on the right and cleft on the left. The travelers are but specks in the lower-right corner, dwarfed by nature and seemingly insignificant in comparison. Fan K'uan's is not a warning of the destructive power of nature, but rather a tribute to its serene majesty. His goal was not to record that which the eye sees, but rather the sensations and perceptions of the experience of nature.

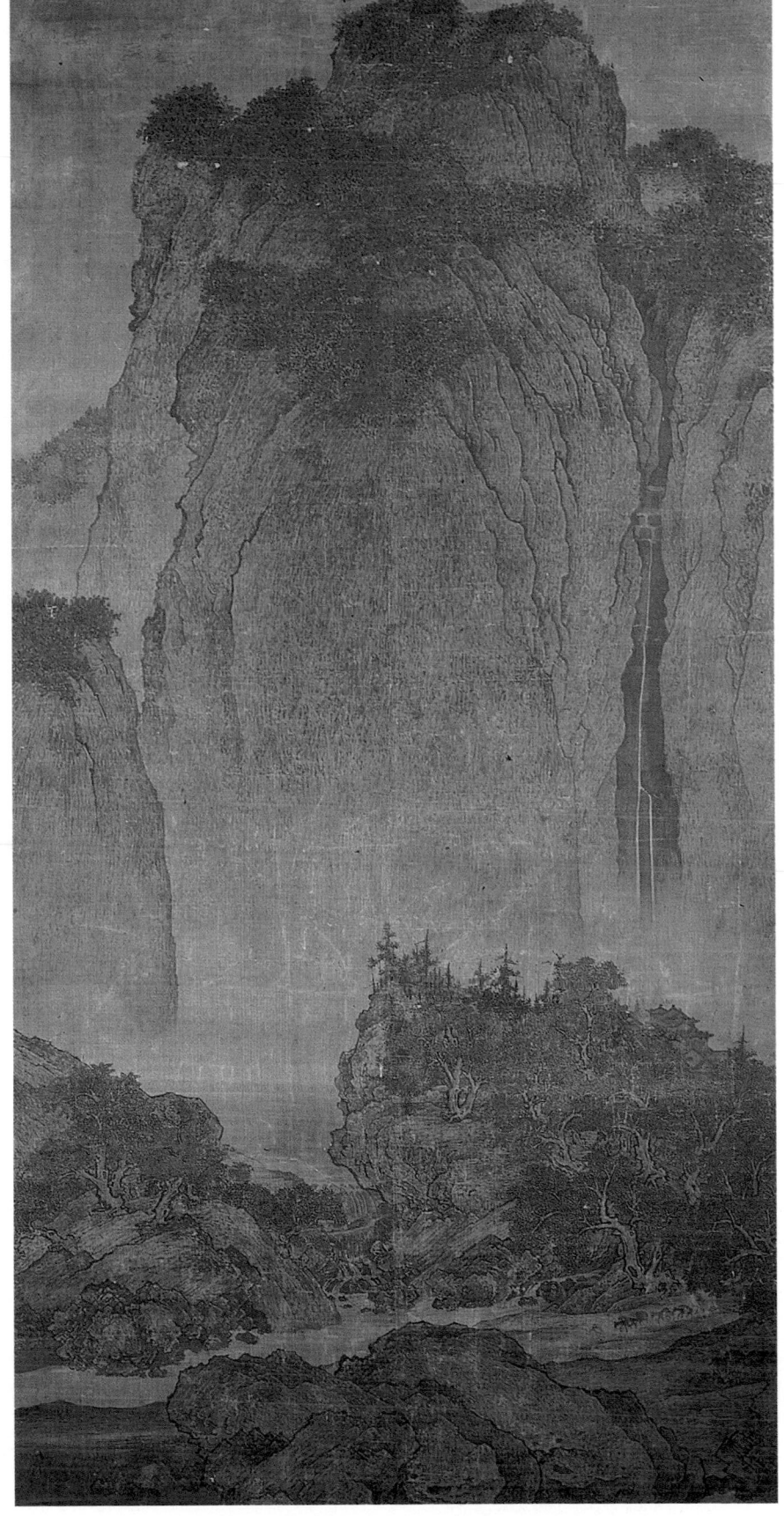

> 16.37 FAN K'UAN, *Travelers among Mountains and Streams* (c. 1000). Hanging scroll, ink and colors on silk; 81¾" high. Collection of the National Palace Museum, Taipei, Taiwan, Republic of China.

1 ft.

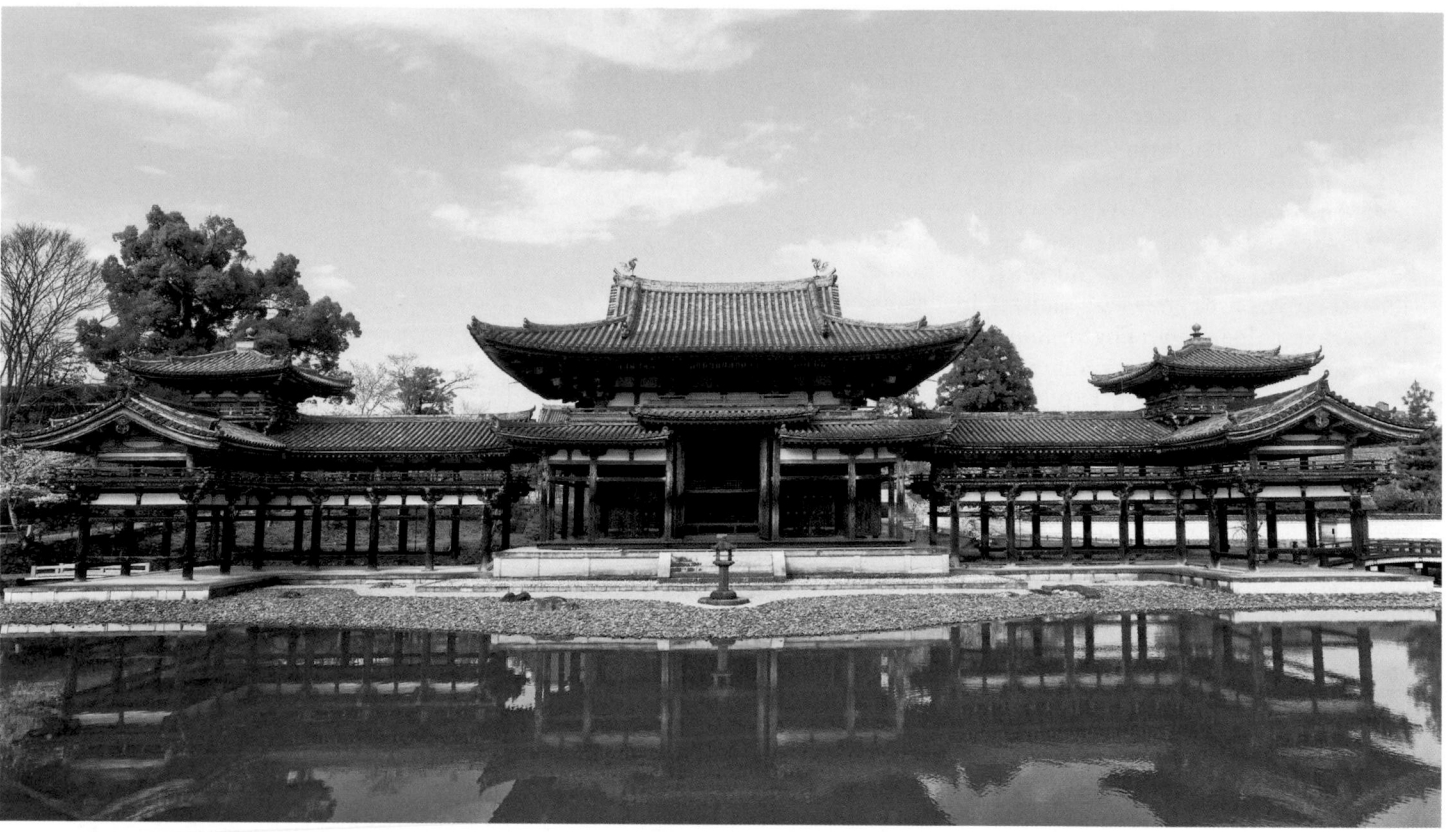

∧ 16.38 **Phoenix Hall (looking west), Byōdō-in, Uji, Kyoto Prefecture, Japan** (Heian period, completed 1053).

Japan

Japan is an island country off the eastern coast of Asia, holding more than 120 million people in an area not quite as large as California (whose population is about 37 million people). The islands were formed from porous volcanic rock, and are thus devoid of hard stone suitable for sculpture and building. Therefore, Japan's sculptural tradition has focused on clay modeling and bronze casting, and its structures have been built from wood.

Ceramic figures and vessels date to the fourth millennium BCE. Archaeological evidence suggests that agricultural communities were developed by 200 CE. Around 400 CE, one of these communities imported scribes from Korea to keep records, because no system of writing as yet existed in Japan. The original chief city had been Nara, laid out in 706 CE in imitation of Chinese urban design. But less than a century later, settlements joined to form a new capital, Heian (now named Kyoto), which remained a center of stability and economic expansion until 1185.

By the beginning of the seventh century, Buddhism had spread to Japan from China and been established as the state religion in Japan. Many sculptors produced wooden and bronze effigies of the Buddha, and Buddhist temples, such as Phoenix Hall (Fig. 16.38) reflected the Chinese style. Phoenix Hall is the main Buddhist temple erected within the Byōdō-in monastery, located in the Kyoto metropolitan area. With its gracefully upward moving, overhanging roofs and its slender wooden columns at ground level, the temple appears to be weightless, floating on the pond before it—creating a Buddhist heaven on earth. The temple derives its name from its shape, which resembles a bird with its wings outspread, as the mythical phoenix. The main bedroom faced south to open upon the sunlight reflected from a pond within a garden. Originally a royal country palace, the hall was converted to a temple to house a gilded statue of the Buddha Amida, who Japanese Buddhists believed had promised salvation for people from all social strata. Smaller images of Buddha are presented as playing musical instruments, heralding worshipers on the path upward.

Shinto, the native religion of Japan, teaches love of nature and the existence of many beneficent gods, who are never symbolized in art or any other visual form. The tension between Shintoism and the influence of Chinese Buddhism always remained an important factor in Japanese religious life. The purpose of the move from Nara to Heian was in part to escape from the domination of Nara's Buddhist priests.

THE PERIOD OF FEUDAL RULE The increasingly remote court life of Kyoto led to internal feuding, and in 1185 a warrior class of **samurai** developed at Kakamura. Samurai followed local aristocratic leaders, who in turn were bound to a shogun—a system like the feudal system that developed in western Europe at about the same time. By the late thirteenth century, when China fell to Mongols, Japan was able to resist two waves of Mongol invasions. Japan was ruled by a **shogun** (abbreviation of "barbarian-suppressing commander-in-chief") from the twelfth through the fifteenth centuries. But when European arts were flourishing in the Renaissance, Japan, as India had done earlier, fell into an Age of the Warring States, which lasted from 1467 to 1568. Japan was again united in the late sixteenth century. Warriors followed local aristocratic leaders, who in turn were bound to the emperor—a system like the feudal system that developed in western Europe at about the same time.

The landscapes, portraits, and narrative scrolls produced by the Japanese during the late twelfth through the early fourteenth centuries are highly original and Japanese in character. Some of them express the contemplative life of Buddhism, others express the active life of the warrior, and still others express the aesthetic life made possible by love of nature. The Kumano Mandala (Fig. 16.39), a scroll executed at the beginning of the fourteenth century, represents three Shinto shrines. For nearly 2,000 years, wooden Shinto shrines such as those shown in the scroll have been razed every 20 years and replaced by duplicates. The shrines in the mandala are actually several miles apart in mountainous terrain, but the artist collapsed the space between them to permit the viewer an easier visual pilgrimage. The scroll pays homage to the unique Japanese landscape in its vivid color and rich detail. The several small figures of the seated Buddha portrayed within testify to the Japanese reconciliation of disparate spiritual influences. The repetition of forms within the shrines and the procession of the shrines afford the composition a wonderful rhythm and unity. A **mandala** is a religious symbol of the design of the universe. It seems as though the universe of the shrines of the Kumano Mandala must carry on forever—as indeed it did in the minds of the Japanese.

The feudal period also gave rise to an extraordinary realism, as in the thirteenth-century wood portrait statue of the priest Kuya preaching

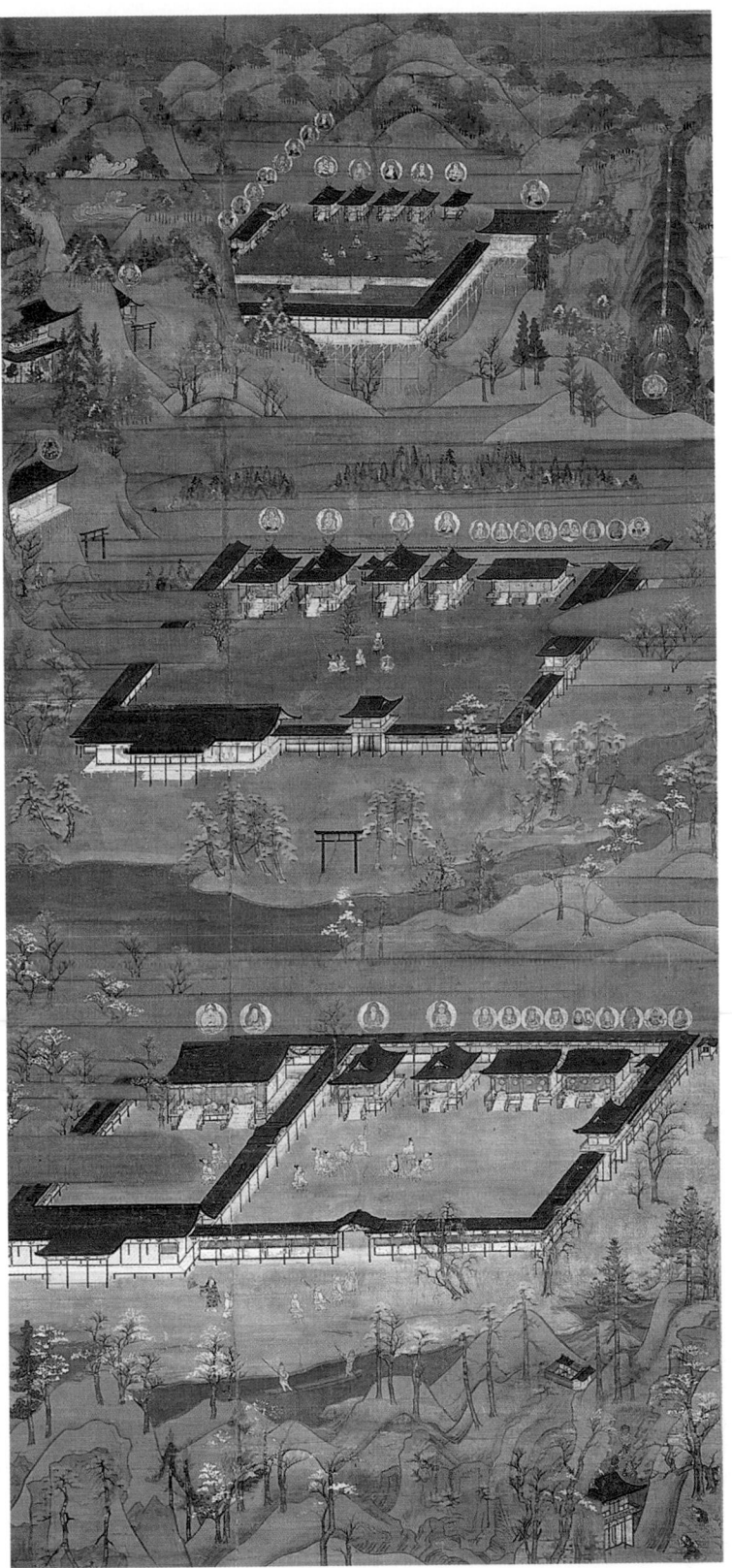

∧ **16.39 Kumano Mandala, Japan** (Kamakura period, c. 1300). Hanging scroll, color on silk; 53¾" × 24⅜". The Cleveland Museum of Art, Cleveland, Ohio.

1 ft.

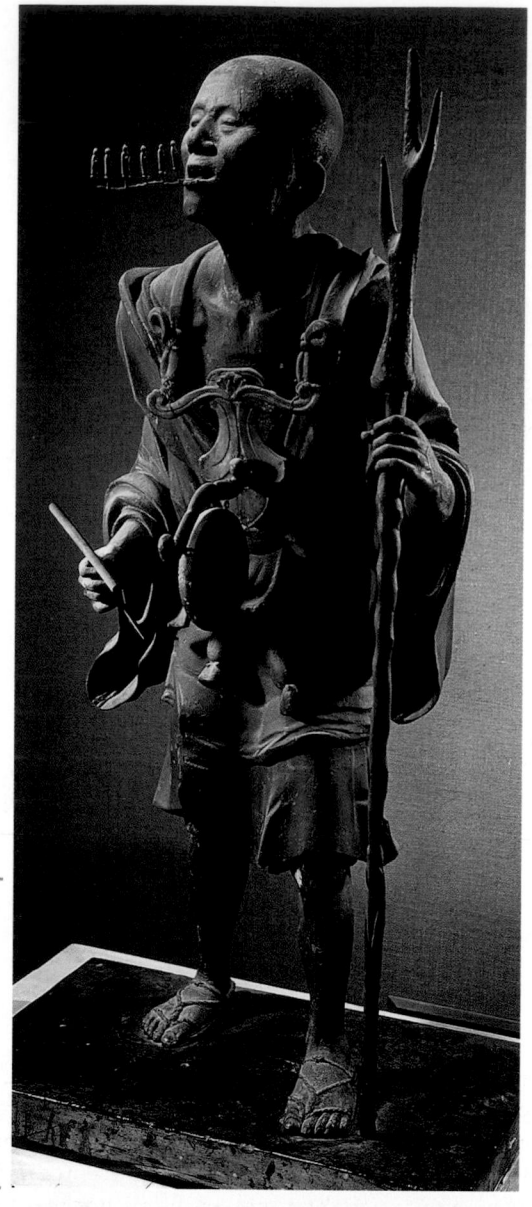

< 16.40 Kosho, portrait statue of the priest Kuya preaching, Roku-haramitsuji, Kyoto, Japan (Kamakura period, early 13th century). Painted wood with inlaid eyes, approximately 46' high.

1 ft.

about the Buddha Amida (Fig. 16.40). From the stance of the figure and the keen observation of every drapery fold to the crystal used to create the illusion of actual eyes, this sculptor's effort to reproduce reality knew no bounds. The artist even went as far as to attempt to render speech: six tiny images of the Buddha come forth from the sage's mouth, representing the syllables of a prayer that repeats the name of the Buddha. A remarkable balance between the earthly and the spiritual is achieved through the use of extreme realism to portray a religious subject.

Africa

Sub-Saharan Africa consists of the broad expanse of the land south of the Sahara Desert. The religion in sub-Saharan Africa is now primarily Christian, but Native African religions generally involve ancestor worship, deification of rulers, respect for nature—the environment and living creatures—and worship of nature deities. **Animism**, the belief that the world is governed by the workings of nature, underscores most traditional African religion, and ritual and ceremony often pertain to managing illness, warding off death, and controlling natural disasters. A tradition of ancestor worship placed emphasis on the family and, more broadly, on the village community. Three major kingdoms flourished in the Africa of the Middle Ages: Ghana, Bening, and Zimbabwe.

Homer, author of the *Iliad* and the *Odyssey*, referred to ancient Mycenae as "rich in gold." If he had known of the kingdom of Ghana, he probably would have described it in the same way. Largely because of its gold, Ghana grew wealthy, and by around 1000 CE it was likely the largest

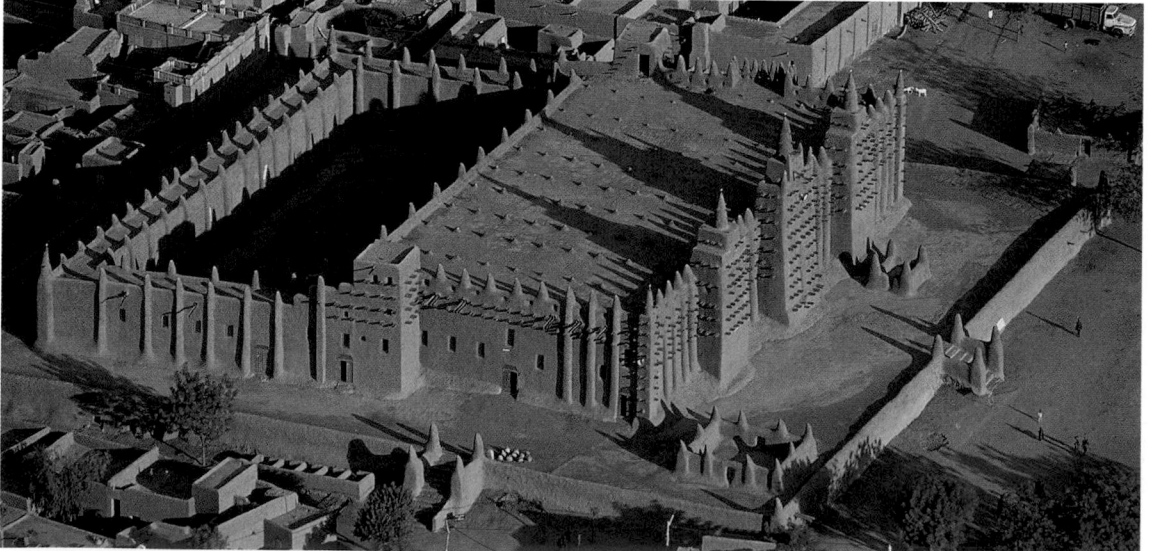

< 16.41 The Great Mosque, Djenné, Mali (13th century). Razed in 1830; rebuilt 1906–1907.

producer of gold in the world. An Arab visitor in 1065 CE numbered the Ghanaian army at 200,000 men. Even so, Ghana's army was defeated by Muslim Berbers before the eleventh century was out, and by 1300 the great kingdom was lost to history.

In the eighth century, North African traders had brought Islam to Ghana, which, due to its prosperity, became a vibrant center of Islamic culture. The plan of the Great Mosque at Djenné in present-day Mali (Fig. 16.41)—which was part of the Ghanaian Empire—like those of all early mosques is based on the model of Muhammad's home in Medina. It has a walled courtyard in front of a wall that faces Mecca. Unlike the stone mosques of the Middle East, however, the mosque at Djenné is built of sun-dried bricks and puddled clay. Wooden poles jutting through the clay support workers who replaster the structure yearly to prevent erosion of the clay. They also provide exterior ornamentation, an aspect of the highly decorative aesthetic of Islamic art and architecture.

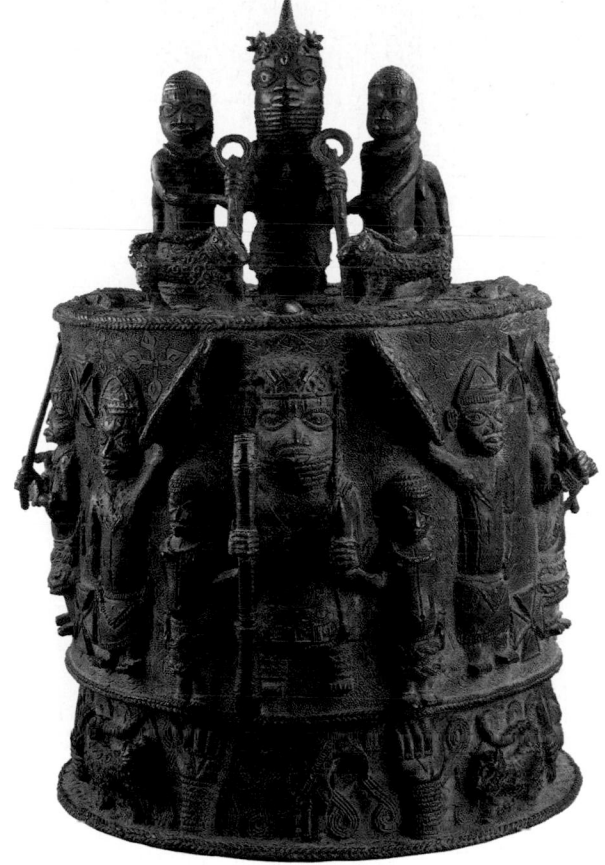

∧ **16.43 Altar to the Hand and Arm, Kingdom of Benin (Nigeria)** (c. 1735–1750). Bronze, 1'5½" high. British Museum, London, England.

> **16.42 Portrait of the Queen Mother Idia** (16th century). From the palace complex at Benin, Kingdom of Benin (Nigeria). Brass, 20½" high. National Museum, Lagos, Nigeria.

1 in.

During Ghana's waning years, the kingdom of Benin was rising within modern-day Nigeria. Benin reached the height of its power and culture between the fourteenth and sixteenth centuries. The eventual demise of the kingdom, in the nineteenth century, was brought about by the massive deportation of its population by Arab and European slave traders.

The kingdom had been ruled by a royal line of kings who had the title of *oba*. The oba's palace was decorated with bronze plaques that portrayed military victories and life at the court. One sculpture in the complex was a portrait of a royal woman with tribal markings and a conical headdress, the Queen Mother Idia (Fig. 16.42). Her son, the oba Esigie, attributed his military successes to what he believed were her magical powers. The portrait adorned one of the sacred altars in Idia's palace. The Benin bronze shown in Figure 16.43 is a royal shrine. The oba is shown two times, dominating accompanying attendants, indicating the importance of the sacred king in Benin life. On this shrine the oba would have offered sacrifices for favors from the gods. On the lid of the shrine, two leopards crouch meekly at the oba's feet, acknowledging the oba's power.

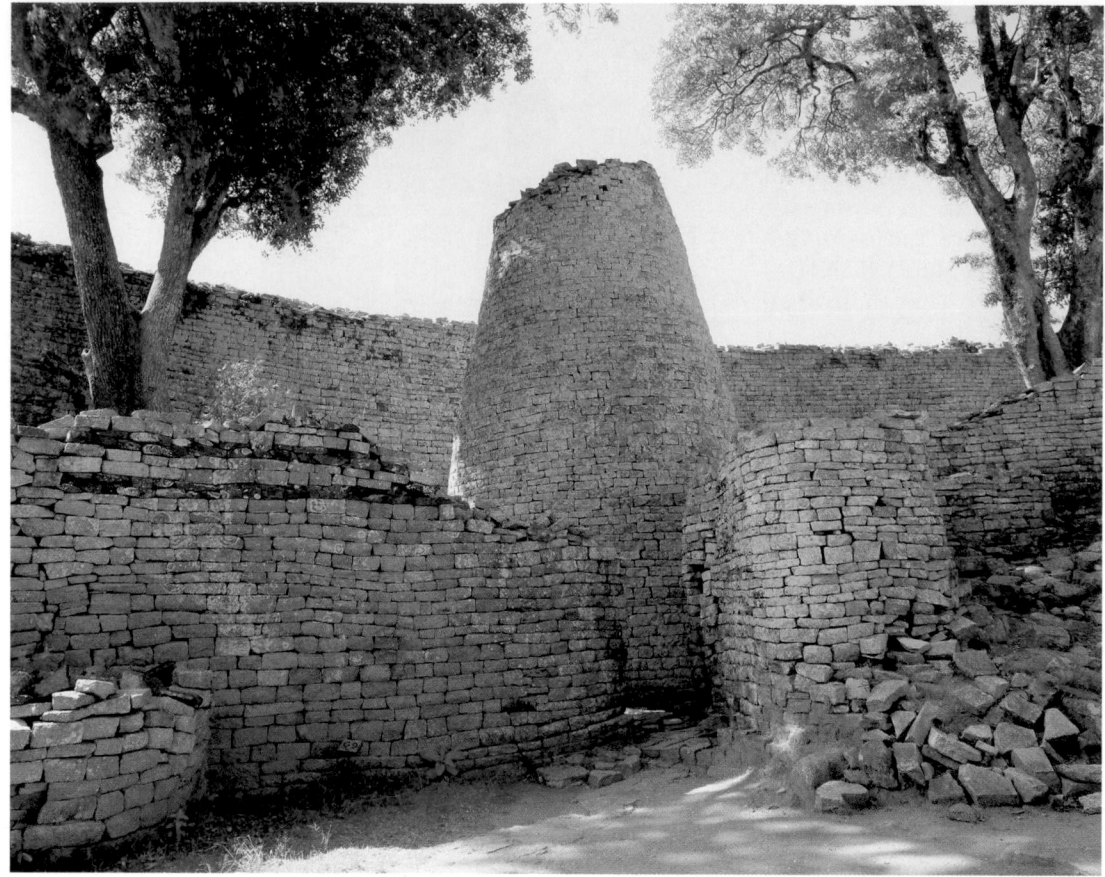

< 16.44 The ancient walls and one of the conical towers showing the inner passage of the Great Enclosure at Great Zimbabwe, Zimbabwe (14th century).

The kingdom of Zimbabwe arose in the south of Africa, with the region first settled in the Stone Age. Around 1300 CE, the rulers erected massive stone buildings surrounded by great walls. One such compound is the Great Zimbabwe (Fig. 16.44). Archaeologists have discovered beads and pottery from the Near and Middle East in the ruins, from even as distant as China. It seems clear that the complex supported a trading empire.

The main building was likely a royal residence. Other structures housed a ceremonial court and the larger ruling class. Archaeologists uncovered a stone carving of an eagle in one of the buildings (Fig. 16.45). The inhabitants of the kingdom may have been the ancestors of the Shona people, who believed that ancestral spirits take the form of birds, especially eagles. The soapstone carving may then represent an ancestral spirit, whose flight transports messages between the human and divine worlds.

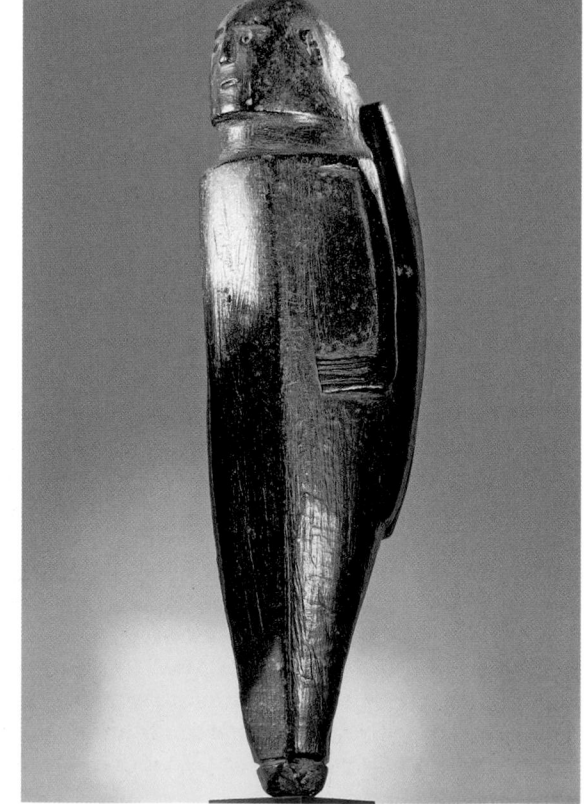

> 16.45 Sculpture of an eagle, Great Zimbabwe, Zimbabwe (c. 1200–1400). Steatite (soapstone) carving. Private collection, New York, New York.

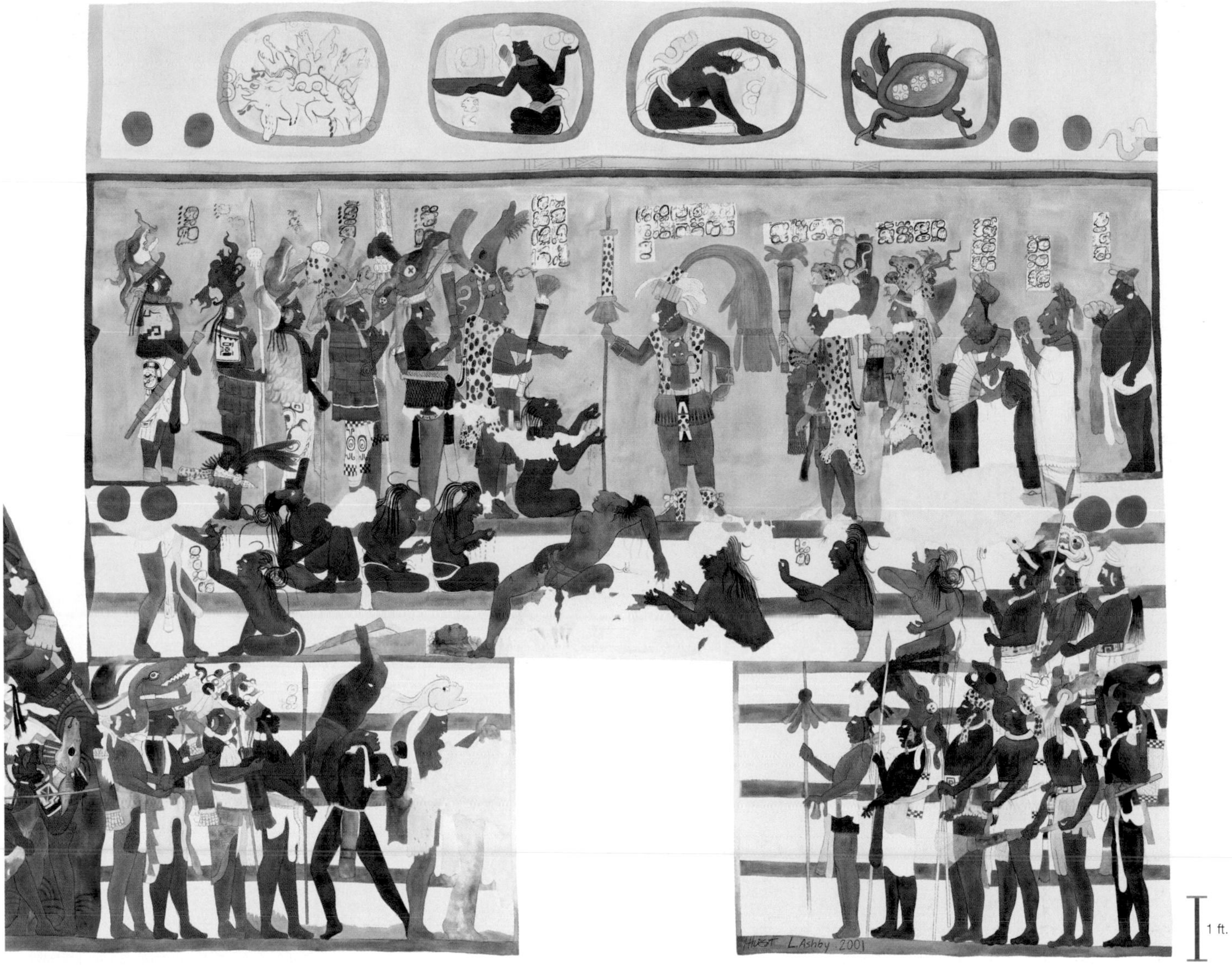

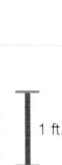

∧ 16.46 **Presentation of captives to Lord Chan Muwan, Room 2 of Structure 1, Bonampak, Mexico, Maya** (c. 790). Mural. 17' × 15'; copy by Heather Hurst at one-half scale. Yale Peabody Museum of Natural History, New Haven, Connecticut.

The Americas

At roughly the same time that the Great Mosque at Damascus and the Mosque at Córdoba were constructed, the Mayan civilization in the Yucatán region of Mexico and the highlands of Guatemala was reaching its glorious peak. The Mayans built many huge limestone structures featuring corbelled vaults, relief carvings depicting rulers and deities, and vividly colored murals commemorating events and illustrating rituals—including human sacrifice. Figure 16.46 is a copy of a badly damaged mural from Bonampak in southeastern Mexico, portraying the offering of captives to a Mayan lord for sacrifice to the gods. Lord Chan Muwan stands in the center of the top of a multistepped platform (likely a pyramid), resplendent

in a feather headdress and jaguar-pelt vest. He holds a ceremonial staff and looks downward at a prisoner who seems to be pleading for his life. Strewn on the stairs directly beneath him are men who have already been slain while others cower in anticipation of their deaths. A strict social hierarchy is portrayed, with nobility on the upper tier, clad in splendid costume, and those of apparently inferior status below. The eye is drawn upward to the center of the composition by the pyramidal shape formed by the scattered prisoners; the figures face the center of the composition, providing symmetry, and the rhythm of the steps provides unity. The subject of human sacrifice is repugnant, yet the composition of the mural shows a classical refinement.

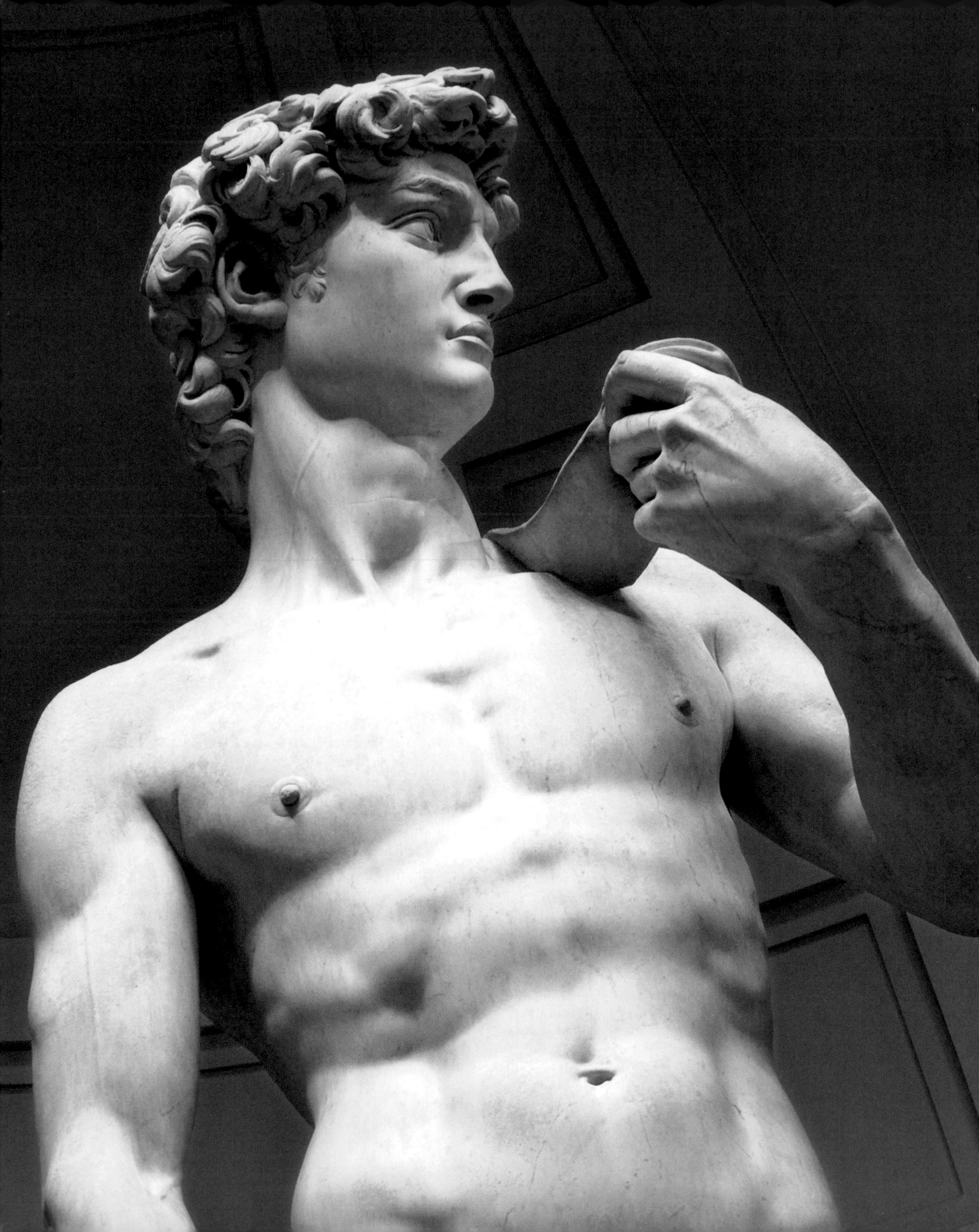

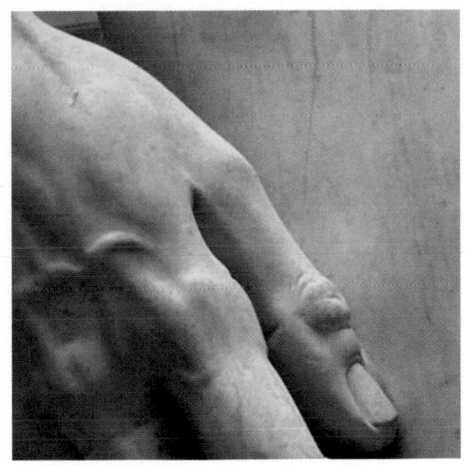

17

THE RENAISSANCE

The fundamental principle will be that all steps of learning should be sought from Nature; the means of perfecting our art will be found in diligence, study, and application.

—LEON BATTISTA ALBERTI

WHILE COLUMBUS brought his ships to the New World in 1492, a 17-year-old Michelangelo Buonarroti was perfecting his skill at rendering human features from blocks of marble. In 1564, the year that Shakespeare was born, Michelangelo died. These are two of the marker dates of the **Renaissance**. *Renaissance* is a French word meaning "rebirth," and the Renaissance in Europe was a period of significant historical, social, and economic events. The old feudal system that had organized Europe during the Middle Ages fell to a system of government based on independent city-states with powerful kings and princes at their helms. The economic face of Europe changed, aided by an expansion of trade and commerce with Eastern countries. The cultural base of Europe shifted from Gothic France to Italy. A plague wiped out the populations of entire cities in Europe and Asia. Speculation on the world beyond, which had so preoccupied the medieval mind, was counterbalanced by a scientific observation of the world at hand. Although Copernicus proclaimed that the sun, and not Earth, was at the center of the solar system, humanity, and not heaven, became the center of all things.

◄ MICHELANGELO, *David* (1501–1504). Detail. Marble, 13½' high. Galleria dell'Accademia, Florence.

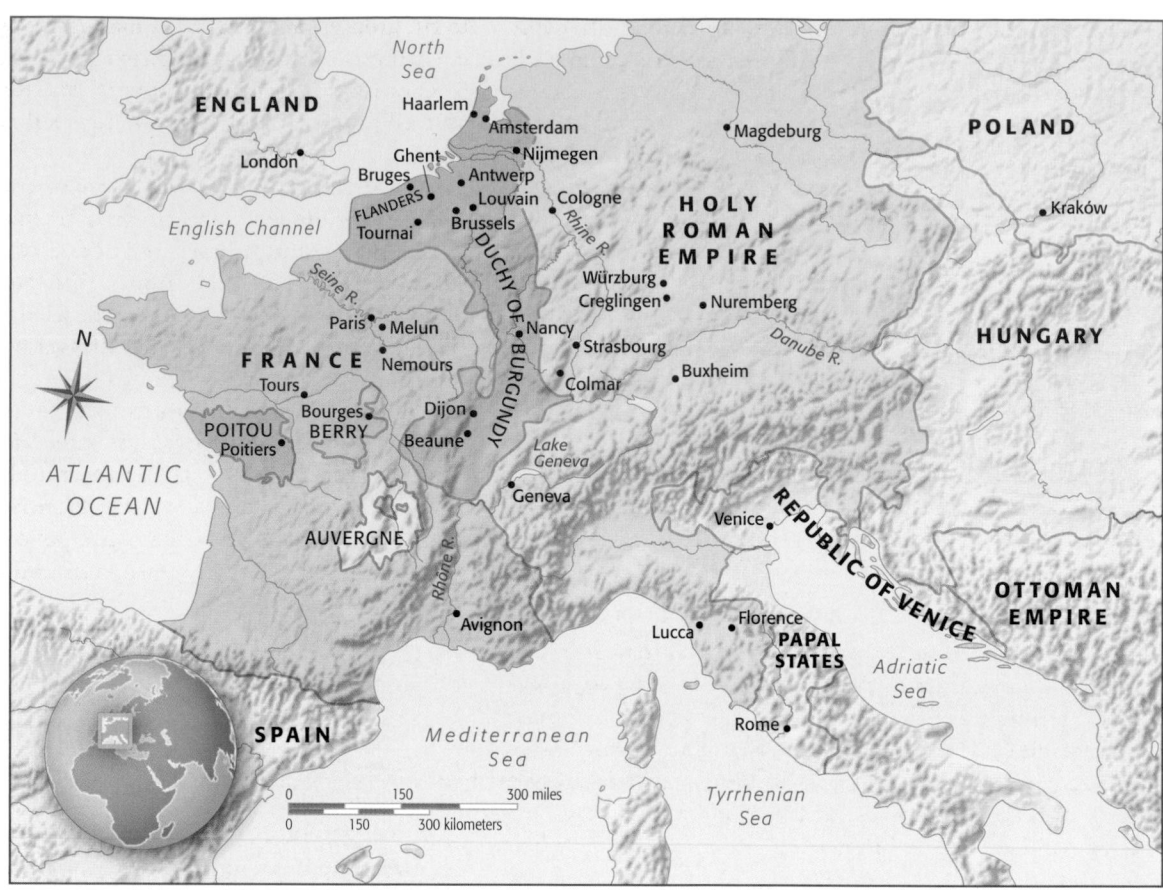

> MAP 17.1 Europe in 1477.

THE RENAISSANCE PERIOD

The Renaissance spans roughly the fourteenth through the sixteenth centuries and is seen by some as the beginning of modern history. During this period, particularly in Italy, we witness a revival of Classical themes in art and literature, a return to the realistic depiction of nature through keen observation, and the revitalization of the Greek philosophy of humanism, in which human dignity, ideas, and capabilities are of central importance.

THE RENAISSANCE

1280	1486	1501	1520	1600
Cimabue paints *Madonna Enthroned* c. 1280–1290	Botticelli paints *The Birth of Venus* c. 1486	Reign of Pope Julius II	Pontormo paints *Entombment* 1525–1528	
Giotto paints his *Madonna Enthroned* c. 1310	Columbus sails to find a western route to India and discovers the Americas 1492	Michelangelo sculpts *David* c. 1501–1504	Titian paints *Venus of Urbino* 1538	
Competition to cast bronzes for Baptistery of Florence 1401–1402	Leonardo da Vinci paints *The Last Supper* 1495–1498	Leonardo paints *Mona Lisa* c. 1503–1505	Catholic Church holds Council of Trent to reform Catholic Church 1545–1563	
Limbourg Brothers create *Les Très Riches Heures du Duc de Berry* 1416		Michelangelo paints ceiling of Sistine Chapel 1508–1512	Anguissola paints *A Game of Chess* 1555	
Massacio paints *Holy Trinity* c. 1428		Raphael paints *The School of Athens* 1510–1511	El Greco paints *The Burial of Count Orgaz* 1586	
Van Eyck paints *Giovanni Arnolfini and His Bride* 1434		Reformation begins in Germany	Tintoretto paints his *The Last Supper* 1592–1594	

Changes, artistic and otherwise, took root all over Europe, but Italy and Flanders (present-day Belgium and the Netherlands) developed into world-class economic and cultural centers in the fifteenth century (see Map 17.1). Given its Classical roots, Italy never quite succumbed to Gothicism and readily introduced elements of Greek and Roman art into its art and architecture. But Flanders was steeped in the medieval tradition of northern Europe and continued to concern itself with the spiritualism of the Gothic era, enriching it with a supreme realism. (It is worth noting that because the word *renaissance* generally refers to the artistic and cultural revival of Classical sources, some art historians no longer use it to describe northern art of this period.)

The difference in attitudes was summed up during the later Renaissance years by one of Italy's great artists, Michelangelo Buonarroti, not entirely without prejudice:

> Flemish painting will, generally speaking, please the devout better than any painting in Italy, which will never cause him to shed a tear, whereas that of Flanders will cause him to shed many. . . . In Flanders they paint with a view to external exactness or such things as may cheer you and of which you cannot speak ill, as for example saints and prophets. They paint stuffs and masonry, the green grass of the fields, the shadows of trees, and rivers and bridges.[1]

Thus, the subject matter of northern artists remained more consistently religious, although their manner of representation was that of an exact, *trompe l'oeil* rendition of things of this world. They used the "trick-the-eye" technique to portray mystical religious phenomena in a realistic manner. The exactness of representation of which Michelangelo spoke originated in **manuscript illumination**, where complicated imagery was reduced to a minute scale. Because this imagery illustrated texts, it was often laden with symbolic meaning. Symbolism was carried into **panel paintings**, where it was fused with a keen observation of nature.

FIFTEENTH-CENTURY NORTHERN PAINTING

Flemish Painting: From Page to Panel

A certain degree of naturalism appeared in the work of the northern book illustrator during the Gothic period. The manuscript illuminator *illuminated* literary passages with visual imagery. As the art of manuscript illumination progressed, these thumbnail sketches were enlarged

to fill greater portions of the manuscript page, eventually covering it entirely. As the text pages became less able to contain this imagery, the northern Renaissance artist shifted to painting in tempera on wood panels.

THE LIMBOURG BROTHERS   One of the most dazzling texts available to illustrate this transfer from minute to more substantial imagery is *Les Très Riches Heures du Duc de Berry*, a Book of Hours illustrated by the Limbourg brothers (born after 1385, died by 1416) during the opening decades of the fifteenth century. Books of Hours were used by nobility as prayer books and included psalms and litanies to a variety of saints. As did most Books of Hours, *Les Très Riches Heures* contained calendar pages that illustrated domestic tasks and social events of the twelve months of the year. In "May" (Fig. 17.1), one of the calendar pages, we witness a parade of aristocratic gentlemen and ladies who have

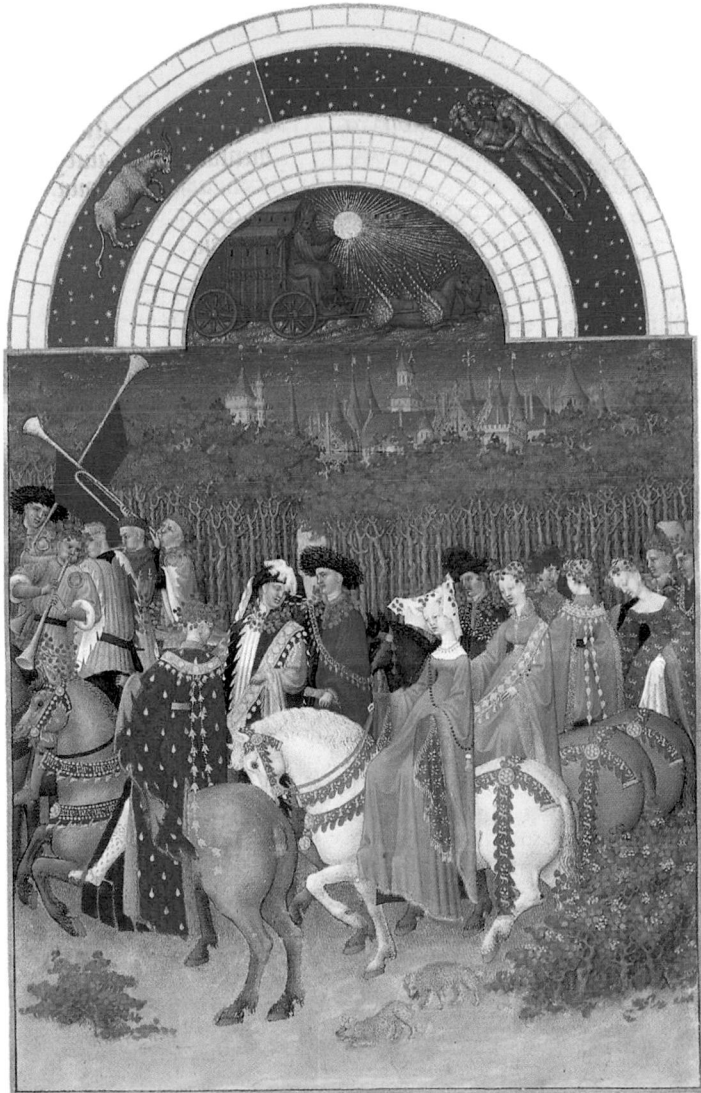

1 in.

⌃ 17.1 LIMBOURG BROTHERS, "May" from *Les Très Riches Heures du Duc de Berry* (1416). Illumination, 8⅞" × 5⅜". Musée Conde, Chantilly, France.

[1] Robert Goldwater and Marco Treves, eds., *Artists on Art* (New York: Pantheon Books, 1972), 68.

> All [Flemish] life was saturated with religion to such an extent that the people were in constant danger of losing sight of the distinction between things spiritual and things temporal.
>
> —JOHAN HUIZINGA

come in their bejeweled costumes of pastel hues to celebrate the first day of May. Complete with glittering regalia and festive song, the entourage romps through a woodland clearing on carousel-like horses. In the background looms a spectacular castle complex, the chateau of Riom.

The calendar pages of *Les Très Riches Heures* are rendered in the **International style**, a manner of painting common throughout Europe during the late fourteenth and early fifteenth centuries. This style is characterized by ornate costumes embellished with gold leaf and by subject matter literally fit for a king, including courtly scenes and splendid processions. The refinement of technique and attention to detail in these calendar pages recall earlier manuscript illumination. These qualities, and a keen observation of the human response to the environment—or in this case the merrymaking—bring to mind Michelangelo's assessment of northern painting as obsessed with representation of the real world through the painstaking rendition of its everyday objects and occurrences.

Although these calendar pages illustrated a holy book, the themes were secular. Fifteenth-century artists tried to reconcile religious subjects with scenes and objects from everyday life, and northern artists accomplished this by using symbolism. Artists would populate ordinary interiors with objects that might bear some spiritual significance. Many, if not most, of the commonplace items might be invested with a special religious meaning. You might ask how you, the casual observer, are supposed to decipher the cryptic meaning lurking behind an ordinary kettle. Chances are that you would be unable to do so without a specialized background. Yet you can enjoy the warm feeling of being invited into someone's home when you look at a northern Renaissance interior and be all the more enriched by the knowledge that there really is something more there than meets the eye.

ROBERT CAMPIN, THE MASTER OF FLÉMALLE Attention to detail and the use of commonplace settings were carried forward in the soberly realistic religious figures painted by Robert Campin, the Master of Flémalle (c. 1378–1444). His *Merode Altarpiece* (Fig. 17.2) is a triptych whose three panels, from left to right, contain the kneeling donors of the altarpiece; an Annunciation scene with the Virgin Mary and the angel Gabriel; and

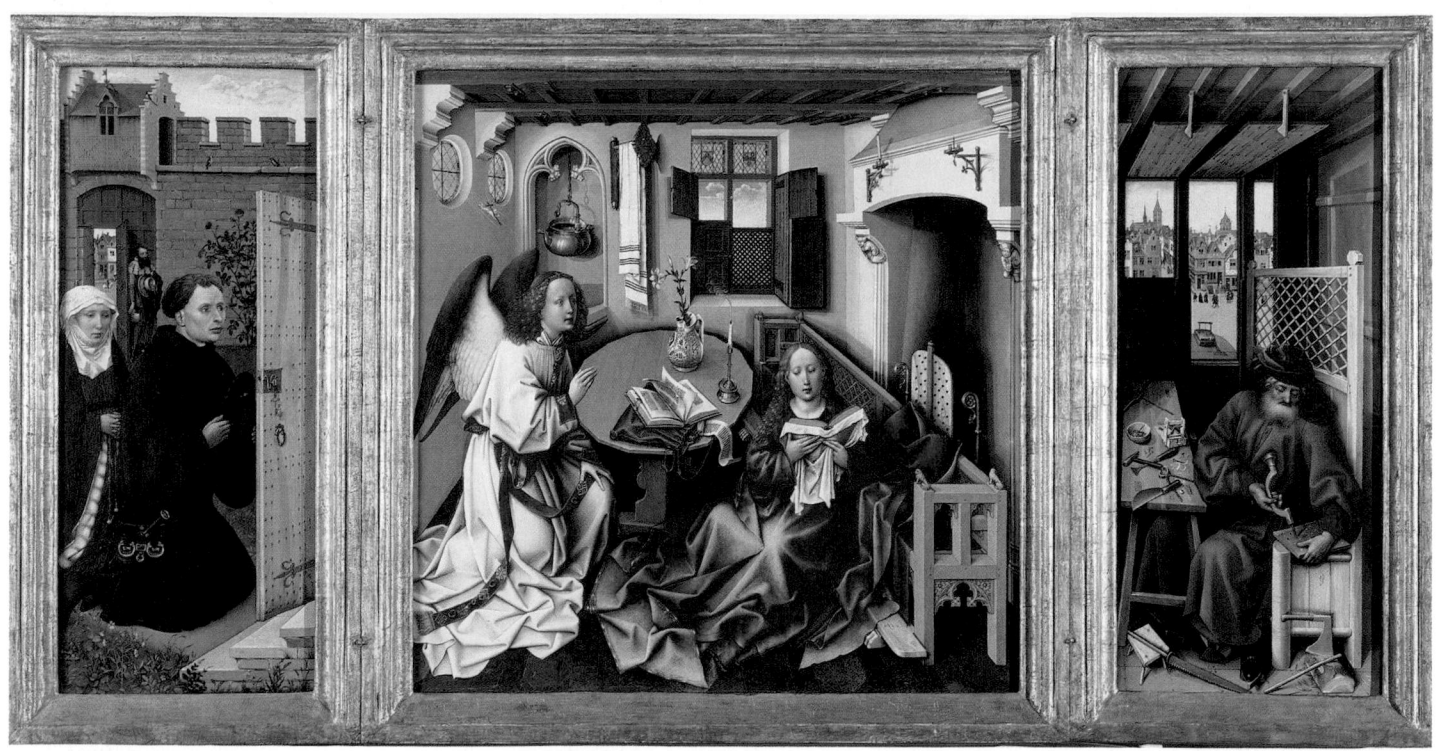

▲ 17.2 ROBERT CAMPIN, *Merode Altarpiece: The Annunciation with Donors and St. Joseph* (c. 1425–1428). Oil on wood. Center: 24¼" × 24⅞"; wings: each 25⅜" × 10⅞". The Metropolitan Museum of Art, The Cloisters, New York.

Joseph, the foster father of Jesus, at work in his carpentry shop. The architectural setting is a typical contemporary Flemish dwelling. The donors kneel by the doorstep in a garden thick with grass and wildflowers, each of which has special symbolic significance regarding the Virgin Mary. Although the door is ajar, it is not clear whether they are witnessing the event inside or whether Campin has used the open door as a compositional device to lead the spectator's eye into the central panel of the triptych.

In any event, we are visually and psychologically coaxed into viewing this most atypical Annunciation. Mary is depicted as a prim and proper middle-class Flemish woman surrounded by the trappings of a typical Flemish household, all rendered in exacting detail. Just as the closed outdoor garden symbolizes the holiness and purity of the Virgin Mary, the items within also possess symbolic meaning. For example, the bronze kettle hanging in the Gothic niche on the back wall symbolizes the Virgin's body—it will be the immaculate container of the redeemer of the Christian world. More obvious symbols of her purity include the spotless room and the vase of lilies on the table. In the upper-left corner of the central panel, a small child can be seen bearing a cross and riding streams of "divine light." The wooden table situated between Mary and Gabriel and the room divider between Mary and Joseph guarantee that the light accomplished the deed. Typically, Joseph is shown as a man too old to have been the biological father of Jesus, although Campin's depiction does not quite follow this tradition. He is gray, but by no means ancient. Jesus's earthly father is busy preparing mousetraps—one on the table and one on the windowsill—commonplace objects that symbolize the belief that Christ was the bait with which Satan would be trapped.

The symbolism in the altarpiece presents a fascinating web for the observer to untangle and interpret. Yet it does not overpower the hard-core realism of the ordinary people and objects. With the exceptions of the slight inconsistency of size and the tilting of planes toward the viewer, Campin offers us a continuous realism that sweeps the three panels. There is no distinction between saintly and common folk; the facial types of the heavenly beings are as individual as the portraits of the donors. Although fifteenth-century viewers would have been aware of the symbolism and the sacredness of the event, they would have also been permitted to become "a part" of the scene, so to speak, and to react to it as if the people in the painting were their peers and just happened to find themselves in extraordinary circumstances.

JAN VAN EYCK We might say that Campin "humanized" his Mary and Joseph in the *Merode Altarpiece*. As religious subjects became more secular in nature and the figures became rendered as "human," an interest in ordinary, secular subject matter sprang up. During the fifteenth century in northern Europe, we have the development of what is known as **genre painting**, painting that depicts ordinary people engaged in run-of-the-mill activities. These paintings make little or no reference to religion; they exist almost as art for art's sake. Yet they are no less devoid of symbolism.

Giovanni Arnolfini and His Bride (Fig. 17.3) was executed by one of the most prominent and significant

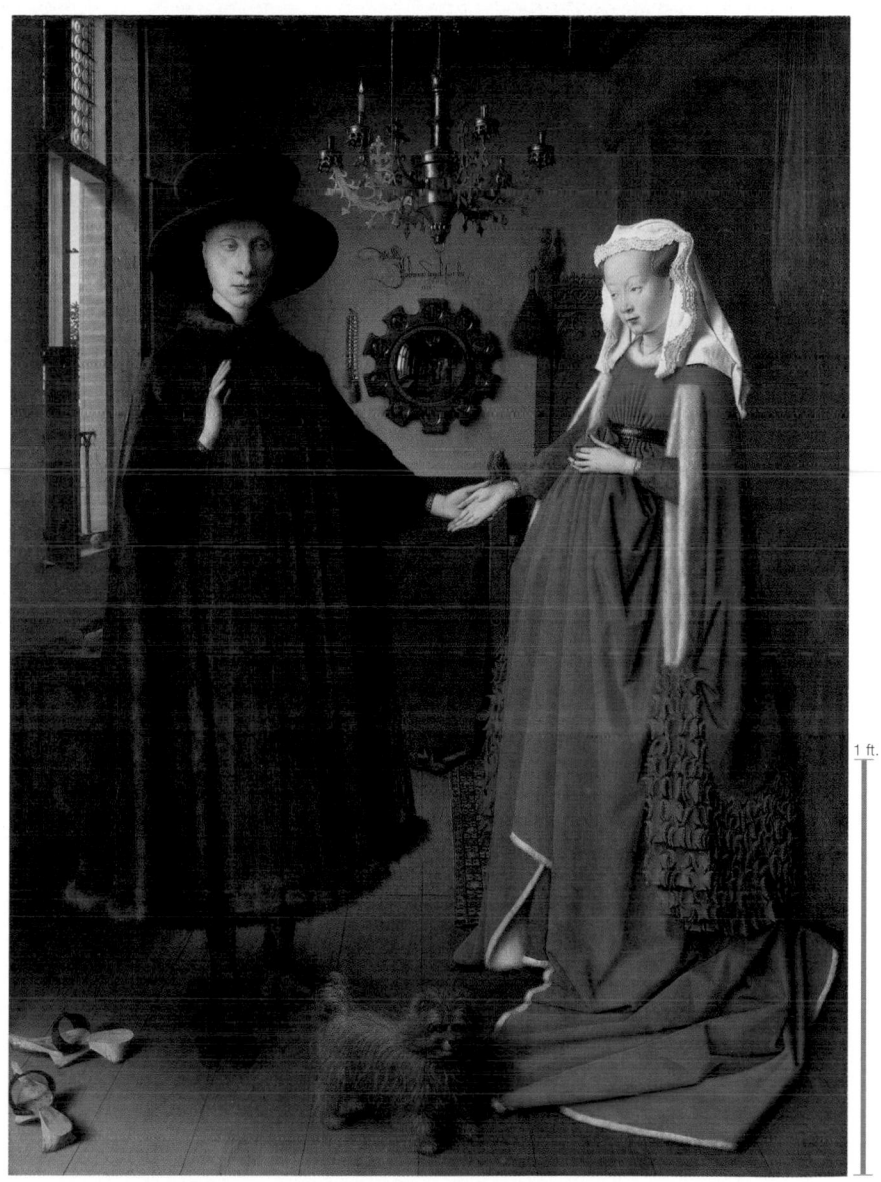

▲ 17.3 **JAN VAN EYCK,** *Giovanni Arnolfini and His Bride* (1434). Oil on wood, 33" × 22½". National Gallery, London, England.

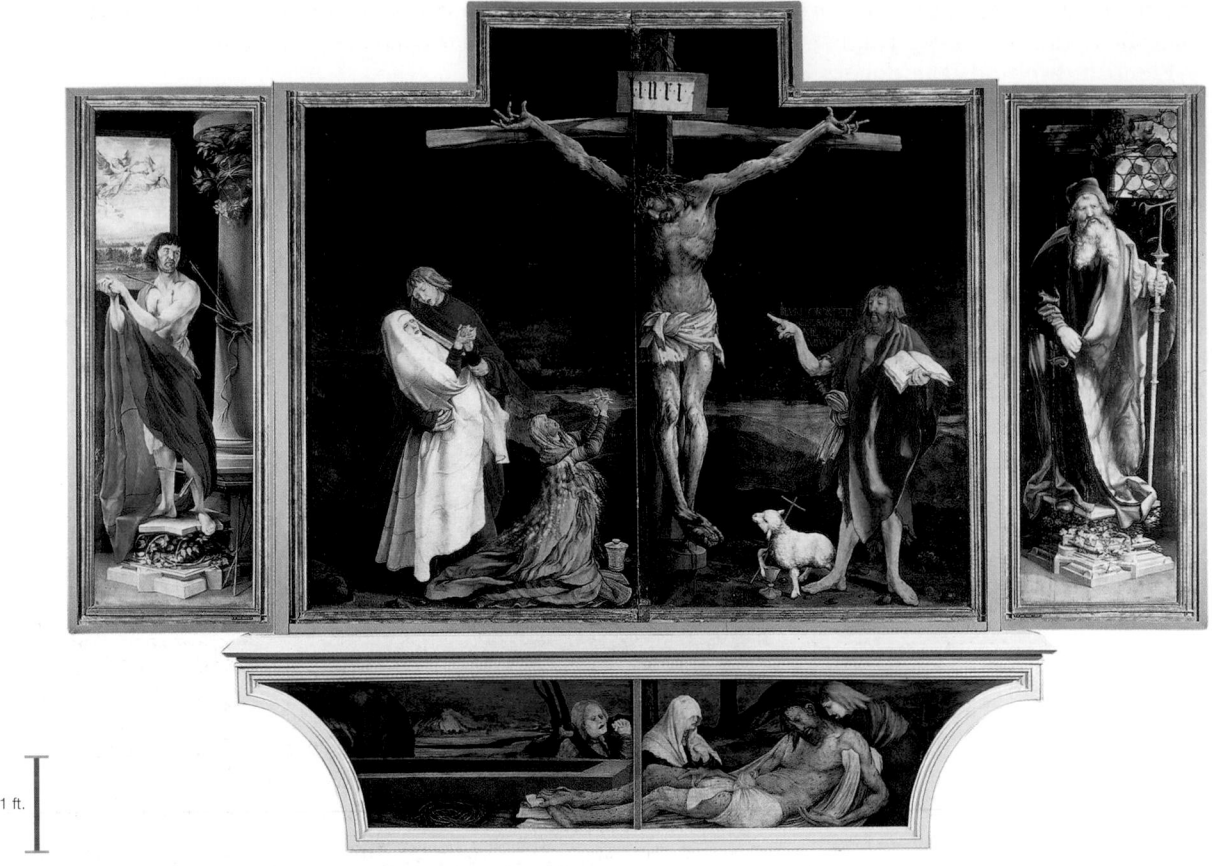

1 ft.

∧ 17.4 **MATTHIAS GRÜNEWALD,** *The Crucifixion,* center panel of *The Isenheim Altarpiece,* exterior (completed 1515). Oil on panel, 8' 10" × 10' 1". Musée d'Unterlinden, Colmar, France.

Flemish painters of the fifteenth century, Jan van Eyck (c. 1395–1441). This unique double portrait was commissioned by an Italian businessman working in Bruges to serve as a kind of marriage contract, or record of the couple's taking of marriage vows in the presence of two witnesses. The significance of such a document—in this case a visual one—is emphasized by the art historian Erwin Panofsky: According to Catholic dogma, the sacrament of matrimony is "immediately accomplished by the mutual consent of the persons to be married when this consent is expressed by words and actions" in the presence of two or three witnesses. Records of the marriage were necessary to avoid lawsuits in which "the validity of the marriage could be neither proved nor disproved for want of reliable witnesses."[2]

Once again we see the northern artist's striking realism and fidelity to detail, offering us exact records of the facial features of the wedding couple. The figures of the two witnesses are reflected in the convex mirror behind the Arnolfinis. Believe it or not, they are Jan van Eyck and his wife, a fact corroborated by the inscription above the mirror: "Jan van Eyck was here." As in most Flemish paintings, the items scattered about are invested with

[2]Erwin Panofsky, "Jan van Eyck's 'Arnolfini' Portrait," *Burlington Magazine* 64 (1934): 117–27.

symbolism relevant to the occasion. The furry dog in the foreground symbolizes fidelity, and the oranges on the windowsill may symbolize victory over death. Giovanni has kicked off his shoes out of respect for the holiness of the ground on which this sacrament takes place. Finally, the finial on the bedpost is an image of St. Margaret, the patroness of childbirth, and around her wooden waist is slung a small whisk broom, a symbol of domesticity. It would seem that Giovanni had his bride's career all mapped out. With Jan van Eyck, Flemish painting reached the height of symbolic realism in both religious and secular subject matter. No one ever quite followed in his footsteps.

German Art

Northern Renaissance painting is not confined to the region of Flanders, and some of the most emotionally striking work of this period was created by German artists. Their work contains less symbolism and less detail than that of Flemish artists, but their message is often more powerful.

MATTHIAS GRÜNEWALD These characteristics of German Renaissance art can clearly be seen in the *Isenheim Altarpiece* (Fig. 17.4) by Matthias Grünewald

(c. 1480–1528), painted more than three-quarters of a century after Jan van Eyck's Arnolfini portrait. The central panel of the German altarpiece is occupied by a tormented representation of the Crucifixion, one of the most dramatic in the history of art. The dead Christ is flanked by his mother, Mary, the apostle John, and Mary Magdalene to the left, and John the Baptist and a sacrificial lamb to the right. These figures exhibit a bodily tension in their arched backs, clenched hands, and rigidly pointing fingers, creating a melodramatic, anxious tone. The crucified Christ is shown with a deadly pallor. His skin appears cancerous, and his chest is sunken with his last breath. His gnarled hands reach painfully upward, stretching for salvation from the blackened sky. We do not find such impassioned portrayals outside Germany during the Renaissance.

ALBRECHT DÜRER We appropriately close our discussion of northern Renaissance art with the Italianate master Albrecht Dürer (1471–1528). His passion for the Classical in art stimulated extensive travel in Italy, where he copied the works of the Italian masters, who were also enthralled with the Classical style. The development of the printing press made it possible for him to disseminate the works of the Italian masters throughout northern Europe.

Dürer's *Adam and Eve* (Fig. 17.5) conveys his admiration for the Classical style. In contrast to other German and Flemish artists who rendered figures, Dürer emphasized the idealized beauty of the human body. His Adam and Eve are not everyday figures of the sort Campin depicted in his Virgin Mary. Instead, the images arise from Greek and Roman prototypes. Adam's young, muscular body could have been drawn from a live model or from Classical statuary. Eve represents a standard of beauty different from that of other northern artists. The familiar slight build and refined facial features have given way to a more substantial and well-rounded

woman. She is reminiscent of a fifth-century BCE Venus in her features and her pose. The symbols associated with the event—the Tree of Knowledge and the Serpent (Satan)—play a secondary role. In *Adam and Eve*, Dürer has chosen to emphasize the profound beauty of the human body. Instead of focusing on the consequences of the event preceding the taking of the fruit as an admonition against sin, we delight in the couple's beauty for its own sake. Indeed, this notion is central to the art of Renaissance Italy.

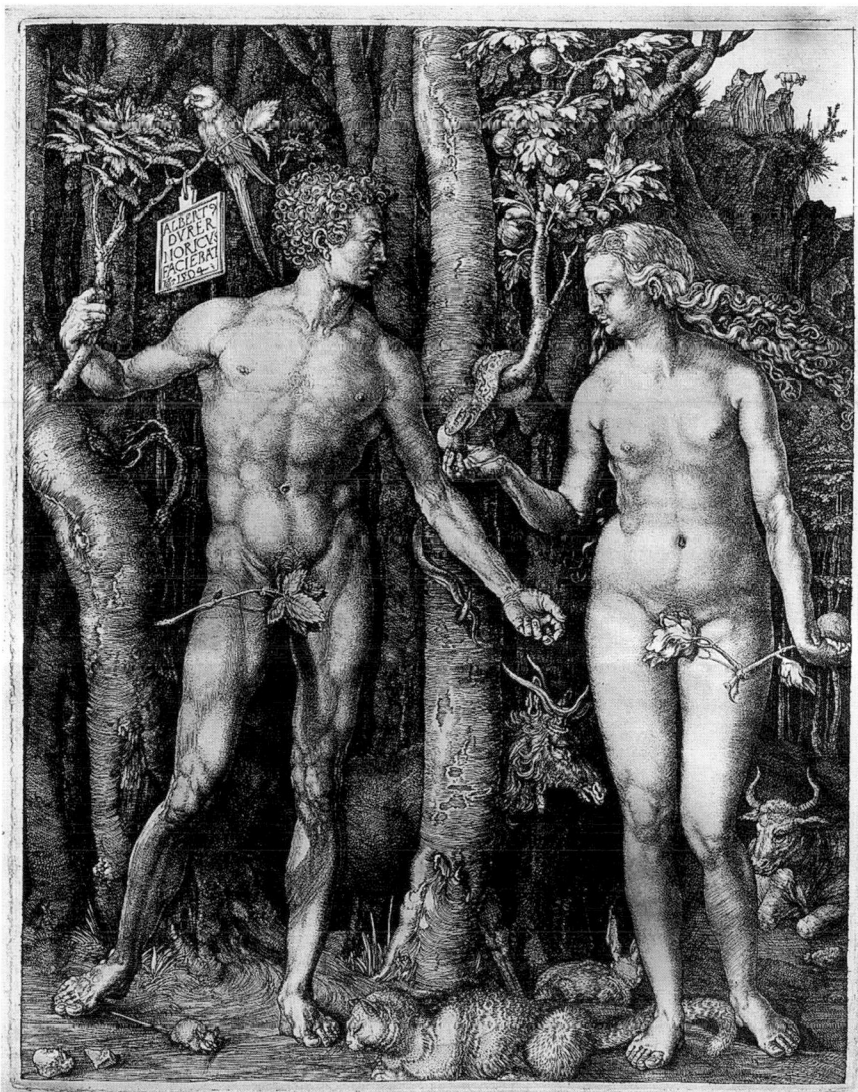

▲ 17.5 **ALBRECHT DÜRER**, *Adam and Eve* (1504). Engraving, 4th state; 9⅞" × 7⅝". The Metropolitan Museum of Art, New York, New York.

THE RENAISSANCE IN ITALY

Early Renaissance

Not only was there a marked difference between northern and Italian Renaissance art, but there were notable differences in the art of various sections of Italy. Florence and Rome witnessed a resurgence of Classicism as Roman ruins were excavated in ancient sites, hillsides, and people's backyards. In Siena, the International style lingered, and in Venice, a Byzantine influence remained strong. There may be several reasons for this diversity, but the most obvious is that of geography. For example, whereas the Roman artist's stylistic roads led to that ancient city, the trade routes in the northeast brought an Eastern influence to works of art and architecture. The Italian Renaissance took root and flourished most successfully in Florence. The development of this city's painting, sculpture, and architecture parallels that of the Renaissance in all of Italy. Throughout the Renaissance, as Florence went, so went the country.

CIMABUE AND GIOTTO Some of the earliest changes from a medieval to a Classical style can be perceived in the painting of Florence during the late thirteenth and early fourteenth centuries, the prime exponents being Cimabue and Giotto. So significant were these artists that Dante Alighieri, the fourteenth-century poet, mentioned both of them in his *Purgatory* of *The Divine Comedy*:

> O gifted men, vainglorious for first place,
> how short a time the laurel crown stays green
> unless the age that follows lacks all grace!
> Once Cimabue thought to hold the field
> in painting, and now Giotto has the cry
> so that the other's fame, grown dim, must yield.[3]

Who were these artists? Apparently they were rivals, although Cimabue (c. 1240–c. 1302) was older than Giotto (c. 1276–c. 1337) and probably had a formative influence on the latter, who would ultimately steal the limelight.

The similarities and differences between the works of Cimabue and Giotto can be seen in two tempera paintings on wood panels depicting the Madonna and Child enthroned. A curious combination of Late Gothic and Early Renaissance styles betrays Cimabue's composition

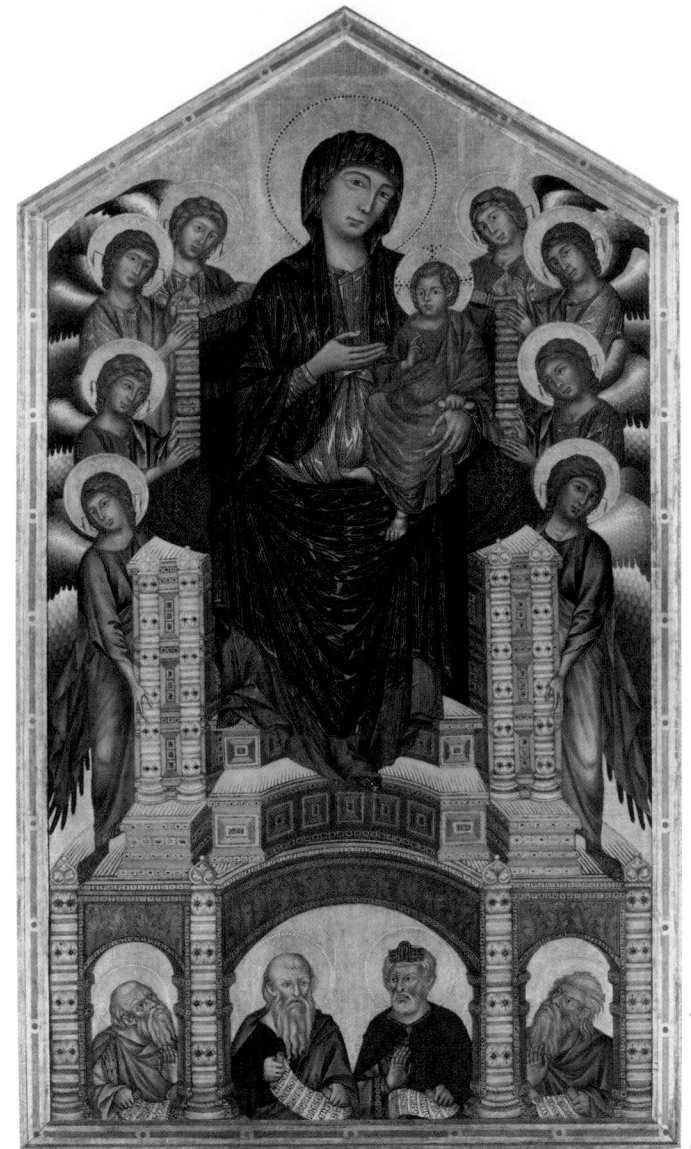

▲ 17.6 CIMABUE, *Madonna Enthroned* (c. 1280–1290). Tempera on wood panel, 12' 7" × 7' 4". Uffizi Gallery, Florence, Italy.

1 ft.

as a transitional work (Fig. 17.6). The massive throne of the Madonna is Roman in inspiration, with column and arch forms embellished with **intarsia**. The Madonna has a corporeal presence that sets her apart from "floating" medieval figures, but the effect is compromised by the unsureness with which she is placed on the throne. She does not sit solidly; her limbs are not firmly planted. Rather, the legs resemble the hinged appendages of Romanesque figures. This characteristic placement of the knees causes the drapery to fall in predictable folds—concentric arcs reminiscent of a more stylized technique. The angels supporting the throne rise parallel to it, their glances forming an abstract zigzag pattern. The resultant

---

[3] From *The Divine Comedy* by Dante Alighieri, trans. John Ciardi. Copyright 1954, 1957, 1959, 1960, 1961, 1965, 1967, 1970 by the Ciardi Family Publishing Trust. Used by permission of W.W. Norton & Company, Inc.

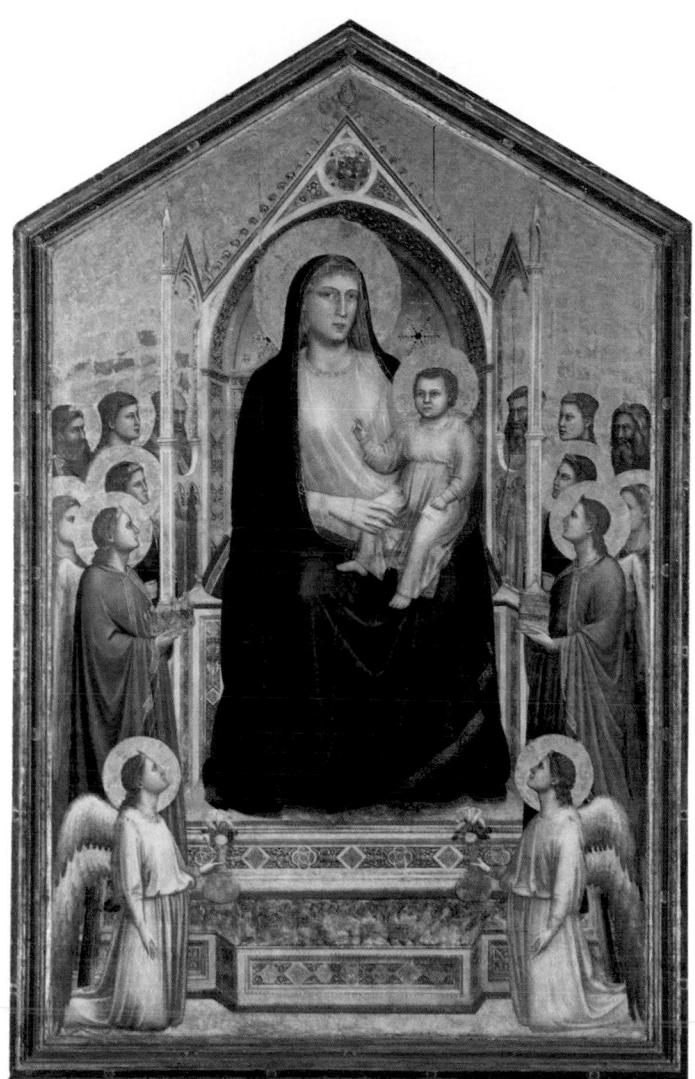

▲ **17.7** GIOTTO, *Madonna Enthroned* (c. 1310). Tempera on wood panel.
10'8" × 6'8", Uffizi Gallery, Florence, Italy.

1 ft.

space. They not only have height and width, as do those of Cimabue, but they also have depth and mass. This is particularly noticeable in the treatment of the angels. Their location in space is from front to rear rather than atop one another as in Cimabue's composition. The halos of the foreground angels obscure the faces of the background attendants, because they have mass and occupy space.

The Renaissance Begins, and So Does the Competition

With Cimabue and Giotto, we witness strides toward an art that was very different from that of the Middle Ages. But artists, like all of us, must walk before they can run, and those strides that express such a stylistic advance from the "cutout dolls" of the Ravenna mosaics and the "hinged marionettes" of the Romanesque era will look primitive in another half century. Because the art of Cimabue and Giotto contains vestiges of Gothicism, their style is often termed proto-Renaissance. But at the dawn of the fifteenth century in Florence, the Early Renaissance began—with a competition.

Imagine workshops and artists abuzz with news of one of the hottest projects in memory up for grabs. Think of one of the most prestigious architectural sites in Florence. Savor the possibility of being known as *the* artist who had cast, in gleaming bronze, the massive doors of the Baptistery of Florence. This landmark competition was held in 1401. There were countless entries, but only two panels have come down to us. The artists had been given a scene from the Old Testament to translate into bronze—the sacrifice of Isaac by his father, Abraham. There were specifications, naturally, but the most obvious is the **quatrefoil** format. Within this space, a certain cast of characters was mandated, including Abraham, Isaac, an angel, and two "extras" who appear to have little or nothing to do with the scene. The event takes place out of doors, where God has commanded Abraham to take his only son and sacrifice him. When they arrive on the scene, Abraham, in loyalty to God, turns the blade to Isaac's throat. At this moment, God sends an angel to stop Abraham from completing the deed.

FILIPPO BRUNELLESCHI AND LORENZO GHIBERTI The two extant panels were executed by Filippo Brunelleschi (c. 1377–1446) and Lorenzo Ghiberti (1378–1455). The obligatory characters, bushes, animals, and altar are present in both, but the placement of these elements, the artistic style, and the emotional energy within each work differ considerably. Brunelleschi's

lyrical arabesque, the flickering color patterns of the wings, and the lineup of unobstructed heads recall the Byzantine tradition, particularly the Ravenna mosaics (see **Fig. 16.3**).

Giotto's rendition of the same theme offers some dramatic differences (**Fig. 17.7**). The overall impression of the *Madonna Enthroned* is one of stability and corporeality instead of instability and weightlessness. Giotto's Madonna sits firmly on her throne, the outlines of her body and drapery forming a solid triangular shape. Although the throne is lighter in appearance than Cimabue's Roman throne—and is, in fact, Gothic, with pointed arches—it, too, seems more firmly planted on the earth. Giotto's genius is also evident in his conception of the forms in three-dimensional

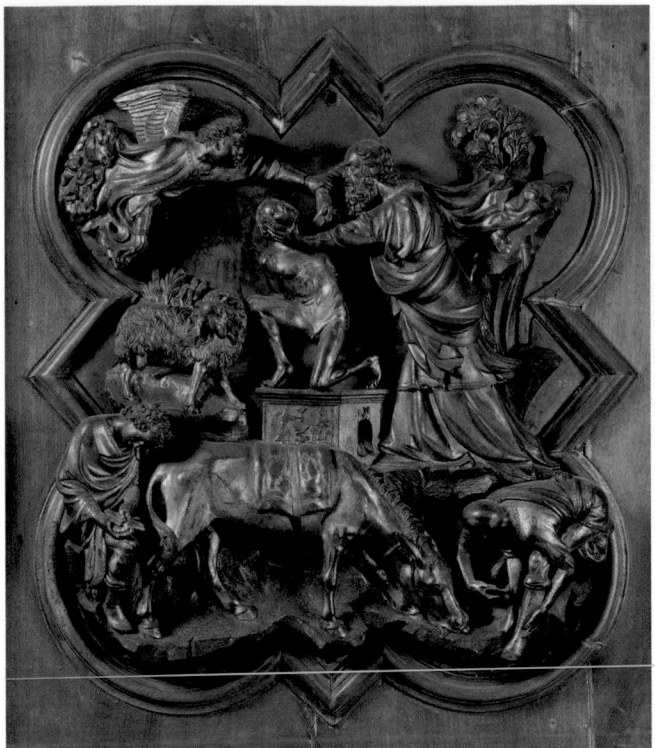

1 in.

▲ **17.8** FILIPPO BRUNELLESCHI, *Sacrifice of Isaac* (1401–1402). Gilt bronze. 21" × 17½", Museo Nazionale del Bargello, Florence, Italy.

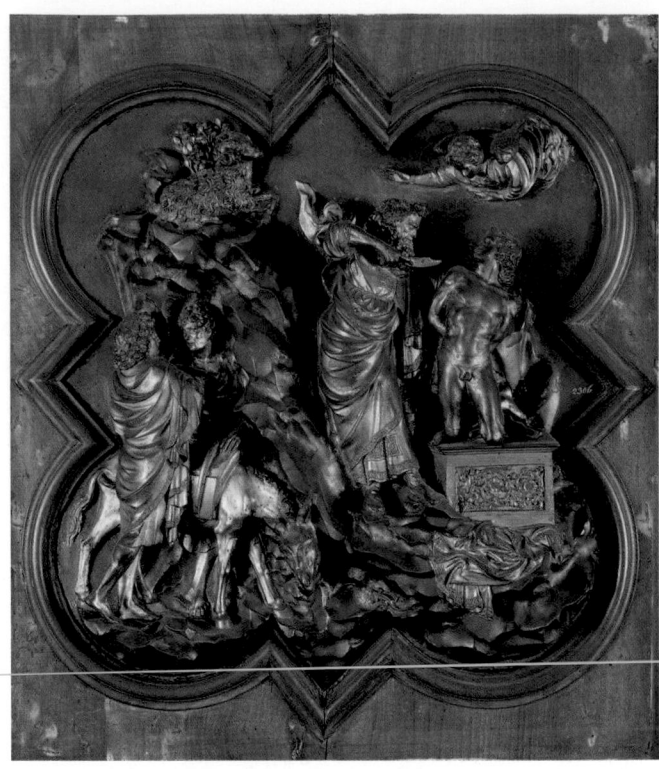

1 in.

▲ **17.9** LORENZO GHIBERTI, *Sacrifice of Isaac* (1401–1402). Gilt bronze. 21" × 17½", Museo Nazionale del Bargello, Florence, Italy.

panel (Fig. 17.8) is divided into sections by strong vertical and horizontal elements, each section filled with objects and figures. In contrast to the rigidity of the format, a ferocious energy bordering on violence pervades the composition. Isaac's neck and body are distorted by his father's grasping fist, and Abraham lunges viciously toward his son's throat with a knife. With similar passion, an angel flies in from the left to grasp Abraham's arm. But this intense drama and seemingly boundless energy are weakened by the introduction of ancillary figures that are given more prominence than the scene requires. The donkey, for example, detracts from Isaac's plight by being placed broadside and practically dead center. Also, one is struck by the staccato movement throughout. Although this choppiness complements the anxiety in the work, it compromises the successful flow of space and tires the eye.

In Lorenzo Ghiberti's panel (Fig. 17.9), the space is divided along a diagonal rock formation that separates the main characters from the lesser ones. Space flows along this diagonal, exposing the figural group of Abraham and Isaac and embracing the shepherd boys and their donkey. The boys and donkey are appropriately subordinated to the main characters but not sidestepped stylistically. Abraham's lower body parallels the rock formation and then lunges expressively away from it in a dynamic counterthrust. Isaac, in turn, pulls firmly away from his father's

forward motion. The forms move rhythmically together in a continuous flow of space. Although Ghiberti's emotion is not quite as intense as Brunelleschi's, and his portrayal of the sacrifice is not quite as graphic, the impact of Ghiberti's narrative is as strong.

It is interesting to note the inclusion of Classicizing elements in both panels. Brunelleschi, in one of his peasants, adapted the Classical sculpture of a boy removing a thorn from his foot, and Ghiberti rendered his Isaac in the manner of the fifth-century sculptor. Isaac's torso, in fact, may be the first nude in this style since Classical times.

Oh, yes—Ghiberti won the competition and Brunelleschi went home with his chisel. The latter never devoted himself to sculpture again but went on to become the first great Renaissance architect. Ghiberti was not particularly modest about his triumph:

> To me was conceded the palm of victory by all the experts and by all . . . who had competed with me. To me the honor was conceded universally and with no exception. To all it seemed that I had at that time surpassed the others without exception, as was recognized by a great council and an investigation of learned men . . . highly skilled from the painters and sculptors of gold, silver, and marble.[4]

[4] E. G. Holt, ed., *Literary Sources of Art History* (Princeton, NJ: Princeton University Press, 1947), 87–88.

The works made before [Masaccio's] day can be said to be painted,
while his are living, real, and natural.

—GIORGIO VASARI

DONATELLO If Brunelleschi and Ghiberti were among the last sculptors to harbor vestiges of the International style, Donatello (c. 1386–1466), the Florentine master, was surely among the first to create sculptures that combined Classicism with realism. In his *David* (see Fig. 17.23), the first life-sized nude statue since Classical times, Donatello struck a balance between the two styles by presenting a very real image of an Italian peasant boy in the guise of a Classical nude figure. David, destined to be the second king of Israel, slew the Philistine giant Goliath with a stone and a sling. Even though Donatello was inspired by Classical statuary, notice that he did not choose a Greek youth in his prime as a prototype for his David. Instead, he chose a barely developed adolescent boy, his hair still unclipped and his arms flaccid for lack of manly musculature. After decapitating Goliath, whose head lies at David's feet, his sword rests at his side—almost too heavy for him to handle. Can such a youth have accomplished such a forbidding task? Herein lies the power of Donatello's statement. We are amazed, from the appearance of this young boy, that he could have done such a deed, much as David seems incredulous as he glances down toward his body. What David lacks in stature he has made up in intellect, faith, and courage. His fate was in his own hands—one of the ideals of the Renaissance man.

MASACCIO The Early Renaissance painters shared most of the stylistic concerns of the sculptors. However, included in their attempts at realism was the added difficulty of projecting a naturalistic sense of three-dimensional space on a two-dimensional surface. In addition to copying from nature and Classical models, these painters developed rules of perspective to depict images in the round on flat walls, panels, and canvases. One of the pioneers in developing systematic laws of one-point linear perspective was Brunelleschi, of Baptistery doors near-fame.

Masaccio's *Holy Trinity* (Fig. 17.10) uses these laws of perspective. In this chapel fresco, Masaccio (1401–1428) creates the illusion of an extension of the architectural space of the church by painting a barrel-vaulted "chapel"

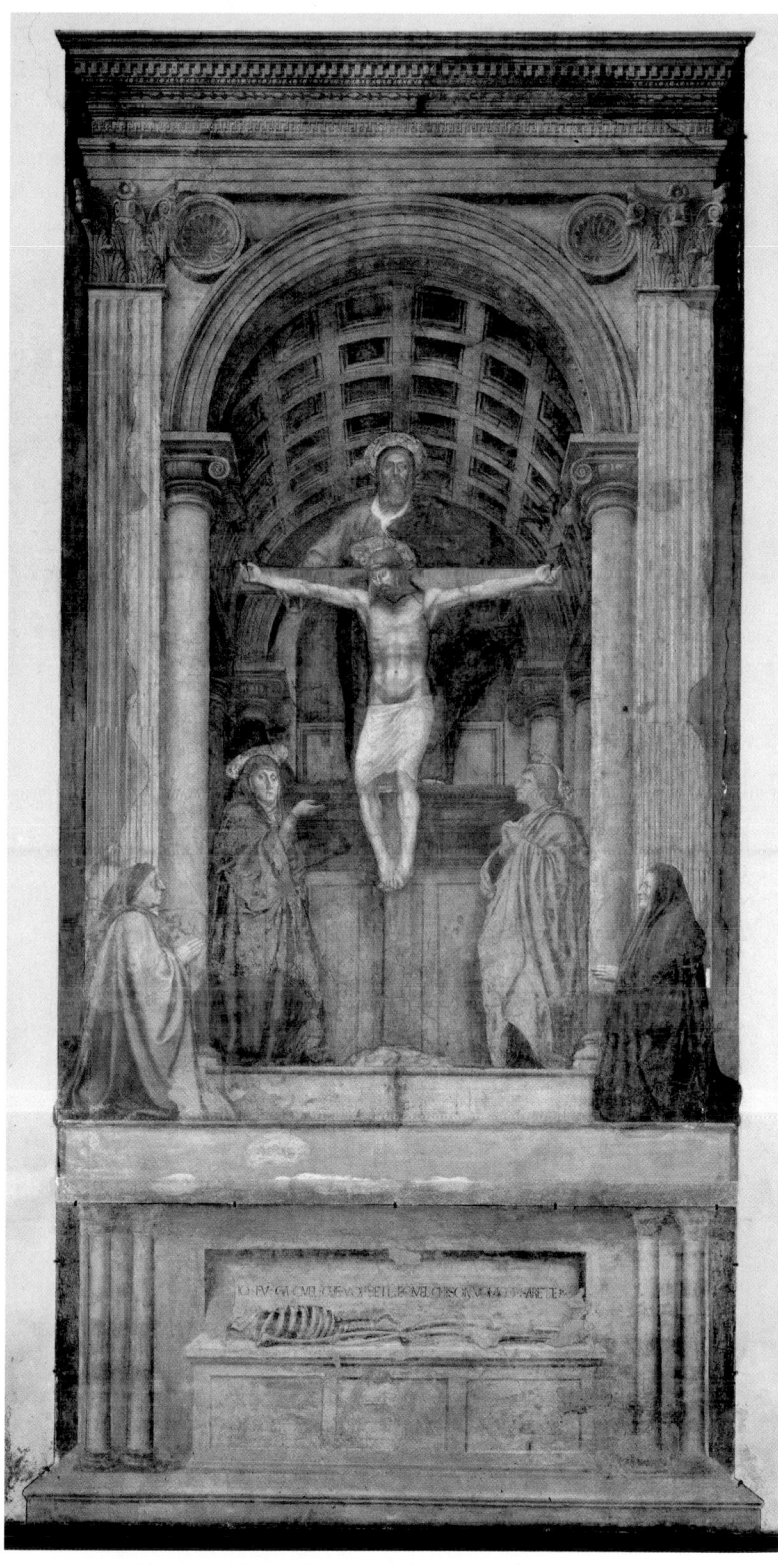

1 ft.

▲ 17.10 **MASACCIO**, *Holy Trinity*, Santa Maria Novella, Florence, Italy (c. 1428). Fresco, 21' × 10'5".

housing a variety of holy and common figures. God the Father supports the cross that bears his crucified son while the Virgin Mary and the apostle John attend. Outside the columns and pilasters of the realistic, Roman-inspired chapel kneel the donors, who are invited to observe the scene. Aside from the *trompe l'oeil* rendition of the architecture, the realism in the fresco is enhanced by the donors, who are given importance equal to that of the "principal" characters, similar to Campin's treatment of the donors in the *Merode Altarpiece* (Fig. 17.2). The architecture appears to extend our physical space, and the donors appear as extensions of ourselves.

FILIPPO BRUNELLESCHI   The revival of Classicism was even more marked in the architecture of the Renaissance. Some twenty years after Brunelleschi's unsuccessful bid for the Baptistery doors project in Florence, he was commissioned to cover the crossing square of the cathedral of Florence with a dome. Interestingly, Ghiberti worked with him at the outset but soon bowed out, and Brunelleschi was left to complete the work alone. It was quite an engineering feat, involving a double-shell dome constructed around twenty-four ribs (see Fig. 16.18A). Eight of these ribs rise upward to a crowning lantern on the exterior of the dome. You might wonder why Brunelleschi, whose architectural models were essentially Classical, would have constructed a somewhat pointed dome reminiscent of the Middle Ages. The fact is that the architect might have preferred a more rounded or hemispherical structure, but the engineering problem required an ogival, or pointed, section, which is inherently more stable. The dome was a compromise between a somewhat Classical style and traditional Gothic building principles.

Renaissance Art at Midcentury and Beyond

ANDREA DEL VERROCCHIO   As we progress into the middle of the fifteenth century, the most important and innovative sculptor is Andrea del Verrocchio (1435–1488). An extremely versatile artist who was trained as a goldsmith, Verrocchio ran an active shop that attracted many young artists, including Leonardo da Vinci. We see in Ver-

rocchio's bronze *David* (see Fig. 17.21), commissioned by the Medici family, a strong contrast to Donatello's handling of the same subject. The Medicis also owned the Donatello *David*, and Verrocchio probably wanted to outshine his predecessor. Although both artists chose to represent David as an adolescent, Verrocchio's hero appears somewhat older and exudes pride and self-confidence rather than a dreamy gaze of disbelief. Whereas Donatello reconciled realistic elements with an almost idealized, Classically inspired torso, Verrocchio's goal was supreme realism in minute details, including orientalizing motifs on the boy's doublet that would have made him look like a Middle Easterner. The sculptures differ considerably also in terms of technique. Donatello's *David* is essentially a closed-form sculpture with objects and limbs centered around an **S-curve** stance; Verrocchio's sculpture is more open, as is evidenced by the bared sword and elbow jutting away from the central core. Donatello's graceful pose has been replaced, in the Verrocchio, by a jaunty **contrapposto** that enhances David's image of self-confidence.

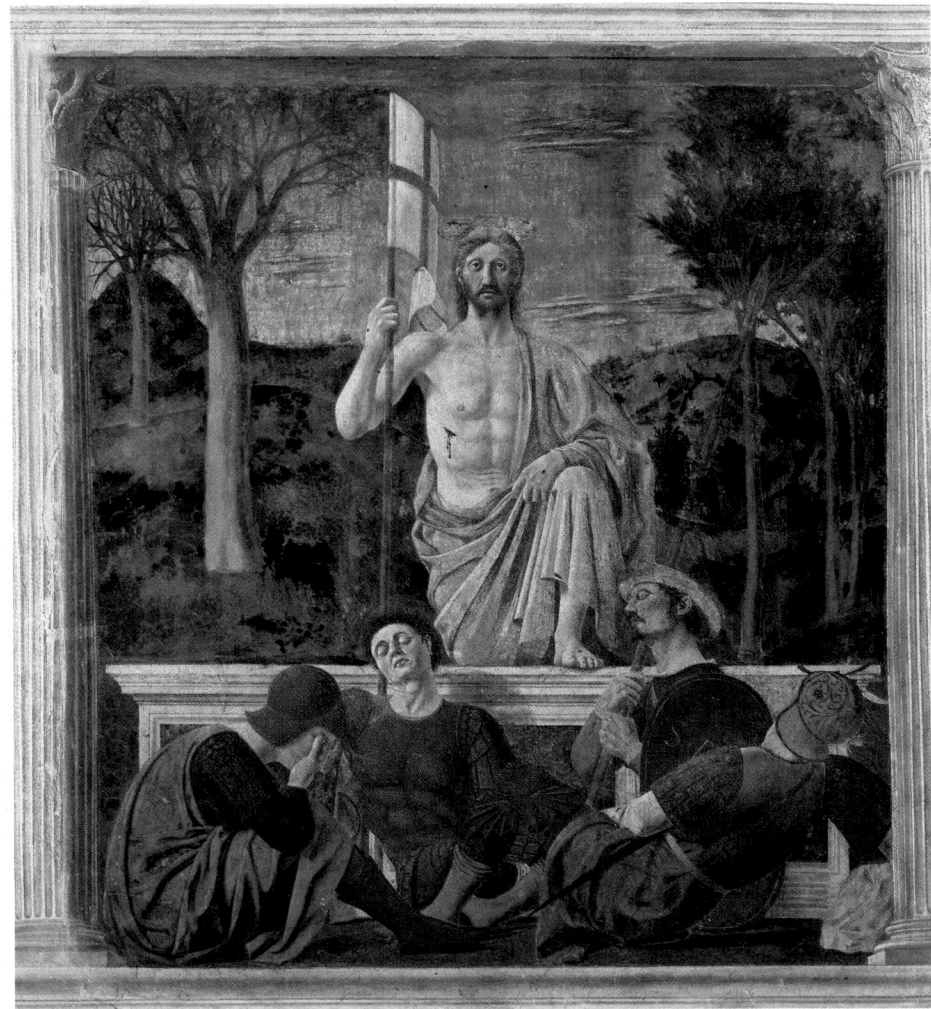

⌃ 17.11 PIERO DELLA FRANCESCA, *Resurrection* (c. late 1450s). Fresco, 7'5" × 6'6½". Town Hall, Borgo San Sepolcro, Italy.

1 ft.

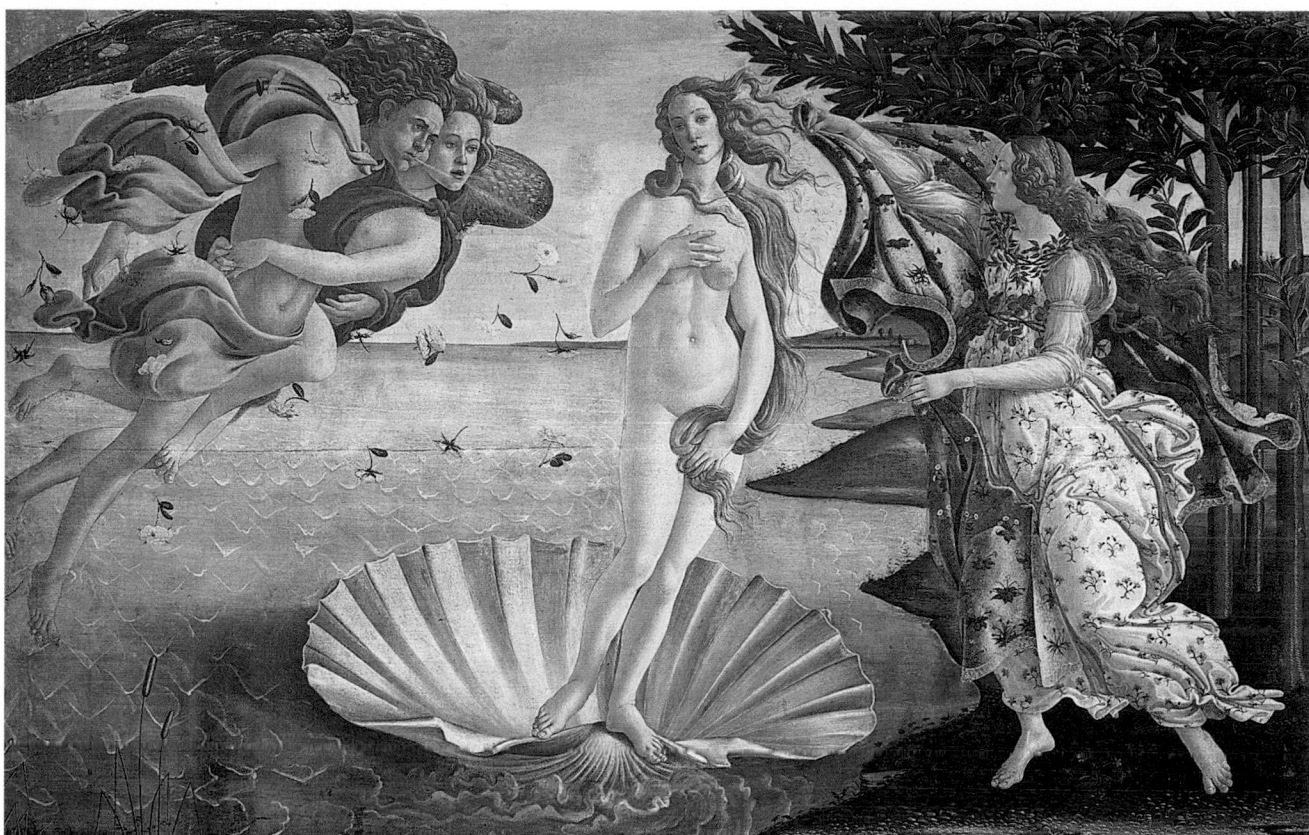

∧ 17.12 **SANDRO BOTTICELLI**, *The Birth of Venus* (c. 1486). Tempera on canvas, 5′8⅞″ × 9′1⅞″. Uffizi Gallery, Florence, Italy.

PIERO DELLA FRANCESCA The artists of the Renaissance, along with the philosophers and scientists, tended to share the sense of the universe as an orderly place that was governed by natural law and capable of being expressed in mathematical and geometric terms. Piero della Francesca (c. 1420–1492) was trained in mathematics and geometry and is credited with writing the first theoretical treatise on the construction of systematic perspective in art. Piero's art, like his scientific thought, was based on an intensely rational construction of forms and space.

His *Resurrection* fresco (Fig. 17.11) for the town hall of Borgo San Sepolcro reveals the artist's obsessions with order and geometry. Christ ascends vertical and triumphant, like a monumental column, above the entablature of his tomb, which serves visually as the pedestal of a statue. Christ and the other figures are constructed from the cones, cylinders, spheres, and rectangular solids that define the theoretical world of the artist. There is a tendency here toward the simplification of forms—not only of people, but also of natural features such as trees and hills. All of the figures in the painting are contained within a triangle—what would become a major compositional device in Renaissance painting—with Christ at the apex. The sleeping figures and the marble sarcophagus provide a strong and stable base for the upper two-thirds of the composition. Regimented trees rise in procession behind Christ, as they never do when nature asserts its random jests; Piero's trees are swept back by the rigid cultivation of scientific perspective. They crown, as ordered, just above the crests of rounded hills. The artist of the Renaissance was not only in awe of nature but also commanded it fully.

SANDRO BOTTICELLI During the latter years of the fifteenth century, we come upon an artistic personality whose style is somewhat in opposition to the prevailing trends. Since the time of Giotto, painters had relied on chiaroscuro, or the contrast of light and shade to create a sense of roundness and mass in their figures and objects, in an effort to render a realistic impression of three-dimensional forms in space. Sandro Botticelli (c. 1444–1510), however, constructed his compositions with line instead of tonal contrasts. His art relied primarily on drawing. Yet when it came to subject matter, his heart lay with his Renaissance peers, for, above all else, he loved to paint mythological themes. Along with other artists and men of letters, his mania for these subjects was fed and perhaps cultivated by the Medici prince Lorenzo the Magnificent, who surrounded himself with Neoplatonists, or those who followed the philosophy of Plato.

One of Botticelli's most famous paintings is *The Birth of Venus* (Fig. 17.12), or, as some art historians would have it,

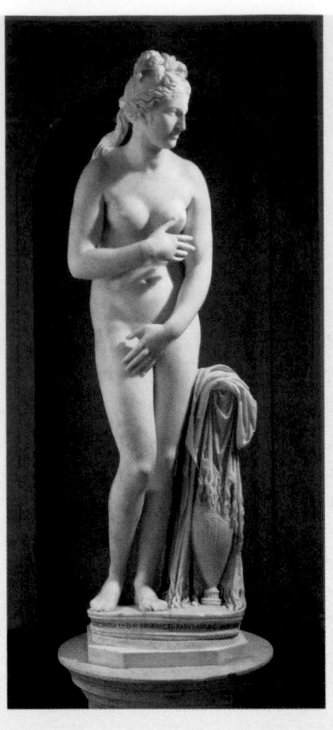

> 17.13 CAPITOLINE VENUS, COPY OF ORIGINAL BY PRAXITELES, FROM ROME (4th Century BCE). Marble, 76" high. Museo Capitolino, Rome, Italy.

architects, the most famous of whom was Vitruvius, and he combined his Classical knowledge with innovative ideas in his grand opus, *Ten Books on Architecture*. One of his most visually satisfying buildings in the great Classical tradition is the Palazzo Rucellai (Fig. 17.14) in Florence. The building is divided by prominent horizontal string courses into three stories, crowned by a heavy cornice. Within each story are apertures enframed by pilasters of different orders. The first-floor pilasters are of the Tuscan order, which resembles the Doric order in its simplicity; the second story uses a composite capital of volutes and acanthus leaves, seen in the Ionic and Corinthian orders, respectively; and the top-floor pilasters are crowned by capitals of the Corinthian order. As in the Colosseum (see Fig. 15.22), this combination of orders gives an impression of increasing lightness as we rise from the lower to the upper stories. This effect is enhanced in Alberti's building by a variation in the masonry. Although the texture remains the same, the upper stories are faced with lighter-appearing smaller blocks in greater numbers. The palazzo's design, with its clear articulation of parts, overall balance of forms, and rhythmic placement of elements in horizontals across the façade, shows a clear understanding of Classical design adapted successfully to the contemporary nobleman's needs.

See more *of Florence in the online Art Tour.*

High Renaissance

The High Renaissance ushered in a new era for some artists—one of respect, influence, fame, and, most important, the power to shape their circumstances. Here is an example: Sometime in 1542, Julius II and Michelangelo Buonarroti were in conflict, and the artist was feeling the brunt of the pope's behavior. As if backing out of his tomb commission and refusing to pay for materials were not enough, the pope laid the last straw by having Michelangelo removed from the Vatican when the artist sought to redress his grievances. Michelangelo let his outrage be known:

> A man paints with his brains and not with his hands, and if he cannot have his brains clear he will come to grief. Therefore I shall be able to do nothing well until justice has been done me. . . . As soon as the Pope [carries] out his obligations towards me I (will) return, otherwise he need never expect to see me again.
>
> All the disagreements that arose between Pope Julius and myself were due to the jealousy of Bramante and of Raffaello da Urbino; it was because of them that he did not proceed with the tomb, . . . and they brought this about in order that I might thereby be ruined. Yet Raffaello was quite right to be jealous of me, for all he knew of art he learned from me.[5]

"Venus on the Half-Shell." The model for this Venus was Simonetta Vespucci, a cousin of Amerigo Vespucci, the navigator and explorer after whom America was named. The composition presents Venus, born of the foam of the sea, floating to the shores of her sacred island on a large scallop shell, aided in its drifting by the sweet breaths of entwined zephyrs. The nymph Pomona awaits her with an ornate mantle and is herself dressed in a billowing, flowered gown. Botticelli's interest in Classicism is evident also in his choice of models for the Venus. She is a direct adaptation of an antique sculpture of this goddess in the collection of the Medici family. Notice how the graceful movement in the composition is evoked through a combination of different lines. A firm horizon line and regimented verticals in the trees contrast with the subtle curves and vigorous arabesques that caress the mythological figures. The line moves from image to image and then doubles back to lead your eye once again. Shading is confined to areas within the harsh, linear, sculptural contours of the figures. Botticelli's genius lay in his ability to utilize the differing qualities of line to his advantage; with this formal element, he created the most delicate of compositions.

LEON BATTISTA ALBERTI You could never accuse Leon Battista Alberti (1404–1472) of false modesty, or of any modesty at all. Like so many other artists of the Renaissance, including Ghiberti, Michelangelo, and Leonardo—and unlike the anonymous European artists of the Middle Ages—he sought fame with conscious conviction.

Some of the purest examples of Renaissance Classicism lie in the buildings Alberti designed. Alberti was among the first to study treatises written by Roman

[5] Robert Goldwater and Marco Treves, eds., *Artists on Art* (New York: Pantheon Books, 1972), 63.

I can make armored cars, safe and unassailable, which will enter the . . . ranks of the enemy with their artillery, and there is no company of men at arms so great that they will not break it. And behind these the infantry will be able to follow quite unharmed and without any opposition. . . . If need shall arise, I can make cannon, mortars, and light ordnance, of very beautiful and useful shapes, quite different from those in common use. . . . Also I can execute sculpture in marble, bronze, and clay, and also painting, in which my work will stand comparison with that of anyone else, who ever he may be.

—LEONARDO DA VINCI (FROM A LETTER OF APPLICATION FOR A JOB)

Although this is only one side of the story (Michelangelo might also have been somewhat jealous of Raphael), this passage offers us a good look at the personality of an artist of the High Renaissance. He was independent yet indispensable—arrogant, aggressive, and competitive.

From the second half of the fifteenth century onward, a refinement of the stylistic principles and techniques associated with the Renaissance can be observed. Most of this significant, progressive work was being done in Florence, where the Medici family played an important role in supporting the arts. At the close of the decade, however, Rome was the place to be, as the popes began to assume the grand role of patron. The three artists who were in most demand—the great masters of the High

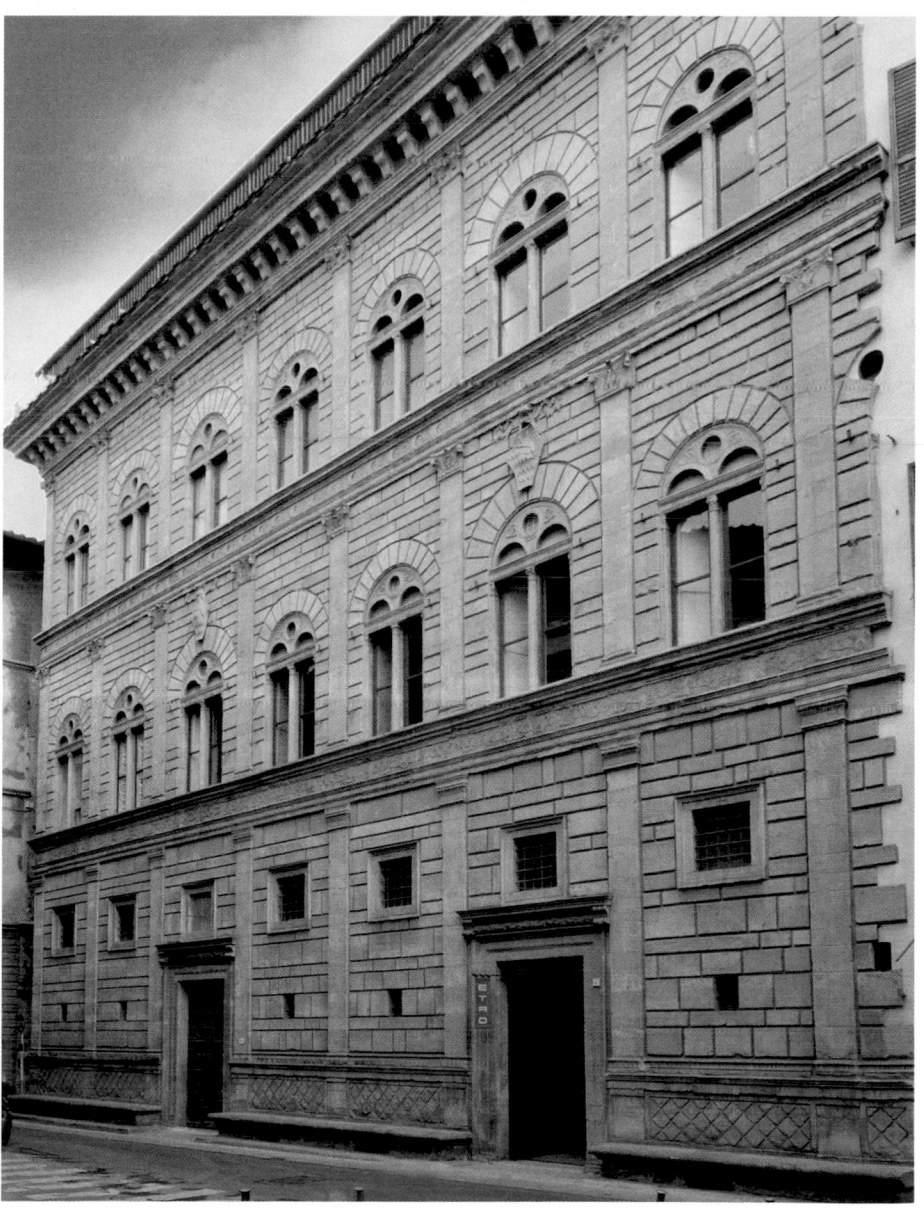

> 17.14 **LEON BATTISTA ALBERTI**, Palazzo Rucellai, Florence (1446–1451).

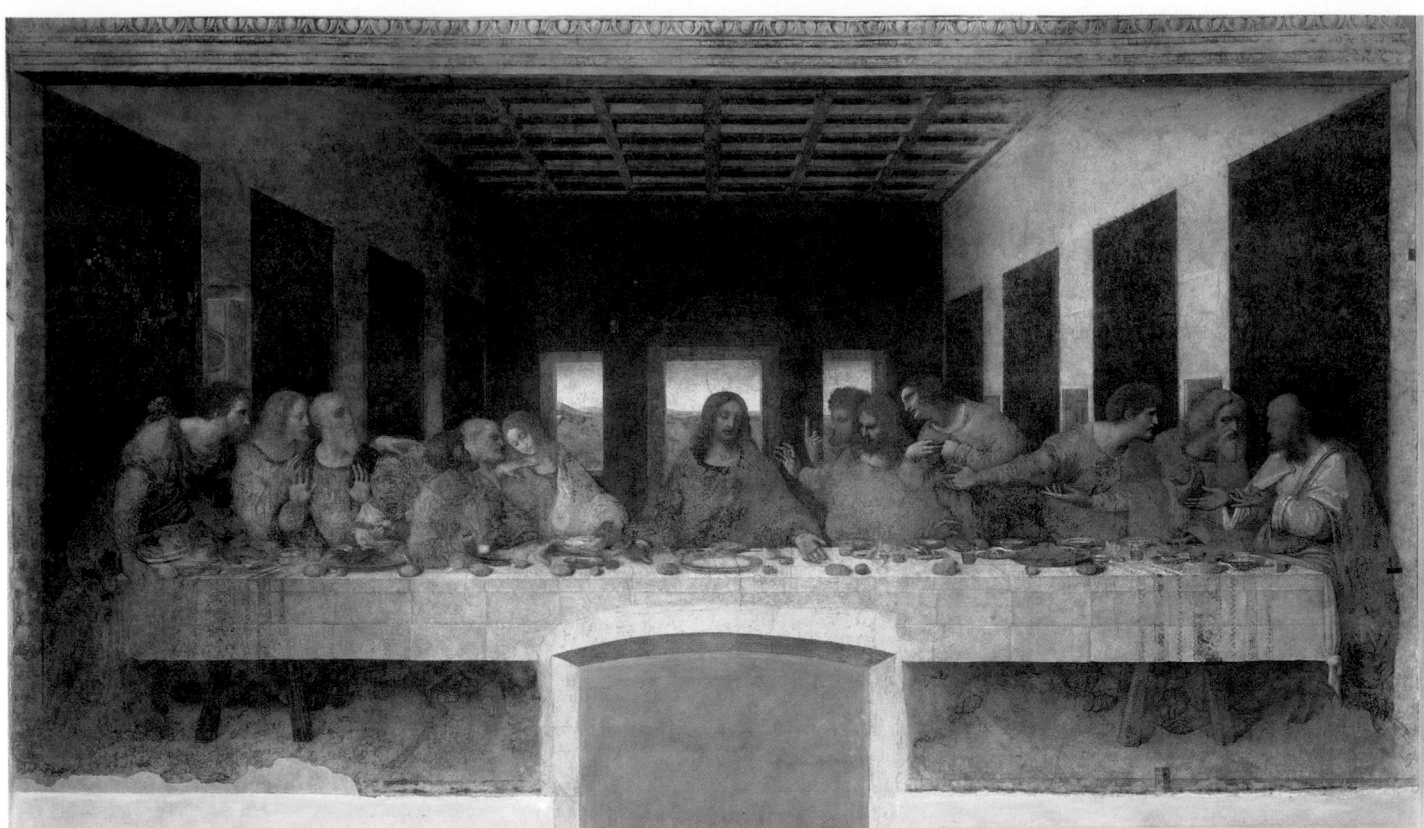

▲ 17.15 **LEONARDO DA VINCI**, *The Last Supper* (1495–1498). Fresco (oil and tempera on plaster), 13'9" × 29'10". Refectory, Santa Maria delle Grazie, Milan, Italy.

Renaissance in Italy—were Leonardo da Vinci, a painter, scientist, inventor, and musician; Raphael, the Classical painter thought to have rivaled the works of the ancients; and Michelangelo, the painter, sculptor, architect, poet, and enfant terrible. Donato Bramante is deemed to have made the most significant architectural contributions of this period. These are the stars of the Renaissance, the artistic descendants of the Giottos, Donatellos, and Albertis, who, because of their earlier place in the historical sequence of artistic development, are sometimes portrayed as but stepping-stones to the greatness of the sixteenth-century artists rather than as masters in their own right.

LEONARDO DA VINCI   If the Italians of the High Renaissance could have nominated a counterpart to the Classical Greek's "four-square man," it most assuredly would have been Leonardo da Vinci (1452–1519). His capabilities in engineering, the natural sciences, music, and the arts seemed unlimited, as he excelled in everything from solving drainage problems (a project he undertook in France just before his death), to designing prototypes for airplanes and submarines, to creating some of the most memorable Renaissance paintings.

The Last Supper (Fig. 17.15), a fresco painting executed for the dining hall of a Milan monastery, stands as one

of Leonardo's greatest works. The condition of the work is poor because of Leonardo's experimental fresco technique—although the steaming of pasta for centuries on the other side of the wall may also have played a role. Nonetheless, we can still observe the Renaissance ideals of Classicism, humanism, and technical perfection now coming to full fruition. The composition is organized through the use of one-point linear perspective. Solid volumes are constructed from a masterful contrast of light and shadow. A hairline balance is struck between emotion and restraint.

The viewer is first attracted to the central triangular form of Jesus sitting among his apostles by orthogonals that converge at his head. His figure is silhouetted against a triple window that symbolizes the Holy Trinity and pierces the otherwise dark back wall. One's attention is held at this center point by the Christ-figure's isolation that results from the leaning away of the apostles. Leonardo has chosen to depict the moment when Jesus says, "One of you will betray me." The apostles fall back reflexively at this accusation; they gesture expressively, deny personal responsibility, and ask, "Who can this be?" The guilty one, of course, is Judas, who is shown clutching a bag of silver pieces at Jesus's left, with his elbow on the table. The two groups of apostles, who sweep dramatically away from Jesus along a horizontal line, are subdivided into four smaller groups of three that tend to moderate the rush of the eye out from the center. The viewer's eye is wafted outward and then coaxed back inward through the "parenthetic" poses of the apostles at either end. Leonardo's use of strict rules of perspective and his graceful balance of motion and restraint underscore the artistic philosophy and style of the Renaissance.

Although Leonardo does not allow excessive emotion in his *Last Supper*, the reactions of the apostles seem

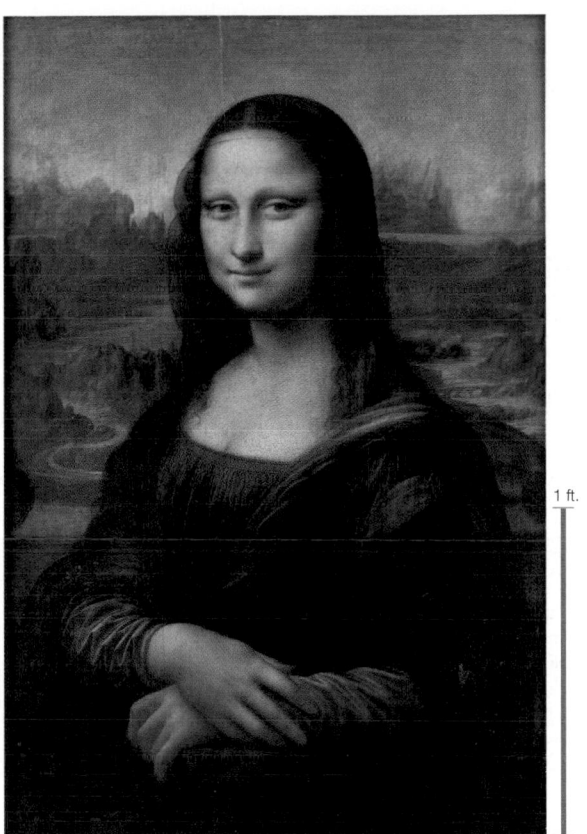

▲ **17.17** **LEONARDO DA VINCI**, *Mona Lisa* (c. 1503–1505). Oil on wood panel, 30¼" × 21". Louvre Museum, Paris, France.

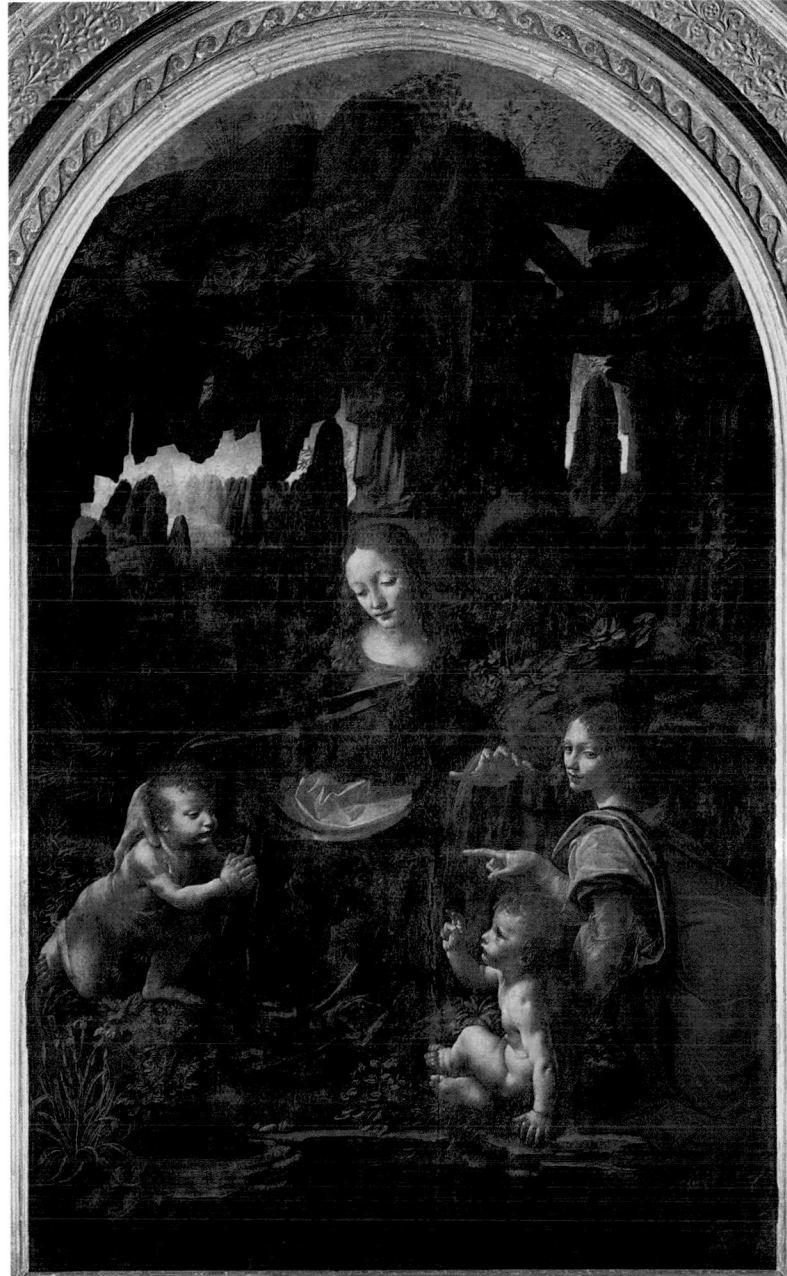

▲ **17.16** **LEONARDO DA VINCI**, *Madonna of the Rocks* (c. 1483). Oil on panel, transferred to canvas; 78½" × 48". Louvre Museum, Paris, France.

genuinely human. This spirit is also captured in *Madonna of the Rocks* (Fig. 17.16). Mary is no longer portrayed as the queen of heaven, but as a mother. She is human; she is "real."

The soft, hazy atmosphere and dreamy landscape of *Madonna of the Rocks*, and the chiaroscuro that so realistically defines the form of the subtly smiling Virgin Mary, were still in Leonardo's pictorial repertory when he created what is arguably the most famous portrait in the history of art—the *Mona Lisa* (Fig. 17.17). An air of mystery pervades the work—from her entrancing smile and intense gaze to her real identity and the location of the landscape behind her. With the *Mona Lisa*, Leonardo altered the nature of portrait painting for centuries, replacing the standard profile view of a sitter to one in which a visual dialogue could be established between the subject and the observer.

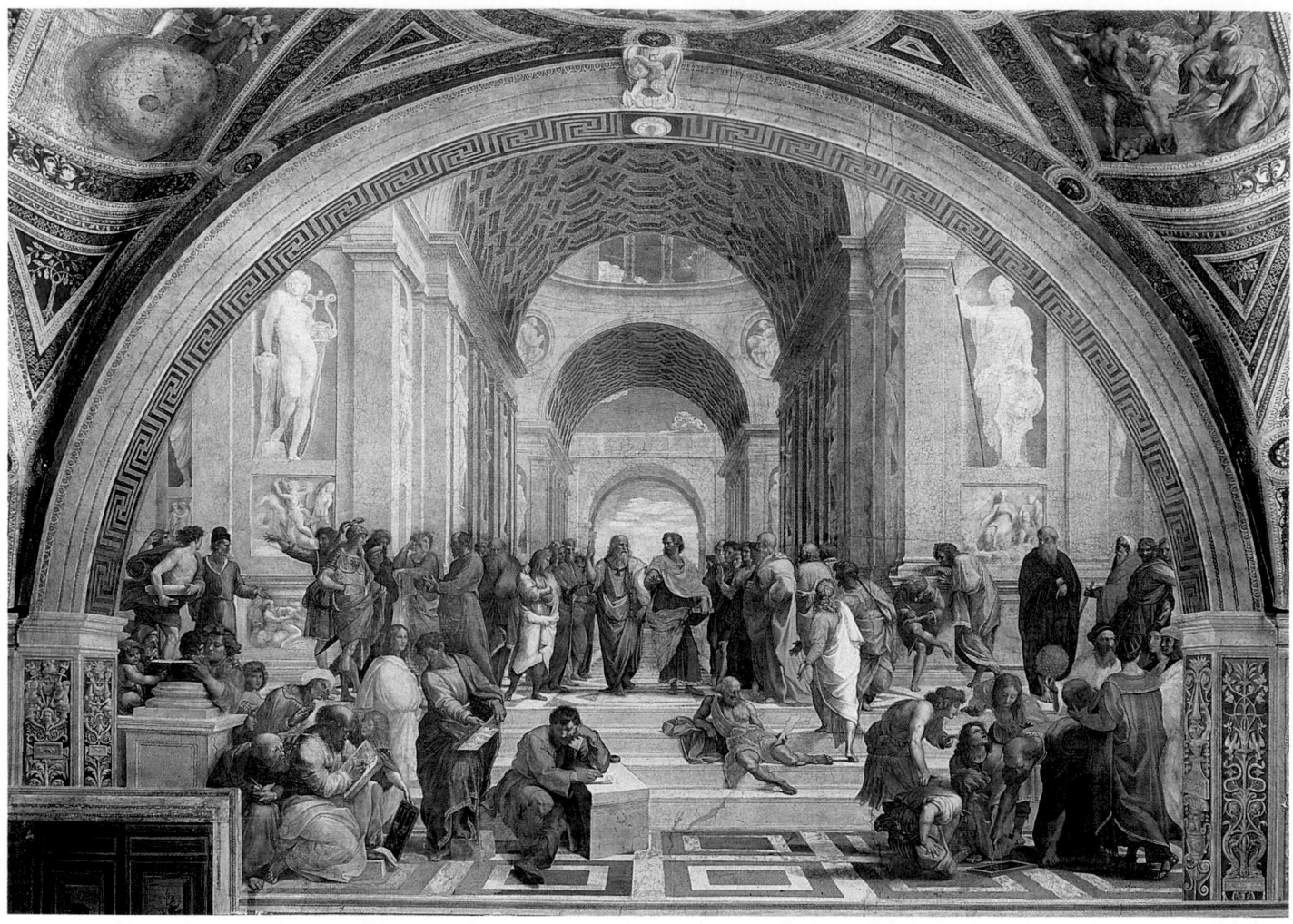

∧ **17.18A** **RAPHAEL**, *The School of Athens* (1510–1511). Fresco, 26' × 18'. Stanza della Segnatura, Vatican, Rome, Italy.

RAPHAEL SANZIO   A younger artist who assimilated the lessons offered by Leonardo, especially on the humanistic portrayal of the Madonna, was Raphael Sanzio (1483–1520). As a matter of fact, Michelangelo was not far off base in his accusation that Raphael copied from him, for the younger artist freely adopted whatever suited his purposes. Raphael truly shone in his ability to combine the techniques of other masters with an almost instinctive feel for Classical art. He rendered countless canvases depicting the Madonna and Child along the lines of Leonardo's *Madonna of the Rocks*. Raphael was also sought after as a muralist. Some of his most impressive Classical compositions, in fact, were executed for the papal apartments in the Vatican.

The commission came from Pope Julius, and to add fuel to Michelangelo's fire, was executed at the same time Michelangelo was at work on the Sistine Chapel ceiling. For the Stanza della Segnatura, the room in which the highest papal tribunal was held, Raphael painted *The*

School of Athens (Fig. 17.18A), one of four frescoes designed within a semicircular frame. In what could be a textbook exercise of one-point linear perspective, Raphael crowded a veritable "who's who" of Classical Greece convening beneath a series of barrel-vaulted archways. The figures symbolize philosophy, one of the four subjects deemed most valuable for a pope's education. (The others were law, theology, and poetry.) The members of the gathering are divided into two camps representing opposing philosophies and are led, on the right, by Aristotle and on the left, by his mentor, Plato. Corresponding to these leaders are the Platonists, whose concerns are the loftier realm of Ideas (notice Plato pointing upward), and the Aristotelians, who are more in touch with matters of the earth, such as natural science. Of particular interest are the possible "portraits" of Raphael's contemporaries who have been cast in a variety of roles. Some identifications that have been proposed include Hericlitus in the left center foreground, resting his face on his hand (almost

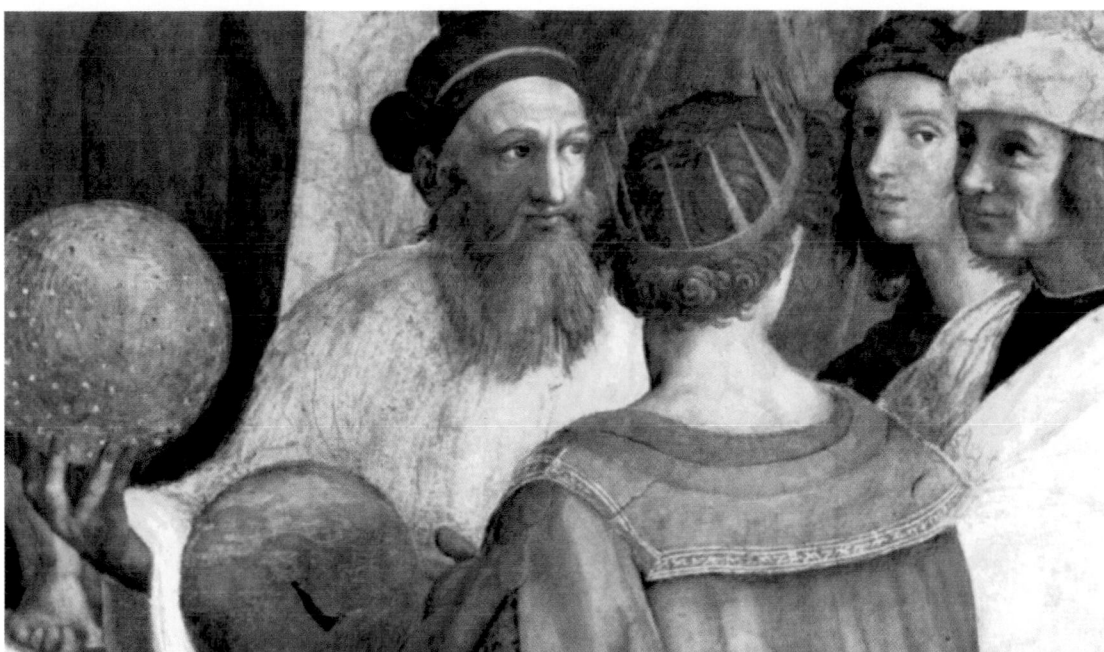

◁ 17.18B **RAPHAEL,**
The School of Athens
(1510–1511). Fresco
(detail), 26' × 18'. Stanza
della Segnatura, Vatican,
Rome, Italy.

certainly Michelangelo); Euclid bending over a slate tablet with a compass in the extreme left foreground (perhaps the architect, Bramante); Plato (Leonardo da Vinci) and Aristotle (Guiliano da Sangallo, the architect who worked with Raphael on St. Peter's); and Raphael himself (looking toward us from the extreme right group) in the guise, perhaps, of the renowned ancient Greek painter, Apelles (see Fig. 17.18B). It bears noting that Raphael assigned himself to the group allied with the rationalist philosophy of Aristotle.

As in *The Last Supper* by Leonardo, our attention is drawn to the two main figures by **orthogonals** leading directly to where they are silhouetted against the sky breaking through the archways. The diagonals that lead toward a single horizon point are balanced by strong horizontals and verticals in the architecture and figural groupings, lending a feeling of Classical stability and predictability. Stylistically, as well as iconographically, Raphael has managed to balance opposites in a perfectly graceful and logical composition.

MICHELANGELO BUONARROTI Of the three great Renaissance masters, Michelangelo (1475–1564) is probably most familiar to us. During the 1964 World's Fair in New York City, hundreds of thousands of culture seekers and devout pilgrims were trucked along a conveyor belt for a brief glimpse of his *Pietà* at the Vatican Pavilion. A year later, actor Charlton Heston (who seems to bear a striking resemblance to the artist) reprised the tumultuous relationship between artist and patron and the traumatic physical experience surrounding the

painting of the Sistine ceiling in the Hollywood film, *The Agony and the Ecstasy*. These two works stand as symbols of the breadth and depth of Michelangelo's talents as an artist.

That famed ceiling is the vault of the chapel of Pope Sixtus IV, known as the Sistine Chapel. The ceiling is some 5,800 square feet and is almost 70 feet above the floor. The decorative fresco cycle was commissioned by Pope Julius II, but the iconographic scheme was Michelangelo's. The artist had agreed to the project in order to pacify the temperamental Julius in the hope that the pontiff would eventually allow him to complete work on his mammoth tomb. For whatever reason, we are indeed fortunate to have this painted work from the sculptor's hand. After much anguish and early attempts to populate the vault with a variety of religious figures (eventually more than 300 in all), Michelangelo settled on a division of the ceiling into geometrical "frames" (Fig. 17.19) housing biblical prophets, mythological soothsayers, and Old Testament scenes from Genesis to Noah's flood.

The most famous of these scenes is *The Creation of Adam* (Fig. 17.20). As Leonardo had done in *The Last Supper*, Michelangelo chose to communicate the event's most dramatic moment. Adam lies on the Earth, listless for lack of a soul, while God the Father rushes toward him amid a host of angels, who enwrap him in a billowing cloak. The contrasting figures lean toward the left, separated by an illuminated diagonal that provides a backdrop for the Creation. Amid an atmosphere of sheer electricity, the hand of God reaches out to spark spiritual life into Adam—but does not touch him!

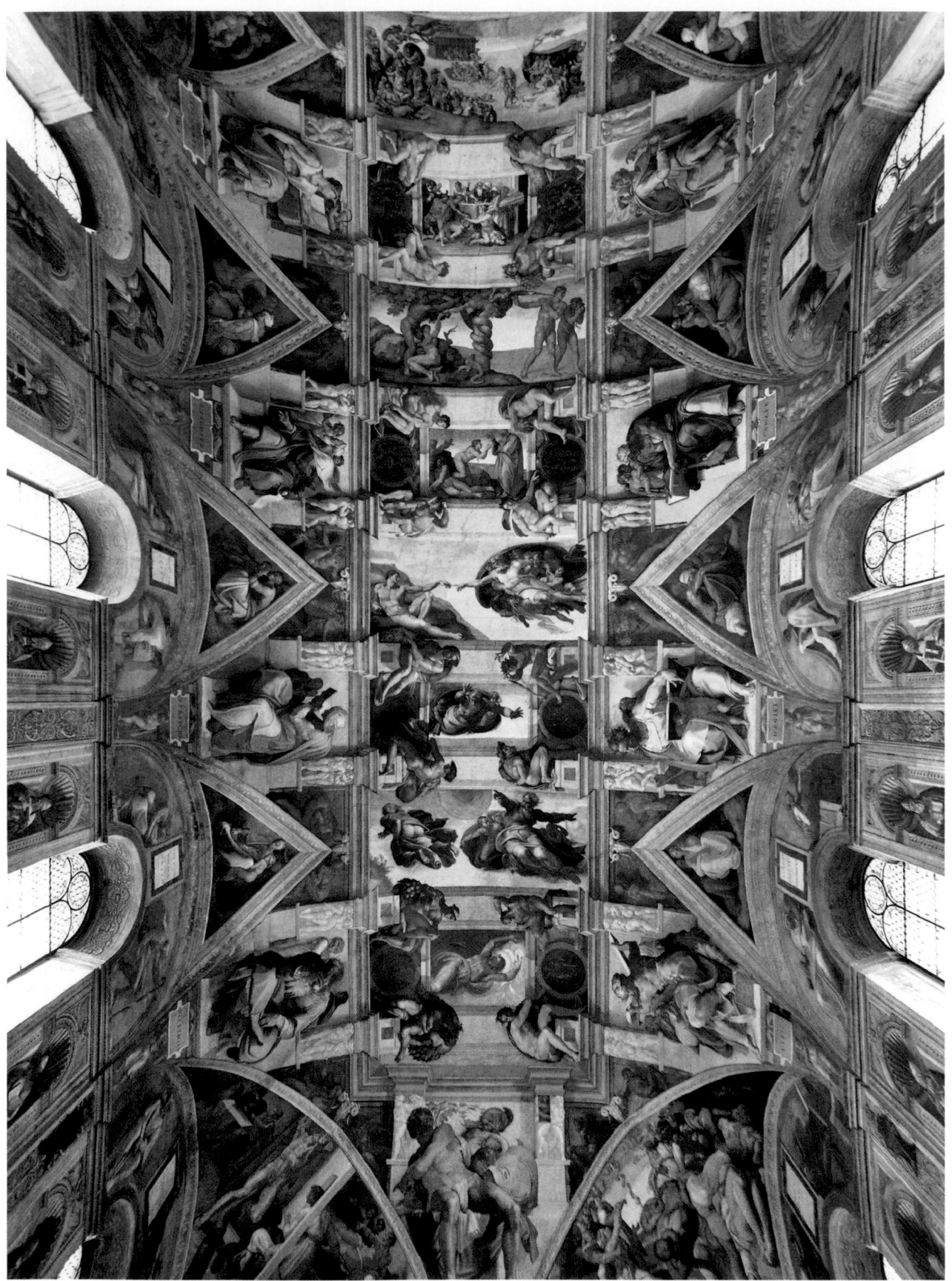

∧ **17.19 MICHELANGELO, The Sistine Chapel in the Vatican, Rome** (1508–1512). 5,800 sq. ft. Vatican Museum, Rome, Italy.

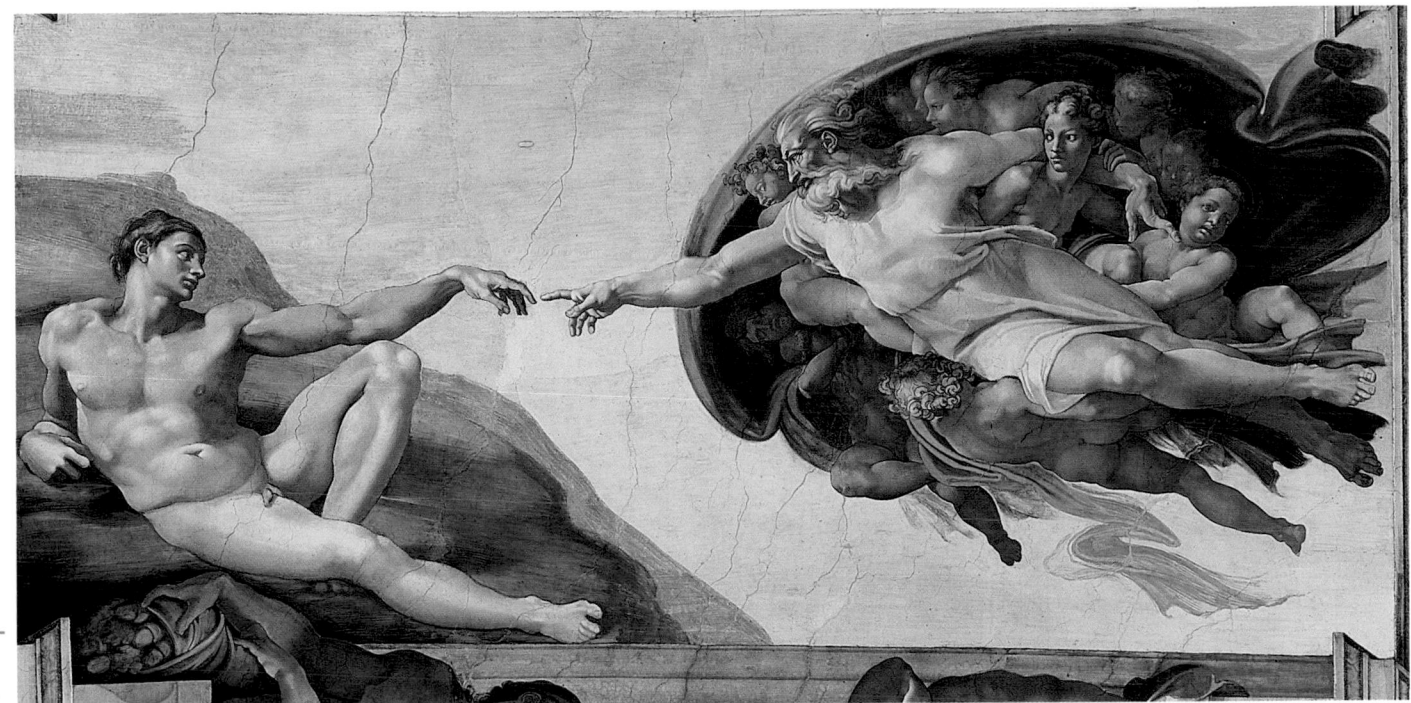

∧ 17.20 MICHELANGELO, *The Creation of Adam* (1508–1512). Detail from the ceiling of the Sistine Chapel in the Vatican, Rome, Italy, Fresco, 9' 2" × 18' 8".

In some of the most dramatic negative space in the history of art, Michelangelo has left it to the spectator to complete the act. In terms of style, Michelangelo integrated chiaroscuro with Botticelli's extensive use of line. His figures are harshly drawn and muscular with almost marble-like flesh. In translating his sculptural techniques to a two-dimensional surface, the artist has conceived his figures in the round and has used the tightest, most expeditious line and modeling possible to render them in paint.

It is clear that Michelangelo saw himself more as a sculptor than as a painter. The "sculptural" drawing and modeling in *The Creation of Adam* attest to this. When Michelangelo painted the Sistine Chapel ceiling, he was all of 33 years old, but he began his career some twenty

CONNECTIONS Who is the woman in Michelangelo's *Creation of Adam* tucked under the left arm of God? She is the third most prominent figure in the composition, occupying a niche between the muscular body of God the Father and a child whose shoulder He touches. For some time it was assumed that the woman is Eve, waiting in the wings, so to speak, to be created from Adam's side. A new theory posits that the woman, rather, is the Virgin Mary and that the child to her side is Jesus. How does that theory impact the narrative of the painting? Why might Michelangelo have placed Mary and Jesus with God in this cocoon of whirling drapery?

years earlier as an apprentice to the painter Domenico Ghirlandaio (1449–1494). His reputation as a sculptor, however, was established when, at the age of 27, he carved the 13½-foot-high *David* (see Fig. 17.23) from a single piece of almost unworkable marble. Unlike the *David*s of Donatello and Verrocchio, Michelangelo's hero is not shown after conquering his foe. Rather, David is portrayed as a most beautiful animal preparing to kill—not by savagery and brute force but by intellect and skill. Upon close inspection, the tensed muscles and the furrowed brow negate the first impression that this is a figure at rest. David's sling is cast over his shoulder, and the stone is grasped in the right hand, the veins prominent in anticipation of the fight.

Michelangelo's *David* is part of the Classical tradition of the "ideal youth" who has just reached manhood and is capable of great physical and intellectual feats. Like Donatello's *David*, Michelangelo's sculpture is closed in form. All of the elements move tightly around a central axis. Michelangelo has been said to have sculpted by first conceptualizing the mass of the work and then carefully extracting all of the marble that was not part of the image. Indeed, in the *David*, it appears that he worked from front to back instead of from all four sides of the marble block, allowing the figure, as it were, to "step out of" the stone. The identification of the figure with the marble block provides a dynamic tension in Michelangelo's work, as the forms try at once to free themselves from and succumb to the binding dimensions.

COMPARE & CONTRAST
The *Davids* of Donatello, Verrocchio, Michelangelo, and Bernini

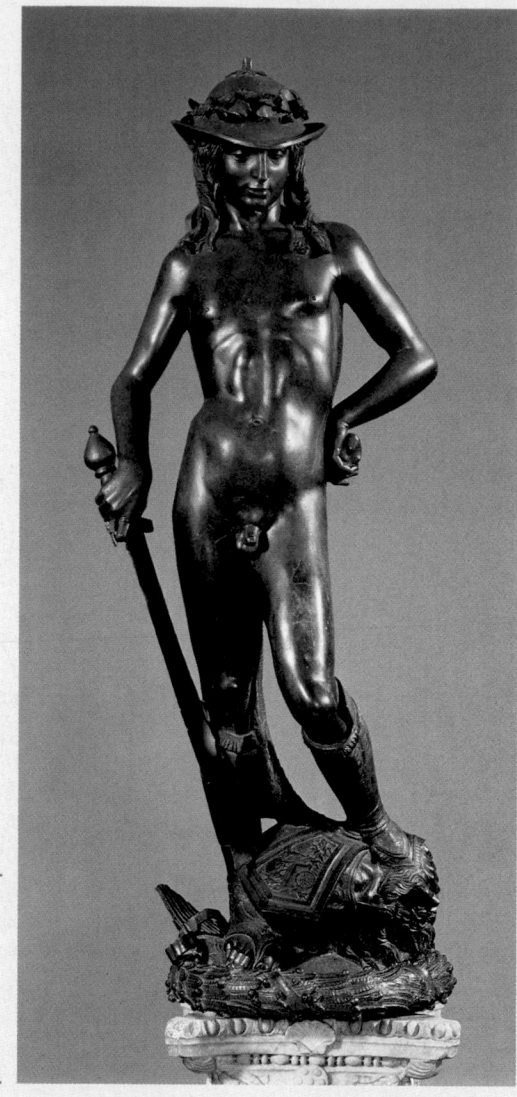

∧ **17.21 DONATELLO,** *David* (1408). Bronze, 5'2" high.
Museo Nazionale del Bargello, Florence, Italy.

SOMETIME SOON AFTER THE year 1430, a bronze statue of *David* (Fig. 17.21) stood in the courtyard of the house of the Medici. The work was commissioned of Donatello by Cosimo de' Medici himself, the founding father of the Republic of Florence. It was the first freestanding, life-sized nude since Classical antiquity, poised in the same contrapposto stance as the victorious athletes of Greece and Rome. But soft, and somehow oddly unheroic. And the incongruity of the heads: David's boyish, expressionless face, framed by soft tendrils of hair and shaded by a laurel-crowned peasant's hat; Goliath's tragic, contorted expression, made sharper by the pentagonal helmet and coarse, disheveled beard. Innocence and evil.

The weak triumphing over the strong. The city of Florence triumphing over the aggressive dukes of Milan? *David* as a civic-public monument.

In the year 1469, Ser Piero from the Tuscan town of Vinci moved to Florence to become a notary. He rented a house on the Piazza San Firenze, not far from the Palazzo Vecchio. His son, who was a mere 17 years old upon their arrival, began an apprenticeship in the Florentine studio of the well-known artist Andrea del Verrocchio. At that time, Verrocchio was at work on a bronze sculpture of the young *David* (Fig. 17.22). Might the head of this fine piece be a portrait of the young Leonardo da Vinci?

For many years, a block of marble lay untouched, tossed aside as unusable, irretrievable evidence of a botched attempt to carve a human form. It was 18 feet high. A 26-year-old sculptor, riding high after the enormous success of his figure of the Virgin Mary holding

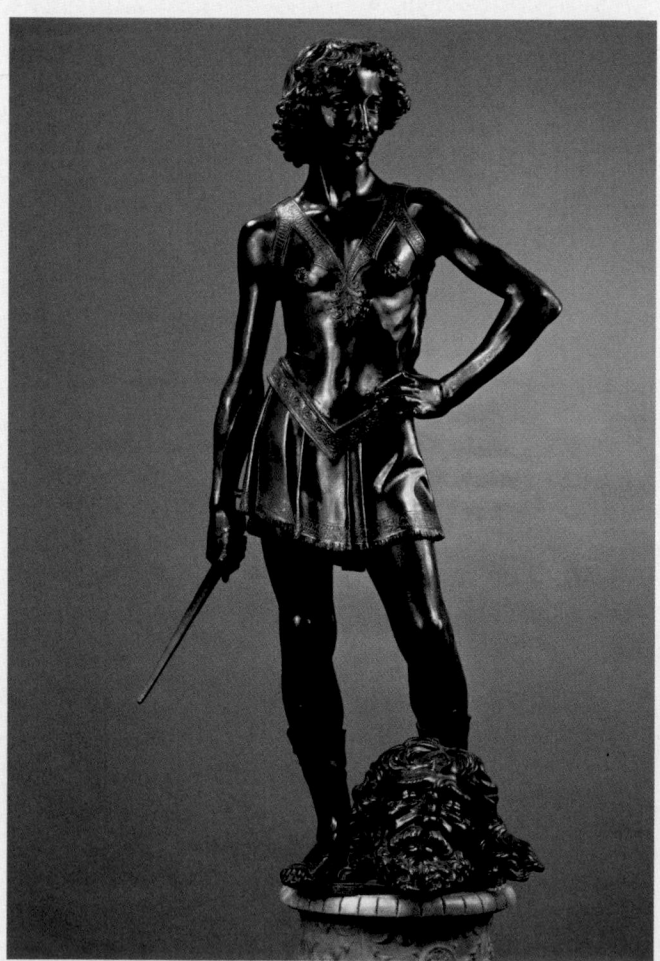

∧ **17.22 ANDREA DEL VERROCCHIO,** *David* (c. 1470). Bronze, 49⅝" high.
Museo Nazionale del Bargello, Florence, Italy.

the dead Christ, decided to ask for the piece. The wardens of the city in charge of such things let the artist have it. What did they have to lose? Getting anything out of it was better than nothing. So this young sculptor named Michelangelo measured and calculated. He made a wax model of David with a sling in his hand. And he worked on his *David* (**Fig. 17.23**) continuously for some three years until, a man named Vasari tells us, he brought it to perfect completion—without letting anyone see it.

A century later, a 25-year-old sculptor stares into a mirror at his steeled jaw and determined brow. A contemporary source

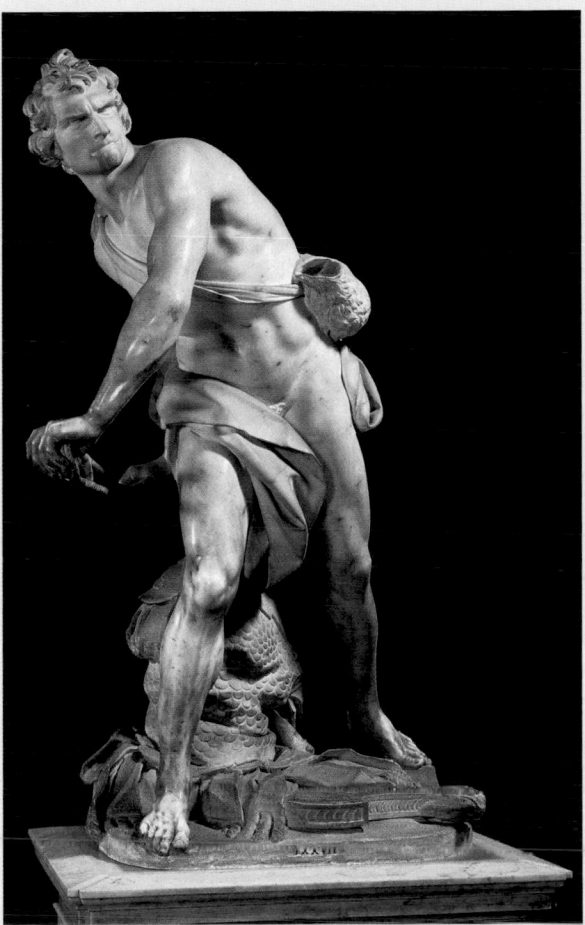

▲ 17.24 **GIANLORENZO BERNINI,** *David* (1623). Marble, 6'7" high. Borghese Gallery, Rome, Italy.

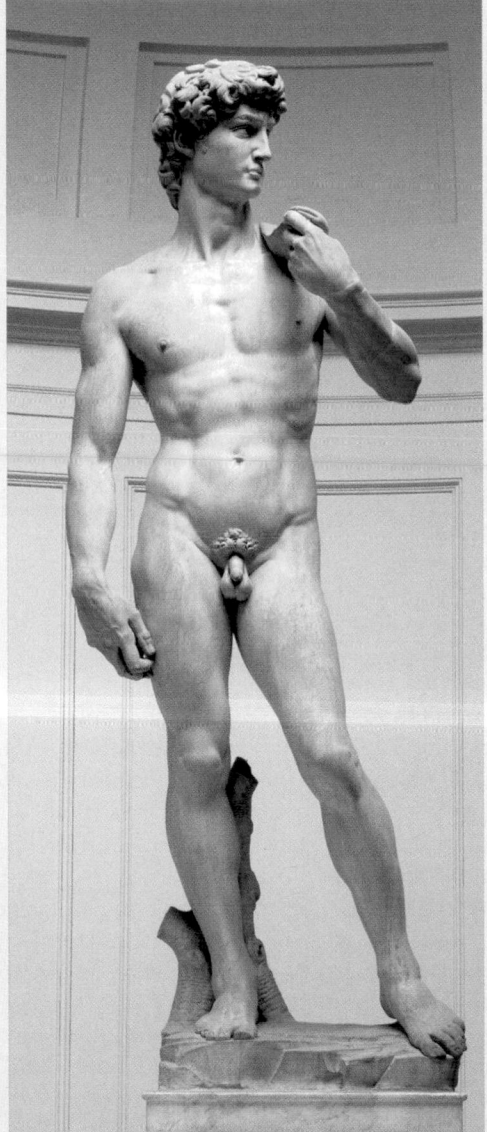

▲ 17.23 **MICHELANGELO,** *David* (1501–1504). Marble, 17' high. Galleria dell'Accademia, Florence, Italy.

tells us that on this day, perhaps, the mirror is being held by Cardinal Maffeo Barberini while Bernini transfers what he sees in himself to the face of his *David* (**Fig. 17.24**). Gianlorenzo Bernini: sculptor and architect, painter, dramatist, composer. Bernini, who centuries later would be called the undisputed monarch of the Roman High Baroque, identifying with David, whose adversary is seen only by him.

The great transformation in style that occurred between the Early Renaissance and the Baroque can be followed in the evolution of David. Look at them: A boy of 12, perhaps, looking down incredulously at the physical self that felled an unconquerable enemy; a boy of 14 or 15, confident and reckless, with enough adrenaline pumping to take on an army; an adolescent on the brink of adulthood, captured at that moment when, the Greeks say, sound mind and sound body are one; and another full-grown youth at the threshold of his destiny as king.

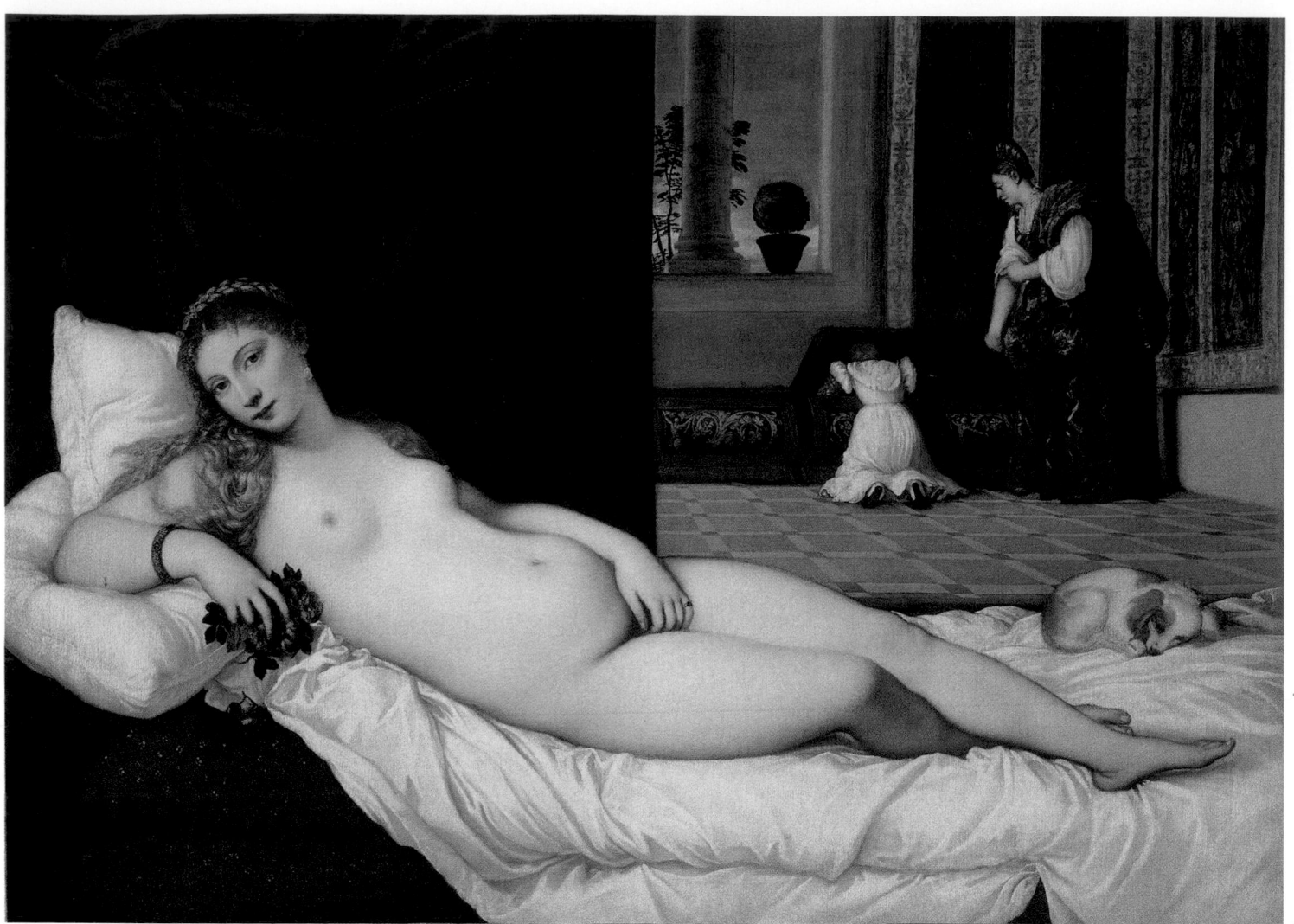

1 ft.

∧ 17.25 TITIAN, *Venus of Urbino* (1538). Oil on canvas, 47" × 65". Uffizi Gallery, Florence, Italy.

High and Late Renaissance in Venice

The artists who lived and worked in the city of Venice were the first in Italy to perfect the medium of oil painting that we witnessed with van Eyck in Flanders. Perhaps influenced by the mosaics in St. Mark's Cathedral, perhaps intrigued by the dazzling colors of imports from Eastern countries into this maritime province, the Venetian artists sought the same clarity of hue and lushness of surface in their oil-on-canvas works. In the sixteenth century, Venice would come to figure as prominently in the arts as Florence had in the fifteenth.

TITIAN   Although he died in 1576, almost a quarter century before the birth of the Baroque era, the Venetian master Tiziano Vecellio (b. 1477)—called Titian—had more in common with the artists who would follow him than with his Renaissance contemporaries in Florence and Rome. Titian's pictorial method differed from those of Leonardo, Raphael, and Michelangelo in that he was foremost a painter and colorist rather than a draftsman or sculptural artist. He constructed his compositions by means of colors and strokes of paint and layers of varnish rather than by line and chiaroscuro. A shift from painting on wood panels to painting on canvas occurred at this time, and with it a change from tempera to oil paint as the preferred medium. The versatility and lushness of oil painting served Titian well, with its vibrant, intense hues and its more subtle, semitransparent glazes.

Titian's *Venus of Urbino* (Fig. 17.25) is one of the most beautiful examples of the glazing technique. The composition was painted for the duke of Urbino, from which its title derives. Titian adopted the figure of the reclining

> [Titian] made the promise of a figure appear in four brushstrokes. [Then] he used to turn his pictures to the wall and leave them there without looking at them, sometimes for several months. When he wanted to apply his brush again, he would examine them . . . to see if he could find any faults. . . . In this way, working on the figures and revising them, he brought them to the most perfect symmetry that the beauty of art and nature can reveal. [So] he gradually covered those essential forms with living flesh, bringing them . . . to a state in which they lacked only the breath of life.
>
> —PALMA IL GIOVANE, CONTEMPORARY OF TITIAN

Venus from his teacher Giorgione, and it has served as a model for many compositions since that time. In the foreground, a nude **Venus pudica** rests on voluptuous pillows and sumptuous sheets spread over a red brocade couch. Her golden hair, complemented by the delicate flowers she grasps loosely in her right hand, falls gently over her shoulder. A partial drape hangs in the middle ground, providing a backdrop for her upper torso and revealing a view of her boudoir. The background of the composition includes two women looking into a trunk—presumably handmaidens—and a more distant view of a sunset through a columned veranda. Rich, soft tapestries contrast with the harsh Classicism of the stone columns and inlaid marble floor.

Titian appears to have been interested in the interaction of colors and the contrast of textures. The creamy white sheet complements the radiant golden tones of the body of Venus, built up through countless applications of glazes over flesh-toned pigment. Her sumptuous roundness is created by extremely subtle gradations of tones in these glazes rather than the harshly sculptural chiaroscuro that Leonardo or Raphael might have used. The forms evolve from applications of color instead of line or shadow. Titian's virtuoso brushwork allows him to define different textures: the firm yet silken flesh, the delicate folds of drapery, the servant's heavy cloth dress, the dog's soft fur. The pictorial dominance of these colors and textures sets the work apart from so many examples of Florentine and Roman painting. It appeals primarily to the senses rather than to the intellect.

Titian's use of color as a compositional device is significant. We have already noted the drape, whose dark color forces our attention on the most important part of the composition—Venus's face and upper torso. It also blocks out the left background, encouraging viewers to narrow their focus on the vista in the right background. The forceful diagonal formed by the looming body of Venus is balanced by three elements opposite her: the little dog at her feet and the two handmaidens in the distance. They do not detract from her because they are engaged in activities that do not concern her or the spectator. The diagonal of her body is also balanced by an intersecting diagonal that can be visualized by integrating the red areas in the lower-left and upper-right corners. Titian thus subtly balances the composition in his placement of objects and color areas.

TINTORETTO   Perhaps no other Venetian artist anticipated the Baroque style so strongly as Jacopo Robusti, called Tintoretto, or "little dyer," after the profession of his father. Supposedly a pupil of Titian, Tintoretto (1518–1594) emulated the master's love of color, although he combined it with a more linear approach to constructing forms. This interest in draftsmanship was culled from Michelangelo, but the younger artist's compositional devices went far beyond those of the Florentine and Venetian masters. His dynamic structure and passionate application of pigment provide a sweeping, almost frantic, energy within compositions of huge dimensions.

Tintoretto's painting technique was unique. He arranged doll-like figures on small stages and hung his flying figures by wires in order to copy them in correct perspective on sheets of paper. He then used a grid to transcribe the figures onto much larger canvases. Tintoretto primed the entire canvas with dark colors. Then he quickly painted in the lighter sections. Thus, many of his paintings appear very dark, except for bright patches of radiant light. The artist painted extremely quickly, using broad areas of loosely swathed paint. John Ruskin, a nineteenth-century art critic, is said to have suggested that Tintoretto painted with a broom.[6] Although this is unlikely, Tintoretto had certainly come a long way from the sculptural, at times marble-like, figures of the High Renaissance and the painstaking finish of Titian's glazed *Venus of Urbino*. This loose brushwork and dramatic white spotlighting on a dark ground anticipate the Baroque style.

---

[6] Frederick Hartt, *History of Italian Renaissance Art*, 2nd ed. (Englewood Cliffs, NJ: Prentice Hall; New York: Harry N. Abrams, 1979), 615.

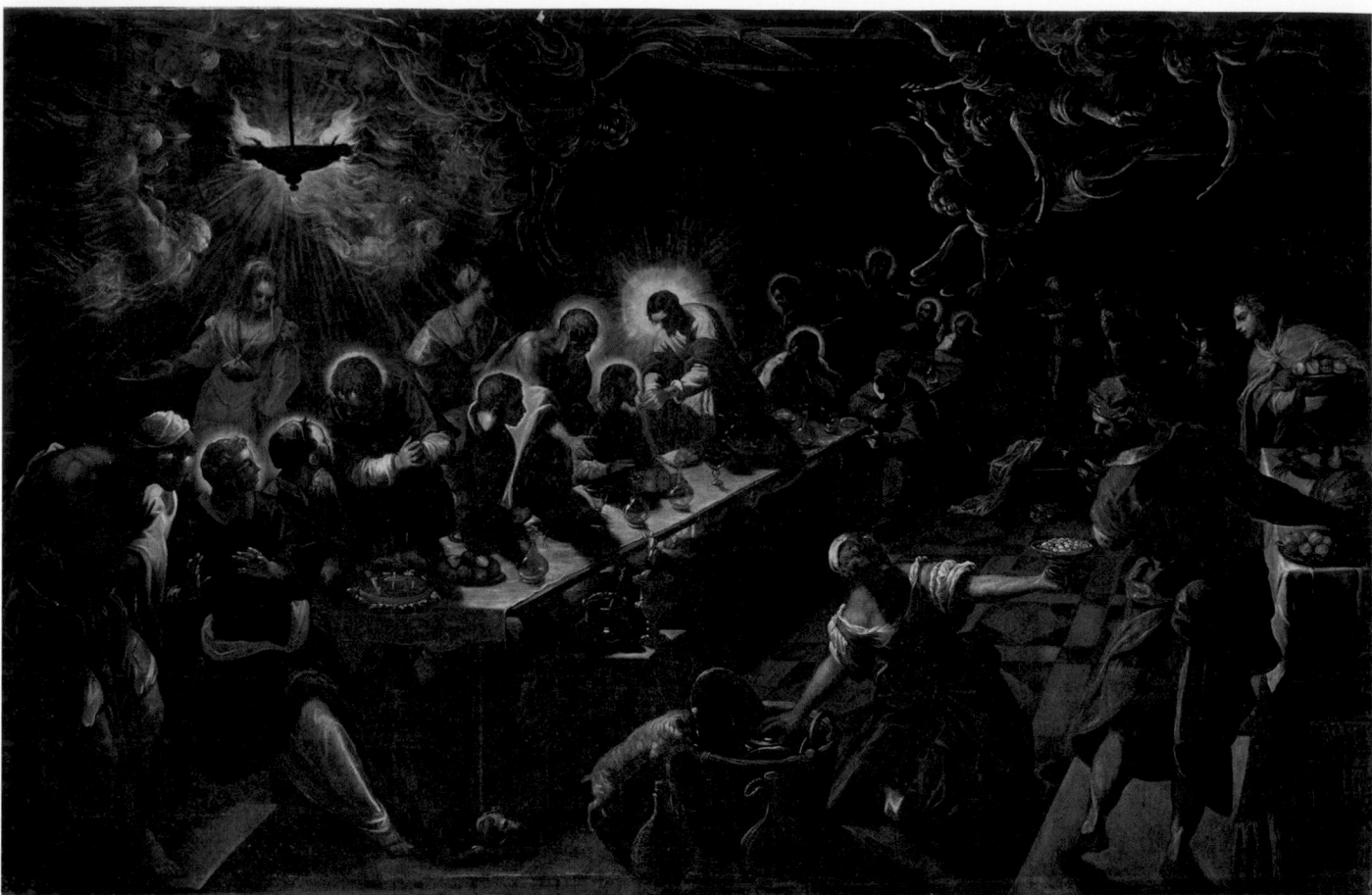

1 ft.

∧ 17.26 **TINTORETTO,** *The Last Supper* (1592–1594). Oil on canvas, 12′ × 18′8″. San Giorgio Maggiore, Venice, Italy.

The Last Supper (Fig. 17.26) seals his relationship to the later period. A comparison of this composition with Leonardo's *The Last Supper* (see Fig. 17.15) will illustrate the dramatic changes that had taken place in both art and the concept of art over almost a century. The interests in motion, space, and time; the dramatic use of light; and the theatrical presentation of subject matter are all present in Tintoretto's *The Last Supper*. We are first impressed by the movement. Everything and everyone are set into motion: people lean, rise up out of their seats, stretch, and walk. Angels fly and animals dig for food. The space, sliced by a sharp, rushing diagonal that goes from lower left toward upper right, seems barely able to contain all of this commotion, but this cluttered effect enhances the energy of the event.

Leonardo's obsession with symmetry, along with his balance between emotion and restraint, yields a composition that appears static in comparison to the asymmetry and overpowering emotion in Tintoretto's canvas. Leonardo's apostles seem posed for the occasion when contrasted with Tintoretto's spontaneously gesturing figures. A particular moment is captured. We feel that if we were to look away for a fraction of a second, the figures would have changed position by the time we looked back!

The timelessness of Leonardo's figural poses has given way to a seemingly temporary placement of characters. The moment that Tintoretto has chosen to depict also differs from Leonardo's. The Renaissance master chose the point at which Jesus announced that one of his apostles would betray him. Tintoretto, on the other hand, chose the moment when Jesus shared bread, which symbolized his body as the wine stood for his blood. This moment is commemorated to this day during the celebration of Mass in the Roman Catholic faith. Leonardo chose a moment signifying death, Tintoretto a moment signifying life, depicted within an atmosphere that is teeming with life.

HIGH AND LATE RENAISSANCE OUTSIDE ITALY

EL GRECO The Late Renaissance outside Italy brought us many different styles, and Spain is no exception. Spanish art polarized into two stylistic groups of religious painting: the mystical and the realistic. One painter was able to pull these opposing trends together in a unique pictorial method. El Greco (1541–1614), born Domeniko Theotokopoulos in Crete, integrated many styles into his work. As a young man, he traveled to Italy, where he encountered the works of the Florentine and Roman masters, and he was for a time affiliated with Titian's workshop. The colors that El Greco incorporated into his paintings suggest a Venetian influence, and the distortion of his figures and use of an ambiguous space speak for his interest in Mannerism, which is discussed later.

These pictorial elements can clearly be seen in one of El Greco's most famous works, *The Burial of Count Orgaz* (Fig. 17.27). In this single work, El Greco combines mysticism and realism. The canvas is divided into two halves by a horizontal line of white-collared heads, separating "heaven" and "earth." The figures in the lower half of the composition are somewhat elongated, but well within the bounds of realism. The heavenly figures, by contrast, are extremely attenuated and seem to move under the influence of a sweeping, dynamic atmosphere. It has been suggested that the distorted figures in El Greco's paintings might have been the result of astigmatism in the artist's eyes, but there is no convincing proof of this.

For example, at times El Greco's figures appear no more distorted than those of other Mannerists. Heaven and earth are disconnected psychologically but joined convincingly in terms of composition. At the center of the rigid, horizontal row of heads that separates the two worlds, a man's upward glance creates a path for the viewer into the upper realm. This compositional device is complemented by a sweeping drape that rises into the upper half of the canvas from above his head, continuing to lead the eye between the two groups of figures, left and right, up toward the image of the resurrected Christ. El Greco's color scheme also complements the worldly and celestial habitats. The colors used in the costumes of the earthly figures are realistic and vibrantly Venetian, but the colors of the upper half of the composition are of discordant hues, highlighting the otherworldly nature of the upper canvas. The emotion is high-pitched and exaggerated by the tumultuous atmosphere. This emphasis on emotionalism links El Greco to the onset of the Baroque era. His work contains a dramatic, theatrical flair, one of the hallmarks of the seventeenth century.

PIETER BRUEGEL THE ELDER During the second half of the sixteenth century in the Netherlands, changes in the subject matter of painting were taking place that would affect the themes of artists working in northern Europe during the Baroque period. Scenes of everyday life involving ordinary people were becoming more popular. One of the masters of this genre painting was Pieter Bruegel the Elder (c. 1520–1569), whose compositions focused on human beings in relation to nature and the life and times of plain Netherlandish

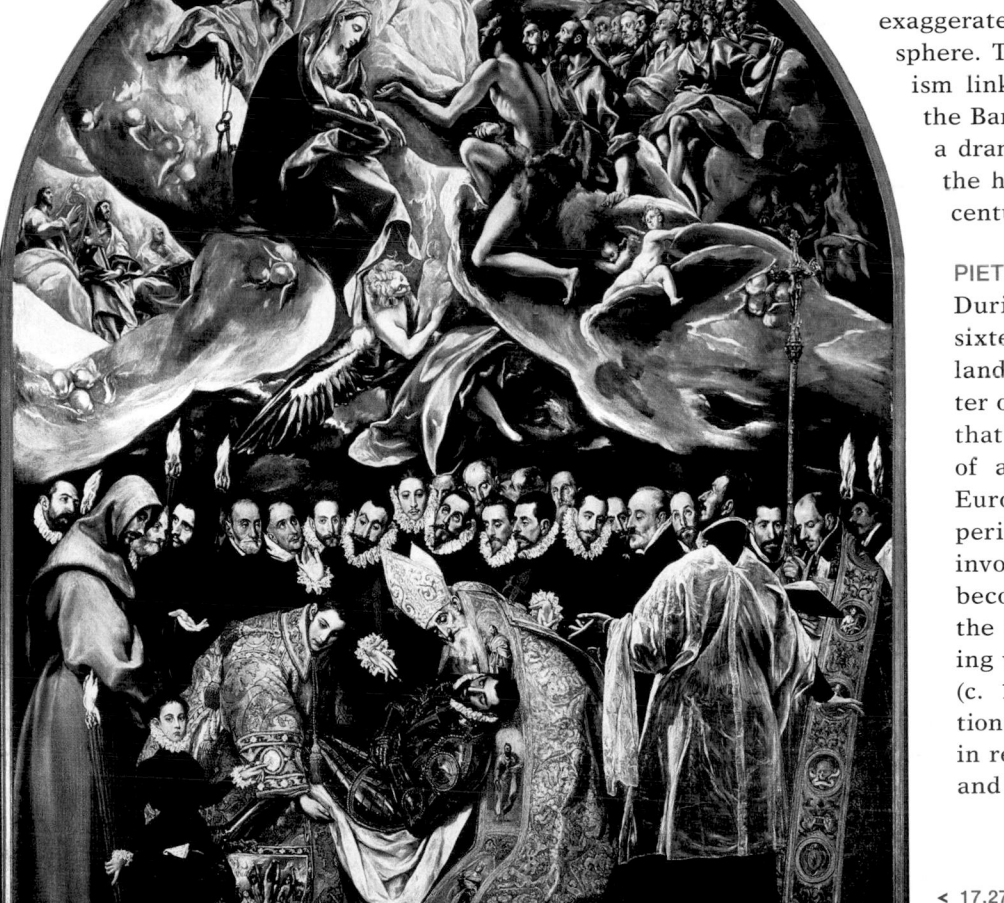

1 ft.

◀ 17.27 EL GRECO, *The Burial of Count Orgaz* (1586). Oil on canvas, 16' × 11' 10". Santo Tome, Toledo, Spain.

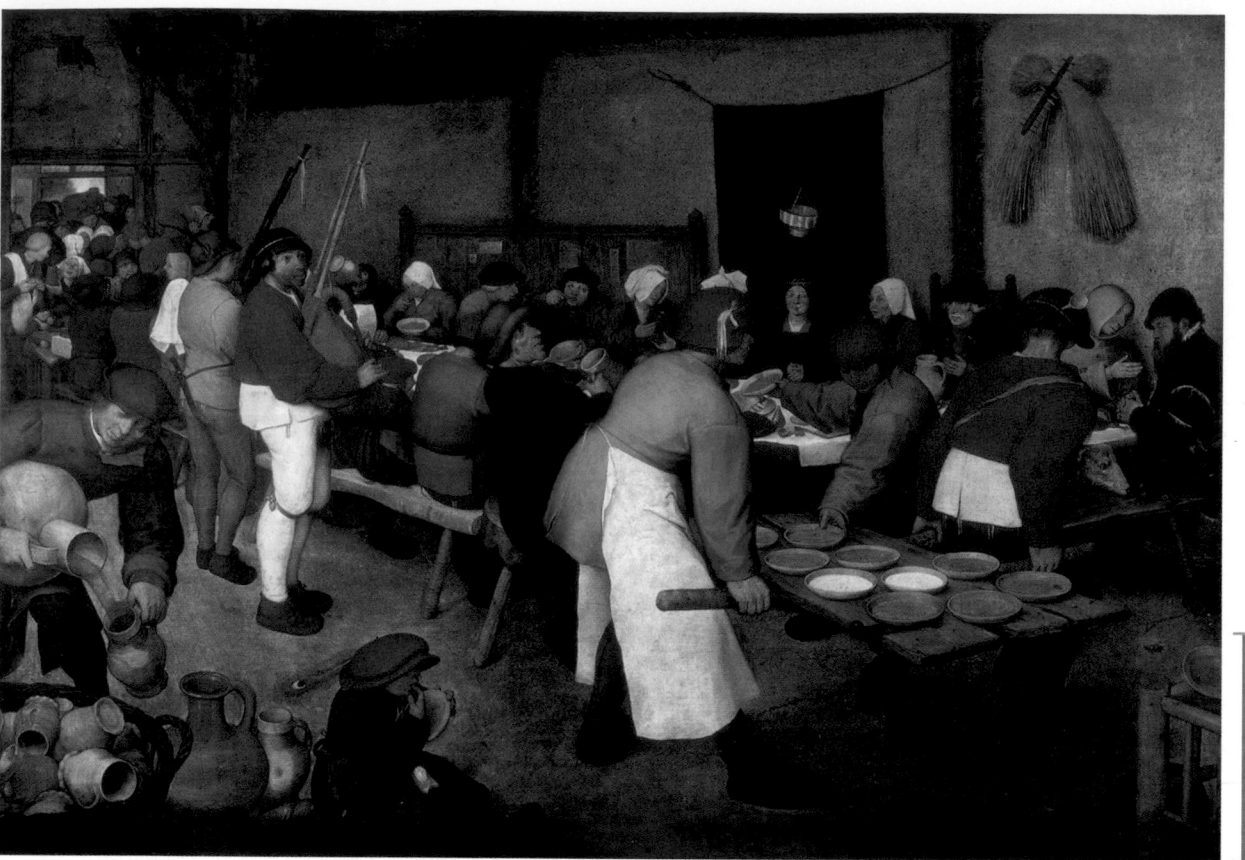

^ 17.28 **PIETER BRUEGEL THE ELDER**, *The Peasant Wedding* (1568). Oil on wood, 45" × 64½". Kunsthistoriches Museum, Vienna, Austria.

folk. *The Peasant Wedding* (Fig. 17.28) is a good example of Bruegel's slice-of-life canvases. The painting transports us to a boisterous hall, where food and drink flow in abundance, and music and merriment raise the rafters. The viewer's experience of this event relies on the degree to which the artist conveys the sense of noise, of laughter, of celebration. The circular rims of soup bowls are echoed in the spherical caps of the peasants and the mouths of the stacked, earthenware pitchers. In a sea of confusion, this simple repetitive element provides visual unity and guides the path of the eye. There is no hidden message here, no religious fervor, no battle between mythological giants. Human activities are presented as sincere and viable subject matter. There are few examples of such painting before this time, but genre painting will play a principal role in the works of Netherlandish artists during the Baroque period.

MANNERISM

During the Renaissance, the rule of the day was to observe and emulate nature. Toward the end of the Renaissance and before the beginning of the seventeenth century,

this rule was suspended for a while, during a period of art that historians have named Mannerism. Mannerist artists abandoned copying directly from nature and copied art instead. Works thus became "secondhand" views of nature. Line, volume, and color no longer duplicated what the eye saw but were derived instead from what other artists had already seen. Several characteristics separate **Mannerist art** from the art of the Renaissance and the Baroque periods: distortion and elongation of figures; flattened, almost two-dimensional space; lack of a defined focal point; and the use of discordant pastel hues.

JACOPO PONTORMO   A representative of early Mannerism, Jacopo Pontormo (1494–1557) used most of its stylistic principles. In *Entombment* (Fig. 17.29), we witness a strong shift in direction from High Renaissance art, even though the painting was executed during Michelangelo's lifetime. The weighty sculptural figures of Michelangelo, Leonardo, and Raphael have given way to less substantial, almost weightless, forms that balance on thin toes and ankles. The limbs are long and slender in proportion to the torsos, and the heads are dwarfed by billowing robes. There is a certain innocent beauty in the arched eyebrows of the haunted faces and in the nervous glances that dart this way and that past the boundaries of the canvas. The figures are pressed against the picture plane, moving within a very limited space. Their weight seems to be thrust outward toward the edges of the composition and away from the almost void center. The figures' robes are composed of odd hues, departing drastically in their soft pastel tones from the vibrant primary colors of the Renaissance masters.

The weightlessness, distortion, and ambiguity of space create an almost otherworldly feeling in the composition, a world in which objects and people do not come under an earthly gravitational force. The artist accepts this "strangeness" and makes no apologies for it to the viewer. The ambiguities are taken in stride. For example, note that the character in a turban behind the head of the dead Jesus does not appear to have a body—there is really no room for it in the composition. And even though a squatting figure in the center foreground appears to be balancing Christ's torso on his shoulders after having taken him down from the cross a moment before, there is no cross in sight! Pontormo seems to have been most interested in elegantly rendering the high-pitched emotion of the scene. Iconographic details and logical figural stances are irrelevant.

SOFONISBA ANGUISSOLA Sofonisba Anguissola (1532–1625) had a highly successful art practice and was the first Italian woman artist of international standing, having, among other things, risen to the position of court painter to Philip II of Spain. She was born into a noble family in the northern Italian city of Cremona and, as was key with many women artists prior to the nineteenth century, had a father who enabled her talents and supported her education in the arts. Anguissola traveled widely and was introduced to important contemporary art-

ists including Michelangelo and Anthony van Dyck, the renowned Flemish painter.

Most of Anguissola's large body of work reflects the regional, realistic style of Cremona rather than the Mannerist stylizations that were popular elsewhere in

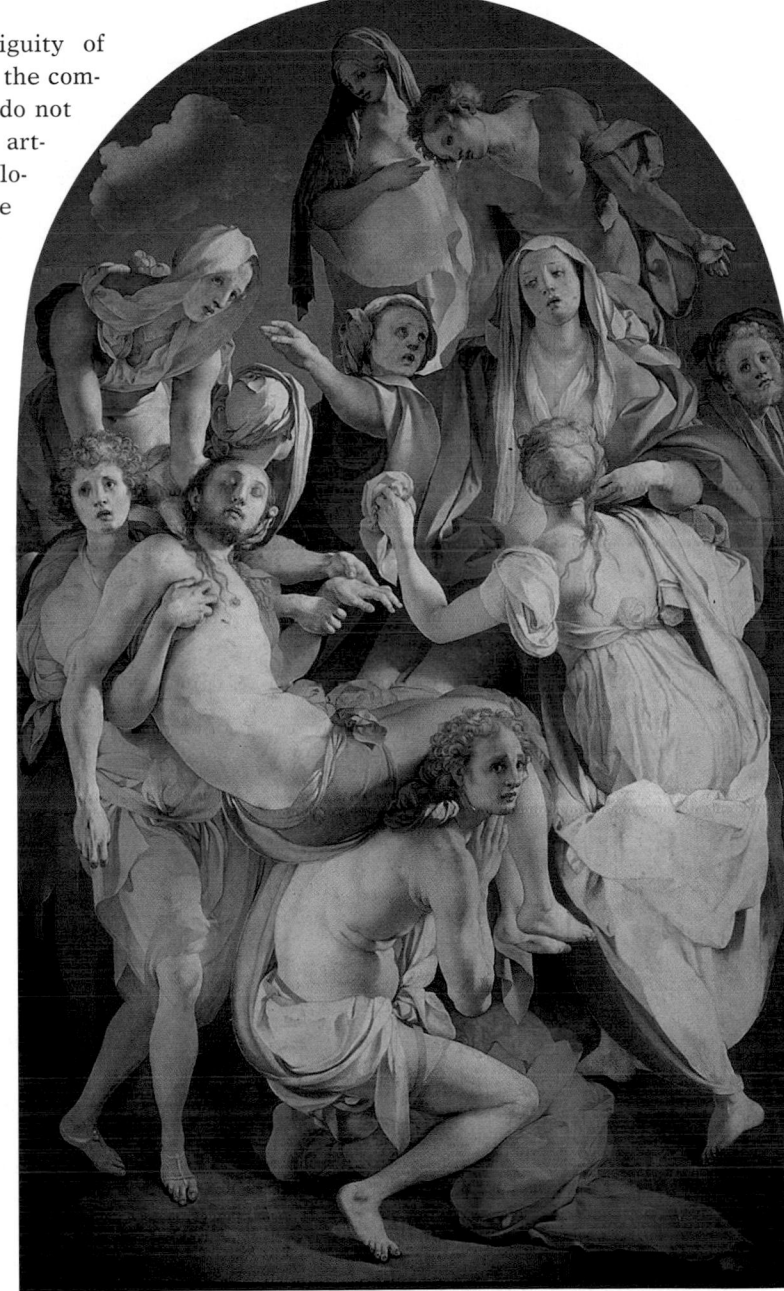

> 17.29 JACOPO PONTORMO, *Entombment of Christ* (1525–1528). Oil on panel, 10'3" × 6'4". Capponi Chapel, Santa Felicitá, Florence, Italy.

1 ft.

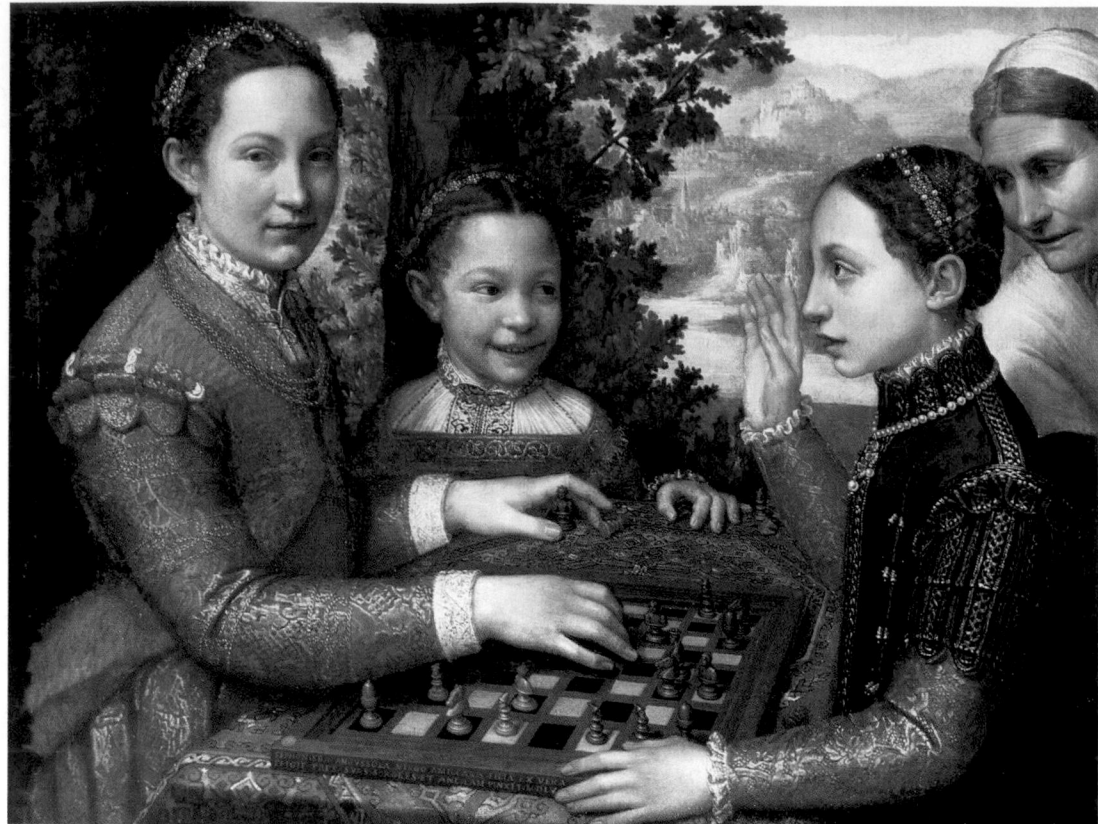

◄ 17.30 SOFONISBA ANGUISSOLA, *A Game of Chess* (1555). Oil on canvas, 28¼" × 38¼". National Museum in Poznan, Poland.

1 ft.

Italy; she had in common with contemporary Flemish portrait painters a taste for meticulous detail. *A Game of Chess* (Fig. 17.30), painted in 1555 when the artist was only 23, is a group portrait of three of the artist's sisters playing chess while a nanny-servant looks on. The brocade fabric of their elaborate dresses and the patterned tablecloth attest to the family's affluence and gentility, although the girls are anything but stilted in their behavior. The oldest, Lucia, looks up from the game to meet our gaze, self-assured and poised. Her sister Minerva seems to try to catch her attention, her hand raised and her lips slightly parted as if about to speak. The youngest looks on, her face brimming with joy, it seems, that Minerva appears to be losing the game. Animated gestures and facial expressions combine to create a work that is less a formal portrait than an absolutely natural and believable scene. Anguissola pushes beyond mere representation to suggest the personalities of her sisters and the relationship among them. This easy, conversational quality will become a familiar characteristic of group portraiture in the seventeenth century, particularly in the north.

The artists from the second half of the sixteenth century through the beginning of the seventeenth century all broke away from the Renaissance tradition in one way or another. Some were opposed to the stylistic characteristics of the Renaissance and turned them around in an inventive style called Mannerism. Others, such as

Titian and Tintoretto, emphasized the painting *process*, constructing their compositions by means of stroke and color rather than line and shadow. Still others combined an implied movement and sense of time in their compositions, foreshadowing some of the concerns of the artist in the Baroque period. The High and Late Renaissance witnessed artists of intense originality who provide a fascinating transition between the grand Renaissance and the dynamic Baroque.

THE WIDER WORLD

India

During the Renaissance era in western Europe, India was separating into a jumble of kingdoms ruled by feuding Hindu warriors. Inability to form a united government left India vulnerable to outside forces, and in 1526, Babur (1483–1530), an Islamic Afghan chieftain, won control over most of northern India. His grandson Akbar (1542–1605) extended Muslim rule to most of India and Afghanistan. Akbar's **Mughal Empire** (meaning "descending from Mongols") lasted until the British seized control of India in the eighteenth century. Unlike Muslim rulers elsewhere, he did not impose his Islamic faith on his subjects. He married a Hindu princess and

1279	1488	1500	1526	1707
Fall of Song Dynasty in China 1279	Dry-landscape garden at Ryoanji in Kyoto, Japan, c. 1488	Inka civilization builds mountain fortress Machu Picchu in modern-day Peru c. 1500	Mughal Dynasty in India 1526–1707	
Aztecs build their capital, Tenochtitlán, on site of Mexico City c. 1325	Sesshu Toyo paints splashed-ink landscapes in China c. 1495	The Spaniard Hernán Cortes conquers the Aztec Empire c. 1519	Momoyama period in Japan 1573–1615	
Beginning of Ming Dynasty in China 1368	Inka Empire blossoms during 15th century in western South America		Erection of Taj Mahal in India 1632–1647	
Muromachi period in Japan 1333–1573; flowering of Zen Buddhism			End of Ming Dynasty in China 1644	
Erection of Forbidden City in Beijing (begun 15th century)				

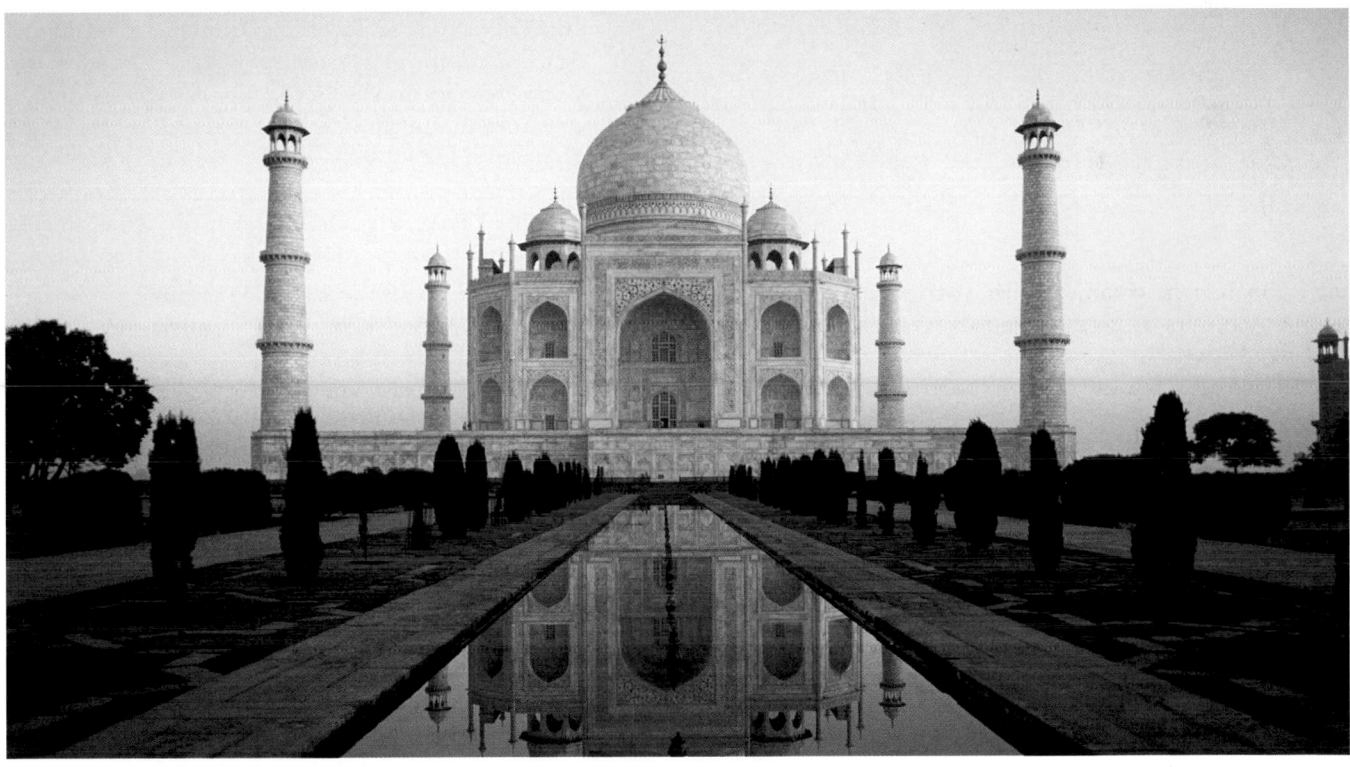

▲ 17.31 **Taj Mahal and gardens (looking north), Agra, India** (1632–1647).

allowed Hindu women at court to practice their religion openly.

Akbar was a great patron of the arts and, under his successors, Mughal architects and painters devised a style that combined aspects of Hindu and Middle Eastern traditions. The best-known Mughal building—visited by architects, art historians, and tourists from around the world—is the Taj Mahal at Agra, built by Shah Jahan (Fig. 17.31). The building's unique appeal reflects, in part, its proportions: the height and width of the central structure are equal; the dome and the central façade on which it sits are equal in height. The Taj Mahal is both a tomb and monument for his favorite wife Arjumand Banu Begum, who was famed for her charity and her beauty. Signature Mughal mausoleum features include a crown-shaped dome set on a cube-shaped structure, towing minarets, and a reflecting pool surrounded by elaborate, precisely plotted gardens and fountains.

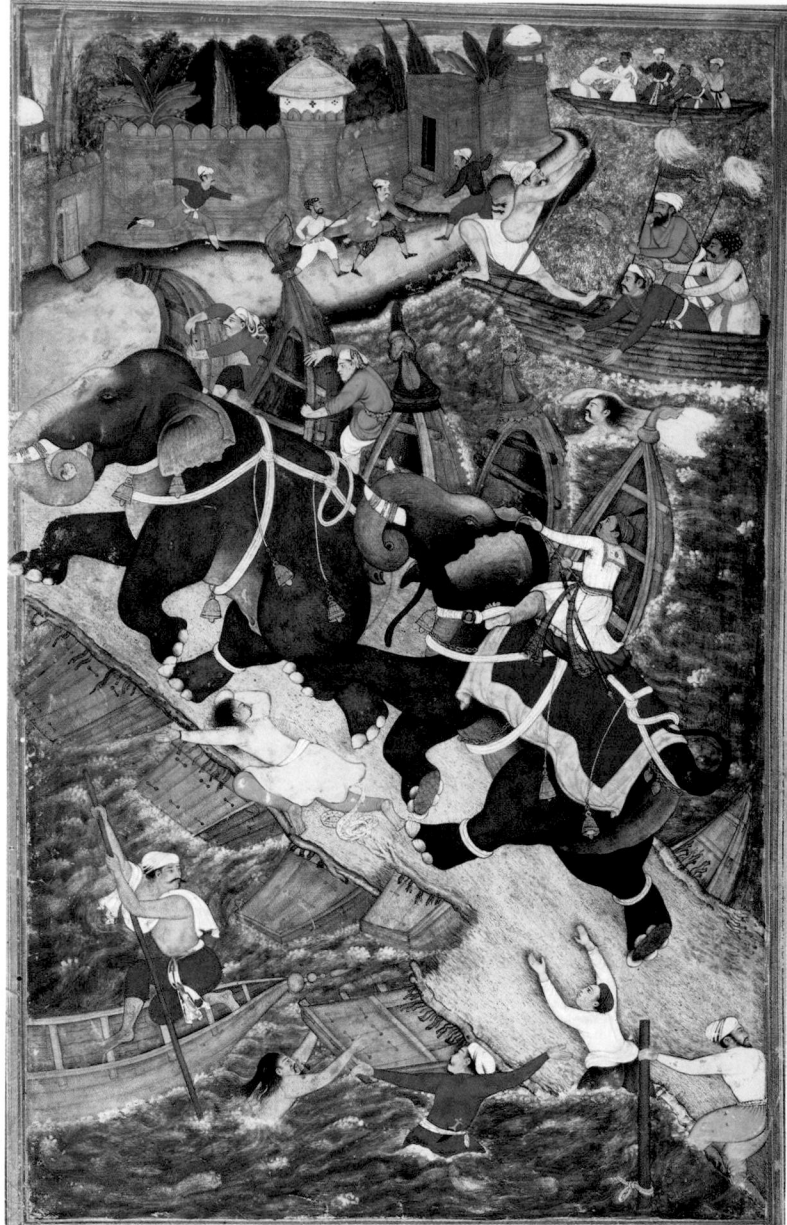

< **17.32 BASAWAN AND CHATAR MUNI,** *Akbar and the Elephant Hawai* (c. 1590). Folio 22 from the *Akbar-nameh* (*History of Akbar*) by Abul al-Fadl. Opaque watercolor on paper, 1'1⅞" × 8¾". Victoria and Albert Museum, London, England.

Nearly all Mughal painting consists of book illustrations or miniatures and unlike Hindu and Buddhist art, features secular subjects. Scenes of courtly life are common, as are depictions of historical events. Figure 17.32 illustrates an episode in the life of Akbar when, at the age of 19, the elephant he was riding charged after another, destroying a bridge. The emperor maintains control over his beast—symbolizing his success at governing the state.

China

In 1279, a year or so before Cimabue painted his *Madonna Enthroned* (see Fig. 17.6) in Florence, the Song Dynasty in China fell before Mongol invaders from the north and was replaced by the Yuan Dynasty (1279–1368) under Kublai Khan. You may recall his name in the context of the travels of Marco Polo, who visited with the Khan during his sweep through Asia. Nearly a century later, a peasant revolt brought on by continued oppression coupled with a series of devastating floods, drove the last Mongol emperor out of Beijing; the Ming Dynasty was born in 1368 and would last nearly three centuries, to 1644.

The Ming Dynasty is associated with grand architecture projects including the Forbidden City, a vast imperial palace, and landscape architecture such as the gardens of Suzhou in which the impression of informality in nonetheless

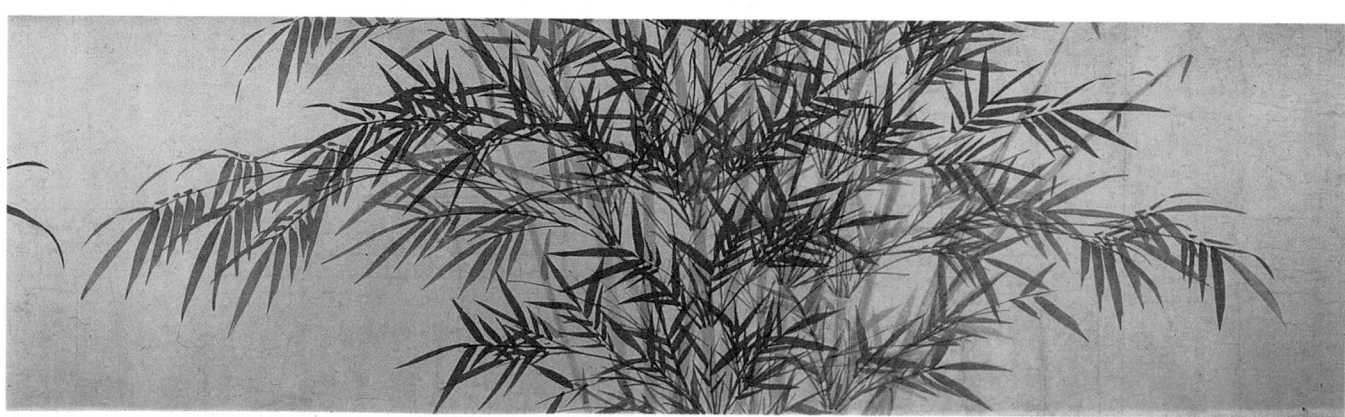

ᴧ **17.33 LI K'AN, Ink** *Bamboo* **section** (Yuan Dynasty, 1308). Handscroll, ink on paper; 14¾" × 93½". The Nelson-Atkins Museum of Art, Kansas City, Missouri.

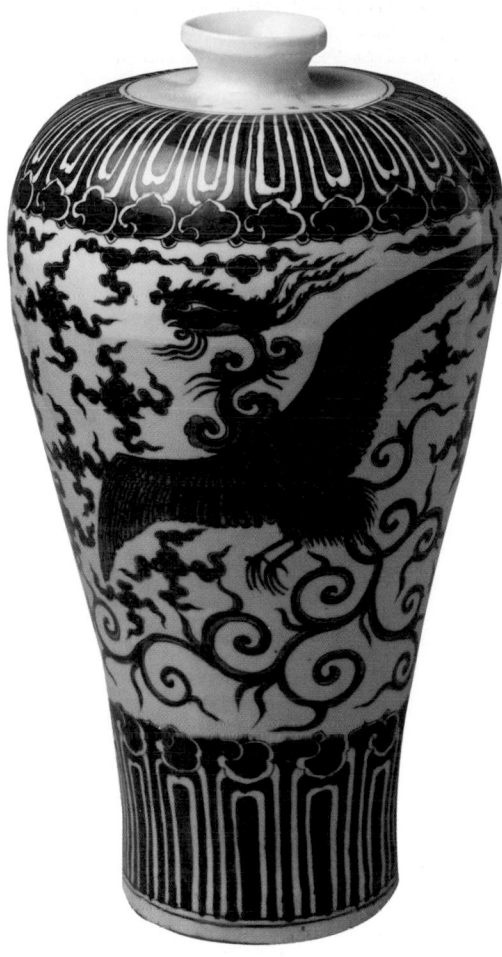

of foliage, crisply defined, leap toward the foreground while others, behind, seem to melt into mist—symphony of calligraphic brushwork. This delicacy is also evident in a blue-and-white porcelain Ming vase (Fig. 17.34). The making of vases such as these was an art form passed from father to son, and was often one of collaboration between expert potters and painters. The vase was decorated using an underglaze-painting technique—a cobalt-based pigment, probably imported from Iran, under a transparent glaze. Blue and white were favorite colors of the Ming court.

Porcelain vases are only one example of the courtly taste for lavishly decorated objects. Among some of the most impressive—technically speaking—were furniture and other objects crafted from lacquered wood. **Lacquer** is produced from the sap or resin of sumac trees, heated to a consistency that can be applied to a surface in layers with a brush. The technique is both time- and labor-intensive, but when dry, the surface is lustrous and hard and can be carved with intricate detail (Fig. 17.35).

The grandest architectural project of the Ming Dynasty was the Forbidden City in Beijing—in essence a "city within a city" that served as the imperial palace and home to the emperor. A chain of buildings constructed of wood—with courtyards interspersed—were placed along a north–south axis; the "backs" of the buildings faced north, "turning away from evil," that is, away from the direction from which the Mongols had invaded. The

ᴧ **17.34 Vase in meiping shape with phoenix** (Ming Dynasty). Porcelain painted with cobalt blue under transparent glaze (Jingdezhen ware); 25⅛" high, 13½" maximum diameter. Metropolitan Museum of Art, New York, New York.

compulsively designed. Ming painters continued the Song tradition of landscape painting in addition to portraits and historical subjects. The dynasty is also known for its ceramics and furniture and objects fashioned of lacquered wood.

Li K'an's fourteenth-century ink-on-paper painting, *Bamboo* (Fig. 17.33), created during the period between the Song and Ming Dynasties, possesses an exceptionally delicate beauty stemming from the subtlest variations in line and value. Velvety black sprays

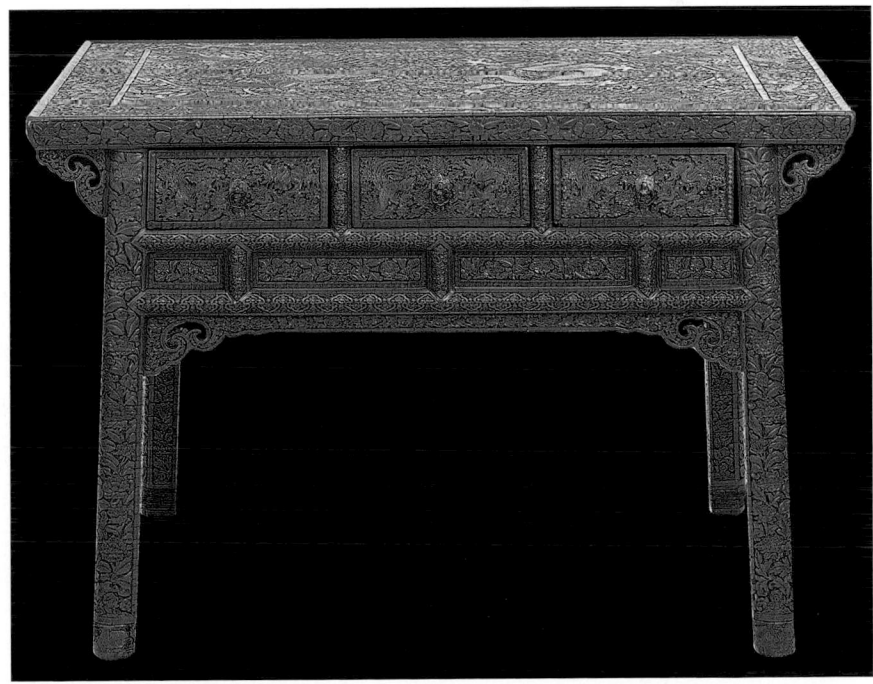

> **17.35 Table with drawers** (Ming Dynasty, c. 1426–1435). Carved red lacquer on a wood core, 3' 11" long. Victoria and Albert Museum, London, England.

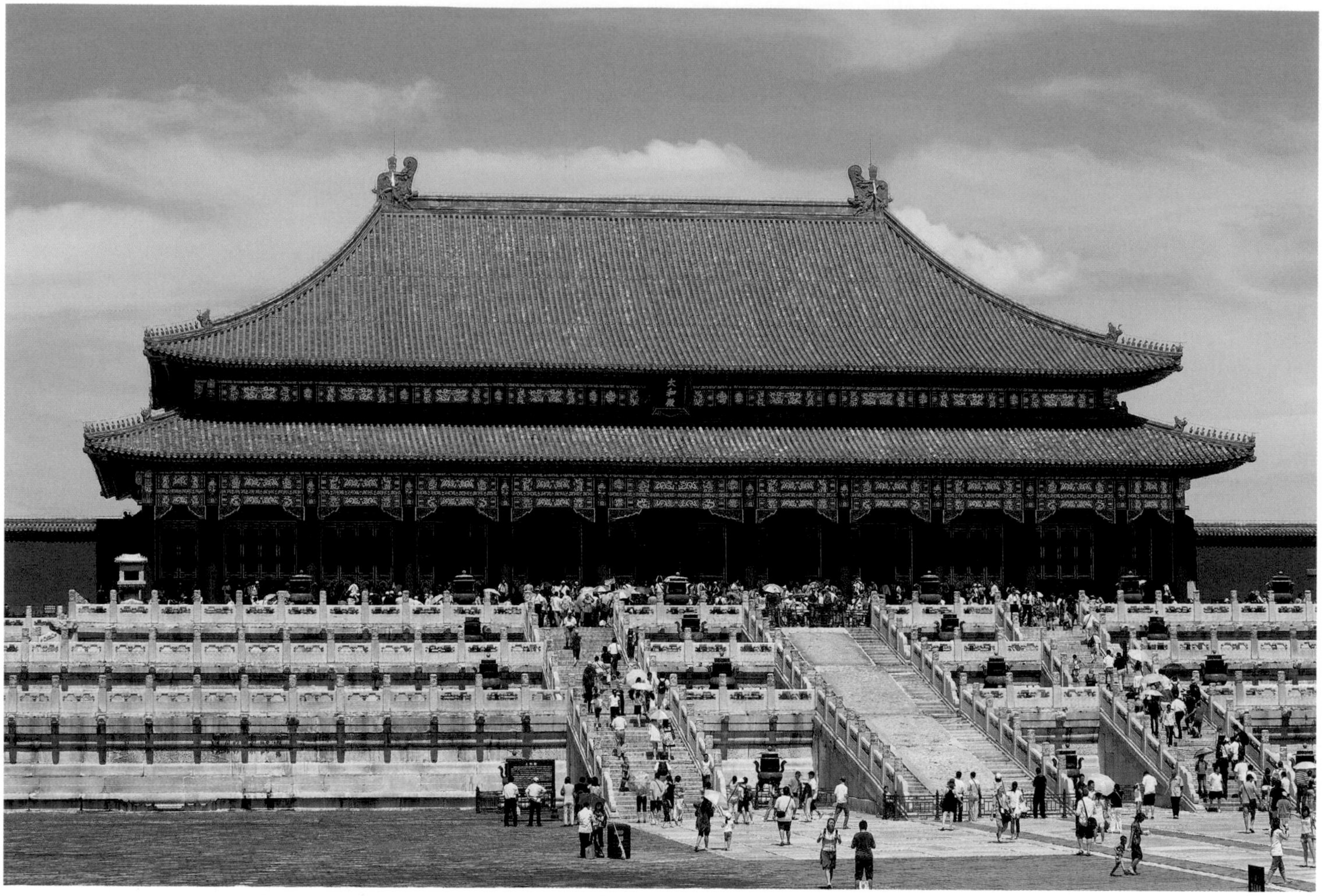

![Hall of Supreme Harmony](...)

∧ 17.36 **Hall of Supreme Harmony (looking north), Forbidden City, Beijing, China** (Ming Dynasty, 15th century and later).

Hall of Supreme Harmony (Fig. 17.36), where the emperor received visitors, is the largest of these. The curved roof—decorated with carvings of animals from Chinese myths—is supported by twenty-four columns carved from mammoth tree trunks that were barged hundreds of miles down the Yangtze River from Sichuan Province in the west. A marble staircase ascends on the exterior of the building and, once inside, another leads to a platform that provides an appropriately elevated, lush setting for the imperial throne of the "Son of Heaven."

Japan

While western Europe was experiencing the Renaissance, Japan was in the so-called Muromachi period (1333–1573), named after the location where the military government—the shogunate—was based. The Muromachi was followed by the Momoyama period (1573–1615), during which three successive warlords ruled Japan.

Numerous **Zen** Buddhist monasteries, temples, and gardens testify to the flowering of the religion during the Muromachi period. Temples served as learning centers where members of the Samurai warrior elite were just as likely to study the teachings of the Buddha as were aristocrats and merchants. Temples also played a vital role in

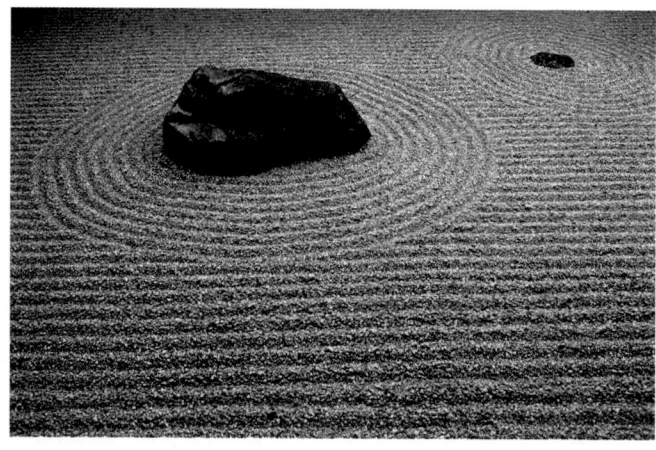

∧ 17.37 **Karesansui (dry-landscape) garden, Ryoanji, Kyoto, Japan** (Muromachi period, c. 1488).

the understanding and preservation of culture—particularly of the arts and literature.

Temple gardens provided Zen Buddhist monks with serene spaces for meditation and ambulation. Some gardens were planted with moss and other greenery while others—"dry-landscape" gardens such as the garden of the Peaceful Dragon Temple (Fig. 17.37)—are designed with areas of gravel that are dotted, here and there, with rocks of interesting shapes and varying sizes. Monks tend to the gardens daily, carefully raking the gravel into linear patterns that evoke rippling water. Their precision reflects the Zen Buddhist emphasis on personal discipline.

The Muromachi era artist Sesshu Toyo traveled to China where he studied the art and architecture of the contemporaneous Ming Dynasty firsthand. His paintings, inspired by the topography of China, were rendered in *haboku*, or splashed-ink style, in which broad ink brushstrokes are applied to paper or silk. Sesshu Toyo's landscape, shown in Figure 17.38, was created at the same time as Leonardo da Vinci was working on his fresco *The Last Supper*. The landscape features a blend of technical mastery and spontaneity that imparts both delicacy and vigor. Just as in Li K'an's painting of bamboo, closer objects the impression of receding space is created by contrasting detailed imagery in the foreground with hazy impressions in the background.

Hasegawa Tohaku's *Pine Forest* (Fig. 17.39), painted during the Momoyama period, is a fine example of the decorative, multipanel folding screens that were used by warlords in their fortified palaces. Also reminiscent of Li K'an's study of bamboo (see Fig. 17.33), *Pine Forest* is a painting in which the stunning simplicity and sensuousness of plant life comprise

the subject. The illusion of depth—and of dreamy mists—is evoked through subtle gradations of value and texture as well as overlapping and relative size. Without foreground or background per se, there is no point of reference from which we can infer the scale of the trees; their monumentality is implied. Groupings of trees within each screen balance one another, and the overall composition suggests the infinite directional strivings of nature to find form and express itself.

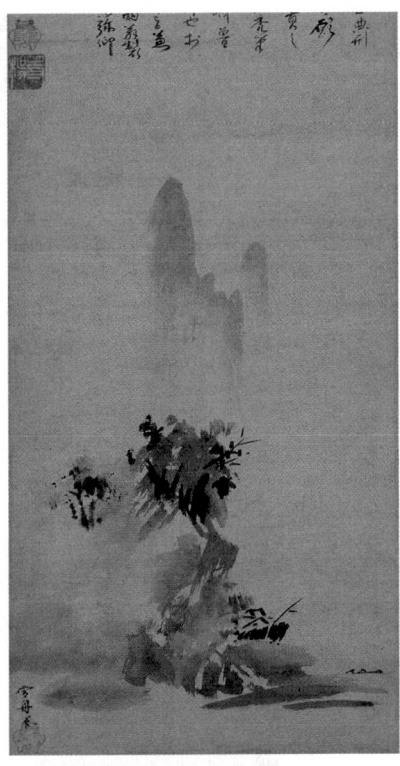

▲ 17.38 SESSHU TOYO, Splashed-ink (haboku) landscape (Muromachi period, 1495). Detail of the lower part of a hanging scroll. Ink on paper; full scroll 4'10¼" × 1'⅞", detail 4½" high. Tokyo National Museum, Tokyo, Japan.

The Americas

Circa 1325 CE, during the formative years of the European Renaissance, the Aztecs of central Mexico, who had been

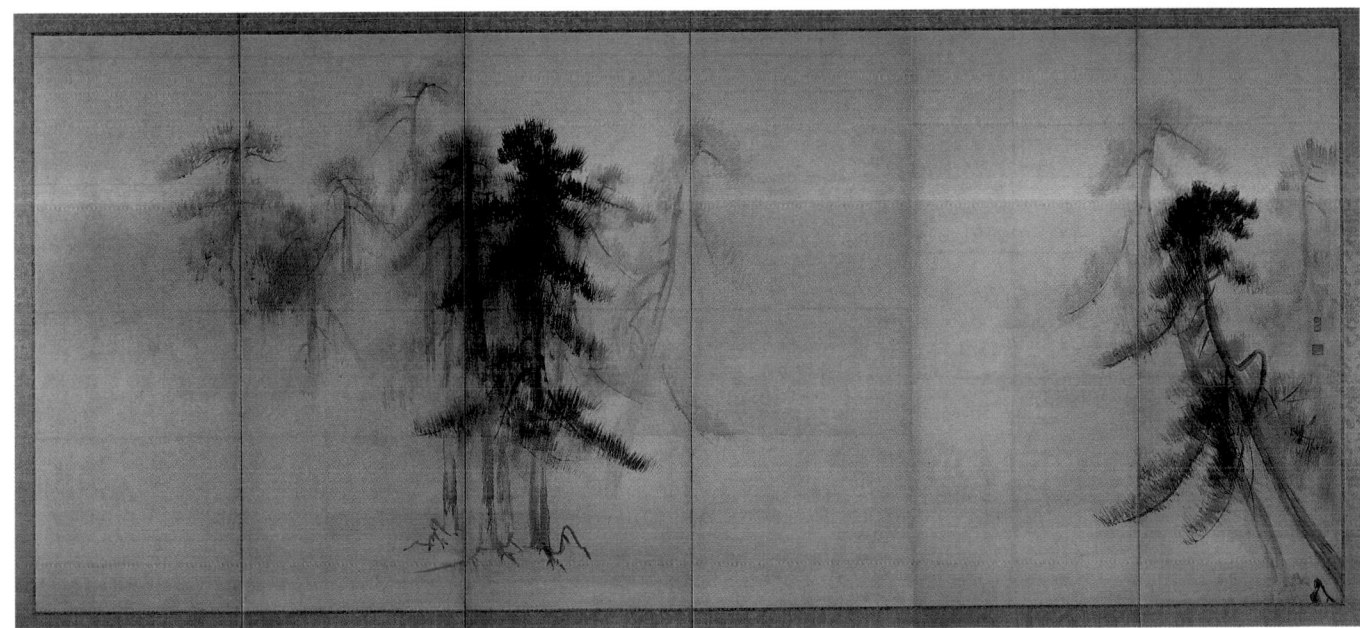

▲ 17.39 HASEGAWA TOHAKU, *Pine Forest* (Momoyama period, late 16th century). One of a pair of six-panel screens. Ink on paper, 5' 1⅜" × 11' 4". Tokyo National Museum, Tokyo, Japan.

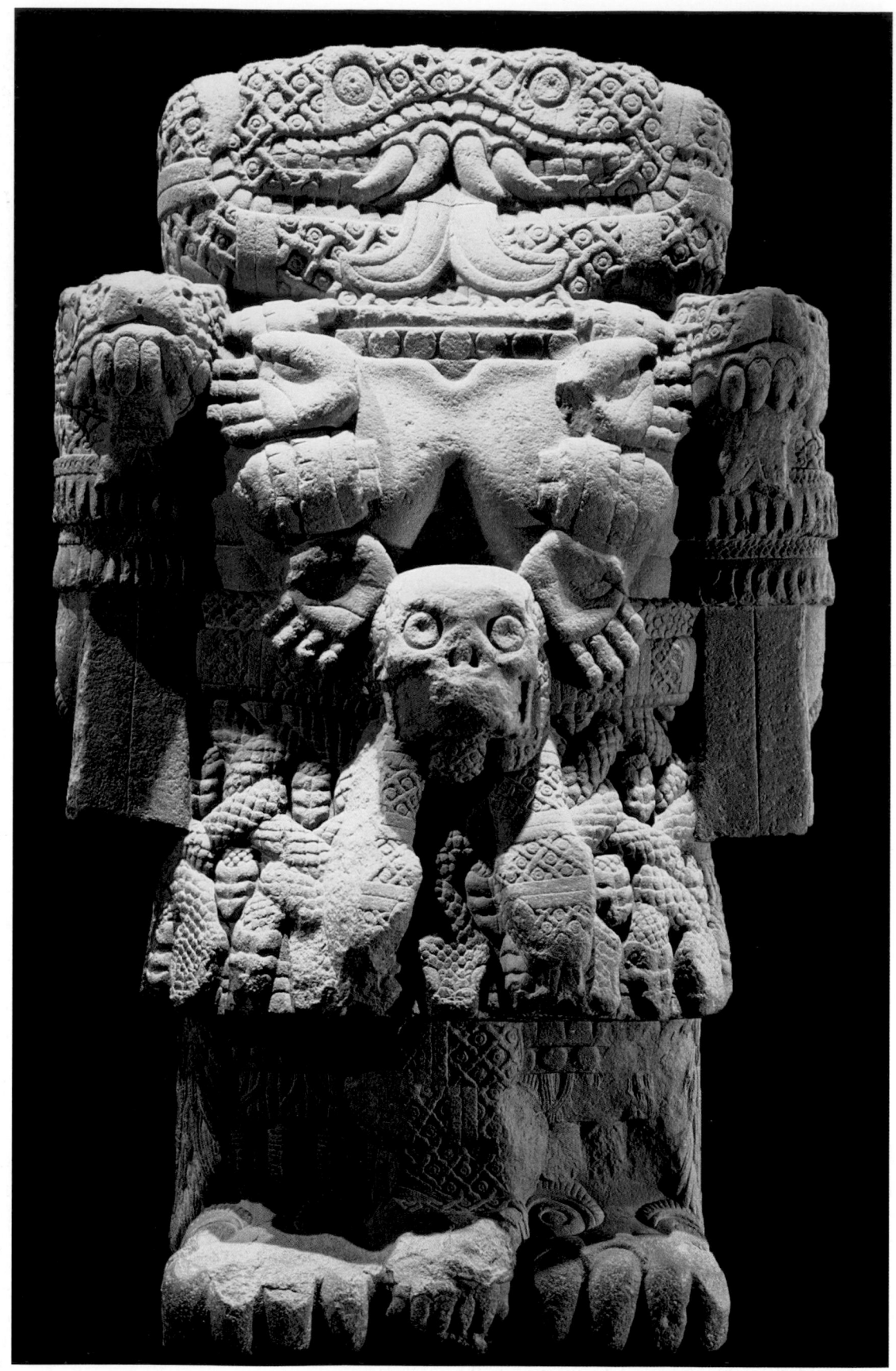

1 ft.

∧ **17.40 Coatlicue, from Tenochtitlán, Mexico City** (Aztec, c. 1487–1520). Andesite. 11'6" high. Museo Nacional de Anthropologia, Mexico City, Mexico.

a group of meager nomads, built their capital, Tenochtitlán, on the site of modern-day Mexico City. Once established, the Aztec civilization would be famous for its advances in mathematics and engineering, along with monumental architecture, and infamous for its cruel subjugation of peoples from surrounding tribes. Prisoners of war fell victim to the ritual of human sacrifice intended to appease the sun god, who was believed to have sacrificed himself in the creation of the human species. It is not surprising that in the early part of the sixteenth century, the Spanish explorer-invaders found many Aztec neighbors more than eager to help them in their conquest of Mexico. The Aztecs also helped seal their own fate by initially treating the Spaniards, who they believed were descended from Quetzalcóatl, with great hospitality. The Spaniards did not rush to disabuse their hosts of this notion and were thus able to creep into the hearts of the Aztecs within the Trojan horse of mistaken identity.

Coatlicue was the Aztec "Mother of Gods," associated with the Earth and the cycle of birth, death, and rebirth. The compact, monumental stone effigy in Figure 17.40 depicts the goddess as symbol of creation and destruction (the Earth gives but also takes away). She wears a skirt of carved serpents, representing fertility, and a necklace of severed hands, hearts, and skulls. Scholars offer different interpretations of the uppermost part of the sculpture. Some read it as Coatlcue's head, composed of the heads of two facing snakes, whose eyes and fangs become her own. Others have said that the sculpture portrays a decapitated Coatlicue in which snakes coil out of her severed neck. This interpretation more directly references one of two myths, in which one of Coatlicue's 400 children called upon her siblings to kill their mother. The ferocity of the imagery, incised and carved in relief, was typical of pre-Columbian societies.

The nomadic roots of the Inka are similar to that of the Aztecs, and like them, the Inka created an extraordinary civilization. Established in the Andes Mountains in what is today southern Peru around 1000 CE, their empire eventually stretched from Ecuador to Chile. The native arts of the Inka include massive pyramid-shaped

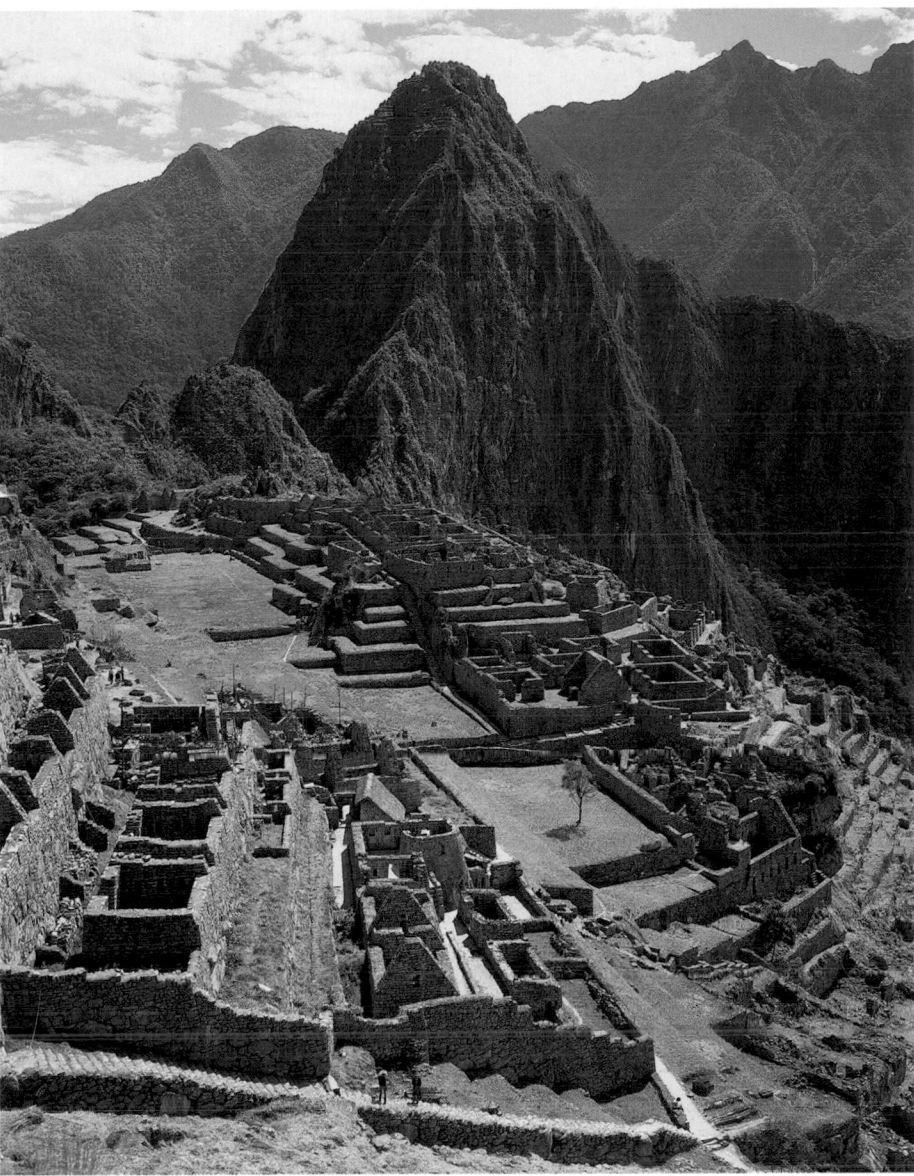

▲ 17.41 View of Machu Picchu (looking northwest), Urubamba Valley, Peru (Inka, 1490–1530).

platforms for what were wooden temples; stone relief carvings, mostly in the form of architectural embellishment; ceramic wares; and wall painting.

Figure 17.41 shows the grand ruins of Machu Picchu, the Inka fortress situated dramatically between two colossal mountain peaks. Constructed around 1500 CE, the civil engineering of the fortress and urban plan rival those for which the Romans were famous. The great, straight "Royal Road of the Mountains"—the main line of communication—was 30 feet wide and walled for its entire 3,750 miles; it had no parallel in Europe. Against the magnificence of the natural landscape, the dry masonry walls, constructed of precisely carved and fitted stones, are a testament to humans' relationship to and control over nature.

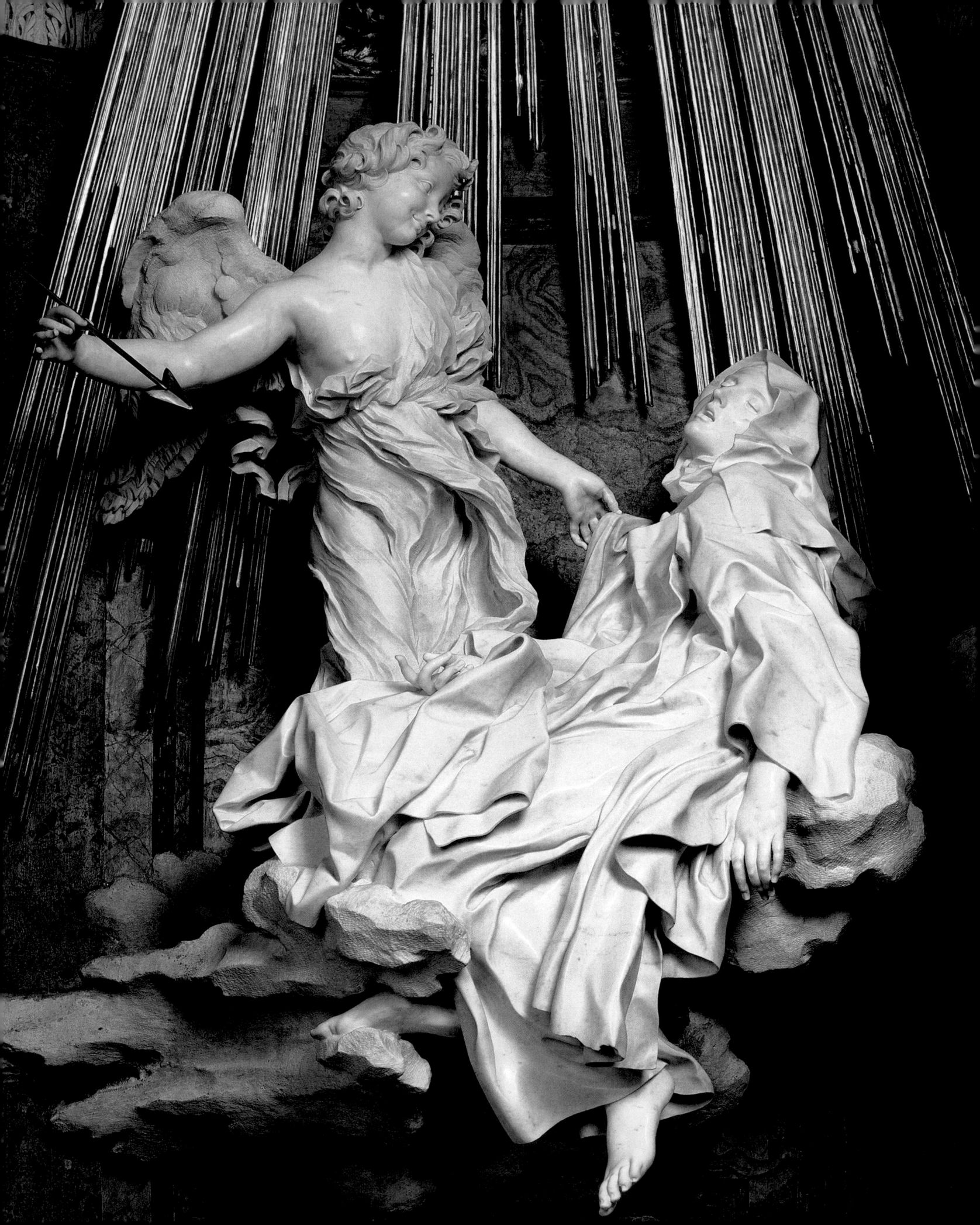

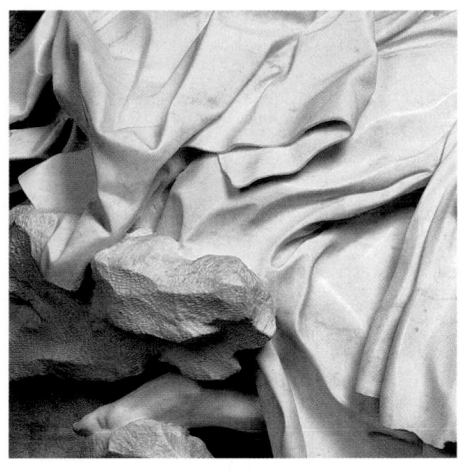

18

THE BAROQUE ERA

Nature, and Nature's laws lay hid in night.
God said: "Let Newton be!" and all was Light!

— ALEXANDER POPE

THE BAROQUE period spans roughly the years from 1600 to 1750. Like the Renaissance, which preceded it, the Baroque period was an age of genius in many fields of endeavor. Sir Isaac Newton derived laws of motion and of gravity that have only recently been modified by the discoveries of Einstein. The achievements of Galileo and Kepler in astronomy brought the vast expanses of outer space into sharper focus. The Pilgrims also showed an interest in motion when, in 1620, they put to sea and landed in what is now Massachusetts. Our founders had a certain concern for space as well—they wanted as much as possible between themselves and their English oppressors.

The Baroque period in Europe included a number of post-Renaissance styles that do not have all that much in common. On the one hand, there was a continuation of the Classicism and naturalism of the Renaissance. On the other hand, a far more colorful, ornate, painterly, and dynamic style was born. If one name had to be applied to describe these different directions, it is just as well that that name is **Baroque**—for the word is believed to derive from the Portuguese *barroco*, meaning "irregularly shaped pearl." The Baroque period was indeed irregular in its stylistic tendencies, and it also gave birth to some of the most treasured pearls of Western art.

Motion and space were major concerns of the Baroque artists, as they were of the scientists of the period. The concept of time, a dramatic use of light, and a passionate theatricality complete the list of the five most important characteristics of Baroque art, as we will see throughout this chapter.

◄ GIANLORENZO BERNINI, *The Ecstasy of St. Theresa* (1645–1652). Marble; height of group approximately 11' 6". Cornaro Chapel, Santa Maria della Vittoria, Rome, Italy.

THE BAROQUE PERIOD IN ITALY

The Baroque era was born in Rome, some say in reaction to the spread of Protestantism resulting from the Reformation. Even though many areas of Europe were affected by the new post-Renaissance spirit (see Map 18.1 on page 394), it was more alive and well and influential in Italy than elsewhere—partly because of the strengthening of the papacy in religion, politics, and patronage of the arts. During the Renaissance, the principal patron of the arts was the infamous Pope Julius II. However, during the Baroque era, a series of powerful popes—Paul V, Urban VIII, Innocent X, and Alexander VII—assumed this role. The Baroque period has been called the Age of Expansion, following the Renaissance Age of Discovery, and this expansion is felt keenly in the arts.

St. Peter's

The expansion and renovation of St. Peter's Cathedral in Rome is an excellent project with which to begin our discussion of the Baroque in Italy, for three reasons: The building expresses the ideals of the Renaissance, stands as a hallmark of the Baroque style, and brings together work by the finest artists of both periods—Michelangelo and Bernini. The major change in the structure of St. Peter's was from the central Greek cross plans of Bramante and Michelangelo to a longitudinal Latin cross plan (Fig. 18.1). Thus, three bays were added to the nave between the domed crossing and the façade. The architect Carlo Maderno was responsible for this task as well as the design for the new façade, but the job of completing the project fell into the hands of the most significant sculptor of the day, Gianlorenzo Bernini.

Gianlorenzo Bernini

Gianlorenzo Bernini (1598–1680) made an extensive contribution to St. Peter's as we see it today, both to the exterior and the interior. In his design for the **piazza** of St. Peter's, visible in the aerial view (Fig. 18.2), Bernini had constructed two expansive arcades extending from the façade of the church and culminating in semicircular "arms" enclosing an oval space. This space, the piazza, was divided into trapezoidal "pie sections," in the center of which rises an Egyptian obelisk. The Classical arcades, true in details to the arts that inspired them, stretch outward into the surrounding city, as if to welcome worshipers and cradle them in spiritual comfort. The curving arms, or arcades, are composed of two double rows of columns with a path between, ending in Classical pedimented "temple fronts." In the interior of the cathedral,

SEVENTEENTH AND EIGHTEENTH CENTURIES IN THE WEST

1600	1621	1648	1679	1800
Caravaggio paints *The Conversion of St. Paul* 1600–1601	Teresa of Ávila is canonized by Pope Gregory XV 1622	The Counter-Reformation ends 1648	The Declaration of Independence 1776	
Galileo invents and improves telescopes 1609	New St. Peter's is consecrated by Pope Urban VIII 1626	Velázquez paints *Las Meninas* 1656	Reign of Louis XVI and Marie-Antoinette 1774–1792	
Rubens paints *The Rape of the Daughters of Leucippus* 1617	Louis XIV, the Sun King, ascends the French throne 1643	Rembrandt paints *Syndics of the Drapers' Guild* 1661–1662	The American Revolutionary War 1778–1783	
Kepler reveals his laws of planetary motion 1619	Galileo is found guilty of heresy and forced to recant his discovery that the sun is the center of the solar system 1633	Borromini designs San Carlo alle Quattro Fontane 1665–1667	Vigée-Lebrun paints *Marie Antoinette and Her Children* 1781	
Gentileschi paints *Judith Decapitating Holofernes* 1620	Poussin paints *The Rape of the Sabine Women* 1636–1637	Construction of the Palace of Versailles begins 1669	The French Revolution begins 1789	
Puritans set sail for North America on the *Mayflower* 1620	Bernini sculpts *The Ecstasy of St. Theresa* 1645–1652	Construction of the New St. Paul's Cathedral begins 1675	Execution of Louis XVI and Marie-Antoinette 1793	
		Baciccio paints *Triumph of the Sacred Name of Jesus* 1676–1679		

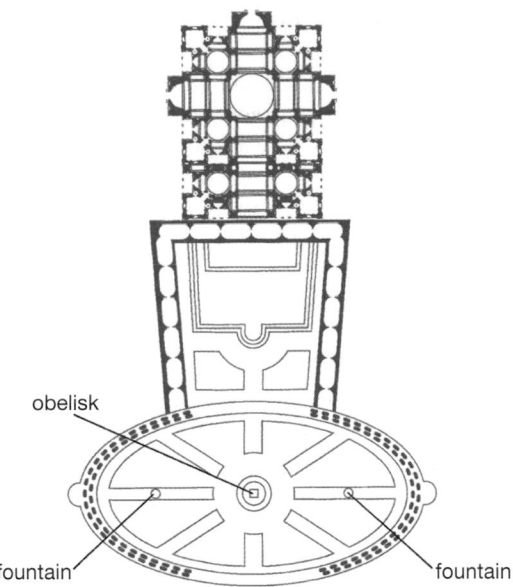

obelisk

fountain   fountain

▲ 18.1 **Plan of St. Peter's Cathedral, Vatican City, Rome, Italy** (1605–1613).

still in a Classical contrapposto stance, but rather extends into the surrounding space away from a vertical axis. This movement outward from a central core forces the viewer to take into account both solids and voids—that is, both the form and the spaces between and surrounding the forms—to appreciate the complete composition. We must move around the work to understand it fully, and as we move, the views of the work change radically.

We may compare the difference between Michelangelo's *David* and Bernini's *David* to the difference between Classical and Hellenistic Greek sculpture. The movement out of Classical art into Hellenistic art was marked by an extension of the figure into the surrounding space, a

beneath Michelangelo's great dome, Bernini designed a bronze canopy to cover the main altar. In the apse, Bernini combined architecture, sculpture, and stained glass in a brilliantly golden display for the Cathedra Petri, or Throne of St. Peter. Through his many other sculptural contributions to St. Peter's, commissioned by various popes, Bernini's reputation as a master is solidified.

Bernini's *David* (see Fig. 17.24) testifies to the artist's genius and illustrates the dazzling characteristics of Baroque sculpture. This David is remarkably different from those of Donatello, Verrocchio, and Michelangelo. Three of the five characteristics of Baroque art are present in Bernini's sculpture: motion (in this case, implied), a different way of looking at space, and the introduction of the concept of time. The Davids by Donatello and Verrocchio were figures at rest after having slain their Goliaths. Michelangelo, by contrast, presented David before the encounter, with the tension and emotion evident in every vein and muscle, bound to the block of marble that had surrounded the figure. Bernini does not offer David before or after the fight, but instead in the process of the fight. He has introduced an element of time in his work. As in *The Last Supper* by Tintoretto (see Fig. 17.26), we sense that David would have used his weapon if we were to look away and then back. We, the viewers, are forced to complete the action that David has begun for us.

A new concept of space comes into play with David's positioning. The figure no longer remains

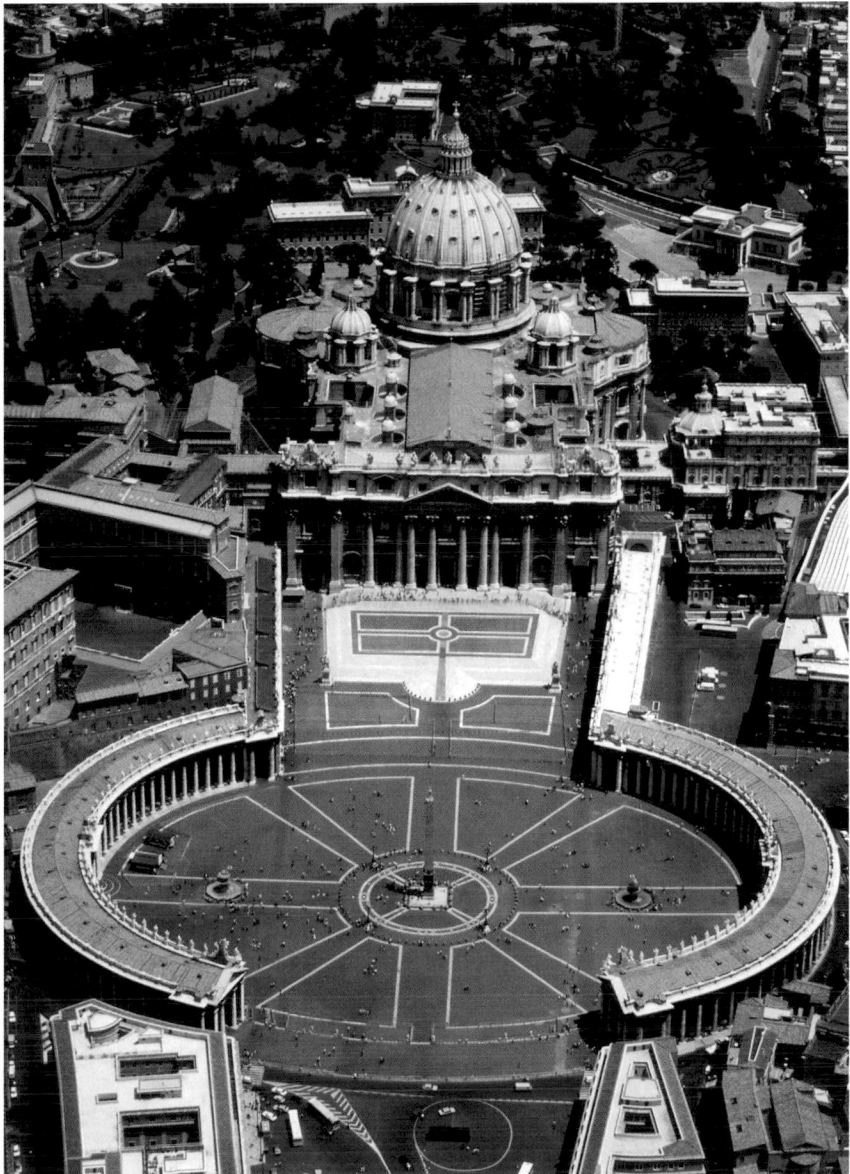

▲ 18.2 **GIANLORENZO BERNINI, Piazza of St. Peter's.** St. Peter's Square, Vatican City, Rome, Italy.

It's pure mockery of realism. It's a lie. It's a stage setting. The same as . . . in films.
Put me a spotlight to the right and another on the left.

—PABLO PICASSO, WHEN ASKED WHETHER CARAVAGGIO WAS A REALIST

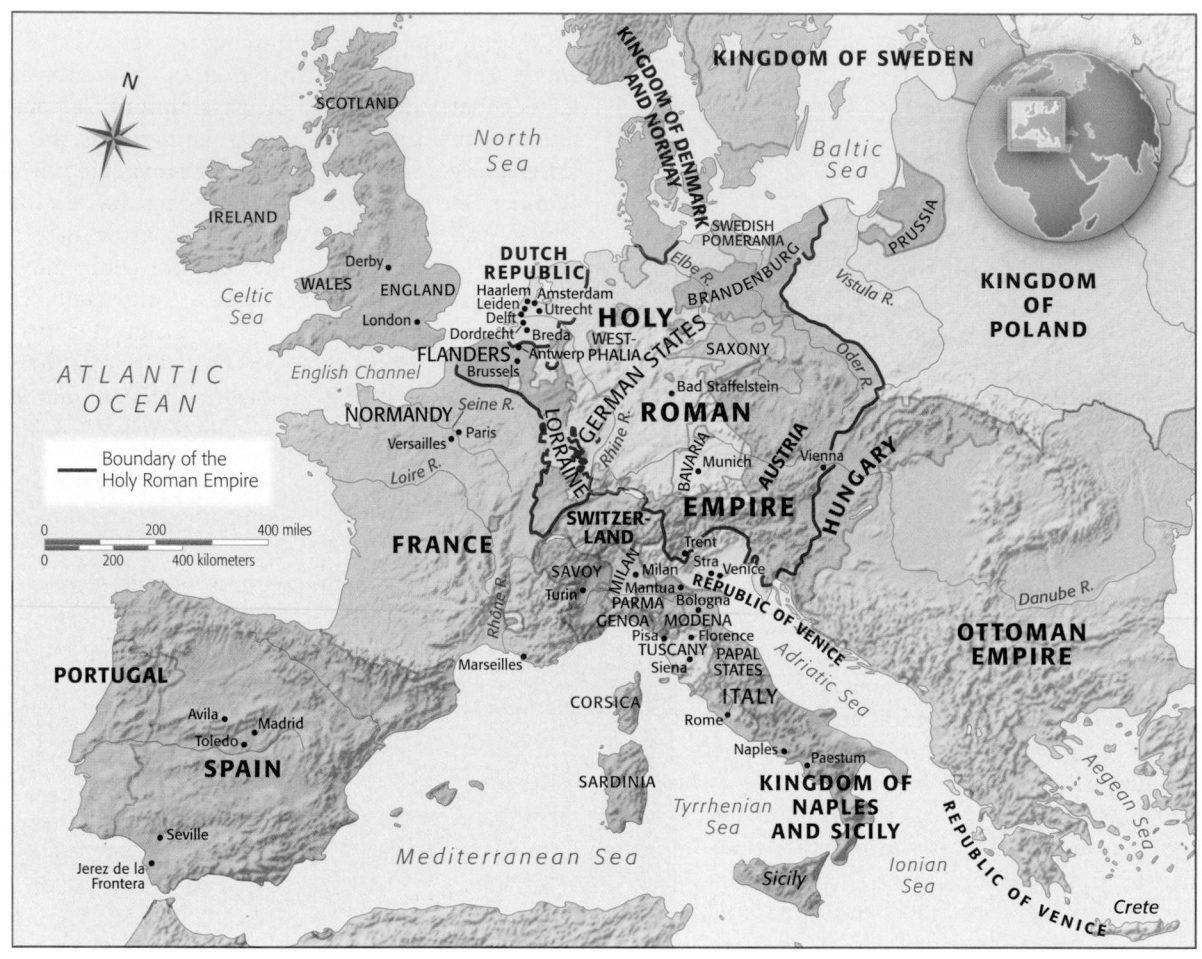

∧ MAP 18.1 Europe in 1648.

sense of implied movement, and a large degree of theatricality. The time-honored balance between emotion and restraint coveted by the Classical Greek artist as well as the Renaissance master had given way in the Hellenistic and Baroque periods to unleashed passion.

Uncontrollable passion and theatrical drama might best describe Bernini's *The Ecstasy of St. Theresa* (Fig. 18.3), a sculptural group executed for the chapel of the Cornaro family in the church of Santa Maria della Vittoria in Rome. The sculpture commemorates a mystical event

involving St. Theresa, a Carmelite nun who believed that a pain in her side was caused by an angel of God stabbing her repeatedly with a fire-tipped arrow. Her response combined pain and pleasure, as conveyed by the sculpture's submissive swoon and impassioned facial expression. Bernini summoned all of his sculptural powers to execute these figures and combined the arts of architecture, sculpture, and painting to achieve his desired theatrical effect. Notice the way in which Bernini described vastly different textures with his sculptural tools: the

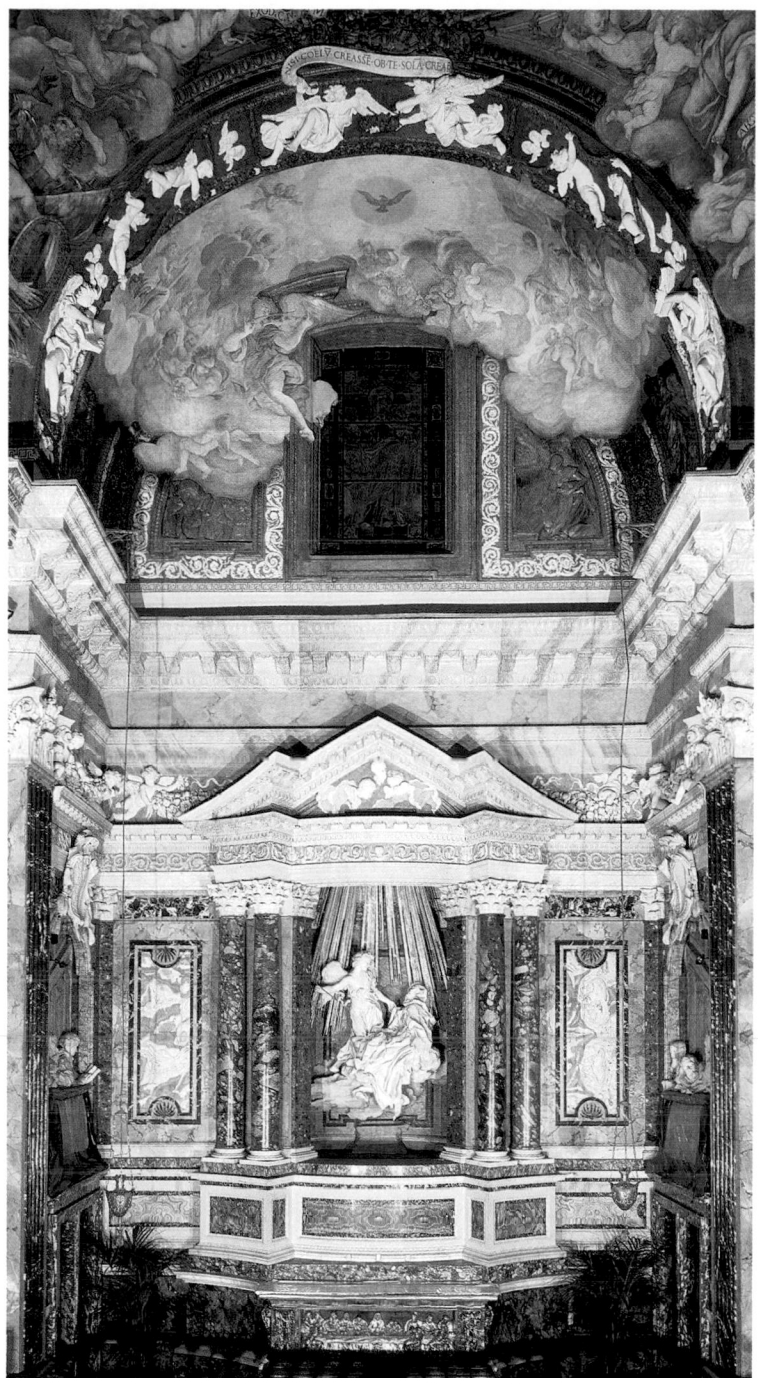

▲ 18.3 GIANLORENZO BERNINI, *The Ecstasy of St. Theresa* (1645–1652). Marble; height of group approximately 11' 6". Cornaro Chapel, Santa Maria della Vittoria, Rome, Italy.

sculptures of the likenesses of members of the Cornaro family in theater boxes to the left and right. They observe, gesture, and discuss the scene animatedly as would theatergoers. The fine line between the rational and the spiritual that so interested the Baroque artist was presented by Bernini in a tactile yet illusionary masterpiece of sculpture.

Caravaggio

This theatrical drama and passion had its counterpart in Baroque painting, as can be seen in the work of Michelangelo de Merisi, called Caravaggio (1573–1610). Unlike Bernini's somewhat idealized facial and figural types, the models for Caravaggio came directly from those around him. Whereas Bernini could move in the company of popes and princes, Caravaggio was more comfortable with the outcasts of society. In a way he was one of them, having a police record for violent assaults. Caravaggio chose lower-class models for his shocking painting *The Conversion of St. Paul* (Fig. 18.4). The artist

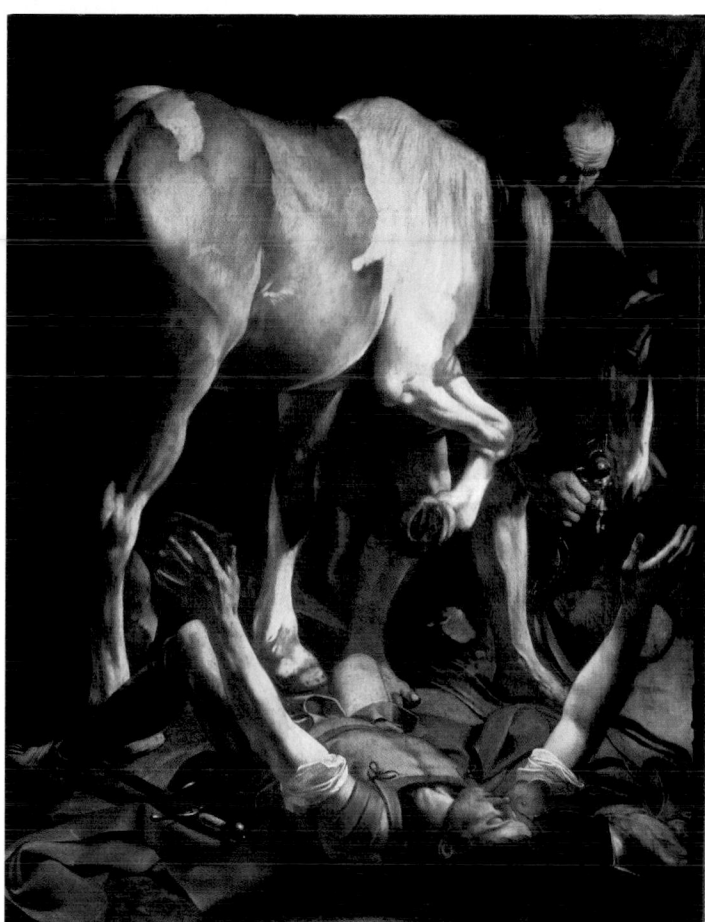

▲ 18.4 CARAVAGGIO, *The Conversion of St. Paul* (1600–1601). Oil on canvas, 90" × 69". Santa Maria del Popolo, Rome, Italy.

roughly textured clouds, the heavy folds of St. Theresa's woolen garment, the diaphanous "wet-look" drapery of the angel (see chapter-opening image). "Divine" rays of glimmering bronze—illuminated by a hidden window—shower down on the figures, as if emanating from the painted ceiling of the chapel. Bernini enhanced this self-conscious theatrical effect by including marble the night, resulting in an exaggerated chiaroscuro called tenebrism.

Tenebrism, translated as "dark manner," is characterized by an often small and concentrated light source within the painting or what appears to be an external "spotlight" directed at specific points in the composition. The effect is harsh and theatrical, as if the events were playing out onstage and being lit from above. The lighting technique of tenebrism was used broadly by Italian Baroque painters but is seen throughout European painting at this time.

Artemisia Gentileschi

One of Caravaggio's foremost contemporaries was Artemisia Gentileschi (1593–c. 1652). Her father, the painter Orazio Gentileschi, who enjoyed much success in Rome, Genoa, and London, recognized and supported Artemisia's talents. Although one of her father's choices for her ended in disaster—an apprenticeship with a man who ultimately raped her—Artemisia came to develop a personal, dramatic, and impassioned Baroque style. Her work bears similarities to that of Caravaggio, her own father, and others working in Italy at that moment, but it often stands apart in the emphatic rendering of its content or in its reconsideration and revision of subjects commonly represented by sixteenth- and seventeenth-century artists.

Consider, for example, her painting of the biblical story of Susannah and the Elders (Fig. 18.5). Most of artists of Artemisia's day rendered Susannah as beautiful and sensual— a feast for the eyes. A painting by Tintoretto shows her with perfume bottles, jewels, and pearls, bathing in a sumptuous, fertile garden. Susannah admires herself in a mirror.

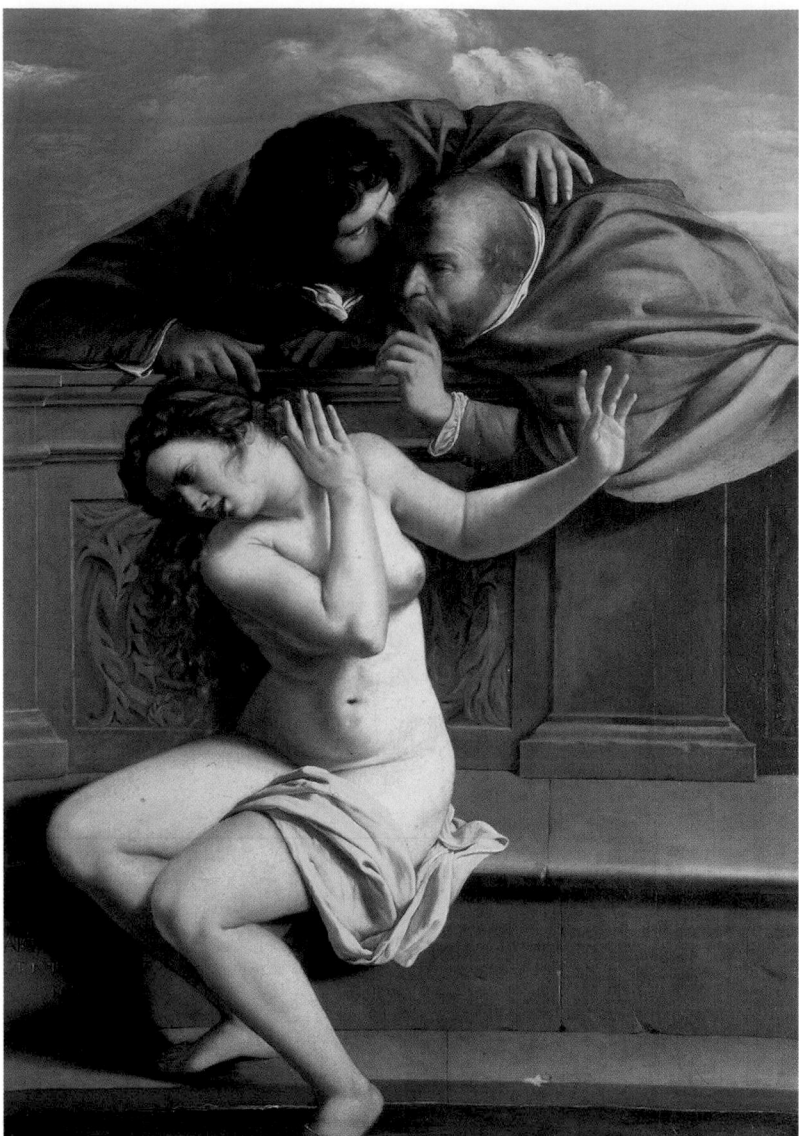

▲ 18.5 **ARTEMISIA GENTILESCHI**, *Susannah and the Elders* (1610). Oil on canvas, 66⅞" × 46⅞". Kunstsammlungen Graf von Schonborn, Wiesentheid, Germany.

marked the dramatic moment when Paul, persecuting Christians in the name of the Roman Empire, was confronted with his actions and, in response, changed the course of his life. Thrown from his horse and blinded by a bright light, Paul professed to have heard a voice asking why he engaged in murderous persecution. The voice, that of Jesus according to Paul, directed him to proceed to Damascus, where he was cured of his blindness and began to preach the tenets of Christianity. Very much in the Baroque spirit, Caravaggio chose to focus on the exact moment when Paul was thrown from his horse. He lies flat on his back, eyelids shut, arms groping in the darkness of his blindness. Paul looks as if he might be trampled by his horse, except for the rugged yet calming hands of a man nearby. A piercing light flashes upon the scene, spotlighting certain parts and casting others into

Is Tintoretto suggesting that Susannah played some role in her seduction? Is he turning us, the spectators, into voyeurs such as those who menaced her? Gentileschi's *Susannah and the Elders* also tells Susannah's story, but Tintoretto's lush garden setting is replaced by a compressed space in which Susannah twists and turns her body to fend off the threatening, sleazy elders. There is nothing sensual about her contorted face and her nakedness against the harsh, cold stone. As one of the men gestures "Shhhhhh! You'd better not say a word!" Susannah finds herself trapped in a claustrophobic space—between her seducers, the stone, and us. If our eyes focus on Susannah, they focus on her anguish. The nearby Compare + Contrast feature compares renderings of a biblical heroine by Caravaggio and Artemisia.

COMPARE & CONTRAST
Two Views of Judith's Biblical Encounter with Holofernes

CONSIDER THE ROUGHLY CONTEMPORARY paintings of *Judith and Holofernes* by Caravaggio (**Fig. 18.6**) and *Judith Decapitating Holofernes* by Gentileschi (**Fig. 18.7**). Both works reference the biblical story of the heroine Judith, who rescues her oppressed people by decapitating the tyrannical Assyrian general Holofernes. She steals into his tent under the cover of night and pretends to respond to his seductive overtures. When he is besotted, with her and with drink, she uses his own sword to cut off his head. Both paintings are prime examples of the Baroque style—vibrant palette, dramatic lighting, an impassioned subject heightened to excess by our coming face-to-terrified-face with a man at the precise moment of his bloody execution. But consider the differences: How would you compare Gentileschi's image of Judith with Caravaggio's? Look at the delicacy of Judith's demeanor and the disgust in her facial expression. Now observe Gentileschi's Judith—determined, strong, physically and emotionally committed to the task. In Caravaggio's painting, Holofernes is caught unaware and falls victim in his compromised, drunken state. Gentileschi's tyrant snaps out of his wine-induced stupor and struggles for his life. He pushes and fights and is ultimately overpowered by a righteous woman. What, if any, gender differences can you interpret in these renderings?

Gentileschi's *Judith Decapitating Holofernes* is one of her most studied and violent paintings. She returned to the subject repeatedly in many different versions, leading some historians to suggest that her seeming obsession with the story signified her personal struggle in the wake of her rape and subsequent trial of her accuser, during which she was tortured in an attempt to verify the truth of her testimony. Do you think that this context is essential to understanding Gentileschi's work?

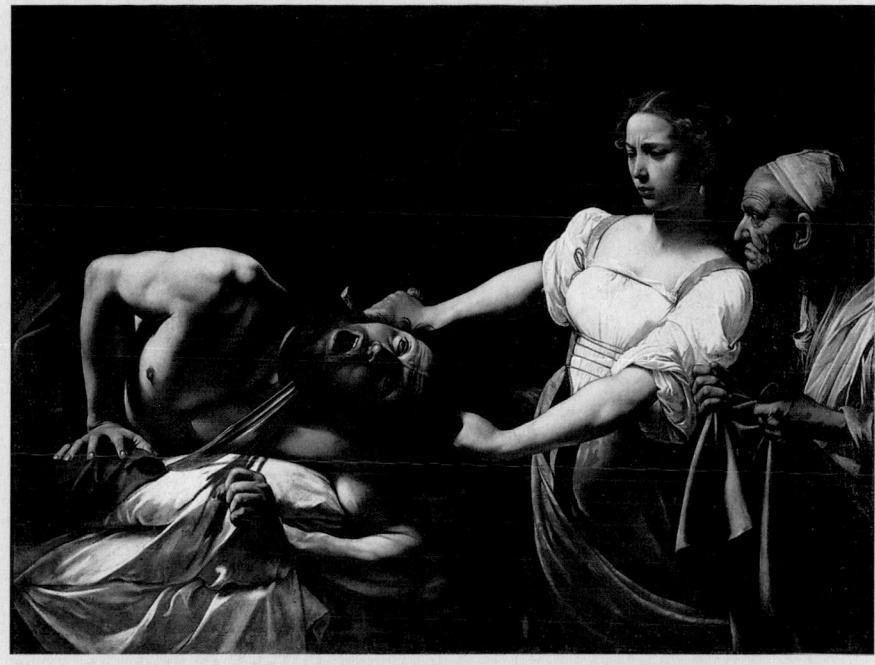

1 ft.

∧ **18.6 CARAVAGGIO,** *Judith and Holofernes* (c. 1598). Oil on canvas, approximately 56¼" × 76¾". Galleria Nazionale d'Arte Antica, Palazzo Barberini, Rome, Italy.

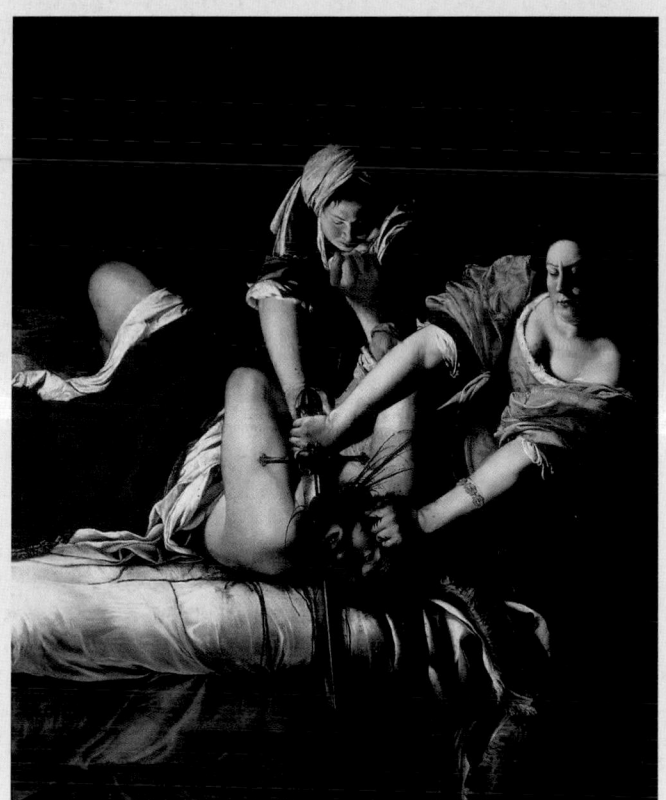

1 ft.

➤ **18.7 ARTEMISIA GENTILESCHI,** *Judith Decapitating Holofernes* (c. 1620). Oil on canvas, 72½" × 55¾". Uffizi Gallery, Florence, Italy.

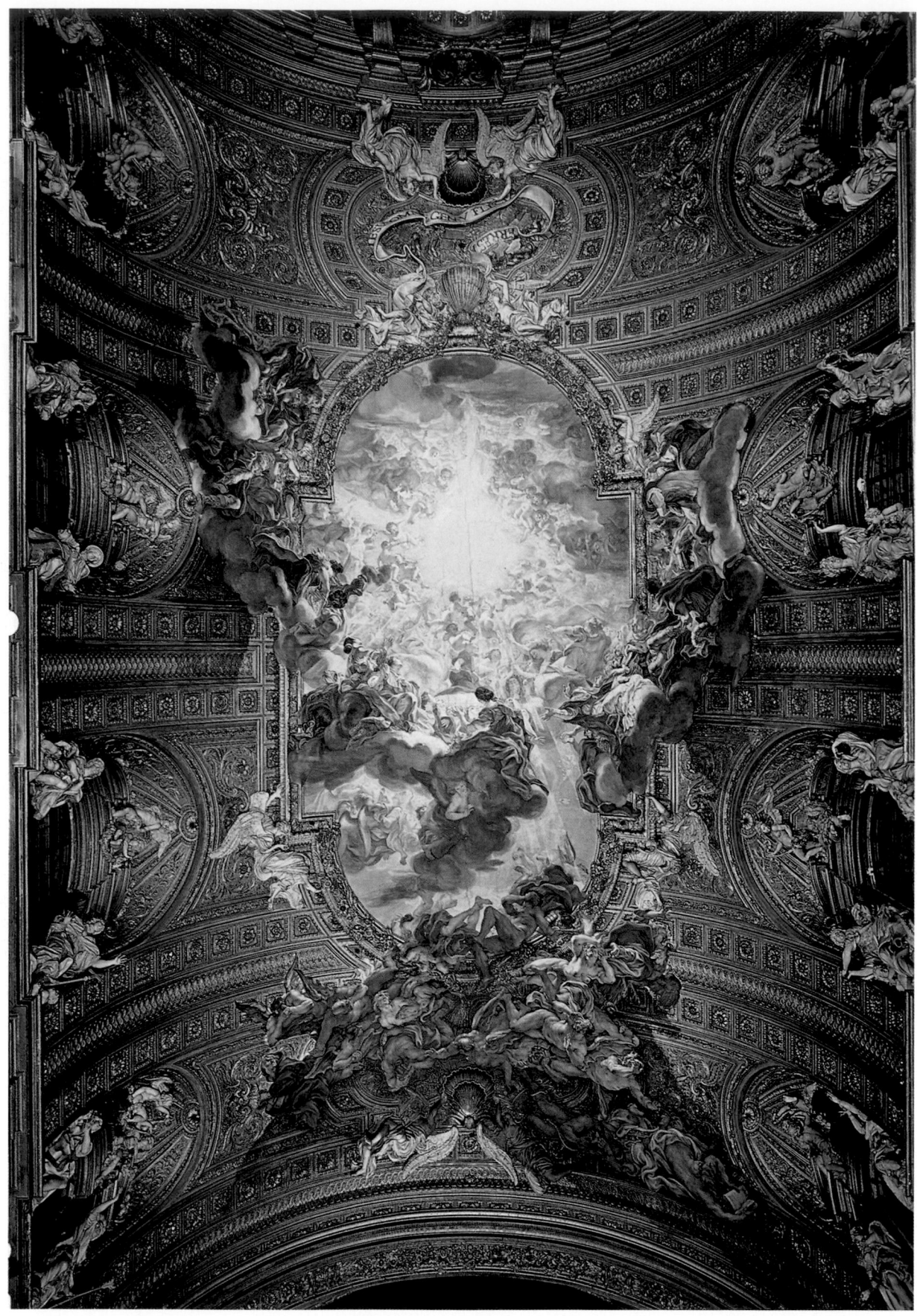

< 18.8 BACICCIO, *Triumph of the Sacred Name of Jesus* (1676–1679). Ceiling fresco. Il Gesu, Rome, Italy.

Baroque Ceiling Decoration

The Baroque interest in combining the arts of painting, sculpture, and architecture found its home in the naves and domes of churches and cathedrals, as artists used the three media to create an unsurpassed illusionistic effect. Unlike Renaissance ceiling painting, as exemplified by Michelangelo's decoration for the Sistine Chapel, the space was not divided into "frames" with individual scenes. Rather, the Baroque artist created the illusion of a ceiling vault open to the heavens with figures flying freely in and out of the church. Baciccio's *Triumph of the Sacred Name of Jesus* (Fig. 18.8) is an energetic display of figures painted on plaster that spill out beyond the gilded frame of the ceiling's illusionistic opening. The *trompe l'oeil* effect is achieved by combining these painted figures with white stucco–modeled sculptures and a gilded stucco ceiling. Attention to detail is remarkable, from the blinding light of the heavens to the deep shadows that would be cast on the ceiling by the painted forms. Saints and angels fly upward toward the light, while sinners are banished from the heavens to the floor of the church. Artists such as Baciccio and their patrons spared no illusionistic device to create a total, mystical atmosphere.

Francesco Borromini

Although it is difficult to imagine an architect incorporating the Baroque elements of motion, space, and light in buildings, this was accomplished by the great seventeenth-century architect Francesco Borromini (1599–1667). His San Carlo alle Quattro Fontane (Fig. 18.9) shows that the change from Renaissance to Baroque architecture was one from the static to the organic. Borromini's façade undulates in implied movement complemented by the concave entablatures of the bell towers on the roof. Light plays across the plane of the façade, bouncing off the engaged columns, while leaving the recessed areas in darkness. The stone seems to breathe because of the **plasticity** of the design and the innovative use of light and shadow. The interior is equally alive, consisting of a large oval space surrounded by rippling concave and convex walls. For the first time since we examined the Parthenon (see Fig. 15.9), we appreciate a building first as sculpture and only second as architecture.

See more of Rome in the online Art Tour.

THE BAROQUE PERIOD OUTSIDE ITALY

Baroque characteristics were also found in the art of other areas of Europe. Artists of Spain and Flanders adopted the Venetian love of color, and with their application of paint in loosely brushed swaths, they created an energetic motion in their compositions. Northern artists had always been interested in realism, and during the Baroque period, they carried this emphasis to an extreme and used innovative pictorial methods to that end. Paintings of everyday life and activities became

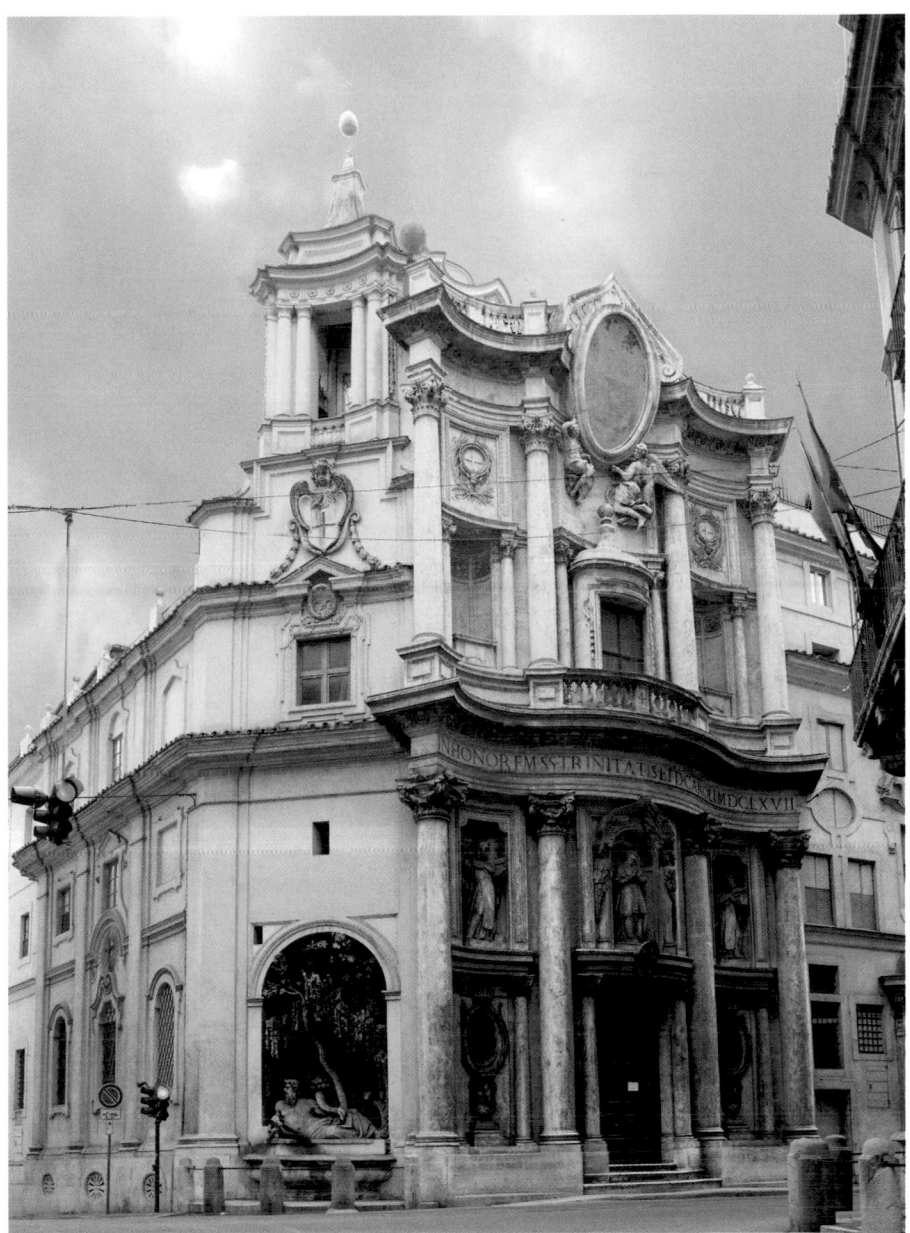

The façade (looking south).

⋀ 18.9 FRANCESCO BORROMINI, San Carlo alle Quattro Fontane, Rome, Italy (1665–1667).

> Las Meninas, what a picture! What realism! There you have the true painter of reality.
>
> —PABLO PICASSO

the favorite subjects of Dutch artists, who followed in Bruegel's footsteps and perfected the art of genre painting. The Baroque movement also extended into France and England, but there it often manifested in a strict adherence to Classicism. The irregularity of styles suggested by the term *baroque* is again apparent.

Spain

Spain was one of the wealthiest countries in Europe during the Baroque era—partly because of the influx of riches from the New World—and the Spanish court was lavish in its support of the arts. Painters and sculptors were imported from different parts of Europe for royal commissions, and native talent was cultivated and treasured.

DIEGO VELÁZQUEZ Diego Velázquez (1599–1660) was born in Spain and rose to the position of court painter and confidant of King Philip IV. Although Velázquez relied on Baroque techniques in his use of Venetian colors, highly contrasting lights and darks, and a deep, illusionistic space, he had contempt for the idealized images that accompanied these elements in the Italian art of the period. Like Caravaggio, Velázquez preferred to use common folk as models to assert a harsh realism in his canvases. Velázquez brought many a mythological subject down to earth by portraying ordinary facial types and naturalistic attitudes in his principal characters. Nor did he restrict this preference to paintings of the masses. Velázquez adopted the same genre format in works involving the royal family, such as the famous *Las Meninas* (Fig. 18.10). The huge canvas is crowded with figures engaged in different tasks. Las meninas, "the maids of honor," are attending the little princess Margarita, who seems dressed for a portrait-painting session. She is being entertained by the favorite members of her entourage, including two little people and an oversized dog.

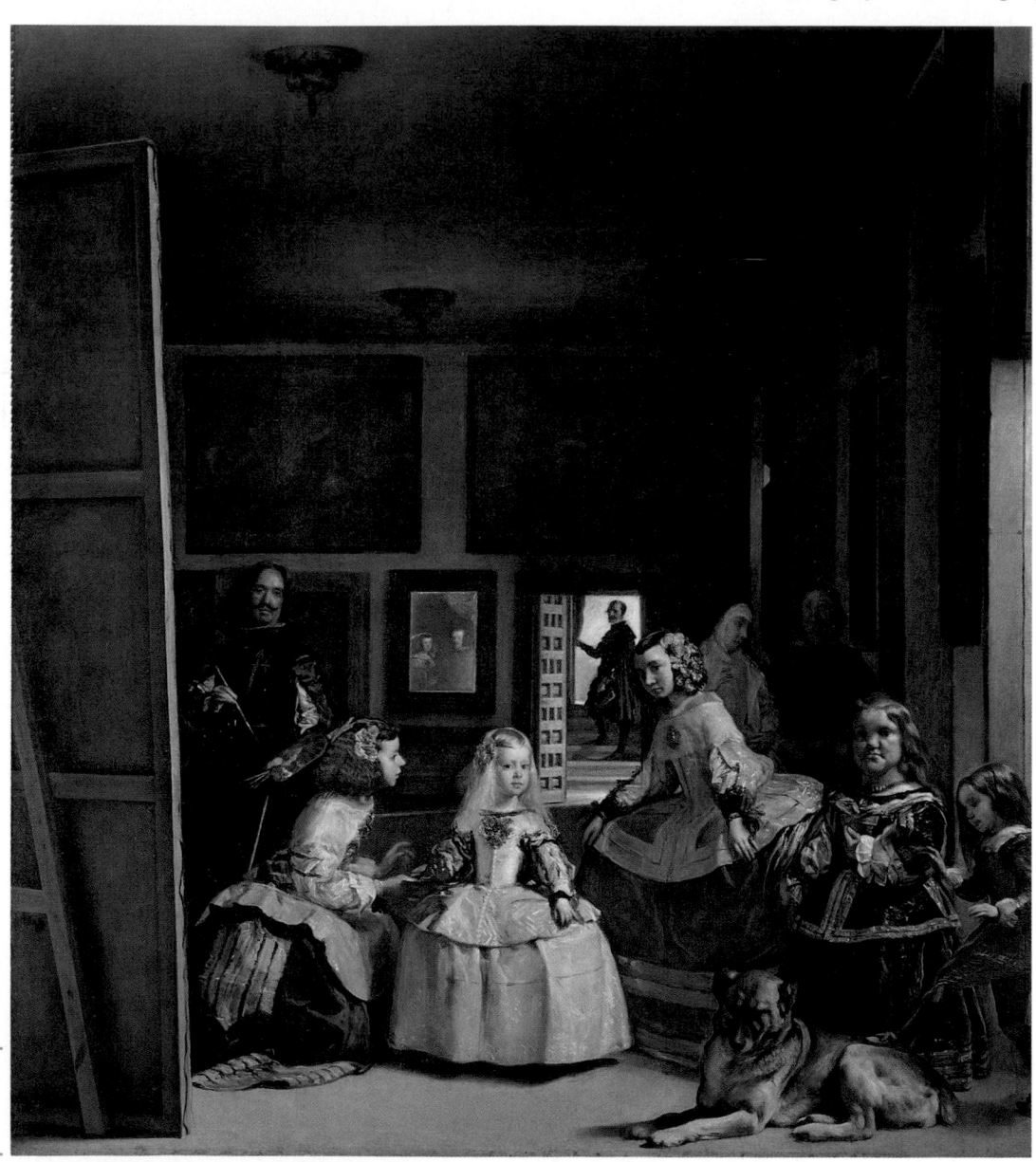

∧ 18.10 DIEGO VELÁZQUEZ, *Las Meninas (The Maids of Honor)* (1656). Oil on canvas, 10' 5" × 9' ¾". Prado Museum, Madrid, Spain.

1 ft.

We suspect that they are keeping her company while the artist, Velázquez, paints before his oversized canvas.

Is Velázquez, in fact, supposed to be painting exactly what we see before us? Some have interpreted the work in this way. Others have noted that Velázquez would not be standing behind the princess and her attendants if he were painting them. Moreover, on the back wall of his studio, we see the mirror images of the king and queen standing next to one another with a red drape falling behind. Because we do not actually see them in the flesh, we may assume that they are standing in the viewer's position, before the canvas and the artist. Is the princess being given a few finishing touches before joining her parents in a family portrait? We cannot know for sure. The reality of the scene has been left a mystery by Velázquez, just as has the identity of the gentleman observing the scene from an open door in the rear of the room. It is interesting to note the prominence of the artist in this painting of royalty. It makes us aware of his importance to the court and to the king in particular. Recall the portrait of Raphael in *The School of Athens* (see Fig. 17.10). Raphael's persona is almost furtive by comparison.

Velázquez pursued realism in technique as well as in subject matter. Building upon the Venetian method of painting, Velázquez constructed his forms from a myriad of strokes that capture light exactly as it plays over a variety of surface textures. Upon close examination of his paintings, we find small distinct strokes that hover on the surface of the canvas, divorced from the very forms they are meant to describe. Yet from a few feet away, the myriad brushstrokes evoke an overall impression of silk or fur or flowers. Velázquez's method of dissolving forms into small, roughly textured brushstrokes that recreate the play of light over surfaces would be the foundation of a movement called Impressionism some two centuries later. In his pursuit of realism, Velázquez truly was an artist before his time.

Flanders

After the dust of Martin Luther's Reformation had settled, the region of Flanders was divided. The northern sections, now called the Dutch Republic (present-day Holland), accepted Protestantism, whereas the southern sections, still called Flanders (present-day Belgium), remained Catholic. This separation more or less dictated the subjects that artists rendered in their works. Dutch artists painted scenes of daily life, carrying forward the tradition of Bruegel, whereas Flemish artists continued

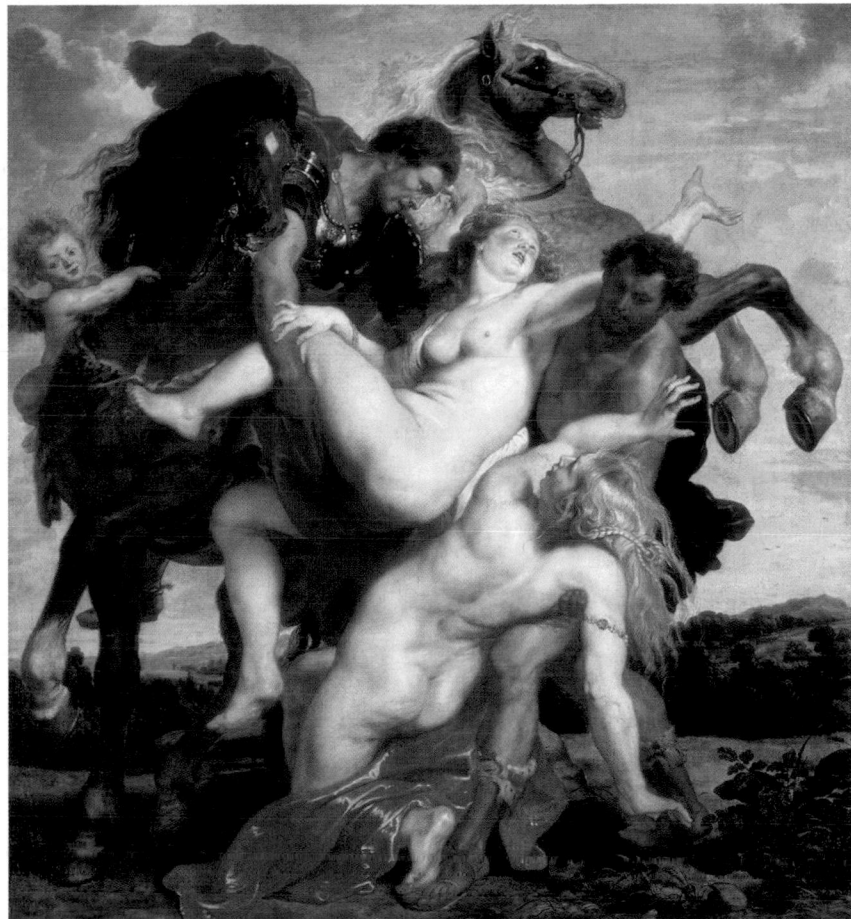

▲ 18.11 PETER PAUL RUBENS, *The Rape of the Daughters of Leucippus* (1617). Oil on canvas, 7'3" × 6'10".

painting the religious and mythological scenes already familiar to us from Italy and Spain.

PETER PAUL RUBENS Even the great power and prestige held by Velázquez were exceeded by the Flemish artist Peter Paul Rubens (1577–1640). One of the most sought-after artists of his time, Rubens was an ambassador, diplomat, and court painter to dukes and kings. He ran a bustling workshop with numerous assistants to help him complete commissions. Rubens's style combined the sculptural qualities of Michelangelo's figures with the painterliness and coloration of the Venetians. He also emulated the dramatic chiaroscuro and theatrical presentation of subject matter we found in the Italian Baroque masters. Much as had Dürer, Rubens admired and adopted from his southern colleagues. Although Rubens painted portraits, religious subjects, and mythological themes, as well as scenes of adventure, his canvases were always imbued with the dynamic energy and unleashed passion we link to the Baroque era.

In *The Rape of the Daughters of Leucippus* (Fig. 18.11), Rubens recounted a tale from Greek mythology in which two mortal women were seized by the twin sons of Zeus, Castor and Pollux. The action in the composition is described by the intersection of strong diagonals and verticals that stabilize the otherwise unstable composition. Capitalizing on the Baroque "stop-action" technique, which depicts a single moment in an event, Rubens placed his struggling, massive forms within a diamond-shaped structure that rests in the foreground on a single point—the toes of a single man and woman. Visually, we grasp that all this energy cannot be supported on a single point, so we infer continuous movement. The action has been pushed up to the picture plane, where the viewer is confronted with the intense emotion and brute strength of the scene. Along with these Baroque devices, Rubens used color and texture much in the way the Venetians used it. The virile sun-tanned arms of the abductors contrast strongly with the delicately colored flesh of the women. The soft blond braids that flow outward under the influence of all of this commotion correspond to the soft, flowing manes of the overpowering horses.

Holland

The grandiose compositional schemes and themes of action executed by Rubens could not have been further removed from the concerns and sensibilities of most seventeenth-century Dutch artists. Whereas mysticism and religious naturalism flourished in Italy, Flanders, and Spain amid the rejection of Protestantism and the invigorated revival of Catholicism, artists of the Low Countries turned to secular art, abiding by the Protestant mandate that humans not create false idols. Not only did artists turn to scenes of everyday life, but the collectors of art were everyday folk. In the Dutch quest for the establishment of a middle class, aristocratic patronage was lost, and artists were forced to peddle their wares in the free market. Landscapes, still lifes, and genre paintings were the favored canvases, and realism was the word of the day. Although the subject matter of Dutch artists differed radically from that of their colleagues elsewhere in Europe, the spirit of the Baroque, with many, if not most, of its artistic characteristics, was present in their work.

REMBRANDT VAN RIJN The golden-toned, subtly lit canvases of Rembrandt van Rijn (1606–1669) possess a certain degree of timelessness. Rembrandt concentrates on the personality of the sitter or the psychology of a particular situation rather than on surface characteristics. This introspection is evident in all of Rembrandt's works, whether religious or secular in subject, landscapes or portraits, drawings, paintings, or prints.

Rembrandt painted many self-portraits that offer us an insight into his life and personality. In a self-portrait at the age of 46 (Fig. 18.12), Rembrandt paints an image of himself as a self-confident, well-respected, and sought-after artist who stares almost impatiently out toward the viewer. It is as if he had been caught in the midst of working and has but a moment for us. It is a powerful image, with piercing eyes, thoughtful brow, and determined jaw that betray a productive man who is more than satisfied with his position in life. All of this may seem obvious, but notice how few clues he gives us to reach these conclusions about his personality. He stands in an undefined space with no props that reveal his identity. The figure is cast into darkness; we can hardly discern his torso and hands resting

▲ 18.12 **REMBRANDT VAN RIJN,** *Self-Portrait* (1652). Oil on canvas, 45" × 32". Kunsthistorisches Museum, Vienna, Austria.

1 ft.

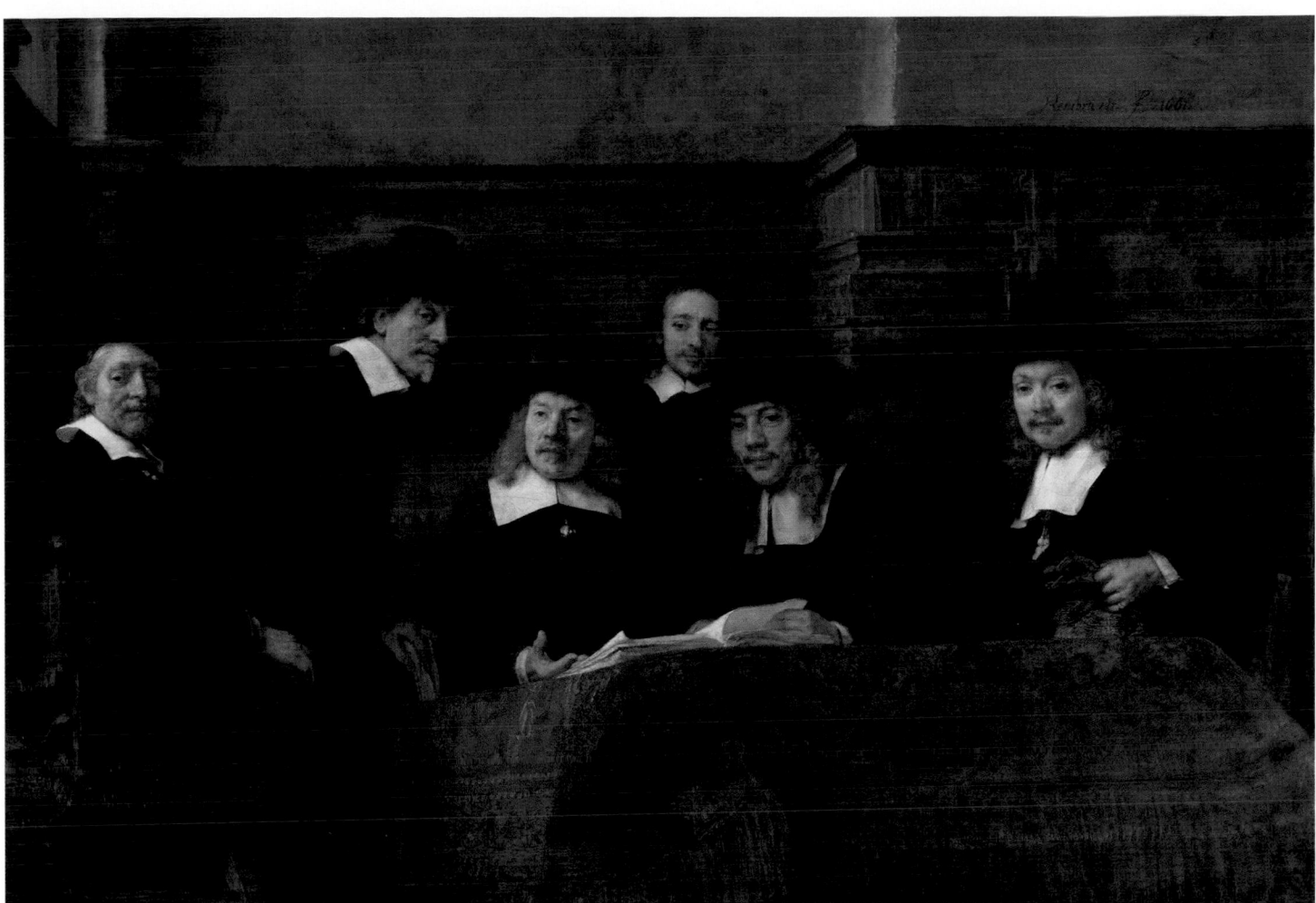

1 ft.

▲ 18.13 **REMBRANDT VAN RIJN,** *Syndics of the Drapers' Guild* (1661–1662). Oil on canvas, 72⅞" × 107⅛". Rijksmuseum, Amsterdam, Netherlands.

in the sash around his waist. The penetrating light in the canvas is reserved for just a portion of the artist's face. Rembrandt gives us a minute fragment with which he beckons us to complete the whole. It is at once a mysterious and revealing portrayal that relies on a mysterious and revealing light.

Rembrandt also painted large group portraits. In his *Syndics of the Drapers' Guild* (Fig. 18.13), which you may recognize from the cover of Dutch Masters's cigar boxes, we, the viewers, become part of a scene involving Dutch businessmen. Bathed in the warm light of a fading sun that enters the room through a hidden window to the left, the men appear to be reacting to the entrance of another person. Some rise in acknowledgment. Others seem to smile. Still others gesture to a ledger as if to explain that they are gathering to "go over the books." Even though the group operates as a whole, the portraits are highly individualized and in themselves complete. As in his self-portrait, Rembrandt concentrates his light on the heads of the sitters, from which we, the viewers, gain insight into their personalities. The haziness that surrounds

Rembrandt's figures is born from his brushstrokes and his use of light. Rembrandt's strokes are heavily loaded with pigment and applied in thick impasto.

As we saw in the painterly technique of Velázquez, Rembrandt's images are more easily discerned from afar than from up close. As a matter of fact, Rembrandt is reputed to have warned viewers to keep their "nose" out of his painting because the smell of paint was bad for them. We can take this to mean that the technical devices Rembrandt used to create certain illusions of realism are all too evident from the perspective of a few inches. Above all, Rembrandt was capable of manipulating light. His is a light that alternately constructs and destructs, that alternately bathes and hides from view. It is a light that can be focused as unpredictably, and that shifts as subtly, as the light we find in nature. Although Rembrandt was sought after as an artist for a good many years and was granted many important commissions, he fell victim to the whims of the free market. The grand master of the Dutch Baroque died at the age of 63, out of fashion and penniless.

JAN VERMEER   If there is a single artist who typifies the Dutch interest in painting scenes of daily life, the commonplace narratives of middle-class men and women, it is Jan Vermeer (1632–1675). Although he did not paint many pictures and never strayed from his native Delft, his precisely sketched and pleasantly colored compositions made him well respected and influential in later centuries.

Young Woman with a Water Jug (Fig. 18.14) exemplifies Vermeer's subject matter and technique. In a tastefully underfurnished corner of a room in a typical middle-class household, a woman stands next to a rug-covered table, grasping a water jug with one hand and, with the other, opening a stained-glass window. A blue cloth has been thrown over a brass and leather chair, a curious metal box sits on the table, and a map adorns the wall. At once we are presented with opulence and simplicity. The elements in the composition are perfectly placed. One senses that their position could not be moved even a fraction of an inch without disturbing the composition. Pure colors and crisp lines grace the space in the painting rather than interrupt it. Every item in the painting is of a simple, almost timeless form and corresponds to the timeless serenity of the porcelain-like image of the woman. Her simple dress and starched collar and bonnet epitomize grace and serenity.

We might not see this as a Baroque composition if it were not for three things: a single source of light bathing the elements in the composition, the genre subject, and a bit of mystery surrounding the moment captured by Vermeer. What is the woman doing? She has opened the window and taken a jug into her hand at the same time, but we will never know for what purpose. Some have said that she may intend to water flowers at a window box. Perhaps she was in the midst of doing something else and paused to investigate a noise in the street. Vermeer gives us a curious combination of the momentary and the eternal in this almost photographic glimpse of everyday Dutch life.

France

During the Baroque period, France, under the reign of the "Sun King," Louis XIV, began to replace Rome as the center of the art world. The king preferred Classicism. Thus did the country, and painters, sculptors, and architects alike created works in this vein. Louis XIV guaranteed adherence to Classicism by forming academies of art that perpetuated this style. These academies were art schools of sorts, run by the state, whose faculties were populated by leading proponents of the Classical style. When we examine European art during the Baroque period, we thus perceive a strong stylistic polarity. On the one hand, we have the exuberant painterliness and high drama of Rubens and Bernini, and on the other hand, a reserved Classicism that hearkens back to Raphael.

NICOLAS POUSSIN   The principal exponent of the Classical style in French painting was

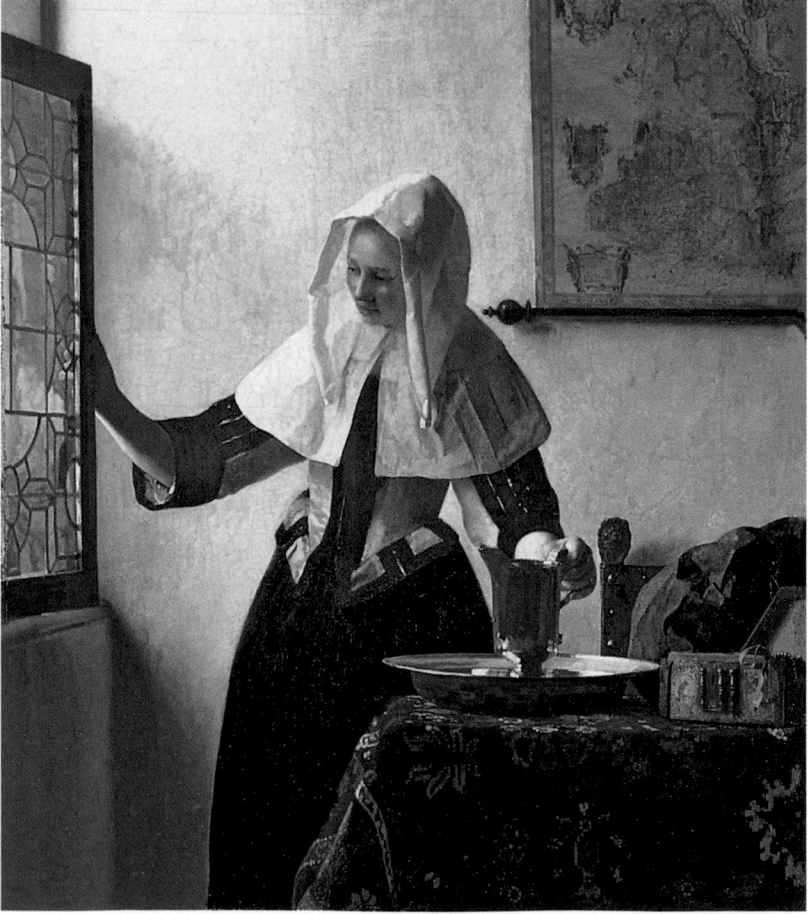

1 in.

◄ 18.14 JAN VERMEER, *Young Woman with a Water Jug* (c. 1665). Oil on canvas, 18" × 16". The Metropolitan Museum of Art, New York, New York.

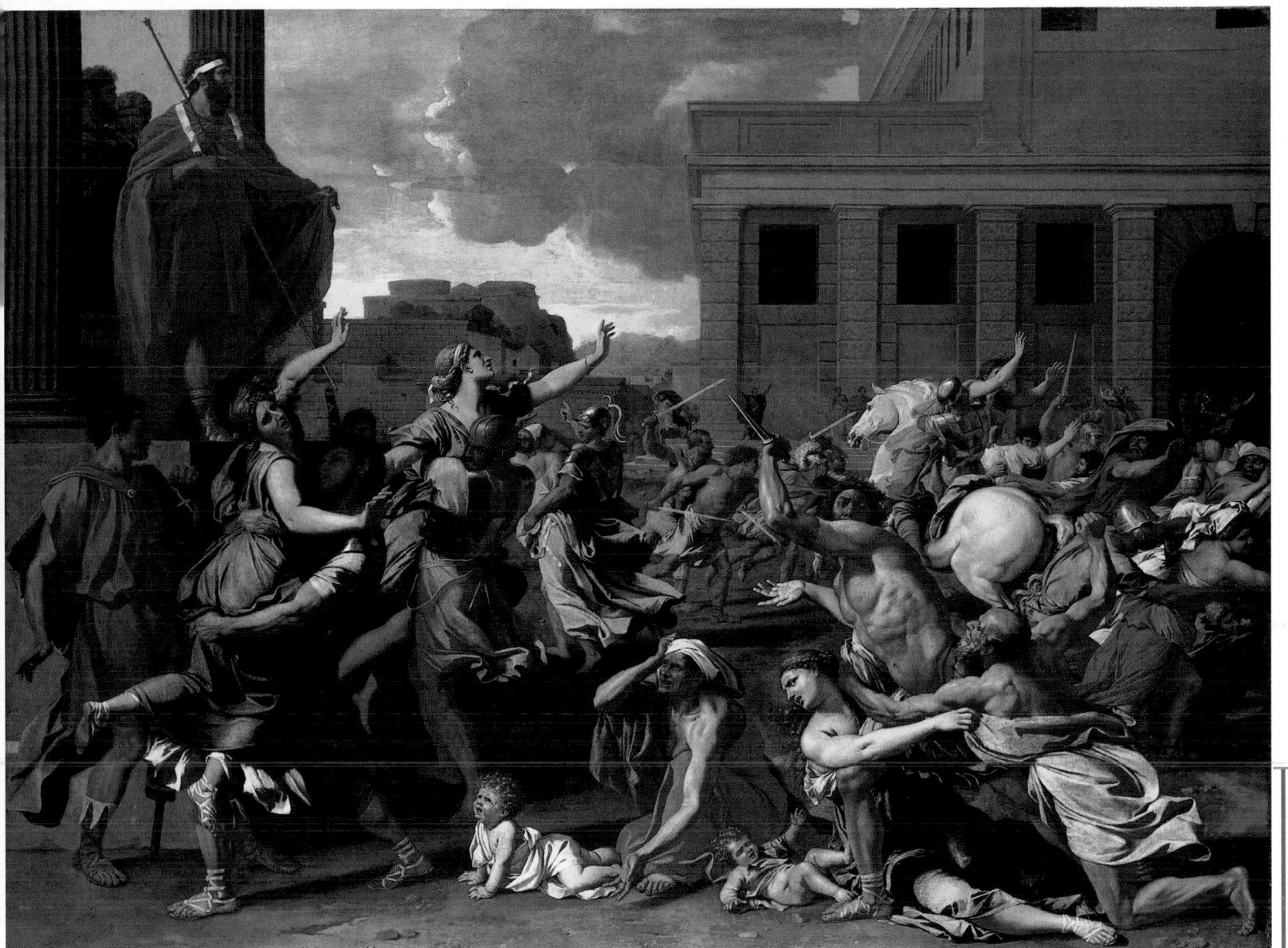

▲ 18.15 **NICOLAS POUSSIN,** *The Rape of the Sabine Women* (c. 1636–1637). Oil on canvas, 60⅞" × 82⅝". The Metropolitan Museum of Art, New York, New York.

1 ft.

Nicolas Poussin (1594–1665). Although he was born in France, Poussin spent much of his life in Rome, where he studied the works of the Italian masters, particularly Raphael and Titian. Although his *Rape of the Sabine Women* (Fig. 18.15) was painted four years before he was summoned back to France by the king, it illustrates the Baroque Classicism that Poussin would bring to his native country. The flashy dynamism of Bernini and Rubens gives way to a more static, almost staged motion in the work of Poussin. Harshly sculptural,

Raphaelesque figures thrust in various directions, forming a complex series of intersecting diagonals and verticals. The initial impression is one of chaos, of unrestrained movement and human anguish. But as was the case with the Classical Greek sculptors and Italian Renaissance artists, emotion is always balanced carefully with restraint. For example, the pitiful scene of the old woman in the foreground, flanked by crying children, forms part of the base of a compositional triangle that stabilizes the work and counters excessive emotion.

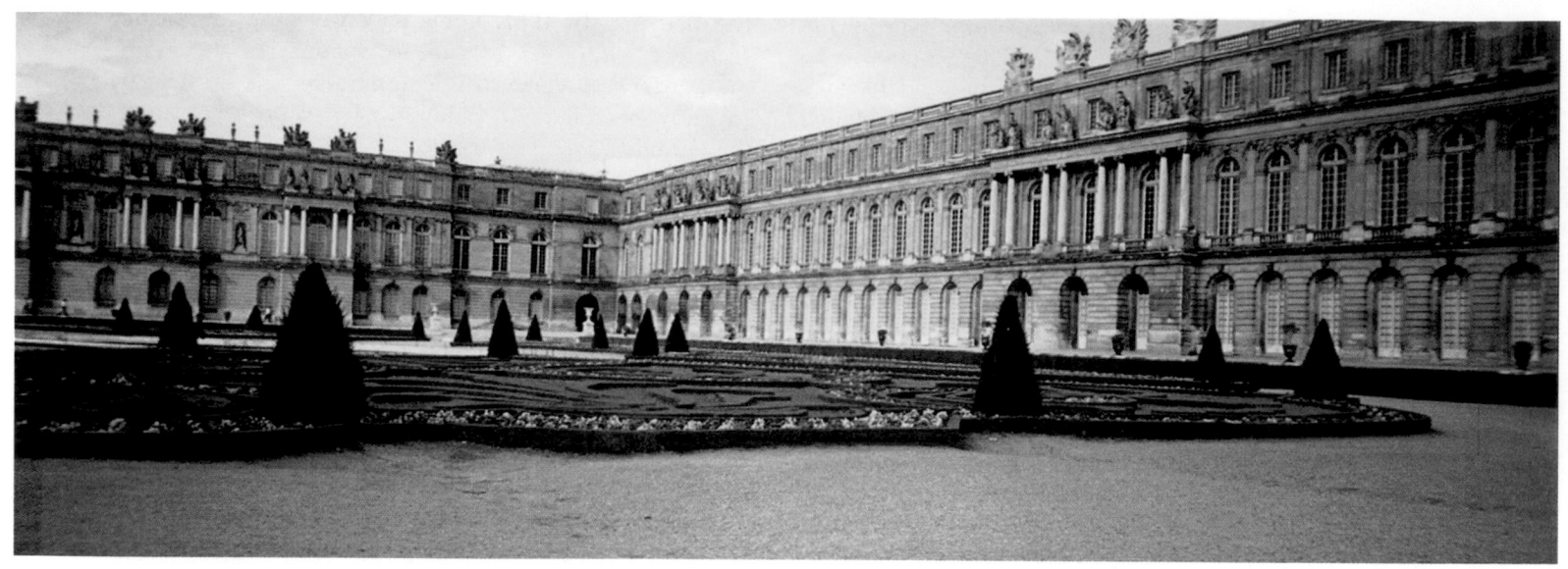

∧ 18.16 LOUIS LE VAU AND JULES HARDOUIN-MANSART, Palace of Versailles, exterior (begun 1669). Versailles, France.

If one draws a vertical line from the top of her head upward to the top border of the canvas, one encounters the apex of this triangle, formed by the swords of two Roman abductors. The sides of the triangle, then, are formed by the diagonally thrusting torso of the muscular Roman in the right foreground, and the arms of the Sabine women on the left, reaching hopelessly into the sky. This compositional triangle, along with the Roman temple in the right background that prevents a radically receding space, are Renaissance techniques for structuring a balanced composition. Poussin used these, along with a stagelike, theatrical presentation of his subjects, to reconcile the divergent styles of the harsh Classical and the vibrant Baroque.

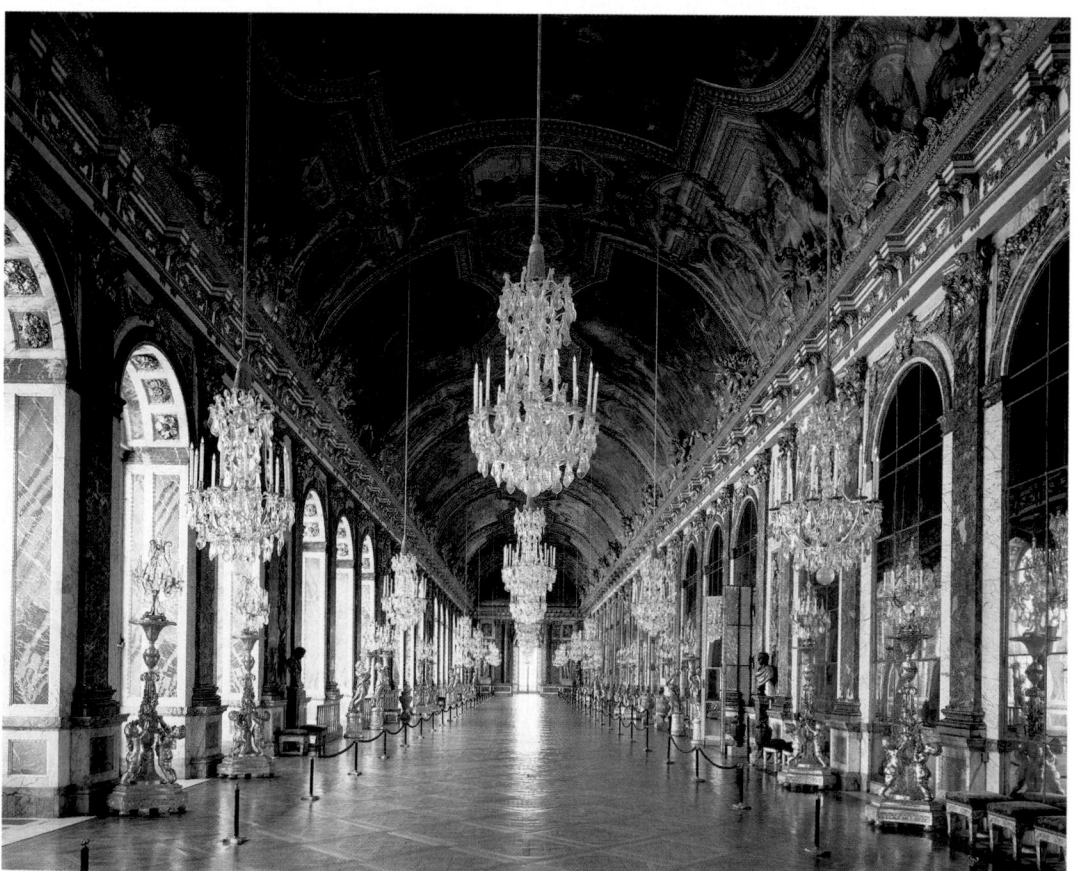

> 18.17 LOUIS LE VAU AND JULES HARDOUIN-MANSART, Palace of Versailles, Hall of Mirrors (c. 1680). Versailles, France.

Polar opposites in style occur in other movements throughout the history of art. It will be important to remember this aspect of the Baroque, because in later centuries we will encounter the polarity again, among artists who divide themselves into the camps Poussiniste and Rubeniste.

VERSAILLES King Louis XIV's taste for the Classical extended to architecture, as seen in the Palace of Versailles. Originally the site of the king's hunting lodge, the palace and surrounding area just outside Paris were converted by a host of artists, architects, and landscape designers into one of the grandest monuments to the French Baroque (Fig. 18.16). In their tribute to Classicism, the architects Louis Le Vau (1612–1670) and Jules Hardouin-Mansart (1646–1708) divided the horizontal sweep of the façades into three stories. The structure was then divided vertically into three major sections, and these were in turn subdivided into three additional sections. The windows march along the façade in a rhythmic beat, accompanied by rigid pilasters that are wedged between the strong horizontal bands that delineate the floors. A balustrade tops the palace, further emphasizing the horizontal sweep while restraining any upward movement suggested by the building's vertical members. The divisions into Classically balanced threes and the almost obsessive emphasis on the horizontal echo the buildings of Renaissance architects. The French had come a long way from the towering spires of their glorious Gothic cathedrals!

The Hall of Mirrors The king began construction of the stunning Hall of Mirrors—the palace's central gallery—in 1678 (Fig. 18.17). Seventeen arches across the hall from seventeen windows each house twenty-one mirrors. At the time mirrors were luxury items, and the best mirrors were made in Venice, Italy. But since it was required that all materials and objects in the palace be made in France, Venetian glass makers were imported to France. The arches are separated by marble pilasters whose gilded capitals bear symbols of France, such as the fleur-de-lis. The Hall served family functions such as being the venue for royal marriages, and royal functions such as being where the king met with ambassadors. The Hall still hosts receptions for visiting royalty, presidents, and prime ministers. But today it is just as likely to serve as a gallery space for contemporary artists.

The Gardens In 1661, Louis XIV gave the landscape architect André Le Nôtre the commission to create the gardens of Versailles. The gardens are the visual pathway between the palace and a waterway called the Grand Canal. They consist of a series of fountains, ponds, and green spaces (Fig. 18.18). Many of the tropical plants are potted because they are brought indoors for the French winter. Critics and tourists alike find the gardens to be as beautiful and compelling as the palace itself.

England

The Baroque in England had a different flavor from that in the European continent, in part because it was not dominated by an absolute monarchy as it was, for example, in France. Instead, England's Common Law and Parliament coexisted with a limited monarchy. Also, unlike other countries, England was also home to a variety of religious groups—including Anglicans and other Protestants, and Catholics. As in Holland, the Baroque era in England witnessed a burgeoning of trade, made possible by the nation's status as a maritime power.

England's most significant contribution to the arts in the seventeenth and early eighteenth centuries was in the realm of architecture. The architect Sir Christopher Wren (1632–1723) was heavily influenced by Italian Baroque architecture, which combined the regimentation and clarity of classical elements with occasional, unpredictable shapes or rhythms. Solicited by King Charles II to renovate St. Paul's Cathedral—a Gothic structure—his

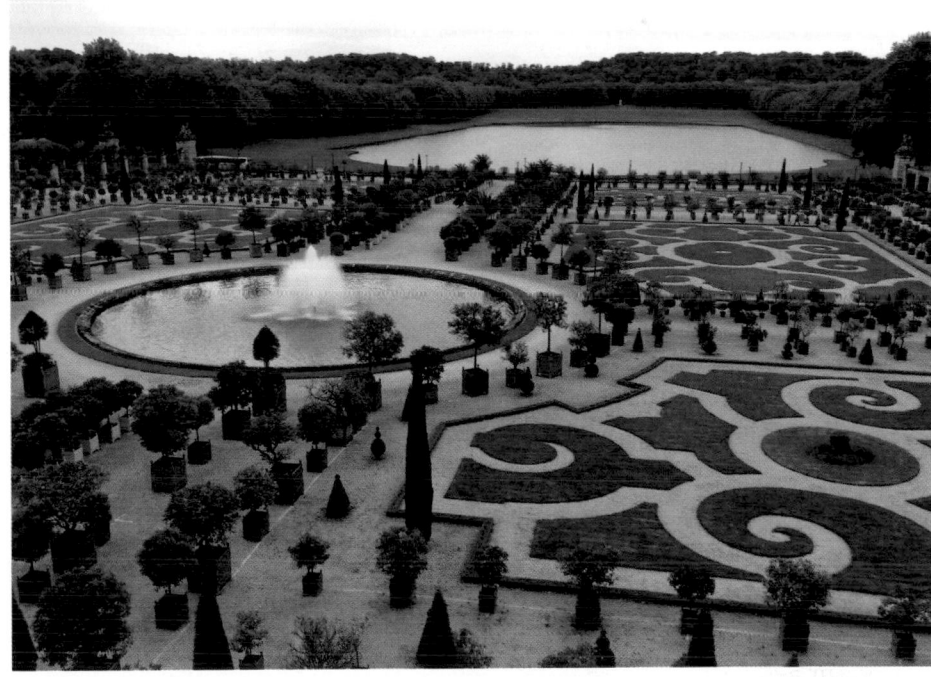

▲ 18.18 ANDRÉ LE NÔTRE, LOUIS LE VAU, AND JULES HARDOUIN-MANSART, Gardens of the Palace of Versailles, Versailles, France.

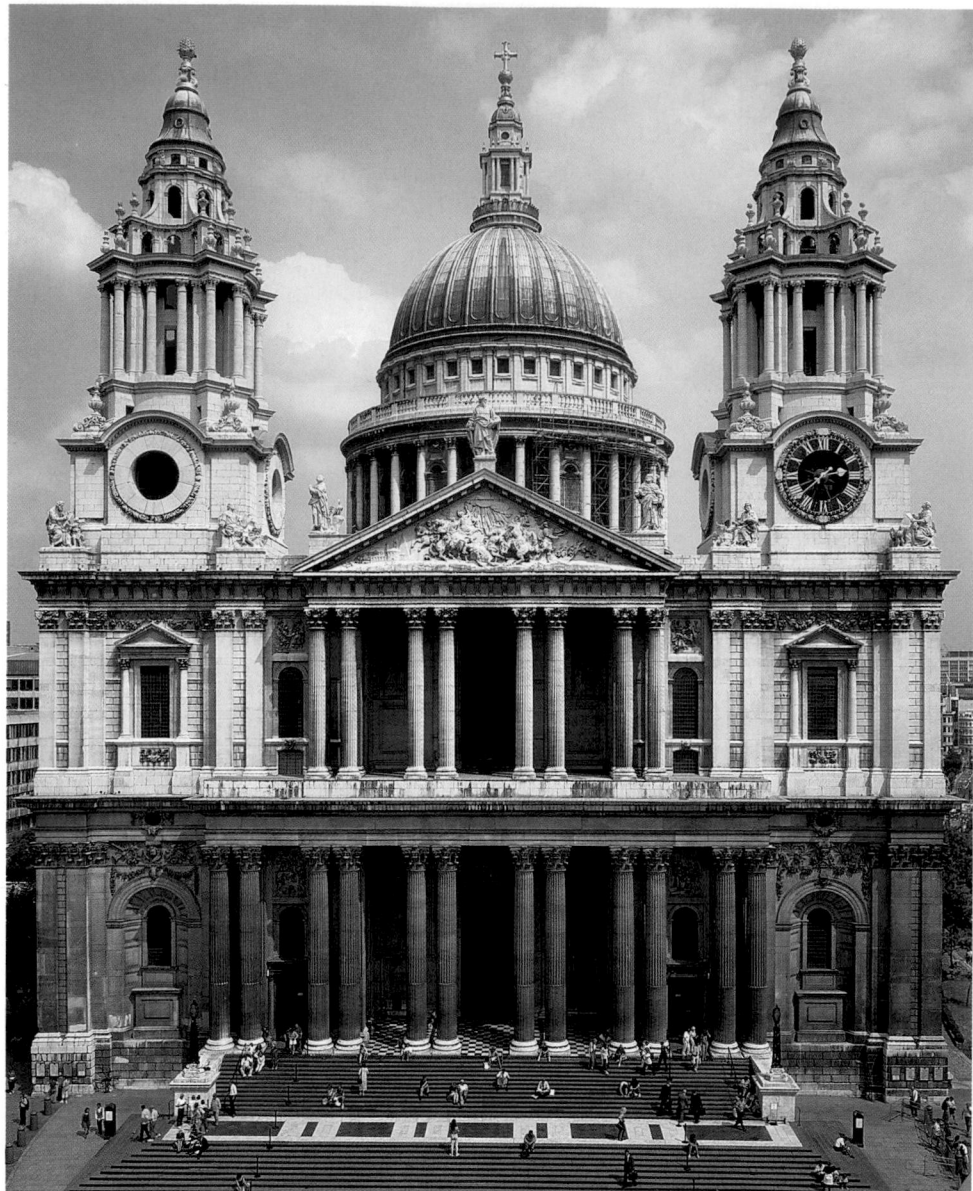

plans for the project were in place when the devastating fire of London in 1666 consumed the old building. The new St. Paul's (Fig. 18.19) stands as Wren's masterpiece and the most beloved structure in London. Influenced by Italian and French Baroque architecture, Wren reconciled the problematic relationship of the classical pedimented façade to hemispherical dome that we first encountered in the Baroque expansion of St. Peter's in Rome. He did this by placing tall bell towers on either side of the façade to soften the visual transition from the horizontal emphasis of the two-storied elevation to the vertical rise of the massive dome a nave's-length away. Wren's design stands midway between the organic, flowing designs of the Italian Baroque and the strict classicism of the French Baroque architects, integrating both in a reserved, but not rigid, composition. The double-columned, two-tiered portico is French Baroque in style, and the upper level of

the bell towers (topped by pineapples—symbols of peace and prosperity) are similar to those found on Borromini's churches, such as San Carlo alle Quattro Fontane (see Fig. 18.9) in Rome.

The dome of St. Paul's is the world's second-highest at 361 feet (St. Peter's is highest). Inside the dome is the so-called Whispering Gallery; visitors who whisper against its walls can be heard on the opposite side of the dome. The interior is richly embellished with marble inlays, frescoes, mosaics, and wrought iron. Aside from its stature as an architectural masterpiece, St. Paul's holds a valuable place in British memory. Winston Churchill took extraordinary measures to protect the church from the Nazi bombing raids—the Blitz—of World War II. It survived amid a virtually ruined city.

See more of London in the online Art Tour.

THE ROCOCO

We have roughly dated the Baroque period from 1600 to 1750. However, art historians have recognized a more distinct style within the Baroque that began shortly after the dawn of the eighteenth century. This **Rococo** style strayed further from Classical principles than did the Baroque. It is more ornate and characterized by sweetness, gaiety, and light. The courtly pomp and reserved Classicism of Louis XIV were replaced with a more delicate and sprightly representation of the leisure activities of the upper class.

The early Rococo style appears as a refinement of the painterly Baroque in which Classical subjects are often rendered in wispy brushstrokes that rely heavily on the Venetian or Rubensian palette of luscious golds and reds. The later Rococo period, following midcentury, is more frivolous in its choice of subjects (that of love among the very rich), palette (that of the softest pastel hues), and brushwork (the most delicate and painterly strokes).

Jean-Honoré Fragonard

Jean-Honoré Fragonard (1732–1806) is one of the finest representatives of the Rococo style, and his painting *Happy Accidents of the Swing* (Fig. 18.20) is a prime example of the aims and accomplishments of the Rococo artist. In the midst of a lush green park, whose opulent foliage was no doubt inspired by the Baroque, we are offered a glimpse of the "love games" of the leisure class. A young, though not-so-innocent, maiden, with petticoats billowing beneath her sumptuous pink dress, is being swung by an unsuspecting bishop high over the head of her reclining gentleman friend, who seems delighted with the view. The subjects' diminutive forms and rosy cheeks make them doll-like, an image reinforced by the idyllic setting. This is eighteenth-century life at its finest—pampered by subtle hues, embraced by lush textures, and bathed by the softest of lights. Unfortunately, this was all a mask for life at its worst. As the ruling class

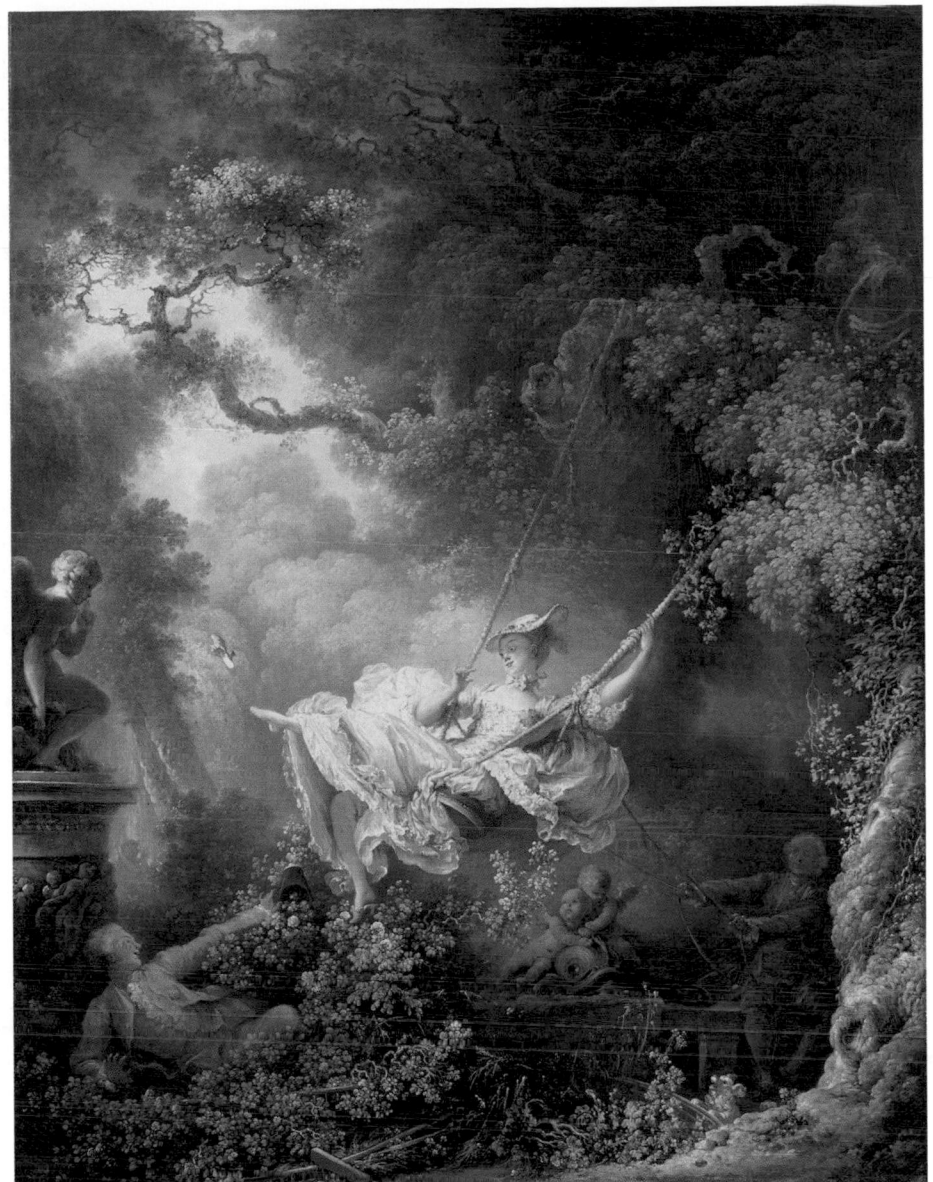

▲ 18.20 JEAN-HONORÉ FRAGONARD, *Happy Accidents of the Swing* (1767). Oil on canvas, 31⅞" × 25⅜". The Wallace Collection, London, England.

1 ft.

continued to ignore the needs of the common people, the latter were preparing to rebel.

Élisabeth Vigée-Lebrun

Whereas Rembrandt epitomizes the artists who achieve recognition after death, Élisabeth Vigée-Lebrun (1755–1842) was a complete success during her lifetime. The daughter of a portrait painter, she received instruction and encouragement from her father and his colleagues from an early age. As a youngster she also studied paintings in the Louvre and was particularly drawn to the works of Rubens. By the time she reached her early twenties, she commanded high prices for her portraits and was made an official portrait painter for Marie

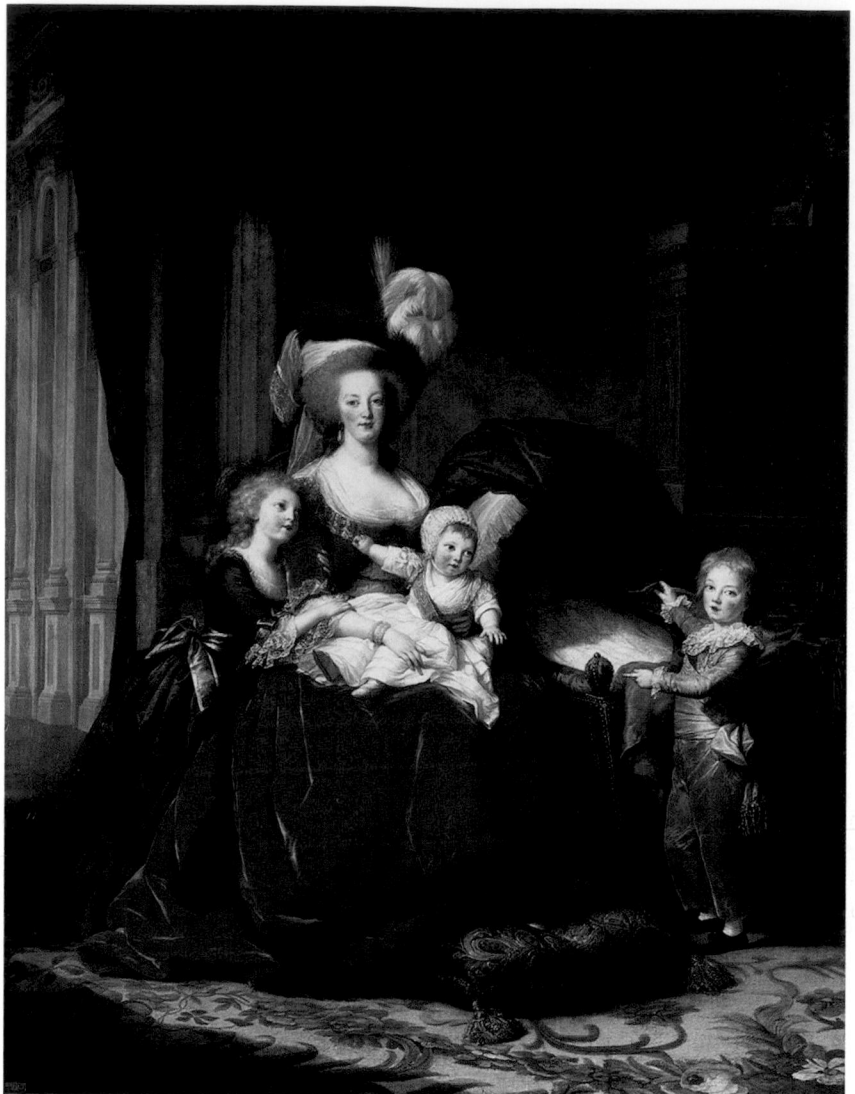

Madonna and Child (see Chapter 17), at once creating a sympathetic portrait of a mother and her children and, subliminally, asserting their divine right. Even amid the opulence at Versailles, Marie Antoinette displays her children as her real jewels. The young dauphin to the right, set apart as the future king, points to an empty cradle that might have originally contained the queen's fourth child, an infant who died two months before the painting was scheduled for exhibition.

The French populace, of course, was not persuaded by this portrait or by other public relations efforts to paint the royal family as accessible and sympathetic. The artist, in fact, did not exhibit her painting as scheduled for fear that the public might destroy it. Two years after the painting was completed, the convulsions of the French Revolution shook Europe and the world. The royal family was imprisoned and then executed. More than the royal family had passed into history, and more than democracy was about to be born. Modern art was also to be ushered into this brave new world.

∧ 18.21 ÉLISABETH VIGÉE-LEBRUN, *Marie Antoinette and Her Children* (1781). Oil on canvas, 8' 8" × 6' 10". Palace of Versailles, Versailles, France.

Enlightenment, Revolution, the Scientific, and the Natural

Antoinette, the Austrian wife of Louis XVI. Neither Marie Antoinette nor her husband survived the French Revolution, but Vigée-Lebrun's fame spread throughout Europe, and by the end of her career, she had created some 800 paintings.

Marie Antoinette and Her Children (Fig. 18.21) was painted nearly a decade after Vigée-Lebrun had begun to paint the royal family. In this work, she was commissioned to counter the antimonarchist sentiments spreading throughout the land by portraying the queen as, first and foremost, a loving mother. True, the queen is set within the imposing Salon de la Paix at Versailles, with the famous Hall of Mirrors to the left and the royal crown atop the cabinet on the right. True, the queen's enormous hat and voluminous skirts create a richness and monumentality to which the common person could not reasonably aspire. But the triangular composition and the child on the lap are reminiscent of Renaissance images of the

The aristocratic culture reflected in the Rococo style may symbolize the late eighteenth century in France, but it was not the only game in town. Enlightenment views and philosophies, which rejected the stranglehold of religion and superstition and promoted scientific inquiry and critical thinking about the world and the human condition, went hand in hand with revolutions in France and America. Many historical personalities are associated with the Enlightenment—France's René Descartes, England's Isaac Newton and John Locke, America's Benjamin Franklin and Thomas Jefferson. But the opposing viewpoints of the Enlightenment—the scientific versus the natural—are represented by, respectively, Voltaire (1694–1778) and Jean-Jacques Rousseau (1712–1778). Voltaire held that science and rationalism held the key to the improvement of the human condition, whereas Rousseau believed that feeling and emotions trumped reason and that the return to the natural, or the "primitive state," would lead to the salvation of humankind. Rousseau's philosophy was translated into the pictorial

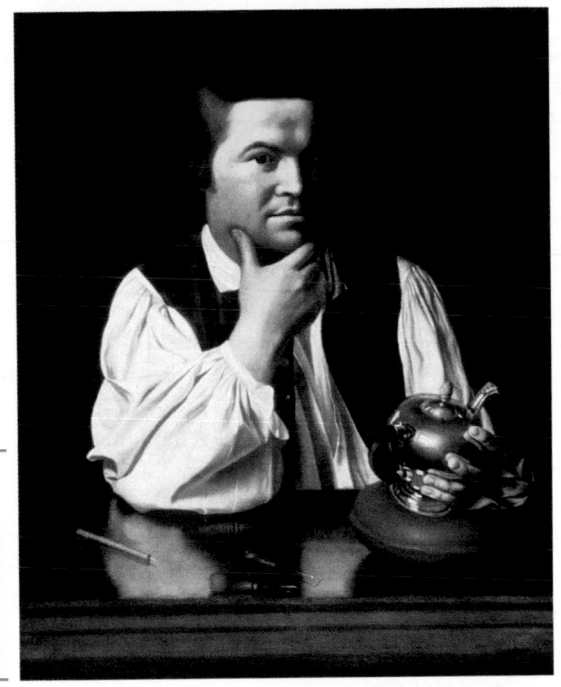

1 ft.

∧ 18.22 JOHN SINGLETON COPLEY, *Portrait of Paul Revere* (c. 1698–1770). Oil on canvas, 2' 11⅛" × 2' 4". Museum of Fine Arts, Boston, Massachusetts.

Copley combined English naturalism with an American taste for realism and simplicity. His *Portrait of Paul Revere* (Fig. 18.22), the silversmith-turned-revolutionary hero, has a directness of expression and an unpretentious gaze. Yet Revere conducts as assertive, visual dialogue with the viewer. Tools at hand, he ponders the teapot on which he is working and raises his head momentarily from the task to acknowledge the visitor, the patron, the observer. The artist uses a harsh linear style. The lighting is dramatic and the textures are purposefully distinct and different from one another (the soft folds of Revere's shirtsleeves against his sculptural arms; the warm wood surface of his worktable against the gleaming metal of his teapot). It is tempting to read Copley's approach as one that reflects American values and sensibilities. Like some other American-born artists of his generation, however, he moved to London, where he adapted his style to the British taste.

THE WIDER WORLD

During the seventeenth and eighteenth centuries, western European nations penetrated the empires and kingdoms of the East. By the end of the Baroque era, Britain had all but grasped complete control of India and, along with other European powers, established trade with China. Only Japan resisted the allure of Europe—and its might. But as we will see in the next chapter, Japan eventually succumbed to an external power several thousand miles to its east—the United States of America.

arts in England and America in works by painters such as Thomas Gainsborough (1727–1788) and John Singleton Copley (1738–1815). It also contributed to the demise of the Rococo, which represented an "artificial" rather than a "natural" state of being.

America offered a new twist in portraiture, perhaps best represented by John Singleton Copley of Massachusetts.

SEVENTEENTH AND EIGHTEENTH CENTURIES IN THE EAST

BEFORE 1600	1600	1700	1800 AND AFTER
Beginning of Mughal Empire in India 1526	Formation of British East India Company 1600	End of Nayak Dynasty in India 1736	End of Mughal Empire in India 1857
Beginning of Nayak Dynasty in India 1529	Gopuras of the Great Temple at Madurai, India completed in 17th century	Japan resists influence from the West in 18th century	Beginning of British hegemony over India 1858
	Beginning of Edo period in Japan 1615	Shitao paints *Riverbank of Peach Blossoms* c. 1700	End of Edo period in Japan 1868
	Construction of Katsura Imperial Villa, Kyoto, Japan, 1620–1663	Thousand Flowers vase 1736–1795	End of Qing Dynasty in China 1911
	Qing Dynasty begins in China 1644	Painting of *Krishna and Radha in a Pavillion* c. 1760	
	East India Company arrives in China 1689	Utamaro prints *Midnight: The Hours of the Rat; Mother and Sleepy Child* c. 1790	

India

The British began their incursion into India in 1613 with the establishment of a trading post under the banner of the East India Company. Just two years later, in 1615, the Hindu (Rajput) rulers in the northwestern part of the country succumbed to the forces of the ever-expanding Mughal Empire—an empire that already ruled over vast territories. The Mughal emperor Jahangir granted the British additional trading rights, and by the time the British defeated a weakened Mughal emperor in 1757 to become the rulers of Bengal, their trading posts had expanded throughout India. The East India Company was disbanded 100 years later, in 1858, but in the same year, the British government took complete control of India, including modern-day Pakistan, Bangladesh, and much of Afghanistan.

Despite Mughal supremacy in northern India, much of the south remained Hindu. The Nayak Dynasty (1529–1736) constructed some of the most elaborate Hindu temple complexes, graced with majestic gateway towers called **gopuras**. Figure 18.23 shows a grouping at the Great Temple at Madurai at the southernmost tip of the Indian peninsula. Gopuras are four-sided, pyramidal-shaped structures comprised of multiple levels that decrease in size from the ground up (wedding-cake style) and are capped by barrel-vaulted roofs. The outer surfaces of the gopuras are entirely covered with stucco sculptures depicting Hindu deities and their entourages—all rendered in exceptionally vivid hues. The stunning freshness of the coloration on these more-than-300-year-old towers is attributed to the practice of refreshing the paint every 12 years when the temple is reconsecrated. The detail shown in Figure 18.24 portrays the god Shiva—the

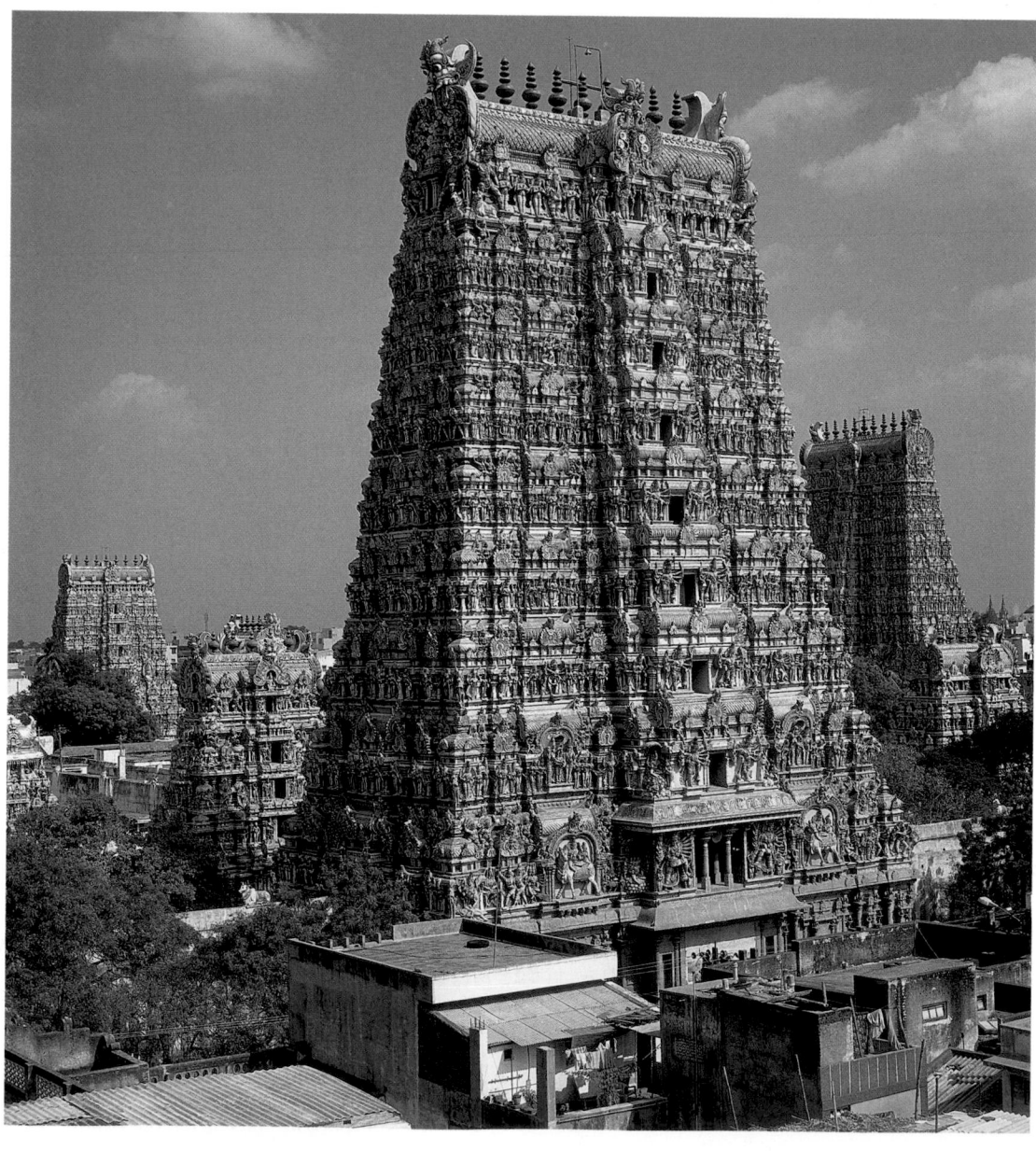

< 18.23 Outermost gopuras of the Great Temple (looking southeast), Madurai, India (completed 17th century).

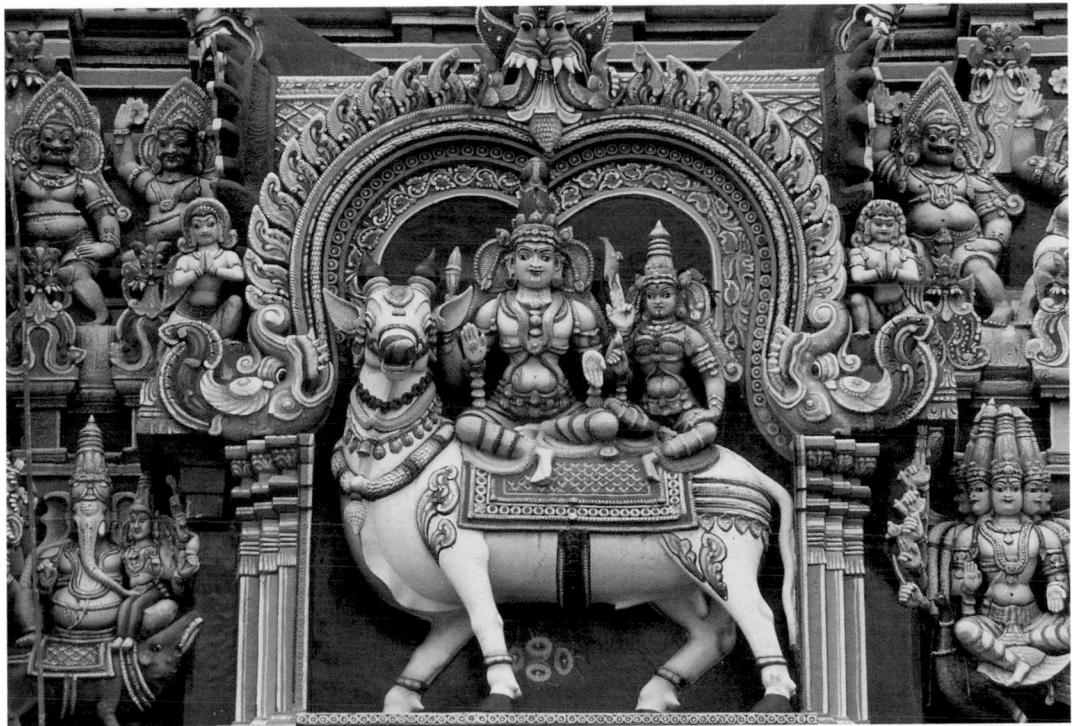

◀ 18.24 Shiva and Parvati riding Nandi, detail of one of the inner gopuras of the Great Temple, Madurai, India (remodeled in the 17th century).

Destroyer and Transformer—and his wife Parvati riding Nandi, the white bull that serves as Shiva's mount.

A small watercolor painting from the northern Punjab Hills at the feet of the Himalayas offers us a glimpse of the style and subjects characteristic of much Rajput painting. Although it shares some characteristics of the paintings of Mughal courtly life, the sensuality and eroticism of the figures place it squarely within a Hindu aesthetic. In this depiction of one of Krishna's liaisons, the Blue God fondles the breasts of his consort, Radha, as the two cuddle, naked, in a brilliantly colored garden pavilion (Fig. 18.25).

China

By the early seventeenth century, control of China slipped from the hands of the Ming emperors as the government bureaucracy grew evermore corrupt and popular uprisings became rampant. In 1628, rebellion drove the last Ming emperor to commit suicide. The situation was ripe for invaders from Manchuria who established the new Qing Dynasty (1644–1911) under the emperor Kangxi. He began to make tentative contacts abroad and, as in India, European traders established operations in China: the British East India Company arrived in 1689. In the same year, Kangxi signed a treaty with Peter the Great of Russia, to collar the expanding Russian Empire. He also

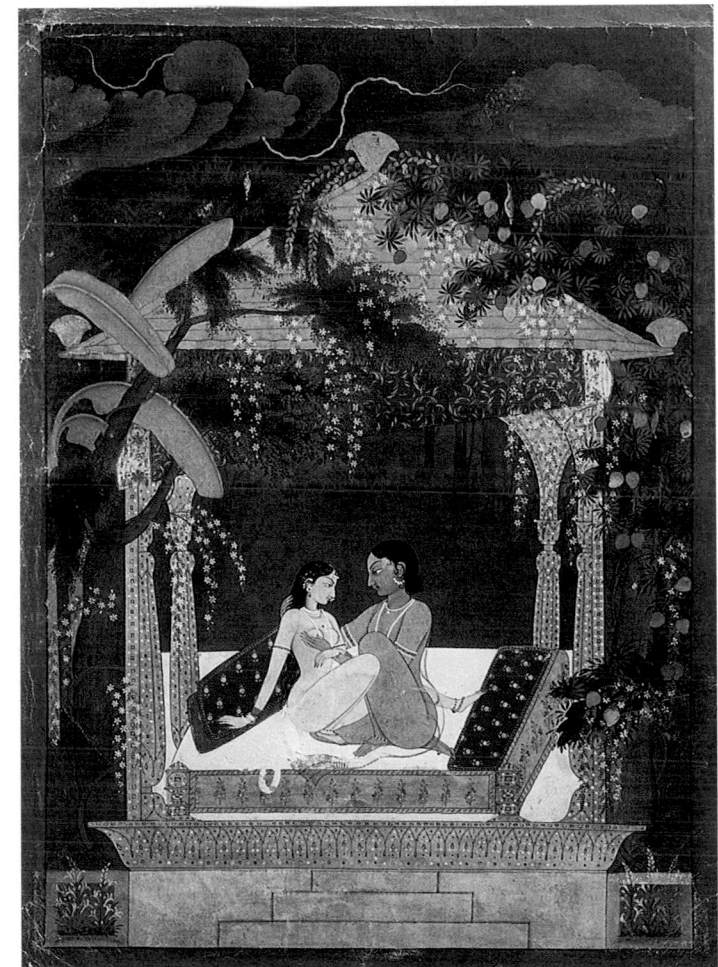

▶ 18.25 *Krishna and Radha in a Pavillion* (c. 1760). Opaque watercolor on paper, 11⅛" × 7¾". National Museum, New Delhi, India.

1 in.

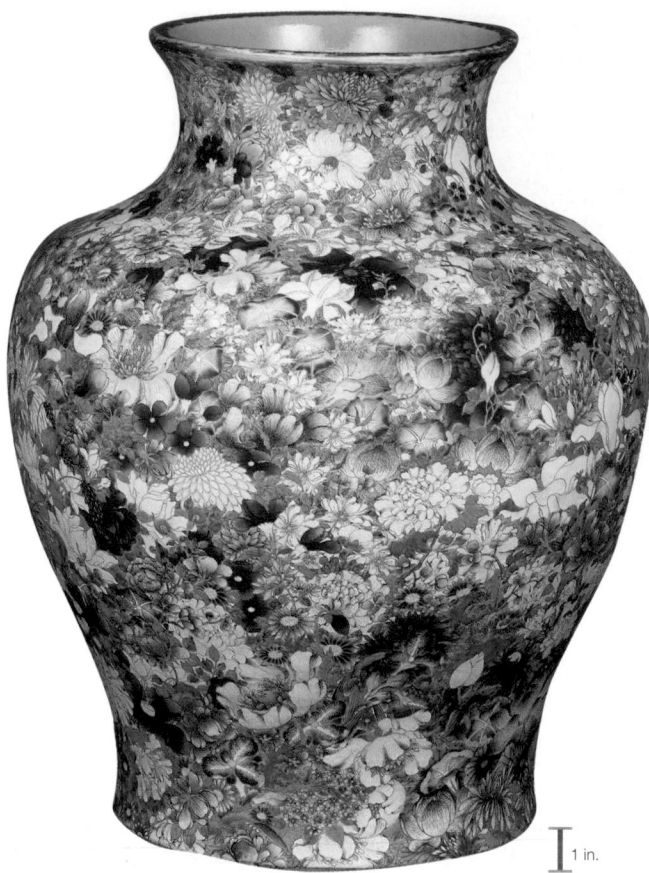

▲ 18.26 *Thousand Flowers vase* (Qianlong period, Qing Dynasty, 1736–1795). Porcelain, color enamels; 18⅞" × 14¼". Musée national des arts asiatiques Guimet, Paris, France.

promoted the introduction of western European arts and education but, supporting Confucianism, drew the line at the import of Christianity.

Qing potters built on the achievements of their Ming Dynasty counterparts, further developing more complex glazing techniques that produced brilliant and varied colors. The Thousand Flowers vase (Fig. 18.26) is more complex in design than earlier Ming Dynasty vases; blooms and petals weave and overlap in an intricate, continuous pattern.

The Qing artist Shitao (1641–1707), who became a Buddhist monk at the age of 20, experimented with new approaches to painting, applying rhythmic lines with several strokes of ink or dabbing transparent color to suggest fields of blossoms or distant mountains fading into atmospheric haze. *Riverbank of Peach Blossoms* (Fig. 18.27) has an abstract quality; short, parallel black lines, along with splotches of red and pink and green, merge to create the impression of flowering trees along the water's edge. The part of the paper left untouched between the plants and the mountain in the distance creates a dramatic sense of space.

➤ 18.27 SHITAO, *Riverbank of Peach Blossoms* (c. 1700). Leaf C from Wilderness Colors, an album of 12 paintings, ink and color on paper; 10⅞" × 8½". The Metropolitan Museum of Art, New York, New York.

Japan

The Momoyama period ended in 1615, after which Japan entered into an era of political stability—the Edo period—which would last for more than 250 years. The city of Edo, a fishing village during the period of the Renaissance in the West, grew into a metropolis known today as Tokyo. The reign of the Tokugawa shogunate, with its 300 local feudal lords, maintained a strict social hierarchy within and embraced a policy of isolation with regard to foreign powers. Yet merchants were free to create and reap the benefits of Japan's economic growth and the court showed great support for the visual and literary arts.

During the early years of the Edo period, the prince Toshihito undertook the development of a country villa whose style would become widespread in Japan and an inspiration for architecture in the west, particularly the United States. The villa (Fig. 18.28) doesn't seek to impress with layer upon layer of upward-reaching fortifications. Instead, it relaxes us with its gentle relationship to the greenery and water, and with its simplified geometric shapes and sweeping but straight rooflines which could just as easily have been designed in the twentieth or twenty-first century. The message is of peace and oneness with nature—not of power. The villa complex took more than forty years to complete, with its many teahouses and residential dwellings. All in all, it looks familiar and comfortable as well as elegant and refined.

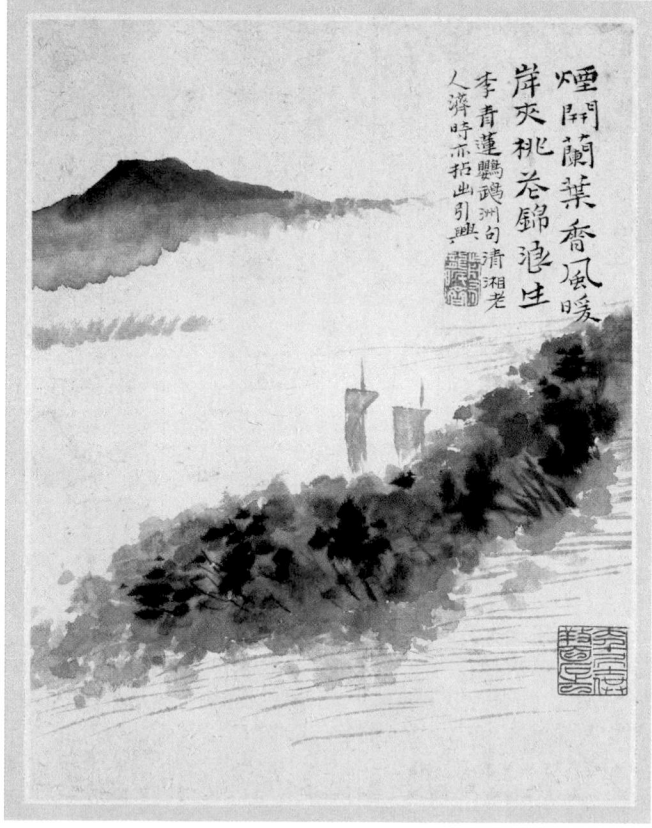

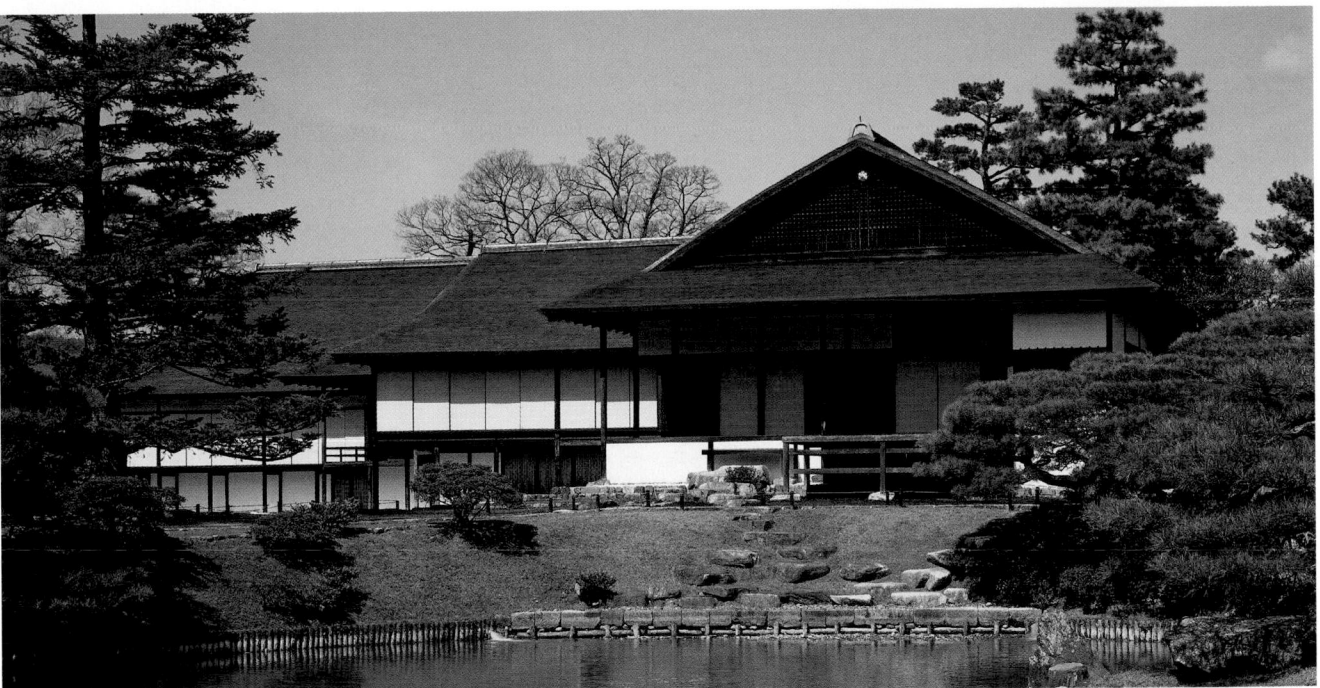

◄ 18.28 East façade of the Katsura Imperial Villa, Kyoto, Japan (Edo period, 1620–1663).

The woodblock print was another significant artistic development of the Edo period, a technique, along with painting, that was employed widely for the depiction of so-called *ukiyo-e* themes including brothel scenes, theatrical images, and domestic settings. Kitagawa Utamaro (1753–1806), perhaps the most widely known ukiyo-e artist in the West, portrayed sensuous images of beautiful women as well as genre (everyday life) subjects including mothers and children. In the polychrome print shown in Figure 18.29, panels of a fine mosquito net part to reveal a mother who scoops up her wriggling, crying baby in the middle of the night. The curving lines that define the simple, flat shapes of her kimono move the eye along a zigzag path, creating a lively energy that contrasts the sweet serenity of the moment. Intimate scenes such as these are indicative of the emphasis on the individual that emerged during the Edo period.

▲ 18.29 KITAGAWA UTAMARO, *Midnight: The Hours of the Rat; Mother and Sleepy Child* (Edo period, 1615–1868). Polychrome woodblock print, 14⅜" high, 9⅝" wide. Metropolitan Museum of Art, New York, New York.

1 in.

CONNECTIONS

Mary Cassatt, as were her fellow French Impressionist artists, was enthralled by the Japanese prints that made their way to Paris in the latter nineteenth century. The economy of line, simple shapes, and flat areas of color and pattern characteristic of Utamaro's woodcut are evident, here, in Cassatt's print of a mother and her child (Fig. 18.30) and in many others portraying women in sparse, intimate interiors.

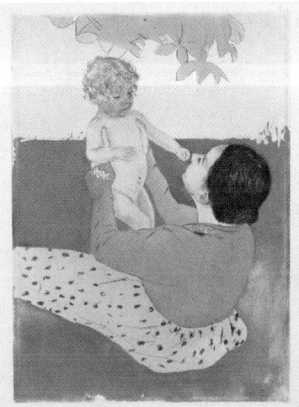

▲ 18.30 MARY CASSATT, *Under the Horse-Chestnut Tree* (1896–1897). Drypoint and aquatint in colors, 20" × 15⅞". Museum of Fine Arts, Houston, Texas.

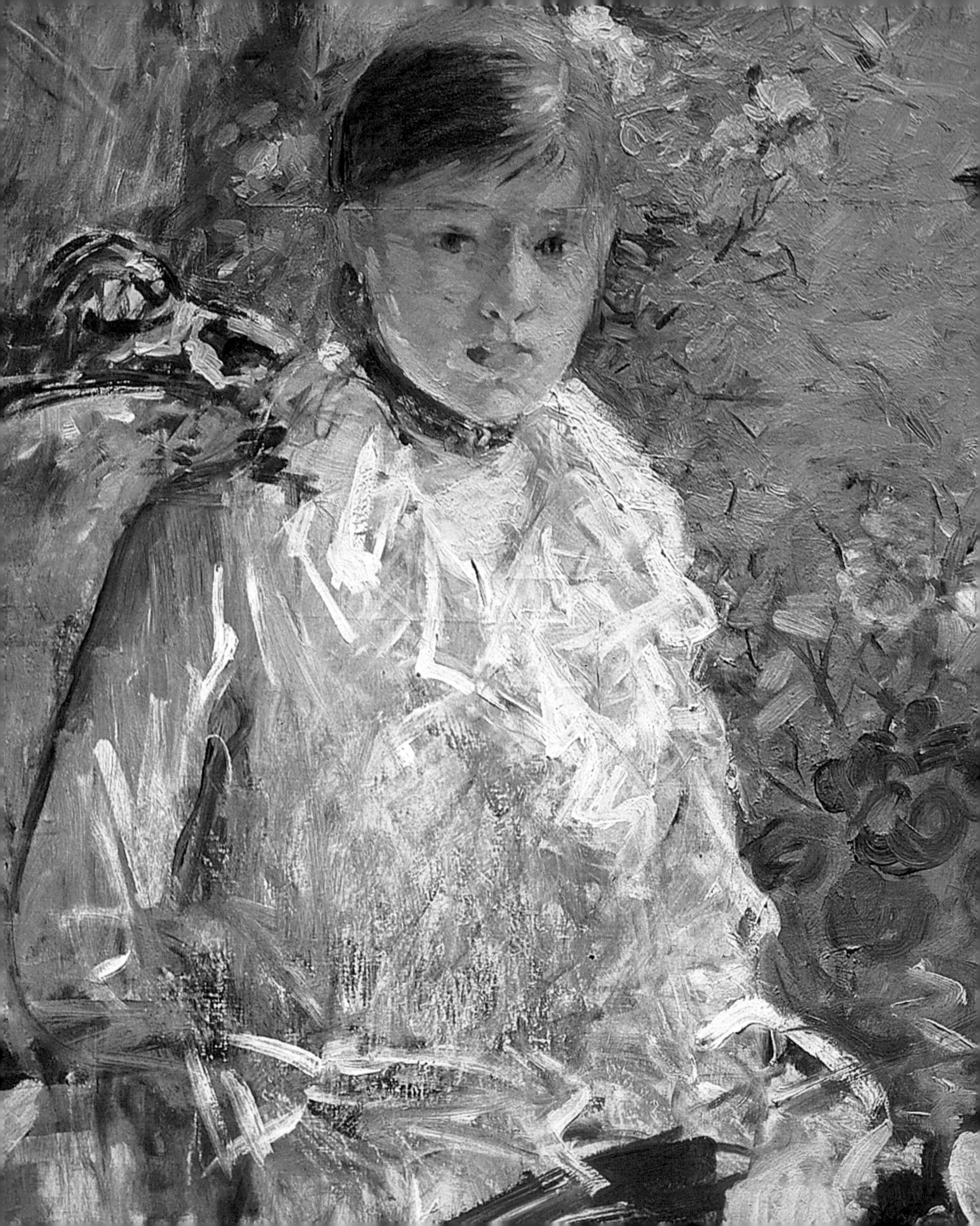

19

THE MODERN ERA

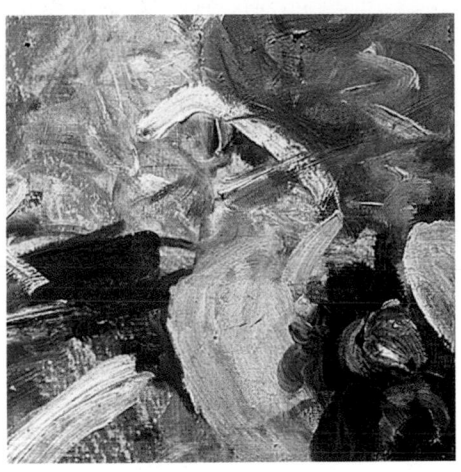

Most painting in the European tradition was painting the mask. Modern art rejected all that. Our subject matter was the person behind the mask.

— ROBERT MOTHERWELL

HISTORIANS OF modern art have repeatedly posed the question, "When did modern art begin?" Some link the beginnings of modern painting to the French Revolution in 1789. Others have chosen 1863, the year of a landmark exhibition of "modern" painting in Paris.

Another issue of interest has been "Just what is modern about modern art?" The artists of the mid-fifteenth century looked upon their art as modern. They chose new subjects, materials, and techniques that signaled a radical change from a medieval past. Their development of one-point linear perspective altered the face of painting completely. From our perspective, modern art begins with the changes in the representation of space as introduced by artists of the late eighteenth century. Unlike the Renaissance masters, who sought to open up endless vistas within the canvas, the artists of the latter 1700s thrust all of the imagery toward the **picture plane**. The flatness or two-dimensionality of the canvas surface was asserted by the use of **planar recession** rather than **linear recession**. Not all artists of the eighteenth and nineteenth centuries abided by this novel treatment of space, but with this innovation, the die was cast for the future of painting. In short, what was *modern* about the modern art of the eighteenth century in France was its concept of space. In a very real sense, the history of modern art is the history of two differing perceptions and renderings of that space.

As we will see in this chapter, the flattening of pictorial space begins in the late eighteenth century with Jacques-Louis David and *Neoclassicism. Romanticism* followed closely in its wake, at times displaying stylistic continuity with its predecessor and at

◄ BERTHE MORISOT, *Young Girl by the Window* (1878). Oil on canvas, 29¹⁵⁄₁₆" × 24". Musée Fabre, Montpellier, France.

417

times diametrically opposing it. We will discuss the survival of Academic painting in the nineteenth century and consider the relationship between art, politics, and social consciousness. In the mid-nineteenth century, change was everywhere. *Realist* artists rejected the content of Academic art and took to the subjects of life around them. The *Impressionists* rejected the isolation of the artist's studio and took to the outdoors to paint, recording the fleeting optical impressions of light and atmosphere. The new medium of photography experienced technical strides, and its growing familiarity had a marked influence on later-nineteenth-century painting. Paris had become the center of the art world.

NEOCLASSICISM

Modern art declared its opposition to the whimsy of the late Rococo style with **Neoclassical art**. The Neoclassical style is characterized by harsh sculptural lines, a subdued palette, and for the most part, planar instead of linear recession into space. The subject matter of Neoclassicism was inspired by the French Revolution and designed to heighten moral standards. The new morality sought to replace the corruption and decadence of Louis XVI's France. The Roman Empire was often chosen as the model to emulate. For this reason, the artists of the Napoleonic era imitated the form and content of Classical works of art. This interest in antiquity was fueled by contemporaneous archeological finds at sites such as Pompeii, as well as by numerous excavations in Greece.

Neoclassical Painting

JACQUES-LOUIS DAVID   The sterling proponent of the Neoclassical style and official painter of the French Revolution was Jacques-Louis David (1748–1825). David literally gave postrevolutionary France a new look. He designed everything from clothing to coiffures. David also set the course for modern art with a sudden and decisive break from the ornateness and frivolity of the Rococo.

In *The Oath of the Horatii* (Fig. 19.1), David portrayed a dramatic event from Roman history to heighten French patriotism and courage. Three brothers prepare to fight an enemy of Rome, swearing an oath to the empire on swords upheld by their father. To the right, their mother and other relatives collapse in despair. They weep for the men's safety but are also distraught because one of the enemy men is engaged to a sister of the Horatii. Family is pitted against family in a conflict that no one can win. Such a subject could descend into pathos, but David controlled any tendency toward sentimentality by reviving the Classical balance of emotion and restraint. The emotionality of the theme is countered by David's cool rendition of forms. The elements of the composition further work to harness emotionalism. Harsh sculptural lines

NINETEENTH-CENTURY WESTERN ART

1800–1815	1815–1840	1840–1870	1870–1880	1880–1890	1890–1900
David paints in the Neoclassical style	Romanticism focuses on subjective emotion and intuition	Courbet and other Realists argue that painters must paint people and events of their own time	Monet and other Impressionists exhibit their work	Manet paints in the Impressionist style	Toulouse-Lautrec paints decadent nightlife with its glaring light and masklike faces
Napoleon appoints David as First Painter of the Empire and imports Italian sculptor Canova	Gericault paints his politically devastating *Raft of the Medusa*	Manet receives hostile reception because of nude subject matter and nonillusionistic style	Impressionists capture instantaneous representations of atmospheric changes	Seurat develops Pointillism	Expatriate Mary Cassatt paints mainly women and children
Ingres bridges Neoclassicism and Romanticism	Delacroix paints *Liberty Leading the People* with vibrant color and bold brushstrokes		Renoir paints *Le Moulin de la Goulette*	Van Gogh emphasizes the expressive power of color and distorted forms	Art Nouveau movement emerges
			European artists collect Japanese prints	Rodin is commissioned to create a sculpture commemorating the Burghers of Calais	

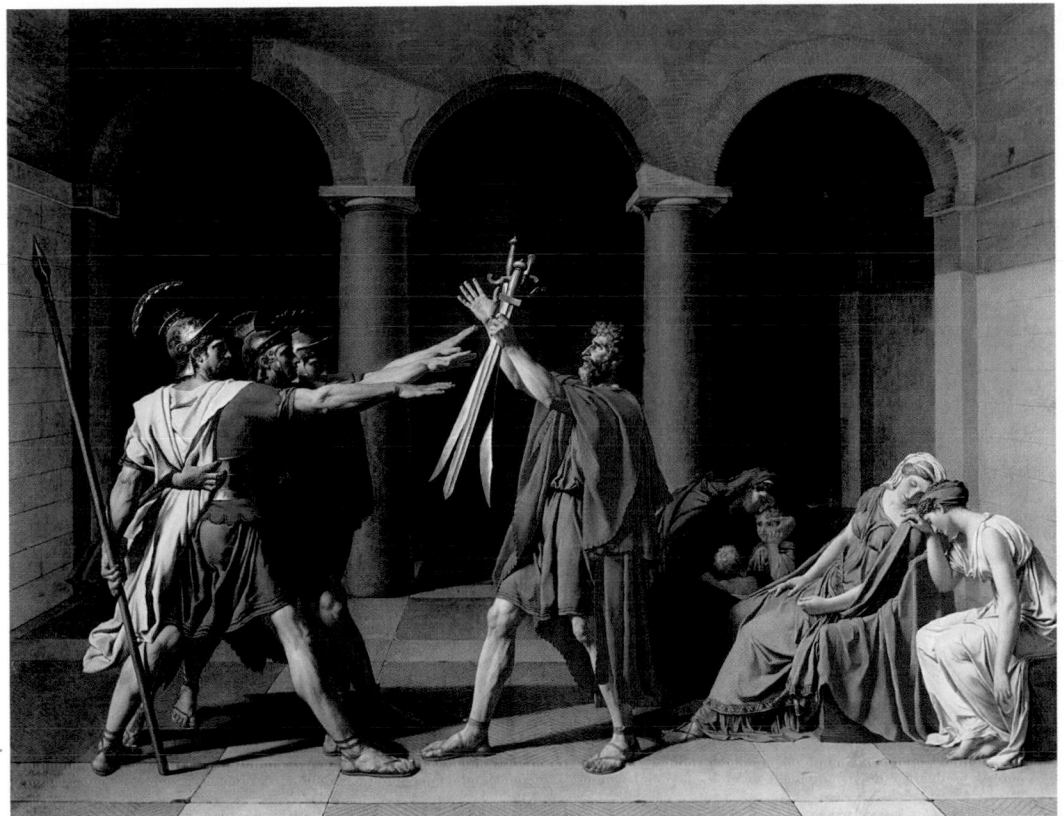

1 ft.

▲ 19.1 JACQUES-LOUIS DAVID, *The Oath of the Horatii* (1784). Oil on canvas, 11' × 14'. Louvre Museum, Paris, France.

David was one of the leaders of the French Revolution, and his political life underwent curious turns. Although he painted *The Oath of the Horatii* for Louis XVI, he supported the faction that deposed him. Later he was to find himself painting a work commemorating the coronation of Napoleon. Having struggled against the French monarchy and then living to see it restored, David chose to spend his last years in exile in Brussels.

ANGELICA KAUFFMAN
Angelica Kauffman (1741–1807) was another leading Neoclassical painter, an exact contemporary of David. Born in Switzerland and educated in the Neoclassical circles

define the figures and setting. The palette is reduced to muted blues and grays, with an occasional splash of deep red. Emotional response is barely evident in the idealized Classical faces of the figures.

Several Classical devices in David's compositional format also function to balance emotion and restraint. The figural groups form a rough triangle. Their apex—the clasped swords of the Horatii—is the most important point of the composition. In the same way that Leonardo used three windows in his *Last Supper*, David silhouetted his dramatic moment against the central opening of three arches in the background. David further imitated Renaissance canvases by presenting cues for a linear perspective in the patterning of the floor. But unlike six-teenth-century artists, David led his **orthogonals** into a flattened space instead of a vanishing point on a horizon line. The closing off of this background space forces the viewer's eye to the front of the picture plane, where it encounters the action of the composition and the canvas surface. No longer does the artist desire to trick observers into believing they are looking through a window frame into the distance. Now the reality of the two-dimensionality of the canvas is asserted.

in Rome, Kauffman was responsible for the dissemination of the style in England. She is known for her portraiture, history painting, and narrative works such as *The Artist in the Character of Design Listening to the Inspiration of Poetry* (Fig. 19.2). In this allegorical work, Kauffman paints her

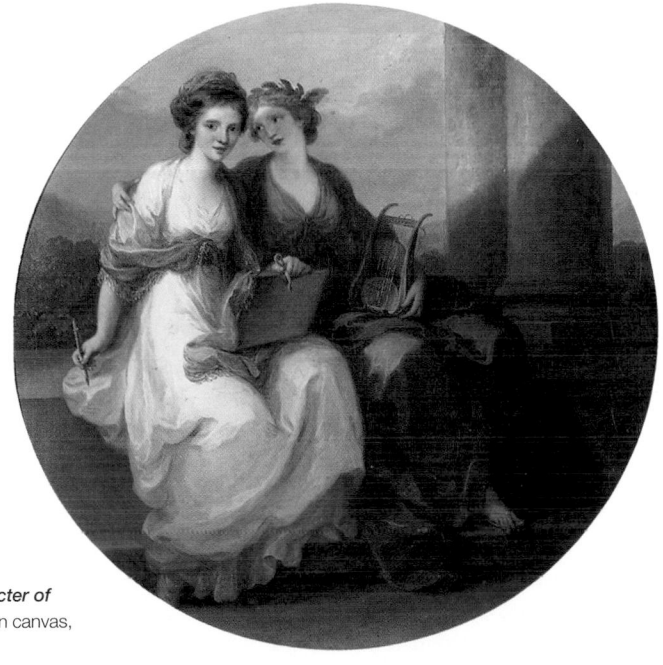

> 19.2 ANGELICA KAUFFMAN, *The Artist in the Character of Design Listening to the Inspiration of Poetry* (1782). Oil on canvas, D: 24". Kenwood House, Hampstead, London, England.

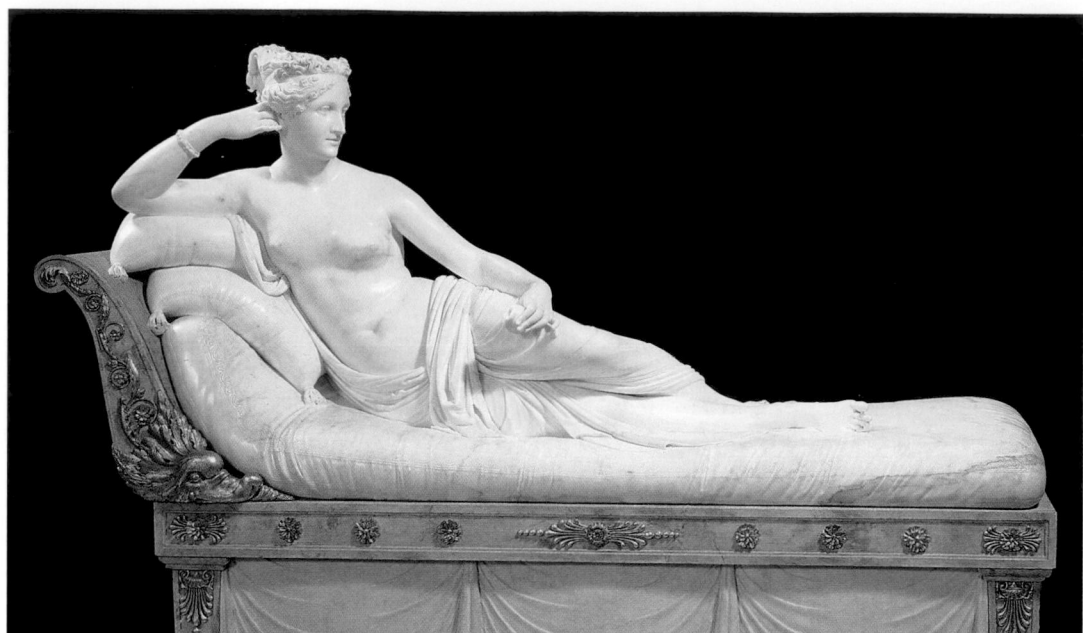

own features in the person of the muse of design, who is listening attentively with paper and pencil in hand to her companion, the muse of poetry. Poetry's idealized facial features, along with the severe architecture, classically rendered drapery, and rich palette, place the work firmly in the Neoclassical style.

JEAN-AUGUSTE-DOMINIQUE INGRES David abstracted space by using planar rather than linear recession. His most prodigious student, Jean-Auguste-Dominique Ingres (1780–1867), created sensuous, though pristinely Classical, compositions in which line functions as an abstract element. Above all else, Ingres was a magnificent draftsman.

Ingres's work is a combination of harsh linearity and sculptural smoothness on the one hand, and delicacy and sensuality on the other. His *Grande Odalisque* (Fig. 19.7 in the nearby Compare + Contrast feature) portrays a Turkish harem mistress in the tradition of the great reclining Venuses of the Venetian Renaissance. Yet how different it is, for example, from Titian's *Venus of Urbino*! (See the Compare + Contrast feature later in the chapter.) The elongation of her spine, her attenuated limbs, and odd fullness of form recall the distortions and abstractions of Mannerist art. In the *Grande Odalisque*, Ingres also delights in the differing qualities of line. The articulation of heavy drapery contrasts markedly with the staccato treatment of the bed linens and the languid, sensual lines of the mistress's body. Like David's, Ingres's forms are smooth and sculptural, and his palette is muted. Ingres also flattens space in his composition by placing his imagery in the foreground, as in a relief.

Ingres's exotic nudes were a popular type of imagery in the late eighteenth century, but other artists often rendered such subjects quite differently. The popular style during this period was similar to that of the Baroque era. On the one hand were artists such as David and Ingres, who represented the linear style. On the other hand were artists whose works were painterly. The foremost proponents of the painterly style were Géricault and Delacroix. The linear artists, called **Poussinistes**, followed in the footsteps of Classicism with their subdued palette and emphasis on draftsmanship and sculptural forms. The painterly artists, termed the **Rubenistes**, adopted the vibrant palette and aggressive brushstroke of the Baroque artist. The two factions argued vehemently about the merits and the shortcomings of their respective styles. No artists were more deeply entrenched in this feud than the leaders of the camps, Ingres and Delacroix.

Neoclassical Sculpture

The principles of Neoclassicism were embraced by sculptors working in France, England, and the United States. It was the style of choice for official portraits, relief sculptures, and monuments of all sorts. Antonio Canova (1757–1822), trained in Italy, wrote of having to "[sweat] day and night over the Greek models, imbibing their style, turning it into one's own blood." He became the sculptor to Napoleon Bonaparte and was responsible for numerous portraits of the emperor and members of his family, including his sister, Pauline Borghese (Fig. 19.3). Just as Napoleon chose a Zeus-like pose for his coronation painting by Ingres, Pauline had herself portrayed as the goddess of love—Venus. The reclining figure clearly references Classical Greek prototypes, although his is a combination of realism and idealism. Pauline's face has the character of a portrait, however modified or improved, and the finely carved details of the elaborate lounge can almost be described as **trompe l'oeil.**

Neoclassical Architecture

In the late eighteenth and nineteenth centuries, Neoclassicism also dominated architectural design in France, England, and America. The architects and visionaries of the U.S. capital—Thomas Jefferson included—embraced Classical models for their aesthetic beauty and simplicity. The reference to ancient Greece also befitted the young democracy. From Pierre Charles L'Enfant's plan for Washington, D.C., with its radiating boulevards, geometric spaces, and vistas culminating in Classical monuments, to Cass Gilbert's design of the U.S. Supreme Court Building (see Fig. 1.2), the city was awash in the serenity and monumentality of columns, pediments, and pristine marble facades. Latrobe especially was a stickler for purity of Greek forms. He combined elements of the **Ionic order** for the Senate chamber and **Corinthian** capitals for the House of Representatives. Also of interest is Latrobe's contribution to the White House—an oval room

with a columned portico that would come to symbolize the hub of presidential power.

ROMANTICISM

Both Neoclassicism and **Romanticism** reflected the revolutionary spirit of the times. Neoclassicism emphasized restraint of emotion, purity of form, and subjects that inspired morality, whereas Romantic art sought extremes of emotion enhanced by virtuoso brushwork and a brilliant palette. The two major proponents of the romantic style in France were Théodore Géricault and Eugène Delacroix.

THÉODORE GÉRICAULT   The depiction of nature as unpredictable and uncontrollable—in the words of the French philosopher Denis Diderot, as stunning the soul and imprinting feelings of terror—was a favorite theme of the Romantic artist. Many French and British paintings of the period reveal a particular fascination with the destructive power of nature at sea, perhaps none as intensely as Théodore Géricault's *Raft of the Medusa* (Fig. 19.4). Based

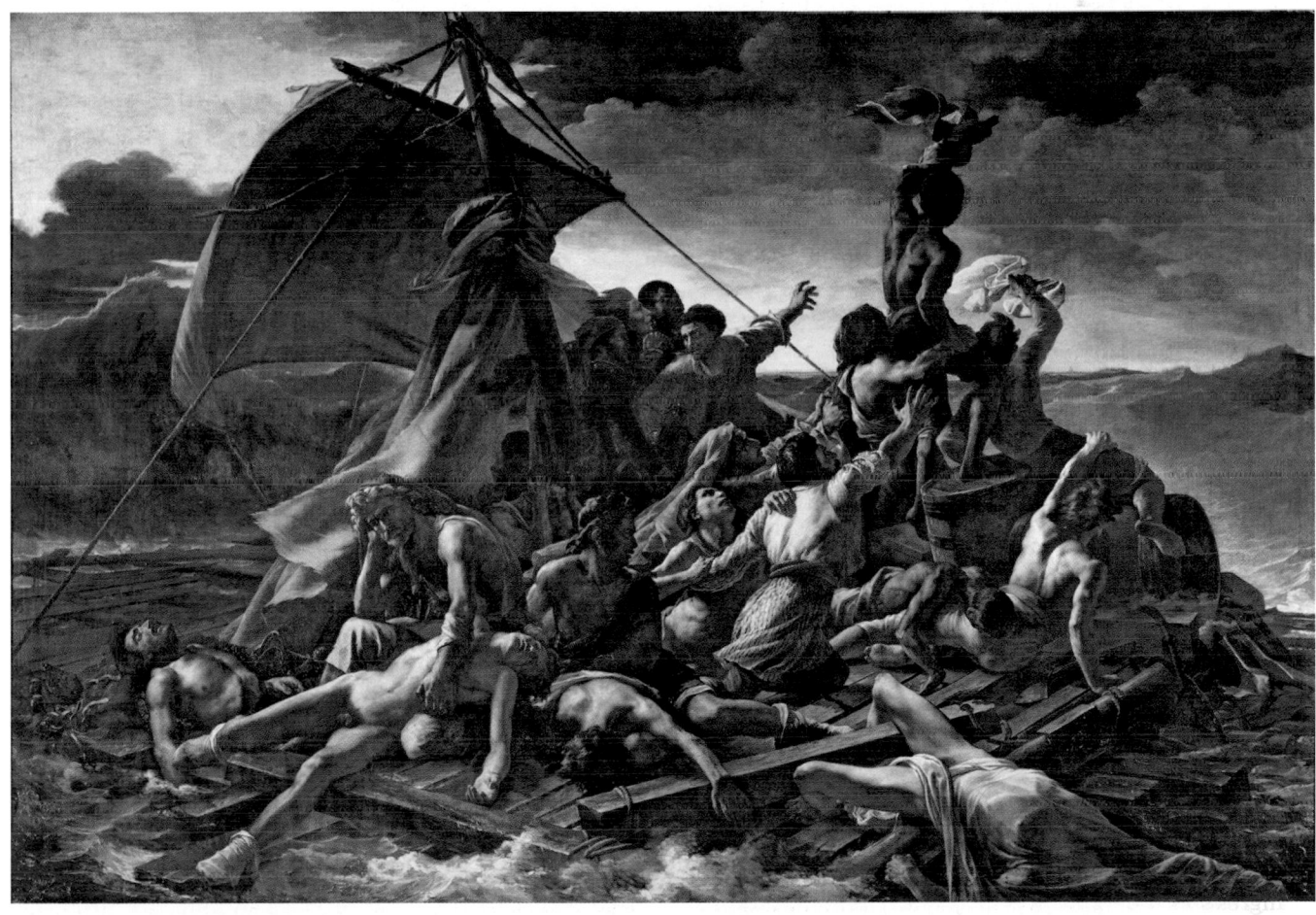

1 ft.

▲ 19.4 **THÉODORE GÉRICAULT,** *Raft of the Medusa* (1818–1819). Oil on canvas, approximately 16' × 23'. Louvre, Paris, France.

> The first virtue of a painting is to be a feast for the eyes.
>
> —EUGÈNE DELACROIX

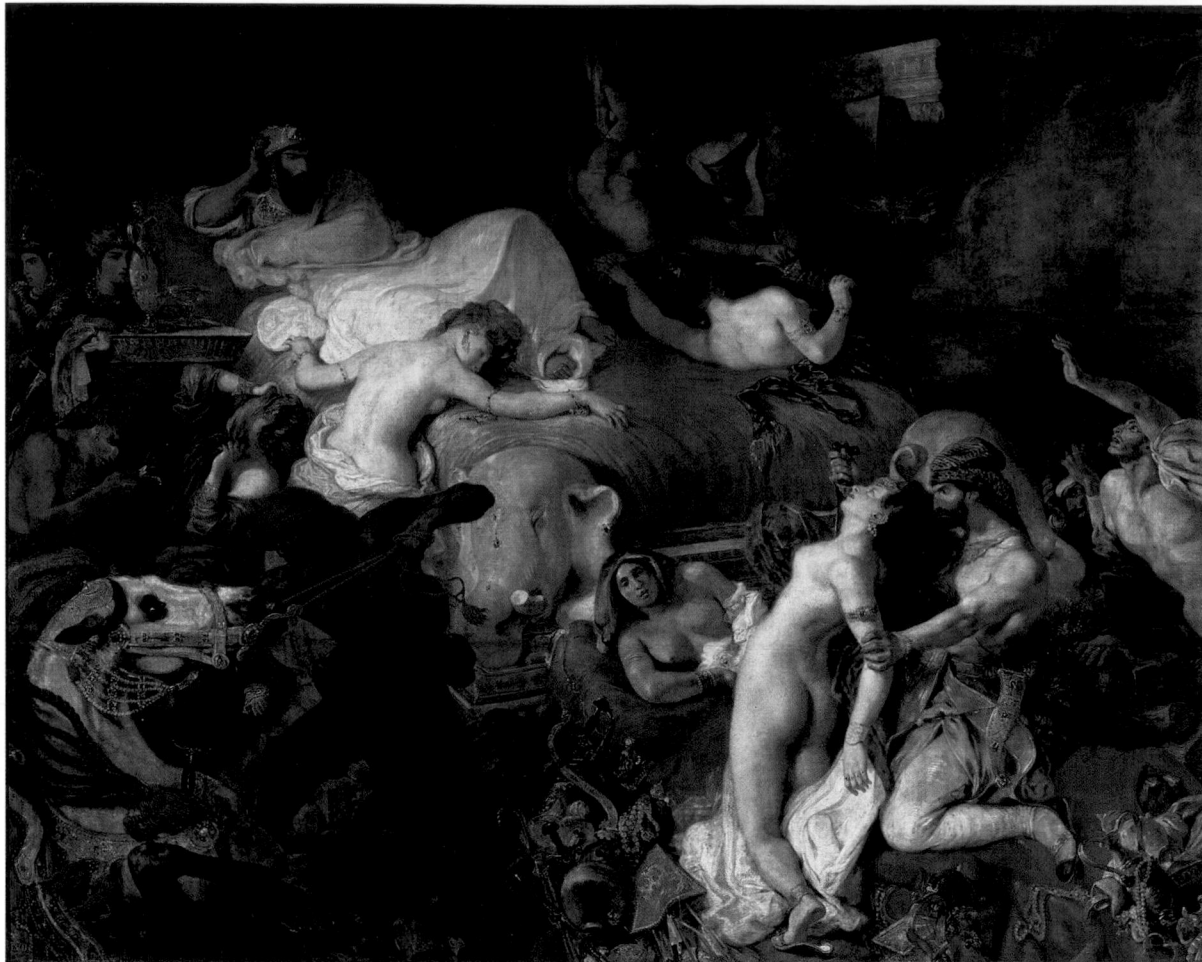

1 ft.

on a shipwreck off the coast of West Africa in 1816, during which a makeshift raft laden with Algerian immigrants was set adrift by the captain and crew of the crippled French ship, *Medusa*, the painting is viewed as Géricault's most controversial and political work.

Like many of his liberal contemporaries, Géricault (1791–1824) opposed the French monarchy and used the tragedy of the *Medusa* to call attention to the mismanagement and ineffectual policies of the French government, as well as the practice of slavery. The plight of the survivors and victims of the *Medusa* became a national scandal, and Géricault's authentic documentation—based on interviews with survivors and visits to the morgue—was intended as a direct attack on the government. The powerful composition is full of realistic detail and explores the full gamut of human emotion under extreme hardship and duress. Much of the drama of Géricault's composition occurs along a diagonal configuration of figures, from the corpse in the lower left that will soon slip into

the dark abyss of the ocean, upward along a crescendo that culminates in the muscular torso of a black man waving a flag toward a barely visible rescue ship on the horizon. The fractured raft is tossed about mercilessly by the winds and waves; humans battle against nature, and their own, for sheer survival.

EUGÈNE DELACROIX The most famous Rubeniste—and Ingres's archrival—was Eugène Delacroix (1798–1863). Whereas Ingres believed that a painting was nothing without drawing, Delacroix advocated the spontaneity of painting directly on a canvas without the tyranny of meticulous preparatory sketches. Ingres believed that color ought to be subordinated to line, but Delacroix maintained that compositions should be constructed of color. Their contrasting approaches to painting can be seen clearly in the *Odalisque* by each artist (Figs. 19.7 and 19.8 in the Compare + Contrast feature), fine examples of the difference between the Neoclassical and Romantic styles.

One of Delacroix's most dynamic statements of the Romantic style occurs in one of his many compositions devoted to the more exciting themes from literary history. *The Death of Sardanapalus* (Fig. 19.5), inspired by a tragedy by Lord Byron, depicts the murder-suicide of an Assyrian king who, rather than surrender to his attackers, set fire to himself and his entourage. All of the monarch's earthly possessions, including concubines, servants, and Arabian stallions, are heaped upon his lavish gold and velvet bed, now turned funeral pyre. The chaos and terror of the event are rendered by Delacroix with all the vigor and passion of a Baroque composition.

The explicit contrast between the voluptuous women and the brute strength of the king's executioners brings to mind *The Rape of the Daughters of Leucippus* by Rubens (see Fig. 18.11). Arms reach helplessly in all directions, and backs arch in hopeless defiance or pitiful submission before the passive Sardanapalus. Delacroix's unleashed energy and assaulting palette were strongly criticized by his contemporaries, who felt that there was no excuse for such a blatant depiction of violence. But his use of bold colors and freely applied pigment, along with the

observations on art and nature that he recorded in his journal, were an important influence on the young artists of the nineteenth century who were destined to transform artistic tradition.

FRANCISCO GOYA Ironically, the man considered the greatest painter of the Neoclassical and Romantic periods belonged to neither artistic group. He never visited France, the center of the art world at the time, and he was virtually unknown to painters of the late eighteenth and early nineteenth centuries. Yet his paintings and prints foreshadowed the art of the nineteenth-century Impressionists. Francisco Goya (1746–1828) was born in Spain and, except for an academic excursion to Rome, spent his life there. He enjoyed a great reputation in his native country and was awarded many important commissions, including religious frescoes and portraits of Spanish royalty.

But Goya is best known for his works with political overtones, ranging from social satire to savage condemnation of the disasters of war. One of his most famous depictions of war is *The Third of May, 1808* (Fig. 19.6). The painting commemorates the massacre of the peasant-citizens of

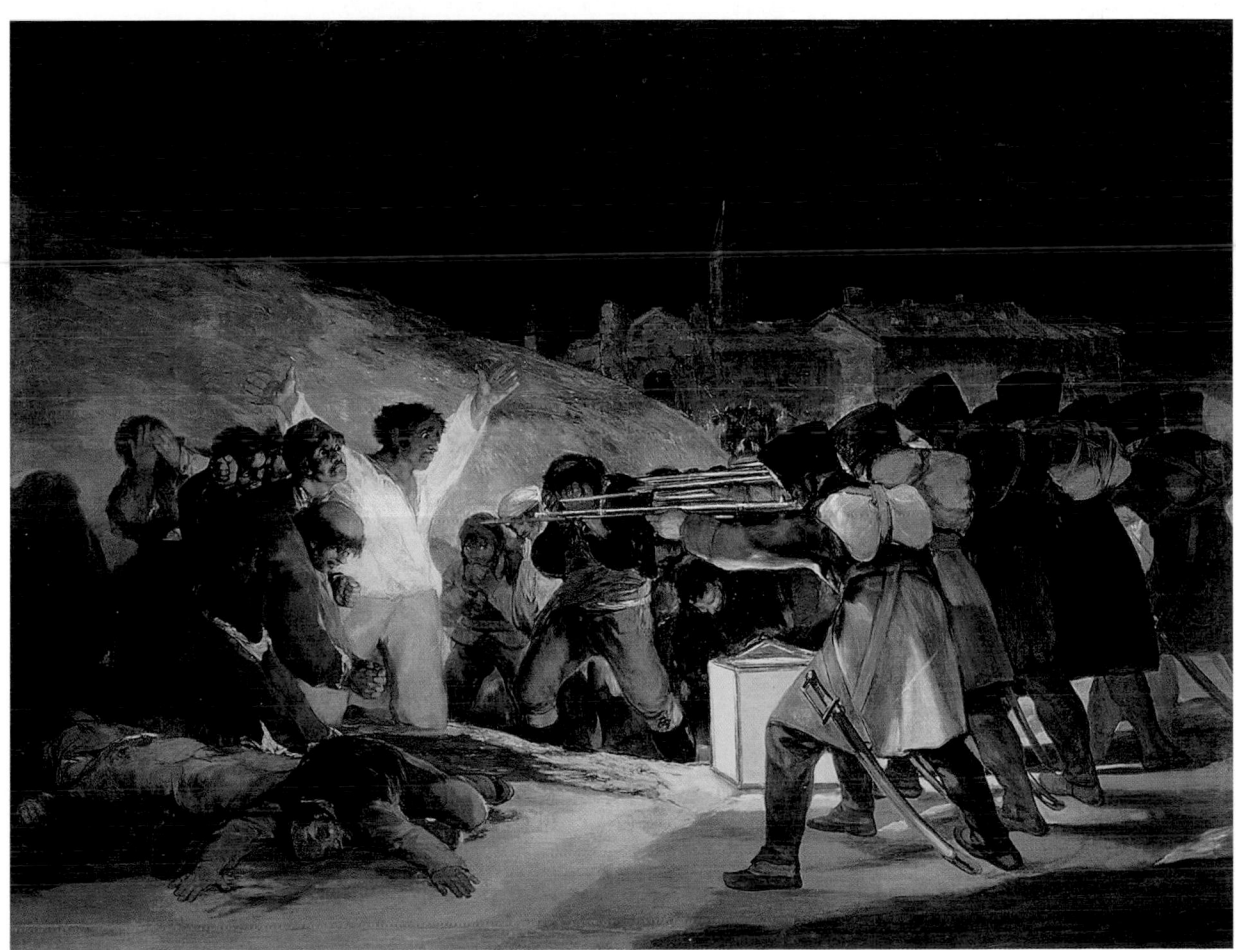

1 ft.

∧ 19.6 FRANCISCO GOYA, *The Third of May, 1808* (1814–1815). Oil on canvas, 8' 9" × 13' 4". Prado Museum, Madrid, Spain.

COMPARE & CONTRAST

Ingres's *Grande Odalisque* with Delacroix's *Odalisque*

COMPARE-AND-CONTRAST EXERCISES are often used to stimulate a student's powers of visual recognition and discrimination, to test the student's ability to characterize and categorize, and to force the student to think critically about the content and context of the work. If put together just right, they ought also to act as a springboard for discussion of issues that push beyond the discipline of art. Tall order? You bet.

You can write paragraphs on the stylistic differences alone between the *Odalisque* paintings by Ingres (**Fig. 19.7**) and by Delacroix (**Fig. 19.8**). They are arch examples of the contrast between a linear and painterly approach to the same subject; they offer clear evidence of the "battle" between the Poussinistes and the Rubenistes during the Romantic period (those whose draftsmanship was inspired by the Classical Baroque artist Nicolas Poussin versus those who "went to school" on the Flemish Baroque painter Peter Paul Rubens). On the other hand, they have one very important thing in common: Both bespeak an enormous fascination with the exotic, with the "Orient," with the *other;* a seemingly insatiable fascination not only with the trappings of an exotic *sens*uality—turbans, silken scarves, peacock feathers, opium pipes—but with what was perceived as an unrestrained and exotic *sexuality*. These two works are in abundant company in nineteenth-century France. Can you do a bit of research and find out what circumstances (historical, political, and sociological) prevailed at this moment in time that might have led to a market for such paintings? Why did these very different artists find the same subject so captivating, so fashionable?

Nineteenth-century art historian and feminist scholar Linda Nochlin has suggested that such paintings speak volumes about contemporary ideology and gender discourse:

> the ways in which representations of women in art are founded upon and serve to reproduce indisputably accepted assumptions held by society in general, artists in particular, and some artists more than others about men's power over, superiority to, difference from, and necessary control of women, assumptions which are manifested in the visual structures as well as the thematic choices of the pictures in question.

Among several that Nochlin lists are assumptions about women's weakness and passivity and availability to satisfy men's sexual needs.

The works in this feature also speak to the tradition of the reclining nude in Western art. In another Compare + Contrast feature

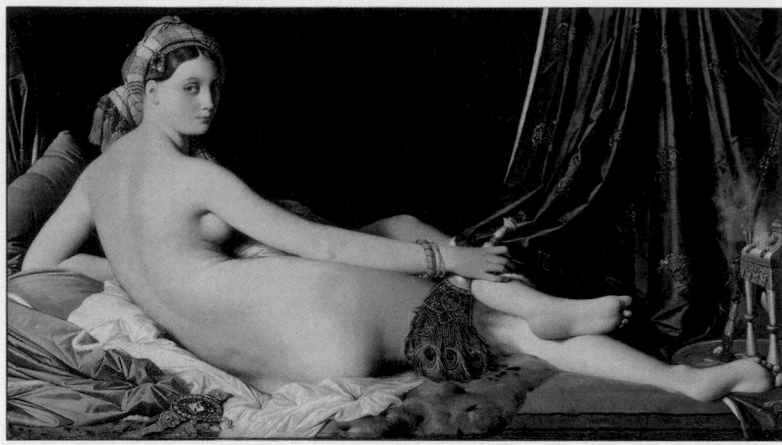

▲ **19.7** JEAN-AUGUSTE-DOMINIQUE INGRES, *Grande Odalisque* (1814). Oil on canvas, 35¼" × 63¾". Louvre Museum, Paris, France.

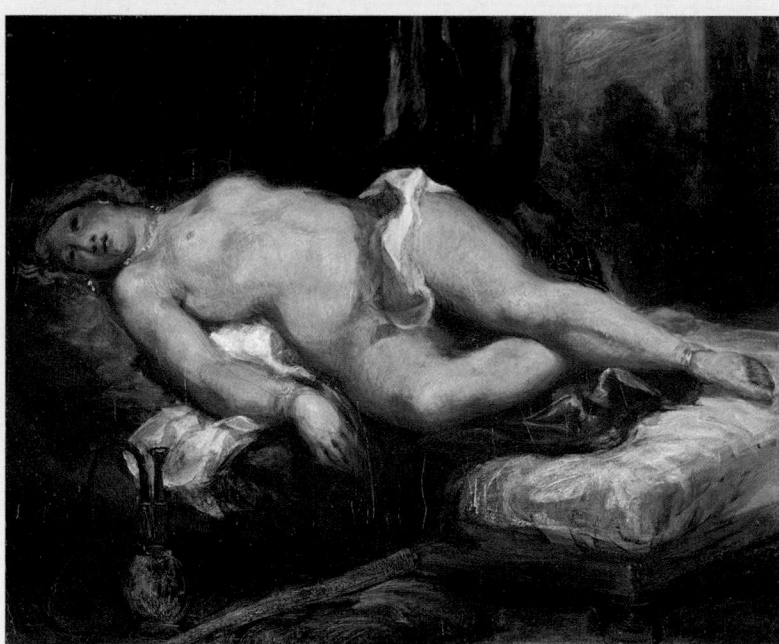

▲ **19.8** EUGÈNE DELACROIX, *Odalisque* (1845–1850). Oil on canvas, 14⅞" × 18¼".

in this chapter, you can see some other examples of this tradition and are asked for whose "gaze" you think they were intended. In fact, the concept of the "male gaze" has been central to feminist theory for the past decade. In a landmark article written in 1973, the filmmaker Laura Mulvey explained the roles of the viewer and the viewed in art, literature, and film this way: Men are in the position of looking, and women are "passive, powerless objects of their controlling gaze."

Madrid after the city fell to the French. Reflecting the procedures of Velásquez and Rembrandt—two Baroque masters whom Goya acknowledged as influential in the development of his style—Goya focuses the viewer's attention on a single moment in the violent episode. A Spaniard thrusts his arms upward in surrender to the bayonets of the faceless enemy. The brusqueness of the application of pigment corresponds to the harshness of the subject. The dutiful and regimented procedure of the executioners, dressed in long coats, contrasts visually and psychologically with the expressions of horror, fear, and helplessness on the faces of the ragtag peasants. The emotion is heightened by the use of acerbic tones and by a strong chiaroscuro that illuminates the pitiful victims while relegating all other details to darkness.

Goya devoted much of his life to the graphic representation of man's inhumanity to man. Toward the end of his life, he was afflicted with deafness and plagued with bitterness and depression over the atrocities he had witnessed. These feelings were manifested in macabre paintings and lithographs, which presaged the style of the great painters of the nineteenth century.

The Academy

Ingres's paintings spoke of a calm, though exotic, Classicism. Delacroix retrieved the dynamism of the Baroque. Goya swathed his canvases with the spirit of revolution. Ironically, the style of painting that had the least impact on the development of modern art was the most popular type of painting in its day. This was **Academic art**, so called because its style and subject matter were derived from conventions established by the Academie Royale de Peinture et de Sculpture in Paris.

Established in 1648, the Academy had maintained a firm grip on artistic production for more than two centuries. Many artists steeped in this tradition were followers rather than innovators, and the quality of their production left something to be desired. Some, however, like David and Ingres, worked within the confines of a style acceptable to the Academy but rose above the generally rampant mediocrity.

ADOLPHE WILLIAM BOUGUEREAU One of the more popular and accomplished

Academic painters was Adolphe William Bouguereau (1825–1905). Included among his oeuvre are religious and historical paintings in a grand Classical manner, although he is most famous for his meticulously painted nudes and mythological subjects. *Nymphs and Satyr* (Fig. 19.9) is nearly photographic in its refined technique and attention to detail. Four sprightly and sensuous wood nymphs corral a hesitant satyr and tug him into the water. Their innocent playfulness would have appealed to the Frenchman on the street, although the saccharine character of the subject matter and the extreme light-handedness with which the work was painted served also as a model against which the new wave of painters rebelled.

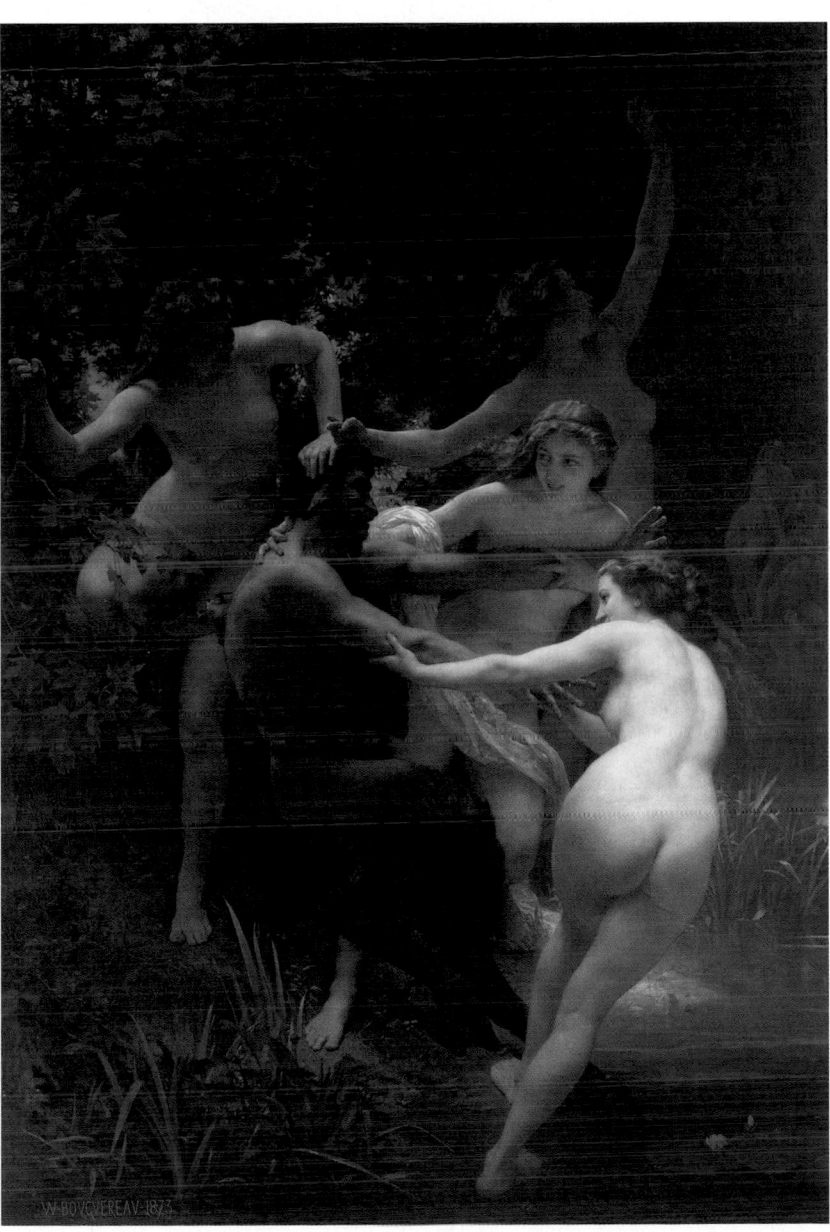

▲ 19.9 **ADOLPHE WILLIAM BOUGUEREAU,** *Nymphs and Satyr* (1873). Oil on canvas, 102⅜" × 70⅞". Sterling and Francine Clark Art Institute, Williamstown, Massachusetts.

1 ft.

> To record the manners, ideas, and aspects of the age as I myself saw them—to be a man
> as well as a painter—in short to create a living art—that is my aim.
>
> —GUSTAVE COURBET

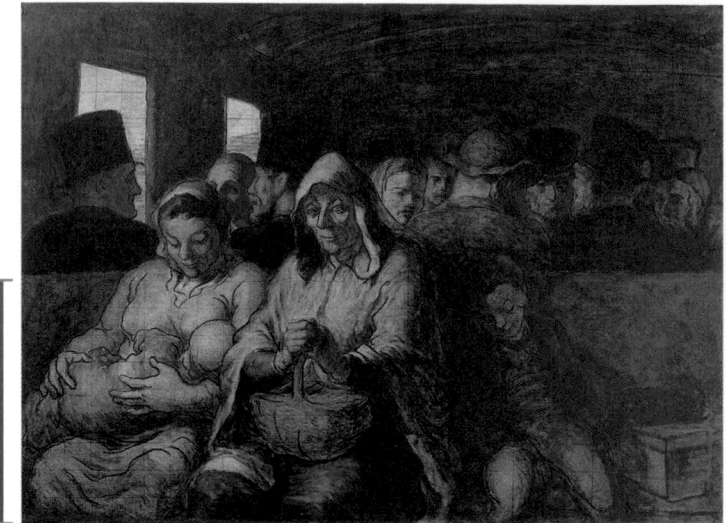

▲ 19.10 HONORÉ DAUMIER, *The Third-Class Carriage* (c. 1862). Oil on canvas, 25¾" × 35½". The Metropolitan Museum of Art, New York, New York.

REALISM

The "modern" painters of the nineteenth century objected to Academic art on two levels: The subject matter did not represent real life; nor did the manner in which the subjects were rendered reflect reality as it was observed by the naked eye.

The modern artists chose to depict subjects that were evident in everyday life. The way in which they rendered these subjects also differed from that of Academic painters. They attempted to render on canvas objects as they saw them—**optically**—rather than as they knew them to be—**conceptually**. In addition, they respected the reality of the medium they worked with. Instead of using pigment merely as a tool to provide an illusion of three-dimensional reality, they emphasized the two-dimensionality of the canvas and asserted the painting process itself. The physical properties of the pigments were highlighted. Artists who took these ideas to heart were known as the Realists. They include Honoré Daumier and two painters whose work stands on the threshold of the Impressionist movement: Gustave Courbet and Édouard Manet.

HONORÉ DAUMIER Of all of the modern artists of the mid-nineteenth century, Honoré Daumier (1808–1879) was perhaps the most concerned with bringing to light the very real subject of the plight of the masses. Daumier worked as a caricaturist for Parisian journals, and he used his cartoons to convey his disgust with the monarchy and contemporary bourgeois society. His public ridicule of King Louis Philippe landed him in prison for six months.

One of Daumier's most famous compositions is *The Third-Class Carriage* (Fig. 19.10). His caricaturist style is evident in the flowing dark outlines and exaggerated features and gestures. The peasants are crowded into the car, their clothing poor and rumpled, their faces wide and expressionless. They contrast markedly with bourgeois commuters, whose felt top hats tower above the kerchiefed heads. Wrapped up in their own thoughts and disappointments, they live their quite ordinary lives from day to day, without significance and without notice.

GUSTAVE COURBET The term *realist*, when it applies to art, is synonymous with Gustave Courbet (1819–1877). Considered to be the "father" of the Realist movement, Courbet used the term *realism* to describe his own work and even issued a manifesto on the subject.

Paintings such as *The Stone-Breakers* (Fig. 19.11) were the objects of public derision. Courbet was moved to paint the work after seeing an old man and a young boy breaking stones on a roadside. So common a subject was naturally criticized by contemporary critics, who favored

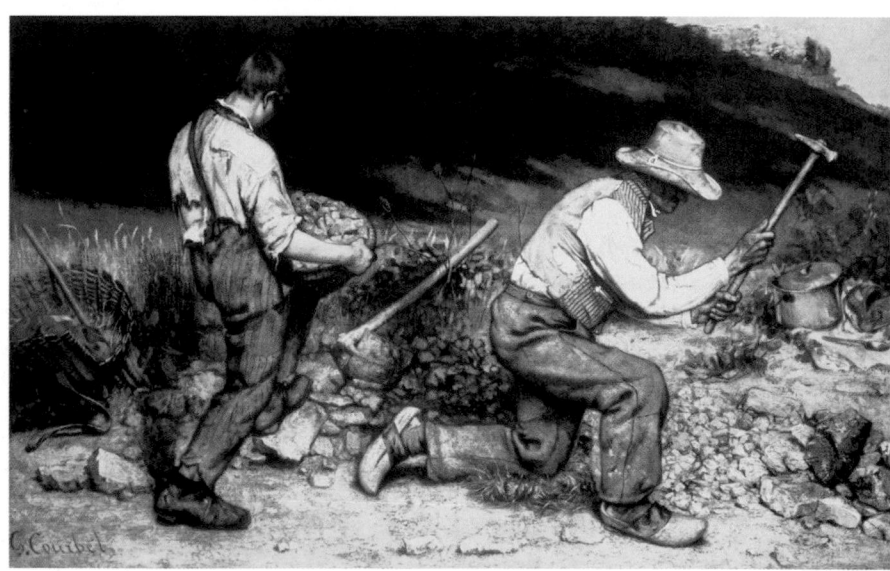

▲ 19.11 GUSTAVE COURBET, *The Stone-Breakers* (1849). Oil on canvas, 63" × 102". Formerly Staatliche Kunstsammlungen, Dresden (destroyed in World War II). Galerie Neue Meister, Dresden, Germany.

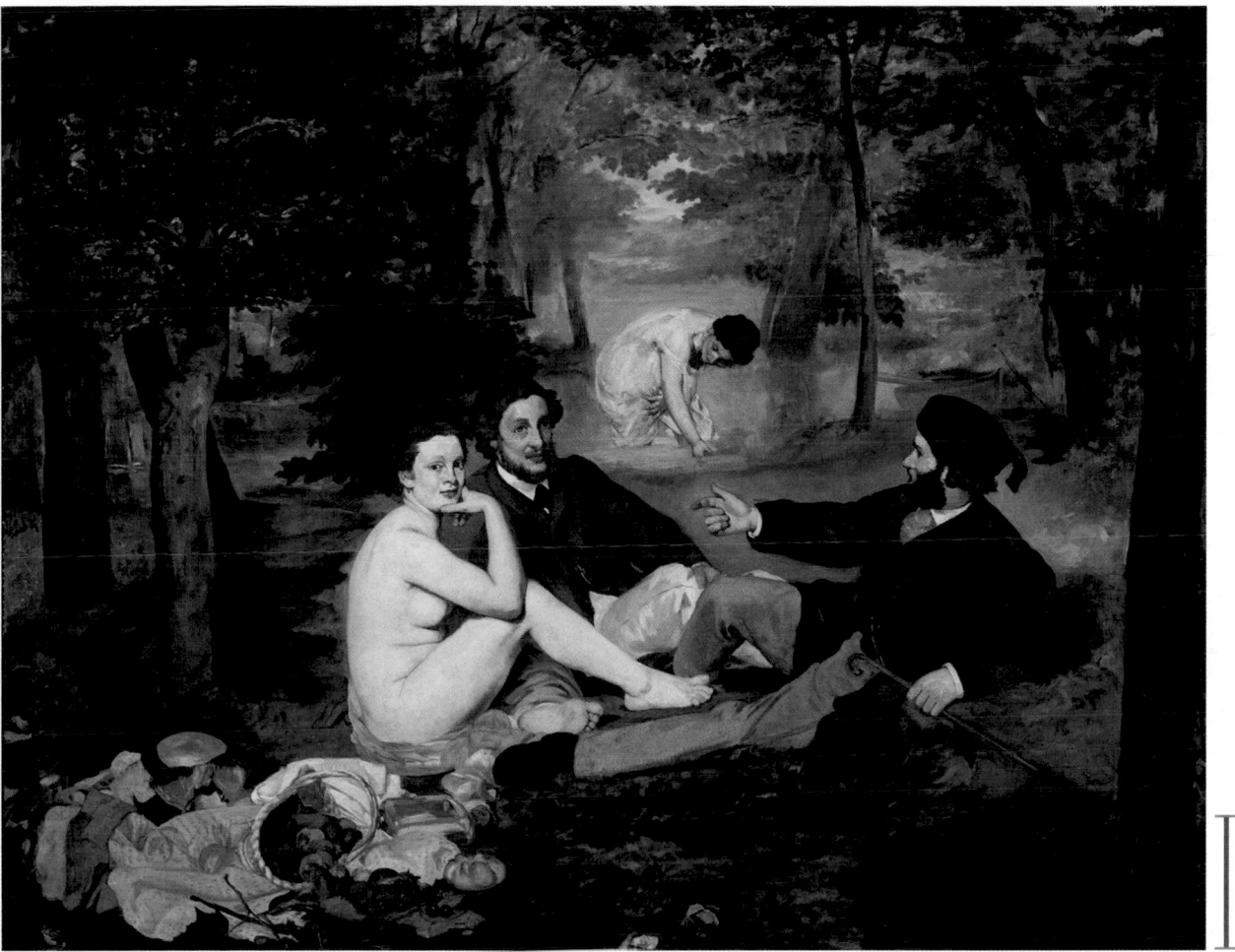

1 ft.

˄ **19.12** ÉDOUARD MANET, *Le Déjeuner sur l'Herbe (Luncheon on the Grass)* (1863). Oil on canvas, 7' × 8' 1". Musée d'Orsay, Galerie Nationale du Jeu de Paume, Paris, France.

mythological or idealistic subjects. It was not only the artist's subject matter, however, that the critics found offensive. They also spurned his painting technique. Although his choice of colors was fairly traditional—muted tones of brown and ocher—their quick application with a palette knife resulted in a coarsely textured surface that could not have been further removed from the glossy finish of an Academic painting. Curiously, although Courbet believed that this type of painting was more realistic than that of the salons, in fact the reverse is closer to the truth. The Academic painter strove for what we would today consider to be an almost photographically exact representation of the figure, whereas Courbet attempted quickly to jot down his impressions of the scene in an often spontaneous flurry of strokes. Despite Courbet's advocacy of hard-core realism, the observer of *The Stone-Breakers* is presented ultimately with the artist's subjective view of the world.

ÉDOUARD MANET

Courbet's painting may have laid the groundwork for Impressionism, but he was not to be a part of the new wave. His old age brought conservatism, and with it

disapproval of the younger generation's painting techniques. One of the targets of Courbet's derision was Édouard Manet (1832–1883). Yet according to some art historians, Manet is the artist most responsible for changing the course of the history of painting.

What was modern about Manet's painting was his technique. Instead of beginning with a dark underpainting and building up to bright highlights—a method used since the Renaissance—Manet began with a white surface and worked to build up dark tones. This approach lent a greater luminosity to the work, one that duplicated sunlight as closely as possible. Manet also did not model his figures with a traditional chiaroscuro. Instead, he applied his pigments flatly and broadly. With these techniques, he attempted to capture an impression of a fleeting moment, to duplicate on canvas what the eye would perceive within that collapsed time frame.

All too predictably, these innovations met with disapproval from critics and the public alike. Manet's subjects were found to be equally abrasive. One of his most shocking paintings, *Le Déjeuner sur l'Herbe (Luncheon on the Grass)* (Fig. 19.12), stands as a pivotal work in the rise of the Impressionist movement. Manet's luncheon takes

COMPARE & CONTRAST

Titian's *Venus of Urbino,* Manet's *Olympia,* Gauguin's *Te Arii Vahine,* and Valadon's *The Blue Room*

"WE NEVER ENCOUNTER the body unmediated by the meanings that cultures give to it." Right out of the starting gate, can you challenge yourself to support or contest this statement with reference to the four works in this exercise? The words are Gayle Rubin's, and they can be found in her essay "Thinking Sex: Notes for a Radical Theory of the Politics of Sexuality." Which of these works, in your view, are about "thinking sex"? Which address the "politics of sexuality"?

Titian's reclining nude (**Fig. 19.13**) was commissioned by the duke of Urbino for his private quarters. There was a considerable market for erotic paintings in the sixteenth century. One point of view maintains that many of the "great nudes" of Western art were, in essence, created for the same purpose as the pinup. Yet there is also no doubt that this particular reclining nude has had an undisputed place in the canon of great art. And this much, at least, has been reaffirmed by the reinterpretations and revisions the work has inspired into contemporary times.

One of the first artists to use Titian's *Venus* as a point of departure for his own masterpiece was Édouard Manet. In his *Olympia* (**Fig. 19.14**), Manet intentionally mimicked the Renaissance composition as a way of challenging the notion that modern art lacked credibility when brought face-to-face with the "old masters." In effect, Manet seemed to be saying, "You want a Venus? I'll give you a Venus." And just where do you find a Venus in nineteenth-century Paris? In the bordellos of the Parisian demimonde. What do these paintings have in common? Where do they depart? What details does Titian use to create an air of innocence and vulnerability? What details does Manet use to do just the opposite?

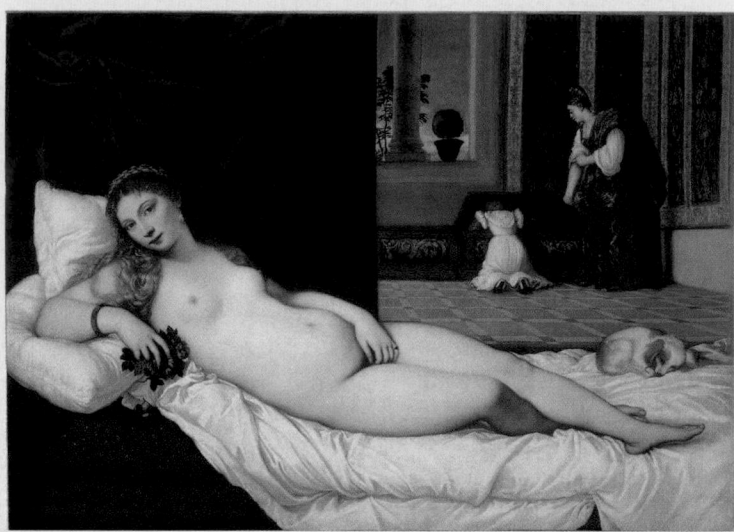

∧ **19.13 TITIAN,** *Venus of Urbino* (1538). Oil on canvas, 47" × 65". Uffizi Gallery, Florence, Italy.

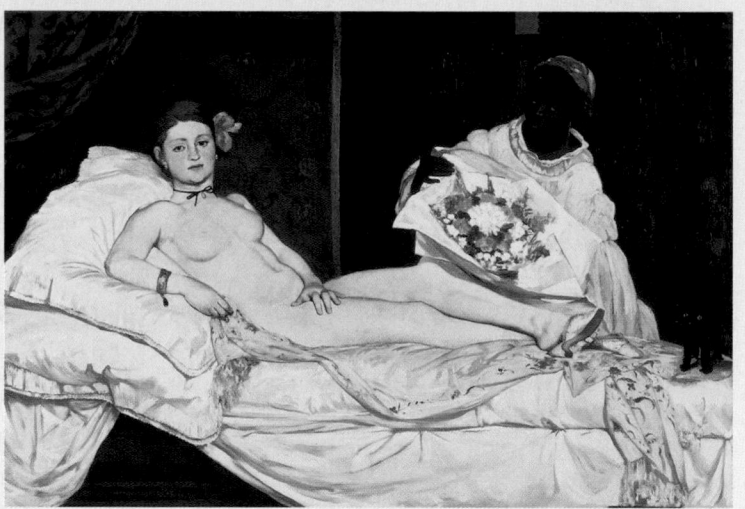

∧ **19.14 ÉDOUARD MANET,** *Olympia* (1863–1865). Oil on canvas, 51⅜" × 74¾". Musée d'Orsay, Paris, France.

Paul Gauguin, the nineteenth-century French painter who moved to Tahiti, was also inspired by the tradition of the Western reclining nude in the creation of *Te Arii Vahine (The Noble Woman)* (**Fig. 19.15**). The artist certainly knew Manet's revision of the work; in fact, he had a photograph of *Olympia* tacked on the wall of his hut. How does this Tahitian Venus fit into the mix? All three of these works have a sense of self-display. In which do the women solicit our gaze? Refuse our gaze? How do the stylistic differences influence our interpretation of the women and our relationship to them? How is the flesh modeled in each work? What overall effects are provided by the different palettes? And the $64,000 question: Are these paintings intended for the "male gaze," "the female gaze," or both?

Suzanne Valadon would probably say that such an image is *not* one that appeals equally to men and women. More to the point, Valadon would argue that the painting of such subjects is not at all of interest to women artists. Perhaps this belief was the incentive behind her own revision of the reclining nude: *The Blue Room* (**Fig. 19.16**). With this work, she seems to be informing the world that when women relax, they really *don't* look like the Venuses of Titian, or Manet, or Gauguin. Instead, they get into their loose-fitting clothes, curl up with a good book, and sometimes treat themselves to a bit of tobacco.

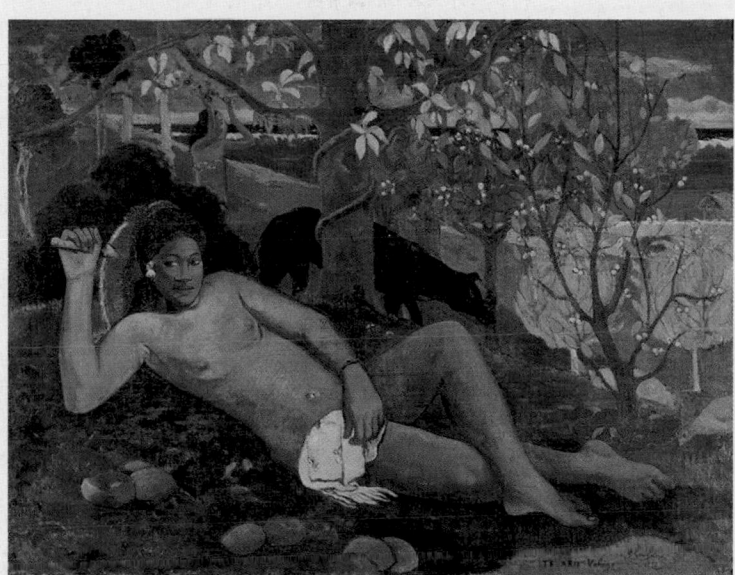

∧ **19.15 PAUL GAUGUIN,** *Te Arii Vahine (The Noble Woman)* (1896). Oil on canvas, 38 ⁹⁄₁₆" × 51 ³⁄₁₆". Pushkin Museum, Moscow, Russia.

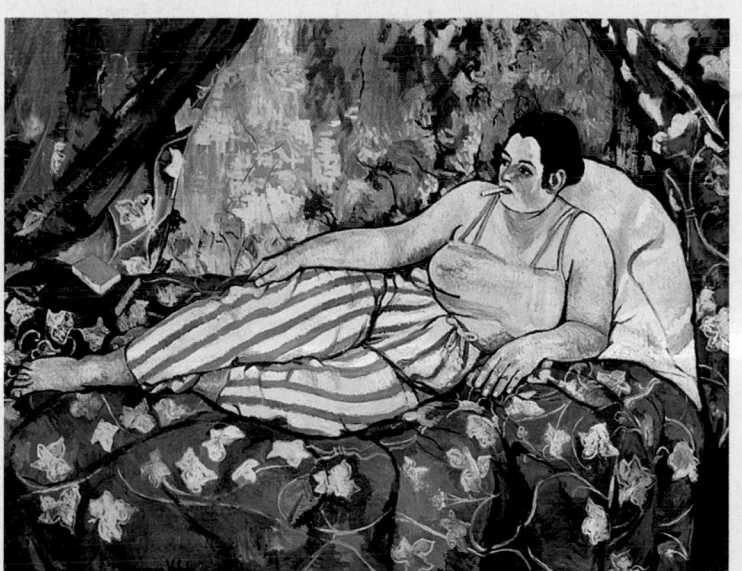

∧ **19.16 SUZANNE VALADON,** *The Blue Room* (1923). Oil on canvas, 35 ½" × 45 ⅝". Musée National d'Art Moderne, Centre Georges Pompidou.

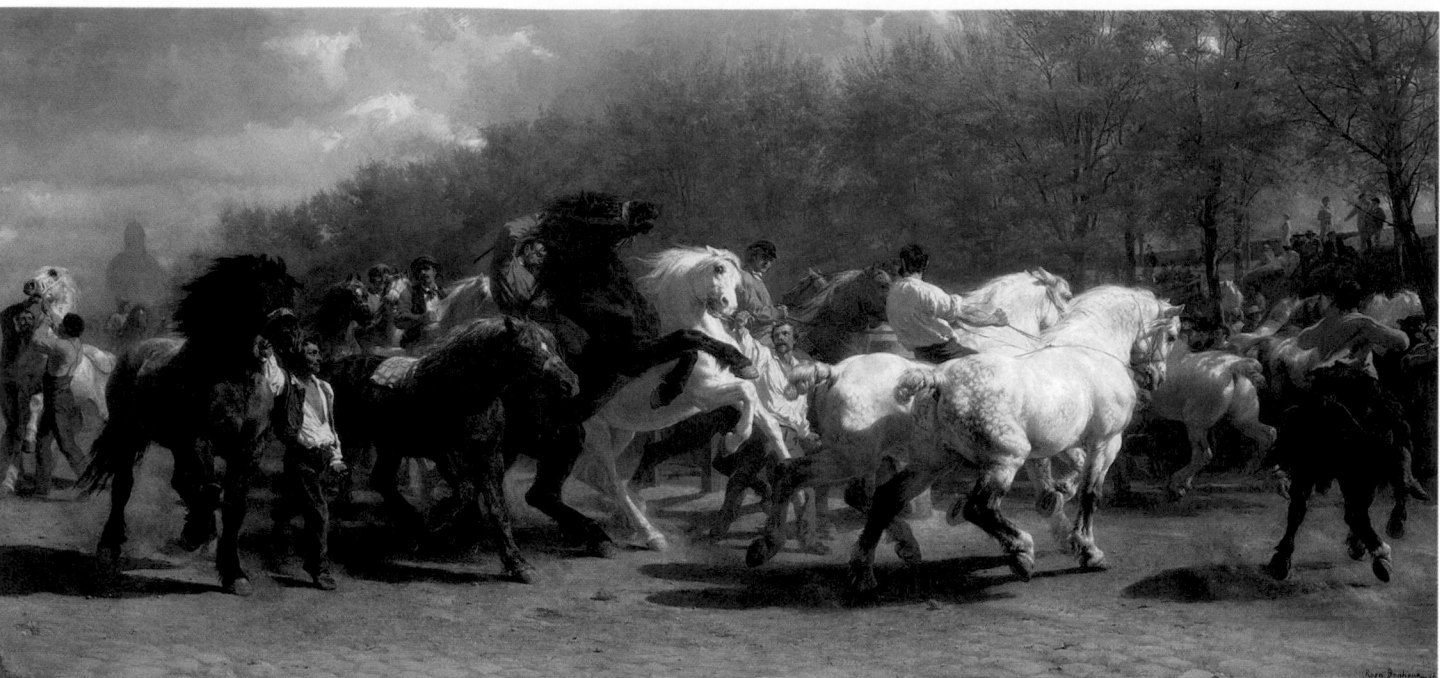

1 ft.

▲ **19.17 ROSA BONHEUR,** *The Horse Fair* (1853). Oil on canvas, 8' ¼" × 16' 7 ½".The Metropolitan Museum of Art, New York, New York.

place in a lush woodland setting. Its guests are ordinary members of the French middle class. It is culled from a tradition of Venetian Renaissance **pastoral** scenes common to the masters Giorgione and Titian. The composition is rather traditional. The figural group forms a stable pyramidal structure that is set firmly in the middle ground of the canvas. In fact, the group is derived from an engraving by Marcantonio Raimondi, *The Judgment of Paris,* after a painting by Raphael.

What was so alarming to the Parisian spectator, and remains so to this day, is that there is no explanation for the behavior of the picnickers. Why are the men clothed and the women undraped to varying degrees? Why are the men chatting between themselves, seemingly unaware of the women? The public was quite used to the painting of nudes, but they were not prepared to witness one of their fold—an ordinary citizen—displayed so shamefully on such a grand scale. The painting was further intolerable because the seated woman meets the viewer's stare, as if the viewer had intruded on their gathering in a voyeuristic fashion.

Viewers expecting another pastoral scene replete with nymphs and satyrs got, instead, portraits of Manet's model (Victorine Meurend), his brother, and a sculptor friend. In lieu of a highly polished Academic painting, they found a broadly brushed application of flat, barely modeled hues that sat squarely on the canvas with no regard for illusionism. With this shocking subject and unconventional technique, Modernism was on its way.

Manet submitted the work to the 1863 Salon, and it was categorically rejected. He and other artists whose works were rejected that year rebelled so vehemently

that Napoleon III allowed them to exhibit their work in what was known as the *Salon des Réfusés*, or Salon of the Rejected Painters. It was one of the most important gatherings of **avant-garde** painters in the century.

Although Manet was trying to deliver a message to the art world with his *Déjeuner*, it was not his wish to be ostracized. He was just as interested as the next painter in earning recognition and acceptance. Commissions went to artists whose style was sanctioned by the academics, and painting salon pictures was, after all, a livelihood. Fortunately, Manet had the private means by which he could continue painting in the manner he desired.

Manet was perhaps the most important influence on the French Impressionist painters, a group of artists who advocated the direct painting of optical impressions. *Déjeuner* began a decade of exploration of these new ideas that culminated in the first Impressionist exhibition of 1874. Although considered by his followers to be one of the Impressionists, Manet declined to exhibit with that avant-garde group. A quarter of a century later, only seventeen years after his death, Manet's works were shown at the prestigious Louvre Museum.

ROSA BONHEUR   Rosa Bonheur (1822–1899) was one of the most successful artists working in the second half of the nineteenth century. In terms of style, she is most closely related to Courbet and the other Realist painters, although for the most part she shunned human subjects in favor of animals—domesticated and wild. She was an artist who insisted on getting close to her subject; she reveled in working "in the trenches." Bonheur was seen

> I have no other wish than a close fusion with nature, and I desire no other fate than to have worked and lived in harmony with her laws. Beside her grandeur, her power, and her immortality, the human creature seems but a miserable atom.
>
> —CLAUDE MONET

in men's clothing and hip boots, plodding through the bloody floors of slaughterhouses in her struggle to understand the anatomy of her subjects.

The Horse Fair (Fig. 19.17) is a panoramic scene of extraordinary power, inspired by the Parthenon's horsemen frieze. The dimensions—more than twice as long as it is high—compel the viewer to perceive the work as just a small portion of a vast scene in which continuation of action beyond the left and right borders of the canvas is implied. The dramatic contrasts of light and dark underscore the struggle between man and beast, while the painterly brushwork heightens the emotional energy in the painting. *The Horse Fair* was an extremely popular work, which was bought widely in engraved reproductions, cementing Bonheur's fame and popularity.

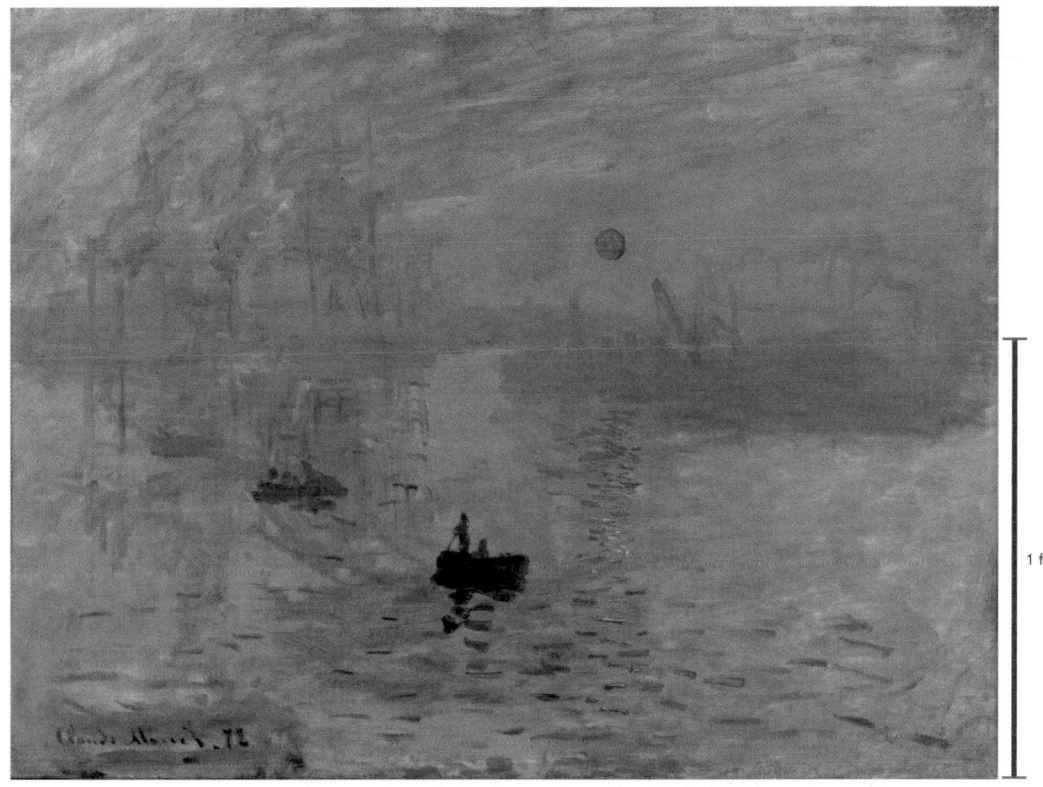

▲ 19.18 CLAUDE MONET, *Impression: Sunrise* (1872). Oil on canvas, 19½" × 25½". Musée Marmottan, Paris, France.

IMPRESSIONISM

While Bonheur won quick acceptance by the Academy, a group of younger artists were banding together against the French art establishment. Suffering from lack of recognition and vicious criticism, many of them lived in abject poverty for lack of commissions. Yet they stand today as some of the most significant, and certainly among the most popular, artists in the history of art. They were called the **Impressionists**. The very name of their movement was coined by a hostile critic and intended to malign their work. The word *impressionism* suggests a lack of realism, and realistic representation was the standard of the day.

The Impressionist artists had common philosophies about painting, although their styles differed widely. They all reacted against the constraints of the Academic style and subject matter. They advocated painting outdoors and chose to render subjects found in nature. They studied the dramatic effects of atmosphere and light on people and objects and, through a varied palette, attempted to duplicate these effects on canvas.

Through intensive investigation, they arrived at awareness of certain visual phenomena. When bathed in sunlight, objects are optically reduced to facets of pure color. The actual color—or local color—of these objects is altered by different lighting effects. Solids tend to dissolve into color fields. Shadows are not black or gray but a combination of colors.

Technical discoveries accompanied these revelations. The Impressionists duplicated the glimmering effect of light bouncing off the surface of an object by applying their pigments in short, choppy strokes. They juxtaposed complementary colors such as red and green to reproduce the optical vibrations perceived when one is looking at an object in full sunlight. Toward this end, they also juxtaposed primary colors such as red and yellow to produce, in the eye of the spectator, the secondary color orange.

CLAUDE MONET The most fervent follower of Impressionist techniques was the painter Claude Monet (1840–1926). His canvas *Impression: Sunrise* (Fig. 19.18) inspired the epithet *impressionist* when it was exhibited at the first Impressionist exhibition in 1874. Fishing vessels

One morning, one of us, lacking black, used blue: Impressionism was born.

—PIERRE-AUGUSTE RENOIR

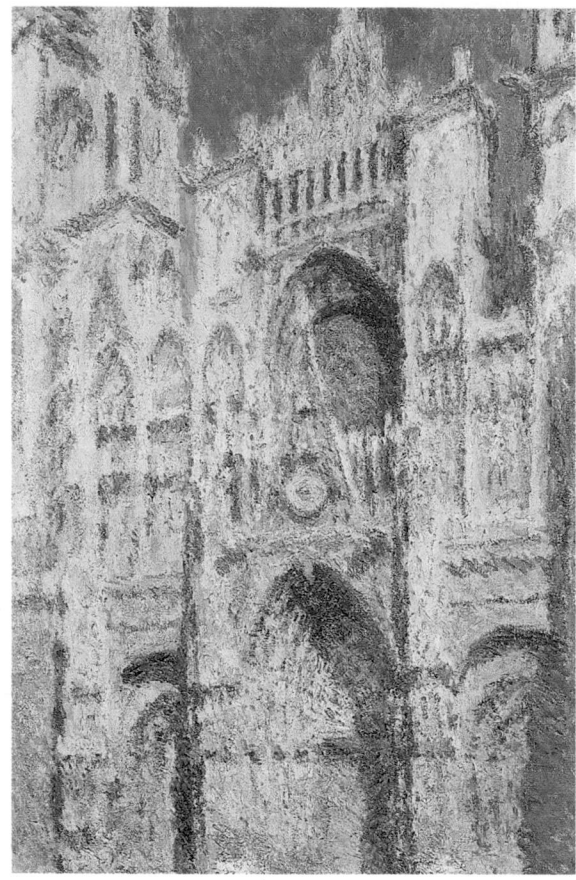

<◄ 19.19 CLAUDE MONET, *Rouen Cathedral* (1894). Oil on canvas, 39¼" × 25⅞". The Metropolitan Museum of Art, New York, New York.

1 ft.

seasons and times of day. The harsh stone façade of the cathedral dissolves in a bath of sunlight, its finer details obscured by the bevy of brushstrokes crowding the surface. Dark shadows have been transformed into patches of bright blue and splashes of yellow and red. With these delicate touches, Monet has recorded for us the feeling of a single moment in time. He offers us his impressions as eyewitness to a set of circumstances that will never be duplicated.

PIERRE-AUGUSTE RENOIR   Most Impressionists counted among their subject matter landscape scenes or members of the middle class enjoying leisure-time activities. Of all the Impressionists, however, Pierre-Auguste Renoir (1841–1919) was perhaps the most significant figure painter. Like his peers, Renoir was interested primarily in the effect of light as it played across the surface of objects. He illustrated his preoccupation in one of the most wonderful paintings of the Impressionist period, *Le Moulin de la Galette* (Fig. 19.20). With characteristic feathery strokes, Renoir communicated all of the charm and

sail from the port of Le Havre toward the morning sun, which rises in a foggy sky to cast its copper beams on the choppy, pale blue water. The warm blanket of the atmosphere envelops the figures, their significance having paled in the wake of nature's beauty.

The dissolution of surfaces and the separation of light into its spectral components remain central to Monet's art. They are dramatically evident in a series of canvases depicting *Rouen Cathedral* (Fig. 19.19) from a variety of angles, during different

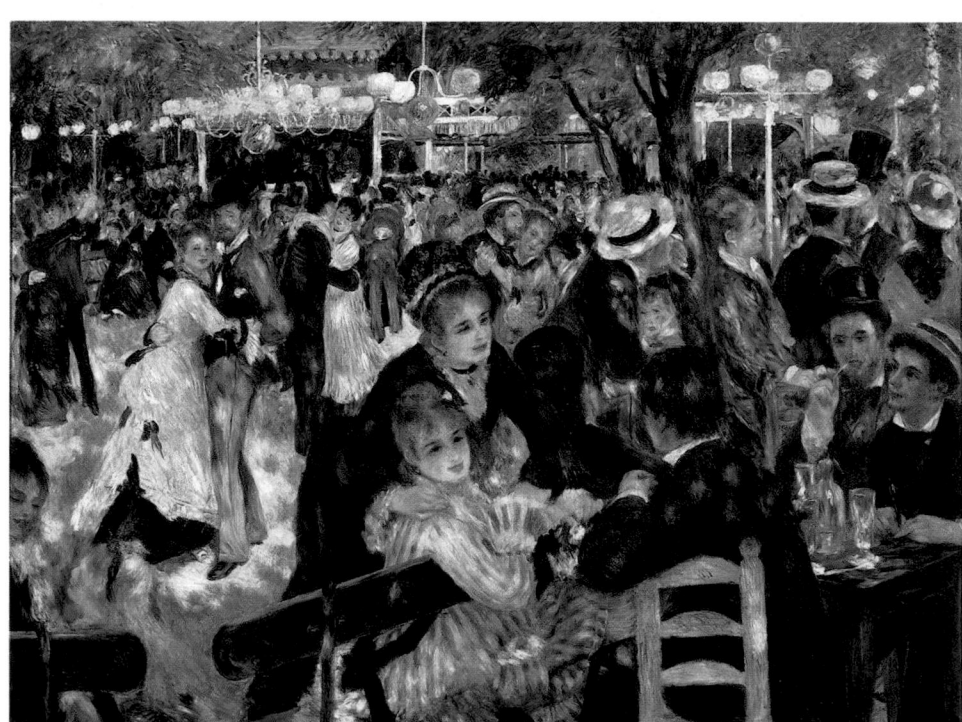

> 19.20 PIERRE-AUGUSTE RENOIR, *Le Moulin de la Galette* (1876). Oil on canvas, 51½" × 69". Musée d'Orsay, Paris, France.

1 ft.

gaiety of an afternoon dance. Men and women caress and converse in frocks that are dappled with sunlight filtering through the trees. All of the spirit of the event is as fresh as if it were yesterday. From the billowing skirts and ruffled dresses to the rakish derbies, top hats, and skimmers, Renoir painted all of the details that imprint forever such a scene upon the mind.

BERTHE MORISOT Like other Impressionists, Berthe Morisot (1841–1895) exhibited at the Salon early in her career, but she surrendered the safe path as an expression of her allegiance to the new. Morisot was a granddaughter of the eighteenth-century painter Jean-Honoré Fragonard (see Chapter 18) and the sister-in-law of Édouard Manet. Manet painted her quite often. In fact, Morisot is the seated figure in his painting *The Balcony.*

In Morisot's *Young Girl by the Window* (Fig. 19.21), surfaces dissolve into an array of loose brushstrokes, applied, it would seem, at a frantic pace. The vigor of these strokes contrasts markedly with the tranquility of the woman's face. The head is strongly modeled, and several structural lines, such as the back of the chair, the contour of her right arm, the blue parasol astride her lap, and the vertical edge of drapery to the right, anchor the figure in space. Yet in this, as in most of Morisot's works, we are most impressed by her ingenious ability to suggest complete forms through a few well-placed strokes of pigment.

EDGAR DEGAS We can see the vastness of the aegis of Impressionism when we look at the work of Edgar Degas (1834–1917), whose approach to painting differed considerably from that of his peers. Degas, like Morisot, had exhibited at the Salon for many years before joining the movement. He was a superb draftsman who studied under Ingres. While in Italy, he copied the Renaissance masters. He was also intrigued by Japanese prints and the new art of photography.

The Impressionists, beginning with Manet, were strongly influenced by Japanese woodcuts, which were becoming readily available in Europe, and oriental motifs appeared widely in their canvases. They also adopted certain techniques of spatial organization found in Japanese prints, including the use of line to direct the viewer's eye to different sections of the work and to divide areas of the essentially flattened space. They found that the patterning and flat forms of oriental woodcuts complemented similar concerns in their own painting. Throughout the Impressionist period, and even more so in the

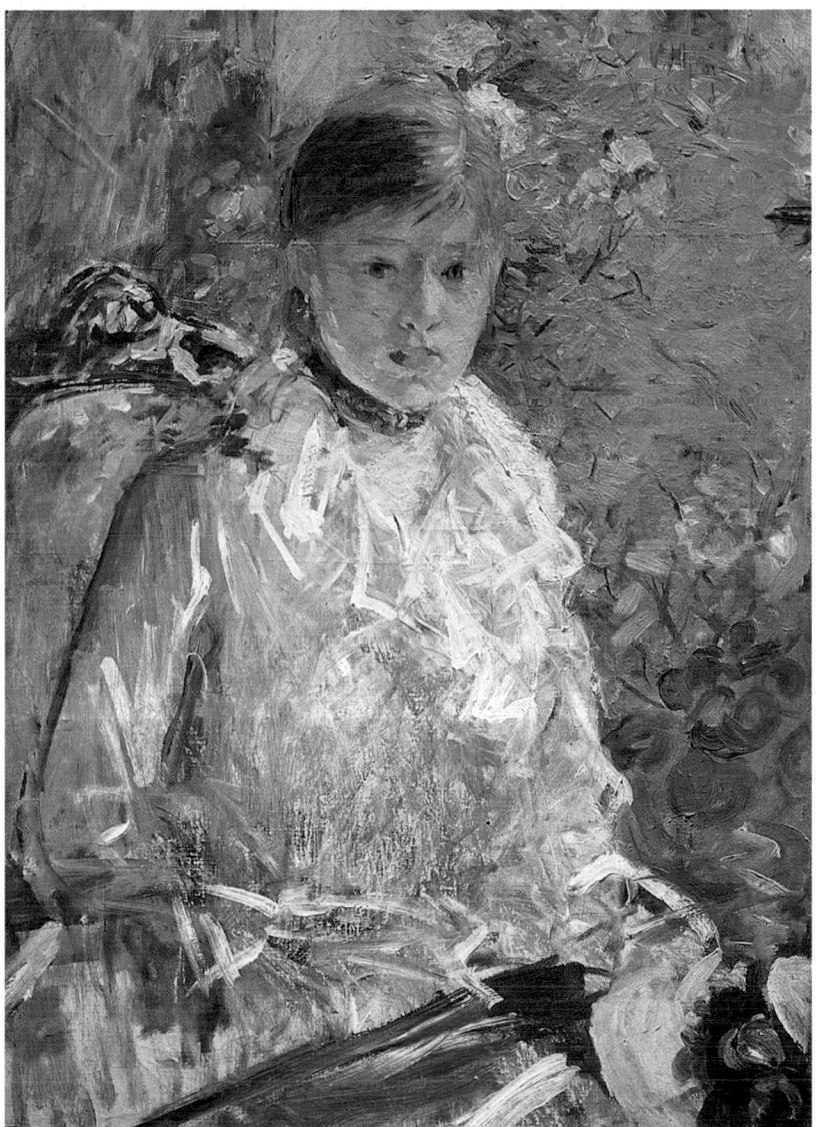

▲ 19.21 **BERTHE MORISOT,** *Young Girl by the Window* (1878). Oil on canvas, 29 15/16" × 24". Musée Fabre, Montpellier, France.

1 ft.

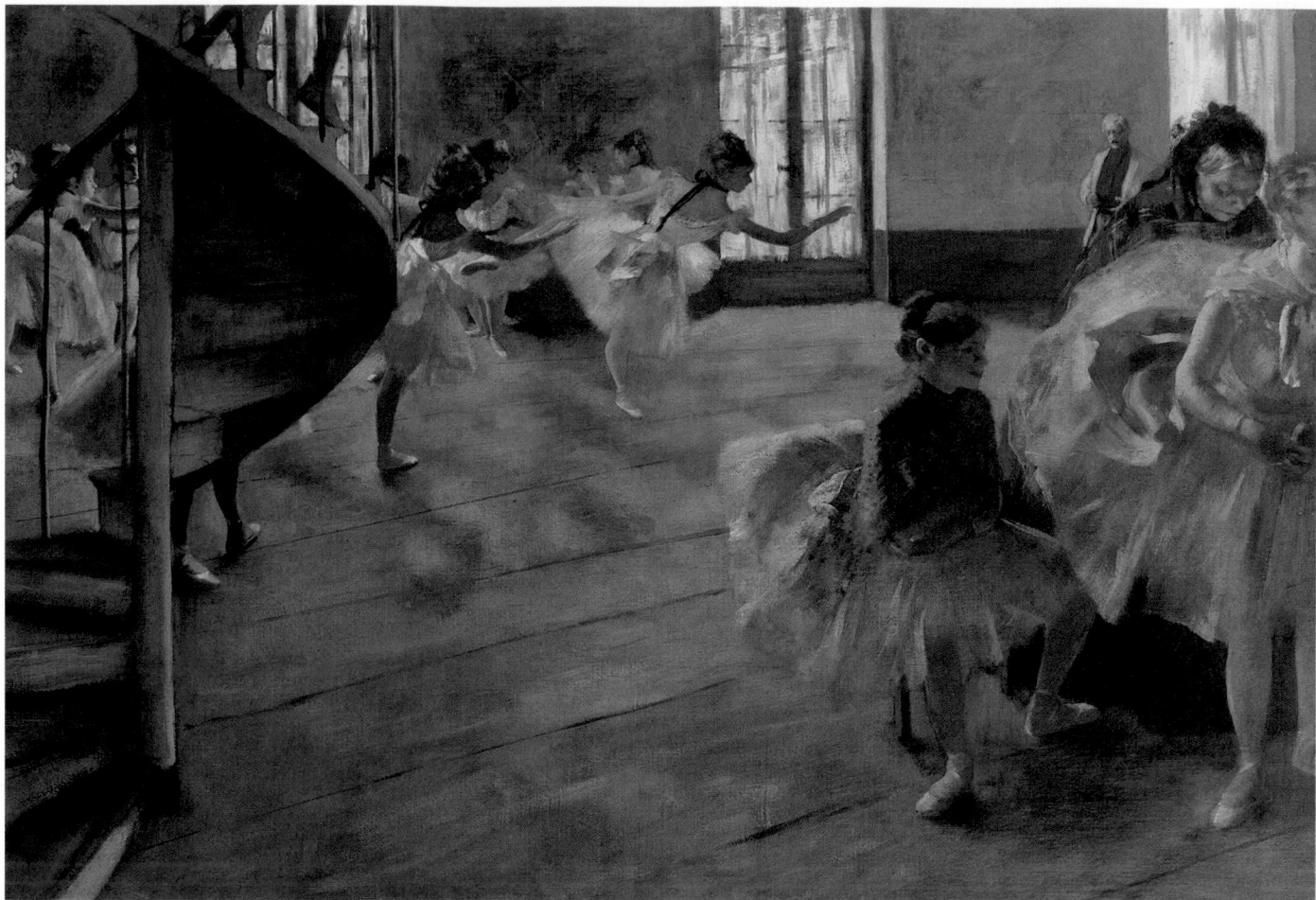

1 ft.

▲ 19.22 EDGAR DEGAS, *The Rehearsal (Adagio)* (1877). Oil on canvas, 26" × 39⅜". The Burrell Collection, Culture and Sport Glasgow (Museums), Scotland.

Postimpressionist period, the influence of Japanese artists remained strong.

Degas was also strongly influenced by the developing art of photography, and the camera's exclusive visual field served as a model for the way in which he framed his own paintings. *The Rehearsal (Adagio)* (Fig. 19.22) contains elements both of photographs and of Japanese prints. Degas draws us into the composition with an unusual and vast off-center space that curves around from the viewer's space to the background of the canvas. The diagonals of the floorboards carry our eyes briskly from outside the canvas to the points at which the groups of dancers congregate. The imagery is placed at eye level so that we feel we are part of the scene. This feeling is enhanced by the fact that our "seats" at the rehearsal are less than adequate; a spiral staircase to the left blocks our view of the ballerinas. In characteristic camera fashion, the borders of the canvas slice off the forms and figures in a seemingly arbitrary manner. Although it appears as if Degas has failed to frame his subject correctly or has accidentally cut off the more important parts of the scene, he carefully planned the placement of his imagery. These techniques are what render his asymmetrical compositions so dynamic and, in the spirit of Impressionism, so immediate.

POSTIMPRESSIONISM

The Impressionists were united in their rejection of many of the styles and subjects of the art that preceded them. These included Academic painting, the emotionalism of Romanticism, and even the depressing subject matter of some of the Realist artists. During the latter years of the nineteenth century, a group of artists who came to be called **Postimpressionists** were also united in their rebellion against that which came before them—in this case, Impressionism. The Postimpressionists were drawn together by their rebellion against what they considered an excessive concern for fleeting impressions and a disregard for traditional compositional elements.

Although they were united in their rejection of Impressionism, their individual styles differed considerably.

Postimpressionists fell into two groups that in some ways parallel the stylistic polarities of the Baroque period as well as the Neoclassical–Romantic period. On the one hand, the work of Georges Seurat and Paul Cézanne had at its core a more systematic approach to compositional structure, brushwork, and color. On the other hand, the lavishly brushed canvases of Vincent van Gogh and Paul Gauguin coordinated line and color with symbolism and emotion.

GEORGES SEURAT At first glance, the paintings by Georges Seurat (1859–1891), such as *A Sunday Afternoon on the Island of La Grande Jatte* (Fig. 19.23), have the feeling of Impressionism "tidied up." The small brushstrokes are there, as are the juxtapositions of complementary colors. The subject matter is entirely acceptable within the framework of Impressionism. However, the spontaneity of direct painting found in Impressionism is relinquished in favor of a more tightly controlled, "scientific" approach to painting.

Seurat's technique has also been called **Pointillism**, after his application of pigment in small dabs, or points, of pure color. Upon close inspection, the painting appears to be a collection of dots of vibrant hues—complementary colors abutting one another, primary colors placed side-by-side. These hues intensify or blend to form yet another color in the eye of the viewer, who beholds the canvas from a distance.

Seurat's meticulous color application was derived from the color theories and studies of color contrasts by the scientists Hermann von Helmholtz and Michel-Eugène Chevreul. He used these theories to restore a more intellectual approach to painting that countered nearly two decades of works that focused wholly on optical effects.

PAUL CÉZANNE From the time of Manet, there was a movement away from a realistic representation of subjects toward one that was abstracted. Early methods of abstraction assumed different forms. Manet used a flatly painted form, Monet a disintegrating light, and Seurat a

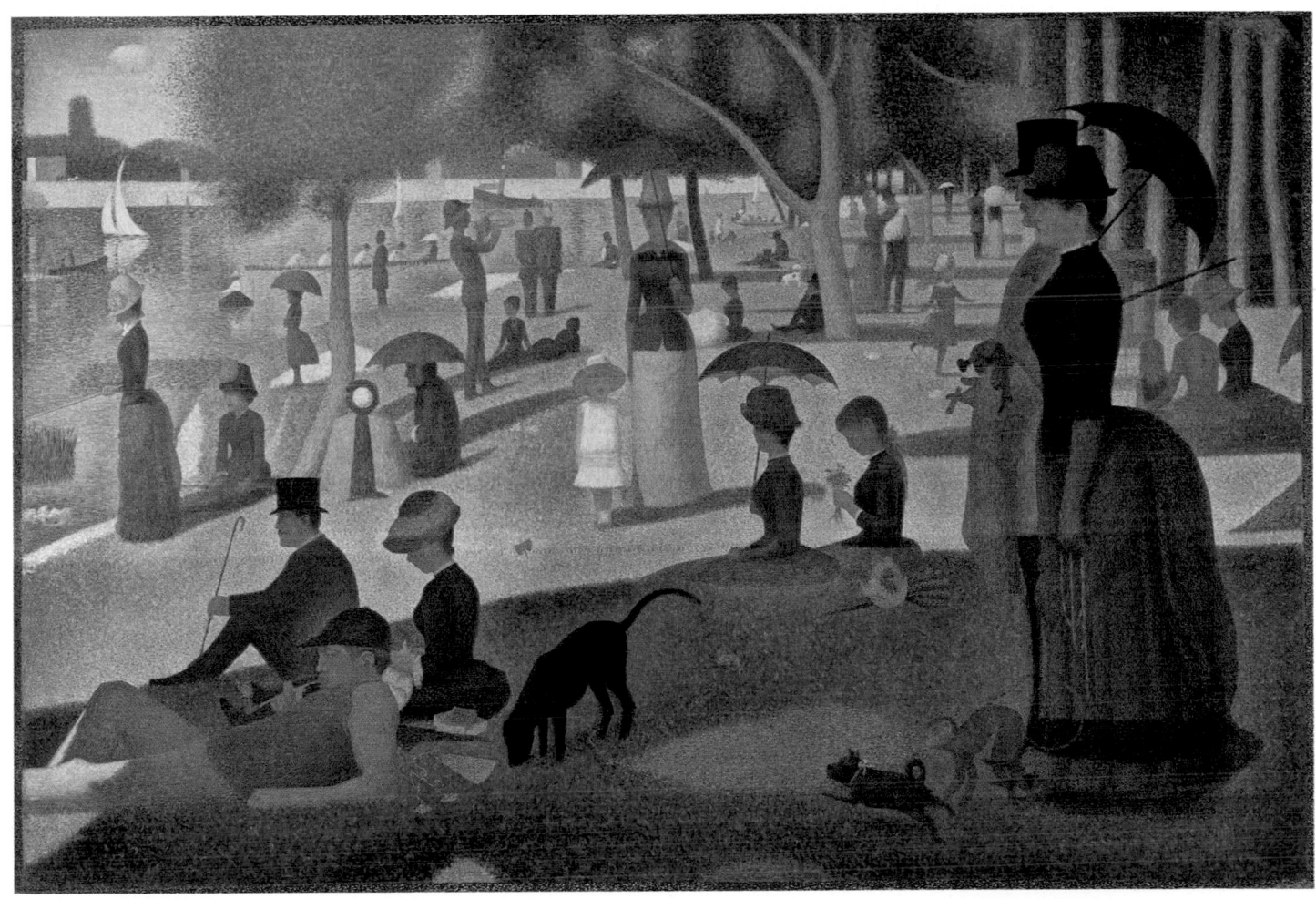

1 ft.

∧ 19.23 GEORGES SEURAT, *A Sunday Afternoon on the Island of La Grande Jatte* (1884–1886). Oil on canvas, 81" × 120⅜". The Art Institute of Chicago, Chicago, Illinois.

> The same subject seen from a different angle gives a subject for study of the highest interest and so varied that I think I could be occupied for months without changing my place, simply bending a little more to the right or left.
>
> —PAUL CÉZANNE

tightly painted and highly patterned composition. Paul Cézanne (1839–1906), a Postimpressionist who shared with Seurat an intellectual approach to painting, is credited with having led the revolution of abstraction in modern art from those first steps.

Cézanne's method for accomplishing this radical departure from tradition did not disregard the old masters. Although he allied himself originally with the Impressionists and accepted their palette and subject matter, he drew from old masters in the Louvre and desired somehow to reconcile their lessons with the thrust of Modernism, saying, "I want to make of Impressionism something solid and lasting like the art in the museums." Cézanne's innovations include a structural use of color and brushwork that appeals to the intellect, and a solidity of composition enhanced by a fluid application of pigment that delights the senses.

Cézanne's most significant stride toward Modernism, however, was a drastic collapsing of space, seen in works such as *Still Life with Basket of Apples* (Fig. 19.24). All of the imagery is forced to the picture plane. The tabletop is tilted toward us, and we simultaneously view the basket, plate, and wine bottle from front and top angles. Cézanne did not paint the still-life arrangement from one vantage point either. He moved around his subject, painting not only the objects but also the relationships between them. He focused on solids as well as on the void spaces between two objects. If you run your finger along the tabletop in the background of the painting, you will see that it is not possible to trace a continuous line. This discontinuity follows from Cézanne's movement around his subject. Despite this spatial inconsistency, the overall feeling of the composition is one of completeness.

Cézanne's painting technique is also innovative. The sensuously rumpled fabric and lusciously round fruits are constructed of small patches of pigment crowded within dark outlines. The apples look as if they would roll off the table, were it not for the supportive facets of the tablecloth.

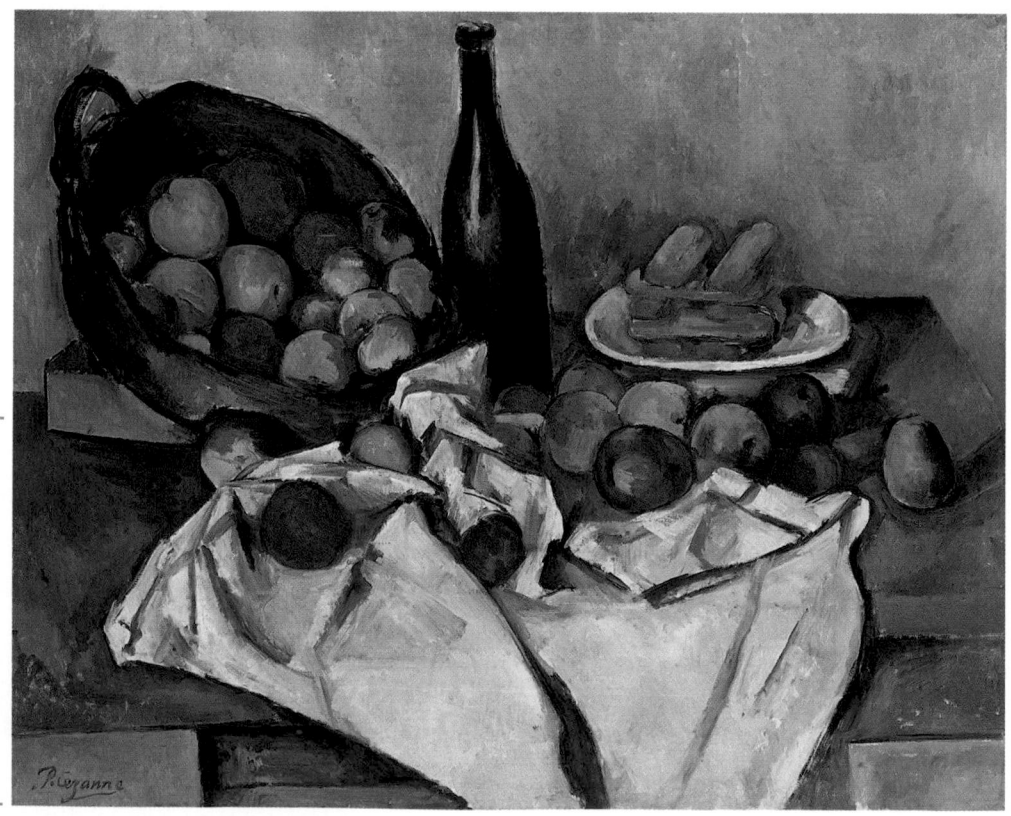

1 ft.

◄ 19.24 PAUL CÉZANNE, *Still Life with Basket of Apples* (c. 1895). Oil on canvas, 2' ⅜" × 2' 7". The Art Institute of Chicago, Chicago, Illinois.

◄ 19.25 VINCENT VAN GOGH, *Starry Night* (1889). Oil on canvas, 29" × 36¼". The Museum of Modern Art, New York, New York.

1 ft.

Cézanne can be seen as advancing the flatness of planar recession begun by David more than a century earlier. Cézanne asserted the flatness of the two-dimensional canvas by eliminating the distinction between foreground and background, and at times merging the two. This was perhaps his most significant contribution to future modern movements.

VINCENT VAN GOGH   One of the most tragic and best-known figures in the history of art is the Dutch Postimpressionist Vincent van Gogh (1853–1890). We associate him with bizarre and painful acts, such as the mutilation of his ear and his suicide. With these events, as well as his tortured, eccentric painting, he typifies the impression of the mad, artistic talent. Van Gogh also epitomizes the cliché of the artist who achieves recognition only after death: just one of his paintings was sold during his lifetime.

"Vincent," as he signed his paintings, decided to become an artist only ten years before his death. His most beloved canvases were created during his last twenty-nine months. He began his career painting in the dark manner of the Dutch Baroque, only to adopt the Impressionist palette and brushstroke after he settled in Paris with his brother Theo. Feeling that he was a constant burden on his brother, he left Paris for Arles, where

he began to paint his most significant Postimpressionist works. Both his life and his compositions from this period were tortured, as Vincent suffered from what may have been bouts of epilepsy and mental illness. He was eventually hospitalized in an asylum at Saint-Rémy, where he painted the famous *Starry Night* (Fig. 19.25).

In *Starry Night,* an ordinary painted record of a sleepy valley town is transformed into a cosmic display of swirling fireballs that assault the blackened sky and command the hills and cypresses to undulate to their sweeping rhythms. Vincent's palette is laden with vibrant yellows, blues, and greens. His brushstroke is at once restrained and dynamic. His characteristic long, thin strokes define the forms but also create the emotionalism in the work. He presents his subject not as we see it, but as he would like us to experience it. His is a feverish application of paint, an ecstatic kind of drawing, reflecting at the same time his joys, hopes, anxieties, and despair. Vincent wrote in a letter to his brother Theo, "I paint as a means to make life bearable. . . . Really, we can speak only through our paintings."

PAUL GAUGUIN   Paul Gauguin (1848–1903) shared with van Gogh the desire to express his emotions on canvas. But whereas the Dutchman's brushstroke was the primary means to that end, Gauguin relied on broad areas

A CLOSER LOOK

Why Did van Gogh Cut Off His Ear?

TWO DAYS BEFORE CHRISTMAS 1888, the 35-year-old Vincent van Gogh cut off the lower half of his left ear (Fig. 19.26). He took the ear to a brothel, asked for a prostitute by the name of Rachel, and handed it to her. "Keep this object carefully," he said. How do we account for this extraordinary event? Over the years, many explanations have been advanced. Many of them are psychoanalytic in nature.* That is, they argue that van Gogh fell prey to unconscious primitive impulses.

As you consider the following suggestions, keep in mind that van Gogh's bizarre act occurred many years ago, and that we have no way today to determine which, if any, of them is accurate. Perhaps one of them cuts to the core of van Gogh's urgent needs; perhaps several of them contain a kernel of truth. But it could also be that all of them fly far from the mark. In any event, here are the explanations suggested in the *Journal of Personality and Social Psychology:*[†]

- Van Gogh was frustrated by his brother's engagement and his failure to establish a close relationship with Gauguin. The aggressive impulses stemming from the frustrations were turned inward and expressed in self-mutilation.
- Van Gogh was punishing himself for experiencing homosexual impulses toward Gauguin.
- Van Gogh identified with his father, toward whom he felt resentment and hatred, and cutting off his own ear was a symbolic punishment of his father.
- Van Gogh was influenced by the practice of awarding the bull's ear to the matador after a bullfight. In effect, he was presenting such an "award" to the lady of his choice.
- Van Gogh was influenced by newspaper accounts of Jack the Ripper, who mutilated prostitutes. Van Gogh was imitating the "ripper," but his self-hatred led him to mutilate himself rather than others.
- Van Gogh was seeking his brother's attention.
- Van Gogh was seeking to earn the sympathy of substitute parents. (The mother figure would have been a model he had recently painted rocking a cradle.)
- Van Gogh was expressing his sympathy for prostitutes, with whom he identified as social outcasts.

- Van Gogh was symbolically emasculating himself so that his mother would not perceive him as an unlikable "rough" boy. (Unconsciously, the prostitute was a substitute for his mother.)
- Van Gogh was troubled by auditory hallucinations (hearing things that were not there) as a result of his mental state. He cut off his ear to put an end to disturbing sounds.
- In his troubled mental state, van Gogh may have been acting out a biblical scene he had been trying to paint. According to the New Testament, Simon Peter cut off the ear of the servant Malchus to protect Christ.
- Van Gogh was acting out the Crucifixion of Jesus, with himself as victim.

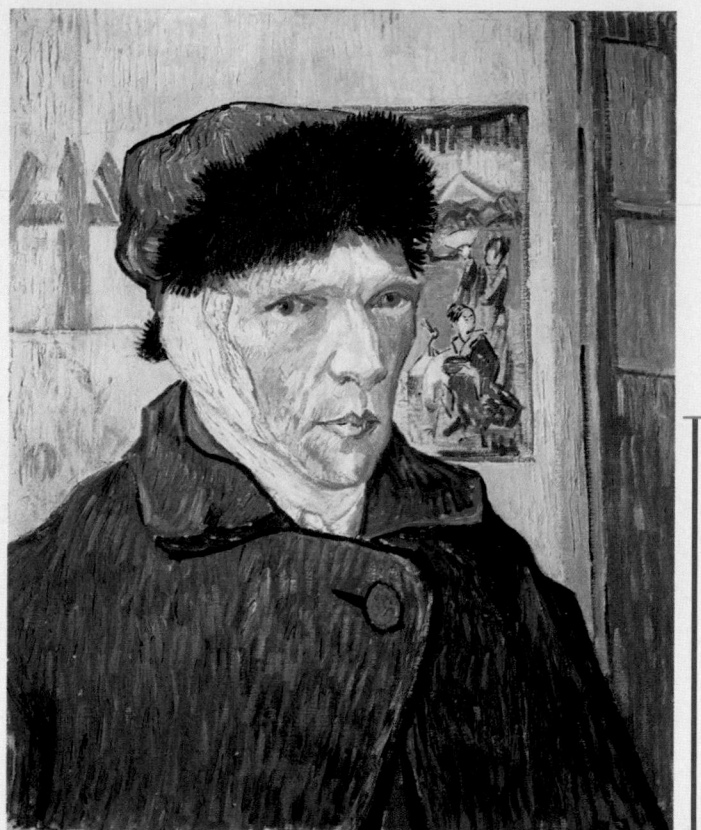

1 ft.

ʌ 19.26 VINCENT VAN GOGH, *Self-Portrait with Bandaged Ear* (1889–1890). Oil on canvas, 23⅝" × 19¼". The Courtauld Gallery, London, England.

---

* William McKinley Runyan, *Journal of Personality and Social Psychology* June 1981.

† Ibid.

> # Art is either plagiarism or revolution.
> —PAUL GAUGUIN

of intense color to transpose his innermost feelings to canvas.

Gauguin, a stockbroker by profession, began his artistic career as a weekend painter. At age 35, he devoted himself full time to his art, leaving his wife and five children to do so. Gauguin identified early with the Impressionists, adopting their techniques and participating in their exhibitions. But Gauguin was a restless soul. Soon he decided to leave France for Panama and Martinique, primitive places where he hoped to purge the civilization from his art and life. The years until his death were spent between France and the South Seas, where he finally died of syphilis five years after a failed attempt to take his own life.

Gauguin developed a theory of art called **Synthetism**, in which he advocated the use of broad areas of unnaturalistic color and primitive or symbolic subject matter. His *Vision after the Sermon (Jacob Wrestling with the Angel)* (Fig. 19.27), one of the first canvases to illustrate his theory, combines reality with symbolism. After hearing a sermon on the subject, a group of Breton women believed they had a vision of Jacob, ancestor of the Hebrews, wrestling with an angel. In a daring composition that cancels pictorial depth by thrusting all elements to the front of the canvas, Gauguin presented all details of the event, actual and symbolic. An animal in the upper left portion

of the canvas walks near a tree that interrupts a bright vermilion field with a slashing diagonal. The Bible tells us that Jacob had wrestled with an angel on the banks of the Jabbok River in Jordan. Caught, then, in a moment of religious fervor, the Breton women may have imagined the animal's four legs to have been those of the wrestling couple, and the tree trunk might have been visually analogous to the river.

Gauguin's contribution to the development of modern art lay largely in his use of color. Writing on the subject, he said, "How does that tree look to you? Green? All right, then use green, the greenest on your palette. And that shadow, a little bluish? Don't be afraid. Paint it as blue as you can." He intensified the colors he observed in nature to the point where they became unnatural. He exaggerated his lines and patterns until they became abstract. He learned these lessons from the primitive surroundings of which he was so fond. They were his legacy to art.

HENRI DE TOULOUSE-LAUTREC   Henri de Toulouse-Lautrec (1864–1901), along with van Gogh, is one of the best-known nineteenth-century European artists—both for his art and for the troubled aspects of his personal life. Born into a noble French family, Toulouse-Lautrec broke his legs during adolescence, and they failed to develop correctly. This deformity resulted in alienation from his

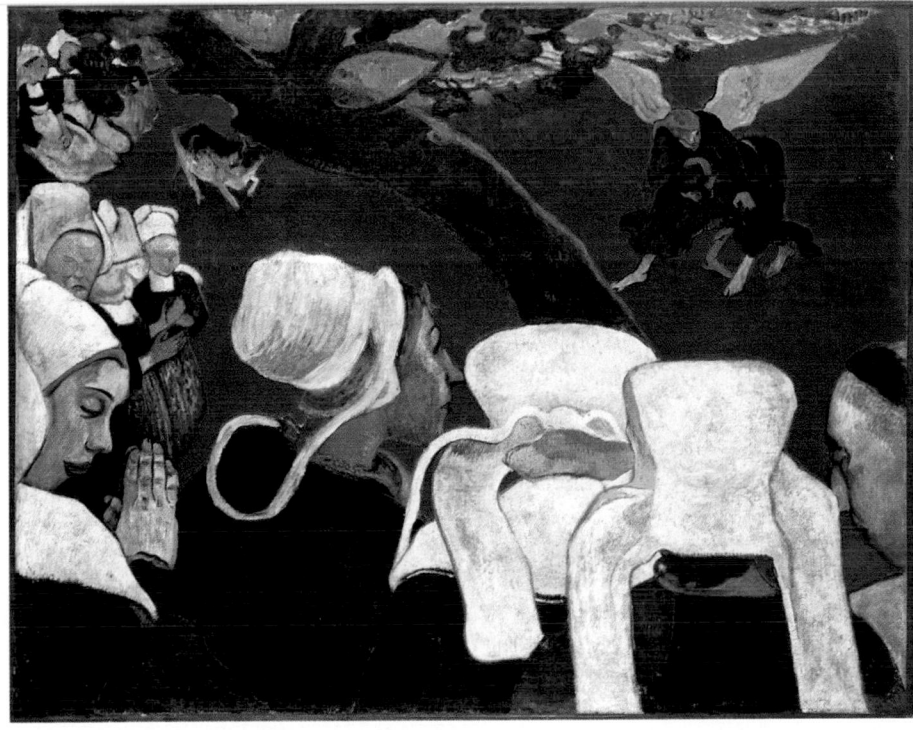

1 ft.

< 19.27 PAUL GAUGUIN, *Vision after the Sermon (Jacob Wrestling with the Angel)* (1888). Oil on canvas, 28¾" × 36½". National Gallery of Scotland, Edinburgh, Scotland.

The sky was suddenly blood-red—I stopped and leaned against the fence, dead tired. I saw the flaming clouds like blood and a sword—the bluish-black fjord and town—my friends walked on—I stood there, trembling with anxiety—and I felt as though Nature were convulsed by a great unending scream.

—EDVARD MUNCH

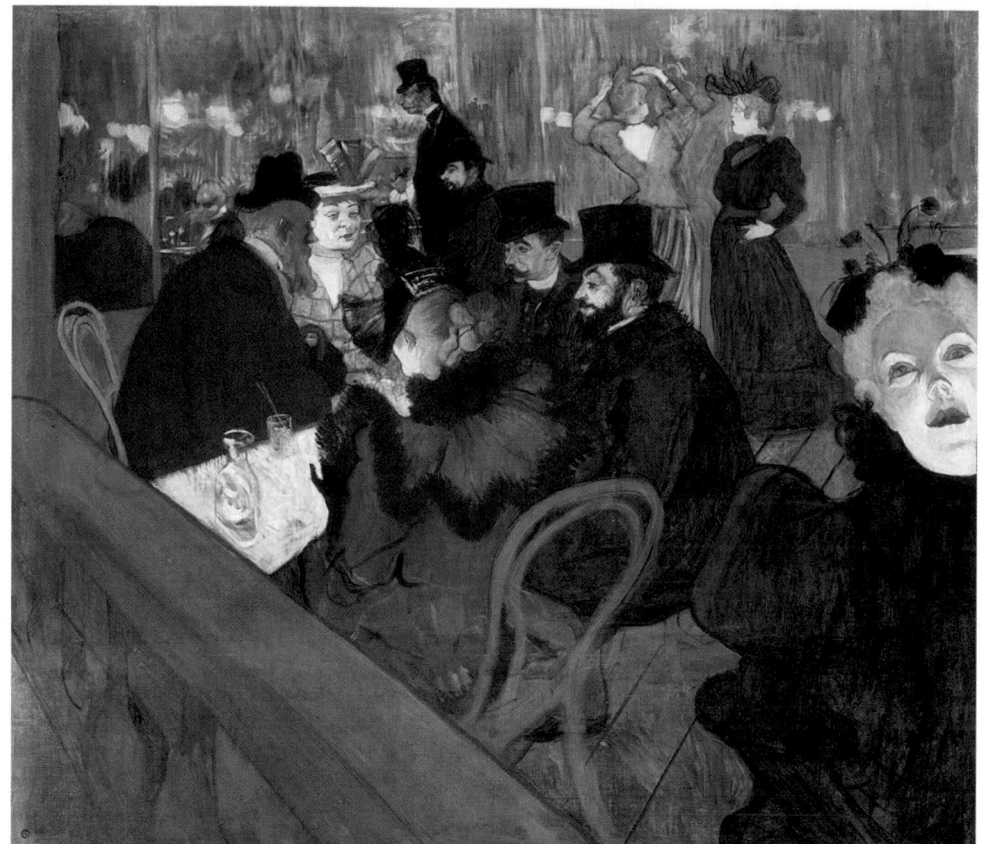

∧ **19.28** HENRI DE TOULOUSE-LAUTREC, *At the Moulin Rouge* (1892). Oil on canvas, 4' × 4' 7". The Art Institute of Chicago, Chicago, Illinois.

1 ft.

family. He turned to painting and took refuge in the demimonde of Paris, at one point taking up residence in a brothel. In this world of social outcasts, Toulouse-Lautrec, the dwarflike scion of a noble family, apparently felt at home.

He used his talents to portray life as it was in this cavalcade of cabarets, theaters, cafés, and bordellos—sort of seamy, but also vibrant and entertaining, and populated by "real" people. He made numerous posters to advertise cabaret acts and numerous paintings of his world of night and artificial light. In *At the Moulin Rouge* (Fig. 19.28), we find something of the Japanese-inspired oblique perspective we found earlier in his poster work. The extension of the picture to include the balustrade on the bottom and the heavily powdered entertainer on the right is reminiscent of those "poorly cropped snapshots" of Degas, who had influenced Toulouse-Lautrec. The fabric of the entertainer's dress is constructed of fluid Impressionistic

brushstrokes, as are the contents of the bottles, the lamps in the background, and the amorphous overall backdrop—lost suddenly in the unlit recesses of the Moulin Rouge. But the strong outlining, as in the entertainer's face, marks the work of a Postimpressionist.

The artist's palette is limited and muted, except for a few accents, as found in the hair of the woman in the center of the composition and the bright mouth of the entertainer. The entertainer's face is harshly sculpted by artificial light from beneath, rendering the shadows a grotesque but not ugly green. The green and red mouth clash, of course, as green and red are complementary colors, giving further intensity to the entertainer's masklike visage. But despite her powdered harshness, the entertainer remains human—certainly as human as her audience. Toulouse-Lautrec was accepting of all his creatures, just as he hoped that they would be accepting of him. The artist is portrayed within this work as well, his bearded profile facing left, toward the upper part of the composition, just left of center—a part of things, but not at the heart of things, certainly out of the glare of the spotlight. There, so to speak, the artist remained for many of his brief thirty-seven years.

See more of Paris in the online Art Tour.

EXPRESSIONISM

A polarity existed in Postimpressionism that was like the polarity of the Neoclassical–Romantic period. On the one hand were artists who sought a more scientific or intellectual approach to painting. On the other were artists whose works were more emotional, expressive, and laden with symbolism. The latter trend was exemplified by van Gogh and particularly Gauguin. These artists used color

Where do all the women who have watched so carefully over the lives of their beloved ones
get the heroism to send them to face the cannon?

—KÄTHE KOLLWITZ

and line to express their inner feelings. In their vibrant palettes and bravura brushwork, van Gogh and Gauguin foreshadowed **Expressionism**.

EDVARD MUNCH The Expressionistic painting of Gauguin was adopted by the Norwegian Edvard Munch (1863–1944), who studied the Frenchman's works in Paris. Munch's early work was Impressionistic, but during the 1890s, he abandoned a light palette and lively subject matter in favor of a more somber style that reflected an anguished preoccupation with fear and death.

The Scream (Fig. 19.29) is one of Munch's best-known works. It portrays the pain and isolation that became his central themes. A skeletal figure walks across a bridge toward the viewer, cupping his ears and screaming. Two figures in the background walk in the opposite direction, unaware of or uninterested in the sounds of desperation

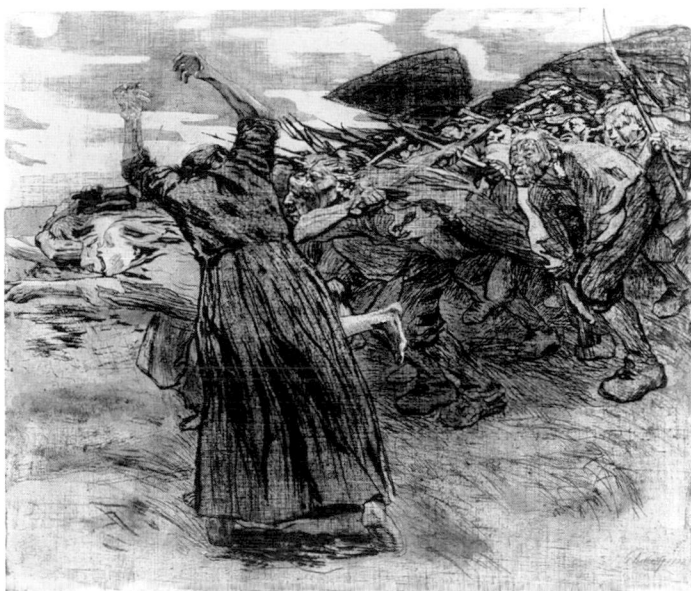

∧ **19.30 KÄTHE KOLLWITZ,** *The Outbreak* (1903). Plate no. 5 from *The Peasants' War.* Etching, dry point, aquatint, and softground. 8" × 9 1/10". Library of Congress, Prints and Photographs Division.

piercing the atmosphere. Munch transformed the placid landscape into one that echoes in waves the high-pitched tones that emanate from the sunken head. We are reminded of the swirling forms of van Gogh's *Starry Night*, but the intensity and horror pervading Munch's composition speak of his view of humanity as being consumed by an increasingly dehumanized society.

KÄTHE KOLLWITZ It is not often in the history of art that we find two artists whose backgrounds are so similar that we can account for just about every variable except for personality when comparing their work. But such is the case with Edvard Munch and Käthe Kollwitz (1867–1945). They were born and died within a few years of each other. They both lived through two world wars; Kollwitz lost a son in World War I and a grandson in World War II. Both are Expressionist artists. Yet their choice of subjects speaks of their idiosyncratic concerns. Whereas Munch looked for symbols of isolation that would underscore his own sense of loneliness, or themes of violence and perverse sexuality that reflected his own psychological problems, Kollwitz sought universal symbols for inhumanity, injustice, and humankind's destruction of itself.

The Outbreak (Fig. 19.30) is one of a series of seven prints by Kollwitz representing the sixteenth-century Peasants' War. In this print, Black Anna, a woman who

∧ **19.29 EDVARD MUNCH,** *The Scream* (1893). Casein on paper, 35 1/2" × 28 2/3". National Gallery, Oslo, Norway.

led the laborers in their struggle against their oppressors, incites an angry throng of peasants to action. Her back is toward us, her head down, as she raises her gnarled hands in inspiration. The peasants rush forward in a torrent, bodies and weapons lunging at Anna's command. Although the work records a specific historical incident, it stands as an inspiration to all those who strive for freedom against the odds. There are few more forceful images in the history of art.

The styles of these early Expressionists would be adopted in the twentieth century by younger German artists who shared their view of the world. Many revived the woodcut medium to complement their expressive subjects. This younger generation of artists worked in various styles, but collectively were known as the Expressionists. We will examine their work in Chapter 20.

AMERICAN EXPATRIATES

Until the twentieth century, art in the United States remained fairly provincial. Striving artists of the eighteenth and nineteenth centuries would go abroad for extended pilgrimages to study the old masters and mingle with the avant-garde. In some cases, they immigrated to Europe permanently. These artists, among them Mary Cassatt and James Abbott McNeill Whistler, are called the American Expatriates.

MARY CASSATT Mary Cassatt (1844–1926) was born in Pittsburgh but spent most of her life in France, where she was part of the inner circle of Impressionists. The artists Manet and Degas, photography, and Japanese prints influenced Cassatt's early career. She was a figure painter whose subjects centered on women and children.

A painting such as *The Boating Party* (Fig. 19.31), with its flat planes, broad areas of color, and bold lines and shapes, illustrates Cassatt's interest and skill in merging French Impressionism with elements of Japanese art. Like many of her contemporaries in Paris, she became aware of Japanese prints and art objects after trade was established between Japan and Europe in the mid-nineteenth century. In their solidly constructed compositions and collapsed space, Cassatt's lithographs, in particular, stand out from the more ethereal images of other Impressionists.

JAMES ABBOTT MCNEILL WHISTLER In the same year that Monet painted his *Impression: Sunrise* and launched the movement of Impressionism, the American artist James Abbott McNeill Whistler (1834–1903) painted one of the best-known compositions in the history of art. Who among us has not seen "Whistler's Mother," whether on posters, billboards, or television commercials? *Arrangement in Black and Gray: The Artist's Mother* (Fig. 19.32) exhibits a combination of candid realism and abstraction that indicates two strong influences on Whistler's art: Courbet and Japanese prints. Whistler's mother is silhouetted against a quiet backdrop in the right portion of the composition. The strong contours of her black dress are balanced by an oriental drape and simple rectangular picture on the left. The subject is rendered in a harsh realism reminiscent of northern Renaissance portrait painting. However, the composition is seen first as a logical and pleasing arrangement of shapes in tones of black, gray, and white that work together in pure harmony.

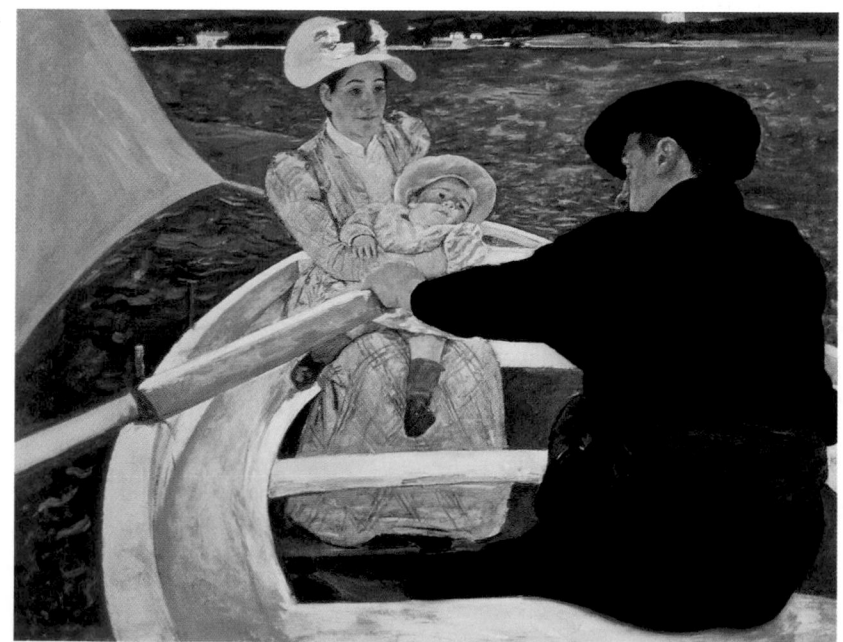

> 19.31 MARY CASSATT, *The Boating Party* (1893–1894). Oil on canvas, 35½" × 46⅛". National Gallery of Art, Washington, D.C.

1 ft.

> Well, not bad, but there are decidedly too many of them, and they are not very well arranged.
> I would have done it differently.
> —JAMES ABBOTT MCNEILL WHISTLER, WHEN ASKED WHETHER THE STARS WERE BEAUTIFUL ONE EVENING

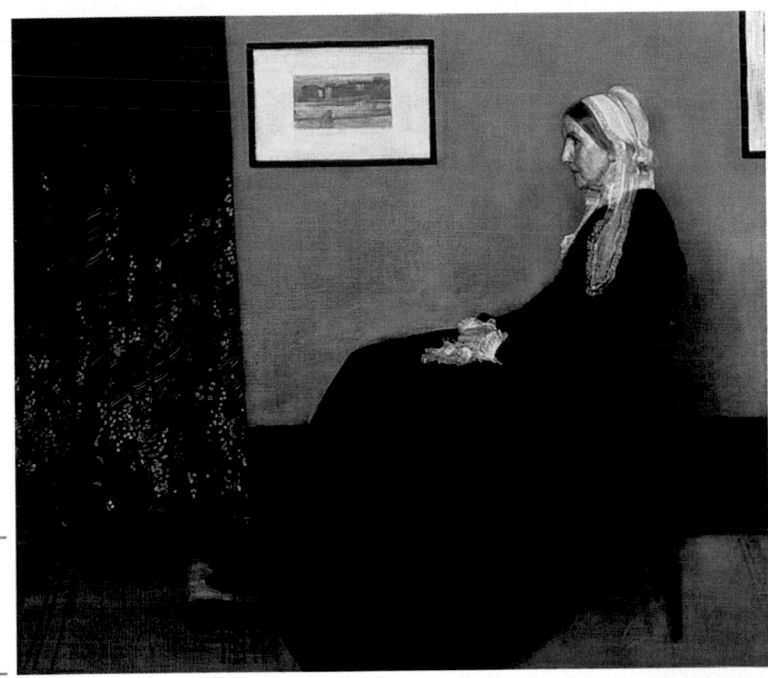

< 19.32 JAMES ABBOTT MCNEILL WHISTLER, *Arrangement in Black and Gray: The Artist's Mother* (1871). Oil on canvas, 57" × 64 ½". Louvre Museum, Paris, France.

1 ft.

colleagues and ultimately forced his resignation from a teaching post at the Pennsylvania Academy of Art.

The Gross Clinic—no pun intended—depicts the surgeon Dr. Samuel Gross operating on a young boy at the Jefferson Medical College in Philadelphia. Eakins thrusts the brutal imagery to the foreground of the painting, spotlighting the surgical procedure and Dr. Gross's bloody scalpel, while casting the observing medical students in the background into darkness. The painting was deemed so shockingly realistic that it was rejected by the jury for an exhibition. Part of the impact of the work lies in the contrast between the matter-of-fact discourse of the surgeon and the torment of the boy's mother. She sits in the

AMERICANS IN AMERICA

While Whistler and Cassatt were working in Europe, several American artists of note remained at home working in the Realist tradition. This realism can be detected in figure painting and landscape painting, both of which were tinted with Romanticism.

THOMAS EAKINS   The most important American portrait painter of the nineteenth century was Thomas Eakins (1844–1916). Although his early artistic training took place in the United States, his study in Paris with painters who depicted historical events provided the major influence on his work. The penetrating realism of a work such as *The Gross Clinic* (Fig. 19.33) stems from Eakins's endeavors to become fully acquainted with human anatomy by working from live models and dissecting corpses. Eakins's dedication to these practices met with disapproval from his

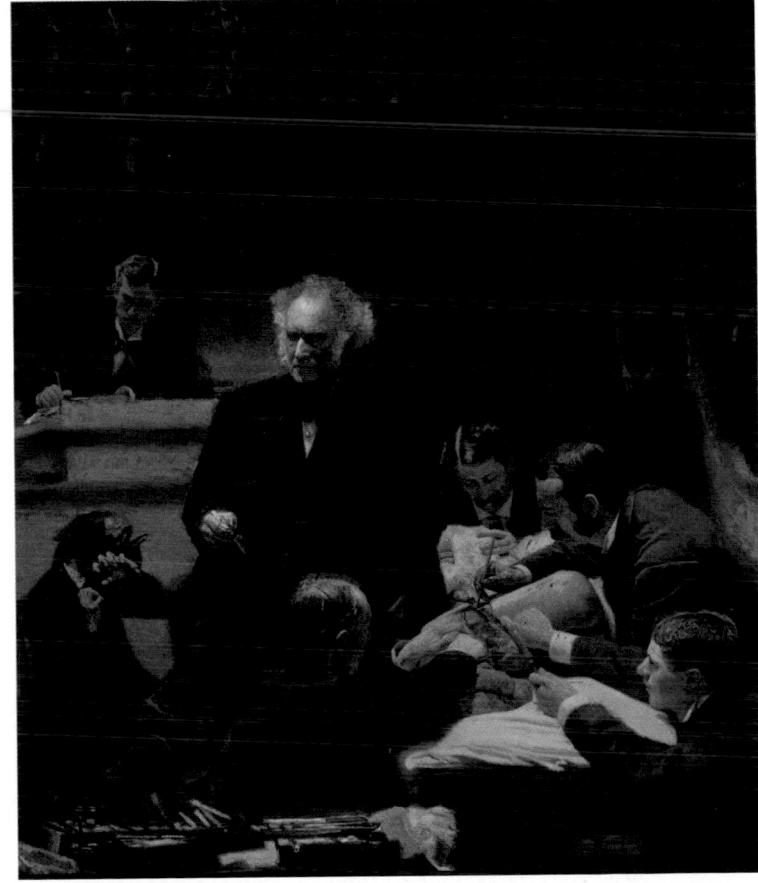

> 19.33 THOMAS EAKINS, *The Gross Clinic* (1875). Oil on canvas, 96" × 78". The Philadelphia Museum of Art, Philadelphia, Pennsylvania.

1 ft.

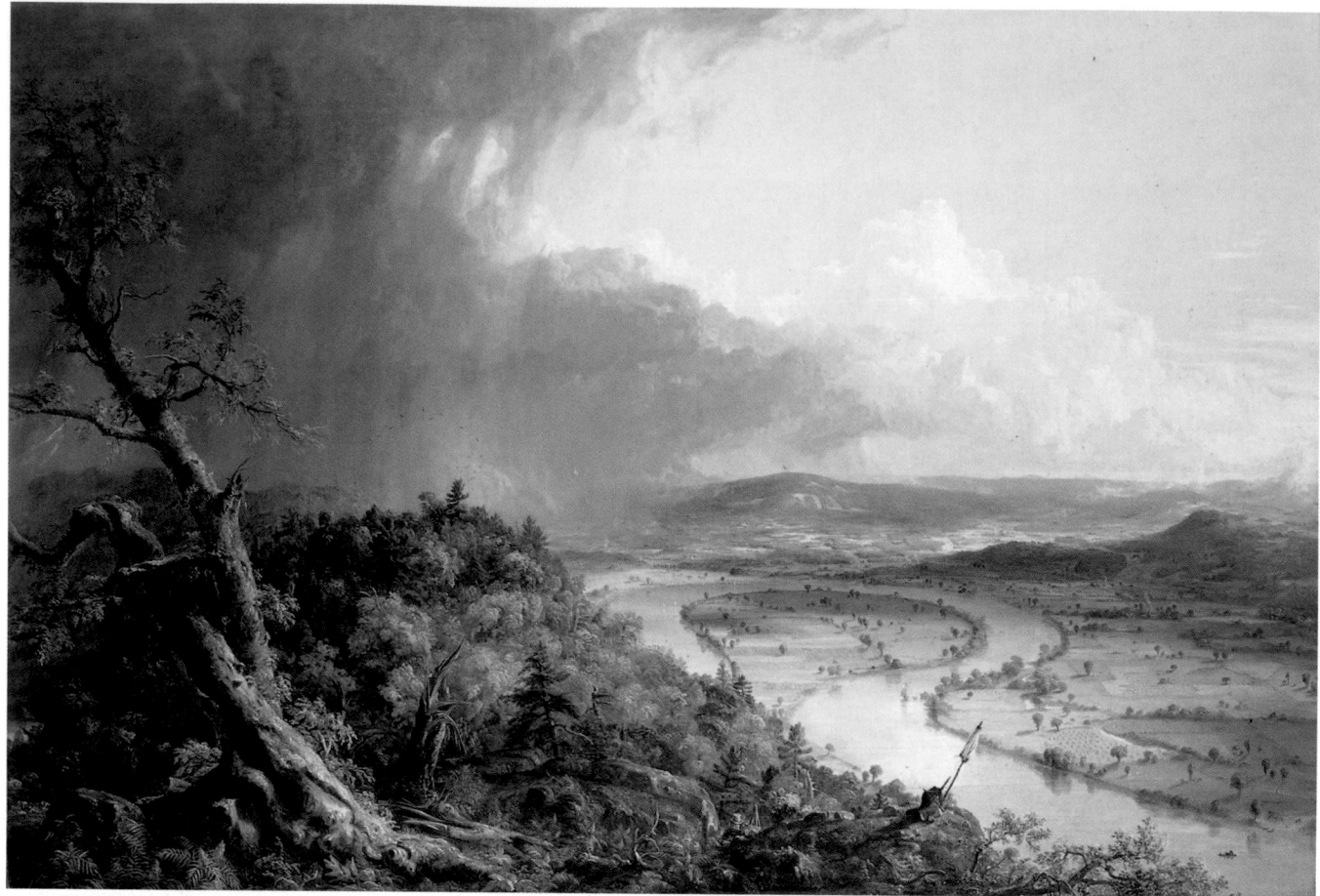

1 ft.

∧ 19.34 **THOMAS COLE**, *The Oxbow (Connecticut River near Northampton)* (1836). Oil on canvas, 51 ½" × 76". The Metropolitan Museum of Art, New York, New York.

lower left corner of the painting, shielding her eyes with whitened knuckles. In brush technique, Eakins is close to the fluidity of Courbet, although his compositional arrangement and dramatic lighting are surely indebted to Rembrandt.

Eakins devoted his career to increasingly realistic portraits. Their haunting veracity often disappointed sitters who would have preferred more flattering renditions. The artist's passion for realism led him to use photography extensively as a point of departure for his paintings as well as an art form in itself. Eakins's style and ideas influenced American artists of the early twentieth century who also worked in a Realist vein.

THOMAS COLE   During the nineteenth century, American artists turned, for the first time, from the tradition of portraiture to landscape painting. Inspired by French landscape painting of the Baroque period, these artists fused this style with a pride in the beauty of their native United States and a Romantic vision that was embodied in the writings of James Fenimore Cooper.

One such artist was Thomas Cole (1801–1848), who was born in England and immigrated to the United States at the age of 17. Cole was always fond of landscape painting and settled in New York, where there was a ready audience for this genre. Cole became the leader of the **Hudson River School**—a group of artists whose favorite subjects included the scenery of the Hudson River Valley and the Catskill Mountains in New York State.

The Oxbow (Fig. 19.34) is typical of such paintings. It records a natural oxbow formation in the Connecticut River Valley. Cole combines a vast, sun-drenched space with meticulously detailed foliage and farmland. There is a contrast in moods between the lazy movement of the river, which meanders diagonally into the distance, and the more vigorous diagonal of the gnarled tree trunk in the left foreground. Half of the canvas space is devoted to the sky, whose storm clouds roll back to reveal rays of intense light. These atmospheric effects, coupled with our "crow's-nest" vantage point, magnify the awesome grandeur of nature and force us to contemplate the relative insignificance of humans.

A CLOSER LOOK

Weaving Together Biblical and Personal Stories

IN 1859, HARRIET BEECHER STOWE, renowned author of *Uncle Tom's Cabin,* described the quilting bee:

> The day was spent in friendly gossip as they rolled and talked and laughed. . . . One might have learned in that instructive assembly how best to keep moths out of blankets; how to make fritters of Indian corn undistinguishable from oysters; how to bring up babies by hand; how to mend a cracked teapot; how to take grease from a brocade; how to reconcile absolute decrees with free will; how to make five yards of cloth answer the purpose of six; and how to put down the Democratic party.[*]

Many years later, an author on quiltmaking quoted her great-grandmother: "My whole life is in that quilt. It scares me sometimes when I look at it. All my joys and all my sorrows are stitched into those little pieces."[†]

The art of quiltmaking was clearly not only an acceptable vehicle for women's artistic expression but also an arena for consciousness raising on the practical and political problems of the day. Beyond this, the object recorded family history, kept memory alive, and ensured the survival of the matriarch/quilter through that historical record.

Toward the end of the nineteenth century, African American quilter Harriet Powers created her *Bible Quilt.* Its fifteen squares of cotton appliqué weave together stories from the Bible with significant events from the family and community of the artist (**Fig. 19.35**).

For example, reading left to right, the fourth square is a symbolic depiction of Adam and Eve in the Garden of Eden. A serpent tempts Eve beneath God's all-seeing eye and benevolent hand. In the sixth square, Jonah is swallowed by a whale. The last square is a stylized depiction of the Crucifixion. Amid the religious subjects are records of meaningful days. For example, the eleventh square was described by Powers as "Cold Thursday,"

> February 10, 1895. A woman is shown frozen at a gateway while at prayer. Icicles form from the breath of a mule. All bluebirds are killed.[‡]

The thirteenth square includes an "independent" hog that was said to have run 500 miles from Georgia to Virginia, and the fourteenth square depicts the creation of animals in pairs.

Unity in the quilt is created by a subtle palette of complementary hues and by simple, cutout shapes that define celestial orbs, biblical and familial characters, and biblical and local animals. The quilt has an arresting combination of widely known themes and private events known to the artist and her family. The juxtaposition establishes an equivalence between biblical and personal stories. The work personalizes the religious events and imbues the personal and provincial events with universal meaning.

Because of the hardness of the times, the artist sold the quilt for five dollars.[§]

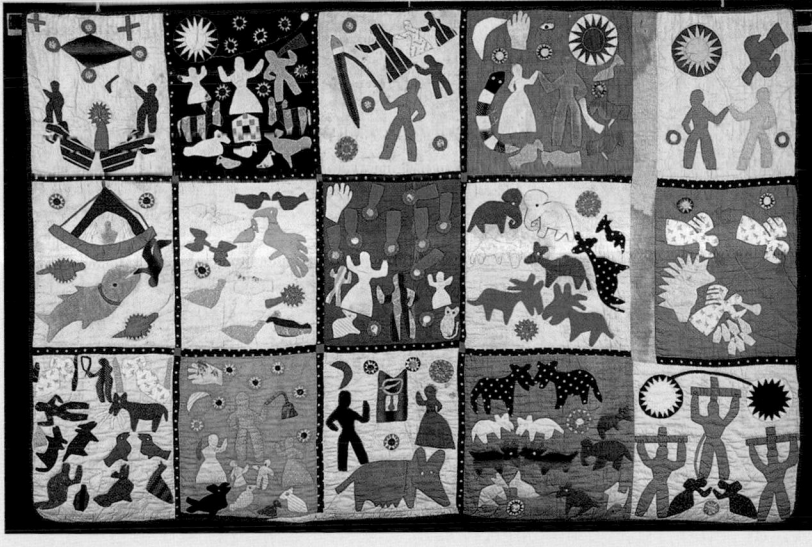

< **19.35 HARRIET POWERS,** *Bible Quilt: The Creation of the Animals* (1895–1898). Pieced, appliquéd, and printed cotton embroidered with cotton and metallic yarn; 69" × 105". Museum of Fine Arts, Boston, Massachusetts.

1 ft.

---

[*] Harriet Beecher Stowe, *The Minister's Wooing* (New York: Derby and Jackson, 1859).

[†] Marguerite Ickis, *The Standard Book of Quiltmaking and Collecting* (New York: Dover, 1960).

[‡] Harriet Powers. Pictorial Quilt. Museum of Fine Arts, Boston. http://www.mfa.org/collections/object/pictorial-quilt-116166.

[§] In Mirra Bank, *Anonymous Was a Woman* (New York: St. Martin's Press, 1979), 118.

The only thing is to see.

—AUGUSTE RODIN

THE BIRTH OF MODERN SCULPTURE

Some of the most notable characteristics of modern painting include a newfound realism of subject and technique; a more fluid, or impressionistic handling of the medium; and a new treatment of space. Nineteenth-century sculpture, for the most part, continued stylistic traditions that artists saw as complementing the inherent permanence of the medium with which they worked. It would seem that working on a large scale with materials such as marble or bronze was not well suited to the spontaneous technique that captured fleeting impressions. One nineteenth-century artist, however, changed the course of the history of sculpture by applying to his work the very principles on which modern painting was based, including Realism, Symbolism, and Impressionism—Auguste Rodin.

AUGUSTE RODIN   Auguste Rodin (1840–1917) devoted his life almost solely to the representation of the

human figure. His figures were imbued with a realism so startlingly intense that he was accused of casting the sculptures from live models. (It is interesting to note that casting of live models is used today without criticism.)

Rodin's *The Burghers of Calais* (Figs. 19.36 and 19.37) represents all of the innovations of Modernism thrust into three dimensions. The work commemorates a historical event in which six prominent citizens of Calais offered their lives to the conquering English so that their fellow townspeople might be spared. They present themselves in coarse robes with nooses around their necks. Their psychological states range from quiet defiance to frantic desperation. The reality of the scene is achieved in part by the odd placement of the figures. They are not a symmetrical or cohesive group. Rather, they are a scattered collection of individuals, who were meant to be seen at street level. Captured as they are, at a particular moment in time, Rodin ensured that spectators would partake of the tragic emotion of the scene for centuries to come.

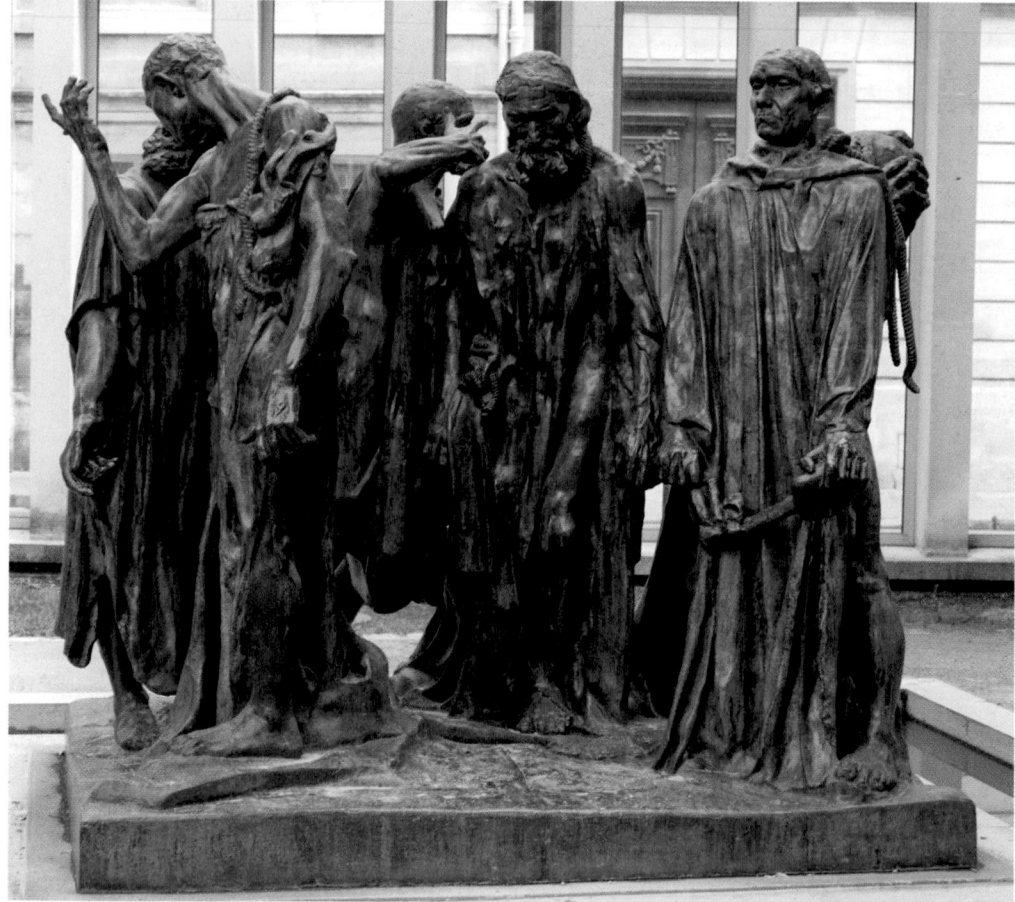

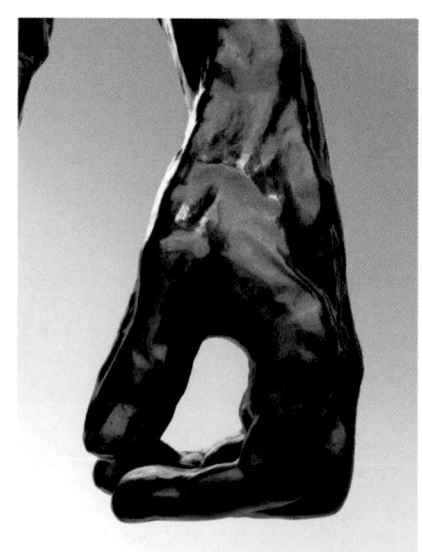

∧ 19.36 **AUGUSTE RODIN,** *The Burghers of Calais* (1884–1895). Bronze, 79⅜" × 80⅞" × 77⅛". Hirshhorn Museum and Sculpture Garden. Smithsonian Institution, Washington, D.C.

∧ 19.37 *The Burghers of Calais.* Detail of hand.

ART NOUVEAU

In looking at examples of French, Norwegian, and American art of the nineteenth century, we witnessed a collection of disparate styles that reflected the artists' unique situations or personalities. Given the broad range of circumstances that give rise to a work of art, it would seem unlikely that a cross-cultural style could ever evolve. However, as the nineteenth century turned to the twentieth, there arose a style called **Art Nouveau** whose influence extended from Europe to the United States. Its idiosyncratic characteristics could be found in painting and sculpture, as well as architecture, furniture, jewelry, fashion, and glassware.

Art Nouveau is marked by a lyrical linearity, the use of symbolism, and rich ornamentation. There is an overriding sense of the organic in all of the arts of this style, with many of the forms, such as those in Victor Horta's (1861–1947) foyer and staircase of the Tassel House (Fig. 19.38), reminiscent of exotic plant life. Antoni Gaudí's (1852–1926) apartment house in Barcelona, Spain (Fig. 19.39), shows an obsessive avoidance of straight lines and flat surfaces. The material looks as if it had grown in place or hardened in malleable wood forms, as would cement, in actuality, it is cut stone. The rhythmic roof is wavelike, and the chimneys seem dispensed like shaving cream or soft ice cream. Nor are any two rooms on a floor alike. This multistory organic hive is clearly the antithesis of the steel-cage construction that was coming into its own at the same time.

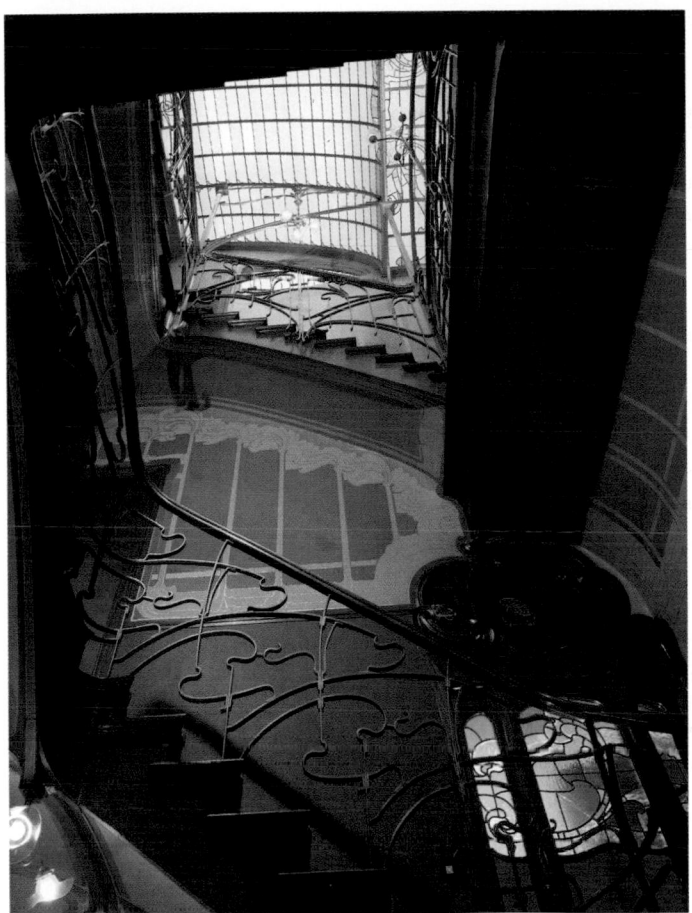

▲ 19.38 VICTOR HORTA, Interior of the *Tassel House*, Brussels, Belgium (1893).

Rodin preferred modeling soft materials to carving because they enabled him to achieve highly textured surfaces that captured the play of light, much as in an Impressionist painting. As his career progressed, Rodin's sculptures took on an abstract quality. Distinct features were abandoned in favor of solids and voids that, together with light, constructed the image of a human being. Such works were outrageous in their own day—audacious and quite new. Their abstracted features set the stage for yet newer and more audacious art forms that would rise with the dawn of the twentieth century.

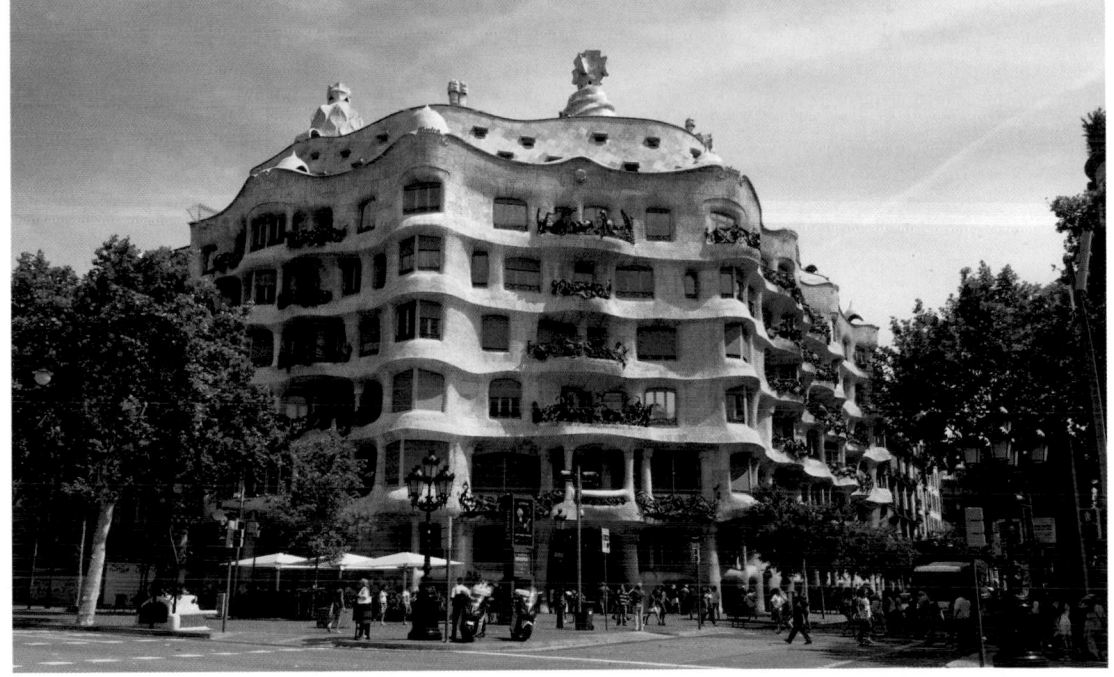

▲ 19.39 ANTONI GAUDÍ, Casa Mila Apartment House, Barcelona, Spain (1905–1907).

Art Nouveau originated in England. It was part of an arts-and-crafts movement that arose in rebellion against the pretentiousness of nineteenth-century art. Although it continued into the early years of the twentieth century, the style disappeared with the onset of World War I. At that time, art began to reflect the needs and fears of humanity faced with self-destruction.

THE WIDER WORLD

The wider world in the nineteenth century is defined, in many, many cases by the expansionism of colonial empires and their effect on indigenous cultures. In the arts, that effect can be detected in the mixing of indigenous and colonial styles and, sometimes, in the continued adherence to traditions in spite of the encroachment of the West. The Wider World section in this chapter begins with Africa and moves east until we get reach the Americas.

Africa

It is only in the nineteenth-century—concurrent with the European conquest of Africa—that anthropologists and other scholars began to consider sculpture and other objects that were created by Africans for commemorative or ritualistic purposes as "art." The march of colonialism in Africa yield so-called "primitive" works of art that appeared in European museum collections and on the open art-market (some of it was looted and some was legitimately purchased). At the beginning of the twentieth century, avant-garde European artists began to

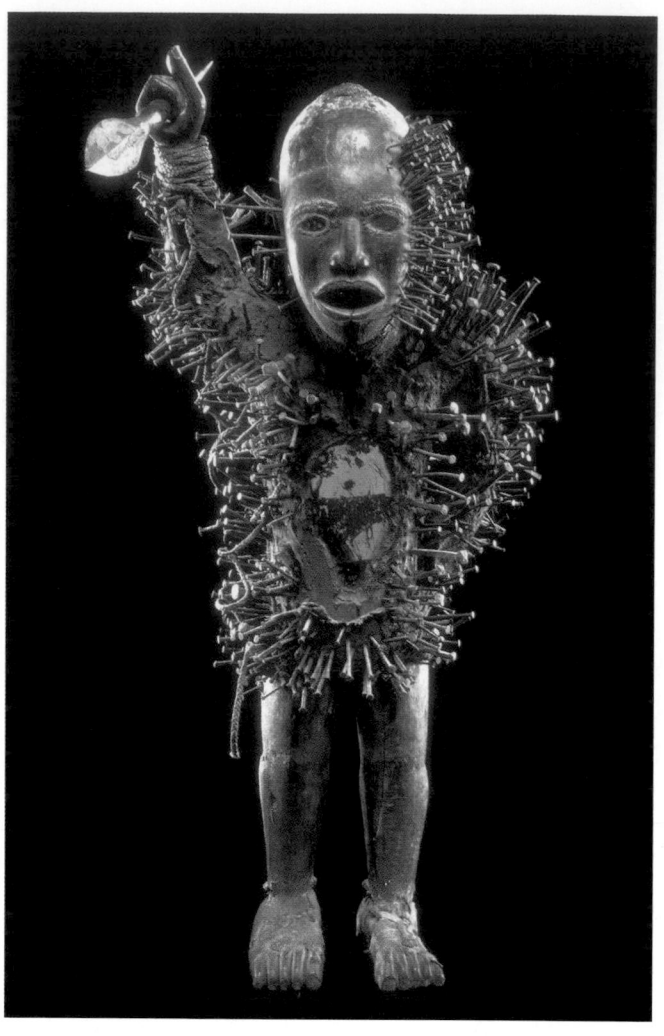

∧ **19.40** *Nkisi N'Kondi* **(hunter figure),** Democratic Republic of Congo (collected before 1905). Wood, nails, iron, fabric; 38³⁄₁₆" high.

NINETEENTH-CENTURY ART IN THE WIDER WORLD

1800–1850	1850–1875	1875–1900
Inuit and Northwest Coast Indians fashion elaborate masks for rituals	U.S. Commodore Perry opens trade with Japan in 1853	In 1877 Queen Victoria becomes empress of India
Oceanic art forms include sculptures and masks of ancestors and deities, painted wood prow ornaments, and communal men's houses	Hiroshige prints the woodblock *Sudden Shower over Shin-Ōhashi Bridge and Atake* in 1857	Victoria Terminus is constructed in India, 1879–1887
Hokusai prints the woodblock of *The Great Wave* in Japan in 1831	In Japan, the Edo period ends in 1868 and the Meiji period begins	The Meiji period brings Japan into the industrial age, creates an elected parliament, and institutes universal education
	The Meiji period introduces Western styles and art techniques to Japan	Congolese artists create power figures with hammered nails to ward off evil
	The French establish the Second Mexican Empire in 1862 with Austrian Ferdinand Maximilian	Yombe and Dogon sculptors carve wood groups of mothers and children or of men and women
	Emperor Maximilian is executed in 1867	

collect pieces of African statuary and masks and began to incorporate some of their formal elements into their paintings and sculpture. Of course, these artists—and collectors and museum curators—were looking at these African pieces from a perspective that had little or nothing to do with their original purposes. It also bears reminding that Africa is an expansive continent with many nations and ethnic groups and the art and artifacts are equally widely diverse in style and function. Thus, any examples we may discuss represent just the smallest fraction of the wealth of material from which we may choose.

Africans created sacred objects (and still do), among other reasons, to honor ancestors and rulers, to beseech and propitiate spirits, and to serve as mediators between living and the dead, between humans and the powers beyond them. The function of a nail figure like *Nkisi N'Kondi* (Fig. 19.40) from the Kongo might be as broad as protecting a village from enemies or as specific as solving villagers' disputes or punishing ordinary evil-doers.

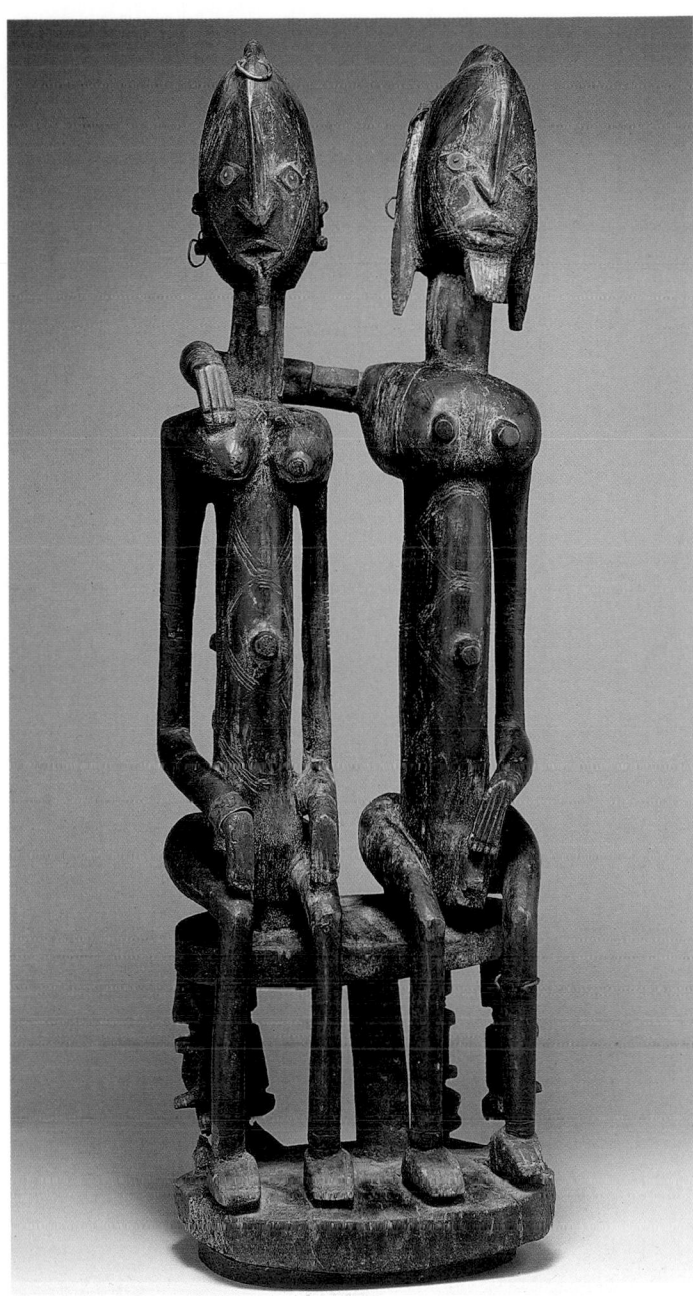

∧ 19.42 **Ancestral couple,** Dogon, Mali (c. 1800–1850). Wood, 2' 4" high. Metropolitan Museum of Art, New York, New York.

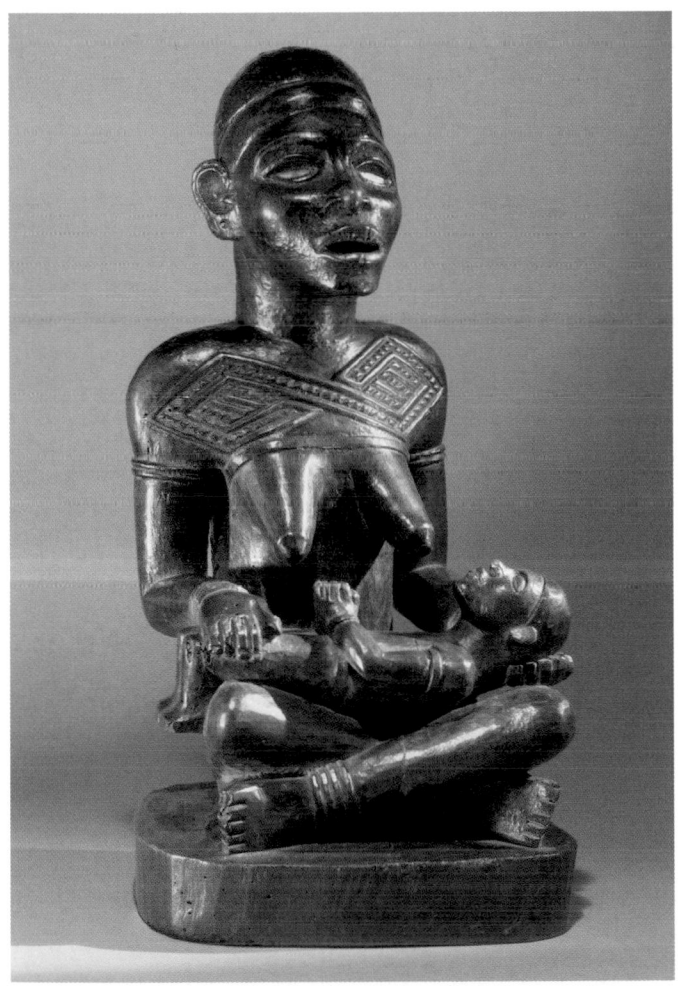

∧ 19.41 **Yombe mother and child (pfemba),** Kongo, Democratic Republic of Congo (late 19th century). Wood, glass, glass beads, brass tacks, and pigment, 10⅛" high. National Museum of African Art, Washington, D.C.

Power figures are riddled with nails or other sharp implements and can take human or animal form.

The mother and child image (*pfemba*) is a common one in African art (Fig. 19.41). An example from the Yombe, also peoples of the Republic of Congo, is typical: a beautiful woman adorned with jewelry, body scarification, and sharpened teeth sits cross-legged with an infant cradled in her lap. Her regal bearing suggests that she likely represents an important maternal ancestor.

The seated couple (Fig. 19.42) from the Dogon people of Mali in the western part of the continent represents

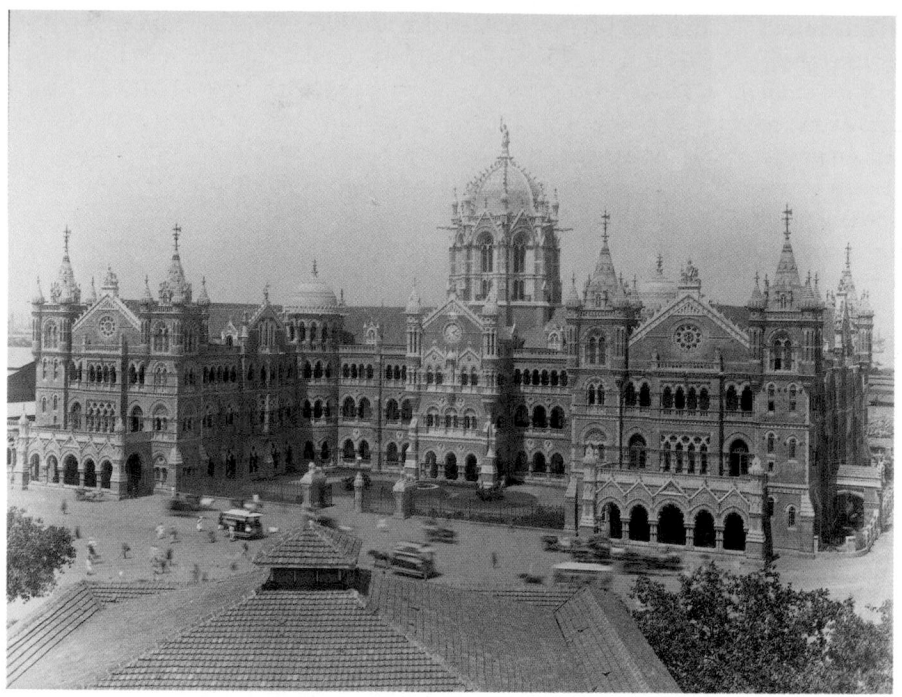

▲ 19.43 FREDERICK W. STEVENS, Victoria Terminus (now Chhatrapati Shivaji Terminus), Mumbai (Bombay), India (1879–1887). Albumen silver print from glass negative, 7³⁄₁₆" × 9⁵⁄₁₆". Metropolitan Museum of Art, New York, New York.

Revival architecture popular in Europe and the U.S. but its motifs and details—as well as the sandstone construction—are unmistakably "local." The station is only one example of the **hybridization**—or fusion of styles east and west—evident in India during colonial rule. Subtly-pointed arches frame the arcades and windows of the railway station, calling to mind architecture such as the Cathedral of Florence (see Fig 16-18), although the meandering floor plan bears close resemblance to Indian palace designs; medieval turrets are juxtaposed with domes and minaret shapes that are consistent with those found in subcontinent Hindu and Mughal architecture. As we have seen in other examples of architecture in India, the exterior of the Terminus is embellished with carvings of allegorical figures, gargoyles, animals and plants, portraits, and other human faces.

The blend of European and indigenous art forms also can be seen in a portrait of Maharaja Jaswant Singh, a

another common image in African art. Although it is not entirely clear why this statue was created, a few details suggest that gender roles are an important part of the piece. The male figure places his arm around the female as if to protect her, touching her breast. Although it cannot be seen from this perspective in the photograph, the man has a quiver on his back that suggests he provides for the family, and the woman carries a baby on hers. Unlike the more naturalistic, rounded forms of the Yombe statue, these abstract figures are stick-like, and details such as the breasts, hands, hair, noses, and more are highly stylized.

India

Through out the nineteenth century, India remained under the hegemony of Britain, whose influence extended to the arts and architecture. Victoria Terminus (designed by the British architect, Frederick W. Stevens during the Victorian Era of the late nineteenth century and renamed Chhatrapti Shivaji Terminus in 1996 to honor the founder of the Maratha Empire) (Fig. 19.43), exhibits a strong stylistic connection to nineteenth-century Italianate Gothic

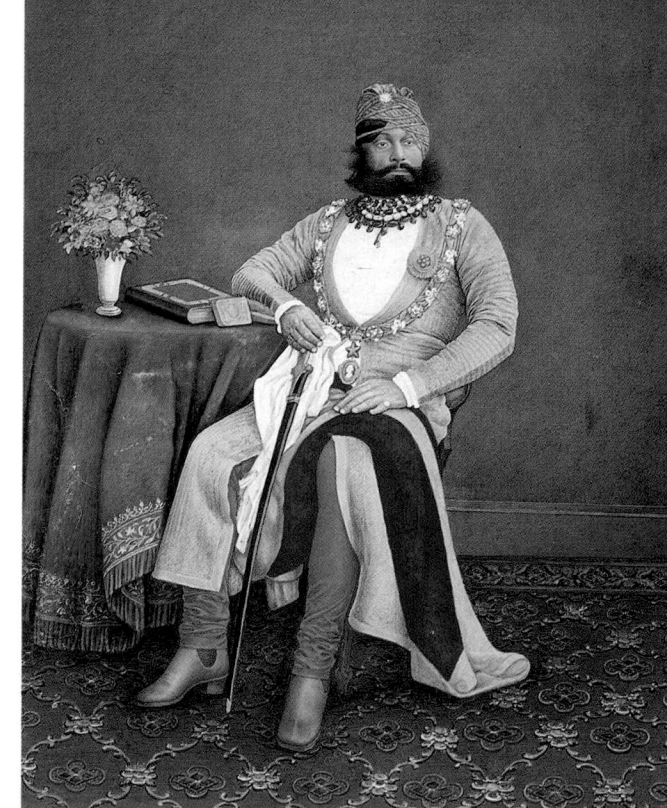

▷ 19.44 **Maharaja Jaswant Singh of Marwar** (c. 1880). Opaque watercolor on paper, 1' 3½" × 11⅝". Brooklyn Museum, Brooklyn, New York.

1 in.

local ruler of Jodhpur in Rajasthan (Fig. 19.44), painted in the late 1800s. The pose—that of a refined and relaxed Englishman amid the standard props of a conventional continental portrait—places the portrait unmistakably in India's colonial period. And yet, the artist has taken great pains to distinguish his sitter from his Western counterparts—from his turbaned head and curly beard to his magnificent emerald bib necklace. The brushwork in this small portrait is fine and meticulous, as it is in traditional Indian miniature painting. The artist captures the detail of the Maharaja's face and clothing with exceptional realism, conveys a presence of power and grandeur.

Japan

During the nineteenth century, the Edo period—with its shogun rule—drew to a close (1868) and the Meiji period began (1868–1912). Japan had remained insular throughout the Edo period, resisting trade with the West—and its influences. But in 1853, U.S. Commodore Matthew Perry sailed into Tokyo harbor with a small fleet and demanded that Japan open trade with the West. Navies from other Western nations followed, and during the middle-to-late 1850s, Japan signed trade treaties with several Western powers and Russia. The Meiji emperor (*Meiji* translates as "enlightened rule") followed the treaties with measures to modernize Japan and within some forty years, the nation boasted universal education, a constitution with an elected parliament, a bureaucracy that would survive a change of ministers, modern communication and transportation, and a strong army and navy. This was not the Japan that had winced at Commodore Perry's threat of force. This was the Japan that would, in a few years, rout an expansionist Russia in the Russo-Japanese War of 1905.

During the Edo period, the innovative woodblock technique made it possible for artists like Katsushika Hokusai (1760–1849) to create multiple copies of prints for a growing audience of collectors. His image of a monstrous crashing wave with a distant, diminutive, but enduring Mount Fuji is one of the best-known Japanese works of art in the West (Fig. 19.45). The

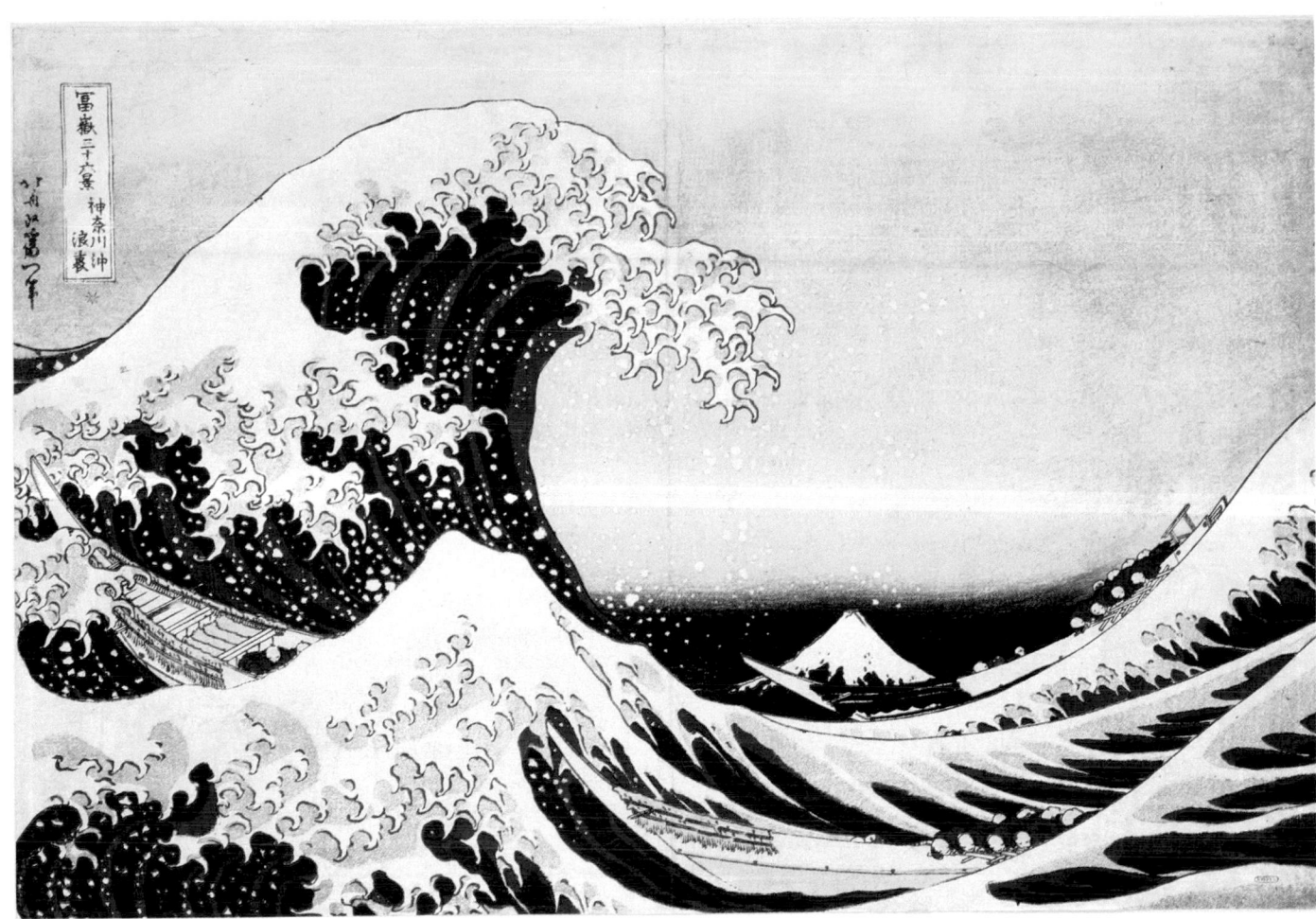

1 ft.

∧ **19.45 KATSUSHIKA HOKUSAI,** *Under the Wave off Kanagawa* (also known as *The Great Wave*) (Edo period, c. 1831). Polychrome woodblock print, 97¾" × 145¾". Musée national des arts asiatiques Guimet, Paris, France.

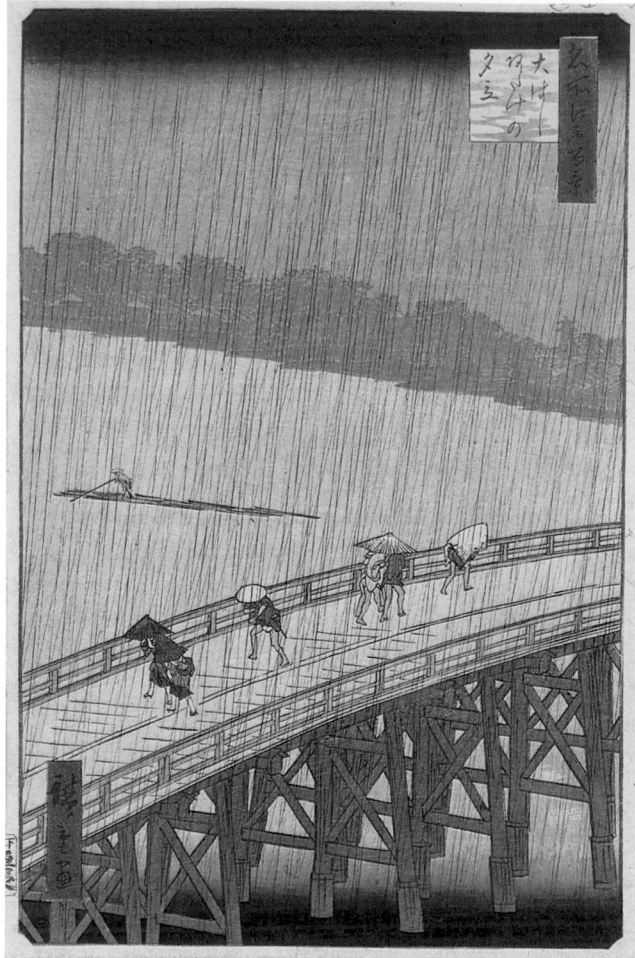

▲ 19.46 ANDO HIROSHIGE, *Sudden Shower over Shin-Ōhashi Bridge and Atake* (1857). Color woodblock print, 13⅞" × 9⅛". The Cleveland Museum of Art, Cleveland, Ohio.

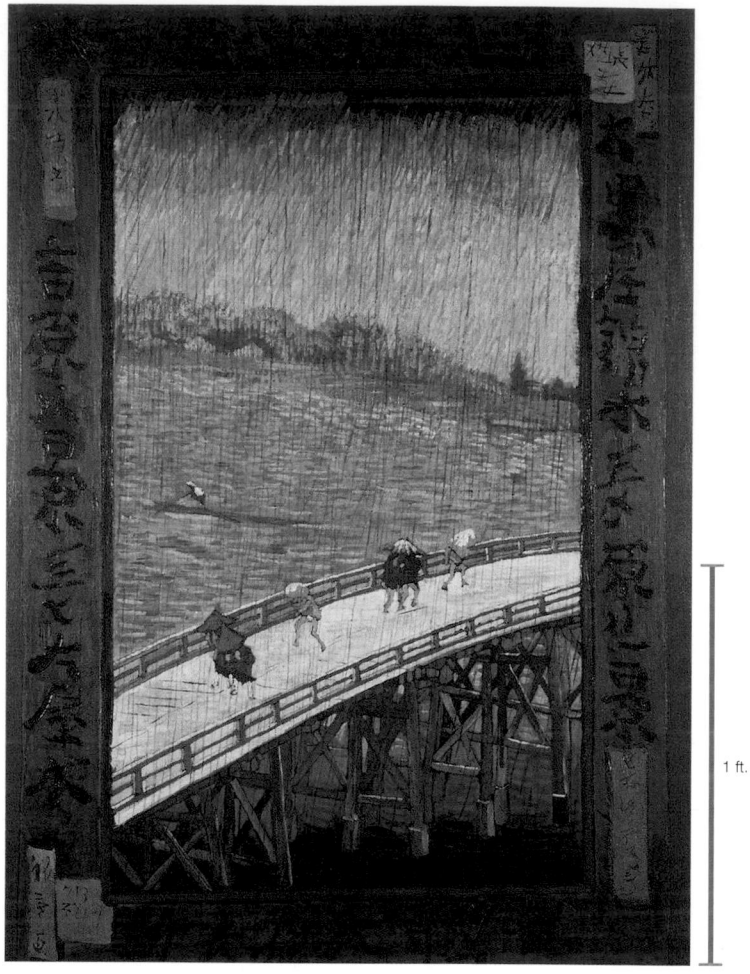

▲ 19.47 VINCENT VAN GOGH, *Bridge in the Rain, copy after Ando Hiroshige* (1887). Oil on canvas, 28¾" × 18¼". Van Gogh Museum, Amsterdam, Netherlands.

ominous claws of the whitecap seem certain to capsize the trading boats below and drown the sailors, who bend to gouge their oars into the rough waters to try to propel themselves past the wave. The vantage point from which we observe the unfolding drama is low in the water, such that we may feel vulnerable to the wave ourselves.

The opening of trade between Japan and the West revealed new artistic worlds to the artists of Western Europe as Japanese prints and objets d'art flowed into Paris and other cities. (Edgar Degas, in fact, hung a bathhouse scene by Torii Kiyonaga in his bedroom and Manet incorporated one by Utagawa Kuniaki II in his portrait of the French writer, Emile Zola.) Modern artists were intrigued by the flatness of space, decorative patterns, brilliant palette, and off-center compositions in Japanese woodcuts such as Hiroshige's *Sudden Shower*

over Shin-Ōhashi Bridge and Atake (Fig. 19.46). Vincent Van Gogh copied the image in an oil painting, adding a decorative frame complete with calligraphy (Fig. 19.47). The ordinariness of Japanese subjects also struck a chord among the Modernists, who were trying to escape the grip of Academic Art.

Japanese artists studied with western artists living in Japan, and some Japanese artists visited cultural enters in Europe. In his portrait of an oiran—a woman of pleasure—Takahashi Yuichi (Fig. 19.48) forgoes the flat, unmodulated features of a typical idealized Japanese woman (see Fig. 18.29) in favor of painting techniques more characteristic of his late-nineteenth-century peers. Yuichi painted his portrait in 1872, less than 10 years after Edouard Manet submitted his scandalous *Olympia* (see Fig. 19.14) to the Salon des Réfusés in Paris.

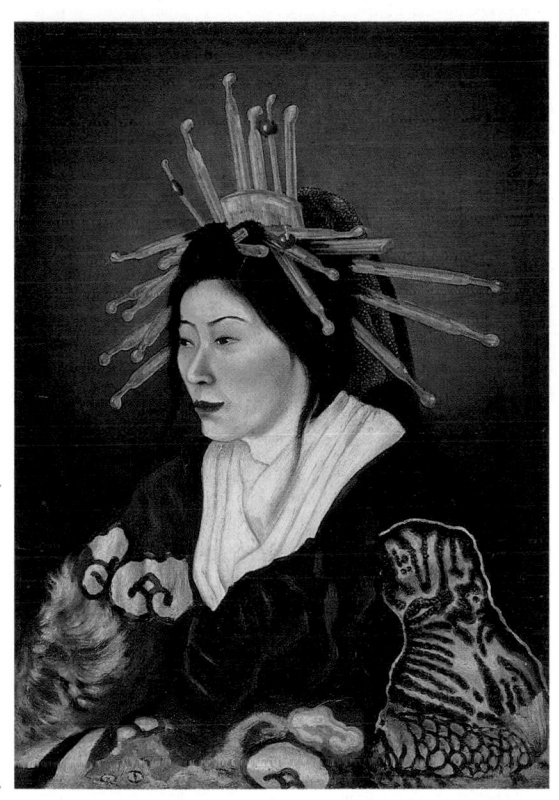

◄ 19.48 **TAKAHASHI YUICHI**, *Oiran (Grand Courtesan)* (Meiji period, 1872). Oil on canvas, 2' 6½" × 1' 9⅝". Musée national des arts asiatiques Guimet, Paris, France.

1 ft.

Oceania

For some of us, the words, "South Pacific" bring to mind the famed Rodgers and Hammerstein 1949 musical (made into a Hollywood feature film in 1958) about U.S. naval forces engaged in the South Pacific during World War II. It was based on stories in a novel by James Michener called *Tales of the South Pacific.* For most of us, the words conjure a picture of exotic life in warm tropical climates on exotic islands (and tourist destinations) such as Tahiti. The cultures of Oceania go back centuries—indeed millennia—although the West's consciousness of them only goes back as far as the early 1500s when European exploration got its real footing (think of the Columbus expedition in 1492 or Cortez's conquest of Mexico in 1519). The division of the territory collectively known as Oceania, however, only dates back to the first third of the nineteenth century; it includes the islands of Micronesia, Melanesia, and Polynesia—which also includes New Zealand.

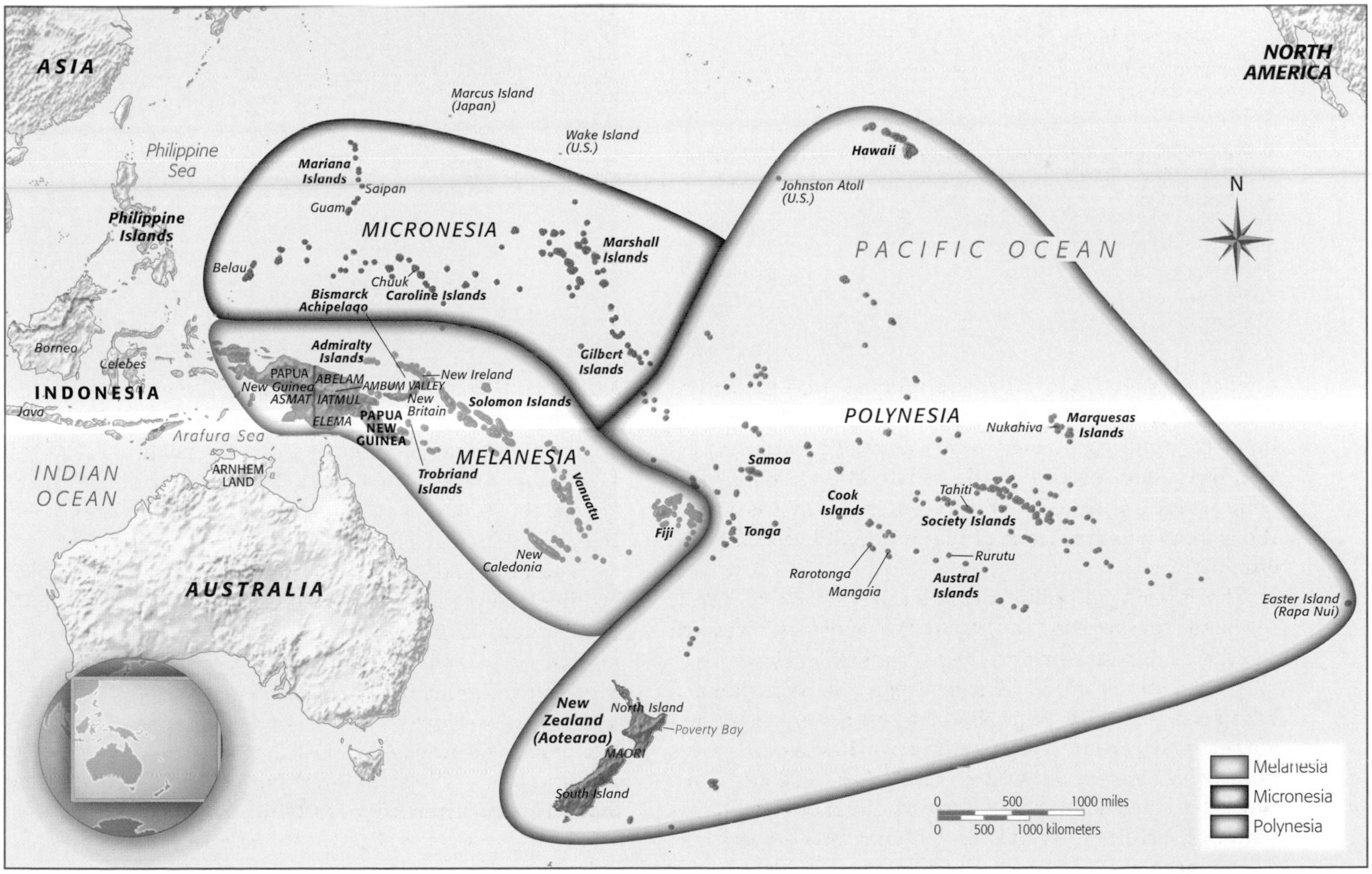

▲ **MAP 19.1** Oceania.

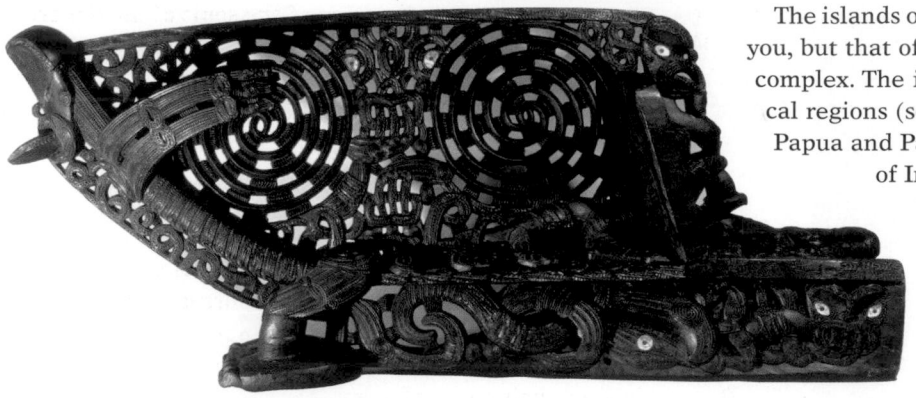

▲ 19.49 **WIREMU KINGI TE RANGITAKE, CHIEF OF THE TE ATI AWA,** *Tauihu* **(war canoe prow)** (early 19th century). Carving.

The canoe was the basic means of transportation and communication among the Oceanic peoples who fitted the prows of their vessels with fearsome-looking figures intended to strike fear into the hearts of enemies and what they believed to be the ominous spirits of the seas. The canoe prow (Fig. 19.49) carved by the Polynesian Maori of New Zealand possesses an intricacy and vitality that is characteristic of their wooden sculptures as well as their body art (Fig. 19.50).

The islands of New Zealand may be better known to you, but that of New Guinea is much larger and more complex. The island is divided into three geographical regions (see map); Papua New Guinea and West Papua and Papua—provinces that are actually part of Indonesia (the archipelago to the west). The carved wooden poles in Figure 19.51 were created by the Asmat peoples of Papua, who inhabit the southwest coastal region of the island. A close look at the poles reveals closely carved figures stacked one on top of the other; projections with airy, decorative openwork extend from the abdomens of the topmost figures. Carved from a single mangrove tree, the poles, whose sharpened points were thrust into the ground, are related to a once-common practice of headhunting to avenge the death of community men by enemies. These poles date from the mid-20th century; headhunting ended in the 1960s.

The Uli figure from Papua New Ireland (Fig. 19.52) represents an ancestral ruler and was used in rites intended

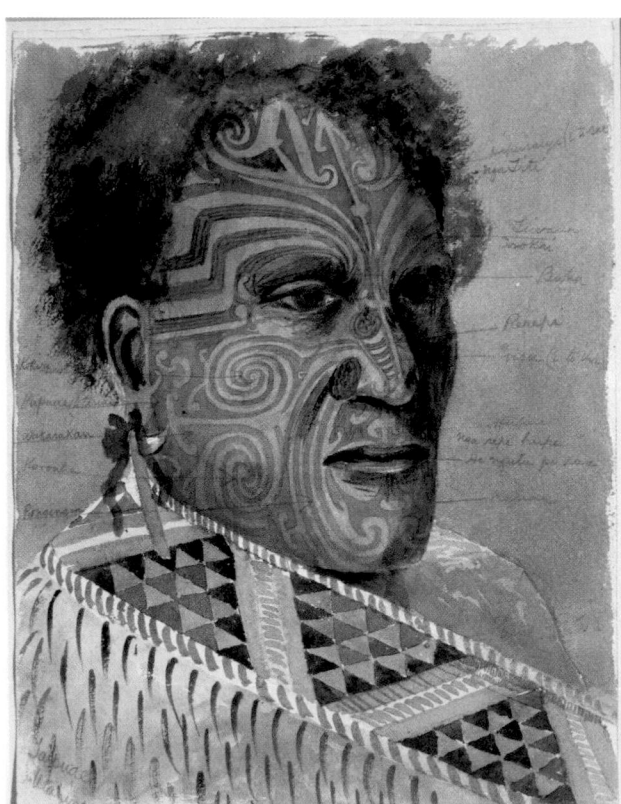

▲ 19.50 **THOMAS RYAN,** *Tapuae* (late 19th century). Watercolor on paper.

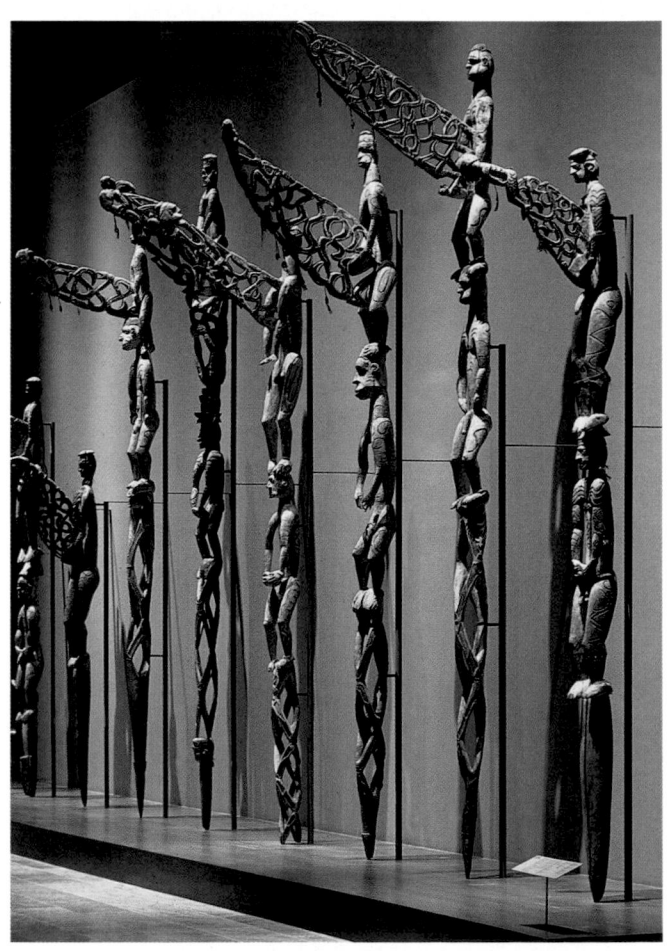

▲ 19.51 *Ancestor poles,* New Guinea (19th century). Wood, paint, and fiber. Height of tallest pole: 17'11". The Metropolitan Museum of Art, New York, New York.

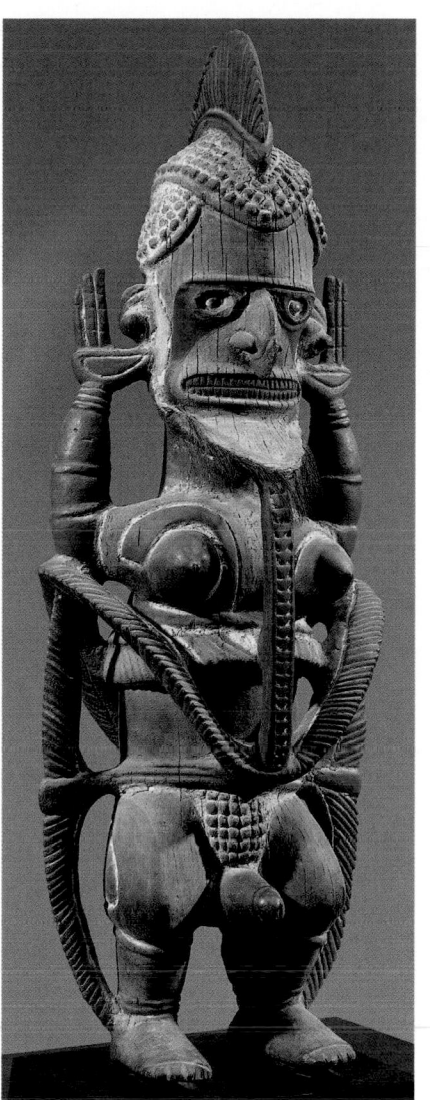

to smooth the transmigration of the souls of the departed to the realm of the dead. As the Uli statue "presided," skulls of deceased ancestors were unearthed then reinterred with fresh plants. Like most similar rites found around the world, a subtext was to reinvigorate the social connectedness and common purpose of the community. This Uli figure as many others is androgynous; it has a man's genitals and a woman's breasts. In terms of stereotypical gender roles, the figure has the fierceness of the warrior along with the capacity to nurture his people.

The cultures of Oceania are numerous and highly diverse. Students are encouraged to explore them more fully on their own; unfortunately, adequate coverage of the history of the region is impossible in a book of this scope.

The Americas

During the nineteenth century, the Americas—including the American Southwest and Great Plains as well as Central America and the Caribbean—continued to be impacted by European contact, conquest, and colonial ambitions.

The Navajo people of the American Southwest, using weaving techniques learned from their Pueblo neighbors along with European synthetic dyes (as opposed to traditional dyes derived from plants), fed a growing appetite for their textiles among the first groups of tourists.

The Native Americans of the Great Plains, living a nomadic existence after their communities were destroyed by settlers, created nature and war paintings on buffalo hide that incorporated some European stylistic, along with assorted leather garments, accessories, and portable objects embellished with beads and feathers. A painted muslin tipi lining from the Crow peoples of the Sioux nation (Fig. 19.53) depicts the deadly combat

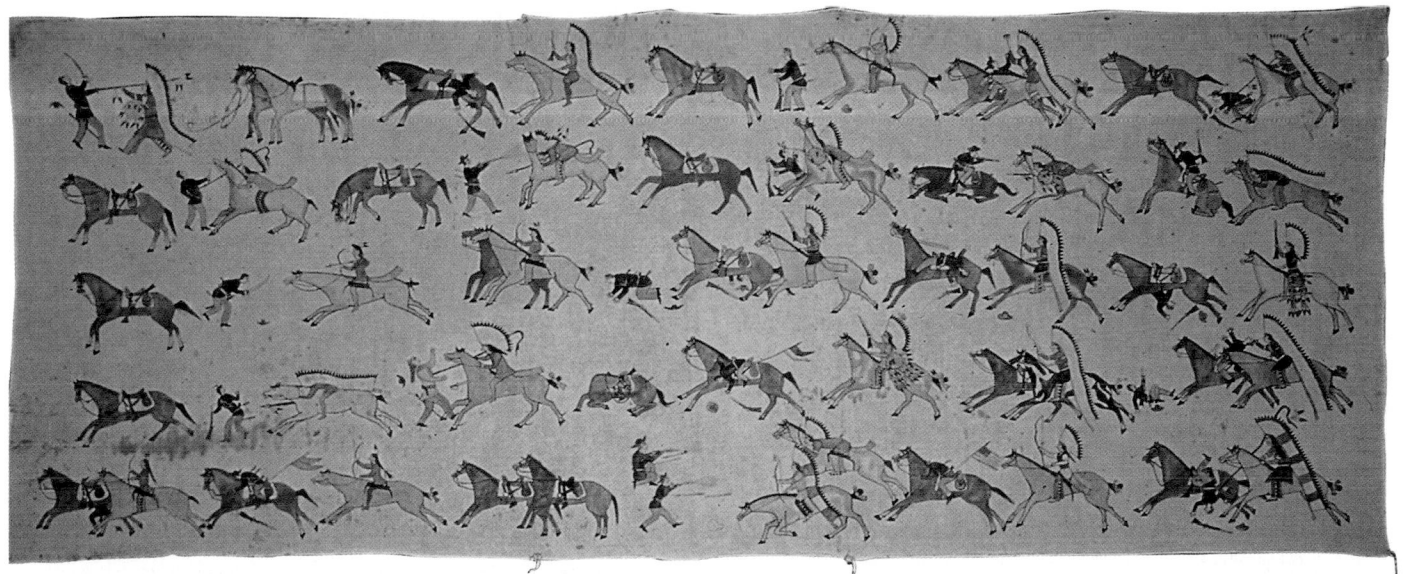

1 ft.

⋏ **19.53 _Custer's Last Stand_** (late 19th century). Teepee lining. Painted muslin, 35" × 85". National Museum of Natural History, Department of Anthropology, Smithsonian Institution, Washington, D.C.

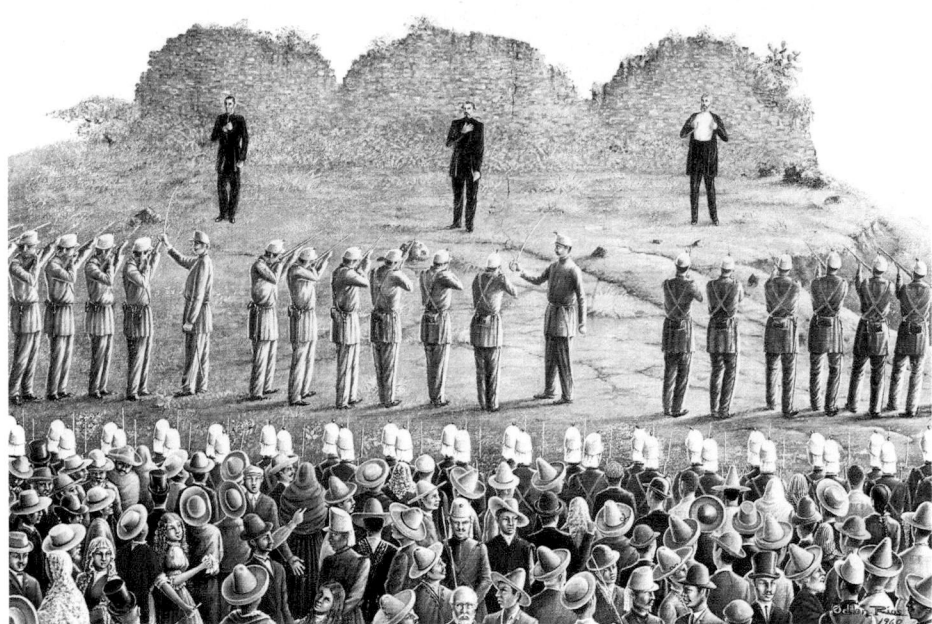

<
19.54 *The Execution of Maximilian I.*
(Mexican School, 19th century). Oil on canvas.
Museo Nacional de Historia, Castillo de
Chapultepec, Mexico.

between the Native Americans and U.S. cavalry under the leadership of General George Custer in the Battle of Little Bighorn during the Great Sioux War of 1878. Custer's forces (most are dead or dismounted) are met on the battlefield by superior opponents who advance rhythmically from the right, shooting arrows as they ride.

In Mexico, the shackles of Spanish rule were broken, and although the nation won independence, it entered a period of disarray that ended only with the radical reforms, separation of church and state, and new constitution established under the leadership of Benito Juarez. At the same time, Mexico lost nearly half of its territory (stretching from Texas to California) by the mid-nineteenth century and, in the opening decade of the twentieth, it would be on the threshold of a revolution. One of the seminal events of the period was the French Intervention in Mexico (1862) that forced Juarez into exile and established (very temporarily) the Second Mexican Empire with Austrian Ferdinand Maximilian appointed as emperor by France's Napoleon III. Maximilian and his loyalist Mexican forces would fall in May of 1867, and, one month later, he would be executed by firing squad on Juarez's order. An oil-on-canvas painting by an artist from the Mexican school portrays the execution (Fig. 19.54). The composition is divided into thirds: Maximilian (in the right background baring the white of his shirt) and two loyalists (with their hands on their hearts) stand tall before rigid lines of rifled soldiers and helmeted guards separating the soon-to-be victims from the crowd of assorted, ordinary Mexicans who have come witness the act. The simple shapes and bright, flat colors of the people in the foreground are a preview of a similar stylistic approach that would characterize the work of the internationally acclaimed Mexican muralists of the twentieth century.

At the very end of the nineteenth century, the Spanish would be driven from Cuba after the breakout of its final independence war in 1895 although throughout most of the century, it maintained a largely white or mulatto (mixed) population—the result of aggressive efforts on the part of the Spanish to "whiten" the Cuban population with waves of immigrants. Adding to the island's mixed heritage were black slaves and free blacks as well as Chinese immigrants who took the place of slave laborers when the institution was abolished in the late 1880s. Among the genres of Cuban painting during this period are views of colonialized Havana, rural landscapes intended to illustrate the progress of the sugar industry on the island, exotic vegetation in the tropical sunlight, and scenes of local customs that juxtapose white Hispanic privilege and "savage" rituals connected to the indigenous and African traditions.

The arrival of European explorers in the Northwest coastal regions of North America (such as what is now Vancouver, British Columbia, Canada and Alaska) did not have the impact on the Native American peoples that it did elsewhere in the wider world. Much of the indigenous population remained isolated during the nineteenth

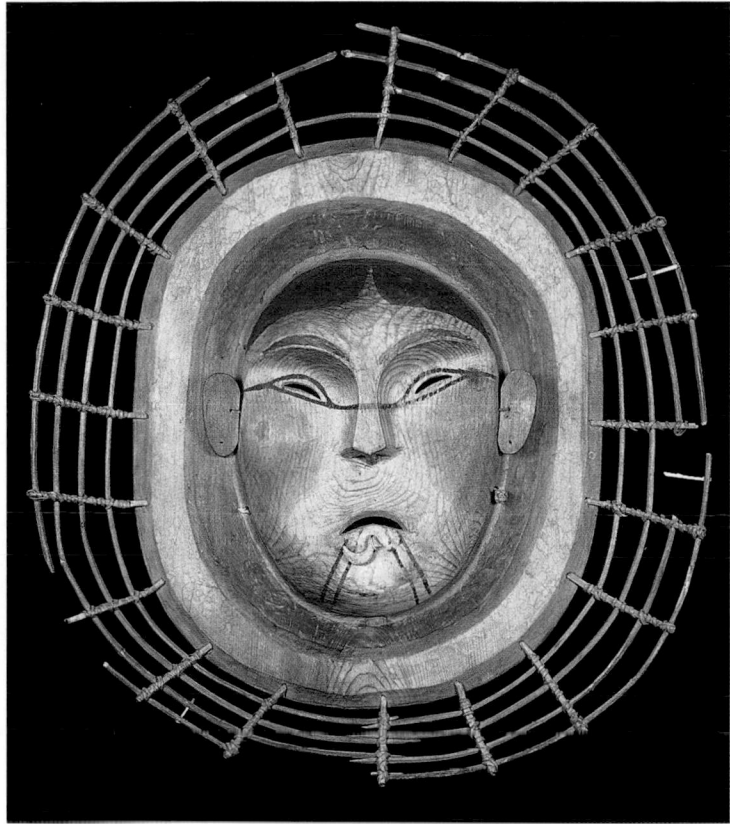

▲ **19.55 Eskimo mask representing a moon goddess** (before 1900). Phoebe A. Hearst Museum of Anthropology. The University of California at Berkeley, Berkeley, California.

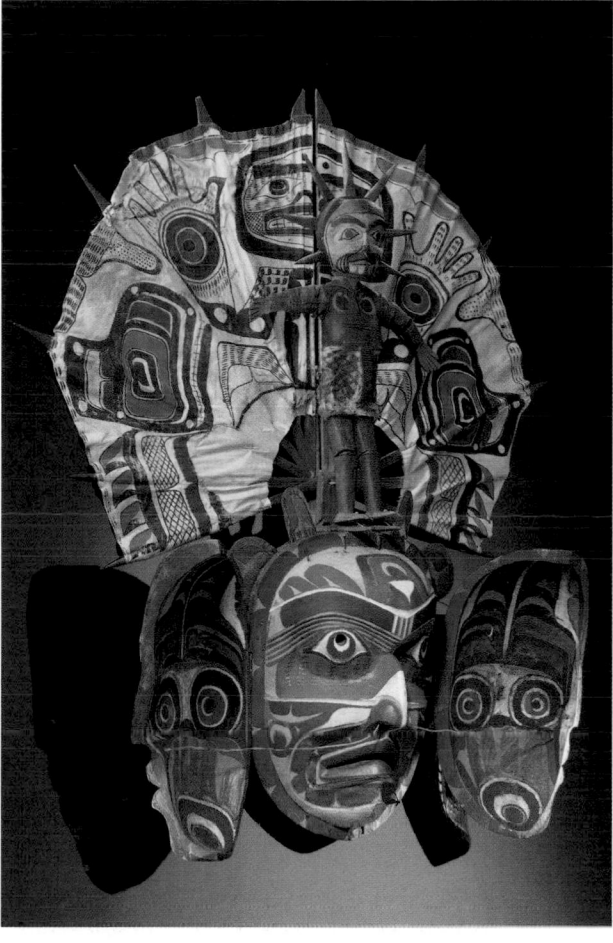

▲ **19.56 Transformation mask representing the sun** (1870–1910). Wood, paint, cotton cloth, metal hinges, iron nails, sinew, cotton cord/cordage; 46" × 52". Smithsonian, National Museum of the American Indian.

century, their traditions and art forms intact. Eskimo, or Inuit, sculpture often exhibits a simplicity and elegant refinement, as in a mask representing a moon goddess (Fig. 19.55). Such masks, worn by shamans in ritual ceremonies, were carved of ivory or wood; some had movable parts that added to the realism of the image.

The carved wood and muslin Kwakwaka'wakw (Kwakiutl) "transformation mask" representing the sun and other spirits (Fig. 19.56), is vividly painted with abstract human and animal forms. Like the Inuit moon goddess mask, it too has movable parts. When the string

hanging from the inner mask is pulled, the two profiles to the sides are drawn together, forming another mask. It is an extraordinary composition that features the symmetry, balance, and repetition characteristic of Northwest Coast style. As is often the case in ethnographic art, the embellishment of the work reflects traditional body decoration, such as painting, tattooing, or scarification.

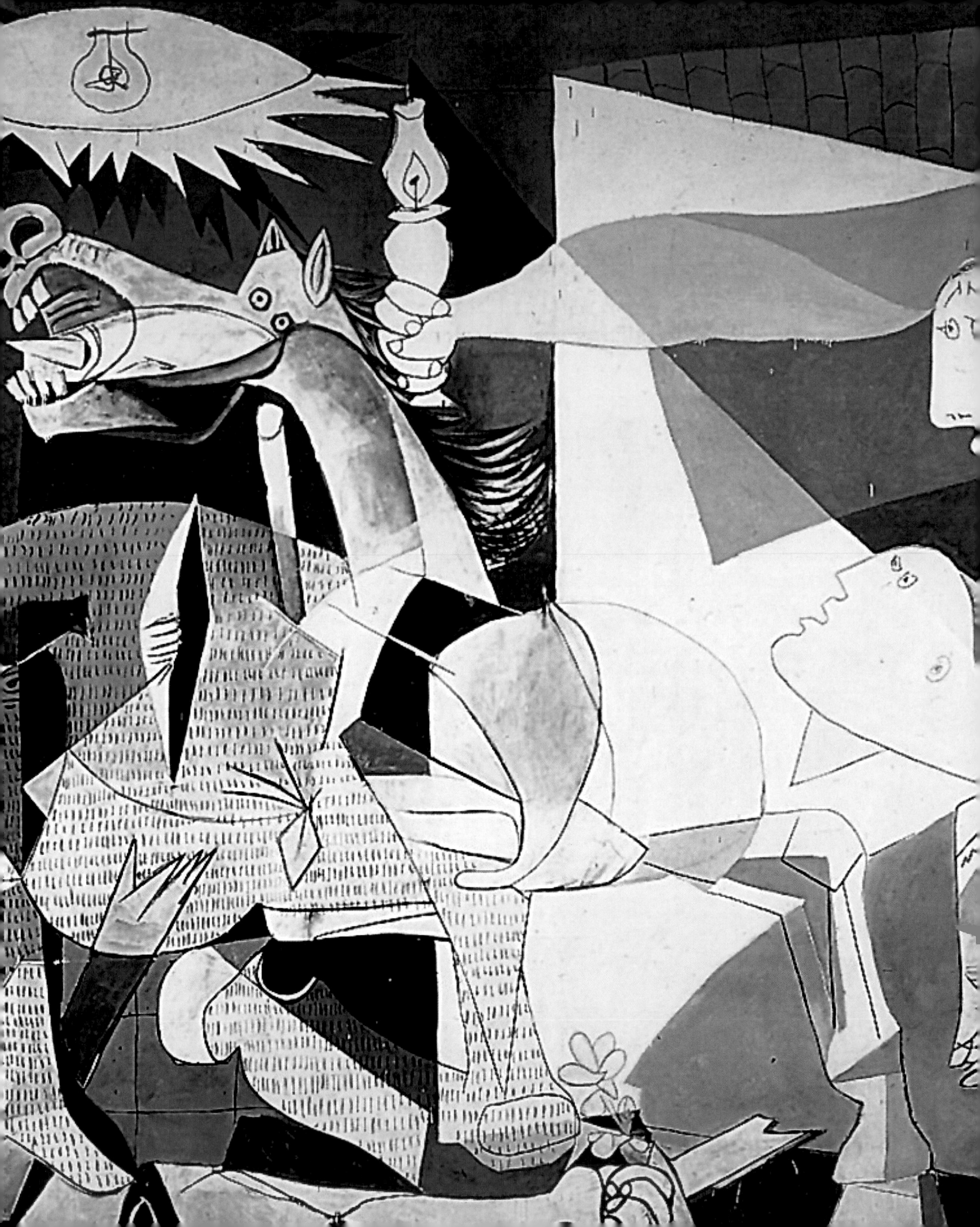

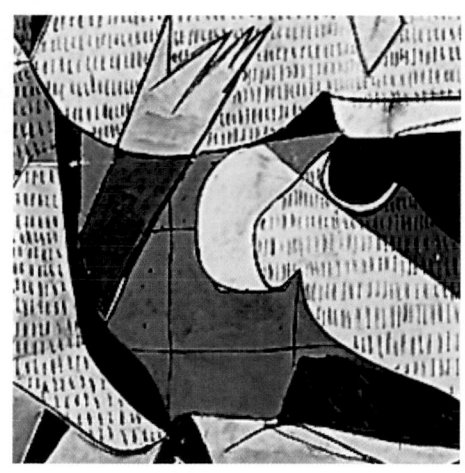

20

THE TWENTIETH CENTURY: THE EARLY YEARS

When people ask me to compare the 20th century to older civilizations, I always say the same thing: "The situation is normal."

—WILL DURANT

IT COULD be said that the art world has been in a state of perpetual turmoil for the last hundred years. All of the important movements that were born during the late nineteenth and early twentieth centuries met with the hostile, antiseptic gloves of critical disdain. When Courbet's paintings were rejected by the 1855 Salon, he set up his own Pavilion of Realism and pushed the Realist movement on its way. Just eight years later, rejection by the Salon jury prompted the origin of the Salon des Réfusés, an exhibition of works including those of Manet. These ornery French artists went on to found the influential Impressionist movement. The very name—*Impressionism*—was coined by a hostile critic who degraded their work as mere "impressions," sort of quick and easy sketches of the painter's view of the world. Impressionism ran counter to the preferred illusionistic realism of Academic painting.

The opening years of the twentieth century saw no letup to these scandalous entrées into the world of modern art. In 1905, the Salon d'Automne—an independent exhibition so named to distinguish it from the Academic salons that were traditionally held in the spring—brought together the works of an exuberant group of French avant-garde artists who assaulted the public with a bold palette and distorted forms. One art critic who peeked in on the show saw a Renaissance-type sculpture surrounded by these blasphemous forms. He was sufficiently unnerved by the juxtaposition to exclaim, "Donatello au milieu des fauves!" (that is, "Donatello among the wild beasts!"). With what pleasure, then, the artists adopted as their epithet "The Fauves." After all, it was a symbol of recognition.

◄ PABLO PICASSO, *Guernica* (1937). Oil on canvas, 11'6" × 25'8". Museo Nacional Centro de Arte Reina Sofia, Madrid, Spain.

459

THE FAUVES

In some respects, **Fauvism** was a logical successor to the painting of van Gogh and Gauguin. Like these Postimpressionists, the Fauvists also rejected the subdued palette and delicate brushwork of Impressionism. They chose their color and brushwork on the basis of their emotive qualities. Despite the aggressiveness of their method, however, their subject matter centered on traditional nudes, still lifes, and landscapes.

What set the Fauves apart from their nineteenth-century predecessors was their use of harsh, nondescriptive color; bold linear patterning; and a distorted form of perspective. They saw color as autonomous, a subject in and of itself, not merely an adjunct to nature. Their vigorous brushwork and emphatic line grew out of their desire for a direct form of expression, unencumbered by theory. Their skewed perspective and distorted forms were also inspired by the discovery of ethnographic works of art from Africa, Polynesia, and other ancient cultures.

ANDRÉ DERAIN One of the founders of the Fauvist movement was André Derain (1880–1954). In his *London Bridge* (Fig. 20.1), we find the convergence of elements of nineteenth-century styles and the new vision of Fauvism. The outdoor subject matter is reminiscent of

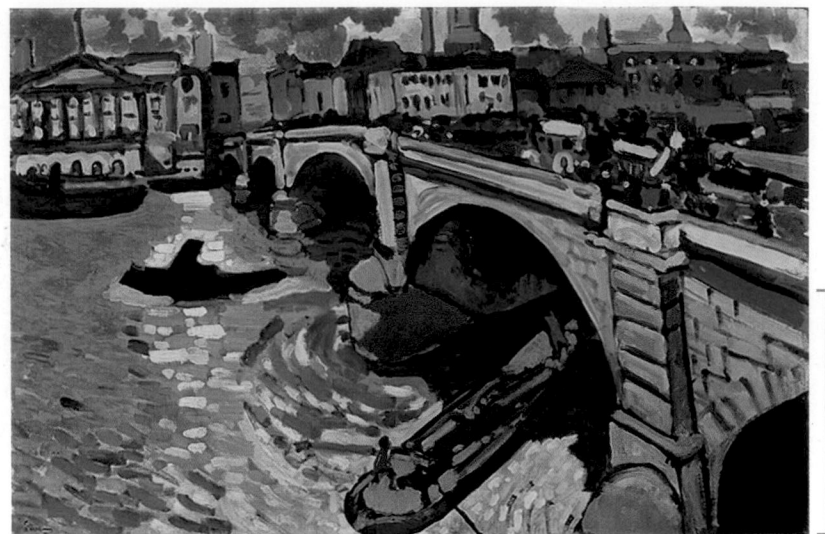

▲ 20.1 **ANDRÉ DERAIN,** *London Bridge* (1906). Oil on canvas, 26" × 39". The Museum of Modern Art, New York, New York.

1 ft.

Impressionism (Monet, in fact, painted many renditions of Waterloo Bridge in London), and the distinct zones of unnaturalistic color relate the work to Gauguin. But the forceful contrasts of primary colors and the delineation of forms by blocks of thickly applied pigment speak of something new.

Nineteenth-century artists emphasized natural light and created their shadows from color components. Derain and the Fauvists evoked light in their canvases solely with color contrasts. Fauvists tended to negate shadow

TWENTIETH CENTURY: THE EARLY YEARS IN EUROPE AND THE UNITED STATES

1900–1910	1910–1920	1920–1929	1929–1945
The Fauves, including Matisse, use color expressively rather than descriptively	Picasso and Braque develop Cubism	Following World War I, German *Neue Sachlichkeit* (New Objectivity) artists depict the horrors of war	Mondrian paints *Composition No. II with Red, Blue, Black, and Yellow* in 1929
German Expressionists produce painting with distorted forms and color	Italian Futurists depict dynamic motion and modern technology	Surrealists seek to use automatism to express the unconscious mind in art	O'Keeffe paints *White Iris* in 1930
African masks influence Picasso and others to set aside traditional styles of representation	Dadaists produce irreverent artworks	Mondrian and other De Stijl artists use primary colors and simple geometric forms to create pure plastic art	Dalí paints *The Persistence of Memory* in 1931
Picasso paints *Les Demoiselles d'Avignon* in 1907	The Armory show brings avant-garde European work to the United States	Brancusi sculpts *Bird in Space*	Picasso paints *Guernica* in 1937
		Bauhaus adherents promote the unity of art, architecture, and design	For the United States, World War II begins in 1941 and ends in 1945

> My choice of colors does not rest on any scientific theory; it is based on observation, on feeling, on the very nature of each experience.
>
> —HENRI MATISSE

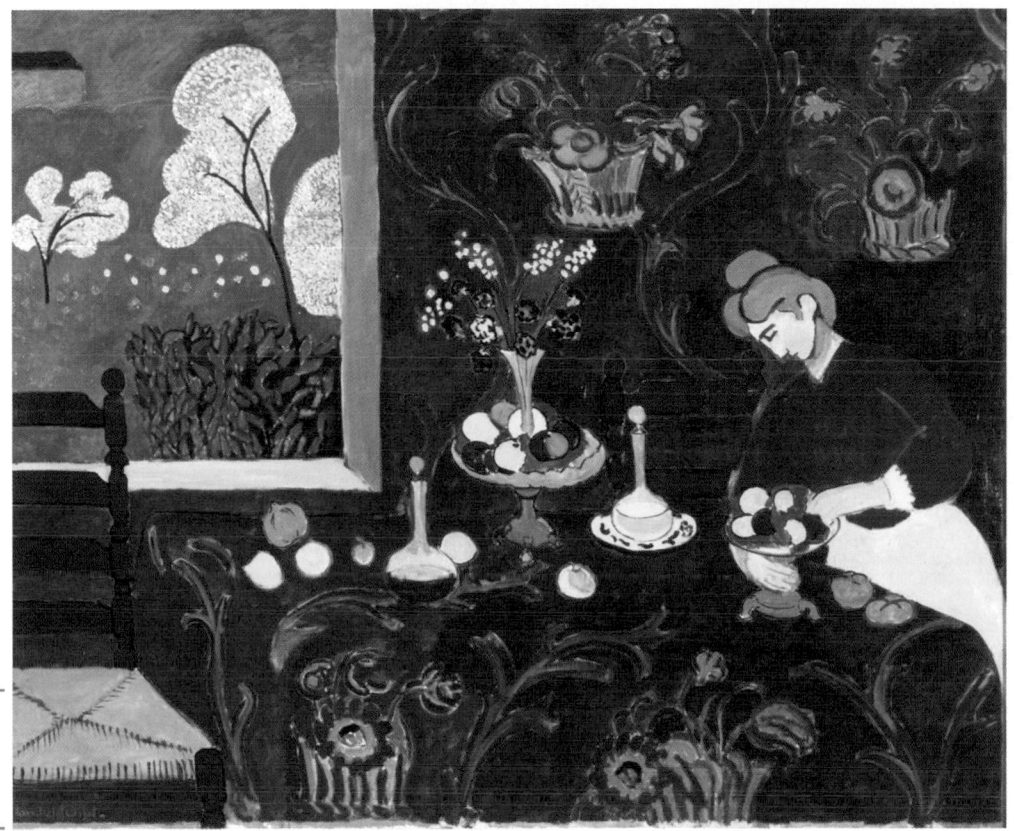

▲ 20-2 HENRI MATISSE, *Red Room (Harmony in Red)* (1908–1909). Oil on canvas, 69¾" × 85⅞". The Hermitage, St. Petersburg, Russia.

1 ft.

Bouguereau (see Fig. 19.9), and from copying old masters in the Louvre. His loose brushwork was reminiscent of Impressionism, and his palette was inspired by the color theories of the Postimpressionists. In 1905, he consolidated these influences and painted several Fauvist canvases in which, like Derain, he used primary color as a structural element. These canvases were exhibited with those of other Fauvists at the Salon d'Automne of that year.

In his post-Fauvist works, Matisse used color in a variety of other ways: structurally, decoratively, sensually, and expressively. In his *Red Room (Harmony in Red)* (Fig. 20.2), all of these qualities of color are present. A vibrant palette and curvilinear shapes create the gay mood of the canvas. The lush red of the wallpaper and tablecloth absorb the viewer in their brilliance. The arabesques of the vines create an enticing surface pattern.

altogether. Whereas Gauguin used color areas primarily to express emotion, the Fauvist artists used color to construct forms and space. Although Derain used his bold palette and harsh line to render his emotional response to the scene, his bright blocks of pigment also function as building facades. Derain's oblong patches of color define both stone and water. His thickly laden brushstroke constructs the contour of a boat and the silhouette of a fisherman.

HENRI MATISSE Along with Derain, Henri Matisse (1869–1954) brought Fauvism to the forefront of critical recognition. Yet Matisse was one of the few major Fauvist artists whose reputation exceeded that of the movement. Matisse started law school at the age of 21, but when an illness interrupted his studies, he began to paint. Soon thereafter, he decided to devote himself totally to art. Matisse's early paintings revealed a strong and traditional compositional structure, which he gleaned from his first mentor, Adolphe William

A curious contest between flatness and three dimensions in *Red Room* characterizes much of Matisse's work. He crowds the table and wall with the same patterns. They seem to run together without distinction. This jumbling of patterns propels the background to the picture plane, asserting the flatness of the canvas. The two-dimensionality of the canvas is further underscored by the window in the upper left, which is rendered so flatly that it suggests a painting of a garden scene instead of an actual view of a distant landscape. Yet for all of these attempts to collapse space, Matisse counteracts the effect with a variety of perspective cues: the seat of the ladder-back chair recedes into space, as does the table; and the dishes are somewhat foreshortened, combining frontal and bird's-eye views.

Matisse used line expressively, moving it rhythmically across the canvas to complement the pulsing color.

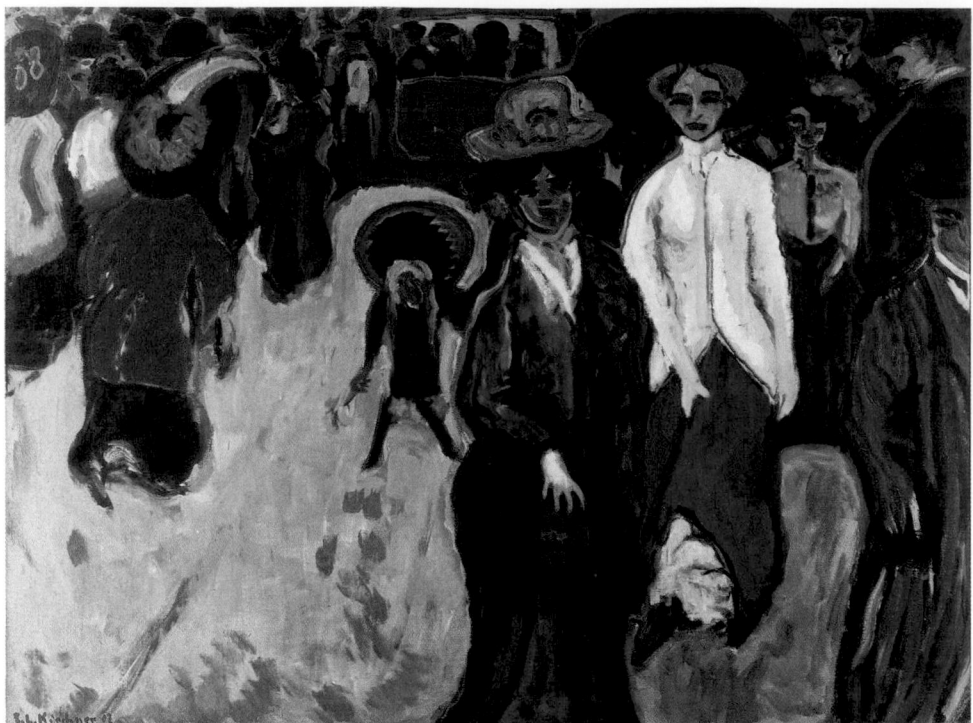

◀ 20.3 **ERNST LUDWIG KIRCHNER**, *Street, Dresden* (1908; reworked 1919; date on painting 1907). Oil on canvas, 59¼" × 78⅞". Museum of Modern Art, New York, New York.

1 ft.

Although the structure of *Red Room* remains assertive, Matisse's foremost concern was to create a pleasing pattern. Matisse insisted that painting ought to be joyous. His choice of palette, his lyrical use of line, and his brightly painted shapes are all means toward that end. He even said of his work that it ought to be devoid of depressing subject matter, that his art ought to be "a mental soother, something like a good armchair in which to rest."[1]

Although the colors and forms of Fauvism burst explosively on the modern art scene, the movement did not last very long. For one thing, the styles of the Fauvist artists were very different from one another, so the members never formed a cohesive group. After about five years, the Fauvist qualities began to disappear from their works as they pursued other styles. Their disappearance was, in part, prompted by a retrospective exhibition of Cézanne's paintings held in 1907, which revitalized an interest in this nineteenth-century artist's work. His principles of composition and constructive brush technique were at odds with the Fauvist manifesto.

While Fauvism was descending from its brief, colorful flourish in France, related art movements, termed *expressionistic*, were ascending in Germany.

---

[1] Robert Goldwater and Marco Treves, eds., *Artists on Art* (New York: Pantheon Books, 1972), 413.

EXPRESSIONISM

Expressionism is the distortion of nature—as opposed to the imitation of nature—to achieve a desired emotional effect or representation of inner feelings. According to this definition, we have already seen many examples of this type of painting. The work of van Gogh and Gauguin would be clearly expressionistic, as would the paintings of the Fauves. Even Matisse's *Red Room* distorts nature or reality in favor of a more intimate portrayal of the artist's subject, colored, as it were, by his emotions. Edvard Munch and Käthe Kollwitz were Expressionistic artists who used paintings and prints as vehicles to express anxieties, obsessions, and outrage.

Three other movements of the early twentieth century have been termed expressionistic: *Die Brücke* (The Bridge), *Der Blaue Reiter* (The Blue Rider), and *Neue Sachlichkeit* (New Objectivity). Although very different from one another in the forms they took, these movements were reactions against Impressionism and Realism. They also sought to communicate the inner feelings of the artist.

Die Brücke (The Bridge)

Die Brücke (The Bridge) was founded in Dresden, Germany, at the same time that Fauvism was afoot in France. The artists who began the movement chose the name *Die Brücke* because, in theory, they saw their movement as

◁ 20.4 **WASSILY KANDINSKY**, *Sketch I for Composition VI* (1913). Oil on canvas, 76⅖" × 115⁷⁄₁₀". Hermitage Museum, St. Petersburg, Russia.

1 ft.

bridging several disparate styles. The aim was to symbolize the artists' desire to connect "all the revolutionary and fermenting elements" that rejected academic and other "fashionable" (socially or culturally acceptable) artforms. But Die Brücke, like Fauvism, was short-lived because of the lack of cohesion among its proponents. Still, Die Brücke artists showed some common interests in techniques and subject matter that ranged from boldly colored landscapes and cityscapes to horrific and violent portraits. Their emotional upheaval may, in part, have reflected the mayhem of World War I and the years leading up to it.

ERNST LUDWIG KIRCHNER Ernst Ludwig Kirchner (1880–1938) was one of the founding members of Die Brücke. Many German Expressionist works, such as Kirchner's *Street, Dresden* (Fig. 20.3) feature themes of isolation and alienation. Agitated brushwork and unnatural color schemes suggest turbulence and uncertainty. The inhabitants of Kirchner's crowded street do not interact, but rather seem lost in their own thoughts as they rush to and fro. In spite of their common circumstances, they are each alone in carrying the weight of their emotional lives. Kirchner portrays, with these masked "automatons," an acute sense of alienation gripping society early in the twentieth century.

Der Blaue Reiter (The Blue Rider)

Emotionally charged subject matter, often radically distorted, was the essence of Die Brücke art. **Der Blaue Reiter (The Blue Rider)** artists—who took their group name from a painting of that title by Wassily Kandinsky, a major proponent—depended less heavily on content to communicate feelings and evoke an emotional response from the viewer. Their work focused more on the contrasts and combinations of abstract forms and pure colors. In fact, the work of Der Blaue Reiter artists, at times, is completely without subject and can be described as non-objective, or abstract. Whereas Die Brücke artists always used nature as a point of departure, Der Blaue Reiter art sought to free itself from the shackles of observable reality.

WASSILY KANDINSKY One of the founders of Der Blaue Reiter was Wassily Kandinsky (1866–1944), a Russian artist who left a career in law to become an influential abstract painter and art theorist. During numerous visits to Paris early in his career, Kandinsky was immersed in the works of Gauguin and the Fauves and was inspired to adopt the Fauvist idiom. The French experience opened his eyes to color's powerful capacity to communicate the artist's inmost psychological and spiritual concerns. In his seminal essay "Concerning the Spiritual in Art" he examined this capability and discussed the psychological effects of color on the viewer. Kandinsky further analyzed the relationship between art and music in this study.

Early experiments with these theories can be seen in works such as *Sketch I for Composition VI* (Fig. 20.4), in free flow of unconscious thought. *Composition VI* and other works of this series underscore the importance of Kandinsky's early Fauvist contacts in their vibrant palette, broad brushstrokes, and dynamic movement, and they also stand as harbingers of a new art unencumbered by referential subject matter.

For Kandinsky, color, line, and shape were subjects in themselves. They were often rendered with a spontaneity born of the psychological process of free association. At this time, free association was also being explored by the founder of psychoanalysis, Sigmund Freud, as a method of mapping the geography of the unconscious mind.

Neue Sachlichkeit (New Objectivity)

As World War I drew to a close and World War II loomed on the horizon, different factions of German Expressionism could be observed. Some artists, such as Max Beckmann (1884–1950), calling themselves the **Neue Sachlichkeit (New Objectivity)**, reacted to the horrors and senselessness of wartime suffering with an art that commented bitterly on the bureaucracy and military with ghastly visions of human torture. Dread occupies every nook and cranny of Figure 20.5, from the amputated and bandaged hands of the man in red stripes to the blinded street musician and maimed harlequin. Are these marionettes from some dark comedy or human puppets locked in a world of manipulation and hopelessness?

CUBISM

The history of art is colored by the tensions of stylistic polarities within given eras, particularly the polarity of an intellectual versus an emotional approach to painting. Fauvism and German Expressionism found their roots in Romanticism and the emotional expressionistic work of Gauguin and van Gogh. The second major art movement of the twentieth century, **Cubism**, can trace its heritage to Neoclassicism and the analytical and intellectual work of Cézanne.

Cubism is an offspring of Cézanne's geometrization of nature and his abandonment of scientific perspective, his rendering of multiple views, and his emphasis on the two-dimensional canvas surface. Picasso, the driving force behind the birth of Cubism, and perhaps the most significant artist of the twentieth century, combined the pictorial methods of Cézanne with

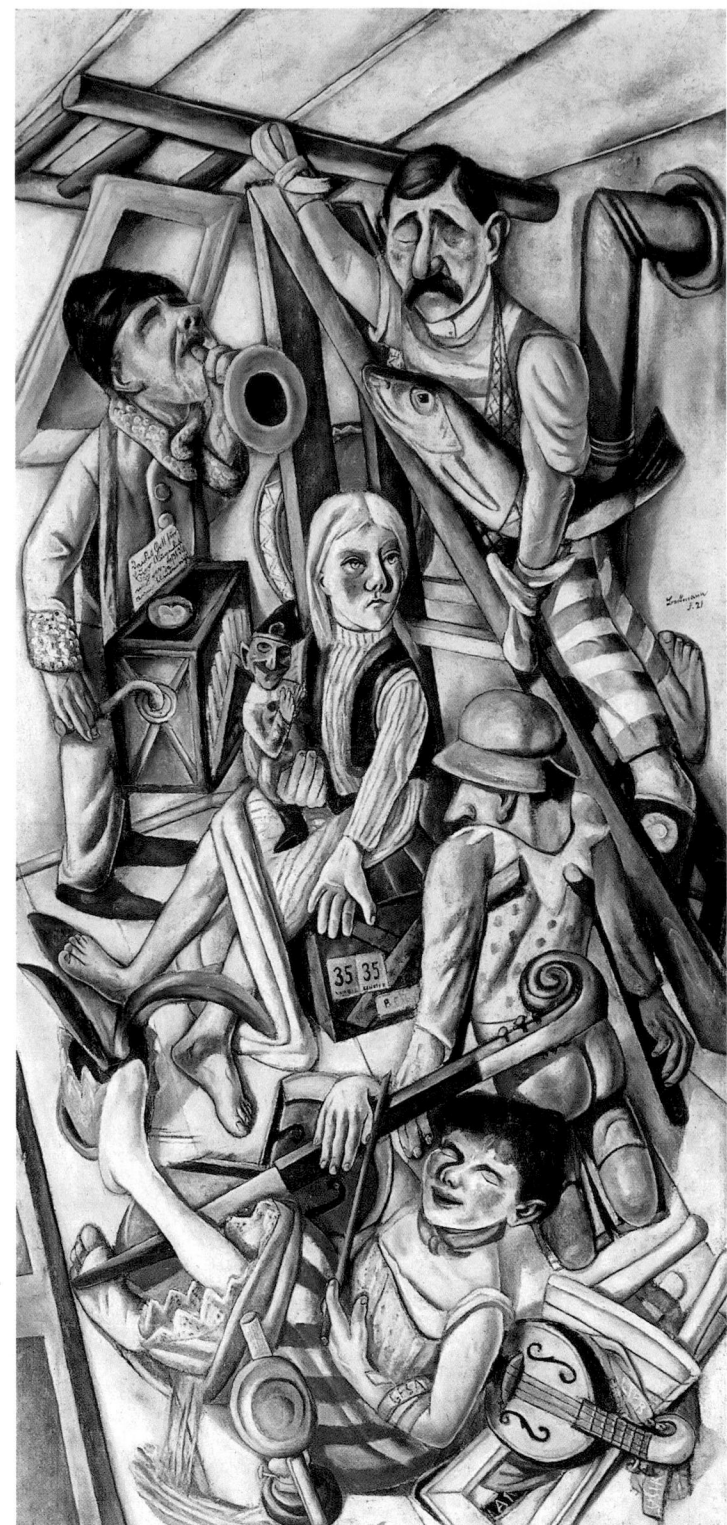

⌃ 20.5 **MAX BECKMANN,** *The Dream* (1921). Oil on canvas, 73⅛" × 35". The Saint Louis Art Museum, Saint Louis, Missouri.

1 ft.

which bold colors, lines, and shapes tear dramatically across the canvas in no preconceived fashion. The pictorial elements flow freely and independently throughout the painting, reflecting, Kandinsky believed, the

Cubism is like standing at a certain point on a mountain and looking around. If you go higher, things will look different; if you go lower, again they will look different. It is a point of view.
—JACQUES LIPCHITZ

I paint objects as I think them, not as I see them.
—PABLO PICASSO

formal elements from native African, Oceanic, and Iberian sculpture.

PABLO PICASSO   Pablo Ruiz y Picasso (1881–1973) was born in Spain, the son of an art teacher. As an adolescent, he enrolled in the Barcelona Academy of Art, where he quickly mastered the illusionistic techniques of the realistic Academic style. By the age of 19, Picasso was off to Paris, where he remained for more than forty years—introducing, influencing, or reflecting the many styles of modern French art.

Picasso's first major artistic phase has been called his Blue Period. Spanning the years 1901 to 1904, this work is characterized by an overall blue tonality, a distortion of the human body through elongation reminiscent of El Greco and Toulouse-Lautrec, and melancholy subjects consisting of poor and downtrodden individuals engaged in menial tasks or isolated in their loneliness. *The Old Guitarist* (Fig. 20.6) is but one of these haunting images. A contorted, white-haired man sits hunched over a guitar, consumed by the tones that emanate from what appears to be his only possession. The eyes are sunken in the skeletal head, and the bones and tendons of his hungry frame protrude. We are struck by the ordinariness of poverty, from the unfurnished room and barren window view (or is he on the curb outside?) to the uneventfulness of his activity and the insignificance of his plight. The monochromatic blue palette creates an unrelenting, somber mood. Tones of blue eerily echo the ghostlike features of the guitarist.

Picasso's Blue Period was followed by works that were lighter both in palette and in spirit. Subjects from this so-called Rose Period were drawn primarily from circus life and rendered in tones of pink. During this second period, which dates from 1905 to 1908, Picasso was inspired by two very different art styles. He, like many artists, viewed and was strongly influenced by the Cézanne retrospective exhibition held at the Salon d'Automne in 1907. At about that time, Picasso also became aware of the formal properties of ethnographic art from Africa, Oceania, and Iberia, which he viewed at the Musée de l'Homme. These two art forms, which at first glance might appear dissimilar, had in common a fragmentation, distortion, and abstraction of form that were

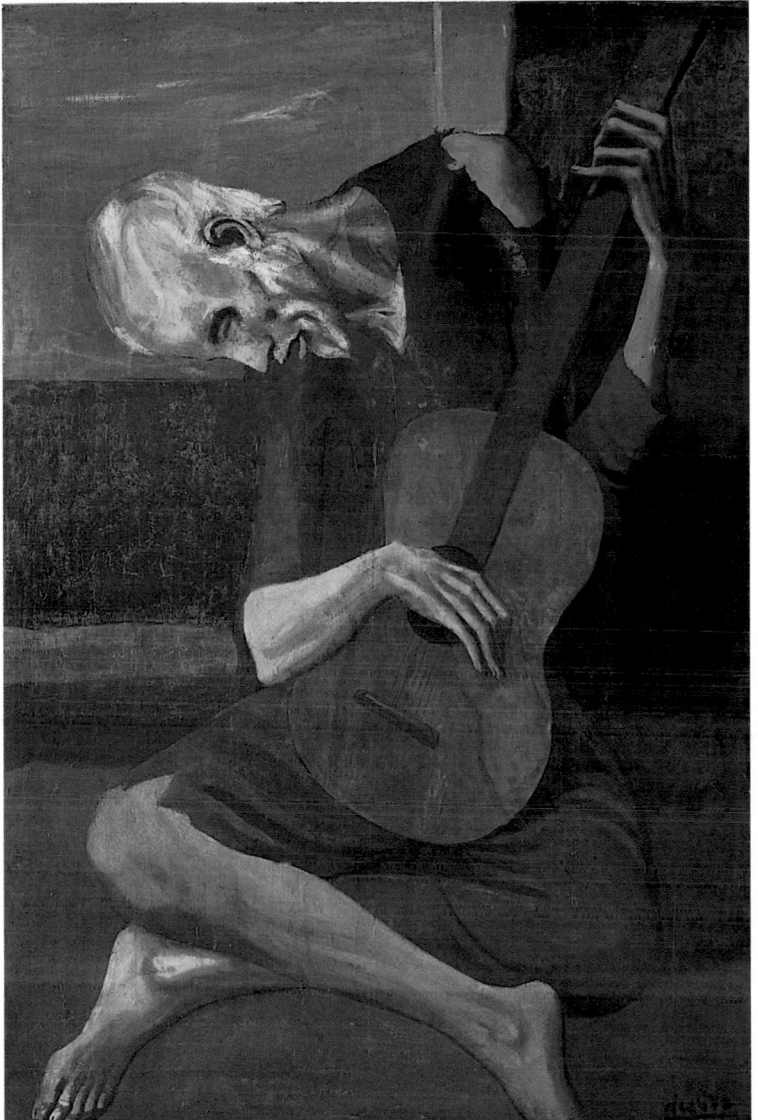

▲ 20.6 **PABLO PICASSO,** *The Old Guitarist* (1903). Oil on canvas, 47¾" × 32½. The Art Institute of Chicago, Chicago, Illinois.

1 ft.

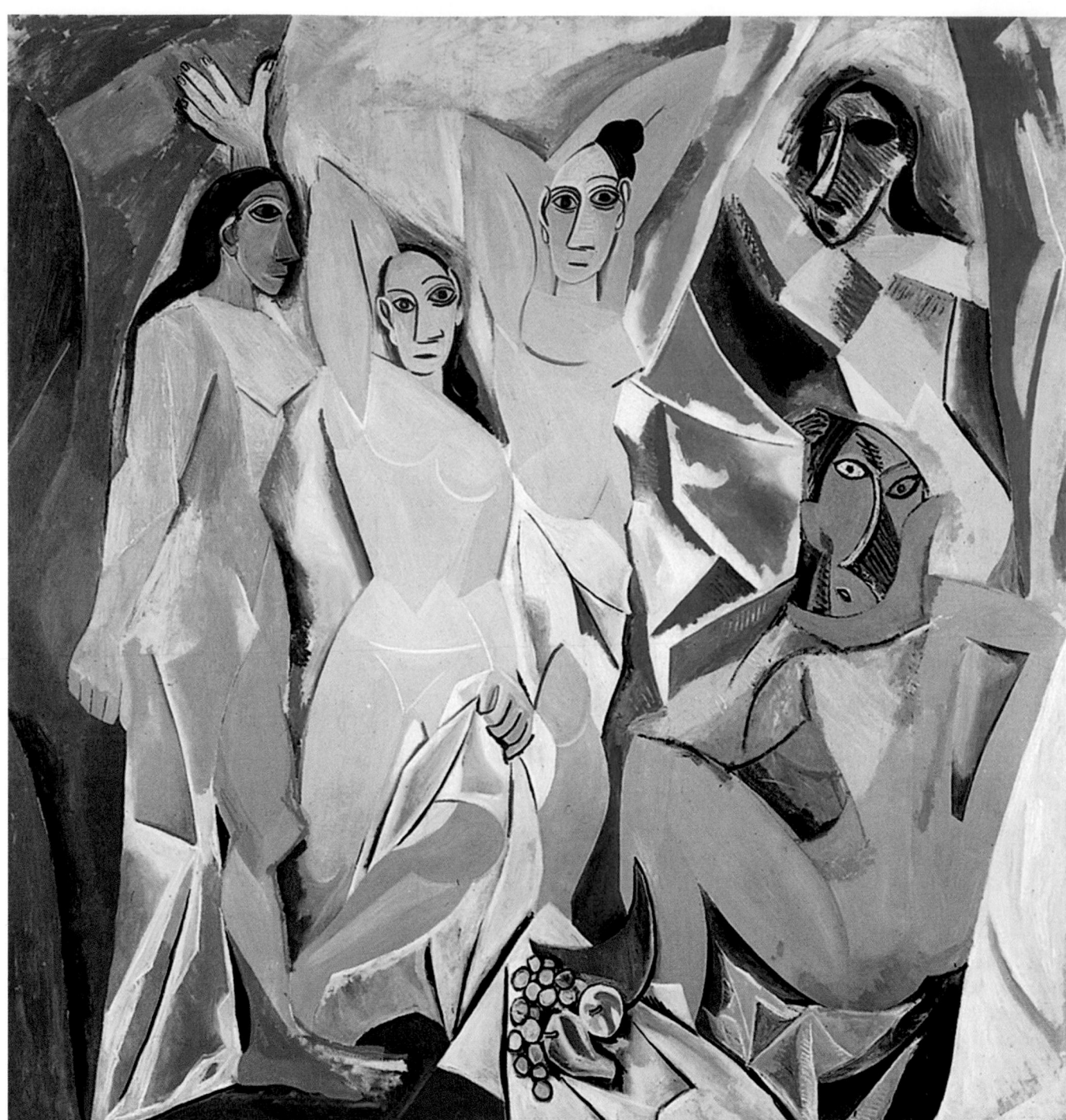

1 ft.

▲ **20.7** **PABLO PICASSO,** *Les Demoiselles d'Avignon* (1907). Oil on canvas, 8' × 7'8". The Museum of Modern Art, New York, New York.

adopted by Picasso in works such as *Les Demoiselles d'Avignon* (Fig. 20.7).

This startling, innovative work, still primarily pink in tone, depicts five women from Barcelona's red-light district. They line up for selection by a possible suitor who stands, as it were, in the position of the spectator. The faces of three of the women are primitive masks. The facial features of the other two have been radically simplified by combining frontal and profile views.

The thick-lidded eyes stare stage front, calling to mind some of the Mesopotamian votive sculptures we saw in Chapter 14.

The bodies of the women are fractured into geometric forms and set before a background of similarly splintered drapery. In treating the background and the foreground imagery in the same manner, Picasso collapses the space between the planes and asserts the two-dimensionality of the canvas surface in the manner of Cézanne. In some

CONNECTIONS In the early years of the twentieth century, Picasso saw an exhibition of the native art of African peoples in Paris. It would have a lasting impression on his art. Compare the facial features of Picasso's *Les Demoiselles d'Avignon* with those of an African mask like the ones he may have seen in Paris (Fig. 20.8). What lines and shapes has Picasso adopted? What other conventions or stylizations of African art has he used?

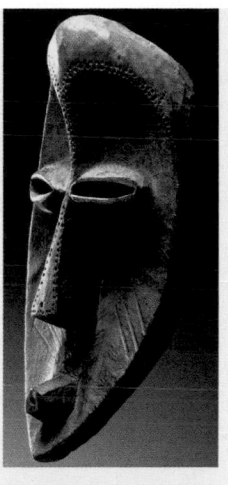

∧ 20.8 **Mask, Etumbi region, Republic of Congo.** Wood, 14" high.

the most basic reality involved consolidating optical vignettes instead of reproducing fixed images with photographic accuracy.

GEORGES BRAQUE During the analytic phase of Cubism, which spanned the years from 1909 to 1912, the works of Picasso and Braque were very similar. The early work of Georges Braque (1882–1963) graduated from Impressionism to Fauvism to more structural compositions based on Cézanne. He met Picasso in 1907, and from then until about 1914, the artists worked together toward the same artistic goals.

The theory of Analytic Cubism reached the peak of its expression in 1911 in works such as Braque's *The Portuguese* (Fig. 20.9). Numerous planes intersect and congregate at the center of the canvas to form a barely

radical passages, such as the right leg of the leftmost figure, the limb takes on the qualities of drapery, masking the distinction between figure and ground. The extreme faceting of form, the use of multiple views, and the collapsing of space in *Les Demoiselles* together provided the springboard for **Analytic Cubism**, cofounded with the French painter Georges Braque in about 1910.

Analytic Cubism

The term *Cubism*, like so many others, was coined by a hostile critic. In this case, the critic was responding to the predominance of geometrical forms in the works of Picasso and Braque. *Cubism* is a limited term in that it does not adequately describe the appearance of Cubist paintings, and it minimizes the intensity with which Cubist artists analyzed their subject matter. It ignores their most significant contribution—a new treatment of pictorial space that hinged upon the rendering of objects from multiple and radically different views.

The Cubist treatment of space differed significantly from that in use since the Renaissance. Instead of presenting an object from a single view, assumed to have been the complete view, the Cubists, like Cézanne, realized that our visual comprehension of objects consists of many views that we perceive almost at once. They tried to render this visual "information gathering" in their compositions. In their dissection and reconstruction of imagery, they reassessed the notion that painting should reproduce the appearance of reality. Now the very reality of appearances was being questioned. To Cubists,

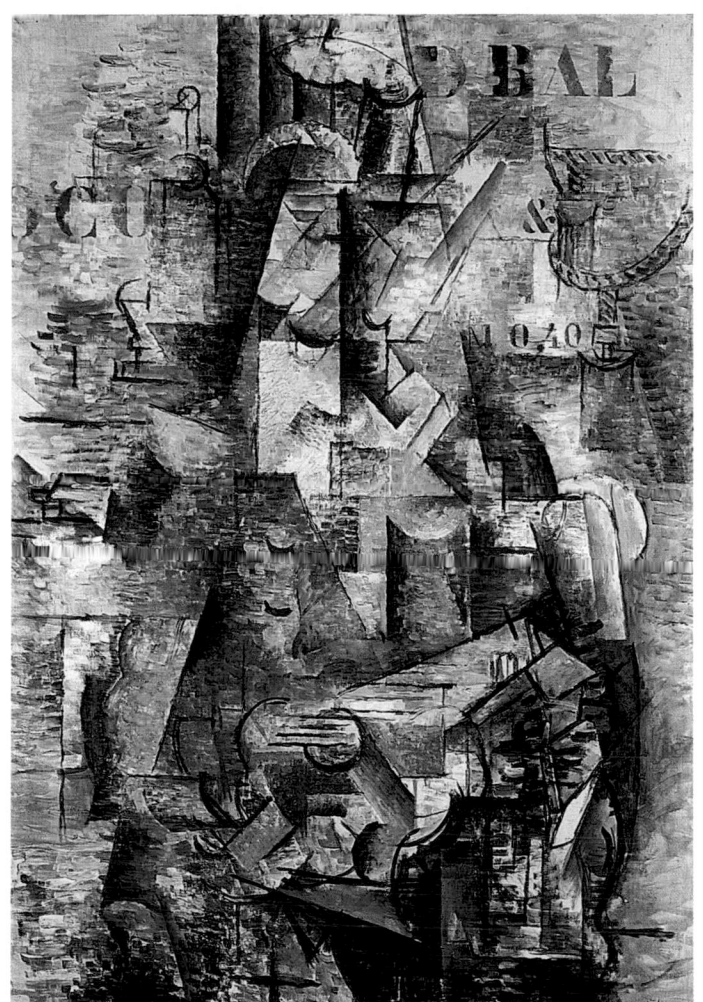

1 ft.

∧ 20.9 **GEORGES BRAQUE,** *The Portuguese* (1911). Oil on canvas, 45½" × 31½". Oeffentliche Kunstsammlung, Kunstmuseum, Basel, Switzerland.

Synthetic Cubism

Picasso and Braque did not stop with the inclusion of precisely printed words and numbers in their works. They began to add characters cut from newspapers and magazines, other pieces of paper, and found objects such as labels from wine bottles, calling cards, theater tickets—even swatches of wallpaper and bits of rope. These items were pasted directly onto the canvas in a technique Picasso and Braque called *papier collé*—what we know as **collage**. The use of collage marked the beginning of the synthetic phase of Cubism.

Some **Synthetic Cubist** compositions, such as Picasso's *The Bottle of Suze* (Fig. 20.10), are constructed entirely of found elements. In this work, newspaper clippings and opaque pieces of paper function as the shifting planes that hover around the aperitif label and define the bottle and glass. These planes are held together by a sparse linear structure much in the manner of Analytic Cubist works. In contrast to Analytic Cubism, however, the emphasis is on the form of the object and on constructing instead of disintegrating that form. Color reentered the compositions, and much emphasis was placed on texture, design, and movement.

After World War I, Picasso and Braque no longer worked together, and their styles, although often reflective of the Cubist experience they shared, came to differ markedly. Braque, who was severely wounded during the war, went on to create more delicate and lyrical still-life compositions, abandoning the austerity of the early phase of Cubism. Although many of Picasso's later works carried forward the Synthetic Cubist idiom, his artistic genius and versatility became evident after 1920, when he began to move in radically different directions. These new works were rendered in Classical, Expressionist, and Surrealist styles.

When civil war gripped Spain, Picasso protested its brutality and inhumanity through highly emotional works such as *Guernica* (Fig. 20.11). This mammoth mural, painted for the Spanish Pavilion of the Paris International Exposition of 1937, broadcast to the world the carnage of the German bombing of civilians in the Basque town of Guernica. The painting captures the event in gruesome details, such as the frenzied cry of one woman trapped in rubble and fire and the pale fright of another woman who tries in vain to flee the conflagration. A terrorized horse rears over a dismembered body, while an anguished mother embraces her dead child and wails futilely. Innocent lives are shattered into Cubist planes that rush and intersect at myriad angles, distorting and fracturing the imagery. Confining himself to a palette of harsh blacks, grays, and whites, Picasso expressed, in his words, the "brutality and darkness" of the age.

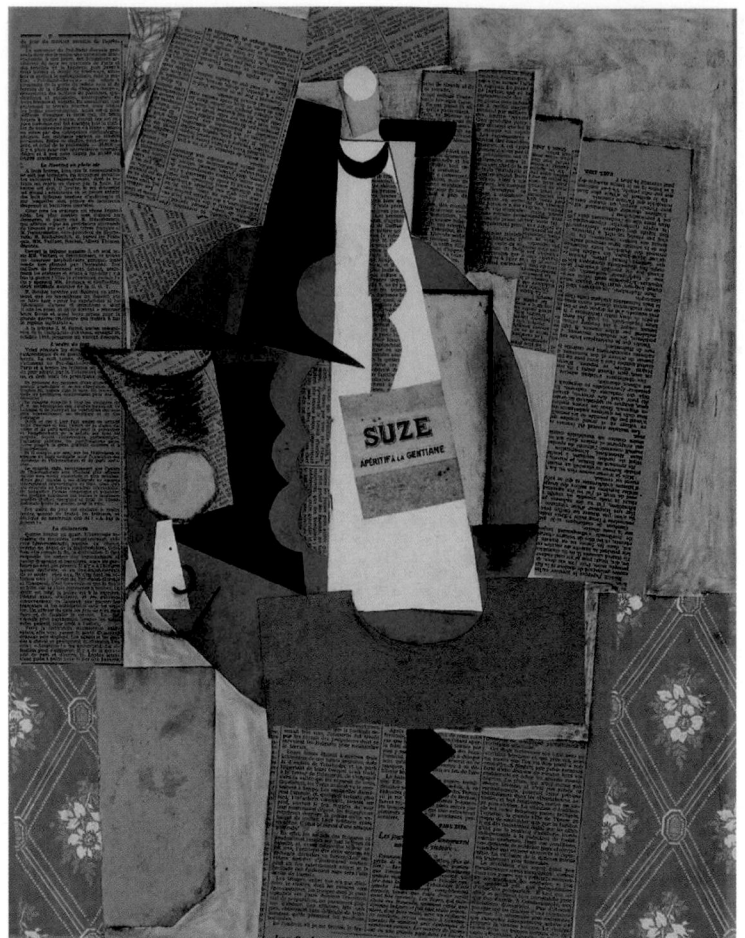

1 ft.

∧ 20.10 **PABLO PICASSO**, *La bouteille de Suze (Bottle of Suze)* (1912). Pasted papers, gouache, and charcoal; 25¾ × 19¾". Mildred Lane Kemper Art Museum, Washington University in St. Louis, Missouri. University purchase, Kende Sale Fund, 1946.

perceptible triangular human figure, which is alternately constructed from and dissolved into the background. There are only a few concrete signs of its substance: dropped eyelids, a mustache, the circular opening of a stringed instrument. The multifaceted, abstracted form appears to shift position before our eyes, simulating the time lapse that would occur in the visual assimilation of multiple views. The structural lines—sometimes called the *Cubist grid*—that define and fragment the figure are thick and dark. They contrast with the delicately modeled short, choppy brushstrokes of the remainder of the composition. The monochromatic palette, chosen not to interfere with the exploration of form, consists of browns, tans, and ochers.

Although the paintings of Picasso and Braque were almost identical at this time, Braque first began to insert words and numbers and to use *trompe l'oeil* effects in portions of his Analytic Cubist compositions. These realistic elements contrasted sharply with the abstraction of the major figures and reintroduced the nagging question, "What is reality and what is illusion in painting?"

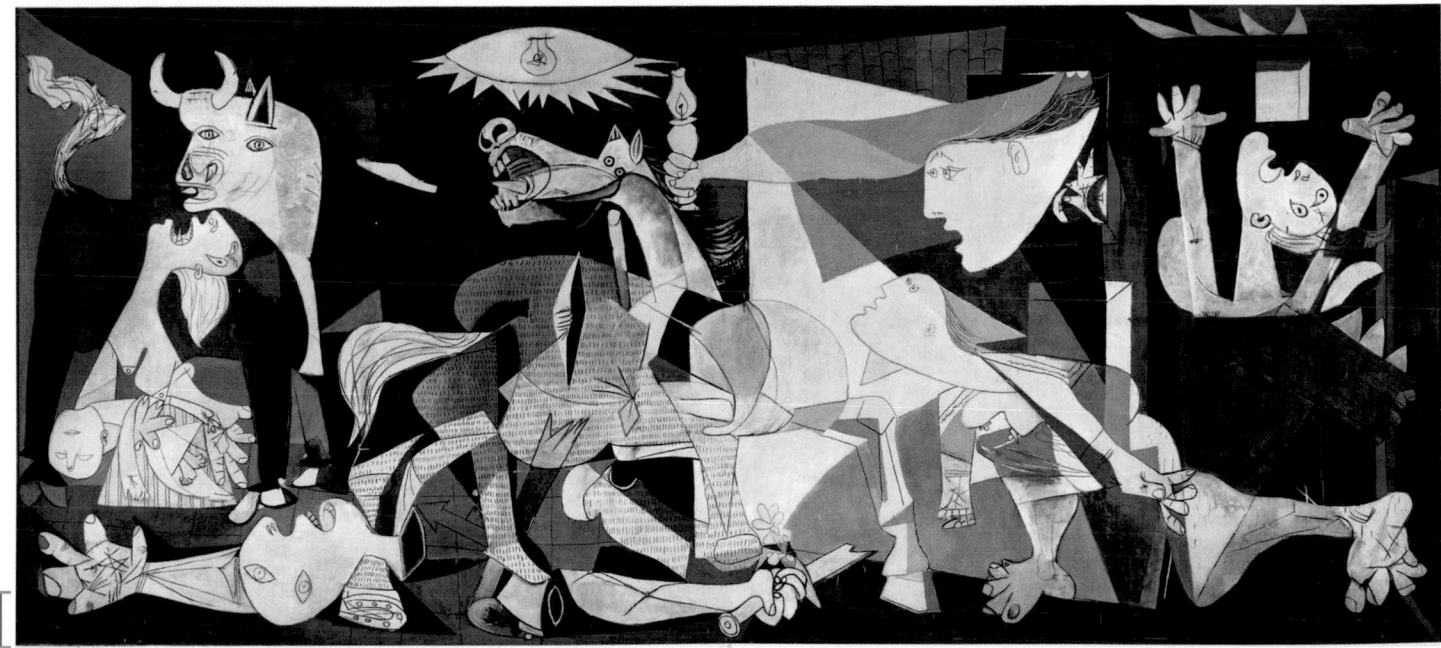

^ **20.11 PABLO PICASSO,** *Guernica* (1937). Oil on canvas, 11'6" × 25'8". Museo Nacional Centro de Arte Reina Sofía, Madrid, Spain.

Cubist Sculpture

Cubism was born as a two-dimensional art form cubist artists attempted to render on canvas the manifold aspects of their subjects as if they were walking around three-dimensional forms and recording every angle. The attempt was successful, in part, because they recorded these views with intersecting planes that allowed viewers to perceive the many sides of the figure.

JACQUES LIPCHITZ Because cubist artists were trying to communicate all of the visual information available about a particular form, they were handicapped, so to speak, by the two-dimensional surface. In some ways, the medium of sculpture was more natural to Cubism, because a viewer could actually walk around a figure to assimilate its many facets. The "transparent" planes that provided a sense of intrigue in Analytical Cubist paintings were often translated as flat solids, as in Jacques Lipchitz's (1891–1964) *Still Life with Musical Instruments* (Fig. 20.12).

ALEXANDER ARCHIPENKO One of the innovations in Cubist sculpture was the three-dimensional interpenetration of Cubist planes, as implied in Lipchitz's relief. Another was the use of void space as solid form, as seen in *Walking Woman* (Fig. 20.13) by Alexander Archipenko (1887–1964). True to Cubist principles, the figure

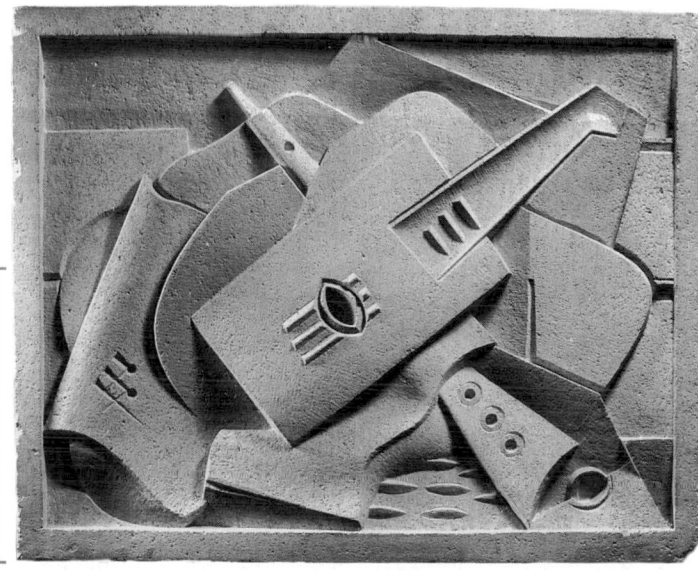

^ **20.12 JACQUES LIPCHITZ,** *Still Life with Musical Instruments* (1918). Stone relief, 22½" × 28". Marlborough Gallery, New York, New York.

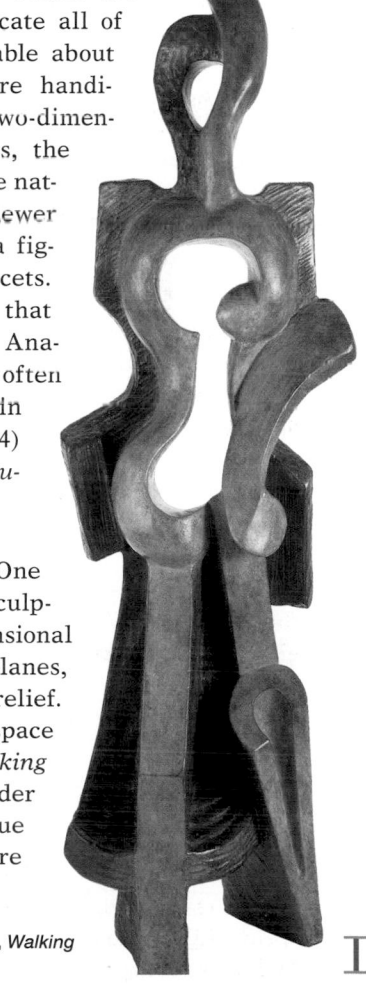

> **20.13 ALEXANDER ARCHIPENKO,** *Walking Woman* (1912). Bronze, 26½" high.

> Everything moves, everything runs, everything turns swiftly. The figure in front of us never is still, but ceaselessly appears and disappears. Owing to the persistence of images on the retina, objects in motion are multiplied, distorted, following one another like waves through space. Thus a galloping horse has not four legs; it has twenty.
>
> —UMBERTO BOCCIONI

is fragmented; the contours are broken and dislocated. But what is new here are the open spaces of the torso and head, now as much a part of the whole as the solid forms of the composition. Although there is a good degree of abstract simplification in the figure, the overall impression of the forms prompts recognition of the humanity of the subject.

FUTURISM

Several years after the advent of Cubism, a new movement sprang up in Italy under the leadership of poet Filippo Marinetti (1876–1944). **Futurism** was introduced angrily by Marinetti in a 1909 manifesto that called for an art of "violence, energy, and boldness" free from the "tyranny of . . . harmony and good taste."[2] In theory, Futurist painting and sculpture were to glorify the life of today, "unceasingly and violently transformed by victorious science." In practice, many of the works owed much to Cubism.

UMBERTO BOCCIONI An oft-repeated word in Futurist credo is **dynamism**, defined as the theory that force or energy is the basic principle of all phenomena. The principle of dynamism is illustrated in Umberto Boccioni's (1882–1916) *Dynamism of a Soccer Player*. Irregular, agitated lines communicate the energy of movement. The Futurist obsession with illustrating images in perpetual motion also found a perfect outlet in sculpture. In works such as *Unique Forms of Continuity in Space* (Fig. 20.14), Boccioni, whose forte was sculpture, sought to convey the elusive surging energy that blurs an image in motion, leaving but an echo of its passage. Although it retains an overall figural silhouette, the sculpture is devoid of any representational details. The flamelike

< 20.14 UMBERTO BOCCIONI, *Unique Forms of Continuity in Space* (1913). Bronze (cast 1931), 43⅞" × 34⅞ × 15¾". The Museum of Modern Art, New York, New York.

curving surfaces of the striding figure do not exist to define movement; instead, they are a consequence of it.

GIACOMO BALLA The Futurists also suggested that their subjects were less important than the portrayal of the "dynamic sensation" of the subjects. This declaration manifests itself fully in Giacomo Balla's (1871–1958) pure Futurist painting, *Street Light* (Fig. 20.15). The light of the lamp pierces the darkness in reverberating circles; V-shaped brushstrokes simultaneously fan outward from the source and point toward it, creating a sense of constant movement. The palette consists of complementary colors that forbid the eye to rest. All is movement; all is sensation.

Cubist and Futurist works of art, regardless of how abstract they might appear, always contain vestiges of representation, whether they be unobtrusive details like an eyelid or mustache, or an object's recognizable contours. Yet with Cubism, the seeds of abstraction were planted. It was just a matter of time until they would find fruition in artists who, like Kandinsky, would seek pure form unencumbered by referential subject matter.

EARLY-TWENTIETH-CENTURY ABSTRACTION IN THE UNITED STATES

The Fauvists and German Expressionists had an impact on art in the United States as well as Europe. Although the years before the First World War in America were

[2] F. T. Marinetti, "The Foundation and Manifesto of Futurism," in *Theories of Modern Art*, ed. Herschel B. Chipp, 284–88 (Berkeley: University of California Press, 1968).

> I said to myself—I'll paint what I see—what the flower is to me but I'll paint it big and they will be surprised into taking the time to look at it—I will make even busy New Yorkers take time to see what I see of flowers.
>
> —GEORGIA O'KEEFFE

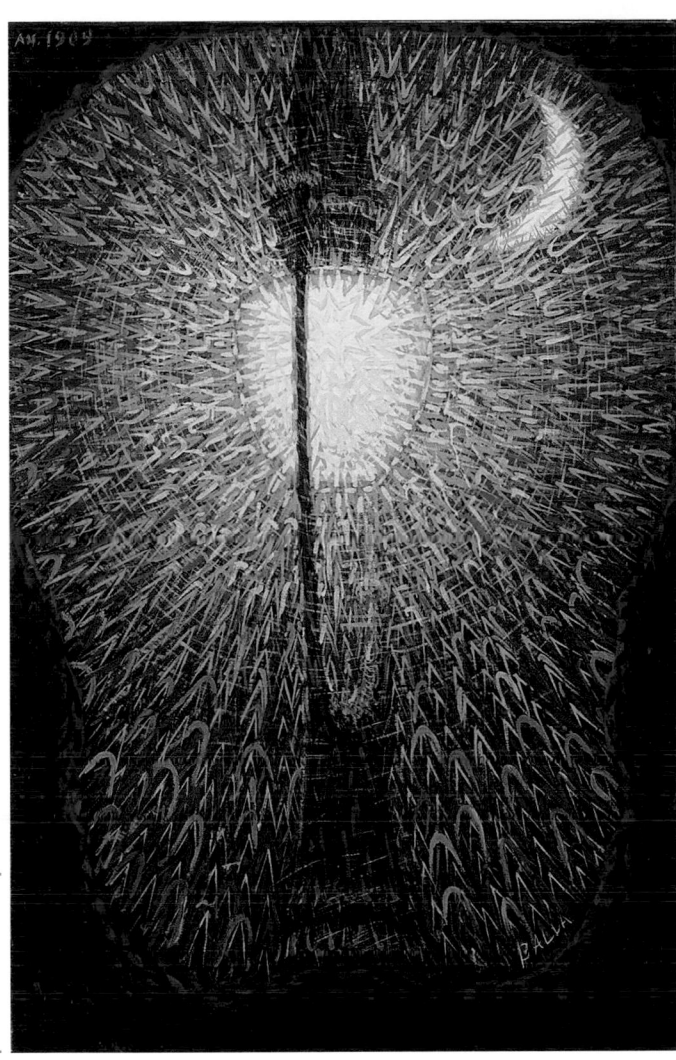

▲ 20.15 GIACOMO BALLA, *Street Light* (1909). Oil on canvas, 68¾" × 45¼". The Museum of Modern Art, New York, New York.

Georgia O'Keeffe was among the artists supported by Stieglitz.

GEORGIA O'KEEFFE Throughout her long career, Georgia O'Keeffe (1887–1986) painted many subjects, from flowers to city buildings to the skulls of animals baked white by the sun of the desert Southwest. In each case, she captured the essence of her subjects by simplifying their forms. In 1924, the year O'Keeffe married Stieglitz, she began to paint enlarged flower pictures such as *White Iris* (Fig. 20.16). In these paintings, she magnified and abstracted the details of her botanical subjects, so that often a large canvas was filled with but a fragment of the intersection of petals. These flowers have a yearning, reaching, organic quality, and her botany seems to function as a metaphor for

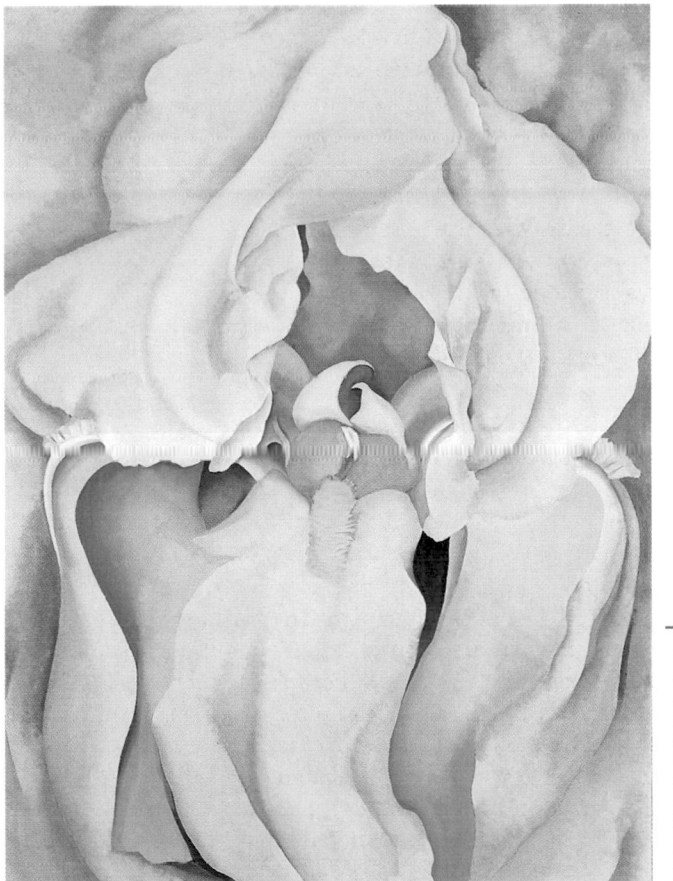

▲ 20.16 GEORGIA O'KEEFFE, *White Iris* (1930). Oil on canvas, 40" × 30". Virginia Museum of Fine Arts, Richmond, Virginia.

marked by an adherence to Realism and subjects from everyday rural and urban life, a strong interest in European Modernism was brewing.

291 Gallery

The American photographer Alfred Stieglitz propounded and supported the development of abstract art in the United States by exhibiting modern European works, along with those of American artists who were influenced by the Parisian avant-garde—Picasso, Matisse, and others—in his 291 gallery (at 291 Fifth Avenue in New York).

The Armory Show

Between 1908 and 1917, Stieglitz brought to 291—and thus to New York City—European Modernists, the likes of Toulouse-Lautrec, Cézanne, Matisse, Braque, and Brancusi. In 1913, the sensational Armory Show—the International Exhibition of Modern Art held at the 69th Regiment Armory in New York City—assembled works by leading American artists and an impressive array of Europeans ranging from Goya and Delacroix to Manet and the Impressionists; from van Gogh and Gauguin to Picasso and Kandinsky. There were many more American than European works exhibited, but the latter dominated the show—raising the artistic consciousness of the Americans while, at the same time, raising some eyebrows. The most scandalous of the Parisian works, Marcel Duchamp's *Nude Descending a Staircase #2* (see Fig. 20.24), was dismissed as a "pile of kindling wood." But the message to American artists was clear: Europe was the center of the art world—for now.

CHARLES DEMUTH In the years following the Armory Show, American artists explored abstraction to new heights, finding ways to maintain a solid sense of subject matter in combination with geometric fragmentation and simplification. Charles Demuth (1883–1935) was one of a group of artists called "Cubo-Realists" or "Precisionists" who overlaid stylistic elements from Cubism and Futurism on authentic American imagery. *My Egypt* (Fig. 20.17) is a precise rendition of a grain elevator in Demuth's hometown of Lancaster, Pennsylvania. Diagonal lines—contradictory rays of light and shadow—sweep across the solid surfaces and lessen the intensity of the stonelike appearance of the masses. The shapes in *My Egypt* are reminiscent of limestone monoliths that form the gateways to ancient temple complexes such as that at Karnak in Egypt. The viewer cannot help being drawn to Demuth's title, which acknowledges the association of the architectural forms and, at the same time, asserts a sense of American pride and history in the possessive

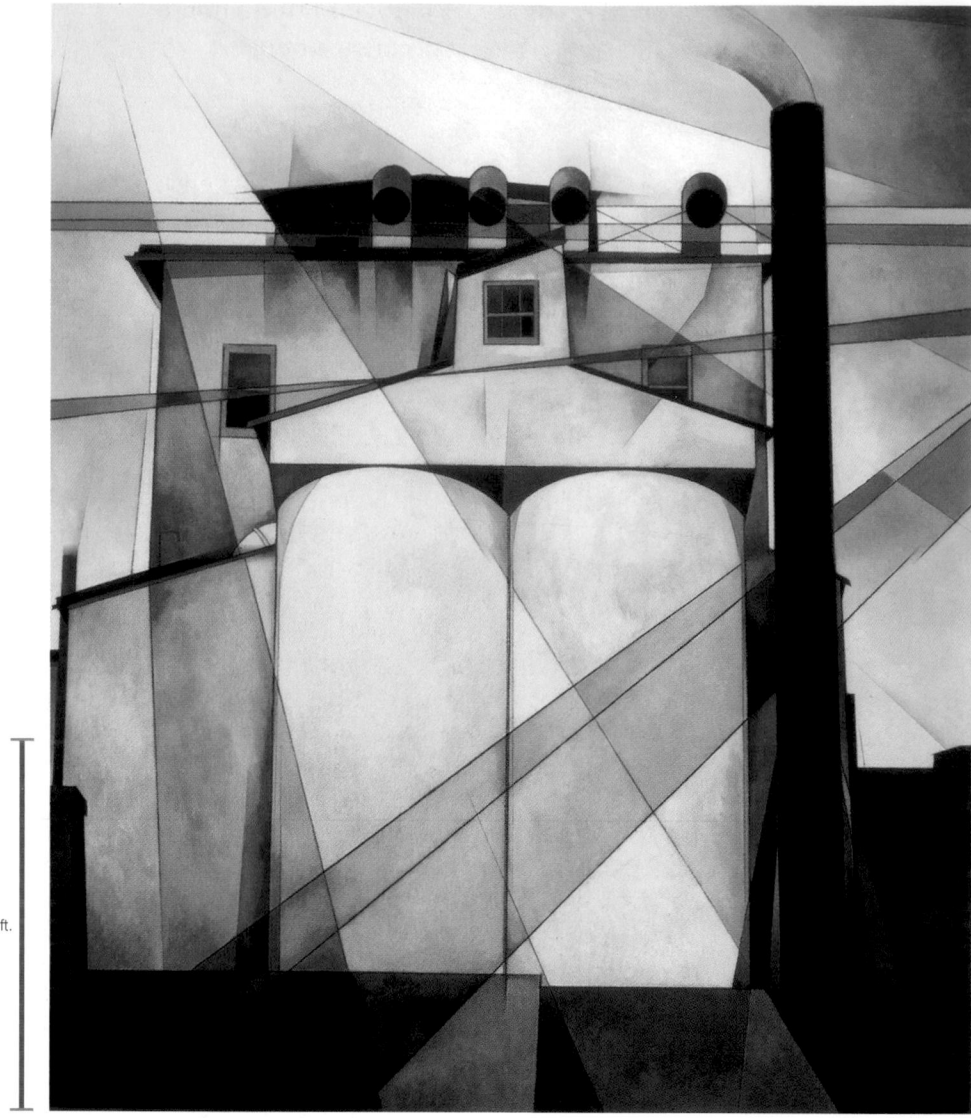

1 ft.

▲ **20.17 CHARLES DEMUTH,** *My Egypt* (1927). Oil on composition board, 35¾" × 30". Whitney Museum of American Art, New York, New York.

zoology. That is, her plants are animistic; they seem to grow because of will, not merely because of the blind interactions of the unfolding of the genetic code with water, sun, and minerals.

And although O'Keeffe denied any attempt to portray sexual imagery in these flowers (those who saw it, she said, were speaking about themselves and not her), the edges of the petals, in their folds and convolutions, are frequently reminiscent of parts of the female body. The sense of will and reaching renders these petals active rather than passive in their implied sexuality, so they seem symbolically to express a feminist polemic. This characteristic might be one of the reasons that O'Keeffe was "invited" to Judy Chicago's *Dinner Party* (see Fig. 21.35).

> All painting is composed of line and color. Line and color are the essence of painting.
> Hence they must be freed from their bondage to the imitation of nature
> and allowed to exist for themselves.
> —PIET MONDRIAN

adjective *My*. It seems to reflect the desire on the part of the American artist to be conversant and current with European style while maintaining a bit of chauvinism about subjects that have meaning to their own time and place.

EARLY-TWENTIETH-CENTURY ABSTRACTION IN EUROPE

The second decade of the twentieth century witnessed the rise of many dynamic schools of art in Europe. Two of these—**Constructivism** and **De Stijl**—were dedicated to

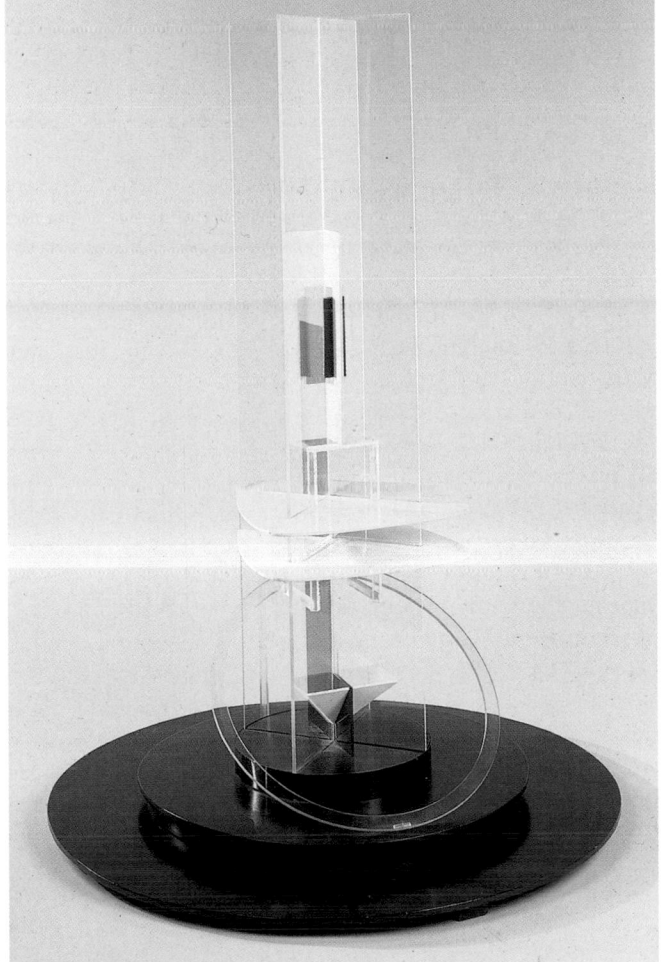

▲ 20.18 **NAUM GABO,** *Column* (c. 1923). Perspex, wood, metal, glass; 41½" × 29" × 29". The Solomon R. Guggenheim Museum, New York, New York.

1 ft.

pure abstraction, or nonobjective art. Nonobjective art differs from the abstraction of Cubism or Futurism in its total lack of representational elements. It does not use nature or visual reality as a point of departure; it has no subject other than that of the forms, colors, and lines that compose it. In nonobjective art, the earlier experiments in abstracting images by Cézanne and then by the Cubists reached their logical conclusion. Kandinsky is recognized as the first painter of pure abstraction, although several artists were creating nonobjective works at about the same time.

Whereas nonobjective painting was the logical outgrowth of Analytic Cubism, Cubist collage gave rise to Constructivist sculpture. Born in Russia, Constructivism challenged the traditional sculptural techniques of carving and casting that emphasized mass rather than space. De Stijl (in English, "the style") was born in Holland. Followers of the movement, such as Theo van Doesburg and Piet Mondrian, reduced visual composition to form and color.

NAUM GABO Naum Gabo (1890–1977), a Constructivist sculptor, challenged the ascendance of mass over space by creating works in which intersecting planes of metal, glass, plastic, or wood defined space. The nonobjective *Column* (Fig. 20.18) exudes a high-tech feeling. It is somewhat reminiscent of magnetic fields, of things plugged in, or even of the skyscrapers that are being imagined as this page is being written—a theme that would be revisited by the **Deconstructivist architects** toward the end of the twentieth century and the early years of the twenty-first century. But the subject of the work consists of the constructed forms themselves. The column is suggested by intersecting planes that interact with the surrounding space; it does not envelop space, and—true to the Constructivist aesthetic—it denies mass and weight. The beauty of *Column* is found in the purity of its elements and in the contrasts between horizontal and vertical elements and translucent and opaque elements.

PIET MONDRIAN Influenced by Vincent van Gogh, fellow Dutch painter Piet Mondrian (1872–1944) began his career as a painter of Impressionistic landscapes. In 1910, he went to Paris and was immediately drawn to the geometricism of Cubism. During the war years, when he was back in Holland, his studies of Cubist theory led him to reduce his forms to lines and planes and his palette to the primary colors and black and white. These limitations, Mondrian believed, permitted a more universally comprehensible art. Mondrian

1 in.

▲ 20.19 PIET MONDRIAN, *Composition II, with Red, Blue, Black and Yellow* (1929). Oil on canvas, 45 × 45 cm. National Museum, Belgrade, Yugoslavia.

developed his own theories of painting that are readily apparent in works such as *Composition No. II with Red, Blue, Black, and Yellow* (Fig. 20.19):

> Painting occupies a plane surface. The plane surface is integral with the physical and psychological being of the painting. Hence the plane surface must be respected, must be allowed to declare itself, must not be falsified by imitations of volume. Painting must be as flat as the surface it is painted on.[3]

Mondrian's obsessive respect for the two-dimensionality of the canvas surface is the culmination of the integration of figure and ground begun with the planar recession of Jacques-Louis David (see Fig. 19.1). No longer was it necessary to tilt tabletops or render figure and ground with the same brushstrokes and palette to accomplish this task. Canvas and painting, figure and ground were one.

CONSTANTIN BRANCUSI The universality sought by Mondrian through extreme simplification can also be seen in the sculpture of Constantin Brancusi (1876–1957). Yet unlike Mondrian's, Brancusi's works, however abstract they appear, are rooted in the figure. Brancusi was born in Romania thirteen years after the

---

[3] Robert Goldwater and Marco Treves, eds., *Artists on Art* (New York: Pantheon Books, 1972), 426.

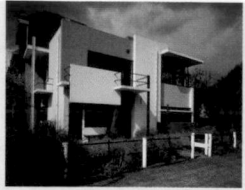

CONNECTIONS If Mondrian's views had been a theory of architecture, perhaps they would have found expression in works such as Gerrit Rietveld's Schröder House, which was built early in the twentieth century but continues to inspire architects today. Here there is an almost literal translation of geometry and color to architecture. Broad expanses of white concrete intersect to define the strictly rectilinear dwelling, or appear to float in superimposed planes. As in a Mondrian painting, these planes are accented by black verticals and horizontals in supporting posts or window mullions. The surfaces are unadorned, like the color fields of a Mondrian.

▲ Gerrit Rietveld's Schröder House (Fig. 2.18)

Salon des Réfusés. After an apprenticeship as a cabinetmaker and studies at the Bucharest Academy of Fine Arts, he traveled to Paris to enroll in the famous École des Beaux-Arts. In 1907, Brancusi exhibited at the Salon d'Automne, leaving favorable impressions of his work.

Brancusi's work, heavily indebted to Rodin at this point, grew in a radically different direction. As early as 1909, he reduced the human head—a favorite theme he would draw upon for years—to an egg-shaped form with sparse indications of facial features. In this, and in other abstractions such as *Bird in Space* (Fig. 20.20), he reached for the essence of the subject by offering the simplest contour that, along with a descriptive title, would fire recognition in the spectator. *Bird in Space* evolved from more representational versions into a refined symbol of the cleanness and solitude of flight.

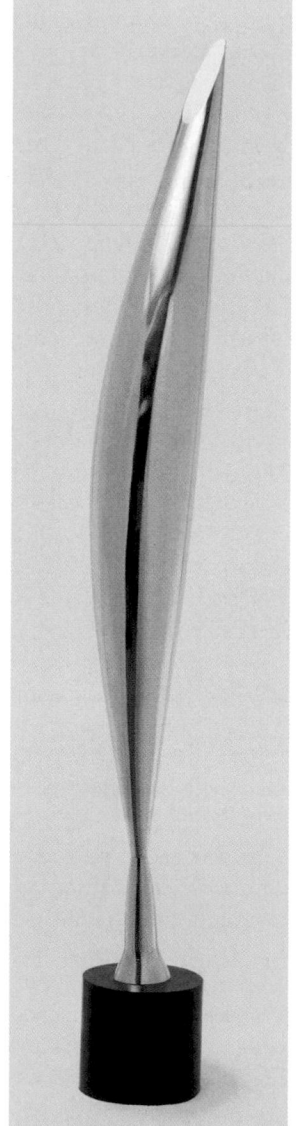

1 ft.

▸ 20.20 CONSTANTIN BRANCUSI, *Bird in Space* (c. 1928). Bronze (unique cast), 54" high. Philadelphia Museum of Art, Philadelphia, Pennsylvania.

FANTASY

Throughout the history of art, most critics and patrons have seen the accurate representation of visual reality as a noble goal. Those artists who have departed from this goal, who have chosen to depict their personal worlds of dreams or supernatural fantasies, have not had it easy. Before the twentieth century, only isolated examples of what we call **Fantastic art** could be found. The early 1900s, however, saw many artists exploring fanciful imagery and working in styles as varied as their imaginations.

How do we describe Fantastic art? The word *fantastic* derives from the Greek *phantastikos*, meaning "the ability to represent something to the mind" or "to create a mental image." *Fantasy* is further defined as "unreal, odd, seemingly impossible, and strange in appearance." Fantastic art, then, is the representation of incredible images from the artist's mind. At times the images are joyful reminiscences; at times, horrific nightmares. They may be capricious or grotesque.

PAUL KLEE One of the most whimsical yet subtly sardonic of the Fantastic artists is Paul Klee (1879–1940). Although influenced early in his career by nineteenth-century artists such as Goya, who touched upon fantasy, Klee received much of his stylistic inspiration from Cézanne. In 1911, he joined Der Blaue Reiter, where his theories about intuitive approaches to painting, growing abstraction, and love of color were well received.

A certain innocence pervades Klee's idiosyncratic style. After abandoning representational elements in his art, Klee turned to ethnographic and children's art, seeking a universality of expression in their extreme simplicity. Many of his works combine a charming naïveté with wry commentary. *Twittering Machine* (Fig. 20.21), for example, offers a humorous contraption composed of four fantastic birds balanced precariously on a wire attached to a crank. The viewer who is motivated to piece together the possible function of this apparatus might assume that turning the crank would result in the twittering suggested by the title.

In this seemingly innocuous painting, Klee perhaps satirizes contemporary technology, in which machines may sometimes seem to do little more than express the whims and ego of the inventor. But why a machine that twitters? Some have suggested a darker interpretation in which the mechanical birds are traps to lure real birds to a makeshift coffin beneath. Such gruesome doings might in turn symbolize the entrapment of humans by their own existence. In any event, it is evident that Klee's simple, cartoonlike subjects may carry a mysterious and rich iconography.

GIORGIO DE CHIRICO Equally mysterious are the odd juxtapositions of familiar objects found in the works of Giorgio de Chirico (1888–1978). Unlike Klee's figures, de Chirico's are rendered in a realistic manner. De Chirico attempted to make the irrational believable. His subjects are often derived from dreams, in which ordinary objects are found in extraordinary situations. The realistic technique tends to heighten the believability of these events and imparts a certain eeriness characteristic of dreams or nightmares. Part of the intrigue of de Chirico's subjects lies in their ambiguity and in the uncertainty of the outcome. Often we do not know why we dream what we dream. We do not know how the strange juxtapositions occur, nor how the story will evolve. We may now and then "save" ourselves from danger by awakening.

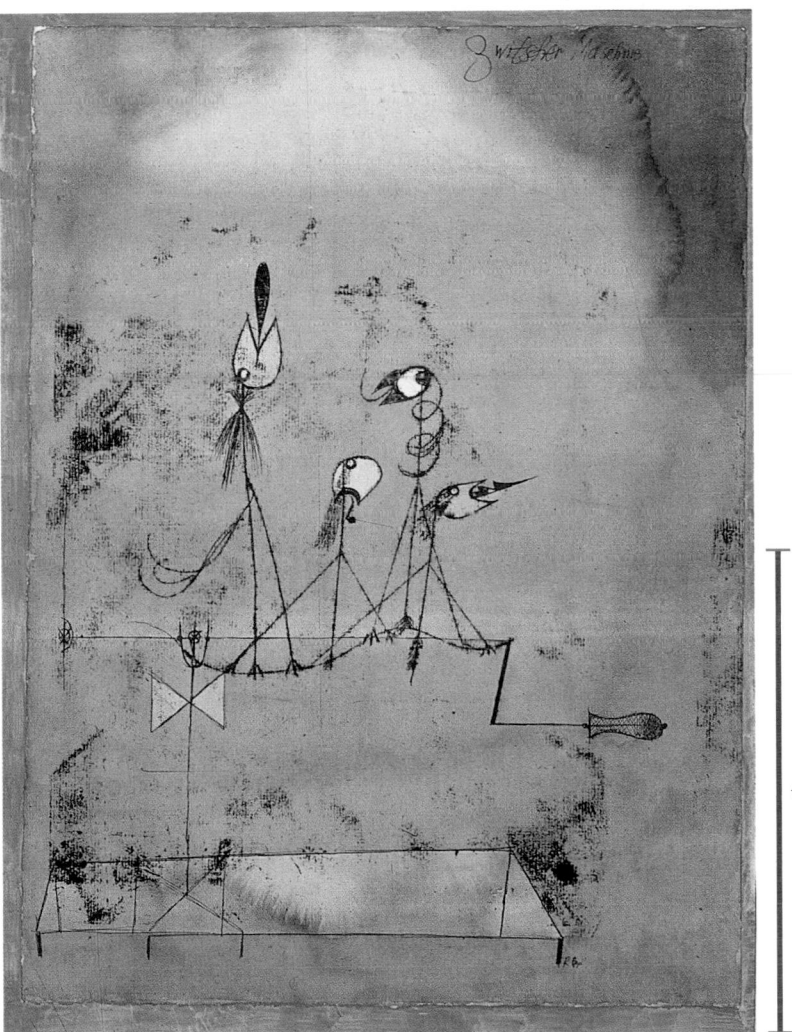

1 ft.

∧ 20.21 PAUL KLEE, *Twittering Machine* (1922). Watercolor, pen and ink; 25¼" × 19". The Museum of Modern Art, New York, New York.

> The most important thing about Dada, it seems to me, is that Dadaists despised what is commonly regarded as art, but put the whole universe on the lofty throne of art.
>
> —JEAN ARP

The intrigues of the dream world are captured by de Chirico in works such as *Piazza d'Italia* (Fig. 20.22). Some of his favorite images—icy arcades, deserted piazzas, a distant locomotive with a suspended puff of smoke rising from the engine car—provide a backdrop for an encounter between two figures at the far end of a diagonal zone of sunlight that connects them to the monumental sculpture resting in the square. We are drawn into a disturbing, dreamlike atmosphere that, in its juxtaposition of familiar shapes with unsettling presences, suggests a certain banality of danger. We perceive an overriding sense of doom for no apparent reason other than that we bring our own fears and superstitions to our interpretation of the painting.

DADA

In 1916, during World War I, an international movement arose that declared itself against art. Responding to the absurdity of war and the insanity of a world that gave rise to it, the Dadaists declared that art—a reflection of this sorry state of affairs—was stupid and must be destroyed. Yet to communicate their outrage, the Dadaists created works of art! This inherent contradiction spelled the

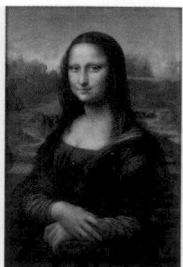

CONNECTIONS If you were asked to close your eyes and think of the most famous work of art in all of history, what would you say? Odds are that the first piece to come up on your memory screen would be none other than the *Mona Lisa*. Her portrait has captivated poets and lyricists, museumgoers, and artists for centuries. Simply put, her face has been everywhere.

⌃ Leonardo's *Mona Lisa* (Fig. 17.17)

eventual demise of their movement. Despite centers in Paris, Berlin, Cologne, Zurich, and New York City, Dada ended with a whimper in 1922.

The name **Dada** was supposedly chosen at random from a dictionary. It is an apt epithet. The nonsense term describes nonsense art—art that is meaningless, absurd, unpredictable. Although it is questionable whether this catchy label was in truth derived at random, the element of chance was important to the Dada art form. Dada poetry, for example, consisted of nonsense verses of random word combinations. Some works of art, such as the Dada collages, were constructed of materials found

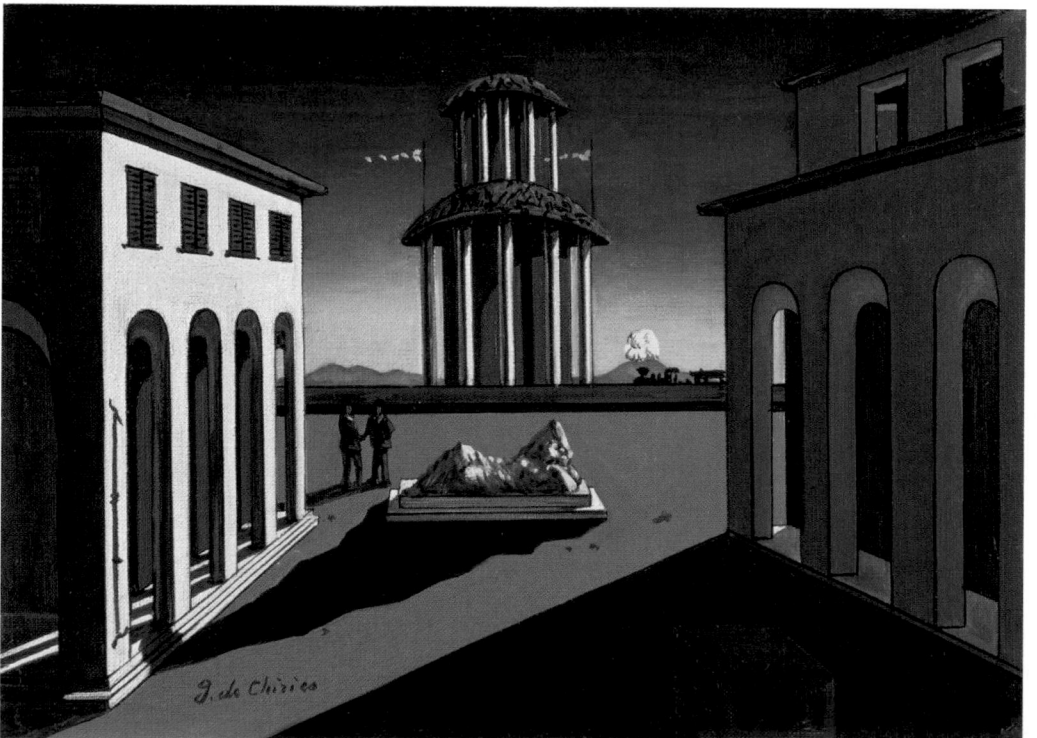

< 20.22 GIORGIO DE CHIRICO, *Piazza d'Italia* (1913). Oil on canvas, 9⅞" × 13⅞". Art Gallery of Ontario, Toronto, Canada.

1 in.

the Dada movement was the notion that the museums of the world are filled with "dead art" that should be "destroyed." Why do you imagine Duchamp would have used the image of the *Mona Lisa* to convey something of this philosophy? Duchamp was certainly a capable enough draftsman to have rendered his own copy of the *Mona Lisa*.

Duchamp's *Nude Descending a Staircase (No. 2)* (Fig. 20.24) reflects the styles of Cubism and Futurism. In effect, the painting simulates the passage of time by creating multiple exposures of a machine-tooled figure walking down a flight of stairs. The overlapping of shapes and the repetition of linear patterns blur the contours of the figure. Even though the *New York Times* art critic

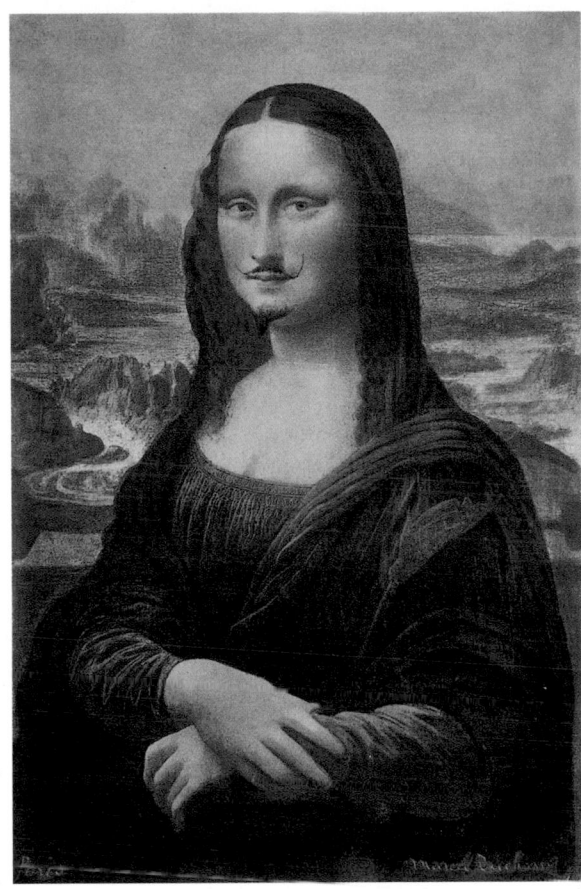

1 in.

▲ 20.23 MARCEL DUCHAMP, *Mona Lisa (L.H.O.O.Q.)* (1919). Rectified readymade; pencil on a reproduction. 7¾" × 4⅞". Philadelphia Museum of Art, Philadelphia, Pennsylvania.

by chance and mounted randomly. Yet however meaningless or unpredictable the poets and artists intended their products to be, in reality they were not. In an era dominated by the doctrine of psychoanalysis, the choice of even nonsensical words spoke something at least of the poet. Works of art supposedly constructed in random fashion also frequently betrayed the mark of some design.

MARCEL DUCHAMP   To advertise their nihilistic views, the Dadaists assaulted the public with irreverence. Not only did they attempt to negate art, but they also advocated antisocial and amoral behavior. Marcel Duchamp summed up the Dada sensibility in works such as *Mona Lisa (L.H.O.O.Q.)* (Fig. 20.23), in which he impudently defiled a color print of Leonardo da Vinci's masterpiece with a mustache and goatee. Beneath the image of the banker's wife is Duchamp's irreverent explanation of that enigmatic smile: If you read the letters aloud with their French pronunciation, using a slurred, legato style, the sound your ears will hear is "elle a chaud au cul." (Rough PG-13-rated translation: "She is hot in the pants.") Part of the underlying philosophy of

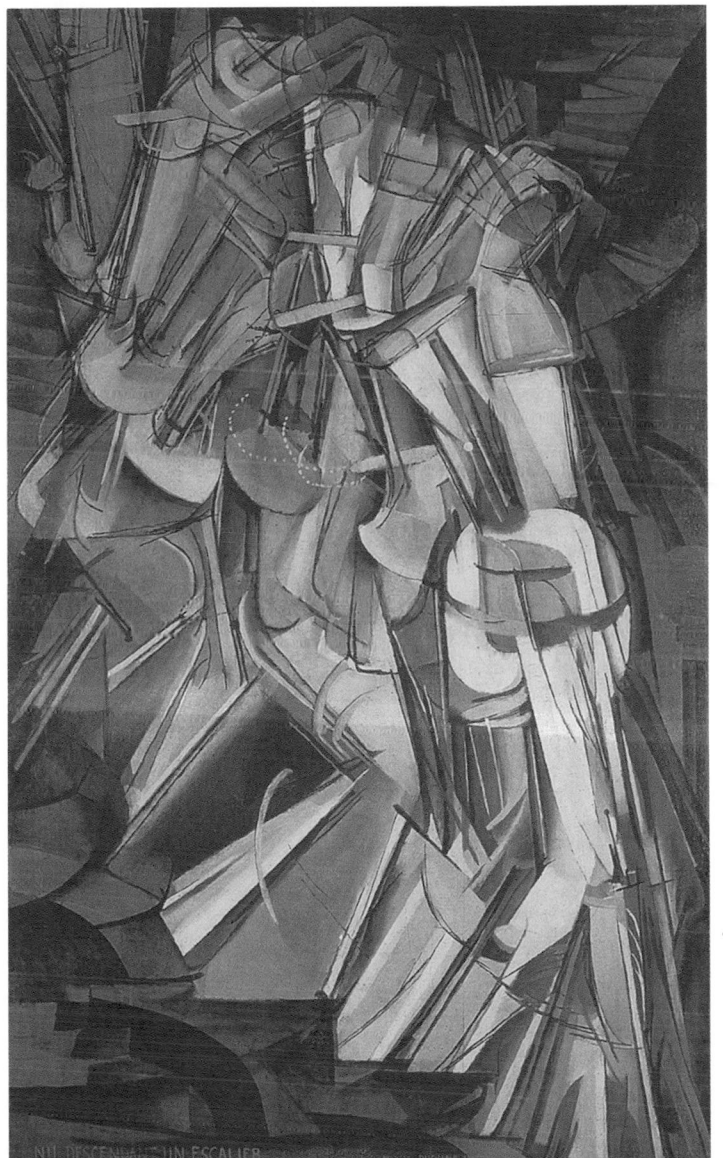

1 ft.

▲ 20.24 MARCEL DUCHAMP, *Nude Descending a Staircase (No. 2)* (1912). Oil on canvas, 57⅞" × 35⅛". Philadelphia Museum of Art, Philadelphia, Pennsylvania.

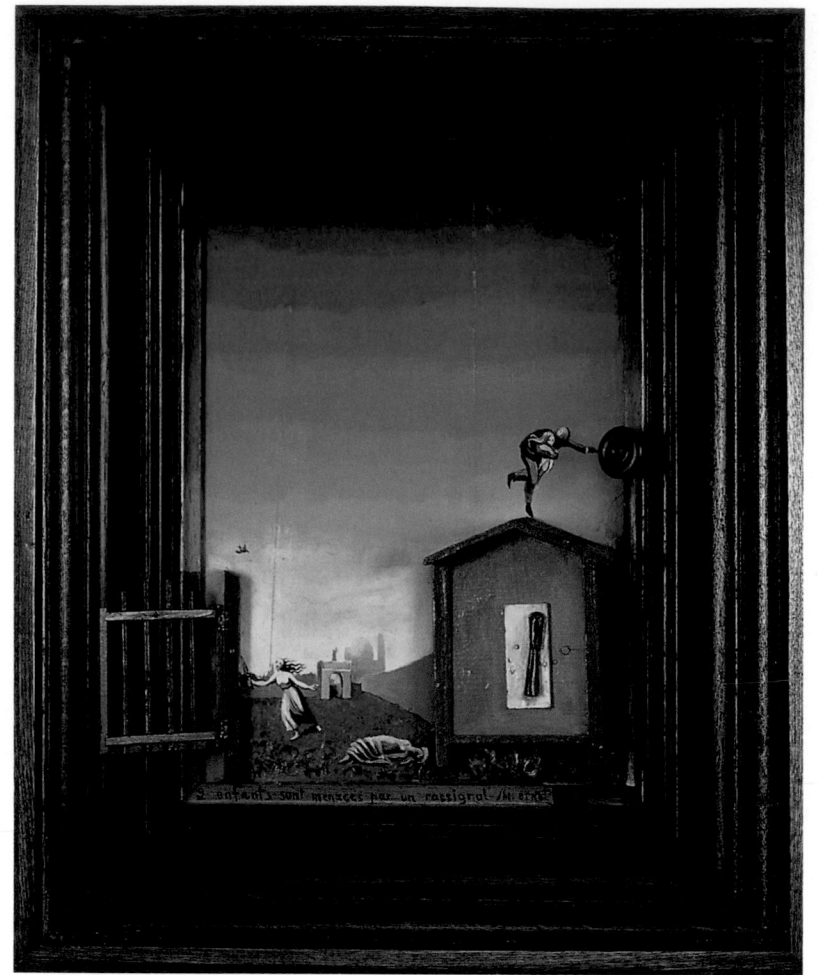

1 ft.

▲ 20.25 MAX ERNST, *Two Children Are Threatened by a Nightingale* (1924). Oil on wood with wood construction, 27 ½" × 22 ½" × 4 ½". The Museum of Modern Art, New York, New York.

literary groups engaged in **automatic writing**, in which the mind was to be purged of purposeful thought, and a series of free associations were then to be expressed with the pen. Words were not meant to denote their literal meanings but to symbolize the often seething contents of the unconscious mind. Eventually the Surrealist writers broke from the Dadaists, believing that the earlier movement was becoming too academic. Under the leadership of the poet André Breton, they defined their movement as follows in a 1924 manifesto:

Surrealism, noun, masc., pure psychic automatism by which it is intended to express either verbally or in writing, the true function of thought. Thought dictated in the absence of all control exerted by reason, and outside all aesthetic or moral preoccupations.

Encycl. Philos. Surrealism is based on the belief in the superior reality of certain forms of association heretofore neglected, in the omnipotence of the dream, and in the disinterested play of thought. It leads to the permanent destruction of all other psychic mechanisms and to its substitution for them in the solution of the principal problems of life.

From the beginning, Surrealism expounded two very different methods of working. **Illusionistic Surrealism,** exemplified by artists such as Salvador Dalí and Yves Tanguy, rendered the irrational content, absurd juxtapositions, and metamorphoses of the dream state in a highly illusionistic manner. The other, called **Automatist Surrealism,** was a direct outgrowth of automatic writing and was used to divulge mysteries of the unconscious through abstraction. The Automatist phase is typified by Joan Miró and André Masson.

SALVADOR DALÍ   Modesty was not his strong suit. One of the few "household names" in the history of art belongs to a leading Surrealist figure, the Spaniard Salvador Dalí (1904–1986). His reputation for leading an unusual—one could say surrealistic—life would seem to precede his art, for many not familiar with his canvases had seen Dalí's outrageous mustache and knew of his shenanigans. Once as a guest on the Ed Sullivan television show, he threw open cans of paint at a huge canvas.

Dalí began his painting career, however, in a somewhat more conservative manner, adopting, in turn, Impressionist, Pointillist, and Futurist styles. Following these forays into contemporary styles, he sought academic training at the Academy of Fine Arts in Madrid.

Julian Street labeled the painting "an explosion in a shingle factory," it symbolized the dynamism of the modern machine era.

Fortified by growing interest in psychoanalysis, Dada, with some modification, would provide the basis for a movement called Surrealism that began in the early 1920s. Like Max Ernst's Dada composition, *Two Children Are Threatened by a Nightingale* (Fig. 20.25), some Surrealist works offer irrational subjects and the chance juxtaposition of everyday objects. These often menacing paintings also incorporate the Realistic technique and the suggestion of dream imagery found in Fantastic art.

SURREALISM

Surrealism began as a literary movement after World War I. Its adherents based their writings on the nonrational, and thus they were naturally drawn to the Dadaists. Both

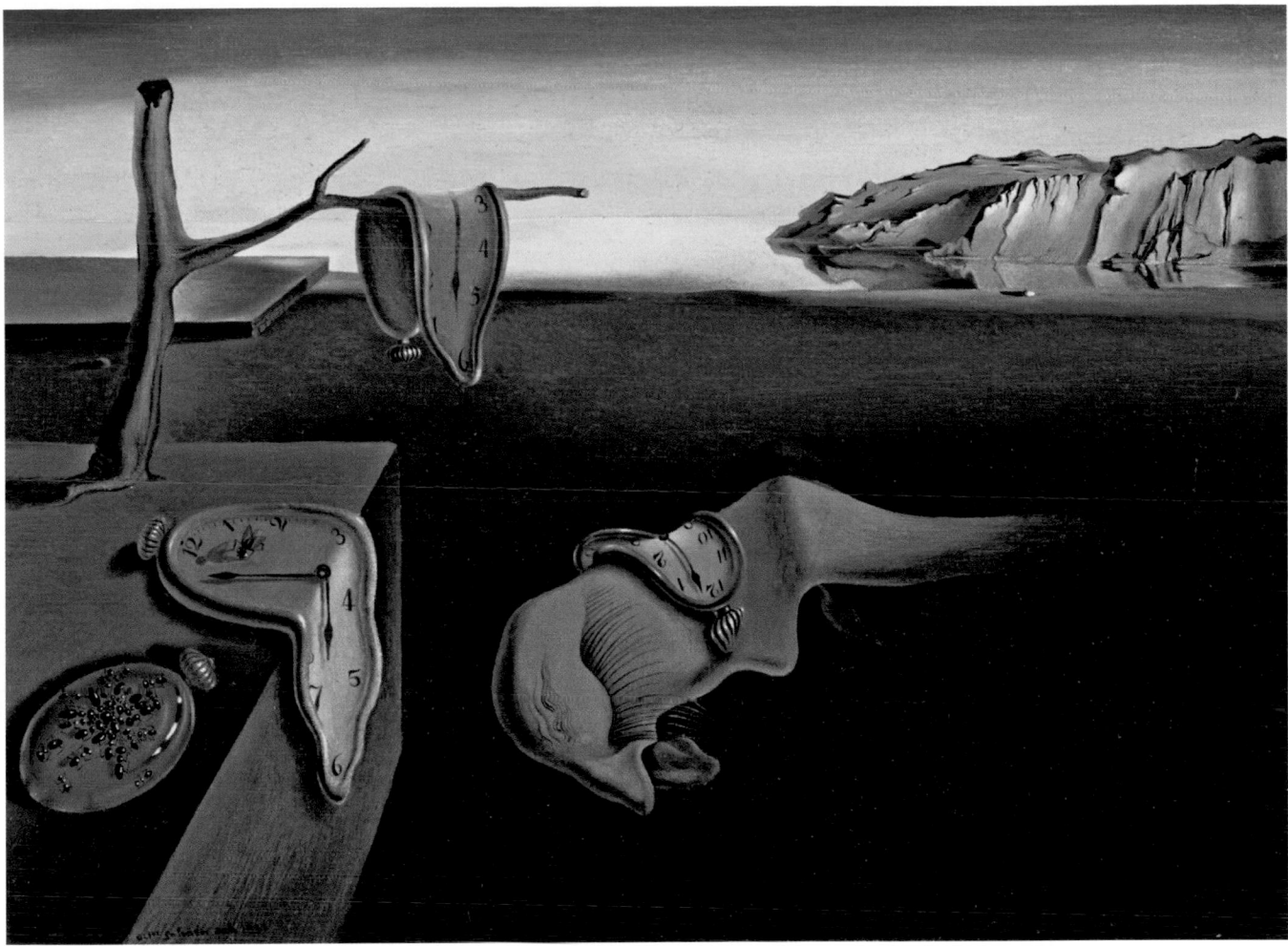

▲ 20.26 SALVADOR DALÍ, *The Persistence of Memory* (1931). Oil on canvas, 9½" × 1' 1". The Museum of Modern Art, New York, New York.

This experience steeped him in a tradition of illusionistic realism that he never abandoned.

In *The Persistence of Memory* (Fig. 20.26), the drama of the dreamlike imagery is enhanced by Dalí's *trompe l'oeil* technique. Here, in a barren landscape of incongruous forms, time, as all else, has expired. A watch is left crawling with insects like scavengers over carrion; three other watches hang limp and useless over a rectangular block, a dead tree, and a lifeless, amorphous creature that bears a curious resemblance to Dalí. The artist conveys the world of the dream, juxtaposing unrelated objects in an extraordinary situation. But a haunting sense of reality threatens the line between perception and imagination. Dalí's is, in the true definition of the term, a surreality—or reality above and beyond reality.

JOAN MIRÓ   Not all of the Surrealists were interested in rendering their enigmatic personal dreams. Some found this highly introspective subject matter meaningless to the observer and sought a more universal form of expression. The Automatist Surrealists believed that the unconscious held such universal imagery, and through spontaneous, or automatic, drawing, they attempted to reach it. Artists of this group, such as Joan Miró (1893–1983), sought to eliminate all thought from their minds and then trace their brushes across the surface of the canvas. The organic shapes derived from intersecting skeins of line were believed to be unadulterated by conscious thought and thus drawn from the unconscious. Once the basic designs had been outlined, a conscious period of work could follow in which the artist intentionally applied his or her craft to render them in their final form. But because no conscious control was to be exerted to determine the early course of the designs, the Automatist method was seen as spontaneous, as employing chance and accident. Needless to say, the works are abstract, although some shapes are amoebic.

Miró was born near Barcelona and spent his early years in local schools of art learning how to paint like the French Modernists. He practiced several styles ranging from Romanticism to Realism to Impressionism, but

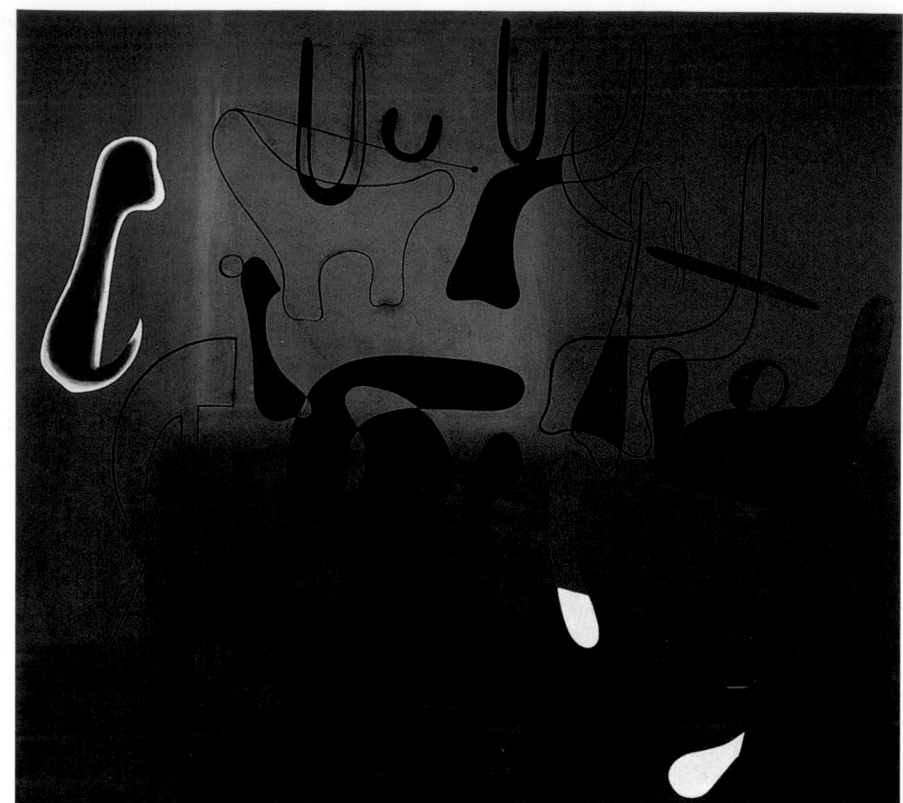

> **20.27** JOAN MIRÓ, *Painting* (1933). Oil on canvas, 68½" × 77¼". The Museum of Modern Art, New York, New York.

1 ft.

Cézanne and van Gogh seem to have influenced him most. In 1919, Miró moved to Paris, where he was receptive to different art styles. The work of Matisse and Picasso, along with the primitive innocence of Rousseau, found their way into his canvases. Coupled with a rich native iconography and an inclination toward fantasy, these different elements would shape Miró's unique style.

Miró's need for spontaneity in communicating his subjects was compatible with Automatist Surrealism, although the whimsical nature of most of his subjects often appears at odds with that of other members of the movement. In *Painting* (Fig. 20.27), meandering lines join or intersect to form the contours of clusters of organic figures. Some of these shapes are left void to display a nondescript background of subtly colored squares. Others are filled in with sharply contrasting black, white, and bright red pigment. In this work, Miró applied Breton's principles of **psychic automatism** in an aesthetically pleasing, decorative manner.

By 1930, Surrealism had developed into an international movement, despite the divorce of many of the first members from the group. New adherents exhibiting radically different styles kept the movement alive.

FIGURATIVE ART IN THE UNITED STATES

Although most of the groundbreaking artists in the United States and Europe were creating abstract art, some artists chose to continue to work with **figurative art**. The term *figurative* does not refer only to human or animal figures, but to any art that contains strong references to people and objects in the real world. Two such artists working in the Depression era and during World War II were Grant Wood and Edward Hopper.

GRANT WOOD Grant Wood (1891–1942) was a proponent of a style known as Midwestern Regionalism. He trained in Europe during the 1920s, but rather than returning home with the latest developments in European abstract art, he was drawn to the realism of sixteenth-century German and Flemish artists.

The weatherworn faces and postcard-perfect surroundings in Grant Wood's *American Gothic* (Fig. 20.28) suggest the duality of rural life in the modern United States—hardship and serenity. The painstakingly realistic portrait is also one of our more commercialized works of art; images derived from it have adorned boxes of breakfast cereal, greeting cards, and numerous other products. Note the repetition of the pitchfork pattern in the man's shirtfront, the upper-story window of the house, and the plant on the porch. He is very much tied to his environment. Were it not for the incongruously spry curl falling from the woman's otherwise tucked-tight hairdo, we might view this composition—as well as the sitters therein—as solid, stolid, and monotonous.

EDWARD HOPPER Edward Hopper (1882–1967) was also a realist painter who took commonplace subjects, but unlike Wood, he often made them into metaphors for rootlessness and loneliness. He was fascinated by bleak New England architectural vistas that were either bereft of people or emptied of people by the

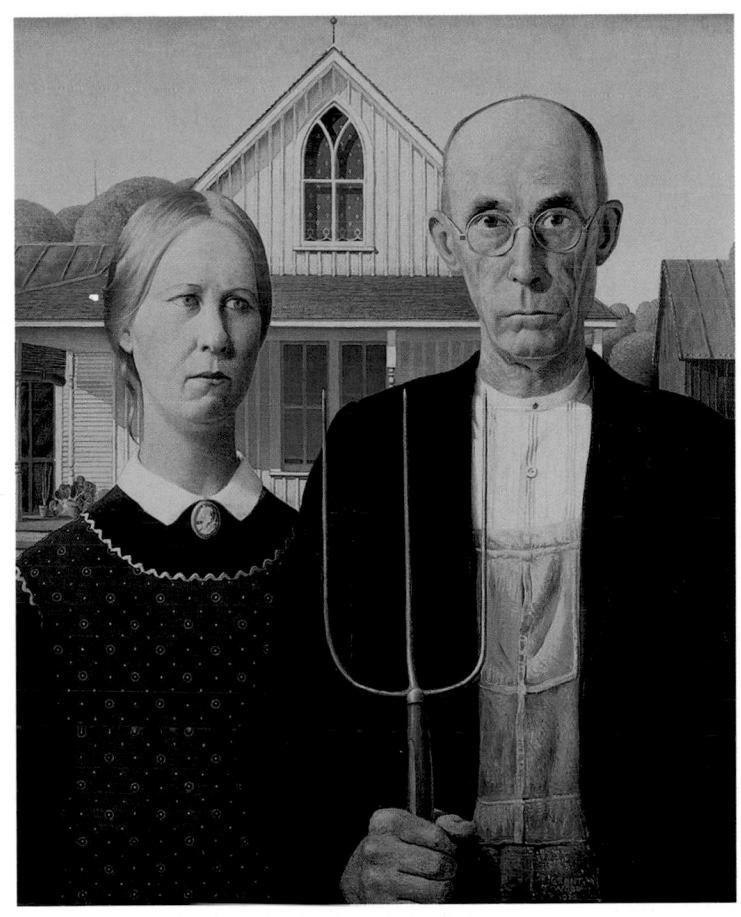

< 20.28 GRANT WOOD, *American Gothic* (1930). Oil on beaverboard, 30¾" × 25¾". Art Institute of Chicago, Chicago, Illinois.

1 ft.

artist. Yet he often used strong light playing off these buildings.

The architecture, hairstyles, hats, and shoulder pads—even the price of cigars (only five cents)—all set Hopper's *Nighthawks* (Fig. 20.29) in an unmistakably American city during the late 1930s or 1940s. The subject is commonplace and uneventful, though somewhat eerie. There is a tension between the desolate spaces of the vacant street and the corner diner. Familiar objects become distant. The warm patch of artificial light seems precious, even precarious, as if night and all its troubled symbols are threatening to break in on disordered lives. Hopper uses a specific sociocultural context to communicate an unsettling, introspective mood of aloneness, of being outside the mainstream of experience. That mainstream of experience at the time of the painting was World War II. We might very well wonder what these people are doing here when so many others are in uniform or otherwise engaged in the war effort.

See more *of Chicago in the online Art Tour.*

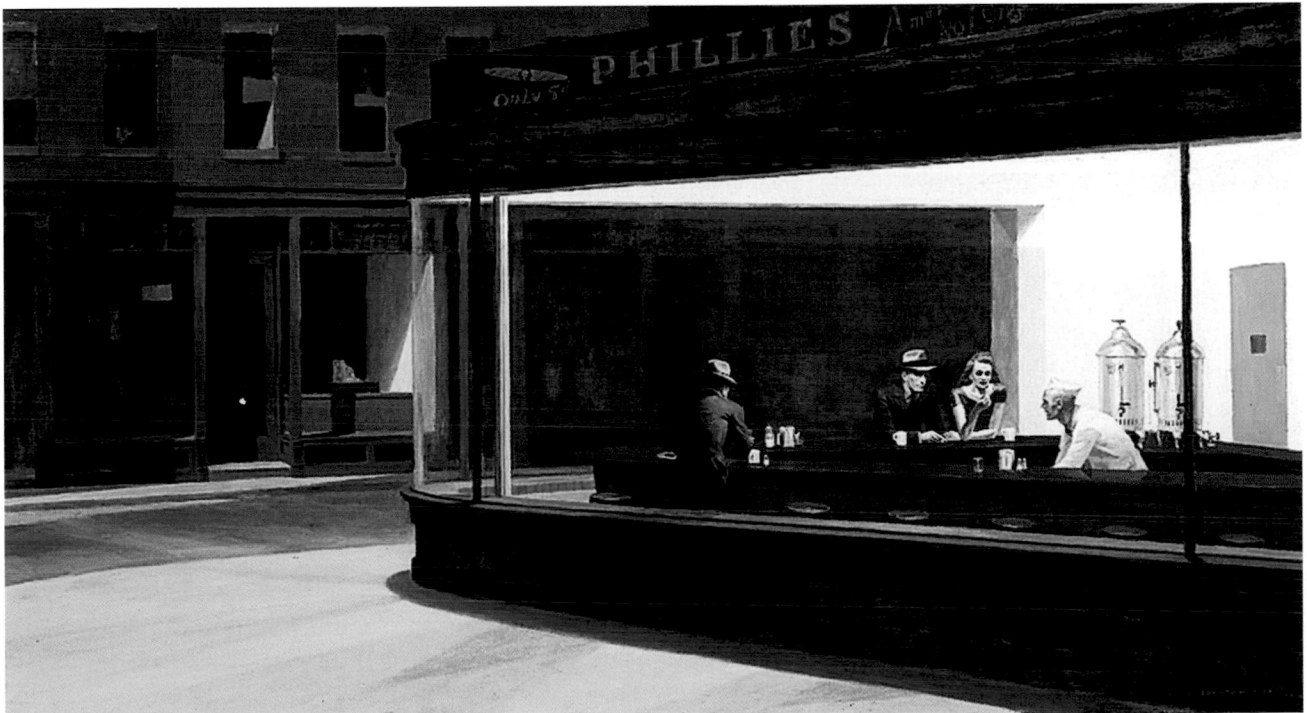

1 ft.

▲ 20.29 EDWARD HOPPER, *Nighthawks* (1942). Oil on canvas, 33⅛" × 60". Art Institute of Chicago, Chicago, Illinois.

THE HARLEM RENAISSANCE

Also in the early part of the twentieth century, a cultural movement was taking root in a section of New York City known as Harlem. There, a concentration of African American writers, artists, intellectuals, and musicians produced such a conspicuous body of specifically African American work that the movement became known as the **Harlem Renaissance**. There were artists such as Hale Woodruff, Sargent Johnson, Augusta Savage, Romare Bearden, Aaron Douglas, and Jacob Lawrence.

AARON DOUGLAS Aaron Douglas (1899–1979) was born in Kansas and died in Tennessee, but beginning in his 20s he played a leading role in the Harlem Renaissance. At first he found work as a magazine illustrator, but soon he became known for his paintings that depicted the cultural history of African Americans. One of his aims, as those of the Harlem Renaissance in general, was to cultivate black pride.

Noah's Ark (Fig. 20.30) translates a biblical story into a work that speaks to African American sensibilities. It expresses Douglas's powerful vision of the great flood.

Animals enter the ark in pairs as lightning flashes about them, and the sky turns a hazy gray-purple with the impending storm. African men, rendered in rough-hewn profile, ready the ark and direct the action in a dynamically choreographed composition that takes possession of and personalizes the biblical event for Douglas's race and culture.

JACOB LAWRENCE Born in New Jersey, Jacob Lawrence (1917–2000) moved to Harlem with his family as a teenager. He, like Aaron Douglas, would bring features reminiscent of African masks into his paintings. His best-known works address themes such as slavery, African American migration northward from the South, Harlem lifestyles, and World War II.

Lawrence used assertive sticklike diagonals to give the slave children in his painting *The Life of Harriet Tubman, No. 4* (Fig. 20.31) a powerful sense of movement and directionality. While the horizon line provides a somewhat stable world, the brightly clad children perform acrobatic leaps, their branchlike limbs akin to the wood above. The enduring world implied by the horizon is shattered by the agitated back-and-forth of the brushed lines that define ground and sky. Such turmoil presumably awaits the children once they mature and realize their lot in life.

∧ 20.30 **AARON DOUGLAS**, *Noah's Ark* (c. 1927). Oil on Masonite, 48" × 36". Carl Van Vechten Gallery of Fine Arts, Fisk University, Nashville, Tennessee.

THE BAUHAUS

The early part of the twentieth century also saw numerous innovations in architecture, including those of the American Frank Lloyd Wright (see Fig. 13.18). The German architect Walter Gropius (1883–1969) and his followers brought several principles to modern architecture, amplifying the concepts that "form follows function" and that "less is more." Gropius relied on basic forms, such as the rectangular solid, and diligently avoided ornamentation and embellishment. For Gropius, an overriding emphasis was on simplicity and on the economical use of space and time, materials, and money.

In 1919, Gropius became director of the Weimar School of Arts and Crafts. He renamed the school Das Staatliche Bauhaus, or "Building House of the State," referred to simply as The Bauhaus. Gropius believed that his vision was a doorway to the future of art and architecture, training architects, artists, designers, and craftspersons. Because of political conflicts, Gropius moved his school to Dessau in 1925 and designed its new home (Fig. 20.32). Design and carpentry were integral to the Bauhaus curriculum, and Gropius had students and faculty create the furnishings for the building. Ludwig Miës van der Rohe (1886–1969) became director of the Bauhaus in 1928 and moved the school to Berlin.

The Nazis shut down the Bauhaus in 1933, and some of its faculty fled to the United States, Gropius and Miës

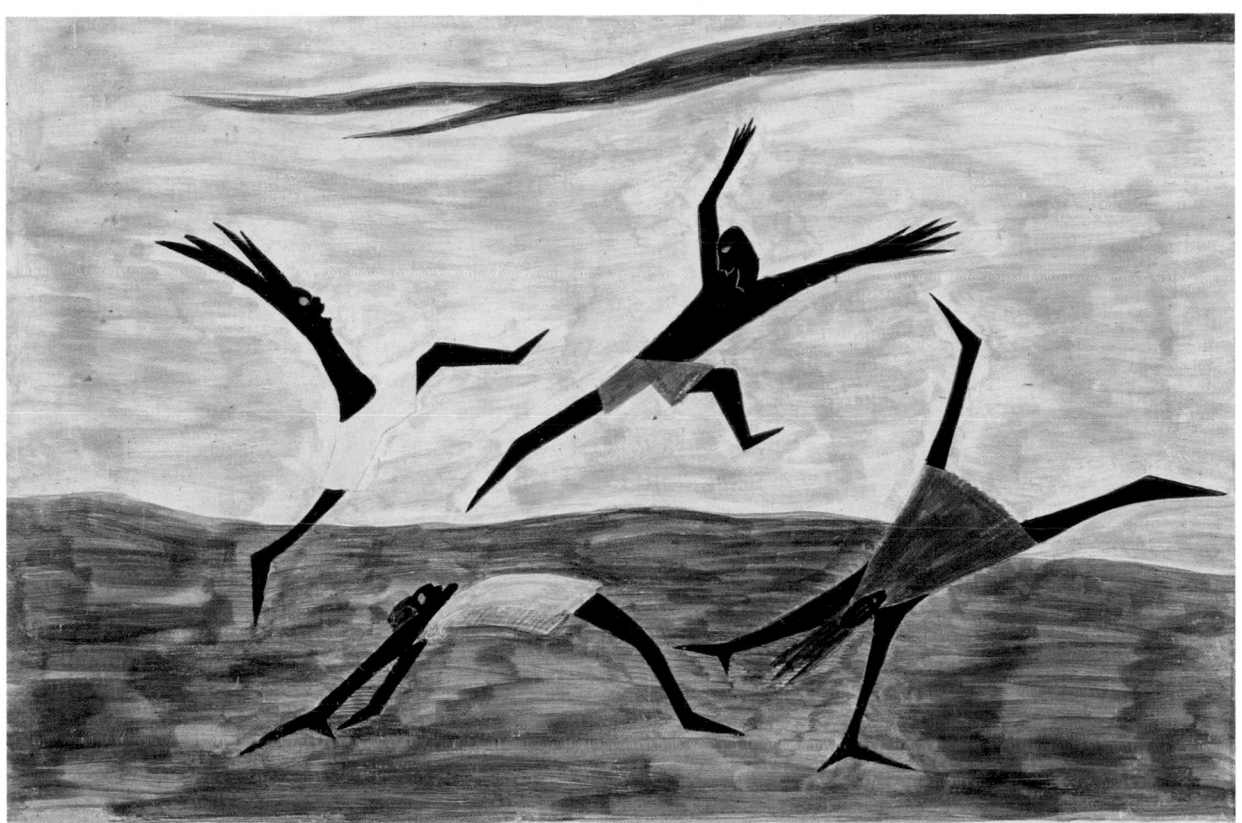

∧ **20.31 JACOB LAWRENCE,** *The Life of Harriet Tubman,* No. 4 (1939–1940). Casein tempera on gessoed hardboard, 12" × 17⅞". Hampton University Museum, Hampton, Virginia.

van der Rohe among them. Gropius became chair of architecture at the Harvard University Graduate School of Design, and Miës chaired the architecture department of the school that would become the Illinois Institute of Technology. During its short life of fifteen years, the Bauhaus gave birth to designers and designs that would shape much of the remaining two-thirds of the twentieth century. In the following chapter, we will see Miës's Farnsworth House (see Fig. 21.52), a single-story residential design. Miës's Seagram Building on New York's Park

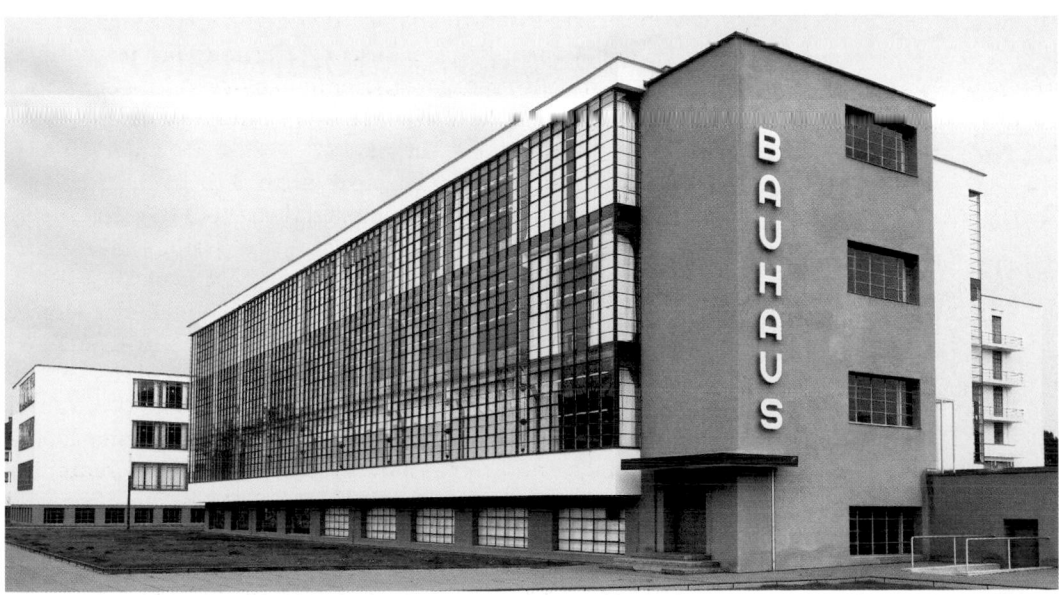

∧ **20.32 WALTER GROPIUS,** Shop Block, The Bauhaus, Dessau, Germany. (1925–1926).

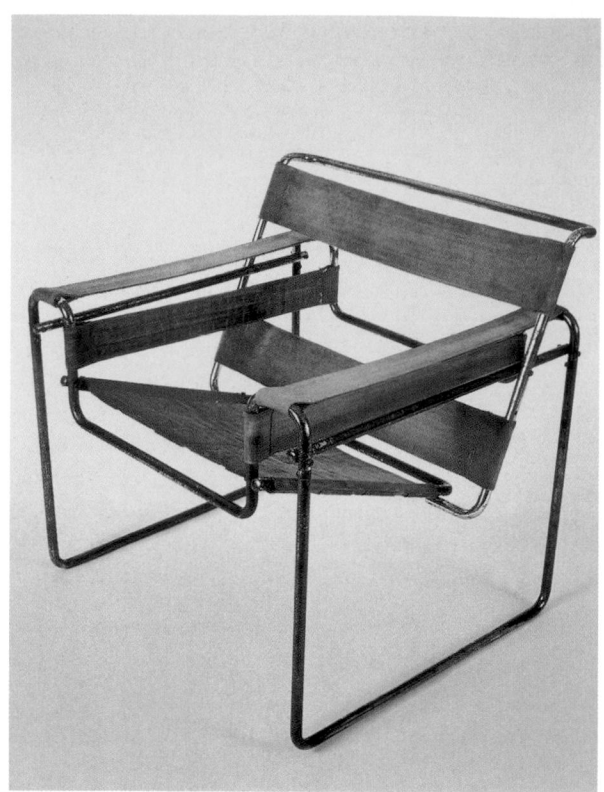

∧ 20.33 MARCEL BREUER, Tubular steel chair (1925).

midair on cloth or leather slings attached to steel tubing. The concept behind the chair is the use of simple shapes, but the result is actually quite complex. Bauhaus furniture, especially Breuer chairs of various kinds, remain popular to this day and are visible on many websites. Like Gropius, Breuer also moved to the United States and taught at Harvard University.

As the decade of the 1930s evolved, Adolf Hitler rose to power, and war once again threatened Europe. Hitler's ascent drove not only architects, but also refugee artists of the highest reputation to the shores of the United States. Among them were the leading figures of Abstraction and Surrealism, two divergent styles that would join to form the basis of an avant-garde American painting. The center of the art world had moved to New York.

THE WIDER WORLD
Japan

The Meiji period ended in 1912 and was followed by the short-lived, democratic, Taisho period. That too ended, in 1926; the Showa period (1926–1989) followed, named for the Showa emperor, Hirohito. The Meiji period witnessed two wars at the turn of the century: the first against the Chinese (1903), waged primarily for control over Korea, and the second—the Russo-Japanese War (1904–1905)—waged this time over control of Korea and Manchuria. Under Hirohito, Japan descended into totalitarianism, militarism, and racism, leading to their invasion of China in 1937. Four years later, Hirohito ordered

Avenue also has glass curtain walls, but is more compact, less soaring in appearance.

Marcel Breuer's (1902–1981) tubular steel chair (Fig 20.33) is an example of Bauhaus furniture. Gone are the overstuffed cushions. The sitter is suspended in

TWENTIETH CENTURY: THE EARLY YEARS IN THE WIDER WORLD

1900–1926	1926–1940	1940–1950
Japan is victorious in the Russo-Japanese War (1904–1905)	In Japan, the Showa period begins in 1926, with Hirohito as emperor	Japan attacks Pearl Harbor, bringing the United States into the war in 1941
In China, the Qing Dynasty is brought down by republican forces in 1911	Civil War breaks out in China between the People's Republic of China and the Communist Party of China in 1927; both sides use art as propaganda	United States drops atom bombs on Hiroshima and Nagasaki, leading to Japanese surrender in 1945
In Japan, the Meiji period ends in 1912		Civil War resumes in China in 1946, ending in 1950, with the Communist Party controlling the mainland and the Republic of China controlling the island of Taiwan
The Taisho period extends from 1912 to 1926	World War II breaks out in the Pacific as Japan invades China in 1937	
Japan and China exchange art students	Japanese and Chinese artists continue to create landscapes	Kahlo paints Surrealistic self-portraits
African masks and other works influence European artists	Rivera paints murals in Mexico	
Native American artists fashion practical and ceremonial craft objects		
Oceanic artists make canoe prows and ancestor poles		

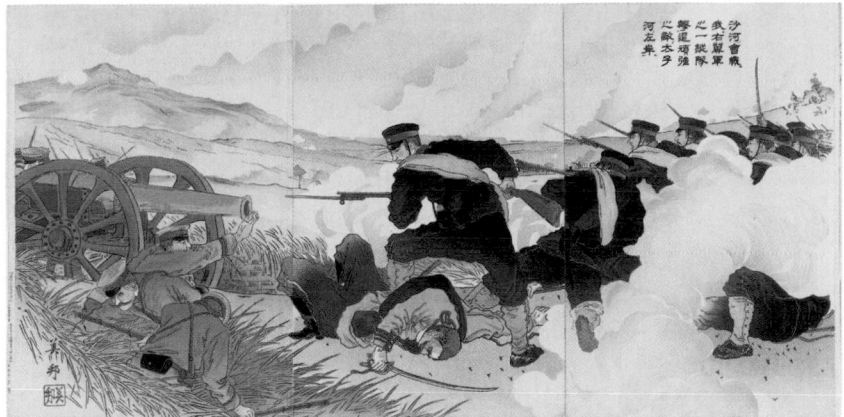

The same war is represented from a radically different perspective by Suzuki Kason (Fig. 20.35)—that of a solitary, melancholic woman, perhaps waiting for her love to return from war, perhaps anticipating the worst. Her stylized visage and emotional restraint reflect the form of the *ukiyo-e* artist two centuries earlier, although her concern is palpable. Against a scene from a bloody battle pinned to the wall behind her, she gnaws at a handkerchief as she looks down

the bombing of the United States' naval fleet stationed in Pearl Harbor, thereby entering into a war with the U.S. That war—World War II—ended in 1945 after the U.S. dropped atom bombs on the cities of Hiroshima and Nagasaki. In the aftermath, the U.S. occupied Japan for seven more years.

During the early part of the century, Japanese artists portrayed contrasting aspects of the Japanese psyche: the warrior side, with its enduring samurai traditions, and the temperate side, meditative, at one with nature. A woodblock triptych by Hirose Yoshikune depicting combat along a 37-mile front during the Russo-Japanese war (1904–1905) (Fig. 20.34) shows Japanese troops advancing inexorably, bayonets engaged. Russians are either dead or begging for mercy, their cannon no match for the fearless Japanese foot soldier. Delicate, transparent plumes of the palest wash rise from an unseen battlefield in the distance, while opaque, white smoke envelops the uniformed front line warriors like a cloud of death.

at a newspaper in her lap. There is a certain timelessness to this image. She represents an everywoman of the centuries, waiting anxiously at home while her man goes off to war.

The grim context of these two works makes Suzuki Shonen's monochromatic scroll painting, *Fireflies at Uji River*, seem ominous (Fig. 20.36). In reality, it is a mystical, almost

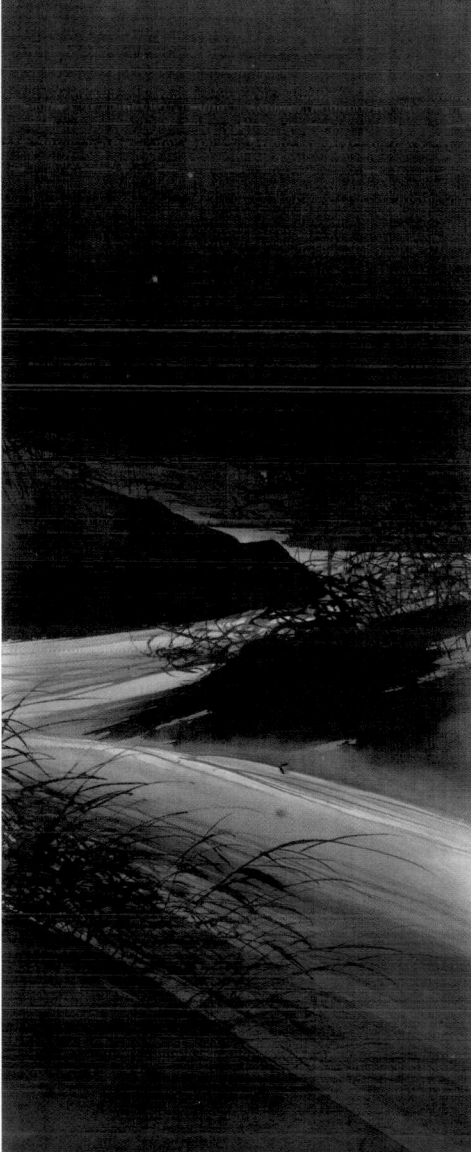

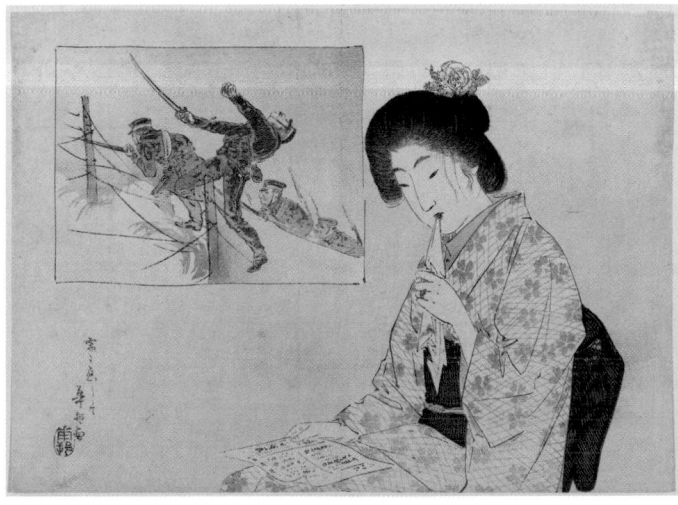

CONNECTIONS Just a bit less than a century before Yoshikune painted his scene from the Battle of the Sha River, Spain's Francisco Goya painted his *Third of May, 1808*, bringing voice to the atrocities committed against his fellow Spaniards by Napoleon Bonaparte's

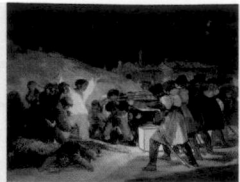

▲ Goya's *Third of May, 1808* (Fig. 19.6)

French soldiers over the course of two days. Considered by some to be the "first modern painting" in the history of art, Goya forgoes the typical glorification and heroism of war and focuses on rather on "Man's inhumanity to man."

the twentieth century, despite political turmoil, Chinese landscape painting continued to thrive. Wang Zhen's ink and brush painting (Fig. 20.37) of a bird and blossoms aestheticizes the stillness of nature. An egret with a wary eye stands firmly on a mountain rock whose cloud-like shape and texture belie its actual mass. Foreground and background are largely established by detail and tone. The pale-colored, softly rounded shapes of distant hills provide a simple setting for the angular, splintery bark of an aged plum tree and the avian specimen standing guard over its precious blossoms.

magical, slice of nature that illustrates a passage from a popular Japanese novel, *The Tale of Genji*, written some 900 years earlier. Under the cover of velvety darkness, a young would-be suitor secretly strains to hear the conversation between two young women, but to no avail, as the river's powerful rushing waters drown out their voices. Broad zig-zag brushstrokes convey the current's swooshing sounds and transport us into the dreamy darkness, illuminated only by the dancing specks of fireflies.

During World War II, Japanese artists came under the control of the government, which enlisted them to record events of the hostilities and to glorify the militarism that swept the country. Many joined Japan's armed forces and did so willingly.[4]

China

Within a decade after the Japanese war with the Chinese (the Sino-Japanese War) that pitted Meiji Japan against Qing Dynasty China, the Revolution of 1911 (Xinhai Revolution) brought an end to Qing imperial rule and the establishment of the Republic of China. But China was soon riven by civil war between nationalist Republic, led by Chiang Kai-Shek, and the Communist Party of China, led by Mao Zedong (also known as Mao Tse-tung). During World War II, hostilities were suspended as members of both parties fought the Japanese but, by mid-century, it resumed; Mao, victorious, became the leader of the People's Republic of China and the nationalists retreated to Taiwan.

Prior to World War II, it was common for Chinese art students to go to Japan to study, and many Japanese students traveled to China for the same reason, although some purists held that traditional Chinese landscape painting was the highest form of art in the world and the notion of studying art in Japan was as silly as going there to learn how to cook Chinese food.[5] In the early years of

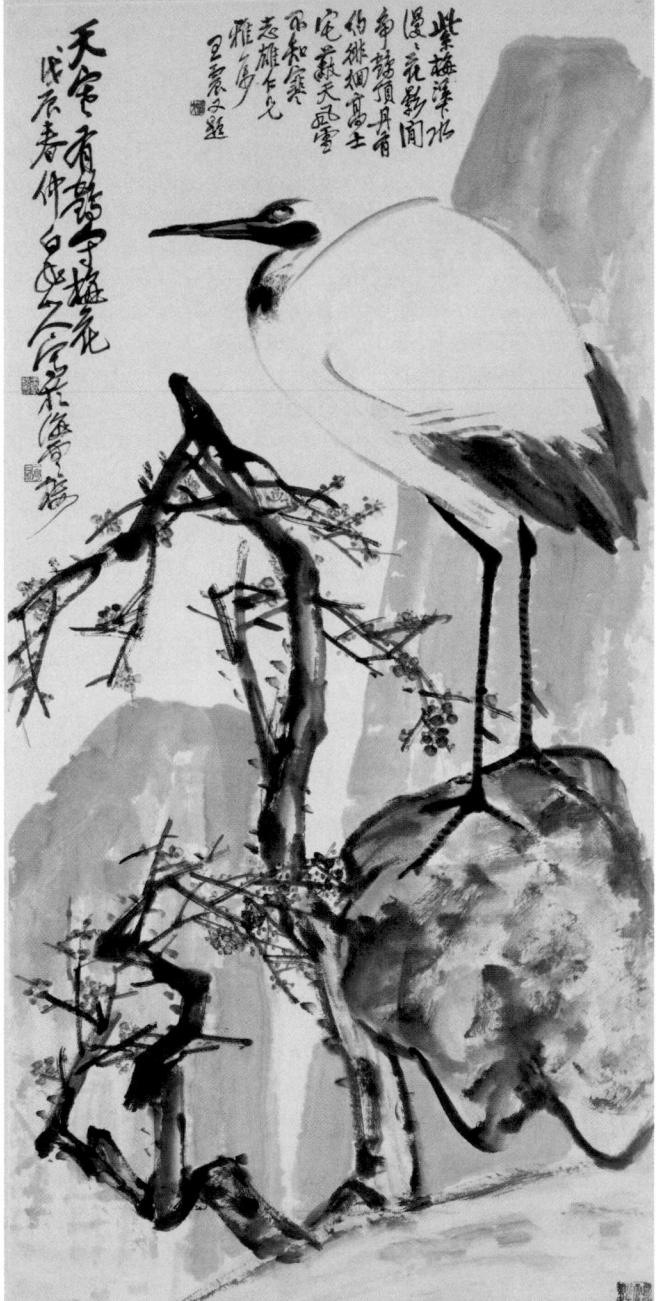

1 ft.

▲ 20.37 **WANG ZHEN (1866–1938).** *Crane and Plum Blossoms.* Hanging scroll, ink and color on paper; 53⅜" × 26⁷⁄₁₀". Private collection.

---

[4] Asato Ikeda, "Japan's Haunting War Art: Contested War Memories and Art Museums," *disClosure* 18 (April 2009), 5–32.

[5] Michael Sullivan, *The Arts of China* (Berkeley: University of California Press, 1999).

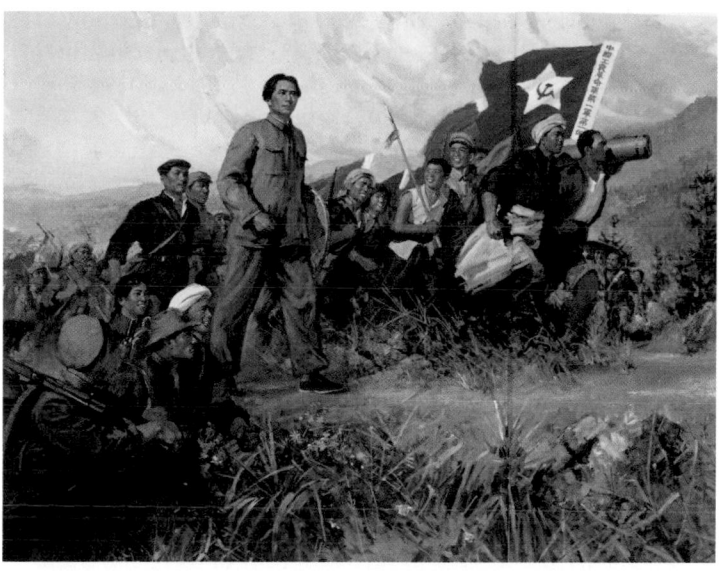

∧ **20.38** *Mao Zedong (1893–1976) marching toward the Jing Gang Mountains in October 1927* (20th century). Chinese School, color lithograph. Private collection.

The Communist Party of China, like Western nations and other nations of the East, produced its share of propaganda. In September 1927, in the early days of the revolution, the Communist Party launched an uprising in Nanking. The lithograph shown in Figure 20.38 portrays Mao's march to nearby mountains, where he established the first revolutionary base in the countryside. A young, virile, idealized Mao leads his adoring followers forward and upward, the Communist flags aloft proclaiming victory and solidarity.

Africa

Ritual and ceremonial objects produced by African peoples during this period exhibit the remarkable continuity of traditions established over centuries. The carved and painted wooden doors from a shrine in the Yoruba Ikere palace (Fig. 20.39), the residence of the king, depict a historical narrative documenting the 1897 meeting of the Yoruba king and Major W.R. Reeve-Tucker of the British Empire. Opposite one another in the second register down from the top, we find the king enthroned with his wife behind him (left), and we see Reeve-Tucker being transported for a royal audience in a sling-style litter by two attendants. It is noteworthy that hierarchical scale has been employed; the king is much larger than his British visitor (see Chapter 6 on "Principles of Design"). The figures, angular and stylized, are carved in such high relief that some (such as the three figures in the lowest register of the right door) seem barely attached to the door. In most sections, a geometric-patterned background adds a rich, tapestry-like quality to the work.

One of the remarkable things about the shrine doors is that we know the name of the artist who carved them:

Olowe of Ise. At the same time that Europe was in the run-up to the First World War, Olowe was employed in the royal palace (1910–1914). Although the doors were given to the British in the 1920s (they are in the British Museum in London), the identity of Olowe was not discovered until decades later. It turns out that he was the most famous artist of his time and place.

The Yoruba are known for their mix of old and new in fanciful objects crafted for religious or ceremonial purposes. Among these objects are masks and headdresses, which are used in performances (masquerades) that are somewhere between theatre and ritual, and often include elements of social commentary.

Masks and headdresses are found in several regions of Africa, and their symbolism is as widely varied as their style. The simplest of these, such as the

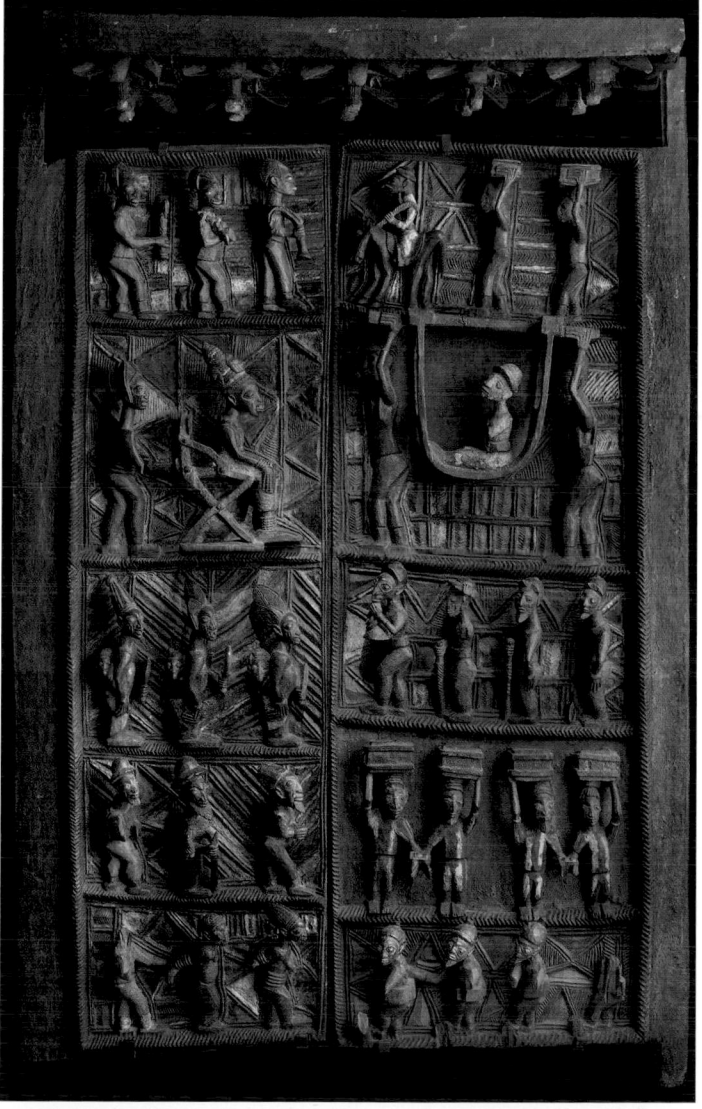

∧ **20.39** OLOWE OF ISE, *Doors from the shrine of the king's head in the royal palace, Ikere, Yoruba, Nigeria* (1910–1914). Painted wood, 6' high. British Museum, London, England.

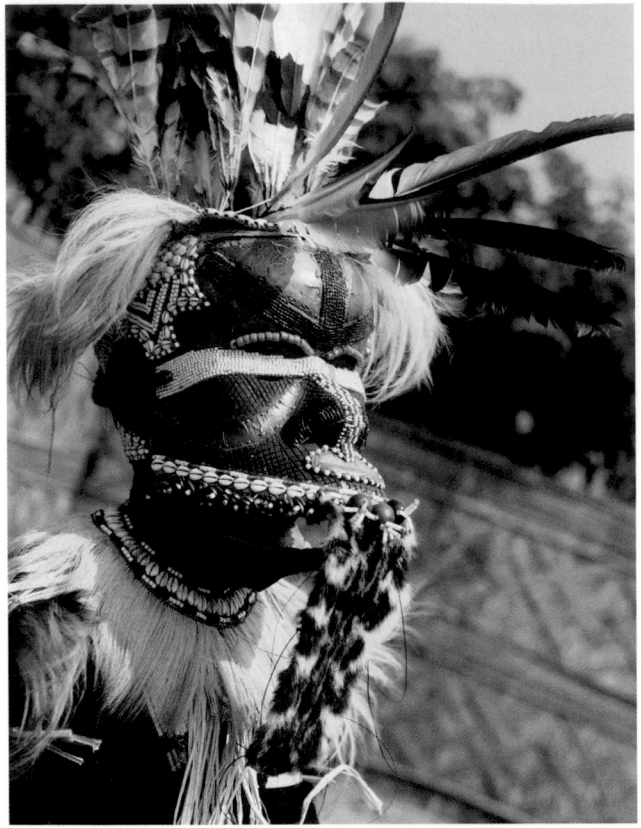

Etumbi mask (see Fig. 20.8), have facial features resolved into abstract geometric shapes. They are also sometimes punched and slashed with markings and patterns intended to denote body scarification. More intricate pieces might be embellished with brass, shells, beads, seeds, feathers, and furs. A helmet mask from the Kuba people of Congo (Fig. 20.40) represents "Bwoom," one of three characters that are central to Kuba creation myths. Bwoom, who signifies the indigenous peoples, has a jutting chin and protruding forehead, alluding to his pygmy form. Such masquerades were a component of royal initiation ceremonies. This particular photograph was taken around 1950.

Mexico

The continuity of local, traditional art forms, at times accompanied by social commentary, is one common thread among artists working in very different parts of the world during the first half of the twentieth century. Another is the blending of Western and Non-Western motifs and styles. In this context, it is interesting to look at Mexico—particularly at a generation of mural painters who channeled the indigenous artistic traditions of Pre-Hispanic Mexico in modern works with epic historical narratives and powerful social and political criticism. Diego Rivera (1886–1957) is one of them, along with Jose Clemente Orozco, David Alfaro Siqueiros, and many others.

After the Mexican Revolution, which started in 1910 and ended around 1920, the government established a public mural program to glorify the revolution, promote its ideals, and create pride in Mexico's *mestizo* (mixed) Spanish and indigenous heritage. Rivera, who had spent eight years in Paris and had studied Renaissance frescos in Italy, came back to his native Mexico and incorporated these influences

∧ 20.40 Bwoom helmet mask, Kuba, Democratic Republic of Congo, 19th–20th centuries (photograph c. 1950). Wood, brass, cowrie shells, beads, seeds, 13" high. Royal Museum for Central Africa, Tervuren, Belgium.

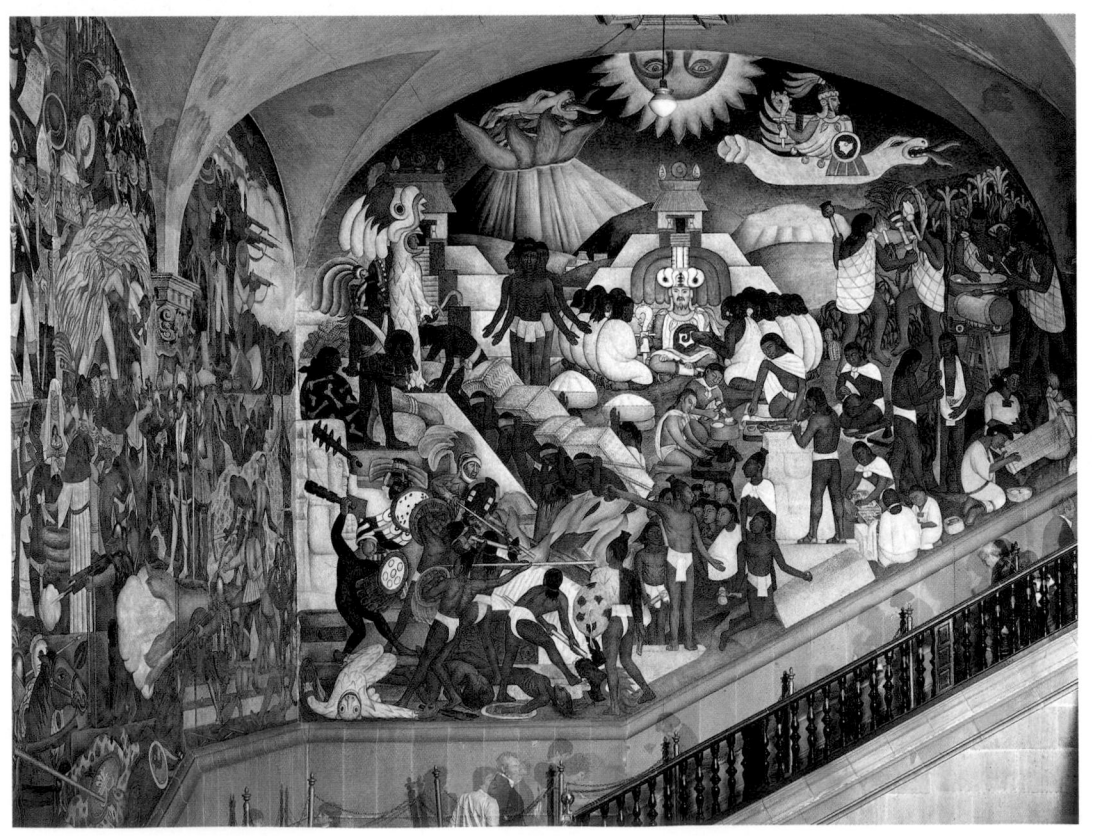

< 20.41 DIEGO RIVERA, *Ancient Mexico* (1929–1935). Detail of history of Mexico, fresco in the Palacio Nacional, Mexico City, Mexico.

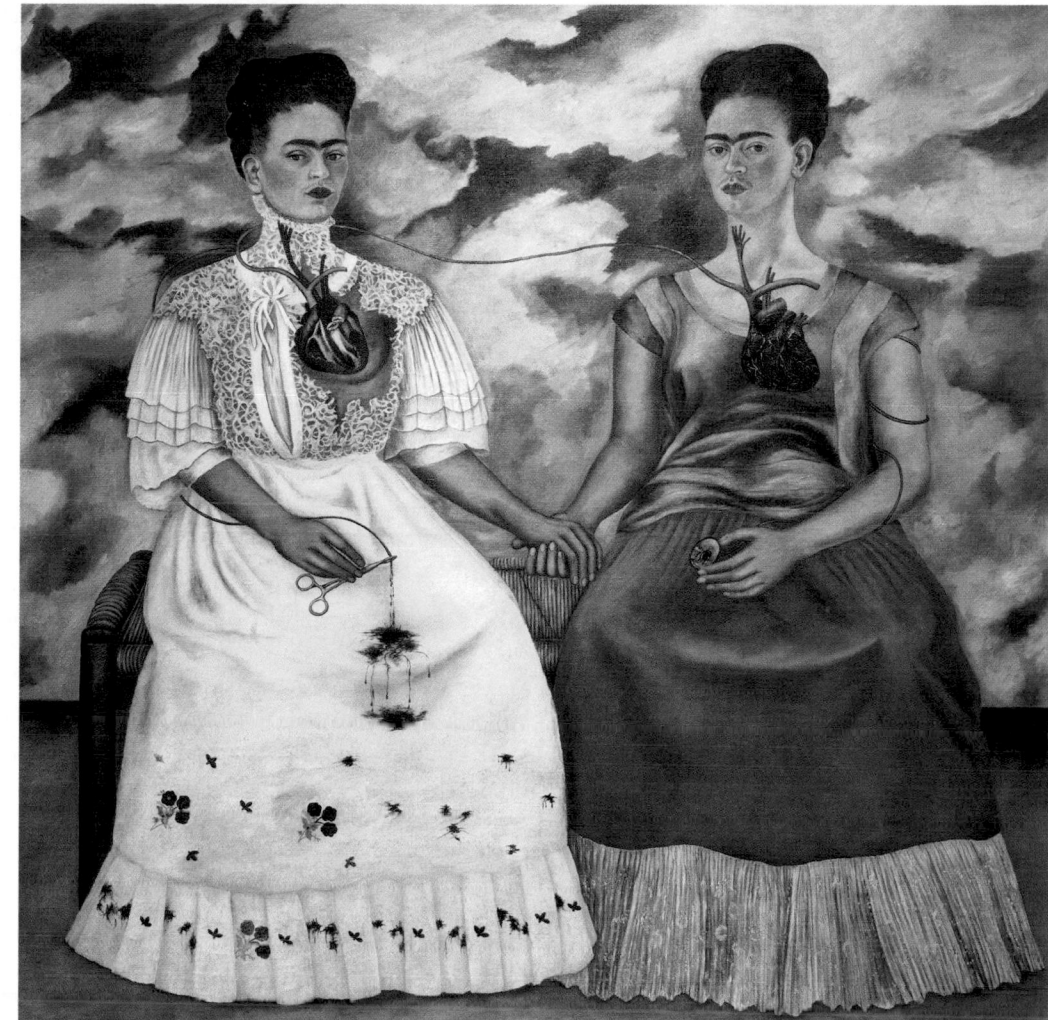

> 20.42 FRIDA KAHLO, *The Two Fridas* (1939). Oil on canvas, 67 11/16" × 67 11/16". Museo de Arte Moderno, Mexico City, Mexico.

into a new, national style that was heavy with elements drawn from ancient Mexico. His fresco cycle for the main stairwell of the Palacio Nacional in Mexico City (1929–1951) is a sweeping historical narrative that played a large role in establishing what would become a national Mexican style with its large, simplified shapes and palette inspired by ancient, native murals. In the section of the murals depicting the *History of Mexico* (see Fig. 20.41) illustrated here, Rivera represented the conflict between indigenous Mexicans and the Spanish conquerors. The blonde, blue-eyed figure sitting cross-legged in the center, wearing a bright green headdress, is Quetzalcoatl, god of the Toltecs, Mayans, and Aztecs who was considered to be the creator of books, knowledge, and arts, as well as death and resurrection (note the artisans working at his feet to the right). Behind him are the pyramids of pre-Hispanic Mexico and, directly above, a child-like representation of the sun shines down—the upside-down positioning symbolizing the decline of the ancient cultures. Other figures include some bringing tribute, farmers planting corn, ceremonial dancers, and warriors. The compressed space, tight overlapping, and repetitive shapes create a vibrant pattern that keeps the eye dancing over the surface.

Although quite different in her approach, Rivera's contemporary (and, for some years, wife), Frida Kahlo (1907–1954) created a body of work that was sometimes political, sometimes nationalistic, and always highly personal. Born to a Mexican mother and German father, Kahlo's mixed heritage was a centerpiece of her iconography, weighted, most often, in favor of her Mexican roots. In her extraordinary double portrait, *The Two Fridas* (Fig. 20.42), the artist shows herself in both a European-style lace dress and a traditional, indigenous Zapotec garment. The two Fridas, seated before a turbulent sky, are connected by blood—an artery that runs from one exposed heart to the other. Drops of red that trickle from the clamped end of the blood vessel form Rorschach-like stains that seem to transform into blossoms and cherries at the hem of her skirt. Her intent gaze and serious expression are an indication of her own physical suffering (she survived an accident that left her in unbearable pain for the rest of her life) and the travails of her people. Kahlo's marriage was also painful. She once told a friend, "I have suffered two serious accidents in my life, one in which a streetcar ran over me. . . . The other accident was Diego."[6]

---

[6] Frida Kahlo, quoted in Martha Zamora, *Frida Kahlo: The Brush of Anguish* (San Francisco: Chronicle Books, 1990), 37.

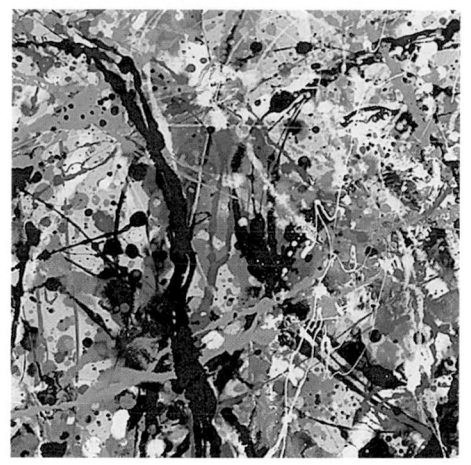

21

THE TWENTIETH CENTURY: POSTWAR TO POSTMODERN

Being an artist now means to question the nature of art.

— JOSEPH KOSUTH

THE OFT-REPEATED quote "May you live in interesting times" captures the appreciation of stimulation and novelty, perhaps even at the expense of tranquility. When it comes to contemporary art, we live in nothing if not interesting times. Louise Bourgeois, who was born in 1911 and continued to work avidly into her 90s, noted that "there are no settled ways"; there is "no fixed approach." Never before in history have artists experimented so freely with so many mediums, such different styles, such a wealth of content. Never before in history have works of art been so accessible to so many people. Go to "Google Images," and the world of art and artists is but a click away.

In this chapter, we discuss painting, sculpture, architecture, and other works that have appeared since the end of World War II—the art of recent times and of today. After the war, the center of the art world shifted to America following its long tenure in France and Germany as waves of immigrant artists settled largely in New York. Among them were Marcel Duchamp, Fernand Léger, Josef Albers, and Hans Hofmann. The Federal Art Project of the U.S. Works Progress Administration (WPA) had also nourished the New York artist community during the Great Depression. This group included Arshile Gorky, Willem de Kooning, Jack Tworkov, James Brooks, Philip Guston, and Stuart Davis, among many others.

< JACKSON POLLOCK, *One (Number 31, 1950)* (1950). Oil and enamel paint on canvas, 8' 10" × 17' 5⅝". The Museum of Modern Art, New York, New York.

THE NEW YORK SCHOOL

At mid-twentieth century, experiments in earlier nonobjective painting, the colorful distortions of Expressionism, the geometric abstraction of Cubism, the Automatist processes of Surrealism, and a host of other influences—including Zen Buddhism and psychoanalysis—were palpable in the developing styles of New York City artists. From this crucible, **Abstract Expressionism** emerged. Like other art movements perceived as radical, critics reacted to it with both intrigue and skepticism. Writing in *The New Yorker* in 1945, Robert M. Coates commented:

> [A] new school of painting is developing in this country. It is small as yet, no bigger than a baby's fist, but it is noticeable if you get around to the galleries much. It partakes a little of Surrealism and still more of Expressionism, and although its main current is still muddy and its direction obscure, one can make out bits of Hans Arp and Joan Miró floating in it, together with large chunks of Picasso and occasional fragments of [African American] sculptors. It is more emotional than logical in expression, and you may not like it (I don't either, entirely), but it can't escape attention.[1]

Spontaneity, gestural brushstrokes, nonobjective imagery, and fields of intense color characterize Abstract Expressionism. Many canvases are quite large, which, at any proximity, seems to envelop the viewer in the artist's distinct pictorial world. Some lines and shapes seem to reference Asian calligraphy, but their rendering is expansive and muscular compared with the more circumscribed and gentle brushstrokes of Chinese and Japanese artists.

Action Painting: Focus on Gesture

For some Abstract Expressionists, such as Jackson Pollock and Willem de Kooning, the gestural application of paint emerged as the most important aspect of their work. For others, it was the structure and saturated palette of the color field.

JACKSON POLLOCK

> Pollock's talent is volcanic. It has fire. It is unpredictable. It is undisciplined. It spills itself out in a mineral prodigality not yet crystallized. It is lavish, explosive, untidy. . . . What we need is more young men who paint from inner compulsion without an ear to what the critic or spectator may feel—painters who will risk spoiling a canvas to say something in their own way. Pollock is one.[2]

Jackson Pollock (1912–1956) is probably the best known of the Abstract Expressionists. Photographs or motion pictures of the artist energetically dripping and splashing paint across his huge canvases (Fig. 21.1) are familiar to

---

[1] Robert M. Coates, "The Art Galleries," *The New Yorker*, May 26, 1945, 68.

[2] Clement Greenberg, quoted in Introduction to catalog of an exhibition, "Jackson Pollock," Art of This Century Gallery, New York, November 9–27, 1943.

1945–1960	1960–1980	1980–
World War II ends in 1945 and many European artists emigrate to New York	Smith and Judd create geometrically pure sculptures	The Guerrilla Girls challenge male dominance of the art world
Abstract Expressionism begins; Pollock engages in action painting	Moore straddles realism and abstraction in his figurative sculptures	Ringgold quilts *Tar Beach*
Modern architects design the Farnsworth House, the Notre-Dame-du-Haut chapel, and the Seagram Building	Minimalism begins	Neo-Expressionism begins
	Pop artist Andy Warhol is at his height	Postmodern architects design the AT&T Building and the Humana Building
Rothko and Frankenthaler engage in color-field painting	John Lennon and Yoko Ono perform *Bagism*	Artists such as Kara Walker and Quick-to-See Smith protest the U.S. history of slavery and expropriation of Native American lands
Hamilton's collage spurs development of Pop Art	Conceptual art movement begins	
	Photorealism begins	
Rauschenberg innovates combine painting	Feminist art is ignited by Schapiro and Chicago	Deconstructivists design the Guggenheim Museum in Bilbao, the Stata Center, Dancing Towers, and the transportation hub for the World Trade Center
	New Image painting begins	
	Piano and Rogers design the Pompidou Center	Abramović performs *The Artist Is Present*

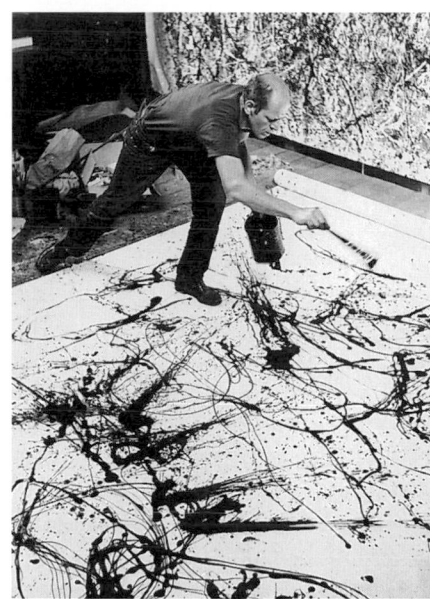

Born in Cody, Wyoming, Pollock came to New York to study with Thomas Hart Benton at the Art Students League. The 1943 quote from Clement Greenberg shows the impact that Pollock made at an early exhibition of his work. His paintings of this era frequently depicted actual or implied figures that were reminiscent of the abstractions of Picasso and, at times, of Expressionists and Surrealists.

Pollock's drip paintings of the late 1940s and early 1950s made several innovations that would be mirrored and developed in the work of other Abstract Expressionists. Foremost among these was the use of an overall gestural pattern barely contained by the limits of the canvas. In *One* (Fig. 21.2), the surface is an unsectioned, unified field. Overlapping skeins of paint create dynamic webs that project from the picture plane, creating an illusion of infinite depth. In Pollock's best work, these webs seem to be composed of energy that pushes and pulls the monumental tracery of the surface.

Pollock was in psychoanalysis at the time he executed his great drip paintings. He believed strongly in the role of the unconscious mind, of accident and spontaneity, in the creation of art. He was influenced not only by the intellectual impact of the Automatist Surrealists but also by what must have been his impression of walking hand in hand with his own unconscious forces through the realms of artistic expression. Before his untimely death in a car crash in 1956, Pollock had returned to figural paintings that were heavy in impasto and predominantly black.

many people. Pollock would walk across the surface of the canvas as if controlled by primitive impulses and unconscious ideas. Accident became a prime compositional element in his painting. Art critic Harold Rosenberg coined the term **action painting** in 1951 to describe the outcome of such a process—a painting whose surface implied a strong sense of activity, as created by the signs of brushing, dripping, or splattering of paint.

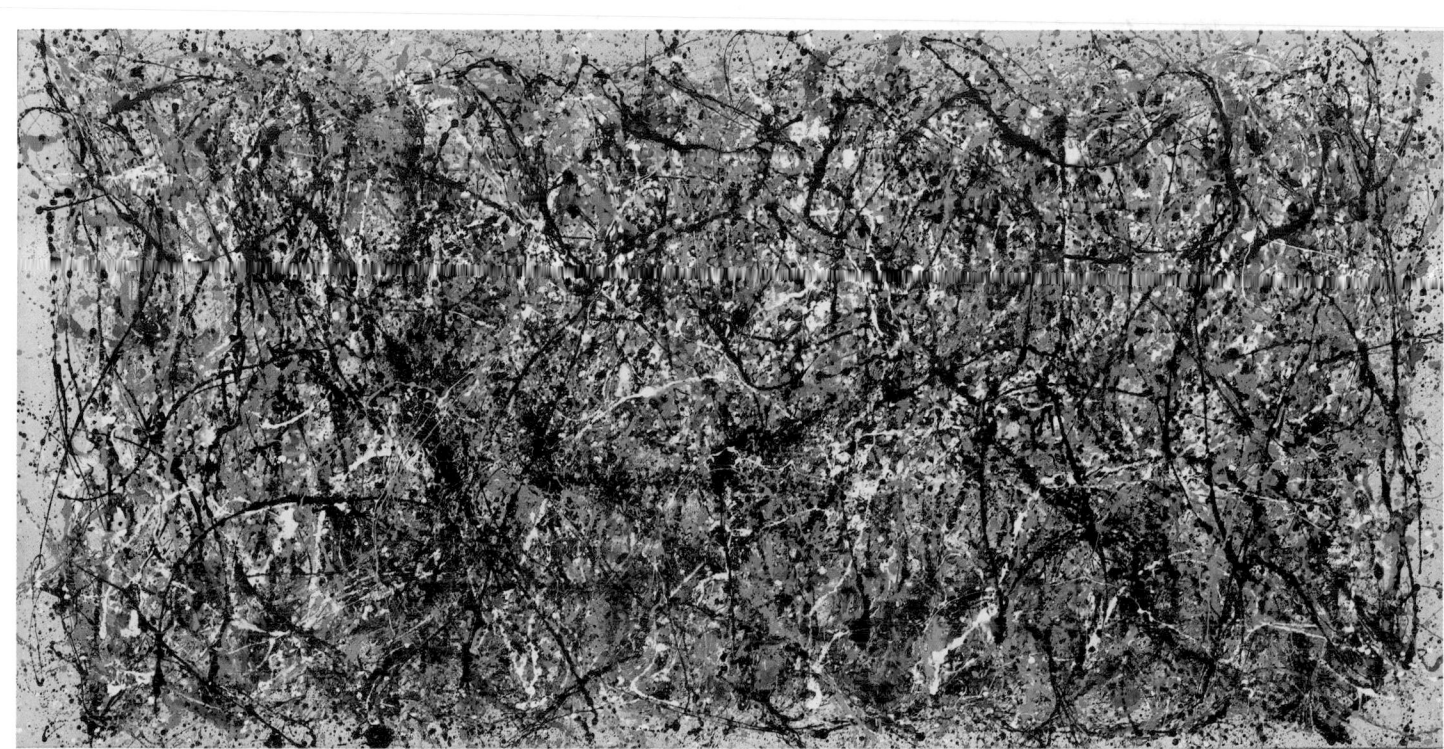

▲ 21.2 **JACKSON POLLOCK,** *One (Number 31, 1950)* (1950). Oil and enamel paint on canvas, 8' 10" × 17' 5⅝". The Museum of Modern Art, New York, New York.

I merge what I call the organic with what I call abstract.

—LEE KRASNER

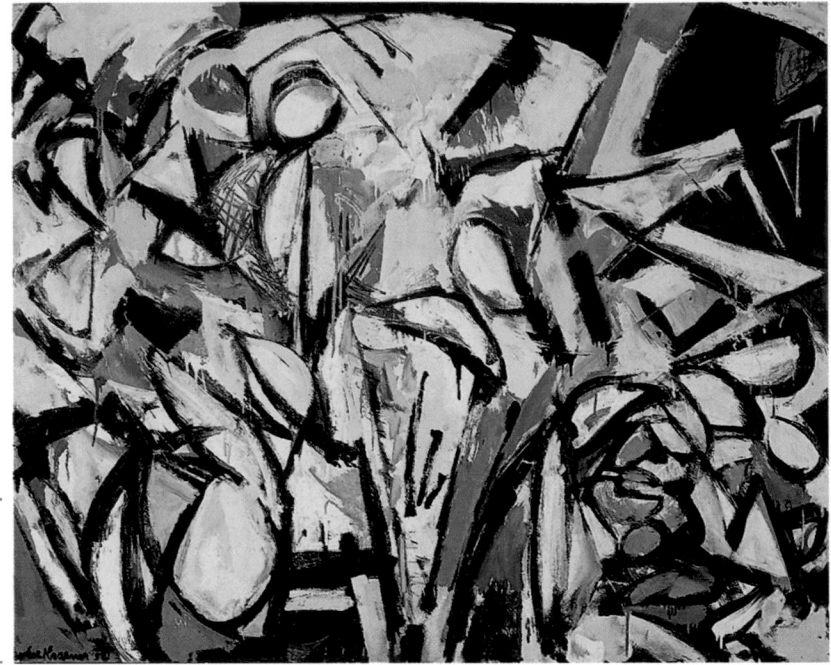

∧ **21.3 LEE KRASNER,** *Easter Lilies* (1956). Oil on cotton duck, 48¼" × 60⅛". Private collection.

LEE KRASNER Lee Krasner (1908–1984) was one of only a few women in the mainstream of Abstract Expressionism. Yet, despite her originality and strength as a painter, her work, until fairly recently, had taken a critical backseat to that of her famous husband—Jackson Pollock. She once noted:

> I was not the average woman married to the average painter. I was married to Jackson Pollock. The context is bigger and even if I was not personally dominated by Pollock, the whole art world was.[3]

Krasner had a burning desire to be a painter from the time she was a teenager and received academic training at some of the best art schools in the country. She was influenced by artists of diverse styles, including Picasso, Mondrian, and the Surrealists. Most important, like Pollock and the other members of the Abstract Expressionist school, she was exposed to the work of many European émigrés who came to New York in the 1930s and 1940s.

Both Pollock and Krasner experimented with allover compositions around 1945, but her work was smaller in scale and exhibited much more

control. Even after 1950, when Krasner's style became much freer and her canvases larger, the accidental nature of Pollock's style never took hold of her own. Rather, Krasner's compositions might be characterized as a synthesis of choice and chance.

Easter Lilies (Fig. 21.3) was painted in 1956, the year of Pollock's fatal automobile accident. The jagged shapes and bold black lines against the muddied greens and ochers render the composition dysphoric; yet in the midst of all that is harsh are the recognizable contours of lilies, whose bright whites offer a kind of hope in a sea of anxiety. Krasner once remarked of her work, "My painting is so autobiographical, if anyone can take the trouble to read it."[4]

WILLEM DE KOONING Born in Rotterdam, Holland, Willem de Kooning (1904–1997) immigrated to the United States in 1926, where he joined the other forerunners of Abstract Expressionism. Until 1940, de Kooning painted figures and portraits. His first abstractions exhibit Picasso's influence. But, as the 1940s progressed, de Kooning's compositions consistently featured a clash of the organic shapes and harsh, jagged

---

[4] Lee Krasner, in Cindy Nemser, "A Conversation with Lee Krasner," *Arts Magazine* 47 (April 1973): 48.

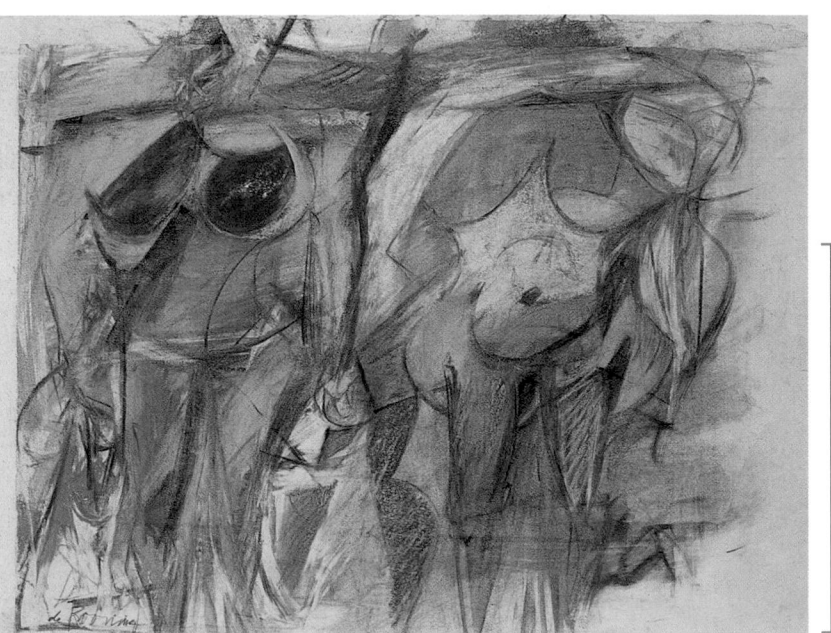

∧ **21.4 WILLEM DE KOONING,** *Two Women's Torsos* (1952), Pastel drawing. 18⅞" × 24". The Art Institute of Chicago. The Art Institute of Chicago, Illinois.

---

[3] Lee Krasner, in Roberta Brandes Gratz, "Daily Close-Up—After Pollock," *New York Post*, December 6, 1973.

> [A critic] thought that American painting couldn't be abstract—it wasn't American.
>
> —WILLEM DE KOONING

lines, reflecting "the age of anxiety" about which W. H. Auden wrote in his Pulitzer Prize–winning poem by the same name set in 1940s New York City.

De Kooning is perhaps best known for his series of paintings of women, which began in 1950. In contrast to the appealing figurative works of an earlier day, many of his abstracted women are frankly overpowering and repellent. Faces are frequently resolved into skull-like masks reminiscent of ancient fertility figures; they assault the viewer from a loosely brushed backdrop of tumultuous color. Perhaps they portray what was a major psychoanalytic dilemma during the 1950s—how women could be at once seductive, alluring, and castrating.

The subjects of *Two Women's Torsos* (Fig. 21.4) are among the more suggestive of the series. Richly curved pastel breasts swell from a sea of spontaneous brushstrokes that here and there violently obscure the imagery. The result is a freewheeling eroticism. A primal urge has been cast loose in space, pushing and pulling against the picture plane. But de Kooning is one of the few Abstract Expressionists who never completely surrendered figurative painting.

JOAN MITCHELL   The intense physicality of action painting had the effect of masculinizing the abstract expressionist movement and artist statements at the time did little to dispel that notion. Pollock, for example, famously referred to his canvas as an arena. The "boys' club" image was underscored by appearances. About the same time that Joan Mitchell (1925–1992) painted *Cercando un Ago* (Fig. 21.5), twenty-eight artists considered the leading figures in New York painting were brought together for

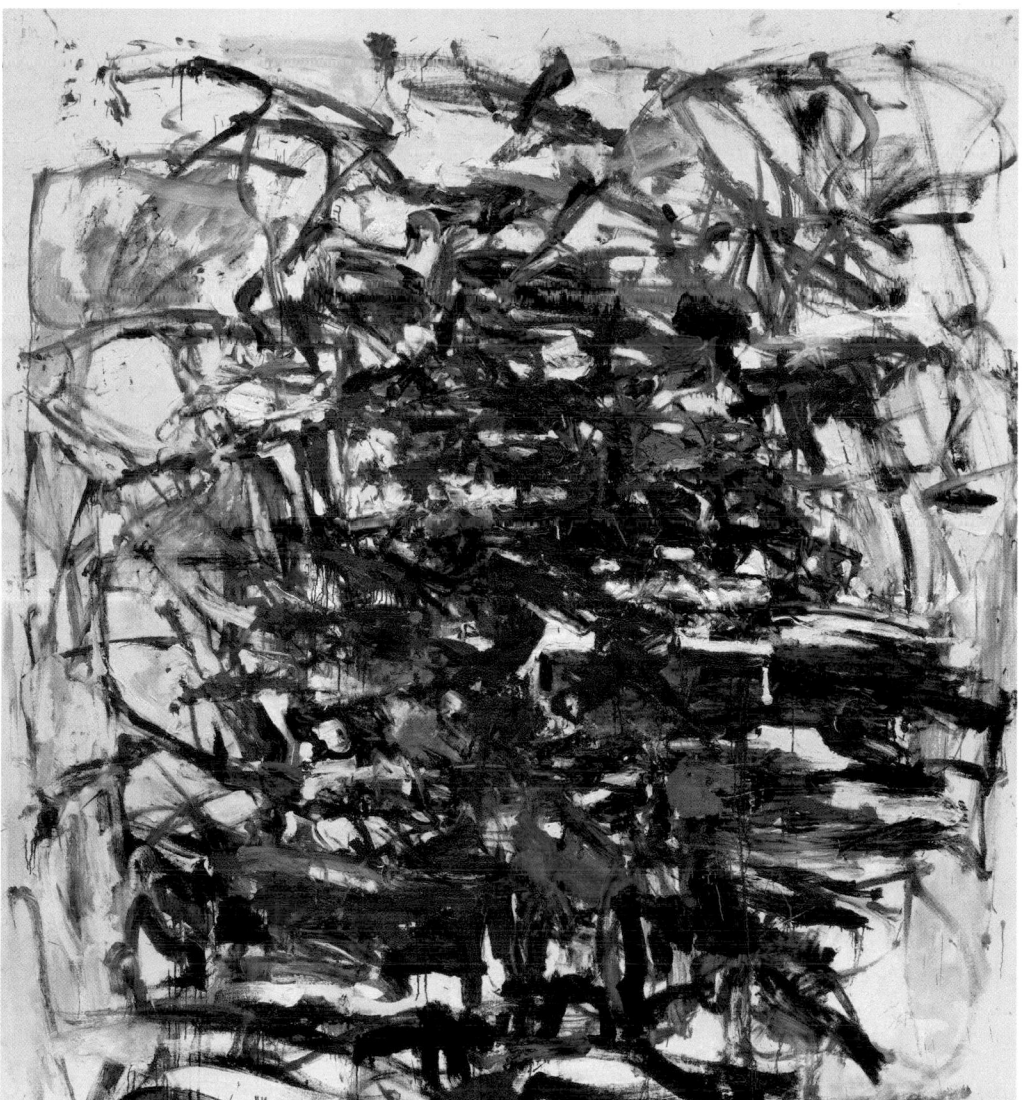

> 21.5 **JOAN MITCHELL,** *Cercando un Ago* (1957). Oil on canvas, 94 ⅛" × 87 ⅝". Collection of the Joan Mitchell Foundation, New York, New York.

1 ft.

MARK ROTHKO (1903–1970) worked in many styles during his lifetime. His early work, like that of many twentieth-century artists, was largely in a realistic vein. By the time he was 40 years old, he showed an interest in Surrealism. But within a few years, he was painting the Abstract Expressionist color-field paintings with which he is mainly associated.

He painted *Number 22* (**Fig. 21.6**) in 1949, at about the time a critic remarked that his work tended to evoke the color patterns of French Impressionists and to create "lovely moods." The realistic images of his early days and the symbols of his Surrealistic days were replaced with large, abstract fields of color, which were more or less vertically stacked. Here Rothko uses a high-key palette with intensely saturated color. The values in *Number 22* are bold, jaunty, hot, and abrasive. We observe the work of an innovative 46-year-old painter coming into his own—creating his mature style, being invited to teach in academies across the country, and receiving some critical acclaim. The light values seem to imbue the work with boisterous emotion and life. Rothko was developing his signature image of "floating" rectangles that continued to be his model throughout his life's work. The canvases consisted solely of these shapes, stacked one atop the other, varying in width and height and hue, their edges softened with feathered strokes that created the illusion of subtle vibration. By not referring to any specific visual experience, the high-key values of these nonobjective works seem to suggest a divine, spiritual presence. The luminosity of *Number 22* is perhaps suggestive of the birth of the universe. The red band in the middle is reminiscent of a horizon line, but all is aglow and alive.

Light that earlier had been reflected became trapped in his canvases. Despite public acclaim, Rothko suffered from depression during his last years. In 1968, he was diagnosed as having heart disease, and one year later his second marriage was in ruins. His paintings of the later years may be an expression of the turmoil and the fading spark within. Compare *Number 22* to a work Rothko painted some twenty years later: *Black on Grey* (**Fig. 21.7**). The painting reveals one of the most dramatic and resonant uses of black in the history of abstract painting. Toward the end of the 1960s, Rothko began to simplify his color fields, stretching his rectangles out to the very edges of the canvas and effectively dividing the surface into two simple fields. He also reduced his palette to low-key values—particularly grays, browns, and black. In Rothko's last painting, *Black on Grey*, created just before he took his own life in his studio on February 25, 1970, black and gray merge at a horizon punctuated by a dull light. Darkness falls heavily on the mottled gray field; note that the title, *Black on Grey*, underscores the symbolism of the encroaching of death. It is as if he has brought his life, and his life's work, to a close. The spiritual presence has flickered out.

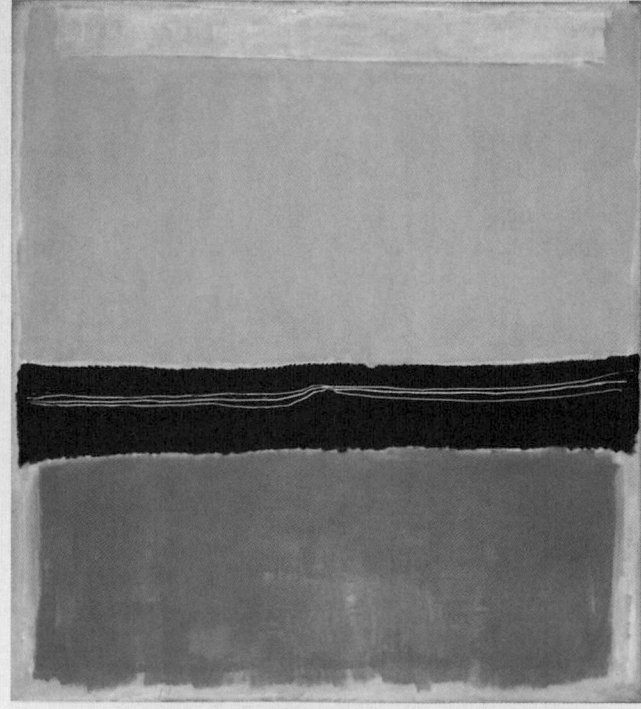

▲ **21.6 MARK ROTHKO,** *Number 22* (1949). Oil on canvas, 117" × 107 ⅛". The Museum of Modern Art, New York, New York.

▲ **21.7 MARK ROTHKO,** *Black on Grey* (1970). Acrylic on canvas, 80 ¼" × 69". The Solomon R. Guggenheim Museum, New York, New York.

a photograph; only one was a woman—a painter named Hedda Sterne—whose work, though gestural, was much less aggressive in character than that of her male colleagues. Mitchell did not pose in the photograph, but she is widely considered to have been the most important woman to work in the gestural idiom of Abstract Expressionism of the 1950s. Her sweeping brushstrokes, liberal use of color, and intense, raw energy create a sense of urgency and a mood of turbulence.

Color-Field Painting

For some Abstract Expressionists, action painting held little interest as they focused on simple shapes and fields of saturated hues, essentially devoid of gesture and emotional content. Their often-large canvases, comprised of subtle modulations of color that create a vibrating or pulsating effect on the eyes, envelop the viewer, and provide a unique sensory experience to those who submit.

MARK ROTHKO   Mark Rothko (1903–1970) painted lone figures in urban settings in the 1930s and biomorphic Surrealistic canvases throughout the early 1940s. Later in that decade, he began to paint the large, floating, hazy-edged color fields for which he is renowned. During the 1950s, the color fields consistently assumed the form of rectangles floating above one another in an atmosphere defined by subtle variations in tone and gesture, as in Figure 21.6. The large scale of these canvases absorbs the viewer in color.

Early in his career, Rothko had favored a palette of pale hues. During the 1960s, however, his works grew somber. Reds that earlier had been intense, warm, and sensuous were now awash in deep blacks and browns and took on the appearance of worn cloth. Oranges and yellows were replaced by grays and black, as we see in the nearby Compare + Contrast feature.

HELEN FRANKENTHALER   Helen Frankenthaler (1928–2011) was described by fellow artist, Kenneth Noland, as a "bridge between Pollock and what was possible." Frankenthaler's approach was less about extending the inner world of the artist into the outer through gesture, and more about exploring the connection between color and surface—indeed the literal integration of the two. By pooling and spreading expanses of diluted paint on unprimed canvas in what she labeled her "soak stain" technique, Frankenthaler's translucent veils of color seeped into the fibers of the canvas, softening the edges of the colorful floating shapes. Intermittent flowing lines, splotches, and splatters of paint keep our eyes attuned to the decorative surface. In paintings such as *The Bay* (Fig. 21.8), the canvas and image are now literally one.

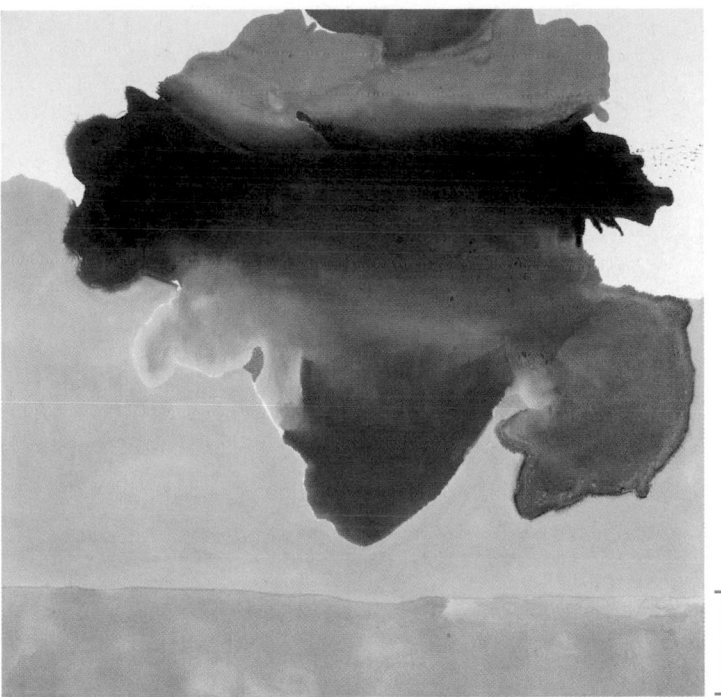

▲ 21.8 HELEN FRANKENTHALER, *The Day* (1063). Acrylic on canvas, 80¼" × 81¾". Detroit Institute of Arts, Detroit, Michigan.

Constructed Sculpture and Assemblage

True experimentation in the medium of sculpture came with the advent of the twentieth century, and contemporary sculptors owe much to the trail-blazing predecessors who embraced unorthodox materials and processes. Constructed sculpture was added to the lexicon of technique as artists built often-large-scale works from pieces of wood or welded shapes of steel. Components of constructed sculpture may include materials such as rods, bars, tubes, planks, dowels, blocks, fabric, wire, thread, glass, plastic, and machined geometric solids. As with many contemporary painters, sculptors were eager to emphasize surfaces and explored varied ways to add to them the artist's gesture. Also as with abstract expressionist paintings, many of their works bore little or no resemblance to objects in the visible world.

Assemblage refers to works that are constructed, but from found objects. Marcel Duchamp, the early twentieth-century Dada artist, assembled his *ready-mades* from

CONNECTIONS Louise Nevelson's wooden assemblages of found objects and jigsawed pieces of wood assume meanings that are more than the sum of their parts.

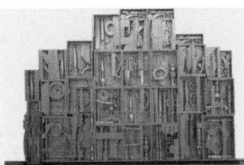

Nevelson's wooden assemblages (Fig. 11.11)

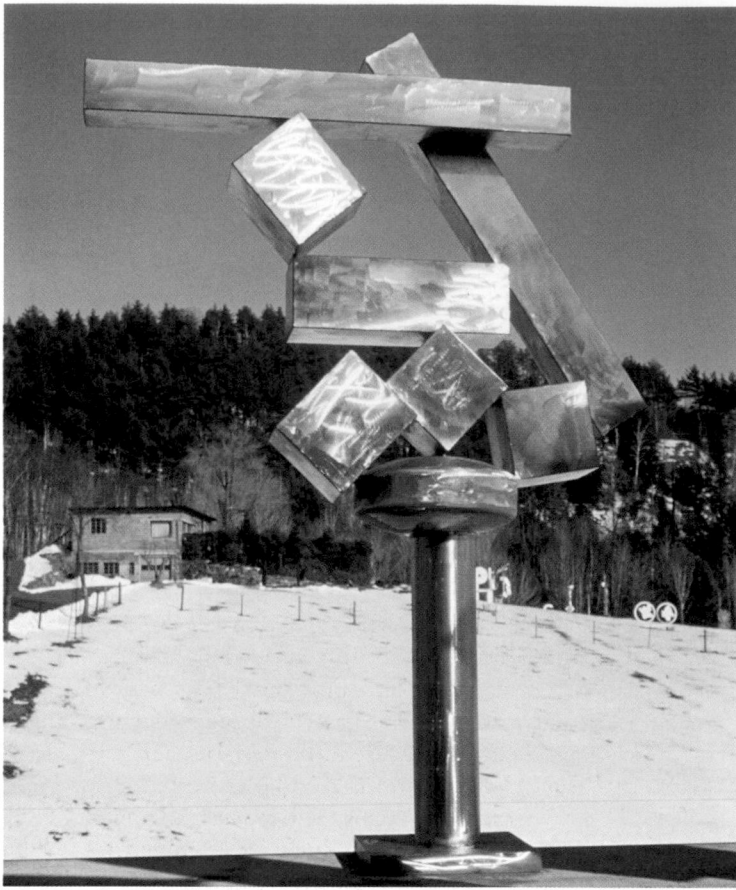

∧ 21.9 DAVID SMITH, *Cubi XVIII* (1964). Stainless steel.

actual objects; one piece consisted of a wire birdcage filled with marble "sugar cubes" and a cuttlebone.

DAVID SMITH David Smith (1906–1965) began his career in the 1940s with figurative sculpture, but his approach to art making in the 1950s can best be described as "drawing in space" with steel. Even as his work shifted to cubes and planes of steel arranged in provocative combinations (Fig. 21.9), his signature burnishing of their highly reflective surfaces imparts a gestural quality similar to that found in Abstract Expressionist paintings.

NANCY GRAVES Smith's influence can be seen in the welded objects and steel shapes that characterize the work of Nancy Graves (1939–1995), although the whimsical nature of her imagery departs from his stolid geometry. *Tarot* (Fig. 21.10) (the word refers to a set of allegorical cards used in fortune-telling) is an assemblage of sundry human-made and natural elements—strange flowers, lacy plants, noodles, dried fish, lampshades, tools and machinery, even packing materials. The spirit of the piece derives from the

juxtapositions and coloration. Graves focused much of her attention on the development of polychrome (multicolored) patinas with poured acrylic and baked enamel.

JUDY PFAFF Described by the *New York Times* art critic Roberta Smith as a "collagist in space," Judy Pfaff's (b. 1946) sculptures and installations (such as *3D*; see Fig. 2.31) are constructed with all manner of materials and objects. *Said the Spider to the Fly* (Fig. 22.11) seems to tumble from the wall into the gallery space, drawing the viewer into a thicket of wood, wire, and paper flowers. Appropriating the opening line of an early-nineteenth-century poem by the same title—"Will you walk into my parlour? Said the Spider to the Fly"— Pfaff juxtaposes seductive shapes and textures with a forbidding, sinister blackness to contemporize a classic cautionary tale.

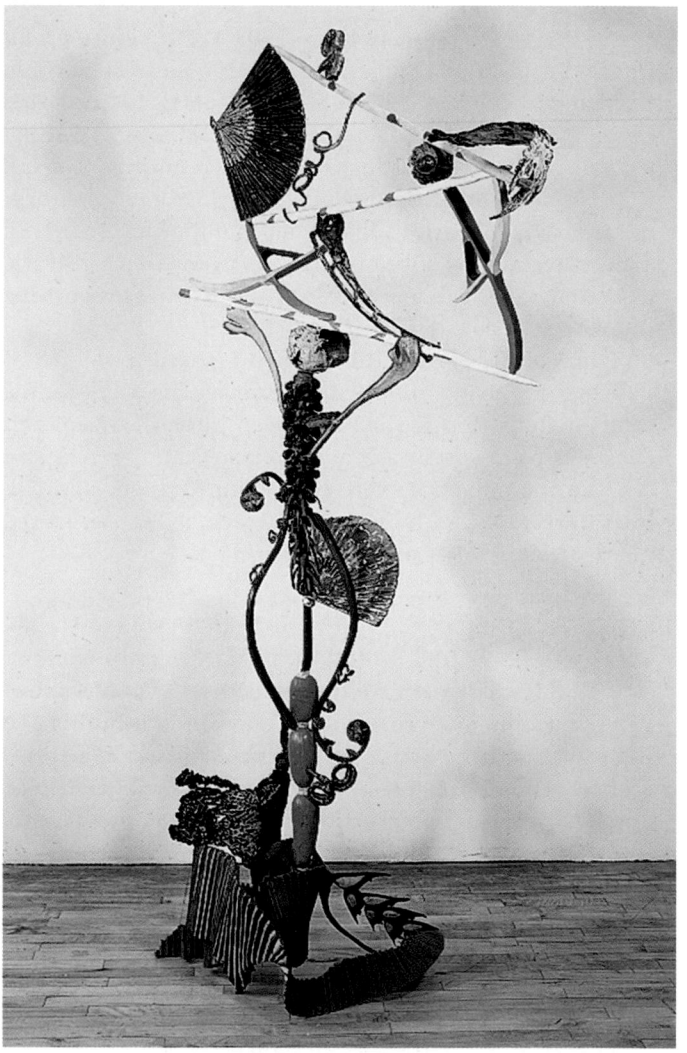

∧ 21.10 NANCY GRAVES, *Tarot* (1984). Bronze with polychrome patina and enamel, 88" × 49" × 20". Private collection.

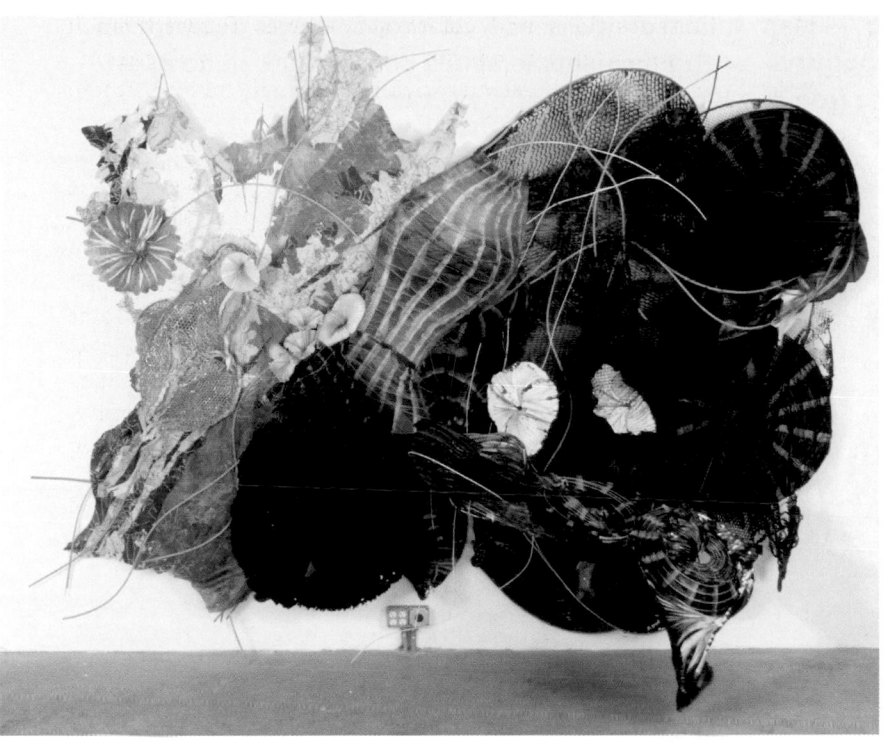

▲ 21.11 **JUDY PFAFF**, *Said the Spider to the Fly* (2010). Paper, wood, wire and rod, artificial flowers; 128" × 162" × 48".

FIGURATION AND ABSTRACTION IN THE POSTWAR YEARS

Although abstract and nonobjective art dominated the American art scene in the 1940s and 1950s, these were not exclusive idioms. Some artists remained strong in their commitment to the figure, to nature, or visible reality, even as they integrated some elements of the New York School.

Focus on the Figure

In the thick of Abstract Expressionism, and in the decade following, when artists sought to create new forms of expression within its canon, the painter Francis Bacon and the sculptor Henry Moore straddled the space between figurative art and abstraction in idiosyncratic ways.

FRANCIS BACON Many of the figurative canvases of British artist Francis Bacon (1909–1992) rework themes by masters such as Giotto, Rembrandt, and van Gogh. But Bacon's personalized interpretation of history is expressionistically distorted by what must be a very raw response to the quality of contemporary life.

Figure with Meat (Fig. 21.12) is one of a series of paintings from the 1950s in which Bacon reconstructed

Velázquez's portrait of Pope Innocent X. The tormented, openmouthed figure is partially obscured, as if seen through a curtain or veil. The brilliantly composed slabs of beef, which stand like totems richly threaded with silver and gold, replace ornamental metalwork posts that rise from the back corners of the papal throne in the Velázquez portrait. Profiles can be seen in the sides of beef, and a goblet of noble proportions is constructed from the negative space between them. The bloody whisperings shared by the profiles are anybody's guess. Whereas the background of Velázquez's subject was a textured space of indefinite depth, Bacon's seated figure and the sides of beef are set by single-point perspective within an abstract black box.

HENRY MOORE Henry Moore (1898–1986) had a long and prolific career that spanned the seven decades since the 1920s, but we introduce him at this point because, despite his productivity, his influence was not generally felt until after World War II.

In the late 1920s, Moore was intrigued by the massiveness of stone. In an early effort to be true to his material, he executed blocky reclining figures reminiscent of the Native American art of Mexico. In the

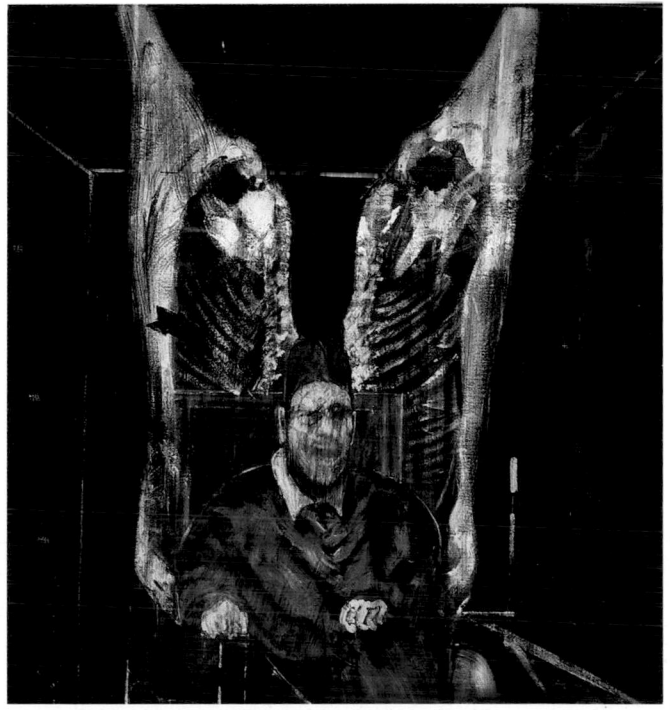

1 ft.

▲ 21.12 **FRANCIS BACON**, *Figure with Meat* (1954). Oil on canvas, 50⅞" × 48". The Art Institute of Chicago, Chicago, Illinois.

> The sensitive observer of sculpture must . . . learn to feel shape simply as shape, not as description or reminiscence. He must, for example, perceive an egg as a simple single solid shape, quite apart from its significance as food, or from the literary idea that it will become a bird.
>
> —HENRY MOORE

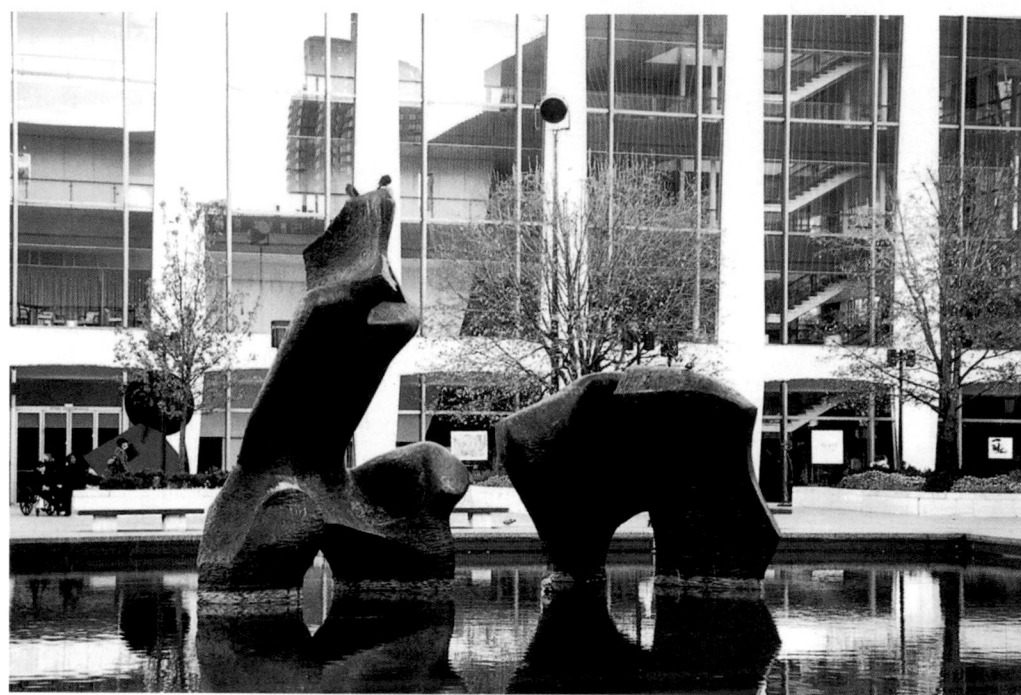

< 21.13 HENRY MOORE, *Reclining Figure, Lincoln Center* (1963–1965). Bronze; 16' high, 30' wide. Lincoln Center for the Performing Arts, New York, New York.

1930s, Moore turned to bronze and wood and was also influenced by Picasso. His figures became abstracted and more fluid. Voids opened up, and air and space began to flow through his works.

At mid-twentieth century, Moore's works received the attention they deserve. He continued to produce figurative works, but he also executed a series of abstract bronzes in the tradition of his early reclining figures, such as the one at Lincoln Center for the Performing Arts in New York City (Fig. 21.13). No longer as concerned about limiting the scope of his expression because of material, he could now let his bronzes assume the massiveness of his earlier stonework. However, his continued exploration of abstract biomorphic shapes and his separation and opening of forms created a lyricism that was lacking in his earlier sculptures.

Abstraction

Another approach to abstraction took root in the wake of Abstract Expressionism, one that was far more precise and controlled, emphasizing the purity of form and asserting the two-dimensionality of the canvas surface.

FRANK STELLA Largely credited as the key figure in hard-edge geometric abstraction in American art of the postwar period, Frank Stella subscribed to the notion that, in his words, "What you see is what you see." His *Mas o Menos* (Fig. 21.14), Spanish for "more or less," is an example of his signature nonobjective works in which the imagery—in this case, lines—is derived from the shape of the perimeter of the canvas. Beginning with the outer edges of the two-dimensional surface, he echoed the contours in a zigzag pattern. Image is connected to object (the physical canvas) as never before.

It is difficult to imagine work farther removed from that of the Abstract Expressionists. There is no gestural brushwork. There is no sense of existential anxiety. The spontaneous gives way to the methodical; intellectual discipline overrides the submission to primal impulses that might be rising to the surface of consciousness.

ELIZABETH MURRAY Shaped canvases such as Stella's challenged yet another convention in painting and marked the first step in obscuring the boundaries between painting, sculpture, and installation. Elizabeth Murray (1940–2007), a shaped-canvas artist of a more recent generation, coupled abstract (more precisely, bio-

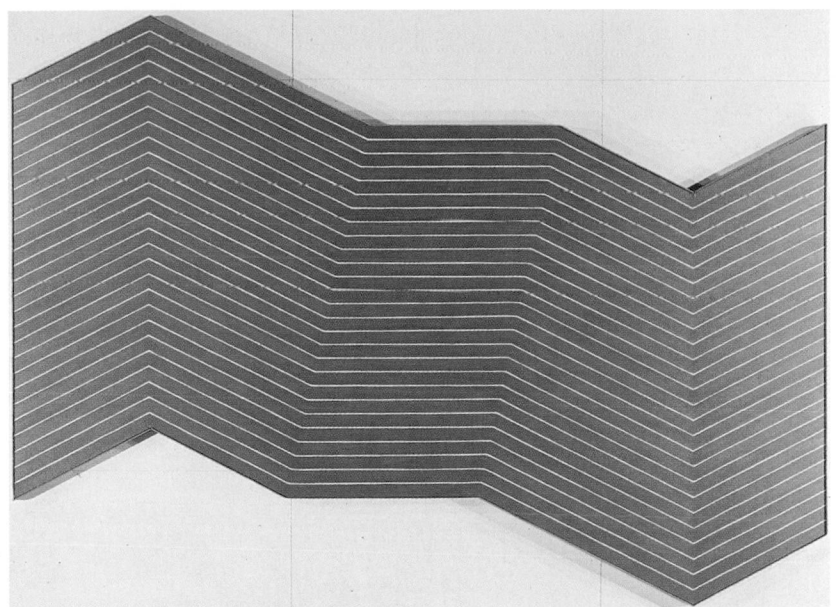

< 21.14 **FRANK STELLA**, *Mas o Menos (More or Less)* (1964). Metallic powder in acrylic emulsion on canvas, 118" × 164 ½". Musée National d'Art Moderne, Centre Georges Pompidou, Paris, France.

morphic) shapes with shaped canvases, often penetrating the flat plane or layering—in the manner of sculptural relief—multiple painted pieces. The effect is one in which the whole is simultaneously fragmented and patched together. *Sail Baby* (Fig. 21.16) is comprised of three large, shaped canvases, individual and, at the same time, linked—pieces in a puzzle, so to speak, that together construct the image of an ordinary teacup. Murray has explained that the painting functions as a narrative: "[It is] about my family. It's about myself and my brother and

my sister, and I think, it is also about my own three children, even though Daisy [Murray's youngest daughter] wasn't born yet."[5] Though essentially an abstract work, its references to human experience—the content—sets Murray apart from Stella, Kenneth Noland (see Fig. 8.8) and other earlier pioneers of shaped-canvas art.

[5] *Elizabeth Murray: Paintings and Drawings*, exhibition catalog organized by Sue Graze and Kathy Halbreich, essay by Roberta Smith (New York: Abrams, in association with the Dallas Museum of Art and the MIT Committee on the Visual Arts, 1987), 64.

CONNECTIONS For the ancient Greek painter, as for contemporary users of the shaped canvas, the shape of a vessel often governed the overall design of the painted imagery (Fig. 21.15), as in a small black-figure cup in which concentric circles of delicate vine tendrils echo the roundness of the perimeter.

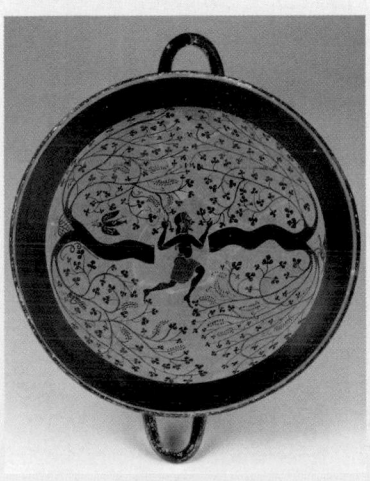

< 21.15 Ionic black-figure cup, "Cup of the Bird Catcher" (c. 550 BCE).

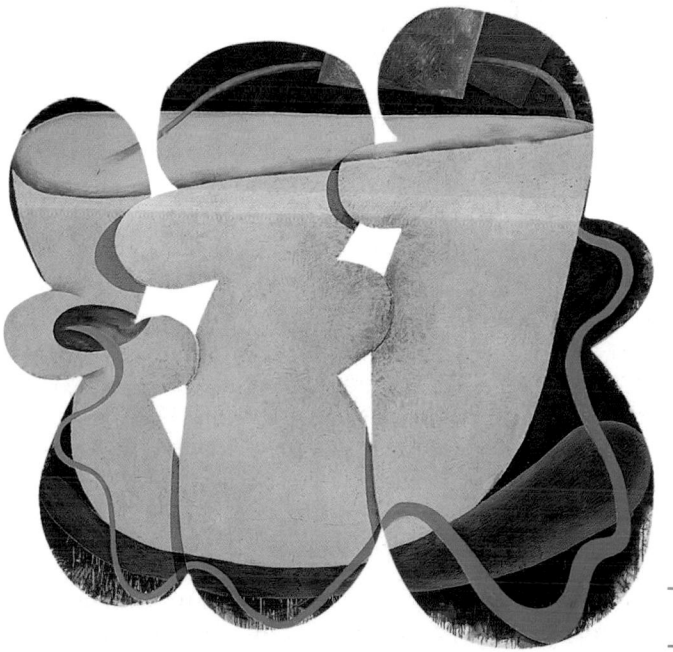

∧ 21.16 **ELIZABETH MURRAY**, *Sail Baby* (1983). Oil on canvas, 126" × 135". Walker Art Center, Minneapolis, Minnesota.

ART OF THE SIXTIES AND SEVENTIES

The art of the 1960s and the 1970s could not appear to be more dichotomous. On the one hand, a group of artists emerged who, in the words of Robert Rauschenberg, sought to work "in the gap between art and life." These Pop artists incorporated found objects (as did Marcel Duchamp and other Dada artists) and images of contemporary culture into their compositions, blurring the distinction between the fine art object and the stuff of everyday life. On the other hand were artists like Donald Judd, who focused on what he called creating "specific objects," which were typically geometric and which ranged from single, simple cubes to works consisting of a series of repeated, identical, industrial-looking forms arranged on the principle of "one thing after another") (see Fig. 21.27). Then there were the conceptual artists, for whom the object—if it was produced at all—was merely the visible embodiment of what existed in the artist's mind. Though very different in style and in aims, the movements of the 1960s and 1970s had at least one thing in common: the desire to eliminate the emotionalism, exclusivity, and egocentricity of Abstract Expressionism.

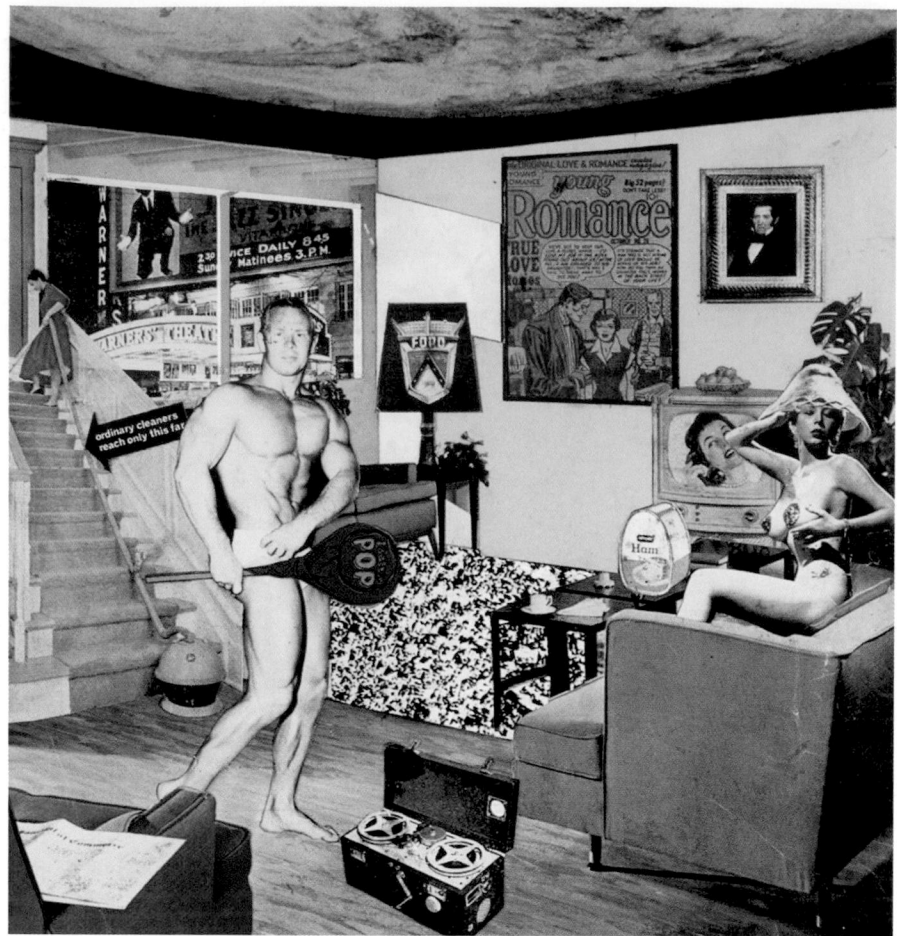

∧ 21.17 **RICHARD HAMILTON**, *Just What Is It That Makes Today's Homes So Different, So Appealing?* (1956). Collage, 10¼" × 9¾". Kunsthalle Tubingen, Tubingen, Germany.

1 in.

Pop Art

If one were asked to choose the contemporary art movement that was most enticing, surprising, controversial, and also exasperating, one might select **Pop Art**. The term *Pop* was coined by English critic Lawrence Alloway in 1954 to refer to the universal images of "popular culture," such as movie posters, billboards, magazine and newspaper photographs, and advertisements. Pop Art, by its selection of commonplace and familiar subjects—subjects that are already too much with us—also challenges commonplace conceptions about the meaning of art.

Whereas many artists have strived to portray the beautiful, Pop Art intentionally depicts the mundane.

Whereas many artists represent the noble, stirring, or monstrous, Pop Art renders the commonplace, the boring. Whereas other forms of art often elevate their subjects, Pop Art is frequently matter-of-fact. One tenet of Pop Art is that the work should be so objective that it does not show the "personal signature" of the artist. This maxim contrasts starkly, for example, with the highly personalized gestural brushstroke found in Abstract Expressionism.

RICHARD HAMILTON Despite the widespread view that Pop Art developed purely in the United States, it actually originated during the 1950s in the United Kingdom. British artist Richard Hamilton (1922–2011), one of its creators, had been influenced by Marcel Duchamp's idea that the mission of art should be to destroy the normal meanings and functions of art.

Hamilton's tiny collage *Just What Is It That Makes Today's Homes So Different, So Appealing?* (Fig. 21.17) is one of the earliest and most revealing Pop Art works.

It functions as a veritable time capsule for the 1950s, a decade during which the speedy advance of technology finds everyone buying pieces of the American dream. What is that dream? Comic books, TVs, movies, and tape recorders; canned hams and TV dinners; enviable physiques; Tootsie Pops; and vacuum cleaners that finally let the "lady of the house" clean all the stairs at once. It is easy to read satire and irony into Hamilton's work, but his placement of these objects within the parameters of art encourages us to truly *see* them instead of just coexisting with them.

ROBERT RAUSCHENBERG American Pop artist Robert Rauschenberg (1925–2008) studied in Paris and then with Josef Albers and others at the renowned Black Mountain College in North Carolina. Before developing his own Pop Art style, Rauschenberg experimented with loosely and broadly brushed Abstract Expressionist canvases. He is best known, however, for introducing a construction referred to as the **combine painting**, in which stuffed animals, bottles, articles of clothing and furniture, and scraps of photographs are attached to the canvas.

Rauschenberg's *The Bed* (Fig. 21.18) is a paint-splashed quilt and pillow, mounted upright on a wall as any painting might be. Here the artist toys with the traditional relationships between materials, forms, and content. The content of the work is actually its support; rather than a canvas on a stretcher, the quilt and pillow are the materials on which the painter drips and splashes his pigments. Perhaps even more outrageous is Rauschenberg's 1959 work *Monogram*, in which a stuffed ram—an automobile tire wrapped around its middle—is mounted on a horizontal base that consists of scraps of photos and prints and loose, gestural painting.

JASPER JOHNS Jasper Johns (b. 1930) was Rauschenberg's classmate at Black Mountain College, and their appearance on the New York art scene was simultaneous. Johns' early work also integrated the overall gestural brushwork of the Abstract Expressionists with the use of found objects, but unlike Rauschenberg, Johns soon made the object central to his compositions. His works frequently portray familiar objects, such as numbers, maps, color charts, targets, and flags, integrated into a unified field by thick gestural brushwork.

One "tenet" of Pop Art, as noted, is that imagery is to be presented objectively, that the personal signature of the artist is to be eliminated. That principle must be modified if we are to include within Pop the works of Rauschenberg, Johns, and others, for many of them immediately betray their devotion to expressionistic

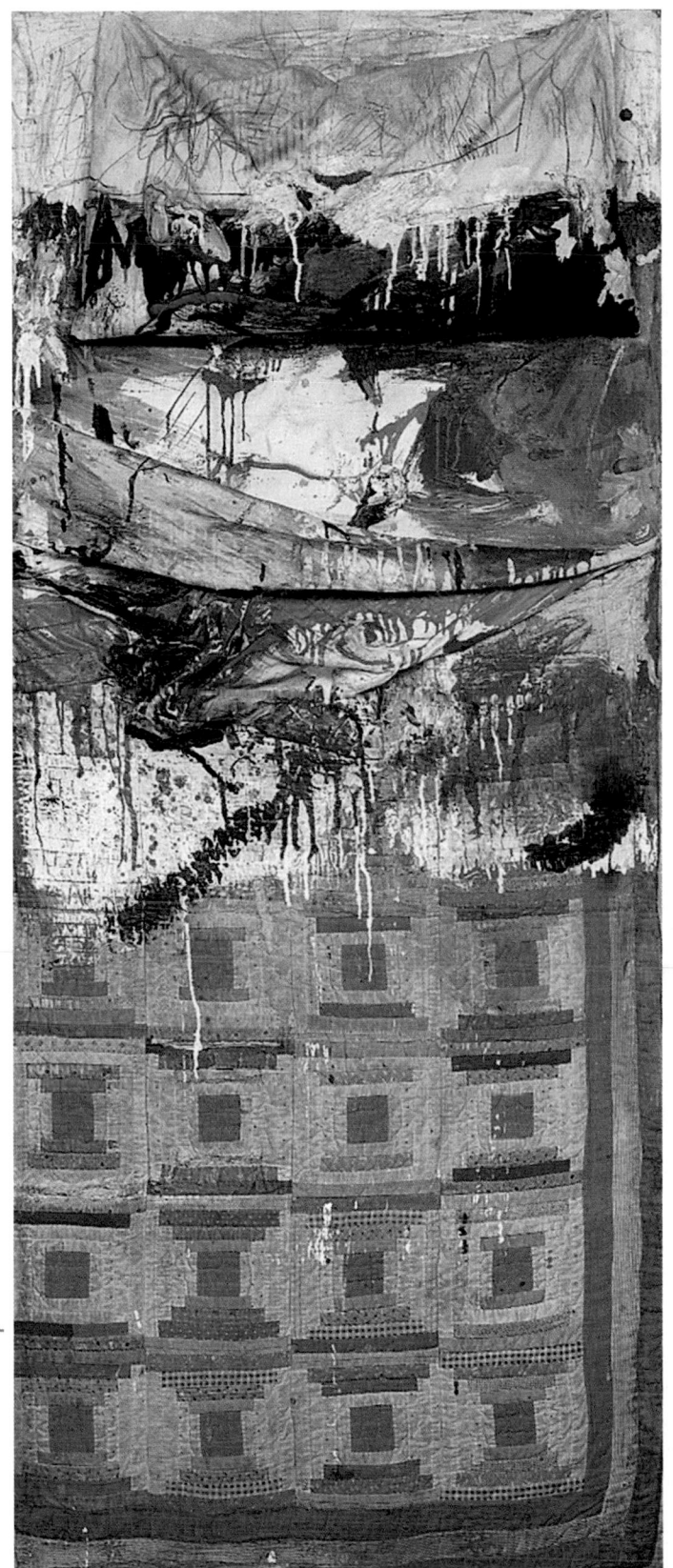

1 ft.

∧ 21.18 ROBERT RAUSCHENBERG, *The Bed* (1955). Combine painting: oil and pencil on pillow, quilt, and sheet on wood supports. 75 ¼" × 31 ½" × 6 ½". The Museum of Modern Art, New York, New York.

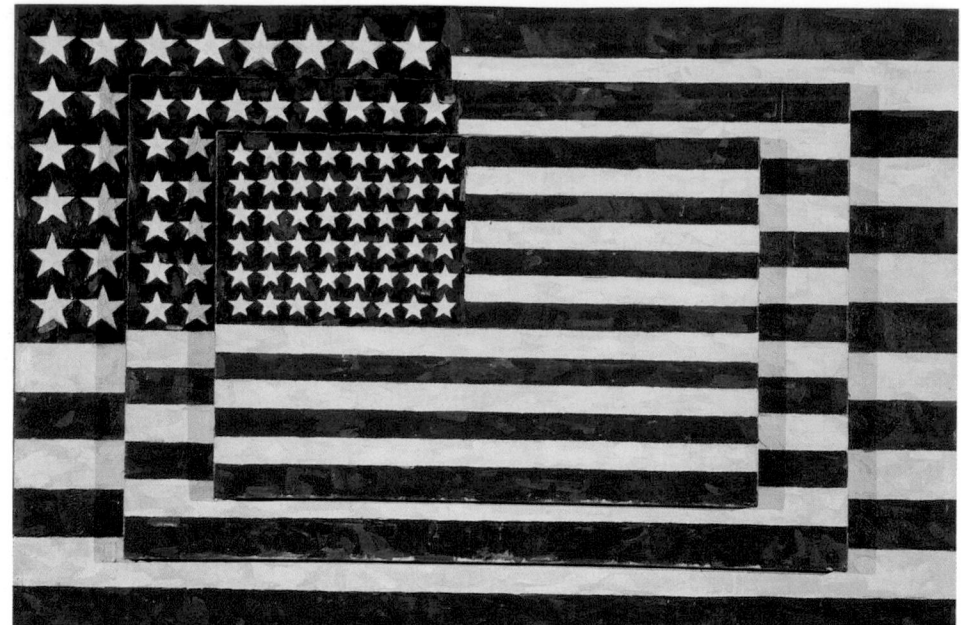

1 ft.

◄ **21.19 JASPER JOHNS,** *Three Flags* (1958). Encaustic on canvas. 30⅞" × 45½" × 5". Whitney Museum of American Art, New York, New York.

brushwork. Johns's *Three Flags* (Fig. 21.19) was painted with encaustic (a combination of liquid wax and pigment) and newsprint on three superimposed canvases of increasing size. The result yields a distinct surface texture that informs the viewer that she or he is not looking at a painting and not at actual machine-made flags. The work requires the viewer to take a new look at a most familiar object.

ANDY WARHOL Andy Warhol (1928–1987) once earned a living designing packages and Christmas cards. Today he epitomizes the Pop artist in the public mind. Just as Campbell's soups represent bland, boring nourishment, Andy Warhol's appropriation of soup cans, his hackneyed portraits of celebrities, his Brillo boxes, and his Coca-Cola bottles (Fig. 21.20) elicit comments that contemporary art has become bland and boring and that there is nothing much to be said about it. Warhol also evoked contempt here and there for his underground movies, which have portrayed sleep and explicit eroticism (*Blue Movie*) with equal disinterest. Even his shooting (from which he recovered) by a disenchanted actress seemed to evoke yawns and a "What-can-you-expect?" reaction from the public.

Warhol painted and printed much more than industrial products. During the 1960s, he reproduced multiple photographs of disasters from newspapers.

► **21.20 ANDY WARHOL,** *Green Coca-Cola Bottles* (1962). Synthetic polymer, silkscreen ink, and graphite on canvas. 82⅜" × 57". Whitney Museum of American Art, New York, New York.

1 ft.

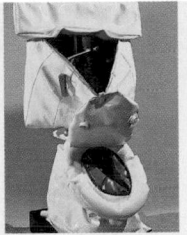

∧ Oldenburg's *Soft
Toilet* (**Fig. 11.21**)

He executed a series of portraits of public figures such as Marilyn Monroe and Jackie Kennedy in the 1960s, and he turned to portraits of political leaders such as Mao Zedong in the 1970s. Although his silkscreens have at least in their technique met the Pop Art objective of obscuring the personal signature of the artist, his compositions and his expressionistic brushing of areas of his paintings achieved an individual stamp.

It could be argued that other Pop artists owe some of their popularity to the inventiveness of Andy Warhol. Without Warhol, Pop Art might have remained a quiet movement, one that might have escaped the notice of the art historians of the new millennium.

GEORGE SEGAL During the 1960s, George Segal (1926–2000) achieved renown as a Pop Art sculptor, casting his figures in plaster from live models, including his friends, and then setting them within eerily decontextualized tableaux constructed of found objects—a Coke machine, pieces of a pickup truck, a movie theater marquis, one-way street signs, and such. Surrounded by ordinary symbols of their day and age, his figures project a mood of isolation and detachment. Segal's work extends beyond museum and gallery spaces into the realm of public art. One of his most acclaimed, and haunting, pieces depicts a somber bread line that symbolizes the despair of the Great Depression of the 1930s in America; it can be seen in Washington, D.C., where it is part of the Franklin Delano Roosevelt Memorial. FDR is credited with establishing government programs that ameliorated the devastating effects of the deep and protracted economic downturn. Segal also used the platform of his celebrity to call attention to gay liberation and gay rights in an outdoor installation in Christopher Park in New York City. Commissioned by an art patron, the piece (Fig. 21.21)

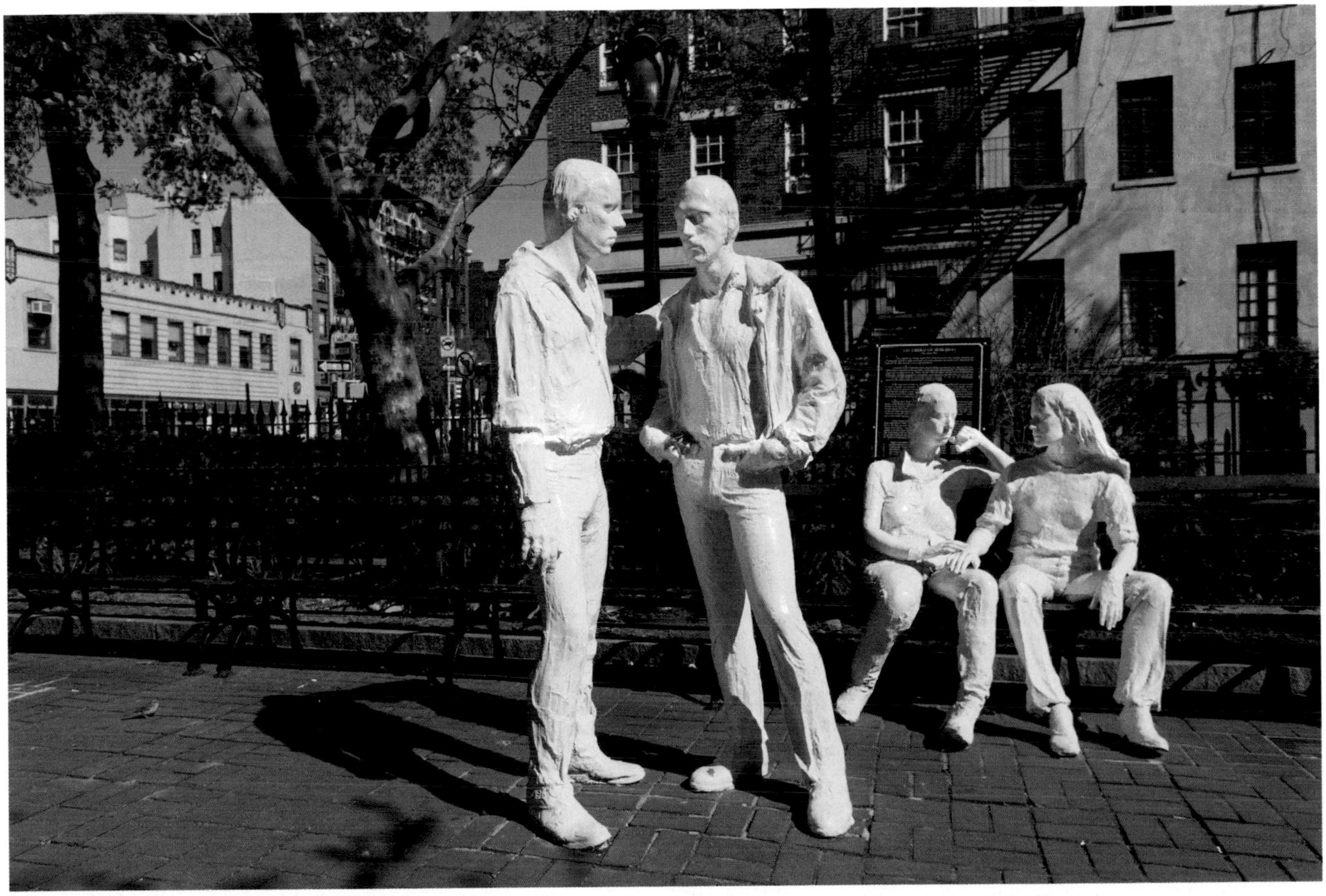

∧ **21.21 GEORGE SEGAL**, *Gay Liberation* (inaugurated in Greenwich Village in 1992). Bronze, covered in white lacquer; life-sized. Christopher Park, Greenwich Village, New York.

commemorates the Stonewall riots in Greenwich Village in which members of the gay community engaged in violent protests against a raid on the Stonewall Inn by Manhattan police. The spontaneous events are seen as a catalyst in the fight for lesbian, gay, bisexual, and transgender (LGBT) rights.

Realism and Photorealism

Realism, or the rendering of subjects with precision, is firmly rooted in the long realistic tradition in the arts. But as a movement that first gained major recognition during the early 1970s, **photorealism** represents a new endeavor to depict subjects with sharp, photographic precision. Photorealism also owes some of its impetus to the Pop artist's objective portrayal of familiar images. It is also in part a reaction to the expressionistic and abstract movements of the twentieth century. That is, photorealism permits artists to do something that is very new to the eye even while they are doing something very old.

ALICE NEEL One of the most dramatic figurative painters of the era was a portrait painter named Alice Neel (1900–1984). The designation "portraitist," however, in no way prepares the viewer for the radical nature of Neel's work. She took no commissions but rather handpicked her sitters from all strata of society and often painted them in the nude, or seminude. The drama, curiously, lies in the very *un*dramatic character of her work—stark, unflinching realism. Neel's sitters were wildly diverse (from painter Andy Warhol to her housekeeper, Carmen), but her harsh style remained constant, as did her belief that she could convey something of a person's inner self through a meticulous rendering of its physical embodiment (see Fig. 21.22).

AUDREY FLACK Audrey Flack (b. 1931) was born in New York and studied at the High School of Music and Art, at Cooper Union, and at Yale University's Graduate School. During the 1950s, she showed figure paintings that were largely ignored, in part because of the popularity of Abstract Expressionism, in part because women artists, in general, had not been privy to the critical attention that their male colleagues had received. Yet throughout these years, she persisted in a sharply realistic, or *trompe l'oeil* style. Her illusionistically real canvases often result from a technique involving the projection of color slides onto her canvases, which she then sketches and paints in detail. Since the 1970s, Flack's focus has largely shifted away from the human figure to richly complex still life arrangements.

One of Flack's best-known works from the 1970s is *World War II (Vanitas)* (Fig. 21.23), a painting that

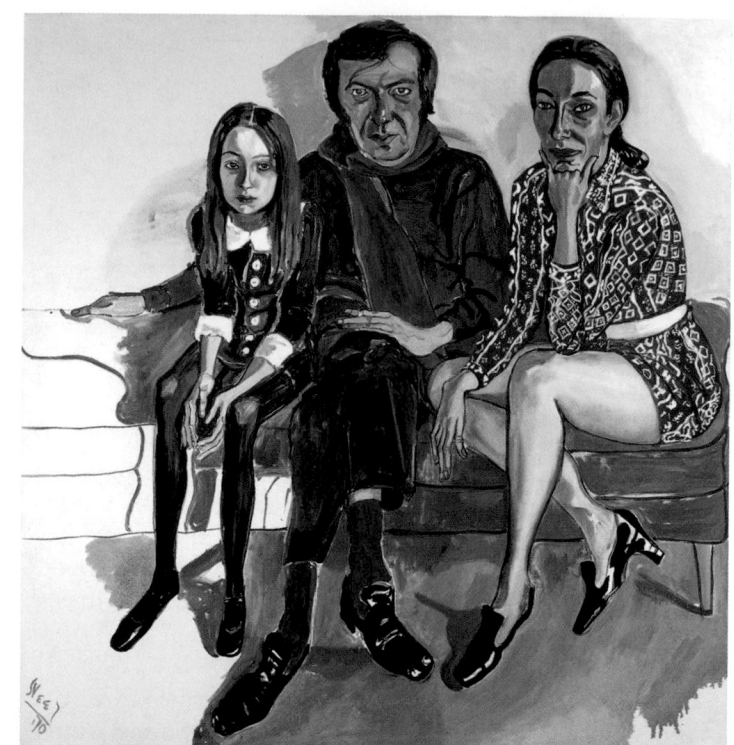

▲ 21.22 ALICE NEEL, *The Family (John Gruen, Jane Wilson, and Julia)* (1970). Oil on canvas, 4' 11⅞" × 5'. Museum of Fine Arts, Houston, Texas.

combines Margaret Bourke-White's haunting photo *The Living Dead of Buchenwald April 1945* (see Fig. 10.13) with ordinary objects that teem with life—pastries, fruit, a teacup, a candle, a string of pearls. The subtitle of the work, *Vanitas*, refers to a type of still life frequently found in the sixteenth and seventeenth centuries. The content was selected specifically to encourage the viewer to meditate on death as the inescapable end to human life. Flack's items are all the more poignant in their juxtaposition because they suggest lives cut short—abruptly and drastically—by Hitler's Holocaust. The painting further functions as a memorial to those who perished at the hands of the Nazis and as a tribute to survivors. Flack is fascinated by the ways in which objects reflect light, and in this painting and others she uses an airbrush to create a surface that imitates the textures of these objects. She layers primary colors in transparent glazes to produce the desired hues without obvious brushstrokes. The resulting palette is harsh and highly saturated, and the sense of realism is stunning.

DUANE HANSON Duane Hanson (1925–1996) was reared on a dairy farm in Minnesota. His *Tourists* (Fig. 21.24) is characteristic of the work of several contemporary sculptors in that it uses synthetic substances such as liquid polyester resin to closely approximate the visual and

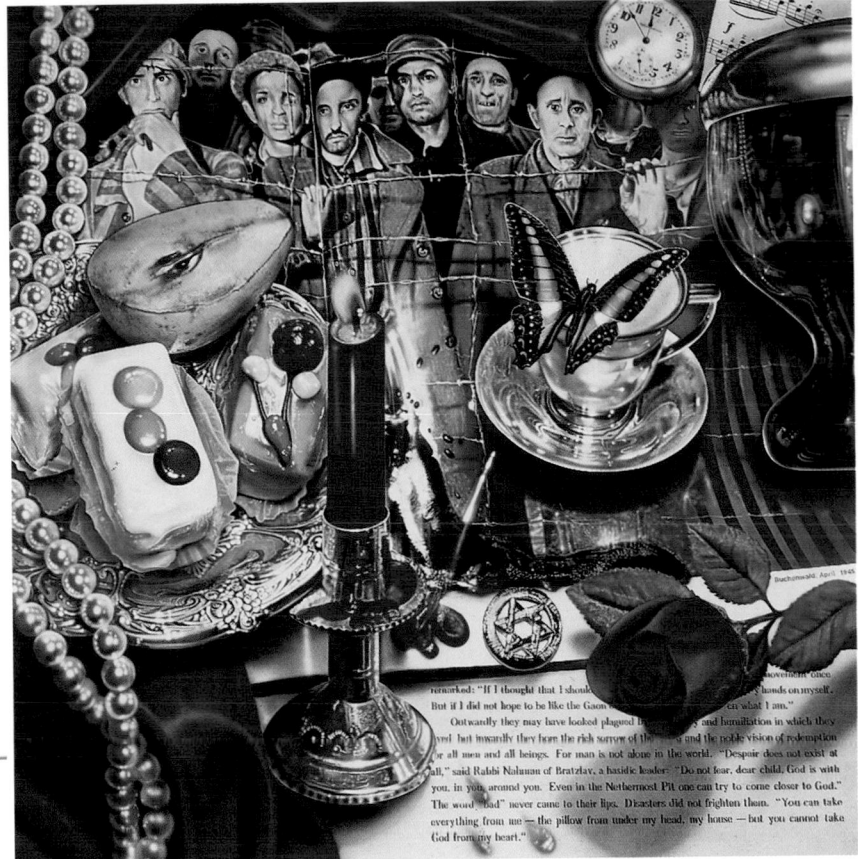

1 ft.

tactile qualities of flesh. Such literal surfaces
allow the artist no expression of personal signature. In the presence of a Hanson figure, or a
John De Andrea nude, viewers watch for the rising and falling of the chest. They do not wish to
stare too hard or to say something careless on
the off-chance that the sculpture is real. There is
an electricity in gallery storerooms where these
sculptures coexist in waiting. One tries to decipher which ones will get up and walk away.

Duane Hanson's liberal use of off-the-rack
apparel and objects such as "stylish" sunglasses,
photographic paraphernalia, and shopping bags

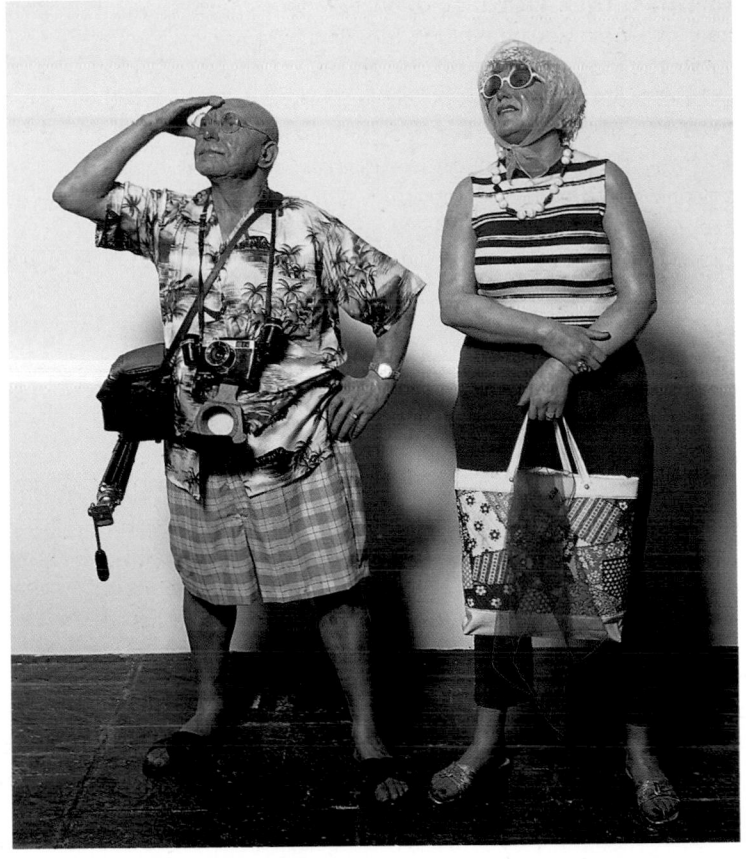

► **21.24 DUANE HANSON, *Tourists*** (1970). Polyester resin/fiberglass,
life-sized; man, 5' high; woman 5'4" high.

gave these figures a caustic, satirical edge. But not all of Hanson's sculptures are lighthearted. Like Warhol, Hanson also portrayed disasters, such as death scenes from the conflict in Vietnam. In his later work, the artist focused more on the psychological content of his figures, as expressed by tense postures and grimaces.

CHUCK CLOSE Chuck Close (b. 1940) is best known for his innovative methods of painting the face, especially in his large-scale paintings that are based on photographs. He typically used a grid technique to enlarge photographs, which tend to portray their subjects without mercy, and to transfer them to the painted canvas, grid by grid. His painstakingly rendered *Big Self-Portrait* (Fig. 21.25) took four months to complete and measures nearly 9' by 7'. With his unkempt hair, both on his head and on his chest, and his brazenly jutting cigarette, he seems to be clearly saying "This is me. Take it or leave it." The cigarette and some of his hair, by the way, were blurry in the photograph, and so Close painted them somewhat "out of focus." Always experimenting with his methods, in the 1980s Close played with Pointillism. He has also used daguerreotypes and thumbprints to render his realistic images.

Minimalism

Minimalists sought to reduce their ideas to their simplest forms. They created geometric shapes or progressions of shapes or lines using minimal numbers of formal elements—for example, the minimum amounts of colors

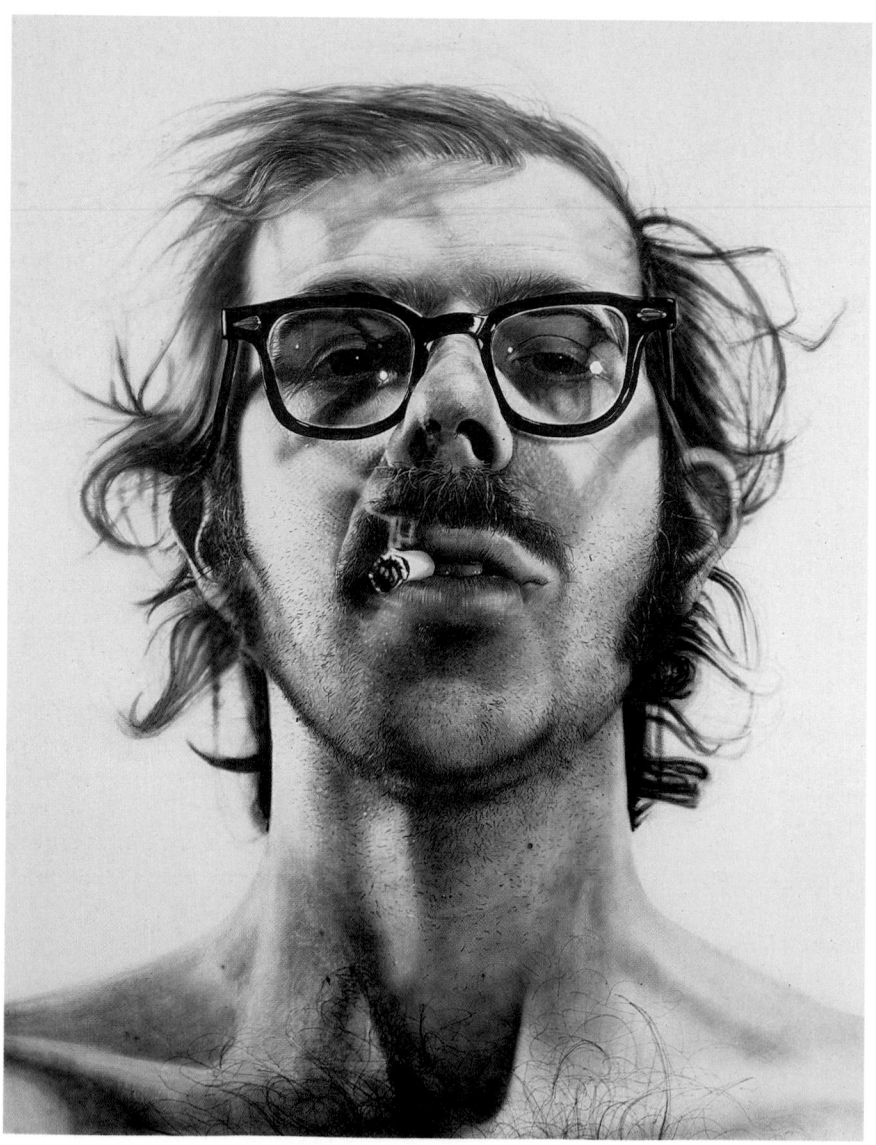

1 ft.

◀ **21.25 CHUCK CLOSE,** *Big Self-Portrait*
(1967–1968). Acrylic on canvas, 107½" × 83½".
Collection Walker Art Center, Minneapolis,
Art Center Acquisition Fund, 1969.

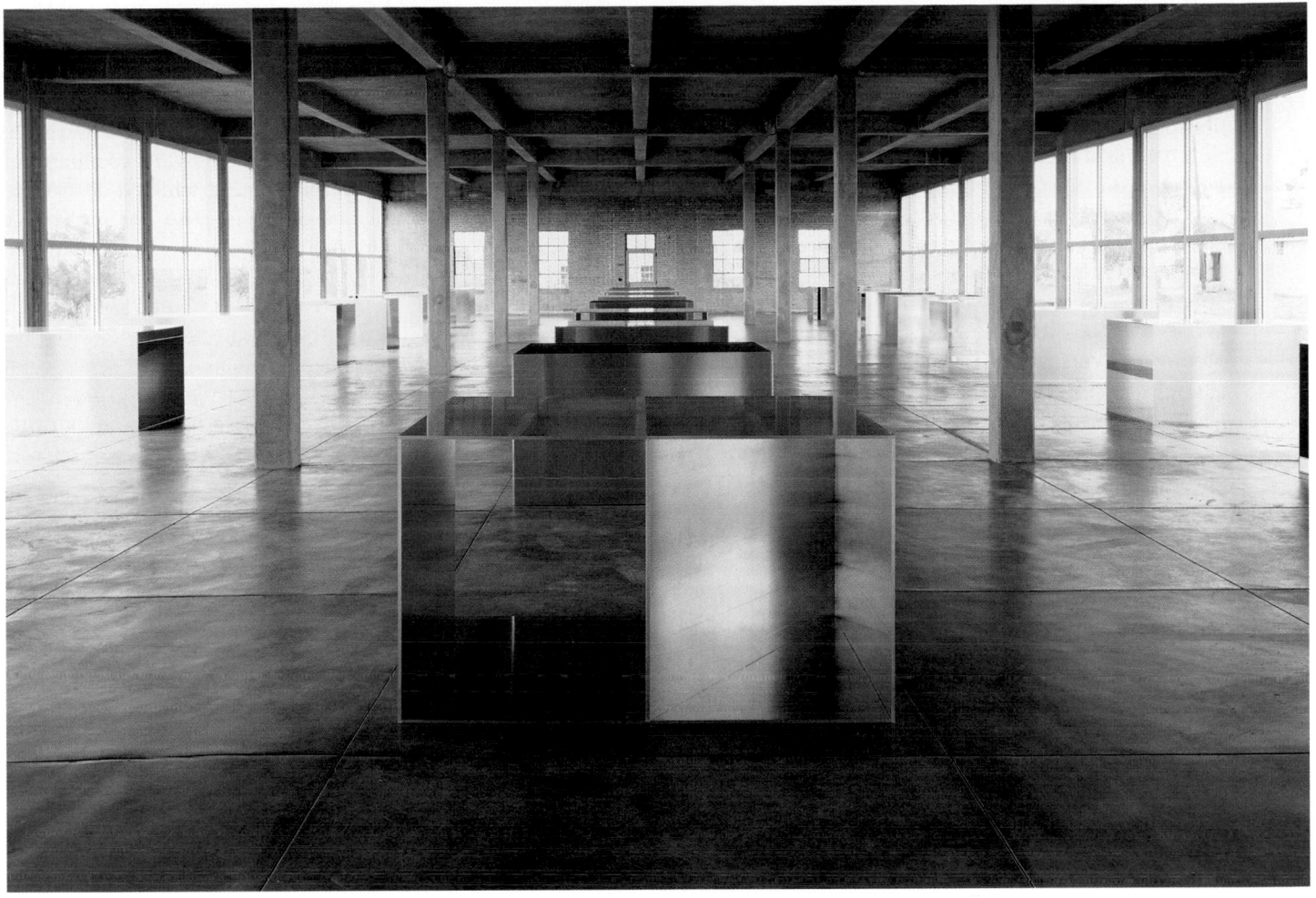

∧ 21.26 **DONALD JUDD,** *100 Untitled Works in Mill Aluminum* (1982–1983). Interior detail. Machined aluminum boxes housed in abandoned buildings (renovated by Judd) on the former U.S. Army base Fort D. A. Russell, Marfa, Texas.

and textures. Nor did they attempt to represent objects. Their school of art is called **Minimalism**.

Frank Stella, as noted, is a founder of the Minimalist school. His *Mas o Menos* (see Fig. 21.14) represents no object in the real world, repeats basic lines, and is rendered in a single color. Except for the fact that both are abstract, one would be hard-pressed to imagine a style of art farther removed from Abstract Expressionism.

DONALD JUDD Sculptor Donald Judd (1928–1994) brought Minimalism into three dimensions. He chose shapes and materials that were pure and simple, mounted on walls or set on the floor in a steady, evenly spaced pattern. The installation at the North Artillery Shed (Fig. 21.26) features 100 identical metal boxes housed in two former military artillery sheds. Although they are absolutely identical, the impression is somewhat more varied because Judd opened one or more panels,

not necessarily the corresponding ones. As light streams through the windows and reflects off the surfaces, the boxes cast shadows of various lengths on the floor and on each other.

Judd's shapes and materials are fabricated in factories from industrial or nontraditional materials. Because skilled workers (and not the artist) created Minimalist works according to the artist's specifications, the traditional relationship between the idea of art and its literal creation—as we will see in the discussion of conceptual art—is subverted.

Performance Art

Amid the strains of Pop and Minimalism in the mid-1960s, an even more unconventional genre appeared: **performance art.** Concurrent with the emergence of conceptualism, performance art privileged action over object, public spaces over museum settings, the impermanent over the permanent, and, often, audience participation over passive spectatorship. Most of the pioneering work in performance art is memorialized only in still photographs, if at all. It is not until relatively recently that performance pieces have been consistently videotaped or digitally recorded. Today, a subgenre of performance art is performance video; such works are scripted and often feature elaborate staging and special effects.

We can actually trace the roots of performance art to the late 1950s and early 1960s in spontaneous events termed *Happenings*. These "pieces" would sometimes be the result of interactions between the artist-performer and the audience. Allan Kaprow (1927–2006), an early proponent of this performance genre, said, "The line between art and life should be kept as fluid, and perhaps as indistinct as possible." In his 1964 Happening, *Household*, women gathered around to lick jam that had been slathered over a car; in *Fluids*, organized three years later, volunteers assembled a rectangular enclosure with blocks of ice (Fig. 21.27 is a photograph of a recreation of the event in Los Angeles, two years after Kaprow's death). Occasionally Happenings were scripted, although as a participatory form of new media art, the outcomes could never be the same.

JEAN TINGUELY   Another early piece that was seminal in the rise of performance art was *Homage to New York* (Fig. 21.28) by the Swiss kinetic sculptor Jean Tinguely (1925–1991). Staged in the outdoor sculpture garden of the Museum of Modern Art in New York City on March 16, 1960, from 6:30 to 7:00 p.m., the centerpiece of the event was a twenty-three-foot-long, twenty-seven-foot-high contraption constructed of objects including a meteorology balloon filled with colored gas, a bathtub, a piano, a go-cart, bicycle wheels, and various electrical motors. Billed as "a self-constructing and self-destroying work of art" on the invitation for the one-night-only performance, the motorized behemoth, during its 27-minute life span, spun, clinked, sparked, and would have utterly self-destructed had not some unexpected flames led to an intervention by the New York City Fire Department. The fact that the piece did not reach completion per se, on the other hand, was of no concern to the artist whose Dada sensibility would dictate that this unpredicted turn of events ultimately became part of the work.

Tinguely also satirized the utilization of random movement in creating works of art in his series titled *Métamatics*. The individual "drawing machines" were kinetic sculptures—table-top stabiles rigged with weights and balances—that produced, through the movement of parts, an "automatic" drawing. The dates of the series—1955 to 1959—coincide with paintings by Jackson Pollock and other Abstract Expressionists who worked under the influence of Automatism.

YOKO ONO   Yoko Ono (b. 1933) is perhaps most familiar to most of us as the wife of Beatles singer-songwriter John Lennon, although she had already had an established career as an influential conceptual and performance artist well before they met. Her participatory work, *Cut Piece*, in fact, is considered one of the earliest feminist artworks. First staged in Tokyo in 1964, Ono walked to the center of a stage in a black dress, knelt down, placed scissors on the floor next to her, and spoke one word to the audience: "Cut." People ascended the stage and did so in turn, cutting away pieces of her clothing right down to her skin. As the blades of the scissors got closer to her body, the act became more and more threatening. Critics came to view this piece—in which Ono tackled the perception of the body as an object and its use as a medium—as one that was groundbreaking in its melding of performance, conceptual, and feminist art.

Ono and Lennon collaborated on a number of performance pieces, the most famous of which were part of their late 1960s peace campaign.

∧ 21.27 **Recreation of Allan Kaprow's** *Fluids* (April 25–27, 2008). One of twenty rectangular enclosures of ice blocks, each measuring approximately 30' long, 10" wide, and 8' high. Los Angeles County Museum of Art, Los Angeles, California.

The only stable thing is movement.
—JEAN TINGUELY

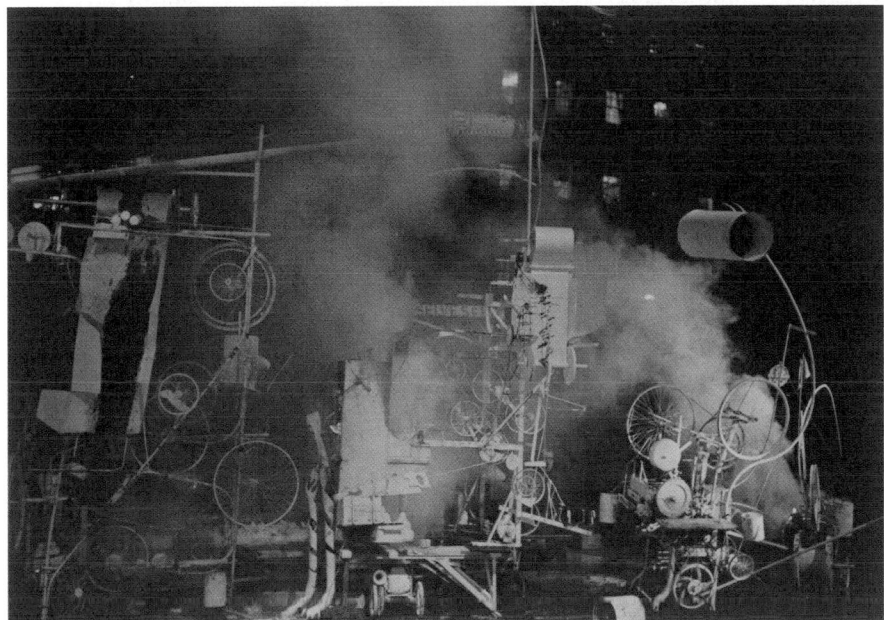

Bagism (Fig. 21.29) is an example intended to erase distinctions among individuals and, in so doing, erase prejudice—gender, race, or class—and promote tolerance.

MARINA ABRAMOVIĆ As the bare steel of the scissors touched Ono's warm flesh during *Cut Piece*, the awareness of the vulnerability of her body grew more disconcerting and disturbing—for her and for her audience. Marina Abramović (b. 1946) has created a career using her body, herself as subject and medium, testing the limits of the physical and psychological as well as pushing the limits of the performer–audience relationship. Her earliest performance works inflicted paint and injury: in one, she jabbed a knife rhythmically between her fingers, which were splayed on a table, pausing to pick up a new knife (there were twenty in all) every time she drew blood. Another collaborative piece with Uwe Laysiepen (Ulay) called *Breathing In/Breathing Out* had the two artists, their open mouths joined, breathing each other's carbon dioxide until their lungs were filled and they fell unconscious. The premise of that piece was the notion that persons could be absorbed into one

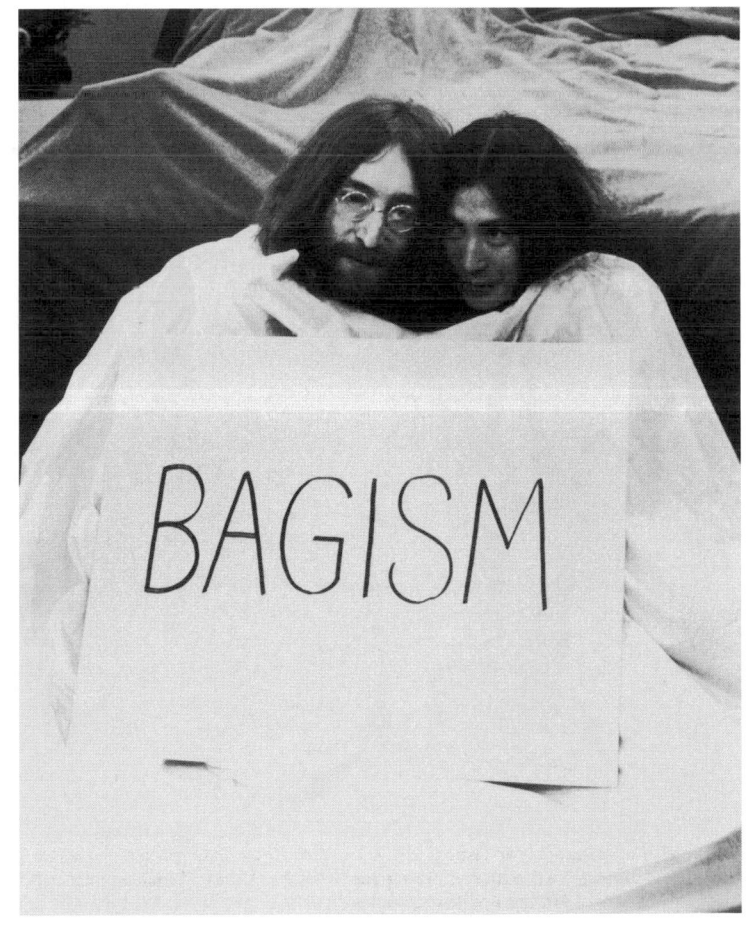

> 21.29 Yoko Ono and John Lennon in a Bagism way in April 1969.

another to such an extent that both would eventually be destroyed.

By the measure of these works, *The Artist Is Present* (Fig. 21.30) would seem quite tame. The piece, which was performed at the Museum of Modern Art from March 14 to May 31, 2010, nonetheless took immeasurable focus and endurance. Abramović sat still and silent at a table in the museum's atrium for a total of 736 hours and 30 minutes, during which time museumgoer participants were passively invited, one at a time, to sit across from her for as long as they wanted to during the museum's regular hours of operation. The performance piece was one part of a major retrospective of the artist's larger body of work.

Conceptual Art

We began this chapter with a statement from Joseph Kosuth that being an artist in our times means challenging what is meant by *art*. Traditionally speaking, an artist has been expected to master his or her craft, be it painting, sculpting, architecture, filmmaking—whatever is the chosen medium. Yet we also noted that many painters forgo the brushstroke; Frankenthaler, for example, poured paint on canvas. Some artists have used found objects; Duchamp took a urinal, flopped it over on its back, labeled it *Fountain*, and the art world generally concedes that it is art. Michelangelo wrote that he conceptualized the figures in blocks of stone and used the chisel to release them. But where, then, in Michelangelo lies the art? In the artist's mind or in the carved product? The **conceptual art** movement, which began in the 1960s, asserts that art does in fact lie in the mind of the artist; the visible or audible or palpable product is merely an expression of the artist's idea.

JOSEPH KOSUTH   The charge Kosuth (b. 1945) gave to himself to change the meaning of art led to the creation of works such as *One and Three Hammers* and *One and Three Chairs* (Fig. 21.31). Each of these works has three parts: the object itself, a photograph of the object, and the dictionary definition of the object. The artist displays what he considers to be the concept of "chairness" as it exists in his mind. It is not in the execution of the art that the art exists. We see no exquisite drawing or painting. We do not even have a found object that is converted into art; the chair is a chair. The photograph is unremarkable. The definition is . . . the definition. (As Stella remarked about his own work: "What you see is what you see.")

BARBARA KRUGER   Barbara Kruger's (b. 1945) *Untitled (We Don't Need Another Hero)* (Fig. 21.32) confronts her male and female viewers with stereotypical epithets for the "dominant sex," seeming to criticize females for feeding male expectations as much as males for having them. In the work, Kruger appropriates a Norman Rockwell illustration to depict the "innocence" of gender ideology—in this case, the requisite fawning of a little girl over the budding muscles of her male counterpart. Kruger violates the innocuous vignette with a cautionary band blazing the words *We don't need another hero*. As a piece of conceptual art, the method of the photographic silkscreen prioritizes the *idea* of the work over the object. It emphasizes the artist's thinking and deemphasizes traditional artistic techniques. Much of Kruger's work has been political, emphasizing issues relating to feminism and power. The representation of the opposition between strength and weakness, traditional masculine and feminine gender roles, is confronted and replaced with the gender discourse of a more socially aware era.

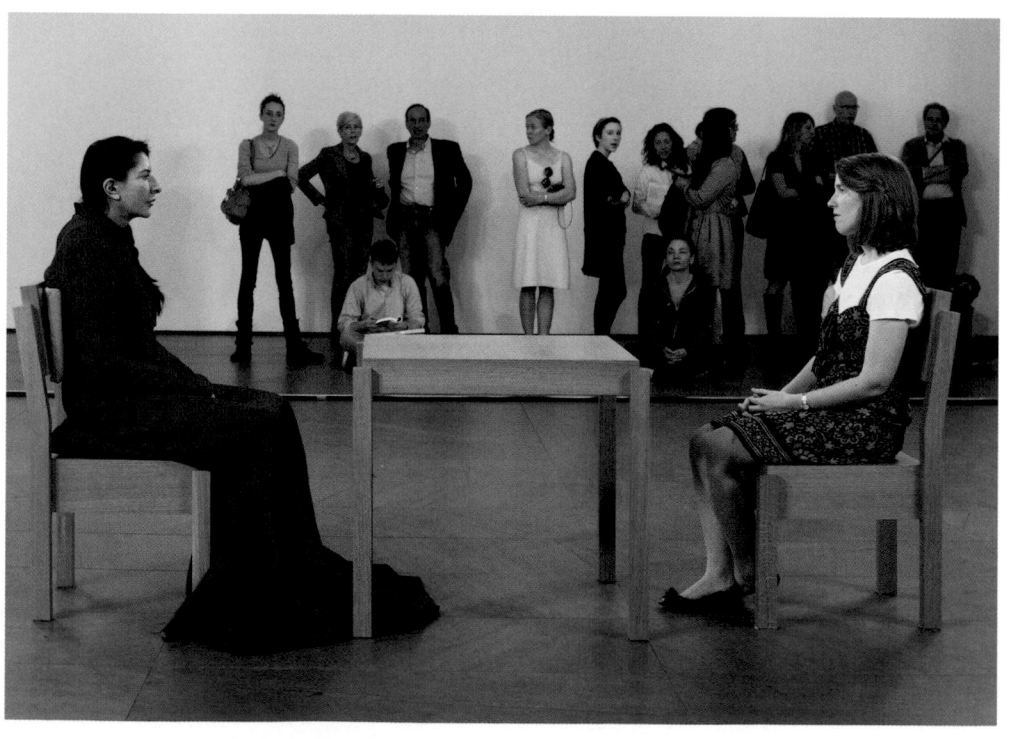

∧ **21.30 MARINA ABRAMOVIĆ,** *The Artist Is Present* (2010). The Museum of Modern Art, New York, New York.

In conceptual art the idea or concept is the most important aspect of the work. When an artist uses a conceptual form of art, it means that all of the planning and decisions are made beforehand and the execution is a perfunctory affair. . . . This kind of art is . . . usually free from the dependence on the skill of the artist as a craftsman.

—SOL LEWITT

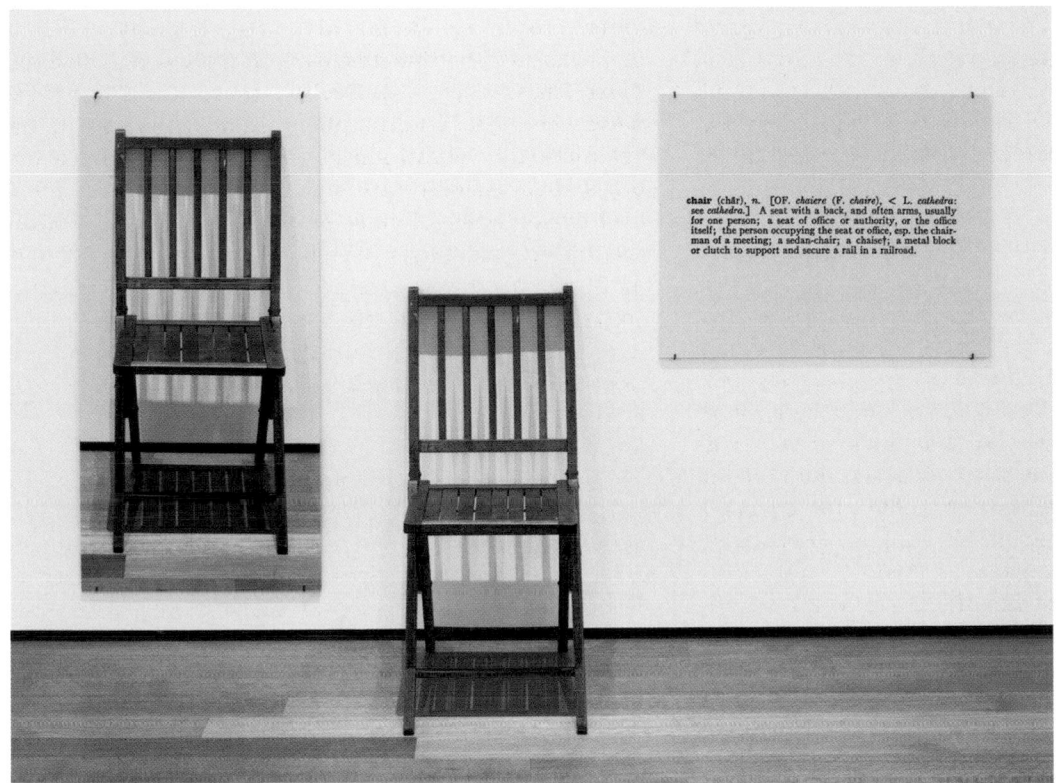

< 21.31 JOSEPH KOSUTH, *One and Three Chairs* (1965). Wooden folding chair, mounted photograph of a chair, and mounted photographic enlargement of the dictionary definition of *chair*. Chair: 32⅜" × 14⅞" × 20⅞"; photographic panel: 36" × 24⅛"; text panel: 24" × 24⅛". Museum of Modern Art, New York, New York.

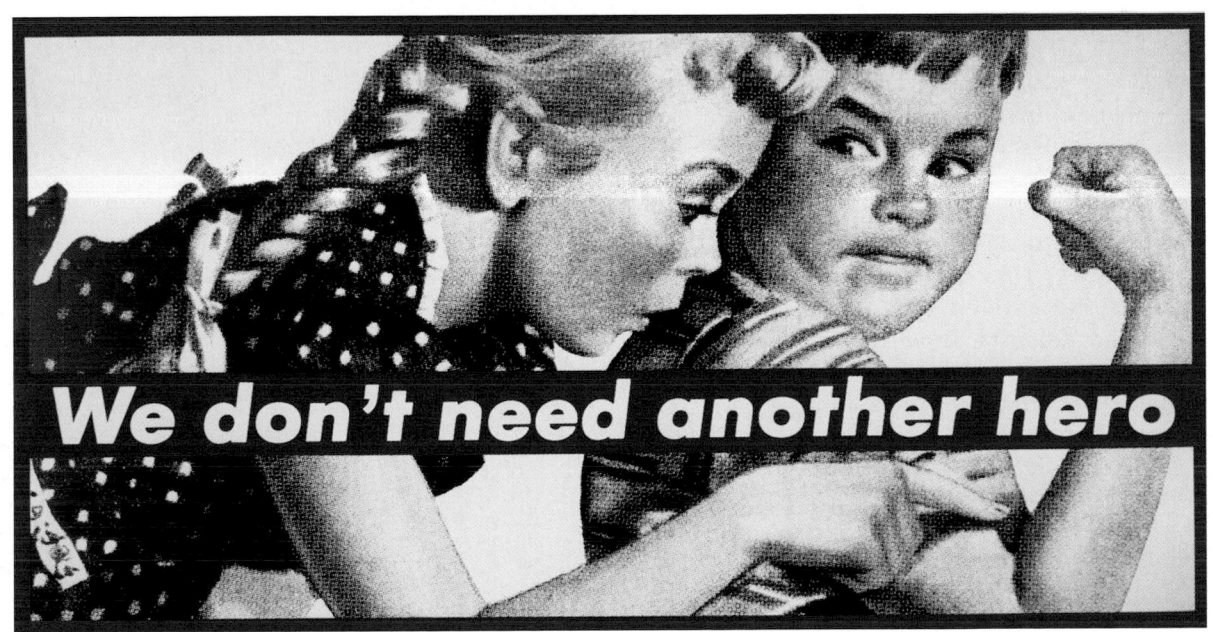

∧ 21.32 BARBARA KRUGER, *Untitled (We Don't Need Another Hero)* (1987). Photographic silkscreen, vinyl; 109" × 210". Mary Boone Gallery, New York, New York.

1 ft.

If it were customary to send little girls to school and to teach them the same subjects as are taught to boys, they would learn just as fully and would understand the subtleties of all arts and sciences.
—CHRISTINE DE PISAN, *CITÉ DES DAMES,* 1405

ART, IDENTITY, AND SOCIAL CONSCIOUSNESS

Art has always reflected the society in which it was created, but today the individual would appear to be paramount, and artists are just as likely to use art to express who they are as people, or members of various ethnic groups, or women, and how they react to the societies in which they find themselves.

Feminist Art

While on the East Coast Pop Art was on the wane and photorealism on the rise, Happenings on the West Coast were about to change the course of women's art, history, and criticism.

JUDY CHICAGO AND MIRIAM SCHAPIRO   In 1970, a midwestern artist named Judy Gerowitz (b. 1939)—who would soon call herself Judy Chicago—initiated a feminist studio art course at Fresno State College in California. One year later, she collaborated with artist Miriam Schapiro (b. 1923–2015) on a feminist art program at the California Institute of Arts in Valencia. Their interests and efforts culminated in another California project—a communal installation in Hollywood called *Womanhouse.* Teaming up with students from the University of California, Chicago and Schapiro refurbished each room of a dilapidated mansion in a theme built around women's experiences: The "Kitchen," by Robin Weltsch, was covered with breast-shaped eggs; the "Menstruation Bathroom," by Chicago, included the waste products of female menstruation cycles in a sterile white environment.

Another room in *Womanhouse* housed a child-sized doll house, in which Miriam Schapiro and Sherry Brody juxtaposed mundane and frightening objects to effect a kind of black humor (Fig. 21.33). The now-famous installation became a much-needed hub for area women's groups and was the impetus for the founding a year later of the Los Angeles Women's Building, which remains active today.

Womanhouse called attention to women artists, their wants, their needs. In some ways, it was an expression of anger toward the injustice of art-world politics that many women artists experienced—lack of attention by critics, curators, and historians; pressure to work in canonical styles. It announced to the world, through shock and exaggeration, that men's subjects are not

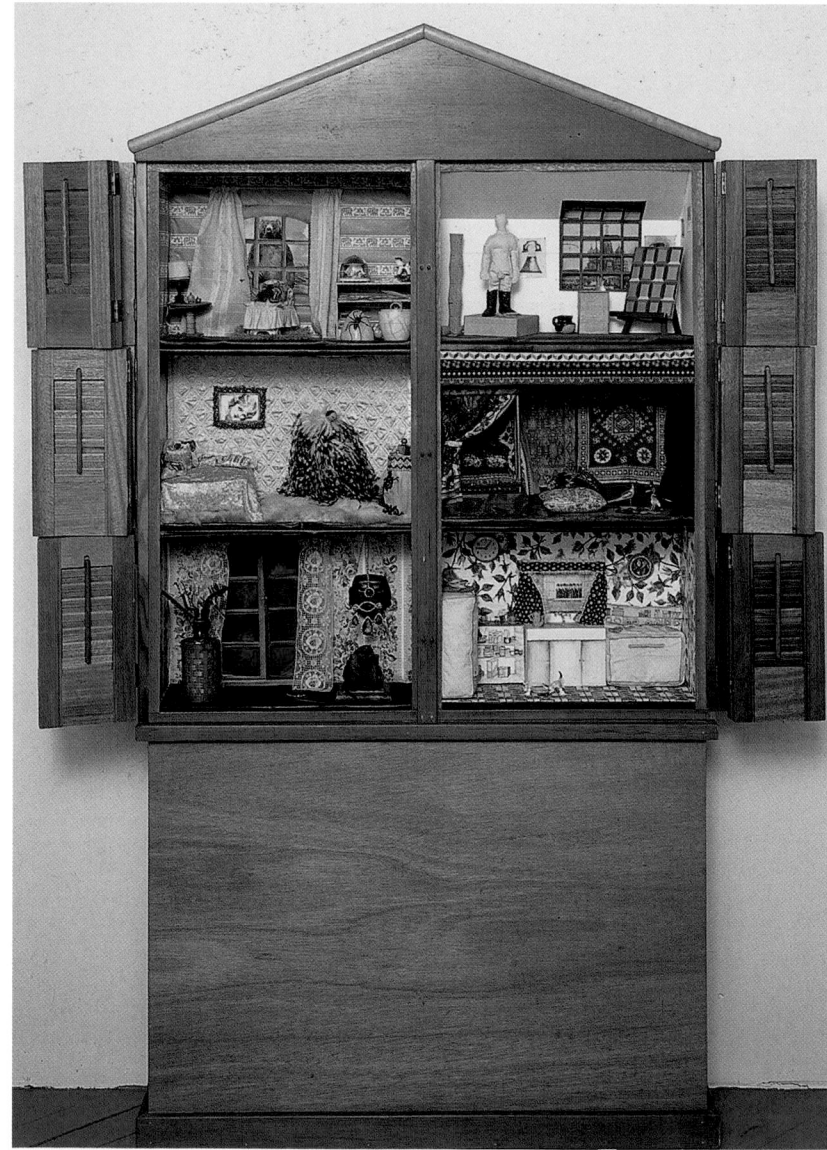

⌃ 21.33 **MIRIAM SCHAPIRO IN COLLABORATION WITH SHERRY BRODY,** *The Doll House* (1972). Mixed media, 84" × 40" × 41". Smithsonian American Art Museum, Washington, D.C.

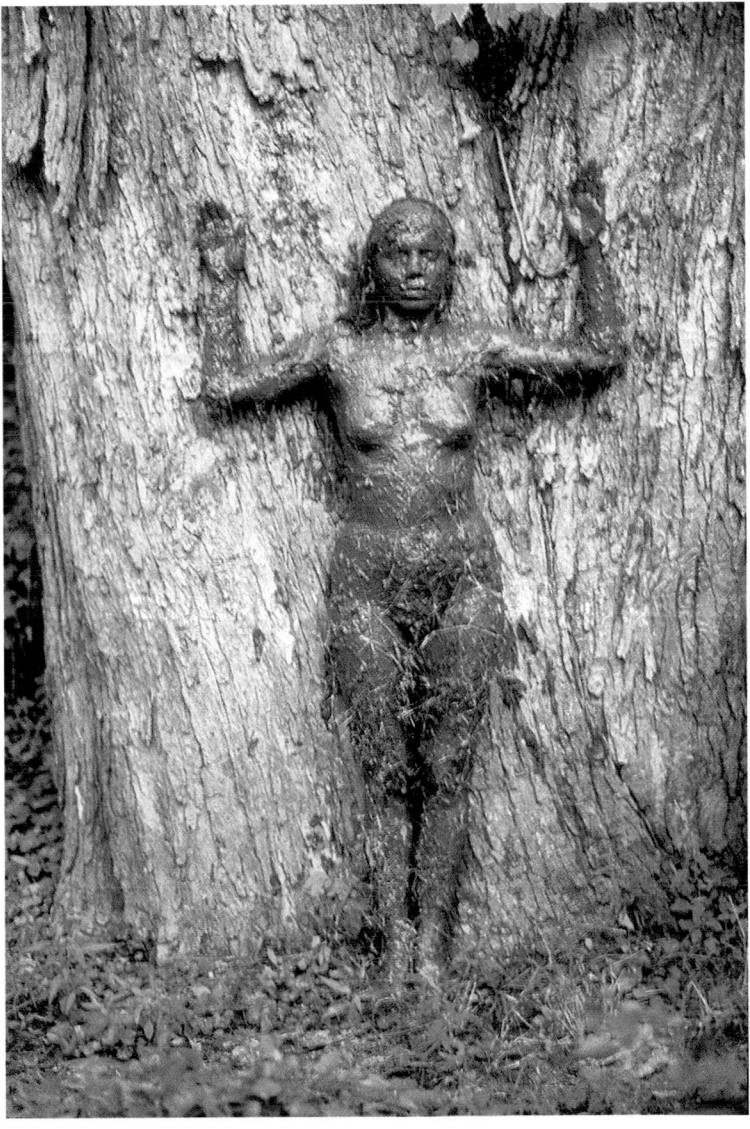

value of its extraordinary contrasts of texture. In this performance piece, feminist artist Ana Mendieta (1948–1985) presented her own body, draped in mud (an "earth–body sculpture"), against the craggy bark of a tree. Like some women artists, she shunned painting, especially abstract painting, as historically inundated with male values. Mendieta tied her flesh and blood, instead, across time and cultures, to the ancient myths of the earth mother goddesses.

necessarily of interest to women; that women's experiences, although not heroic in the masculine sense of the term, are significant. And perhaps of most importance, particularly in light of the subsequent careers of its participants, the exhibition exalted women's ways of working.

Chicago has since become renowned for her installation *The Dinner Party* (Fig. 21.34), in which the lines between life and death, and between place and time, are temporarily dissolved. The idea for this multimedia work, which was constructed to honor and immortalize history's notable women, revolves around a fantastic dinner party, where the guests of honor are seated before place settings designed to reflect their personalities and accomplishments. Chicago and numerous other female artists have invested much energy in alerting the public to the significant role of women in the arts and society.

ANA MENDIETA Much of the impact of *Arbol de la Vida (Tree of Life), no. 294* (Fig. 21.35) is related to the shock

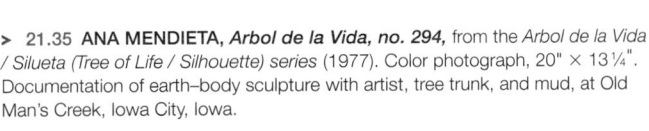

> 21.35 **ANA MENDIETA**, *Arbol de la Vida, no. 294,* from the *Arbol de la Vida / Silueta (Tree of Life / Silhouette) series* (1977). Color photograph, 20" × 13¼". Documentation of earth–body sculpture with artist, tree trunk, and mud, at Old Man's Creek, Iowa City, Iowa.

A CLOSER LOOK

Guerrilla Girls Warfare

DURING THE 1980S, something of a backlash against inclusion of women and ethnic minorities in the arts could be observed.[6] For example, a 1981 London exhibition, *The New Spirit in Painting*, included no women artists. A 1982 Berlin exhibition, *Zeitgeist*, represented 40 artists, but only 1 was a woman. The 1984 inaugural exhibition of the Museum of Modern Art's remodeled galleries, *An*

---

[6] Whitney Chadwick, *Women, Art, and Society* (London and New York: Thames and Hudson, 1990).

International Survey of Recent Painting and Sculpture, showed the works of 165 artists, only 14 of whom were women. The New York exhibition *The Expressionist Image: American Art from Pollock to Now* included the works of 24 artists, only 2 of whom were women. And so it goes.

To combat this disturbing trend, an anonymous group of women artists banded together as the Guerrilla Girls. The group appeared in public with gorilla masks and proclaimed themselves to be the "conscience of the art world." They mounted posters on buildings in Manhattan's SoHo district, one of the most active centers of the art world of the day. They took out ads of protest.

Figure 21.36 shows one of the Guerrilla Girls' posters. This particular poster sardonically notes the "advantages" of being a woman artist in an art world that, despite the "liberating" trends of the postfeminist era, continues to be dominated by men. It also calls attention to the blatant injustice of the relative price tags on works by women and men. A 1993 cover story for the *New York Times Magazine* pictures the "Art World All-Stars" of dealer Arnold Glimcher (**Fig. 21.37**). Women artists and artists of color are conspicuous by their absence. Note that at this writing, the inequity persists.

THE ADVANTAGES OF BEING A WOMAN ARTIST:

Working without the pressure of success.
Not having to be in shows with men.
Having an escape from the art world in your 4 free-lance jobs.
Knowing your career might pick up after you're eighty.
Being reassured that whatever kind of art you make it will be labeled feminine.
Not being stuck in a tenured teaching position.
Seeing your ideas live on in the work of others.
Having the opportunity to choose between career and motherhood.
Not having to choke on those big cigars or paint in Italian suits.
Having more time to work after your mate dumps you for someone younger.
Being included in revised versions of art history.
Not having to undergo the embarrassment of being called a genius.
Getting your picture in the art magazines wearing a gorilla suit.

Please send $ and comments to: **GUERRILLA GIRLS** CONSCIENCE OF THE ART WORLD
Box 1056 Cooper Sta. NY, NY 10276

WHEN RACISM & SEXISM ARE NO LONGER FASHIONABLE, WHAT WILL YOUR ART COLLECTION BE WORTH?

The art market won't bestow mega-buck prices on the work of a few white males forever. For the 17.7 million you just spent on a single Jasper Johns painting, you could have bought at least one work by all of these women and artists of color:

Bernice Abbott	Elaine de Kooning	Dorothea Lange	Sarah Peale
Anni Albers	Lavinia Fontana	Marie Laurencin	Ljubova Popova
Sofonisba Anguissola	Meta Warrick Fuller	Edmonia Lewis	Olga Rosanova
Diane Arbus	Artemisia Gentileschi	Judith Leyster	Nellie Mae Rowe
Vanessa Bell	Marguérite Gérard	Barbara Longhi	Rachel Ruysch
Isabel Bishop	Natalia Goncharova	Dora Maar	Kay Sage
Rosa Bonheur	Kate Greenaway	Lee Miller	Augusta Savage
Elizabeth Bougereau	Barbara Hepworth	Lisette Model	Varvara Stepanova
Margaret Bourke-White	Eva Hesse	Paula Modersohn-Becker	Sophie Taeuber-Arp
Romaine Brooks	Hannah Hoch	Tina Modotti	Alma Thomas
Julia Margaret Cameron	Anna Huntingdon	Berthe Morisot	Marietta Robusti Tintoretto
Emily Carr	May Howard Jackson	Grandma Moses	Suzanne Valadon
Rosalba Carriera	Frida Kahlo	Gabriele Münter	Remedios Varo
Mary Cassatt	Angelica Kauffmann	Alice Neel	Elizabeth Vigée Le Brun
Constance Marie Charpentier	Hilma af Klint	Louise Nevelson	Laura Wheeling Waring
Imogen Cunningham	Kathe Kollwitz	Georgia O'Keeffe	
Sonia Delaunay	Lee Krasner	Meret Oppenheim	

Information courtesy of Christie's, Sotheby's, Mayer's International Auction Records and Leonard's Annual Price Index of Auctions

Please send $ and comments to: **GUERRILLA GIRLS** CONSCIENCE OF THE ART WORLD
Box 1056 Cooper Sta. NY, NY 10276

∧ 21.36 GUERRILLA GIRLS, *Poster* (c. 1987). www.guerillagirls.com.

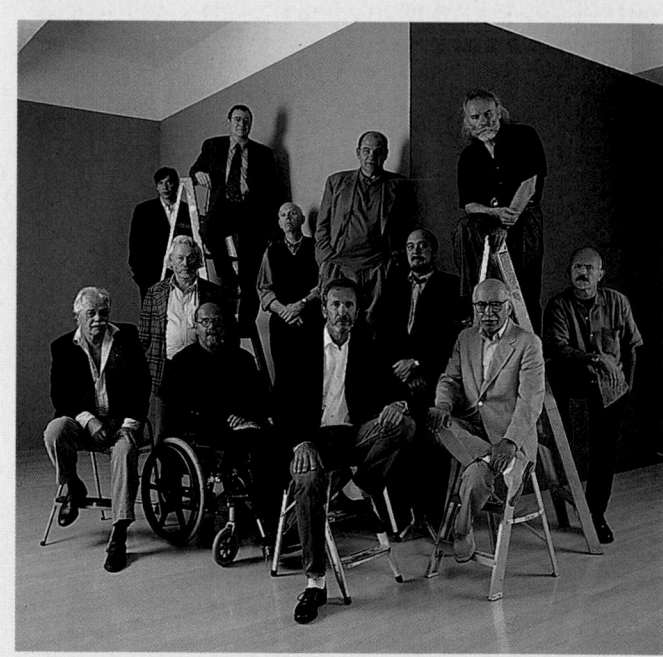

∧ 21.37 Arnold Glimcher and His Art World All-Stars. Used on the cover of the *New York Times Magazine* (October 3, 1993).

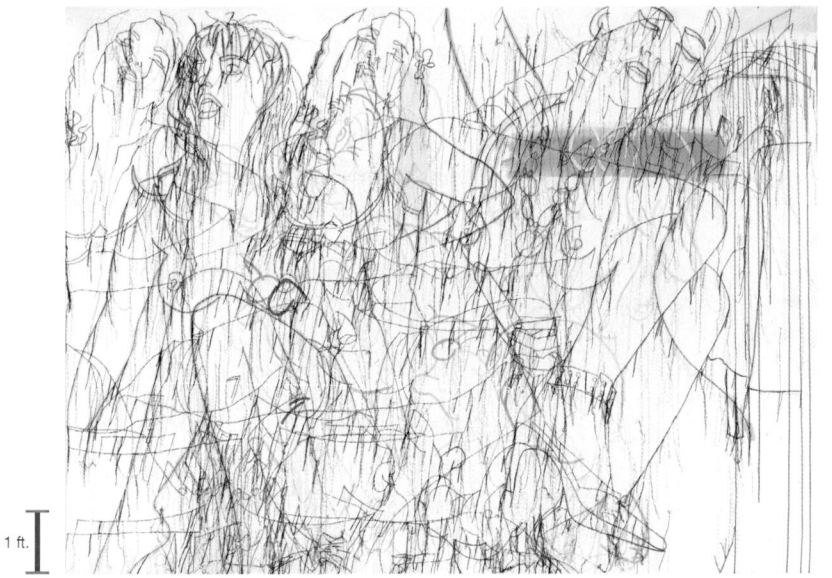

▲ 21.38 GHADA AMER, *Knotty but Nice* (2005). Acrylic, embroidery, and gel medium on canvas; 108" × 144".

Sexual Identity

As women have sought to express their individuality and social concerns through art, so have members of the LGBT community.

ROBERT MAPPLETHORPE   Photographer Robert Mapplethorpe (1946–1989) created many black-and-white images of people struggling in a world that was hostile toward them because of their sexual identity. He grabbed that world and shook it, using his photographic skills and stylized, formalist aesthetic to capture a range of portrait and still life images, male and female nudes, and, infamously, explicit erotic practices connected with underground sadomasochism and bondage in the explosion of gay culture in the late 1960s and early 1970s.

GHADA AMER   Egyptian American artist **Ghada Amer** (b. 1963) is known for her drawings, paintings, sculptures, and gardens. Amer left her home country as a child and moved with her family to France. She now lives and works in New York. Amer's works comment on the mindless devastation of war, the clash of cultures, the subjection of women in domestic roles, male domination of the art world, the historic arts practiced mainly by women, and perhaps most uniquely, her celebration of women's sexuality. As in *Knotty but Nice* (Fig. 21.38), many of her works confront the viewer with idealized, stereotypical European American women in erotic poses that are gleaned from pornographic magazines. Although they appear to openly present themselves to the viewer, Amer's women are not so readily grasped. The viewer searches, sometimes in vain, for exposed genitals in the entangling embroidery. Why is the work feminist? Part of the answer may be that it trumpets the fact that women, like men, can enjoy sex, but also suggests that male gazers can be predatory.

Amer writes that "The history of art was written by men, in practice and in theory. Painting has a symbolic and dominant place inside this history, and in the twentieth century it became the major expression of masculinity, especially through abstraction. For me, the choice to be mainly a painter and to use the codes of abstract painting . . . is occupying a territory that has been denied to women historically. . . . [but] I integrate in this male field a feminine universe: that of sewing and embroidery."[7]

Mapplethorpe worked primarily with black-and-white photography and his images derive their drama from harsh value contrast. *Ken Moody and Robert Sherman* (Fig. 21.39), a double-profile portrait, is one of several gelatin silver print photographs featuring the couple in which formal elements and design principles—shape, line, light, rhythm, and repetition—comprise the primary aspect of the work.

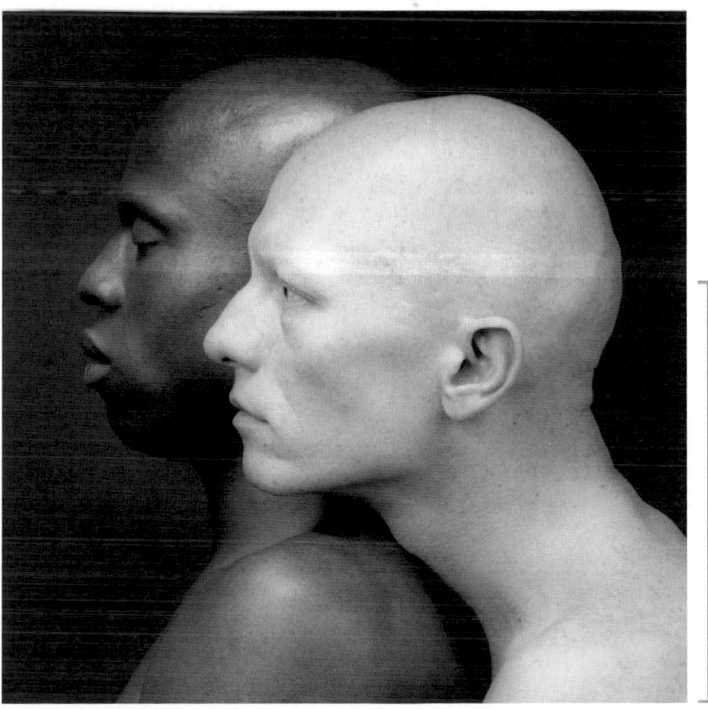

▲ 21.39 ROBERT MAPPLETHORPE, *Ken Moody and Robert Sherman* (1984). Platinum print, A.P. ⅟₁, edition of 10; 19½" × 19⅝". Solomon R. Guggenheim Museum, New York, New York.

[7] Ghada Amer "Feminist Artist Statement." Elizabeth A. Sackler Center for Feminist Art: Feminist Art Base: Ghada Amer. www.brooklynmuseum.org/eascfa/feminist_art_base/gallery/ghada_amer.php (accessed February 12, 2015).

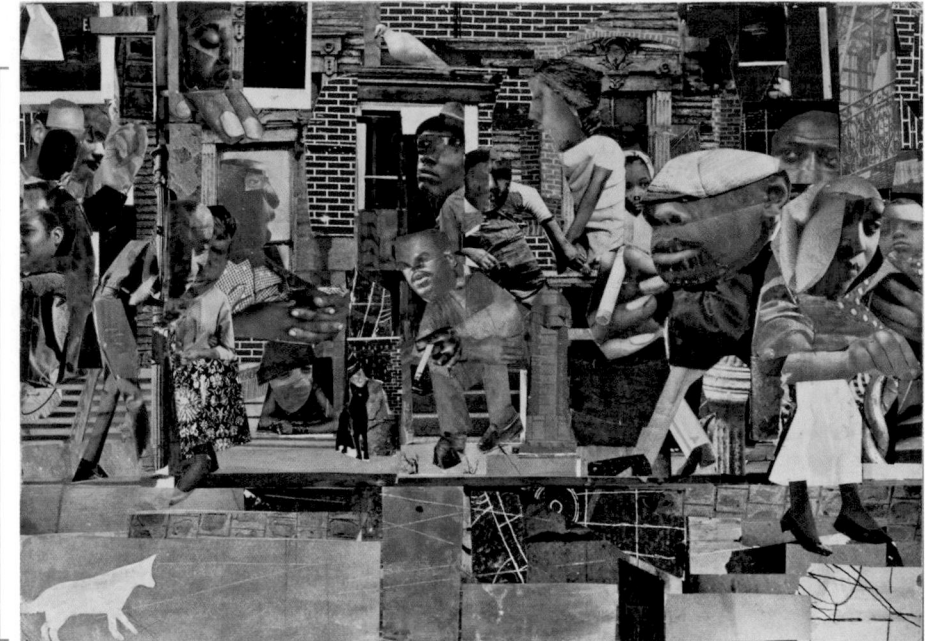

1 ft.

∧ 21.40 **ROMARE BEARDEN,** *The Dove* (1964). Cut-and-pasted paper, gouache, pencil, and colored pencil on cardboard. 13⅜" × 18¾". Museum of Modern Art, New York, New York.

Racial and Ethnic Identity

The postwar era in the United States was marked by the increasing, searing exposure of the inequality between races. In his poem "Will V-Day Be Me-Day Too? A Negro Fighting Man's Letter to America," Harlem poet Langston Hughes drew attention to the bitter irony felt by African American soldiers who fought, with white soldiers, during World War II, only to return home to the status quo of Jim Crow laws, segregation, and inequality. The dominant art movements of the 1950s and 1960s were, as noted, almost exclusively white male: Few if any women artists or artists of color working in the mainstream idioms became familiar names, much less those whose visual images articulated racial and cultural difference. What follows is a look at some ways in which artists in the second half of the twentieth century explored identity through visual representation.

ROMARE BEARDEN Born to middle-class parents, African American artist Romare Bearden (1914–1988) attended the Art Students League and New York University in the 1940s. He believed that African Americans should create their own art form, just as they had developed musical styles such as jazz and the blues. In the Harlem of the 1960s, he arrived at his signature style, which combined painting and collage. A work such as *The Dove* (Fig. 21.40) represents a synthesis of Cubism and Abstract Expressionism, constructed through the lens of the African American experience. We are drawn into a Harlem street scene composed of clipped, irregularly shaped

fragments of photographs—varying in scale and density—pasted onto a regimented backdrop that feels almost like a Cubist grid. The imagery spreads across the field uniformly, with no particular focal point—much the way Abstract Expressionists created their all-over compositions. As in viewing a Pollock painting, we experience the tension between surface and depth: the overlapping lines in *One* (see Fig. 21.2) draw us into the compressed space of the painting and then fix our gaze again on the surface. In *The Dove*, the clarity of some images in relation to others, and the shifts and subversions of scale, lead us to believe that some figures are near and others are distant. Works such as *The Dove* reflect Bearden's desire to capture flashes of memory that read like a scrapbook of consciousness and experience particular to his own life—from his childhood in North Carolina to his life and work in Harlem. The writer and literary critic Ellison wrote of Bearden's art:

> Bearden's meaning is identical with his method. His combination of technique is in itself eloquent of the sharp breaks, leaps in consciousness, distortions, paradoxes, reversals, telescoping of time and surreal blending of styles, values, hopes and dreams which characterize much of [African] American history.[8]

FAITH RINGGOLD Faith Ringgold was born in New York City's Harlem neighborhood in 1930 and educated in the public schools of New York City. Raised with a social conscience, she painted murals and other works inspired by the civil rights movement in the 1960s, and a decade later took to feminist themes after her exclusion from an all-male exhibition at New York's School of Visual Arts. Ringgold's mother, a fashion designer, was always sewing, the artist recalls, and at this time the artist turned to sewing and related techniques—needlepoint, beading, braided ribbon, and sewn fabric—to produce soft sculptures.

More recently, Ringgold has become known for her narrative quilts, such as *Tar Beach* (Fig. 21.41), which combine traditions common to African Americans and women—storytelling and quilting. Here Ringgold tells

---

[8] Ralph Ellison, introduction to *Romare Bearden: Paintings and Projections* (Albany, NY: The Art Gallery at the State University of New York, 1968).

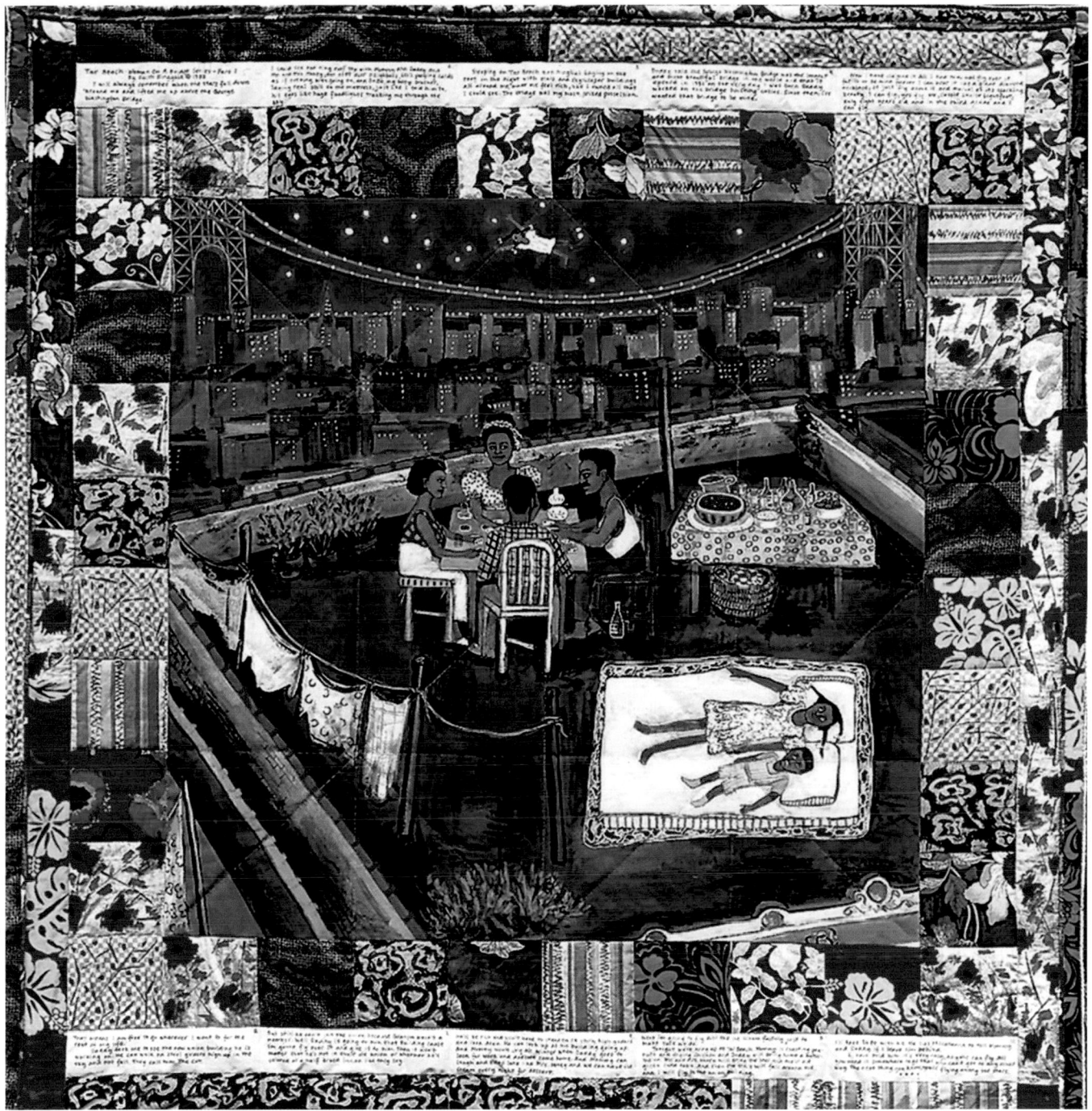

▲ 21.41 **FAITH RINGGOLD**, *Tar Beach* (1988). Acrylic on canvas, bordered with printed, painted, quilted, and pieced cloth. 74⅝" × 68½". Solomon R. Guggenheim Museum, New York, New York.

the story of life and dreams on a tar-covered rooftop. *Tar Beach* is a painted patchwork quilt that stitches together the artist's memories of family, friends, and feelings while growing up in Harlem. Ringgold is noted for her use of materials and techniques associated with women's traditions as well as her use of narrative or storytelling, a strong tradition in African American families. A large, painted square with images of Ringgold, her brother, her parents, and her neighbors dominates the quilt and is framed with brightly patterned pieces of fabric. Along the top and bottom are inserts crowded with Ringgold's written description of her experiences. This wonderfully innocent and joyful monologue begins:

I will always remember when the stars fell down around me and lifted me up above the George Washington Bridge.

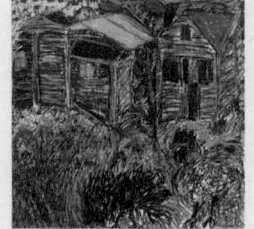
Basquiat's origins as an artist were not propitious. The themes, symbols, and strokes for which he is known first appeared on downtown New York City walls as graffiti. With Andy Warhol as a mentor, he brought his own complex form of collage to canvas, combining photocopies, drawing, and painting in intricate and overworked layers. In virtually all of Basquiat's art, there is a complex iconography at work. References to the black experience—from slavery and discrimination (Fig. 21.42) to the hard-won successes of African Americans such as jazz musician Charlie Parker or athlete Jesse Owens—pour across the canvases in images, symbols, and strands of text. Basquiat sought to emphasize the process of painting while never losing focus of the essential role of narrative.

JEAN-MICHEL BASQUIAT Jean-Michel Basquiat (1960–1988) was a Haitian Hispanic artist who dropped out of school at 17, rose quickly to fame and fortune in his early twenties, and died at age 27 of a drug overdose. He is now considered to have been one of the most talented artists of his generation, as well as a symbolic casualty of the cycle of work, success, and burnout that characterized the 1980s in the United States.

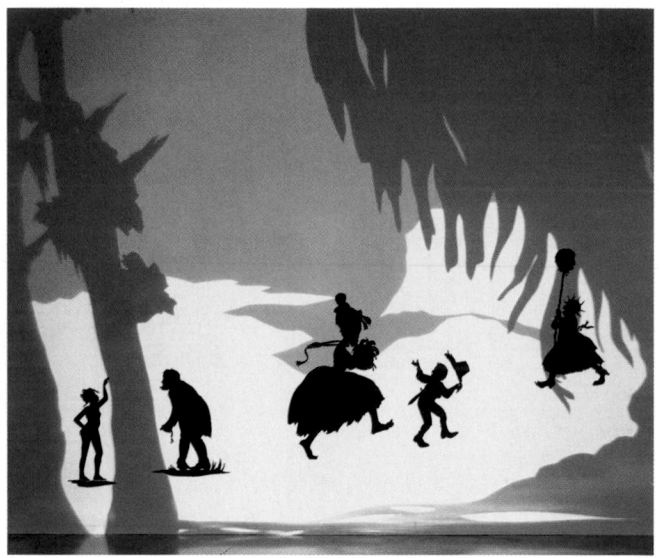

▲ 21.43 **KARA WALKER,** *Insurrection! (Our Tools Were Rudimentary, Yet We Pressed On)* (2000). Installation view (detail). Cut-paper silhouettes and light projections, site-specific dimensions. Solomon R. Guggenheim Museum, New York, New York.

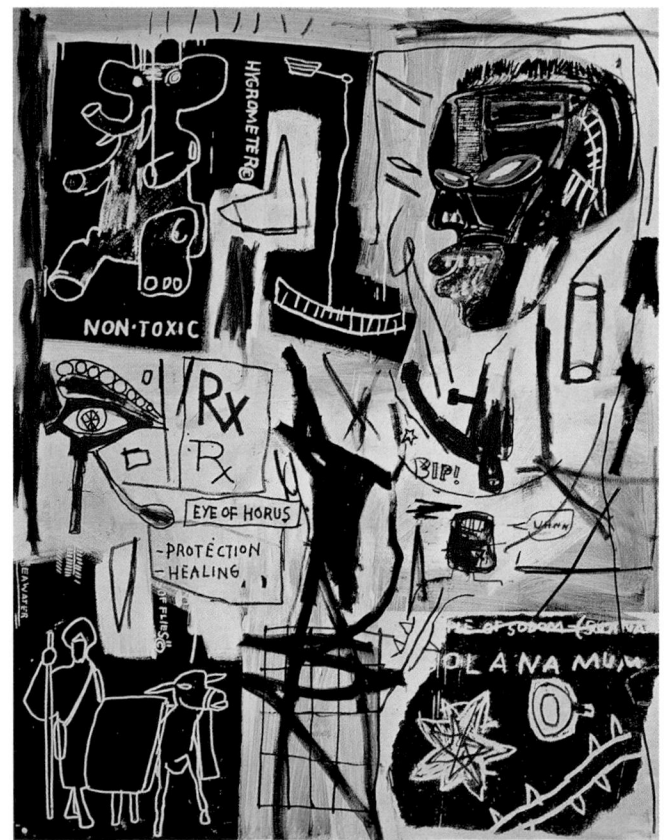

1 ft.

▲ 21.42 **JEAN-MICHEL BASQUIAT,** *Melting Point of Ice* (1984). Acrylic, oil paintstick, and silkscreen on canvas, 86" × 68". The Broad Art Foundation, Santa Monica, California.

KARA WALKER As an African American woman, Kara Walker (b. 1969), has experienced much of her life in terms of black and white and now produces much of her art in this dichotomous palette. She has worked in many mediums, but her life-sized paper cutouts, which are used to silhouette her comments on the often-brutal history of race relations in the United States, have captured the attention of the art world. Her figures are two-dimensional—typically black figures pasted onto white gallery walls—and their flatness seems to echo the stereotyping that prevents people of one background from seeing people of other backgrounds in their full vitality and individualism. *Insurrection! (Our Tools Were Rudimentary, Yet We Pressed On)* (Fig. 21.43) recounts some grisly events taken from the history of slavery in the United States.

COMPARE & CONTRAST

Two Views of *Napoléon Crossing the Alps*

JACQUES-LOUIS DAVID'S PORTRAIT *Napoléon Crossing the Alps* (**Fig. 21.44**) shows a heroic emperor making a nearly impossible ascent with passion and style. Two hundred years later, African American artist Kehinde Wiley (b. 1977) reinvented the David painting, replacing Napoléon with a man of color in street clothes (**Fig. 21.45**). Napoléon sports his rakish bicorn (two-cornered) hat, his cape, and his military boots against a turbulent wintry backdrop. Wiley's anonymous young man models a bandana and sweatbands on his wrists, which are parts of contemporary American hip-hop culture; he adds what appear to be designer fatigues and a swirl of drapery. Wiley also brings the scene indoors with his signature wallpaper backdrop. The craggy rocks are reduced to stage props,

with the history of Alpine crossings carved on them. Note that Wiley adds Hannibal to the list. Interestingly, Wiley keeps the same stallion as in the David. He is believed to be Marengo, the war mount of Napoléon who carried his rider safely through many battles, including the Battles of Austerlitz, Waterloo, and Marengo, from which he was given his name.

What is Wiley trying to accomplish in his contemporary reimagining of the classical painting? Is he commenting on heroism? Why does he replace the emperor with an African American? Why does he add Hannibal to the list of those who have traversed the Alps? Why does he bring the painting indoors?

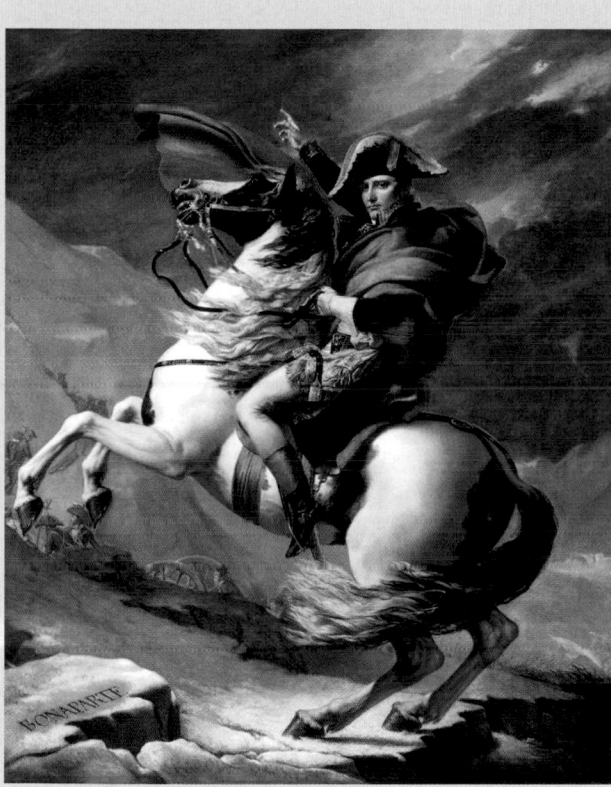

△ 21.44 JACQUES-LOUIS DAVID, *Napoléon Crossing the Alps* (1800). Oil on canvas, 8' 10" × 7' 7". Château de Versailles, Versailles, France.

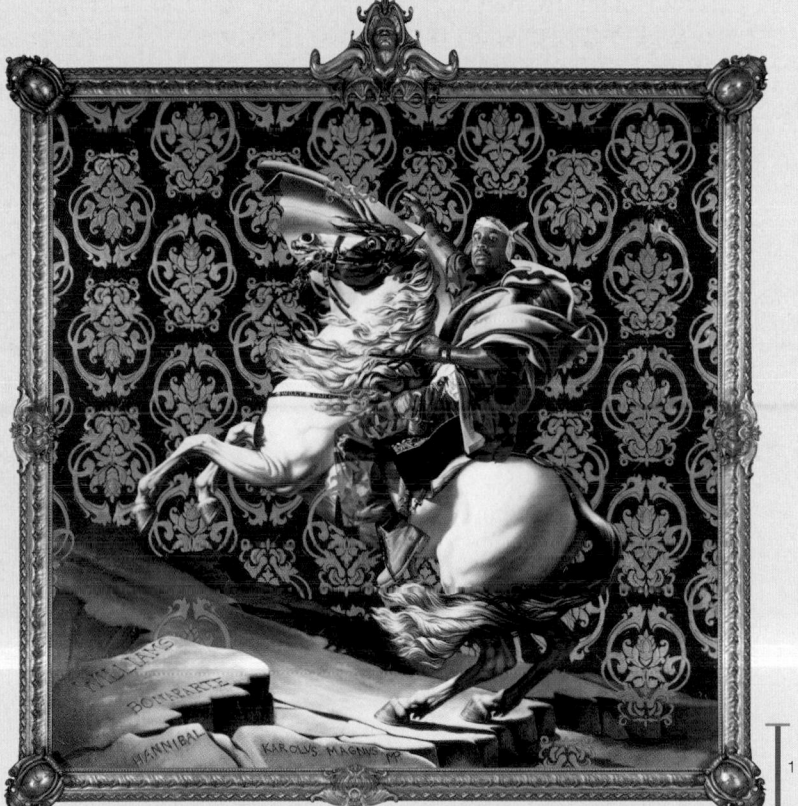

△ 21.45 KEHINDE WILEY, *Napoleon Leading the Army Over the Alps* (2005). Oil on canvas, 9' × 9'. Brooklyn Museum, Brooklyn, New York.

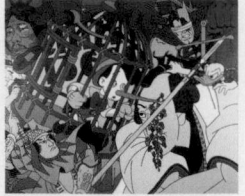

∧ Shimomura's *Untitled* (Fig. 8.13)

A nude slave is propositioned by a plantation owner. A woman with a baby barely escapes being lynched. Elsewhere a group tortures a victim. The piece fills the walls of a large room, where additional shapes are projected onto the walls, and visitors find their own shadows projected among them. Viewers are thus integrated into the haunting works, as if they share in culpability or victimhood. Walker's installations are haunting in their disconnect between the lyrical shadow-puppet display and the dark content of the narrative.

JAUNE QUICK-TO-SEE SMITH Native American artist Jaune Quick-to-See Smith (b. 1940) grew up on the Flathead Indian reservation in Montana. Inspired, in form and process, by the work of Picasso, Paul Klee, and Robert Rauschenberg, the content of her paintings—a full visual vocabulary of Native American images and motifs—reveals her deep connection to her heritage. Created in 1992 on the 500th anniversary of Columbus's arrival in the New World, *Trade (Gifts for Trading Land with White People)* (Fig. 21.46) is a mixed-media composition that the artist referred to as a "non-celebration."[10]

The centerpiece of the more than 14-foot composition is a canoe that hovers, dreamlike, before a background awash in veils of primarily red paint that cannot but evoke the spilling of Native American blood by European conquerors. Peering through the transparent layers are numerous photographs, including exoticized representations of Native Americans by white illustrators and photographers, as well as newspaper clippings reporting conditions past and present—from the murderous events of conquest to the poverty and alcoholism that are rife on modern-day reservations. Strung across the top of the

[10] "A Non-Celebration," *Identity, the Body and the Subversion of Modernism,* Khan Academy. https://www.khanacademy.org/humanities/global-culture/identity-body/identity-body-united-states/a/jaune-quick-to-see-smith-trade-gifts-for-trading-land-with-white-people (accessed February 16, 2015).

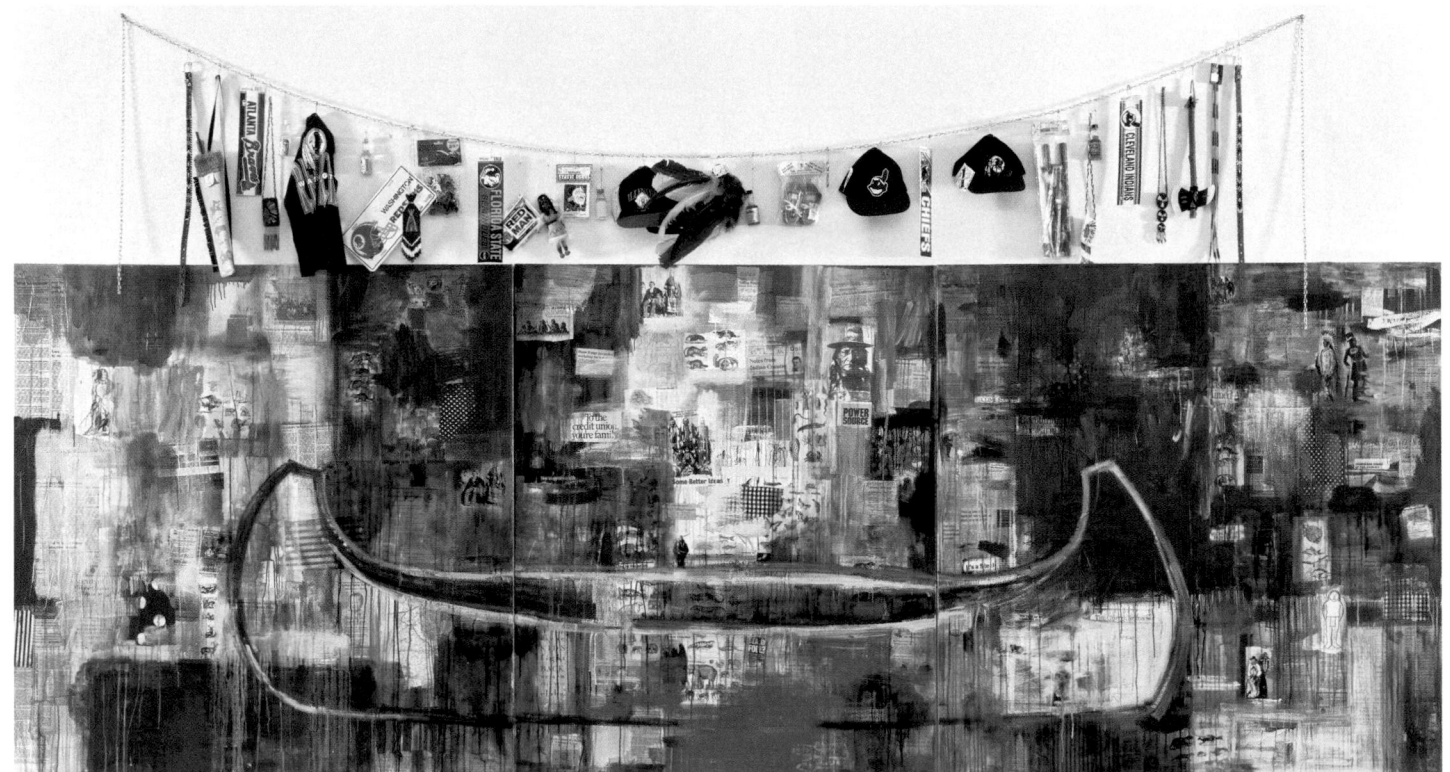

1 ft.

∧ **21.46 JAUNE QUICK-TO-SEE SMITH,** *Trade (Gifts for Trading Land with White People* (1992). Oil and mixed media on canvas, 5' × 14' 2". Chrysler Museum of Art, Norfolk, Virginia.

painting like so many cheap objects from a roadside souvenir stand, we find a toy tomahawk, feather headdress, a quiver and arrows, and strings of beads interspersed with baseball caps and banners bearing the offensive, racist names and logos of U.S. sports teams. The title of the painting, along with the array of trinkets, references the exchange of tribal nation territory for next to nothing by white settlers and offers a suggestion that Native Americans rework the deal by offering "junk" in return for appropriated land.

ART AFTER 1980: SOME DIVERGENT TRENDS

The 1970s witnessed a strong presence of realism in the visual arts that was, in part, a reaction against the introspective and subjective abstract tendencies that had gripped American art since World War II in one form or another. Although Minimalism and conceptualism continued, what seemed to some, to be lost were the acts of making art themselves. The period that followed was marked by a pluralism of artistic styles the reflected the growing pluralism in contemporary society in the wake of the civil rights and feminist movements.

New Image Painting

In 1978, New York's Whitney Museum of American Art mounted a controversial though significant exhibition called *New Image painting*. The participants, including Jennifer Bartlett (b. 1941), Susan Rothenberg (b. 1945), and eight other artists, were doing something very different. They were, in their own way, reconciling the disparate styles of abstraction and representation. The image was central to their compositions, much in the tradition of realist artists. But the images were often so simplified that they conveyed the grandeur of abstract shapes. These images never dominated other aesthetic components of the work, such as color, gesture, texture, or even composition. Rather, they cohabited the work in elegant balance.

JENNIFER BARTLETT Jennifer Bartlett's *Spiral: An Ordinary Evening in New Haven* (Fig. 21.47) combines a painted canvas and several sculptural objects in a virtual maelstrom of imagery that is alternately engulfed by flames and apparently spewed out by the turbulent blaze. In this work, Bartlett includes figurative imagery and explores the use of line and color. The title and the work invite the viewer's speculation as to exactly what has happened to cause the conflagration and how it can possibly represent an "ordinary evening" anywhere. This

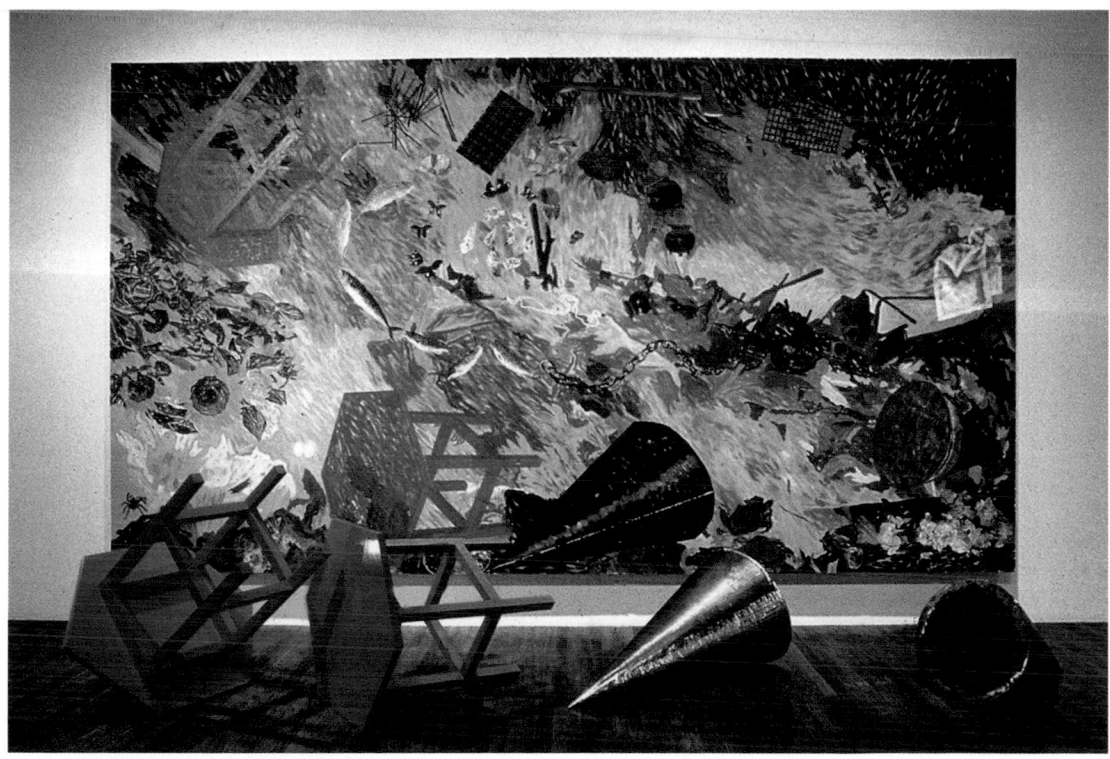

▲ **21.47 JENNIFER BARTLETT,** *Spiral: An Ordinary Evening in New Haven* (1989). Painting: oil on canvas, 108" × 192"; tables: painted wood, 30½" × 32" × 35"; painted wood with steel base, 39½" × 41" × 35"; cones: welded steel, 20" × 30¼" × 21".

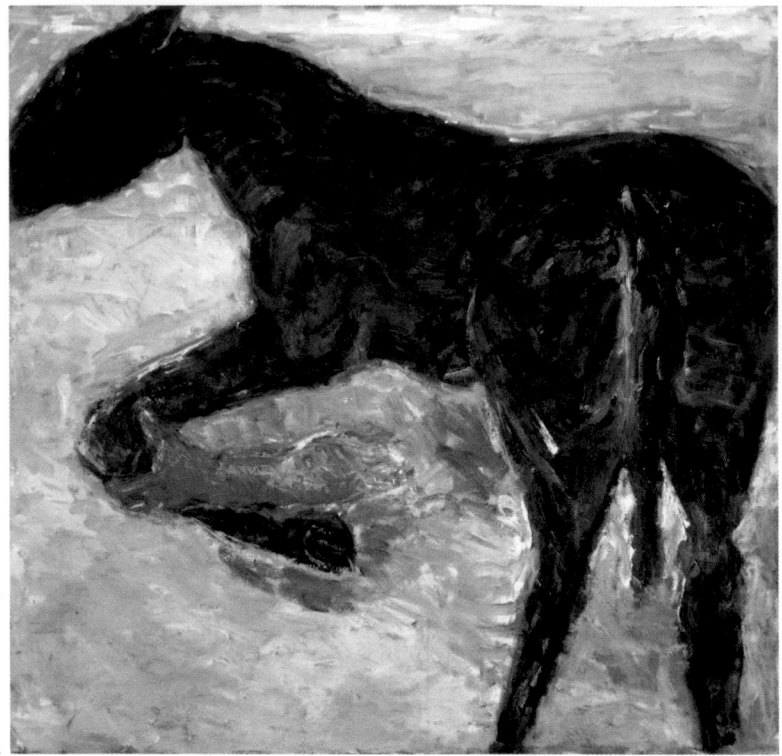

1 ft.

∧ 21.48 **SUSAN ROTHENBERG,** *Chix* (2003). Oil on canvas, 57" × 58 ½". Collection Susan and Leonard Nimoy, Los Angeles, California.

sort of interplay between the verbal and the visual is another hallmark of **New Image painting**. Bartlett combines narrative, conceptual art, representation, and some abstract process painting of the sort we find in Abstract Expressionism.

SUSAN ROTHENBERG Susan Rothenberg's *First Horse* is a small piece that was painted in 1974, some four years before the Whitney Museum exhibition. Since then, the artist has consistently explored the minimalist contours of the horse in relation to the textural field. One of the few artists who maintained a strong connection to the premise of New Image painting, Rothenberg assigns equal weight to structure and image in her compositions. She calls attention to surface, melds the representational and the abstract, and does not reject the potential of narrative. In a recent work titled *Chix* (Fig. 21.48), a fleshy, disembodied forearm emerges from a mélange of painterly brushstrokes to tenderly grasp the front leg of a colt. The tight framing distributes our focus equally on structure and image—on the black and white shapes formed where figure and ground meet as well as the implied, yet open-ended narrative.

Neo-Expressionism

The center of the art world moved to New York in the 1940s for historical as well as artistic reasons. The first-generation Abstract Expressionists developed a style that was viewed worldwide as highly original and influential. They laid claim to the tenet that the *process* of painting was a viable alternative to subject matter. In the early 1980s, a group of artists who were born during the Abstract Expressionist era—though on other shores—wholeheartedly revived the gestural manner and experimentation with materials that the Americans had devised four decades earlier, but with an added dimension. These young German and Italian artists, who came to be called **Neo-Expressionists**, detested painting "about nothing." Born as they were during the darkest years of postwar Europe, when Germany and Italy stood utterly defeated, these artists would mature to portray the bitter ironies and angst of their generation in emotionally fraught images that are rooted in history, literature, and expressionistic art.

ANSELM KIEFER Perhaps the most remarkable of these Neo-Expressionists is the German artist Anselm Kiefer (b. 1945). Kiefer has been able to synthesize an expressionistic painterly style with strong abstract elements in a narrative form of painting that makes multivalent references to German history and culture. The casual observer cannot hope to decipher Kiefer's paintings; they are highly intellectual, obscure, and idiosyncratic. But at the same time, they are overpowering in their scale, their larger-than-life subjects, and their textural, encrusted surfaces.

Kiefer's *Dein Goldenes Haar, Margarethe* (Fig. 21.49) serves as an excellent example of the artist's formal and literary concerns. The title of the work, and others of this series, refers to a poem by Paul Celan titled "Your Golden Hair, Margarete," which describes the destruction of European Jewry through the images of a golden-haired German woman named Margarete and a dark-haired Jewish woman, Shulamith. Against a pale gray blue background, Kiefer uses actual straw to suggest the hair of the German woman, contrasting it with thick black paint that lies charred on the upper canvas, to symbolize the hair of her unfortunate counterpart. Between them a German tank presides over this human destruction, isolated against a wasteland of its own creation. Kiefer here, as often, scrawls his titles or other words across the canvas surface, sometimes veiling them with his textured materials. The materials function as content; they become symbols to which we must emotionally and intellectually respond.

ERIC FISCHL Several American painters responded to European Neo-Expressionism with narrative works that have American references. For example, New York painter Eric Fischl (b. 1948) focused on middle-class life in the

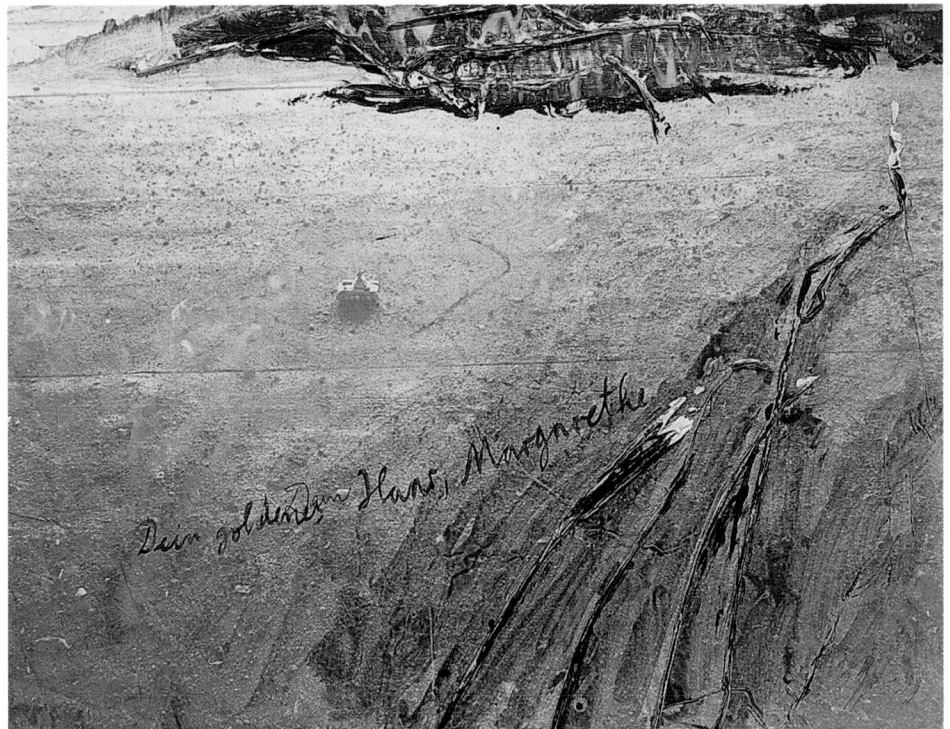

◄ 21.49 ANSELM KIEFER, *Dein Goldenes Haar, Margarethe (Your Golden Hair, Margarete)* (1981). Mixed media on paper, 14" × 18¾".

1 in.

suburbs, including Levittown, Long Island. Fischl's *A Visit To/A Visit From/The Island* (Fig. 21.50) shifts the locale from big-city suburbs to an island vacation setting. While his transported suburbanites blithely bob along in the turquoise waters of the Caribbean, oblivious to anything other than pleasure seeking, their counterparts—native islanders—are drowning in the surf. Fischl is underscoring the bipolar social structure we find in these vacation "paradises"—the affluent tourists versus the poverty-stricken workers. Although Fischl's style can be characterized as a lush realism, in some ways very different from that of the Europeans, he too embraces a narrative format.

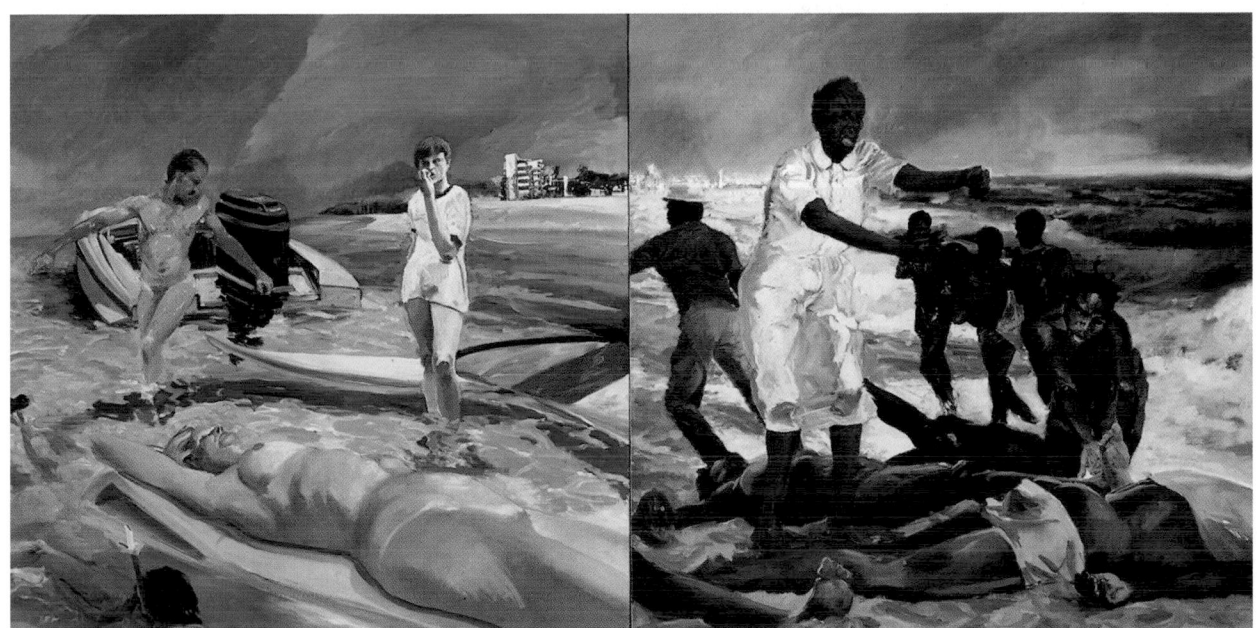

1 ft.

▲ 21.50 ERIC FISCHL, *A Visit To/A Visit From/The Island* (1983). Oil on canvas. Two panels; each panel: 84" × 84". Whitney Museum of American Art, New York, New York.

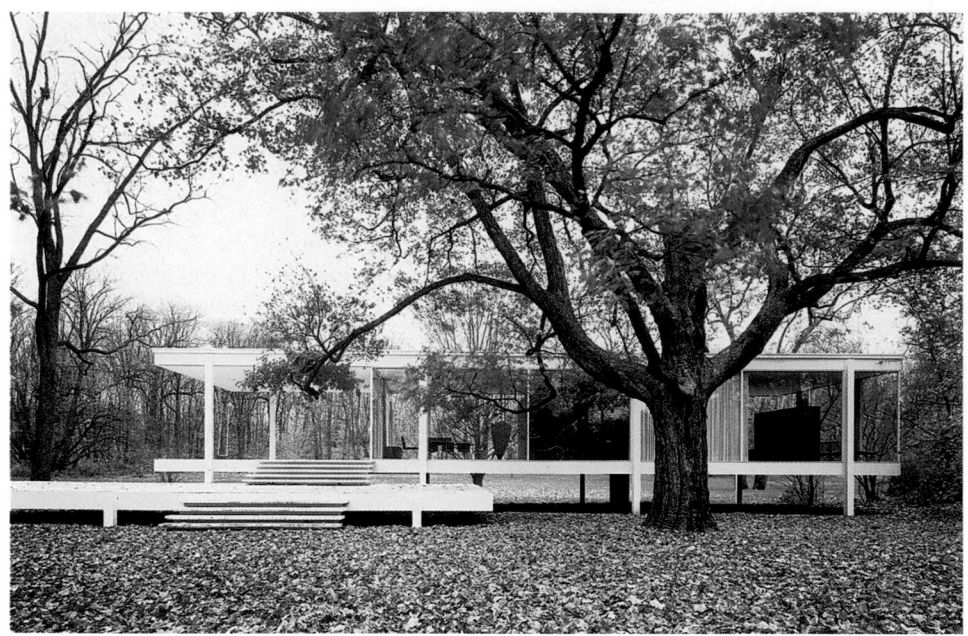

▲ 21.51 LUDWIG MIËS VAN DER ROHE, Farnsworth House, Fox River, Plano, Illinois (1950).

As we see in the differences among Le Corbusier's work, Levittown, Miës van der Rohe's Farnsworth House, and Miës van der Rohe and Philip Johnson's Seagram Building, modernism in architecture never comprised just one style. Rather, it serves as an umbrella term that encompasses the many architectural visions, including those of Frank Lloyd Wright (see Fig. 13.18), Le Corbusier, Miës van der Rohe, Gordon Bunshaft, and many others.

LUDWIG MIËS VAN DER ROHE A rhythmic procession of white steel columns suspends Miës van der Rohe's Farnsworth House (Fig. 21.51) above the Illinois countryside. In its perfect technological elegance, it is in many ways visually remote from its site. Why steel? Less expensive wood could have supported this house of one story and short spans, and wood might have appeared more natural on this sylvan site. The architect's choices can be read as a symbol of our contemporary remoteness from our feral past. Perhaps the architect is suggesting that contemporary technology has freed humankind from victimization at the brutal hand of nature, even as it allows humans to enjoy interaction with nature on an aesthetic level. The Farnsworth House is as beautiful as it is austere in ornamentation. It has platforms, steps, and a glass curtain wall that allows the environment to flow through. The steps and platforms provide access to a less well-ordered world below.

LUDWIG MIËS VAN DER ROHE AND PHILIP JOHNSON   The Seagram Building (see Fig. 21.52), built as the U.S. headquarters for the Canadian distiller Joseph E. Seagram & Sons, was constructed across Park Avenue from its equally famous and equally Modernist neighbor, Lever House (see Fig. 13.16). Designed by Ludwig Miës van der Rohe and Philip Johnson, it is another signature example of the Modernist credo "form ever follows function."

There is no ornamentation. The vertical I beams of bronze-coated steel form a perfectly regular pattern across the elevations of the structure and emphasize its upward reach. Miës, who abhorred irregularity, even specified that the window coverings for the building be uniform, so that from the outside, the windows would never look chaotic or messy. The sharp-edged columns at the entry-level plaza complement the stark grid of the building but also define a softer, transitional space—with trees and fountains—between the chaos of the surrounding city and the austere serenity of the building's interior.

ARCHITECTURE

After World War II, architecture moved in many directions. Some of these were technological advances that allowed architects to literally achieve greater heights, as in the skyscraper, and to create more sculptural forms, as in Le Corbusier's Chapel of Notre-Dame-du-Haut (see Fig. 13.17). Millions of soldiers returned from Europe and the Pacific and established new families, giving birth not only to what we now call the baby boomers, but also to vast housing tracts like Levittown (see Fig. 13.10) that dotted suburbs that had earlier been farms, small towns, or wilderness. All these and more were examples of modern architecture.

Modern Architecture

Modern architecture rejected the ideals and principles of the classical tradition in favor of the experimental forms of expression that characterized many styles of art and literature from the 1860s to the 1970s. *Modernism* also refers to approaches that are ahead of their time. "Modern" suggests, in general, an approach that overturns the past and, by that definition, every era of artists doing something completely new can be considered modern in their time.

Modernism is a concept of art making built on the urge to depict contemporary life and events rather than history. Modernism was a response to industrialization, urbanization, and the growth of capitalism and democracy. Modern architects, like modern artists, felt free to explore new styles inspired by technology and science, psychology, politics, economics, and social consciousness.

In response—or in revolt—by the end of the 1970s, architects continued to create steel-cage structures but drew freely from past styles of ornamentation, including classical columns, pediments, friezes, and a variety of elements we might find in ancient Egypt, Greece, and Rome. The architectural movement was termed **Postmodernism**, and the idea was to once more "warm up" buildings, to link them to the architectural past, to a Main Street of the heart or mind—some sort of mass architectural nostalgia. Postmodernist structures rejected the formal simplicity and immaculate finish of Modernist architecture in favor of whimsical shapes, colors, and patterns. Postmodern architects revived the concept of the decorative in architecture, a practice that was completely antithetical to the purity of Modernism in the twentieth century.

PHILIP JOHNSON AND JOHN BURGEE   One of the most interesting aspects of Postmodern architecture is its appropriation of historical motifs; Philip Johnson's and John Burgee's AT&T Building in New York City, which was subsequently sold to SONY (Fig. 21.53), is one of

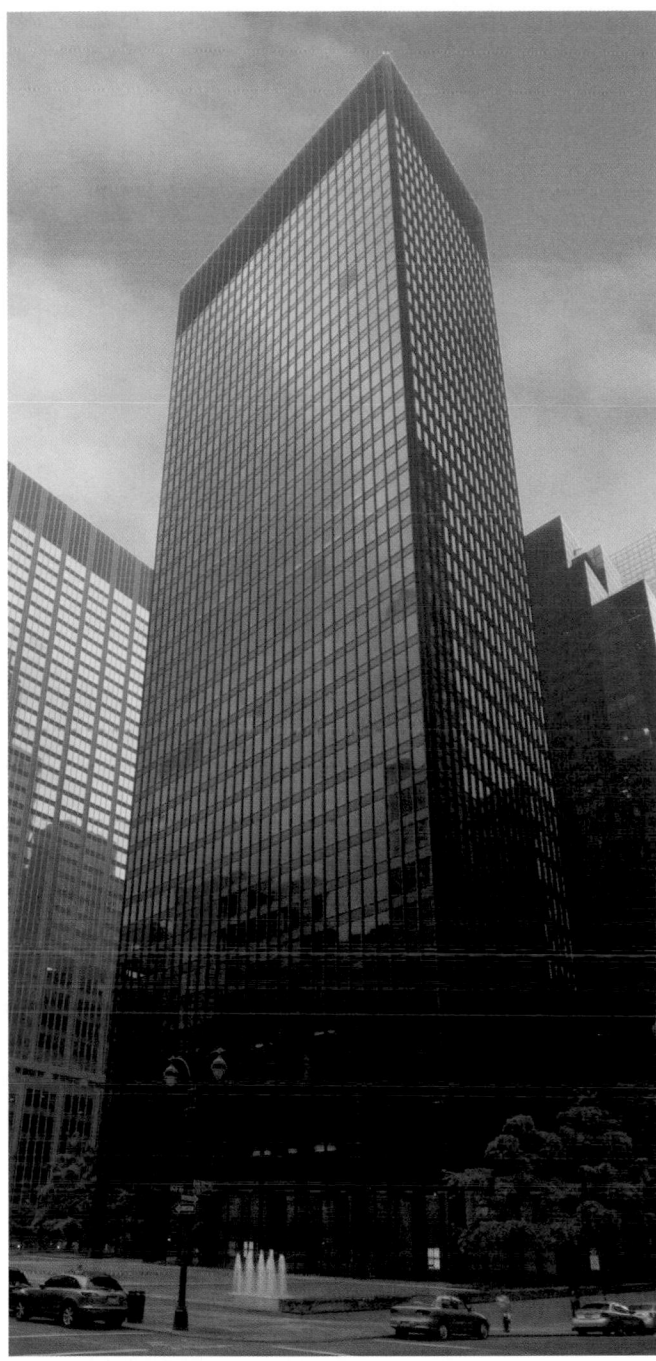

∧ 21.52 LUDWIG MIËS VAN DER ROHE AND PHILIP JOHNSON, Seagram Building, New York, New York (1958).

Postmodern Architecture

By the mid-1970s, the clean Modernist look of buildings such as Lever House was overwhelming the cityscape. Architectural critics began to argue that a national proliferation of steel-cage rectangular solids was threatening to bury the nation's cities in boredom. John Perrault said in 1979, "We are sick to death of cold plazas and 'curtain wall' skyscrapers."

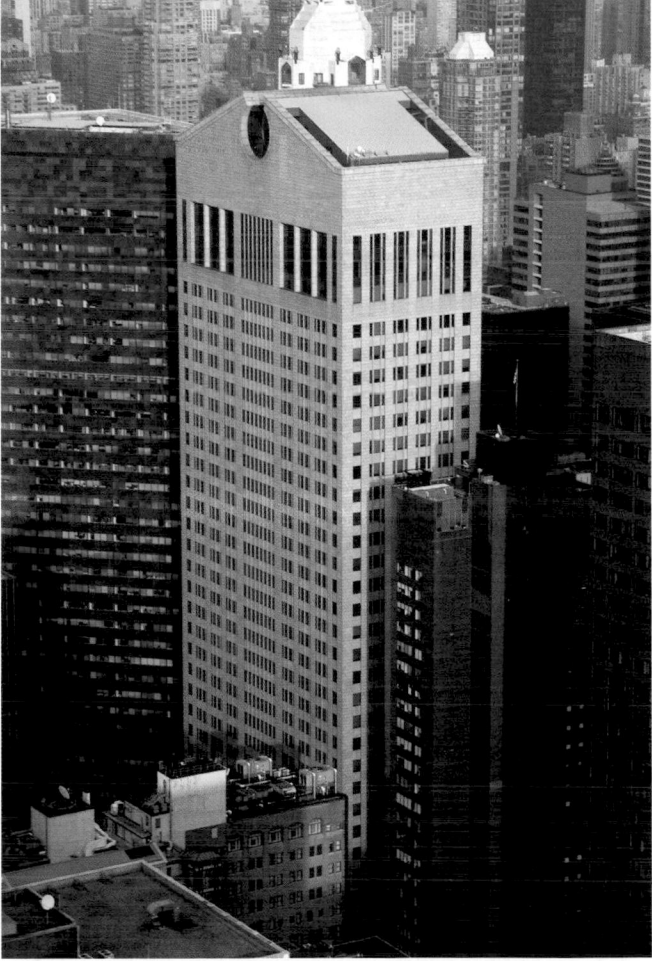

∧ 21.53 BURGEE ARCHITECTS WITH PHILIP JOHNSON. SONY Plaza (formerly AT&T Building), New York, New York (1984).

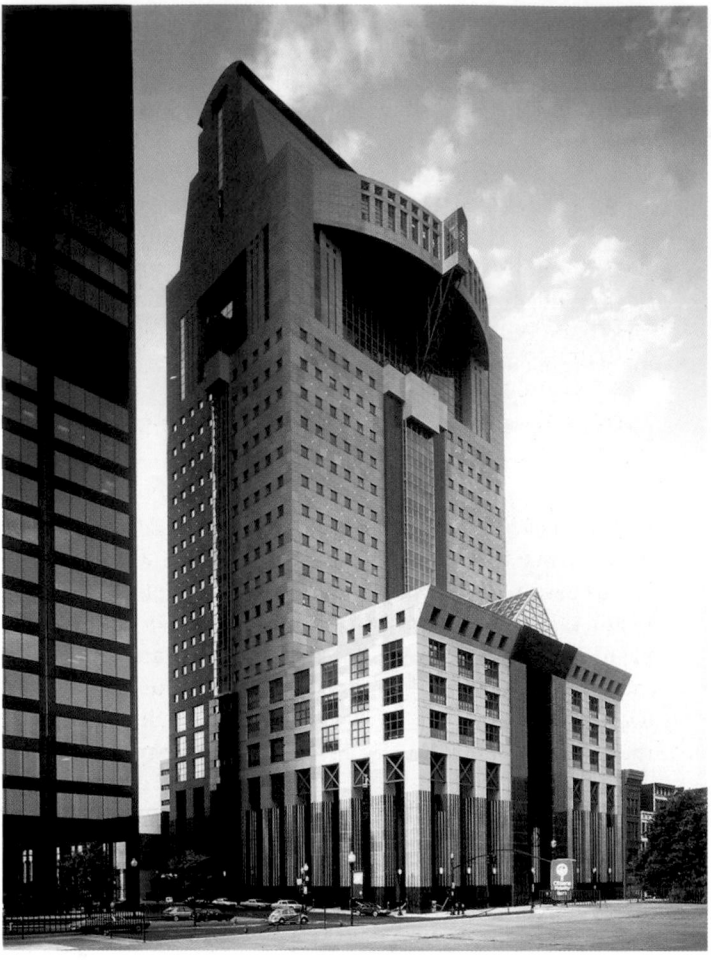

▲ 21.54 MICHAEL GRAVES, Humana Building, Louisville, Kentucky (1985).

the ground. The overall impression recalls the great pylons, or gateways, of Egyptian temple complexes such as the one at Karnak (see Figs. 13.4 and 13.5). The office building is set behind the entry in such a way that the overall contour mimics the blocklike seated body position in ancient statuary (see Fig. 16.10). The curved shape at the top of the front elevation, "adorned" with a projecting rectangle, recalls a pharaonic headdress.

RENZO PIANO AND RICHARD RODGERS   The architects of the Georges Pompidou National Center for Arts and Culture in Paris (Fig. 21.55) were an Italian, Renzo Piano, and a Britisher, Richard Rogers. This genesis, perhaps, is one of the reasons that many Parisians were initially critical of the building, which differs from modern architecture in that it wears its skeleton on the outside. Staid modern buildings, such as the Seagram Building, have a central service core that carries heating and air-conditioning ducts, electricity, and water—and, of course, elevators and stairways. The various pipes that cover these utilities are coded with different colors to enable workers and repair people to readily locate them. The pipes are also coded in—or rather, on—the Pompidou Center, but they are part of the façade of the building and allowed the architects to splash the building with color. Even the elevator is on the outside—a transparent conveyer that delivers a grander view of the city as it delivers its occupants to the upper floors.

the earliest examples. The massive tower sits on a forest of columns, reminiscent—to Johnson—of an Egyptian **hypostyle** hall. Its pale pink façade is punctuated with fenestration, although the prominent stone grid lines regulate the pace of the upward sweep. The building is crowned with a broken roof pediment referencing the Chippendale style that originated with the eighteenth-century British cabinetmaker, Thomas Chippendale. Beneath the ornamentation lies a steel-cage structure, now visually all but disguised.

MICHAEL GRAVES   Michael Graves's Humana Building (Fig. 21.54) also looks to ancient Egypt for its historic reference. Tall, tightly arranged pillars (as in an Egyptian hypostyle hall) and a grid of square windows lighten the otherwise heavy rectangular solids, which seem to anchor the building firmly to

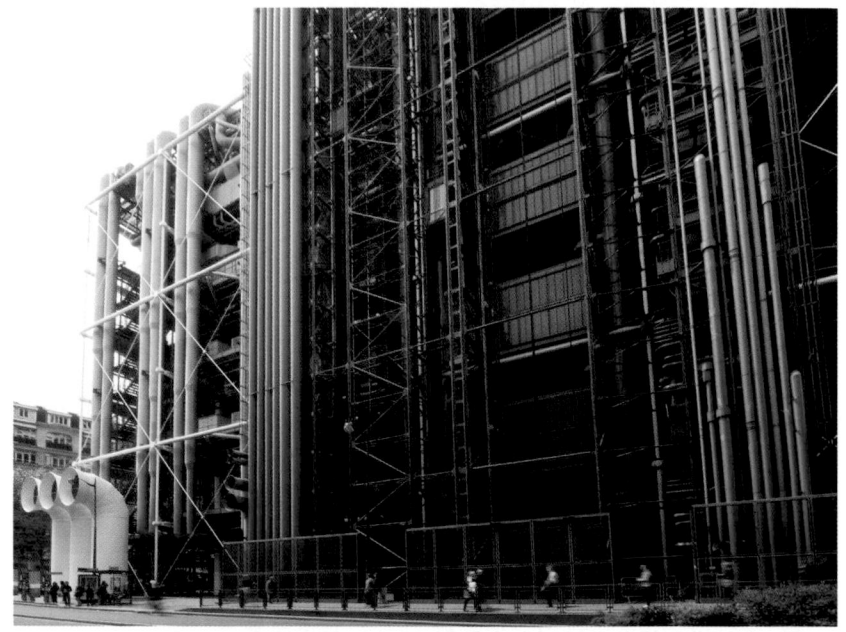

▲ 21.55 RENZO PIANO AND RICHARD ROGERS, Georges Pompidou National Center for Arts and Culture, Paris, France (1977).

> The void is one of the organizing features of the building. . . . It is the cut through German history, Jewish history. It is the extermination of Jews and the deportation of Jews not only from this city but from Germany and from Europe.
>
> —DANIEL LIBESKIND

CONNECTIONS Frank Gehry's Deconstructivist works disorient the viewer by haphazardly presenting planes, volumes, and masses to challenge observer's pre-conceptions about how form should be related to function.

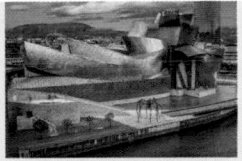

∧ Guggenheim Museum, Bilbao, Spain (**Fig. 2.22**)

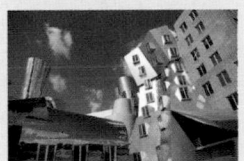

∧ Ray and Maria Stata Center (**Fig. 13.24**)

Deconstructivist Architecture

What we have known as modern architecture is no longer modern, at least not in the sense of relating to the *present*. It's not even Postmodern, if we want to pigeonhole style. As we move forward in the third millennium, the world of architecture seems completely enmeshed in a movement called *Deconstructivism*.

The Deconstructivist movement originated in the 1960s with the ideas of the French philosopher Jacques Derrida. He argued, in part, that literary texts can be read in different ways and that it is absurd to believe that there can be only one proper interpretation. Similarly, in Deconstructivist architectural design, the whole is less important than the parts. In fact, buildings are meant to be seen in bits and pieces. The familiar elements of traditional architecture are taken apart, discarded, or disguised so that what remains seems randomly assembled.

Deconstructivist architects deny the modern maxim that form should follow function. Instead, they tend to reduce their structures to purer geometric forms made possible by contemporary materials, and they make liberal use of color to express emotion. An early (1988) exhibition of Deconstructivist works at the Museum of Modern Art connected Deconstructivist architecture with Cubism and with the Constructivist Russian painting and sculpture of the 1920s (see Naum Gabo's *Column*, **Fig. 20.15**). American architect Philip Johnson contributed to that exhibition at the age of 82, and he was the only architect of note to have been a driving force in the Modern, Postmodern, and Deconstructivist movements.

DANIEL LIBESKIND Although Daniel Libeskind seems to have taken Deconstructivism as a point of departure in his design for the Jewish Museum Department of the Berlin Museum (**Fig. 21.56**), he invested its parts with profound symbolism. The addition is intended to communicate the vastness and also the legacy of things that are not completely visible. Contrary to public opinion, the flesh of architecture is not cladding, insulation, and structure, but the substance of the individual in society and history; a figuration of the inorganic, the body and the soul.

The zigzag, or lightning-bolt, shape of the building resembles a broken Star of David. It was derived mathematically by plotting the Berlin addresses of Jewish writers, artists, and composers who were killed during the Holocaust. The overall design is punctuated by voids that symbolize the absence of Jewish people and culture

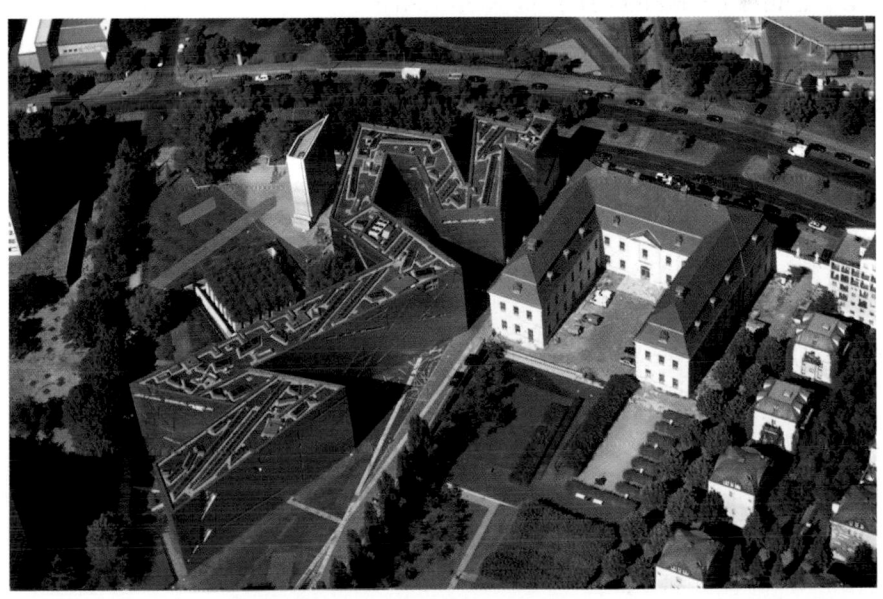

∧ **21.56 DANIEL LIBESKIND**, Extension of the Berlin Museum, Berlin, Germany (1989–1996). Reinforced concrete with zinc façade, 166,840 square feet.

in Berlin. The zinc exterior of the museum is slashed by a linear pattern of windows that was determined by connecting the addresses of German and Jewish Berliners on a map of the museum's neighborhood. The visitor cannot help being struck by the overwhelming sense that every structural, design, and symbolic element—each of which attracts and holds interest—has been informed by the historic circumstances that gave rise to the building.

ZAHA HADID The realm of architecture has not been an easy one for women to crack. When one considers that situation, along with the fact that traditional Islamic

societies in the Middle East often restrict the social and professional roles that women can play, Zaha Hadid's global position as an award-winning and highly sought woman architect becomes especially notable. Hadid was born in Baghdad and educated in London, where she currently resides, but she has had several Middle Eastern commissions, including the Dancing Towers project in Dubai (Fig. 21.57).

The Dancing Towers resemble a choreographed interlacing of abstract torsos. Three towers originate on a common base and then appear to "do their own thing," touching their companion towers here and there on certain levels where the functions of the individual towers overlap—offices, a hotel, residences, leisure facilities, and restaurants. The Dancing Towers evoke the fluidity of the oft-referenced image of the Three Graces in art history, in which a trio of beautiful women intertwine in dance, their collective positions combining to create a single, perfect form.

SANTIAGO CALATRAVA Santiago Calatrava's architecture seems to be going up everywhere: a symphony center in Atlanta; thirty bridges including three that will span the Trinity River in Dallas; a transportation hub for the World Trade Center site; and a residential tower composed of twelve cubes cantilevered from a concrete core overlooking the East River in New York City. *Time* magazine named Calatrava one of the 100 most influential people of 2005, and the American Institute of Architects awarded him their coveted gold medal in the same year.

As we see in the transportation hub (Fig. 21.58), Calatrava—also a sculptor and a painter—has erased the lines between architecture and sculpture. Eero Saarinen's TWA Terminal at New York's Kennedy Airport has been said to look like a bird in flight. So will Calatrava's transportation hub, although it also looks something like the plated spine of a stegosaurus. Most of the hub is actually underground, but it will have a lithesome body of glass and steel at street level, along with two canopies that stretch upward, creating the impression of wings. The practical purpose to the design is to bring abundant natural light down onto the train platform, which is 60 feet below. Calatrava remarked that light is one of his building materials. Although passengers arriving at the hub will be underground, they will be drenched with natural light.

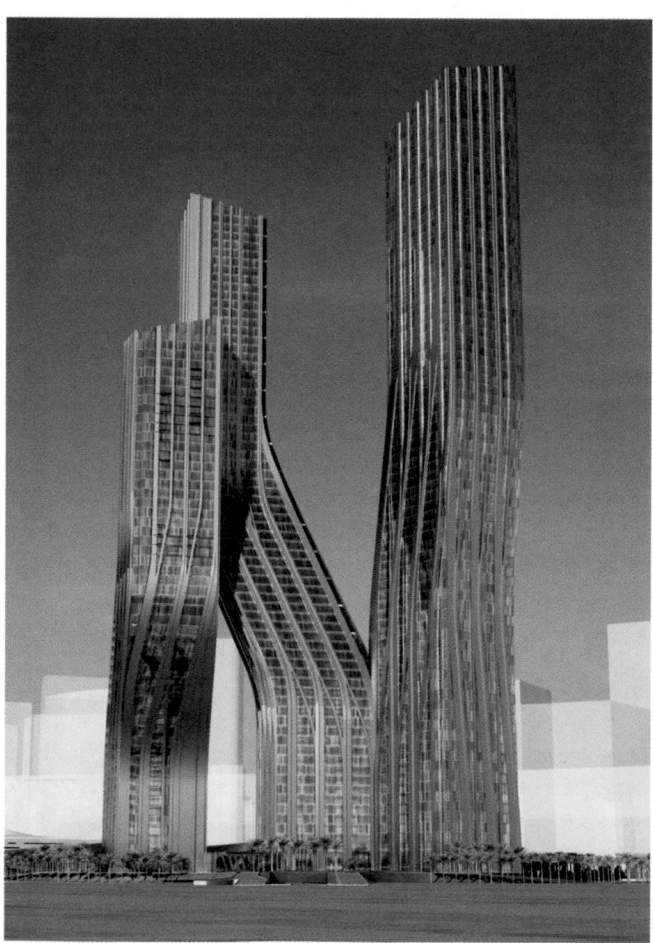

▲ 21.57 ZAHA HADID, *Dancing Towers*, Dubai (2009).

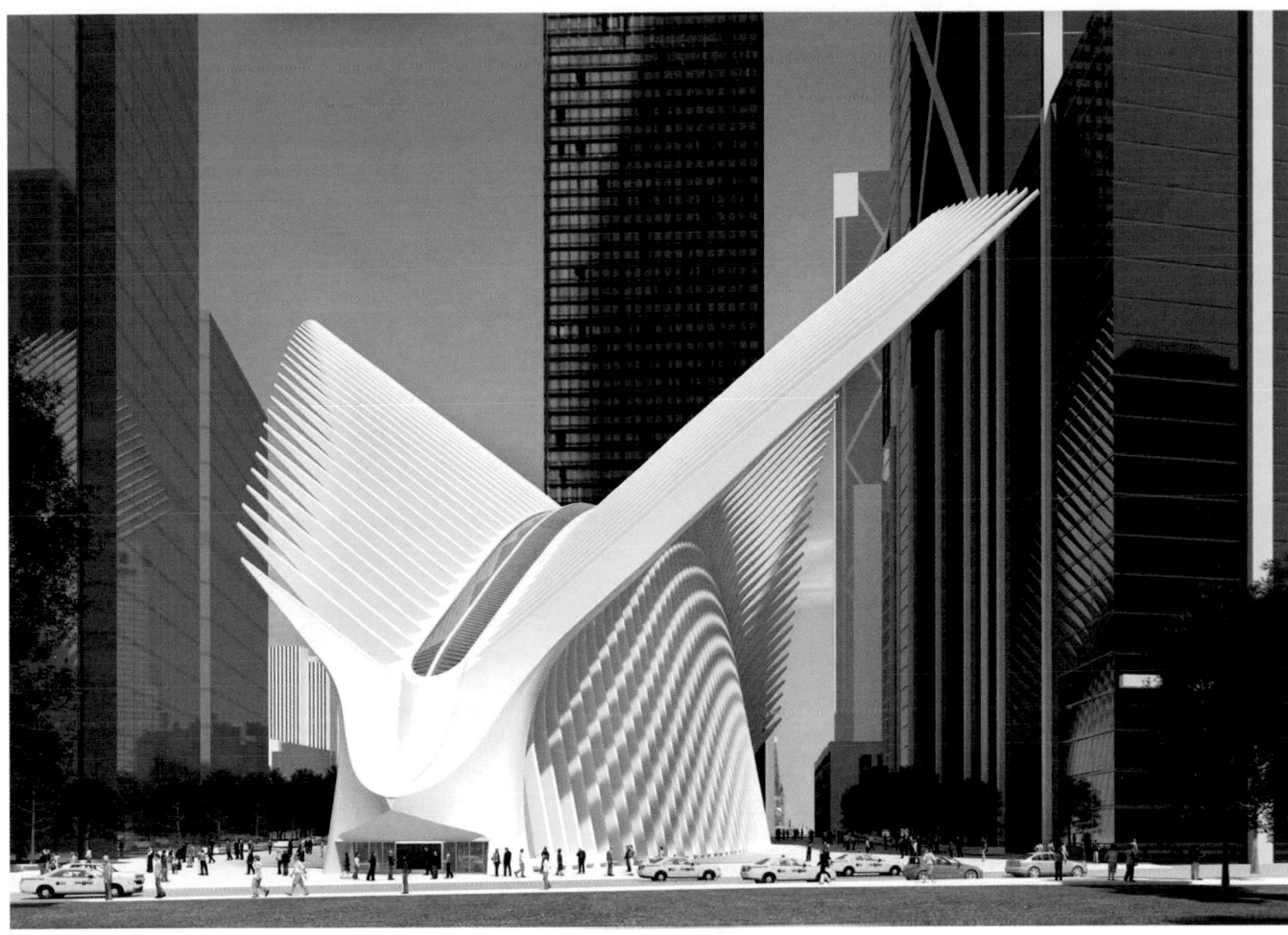

∧ 21.58 SANTIAGO CALATRAVA, World Trade Center Transportation Hub, New York, New York (2015).

THE WIDER WORLD

In the years following World War II, perhaps nowhere in the wider world were political, social, and industrial disruptions so prevalent as in the East—India, China, and Japan. India became an independent nation, only to partition into what is now India and Pakistan; Pakistan would split later into current-day Pakistan and Bangladesh. Mao Zedong's revolutionary grip tightened on China, culminating in his establishment of the People's Republic in 1949—in truth, a Communist dictatorship. Mao brought China from an agrarian culture into the industrial age, sought equality for women, and improved health care. The societal changes aimed at equalization were accompanied by Mao's Cultural Revolution beginning in 1966; schools and cities were emptied of intellectuals who were compelled to work in the fields alongside farmers. One of the artists we discuss, Wu Guanzhong, who was initially inspired by Mao's rise to power, was forced to destroy many of his own paintings and could not return to his career until Mao's death in 1976.

After the surrender of Japan to the Allied Forces during World War II, the United States played the prominent role in converting the country from a militant imperial empire to an enduring democracy, hotbed of invention, and vibrant economic power. This chapter's "Wider World" focuses on the East. In the following chapter our coverage will expand yet wider to include the Middle East, Africa, and Latin America.

We have seen thus far many works by Western artists inspired by their counterparts around the globe. Toward the latter half of the nineteenth century, European artists were enthralled with Japanese ukiyo-e prints; Manet, Monet, Degas, Cassatt, van Gogh—they all copied them. The mania for all things Japanese entered the visual culture of France, inspiring everything from fashion to interior design. Some 100 years earlier, during the Rococo period in France, the taste for Chinese artistic styles and objects—*chinoiserie*—inspired paintings, porcelain, decorative screens, wallpaper, and more. In the early twentieth century artists such as Picasso and Matisse and some of the German Expressionists brought references to

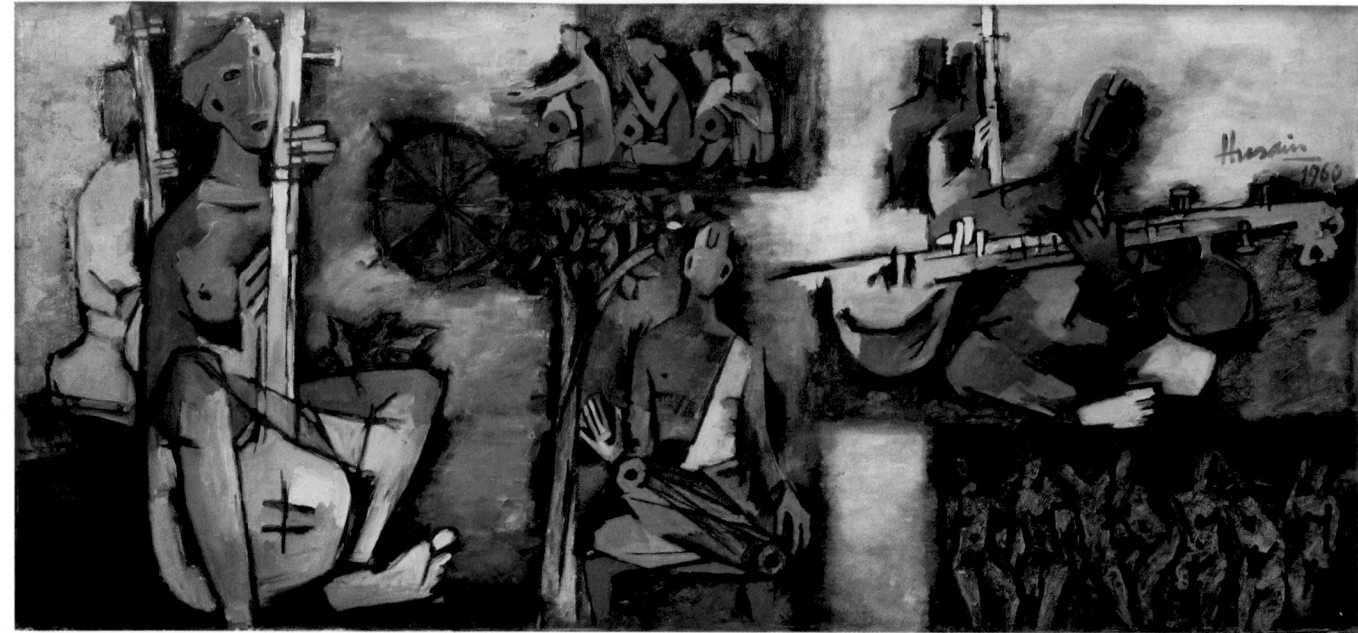

▲ 21.59 MAQBOOL FIDA HUSAIN, *Ragamala Series* (1960). Oil on canvas, 35" × 74". Private collection.

African art into their own imagery. In the postwar years, the influence of the West also can be seen in the work of artists of the East.

India and Pakistan

In 1947 "British India" was dissolved and the Dominion of India gained independence from the United Kingdom. Led by Mahatma Gandhi, whose campaign of rebellion was based on peaceful civil disobedience (and whose model was adopted by Martin Luther King Jr. during the U.S. civil rights movement), India entered its postcolonial period. Gandhi further advocated for the alleviation of the deprivations experienced by India's lowest caste—the

Dalits, or untouchables—and promoted amicable relations between Hindus and Muslims. Yet in the same year the British departed, India broke apart into the sovereign nations of the Union of India (the majority, Hindu) and the Dominion of Pakistan (Muslim).

In Bombay (now Mumbai), in the same year that political independence came to India, Maqbool Fida Husain (1915–2011) and others founded the Marxist-leaning Progressive Artists' Group. Rejecting colonial stylistic idioms that thrived during British rule, the Progressives embraced 20th Century European modernism, including Primitivism, Expressionism, Cubism, and Surrealism. In Husain's *Ragamala Series* (Fig. 21.59), references to these European styles are clear: fragmented form, integration

1945–1960	1960–1980	1980–
World War II ends in 1945	Pakistan partitions into current-day Pakistan and Bangladesh in 1971	Japan and China develop into great industrial and economic powers
The Allies occupy Japan from 1945 to 1952	Wu Hufan paints *Celebrate the Success of Our Glorious Atomic Bomb Explosion!* in 1965	Japan's automobile industry and China's electronics industry gain global prominence
India partitions into India and Pakistan in 1947	Mao Zedong initiates the Cultural Revolution in China in 1966	
The Progressive Artists' Group is initiated in India in 1947	Mao dies in 1976, enabling artists to find more freedom	
Mao Zedong founds the People's Republic of China in 1949		
The Gutai Art Association is founded in Japan in 1954		

1 ft.

⋀ 21.60 **NATVAR BHAVSAR,** *Yosemite IV* (1980). Acrylic on paper, 46" × 42". (1980.227). The Metropolitan Museum of Art, New York, New York, New York.

of foreground and background, mood-evoking color, imagery that spreads from one edge of the canvas to the other. However, Husain's subject matter—drawn from traditional Indian painting—is distinct from that of his European counterparts. Ragamala painting, which combines references to art, poetry, and music (a *raga* is a musical mode) in a single illustration, date back to the sixteenth and seventeenth centuries. As in Husain's piece, moods are evoked in ragamala paintings through, among other things, color. Blended blues and greens create a soothing atmosphere while bits of complementary yellow-orange add a dynamic counterpoint. The "beats

and pulses" of color correspond to the sounds and movements suggested by the musicians, instruments, and dancing figures.

Natvar Bhavsar's (b. 1934) work was also clearly informed by his interaction with the West—in this case, New York City, where he took up residence in the 1960s. Paintings such as *Yosemite IV* (Fig. 21.60) reveal an interest in exploring the color field—as did Rothko and other artists of the New York School. This particular work bears a very "American" reference, but Bhavsar's palette choices were strongly connected to the significant, symbolic role of color in Hindu religion and culture.

China

Just as Western art for many centuries reflected and reinforced Christian belief, so too did virtually all of the art produced under Mao's Communist rule extoll his social and political agenda. As in a propaganda poster from 1970 (Fig. 21.61), the virtues of nationalism, gender-neutral comradeship, and hard work are consistent visual themes.

Just a few years before this poster was created, Wu Hufan (1894–1968) painted one of his most famous scrolls—a homage to China's "glorious" 1964 entry into the world's nuclear "club" whose members, at the time, were limited to the United States, Russia, and the European powers of France and the United Kingdom. As with many Chinese painters, Hufan had concentrated his practice on traditional landscapes with images such as birds and flowers. In fact, critics had noted that for

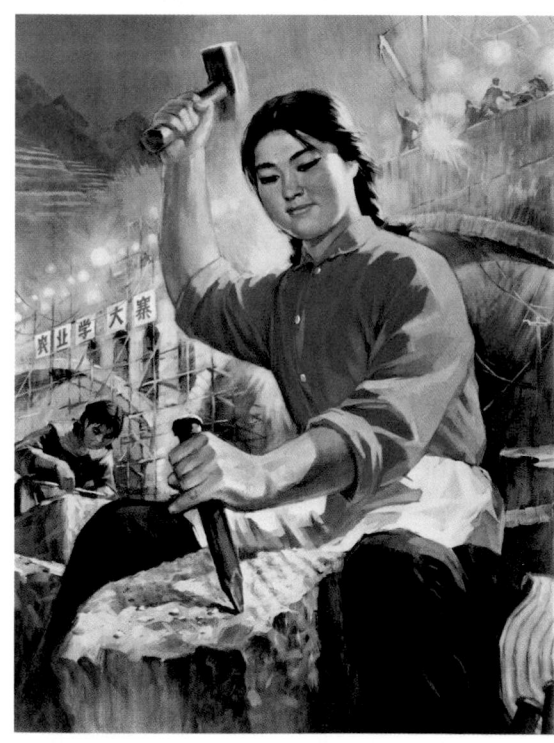

妇女能顶半边天　管教山河换新颜

⌃ 21.61 *"Women hold up half of heaven, and, cutting through mountains and rivers, change to a new attitude"* (1970). Propaganda poster, color lithograph; approximately 30" × 21". Private collection.

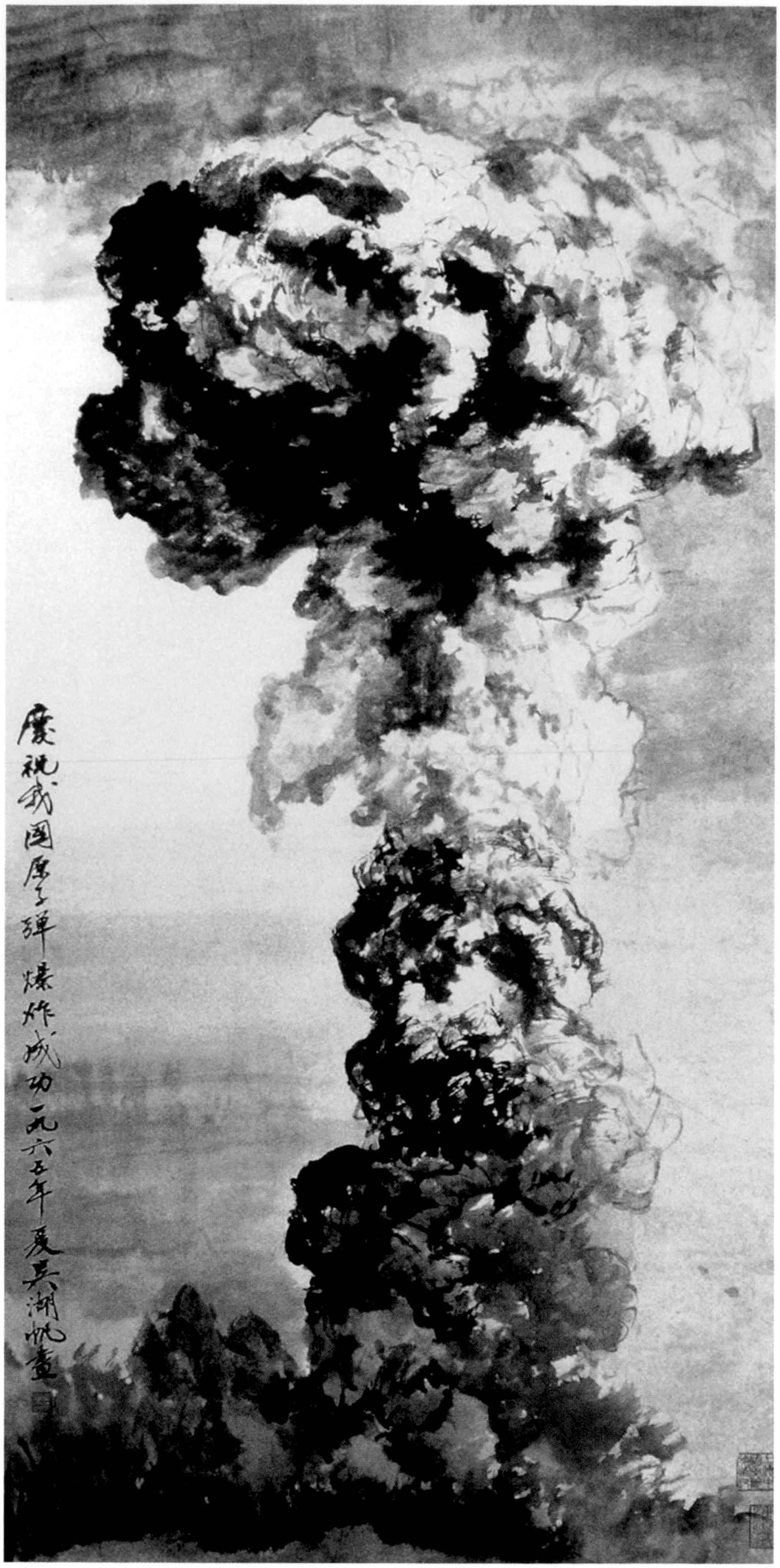

⌃ 21.62 **WU HUFAN**, *Celebrate the Success of Our Glorious Atomic Bomb Explosion!* (1965). Hanging scroll, ink, and color on absorbent paper; 53⅛" × 26⅜".

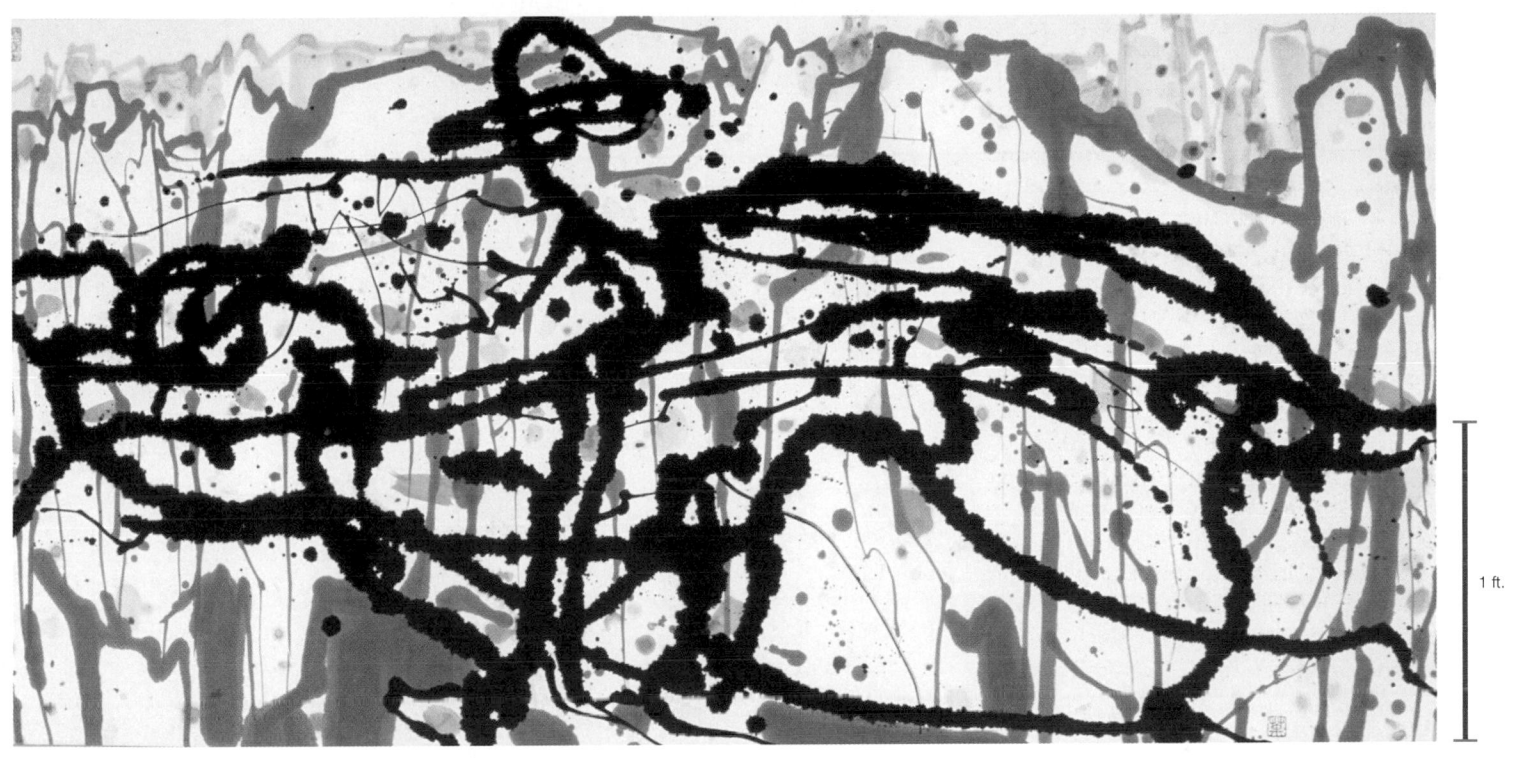

1 ft.

∧ 21.63 WU GUANZHONG, *Pine Spirit* (1984). Chinese ink, color on paper; 27 ½" × 55 ⅛". Spencer Museum of Art, The University of Kansas, Lawrence, Kansas.

most of his life, Hufan's art had steered away from the social and political realities of his day in favor of eternal, beautiful, and mesmerizing scenes of nature. In this context, his 1965 scroll painting *Celebrate the Success of Our Glorious Atomic Bomb Explosion!* (Fig. 21.62) is all the more chilling. Just as his earlier works had been untouched by the incessant warfare and social turmoil of the day, so does his ironic memorialization of China's entry into the "club" seem untouched by the reality of the meaning of the bomb. In this painting, Hufan exchanges the typical, delicate tracery of foliage for the instantly recognizable shape of the mushroom cloud of an atomic bomb explosion. Using the standard format and palette of traditional scroll painting, the artist creates a trope that perverts meaning even as it embraces the familiar. His gestural brushstrokes capture the column of death with no more emotion than they, in other works, conveyed the spirit of nature. The irony does not escape us: a landscape in the wake of an atom bomb is, and remains, dead.

When Beijing-born Wu Guanzhong (1919–2010) traveled to France for his artistic training in 1947, just two years after the victory of the Allies in World War II, Automatist Surrealism was still alive and well, and

the American Abstract Expressionists were gaining momentum on the other side of the Atlantic. His *Pine Spirit* (Fig. 21.63) would seem to be the perfect marriage between these contemporary influences and Chinese landscape painting. Guanzhong's abstract imagery derived from *plein air* sketches that he then modified in the studio, chasing the chimera of the unconscious and marking it with spills and drips and delicate jagged strokes of diluted ink. Like the work of artists of the New York School, *Pine Spirit* is impressive in scale—twice as long as it is high—enveloping viewers and drawing them into its misty, mysterious space. The dramatically dark skein of line at the picture plane functions, at once, as a visual barrier and as an invitation to attempt to explore beneath and beyond.

Japan

At midcentury, Japan had lost the war, and industry and the economy were in a shambles. Yet within a couple of decades, the country managed something of an economic miracle. People were back to work and the nation would go on to produce cars and trucks sold all over the world,

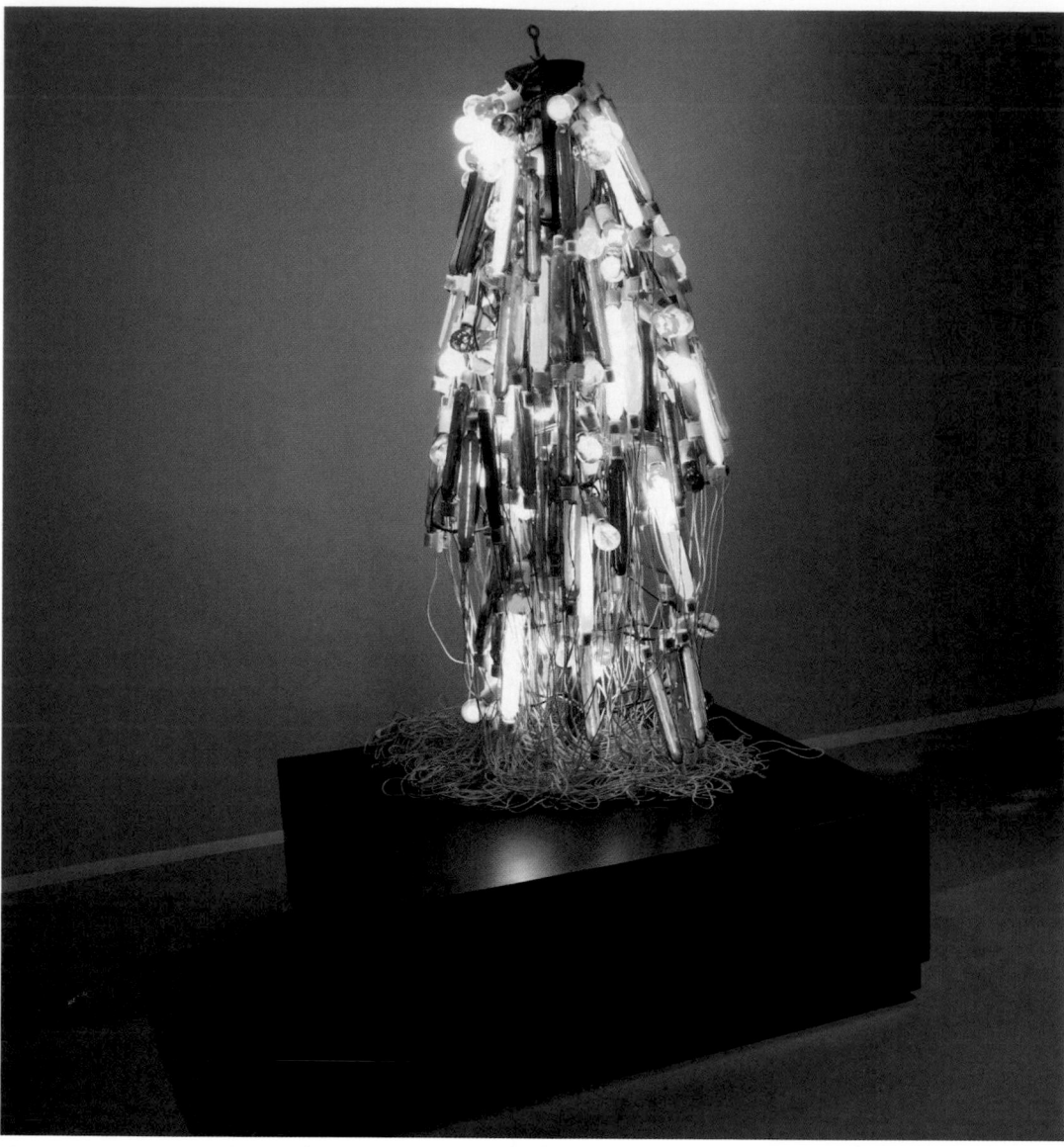

▲ **21.64 ATSUKO TANAKA,** *Electric Dress* (1956; reconstruction 1986). Enamel paint on lightbulbs, electric cords, and control console; 65" × 31½" × 31½". Takamatsu City Museum of Art, Takamatsu, Japan.

along with electronics that would dominate the industry until competition arose from the South Koreans and the Chinese.

Within this setting, the Gutai Art Association—an experimental group founded in 1954, some two years after the Allied postwar occupation of Japan ended—explored new art forms that combined painting with performance and interactive installations. As did many contemporary performance artists elsewhere (although they were much more radical for the era than their Western counterparts), they used their bodies as a way to make permeable the boundaries between the artist and the spectator. A member of the association, Atsuko Tanaka (1932–2005), used unconventional—even intangible—materials in works such as *Electric Dress* (Fig. 21.64), a wearable kimono-like sculpture composed of brightly painted, flickering bulbs

and cathode tubes that envelop and etherealize the body with color and light.

In describing his work in an interview, Jackson Pollock said, "On the floor I am more at ease. I feel nearer, more a part of the painting, since this way I can walk around it, work from the four sides and literally be in the painting."[11] Pollock's comment may just as easily have described the work of Kazuo Shiraga (1924–2008), who used his body—specifically his hands and feet—to create the imagery in his paintings (Fig. 21.65). Shiraga, who was trained in traditional Japanese style, emerged as one of

---

[11] *Possibilities* 1, no. 1 (Winter 1947–1948): 79; as quoted in "Jackson Pollock: Is He the Greatest Living Painter in the United States?," *Life*, August 8, 1949, pp. 42–45.

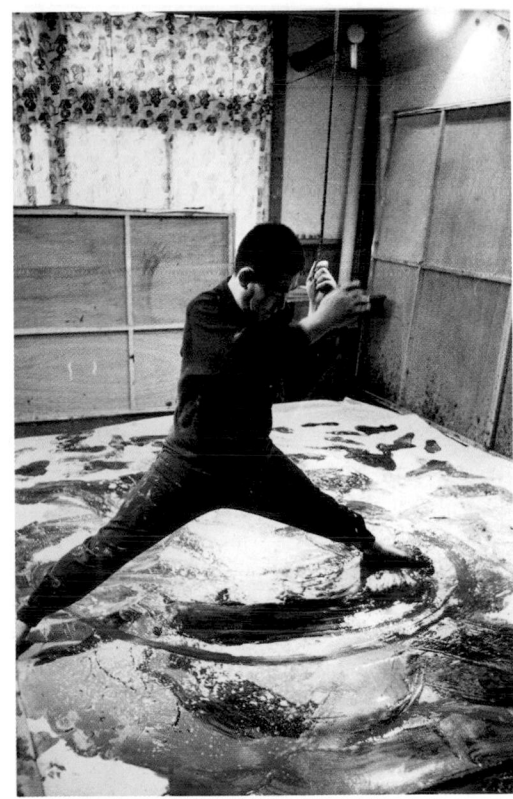

1 ft.

the most celebrated artists of the country's avant-garde, joining the Gutai group in the early 1970s. As did Pollock, he virtually abandoned the brush and the conventional artist–canvas relationship, spilling and dripping paint. But Shiraga radicalized the process by seamlessly weaving performance with painting, using his feet to create "strokes" while hanging from a rope suspended from the ceiling above him (Fig. 21.66). The artist described his intent as exhibiting "traces of action carried out by speed."

< 21.66 Kazuo Shiraga at work.

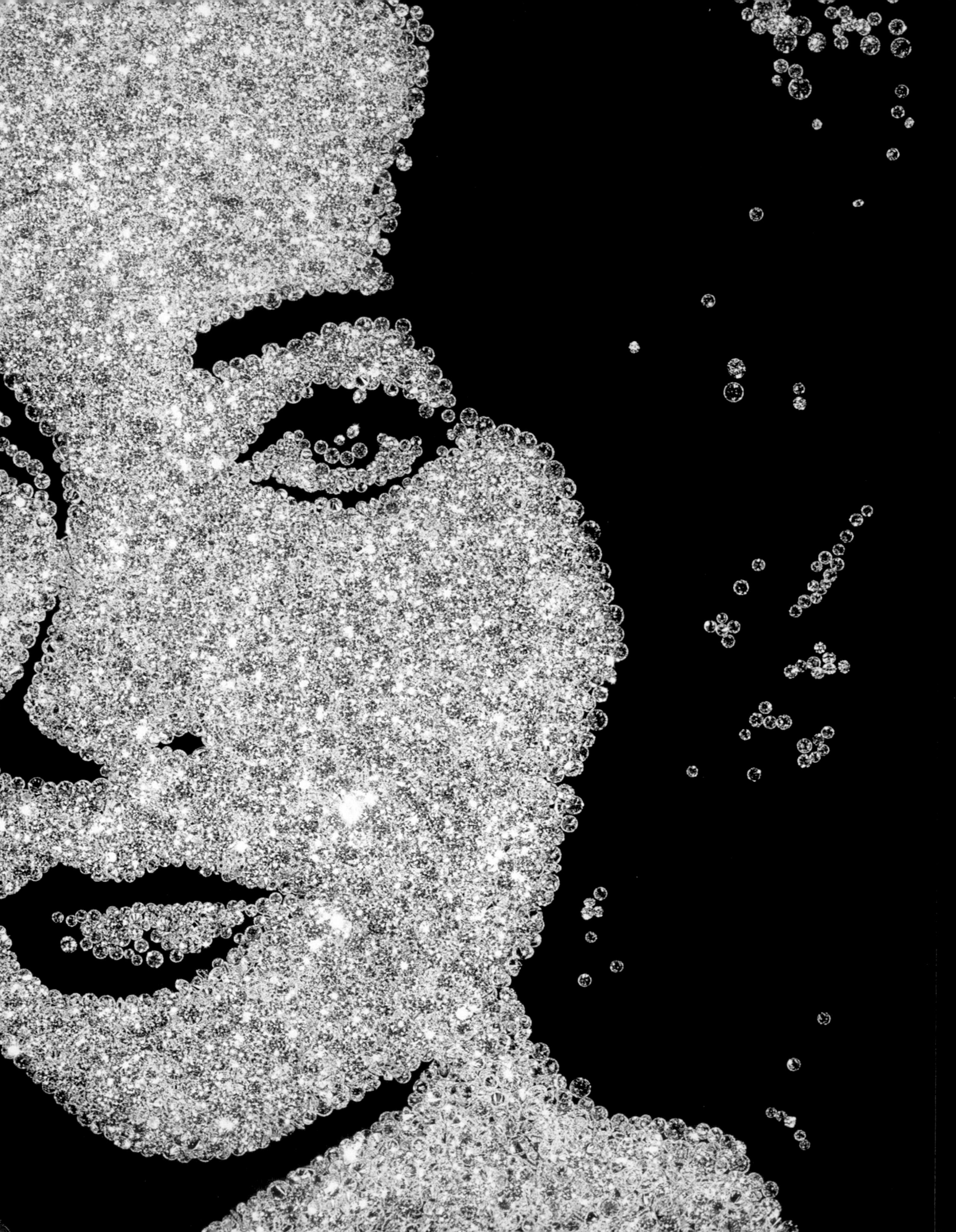

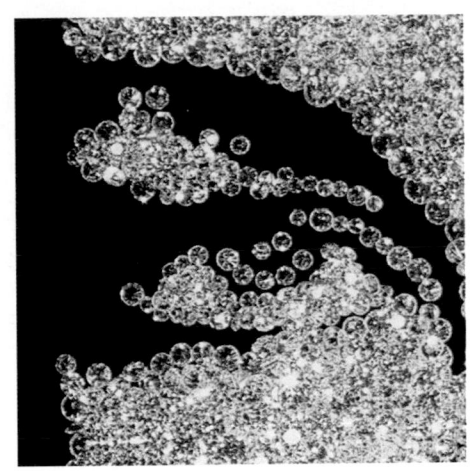

22

ART NOW: A GLOBAL PERSPECTIVE

A few decades back, when the art world was smaller and easier to police, and "international" meant Manhattan and Western Europe, New York more or less dictated what kind of art would be looked at, what ideas would circulate, what would be cool. But this is no longer so. The arena has expanded. Although economically powerful, New York is increasingly just one of many art centers doing their local thing. Most work that turns up in Manhattan galleries has little connection with, or pertinence to, what artists are doing and thinking about in Africa or India or even in the Bronx.

—HOLLAND COTTER[1]

WHEN HOLLAND Cotter wrote these words for his introduction to an exhibition of Caribbean art at the Brooklyn Museum, he stated the facts as he observed them: that it seems no longer meaningful or even valid to be talking about a center of the art world, much less continuing to assign that center to the city of New York. Contemporary art has gone global—in venue, in subject, even in the raw economics of the art market—dovetailing with the phenomenon of globalization that characterizes spheres outside the realm of culture.

---

[1] Holland Cotter, "Caribbean Visions of Tropical Paradise and Protest," *New York Times*, August 31, 2007, F25, F27.

◄ VIK MUNIZ, *Elizabeth Taylor (Diamond Divas)* (2004). Cibachrome print mounted on aluminum, 60" × 43".

GLOBALIZATION

The phenomenon of **globalization** has created a world in which cultures are no longer distant from one another, and people and places are no longer separate. Television and the Internet create an immediacy of communication of visual images as never before; a war around the globe finds its way into living rooms around the clock. "Distant" hurricanes, cyclones, and earthquakes happen everywhere at once. One stock market affects all stock markets. China's air pollution flows into California, and China's toys overflow America's stockings at Christmastime. So too do visual images from various cultures invade the consciousness and the marketplace around the globe as never before. But familiarity and proximity do not necessarily beget understanding and tolerance. Much contemporary art on the global stage is directed toward awareness, understanding, and tolerance.

Art historians and critics have had to find new ways of analyzing and organizing material on the subject of multiculturalism and cross-culturalism in contemporary art. The traditional vocabulary is insufficient. As we consider works of art in the twenty-first century, we will add to our critical rubric concepts such as *hybridity, appropriation,* and *postcolonialism.*

Hybridity

In the visual arts, one of the effects of globalization is **hybridity,** or the mixing of the traditions of different cultures to create new blends and new connections. High art and low culture were historically viewed as antithetical concepts. High art and high culture are associated with classical antiquity and perpetuated through the artistic traditions of the Renaissance. They include art of the Old Masters or compositions by Classical musicians or canonical works of literature, primarily from the West. These classics are associated with elitism; by contrast, low culture has been used derogatorily to describe popular or mass culture. However, some contemporary art has focused particularly on the blurring of boundaries between high art and low culture, with artists such as Takashi Murakami appropriating images from low culture.

As an example of the ways in which globalization has led to an intermingling of the world's cultural icons, Takashi Murakami (b. 1962) has been dubbed Japan's Andy Warhol. As did Andy Warhol, Murakami questions the separation of high art and low culture and draws on consumer culture for his imagery. And, like Warhol, Murakami is vigorously self-promotional, exhibiting his paintings and sculpture at major museums around the world while creating mass-market products ranging from T-shirts and key chains to mouse pads and upscale Louis Vuitton handbags.

As a boy, Murakami fantasized about illustrating Japanese graphic novels called *manga,* which are also hybrids. While illustrated manuscripts have as long and distinguished a history in Japanese art as they do in Western art, their modern form is heavily influenced by American comic books, which infiltrated Japanese culture soon after the end of World War II, when Japan

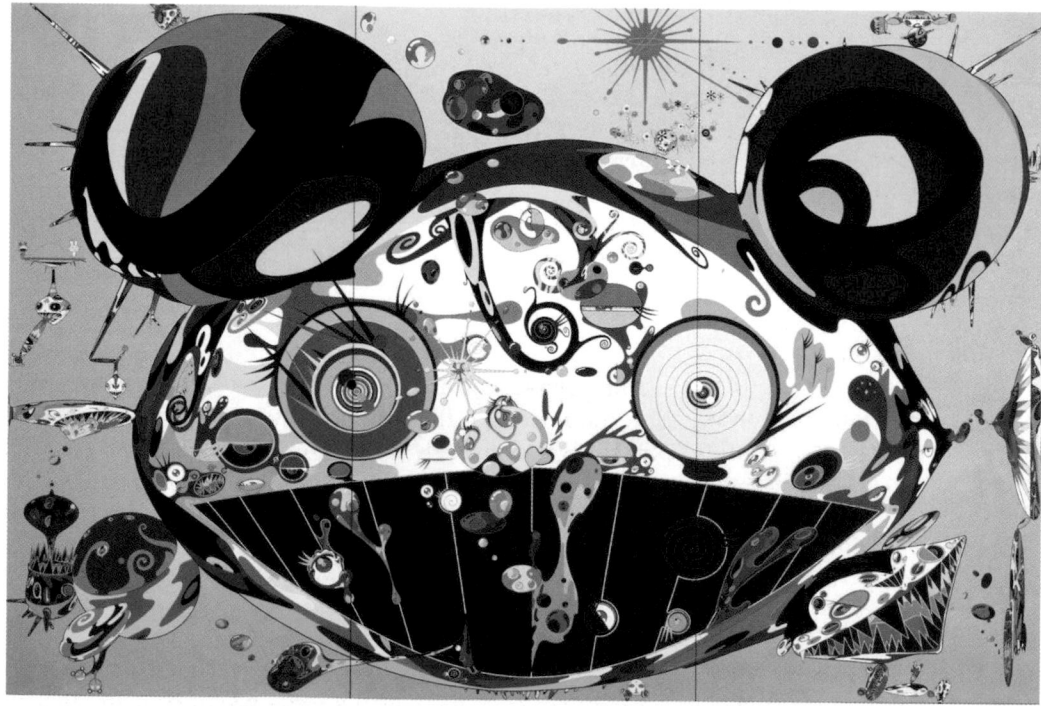

∧ 22.1 **TAKASHI MURAKAMI,** *Tan Tan Bo* (2001). Acrylic on canvas mounted on board, 141¾" × 212⅝" × 2⅝".

540 | CHAPTER 22 *Art Now: A Global Perspective*

was occupied by the United States and American culture became popular.

As a student, Murakami experimented with the large-eyed cartoon figures in the popular *anime* style (a style of animation developed in Japan), but he was also trained in classical Japanese painting techniques. Consequently, his work often aims to reconcile "high art" and "low culture." *Tan Tan Bo* (Fig. 22.1) is filled with cartoon-like imagery rendered in simple, dark outlines filled in with bright colors. The overall shape may resemble a fierce Mickey Mouse, but the artist has dubbed his signature character "Mr. DOB," the artist's large-eared alter ego. Murakami has created a multimedia sensation of Mr. DOB ranging from lithographs to inflatable balloons. In the tradition of "pure" Pop, he makes no distinction between art and merchandise.

Appropriation

Appropriation became part of the lexicon of contemporary art with the advent of Postmodernism in the 1980s. The concept, however, was not a new one; it stretched back to early-twentieth-century art movements such as Cubism and Dada. Appropriation consisted then of borrowed elements. Picasso and Braque, for example, incorporated materials and techniques from the nonart world—newspaper, wallpaper, and wine labels—into their collages; Duchamp used ordinary or familiar objects for his ready-mades, including a urinal and a bicycle wheel. Appropriation in the Postmodern era became a more refined idea, specifically referring to the use of another artist's work as a basis for one's own. Sometimes the new work built on or changed the one appropriated, but at other times, the original image was left unaltered.

Brazilian artist Vik Muniz (b. 1961) is known for using anything to construct the imagery for his photographs—beans, dirt, pepper, caviar, chocolate, peanut butter, sand, and . . . junk. In fact, Muniz created an entire series called *Pictures of Junk* in which he and his assistants meticulously arranged garbage and debris into compositions based on Old Master paintings of mythological figures. Muniz refers to his appropriations as "the worst possible illusion." *Diamond Divas* is a series that subverts his earlier junk aesthetic with the most diametrically opposed material: diamonds. In *Diamond Divas*, Muniz arranged 500 carats of diamonds into the likenesses of film sirens such as Brigitte Bardot, Sophia Loren, and Elizabeth Taylor. *Elizabeth Taylor* (Fig. 22.2) is a second-generation appropriation, based on a 1964 silkscreen by Pop artist Andy Warhol. Warhol based his own image on iconic photographs of the screen legend, taken at the height of her fame after her starring role in the film *Cleopatra*. Taylor, especially, was known for her collection of lavish diamonds, including the famous "Taylor-Burton Diamond," a 69.42-carat

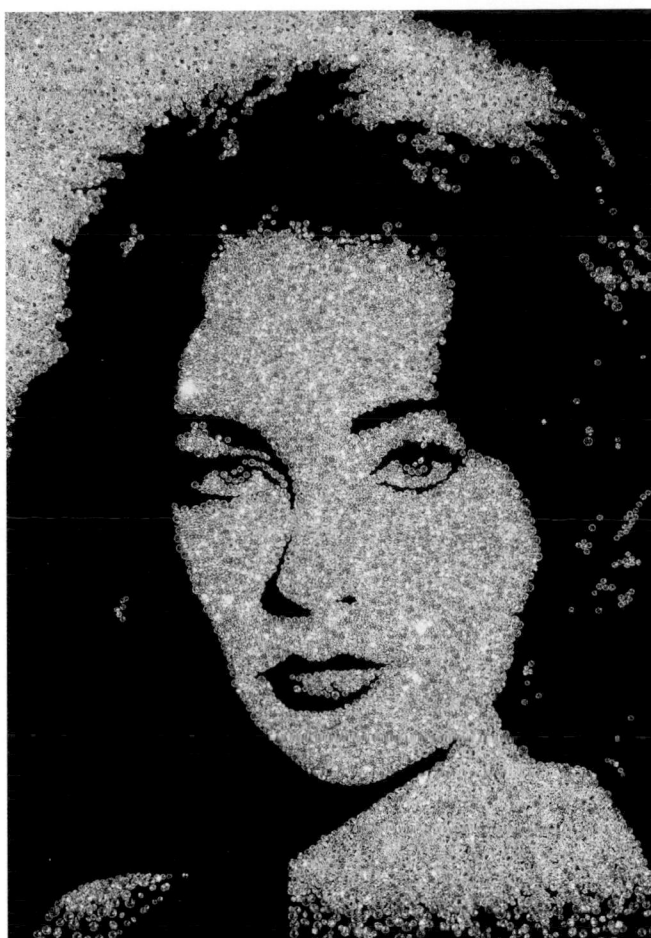

∧ 22.2 VIK MUNIZ, *Elizabeth Taylor (Diamond Divas series)* (2004). Cibachrome print mounted on aluminum, 60" × 43".

pear-shaped stone given to her by her husband, actor Richard Burton. The conspicuous value of the diamonds in the renderings suggests a connection between the actors and their monetary worth to producers in box office returns. Elizabeth Taylor shimmers in a palette of silvery black and white, further suggestive of the so-called silver screen of a bygone cinematic era.

Postcolonialism

Some aspects of globalization in the arts are a reaction to the retreat of the European empires that ruled much of the world through the middle of the twentieth century. The former colonies in the Americas, Africa, the Middle East, and far eastern Asia bear complex relationships with their former rulers—political, economic, ethnic, and of course cultural.

London-based artist Hew Locke was raised in Guyana on the coast of South America. Like Canada, Australia, New Zealand, India, Pakistan, Egypt, and the original American colonies, Guyana was once part of the British Empire. Locke entered his equestrian statue *Sikandar*

INDIA AND PAKISTAN

In the mid-twentieth century, India threw off the yoke of British rule under the leadership of Mahatma Gandhi, who embraced civil disobedience rather than violent, armed rebellion. (Martin Luther King Jr. would adopt his pacifist model during the Civil Rights Movement in the United States.) Gandhi encouraged the boycott of British goods, promoted friendship between Hindus and Muslims, and argued for alleviation of the deprivations experienced by the lowest caste—the untouchables. Gandhi's campaign ultimately led to the Indian Independence Art of 1947 and the British Parliament's partition of British India into the dominions of India and Pakistan.

Contemporary Indian artist Subodh Gupta (b. 1964) was reared in one of the poorest and most violent provinces in India and lives today in New Delhi, a city of economic extremes. Gupta taps into sacred symbols and ancient cultural identity, but his frequent use of found objects connects his work—and message—to twenty-first-century issues and realities. *Silk Route* (Fig. 22.4) emphasizes India's key historic and contemporary role in globalization as an important economic conduit, at the same time illustrating the "current state of India's shifting society, migration, a sense of home and place and the effects and frictions caused by a rapidly globalizing society."[2] The Silk Road refers to a web of ancient trade routes that ran some 4,000 miles through the Indian subcontinent and connected China to the Mediterranean Sea. Caravans of merchants on horses and Bactrian camels moved silk and other luxuries from East to West over perilous terrain—trading cotton, linen, pearls, ivory, spices, perfumes, and much more for commodities such as copper, tin, wool, and wine. Gupta's gleaming, highly polished silvery bowls and utensils conjure the sight of shimmery silken fabrics that so mesmerized the West from the time of Julius Caesar through the era of the Silk Road. Yet piled on top of one another and crowded into the space of a single tabletop, the same glittering objects evoke the overcrowding of cities. They call attention to the societal disconnect between poverty-stricken inner-city life and some of the most critically acclaimed works of contemporary architecture (much of it designed by Western architects) springing up in cities across the globe, particularly in the East. The stacks of utensils move along mechanized tracks carved into the steel table, almost as luggage on an airport conveyer belt. Is world travel in our own era of globalization—and the objects we bring back home to remind us of the people and places we have seen—an echo of the past?

ʌ 22.3 **HEW LOCKE,** *Sikander* (2010). Mixed-media maquette; height of maquette including plinth: approximately 31 ½".

(Fig. 22.3) as a potential occupant of "the fourth plinth"—one of four pedestals designed for heroic sculpture in London's Trafalgar Square. The plinth was left unfinished and today serves as a site for temporary art projects. The name, "Sikandar" references Alexander the Great, but the overall form of the statue is derived from an equestrian monument not far from London's Regent's Park, which honors the "conspicuous bravery" of British Field Marshal, Sir George Stuart White. White commanded nineteenth century imperial campaigns in the Middle East and South Central Asia—including modern-day Afghanistan. Locke's *Sikandar* is no horseback hero in the tradition of other bronze monuments, however. Weighed down by ironic "plundered loot"—plastic trinkets, medals, sabers, charms, votive offerings and more—the conquering hero is chained to his mount, dignified in posture but immobilized by the undignified symbols of conquest and colonialism.

We continue our conversation about global art in the twenty-first century by looking at some places and some artists who contribute to the contemporary contour.

[2] Artes Mundi, Wales International Visual Art Exhibition and Prize, Subodh Gupta, January 20, 2011, www.artesmundi.org/subodh-gupta.

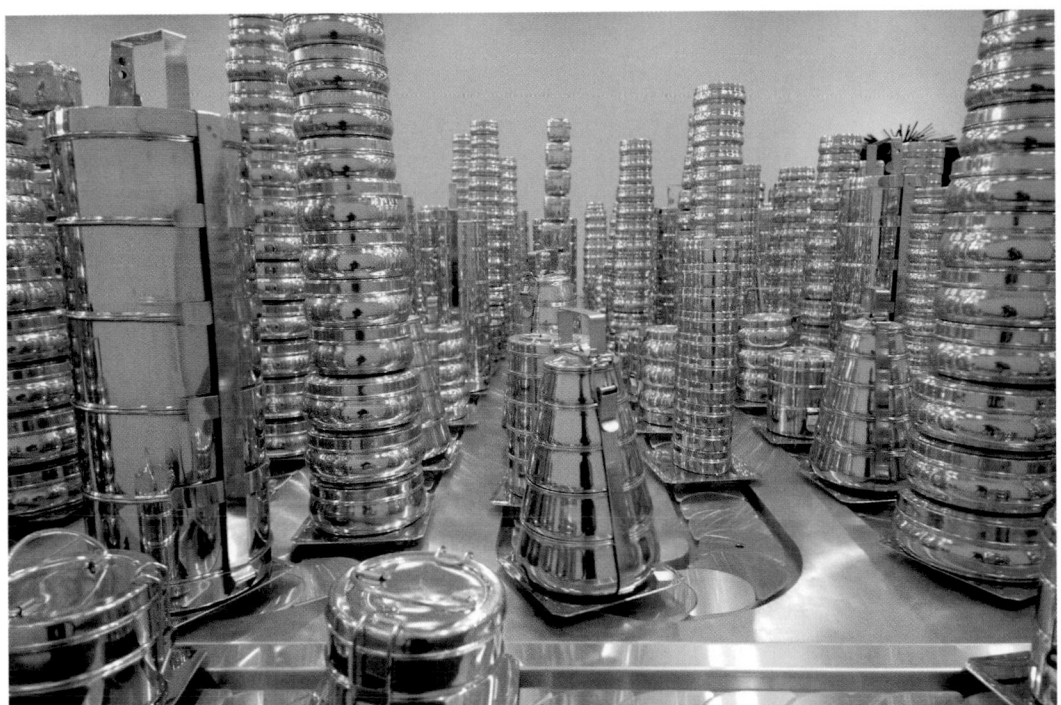

< 22.4 SUBODH GUPTA, *Silk Route* (2007). Detail. Stainless-steel kitchen utensils. BALTIC Centre for Contemporary Art, Gateshead, England.

Pakistan-born Shahzia Sikander was trained in the painstaking methods of Asian/Persian miniature painting and also studied at the Rhode Island School of Design; she now lives and works in the United States. In *Perilous Order* (Fig. 22.5), Sikander casts light on past and present challenges faced by women and gays in the Islamic world, embedding her controversial commentary on hypocrisy regarding homosexuality in a diminutive work of traditional style. The centerpiece of the painting is a profile portrait of the seventeenth-century Mughal emperor Aurangzeb (in actuality, the likeness of one of her friends) who was reputed to be gay and yet enforced Islamic restrictions against, and punishments of, gay Muslims. We see "Aurangzeb" through the hovering, veil-like specter-spirit of a Hindu goddess and surrounded by Hindu nymphs. The rigidity of his profile and the tight frame surrounding it contrast considerably with the sensuality of the female figures, perhaps alluding to the contrast between more liberal Hindu sexuality and the oppressive strictures against it in the Muslim world.

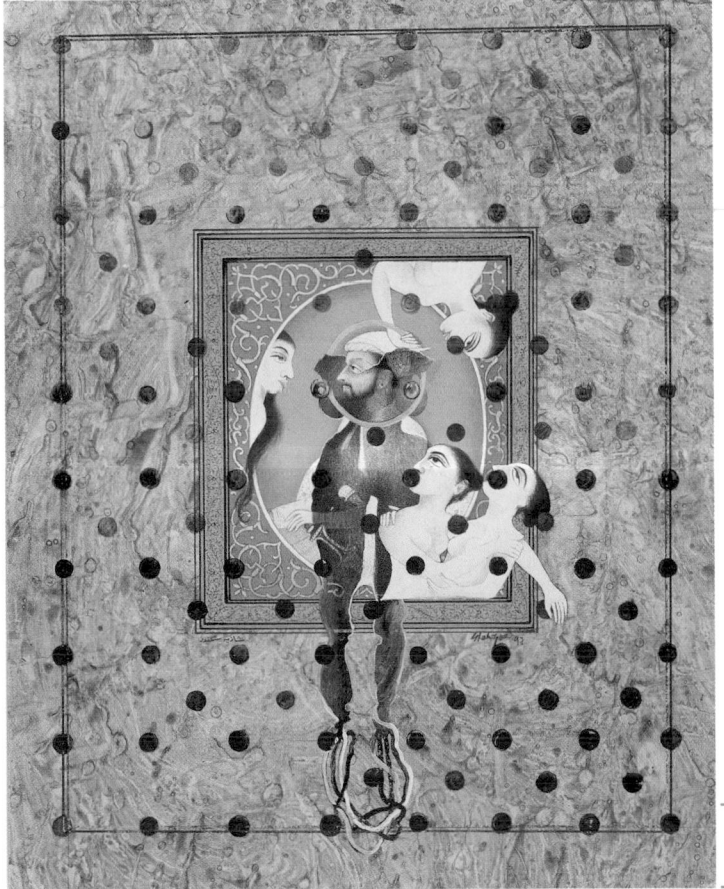

▲ 22.5 **SHAHZIA SIKANDER,** *Perilous Order* (1994–1997). Vegetable color, dry pigment, watercolor, and tea on Wasli paper; 10½" × 8". Whitney Museum of American Art, New York, New York.

CONNECTIONS Prajakta Palav Aher provides a fascinating updated version of Ganesh, a Hindu deity, riding to work on a commuter train.

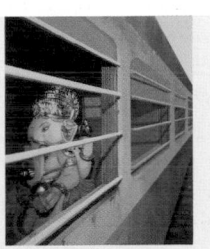

▲ Aher's *Untitled I* (Fig. 16.35)

India and Pakistan | 543

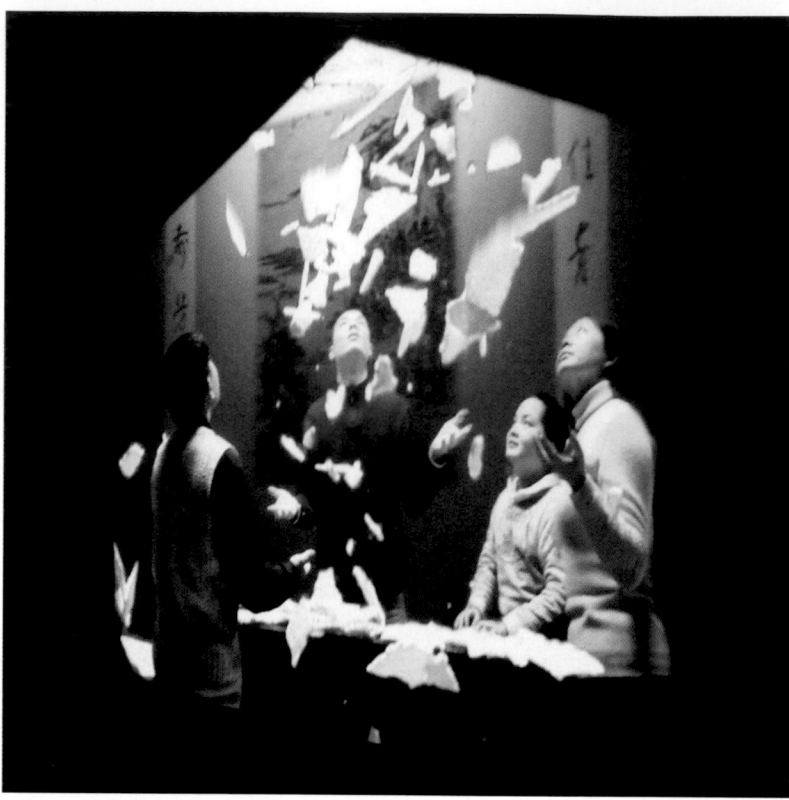

▲ 22.6 WANG GONGXIN, *Our Sky Is Falling In!* (2007). Video. The Tate Gallery, London, England.

CHINA

Virtually all of the art produced under Communist rule exalted the party (under Mao especially), the virtues of hard work, and service for the greater good. But the China that abhorred capitalism in the mid-twentieth century is now a hybrid communist–capitalist system with more than a few billionaires. Contemporary Chinese art, produced in a variety of styles—and no longer necessarily pro-government—sells for millions of dollars in a global art market. Chinese artists are represented by major galleries in London, New York, Paris, and Rome, in addition to Shanghai and Beijing. It is not unheard of for artists who protest too loudly against the Communist Party to wind up with restrictions and lost privileges, but many "commute" freely between the major cities in China and the rest of the world.

Wang Gongxin (b. 1960) is credited with being one of the first artists in China to transform video from a mere recording medium to an art medium. His works have largely focused on the anxieties experienced by ordinary Chinese people as their lives have been transformed by rapid industrialization—with its attendant pollution, relocations, and changes in traditional values. In recent years,

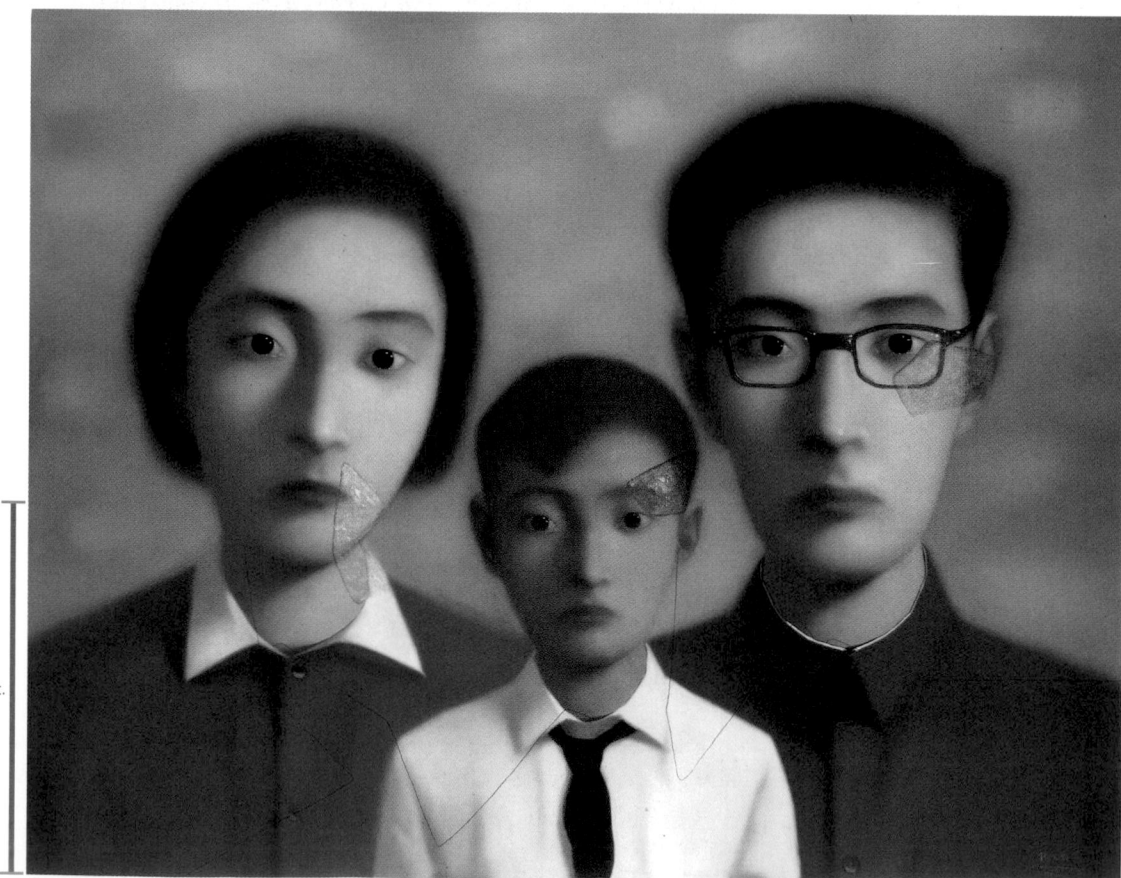

1 ft.

◄ 22.7 ZHANG XIAOGANG, *Big Family* (2003). Lithograph (in an edition of 199), 27½" × 32½".

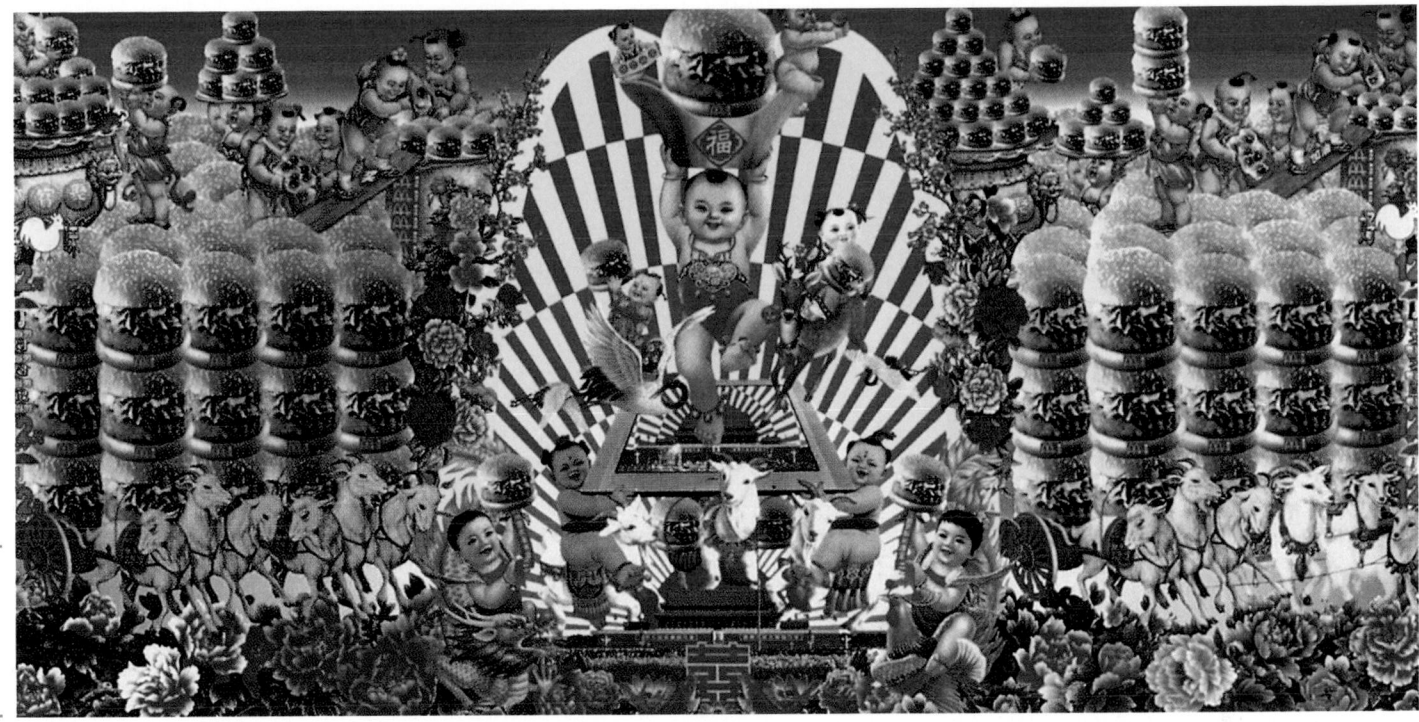

1 ft.

∧ 22.8 LUO BROTHERS, *Welcome to the World Famous Brand* (2000). Collage and lacquer on wood, 49⅝" × 96⅞" × 1³⁄₁₆".

China has experienced an unparalleled economic boom that has led to mushrooming growth of cities, mass migration from rural lands into these cities, and the projection of new economic and military power overseas. *Our Sky Is Falling In!* (Fig. 22.6) portrays an everyday family scene that is suddenly disrupted when the ceiling begins to collapse. The video tells a personal story, but is also a commentary on the helplessness of the individual amid the titanic forces of progress and modernization.

Zhang Xiaogang's (b. 1958) *Big Family* (Fig. 22.7) features a passage of red in a sea of monotonous beige and gray tones. For this Chinese artist, the uniformity of a drab palette reflects the appearance—indeed the lives—of what he calls a typical revolutionary family: "asexual, dressed in Mao suits, their gaze glassy and dismal. . . . They could be clones."[3] Red as a signifier of Chinese Communist culture creates points of narrative and visual emphasis, but there is more to the print than its design elements. The work addresses a truth of contemporary Chinese life: this "big" family is as big as a family has been permitted to get in the overpopulated country, given its one-child policy. Because of sexism—and despite official gender equality—abortion is not uncommon when an early sonogram reveals that a fetus is female. Chinese social critics note that the country has been developing a surplus of males; some have even suggested that women be permitted to have more than one husband.

---

[3] M. Nuridsany, *China Art Now* (Paris: Flammarion, 2004), 114.

Welcome to the World Famous Brand (Fig. 22.8), by the Luo brothers, emphasizes the convergence of consumerism and globalism. It continues the theme of East meets West—or, in this case, West invades East—with Big Macs. Mimicking the garish packaging of Chinese merchandise, the Luo brothers' compositions are often overcrowded, intensely colored, and exuberant in mood. There is so much energy bound up in the imagery that it is almost impossible for the eyes to stop and focus. The "enthroned" baby raising a McDonald's sandwich in the center of the piece becomes the focal point. It is emphasized by the red and yellow bands of lines that look like divine rays emanating from behind the baby, who in turn is bolstered on a floating rectangle by lesser, though no less jubilant, little ones. To the left and right are regimented stacks of burgers riding on chariots pulled by teams of lambs. Brightly colored peonies add to the outrageously festive atmosphere. This formula—enthroned central figure buoyed by devoted onlookers and flanked by symmetrical groups of regimented figures—is standard in religious altarpieces over centuries of art history. The Luo brothers appropriate this formula to sharpen their statement about what we "worship" in contemporary society.

ARCHITECTURE Chinese cities have become boomtowns for contemporary architecture, although—at least for the time being—many of the principal architects involved in the designs for these cities are European and American. Iranian British architect Zaha

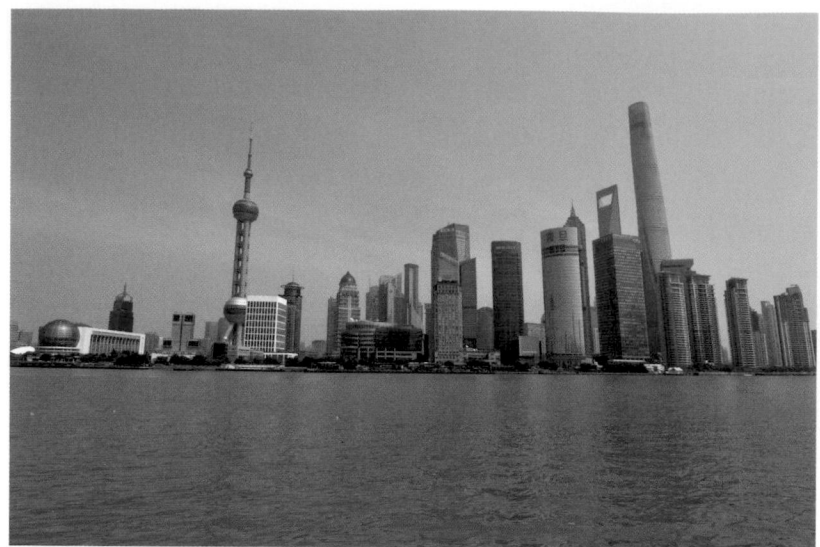

JAPAN

Japanese visual artists maintained the country's strong traditions in printmaking, painting, and ceramics in the latter part of the twentieth century, but it is in film that Japan entered into global pop culture. Perhaps no Japanese film has been so popular and fecund—in its spawning of remakes and sequels—as *Godzilla* (Fig 22.10), directed by Ishiro Honda. Despite its primitive special effects and humble origin, it captured the interest of viewers around the world, giving rise to nearly 30 sequels, comic-book art, and tie-in products such as Godzilla toys and video games. *Godzilla* tells the story of a 400-foot prehistoric monster awakened from the depths of the Pacific by hydrogen-bomb tests. Provoked by depth charges, Godzilla uses his fiery breath to turn Tokyo to toast. Eventually he is killed by another weapon of mass destruction, one that destroys the oxygen in the water around him.

The strength of the film lies in its portrayal of Japanese fears about weapons of mass destruction following World War II and in its personalization of the monster. Although

Hadid has called China "an incredibly empty canvas for innovation." Anthony Fieldman, of the Hong Kong office of architects Skidmore, Owings, and Merrill, has said that in China "you're seeing things that no one in their right mind would build elsewhere." Between the buildup that occurred for the 2008 Beijing Summer Olympics and Shanghai's conglomerate Pudong skyline (Fig. 22.9), it's no wonder that Wang Lu of Beijing-based *World Architecture* magazine has said, "Architecture in China has become like a kung fu film, with all of these giants trying to vanquish each other."

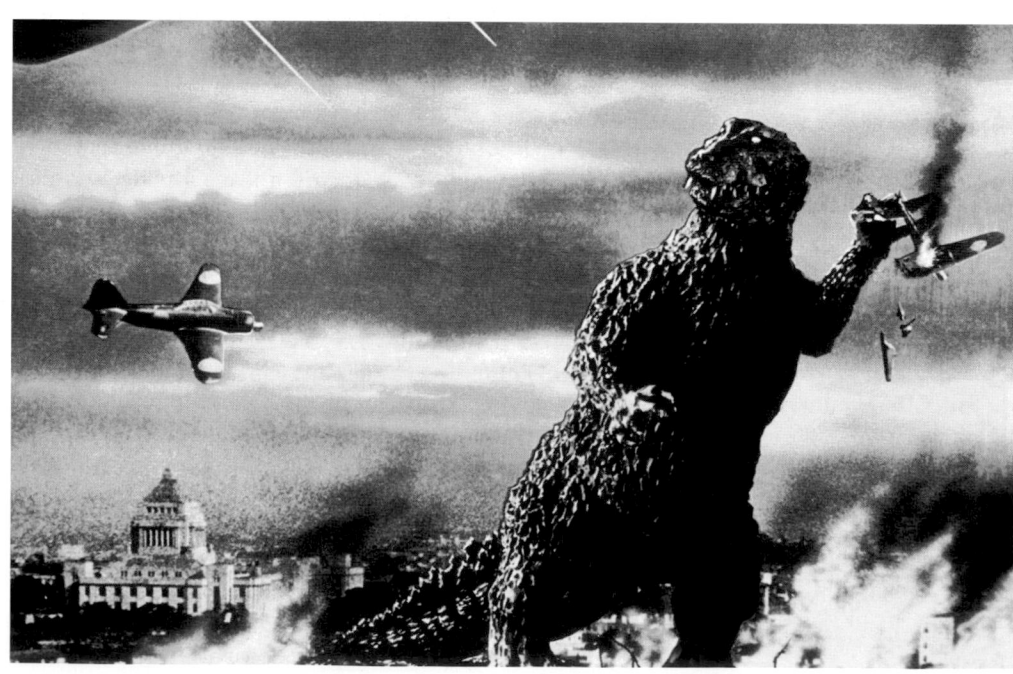

< 22.10 ISHIRO HONDA AND TERRY O. MORSE, Film still from *Godzilla* (1954).

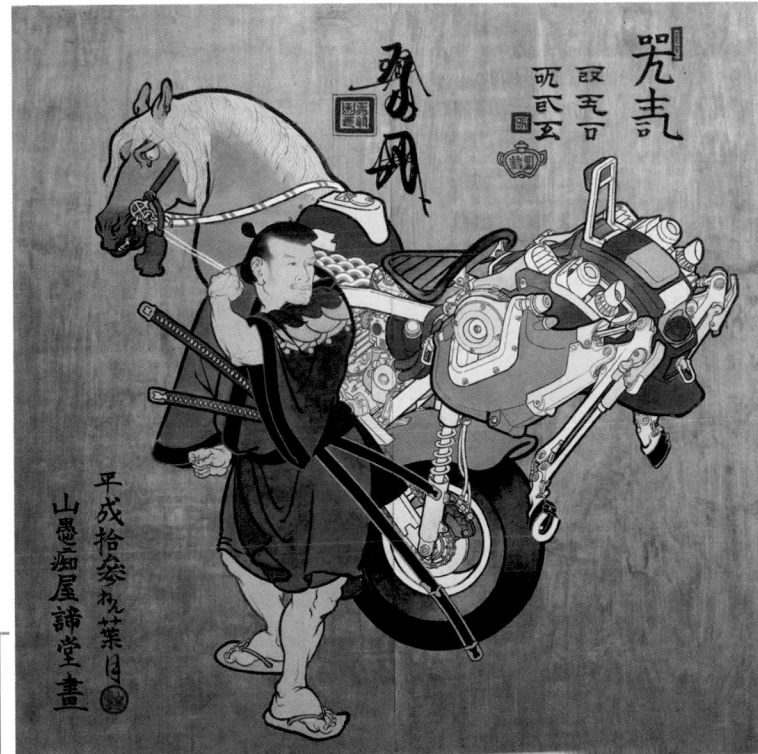

1 ft.

▲ 22.11 **AKIRA YAMAGUCHI**, *Votive Tablet of a Horse* (2001). Oil, varnish on plywood; 71⅞" × 72". Mizuma Art Gallery, Tokyo, Japan.

humans must be saved from Godzilla, Godzilla is also a victim of the nuclear genie that humans have uncorked. The atomic devastation of Hiroshima and Nagasaki horrified the Japanese not only because of the immediate loss of life but also because of the disfigurement of survivors

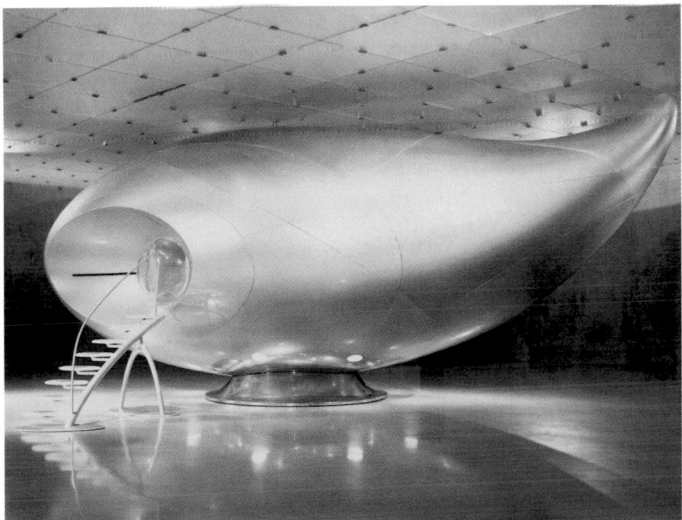

▲ 22.12 **MARIKO MORI**, *Wave UFO* (1999–2003). Brainwave interface, vision dome, projector, computer system, fiber glass, Technogel®, acrylic, carbon fiber, aluminum, magnesium. Dimensions: 194 ¹/₁₀" × 446 ⁹/₂₀" × 207 ¹⁷/₂₀".

and lingering radiation sickness. Was *Godzilla* a not-so-subtle protest film?

Much of contemporary Japanese pop culture is rooted in traditional artistic forms of the past. For example, if you look at the work of Roger Shimomura (see Fig. 8.13), you will make a visual connection easily to the traditional woodblock printmaking aesthetic (see Fig. 9.1). Past and present—historically and stylistically—are often blended in Japanese art.

Akira Yamaguchi (b. 1969) finds many of his sources in historic subject matter and styles, often mixing past and present, West and non-West. One work, painted on a traditional scroll, pairs ancient customers and contemporary sales clerks in a department store. His *Votive Tablet of a Horse* (Fig 22.11) resembles wooden plaques with the image of a sacred white horse that were given as religious offerings to Japanese shrines and temples for many hundreds of years. The horses are believed to have symbolized purity, divine messages, and immortal poets. Yamaguchi replaces the horse's legs with a fantastical combination of motorcycle parts and robotics, as if to supercharge it into a more invincible machine.

Mariko Mori (b. 1967), a photographer, video-artist, and self-described "daughter of Warhol and granddaughter of Duchamp," has been labeled a "cyberchick" and "a cross between a geisha girl and a gidget." Channeling her experience as a former model and fashion design student, Mori has created computer-manipulated self-portraits in futuristic, cyber-couture. Her wide-eyed stare and plastic smile look a bit like a real-life version of Takashi Murakami's cartoon images or manga style (see Fig. 7.20). It is interesting to note that the word, *kawaii*, in Japanese means both "beautiful" and "cute" and that in Japanese pop culture, the notion of cuteness is not "kiss of death" that it is seen to be by artists of other cultures.

Mori's *Wave UFO* (Fig. 22.12) is a futuristic "vehicle" with a pop flair that mixes the mediums of sculpture, architecture, and video to create a transporting, sensory experience for the participant. We use the word *participant* instead of *viewer* because the imagery that appears on the screen within the eye-shaped capsule is determined by connecting a participant's brainwaves to an interactive biofeedback loop. Mori, who has begun to integrate references to Japanese religion and culture into her recent work, alludes to the Buddhist vision of nirvana in *Wave UFO*. She has said that the experience of the piece reveals that "human beings as collective living beings shall unify and transcend cultural differences and national borders through positive and creative evolution."[4]

---

[4] *"Wave UFO" by Mariko Mori in Kunsthaus Bregenz—A "Walk-in" Sculpture and Virtual Voyage in Space*, March 23, 2003, http://www.swissarts.info/en/news_archive_article.php?myeditid=308&langindex=en.

KOREA

The career of Korean-born sculptor and installation artist, Do Ho Suh, is emblematic of the global impact—and internationality—of contemporary artists in the twenty-first century: the geographical scope of his commissions for public projects extends from the West Coast of California to Scandinavia. Suh's art education began in Seoul where he earned bachelor and master degrees in oriental painting; he then received degrees from both the Rhode Island School of Design (RISD) and Yale University. Today, he splits his time between Korea, the U.S., and England. Suh's work, which is heavy in architectural references, centers on themes of "history and biography, longing and belonging, migration and globalization," as noted in a 2015 *Artforum* review of an exhibition in The Contemporary Austin Art Museum. His 2009 installation at the Los Angeles County Museum, *Fallen Star 1/5* (Fig. 22.13) is a powerful, visual articulation of these themes. A replica of the house in Korea in which Suh grew up seems to tumble from the sky and smash into a replica of the Providence, Rhode Island apartment building he lived in in the early 1990s while a student at RISD. Everything—including all of the furnishings, clothing, utensils, appliances, etc., are reproduced at one-fifth scale, coaxing viewers into the role of voyeur as they are drawn into what are very private spaces. The association with the landing of Dorothy's Kansas house in the Munchkin Land from the film, *The Wizard of Oz*, is hard to avoid and, of course, all of the symbolism that goes with it: a stranger, dropped into a strange land. Included in the installation, however, was a parachute. Suh has said that this element (unlike the incident with Dorothy) symbolizes a "semi-soft landing": "Culture shock didn't come as a shock to me. It took a long time."

THE MIDDLE EAST

Contemporary art by artists in or from this region often reflects on the tensions between the secular and the religious within and among societies, particularly as these tensions are interwoven with politics.

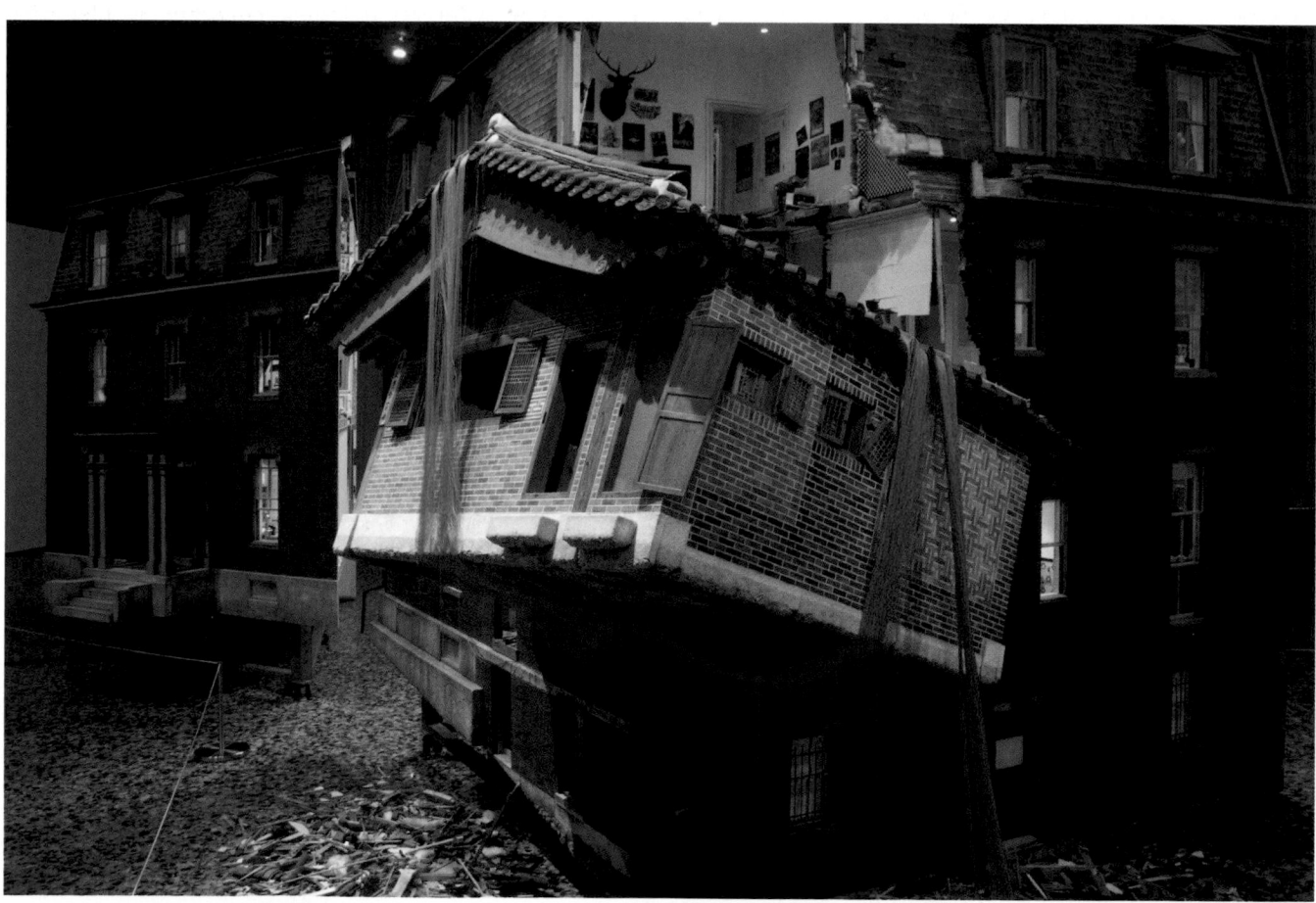

∧ **22.13 DO HO SUH,** *Fallen Star 1/5* (2008–2011). Installation view from the exhibition "Your Bright Future: 12 Contemporary Artist from Korea," MFA Houston, November 21, 2009 through February 14, 2010.

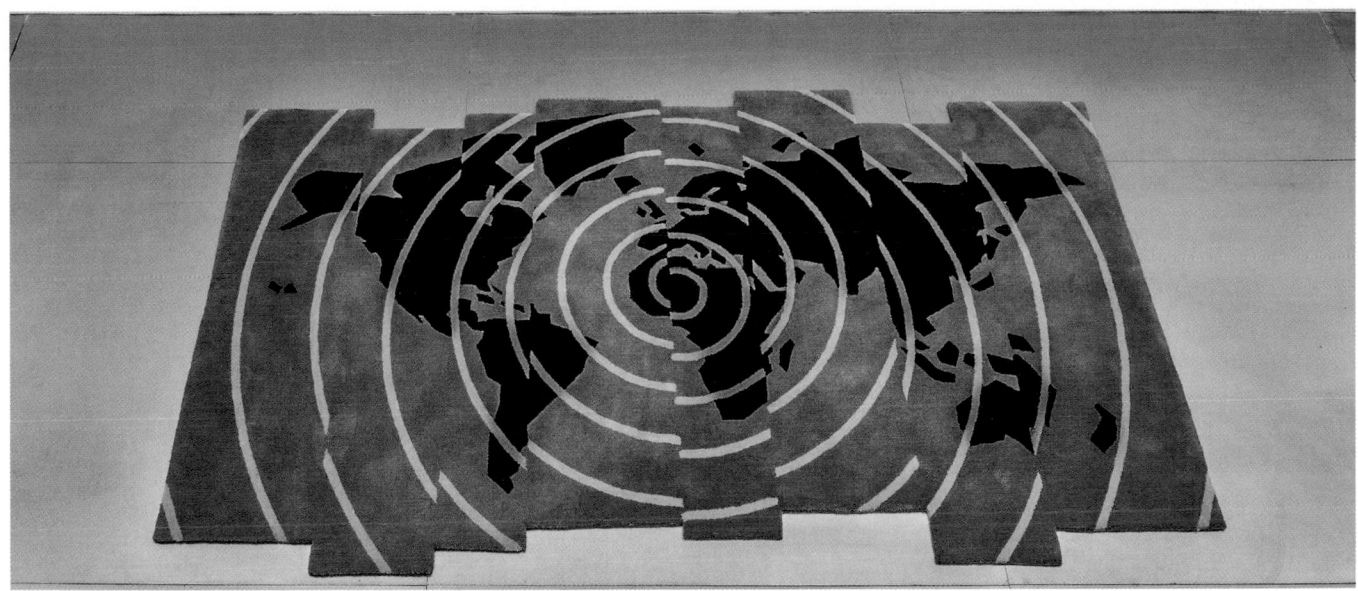

1 ft.

∧ 22.14 **MONA HATOUM,** *Shift* (2012). Wool, 59 1/16 × 102 3/8" in. (150 × 260 cm). © Mona Hatoum. Photo © Murat Germen Courtesy ARTER, Istanbul and White Cube.

Mona Hatoum (b. 1952) was born into a Palestinian family in Beirut, Lebanon, and was on a short trip to London in 1975 when civil war in Lebanon made return impossible. She attended art school in London and has lived and worked in Europe ever since. Throughout the 1980s, Hatoum's favored mediums were video and performance, but since the early 1990s she has focused on sculpture and site- (or location-) specific installation. Her works deal mostly with violence, oppression, and geo-political tensions—common themes in the Middle East. *Shift* (Fig. 22.14), inspired by and produced in Istanbul, is a large wool floor piece that makes an obvious connection to Turkish traditions of carpet weaving. Over eight feet long and almost five feet wide, Hatoum presents a flattened map of the world divided into slightly shifting segments. The map is overlaid with concentric circles representing seismic activity, as if the entire world suffers reverberations—or aftershocks—of explosive situations in any one place.

Shirin Neshat (b. 1957), a native Iranian whose family led Westernized lives before the Islamic revolution of 1979, embraced feminism at an early age, encouraged by a father who insisted that his daughters have the same access as anyone else when it came to education, travel, and experiences. Neshat was in college in California when the revolution began, and she did not return to Iran until 1990. As a

photographer, video-artist, and filmmaker, much of her work has been devoted to issues concerning gender roles in post-revolutionary Islamic society. Neshat's film *Passage* (Fig. 22.15), commissioned by the world-renowned composer Philip Glass, follows the ritual of passage from this world to the next as men carry a shrouded body, women prepare a grave with their bare hands, and a little girl

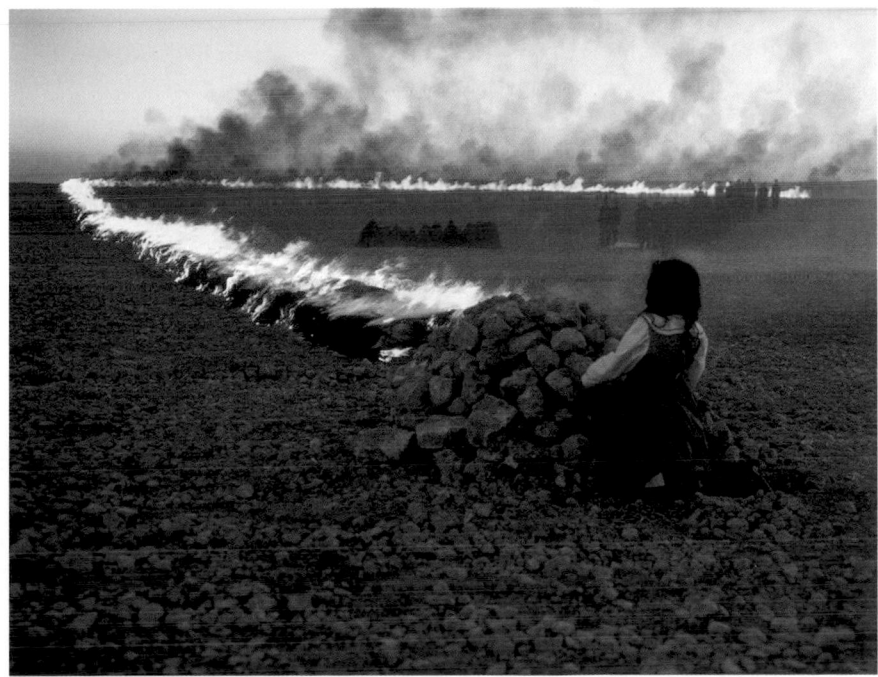

∧ 22.15 **SHIRIN NESHAT, Still from** *Passage* (2001). Color video installation with sound, 00:11:40. Dimensions vary with installation. Number 5 of edition of 6. Solomon R. Guggenheim Museum, New York, New York.

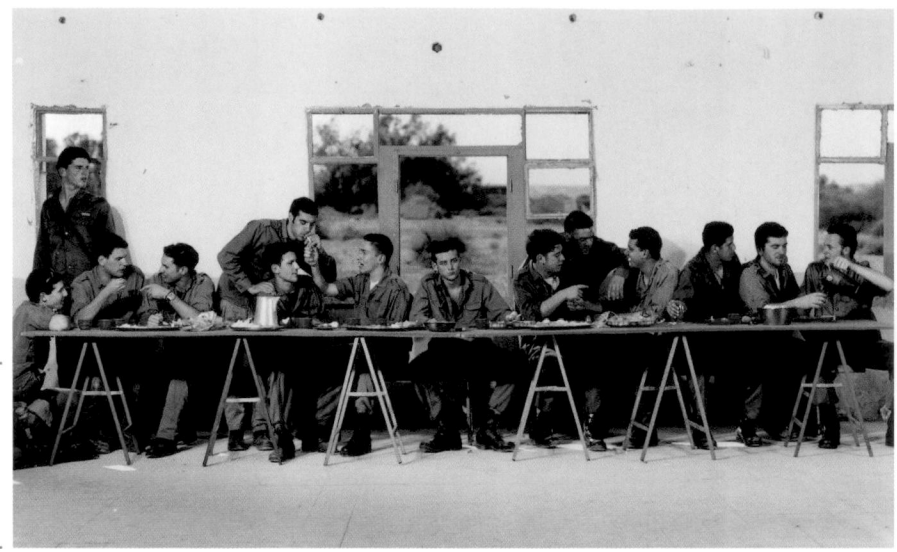

1 ft.

▲ 22.16 **ADI NES,** *Untitled* (1999). Chromogenic print, 35⁷⁄₁₆" × 56¹¹⁄₁₆". The Israel Museum, Jerusalem, Israel.

threat of danger and death embodied in the image of the soldier. In his role of artist as social critic, some of Nes's work is intended to point out the discrepancy between the dream of Israel and certain social realities of contemporary Israel.

Akram Zaatari (b. 1966) was born in Saida, Lebanon, but, unlike many of his peers who were born in the Middle East but have moved to countries in the West, he lives and works in Beirut. For the 2013 Venice Biennale (a biennial international exhibition for which national pavilions are erected), Lebanon chose his video, *Letter to a Refusing Pilot* (Fig. 22.17), as its sole entry. Zaatari's work was inspired by a circulating rumor about an Israeli pilot in 1982 who, rather than follow orders to bomb Saida (the artist's hometown), released his payload into the Mediterranean Sea. The rumor turned out to be true; the pilot, Hagai Tamir, concluded that the building must not be a military target because he had studied architecture and recognized the structure as typical of a hospital or school. The still from the video shows the pilot's digression from his authorized flight plan (denoted by a paper airplane) and heading toward the sea. The title of the video references an essay by the French writer-philosopher Albert Camus, written during World War II. The pilot's challenge of military authority brought to the Zaatari's mind Camus's statement, "I should like to be able to love my country and still love justice."[5]

sets a fire that comes to circumscribe the scene. During one of the film's most abstract and intensely visual passages, Glass's pulsating score juxtaposed with a close-up of the women's thrumming chadors creates a sense of oil bubbling from the desert ground. The ingredients are natural and elemental—sticks, stones, fire, smoke, sand, and dust—and the repetitive movements, chanting, and music form a circle of life, death, and perhaps, rebirth.

Israeli artist Adi Nes (b. 1966) is best known for his hyperstaged photographs of young male actors posing as Israeli soldiers. The artist has said that, as a gay man, he is interested in issues of masculinity and male identity, particularly in a society that prizes—almost mythologizes—physical strength. His single most famous photograph recreates Leonardo da Vinci's fresco, *The Last Supper* (see Fig. 17.14), substituting soldiers at a table in a mess hall for apostles (Fig. 22.16). Aside from the visual pun, Nes draws our attention to the concrete place (Israel) where so many events of the Bible (Hebrew and Christian) are said to have occurred and the links between the larger-than-life aspect of those events and the ordinary plight of individuals struggling to survive in his country today. In Leonardo's version of *The Last Supper*, the apostles react to Jesus's announcement to them that one among them will betray him and that he will die. Despite the laughing and talking going on in Nes's version of the masterpiece, there is an implicit

5 Sfeir-Semler Gallery, "Akram Zaatari," www.sfeir-semler.com/gallery-artists/zaatari/view-work/ (accessed February 18, 2015).

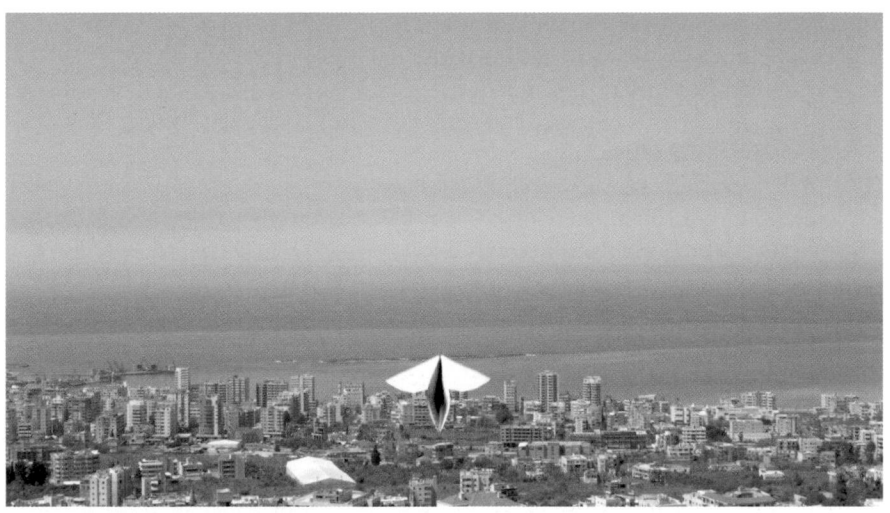

▲ 22.17 **AKRAM ZAATARI,** *Letter to a Refusing Pilot* (2013). Video still. Shown at the Venice Biennial, Lebanon Pavillion, 2013.

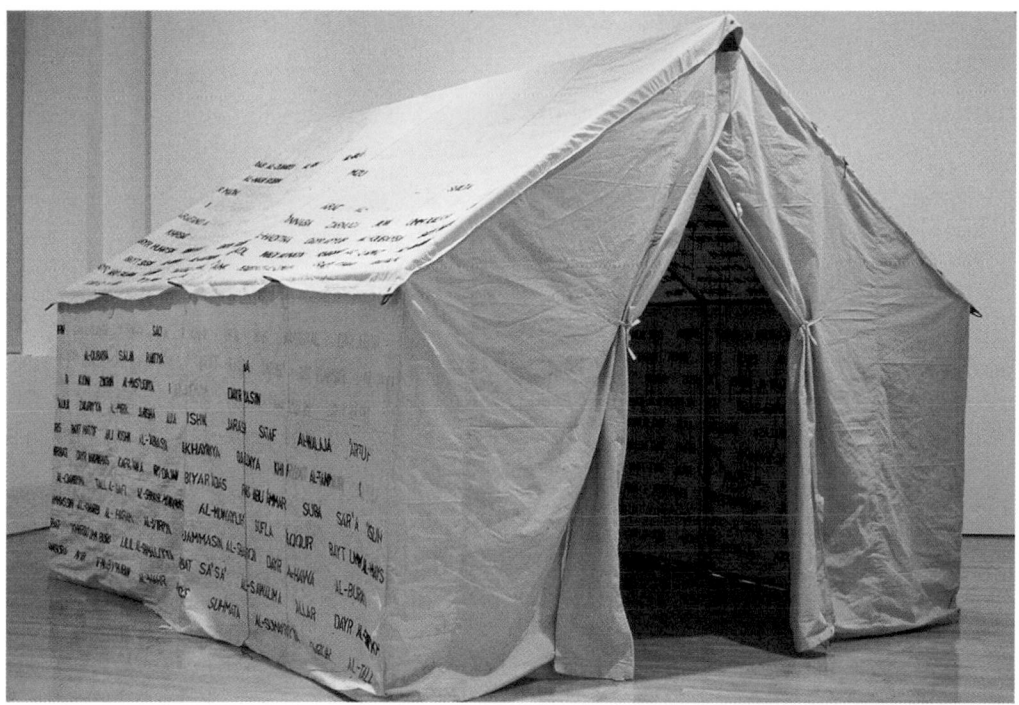

▲ **22.18** EMILY JACIR, *Memorial to 418 Palestinian Villages Destroyed, Depopulated and Occupied by Israel in 1948* (2001). Refugee tent, embroidery thread, daily log of names of people who worked on tent; 8' × 12' × 10'. National Museum of Contemporary Art, Athens, Greece.

Emily Jacir (b. 1970) was born to a Palestinian family in the West Bank city of Bethlehem but was reared in Saudi Arabia. She currently divides her time between Ramallah, in the West Bank, and Rome. Jacir has engaged in numerous acts intended to spotlight the hardships of the Palestinian people; she has secretly filmed the prolonged delays Palestinian workers experience as they try to pass Israeli checkpoints in the West Bank. She has used her own U.S. passport and free-movement status to facilitate communication among Palestinians living in occupied territory who are denied access to their families. Addressing the nature of life under occupation, the hardships, and the almost Darwinian approach to survival, Jacir has placed bogus personal ads in New York's *Village Voice* publication purportedly by Palestinian women in search of Israeli husbands to get residency permits. One of her most literal works is a tent stitched with the names of Palestinian villages (Fig. 22.18) that have been depopulated by Israel over long years of conflict between the two peoples. Tents like these can be seen in refugee camps throughout Gaza.

Wael Shawky (b. 1971), an Egyptian artist who was born, raised, and continues to live and work in Alexandria, has created a body of work that tackles issues of identity—artistic, nationalistic, and religious—and the effects of globalization using narrative and performance. *Cabaret Crusades: The Horror Show Files* (2010), *Cabaret Crusades: The Path to Cairo* (2012), and *Cabaret Crusades: The Secrets of Karbala* (2014) is a trilogy of puppet animations that retells the history of the medieval Crusades from an Arabic perspective (Fig. 22.19). Shawky has said that his use of puppets—some of them 200 years old—contributes to the notion of control. According to the artist, "The work also implies a criticism of the way history has been written and manipulated."

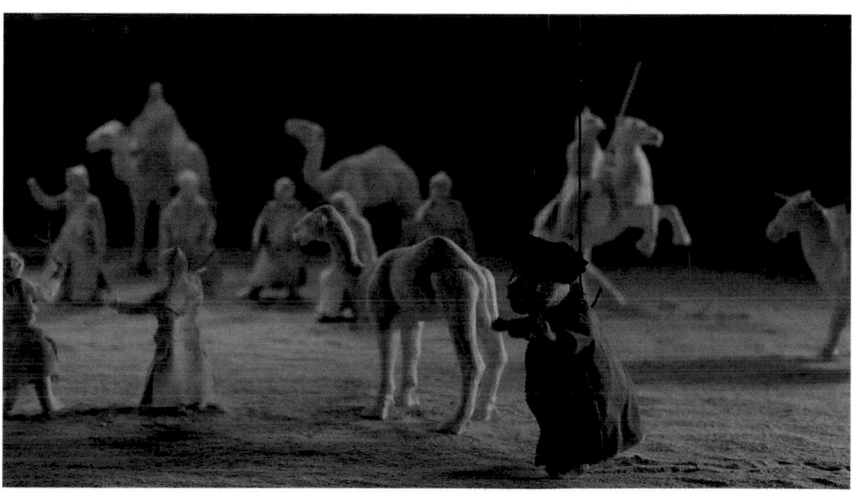

▲ **22.19** WAEL SHAWKY, *Cabaret Crusades: The Path to Cairo* (2012). HD video, color, sound, 58 minutes, film still.

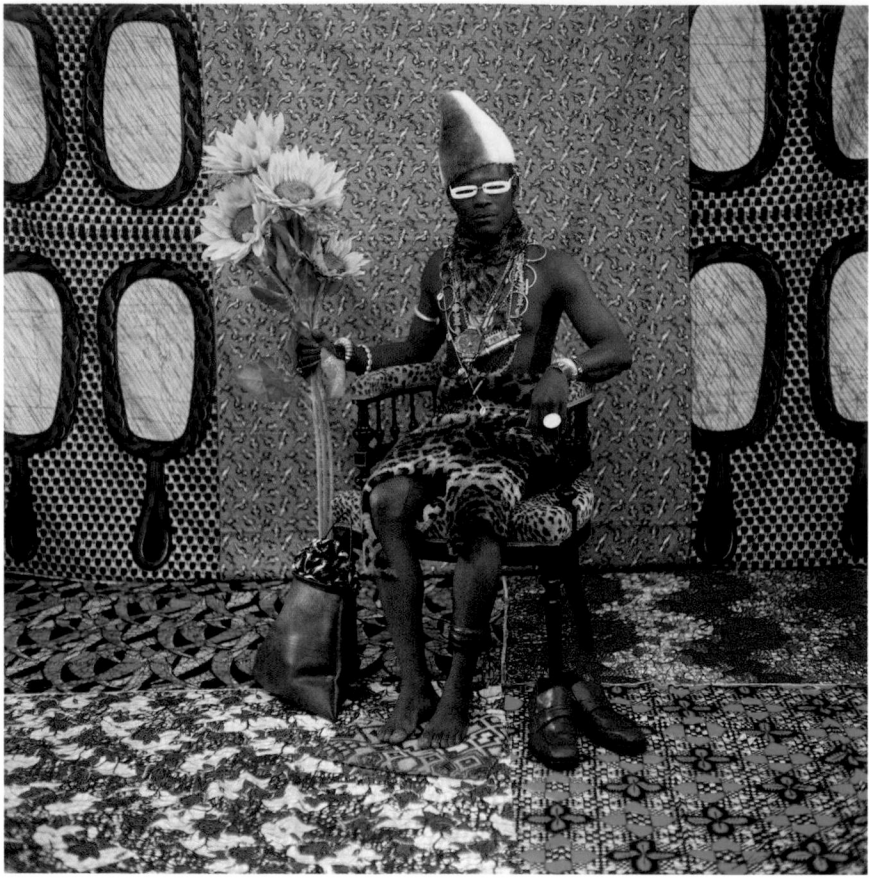

◄ 22.20 **SAMUEL FOSSO**, *The Chief: He Who Sold Africa to the Colonists*, **from *Self-Portraits I-IV*** (1997). C-print photograph, 39¾" × 39¾". Musée National d'Art Moderne, Centre Georges Pompidou, Paris, France.

1 ft.

AFRICA

Contemporary African artists often work with traditional techniques and art forms or combine them with Western references. These hybrid works correspond to the melding of cultures that occurred in Africa as a result of European and Arab colonization and continues to factor into African life today.

El Anatsui (b. 1944) lives and works in Nigeria, but he was born in Ghana, where kente cloth—a silk and cotton textile made of colorful, interwoven strips—originated. This sacred cloth is most certainly the inspiration for his many wall hangings, but rather than weaving pieces of fabric, Anatsui recycles the aluminum wrappings of liquor-bottle caps and other packaging and assembles it all into a facsimile of cloth using copper wire (see Fig. 4.12).

CONNECTIONS Ghana-born artist El Anatsui's wall hangings are immense, evoking tapestries and mosaic murals. At the same time, they serve as a sociopolitical and economic commentary on globalization.

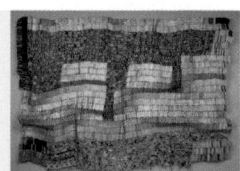

▲ El Anatsui's *Between Earth and Heaven* (**Fig. 4.12**)

Samuel Fosso (b. 1962), of the Central African Republic, began his career as a photographer by taking self-portraits that later morphed into impersonations with sociopolitical messages. For example, some of the most violent slave-runners were Africans themselves who plundered the villages of tribes to capture their victims. In the same way, a number of African chieftains sold their land and slaves to colonialists. In Figure 22.20, we see Fosso in the garb of such a chieftain, adopting the typical pose of a tribal leader of power and prestige. We see him wearing leopard skins and gold jewelry, accouterments far beyond the means of ordinary people. His scepter of sunflowers suggests the ruler's bold seeking of his place in history (and the tribe). In other self-portraits Fosso impersonated Nelson Mandela, Muhammad Ali, and even the American female civil rights activist Angela Davis, who achieved prominence in the 1960s as a member of the Communist Party USA and was associated with the Black Panther Party.

Figure 22.21 is a satirical riff on traditional African ceremonial masks from the "jerry can" series by Romuald Hazoumé (b. 1962). In this series of assemblages, Hazoumé is calling attention to the worldwide shortage of gasoline, the exploitation of Africa's resources, and the economic enslavement of Africans who are forced to ferry the fuel. Assemblages such as these begin with

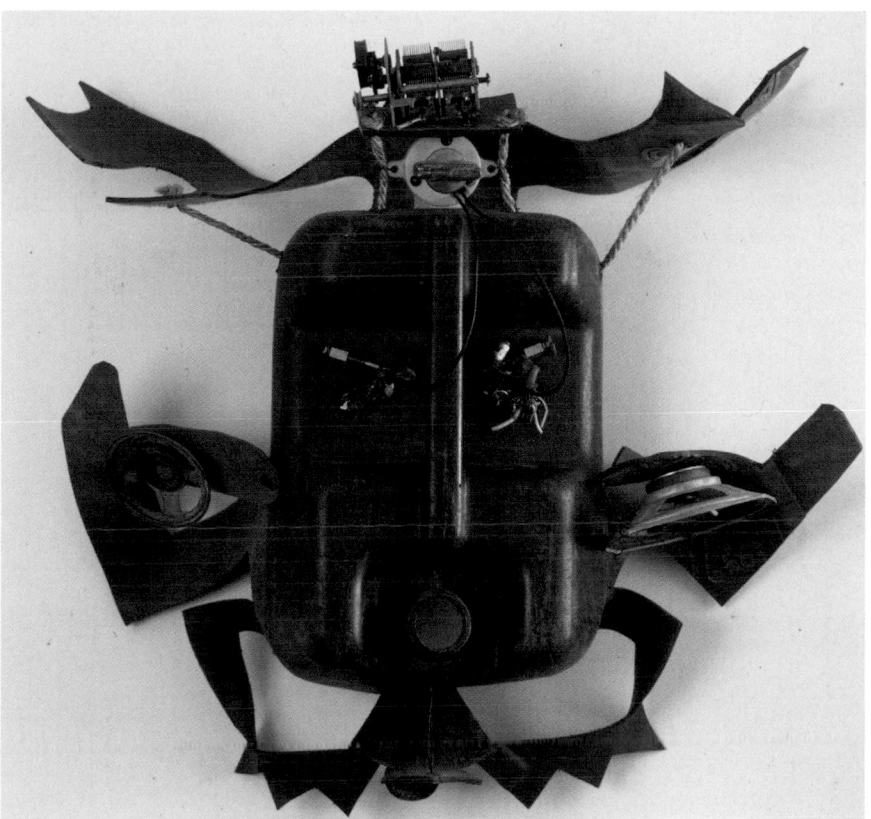

< 22.21 ROMUALD HAZOUMÉ, *Bagdad City* (1992). Brush, speakers, and plastic can. The Contemporary African Art Collection (C.A.A.C. The Pigozzi Collection), Geneva, Switzerland.

what early-twentieth-century European artists called ready-mades—objects there for the taking, which, with little or no manipulation, would take on a character that negated their original purpose. Like Anatsui, Hazoumé calls attention to the effects of global encounters on cultural traditions.

Many of the works of Kenyan artist Wangechi Mutu are also examples of hybridity. She juxtaposes contemporary print models and African objects in politically charged collages that feature women's bodies surrounded by rich, explosive colors, animal prints, botanical elements, and abstract patterns that evoke traditional textiles. In *Mask* (Fig. 22.22), the model becomes an exotic temptress who invokes the sexualized stereotype of the dominatrix and overturns the traditional male–female power relationship. Many of Mutu's works illustrate twisted female anatomy and conditions of deterioration that draw attention to what she describes as the sexualization and neglect of African women by oppressive men. Underneath the stereotype, women are suffering, and Mutu wants her viewers to challenge their assumptions about race, gender, and beauty.

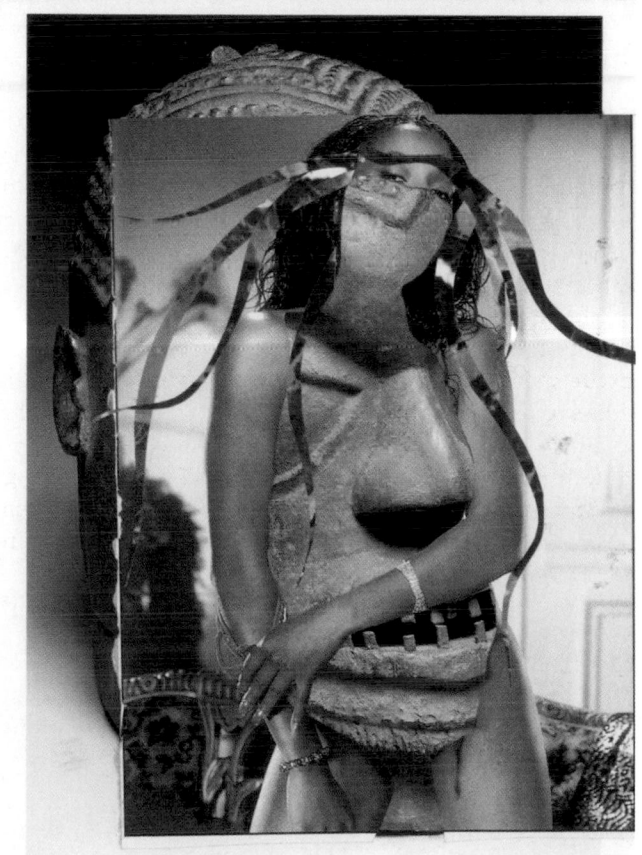

> 22.22 WANGECHI MUTU, *Mask* (2006). Mixed-media collage. Saatchi Gallery, London, England.

COMPARE & CONTRAST

Out of Africa: The Enduring Legacy of the Ceremonial Mask

MASKS OF MYRIAD DESIGNS AND materials play an essential role in the rituals of the traditional peoples of sub-Saharan and West Africa. They typically have religious or spiritual meanings and are the focal piece of masquerades—ceremonial dances performed for events ranging from funerals and initiation rites to social gatherings and entertainment. Mask makers have special status in these societies, and their craft is usually passed down over the generations.

In the early twentieth century, the mask became the quintessential object associated with traditional African culture and was widely collected by European artists, writers, and the intellectual elite (**Fig. 22.23**). Drawn to the straightforwardness, the directness of expression, the rustic carving, and the inherent power of the fundamental forms—untouched and unmediated by the West—young modern artists such as Pablo Picasso and Henri Matisse incorporated aspects of African masks and other objects in their own paintings and sculpture. In his *Head of a Sleeping Woman* (**Fig. 22.24**), Picasso mimicked the geometric rhythms and straightforward features of African objects. He would return to these forms—which he first saw in an exhibition in Paris—throughout his long career.

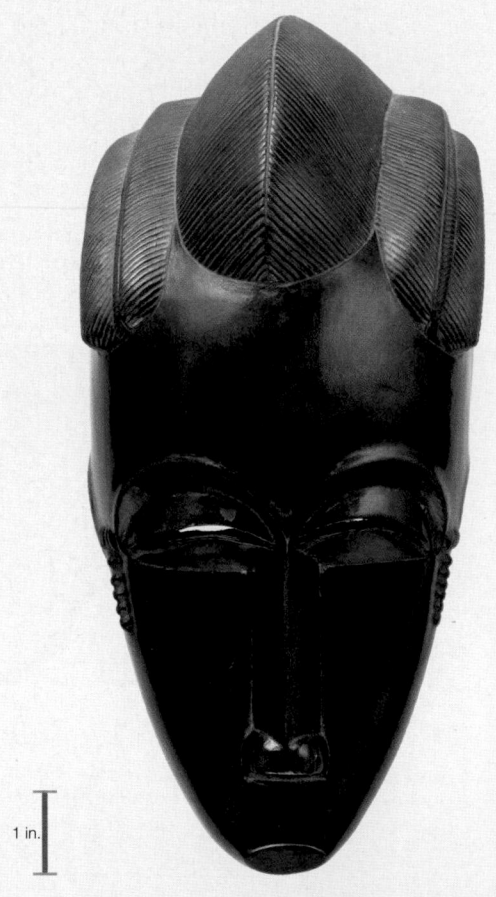

▲ 22.23 **Portrait Mask (Gba gba), Côte D'Ivoire** (before 1913). Wood, 10¼" × 4⅞" × 4⅛". The Metropolitan Museum of Art, New York, New York.

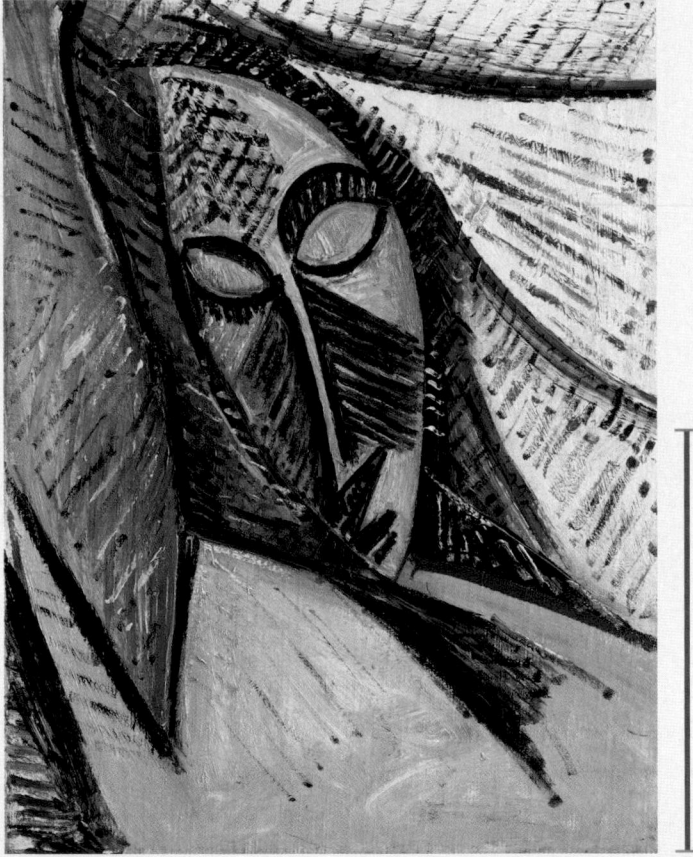

▲ 22.24 **PABLO PICASSO,** *Head of a Sleeping Woman (Study for Nude with Drapery)* (1907). Oil on canvas, 24¼" × 18¾". The Museum of Modern Art, New York, New York.

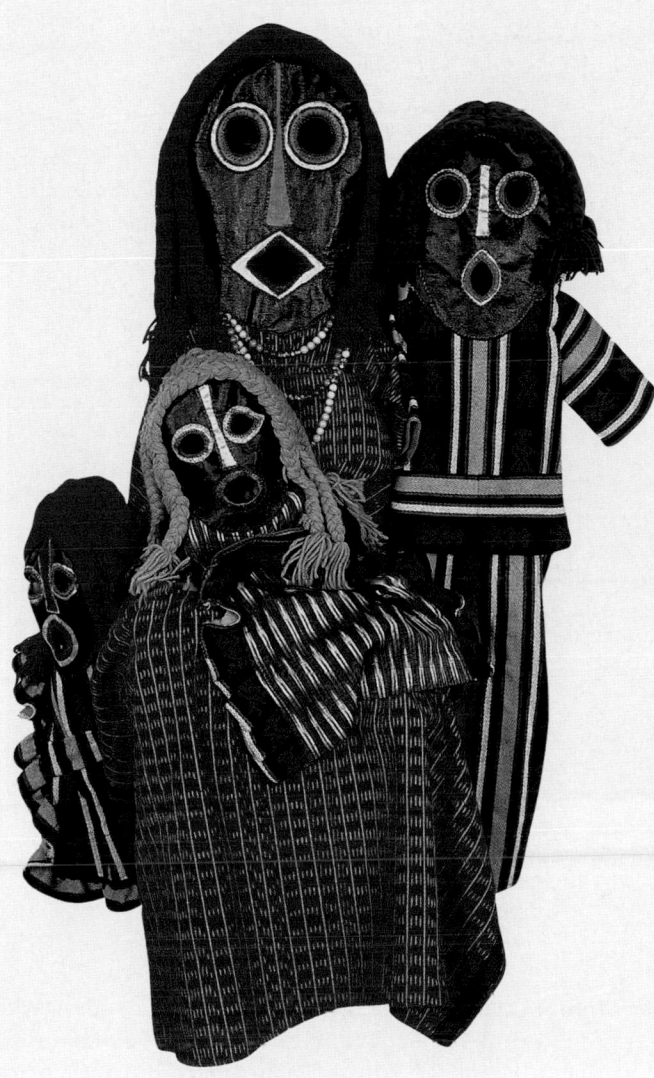

Willie Cole has created masklike sculptures from women's high-heeled shoes that, while captivating in their cleverness, are stocked with multiple references that elicit conflicting emotions. His mask called *Shine* (**Fig. 22.26**) has positive and negative associations. The use of the word *shine* as a derogatory expression for African Americans originated in the early twentieth century, perhaps in reference to shoe shining or polishing, which was a common way for urban black men and boys to eke out a living. At the same time, the word connotes radiance, and indeed, the positioning of the shoes with the heels aimed outward from the central core of the mask can read as rays emanating from a spiritual object. Cole has said, "I want the [masks] to be links between worlds, . . . art that looks like it is from another culture and another time, even though the materials in the work are strictly American."

1 ft.

∧ **22.25 FAITH RINGGOLD,** *Mrs Jones and Family* (1973). Mixed media (embroidery and sewn fabric), 74" × 69".

Contemporary African American artists Faith Ringgold and Willie Cole have also referenced masks in many of their works. Ringgold's *Mrs Jones and Family* (**Fig. 22.25**) is constructed of stitched fabric of traditional kente-cloth patterns with embroidered details. The wedge-shaped noses and open mouths on the heads of the soft-sculpture dolls evoke common features of African masks. In combination, these elements connect the artist to both her African heritage and artistic traditions—like needlework and quilting—among enslaved African women.

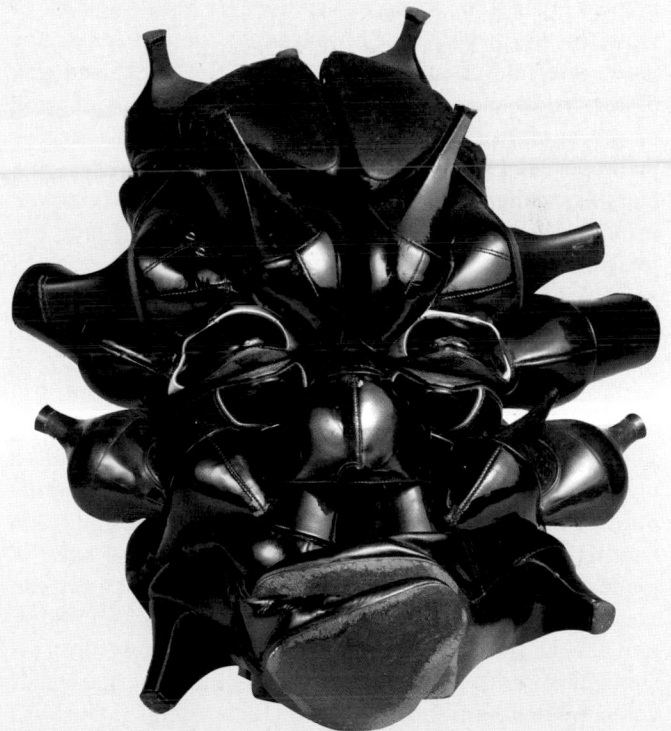

1 in.

∧ **22.26 WILLIE COLE,** *Shine* (2007). Shoes, steel wire, monofilament line, washers, and screws; 15¾" × 14" × 15". The Metropolitan Museum of Art, New York.

THE AMERICAS

For four months in 2014, the Solomon R. Guggenheim museum in New York City hosted an exhibition called *Under the Same Sun: Art from Latin America Today*. It featured works by artists from fifteen countries who share, among other things, a history of colonialism, slavery, and interaction among racial and ethnic groups that has fostered unbreakable ties among Caribbean and Latin American homelands. Even as some natives attempt to leave, tourists from the all over the world descend on the islands and the beaches of these southern paradises, but remain insulated from the harsh realties faced by most local people every day. The art produced by people of and from the Caribbean and Latin America tends to reflect these themes—the residue of colonialism, poverty, political conflict, the northward push, and what life means from day to day.

See more of New York in the online Art Tour.

Much of Cuban artist Alexandre Arrechea's (b. 1970) work is a commentary on the irony that while his country builds its new socialist society, its jewels—like the capital city of Havana—lie in disrepair. *Elementos Arquitectronicos* (Fig. 22.27) is a stunning portrait of a laborer struggling to carry—or at least hold—a stack of whitewashed bricks that obscures his identity. Arrechea uses pictorial and symbolic devices—the hard fired clay of the brick against the man's flesh or the insinuation of the verdant plant life against the decaying stucco— to suggest the workers' struggle and chance at hope in a classless, collectivist society. The faceless man is locked into a task that seems to have no beginning or end; the image is one of quiet desperation.

Haitian artist Jean-Ulrick Désert (b. 1965) has focused many of his projects on the relationship between immigrants and outsiders and their adopted or host countries, some of it growing out of his own experiences. Cultural mixing and identity are also the concepts underlying *The Burqa Project* (Fig. 22.28), in which Désert stitched national flags into burqas and draped them on mannequins. *Burqas* are garments that Muslim women in some countries choose or are forced to wear for the sake of modesty. The flags used in *The Burqa Project* represent the Western countries of Germany, France, the United States, and the United Kingdom and seem to suggest the tensions between religious and national identity that occur when Western and non-Western cultures clash. Outward symbols of allegiance are often perceived as threatening to the homogeneity of nationalism and can lead to legislation (as it did in France) that forbids their use in state institutions (like a public school). The burqa-clad mannequins in Désert's piece offer a tangible resolution to the dilemma of allegiance.

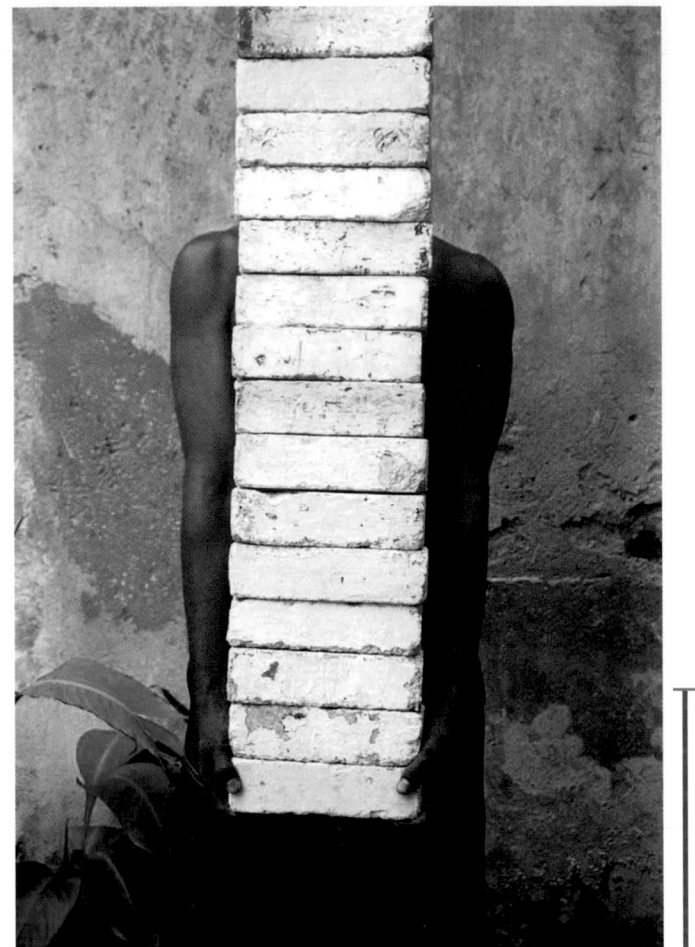

∧ 22.27 **ALEXANDRE ARRECHEA**, *Elementos Arquitectronicos* (2006). Chromogenic print, 43" × 31". Edition 2 of 4, 1AP.

Miguel Luciano (b. 1972) focuses much of his work on the cultural and economic relationship between the Caribbean island of Puerto Rico, where he was born, and the United States. Puerto Rico is a self-governing commonwealth that was ceded to the United States in a treaty with Spain that ended the Spanish-American war at the end of the nineteenth century. Historically, both the United States and Puerto Rico have had wavering feelings about their relationship. In the postwar years, the U.S. Congress was not unanimous in its support of annexation, and even today Puerto Ricans continue to debate the island's political status, between options of statehood, independence, or the commonwealth status quo. Luciano's *Plántano Pride* (Fig. 22.29) shows a Puerto Rican adolescent boy in a universal white T-shirt and culture-specific bling. Sugar, tobacco, and plantains—a banana-like fruit—were once the island's cash crops. The boy poses for the camera with a cocky expression, wearing with pride a symbol associated

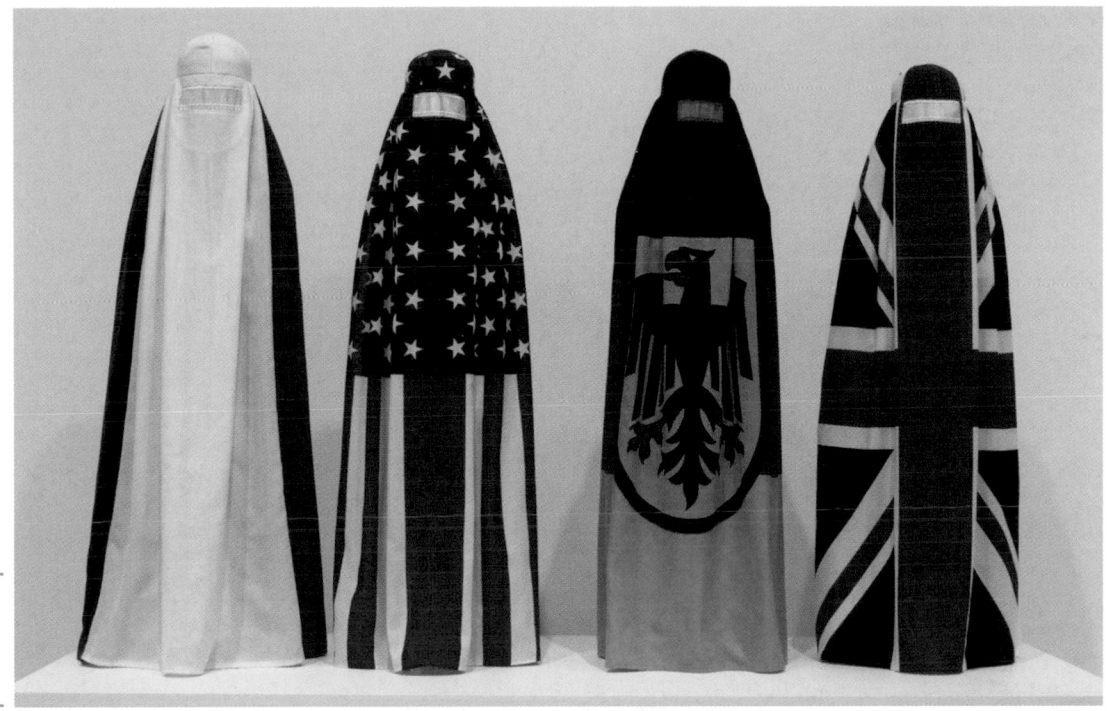

▲ 22.20 JEAN-ULRICK DÉSERT, *The Burqa Project: On the Borders of My Dreams I Encountered My Double's Ghosts* (2001). Flag-textiles, dye, lace; 63" × 118". Installation at Infinite Island, Contemporary Caribbean Art, The Brooklyn Museum New York, New York.

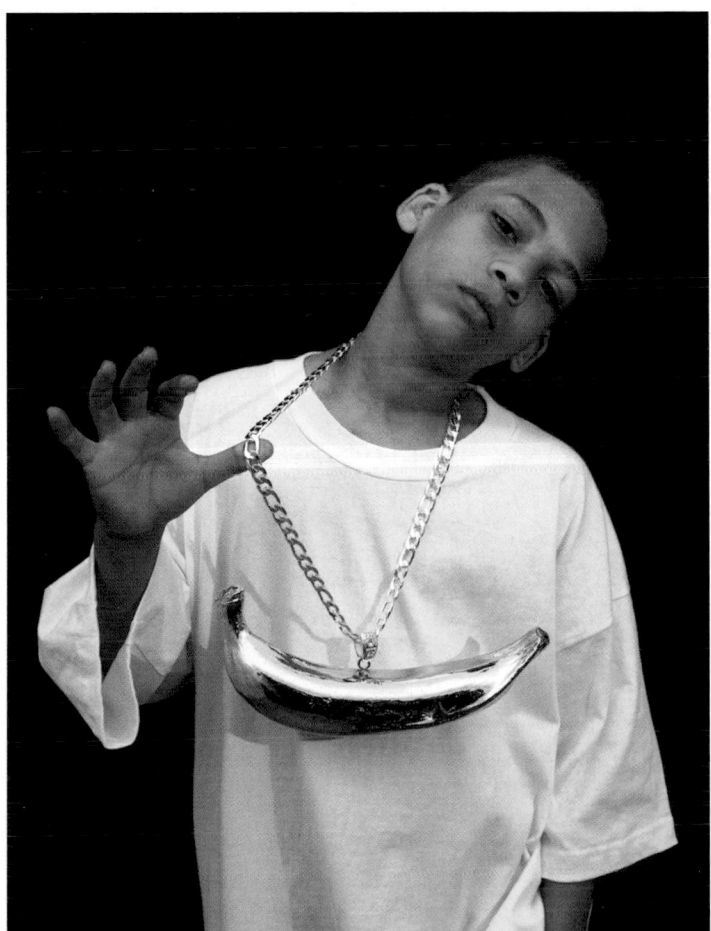

with his country's national identity, but also with American materialism and rap culture. Luciano's work addresses political, economic, and cultural subjugation.

Mexican artist Enrique Chagoya's (b. 1953) paintings and prints chronicle cultural change and exchange. Chagoya, who was born in Mexico City, has recently turned his attention to immigration, a long-standing and unresolved issue between the United States and Mexico. His print titled *Illegal Alien's Guide*

◄ 22.29 MIGUEL LUCIANO, *Plántano Pride* (2006). Chromogenic print (platinum plantain), 40" × 30".

to Critical Theory (Figs. 22.30A and 22.30B) is a satire on his own experience as an immigrant now leading an academic life at California's prestigious Stanford University. A detail of the work features Chagoya as a plucked chicken in a sombrero, peddling a bicycle as fast as he can while spouting a "critically correct" phrase torn from the pages of literary or artistic theory. Playing on the common cardboard placard graphic "Works for food," a talk-bubble next to the artist's head reads: "Works to suggest that the act finally distills into something dense and unknowable." Other details include visual references to pre-Columbian reliefs and wall paintings, particularly from the Mayan civilization. Chagoya says, "My artwork is a conceptual fusion of opposite cultural realities that I have experienced in my lifetime. I integrate diverse elements: from pre-Columbian mythology, western religious iconography, and American popular culture."

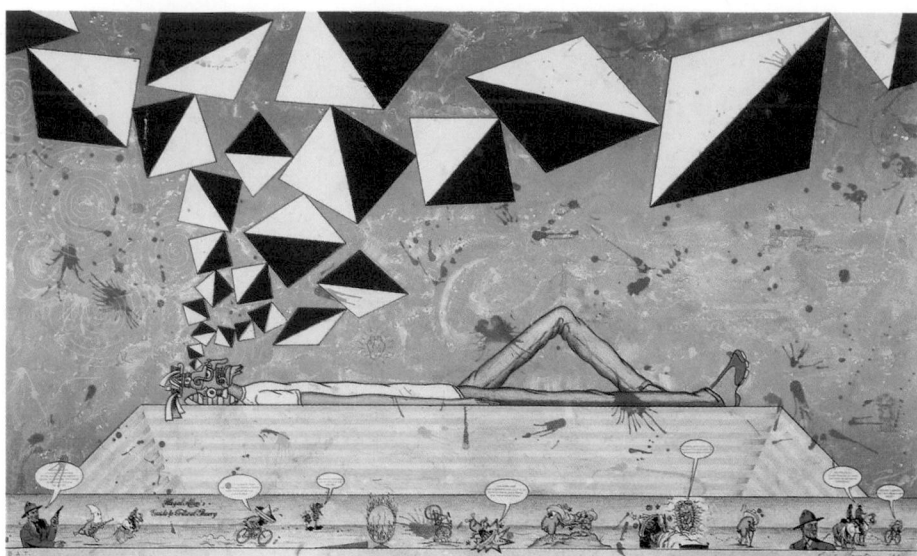

▲ 22.30A ENRIQUE CHAGOYA, *Illegal Alien's Guide to Critical Theory* (2007). Color lithograph, 24" × 40".

Our chapter, and our text, closes with an Argentinian artist included in the Guggenheim show, Amalia Pica, and her work entitled *Stage (as seen on Afghan Star)* (Fig. 22.31). Pica tackles historical injustices (several of her works pertain to absurd and murderous tactics of Argentina's military junta in the 1970s) and extremism past and present. *Stage (as seen on Afghan Star)* is a recreation of a performance stage from the Afghani version of the reality competition TV show, *American Idol*. The televised program symbolized a "taste of democracy" for Afghans

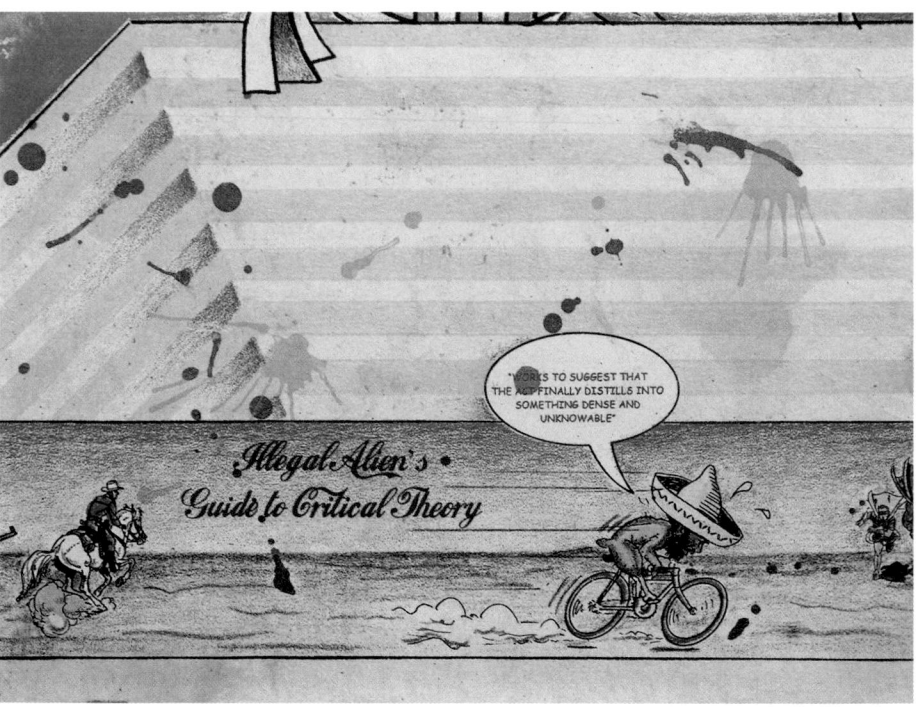

▲ 22.30B ENRIQUE CHAGOYA, Detail of *Illegal Alien's Guide to Critical Theory* (2007).

who got to vote for their favorite singer, even though most still do not own TV sets because the Taliban outlawed them in 1998. In her article in *Aesthetica*, Ruby Beesley noted that Pica's work "engages not only with concepts of freedom of speech and democratic voting processes, but also with the cult of celebrity, and the absurdity of how the vacuous process of voting in a reality television show should have preceded free and fair political elections." This single piece coveys the place of the artists in the contemporary contour, not only in terms of their far-reaching influence in the global art market, but also in terms of the "borderlessness" of their concerns and their desire to use their art to raise the consciousness of their international audiences.

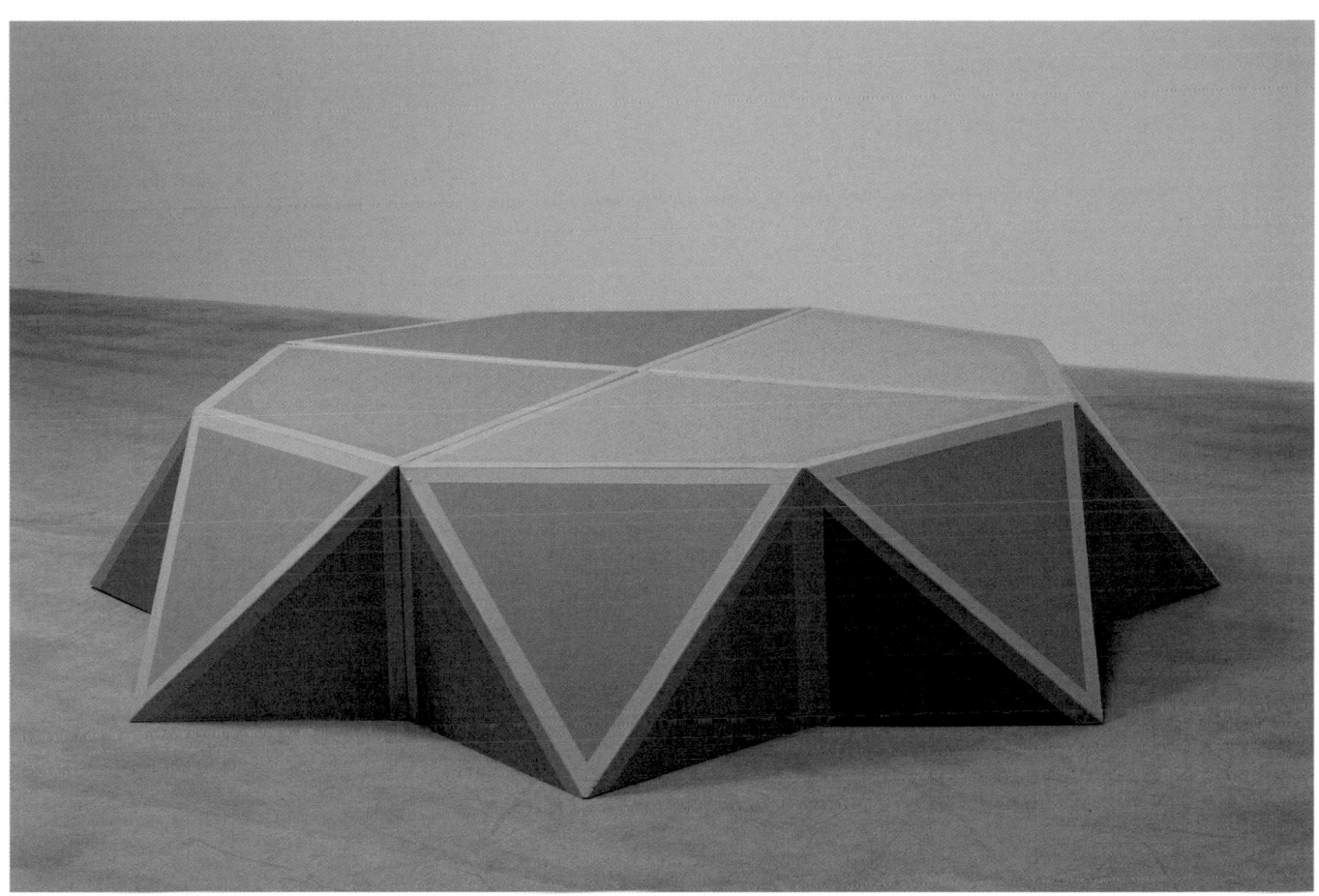

∧ 22.31 **AMALIA PICA,** *Stage (as seen on Afghan Star)* (2011). Cardboard, wood, tape, spotlight; 10" × 110" × 110".

VISUAL GLOSSARY

THEMES & PURPOSES OF ART

WE LEARN HOW TO UNDERSTAND ART by approaching it from many different directions, analyzing it from several points of view—as you are doing in your class and in reading this textbook. Subjects and symbolism, historic and cultural context (the "what" of a work), materials and techniques, elements and design principles (the "how" of a work), all come into play.

Considering the "whys" behind works of art, however, may further enrich our appreciation of art. Why did this building or this piece come into existence? What was its *purpose*? What is the *theme* of this painting, and why was it chosen? What message does the theme convey? Is that message unique? Universal? Art is created for a multitude of reasons, some of which we may never know. But what we do find out will most certainly contribute to a fuller understanding of the works, their makers, the circumstances that surround them, and their reactions to the world in which they live.

The *purposes* of art—the reasons why art exists— range from the mundane (artistic objects used in daily life or structures that contribute to human survival) to the lofty (glorifying the mighty, seeking immortality, protesting racism or war, or encouraging the viewer to take a new look at objects in the environment). The graffitist-turned-cultural-icon, Keith Haring, thought that art should be "something that liberates the soul, provokes the imagination and encourages people to go further." The Irish playwright, George Bernard Shaw, wrote, "Without art, the crudeness of reality would become unbearable." JR, the semi-anonymous French street artist and TED Prize winner, states that the purpose of art is to "turn the world inside out" and to change the way we see it.

Themes in the arts express fundamental ideas and ideals and transmit messages about society, the human condition, and human nature. Themes are distinct from subjects; themes represent "larger" concepts or philosophies embedded in the form and content of a work of art (religious belief, power and politics, sexuality and the body, war and violence).

This visual glossary is a compilation of some of the purposes and themes of art. Most of the works featured in the Visual Glossary appear elsewhere in your book. Figure numbers enable you to readily return to the chapters and read about the works as examples of a particular purpose or theme and, in so doing, perhaps it will change the way you see them.

THE THEMES

Contemporary Life and Popular Culture   562

Fantasy   563

Nature   564

Power, Politics, and the State   565

Race, Ethnicity, Gender, and Social Class   566

Religion   567

Sexuality and the Body   568

Social Consciousness and Protest   569

The Grotesque   570

War and Violence   571

THE PURPOSES

Beauty   572

Glorification and Immortality   573

History and Memory   574

Ideology   575

Pleasure   576

Self-Expression   577

Survival and Well-Being   578

CONTEMPORARY LIFE & POPULAR CULTURE

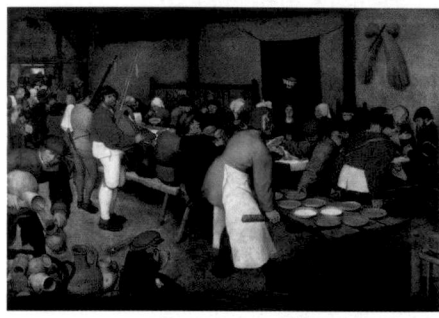

< 17.28 PIETER BRUEGEL THE ELDER. *The Peasant Wedding* (1568).

ALL ART IS CONTEMPORARY. All art was made in its time and in its place. Flemish artist Pieter Bruegel the Elder's *The Peasant Wedding* (Fig. 17.28), for example, was painted in the Netherlands in the middle of the sixteenth century. It shows the common human activities one would expect at a rural wedding—the pies and meats, the peasant pottery, the head coverings, the lantern and wall hangings—all emblems of their time and place. But when we speak now of contemporary art, we are usually talking about art of the last fifty or sixty years, especially the art that continues to speak to us today about the lives we lead and where we lead them. The popular culture of the day is also the subject matter of Pop Art, well expressed in Hamilton's humorous early work in the genre: *Just What Is It That Makes Today's Homes So Different, So Appealing?* (Fig. 21.17). We see the advent of the black-and-white television set. We see the body of a muscleman at a time when comic books were advertising how males could avoid being 97-pound weaklings. We see the obsession with the size of women's breasts. Making the home even more appealing is the vacuum cleaner on the stairs, a labor-saving device intended to free women from traditional drudgery.

Let us also think about the world of

today and how artists represent and express their feelings about that world. Things are changing faster than ever before. New national borders are drawn, new medicines and medical methods come into being, some economies fade while others ascend, and populations move around more easily than ever. In China, where the economy has grown at about 10 percent

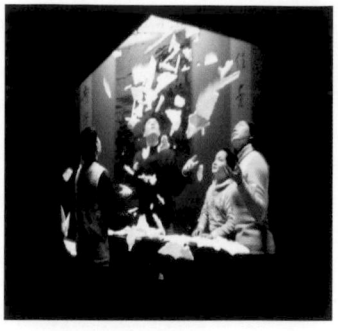

∧ 22.6 WANG GONGXIN. *Our Sky Is Falling In!* (2007).

a year and hundreds of millions have moved from farms into cities, it not surprising that some feel that "our sky is falling in," which happens to the title of a video on the subject (Fig. 22.6). There is globalization. Apple, Coca-Cola, McDonald's, and Starbucks are brands found all over the globe. Apple is the most admired company in the United States and the world's best-known brand. The familiar shape of the iPhone, with its myriad applications under glass, is sought by consumers worldwide (Fig. 11.44).

We are enchanted by the media—film, television, video, video games, photography, the Internet. Millions tune in to popular TV series such as *Game of Thrones*, whether shown on Netflix, Apple TV, or streamed from elsewhere. We are addicted to monster movies, science fiction, and disaster films. We have the *Matrix* series, the *Star Wars* series, and all the offspring of the *Godzilla* film (Fig. 22.10).

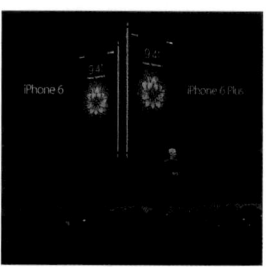

∧ 11.44 Apple CEO Tim Cook presenting the iPhone 6 Plus.

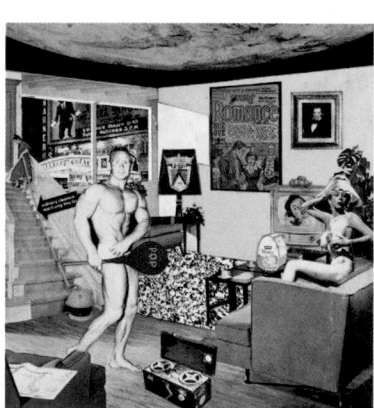

∧ 21.17 RICHARD HAMILTON. *Just What Is It That Makes Today's Homes So Different, So Appealing?* (1956).

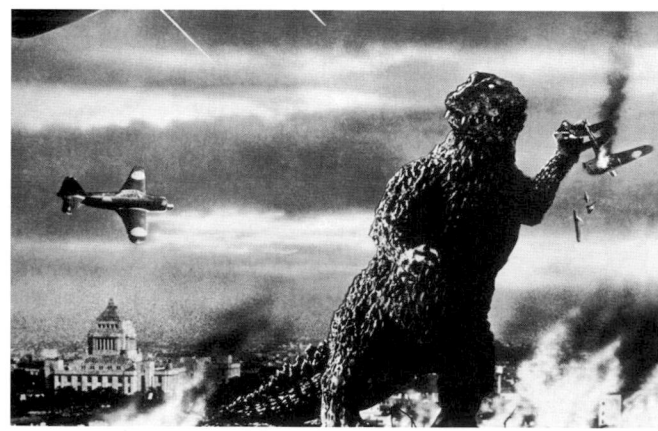

∧ 22.10 ISHIRO HONDA AND TERRY O. MORSE. Film still from *Godzilla* (1954).

FANTASY

THE FRENCH PAINTER ODILON REDON said that there is "a kind of drawing which the imagination has liberated from any concern with the details of reality in order to allow it to serve freely for the representation of things conceived [in the mind]." Art is a vehicle by which artists can express pure imagination and their innermost fantasies.

In Marc Chagall's self-portrait, *I and the Village* (shown here), fleeting memories of life in his native Russian village—reduced to images rich in personal meaning—are assembled like so many pieces of a dreamlike puzzle. Chagall once said of his approach to art that, for him, "a painting is a surface covered with representations of things . . . in which logic and illustration have no importance."

Fantastic art is a broad genre within art history and can be seen in the work of particular artists from various periods in a broad range of styles. What these works have in common are qualities that are mystical or dreamlike (sometimes hallucinogenic) and images that are not realistic, that is, what is represented is out of the realm of actual human experience. By this definition, wildly different artists like Hieronymus Bosch, Matthias Grünewald, and Francisco Goya—all of whom only dabbled in fantasy on occasion—might be listed in the same category as the twentieth-century surrealists whose entire oeuvres were based on fantasy. It is worth noting that fantastic

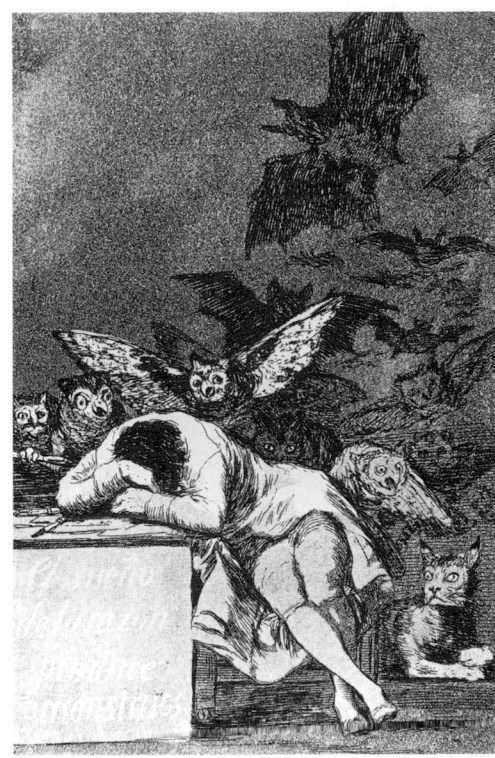

△ FRANCISCO GOYA. *The Sleep of Reason Produces Monsters* (1797–1798).

art very often incorporates the grotesque. In *The Sleep of Reason Produces* Monsters (shown here), Romantic artist Francisco Goya focuses on emotion rather than the intellect and uses the fantastic to probe into the creative imagination. In *The Persistence of Memory* (Fig. 20.26), a Surrealist work, Dalí conveys the world of the dream, juxtaposing unrelated objects in an extraordinary situation.

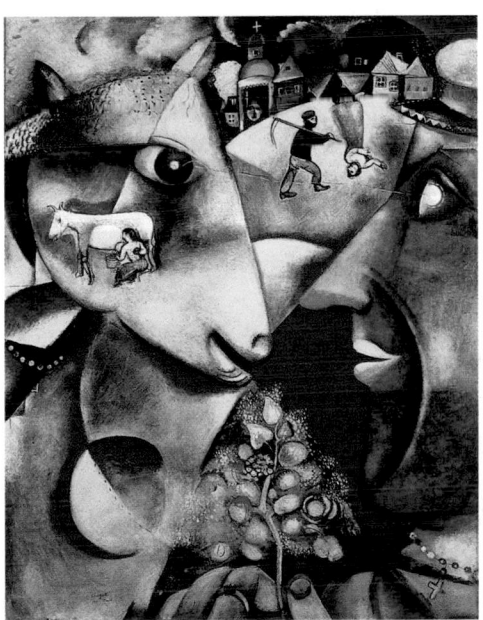

△ MARC CHAGALL. *I and the Village* (1911).

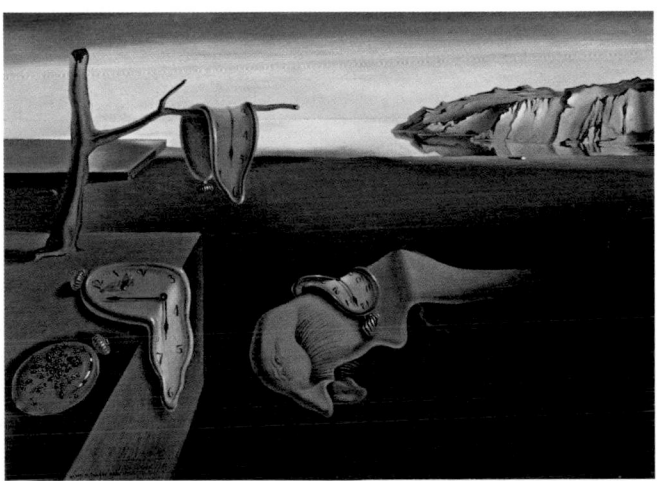

△ 20.26 SALVADOR DALÍ. *The Persistence of Memory* (1931).

NATURE

NATURE REFERS TO THE PHYSICAL WORLD in which plants, animals, landscapes and seascapes, the sources of light and wonder in the skies—and we—all exist. Modern life has enabled us to create barriers between ourselves and some of the negative aspects of nature—barriers such as shelters to keep out snow and rain, and heat and air conditioning to moderate the temperature and humidity to which we are exposed. Yet nature retains it beauty, its bounty, and its wonderment, such that many of us do not feel whole unless we can visit the woods or the seashore.

The Romantic artist Casper David Friedrich was inspired by the glacier-capped mountains of Central Europe to portray a wanderer agaze in wonderment at the vastness and splendor of nature (shown here). Because of our vantage point behind the wanderer, we participate in his sublime experience. Literally at the same time Friedrich was struck by the beauty of nature, another Romantic artist, Théodore Géricault, was captivated by its unpredictability and uncontrollability, as depicted in his painting of a shipwreck—which is also an indictment of the incompetency of the French government, which should have seen to a more efficient rescue of the ship's passengers and crew (Fig. 19.4). Van Gogh reflected his own inner emotionalism in his rendering of the movements of the stars in the sky above a sleepy French village (Fig. 19.25).

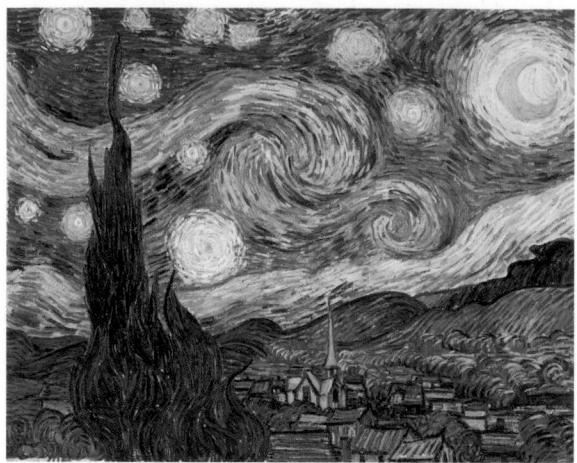

∧ 19.25 VINCENT VAN GOGH. *Starry Night* (1889).

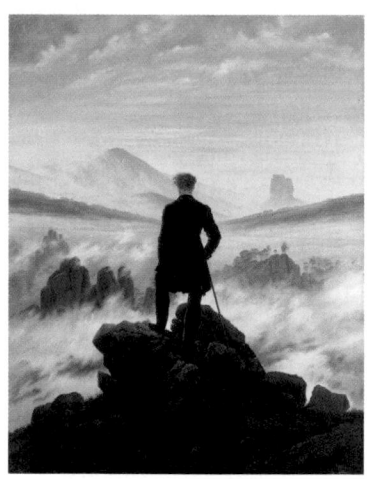

∧ CASPER DAVID FRIEDRICH. *Wanderer Above a Sea of Mist* (1817–1818).

As with Friedrich, there is a connection between the painter and nature, but in van Gogh's case, the connection is defined by the rhythms of swirling fireballs.

Song Dynasty painter Fan K'uan provides viewers with an imaginary journey among pathways nestled among trees and rocks. He portrays vegetation, mountains peaks, and a waterfall in the so-called Monumental style, with nature dwarfing travelers in the lower right of the composition (Fig. 16.37). Japanese printmaker Katsushika Hokusai, like Géricault, portrays the power of nature, with a wave menacing the boats below and threatening to drown the sailors (Fig. 19.45).

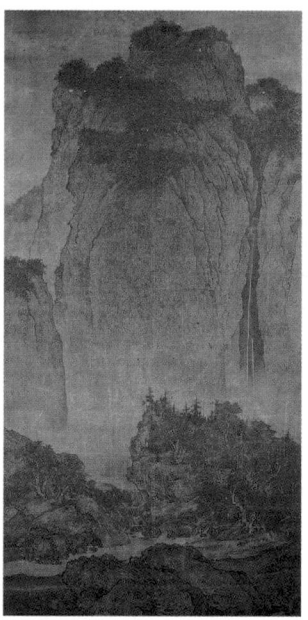

∧ 16.37 FAN K'UAN. *Travelers among Mountains and Streams* (c. 1000).

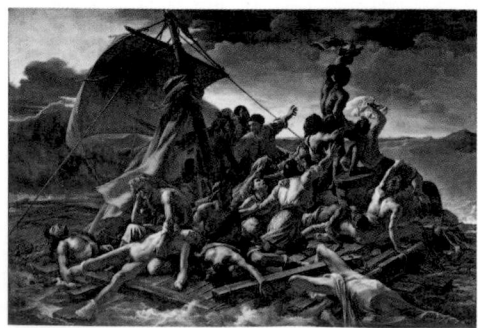

< 19.4 THÉODORE GÉRICAULT. *Raft of the Medusa* (1818–1819).

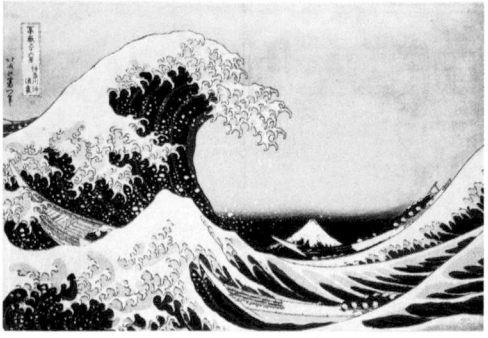

∧ 19.45 KATSUSHIKA HOKUSAI. *Under the Wave off Kanagawa* (also known as *The Great Wave*) (c. 1831).

POWER, POLITICS, & THE STATE

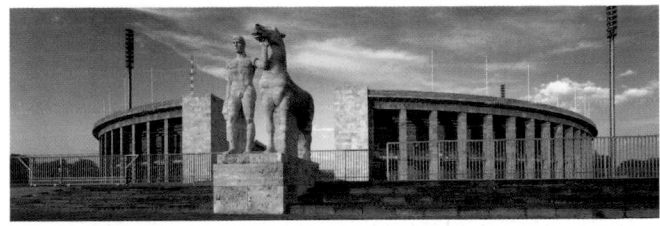

WHEN MICHELANGELO WAS CALLED TO ROME to design a tomb for Pope Julius II (who, upon election to the papacy, took a name that referred to the glorious Julius Caesar), the pope's object was to glorify himself as the Romans had deified their emperors after death, but also to serve as a reminder of his temporal power. It was under Julius—the "warrior pope"—that the Vatican regained control of territories on the Italian peninsula that had been previously lost. In spite of the fact that the role of the papacy was, by definition, one of spiritual leadership, popes throughout the history of the Catholic Church exerted their power as political entities and indeed influenced the course of historical events. Julius's tomb was never completed as intended—a pyramidal structure with forty carved figures that makes an obvious architectural reference to the deified pharaohs of ancient Egypt—but his reputation as an art patron, powerbroker, and head of state lives on.

Art not only reflects the power of the patron whether they are rulers or royalty; art also propagandizes the power and control of the state. With the Parthenon (15.9) we see that Pericles knew well how to use art to communicate and ideologize the principles of the Greeks. Adolf Hitler understood the power of art and architecture to reinforce the racist, nationalistic, and militaristic underpinnings of the Nazi regime, as we see in Werner March's Olympic Stadium (Fig. 15.23).

Politics can also play an outsized role in public projects such as monuments, memorials, and even architecture. One World Trade Center (at one time dubbed the Freedom Tower (Fig. 13.24) is the 1,776-foot structure that now occupies a site adjacent to the twin towers of the World Trade Center that were destroyed by terrorists on September 11, 2001. Its design was fraught with controversy and compromised by assorted political and social agendas. Maya Lin's Vietnam Veterans Memorial (Fig. 11.41) on the Mall in Washington, DC, completed in 1982, is one of the most arresting—and most visited—memorials in the U.S. capital today and yet opposition to the design by public officials and contributors at the outset was strong. The secretary of the interior of the Ronald Reagan administration, James Watt, even initially denied a building permit for the project.

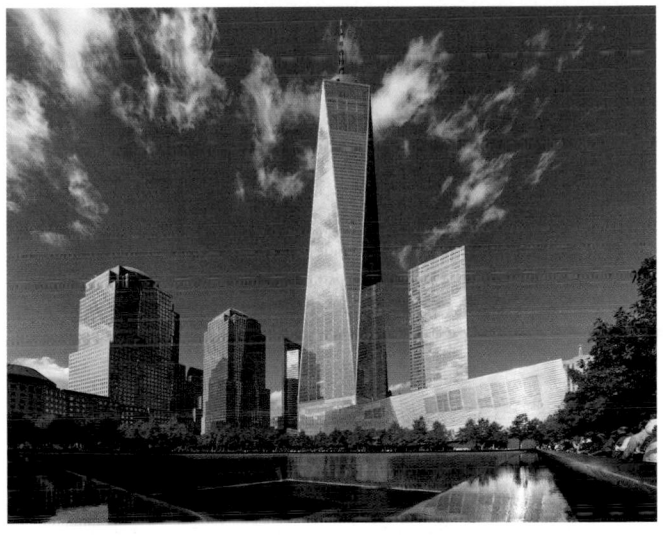

∧ 13.24 New World Trade Center.

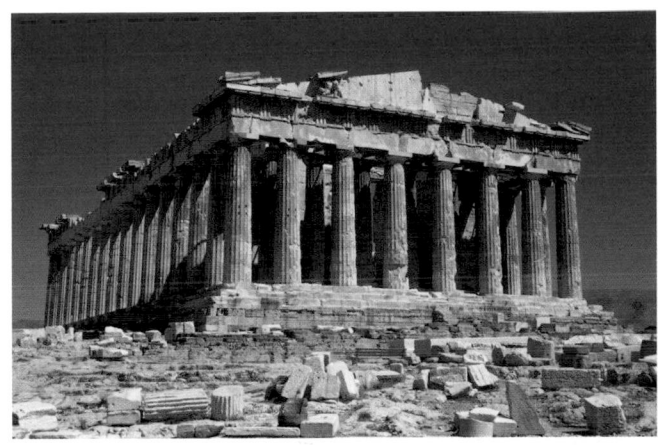

∧ 15.9 **ICTINOS AND CALLICRATES.** The Parthenon on the Acropolis, Athens (448–432 BCE).

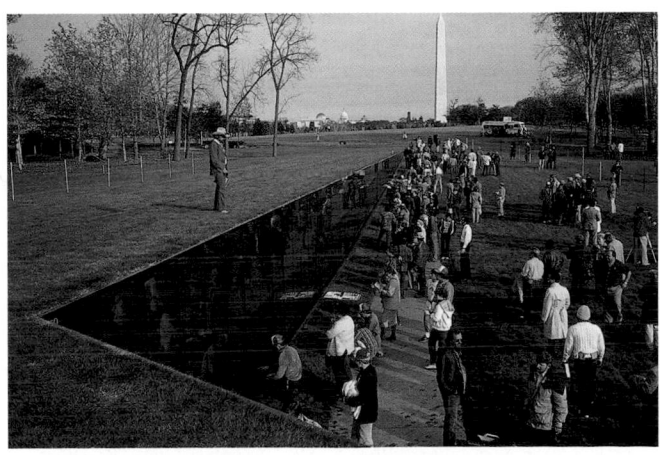

∧ 11.41 **MAYA YING LIN.** Vietnam Veterans Memorial (1982).

RACE, ETHNICITY, GENDER, & SOCIAL CLASS

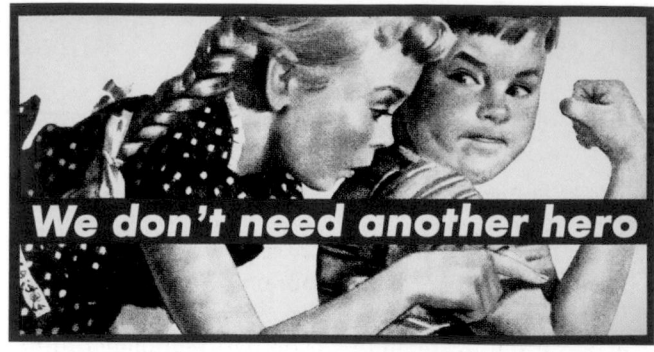

MUCH OF THE HISTORY OF ART reflects the power structures of the privileged and dominant classes—from the Egyptian pharaohs to the royal houses and merchants of Europe. And works of art and architecture play an important role in sustaining the status quo—or subverting it. We see the subjects (or subtexts) of race, ethnicity, gender, and class in works of art from many periods, many places. With themes of identity, "otherness," and inequality we should not be surprised that ideology (one of the purposes of art we discuss in this visual glossary) comes into play—or is confronted.

Contemporary painter Kehinde Wiley brings his unique sensitivities as a gay African American to the reimagining of classical works such as David's painting *Napoleon Crossing the Alps* (Fig. 21.45). As a challenge to Islamic restrictions on gay Muslims, Pakistan-born miniature painter Shahzia Sikander's *Perilous Order* ironically portrays a seventeenth-century Mughal emperor known for his anti-gay policies, yet who was probably himself gay (Fig. 22.5). Barbara Kruger's text works combine a subversive turn of familiar phrases with period black-and-white photos that compel us to consider the ideological hold that words and pictures can have on us even if we are not aware of it (Fig. 21.32).

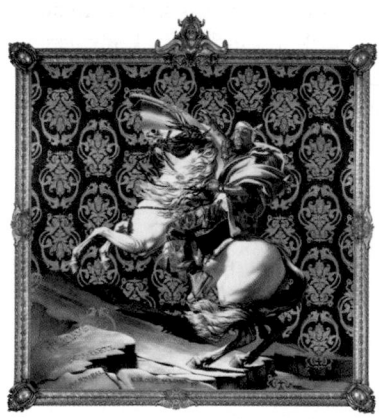

∧ 21.45 **KEHINDE WILEY.** *Napoleon Leading the Army Over the Alps* (2005).

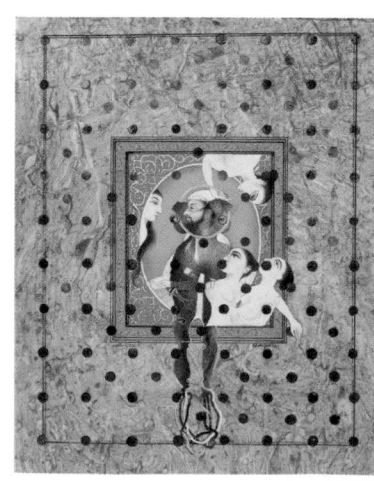

< 22.5 **SHAHZIA SIKANDER.** *Perilous Order* (1994–1997).

Of course, works of art that feature subjects reflecting African life or celebrate women's ways of working or represent the working class, and the like, do not always pose questions about inequality. Miriam Schapiro developed her *femmage* technique combining collage with crochet, embroidery, or quilting—traditional feminine handiwork. Pieter Brueghel, Honoré Daumier, and Edgar Degas showed the labors of the peasants and working classes. In nineteenth-century colonial India, a local ruler, the Maharaja Jaswant Singh, combined his northwestern Indian ethnic heritage with that of a refined English gentleman, adopting the pose and props of a standard colonial portrait with his turbaned head and traditional beard (Fig. 19.44). Dorothea Lange photographed anguished members of the struggling migrant class during the years of the American dust bowl and the Great Depression (Fig. 10.12).

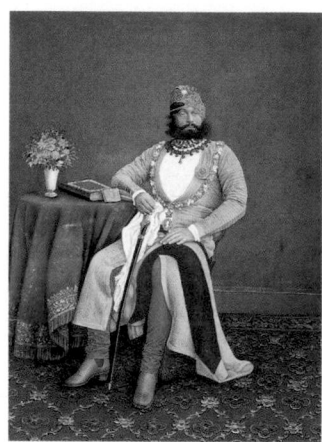

∧ 19.44 *Maharaja Jaswant Singh of Marwar* (c. 1880).

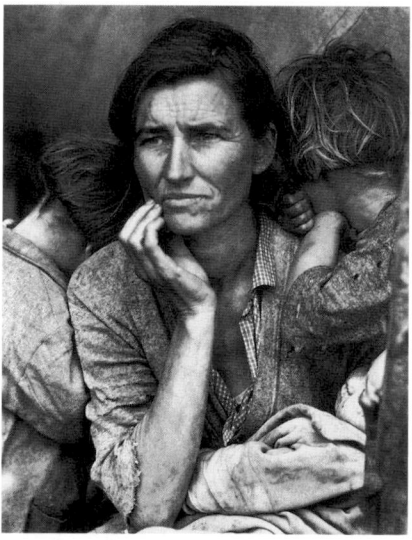

∧ 10.12 **DOROTHEA LANGE.** *Migrant Mother, Nipomo, California* (1936).

RELIGION

NEARLY EVERY CULTURE STUDIED by anthropologists and philosophers has had some form of religion. Aside from providing ways of life, religious strivings have sought to secure, at any point in time, those things that humans have not been able to obtain by their own hands and minds—such as a fertile season for crops, rain, healthy livestock, a solid community, even personal immortality. Religions, in other words, have allowed adherents to transcend the bounds of everyday experience and given life value and meaning. Religions suggest that spiritual work is being done between worshipers and a higher plane of existence to grant peace to the individual and to cement family and communal ties.

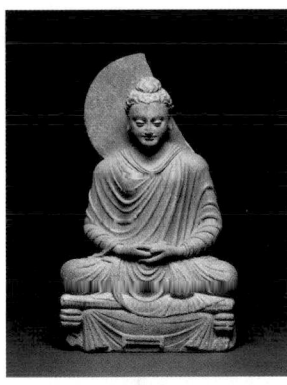

▲ 16.30 Shiva, a main Hindu deity, in the form of Nataraja, the King of Dance (c. 1100).

Animism—or the belief that plants, animals, and inanimate objects possess souls—has thrived among native peoples throughout the planet. Hinduism in the East and Judaism in the West are among the oldest religions. By their standards, Buddhism, Christianity, and Islam are newcomers. The Hindus created stone temples with erotic sculptures, believed to reference the activities of the gods, and fashioned images of the gods themselves (Fig. 16.30). Buddhists sculpted many thousands of images of the Buddha (Fig. 15.39), whereas most Muslims believe that it is improper to portray the face of Muhammed (the Prophet) or to attempt to depict Allah (God). But Islamic mosques, such as the Dome of the Rock in Jerusalem (Fig. 16.21), have amply displayed the glory of the religion. Christians have painted and sculpted religious figures such as Mary and Jesus repeatedly (Fig. 17.7) and erected magnificent cathedrals as places of worship. A well-known image from the Sistine Chapel of the Vatican (Fig. 17.20) portrays the creation of Adam, the origin of humankind on earth, a creation myth believed by the faithful in the three Abrahamic religions, Judaism, Christianity, and Islam. Meanwhile, native peoples have portrayed their own gods, such as Coatlicue, the Aztec "Mother of Gods" (Fig. 17.40)—symbol of creation and destruction worshiped in what is present-day Mexico. She bears a necklace of severed skulls and other body parts, and her head is made of snakes—all trumpeting the fierceness of the Aztec religion and its myths.

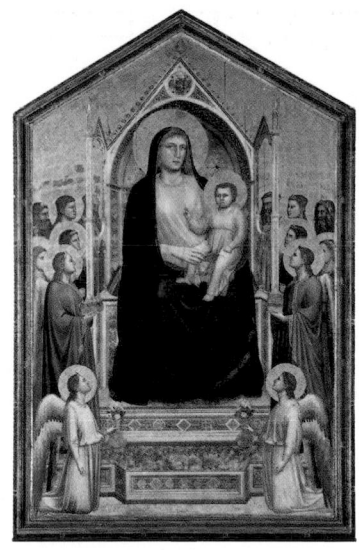

▲ 17.7 GIOTTO. Madonna Enthroned (c. 1310).

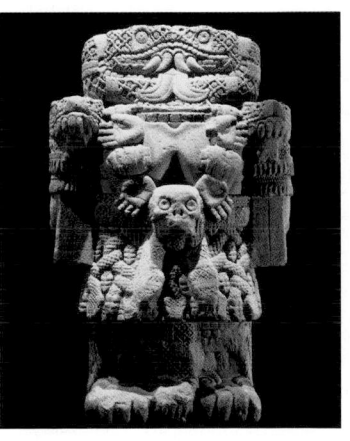

▲ 15.39 Seated Buddha (1st–3rd century CE).

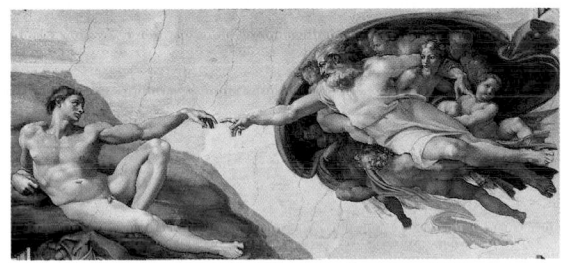

▲ 17.20 MICHELANGELO. The Creation of Adam (1508–1512).

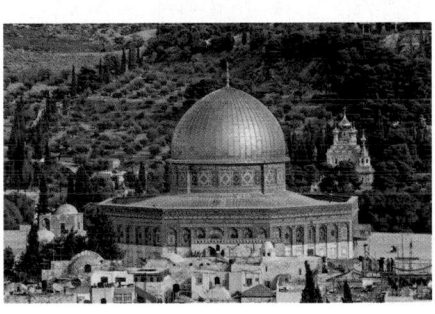

< 16.21 Dome of the Rock, Jerusalem.

< 17.40 Coatlicue, from Tenochtitlán, Mexico City (Aztec, c. 1487–1520).

SEXUALITY & THE BODY

SEXUALITY AND THE HUMAN FORM have always been favorite subjects of artists; however, their purposes and approaches in depicting sexuality and the body have varied. Some artists have distorted the human form to "make a statement." Other artists have sought to be as realistic as possible. Still other artists have afforded something akin to a sculptural nip and tuck here and there to idealize the body, as the Greek sculptor Polykleitos did with his *Spear-Bearer* (Fig. 15.10A) and as Titian did with his voluptuously elongated *Venus of Urbino* (Fig. 17.25).

The so-called Venus of Willendorf (Fig.14.2) is named after the Austrian town in which she was discovered, but she is 25,000–30,000 years old. Her huge, pendulous breasts and her exposed genitalia

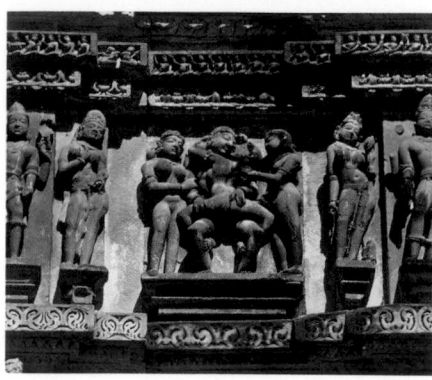

< 16.32 Mithuna reliefs, detail of the north side of the Vishvanatha Temple, Khajuraho, India (c. 1000).

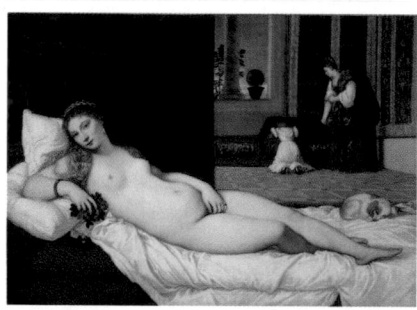

∧ 17.25 **TITIAN**, *Venus of Urbino* (1538).

∧ 15.10A **POLYKLEITOS**, *Doryphoros (Spear-Bearer)* (c. 450–440 bce)

suggest that she has much to do with fertility; perhaps she was carved to earn the favor of deities that might have been thought to aid in human fertility.

The *Winged Victory* (shown here) reveals that some 2,200 years ago the Greeks had a standard for female beauty that is very much like our own. *Winged Victory* may have been carved to celebrate a naval victory, but her "wet look" drapery suggests that the statue was also intended to arrest the gaze of the male viewer.

The relief sculptures that adorn the lower part of the (Hindu) Vishvanatha Temple (Fig. 16.32) show gods or idealized human figures engaged in erotic activity. Hinduism, which is somewhat puritanical today, clearly promoted eroticism about a thousand years ago.

Fragonard's *Happy Accidents of the Swing* suggests sexuality in the context of a garden of delights, occupied by the leisure class (Fig. 18.20). The woman's gentleman friend, or boyfriend, enjoys the view afforded by the woman's billowing undergarments. She is all decked out in pink, the color of cheeks flushing with blood, the color of youth and vitality.

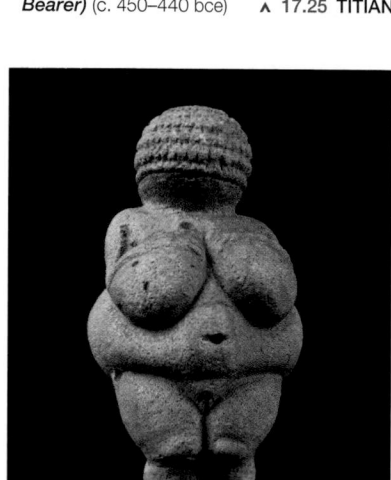

∧ 14.2 **Venus of Willendorf** (c. 28,000–25,000 BCE).

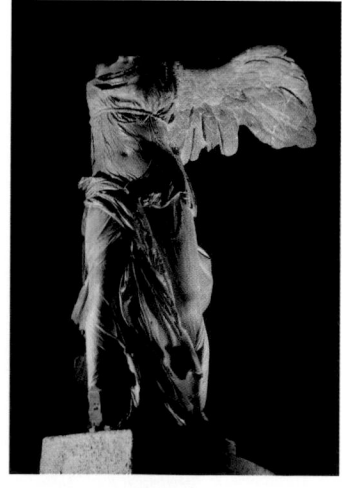

∧ *Winged Victory (Nike of Samothrace)* (c. 190 BCE).

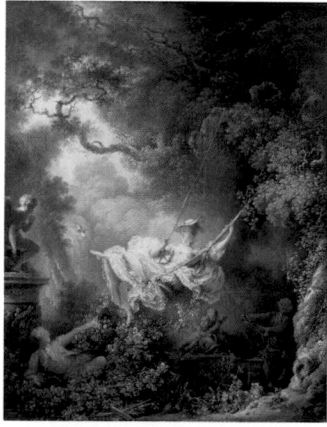

∧ 18.20 **JEAN-HONORÉ FRAGONARD.** *Happy Accidents of the Swing* (1767).

SOCIAL CONSCIOUSNESS & PROTEST

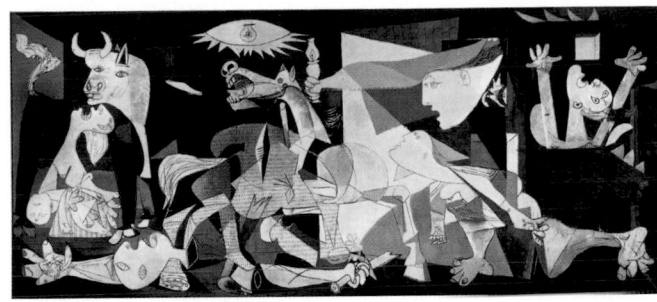

∧ 20.11 **PABLO PICASSO,** *Guernica* (1937).

IN THE MODERN ERA, particularly, it is not unusual to see artists who found the need to take on the bitter struggles against injustices of their times, using their art—and their reputations—to enlighten and persuade others to join their cause.

The Spanish painter Francisco Goya satirized the political foibles of his day and condemned the horrors of war (one of his plates from *The Disasters of War* is shown here). Pablo Picasso drew focus to the German atrocity of bombing a Spanish town in his *Guernica* (Fig. 20.11). Eugene Delacroix painted *Liberty Leading the People* to commemorate the July Revolution of 1830 (shown here); in it, a mixture of people of all classes are united in rising up against injustice—from a bourgeois in a top hat to a young, working-class boy brandishing pistols.

There are many examples of such work in this book. We see the purpose and the power of these images, and we recognize the sense of responsibility the artist must possess with regard to his or her role in society.

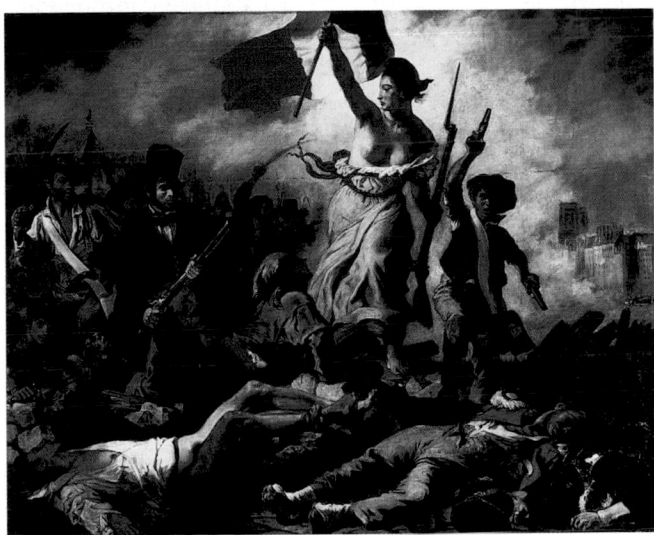

∧ **EUGÈNE DELACROIX.** *Liberty Leading the People* (1830).

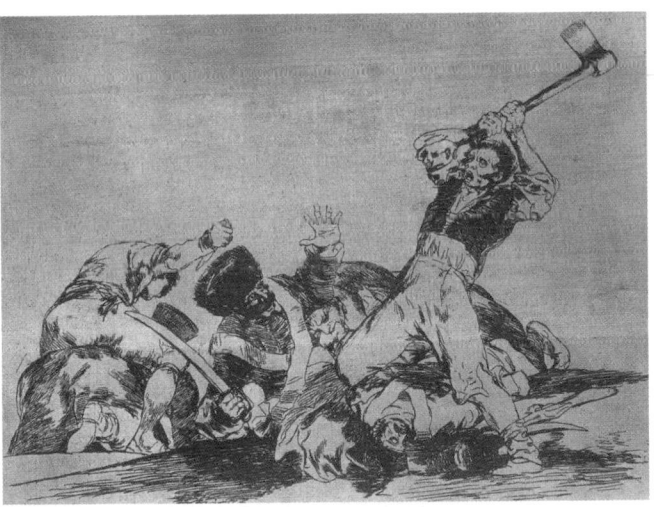

∧ FRANCISCO GOYA. The same (Lo mismo), plate 3 from *The Disasters of War* (1810–1814, pub. 1863 [etching]).

THE GROTESQUE

BEAUTY IS OFTEN THE DEFAULT association when we think of art, and yet, throughout the history of art, artists have employed the grotesque to depict visions of real or imagined horrors. The word *grotesque* has an interesting origin. During the Renaissance, lavishly painted frescoes from the emperor Nero's magnificent residence were discovered in Rome. Raphael himself was reputed to have lowered himself underground by ropes in order to view the spectacular works. Motifs—including masks and satyrs—inspired by this discovery were mimicked in Renaissance painting and referred to as "grotesques," after the word *grotto*, meaning "cave."

Grotesque imagery can inspire fear and terror and can be seen in the depictions of Satan and his companions in depictions of the Last Judgment on the portals of Romanesque cathedrals; in the sadistic, depraved scenes of hell in the paintings of Hieronymus Bosch; or in the ghastly demons in a painted panel of Grünewald's *The Isenheim Altarpiece* (Fig. 17.4).

For modern artists in the early twentieth century, the grotesque imagery of the imagination found its real-life counterpart in the graphic realities of suffering and death during the First World War (Fig. 20.5). Artists Salvador Dalí (Fig. 10.37) and Francis Bacon (Fig. 21.12), though coming from different countries and different artistic premises, effectively used grotesque imagery to draw focus to personal and collective anxieties of the modern era.

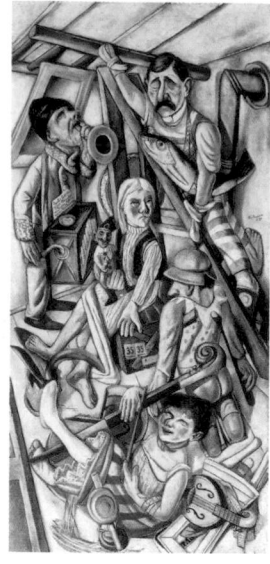

⌃ 20.5 MAX BECKMANN. *The Dream* (1921).

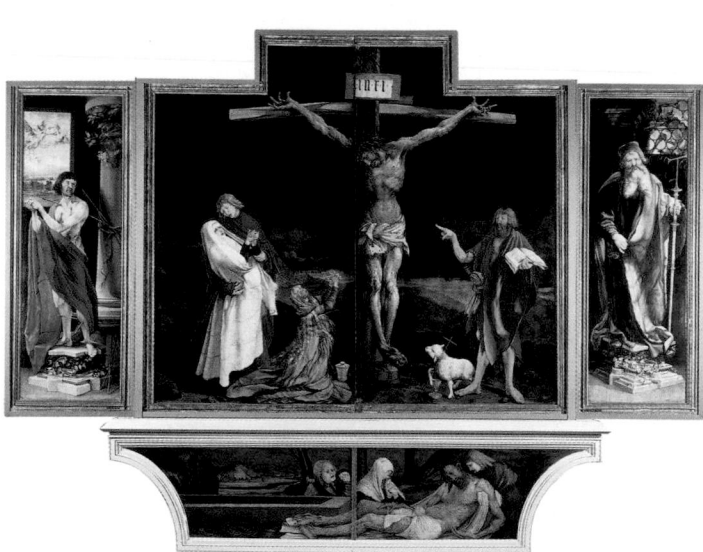

⌃ 17.4 MATTHIAS GRÜNEWALD. *The Crucifixion,* center panel of *The Isenheim Altarpiece,* exterior (completed 1515).

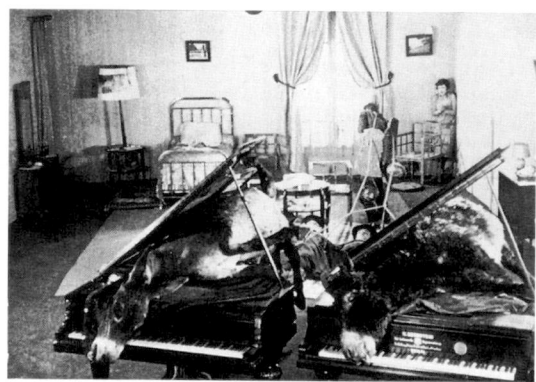

⌃ 10.37 SALVADOR DALÍ AND LUIS BUÑUEL. *Film still from Un Chien Andalou* (1928).

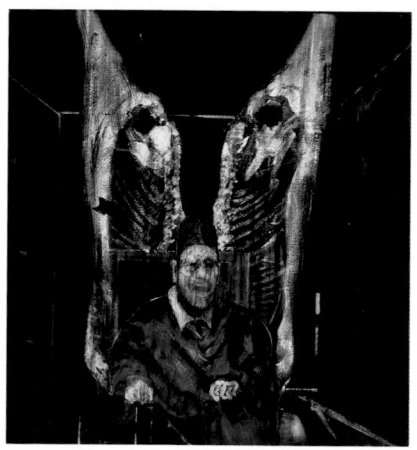

⌃ 21.12 FRANCIS BACON. *Figure with Meat* (1954).

WAR & VIOLENCE

HUMANS ARE CAPABLE OF LOVE, generosity, and altruism. Humans are also capable of the horrors of warfare, murder, and destruction—individual destruction and destruction on a grand scale, as in the attempted genocide of a whole people, to wit, the Turkish genocide of Armenians during World War I and Hitler's genocide of Jews during World War II.

Many artists have glorified warfare, as in Yoskikune's woodblock triptych showing the inexorable advance of Japanese troops during the Russo-Japanese War of 1904–1905 (Fig. 20.34). Wu Hufan paid homage to China's

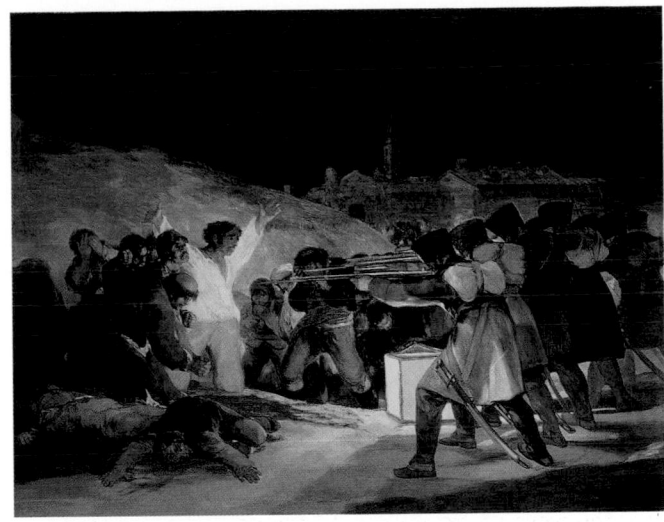

∧ 19.6 FRANCISCO GOYA. *The Third of May, 1808* (1814–1815).

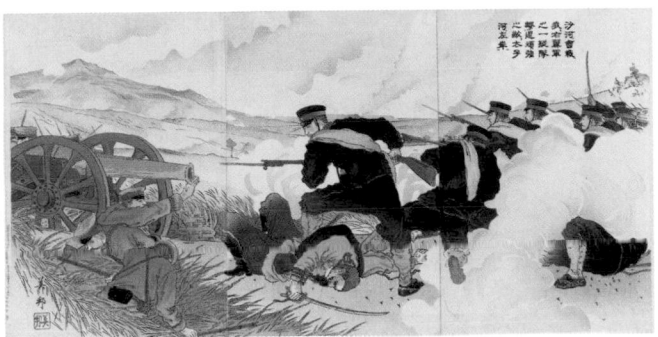

∧ 20.34 HIROSE YOSHIKUNE. "In the Battle of the Sha River, a Company of Our Forces Drives a Strong Enemy Force to the Left Bank of the Taizi River" (1904).

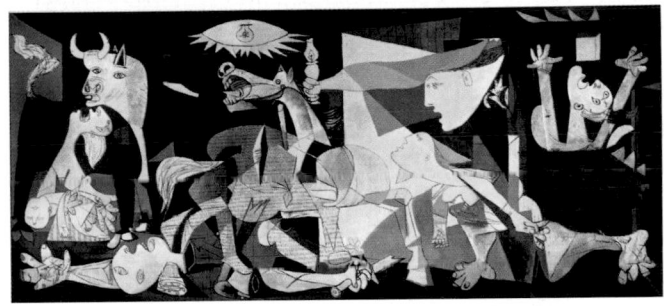

∧ 20.11 PABLO PICASSO. *Guernica* (1937).

"glorious" 1964 entry into the nuclear "club" with a scroll painting that seems untouched by the possibilities of the vast destruction that is wrought by nuclear weapons (Fig. 21.62). Yet many other artists have chosen to emphasize the black underside of the cruelty of war, as in Goya's *Third of May, 1808*, which depicts Napoleon's massacre of Spanish civilians in Madrid, after the city fell to the French (Fig. 19.6). A man raises his arms in a futile gesture of surrender; the bayonets of the faceless enemy foretell his fate. A painting by Picasso shows another massacre of Spanish civilians more than a hundred years later (Fig. 20.11). As a prelude to World War II, the Germans bombed civilians in a town named *Guernica*. We

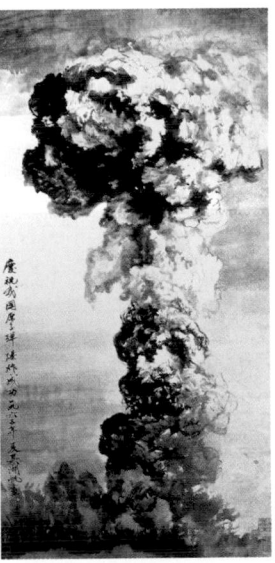

∧ 21.62 WU HUFAN. *Celebrate the Success of Our Glorious Atomic Bomb Explosion!* (1965).

witness a mother crying while she holds her dead child. A frightened horse rears above a dismembered body. Audrey Flack's *World War II (Vanitas)* (Fig. 21.23) incorporates Margaret Bourke-White's photo *The Living Dead of Buchenwald April 1945,* a barbaric outcome of Hitler's war against Jews. Flack combines the photo with everyday objects, further encouraging the viewer to contemplate warfare and death.

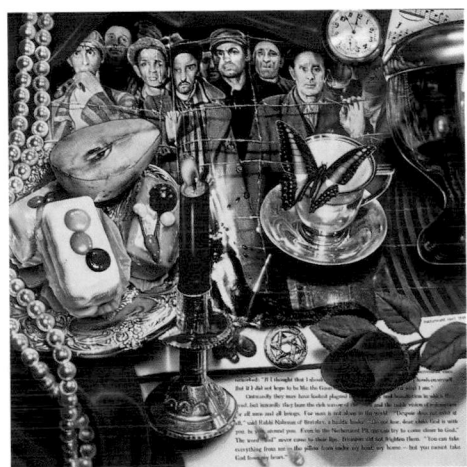

∧ 21.23 AUDREY FLACK. *World War II (Vanitas)* (1976–1977).

571

BEAUTY

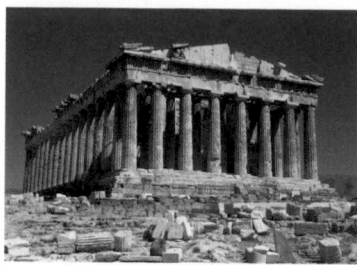

▲ 15.9 ICTINOS AND CALLICRATES.
The Parthenon on the Acropolis, Athens
(448–432 BCE).

IN THE WESTERN TRADITION, the connections among art, beauty, nature, and imitation can be traced to the Greek philosopher, Plato. The Greeks of the Golden Age sought not only to imitate nature by keenly observing it, but, in the pursuit of beauty, they aimed to perfect nature in art. Obsessed with their concept of beauty, they created mathematical formulas for rendering the body to achieve a majesty and perfection beyond that found in nature. The standard of beauty for the Greeks was linked to perfect proportions—whether in architecture, as in the Parthenon (Fig. 15.9) or figurative sculpture, as in Polykleitos's *Spear-Bearer* (Fig. 15.10A).

The idealism of the Greeks—and their notions of beauty—became

< 17.17 LEONARDO DA VINCI. *Mona Lisa* (c. 1503–1505).

the model for artists of the Italian Renaissance, some of whom embraced Platonic ideas and aesthetics. Leonardo da Vinci's *Mona Lisa*—perhaps the most famous painting in the history of Western art—has enchanted generations of viewers with what has been described as an "eternal beauty" (Fig. 17.17). But that beauty is defined in relation to Western notions of the beautiful in general and those of sixteenth-century Italy in particular (see the *Venus of Urbino* (Fig. 17.25)). A quick look at the features in Dutch portraits of the same time period even reveal a quite different standard (Fig. 18.14). And in societies in the wider world, yet other aesthetics prevail; other concepts of beauty are cherished and perpetuated (Fig. 18.29).

< 15.10A POLYKLEITOS. *Doryphoros (Spear-Bearer)* (c. 450–440 BCE).

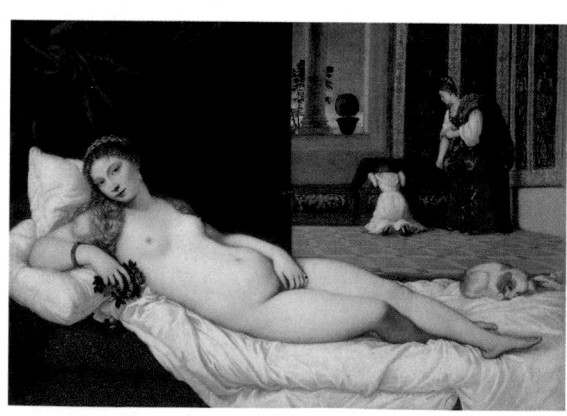

▲ 17.25 TITIAN. *Venus of Urbino* (1538).

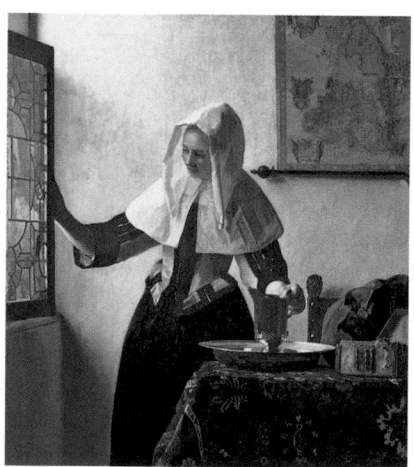

▲ 18.14 JAN VERMEER. *Young Woman with a Water Jug* (c. 1665).

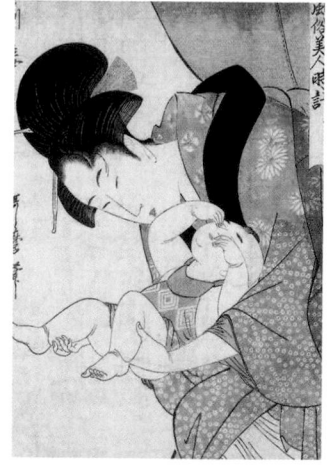

▲ 18.29 KITAGAWA UTAMARO. *Midnight: The Hours of the Rat; Mother and Sleepy Child* (Edo period, 1615–1868).

GLORIFICATION & IMMORTALITY

IN THE FACE OF CERTAIN DEATH, artists (and other people) can defy mortality by creating (or commissioning) works of art that will keep their memory and their accomplishments in the public's consciousness long after they pass. Human beings are the only species conscious of death, and for millennia they have used art to overleap the limits of this life.

The lines between life and death, between place and time, are temporarily dissolved in the renowned installation, *The Dinner Party,* by Judy Chicago (Fig. 21.34). The idea for this mixed-media work, which was constructed to honor and immortalize history's notable women, revolves around a fantastic dinner party, where the guests of honor meet before place settings designed to reflect their personas and achievements.

The desire to immortalize often goes hand-in-hand with the desire to glorify. Some of art history's wealthiest patrons—from the Caesars of ancient Rome and the popes of the Vatican to emperors from around the world—have commissioned artists to create works that glorify their reigns and accomplishments. The Roman emperor Trajan's tomb, 128 feet high, is covered with a continuous spiral relief that recounts his victories in

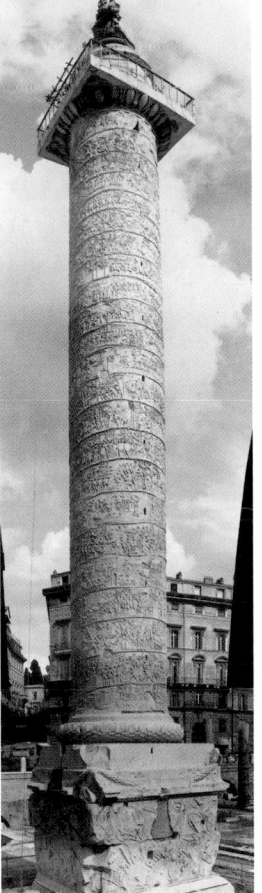

< Column of Trajan, Forum of Trajan (dedicated 112 CE).

military campaigns in great detail (shown here). Centuries later, the French would adapt this design for a column erected to glorify the victories of the emperor, Napoleon Bonaparte.

In China during the early third century BCE, the first emperor of the Qin Dynasty prepared a tomb for himself that was filled not only with treasure, but also with facsimiles of more than 6,000 soldiers and horses, along with bronze chariots (Fig. 15.41). The site was probably intended to recreate the emperor's lavish palace. The sheer manpower that was necessary to create the imperial funerary monument—literally thousands of workers and artists—is a testament to the emperor's wealth, power, and ambition.

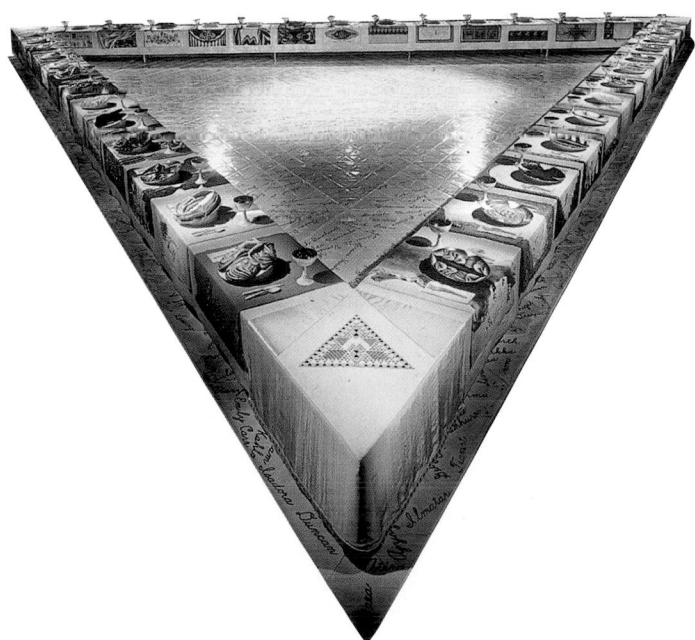

▲ 21.34 **JUDY CHICAGO.** *The Dinner Party* (1974–1979).

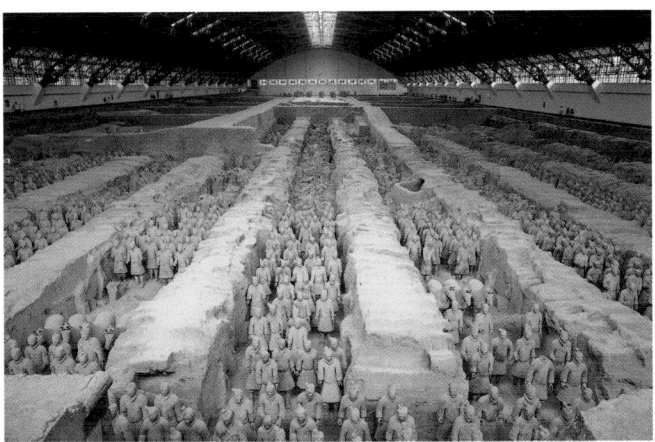

▲ 15.41 **Army of Shi Huangdi (First Emperor) in pits next to his burial mound** (c. 210 BCE , Qin Dynasty).

573

HISTORY & MEMORY

IN WESTERN CULTURE, going back at least to the fifteen century, as noted by Renaissance architect and philosopher Leon Battista Alberti, "history" was considered the noblest subject for the painter. The word history, of course, can be understood as "his (or her) story" rather than a fully objective accounting of the past. History in visual form is no more free of bias than are written narratives. Visual representations of history are best seen as *versions* of historical events that, at the time they were created, were deemed to have great import. The goal of the artist was not simply to record but also to keep the memory of these events in the consciousness of future generations.

Art is a powerful tool for preserving memory—of triumphs and tragedies, of struggle and sacrifice both individual and collective. There is an expression in Latin, "*ars longa, vita brevis,*" which means that art outlasts the brevity of life The endurance of art over time provides comfort by informing us that, through art, events and human experiences will not be forgotten.

For the artist, the responsibility for institutionalizing memory is a weighty one. Memorials require specificity to be meaningful to the survivors of those they commemorate yet, to communicate the impact of loss to even those directly unaffected, must have universality; they must be accessible enough to serve as vehicles for empathy.

The Taj Mahal was commissioned in 1632 by a Mughal emperor to house the tomb of his wife (Fig. 17.31). Flack's *World War II (Vanitas)* (Fig. 21.23), like other works of its kind, is intended to encourage the viewer to meditate on death. Eisenman's Holocaust Memorial (Fig. 11.39) seems to participate in the Jewish custom of placing a stone upon a grave as evidence that the grave has been visited. Florian and Lin's war memorials (Figs. 11.40 and 11.41) show a very different sensibility concerning the meaning of war.

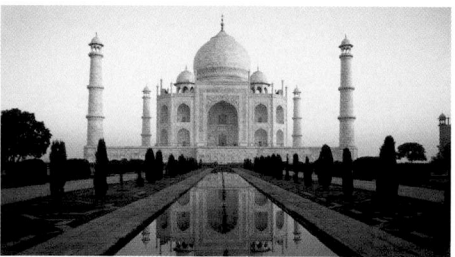

< 17.31 Taj Mahal and gardens (looking north), Agra, India (1632–1647).

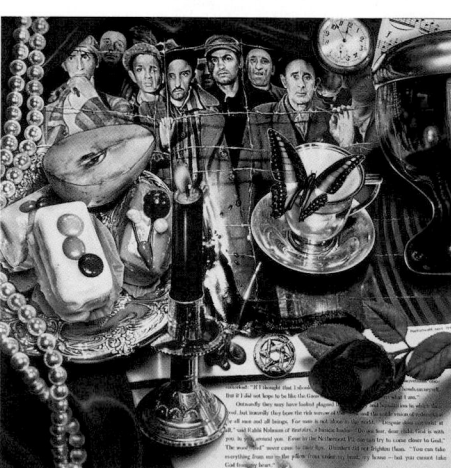

< 21.23 AUDREY FLACK. *World War II (Vanitas)* (1976–1977).

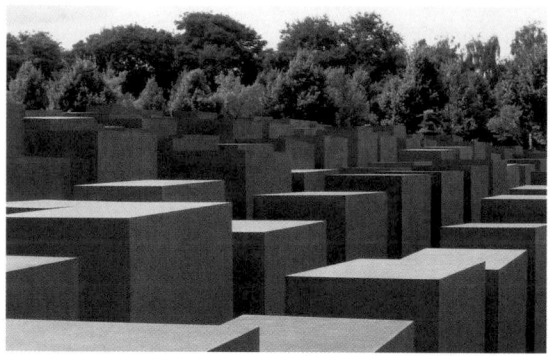

⌃ 11.39 PETER EISENMAN. Holocaust Memorial (2004).

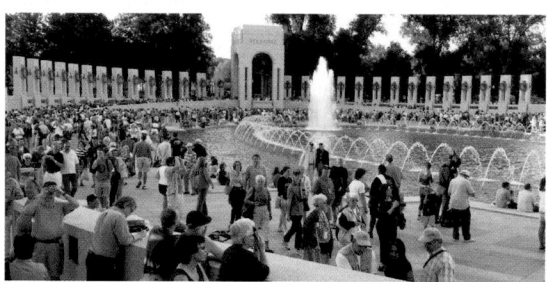

⌃ 11.40 FRIEDRICH ST. FLORIAN. National World War II Memorial (2004).

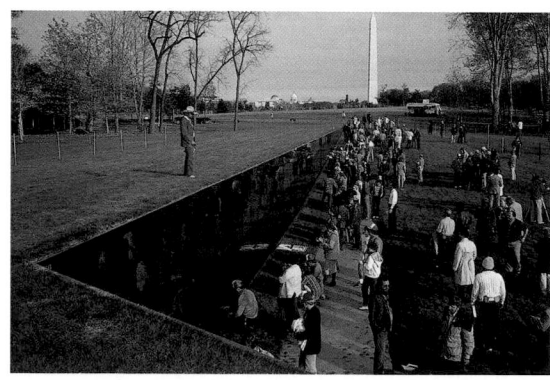

⌃ 11.41 MAYA YING LIN. Vietnam Veterans Memorial (1982).

IDEOLOGY

WORKS OF ART HAVE BEEN USED to reinforce ideologies ranging from the political to the cultural and the sociological. Defined as an organized collection of ideas, ideologies articulate the way societies look at things. These ideas spring from commonly held beliefs or are imposed on members of society by ruling or dominant classes. The degree to which an ideology is perpetuated depends on the degree to which members of a society subscribe to it. The political platforms of Democrats and Republicans in the U.S. two-party system can be characterized as ideological. Communism, which is constructed on the premise of collective ownership of property, is another example of a political ideology. The twentieth-century Chinese Communist propaganda poster shown here (Fig. 21.61) touts the equality of women and men as workers. Cultural and social ideologies such as gender ideology—concerned with societal attitudes toward men and women—and racism can be powerful, deep seeded, and unshakable. Religions by definition are ideologies with tenets of faith to which believers are required to adhere. The Hagia Sophia (Fig. 16.4) was home to two conflicting ideologies: Christianity and then, with minarets added, Islam.

When it comes to ideology and art, images can speak louder than words. Think of representations of Adam and Eve (Fig. 17.5). Every time that you see Eve

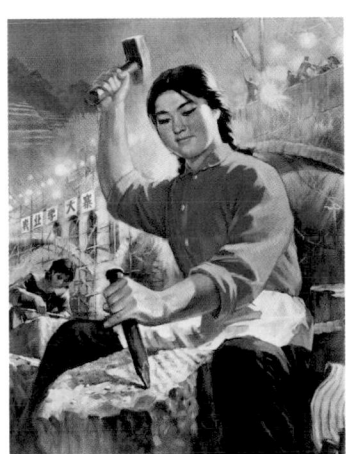

▲ 21.61 "Women hold up half of heaven, and, cutting through mountains and rivers, change to a new attitude" (1970).

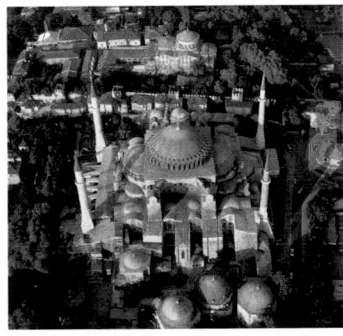

▲ 16.4 ANTHEMIUS OF TRALLES AND ISIDORUS OF MILETUS. Hagia Sophia, Constantinople (modern-day Istanbul), Turkey (532–537).

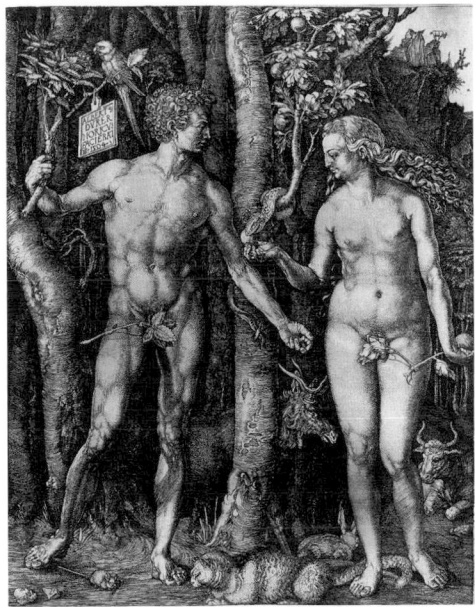

▲ 17.5 ALBRECHT DÜRER. *Adam and Eve* (1504).

tempting Adam with an apple, you are witnessing the representation of an ideology in art, in this case, the view that Eve (and, by extension, women in general) was responsible for humankind's fall from grace and loss of paradise. For hundreds of years, Christianity perpetuated a negative view of women based on this ideological position. Artemisia Gentileschi, rebelling against the stereotype of women as the "weaker" sex, showed a muscular, determined Judith decapitating Holofernes in the biblical tale (Fig. 18.7).

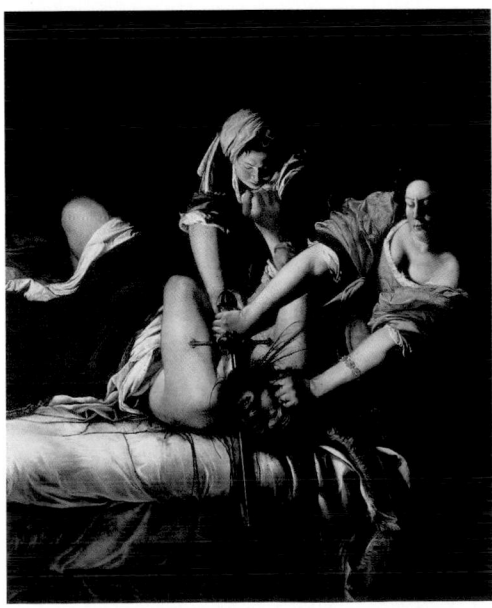

▲ 18.7 ARTEMISIA GENTILESCHI. *Judith Decapitating Holofernes* (c. 1620).

PLEASURE

FROM FRESCOS AND MOSAICS in the homes of wealthy Roman patricians and tapestries that adorned and insulated the cold stone walls of medieval castles, to elaborate fountains that provided focal points for manicured, palatial gardens, whatever other functions they may serve, many works of art are intended for decorative purposes, to create pleasurable and visually interesting environments. The Italian villa of Livia was decorated with lavish gardenscapes (Fig. 15.19A). Pope Julius II com-

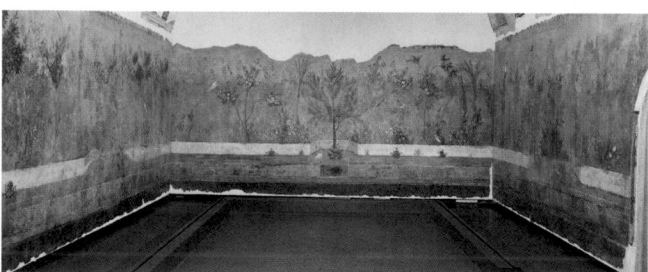

▲ 15.19A Gardenscape, Villa of Livia, Primaporta, Italy (c. 30–20 BCE).

missioned Raphael to decorate an important room in the Vatican papal apartments in *The School of Athens* (Fig. 17.18A). The Medici family of Renaissance Italy commis-

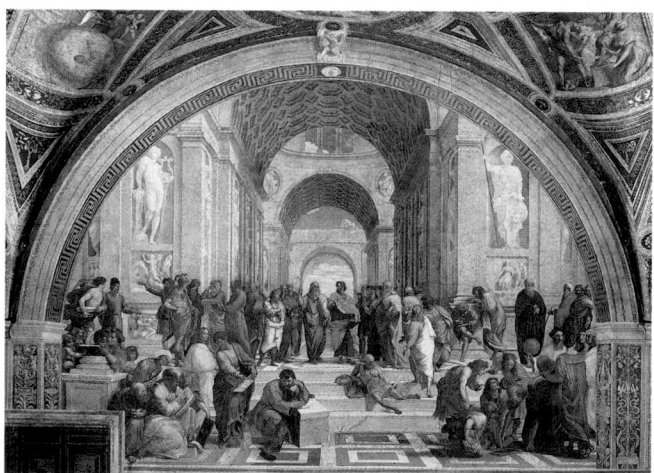

▲ 17.18A RAPHAEL. *The School of Athens* (1510–1511).

sioned not one, but two, sculptures of David to decorate the courtyard of their Florence palazzo (Fig. 17.23); André Le Nôtre designed the grounds of the palace of Versailles for Louis XIV (Fig. 18.18).

Consider, in our day and time, Joyce Kozloff's *Galla Placidia in Philadelphia* (shown here), a mosaic for the Penn Center Suburban Station in Philadelphia. A public work of art commissioned to "beautify" an otherwise humdrum city-scene, it is a riff on the exquisite interior of the fifth-century chapel and

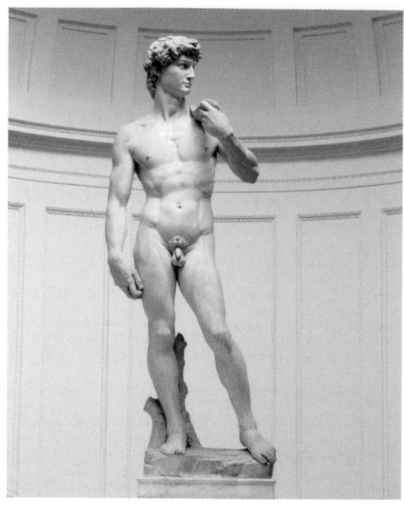

▲ 17.23 MICHELANGELO. *David* (1501–1504).

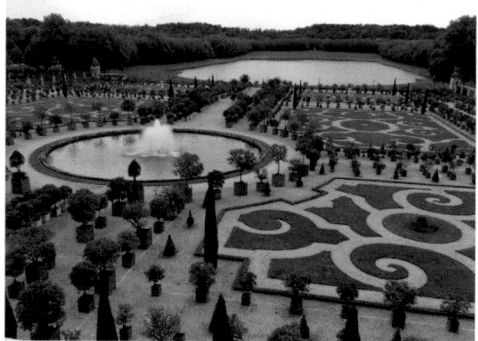

▲ 18.18 ANDRÉ LE NÔTRE, LOUIS LE VAU, and JULES HARDOUIN-MANSART. Gardens of the Palace of Versailles.

burial place of a Byzantine empress in Ravenna, Italy. In fact, underground metro systems throughout the world have become sites for decoration intended to create pleasurable experiences for commuters.

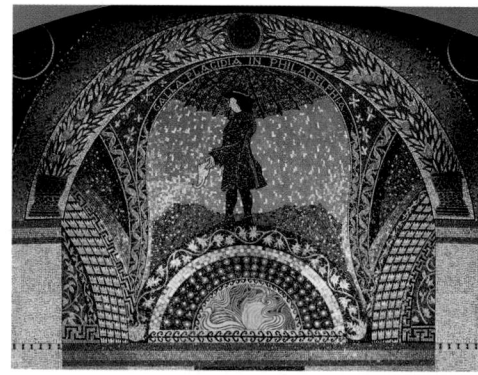

▲ JOYCE KOZLOFF. *Galla Placidia in Philadelphia* (1985).

SELF-EXPRESSION

CREATING WORKS OF ART that are accepted by an audience can lead to an artist's social acceptance and recognition. But sometimes art is created only for the purpose of self-expression—to meet the personal needs of the artist and nothing beyond—with no thought to sale, exhibition, review, or recognition. Such is the story of so-called *outsider art*, a catchall category that has been used to describe works by untrained artists; self-taught artists who have been incarcerated for committing crimes and who use the circumstances of their isolation as a motive for creating; and people who are psychologically compromised and sometimes institutionalized. Works of art by these individuals and others like them are often *not* intended to be seen. Thus, in the purest sense, they come into existence to meet some essential emotional or psychological need of the artist and the artist alone.

Self-portraits are an interesting body of work to consider in this regard. Vincent van Gogh's psychological narrative resides in the brushwork of his alternately joyous and painful self-portraits (Fig. 19.26). Frida Kahlo's traumatic life and deep connection to her Mexican ancestry are inscribed in countless renderings of her unique features and graphic paintings brimming with symbolic images (Fig. 20.42). Those who knew her conjecture that she painted self-portraits "to survive, to endure, and to conquer death." Perhaps it is the process of gazing for long hours into a mirror, into his or her own eyes, that leads to self-insight and ultimately captures the essence of the artist for the viewer. Self-portraiture is a tool with which artists may attempt to unlock their visions of themselves or come to decipher who they are and how they think and feel.

The portrait of the maharaja (Fig. 19.44), painted during the British hegemony over India, reveals the sitter's self-concept as belonging to two opposing cultures. Chuck Close's self-portrait (Fig. 21.25) is (literally) larger than life and has something of a mocking tone. The record of Ana Mendieta's provocative and haunting earth-body work (Fig. 21.35) is suggestive of the artist's desire to express her personal identity and femininity.

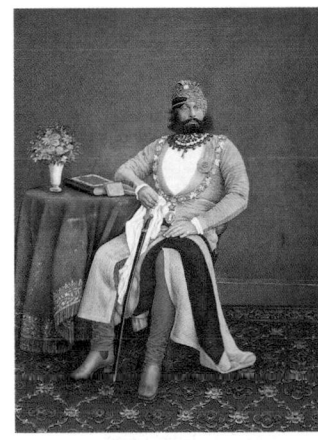

< 19.44 Maharaja Jaswant Singh of Marwar (c. 1880).

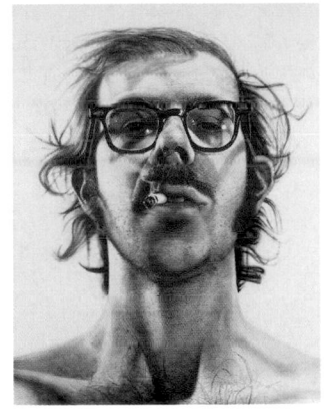

< 21.25 CHUCK CLOSE. *Big Self-Portrait* (1967–1968).

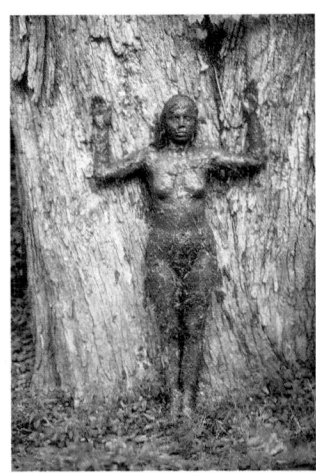

< 21.35 ANA MENDIETA. *Arbol de la Vida, no. 294 (Tree of Life / Silhouette) series* (1977).

^ 19.26 VINCENT VAN GOGH. *Self-Portrait with Bandaged Ear* (1889–1890).

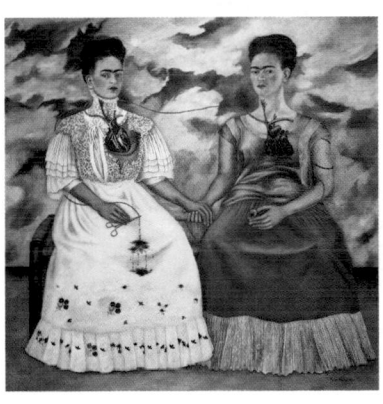

< 20.42 FRIDA KAHLO. *The Two Fridas* (1939).

577

SURVIVAL & WELL-BEING

IN THE FACE OF THREATS posed by the unknown—floods, drought, disease—and in efforts by humans to shape and control their circumstances, images and objects have been perceived to have great power—and still do.

Some of the image-making by human ancestors on cave walls, according to the most recent dating of archaeological finds, dates well into the Paleolithic era, at least 40,000 years (Fig. 14.1). We cannot know for certain why cave paintings such as the one shown here were created; however, it is unlikely that their purposes were merely decorative because most such works have been discovered in the deepest recesses of caves, reachable only with great difficulty. Numerous and conflicting theories have been launched by scholars regarding the purposes of these

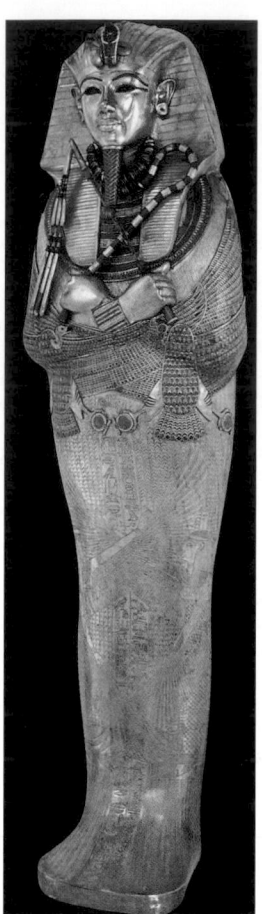

< 14.16 The innermost coffin of the king, from the tomb of Tutankhamen (c. 1323 BCE).

paintings, but most presuppose that they involved magic rituals connected with survival. Similarly, figurines with attributes of the female body associated with fertility and childbearing may have played a role in rituals connected with ensuring the survival of the species and the fertility of the land (Fig. 14.2).

Survival and well-being did not stop necessarily at death's door. Burials in ancient Egypt (Fig. 14.16). The Aegean (Fig. 11.20), and Etruria—only three examples—contained expertly crafted objects of bronze, gold, and terra-cotta that the deceased presumably might find useful in the afterlife.

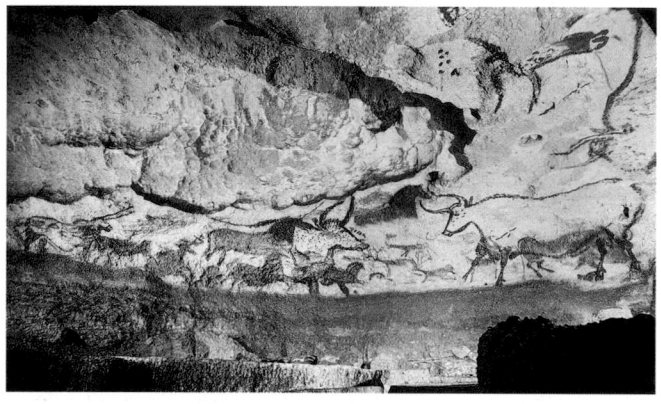

∧ 14.1 Hall of Bulls, Lascaux (Dordogne), France (c. 16,000–14,000 BCE).

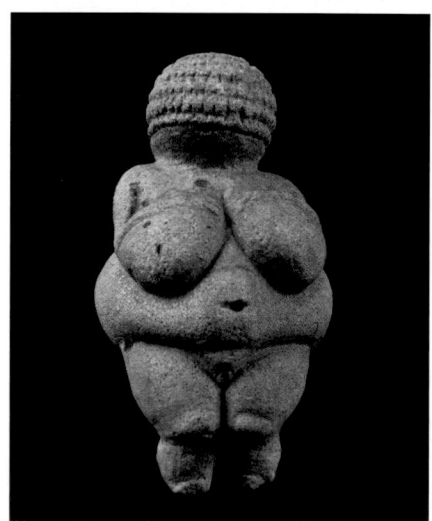

< 14.2 Venus of Willendorf (c. 28,000–25,000 BCE).

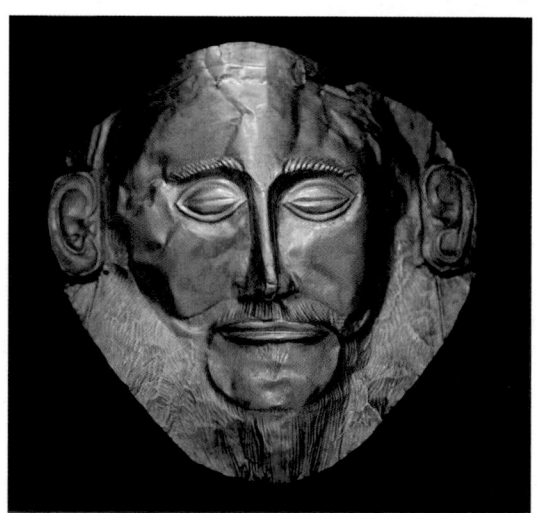

∧ 14.22 *Funerary mask, from Grave Circle A, Mycenae, Greece* (c. 1600–1500 BCE).

GLOSSARY

Note: Figure numbers in blue illustrate the definition.

Abstract art   Works whose shapes are distorted or converted into patterns that may be read by the viewer as interesting in their own right or as representing another vision of a subject. (Fig. 20.20)

Abstract Expressionism   A post-World War II New York City-based art movement that featured two predominant styles—gestural abstraction and color-field (or chromatic) abstraction. The work of Abstract Expressionist artists foregrounded the physical process of artmaking. (Fig. 21.3)

Academic art   A neoclassical, nonexperimental style promoted by the Royal French Academy during the eighteenth and nineteenth centuries. (Fig. 19.9)

Achromatic   Without color.

Action painting   A term that originated in conjunction with Abstract Expressionism that describes a process of painting connected to the artist's physical gesture. Jackson Pollock was described as an action painter; he dripped, flung, and puddled streams of paint onto canvases that were spread on the floor of his studio. (Fig. 21.2)

Actual line   A line that is physically present in a work of art. (Fig. 2.5)

Actual space   The three dimensions (height, width, and depth) in which we live. (Fig. 17.23)

Actual texture   Tactile, physical texture related to the material used to create the work. (Fig. 4.4)

Additive color   Color that is created by mixing colored light. The three primary additive colors are red-orange, blue-violet, and green.

Additive process   In sculpture, adding or assembling materials, as in modeling and constructing. Contrast with *subtractive process*. (Fig. 11.6)

Adobe   Brick that has been dried in the sun rather than fired in a kiln.

Alternate a-b-a-b support system   An architectural support system in which every other nave wall support sends up a supporting rib that crosses the vault as a transverse arch. (Fig. 16.10)

Alternating rhythm   A type of rhythm in which different elements in a work repeat themselves in a predictable order. (Fig. 6.30)

Aluminum   A highly reflective, light, silvery gray metal.

Ambulatory   In a church, a continuation of the side aisles of a *Latin cross plan* into a passageway that extends behind the

choir and apse and allows traffic to flow to the chapels, which are often placed in this area (from *ambulare*, Latin for "to walk").

Amorphous   Without shape; without boundaries. (Fig. 20.26)

Amphitheater   A round or oval open-air theater with an arena surrounded by rising tiers of seats. (Fig. 15.20)

Analogous color scheme   The combination of two or more colors that lie adjacent to one another on the color wheel, tending to create a feeling of harmony. (Fig. 3.21)

Analytic Cubism   The early phase of Cubism (1909–1912) during which objects were dissected or analyzed in a visual information-gathering process and then reconstructed on the canvas. (Fig. 20.9)

Animism   The belief that plants, inanimate objects, and natural events such as rain and wind have souls.

Annunciation   The angel Gabriel's announcement to Mary that she would give birth to Jesus. (Fig. 17.2)

Apocalypse   The ultimate triumph of good over evil foretold in Judeo-Christian writings.

Appropriation   (1) Borrowing elements from the nonart world such as newspapers and wine labels, as by Picasso and Braque. (2) The use of another artist's work as a basis for one's own. (Fig. 22.2)

Apse   A semicircular or polygonal projection of a building with a semicircular dome, especially on the east end of a church. (Fig. 16.1)

Aquarelle   A watercolor technique in which a transparent film of paint is applied to a white, absorbent surface.

Aquatint   An etching technique in which a metal plate is colored with acid-resistant resin and heated, causing the resin to melt. Before printing, areas of the plate are exposed by a needle, and the plate receives an acid bath. Aquatinting can be manipulated to resemble washes. (Fig. 18.30)

Aqueduct   A bridgelike structure that carries a canal or pipe of water across a river or valley (from Latin roots meaning "to carry water"). (Fig. 15.24)

Arbitrary (subjective) color   The use of color that is not normally associated with the subject being depicted.

Arch   A curved or pointed structure consisting of wedge-shaped blocks that span an open space and support the

weight of material above by transferring the load outward and downward over two vertical supports, or piers. (Fig. 15.25)

Archaic period   A period of Greek art dating roughly 660–480 BCE. The term *archaic* means "old" and refers to the art created before the Classical period. (Fig. 15.2)

Architectural-style painting   A style of Roman painting in which walls were painted to create the illusion that doorways and windows open onto a scene such as a landscape or cityscape. (Fig. 15.19B)

Architecture   The art and science of designing aesthetic buildings, bridges, and other structures to help people meet their personal and communal needs. (Fig. 13.18)

Architrave   In architecture, the lower part of an *entablature*, which may consist of one or more horizontal bands. (Fig. 15.4)

Archivolts   In architecture, concentric moldings that repeat the shape of an arch. (Fig. 16.16)

Art Nouveau   A highly ornamental style of the 1890s characterized by floral patterns, rich colors, whiplash curves, and vertical attenuation (French for "new art"). (Fig. 19.38)

Asymmetrical balance   Balance in which the right and left sides of a composition contain different shapes, colors, textures, or other elements and yet are arranged or "weighted" so that the overall impression is one of balance. Contrast with *symmetrical balance*. (Fig. 19.22)

Athena   The Greek goddess of wisdom, skills, and war.

Atmospheric perspective   The creation of the illusion of depth through techniques such as texture gradient, brightness gradient, color saturation, and the use of warm and cool colors; an indistinct or hazy effect produced by distance and the illusion of distance in visual art. Its name derives from recognition that the atmosphere between the viewer and the distant objects (with its water droplets, dust, or pollution) would cause the effect. (Fig. 17.17)

Atrium   A hall or entrance court.

Automatic writing   Writing based on free association, practiced by Dadaists and Surrealists.

Automatist Surrealism   An outgrowth of automatic writing in which the artist attempts to derive the outlines of images from the unconscious through free association. (Fig. 20.27)

Avant-garde   The leaders in new, unconventional movements; the vanguard (from French meaning "advance guard").

Balance   The distribution of the weight, mass, or other elements of a work of art to achieve harmony. (Fig. 6.23)

Balloon framing   In architecture, a wooden skeleton of a building constructed from prefabricated studs and nails. (Fig. 13.8)

Baroque   A seventeenth-century European style characterized by ornamentation, curved lines, irregularity of form, dramatic lighting and color, and exaggerated gestures. (Fig. 18.4)

Barrel vault   A roofed-over space or tunnel constructed as an elongated arch. (Fig. 16.9C)

Basalt   A dark, tough volcanic rock. (Fig. 14.7)

Basketry   See *basket weaving*. (Fig. 12.21)

Basket weaving   The craft of making baskets. Also called *basketry*. (Fig. 12.21)

Bas-relief   Sculpture that projects only slightly from its background (from *bas*, French for "low"). Contrast with *high relief*. (Fig. 14.8)

Batik   The process of making designs in cloth by waxing fabric to prevent dye from coloring certain areas; a cloth or design made in this way.

Bay   In architecture, the area or space spanned by a single unit of vaulting that may be marked off by piers or columns. (Fig. 16.17B)

Binder   A material that binds substances together.

Black-figure painting   A three-stage firing process that gives vases black figures on a reddish ground. In the first, oxidizing phase of firing, oxygen in the kiln turns the vase and slip red. In the second, reducing phase, oxygen is eliminated from the kiln and the vase and slip turn black. In the third, reoxidizing phase, oxygen is reintroduced into the kiln, turning the vase red once more. (Fig. 15.5)

Brightness gradient   The relative degree of intensity in the rendering of nearby and distant objects, used to create an illusion of depth in a two-dimensional work.

Bronze   A yellowish-brown alloy of copper with tin and now and then other elements; used in sculpture for its attractive appearance and resistance to water. (Fig. 15.30)

Buon fresco   True fresco, executed on damp lime plaster. Contrast with *fresco secco*. (Fig. 17.10)

Burin   A pointed cutting tool used by engravers. (Fig. 9.4)

Burnish   To make shiny by rubbing or polishing.

Buttress   To support or prop up construction with a projecting structure, usually built of brick or stone; a massive masonry structure on the exterior wall of a building that presses inward and upward to hold the stone blocks of arches in place. (Fig. 16.14)

Byzantine   A style associated with eastern Europe that arose after 300 CE, the year that Emperor Constantine moved the capital of his empire from Rome to Byzantium and renamed the city Constantinople (present-day Istanbul). The style was concurrent with the Early Christian style in western Europe. (Fig. 16.3)

Calligraphy   Beautiful handwriting; penmanship; ornamental writing with a pen or brush. (Fig. 16.28)

Canon of proportions   A set of rules governing the proportions of the human body as they are to be rendered by artists. (Fig. 15.10A)

Capital   In architecture, the area at the top of the shaft of a column that provides a solid base for the horizontal elements above. Capitals provide decorative transitions between the cylinder of the column and the rectilinear *architrave* above. (Fig. 15.4)

Carolingian   Referring to Charlemagne or his period. Charlemagne was emperor of the Holy Roman Empire from 800 to 814 CE. (Fig. 16.7A)

Carpet page   A page of geometrical ornamentation resembling a carpet, often having repeated animal figures, and placed at the beginnings of the four Gospels in medieval Gospel Books. (Fig. 16.6)

Cartoon   Originally, a preparatory drawing made for a fresco, usually on paper and drawn to scale; a drawing that caricatures or satirizes an event or person of topical interest. (Fig. 7.19)

Carving   In sculpture, the process of cutting away material, such as wood. (Fig. 11.3)

Caste system   A class structure in which one's social position is determined by birth, thereby preventing social mobility.

Casting   The process of creating a form by pouring a liquid material into a mold, allowing it to harden, and then removing the mold. (Fig. 11.8)

Cast iron   A hard alloy of iron containing silicon and carbon that is made by casting.

Catacomb   A vault or gallery in an underground burial place. (Fig. 15.33)

Centering   In architecture, a wooden scaffold used in the construction of an arch.

Central plan   A design for a church or a chapel with a primary central space surrounded by symmetrical areas around each side. Contrast with *longitudinal plan*. (Fig. 16.2)

Ceramics   The art of creating baked clay objects, such as pottery and earthenware. (Fig. 12.3)

Chalk   A form of soft limestone that is easily pulverized and can be used as a drawing implement.

Chiaroscuro   A technique in which subtle gradations of value create the illusion of rounded three-dimensional shapes in space; also termed modeling. From the Italian meaning *light* and *dark*. (Fig. 18.11)

Chromatic   Relating to color or colors.

Clapboard   In architecture, siding composed of thin, narrow boards placed in horizontal, overlapping layers. (Fig. 13.11)

Classical art   Art of the Greek Classical period, spanning roughly 480–400 BCE; also known as Hellenic art (from "Hellas," the Greek name for Greece). (Fig. 15.11)

Clerestory   In a *Latin cross plan*, the area above the *triforium* in the elevation of the nave, which contains windows to provide direct lighting for the vault and nave. (Fig. 16.14)

Coffer   A decorative sunken panel. (Fig. 15.27)

Coiling   A pottery technique in which lengths of rolled clay are wound in a spiral fashion. (Fig. 12.3)

Collage   An assemblage of two-dimensional objects to create an image; works of art in which materials such as paper, cloth, and wood are pasted to a two-dimensional surface, such as a wooden panel or canvas (from *coller*, French for "to paste"). (Fig. 20.10)

Colonnade   A series of columns placed side by side to support a roof or a series of arches. (Fig. 18.2)

Color   The hue of an object, pigment, or light, which is perceived by the eye and produces different sensations in the brain by the manner in which it reflects or emits light.

Color schemes   The use of colors based on knowledge of the ways in which colors interact to produce harmonious or disharmonious compositions. (Fig. 3.19)

Color wheel   The traditional wheel for representing colors of pigments, consisting of twelve colors, including the three primary colors of red, yellow, and blue; the secondary colors of orange, green, and purple; and six tertiary colors. (Fig. 3.10)

Combine painting   A word coined by Pop artist, Robert Rauschenberg, to describe canvases in which found objects were attached to the surface. (Fig. 21.18)

Complementary color scheme The combination of two or more colors that lie across from one another on the color wheel; the combination tends to create feelings of dynamic contrast and disharmony. (Fig. 3.22)

Composite view The combination of different perspectives in a work; also known as *twisted perspective*. (Fig. 5.19)

Composition The organization of the visual elements in a work of art.

Compound pier In Gothic style, a complexly shaped vertical support to which a number of colonnettes (thin half columns) are often attached. (Fig. 16.14)

Compressive strength The degree to which a material can withstand the pressure of being squeezed.

Conceptual Portrayed as a person or object is known or thought (conceptualized) to be; not copied from nature at any given moment. Conceptual figures tend to be stylized rather than realistic.

Conceptual art Also known as idea art, an approach to artmaking that emerged in the 1960s in which the concept of the work takes precedence over the methods and materials used to create it. Conceptual art challenged the traditional view of the artist as a skilled craftsperson or master of a chosen medium. (Fig. 21.31)

Conceptual representation The use of multiple perspectives to depict objects as they are known to be rather than as they are seen from a single vantage point. (Fig. 15.5)

Constructivism A Russian art movement founded in 1913 based on the rejection of conventional sculptural techniques such as carving and casting in favor of assemblages of wood, various metals, and plastics. Space rather than mass were emphasized. (Fig. 20.18)

Conté crayon A wax crayon with a hard texture. (Fig. 7.11)

Content All that is contained in a work of art: the visual elements, subject matter, and underlying meaning or themes.

Contour line A perceived line that marks the edge of a figure as it curves back into space. (Fig. 2.11)

Contrapposto Counterpose; a figure positioned so that the hips and legs turn in a different direction from the shoulders and head. (Fig. 15.13)

Corinthian order The most ornate of the Greek architectural styles, characterized by slender, fluted columns and capitals with an acanthus leaf design. (Fig. 15.20)

Cornice In architecture, a horizontal molding that projects along the top of a wall or a building; the uppermost part of an *entablature*. (Fig. 15.4)

Cosmetic palette A palette for mixing cosmetics, such as eye makeup, with water.

Crayon A small stick of colored wax, chalk, or charcoal.

Crosshatching The creation of shading in a drawing or etching through the use of intersecting sets of parallel lines. (Fig. 9.9)

Cubism A twentieth-century style developed by Picasso and Braque that emphasizes the two-dimensionality of the canvas, characterized by multiple views of an object and the reduction of an image to its essential lines and shapes. (Fig. 20.7)

Cuneiform Wedge-shaped; descriptive of the characters used in ancient Akkadian, Assyrian, Babylonian, and Persian alphabets.

Curvilinear Consisting of a curved line or lines. (Fig. 2.23)

Cyclopean masonry A type of Mycenaean stonework that uses massive limestone boulders, which are fitted together without benefit of mortar. (Fig. 14.21)

Cyclopes Members of a mythical race of one-eyed giants, as the Cyclops Polyphemus in Homer's *Odyssey*.

Dada A post–World War I movement that sought to use art to destroy art, thereby underscoring the paradoxes and absurdities of modern life. (Fig. 20.23)

Deconstructivist architecture A Postmodern approach to the design of buildings that disassembles and reassembles the basic elements of architecture. The focus is on the creation of forms that may appear abstract, disharmonious, and disconnected from the functions of the building. Deconstructivism challenges the view that there is one correct way to approach architecture. (Fig. 21.56)

Der Blaue Reiter (The Blue Rider) A twentieth-century German Expressionist movement that focused on the contrasts between, and combinations of, abstract form and pure color. (Fig. 20.4)

Design The combination of the visual elements of art according to such principles as balance and unity.

De Stijl An early twentieth-century movement that emphasized the use of basic forms, particularly cubes, horizontals, and verticals. (Fig. 20.19)

Diagonal balance The type of balance in which the elements on either side of a diagonally divided pictorial space seem to be about equal in weight, number, or emphasis. (Fig. 6.28)

Diagonal rib In architecture, a *rib* that connects the opposite corners of a groin vault. (Fig. 16.10)

Die Brücke (The Bridge) A short-lived German Expressionist movement characterized by boldly colored landscapes

and cityscapes and by violent portraits. (Fig. 20.3)

Digital photography Photography that stores visual information electronically rather than on film. (Fig. 10.19)

Directional lines Lines that encourage the viewer to visually traverse the area within the boundaries of a work in a certain way.

Direct-metal sculpture Metal sculpture that is assembled by such techniques as welding and riveting rather than *casting*. (Fig. 11.18)

Dome In architecture, a hemispherical structure that is round when viewed from beneath. (Fig. 15.27)

Doric order The earliest and simplest of the Greek architectural styles, consisting of relatively short, squat columns, sometimes unfluted, and a simple, square-shaped capital. The Doric *frieze* is usually divided into *triglyphs* and *metopes*. (Fig. 15.9)

Dot In art, a point that has a measurable size.

Drawing The art of running an implement that leaves a mark over a surface; a work of art created in this manner. (Fig. 7.3)

Dry masonry Brick or stone construction without use of mortar. (Fig. 14.21)

Dry medium Drawing material that does not involve the application of water or other liquids. Contrast with *fluid medium*. (Fig. 7.4)

Drypoint A variation of engraving in which the surface of the matrix is cut with a needle to make rough edges. In printmaking, rough edges make soft rather than crisp lines. (Fig. 9.7)

Dynamism The Futurist view that force or energy is the basic principle that underlies all events, including everything we see. Objects are depicted as if in constant motion, appearing and disappearing before our eyes. (Fig. 20.14)

Earthenware Reddish tan, porous pottery fired at a relatively low temperature (below 2,000°F). (Fig. 12.11)

Eastern Orthodox A form of Christianity dominant in eastern Europe, western Asia, and North Africa.

Emboss To decorate with designs that are raised above a surface.

Embroidery The art of ornamenting fabric with needlework. (Fig. 16.12)

Emphasis The direction of the viewer's eye to a particular area of a composition, thus giving the area visual or conceptual dominance.

Empire period The Roman period from about 27 BCE to 395 CE, when the empire was divided. (Fig. 15.28)

Enamel To apply a hard, glossy coating to a surface; a coating of this type.

Encaustic A method of painting in which the colors in a wax medium are burned into a surface with hot irons. (Fig. 8.2)

Engraving Cutting; in printmaking, an *intaglio* process in which plates of copper, zinc, or steel are cut with a burin and the ink image is pressed onto paper. (Fig. 9.6)

Entablature In architecture, a horizontal structure supported by columns, which, in turn, supports any other element, such as a pediment, that is placed above; from top to bottom, the entablature consists of a *cornice*, a *frieze*, and an *architrave*. (Fig. 15.4)

Entasis In architecture, a slight convex curvature of a column used to provide the illusion of continuity of thickness as the column rises. (Fig. 15.9)

Ephemeral art Works that have a temporary immediacy or are built with the recognition that they will disintegrate. (Fig. 11.32)

Ergonomics The study of the factors that contribute to efficiency in the work environment.

Etching In printmaking, an *intaglio* process in which the matrix is first covered with an acid-resistant ground. The ground is removed from certain areas with a needle, and the matrix is dipped in acid, which eats away at the areas exposed by the needle. These areas become grooves that are inked and printed. (Fig. 9.8)

Expressionism A modern school of art in which an emotional impact is achieved through agitated brushwork, intense coloration, and violent, hallucinatory imagery. (Fig. 20.3)

Extrude To force metal through a die or small holes to give it shape.

Fantastic art The representation of fanciful images, sometimes joyful and whimsical, sometimes horrific and grotesque. (Fig. 20.21)

Fauvism An early-twentieth-century style of art characterized by the juxtaposition of areas of bright colors that are often unrelated to the objects they represent, and by distorted linear perspective (from French for "wild beast"). (Fig. 20.1)

Fenestration The arrangement of windows and doors in a structure, often used to create balance and rhythm as well as light, air, and access. (Fig. 16.15)

Ferroconcrete See *reinforced concrete*. (Fig. 21.56)

Fertile Crescent The arable land lying between the Tigris and Euphrates Rivers in ancient Mesopotamia.

Fertile Ribbon The arable land lying along the Nile River in Egypt.

Fiber A slender, threadlike structure or material that can be woven. (Fig. 12.18)

Fiberglass Fine spun-glass filaments that can be woven into textiles. (Fig. 21.24)

Figurative art Art that represents the likeness of human and other figures. (Fig. 15.28)

Figure A shape in two-dimensional art.

Figure–ground reversal The shifting of viewer perceptions such that what at one moment appears to be the figure in a composition becomes the ground (background), and vice versa. (Fig. 2.31)

Fluid medium Liquid-based drawing material. Contrast with *dry medium*. (Fig. 2.27)

Focal point The main point of interest in a work; the area or part of a composition that seizes and maintains the viewer's attention. (Fig. 6.12)

Foreshortening Diminishing the size of the parts of an object that are represented as farthest from the viewer. Specifically, rendering parts of an object as receding from the viewer at angles oblique to the picture plane so that they appear proportionately shorter than parts of the object that are parallel to the picture plane. (Fig. 17.7)

Forge To form or shape metal (usually heated) with blows from a hammer, press, or other implement or machine.

Form The *how* of a work of art—the general structure and overall organization of a work; also sometimes synonymous with shape in describing three-dimensional works.

Formalism An approach to art criticism that concentrates on the elements and design of works of art rather than on historical factors or the biography of the artist.

Freestanding sculpture Sculpture that is carved or cast in the round, unconnected to a wall, and thereby capable of being viewed in its entirety by walking around it. Freestanding sculpture can also be designed for a niche, which limits the visible portion of the sculpture. (Fig. 15.14)

Fresco A type of painting in which pigments are applied to a fresh, wet plaster surface or wall and thereby become part of the surface or wall (from Italian for "fresh"). (Fig. 17.18A)

Fresco secco Dry fresco; painting executed on dry plaster. Contrast with *buon fresco*.

Frieze In architecture, a horizontal band between the *architrave* and the *cornice* that is often decorated with sculpture. (Fig. 14.9)

Futurism An early-twentieth-century style that portrayed modern machines and the dynamic character of modern life and science. (Fig. 20.15)

Gallery A building or room in which works of art are displayed or sold; also, a space referring to the business in which works of art are sold.

Gauffrage An inkless *intaglio* process. (Fig. 9.12)

Genre painting Simple human representations; realistic figure painting that focuses on themes taken from everyday life. (Fig. 17.3)

Genres Categories of artistic compositions characterized by similarities in style or subject matter.

Geometric period A period of Greek art from about 900 to 700 BCE during which works of art emphasized geometric patterns. (Fig. 15.1)

Geometric shape A shape that is regular, easy to measure, and easy to describe, as distinguished from organic or biomorphic shape, which is irregular, difficult to measure, and difficult to describe.

Gesso Plaster of Paris that is applied to a wooden or canvas support and used as a surface for painting or as the material for sculpture (from Italian for "gypsum").

Globalization In general, the mutual influence of cultures, economies, marketplaces, and current events that were once distant and separate. In art, more specifically the worldwide invasion of visual images and the art marketplace from various cultures into people's consciousness; multiculturalism and cross-culturalism in contemporary art.

Golden Mean The principle that a small part of a work should relate to a larger part of the work in proportion to the manner in which the larger part relates to the whole. (Fig. 6.37)

Golden Rectangle A rectangle based on the *Golden Mean* and constructed so that its width is 1.618 times its height. (Fig. 6.38)

Golden Section Developed in ancient Greece, a mathematical formula for determining the proportional relationship of the parts of a work to the whole. (Fig. 6.37)

Gopuras A monumental tower at the entrance of a Hindu temple, especially in southern India. (Fig. 18.23)

Gothic A western European style developed between the twelfth and sixteenth centuries CE, characterized in architecture by ribbed vaults, pointed arches, flying buttresses, and steep roofs. (Fig. 16.17)

Gouache Watercolor paint that is made opaque by mixing pigments with a particular gum binder. (Fig. 8.12)

Graphic design Design for advertising and industry that includes design elements such as typography and images for communication purposes. (Fig. 9.20)

Graver A cutting tool used by engravers and sculptors. (Fig. 9.4)

Griffin A mythical creature with the body and back legs of a lion, and the head, talons, and wings of an eagle.

Groin vault In architecture, a vault that is constructed by placing *barrel vaults* at right angles so that a square is covered. (Fig. 15.34)

Ground The surface on which a two-dimensional work of art is created; a coat of liquid material applied to a surface that serves as a base for drawing or painting. Also, the background in a composition. See also *figure–ground reversal*.

Gum A sticky substance found in many plants, used to bind pigments as found, for example, in silverpoint, chalk, and pastel drawings.

Gum arabic A gum obtained from the African acacia plant.

Harlem Renaissance A Manhattan cultural movement of the 1920s and 1930s that portrayed and celebrated African American traditions, ways of life, writing, music, performing arts, and visual arts. (Fig. 20.30)

Hatcher An engraving instrument that produces thousands of tiny pits that will hold ink.

Hatching Fine parallel lines drawn or engraved to represent shading. (Fig. 9.3)

Hellenism The culture, thought, and ethical system of ancient Greece. (Fig. 15.14)

Hierarchical scaling The use of size to indicate the relative importance of the objects or people in a composition. (Fig. 14.10A)

High-key value range Describes values heading toward white.

Highlighting The exaggeration or emphasis of light areas in a composition.

High relief Sculpture that projects from its background by at least half its natural depth. Contrast with *bas-relief*. (Fig. 16.32)

Horizontal balance Balance in which the elements on the left and right sides of the composition seem to be about equal in number or visual emphasis. (Fig. 6.27)

Horus The ancient Egyptian sun god. (Fig. 14.10A)

Hudson River School A group of nineteenth-century American artists whose favorite subjects included the scenery of the Hudson River Valley and the Catskill Mountains of New York State. (Fig. 19.34)

Hue Color; the visual sensation created by specific parts of the visible spectrum, enabling us to label it, for example, as red or blue.

Humanism A system of belief in which humankind is viewed as the standard by which all things are measured.

Hybridity In art, the mixing of the traditions of different cultures to create new blends and new connections. (Fig. 22.1)

Iconography The study of themes and symbols—figures and images that, when deciphered, reveal the underlying meaning of a work of art. (Fig. 1.6)

Idealism The representation of forms according to a concept of perfection. (Fig. 15.12)

Illusionistic Surrealism A form of *Surrealism* that renders the irrational content, absurd juxtapositions, and changing forms of dreams in a highly illusionistic manner that blurs the distinctions between the real and the imaginary. (Fig. 20.26)

Illusion of space The suggestion of three dimensions on a two-dimensional surface. (Fig. 5.3)

Imam A prayer leader in a mosque; a religious and temporal ruler of a Muslim community or state.

Impasto Application of a medium such as oil or acrylic paint so that an actual texture is built up on a surface. (Fig. 18.12)

Implied line A line created by a viewer's perceptual tendency to connect a series of points. (Fig. 2.7)

Implied motion Motion that is suggested by the artist rather than actual, as by tightened muscles in statues of human figures or by the use of diagonal lines in compositions. (Fig. 20.14)

Implied space The space or depth suggested by an artist in a two-dimensional work. (Fig. 5.3)

Impressionism A late-nineteenth-century style characterized by the attempt to capture the fleeting effects of light by painting in short strokes of pure color. (Fig. 19.18)

Incise To cut into with a sharp tool.

Intaglio A printing process in which metal plates are incised, covered with ink, wiped, and pressed against paper. The print receives the image of the areas that are below the surface of the matrix. (Fig. 9.1)

Intarsia A style of decorative mosaic inlay.

Intensity Brightness of a color. Pure colors, such as unmixed pigments, are most intense.

International Gothic style A refined style of painting in late-fourteenth-century and early-fifteenth-century Europe characterized by splendid processions and courtly scenes, ornate embellishment, and attention to detail. (Fig. 17.1)

International style A post–World War I school of art and architecture that used modern materials and methods and expressed the view that form must follow function.

Invented texture Texture that makes no reference to real or actual texture.

Investiture The fire-resistant mold used in metal casting.

Ionic order A moderately ornate Greek architectural style introduced from Asia Minor and characterized by spiral scrolls (*volutes*) on capitals and a continuous *frieze*. (Fig. 15.4)

Iron A strong silvery gray metal that is subject to rusting in a moist environment.

Jamb In architecture, the side post of a doorway, window frame, fireplace, and so on. (Fig. 16.19)

Ka figure According to ancient Egyptian belief, an image of a body in which the soul would dwell after death. (Fig. 14.11)

Keystone In architecture, the wedge-shaped stone placed in the top center of an arch to prevent the arch from falling inward.

Kiln An oven used for drying and firing ceramics.

Kinetic sculpture Sculpture that actually moves (as opposed to providing the illusion of movement). (Fig. 5.21)

Kiva A circular, subterranean structure built by Native Americans of the Southwest for community and ceremonial functions. (Fig. 13.2)

Kouros figure The male figure as represented in the sculpture of the geometric and Archaic styles (from Greek for "boy"). (Fig. 15.2)

Krater In ancient Greece, a large wide-mouthed vase, with two handles, that was used primarily to mix wine with water. (Fig. 15.5)

Lamination The process of building up by layers.

Land art Site-specific work that is created or marked by an artist within natural surroundings. (Fig. 11.26)

Lapis lazuli An opaque blue, semiprecious stone.

Latin cross plan A cross-shaped church design in which the nave is longer than the transept. (Fig. 16.10)

Layout In books and other printed matter, the organization of the design elements, such as the fonts and sizing of the type, the use of photographs, and so on. (Fig. 9.20)

Lift-ground etching A technique in which a sugar solution is brushed onto a resin-coated plate, creating the illusion of a brush-and-ink drawing.

Line The element of art created by the connection of points, either actual or implied.

Linear perspective Formal systems developed by artists to portray three-dimensional objects in two-dimensional space; based on the fact that objects appear smaller when they are farther from the viewer; therefore, parallel lines (such as train tracks) appear to converge as they recede from the viewer. (Fig. 17.10)

Linear recession   Depth as perceived through the convergence of lines at specific points in the composition, such as the horizon line. (Fig. 17.10)

Lithography   A surface printing process in which an image is drawn onto a matrix with a greasy wax crayon. When dampened, the waxed areas repel water while the material of the matrix absorbs it. An oily ink is then applied, which adheres only to the waxed areas. When the matrix is pressed against paper, the paper receives the image of the crayon. (Fig. 9.13)

Local color   The hue of an object created by the colors its surface reflects under normal lighting conditions (contrast with *optical color*). Color that is natural rather than symbolic for the depicted objects.

Logo   A distinctive company trademark or signature (short for "logogram" or "logotype"). (Fig. 9.23)

Longitudinal plan   A church design in which the nave is longer than the transept and in which parts are symmetrical against an axis. Contrast with *central plan*. (Fig. 16.10)

Loom   A machine that weaves thread into yarn or cloth.

Lost-wax technique   A bronze-casting process in which an initial mold is made from a model (usually clay) and filled with molten wax. A second, fire-resistant mold is made from the wax, and molten bronze is cast in it. (Fig. 11.5)

Low-key value range   Describes values moving toward black.

Low relief   A projecting image whose overall depth is shallow.

Magazine   In architecture, a large supply chamber.

Mandala   In Hindu and Buddhist traditions, a circular design symbolizing wholeness or unity. (Fig. 16.39)

Mannerist art   A sixteenth-century, post-Renaissance style characterized by artificial poses and gestures, vivid—sometimes harsh—color, and distorted, elongated figures. (Fig. 17.29)

Manuscript illumination   Illustration or decoration of books and letters with pictures or designs. (Fig. 17.1)

Masonry   Construction using stone, brick, concrete block, glass block, stucco, and tile.

Mass   In painting, a large area of one form or color; in three-dimensional art, the bulk of an object.

Matrix   In printmaking, the working surface of the block, slab, or screen. In sculpture, a mold or hollow shape used to give form to a material that is inserted in a plastic or molten state. (Fig. 9.1)

Medium   The material and tools that an artist uses to create a work of art.

Megalith   A huge stone, especially as used in prehistoric construction. (Fig. 14.3)

Mesolithic   Of the Middle Stone Age.

Metalwork   A metal object; the art of making metal objects that are practical or decorative, ranging from delicate, intricate jewelry to bridges, ships, and engine parts. (Fig. 12.23)

Metope   In architecture, the panels containing *relief sculpture* that appear between the *triglyphs* of the Doric *frieze*. (Fig. 15.4)

Mezzotint   A nonlinear engraving process in which the *matrix* is pitted with a *hatcher*.

Mihrab   A niche in the wall of a mosque that faces Mecca and thus provides a focus of worship. (Fig. 16.25)

Minaret   A tall, slender tower of a mosque from which Muslims are called to prayer. (Fig. 16.26)

Minimalism   A non-objective art movement begun in the 1960s that emphasizes the use of pure and simple shapes and materials. (Fig. 21.26)

Modeling   In two-dimensional works of art, the creation of the illusion of depth through the use of light and shade (*chiaroscuro*). In sculpture, the process of shaping a pliable material, such as clay or wax, into a three-dimensional form. (Fig. 18.11)

Modernism   A contemporary style of architecture that deemphasizes ornamentation and uses recently developed materials of high strength. (Fig. 21.52)

Mold   A pattern or matrix for giving form to molten or plastic material; a frame on which something is modeled.

Monochromatic color scheme   A manner of using color in which one (mono) color (chroma) dominates and is sometimes combined with its various tints and shades.

Monotype   In printmaking, a technique in which paint is brushed onto a matrix that is pressed against a sheet of paper, yielding a single print. (Fig. 9.17)

Mortuary temple   An Egyptian temple of the New Kingdom in which the pharaoh worshiped and was worshiped after death. (Fig. 14.13)

Multiple perspectives   The depiction of objects or scenes from more than one vantage point, providing a broader picture than one could obtain from a single vantage point.

Mural   Image(s) painted directly on a wall or intended to cover a wall completely (from *muralis*, Latin for "of a wall"). (Fig. 20.41)

Narthex   A church vestibule that leads to the nave, constructed for use by the catechumens (individuals preparing to be baptized). (Fig. 16.1)

Naturalism   Representation that strives to imitate nature rather than to express intellectual theory. (Fig. 15.12)

Naturalistic style   A style prevalent in Europe during the second half of the nineteenth century that depicted the details of ordinary life.

Nave   The central aisle of a church, constructed for use by the congregation at large. (Fig. 16.10)

Negative shape   Space that is empty or filled with imagery that is secondary to the main objects or figures depicted in the composition. Contrast with *positive shape*.

Neoclassical art   An eighteenth-century revival of Classical Greek and Roman art, characterized by simplicity and straight lines. (Fig. 19.3)

Neo-Expressionism   A violent, figurative style of the second half of the twentieth century that largely revived the German Expressionism of the early twentieth century.

Neolithic   Of the New Stone Age. (Fig. 14.3)

Neue Sachlichkeit   (New Objectivity)   A post–World War I German art movement that rebelled against German Expressionism and focused on the detailed representation of objects and figures. (Fig. 20.5)

Nib   The point of a pen; the split and sharpened end of a quill pen.

Nonobjective art   Art that is abstract and nonrepresentational, that is, does not portray figures or objects from the visible world. (Fig. 21.5)

Nonporous   Not containing pores and thus not permitting the passage of fluids.

Nonrepresentational art   Art that does not represent figures or objects.

Ocher   A dark yellow color derived from an earthy clay.

Oculus   In architecture, a round window, particularly one placed at the apex of a dome (from Latin for "eye"). (Fig. 15.27)

Oil paint   Paint in which pigments are combined with an oil medium. (Fig. 17.3)

One-point perspective   Linear perspective in which a single vanishing point is placed on the horizon. (Fig. 17.10)

Optical color   The depiction of colors as they are perceived under different lighting conditions.

Optical representation   The depiction of objects as they are actually seen from a single vantage point.

Ordered chaos   The artist's depiction of a chaotic subject with a unifying sense of order.

Orthogonal   Composed of right angles.

Outline A line that marks the outer boundaries or contours of a figure or an object. (Fig. 2.10)

Oxidizing phase See *black-figure painting*.

Paint A mixture of a pigment with a vehicle or medium.

Painting The application of a pigment to a surface; a work of art created in this manner. (Fig. 17.12)

Palatine chapel A chapel that is part of a palace. (Fig. 16.7)

Paleolithic The early phase of the Stone Age, beginning 2–2.5 million years ago, and characterized by the earliest known use of stones as tools by the ancestors of *homo sapiens*.

Pan To move a motion picture or video camera from side to side to capture a comprehensive or continuous view of a subject.

Panel painting A painting, usually in tempera but sometimes in oil, whose ground is a wooden panel. (Fig. 17.6)

Panorama An unlimited view in all directions.

Papyrus A writing surface made from the papyrus plant.

Parallel editing In cinematography or video, shifting back and forth from one event or story line to another.

Pastel A drawing implement made by grinding coloring matter, mixing it with gum, and forming it into a crayon. (Fig. 21.4)

Pastoral Relating to idyllic rural life, especially of shepherds and dairymaids.

Patina A fine crust or film that forms on bronze or copper because of oxidation. It usually provides a desirable greenish or greenish blue tint to the metal. (Fig. 11.6)

Patrician A member of the noble class in ancient Rome.

Pediment In architecture, any triangular shape surrounded by *cornices*, especially one that surmounts the *entablature* of the portico façade of Greek temple. The Romans frequently placed pediments without support over windows and doorways. (Fig. 15.4)

Pendentive In architecture, a spherical triangle that fills the wall space between the four arches of a *groin vault* to provide a circular base on which a dome may rest. (Fig. 13.3)

Peplos In Greek Classical Art, a heavy woolen wrap.

Photography The creation of images by exposure of a photosensitive surface to light. (Fig. 10.1)

Photorealism A movement dating from the 1960s in which subjects are rendered with hard, photographic precision. (Fig. 21.23)

Photosensitive Descriptive of a surface that is sensitive to light and therefore capable of recording images.

Photo silkscreen A variation of *serigraphy*, or *silkscreen printing*, that allows the artist to create photographic images on a screen covered with a light-sensitive gel.

Piazza An open public square or plaza. (Fig. 18.2)

Pictograph A simplified symbol of an object or action; for example, a schematized or abstract form of an ancestral image, animal, geometric form, anatomic part, or shape suggestive of a cosmic symbol or microscopic life. (Fig. 14.25)

Pictorial space The illusionary space that, by seeming to recede into the distance from the picture plane, provides a sense of depth in a two-dimensional composition.

Picture plane The flat, two-dimensional surface on which a picture is created. In much Western art, the picture plane is viewed as a window opening onto deep space.

Pier In architecture, a column-like support with a rectilinear rather than cylindrical profile. Piers generally support arches.

Pigment The vehicle for color, be it paint, ink, or another material or substance.

Pilaster In architecture, a decorative element that recalls the shape of a structural *pier*. Pilasters are attached to the wall plane and project very little. They may have all the visual elements of piers, including base, shaft, *capital*, and *entablature*. (Fig. 15.20)

Pile weave A weave in which knots are tied, then cut, forming an even surface. (Fig. 12.18)

Plain weave A weave in which the woof thread passes above one warp fiber and below the next.

Planar recession Perspective in which the illusion of depth is created through parallel planes that appear to recede from the picture plane.

Planographic printing Any method of printing from a flat surface, such as *lithography*. (Fig. 9.13)

Plasticity Capacity of a material to be molded or shaped.

Plebeian class In ancient Rome, the common people.

Plywood Sheets of wood that resist warping because they are constructed of layers glued together with the grain oriented in different directions. (Fig. 22.11)

Pointed arch An arch that comes to a point rather than curves at the top. (Fig. 16.1)

Pointillism A systematic method of applying minute dots of unmixed pigment to the canvas; the dots are intended to be "mixed" by the eye when viewed. Also called "divisionism." (Fig. 19.23)

Pop Art An art style originating in the 1960s that uses commercial and popular images and themes as its subject matter. (Fig. 21.17)

Porcelain A hard, white, translucent, nonporous clay body. The *bisque* is fired at a relatively low temperature and the glaze at a high temperature. (Fig. 12.13)

Portico The entrance facade of a Greek temple, adapted for use with other buildings and consisting of a *colonnade*, *entablature*, and *pediment* (from Greek for "porch"). (Fig. 15.26)

Positive shape The spatial form defined by the objects or figures represented in works of art. Contrast with *negative shape*.

Post-and-beam construction Construction in which vertical elements (posts) and horizontal timbers (beams) are pieced together with wooden pegs. (Fig. 13.8)

Post-and-lintel construction Construction in which vertical elements (posts) are used to support horizontal crosspieces (lintels). Also termed "trabeated structure." (Fig. 14.3)

Postimpressionism A late nineteenth-century French school of painting that rejected the objective naturalism of Impressionism and used form and color in personally expressive ways. (Fig. 19.25)

Postmodernism A contemporary style that arose as a reaction to Modernism and that returns to ornamentation drawn from Classical and historical sources. (Fig. 22.2)

Pottery Pots, bowls, dishes, and similar wares made of clay and hardened by heat; a shop at which such objects are made. (Fig. 12.5)

Poussinistes Those Neoclassical artists who took Nicolas Poussin as their model. Contrast with *Rubenistes*. (Fig. 19.7)

Prefabricate In architecture, to build beforehand at a factory rather than at the building site. (Fig. 13.12)

Pre-Hellenic Of ancient Greece before the eighth century BCE. (Fig. 14.19)

Primary pigment colors Colors of pigments that cannot be created by mixing other colors: red, yellow, and blue pigments. Colors of lights that cannot be created by mixing other lights: red, green, and blue lights.

Print In printmaking, a picture or design made by pressing or hitting a surface with a plate or block; in photography, a photograph, especially one made from a negative. (Fig. 9.7)

Prism A transparent object with triangular ends, usually made of glass, that separates white light passed through it into the visible spectrum.

Progressive rhythm A type of rhythm in which elements in a work change slightly as they move, or progress, toward a defined point in a composition. (Fig. 6.31)

Proportion The size of elements or images within a work of art in relation to each other or to the whole. (Fig. 6.20)

Propylaeum In architecture, a gateway building leading to an open court in front of a Greek or Roman temple; specifically, such a building on the Acropolis.

Proximity Nearness.

Psychic automatism A process of generating imagery through ideas received from the unconscious mind and expressed in an unrestrained manner. (Fig. 20.25)

Psychological line A suggestion of linear direction formed by a viewer's knowledge of relationships in a work of art, such as the relationship between the glance of a person toward an object. (Fig. 2.8)

Public art Works created for public spaces.

Quatrefoil In architecture, a design made up of four converging arcs that are similar in appearance to a flower with four petals.

Radial balance Balance in which the design elements radiate from a center point. (Fig. 6.29)

Radiating chapel An apse-shaped chapel, several of which generally radiate from the *ambulatory* in a *Latin cross plan.* (Fig. 16.9)

Raking cornice A cornice that follows the slop of a pediment or a gable.

Rasp A rough file that has raised points instead of ridges.

Rationalism The belief that ethical conduct is determined by reason; in philosophy, the theory that knowledge is derived from the intellect, without the aid of the senses.

Realism A style characterized by accurate and truthful portrayal of subject matter; a nineteenth-century style that portrayed subject matter in this manner. (Fig. 19.11)

Rectangular bay system A church plan in which rectangular *bays* serve as the basis for the overall design. (Fig. 16.10)

Rectilinear Characterized by straight lines. (Fig. 20.19)

Red-figure technique A style of figurative Greek vase painting that developed at about 520 BCE and replaced black-figure vase painting. Details of the figures were painted, permitting flexibility in the depiction of their forms, movements, and expressions. (Fig. 15.7)

Register A horizontal segment of a structure or work of art. (Fig. 14.10B)

Regular repetition The systematic repetition of the visual elements in a work to create *rhythm.*

Reinforced concrete Concrete that is strengthened by steel rods or mesh. Same as *ferroconcrete.* (Fig. 21.56)

Relative size The size of an object or figure in relation to other objects or figures or the setting. See also *scale.*

Relief printing Any printmaking technique in which the matrix is carved with knives so that the areas not meant to be printed (that is, not meant to leave an image) are below the surface of the matrix. (Fig. 9.2)

Relief sculpture Sculpture that is carved to ornament architecture or furniture, as opposed to *freestanding sculpture.* See also *bas-relief* and *high relief.* (Fig. 17.9)

Renaissance A period spanning the fourteenth and fifteenth centuries CE in Europe. The Renaissance (French for "rebirth") rejected medieval art and philosophy; it first turned to Classical antiquity for inspiration and then developed patterns of art and philosophy that paved the way toward the modern world. (Fig. 17.23)

Reoxidizing phase See *black-figure painting.*

Repetition The use of the same or similar elements over and over again in a composition. (Fig. 20.24)

Republican period The Roman period lasting from the victories over the Etruscans to the death of Julius Caesar (527–509 BCE). (Fig. 15.18)

Rhythm The orderly repetition or progression of the visual elements in a work of art. (Fig. 11.13)

Rib In Gothic architecture, a structural member that reinforces the stress points of *groin vaults.* (Fig. 16.14)

Rococo An eighteenth-century style during the Baroque era that is characterized by lighter colors, greater wit, playfulness, occasional eroticism, and yet more ornate decoration. (Fig. 18.20)

Romanesque style A style of European architecture of the eleventh and twelfth centuries that is characterized by thick, massive walls, the *Latin cross plan*, the use of a *barrel vault* in the *nave*, round arches, and a twin-towered facade. (Fig. 16.9)

Romanticism A nineteenth-century movement that rebelled against academic Neoclassicism by seeking extremes of emotion as enhanced by virtuoso brushwork and a brilliant palette. (Fig. 19.4)

Root Five Rectangle A rectangle whose length is 2.236 (the square root of 5) times its width that can be constructed by rotating the diagonal of a half square left and right. (Fig. 6.39)

Rose window A large circular window in a Gothic church, assembled in segments that resemble the petals of a flower, usually adorned with stained glass and plantlike ornamental work. (Fig. 16.15)

Rubenistes Those Romantic artists who took Peter Paul Rubens as their model. Contrast with *Poussinistes.* (Fig. 19.5)

Samurai A member of a warrior caste in feudal Japan.

Satin weave A weave in which the woof passes above and below several warp threads at a time.

Saturation Another term for the intensity of a color.

Scale The relative size of an object compared to other objects, the setting, or people. (Fig. 6.32)

Sculpture-in-the-round Freestanding sculpture, which may be walked around and thereby viewed from various vantage points. (Fig. 11.6)

Secondary pigment colors Colors created by mixing primary colors.

Serigraphy A printmaking process in which stencils are applied to a screen of silk or similar material stretched on a frame. Paint or ink is forced through the open areas of the stencil onto paper beneath. Also termed *silkscreen printing.* (Fig. 9.16)

Shade A low value of a color, created by the addition of black to a hue.

Shape An area within a composition that has boundaries that separate it from what surrounds it and makes it distinct.

Shogun The title of a chief military commander or military governor of Japan from the twelfth century to the nineteenth century.

Side aisles A lateral aisle of a church or theater, as distinguished from the nave or central aisle. (Fig. 16.10)

Silkscreen printing A printmaking process in which stencils are applied to a screen of silk or similar material stretched on a frame. Paint or ink is forced through the open areas of the stencil onto paper beneath. Also termed *serigraphy.* (Fig. 9.16)

Slip In ceramics, clay that is thinned to the consistency of cream for use in casting, decorating, or cementing.

Soft-ground etching An etching technique in which a ground of softened wax yields effects similar to those of pencil or crayon drawings.

Space The dimensions of height, width, and depth within which objects exist and move; a continuous open area or expanse.

Spiral A curve that radiates from a central point and, revolving around that point, moves progressively farther away; the extension of the Golden Rectangle in a circular manner. (Fig. 6.45)

Squeegee A T-shaped tool with a rubber blade used to remove liquid from a surface. (Fig. 9.1)

Stainless steel Steel that has been alloyed with chromium or other metals to make it virtually immune to corrosion. (Fig. 21.9)

Stamp To impress or imprint with a mark or design.

Steel A hard, tough metal composed of iron, carbon, and other metals, such as nickel or chromium.

Steel cable A strong cable composed of multiple intertwined steel wires.

Steel cage A steel framework of beams and columns designed to carry the loads and stresses of a building to its foundation.

Steel-cage construction A method of building that capitalizes on the strength of steel by piecing together slender steel beams to form the skeleton of a structure. (Fig. 21.52)

Stele (or stelae, pl.) An engraved stone slab or pillar that serves as a grave marker. (Fig. 14.7)

Stippling Drawing or painting small dots or dabs to create shading or a dappled effect.

Stoicism The philosophy that the universe is governed by natural laws and that people should follow virtue, as determined by reason, and remain indifferent to passion or emotion.

Stoneware A ceramic that is fired at 2,300°F–2,700°F. The resulting object is usually gray but can be tan or reddish. Stoneware is nonporous or slightly porous and is used in dinnerware and ceramic sculpture. (Fig. 12.7)

Stupa A dome-shaped Buddhist shrine. (Fig. 15.37)

Style The signature look of an artist's work; the distinctive characteristics of an artist's work and those of a culture and era.

Stylobate A continuous base or platform that supports a row of columns. (Fig. 15.4)

Stylus A pointed, needle-like tool used in drawing, printmaking, making impressions on electronic]media, and so on.

Subject In art, the themes or objects being depicted.

Subtractive color Color that is created by mixing pigments. The subtractive primary colors are red, yellow, and blue pigments.

Subtractive process In sculpture, the removal of material, as in carving. Contrast with *additive process*. (Fig. 11.3)

Subversive texture Texture that is chosen or created by artists to foil or undermine our ideas about the objects that they depict. (Fig. 4.7)

Surrealism A twentieth-century art style whose imagery is believed to stem from unconscious, irrational sources and that therefore takes on *fantastic art* forms. Although the imagery is fantastic, it is often rendered with extraordinary realism. (Fig. 20.26)

Symmetrical balance Balance in which imagery on one side of a composition is mirrored on the other side. Symmetrical balance can be pure, or it can be approximate, in which case the whole of the work has a symmetrical feeling but with slight variations that provide more visual interest than would a mirror image. Contrast with *asymmetrical balance*. (Fig. 6.22)

Symmetry Similarity of form or arrangement on both sides of a dividing line.

Synthetic Cubism The second phase of Cubism, which emphasized the form of the object and constructing rather than disintegrating that form. (Fig. 20.10)

Synthetism Gauguin's theory of art, which advocated the use of broad areas of unnatural color and primitive or symbolic subject matter. (Fig. 19.27)

Tempera A kind of painting in which pigments are mixed with casein, size, or egg—particularly egg yolk—to create a dull finish. (Fig. 17.6)

Temple A building devoted to the worship of a god or gods. (Fig. 15.16)

Tenebrism A technique in which there is very little modeling. The artist moves rapidly from highlighting to deep shadow. (Fig. 18.4)

Tensile strength The degree to which a material can withstand being stretched.

Terra-cotta A hard, reddish brown earthenware used in sculpture and pottery; usually left unglazed. (Fig. 12.10)

Tertiary colors Colors created by mixing primary and secondary colors.

Textile arts Arts and crafts that use plant, animal, or synthetic fibers to make practical or decorative objects, such as carpets, tablecloths, and baskets. (Fig. 12.19)

Texture The surface character of materials as experienced by the sense of touch.

Texture gradient The visual perception of nearby objects as distant objects; a method in two-dimensional works whereby the artist creates the illusion of depth by making objects designated as nearby more detailed in texture.

Throwing (a pot) In ceramics, the process of shaping that takes place on the potter's wheel. (Fig. 12.5)

Tie-dyeing Making designs by sewing or tying folds in cloth to prevent a dye from reaching certain areas.

Tint A high value of a color, created by the addition of white to a hue.

Tone A variety of values created by the addition of gray to a hue.

Transept The "arms" of a *Latin cross plan*, used by pilgrims and other visitors for access to the area behind the crossing square. (Fig. 16.10)

Transversals Lines drawn parallel to the horizon lines.

Transverse rib In architecture, a rib that connects the midpoints of a *groin vault*. (Fig. 16.10)

Tribune gallery In architecture, the space between the *nave* arcade and the *clerestory* that is used for traffic above the side aisles on the second stage of the elevation. (Fig. 16.15)

Triforium In a church, a gallery or arcade in the wall above the arches of the *nave, transept,* or choir. (Fig. 16.14)

Triglyph In architecture, a panel incised with vertical grooves (usually three, hence *triglyph*) that divide the scenes in a Doric *frieze*. (Fig. 15.4)

Trompe l'oeil A painting or other art form that creates such a realistic image that the viewer may wonder whether it is real or an illusion (from French for "fool the eye"). (Fig. 18.8)

Truss A rigid, triangular frame used for supporting structures such as roofs and bridges.

Twill weave A weave with broken diagonal patterns.

Twisted perspective The combination of different perspectives in a work; also known as *composite view*. (Fig. 5.19)

Tympanum Semicircular space above the doors of a cathedral. (Fig. 16.11)

Typography The art of designing, arranging, and setting type for printing.

Umber A kind of earth that has a yellowish or reddish brown color.

Unity The oneness or wholeness of a work of art.

Value The lightness or darkness of a color.

Value contrast The degrees of difference between shades of gray. (Fig. 20.10)

Value pattern The variation in lightness and darkness within a work of art, and the ways in which values are arranged within a composition. (Fig. 3.6)

Vanishing point In linear perspective, a point on the horizon where parallel lines appear to converge.

Vantage point The actual or apparent spot from which a viewer observes an object or picture.

Variety Contrast and diversity; the counterpoint to unity.

Variety within unity   The use of contrast and diversity within an overall harmonious or unified composition.

Vault   In architecture, any series of arches other than an arcade used to create space. See also *barrel vault* and *groin vault*. (Fig. 16.9C)

Vehicle   A liquid such as water or oil with which pigments are mixed for painting.

Veneer   In architecture, a thin layer of high-quality material used to enhance the appearance of the façade of a structure.

Venus   The Roman goddess of beauty; a prehistoric fertility figure, such as the Venus of Willendorf. (Fig. 14.2)

Venus pudica   A Venus with her hand held over her genitals for modesty. (Fig. 15.15)

Vertical balance   Balance in which the elements in the top and bottom of the composition are in balance. (Fig. 6.26)

Vertical positioning   A method of creating the illusion of space by placing objects designated as being farther from the viewer toward the upper edge of the composition.

Visitation   In Roman Catholicism, the visit of the Virgin Mary to Elizabeth; a church feast commemorating the visit. (Fig. 16.20)

Visual balance   The distribution of the elements of a composition such that some elements echo or serve as counterpoints to other elements in a composition.

Visual texture   The illusion of an actual texture. (Fig. 4.2)

Volume   The mass or bulk of a three-dimensional work; the amount of space such a work contains.

Volute krater   A wide-mouthed vessel (krater) with scroll-shaped handles. (Fig. 15.5)

Voussoir   A wedge-shaped stone block used in the construction of an arch.

Warp   In weaving, the threads that run lengthwise in a loom and are crossed by the weft or woof.

Wash   A thin, watery film of paint, especially watercolor, applied with even, sweeping movements of the brush.

Watercolor   A paint with a water medium. Watercolors are usually made by mixing pigments with a gum binder and thinning the mixture with water. (Fig. 8.11)

Weaving   The making of fabrics by the interlacing of threads or fibers, as on a loom. (Fig. 12.18)

Webbing   In architecture, a netlike structure that composes that part of a ribbed vault that lies between the ribs.

Weft   In weaving, the yarns that are carried back and forth across the warp. Also called *woof*.

Weight-shift principle   The situating of the human figure so that the legs and hips are turned in one direction and the chest and arms in another. This shifting of weight results in a diagonal balancing of tension and relaxation. See also *contrapposto*.

Wood engraving   A type of relief printing in which a hard, laminated, nondirectional wood surface is used as the matrix. (Fig. 9.5)

Woodcut   Relief printing in which the grain of a wooden matrix is carved with a knife. (Fig. 9.3)

Woof   See *weft*.

Zen   A Buddhist sect that seeks inner harmony through introspection and meditation. (Fig. 17.37)

Ziggurat   A temple tower in the form of a terraced pyramid, built by ancient Assyrians and Babylonians. (Fig. 14.4A + 14.4B)

CREDITS

CHAPTER 1—Opener: Titled (Art as Idea as Idea) [Art], 1968, Kosuth, Joseph (b. 1945)/Private Collection/Photo © Christie's Images/Bridgeman Images; **1.1:** LatitudeStock/Alamy; **1.2:** B Christopher/Alamy; **1.3:** David Levenson/Alamy; **1.4:** Ganter Schneider; **1.5:** Cercando un Ago, 1957, oil on canvas, 95 × 88.1 in. © Estate of Joan Mitchell; **1.6:** National Gallery, London/Art Resource, NY; **1.7a:** Digital Image © The Museum of Modern Art/Licensed by SCALA/Art Resource, NY; **1.7b:** Digital Image © The Museum of Modern Art/Licensed by SCALA/Art Resource, NY; **1.7c:** Digital Image © The Museum of Modern Art/Licensed by SCALA/Art Resource, NY; **1.7d:** Digital Image © The Museum of Modern Art/Licensed by SCALA/Art Resource, NY; **1.8:** Corbis; **1.9:** © Audrey Flack, Collection of The University of Arizona Museum of Art & Archive of Visual Arts, Tucson; Museum Purchase with Funds Provided By the Edward J. Gallagher, Jr. Memorial Fund; **1.10:** © Jane Antoni, Courtesy Luhring Augustine, NY; **1.11:** Tamaris, France, c. 1885 (oil on canvas), Renoir, Pierre Auguste (1841–1919)/Minneapolis Institute of Arts, MN, USA/Bequest of Mrs. Peter Ffolliott/The Bridgeman Art Library; **1.12:** Photo © Christie's Images/ The Bridgeman Art Library. Art © 2015 The Pollock-Krasner Foundation/Artists Rights Society (ARS), New York; **1.13:** © Art & Language, courtesy of Lisson Gallery, London; **1.14:** RMN-Grand Palais/Art Resource, NY, **1.15:** Art by Andres Serrano/Yvon Lambert, Paris; **1.16:** Image copyright © The Metropolitan Museum of Art. Image source: Art Resource, NY; **1.17:** © 2015 Succession H. Matisse, Paris/Artists Rights Society (ARS), NY. Photo: Archives Henri Matisse and San Francisco Museum of Modern Art; **1.18:** Scala/Art Resource, NY.

CHAPTER 2—Opener: © Judy Pfaff; **2.1:** Gjon Mili/Time Life Pictures/Getty Images; **2.2:** © Kristin Baker; **2.3:** © Sylvia Plimack Mangold. Photo by Bill Orcutt, courtesy Alexander and Bonin; **2.4:** Photo by Hester and Hardaway courtesy of Andrea Rosen Gallery, NY. © Matthew Ritchie; **2.5:** Royal Geographical Society/Alamy; **2.6:** © Sam Gilliam. Courtesy David Kordansky Gallery, Los Angeles, CA. Photography: Fredrik Nilsen; **2.7:** Smithsonian American Art Museum, Washington, DC/Art Resource, NY; **2.8–2.9:** Emily Mary Osborne/Private Collection; **2.10:** The Birth of Venus, c. 1485 (tempera on canvas) (detail of 412), Botticelli, Sandro (Alessandro di Mariano di Vanni Filipepi) (1444/5-1510)/Galleria degli Uffizi, Florence, Italy/Bridgeman Images; **2.11:** Mona Lisa, c. 1503–6 (oil on panel) (detail of 3179), Vinci, Leonardo da (1452–1519)/Louvre, Paris, France/Bridgeman Images; **2.12:** Dunes, Oceano, 1936 (gelatin silver photograph), Weston, Edward Henry (1886–1958)/Art Gallery of New South Wales, Sydney, Australia/Bridgeman Images; **2.13:** Hebe, 1770 (etching), Kauffmann, Angelica (1741–1807)/Private Collection/The Bridgeman Art Library; **2.14:** Cengage Learning; **2.15:** Hampton University Museum, Hampton, VA. Art © Elizabeth Catlett. Licensed by VAGA, New York, NY; **2.16:** Peter Horree/Alamy; **2.17:** Municipal Museum The Hague, The Netherlands; **2.18:** Nathan Willock/VIEW Pictures Ltd/Alamy; **2.19:** Sneferu's Red Pyramid in Dashur (photo)/The Bridgeman Art Library; **2.20:** RMN Grand Palais/Art Resource, NY; **2.21:** CNAC/MNAM/Dist. RMN-Grand Palais/Art Resource, NY; **2.22:** Greenberg Van Doren Fine Art/2015 Artists Rights Society (ARS), New York; **2.23:** JPoore/Cengage Learning; **2.24:** Travel Library Limited/SuperStock; **2.25:** © 2015 Estate of Pablo Picasso/Artists Rights Society (ARS), New York, Digital Image © The Museum of Modern Art/Licensed by SCALA/Art Resource, NY; **2.26:** © Robert Colescott; **2.27:** Dynamism of a Cyclist (Dinamismo di un ciclista) 1913 (oil on canvas), Boccioni, Umberto (1882–1916)/Mattioli Collection, Milan, Italy/The Bridgeman Art Library; **2.28:** © 2015 Estate of Helen Frankenthaler/Artists Rights Society (ARS), New York. Photo: Gagosian Gallery. Photography by Sibila Savage Photography; **2.29:** © Judy Pfaff; **2.30:** The Laundresses (The Ironing) c. 1874–1876 (oil on canvas), Degas, Edgar (1834–1917)/Private Collection/Photo © Christie's Images/The Bridgeman Art Library; **2.31:** Laundresses at Arles, by Paul Gauguin, 1888, 1848–1903/De Agostini Picture Library/G. Dagli Orti/The Bridgeman Art Library; **2.32:** © Andrew Adolphus; **2.33:** Cengage Learning; **2.34:** Michele and Tom Grimm/Alamy; **2.35:** RIEGER Bertrand/Hemis.fr/SuperStock; **2.36:** Swim Ink 2, LLC/Corbis; **2.37:** © Aaron Alex/Alamy.

CHAPTER 3—Opener: Walter Bibikow/Mauritius/SuperStock; **3.1:** Kiyoshi Takahase Segundo/Alamy; **3.2:** Daniel M. Mendelowitz et al. (2007); **3.3:** © Marc Brandenburg. Digital image: The Museum of Modern Art/Licensed by SCALA/Art Resource, NY; **3.4:** Cengage Learning; **3.5:** © Hank Willis Thomas. Courtesy of the artist and Jack Shainman Gallery, New York; **3.6:** Art © David Salle/Licensed by VAGA, New York, NY; **3.7:** St. Joseph, the Carpenter, c. 1640 (oil on canvas), Tour, Georges de la (1593–1652)/Louvre, Paris, France/Bridgeman Images; **3.8:** Photograph © Timothy Hursley; **3.9:** Moviestore Collection Ltd./Alamy; **3.10–3.13:** © Cengage Learning 2015; **3.14:** Art Resource, NY; **3.15–3.17:** © Cengage Learning; **3.18:** Courtesy of Dale Chihuly, Seattle, WA; **3.19:** © Cengage Learning; **3.20:** © Tino Zago. Courtesy OK Harris Gallery, New York; **3.21:** Mark Messersmith. Courtesy of the artist; **3.22:** In the Loge, 1879 (oil on canvas), Cassatt, Mary Stevenson (1844–1926)/Museum of Fine Arts, Boston, Massachusetts, USA/The Hayden Collection—Charles Henry Hayden Fund/Bridgeman Images; **3.23:** The Metropolitan Museum of Art/Art Resource, NY; **3.24:** Credit: The Pine Tree at St. Tropez, 1909 (oil on canvas), Signac, Paul (1863–1935)/Pushkin Museum, Moscow, Russia/The Bridgeman Art Library; **3.25:** © Yinka Shonibare MBE. All Rights Reserved, DACS/ARS, NY 2015.

CHAPTER 4—Opener: Image copyright © The Metropolitan Museum of Art. Image source: Art Resource, NY; **4.1:** Orchard in Blossom, 1880 (oil on canvas), Gogh, Vincent van (1853–1890)/© Scottish National Gallery, Edinburgh/The Bridgeman Art Library; **4.2:** Mulberry Tree, 1889 (oil on canvas), Gogh, Vincent van (1853–1890)/Norton Simon Collection, Pasadena, CA, USA/The Bridgeman Art Library; **4.3:** Photo © Lyndon Douglas Courtesy Barbican Art Gallery; **4.4:** © 2015 Artists Rights Society (ARS), New York/ADAGP, Paris. Digital image: The Bridgeman Art Library; **4.5:** © Lynda Bengalis/Licensed by VAGA, New York, NY; **4.6:** © 2015 Artists Rights Society (ARS), New York/ADAGP, Paris. Digital image: Washington University, St. Louis, USA/Giraudon/The Bridgeman Art Library; **4.7:** Doormat II, 2000–2001 (stainless steel and nickel-plated pins, glue, and canvas) (see also 703511), Hatoum, Mona (b. 1952)/Private Collection/Photo © Christie's Images/Bridgeman Images; **4.8:** © 2015 Artists Rights Society (ARS), New York; **4.9:** Erich Lessing/Art Resource, NY; **4.10:** © 2015 Frank Stella/Artists Rights Society (ARS), New York; **4.11:** Image copyright © The Metropolitan Museum of Art. Image source: Art Resource, NY.

CHAPTER 5—Opener: Study for Loie Fuller (1862–1928) at the Folies-Bergere, 1893 (oil on cardboard), Toulouse-Lautrec, Henri de (1864–1901)/Musee Toulouse-Lautrec, Albi, France/Giraudon/The Bridgeman Art Library; **5.1a:** Copyright Allen Jones. Echo, 2003 (painted steel),

Jones, Allen (b. 1937)/Private Collection/ The Bridgeman Art Library; **5.1b**: Echo, 2003 (painted steel), Jones, Allen (b. 1937)/ Private Collection/Bridgeman Images; **5.2**: Sarah Quill/The Bridgeman Art Library; **5.3**: RMN-Grand Palais/Art Resource, NY; **5.4**: Smithsonian American Art Museum, Washington, DC/Art Resource, NY; **5.5**: Courtesy of the National Museum of Women in the Arts, Washington, DC, Gift of Wallace and Wilhelmina Holladay; **5.6**: Still Life with a Bottle of Olives, 1760 (oil on canvas), Chardin, Jean-Baptiste Simeon (1699–1779)/Louvre, Paris, France/ Giraudon/The Bridgeman Art Library; **5.7**: The Bottle of Banyuls, 1914 (gouache & collage), Gris, Juan (1887–1927)/Kunstmuseum, Bern, Switzerland/Peter Willi/The Bridgeman Art Library; **5.8**: Stained glass window with landscape/De Agostini Picture Library/The Bridgeman Art Library; **5.9**: Gianni Dagli Orti/The Art Archive at Art Resource, NY; **5.10**: Tomas Abad/ Alamy; **5.11**: Photo credit Luc Demers, courtesy of the artist; **5.12**: Alinari/Art Resource, NY; **5.13**: © Cengage Learning 2015; **5.14a**: Erich Lessing/Art Resource, NY; **5.14b**: Erich Lessing/Art Resource, NY; **5.15**: © Cengage Learning 2015; **5.16a**: Erich Lessing/Art Resource, NY; **5.16b**: Erich Lessing/Art Resource, NY; **5.17**: Art Resource, NY; **5.18**: Smithsonian American Art Museum, Washington, DC/ Art Resource, NY/courtesy of The William H. Johnson Foundation for the Arts; **5.19**: © The Trustees of The British Museum/Art Resource, NY; **5.20**: Sprengel Museum/akgimages; **5.21**: © 2015 Calder Foundation, New York/Artists Rights Society (ARS), New York; **5.22**: Jesse Godley, 1884 (gelatin silver print), Eakins, Thomas Cowperthwait (1844–1916)/Philadelphia Museum of Art, Pennsylvania, PA, USA/Gift of Charles Bregler, 1977/The Bridgeman Art Library; **5.23**: © 2015 Artists Rights Society (ARS), New York/SIAE, Rome. Digital image: Galleria d'Arte Moderna, Milan, Italy/Giraudon/The Bridgeman Art Library; **5.24**: © Bridget Riley 2013. Courtesy Karsten Schubert Gallery, London; **5.25a**: Hideki Yoshihara/age Fotostock; **5.25b**: Hideki Yoshihara/age Fotostock; **5.26**: Frieze of Dancers, c. 1895 (oil on fabric), Degas, Edgar (1834–1917)/Cleveland Museum of Art, OH, USA/Gift of the Hanna Fund/The Bridgeman Art Library; **5.27**: © RMN-Grand Palais/Art Resource, NY; **5.28**: akg-images; **5.29**: Study for Loie Fuller (1862–1928) at the Folies-Bergere, 1893 (oil on cardboard), Toulouse-Lautrec, Henri de (1864–1901)/Musee Toulouse-Lautrec, Albi, France/Giraudon/The Bridgeman Art Library; **5.30**: © Dennis Oppenheim. Courtesy of the artist; **5.31**: Add.10546 f.5v Adam and Eve, from the Moutier-Grandval Bible, illuminated in the Carolingian Abbey of St. Martin, Tours,

Latin, c. 834–843 (vellum), French School, (9th century)/British Library, London, UK/© British Library Board. All Rights Reserved.

CHAPTER 6—Opener: © Willie Cole. Courtesy Alexander and Bonin, New York; **6.1:** © Andrew Adolphus; **6.2:** © 1993 Delilah Montoya. Smithsonian American Art Museum, Washington, DC/Art Resource, NY; **6.3:** © Linda Mieko Allen. Courtesy Nancy Hoffman Gallery, New York; **6.4:** © Josiah McElheny. Courtesy Andrea Rosen Gallery, New York; **6.5:** © Andrew Adolphus. Image courtesy of the artist; **6.6:** Brick' screen, 1923–1925 (lacquered wood), Gray, Eileen (1879–1976)/Private Collection/Photo © Christie's Images/The Bridgeman Art Library; **6.7:** © Elliott Erwitt/ Magnum Photos; **6.8:** Whitney Museum of American Art. Jointly owned by the Whitney Museum of American Art, New York, and the Metropolitan Museum of Art; Gift of Ethel Redner Scull 86.6 1a-jj. © 2015 Andy Warhol Foundation for the Visual Arts/Artists Rights Society (ARS), New; **6.9:** © Beverly Buchanan. Courtesy of the artist; **6.10:** Smithsonian American Art Museum, Washington, DC/Art Resource, NY; **6.11:** © Cheltenham Art Gallery & Museums, Gloucestershire, UK/The Bridgeman Art Library; **6.12:** Erich Lessing/Art Resource, NY; **6.13:** © Willie Cole. Courtesy Alexander and Bonin, New York; **6.14:** © RMN-Grand Palais/Art Resource, NY; **6.15:** Jean-Paul, from the series "Splendours II," 1976 (oil on canvas), Fromanger, Gerard (b. 1939)/Private Collection/Giraudon/The Bridgeman Art Library; **6.16:** Heritage Image Partnership Ltd./Alamy; **6.17:** Tate, London/Art Resource, NY; **6.18:** © Eric Fischl. Courtesy of the artist; **6.19:** Courtesy of the artist and Salon 94, New York; **6.20:** Scala/Art Resource, NY; **6.21:** The Drunkenness of Bacchus, 1496–1497 (marble), Buonarroti, Michelangelo (1475–1564)/Museo Nazionale del Bargello, Florence, Italy/ The Bridgeman Art Library; **6.22:** Scala/Art Resource, NY; **6.23:** © Philip Taaffe. Courtesy Raymond Foye, Fine Arts Service Ltd; **6.24:** © William Wegman. Courtesy of the artist; **6.25:** Estate Otto Steinert, Museum Folkwang, Essen; **6.26:** ©Bruce Barnbaum; **6.27:** © 2015 Estate of Kay Sage/Artists Rights Society (ARS), New York. Digital image: Princeton University Art Museum/ Art Resource, NY; **6.28:** © Adil Jain; **6.29:** Victoria & Albert Museum, London/Art Resource, NY; **6.30:** Cosmo Condina/SuperStock; **6.31:** The Philadelphia Museum of Art/Art Resource, NY; **6.32:** George Eastman House; **6.33:** Art Resource; **6.34:** © Gui Borchert. Courtesy of the artist; **6.35:** Private Collection/James Goodman Gallery, New York/The Bridgeman Art Library. © Fernando Botero, courtesy Marlborough Gallery, New York; **6.36:** Photo © Christie's

Images/The Bridgeman Art Library; **6.37:** © Cengage Learning 2015; **6.38:** © Cengage Learning 2015; **6.39:** © Cengage Learning 2015; **6.40:** © Cengage Learning 2015; **6.42:** © Cengage Learning 2015; **6.43:** Exactostock/ SuperStock; **6.44:** Gianni Dagli Orti/The Art Archive at Art Resource, NY; **6.45:** Erich Lessing/Art Resource, NY.

CHAPTER 7—Opener: A study of a woman's hands, c. 1490 (metalpoint, heightening and charcoal on paper), Vinci, Leonardo da (1452–1519)/Royal Collection © Her Majesty Queen Elizabeth II, 2015/ Bridgeman Images; **7.1:** Art Institute of Chicago, Chicago, IL; **7.2:** Courtesy of the artist and Richard Solomon; **7.3:** A study of a woman's hands, c. 1490 (metalpoint, heightening and charcoal on paper), Vinci, Leonardo da (1452–1519)/Royal Collection Trust © Her Majesty Queen Elizabeth II, 2015/Bridgeman Images; **7.4:** Christopher Allsopp, 2012 (pencil on paper), Fowler, Nina (b. 1981)/© Courtesy of the Warden and Scholars of New College, Oxford/ Bridgeman Images; **7.5:** Adrian Piper Research Archive, Collection Eileen and Peter Norton; **7.6:** Digital Image © The Museum of Modern Art/Licensed by SCALA/Art Resource, NY. Courtesy of the artist and Gavin Brown's Enterprise; **7.7:** Rosenwald Collection, 1943.3.5217. Image © 2007 Board of Trustees, National Gallery of Art, Washington, DC. © 2015 Artist's Rights Society (ARS), New York/VG Bild-Kunst, Bonn; **7.8:** Christie's Images/Fine Art/Corbis; **7.9:** Madonna and child, c. 1525 (pencil & red chalk on paper), Buonarroti, Michelangelo (1475–1564)/Casa Buonarroti, Florence, Italy/Bridgeman Images; **7.10:** Digital Image © The Museum of Modern Art/Licensed by SCALA/Art Resource, NY; **7.11:** Digital Image © The Museum of Modern Art/Licensed by SCALA/Art Resource, NY; **7.12a:** Courtesy of Bernice Steinbaum Gallery, Miami, FL; **7.12b:** Courtesy of Bernice Steinbaum Gallery, Miami, FL; **7.13:** Collection of Lois Fichner-Rathus. Courtesy of Bernice Steinbaum Gallery, Miami, FL; **7.14:** Digital Image © The Museum of Modern Art/Licensed by SCALA/Art Resource, NY; **7.15:** Cafe Terrace at Night, September 1888 (reed pen and ink with graphite on laid paper), Gogh, Vincent van (1853–1890)/ Dallas Museum of Art, Texas, USA/The Wendy and Emery Reves Collection/Bridgeman Images; **7.16:** Cafe Terrace, Place du Forum, Arles, 1888 (oil on canvas), Gogh, Vincent van (1853–1890)/Rijksmuseum Kroller-Muller, Otterlo, Netherlands/Bridgeman Images; **7.17:** Drawing of a man seated with left leg resting over right knee (ink on paper), Hokusai, Katsushika (1760–1849)/ Brooklyn Museum of Art, New York, USA/ by exchange/Bridgeman Images; **7.18:** Digital Image © The Museum of Modern Art/Licensed by SCALA/Art Resource, NY;

Hornak/Fine Art/Corbis; **18.20:** © Wallace Collection, London, UK/The Bridgeman Art Library; **18.21:** Erich Lessing/Art Resource, NY; **18.22:** The Granger Collection, NYC; **18.23:** F1 ONLINE/SuperStock; **18.24:** Gerard Degeorge/akg-images; **18.25:** National Museum, New Delhi; **18.26:** © RMN-Grand Palais/Art Resource, NY; **18.27:** Image copyright © The Metropolitan Museum of Art. Image source: Art Resource, NY; **18.28:** Lebrecht Music and Arts Photo Library; **18.29:** Japan: *Midnight: The Hours of the Rat; Mother and Sleepy Child. Kitagawa Utamaro* (1753–1806), c. 1790/Pictures From History/Bridgeman Images; **18.30:** Under the Horse-Chestnut Tree, 1896–1897 (drypoint and aquatint in colors), Cassatt, Mary Stevenson (1844–1926)/Museum of Fine Arts, Houston, Texas, USA/Museum purchase funded by The Brown Foundation, Inc. and the Brown Foundation Accessions Endowment Fu.

CHAPTER 19—Opener: Giraudon/Art Resource, NY; **19.1:** © RMN-Grand Palais/Art Resource, NY; **19.2:** Heritage Images; **19.3:** Scala/Ministero per i Beni e le Attività culturali/Art Resource, NY; **19.4:** Erich Lessing/Art Resource, NY; **19.5:** RMN-Grand Palais/Art Resource, NY; **19.6:** Institut Amatller d'Art Hispanic; **19.7:** Art Resource, NY; **19.8:** Odalisque, c. 1825 (oil on canvas), Delacroix, Ferdinand Victor Eugene (1798–1863)/Fitzwilliam Museum, University of Cambridge, UK/The Bridgeman Art Library; **19.9:** Nymphs and Satyr, 1873 (oil on canvas), Bouguereau, William-Adolphe (1825–1905)/Sterling & Francine Clark Art Institute, Williamstown, Massachusetts, USA/The Bridgeman Art Library; **19.10:** The Metropolitan Museum of Art/Art Resource, NY; **19.11:** The Stone Breakers, 1849 (oil on canvas) (destroyed in 1945), Courbet, Gustave (1819–1877)/Galerie Neue Meister, Dresden, Germany/© Staatliche Kunstsammlungen Dresden/The Bridgeman Art Library; **19.12:** Erich Lessing/Art Resource, NY; **19.13:** Alinari Archives/Fratelli Alinari/Corbis; **19.14:** Erich Lessing/Art Resource, NY; **19.15:** Erich Lessing/Art Resource, NY; **19.16:** CNAC/MNAM/Dist. Réunion des Musées Nationaux/Art Resource, NY; **19.17:** The Metropolitan Museum of Art/Art Resource, NY; **19.18:** Erich Lessing/Art Resource, NY; **19.19:** The Metropolitan Museum of Art/Art Resource, NY; **19.20:** A. DAGLI ORTI/De Agostini Picture Library/Getty Images; **19.21:** Giraudon/Art Resource, NY; **19.22:** Glasgow Art Galleries and Museum; **19.23:** Georges Seurat French, 1859–1891, A Sunday on La Grande Jatte—1884, 1884–1886, Oil on canvas, 81 3/4 × 121 1/4 in. (207.5 × 308.1 cm), Helen Birch Bartlett Memorial Collection, 1926.224, The Art Institute of Chicago. Photography © The Art Institute; **19.24:** The Art Institute of Chicago;

19.25: Digital Image © The Museum of Modern Art/Licensed by SCALA/Art Resource, NY; **19.26:** Self Portrait with Bandaged Ear, 1889 (oil on canvas), Gogh, Vincent van (1853–1890)/© Samuel Courtauld Trust, The Courtauld Gallery, London, UK/The Bridgeman Art Library; **19.27:** The Vision after the Sermon (Jacob wrestling with the Angel) 1888 (oil on canvas), Gauguin, Paul (1848–1903)/© National Gallery of Scotland, Edinburgh, Scotland/The Bridgeman Art Library; **19.28:** The Art Institute of Chicago; **19.29:** Photo: © Erich Lessing/Art Resource, NY © 2015 The Munch Museum/The Munch-Ellingsen Group/Artists Rights Society (ARS), NY; **19.30:** Reproduced from the collections of the Library of Congress, Washington, DC. © 2015 Artists Rights Society (ARS), New York/VG Bild-Kunst, Bonn; **19.31:** National Gallery of Art, Washington DC, USA/Index/The Bridgeman Art Library; **19.32:** James Abbott McNeill Whistler/The Gallery Collection/Corbis; **19.33:** The Philadelphia Museum of Art/Art Resource, NY; **19.34:** The Metropolitan Museum of Art/Art Resource, NY; **19.35:** Museum of Fine Arts, Boston; **19.36:** Vanni/Art Resource, NY; **19.37:** Lois Fichner-Rathus; **19.38:** Erich Lessing/Art Resource, NY; **19.39:** Lois Fichner-Rathus; **19.40:** Musée Barbier-Mueller; **19.41:** Werner Forman/Art Resource, NY; **19.42:** © The Metropolitan Museum of Art/Art Resource, NY; **19.43:** Image copyright © The Metropolitan Museum of Art. Image source: Art Resource, NY; **19.44:** The Brooklyn Museum of Art, 87.234.6; **19.45:** Historical Picture Archive/Corbis; **19.46:** Cleveland Museum of Art; **19.47:** Francis G. Mayer/Corbis; **19.48:** Tokyo National University of Fine Arts and Music; **19.49:** Tauihu, war canoe prow carved by Wiremu Kingi Te Rangitake, chief of the Te Ati Awa/Werner Forman Archive/Bridgeman Images; **19.50:** Tapuae, c. 1900 (w/con paper), Ryan, Thomas (1864–1927)/Private Collection/© Michael Graham-Stewart/Bridgeman Images; **19.51:** © The Metropolitan Museum of Art/Art Resource, NY; **19.52:** Erich Lessing/Art Resource, NY; **19.53:** Catalogue No. E358425, Department of Anthropology, NMNH, Smithsonian Institution; **19.54:** *The Execution of Maximilian I* (1832–1867) (oil on canvas), Mexican School (19th century)/Museo Nacional de Historia, Castillo de Chapultepec, Mexico/Bridgeman Images; **19.55:** Phoebe A. Hearst Museum of Anthropology; **19.56:** Smithsonian, National Museum of the American Indian.

CHAPTER 20—Opener: © 2015 Estate of Pablo Picasso/Artists Rights Society (ARS), NY. Photo: © Erich Lessing/Art Resource, NY; **20.1:** Digital Image © The Museum of Modern Art/Licensed by SCALA/Art Resource, NY. © 2015 Artists Rights Society, New York/ADAGP, Paris; © 2012 Succession H. **20.2:** © 2015 Succession

H. Matisse, Paris/Artists Rights Society (ARS), New York. Photo: Archives Henri Matisse; **20.3:** © The Museum of Modern Art/Licensed by SCALA/Art Resource, NY; **20.4:** Scala/Art Resource, NY; **20.5:** The Saint Louis Art Museum. Bequest of Morton D. May. 841:1983 © 2015 Artists Rights (ARS), New York/VG Bild-Kunst, Bonn; **20.6:** Helen Birth Bartlett Memorial Collection. 1926.253. Photography © The Art Institute of Chicago. © 2015 Estate of Pablo Picasso/Artists Rights Society (ARS), New York; **20.7:** © 2015 Estate of Pablo Picasso/Artists Rights Society (ARS), New York, Digital Image © The Museum of Modern Art/Licensed by SCALA/Art Resource, NY; **20.8:** Musée Barbier-Mueller; **20.9:** © 2015 Artists Rights Society (ARS), NY/ADAGP, Paris. Photo: © Bridgeman-Giraudon/Art Resource, NY; **20.10:** Pablo Picasso, La bouteille de Suze (Bottle of Suze), 1912. Pasted papers, gouache, and charcoal, 25 3/4 × 19 3/4". Mildred Lane Kemper Art Museum, Washington University in St. Louis. University purchase, Kende Sale Fund, 1946; **20.11:** Erich Lessing/Art Resource, NY; **20.12:** © The Estate of Jacques Lipchitz, courtesy Marlborough Gallery, New York; **20.13:** © 2015 Estate of Alexander Archipenko/Artists Rights Society (ARS), New York; **20.14:** The Museum of Modern Art/Licensed by SCALA/Art Resource, NY; **20.15:** The Museum of Modern Art/Licensed by SCALA/Art Resource, NY; **20.16:** Virginia Museum of Fine Arts. Gift of Mr. and Mrs. Bruce Gotwald. Image © Virginia Museum of Fine Arts. Photo by Katherine Wetzel. © 2015 The Georgia O'Keeffe Foundation/Artists Rights Society (ARS), New York; **20.17:** © 2003 Whitney Museum of American Art; **20.18:** The Work of Naum Gabo © Nina & Graham Williams. Photograph by David Heald © The Solomon R. Guggenheim Foundation, NY, 55.1429; **20.19:** Scala/Art Resource, NY; **20.20:** © 2015 Artists Rights Society (ARS), NY/ADAGP, Paris. © Philadelphia Museum of Art/Corbis; **20.21:** © 2015 Artists Rights Society (ARS), NY/VG-Bild Kunst, Bonn. Digital Image © The Museum of Modern Art/Licensed by Scala/Art Resource, NY, 564.1939; **20.22:** Art Gallery of Ontario, Toronto, Canada/Gift of Sam and Ayala Zacks, 1970/ The Bridgeman Art Library; **20.23:** Burstein Collection/CORBIS; **20.24:** Marcel Duchamp (1887–1968), Nude Descending a Staircase (No. 2) (1912), oil on canvas. The Louise and Walter Arensberg Collection, 1950. The Philadelphia Museum of Art/Art Resource, NY. © 2012 Art; **20.25:** © 2015 Artists Rights Society (ARS), NY/ADAGP, Paris. Digital Image © The Museum of Modern Art/Licensed by Scala/Art Resource, NY, 00256.37; **20.26:** The Museum of Modern Art/Licensed by SCALA/Art Resource, NY © Salvador Dali, Artists Rights Society (ARS), New York

2014; **20.27:** © 2015 Artists Rights Society (ARS), NY/ADAGP, Paris. Digital Image © The Museum of Modern Art/Licensed by Scala/Art Resource, NY, 229.1937; **20.28:** Art © Figge Art Museum, successors to the Estate of Nan Wood Graham/Licensed by VAGA, New York, NY Photography © The Art Institute of Chicago,1930.934; **20.29:** © Francis G. Mayer/Corbis; **20.30:** The Carl Van Vechten Gallery of Fine Arts, Fisk University, Nashville, TN; **20.31:** Hampton University Museum, Hampton, VA. © 2015 The Jacob and Gwendolyn Lawrence Foundation, Seattle/Artists Rights Society (ARS), New York; **20.32:** Jonathan Poore/Cengage Learning; **20.33:** DeA Picture Library/Art Resource, NY; **20.34:** [2000.472] Sharf Collection, Museum of Fine Arts, Boston; **20.35:** Museum of Fine Arts, Boston, Jean S. and Frederick A. Sharf Collection. Accession number: 2000.323; **20.36:** Image copyright © The Metropolitan Museum of Art. Image source: Art Resource, NY; **20.37:** Christie's Images Ltd./SuperStock; **20.38:** Mao Zedong (1893–1976) Marching towards the Jing Gang Mountains in October 1927 (color litho), Chinese School (20th century)/Private Collection/Archives Charmet/Bridgeman Images; **20.39:** © Trustees of the British Museum, London; **20.40:** Otto Lang/Corbis; **20.41:** History of Mexico: The Aztec World, 1929 (photo)/Palacio Nacional, Mexico City, Mexico/Dirk Bakker, photographer for the Detroit Institute of Arts/Bridgeman Images; **20.42:** The two Fridas, 1939, by Frida Kahlo (1907–1954), oil on canvas, 172 × 173 cm. Mexico, 20th century., Kahlo, Frida (1907–1954)/Museo de Arte Moderno, Mexico City, Mexico/De Agostini Picture Library/G. Dagli Orti/Bridgeman Images.

CHAPTER 21—Opener: The Museum of Modern Art/Licensed by SCALA/Art Resource, NY; **21.1:** Center for Creative Photography University of Arizona; **21.2:** The Museum of Modern Art/Licensed by SCALA/Art Resource, NY; **21.3:** Artists Rights Society; **21.4:** The Art Institute of Chicago; **21.5:** © Estate of Joan Mitchell Photograph: © Butler Institute of American Art, Youngstown, OH, USA/Gift of Marilynn Meeker, 1986 Courtesy of the Joan Mitchell Foundation, NYC/The Bridgeman Art Library International; **21.6:** Digital Image © The Museum of Modern Art/Licensed by SCALA/Art Resource, NY; **21.7:** The Solomon R. Guggenheim Museum, New York. Gift, The Mark Rothko Foundation, Inc., 1986. 86.3422 © 2015 Kate Rothko Prizel and Christopher Rothko/Artists Rights Society (ARS), New York; **21.8:** Helen Frankenthaler, The Bay, 1963 (acrylic on canvas), 205.1 × 207.7 cm, Detroit Institute of Arts, USA/© DACS/Founders Society Purchase, Dr. & Mrs. Hilbert H. DeLawter Fund/The Bridgeman Art Library International. Art © 2015 Helen Frankenthaler/

Artis; **21.9:** Art Resource, NY © Estate of David Smith/Licensed by VAGA, New York, NY; **21.10:** VAGA (Visual Artists and Galleries Association); **21.11:** JUDY PFAFF; **21.12:** The Art Institute of Chicago; **21.13:** Photograph © Spencer A. Rathus. All rights reserved. Reproduced by permission of the Henry Moore Foundation; **21.14:** © 2015 Frank Stella/Artists Rights Society (ARS), NY. Photo © CNAC/MNAM/Dist./Art Resource, NY; **21.15:** © RMN-Grand Palais/Art Resource, NY; **21.16:** Collection of the Walker Art Center, Minneapolis. Walker Special Purchase Fund, 1984; **21.17:** "Just what is it that makes today's homes so different, so appealing?," 1956 (collage), Hamilton, Richard (1922–2011)/Kunsthalle, Tubingen, Germany/The Bridgeman Art Library; **21.18:** Robert Rauschenberg, Bed, 1955, 6' 3 1/4" × 31 1/2" × 8", Combine painting: oil and pencil on pillow, quilt and sheet on wood supports. Digital Image © The Museum of Modern Art/Licensed by SCALA/Art Resource, NY. Art © Estate of Robert Rauschenberg/L; **21.19: 22.21:** Art © Jasper Johns/Licensed by VAGA, New York, NY. Digital image © Jasper Johns/Bridgeman Art Library; **21.21:** Hemis/Alamy; **21.22:** © SuperStock; **21.23:** Incorporating a portion of Margaret Bourke White's photograph Buchenwald, 1945. © Time, Inc. Photograph courtesy of the Louis K. Meisel Gallery, New York; **21.24:** Courtesy of Mrs. Duane Hanson. Art © Estate of Duane Hanson/Licensed by VAGA, New York, NY; **21.25:** Close, Chuck Big Self Portrait 1967–1968, acrylic on canvas. Collection Walker Art Center Minneapolis. Art Center Acquisition Fund, 1969; **21.26:** Permanent collection the Chinati Foundation, Marfa, Texas. Photograph by Florian Holzherr, 2002. Art © Judd Foundation. Licensed by VAGA, New York, NY; **21.27:** Digital Image © 2008 Museum Associates/LACMA. Licensed by Art Resource, NY; **21.28:** © 2015 Artists Rights Society (ARS), NY/ADAGP, Paris Photo Credit: Digital Image © The Museum of Modern Art/Licensed by SCALA/Art Resource, NY; **21.29:** Keystone-France/Getty Images; **21.30:** Digital Image © (2015) Museum Associates/LACMA. Licensed by Art Resource, NY; **21.31:** Digital Image © The Museum of Modern Art/Licensed by SCALA/Art Resource, NY; **21.32:** Collection of Emily Fisher Landau, New York. Courtesy of Mary Boone Gallery, New York; **21.33:** National American Art Museum, Smithsonian Institution, Washington, DC/Art Resource, NY. © 2007 Miriam Schapiro and Flomenhaft Gallery; **21.34:** © 2015 Judy Chicago/Artists Rights Society (ARS), New York; **21.35:** © The Estate of Ana Mendieta Collection, LLC Courtesy Galerie Lelong, New York; **21.36:** Copyright © Guerrilla Girls. Courtesy www.guerrillagirls.com; **21.37:** Photograph by Lizzie Himmel from the New York Times Sunday Magazine;

21.38: Courtesy of the artist and Cheim & Read Gallery; **21.39:** The Estate of Robert Mapplethorpe; **21.40:** Romare Bearden/Museum of Modern Art; **21.41:** Solomon R. Guggenheim Museum, New York, gift of Mr. and Mrs. Gus and Judith Lieber, 1988, 99.3620. Photograph by David Heald © The Solomon R. Guggenheim Foundation, New York; **21.42:** The Broad Art Foundation, Santa Monica, CA. Photo: Douglas Parker Studio. © 2015 Estate of Jean-Michel Basquiat/Artists Rights Society (ARS), New York/ADAGP, Paris; **21.43:** The Solomon R. Guggenheim Foundation, New York; **21.44:** Napoleon Crossing the Alps on 20th May 1800, 1803 (oil on canvas) (see 184124 for detail), David, Jacques Louis (1748–1825) (workshop of)/Versailles, France/Bridgeman Images; **21.45:** Napoleon Leading the Army Over the Alps © Kehinde Wiley Studio. Used by Permission; **21.46:** Chrysler Museum of Art, Norfolk, VA, Museum Purchase, 93.2, © Jaune Quick-to-See-Smith; **21.47:** Courtesy of the artist and The Pace Gallery; **21.48:** © 2015 Susan Rothenberg/Artists Rights Society (ARS), New York. Courtesy Sperone Westwater, New York; **21.49:** Gagosian Gallery; **21.50:** Collection of the Whitney Museum of American Art, New York. Purchase, with funds from the Louis and Bessie Adler Foundation, Inc., Seymour M. Klein, President, 83.17a-b; **21.51:** Ludwig Mies van der Rohe, Farnsworth House, Plano, Illinois, Exterior view, c. 1945–1951. Gelatin silver print, 8" × 10" (20.3 × 25.4 cm). Mies van der Rohe Archive, gift of the architect. Photograph by Heinrich Blessing. Digital Image © The Museum of Mod; **21.52:** Jonathan Poore/Cengage Learning; **21.53:** Ambient Images Inc./Alamy; **21.54:** MICHAEL GRAVES; **21.55:** Jonathan Poore/Cengage Learning; **21.56:** Studio Daniel Libeskind; **21.57:** Courtesy Zaha Hadid Architects; **21.58:** The Port Authority of NY & NJ; **21.59:** Ragamala Series, 1960 (oil on canvas), Husain, Maqbool Fida (M.F.) (1915–2011)/Private Collection/Photo © Christie's Images/Bridgeman Images; **21.60:** The Metropolitan Museum of Art; **21.61:** © The Bridgeman Art Library; **21.62:** Shanghai Chinese Painting Academy; **21.63:** Spencer Museum of Art, The University of Kansas, Lawrence, Kansas. Museum purchase: Gift of E. Rhodes and Leona B. Carpenter Foundation; **21.64a:** Agencja Fotograficzna Caro/Alamy; **21.64b:** © Atsuko Tanaka/Museum of Contemporary Art, Tokyo; **21.65:** © CNAC/MNAM/Dist. RMN-Grand Palais/Art Resource, NY; **21.66:** Amagasaki Cultural Center.

CHAPTER 22—Opener: Private Collection/Photo © Christie's Images/The Bridgeman Art Library /VAGA; **22.1:** Collection of John A. Smith and Victoria Hughes. Courtesy Tomio Koyama Gallery, Tokyo.

INDEX

NOTE: Page references in **bold** refer to illustrations or photos of art.

A

Abbasid Caliphate. *See* Golden Age of Islam
Abramovic, Marina, 511–512; *The Artist Is Present,* 512, **512**; *Breathing In/Breathing Out,* 511
abstract art, 4, 16–17
Abstract Expressionist era, 492
abstraction, 500–501; in Europe, 473–474; in United States, 470–473
abstract shapes, 29, 33
Academic art, 425
Academy, 425
Achilles (Greek hero), 277
Acropolis, 283, **283**
acrylic painting, 127, 129
action painting, 493
actual lines, 22
actual mass, 28
Adam and Eve (Dürer), 359, **359**
Adams, Ansel: *Moon and Half Dome, Yosemite National Park, California,* 150, 150–151
additive colors, 46, **46**
additive process, 180
adobe, 227
Adolphus, Andrew: *Divergence 2,* 84, **84**; *Sight Lines (Birds),* 86, 87; *Untitled,* 35, **35**
Adoration of the Magi (da Fabriano), **124,** 124–125
Aegean, 265–269; in Crete, 266–267; in Cyclades, 265–266; in Mycenae, 267–269
Aeron Chair (Stumpf and Chadwick), 204, **205**
Africa: map of, **269**; modern art, 447–450; religion in, 348–350
African art: ancient, 269–271; contemporary, 552–555; masks, 467; twentieth-century art, 487–488
Age of the Warring States, 347
Agesander: *Laocoön and His Sons,* 289, 289–290
The Agony and the Ecstasy, 371
Aher, Prajakta Palav: Ganpati Series *Untitled I,* 344, **344,** 543
Akbar, 382–384, **384**
Akbar and the Elephant (Basawan and Chatar Muni), 384, **384**
Akhenaton, 261–262, **262**
Akkad, 253–254
Albers, Josef: *Solo V,* 141, **141**
Alberti, Leon Battista, 353, 366; Palazzo Rucellai, Florence, 366, **367**
Aldred, Cyril, 262
Alexander the Great, 244, 288–289, 308
Alexandria, Egypt: Eastern Harbor, 245, **245**
Alexandros of Antioch-on-the-Meander: *Aphrodite (Venus de Milo),* 290, **290**
Alhambra, 339–340
Allegiance and Wakefulness (Women of Allah) (Neshat), 161–162, **162**
Allen, Linda Mieko: *Atmospherics XIX (ultraviolet),* 84, **85**
Alloway, Lawrence, 502
Altar to the Hand and Arm, Kingdom of Benin (Nigeria), 349
alternate a-b-a-b support system, 324

alternating rhythm, 100
Alvin Ailey American Dance Theater website, 177, **177**
Amarna period, ancient art in, 261–262
ambulatory, 317
Amer, Ghada, 517; *Knotty but Nice,* 517, **517**
American Gothic (Wood), 480
Americas: ancient art in, 311; contemporary art in, 556–559; modern art in, 455–457; religion in, 351; during Renaissance in Europe, 387–389
The Arnolfini Portrait (van Eyck), **10,** 10–11
amorphous shape, 29, 33–34
amphitheaters, 298
analogous color, 50
analytic Cubism, 467–468
Ancestor poles, 454, **454**
Ancestral Couple, **449,** 449–450
ancient art, 247–273; Aegean, 265–269; African, 269–271; Asian, 270, 271–273; Egyptian, 256–264; in India, 270, 272, 273; Mesopotamia, 251–256; prehistoric art, 248–251
Ancient Egypt map, **257**
Ancient Near East map, **251**
Anderson, Wes: *Fantastic Mr. Fox,* 169, **169**
Angel (Salle), 42, **42**
Angel of the Waters (Stebbins), 198, **198**
Angkor Wat, 342, **343**
Anguissola, Sofonisba, 381–382; *A Game of Chess,* 382, **382**
animation, in cinematography, 167–169
animism, 348
Annunciation and Visitation, jamb figures on the right side of the central doorway of the west façade, Reims Cathedral, 332, **332**
Antoni, Janine: *Gnaw,* 12, **12,** 192, **192**
aperture, 152
Aphrodite (Greek goddess), 277
Aphrodite of Melos, 290, **290**
apocalypse, 331
Apollo (Greek god), 277
Apollo and Daphne (Bernini), 179, **180**
Apoxyomenos (Lysippos), 288, **288**
Apple brand icon, 36, **147**
appropriation, 541
apse, 316
aquarelle, 127
aquatint, 140
Ara Pacis (Altar of Peace), 300, 301
arbitrary color, 52
Arbol de la Vida, no. 294 (Mendieta), 515, **515**
Arcadia Revisited (Crash), 130, **130**
Arc de Triomphe, Paris, 229
Archaic period, 276, 278–282; architecture, 278–280; sculpture, 278; vase painting, 280–282
arches, **227,** 229
Archipenko, Alexander, 469–470; *Walking Woman,* **469,** 469–470
architecture, 225–243; Aegean, 268; Archaic period, 278–280; Baroque, 399; cast-iron, 233–234; Chinese, 384–386, 545–546; Christian, 315–318; Classical, 283, 286; Deconstructivist, 529–531; defined, 225; Gothic, 230, 327, 327–331; green buildings, 242–243; Modern, 526–527; Neoclassicism, 421; new materials and visions,

239, 242–243; Old Kingdom, 259–260; Old Kingdom Egypt, 259–260; Postmodern, 527–528; reinforced concrete, 236–238; Renaissance, 366; Roman Empire, 295–300, 304–305; shell, 239; steel-cable, 238–239; steel-cage, 234–236; stone, 226–230; symbolic significance, 5; wood, 230–233
architrave, 279
archivolts, 331
Ardabil Carpet, Iran, 218–219
Armory Show, 472–473
Army of Shi Huangdi (First Emperor), 308–309, **309**
Arneson, Robert: *Jackson Pollock,* 212, **212**
Arnheim, Rudolf, 83
"Arnold Glimcher and Art World All-Stars," 516, **516**
Arrangement in Black and Gray: The Artist's Mother (Whistler), 442–443, **443**
Arrechea, Alexandre, 556; *Elementos Arquitectronicos,* 556, **556**
The Arrival of Spring in Woldgate, East Yorkshire in 2011 (Hockney), 119, **119**
art: content, 4–6; defined, 2–3; form, 7; iconography, 7; mediums and techniques, 12; subject of, 3; visual elements, 8–11
The Artist in the Character of Design Listening to the Inspiration of Poetry (Kauffman), 419, 419–420
The Artist Is Present (Abramovic), 512, **512**
The Artist's Studio (Daguerre), 154, **154**
Art Nouveau, 447–448
Artworks for AIDS exhibition, Seattle, 222
Aryans, 273
Ashurbanipal (King of Assyria), 255
Ashurnasirpal II hunting lions, **255**
Asia, ancient art in, 271–273
assemblages, 185–186
Assyria, 255
asymmetrical balance, 97
Athena (Greek goddess), 277
Athenadorus: *Laocoön and His Sons,* 289, 289–290
Atmospherics XIX (ultraviolet) (Allen), 84, **85**
AT&T Building, New York City (Burgee architects with Johnson), 527, 527–528
At the Concert Européen (Seurat), 112, 113
Augustus (Emperor of Rome), 293, 295, 300
Augustus of Primaporta, 95, **95,** 102, **274–275,** 300, **300**
Aurangzeb, 543
Autobiography: Water/Ancestors, Middle Passage/Family Ghosts (Pindell), 130–131, **131**
automatic writing, 478
Automatist Surrealism, 478, 479
"*Autumn Showers (Shigure)*" (Kason), 485, **485**
Aztecs, 388–389
Aztec Vase #06-1 (Woodman), 213, **213**

B

Babur, 382
Babylonia, 254
Baciccio: *Triumph of the Sacred Name of Jesus,* 398, 399
Bacon, Francis, 499; *Figure with Meat,* 499, **499**
Baghdad, 243–244
Baghdad City (Hazoumé), 553
Bagism (Ono), 511, **511**
Baker, Kristin: *Oculatei Der Boomen,* 20, **20**

balance, 11, 95–96; actual, 96; asymmetrical, 97; diagonal, 98; horizontal, 97; radial, 98–99; symmetrical, 96–97; vertical, 98; visual, 96
Balla, Giacomo, 470; *Girl Running on the Balcony,* 79, 79–80; *Street Light,* 76, 470, **471**
The Ballet Master (Degas), 144, **144**
balloon framing, **232**, 232–233
Bamboo (Li K'an), **384**, 385
Baptistery of Florence competition, 361–362
Barack Obama "Hope" Poster (Fairey), 37, **37**
Barbecue (Fischl), 94, **94**
Barnbaum, Bruce: *Wall with Two Ridges, Lower Antelope Canyon,* 98, **98**
Baroque period, 391–415; in China, 413–414; classicism in, 404, 407; definition of, 391; in England, 407–408; in Flanders, 401–402; in France, 404–407; in Holland, 402–404; in India, 412–413; in Italy, 392–399; in Japan, 414–415; Rococo style in, 409–411; in Spain, 399–401
barrel vault, **227**, 229
Bartlett, Jennifer, 523; *Spiral: An Ordinary Evening in New Haven,* **523**, 523–524
Basawan: *Akbar and the Elephant,* 384, **384**
Baseball Catcher (Yoshihara), 80, **80**
Basilica Nova, Rome, 304–305, **305**
Basilica of St. Peter's, Rome, 313–314, 316, **316**, 392, 393, **393**; Piazza of St. Peter's (Bernini), 393
basket weaving, 220
Basquiat, Jean-Michel, 520; *Melting Point of Ice,* **520**
bas-relief, 180
batik, 220
Battle of Hastings, detail of the Bayeux Cathedral, 325
Battle of Ten Naked Men (Pollaiuolo), **136**, 137
The Battleship Potemkin (Eisenstein), 167, **167**
Bauhaus, 482–484
baumraum treehouse, 231, **231**
bay, 229
The Bay (Frankenthaler), **497**
Bayeux Cathedral, **325**
Bayeux Tapestry, 325, 327; Battle of Hastings detail of, **325**
Bearded Man (Mohenjo-Daro), 273, **273**
Bearden, Romare, 518; *The Dove,* 518, **518**
Beckmann, Max: *The Dream,* 464, **464**
The Bed (Rauschenberg), 130, 503, **503**
Beesley, Ruth, 558
Before the Caves (Frankenthaler), 33, 33–34
Benglis, Lynda: *Morisse,* 58, **58**
Benin, 349
Berard, Ron: *Untitled,* 159, **159**
Berlin Museum extension (Libeskind), 5–6, 529, **529**
Berlin Olympic Stadium, 296, **296**
Bernini, Gianlorenzo, 374–375, 392–395; *Apollo and Daphne,* 179, **180**; *David,* 64, 65, 80, 375, **375**; *The Ecstasy of St. Theresa,* 180, **390–391**, 394–395, **395**
Between Earth and Heaven (El Anatsui), **54–55**, **61**, 552
Bhavsar, Natvar: *Yosemite IV,* 533, **533**
Bible Quilt (Powers), 445, **445**
Big Family (Zhang Xiaogang), **544**, 545
Big Self-Portrait (Close), 508, **508**
binder, 111
Bird, Brad: *The Incredibles,* 168, **168**
Birnbaum, Dara: *Rio Videowall,* 172, **172**
The Birth of Venus (Botticelli), **24**, 24–25, 365, 365–366
bitumen, 154
black-and-white film, 153
Black eggshell pottery (Longshan), **271**

black-figure painting, 280
Black on Grey (Rothko), 496, **496**
Block #43 (Casanovas), 213, **213**, 214
Bloom, Howard, 225
Bloomberg, Michael R., 196
Blossoming Earth (Dubuffet), 57, **57**
Blue Door (Miller), 174, **174**
Blue Period (Wegman), 160, **160**
The Boating Party (Cassatt), 442, **442**
Boccioni, Umberto, 470; *Dynamism of a Cyclist,* 33, **33**; *Dynamism of a Soccer Player,* 470; *The Street Enters the House,* 76, **76**; "Technical Manual of Futurist Painting," 76; *Unique Forms of Continuity in Space,* 76, 470, **470**
Bonaparte, Napoleon, 420
Bonheur, Rosa, 430–431; *The Horse Fair,* **430**, 431
Borchert, Gui: "Nike Restoration," 102
Borromini, Francesco, 399; San Carlo alle Quattro Fontane, Rome, 399, **399**
Botanical Specimen (Talbot), 155, **155**
Botero, Fernando: *Theatre Characters,* 102
Botticelli, Sandro, 365–366; *Birth of Venus,* **24**, 24–25, **365**, 365–366
Bottle (Nealie), **211**, 211–212
The Bottle of Banyuls (Gris), 67, **67**
Bouguereau, Adolphe William, 425, 461; *Nymphs and Satyr,* 425, **425**
Bourgeois, Louise, 491; *Eyes,* 187, **187**; *Portrait of Robert,* 181, **181**
Bourke-White, Margaret, 159; *The Living Dead of Buchenwald,* 157–158, **158**
Boursier-Mougenot, Céleste: *From Here to Ear,* 57, **57**
Bowls (Cooper), **211**, 211–212
Brady, Matthew, 157
Brancusi, Constantin, 474; *Bird in Space,* 474, **474**
Brandenburg, Marc: *Untitled* (2004), 40–41, **41**
Braque, Georges, 467–468; *The Portuguese,* **467**, 467–468
Bravo, Claudio: *Package,* 111, **111**
Breton, André, 478
Breuer, Marcel, 484; tubular steel chair, 484
'Brick' Screen (Gray), 87, **87**
Bridge in the Rain (van Gogh), 452, **452**
Brody, Sherry, 514; *The Doll House,* 514, **514**
bronze, 182, 221
Brooklyn Bridge, **238**, 238–239
Brown, J. Carter, 190
The Brown Sisters (Nixon), 156, **156**
Bruegel, Pieter, the Elder, 379–380; *The Peasant Wedding,* 380, **380**
Brunelleschi, Filippo, 361–362, 364; *Sacrifice of Isaac,* 361–362, **362**
brush and ink, 115–116
Buchanan, Beverly: *4 Shacks with Black-Eyed Susans,* 88, 88–89; *Henriette's Yard,* 114, **114**, 520
Buddha, 307–308, **308**
Buddha, 348
Buddhism, 306–307, 346
Bull-leaping fresco, 267, **267**
Bunshaft, Gordon: Lever House, **235**, 235–236
Buñuel's, Luis: *Un Chien Andalou,* 171, **171**
buon fresco, 123
Burgee, John: AT&T Building, New York City, **527**, 527–528
The Burghers of Calais (Rodin), 446, **446**
The Burial of Count Orgaz (El Greco), 379, **379**
burin, 135, **135**
burnished, 182
The Burqa Project (Désert), 543, **544**
Burton, Tim: *The Corpse Bride,* 168, 168–169

Bust of Queen Nefertiti, 261, **261**
buttressing, 229–230
"Buy War Bonds," 101, **101**
Bwoom helmet mask, 488, **488**
Byodo-in monastery, 346, **346**
By the Sea II (Zakanich), 128, **128**
Byzantine art: San Vitale, Ravenna, 316, 317, **317**, 320

C

The Cabinet of Dr. Caligari (Wiene), 171, **171**
Caesar, Julius, 244
Café (Johnson), 74, **74**
Café Terrace, Place du Forum, Arles (van Gogh), 115
Café Terrace at Night, September 1888 (van Gogh), **113**
Cai Guo-Qiang: *Drawing for Transient Rainbow,* 117, **117**
Caillebotte, Gustave: *Paris Street: Rainy Day,* 73, **73**, 93
Calatrava, Santiago, 107, 530; World Trade Center Transportation Hub, **531**
Calder, Alexander, 186; *Five Swords,* 190; *Little Spider,* 77, **77**, 96
California Institute of Arts, 514
caliph, 334
Callicrates, Parthenon and, 286
calligraphy, 113
Calyx Krater (Euphronios and Euxitheos), **208**
Cambodia, 342
Cambrensis, Giraldus, 320
camera and the human eye compared, **152**
camera obscura, 154, **154**
cameras: film, 152–153; human eye compared to, **152**; in photography, 152
Campana Brothers: *Favela Chair,* 223, **223**
Campin, Robert, 356–357
Canada, 456–457
Canaletto, Giovanni Antonio: *The Rialto Bridge,* 65
canon of proportion: defined, 102; Khafre rendered according to, 259; subverting, 103
Canova, Antonio: *Pauline Borghese as Venus,* **420**, 420–421
Capitoline Venus, 366
Caravaggio, 395–396; *The Conversion of St. Paul,* **395**, 395–396; *Judith and Holofernes,* 397, **397**
Carlos, Don Juan, Count de Montizon: *The Hippopotamus at the Zoological Gardens, Regent's Park,* 101, **101**
Carolingian art, 320–321
carpet page, **319**, 319–320
Carter, Holland, 539
Carter, Howard, 263
Cartier-Bresson, Henri, 80
cartoons, 116
carving, 181
Casa Mila Apartment House, Barcelona (Gaudí), 30, 31, 199, 447, **447**
Casanovas, Claudi: *Block #43,* 213, **213**, 214
Cassatt, Mary, 415, 442; *The Boating Party,* 442, **442**; *In the Loge,* 50, **51**
casting, 181–182, 184
cast-iron architecture, 233–234
catacombs, 304, 315
Cathedral of Saint-Lazare, Autun, France, 324, **324**
Catlett, Elizabeth: *Sharecropper,* 26, **26**
A Cautionary Tale Continuum (Yellow) (Doolan), 189, **189**
ceiling decoration, in Baroque period, 399
Celebrate the Success of Our Glorious Atomic Bomb Explosion! (Hufan), 534, **534**

Cellini, Benvenuto: *Saltcellar of Francis I,* 221, **221**
centering, 229
central plans, 316
Central watchtower, architectural model, Eastern Han Dynasty, **310**
ceramics: clay, methods of working with, 209–210; defined, 209; earthenware, 212–213; glazing in, 211–212; porcelain, 213–214; potter's wheel in, 210–211; stoneware, 213; terra-cotta, 212–213
Cercando un Ago (Mitchell), 6
Ceremonial feathered basket with bead and shell pendants, 220
ceremonial masks, 554–555
Ceremonial vessel (Guang), **271**, 271–272
Cézanne, Paul, 435–437; *Mont Sainte-Victoire Seen from Bibemus Quarry,* 47, **47**; *Still Life with Basket of Apples,* **436**, 436; *The Winding Road,* 128, **128**
Chadwick, Don: *Aeron Chair,* 204, **205**
Chagoya, Enrique, 557–558; *Illegal Alien's Guide to Critical Theory,* 557–558, **558**
chalk, 111–112
chaos, art and, 89, 91
chapel of Notre-Dame-du-Haut (Le Corbusier), **236**
Chaplin, Charlie: *The Great Dictator,* 170, **170**
charcoal, 110–111
Chardin, Jean-Baptiste Simeon: *Still Life with Bottle of Olives,* **67**
Chariots of Fire (Hudson), 164
Charlemagne (Charles the Great), 320
Chartres Cathedral, France, 328–329, **329**
Chatar Muni: *Akbar and the Elephant,* **384**, 384
Che, Hoy y Siempre Movie Poster (Niko), 37, **37**
Chiang Kai-Shek, 486
chiaroscuro, 25, 42–43
Chicago, Judy, 514–515; *The Dinner Party,* 515, **515**; *Womanhouse,* 514
The Chief: He Who Sold Africa to the Colonists, from *Self-Portraits I-IV* (Fosso), **552**
Chihuly, Dale: *Fibri di Como,* **49**; *Glass Flowers,* **38–39**; *Icicle Creek Chandelier,* 216–217, **217**; *Rio delle Torreselle Chandelier,* 216, **216**
Chilkat robe (Jackson), 219, **219**
China, 139; architecture, 384–386, 545–546; Baroque period in, 413–414; contemporary art in, 544–546; Ming Dynasty, 384–386; post–World War II, 531, 534–535; Qin Dynasty, 308–309; religion in, 342–343; twentieth-century art, 486–487
Chinese art: ancient, 271–272; Song Dynasty, 345
chinoiserie, 531
Chix, 523, **523**
Christ as the Good Shepherd, 304, **304**
Christ Crucified between the Two Thieves (Rembrandt), **137**, 137–138
Christian architecture, 315–318
Christian art, 303–304, 319–320
Christianity, 303, 314
Christo: *The Gates, Central Park, New York City,* 196, **196**
Chrysler Building, New York City, 221
Church, Frederic Edwin: *The Heart of the Andes,* 69, **69**
Church and Castle, Mont Saint Michel (Clements), 66, 67
Church of San Vitale, Ravenna, **316**, 317, **317**, 320
Cimabue, 360–361; *Madonna Enthroned,* **360**, 360–361
cinematography, 163–171; animation in, 167–169; defined, 163; editing in, 165–167; fantasy in, 171; propaganda in, 169–170; satire in, 170;

slow motion in, 164–165; social commentary in, 170–171; special effects in, 163; symbolism in, 171
citadel of Mycenae, 268
Citadel ruins (Mohenjo-Daro), **272**
Citrus Express, 203, **203**
clapboard, 233
Classical art, 275–311; the Americas, 311; architecture, 283, 286; Asia, 306–310; defined, 276; Etruscan civilization, 290–292; Greece, 275–290; Rome, 292–305; sculpture, 286–288
clay: methods of working with, 209–210; sculptures, 189
Clements, Gabrielle de Veaux: *Church and Castle, Mont Saint Michel,* 66, 67
clerestory, 230, **327**
cliff dwellings, Mesa Verde, CO, **226**, 227
Close, Chuck: *Big Self-Portrait,* 508, **508**
Cloud Gate (Kapoor), 200, **200**
Cluster of Four Cubes (Rickey), 186
Coates, Robert M., 492
Coatlicue (Aztec goddess), **388**, 389
coiling pottery, 210
Coke bottle, 36
Cole, Thomas, 444; *The Oxbow,* 444, **444**
Cole, Willie: *With a Heart of Gold,* **82–83**, 92, **92**, 98; *Shine,* 185, **555**
Colescott, Robert: *Les Demoiselles d'Alabama: Vestidas,* 32, **32**
collages, 468, 502–503
Colombo, Jorge: *42nd Street,* 175, **175**
colonnades, 261
color, 9, 11, 45–53; additive and subtractive, 46, **46**; arbitrary (subjective), 52; complementary vs. analogous, 50; cool, 47; local, 51–52; optical, 52; properties of, 47–49; schemes, 49–50, **50**; as symbol, 52–53; unifying elements, 85; warm, 47
colored pencil, 110
color film, 153
color reversal film, 153
color wheel, **45**, 45–46
Colossal head, La Venta, Mexico, Olmec, **311**
Colosseum, Rome, 296, **296**, 298–299
Column (Gabo), **473**, 473
Communist Party of China, 486, 487, 531, 544
Competition Entry for New Forum, Les Halles, Paris (Koolhaas), **245**
complementary color, 50
composite view, 75
composition. See design
Composition No. II with Red, Blue, Black, and Yellow (Mondrian), **474**, 474
compound piers, 323, **327**
compressive strength, 229
conceptual art, 425, 512–513
conceptual representation, 73
Confucianism, 310
Confucius, 310
Constantine, 302–303, 304–305, 313–314, 318
Constantinople. *See* Istanbul
constructed sculptures, 184–185
Constructivism, twentieth-century, 473–474
contact print, 155
conté crayon, 112–113
contrapposto, 95
Cook, Tim, 204
cool color, 47, 48
Cooper, Emmanuel: *Bowls,* 211, 211–212
Copley, John Singleton, 411; *Portrait of Paul Revere,* **411**

Coral Nest (McCurdy), **206–207**, **210**
Corinthian capitals, 421
Corinthian orders, 278–279, 298
cornice, 279
Coronation Gospels, 320–321, **321**
The Corpse Bride (Burton), **168**, 168–169
cosmetic palette, 257–258
Counter-Composition of Dissonances (van Doesburg), **26**, 27
Courbet, Gustave, 426–427, 459; *The Stone-Breakers,* **426**, 426–427
Court of the Lions, 339–340, **340**
Cowart, Jack, 217
craft: art world's attitude toward, 207–209; ceramics, 209–214; glass, 214–217; metalwork and jewelry, 221–222; textile arts, 218–220; wood, 222–223
Crane and Plum Blossoms (Wang), 486, **486**
Crash: Arcadia Revisited, 130, **130**
crayon, 112
Crazy Quilt, 89
The Creation of Adam (Michelangelo), 371, 373, **373**
Crete, Aegean art in, 266–267
cross-cutting, 167
crosshatching, 25
The Crossing (Viola), **148–149**, **172**, 173
The Cross-Legged Captive (Michelangelo), **178–179**, 181, **181**
Crow peoples, 455
Crystal Palace, London (Paxton), 234, **234**
Cuba, 456
Cubism, 464–470; analytic, 467–468; defined, 464; Picasso and, 465–467, sculpture, 469–470; synthetic, 468
Cubist grid, 468
Cultural Revolution, 531
"Cup of the Bird Catcher," 501
Custer's Last Stand, 455
Cyclades, Aegean art in, 265–266
Cyclopean masonry, 268
Cyclopes, 268
Cyrus (King of Persia), 255

D

Dada, 183, 476–478
da Fabriano, Gentile: *Adoration of the Magi,* **124**
Daguerre, Louis-Jacques-Mandé: *The Artist's Studio,* 154, **154**
daguerreotype, 154–155
Dali, Salvador, 171, 478–479; *The Persistence of Memory,* 479, **479**; *Un Chien Andalou,* 171, **171**
Danto, Arthur C., 207–208
Dark Age of Greece, 277–278
Daumier, Honoré, 426; *The Third-Class Carriage,* 426, **426**
David (Bernini), 64, 65, 80, 375, **375**, 393
David (Donatello), 363, 364, 374, **374**
David (Michelangelo), **352–353**, 373, 374–375, **375**, 393–394
David (Verrocchio), 64, 65, 364
David, Jacques-Louis, 417, 418–419, 474; *Napoleon Crossing the Alps,* 521, **521**; *The Oath of the Horatii,* 90, **90**, 418–419, **419**
Davie, Karin: *Between My Eye and Heart No. 12,* 126, **126**
da Vinci, Leonardo. *See* Leonardo de Vinci
Davis, Orbert: *Fanfare for Cloud Gate,* 200
Dear Fatherland, Rest Quietly (Bourke-White), 158
The Death of Sardanapalus (Delacroix), **422**, 423
de Brukyner, Tania, 210

de Chirico, Giorgio, 227, 475–476; *The Mystery and Melancholy of the Street,* 475–476; *Piazza d'Italia,* 476, **476**
Deconstructivist architecture, 529–531
decorative end paper, **61**
Degas, Edgar, 433–434; *The Ballet Master,* 144, **144**; *in a Café,* 74, **74**; *Frieze of Dancers,* 80, **81**; *The Laundresses,* 34, **34**; *Small Dancer Aged 14,* 182, **182**
Degas, Edgar: *The Rehearsal (Adagio),* 434, **434**
Dein Goldenes Haar, Margarethe (Kiefer), 524, **524**
Delacroix, Eugène, 108; *The Death of Sardanapalus,* **422,** 423; *Odalisque,* 424, **424**; *Sketches of Tigers and Men in Sixteenth-Century Costume,* 108
della Francesca, Piero: *Resurrection,* 364, 365
de Maria, Walter, 194; *The Lightning Field,* 195, **195**
Demuth, Charles, 472–473; *My Egypt,* **472,** 472–473
Denis, Maurice, 123
Derain, André, 460–461; *London Bridge,* 460, **460**
Der Blaue Reiter (The Blue Rider), 463–464
Derflinger, Johann: *Performance Gender,* 161, **161**
Désert, Jean-Ulrick, 556; *The Burqa Project,* **544,** 556
design, 83–105; defined, 83; emphasis in, 89; focal point in, 11, 91–93; rhythm in, 99–101; scale in, 101–102; unity in, 11, 84–91; variety in, 11, 87–91
De Stijl, 8–9
diagonal balance, 98
diagonal ribs, 324, **327**
Die Brücke (The Bridge), 463–464
digital art, 150, 174–175
digital photography, 153–154
The Dinner Party, Chicago, 515, **515**
Dipylon Vase with funerary scene, 277, 277–278, 280
direct-metal sculptures, 189
Dish with epigraphic decoration, Khurasan, Iran, 339
Diskobolos (Discus Thrower) (Myron), 282, 283
distortion of scale, 102
Divergence 2 (Adolphus), 84, **84**
Dog Toy 4 (Gnome) (Fleury), 192, **192**
The Doll House (Schapiro and Brody), 514, **514**
Dome of the Rock, Jerusalem, 100, **100,** 334, 335, **335**
domes, 227, 229; cathedral of Florence, 364; Hagia Sophia, 318; Pantheon, 299–300
Donatello, 363, 374; *David,* 363, 364, 374, **374**
Doolan, Michael: *A Cautionary Tale Continuum (Yellow),* 189, **189**
Doormat II (Hatoum), 58, **59**
Doors from the shrine of the king's head in the royal palace, Ikare, Yoruba, Nigeria (Olowe of Ise), 487, **487**
Doric order, 278, 279, **280,** 286, 298, 366
Doryphoros (Polykleitos), **284,** 284–285, **285**
dot, 20
Douglas, Aaron, 482; *Noah's Ark,* 482, **482**
The Dove (Bearden), 518, **518**
drawing, 107–119; alternative approaches to, 116–119; categories of, 108; materials, 109–116
Drawing of a man seated with left leg resting over right knee (Hokusai), 115, **115**
The Dream (Beckmann), 464, **464**
Droga (von Rydingsvard), 188, **188**
The Drunkenness of Bacchus (Michelangelo), **95,** 95–96
dry mediums, 109–113; chalk, 111–112; charcoal, 110–111; colored pencil, 110; crayon, 112; metalpoint, 109; pastel, 111–112; pencil, 109–110
Dubuffet, Jean: *Blossoming Earth,* 57, **57**
Duchamp, Marcel, 477–478; *Fountain,* 183, **183**; *Mona Lisa (L.H.O.O.Q.),* 477, **477**; *Nude Descending a Staircase #2,* 477, 477–478
Dunes, Oceano (Weston), 25, **25**

Dura-Europos, 315
Dura-Europos, Synagogue in, **302,** 303; *Fresco of Moses and the Exodus,* **303**
Dürer, Albrecht, 359; *Adam and Eve,* 359, **359**; *Great Piece of Turf,* 57, 127–128
Dynamism of a Cyclist (Boccioni), 33, **33**
Dynamism of a Soccer Player (Boccioni), 470

E

Eakins, Thomas, 443–444; *The Gross Clinic,* **443,** 443–444; *Jesse Godley,* 77, **77**
earthenware, 212–213
Earthrise (NASA), 151, **151**
Eastern Orthodox, 318
East India Company, 412, 413
Echo (Jones), 64, 64–65
The Ecstasy of St. Theresa (Bernini), 180, 390–391, 394–395, **395**
Eddy (Pearlman), **118,** 119
Edgerton, Harold: *Milk Drop Coronet,* 162, **162**
Edison, Thomas Alva, 163
editing, in cinematography, 165–167
Edo period, 414–415
eggshell pottery, 271, **271**
Egyptian architecture, 228
Egypt, map of ancient, **257**
Egyptian art, 256–264; contemporary, 551; in Middle Kingdom, 260; in New Kingdom, 260–264; in Old Kingdom, 256–260
Eiffel Tower, Paris (Eiffel), 234, **234**
85 Lamps Lighting Fixture (Graumans), 204, **205**
Ein-Fuß-Gänger (One-Foot Walker) (Steinert), 97, **97**
Eisenman, Peter: Holocaust Memorial (Berlin), 200–201, **201**
Eisenstein, Sergei: *The Battleship Potemkin,* 167, **167**
El Anatsui: *Between Earth and Heaven,* **54–55,** 58, **61,** 552
Electric Dress (Tanaka), 536
Elementos Arquitectronicos (Arrechea), 556, **556**
El Greco, 378–379
Eliasson, Olafur: *New York City Waterfalls,* 198, **198**
Elizabeth Taylor (Muniz), **538–539,** 541
Ellsworth, David: *Vessel,* 223, **223**
embroidery, 220
Emilio Ambrasz & Associates: *Fukuoka Prefectural International Hall,* 243, **243**
emphasis, in design, 11, 89
emulsion, 153
enameled, 221
encaustic painting, 123–124
The Endurance *by Night* (Hurley), 22, **22**
England, Baroque period in, 407–408; Wren, 407–408
entablature, 279
Entombment of Christ (Pontormo), 380–381, **381**
ephemeral art, 197
equestrian portrait, **301,** 301–302
ergonomics, 204
Ergotimos: *François Vase,* 280, 281, **281**
Ernst, Max, 476; *L'oeil du silence,* 58, **59**; *Two Children Are Threatened by a Nightingale,* 478, **478**
Erwitt, Elliot: *Felix, Gladys, and Rover,* 87, **87**
Eskimo mask representing a moon goddess, 456–457, **457**
Etambi mask, 488
etching, 140–141
Ethel Scull Thirty-Six Times (Warhol), 88, **88**
Ethiopia (Wegman), 97, **97**
Ethnic and racial identity, 518–523
Etruscans, 290–292; architecture, 290–291; sculpture, 291–292

Euclid, 277
Euphronios and Euxitheos: *Calyx Krater,* **208**; *Death of Sarpedon,* 282, **282**
Europe: early medieval, 318–321; twentieth-century abstraction in, 473–474
Europe, maps of: Baroque period, **394**; Renaissance period, **354**
Euxitheos: *Calyx Krater,* **208**; *Death of Sarpedon,* 282, **282**
Evans, Frederick H.: *A Sea of Steps,* **100,** 100–101
Evans, Sir Arthur, 265
Evaristti, Marco: *The Ice Cube Project,* 194–195, **195**
The Execution of Maximilian I, 456, **456**
Exekias: *Achilles and Ajax Playing Dice,* 281, **281**
Expressionism, 16, 440–442, 462–464; Der Blaue Reiter (The Blue Rider), 463–464; Die Brücke (The Bridge), 463–464; Munch, 441; Neue Sachlichkeit (New Objectivity), 464
extruded, 189
Eyes (Bourgeois), 187, **187**

F

Fairey, Shepard: *Barack Obama "Hope" Poster,* 37, **37**
The Fall of Man and the Expulsion from the Garden of Eden (Michelangelo), 104, **104**
The Family (Neel), 506, **506**
Family by the Lotus Pond (Xiaomo), 134–135, **135**
Fanfare for Cloud Gate (Davis), 200
Fan K'uan: *Travelers among Mountains and Streams,* 345, **345**
Fantastic art, 475–476
Fantastic Mr. Fox (Anderson), 169, **169**
fantasy: in cinematography, 171
Farnsworth House (Miës van der Rohe), 483, 526, **526**
Fauvism, 460–462
Favela Chair (Campana Brothers), 223, **223**
Feldman, Anthony, 546
Felix, Gladys, and Rover (Erwitt), 87, **87**
feminist art, 514–517
fenestration, 230
ferroconcrete, 236
Fertile Crescent, 256
Fertile Ribbon, 256
feudalism: in Europe, 321–322; in Japan, 347–348
fibers, in textile arts, 218
Fibri di Como (Chihuly), 49
fifteenth-century northern painting, 355–359; Flemish, 355–358; German, 358–359
figurative art in United States, 480–481
Figure (Leong), **188,** 188–189
figure, in twentieth-century art, 499–500
figure–ground reversals, 35
Figure with Meat (Bacon), 499, **499**
Figurine of a woman from Syros (Cyclades), Greece, **265**
film: black and white, 152–153; color, 153; motion picture, 162–171; negatives, 153
Fireflies over the Uji River (Shonen), 485, 485–486
Firmager, Melvyn: *Untitled,* **222,** 222–223
Fischl, Eric, 524–525; *Barbecue,* 94, **94**; *A Visit To/A Visit From/The Island,* 525, **525**
"Five Pillars" of Islam, 335
Five Swords (Calder), 190
Flack, Audrey: *Marilyn (Vanitas),* 13, **13,** 52; *World War II (Vanitas),* 506, **507**
Flanders: Baroque period in, 401–402; Renaissance period in, 355
The Flatiron Building-Evening (Steichen), **159,** 159–160
Flavin, Dan, 192; *Untitled,* 99, **186,** 186–187

Flemish painting, 355–358; Campin, 356–357; Limbourg brothers, 355–356; van Eyck, 357–358

Fleury, Sylvie: *Dog Toy 4 (Gnome),* 192, **192**

flint glass, 215

Florence Cathedral (Italy), 330, 330–331

fluid mediums, 113, 115–116; brush and ink, 115–116; pen and ink, 113; wash, 115–116

Fluids (Kaprow), **510**

flying buttresses, **227,** 327

Flying horse, from the tomb of Governor-General Zhang, **310**

focal point, in design, 11, 90, 91–95

Follower of Rembrandt: *Head of St. Matthew,* **124**

Forbidden City, 233, 384–386, **386**

Ford, John: *The Grapes of Wrath,* 170–171, **171**

foreshortening, 248

forged, 189

form, 7; shapes and, 27

formalism, 27

42nd Street (Colombo), 175, **175**

Fosso, Samuel: *The Chief: He Who Sold Africa to the Colonists,* from *Self-Portraits I-IV,* **552**

Foster, Sir Norman: Hearst Tower, **242,** 243

Fountain (Duchamp), 183, **183**

4 Shacks with Black-Eyed Susans (Buchanan), 88, 88–89

Four Marilyns (Warhol), 142–143, **143**

Four Quad Cinema (Taaffe), 96, 97

Fowling (Bird-Hunting) Scene, 75, **75**

Fragonard, Jean-Honoré, 409; *Happy Accidents of the Swing,* 409, **409**

France: Baroque period in, 404–407; Gothic architecture in, 328–329

François Vase (Kleitias and Ergotimos), 280, 281, **281**

Frankenthaler, Helen, 497; *The Bay,* **497;** *Before the Caves,* 33, 33–34

free-standing sculptures, 64–65, 180

Fresco of Moses and the Exodus, Dura-Europos synagogue, **303**

fresco painting, 123

fresco secco, 123

frieze, 279

Frieze of Dancers (Degas), 80, **81**

Fromanger, Gerard: *Jean-Paul Sartre,* 92, 92–93

From Here to Ear (Boursier-Mougenot), 57, 57

Frozen, **169**

F-stop, 152

Fukuoka Prefectural International Hall (Emilio Ambrasz & Associates), 243, **243**

Fuller, Buckminster: *United States Pavilion, Expo 67, Montreal, Quebec, Canada,* 230, 239, **239**

Fuller, Loïe, 78

Funerary mask, from Grave Circle A (Mycenae), 268, **268**

Furcron, Mary Lou, 114; photographs of Ms. Mary Lou Furcron's home, **114**

Furedi, Lily: *Subway,* 89, **89**

Furedi, Lily, 292

Futurism, 470

Futurists, 76

G

Gabo, Naum, 473; *Column,* 473, **473**

Gainsborough, Thomas, 411

Galileo Galilei, 391

A Game of Chess (Anguissola), 382, **382**

Gandhi, Mahatma, 542

Ganesh (Hindu god), 343, **344**

Ganpati Series *Untitled I* (Aher), 344, **344**

Gapp, Paul, 202

Gardenscape, Villa of Livia, Primaporta, Italy, **294,** 295, **295**

Gardens of Versailles, 407

Gardner, Alexander: *Home of a Rebel Sharpshooter, Gettysburg,* 157, **157**

Gas Giant (Hashimoto), 192–193, **193**

The Gates, Central Park, New York City (Christo and Jeanne-Claude), 196, **196**

Gateway Arch (Saarinen), 229, **229**

Gaudí, Antoni: Casa Mila Apartment House, Barcelona, 30, **31,** 199, 447, **447;** Parc Guell, hypostyle hall, 199; *Serpent/Salamander,* Parc Guell, **199**

gauffrage, 141

Gauguin, Paul, 437, 439; *Laundresses at Arles,* 34, 34–35; *Te Arii Vahine (The Noble Woman),* 429, **429;** *Vision after the Sermon (Jacob Wrestling with the Angel),* 439, **439**

Gay Liberation (Segal), **505,** 505–506

Gehry, Frank, 529; Guggenheim Museum, Bilbao, 30; Ray and Maria Stata Center, **224–225,** 239, **239,** 242

genre painting, 357

Gentileschi, Artemisia, 396–397; *Judith Decapitating Holofernes,* 397, **397;** *Susannah and the Elders,* 396, **396**

geodesic dome, **227**

Geometric period, 276, 277–278

geometric shapes, 29–30

Georges Pompidou National Center of Art and Culture, Paris, 528, **528**

George Washington (Lichtenstein), **120–121**

George Washington (Stuart), 125, **125**

Géricault, Théodore: *Raft of the Medusa,* 60, 60, 92, **421,** 421–422

German art, 358–359; Dürer, 359; Grünewald, 358–359

Gérome, Jean-Léon: *Pygmalion and Galatea,* **180**

Ghana, 348–349

Ghiberti, Lorenzo, 361–362; *Joseph of Egypt Sold by His Brothers,* 72, **72;** *Sacrifice of Isaac,* 362, **362**

Gilbert, Cass, 421

Gilliam, Sam: *Swing 64,* **22,** 23

Giotto, 360–361; *Lamentation,* **122,** 123; *Madonna Enthroned,* 361, **361**

Giovane, Palma il, 377

Giovanni Arnolfini and His Bride (van Eyck), **357,** 357–358

Girl Running on the Balcony (Balla), 79, 79–80

Glaber, Raoul, 324

glass, 214–217

glassblowing, 214

Glass Flowers (Chihuly), 38–39

glazing, 211–212

Glimcher, Arnold, 516

globalization, 540–542

Gnaw (Antoni), 12, **12,** 192, **192**

Godard, Jean-Luc: *Breathless,* 165, **165**

Godzilla, **546,** 546–547

Golden Age of Islam, 338–340

Golden Autumn (Xuhai), 135, **135**

Golden Mean, 103, **103**

Golden Rectangle, 103, 103–104

Goldsworthy, Andy: *Ice Star,* 194, **194**

gold work, in Aegean art, 268

Google logo, **147**

gopuras, 412, **412**

Gothic art, 327–333; architecture, 230, **327,** 327–331; sculpture, 331–333

gouache, 128

Goya, Francisco, 423; *The Third of May, 1808,* 423, **423,** 425, 486

graffiti style, 130

Grande Odalisque (Ingres), 127, 420, 424, **424**

The Grapes of Wrath (Ford), 170–171, **171**

graphic design, 144–147; defined, 144; layout, 145–147; typography, 145

graphic match, 166

Graumans, Rody: *85 Lamps Lighting Fixture,* 204, **205**

graver, 135

Graves, Michael, 528; Humana Building, Louisville, Kentucky, **528,** 530

Gray, Eileen: *'Brick' Screen,* 87, **87**

gray, shades of, 40–41

"Great Beginnings" spread (Scher), 146, **146**

Great Criticism (Guangyi), 141

The Great Dictator (Chaplin), 170, **170**

Great Mosque at Samarra, 105, **105,** 338, 338–339

Great Mosque of Córdoba, 337, **337**

Great Mosque of Damascus, 335–336, **336**

Great Mosque of Djenné, 348, 349

Great Piece of Turf (Dürer), 57, 127–128

Great Pyramids at Gizeh, 259, 259–260

Great Stupa of Sanchi, India, **307,** 307–308, **308**

Great Temple, Madurai, India, **412**

Great Wall of China, 308–309, **309**

Great Zimbabwe compound, 350, **350**

Greco-Roman art, 292

Greece (ancient), 275–290; Archaic period, 276, 278–282; architecture, 5; Classical art, 276, 283, 286–287; Classical art, early, 276, 282–283; Classical art, late, 276, 287–288; Geometric period, 276, 277–278; Hellenistic art, 276, 289–290; map of, **277**

green buildings, 242–243

Green Coca-Cola Bottles (Warhol), 504, **504**

grid, 84

Gris, Juan: *The Bottle of Banyuls,* 67, **67**

groin vault, 229–230

Gropius, Walter, 482; Shop Block, The Bauhaus, **483**

The Gross Clinic (Eakins), 443, 443–444

ground, 34, 109

Ground Zero, 240–241

Growing Corn (Landacre), 136, **136**

Grünewald, Matthias, 358–359; *The Crucifixion (Isenheim Altarpiece),* **358,** 358–359

Guangyi, Wang: *Great Criticism,* 141–142

Guernica (Picasso), 44, 85, **458–459,** 469

Guerrilla Girls, 516; poster, **516**

Guevara, Che, 37

Guggenheim Museum, Bilbao (Gehry), 30, **31**

gum, 109

gum arabic, 111

Gupta, Subodh, 542; *Silk Route,* **543**

Gutai Art Association, 536

H

Habitat, Expo 67 (Montreal, Quebec, Canada) (Safdie), **238**

haboku, 387

Hadid, Zaha, 530; Dancing Towers, Dubai, 530, **530**

Hagia Sophia, Istanbul, 317, **317,** 339

Hajj, 335

Hall of Bulls in the cave at Lascaux, France, 122, **246–247,** 248, **249**

Hall of Mirrors, Versailles, 407

Hall of Supreme Harmony, 386, **386**

Hamilton, Richard, 502–503; *Just What Is It That Makes Today's Homes So Different, So Appealing?,* **502,** 502–503

Hammurabi's Code of Laws, 254
hand printing, 220
Hands of the Potter, 210
Han Dynasty, 310, **310**
Hanson, Duane, 506–508; *Tourists,* 506–508, **507**
Hardouin-Mansart, Jules: Palace of Versailles, **406**, 407, **407**
Harlem Renaissance, 482
Harvard University Graduate School of Design, 483
Hasegawa Tohaku: *Pine Wood,* 387, **387**
Hashimoto, Jacob: *Gas Giant,* 192–193, **193**
hatching, 25–26
Hatoum, Mona: *Doormat II,* 58, **59**; *Shift,* 549, **549**
Haussmann, Raoul, 244
Hazoumé, Romuald, 552–553; *Baghdad City,* **553**
Head #12 (Samaras), 112, **112**
Head of a Roman, 294, **294**
Head of a Sleeping Woman (Study for Nude with Drapery) (Picasso), 554, **554**
Head of Constantine, 305, **305**
Head of St. Matthew (Follower of Rembrandt), **124**
Hearst Tower (Foster), **242**, 243
The Heart of the Andes (Church), 69, **69**
Hebe (Kauffman), 25, **25**
Heirs Come to Pass, 3 (Lopez), 66, **66**, 92, 93
Hellenism, 275
Hellenistic art, 276, 289–290
Henriette's Yard (Buchanan), 114, **114**
Hermes and Dionysos (Praxiteles), **287**, 287–288
Hershman, Lynn, 174; *Digital Venus,* 174–175, **175**
Herzog & de Meuron: *Beijing Stadium for the 2008 Olympic Games,* 297, **297**
hierarchical scale, 101
High and Late Renaissance, outside of Italy, 378–380
high-key value range, 40
highlighting, 43
high relief, 180
High Renaissance: in Italy: Leonardo da Vinci, 368–369; Michelangelo, 366, 371–375
High Renaissance: Raphael Sanzio, 370–371
Hildegard of Bingen: *"Vision of God's Plan for the Seasons,"* **312–313**, 326, **326**
Hind, Arthur M., 133
Hinduism, 306–307, 340, 342, 344, 412
The Hippopotamus at the Zoological Gardens, Regent's Park (Carlos), 101, **101**
Hirohito, 485
Hiroshige, Ando: *Sudden Shower over Shin-Ohashi Bridge and Atake,* 452, **452**
Hitchcock, Alfred: *Psycho,* 166, **166**
Hitler, Adolf, 170, 296, 484
Hockney, David: *The Arrival of Spring in Woldgate, East Yorkshire in 2011,* 119, **119**
Hokusai, Katsushika: *Drawing of a man seated with left leg resting over right knee,* 115, **115**; *Under the Wave off Kanagawa (The Great Wave),* **451**, 451–452
Holland, Baroque period in, 402–404; Rembrandt, 402–403; Vermeer, 404
Holocaust Memorial, Berlin (Eisenman), 200–201, **201**
Holy Trinity (Masaccio), 363, 363–364
Homage to New York (Tinguely), 510, **511**
Home of a Rebel Sharpshooter, Gettysburg (Gardner), 157, **157**
Homer, 265, 348–349
Hopper, Edward, 480–481; *Nighthawks,* 481, **481**
horizon, 70
horizontal balance, 98

The Horse Fair (Bonheur), **430**, 431
Horta, Victor: Tassel House, Interior of (Brussels), 447, **447**
Household (Kaprow), 510
Hoving, Thomas, 207
Hudson, Hugh: *Chariots of Fire,* 164, **164**
Hudson River School, 444
hues, 48, **49**
Hufan, Wu: *Celebrate the Success of Our Glorious Atomic Bomb Explosion!,* 534, **534**
Hughes, Robert, 184
Huizinga, Johan, 356
Humana Building, Louisville, Kentucky (Graves), 528, **528**
humanism, 276
human models, casting of, 184
Hung Liu: *Untitled,* 139, **139**
Hunt, Richard M., *J.N.A.: Griswold House,* **232**, 233
Hurley, Frank: *The Endurance by Night,* 22, **22**
Husain, Maqbool Fida, **532**, 532–533
hybridity, 540
Hypostyle Hall, Temple of Amen-Re, Karnak, Egypt, **228**

I

The Ice Cube Project (Evaristti), 194–195, **195**
Ice Star (Goldsworthy), 194, **194**
I Ching (Book of Changes), 310
Icicle Creek Chandelier (Chihuly), 216–217, **217**
iconography, 5, 7, 36–37
Ictinos, Parthenon and, **5**, 286
idealism, 276
Iliad (Homer), 265, 348
Illegal Alien's Guide to Critical Theory (Chagoya), 557–558, **558**
Illusionistic Surrealism, 478
illusion of space, 65
imaging: photography, 150–151
imam, 337
impasto, 57
The Imperial Procession, 300–301, **301**
implied lines, 22–23
implied mass, 28
implied space, 65
Impressionism, 431–434, 459; Degas, 433–434; Monet, 431–432; Morisot, 433; Renoir, 432–433
in a Café (Degas), 74, **74**
incised detail, 257
incised lines, 135
The Incredibles (Bird), 168, **168**
India: ancient art in, 270, 272, 273; Baroque period in, 412–413; contemporary art in, 542; modern art in, 450–451; religion in, 340–342, 344; Renaissance era, 382–384
industrial design, 203–205
Ingres, Jean-Auguste-Dominique, 276, 420; *Grande Odalisque,* 127, 420, 424, **424**
Inka, 389
Ink-and-Wash-Painting No. 3 (Lijun), **115**, 115–116
installation artistic medium, 192–193
Insurrection! (Our Tools Were Rudimentary, Yet We Pressed On) (Walker), 520, **520**, 522
intaglio, **134**, 136–138, 140–141
intensity, 49, **49**
Interior of the synagogue, with wall paintings of Old Testament themes, 302
International style, 356
"In the Battle of the Sha River, a Company of Our Forces Drives a Strong Enemy Force to the Left Bank of the Taizi River" (Yoshikune), 485, **485**

In the Loge (Cassatt), 50, **51**
Ionic order, 278, 279, **280**, 298, 421
iPhone, Apple, Inc., 204, **204**
iron, 221
I Saw Three Cities (Sage), 98, **98**
Isenheim Altarpiece (Grünewald), **358**, 358–359
Isfahani, Ali Muhammad Kashigar: *Iranian tabletop,* 98–99, **99**
Islam, 306, 333–340; Golden Age of, 338–340; Umayyad Caliphate, 335–337
Islamic world map (during Umayyad Caliphate), **334**
Israel, 550–551
Istanbul, 317, 339
Italy, Baroque period in, 392–399; Bernini, 392–395; Borromini, 399; Caravaggio, 395–396; ceiling decoration, 399; Gentileschi, 396; St. Peter's in Vatican City, 392
Italy, Gothic architecture in, 330–331
Italy, Renaissance in, 360–378; Alberti, 366; Bernini, 374–375; Botticelli, 365–366; Brunelleschi, 361–362, 364; Cimabue, 360–361; competition and, 361–362; Donatello, 363, 374; early, 360–361; Ghiberti, 361–362; Giotto, 360–361; Leonardo da Vinci, 368–369; Masaccio, 363–364; Michelangelo Buonarroti, 371–375; Piero della Francesca, 365; Raphael Sanzio, 370–371; Tintoretto, 377–378; Titian, 376–377; Verrocchio, 364

J

Jacir, Emily, 551; *Memorial to 418 Palestinian Villages Destroyed, Depopulated and Occupied by Israel,* 551, **551**
Jackson, Dorica: Chilkat robe, 219, **219**
Jackson Pollock (Arneson), 212, **212**
Jacobs, Ferne, 219; *Medusa's Collar,* **219**, 219–220
Jain, Adil: *Two Heads,* 98, **99**
jamb figures: Chartres Cathedral, **331**, 331–332; Reims Cathedral, 332, **332**
Japan: Baroque period in, 414–415; feudal rule, 347–348; following World War II, 535–536; modern art in, 451–452; Muromachi period, 386–387; religion, 346
Japanese art: brush-and-ink medium, 115; film, 546–547; graphic novels, 540–541; Pop culture, 547; shrines, 346; in twentieth century, 484–486
Jar (Martinez and Martinez), 209, **209**
Jeanne-Claude: *The Gates, Central Park, New York City,* 196, **196**
Jean-Paul Sartre (Fromanger), 92, 92–93
Jesse Godley (Eakins), 77, **77**
Jesus, 314
J.N.A.: Griswold House (Hunt), **232**, 233
Johns, Jasper, 503–504; *Three Flags,* 504, **504**
Johnson, Philip: AT&T Building, New York City, **527**, 527–528; Seagram Building, New York City, 483–484, 526–527, **527**
Johnson, William H.: *Café,* 74, **74**
John the Baptist, 336
Jones, Allen: *Echo,* **64**, 64–65
Joseph of Egypt Sold by His Brothers (Ghiberti), 72, **72**
Joseph Stalin Gazing Enigmatically at the Body of V.I. Lenin as It Lies in State in Moscow in the Style of Jackson Pollock (Baldwin and Ramsden), 14, **14**
Judd, Donald, 502; *100 Untitled Works in Mill Aluminum,* 509, **509**
Judith and Holofernes (Caravaggio), 397, **397**

Juicy Salif (Starck), 203, **203**
Julius Caesar, 292–293
Justinian and Attendants, 317, **317**
Just What Is It That Makes Today's Homes So Different, So Appealing? (Hamilton), **502**, 502–503

K

Kadishman, Menashe: *Suspended,* **190**
Kahlo, Frida: *The Two Fridas,* 489, **489**
Kandinsky, Wassily, 463–464; *Composition VI,* 4, **4**, 45; *Sketch I for Composition VII,* **463**, 463–464
Kapoor, Anish: *Cloud Gate,* **200**
Kaprow, Allan, 510; *Fluids,* **510**; *Household,* 510
Karesansui (dry-landscape) garden, **386**
Ka sculptures, 259
Kason, Suzuki: *"Autumn Showers (Shigure),"* 485, **485**
Kath, Gitte: Sydney Paralympics poster, **146**, 146–147
Katsura Imperial Villa, **415**
Katz, Alex: *Red Coat,* 143, **143**
Kauffman, Angelica, 419–420; *The Artist in the Character of Design Listening to the Inspiration of Poetry,* **419**, 419–420; *Hebe,* 25, **25**, **138**, 138–139
Kaufmann House ("Fallingwater") (Wright), **237**, 237–238
Kelley, Gary: *Promotion for the Mississippi Delta Blues Festival,* 108, **108**
Ken Moody and Robert Sherman (Mapplethorpe), 517, **517**
Kepler, 391
Kessler, Jon: *The Palace at 4 a.m.,* 94, **94**
keystone, 229
Khafre, 258–259
Kiefer, Anselm, 524; *Dein Goldenes Haar, Margarethe,* **524**, **524**
kilns, 182
kinetic sculpture, 186
Kinetoscope, 163
King Tut. *See* Tutankhamen (king of Egypt)
Kirchner, Ernst Ludwig: *Street, Dresden,* **462**, 463
kivas, 227
Klee, Paul, 475; *Twittering Machine,* 475, **475**
Kleitias: *François Vase,* 281, **281**
Knossos (palace), 266–267
Knotty but Nice (Amer), 517, **517**
Knowles, Conrad, 210
Kodak, 155
Kollwitz, Käthe, 441–442; *The Mothers,* 142, **142**; *The Outbreak,* **441**, 441–442; *Self-Portrait,* 111, **111**
Koolhaas, Rem, 244; *Competition Entry for New Forum, Les Halles, Paris,* **245**
Kooning, Willem de, 494–495; *Two Women's Torsos,* **494**, 495
Koran. *See* Qur'an
Korea, 548
Kosuth, Joseph, 512; *One and Three Chairs,* 512, **513**; *One and Three Hammers,* 512; *Titled (Art as Idea as Idea),* 3–4
kouros figures, **279**
Krasner, Lee, 494; *Easter Lilies,* 494, **494**
Krishna and Radha in a Pavillion, 413, **413**
Krishna killing the horse demon keshi, **212**, 213
Kroisos, 278, **279**
Kruger, Barbara, 512; *Untitled (We Don't Need Another Hero),* 512, **513**
Kublai Khan, 384
Kumano Mandala, 347, **347**
Kwakwaka'wakw (Kwakiutl) "transformation mask," 457, **457**
Kyoto, 347

L

Lacquer, 385
La Loïe Fuller, Folies-Bergère (PAL), **78**
Lamentation (Giotto), **122**, 123
laminated, 135
lancet, 327
Landacre, Paul: *Growing Corn,* 136, **136**
land art, 194–195
Lange, Dorothea, 159; *Migrant Mother, Nipomo, California,* 157, **157**
Laocoön and His Sons (Athenadorus, Agesander, and Polydorus of Rhodes), **289**, 289–290
Laon Cathedral, France, 4, 328, **328**
lapis lazuli, 252–253
Las Meninas (Velázquez), **400**, 400–401
Last Supper (Tintoretto), 378, **378**
The Last Supper (Leonardo da Vinci), 123, **368**, 368–369, 550
Latin Cross plan, 316
la Tour, Georges de: *Saint Joseph the Carpenter,* 43, **43**
The Laundresses (Degas), 34, **34**
Laundresses at Arles (Gauguin), 34, 34–35
lavender oil, 154
Lawrence, Jacob, 482; *The Life of Harriet Tubman,* 24, 124, 482, **483**
Layamon, 250
layout in graphic design, 145–147
Lebanon, 549
Le Corbusier, 236; chapel of Notre-Dame-du-Haut, **236**, 237
Le Déjeuner sur l'Herbe (Luncheon on the Grass) (Manet), **427**, 427, 430
Le Divan Japonais (Toulouse-Lautrec), 147, **148**
Le Moulin de la Galette (Renoir), **432**, 432–433
L'Enfant, Pierre-Charles: Washington, D.C., plan for, 244, **244**, 421
Leonardo da Vinci, 108, 121, 367, 368–369; *The Last Supper,* 123, **368**, 550; *Madonna of the Rocks,* 369, **369**; *Mona Lisa,* 24, 24–25, 369, **369**, 476; *Proportion of the Human Figure,* 96, 96–97; *A study of a woman's hands,* 106–107, **109**
Leong, Po Shun: *Figure,* **188**, 188–189
Les Demoiselles d'Alabama: Vestidas (Colescott), 32, **32**
Les Demoiselles d'Avignon (Picasso), 32, **32**, 33, **466**, 466–467
Les Halles, 244
Les Très Riches Heures du Duc de Berry (Limbourg brothers), 355, 355–356
Letter to a Refusing Pilot (Zaatari), 550, **550**
Le Vau, Louis: Palace of Versailles, 406, **407**, 407
Lever House, New York City, 235, 235–236
Levine, Sherrie: *Fountains after Duchamp,* 183, **183**
Levittown, 233, **233**
Liber Scivias, 326
Libeskind, Daniel, 5–6, 529–530; Berlin Museum, extension of, 5, 5–6, **529**
Lichtenstein, Roy: *George Washington,* **120–121**, **125**, 125–126
The Life of Harriet Tubman (Lawrence), 24, 124, 482, **483**
light, 39; chiaroscuro and, 42–43; descriptive and expressive properties of, 44–45; sculptures, 186–187; value and, 40–44; visible spectrum, 39, **40**
Light Blue Nursery (Thomas), **22**, 23
The Lightning Field (de Maria), 195, **195**
Lijun, Fang: *Ink-and-Wash-Painting No. 3,* **115**, 115–116

Li K'an: *Bamboo,* 384, 385
Limbourg brothers, 355–356; *Les Très Riches Heures du Duc de Berry,* **355**, 355–356
Lin, Maya Ying: Vietnam Veterans Memorial, 201, **202**, 202–203
Lindisfarne Gospels, carpet page from, **319**, 319–320
linear recession, 417
lines, 9–10, 19–28; actual, 22–23; contour, 24–25; defined, 19; incised, 135; measure of, 20; to outline and shape, 24–25; psychological, 23; to suggest direction and movement, 24; to unify components, 87; value and shape, 25–26
Lion capital, from a column erected by Ashoka, **306**
Lipchitz, Jacques, 465, 469; *Still Life with Musical Instruments,* 469, **469**
lithography, 134, 141–142
Little Spider (Calder), 77, **77**, 96
The Living Dead of Buchenwald (Bourke-White), 157–158, **158**
living rocks, 280
local color, 51–52
Locke, Hew, 541–542; *Sikandar,* 541–542, **542**
L'oeil du silence (Ernst), 58, **59**
logos, 147
Loïe Fuller Dancing (Taber), **78**
London Bridge (Derain), 460, **460**
longitudinal plan, 316
loom, 219
Lopez, Martina: *Heirs Come to Pass, 3,* 66, **66**, **92**, 93
Lord Chan Muwan, 351, **351**
Lost Hindsight (Messersmith), 50, **51**
lost-wax technique, 182, **182**
Louis XIV (king of France), 404, 407
Louis XVI (king of France), 418
Loulou Distracted (Matisse), 138, **138**
low-key value range, 40
low or bas-relief, 180
Luce, Henry, 158
Luciano, Miguel, 556–557
Luhrmann, Baz: *Moulin Rouge,* 74
Lumiére, August: *The Demolition of a Wall,* 163
Lumiére, Louis, 163; *The Demolition of a Wall,* 163; *Young Lady with an Umbrella,* 155, **155**
Lunch II (van Elk), 93, **93**
Luo Brothers: *Welcome to the World Famous Brand,* **545**
Lysippos: *Apoxyomenos,* 288, **288**

M

Macfarlane, Seth: *Ted,* 167
Machu Picchu, Urubamba Valley, Peru, 69, 228, 389, **389**
Madonna and Child (Michelangelo), **111**, 111–112
Madonna Enthroned (Cimabue), **360**, 360–361
Madonna Enthroned (Giotto), 361, **361**
Madonna of the Rocks (Leonardo da Vinci), 369, **369**
magazines, 266
Magnolia and Irises (Tiffany Studios), 68, **68**, 215, **215**
Maharaja Jaswant singh of Marwar, **450**, 450–451
Maid of Honour (Schapiro), 131, **131**
Malevich, Kasimir: *Suprematist Composition,* 93, **93**
Malwiya Minaret, 338, **338**
mandala, 347, **347**
Mandolin and Clarinet (Picasso), 184, **184**
Manet, Édouard, 427–428, 430; *Le Déjeuner sur l'Herbe (Luncheon on the Grass),* 427, **427**, 430; *Olympia,* 426, **426**

manga, 116, **116**, 540–541

Mangold, Sylvia Plimack: *Three Exact Rules,* 20–21, **21**

mannerism, 380–382

manuscript illumination: Carolingian art, 320–321; Flemish painting, 355–356; Renaissance years, 355

Mao Zedong, 486

Mao Zedong (1893–1976) marching toward the Jing Gang Mountains in October 1927, 487, **487**

Mapplethorpe, Robert, 516; *Ken Moody and Robert Sherman,* 517, **517**

Marc (April) (Peyton), 110, **110**

March, Werner: *Olympic Stadium,* Berlin, 296, **296**

Marco Polo, 384

Marcus Aurelius on Horseback, **301**, 301–302, 303

Marie Antoinette and Her Children (Vigée-Lebrun's), 410, **410**

Marilyn (Vanitas) (Flack), 13, **13**

Marinetti, Filippo, 470

Martinez, Maria and Julian: *Jar,* 209, **209**

Masaccio, 363–364; *Holy Trinity,* **363**, 363–364

Mask (Mutu), 553, **553**

masks, ceremonial, 554–555

Mas o Manos (More or Less) (Stella), 501

masonry, 228

mass, 27, 28

match cut, 166

Matisse, Henri, 19, 94, 461–462; *Loulou Distracted,* 138, **138**; *Red Room (Harmony in Red),* **461**, 461–462; *Woman with a Hat,* 16, **17**

Matos, John. *See* Crash

matrix, 134

The Matrix (Wachowski and Wachowski), 165, **165**

Mayans, 351, 558

McCurdy, Jennifer: *Coral Nest,* **206**–207, **210**, 210–211

McElheny, Josiah: *Three Screens for Looking at Abstraction,* 85, **85**

Mecca, 333

Medicis, 367, 374

Medina, 333

mediums, 12

Medusa's Collar, **219**, 219–220

megaliths, 250–251

Meiji period, 484

Melies, Georges, 163

Melting Point of Ice (Basquiat), **520**

Memorial to 418 Palestinian Villages Destroyed, Depopulated and Occupied by Israel (Jacir), 551, **551**

Mendieta, Ana, 515–516; *Arbol de la Vida, no. 294,* **515**

Merode Altarpiece: The Annunciation with Donors and St. Joseph (Campin), **356**, 356–357, 364

Mesopotamia, 251–256. *See also* Near Eastern ancient art; Akkad, 253–254; Assyria, 255; Babylonia, 254; Persia, 255–256; Sumer, 251–253

Messersmith, Mark: *Lost Hindsight,* 50, **51**

metalpoint, 109

metalwork and jewelry, 221–222

Metamorphosis (Ovid), 179

metopes, 279

Metropolitan Museum of Art, New York City, 176; Website home page, **176**

Mexican Revolution, 488

Mexico: ancient art in, 311; Mayan civilization, 351; native arts of, 543–544; postcolonial, 456; twentieth-century art, 488–489

Mezquita-Catedral, 336–337

mezzotint, 140

Michelangelo, 353, 355, 371–375; *The Creation of Adam,* 371, 373, **373**; *The Cross-Legged Captive,* **178**–179, 181, **181**; *David,* **352**–353, 374–375, **375**; *The Drunkenness of Bacchus,* **95**, 95–96; *The Fall of Man and the Expulsion from the Garden of Eden,* 104, **104**; *Pietà,* 371; Sistine Chapel, 193, **372**

Michelangelo de Merisi. *See* Caravaggio

Michelangelo: *Madonna and Child,* **111**, 111–112

Middle East, contemporary art in, 548–551; Egypt, 551; Iran, 549–550; Israel, 550–551

Middle Kingdom, ancient art in, 260

Midnight: The Hours of the Rat; Mother and Sleepy Child (Utamaro), 415, **415**

Midwestern Regionalism, 480

Miës van der Rohe, Ludwig, 482–483, 526; Farnsworth House, 483, **526**; Seagram Building, New York City, 483–484, 528–529, **529**

Migrant Mother, Nipomo, California (Lange), 157, **157**

mihrab, 337

Mihrab from the Madrasa Imami (Isfahan), **337**

Mili, Gjon: *Picasso,* 20, **20**

Milk Drop Coronet (Edgerton), 162, **162**

Miller, Ruane: *Blue Door,* 174, **174**

minaret, 338, **338**

Ming Dynasty, 211, 384–386

Minimalism, 508–509

Minoan civilization, 266

Minos (King of Crete), 266

Miró, Joan, 479–480; *Painting,* 480, **480**

Mitchell, Joan: *Cercando un Ago,* 6; *Untitled,* 495, **495**, 497

Mithuna reliefs, detail of the north side of the Vishvanatha Temple, **342**

mixed media: in paintings, 130–131

modeling, 25, 181

Model Maison d'Artiste (van Doesburg), 27, **27**

Model of a typical Etruscan temple of the sixth century, **291**

Modern architecture, 526–527

Modern art, 417–457; in Africa, 448–450; American Expatriates, 442; Americans in America, 443–444; in the Americas, 455–457; Art Nouveau, 447–448; Expressionism, 440–442; Impressionism, 431–434; in India, 450–451; in Japan, 451–452; Neoclassicism, 418–421; in Oceania, 452–455; Postimpressionism, 434–440; Realism, 426–431; Romanticism, 421–425; sculpture, 446–447

Modigliani, Amedeo: *Young Man with Red Hair,* 103, **103**

Mohenjo-Daro, 272–273

molds in casting, 182

Mona Lisa (Leonardo da Vinci), **24**, 24–25, 369, **369**, 476

Mona Lisa (L.H.O.O.Q.) (Duchamp), 477, **477**

monasticism, 321–322

Mondrian, Piet, 473–474; *Composition No. II with Red, Blue, Black, and Yellow,* 474, **474**

Monet, Claude, 431–432; *Dandy with a Cigar,* 116; *Impression: Sunrise,* **431**, 431–432; *Rouen Cathedral,* 52, **52**, 432, **432**

Mongols, 339

Monier, Jacques, 236

monochromatic color scheme, 50

monotype, 144

Montoya, Delilah: *Los Jovenes (Youth),* 84

Mont Sainte-Victoire Seen from Bibemus Quarry (Cézanne), 47, **47**

monuments, 200–203

Moon and Half Dome, Yosemite National Park, California (Adams), **150**, 150–151

Moore, Henry, 179, 499–500; *Reclining Figure,* Lincoln Center, 500, **500**

Moors, 339–340

Mori, Mariko, 547; *Wave UFO,* **547**

Morisot, Berthe, 433; *Young Girl by the Window,* **416**–417, 433, **433**

Morisse (Benglis), 58, **58**

mortuary temple, 280

Mortuary Temple of Queen Hatshepsut, **260**, 261

mosques: Great Mosque of Córdoba, 337, **337**; Great Mosque of Damascus, 335–336, **336**; Great Mosque of Djenné, **348**, 349; Great Mosque of Samarra, 105, **105**, **338**, 338–339

The Mothers (Kollwitz), 142, **142**

Motherwell, Robert, 121, 417

motion: implied, 80

motion picture film, 162–171

Moulin Rouge (Luhrmann), 74

Mrs. Jones and Family (Ringgold), 555, **555**

Mughal Empire, 382–383, 412

Muhammad, 333–334

Mulberry Tree (van Gogh), 55, **56**

multiple perspectives, 76

Munch, Edvard, 440, 441; *The Scream,* 441, **441**

Muniz, Vik, 541; *Elizabeth Taylor,* **538**–539, 541

Munna Appa's Kitchen (Singh), 127, **127**

Murakami, Takashi, 540–541; *Tan Tan Bo,* **540**

murals, 122–123

Muromachi period, 386–387

Murray, Elizabeth, 500–501; *Sail Baby,* 501, **501**

Muschamp, Herbert, 240

Mutu, Wangechi, 553; *Mask,* 553, **553**

Muybridge, Eadweard, 162–163; *Galloping Horse,* 163, **163**

Mycenae, Aegean art in, 267–269; architecture, 288; gold work, 288

My Egypt (Demuth), **472**, 472–473

Myron: *Diskobolos (Discus Thrower),* **282**, 283

The Mystery and Melancholy of the Street (de Chirico), 475–476

N

Nadar: *Sarah Bernhardt,* 156, **156**

Nakashima, Harumi: *Porcelain Form,* 214, **214**

Nameless and Friendless (Osborne), 23, **23**

Napoleon Crossing the Alps (David), 521, **521**

Napoleon III, 430

Napoleon Leading the Army Over the Alps (Wiley), 521, **521**

Narmer (king of Egypt), 258

Narmer Palette (Egypt), 258, **258**

narthex, 316

NASA photograph: *Earthrise,* 151, **151**

National World War II Memorial, Washington, D.C., **201**, 201–202, 203

Native Americans of Great Plains, 455–456

naturalism, 248; in Akkadian art, 253–254; in Babylonian art, 254; in Classical art, 276; in Egyptian art, 257, 259, 262, 263; in Paleolithic art, 248

naturalistic style, 238

Navajo people, 455

naves, 316, **327**

Nayak Dynasty, 412

Nealie, Chester: *Bottle,* **211,** 211–212
Nebuchadnezzar (king of Babylonia), 255
Neel, Alice: The Family, 506, **506**
Nefertiti: bust of, **261;** relief engraving, **262;**
    translation of, 261, 262
negatives, 153, 155
Neoclassical period, 275
Neoclassicism, 418–421; architecture, 421; David,
    418–419; Ingres, 420; Kauffman, 419–420;
    painting, 418–420; sculpture, 420–421
Neo-Expressionism, 524–525
Neolithic art, 250–251
Neolithic period, 248
Neo-Plasticism, 8–9
Nervi, Pier Luigi: *Palazzo dello Sport,* Rome,
    296–297, **297**
Nes, Adi, 550; *Untitled,* 550, **550**
Neshat, Shirin, 161–162; *Allegiance and
    Wakefulness (Women of Allah),* **162;** *Passage,*
    549, 549–550
Neue Sachlichkeit (New Objectivity), 464
Nevelson, Louise, 185; *Royal Tide IV,* **185,**
    185–186
new brutalism, 237
New Image painting, 523–524
New Kingdom, ancient art in, 260–264
Newton, Sir Isaac, 39, 45–46
New York City Waterfalls (Eliasson), 198, **198**
New York School, 492–498; color field, 497;
    constructed sculpture and assemblage, 497–498;
    gesture, focus on, 492–495, 497
Niepce, Joseph-Nicéphore, 154
Niko: *Che, Hoy y Siempre* Movie Poster, 37, **37**
Nixon, Nicholas: *The Brown Sisters,* 156, **156**
Nkisi N'Kondi (hunter figure), **448,** 449
Noah's Ark (Douglas), 482, **482**
Noland, Kenneth: *Graded Exposure,* 126, **126**
Nolde, Emil, 247
nonobjective art, 4
nonobjective shapes, 29, 33
nonporous vessels, 211
nose ornament, crayfish, Peru, 222, **222**
Number 19 (Pollock), 14, **14**
Number 22 (Rothko), 496, **496**
Nymphs and Satyr (Bouguereau), 425, **425**

O

The Oath of the Horatii (David), 90, **90,** 418–419, **419**
oba, 349
Obama, Barack, 37
Oceania, map of, **453**
Oceanic art, 453–455
ocher, 111
Oculatei Der Boomen (Baker), 20, **20**
oculus, **327**
Odysseus (Greek hero), 277
Odyssey (Homer), 265, 348
oil painting, 125, 127
Oiran (Grand Courtesan) (Yuichi), 452, **453**
O'Keeffe, Georgia, 156, 471–472; *White Iris,* 471,
    471
Oldenburg, Claes: *Soft Toilet,* 191, **191,** 505
The Old Guitarist (Picasso), 160, 465, **465**
Old Kingdom, ancient art in, 256–260;
    architecture, 259–260; sculpture, 257–259
Old St. Peter's, Rome, **315,** 315–316
Olmec civilization, 311
Olowe of Ise: Doors from the shrine of the king's
    head in the royal palace, Ikare, Yoruba,
    Nigeria, 487, **487**

Olympia (Manet), 426, **426**
Olympic Stadium, Berlin, 296, **296**
One (Pollock), **491–492**
One and Three Chairs (Kosuth), 512, **513**
One and Three Hammers (Kosuth), 512
100 Untitled Works in Mill Aluminum (Judd),
    509, **509**
one-point perspective, 70
One World Trade Center (One WTC), 240–241, **241**
Ono, Yoko, 510–511; *Bagism,* 511, **511;** *Cut Piece,*
    510
Oppenheim, Dennis: *Reading Position for a Second
    Degree Burn,* 81, **81**
optical art, 426
optical color, 52
optical representation, 73
Orchard in Blossom (Plum Trees) (van Gogh), 55, **56**
ordered chaos, 91
organic shapes, 30
orthogonals, 70, 371, 419
Osborne, Emily Mary: *Nameless and Friendless,*
    23, **23**
Ottoman Turks, 339
Our Sky Is Falling (Wang), **544,** 544–545
Ourussoff, Jesse, 296
The Outbreak (Kollwitz), **441,** 441–442
Ovid: *Metamorphosis,* 179
Owens, Jesse, 296
The Oxbow (Cole), 444, **444**

P

Package (Bravo), 111, **111**
The Painter and His Model (Picasso), 140, **140**
painting, 121–131; acrylic, 127, 129; encaustic,
    123–124; fresco, 123; gouache, 128; mixed
    media and, 130–131; oil, 125, 127; spray paint,
    130; tempera, 124–125; watercolor, 127
Pakistan: contemporary art in, 543
PAL (Jean De Paleologon), *La Loïe Fuller, Folies-
    Bergère,* 78
The Palace at 4 a.m. (Kessler), 94, **94**
A palace concert, 343, **343**
Palatine Chapel of Charlemagne, 320, **321**
Palazzo dello Sport, Rome (Nervi), 296–297, **297**
Palazzo Ruccllai, Florence (Alberti), 366, **367**
Paleolithic art, 248–250
panel paintings, 355
Panofsky, Erwin, 257
Pantheon, Rome, 230, 299, **299**
papyrus, 113
parallel action editing, 166–167
Parc Güell, hypostyle hall (Gaudí), 199
Paris Street: Rainy Day (Caillebotte), 73, **73,** 93
Parthenon, Athens, **104,** 193, 228, **283,** 286
Pascal's Provincial Letters (Rockburne), 30, **30,** 33
Passage (Neshat), **549,** 549–550
pastel, 111–112
pastoral scenes, 430
patinas, 189
patricians, 293
pattern, 58–59
Pauline Borghese as Venus (Canova), 420–421
Paxton, Sir Joseph: *Crystal Palace,* 234, **234**
Peaceful Dragon Temple, 387
Pearlman, Mia: *Eddy,* 118, 119
pectoral piece from Ordzhonikidze, Russia, **220,**
    221
pediment, 279–280
Pei, I. M.: Pyramid at the Louvre, 29
pen and ink, 113

pencil, 109–110
pendentives, **227,** 317
Penelope (Greek heroine), 277
peplos, 286
Performance art, 509–513
Performance Gender (Derflinger), 161, **161**
Perilous Order (Sikander), **543**
Persepolis, 256
Persia, 255–256
The Persistence of Memory (Dalí), 479, **479**
perspective drawing of objects set at different
    angles, 70
Peru: native arts of, 222, **222**
Petherbridge, Guy, 212
Peyton, Elizabeth: *Marc (April),* 110, **110**
Pfaff, Judy: *3D,* **18–19,** 34, **34,** 193
Phidias, 286
Philosophy, or *The School of Athens* (Raphael), 71,
    71, 401
Phoenix Hall (looking west), Byodo-in, Uji, Kyoto
    Prefecture, Japan, 346, **346**
photogenic drawings, 155
photography, 150–162; as art form, 159–162;
    cameras, 152; defined, 150; digital, 153–154;
    film, 152–153
photography, history of, 154–159; camera
    obscura, 154, **154;** daguerreotype, 154–155;
    heliography, 154; negatives, 155;
    photojournalism, 157–159; photosensitive
    surfaces, 154; portraits, 156
photojournalism, 157–159
photosensitive surfaces, 150, 154
Piano, Renzo: Georges Pompidou National Center
    for Arts and Culture, 528, **528**
piazza, 392
Piazza d'Italia, 476, **476**
Piazza of St. Peter's (Bernini), 393
Pica, Amalia, 558–559; *Stage (as seen on Afghan
    Star),* 558, **559**
Picasso (Miti), 20, **20**
Picasso, Pablo, 3, 4, 20, 32, 140, 185, 283, 294, 394,
    403, 468; Cubism and, 465–467; *Guernica,* 44,
    85, **458–459, 469;** *Head of a Sleeping Woman
    (Study for Nude with Drapery),* 554, **554;** *La
    bouteille de Suze (Bottle of Suze),* 468, **468;** *Les
    Demoiselles d'Avignon,* 32, **32,** 33, **466,** 466–467;
    Mandolin and Clarinet, 184, **184;** *The Old
    Guitarist,* 160, 465, **465;** *The Painter and His
    Model,* 140, **140**
pictorial space, 65
picture plane, 417
Piero della Francesca, 365
Pietà (Michelangelo), 371
pigment, 109
pilasters, 235
pile weaving, 218
Pindell, Howardena: *Autobiography: Water/
    Ancestors, Middle Passage/ Family Ghosts,*
    130–131, **131**
Pine Spirit (Wu), 535, **535**
The Pine Tree at St. Tropez (Signac), **53**
Pine Wood (Hasegawa Tohaku), 387, **387**
pinnacle, **327**
Piper, Adrian: *Self-Portrait Exaggerating My
    Negroid Features,* 110, **110**
Pisan, Christine de, 514
Pissarro, Camille, 107
plain weave, 218
planar recession, 417
planographic printing, 141

Plántano Pride (Luciano), **557**
plasticity, 399
Plato, 208
plebeian class, 293
Pliny the Elder, 214, 288
Plutarch, 283
plywood, 231
Poe, Edgar Allan, 275
pointed arches, 230
pointillism, 435
Pollaiuolo, Antonio: *Battle of Ten Naked Men,* **136,** 137
Pollock, Jackson, 4, 7, 14, 212, 492–493, 536–537; *Number 19,* 14, **14;** *One,* **491–492,** 493, **493**
Polydorus: *Laocoön and His Sons,* **289,** 289–290
Polykleitos, 102, 284–285; *Doryphoros,* **284, 285,** 300
Pomo gift baskets, 220, **220**
Pont du Gard, France, 229, 297, **297**
Pontormo, Jacopo, 380–381; *Entombment of Christ,* 380–381, **381**
Pop art, 502–506
Pope, Alexander, 391
Pope.L., William: *Training Crawl, Lewiston, ME,* 70, **70**
Popova, Liubuv: *Study for a Portrait,* 17, **17**
porcelain, 213–214
Porcelain Form (Nakashima), 214, **214**
Portland Vase, 214–215, **215**
Portrait Mask (Gba gba), 554, **554**
Portrait of Baldassare Castiglione (Raphael), 15, **15,** 43
Portrait of Paul Revere (Copley), 411, **411**
Portrait of the Queen Mother Idia, **349**
Portrait of two brothers, from Sheikh Abada, Egyptian civilization, **123,** 123–124
portraits, 156
The Portuguese (Braque), **467,** 467–468
positive shapes, 34–35
post-and-beam construction, 231, **232**
post-and-lintel construction, **227,** 227–228
postcolonialism, 541–542
Postimpressionism, 434–440; Cézanne, 435–437; Gauguin, 437, 439; Seurat, 435; Toulouse-Lautrec, 439–440; van Gogh, 437, 438
Postmodern architecture, 527–528
potter's wheel, **210,** 210–211
pottery: Golden Age of Islam, 339; Qing, 414
Poussin, Nicolas, 404–407; *Rape of the Sabine Women,* **405,** 405–406
Poussinistes, 420
Powers, Harriet, 445; *Bible Quilt: The Creation of the Animals,* 445, **445**
Praxiteles: *Capitoline Venus,* 366; *Hermes and Dionysos,* **287,** 287–288
Predock, Antoine: Nelson Fine Arts Center, Arizona State University, **43,** 43–44
pre-Hellenic Greece, 265
Prehistoric Aegean, map of, **265**
prehistoric art, 248–251; Neolithic, 250–251; Paleolithic, 248–250
Prehistoric Europe, map of, **248**
Presentation of captives to Lord Chan Muwan, Room 2 of Structure 1, Bonampak, Mexico, Maya, **351**
Principles of design, 11, 83–105
print, 134
printmaking, 133–144; intaglio, **134,** 136–138, 140–141; lithography, **134,** 141–142; monotype, 144; relief printing, **134,** 134–136; serigraphy, **134,** 142–143
processional frieze from the royal audience hall (Persepolis), **256**

Progressive Artists' Group, 532–533
progressive rhythm, 100
propaganda, in cinematography, 169–170
proportion, 102–105; canon of, 102–103; defined, 11; golden mean, golden rectangle, and root five rectangle, 103–104
Proportion of the Human Figure (Leonardo da Vinci), 96, 96–97
Proposition Player (Ritchie), 20–21, **21**
propylaeum, 316
proximity, 84
psychic automatism, 480
Psycho (Hitchcock), 166
psychological lines, 23
public art, 198–200
Pudong New Area, Shanghai, 546, **546**
pure or formal symmetry, 97
purse cover (Sutton Hoo), 319
Puryear, Martin, 207, 208
Pygmalion and Galatea (Gérome), **180**
Pyramid of the Moon, 311
Pyramid of the Sun, 311
pyramids: Pyramid at the Louvre (Pei), 29; Red Pyramid, 28

Q

Qiang, Cai Guo: *Transient Rainbow,* 197, **197**
Qin Dynasty, 308–309
Qing Dynasty, 413–414
quatrefoil, 361
Quill, Sarah: *View Towards the Rialto Bridge,* **65**
quiltmaking, 445
Qur'an, 333–334, **338,** 339

R

Racial and ethnic identity, 518–523
radial balance, 98–99
Radioactive Cats (Skoglund), 160, **160**
Raft of the Medusa (Géricault), 60, **60,** 92, **421,** 421–422
Raft of the Medusa, Part I (Stella), 60, **60**
raking cornice, 279
Ramadan, 335
The Rape of the Daughters of Leucippus (Rubens), **401,** 401–402, 423
Rape of the Sabine Women (Poussin), **405,** 405–406
Raphael, 15, 370–371; *Philosophy,* or *The School of Athens,* 71, **71,** 370, **370, 371,** 401; *Portrait of Baldassare Castiglione,* 15, **15,** 43; *The School of Athens,* 71, **71;** *Stanze della Segnatura,* fresco for, 370
rasp, 187
Rauschenberg, Robert, 502; *The Bed,* 130, 503, **503**
Ray and Maria Stata Center (Gehry), **224–225,** 239, **239,** 242
Reading Position for a Second Degree Burn (Oppenheim), 81, **81**
Realism, 15–16, 417, 426–431, 506–508; Bonheur, 430–431; Courbet, 426–427; Daumier, 426; Manet, 427–430; in sculptures, 179
Reclining Figure, Lincoln Center (Moore), 500, **500**
rectangular bays, 329
Red Coat (Katz), 143, **143**
red-figure technique, 281–282
Red Pyramid, 28
Red Room (Harmony in Red) (Matisse), **461,** 461–462
reducing phase, 280–281
Reeve-Tucker, W. R., 487

registers, 258
regular repetition, 99
The Rehearsal (Adagio) (Degas), 434, **434**
Reims Cathedral, jamb figures of, 332, **332**
reinforced concrete architecture, 236–238
relative size, space and, 101
Relic 130 (Thomas), 209, 209–210
relief printing, **134,** 134–136; woodcut, 134–135; wood engraving, 135–136
relief sculptures, 72, 180
religion, art and: in Roman Empire, 303–304
Rembrandt van Rijn, 402–404; *Christ Crucified between the Two Thieves,* **137,** 137–138; *Self-Portrait,* **402,** 402–403; *Syndics of the Drapers' Guild,* 403, **403**
Renaissance, 275, 353–389; Classicism during, 362, 364, 366, 368, 370, 373; defined, 353; fifteenth-century northern painting, 355–359; High, 366–375; in Italy, 360–366; mannerism, 380–382; outside Italy, high and late, 378–380; in Venice, High and Late, 376–378
Renaissance Europe, map, **354**
Renoir, Pierre-Auguste, 12, 432–433; *Le Moulin de la Galette,* **432,** 432–433; *Tamaris, France,* **12**
reoxidizing phase, 281
repetition, 84–85
Reservoir Dogs (Tarantino), 164, **164**
resolution, 153
Resurrection (della Francesca), **364,** 365
Reynolds, Sir Joshua, 107
Rhode Island School of Design (RISD), 548
rhythm, 11, 99–101
The Rialto Bridge (Canaletto), **65**
ribs, 230
Rickey, George: *Cluster of Four Cubes,* 186
Riefenstahl, Leni: *Triumph of the Will,* 169–170, **170**
Rietveldt, Gerrit: Schröder House, Utrecht, **27,** 27–28, 474
Riley, Bridget: *Gala,* 80, **80**
Ringgold, Faith, 518–519; *Mrs. Jones and Family,* 555, **555;** *Tar Beach,* 519, **519**
Rio delle Torreselle Chandelier (Chihuly), 216, **216**
Rio Videowall (Birnbaum), 172, **172**
Ritchie, Matthew: *Proposition Player,* 20–21, **21**
Rivera, Diego, 193, 488; *History of Mexico,* 488, **488**
Riverbank of Peach Blossoms (Shitao), 414, **414**
Robusti, Jacopo. See Tintoretto
Rockburne, Dorothea: *Pascal's Provincial Letters,* 30, **30**
Rococo style in Baroque period, 409–411; Copley, 411; Enlightenment and, 410–411; Fragonard, 409; Gainsborough, 411; Vigée-Lebrun, 409–410
Rodin, Auguste, 446–447; *The Burghers of Calais,* 446, **446**
Roebling, John A.: Brooklyn Bridge, **238,** 238–239
Roman Empire, 243, **292,** 295–305
Romanesque art, 321–327; architecture, 230, 322–324; sculpture, 324–325; tapestry, 325, 327
Romanticism, 421–423; Academy, 425; Delacroix, 422–424; Géricault's, 421–422; Goya, 423, 425
Rome, 292–305; architecture, 5, 295–300, 304–305; early empire, 295, 298–302; late empire, 302–305; Republican period, 292–295; sculpture, 300–302, 304–305
Root Five Rectangle, 104, **104**
Rosenberg, Harold, 493
Rosetta Stone, 263, **263**
rose window, 328
Rothenberg, Susan, 524; *Chix,* 524, **524**

Rothko, Mark, 496, 497; *Black on Grey*, 496, **496**; *Number 22*, 496, **496**
Rouen Cathedral (Monet), 52, **52**, 432, **432**
Rousseau, Jean-Jacques, 410
"Royal Road of the Mountains," 389
Royal Tide IV (Nevelson), **185**, 185–186
Rubenistes, 420
Rubens, Peter Paul, 401–402
Rubin vase, 35, **35**
Rumi, Jalal al-Din, 313
Running woman, rock painting, Tassili n'Ajjer, Algeria, **270**, 271
Ruskin, John, 234, 237, 377
Russo-Japanese War, 484
Ryan, Thomas: *Tapuae*, 454, **454**

S

Saarinen, Eero: Gateway Arch, 229, **229**
Sacrifice of Isaac (Brunelleschi), 361–362, **362**
Safdie, Moshe: *Habitat, Expo 67 (Montreal, Quebec, Canada)*, 238, **238**
Sage, Kay: *I Saw Three Cities*, 98, **98**
Sail Baby (Murray), 501, **501**
Saint Joseph the Carpenter (de la Tour), 43, **43**
Salle, David: *Angel*, 42, **42**
Salon d'Automne, 459, 465
Salon des Réfusés, 430, 459
Saltcellar of Francis I (Cellini), 221, **221**
Samaras, Lucas: *Head #12*, 112, **112**
samurai, 347
San Carlo alle Quattro Fontane, Rome (Borromini), 399, **399**
Sandwich glass, 215
Santa Maria del Fiori, Florence, 394–395
San Vitale, Ravenna, **316**, 317, **317**, 320
Sarah Bernhardt (Nadar), 156, **156**
sarcophagi, 291
Sarcophagus from Cerveteri, 292, **292**
satin weave, 218
satire, in cinematography, 170
saturation of color, 49
scale, 101–102; defined, 11; distortion of, 102; hierarchical, 101
Scenes from Genesis (Moutier-Grandval Bible), 81, **81**
Schapiro, Miriam, 514–515; *Maid of Honour*, 131, **131**; *Wonderland*, 208, **208–209**
Scher, Paula: "Great Beginnings" spread, 146, **146**
Schindler's List (Spielberg), 44, **44–45**
Schliemann, Heinrich, 265, 268
The School of Athens (Raphael), 71, **71**, 401
Schroeder House, Utrecht (Rietveldt), **27**, 27–28
Schunnemunk Fork (Serra), **189**
The Scream (Munch), 441, **441**
sculpture, 179–192, 497–499; Archaic period, 278; assemblage, 185–186; carving, 181; casting, 181, 184; Classical art, 286–288; constructed, 184–185; Cubism, 469–470; free-standing, 64–65; Gothic art, 331–333; Hellenistic art, 289–290; installation, 192–193; kinetic, 186; light, 186–187; modeling, 181; in modern art, 446–447; Old Kingdom, 257–259; relief, 72; Roman Empire, 300–302, 304–305
sculpture-in-the-round, 180
sculpture materials: clay, 189; metal, 189; stone, 187; unexpected, 191–192; wood, 188–189
sculpture of an eagle, Great Zimbabwe, **350**
Seagram Building, New York City (Miës van der Rohe and Johnson), 483–484, 526–527, **527**

A Sea of Steps (Evans), **100**, 100–101
Seated Buddha, **308**
secondary colors, 46
Segal, George, 184; *Gay Liberation*, **505**, 505–506; *Three Figures and Four Benches*, 184, **184**
Self-Portrait Exaggerating My Negroid Features (Piper), 110, **110**
Self-Portrait (Kollwitz), 110, **110**
Self-Portrait (Rembrandt), **402**, 402–403
Self-Portrait with Bandaged Ear (van Gogh), 438, **438**
Senefelder, Aloys, 141
serigraphy, 142–143, **144**
Serpent/Salamander, Parc Guëll (Gaudî), 199, **199**
Serra, Richard: *Schunnemunk Fork*, **189**
Serrano, Andres: *Nomads series*, **15**, 15–16
Sesshu Toyo: *Splashed-ink (haboku) landscape*, 387, **387**
Seurat, Georges, 39, 435; *At the Concert Européen*, **112**, 113; *A Sunday Afternoon on the Island of La Grande Jatte*, 435, **435**
shades of color, 48
Shang Dynasty, 271–272
Shanghai's Pudong New Area, 546, **546**
shapes: abstract, 33; amorphous, 33–34; defined, 9, 19; expressive potential of, 32; figure–ground relationship of, 35; geometric, 28–30; as icon, 36–37; nonobjective, 33; organic, 30; positive and negative, 34–35
Sharecropper (Catlett), 26, **26**
Shariah, 334
Shawky, Wael, 551; *Cabaret Crusades: The Path to Cairo*, 551, **551**
shell architecture, 239
Sherman, Cindy: *Untitled*, 160–161
Shift (Hatoum), 549, **549**
Shi Huangd, 308–309, **309**
Shimomura, Roger: *Untitled*, 129, **129**, 522
Shine (Cole), 185, **555**
Shinto shrines, 346
Shiraga, Kazuo: *Untitled*, 537, **537**
Shitao: *Riverbank of Peach Blossoms*, 414, **414**
Shiva (Hindu god), 342
Shiva and Parvati riding Nandi, **413**
shogun, 347
Shonen, Suzuki: *Fireflies over the Uji River*, **485**, 485–486
Shonibare, Yinka: *Victorian Couple*, 52–53, **53**
Shop Block, The Bauhaus (Gropius), **483**
shutter, 152
Siddhartha Gautauma, 307
Sight Lines (Birds) (Adolphus), 86
Signac, Paul: *The Pine Tree at St. Tropez*, 53
Signage: for nonsmoking area, **145**; for women's and men's restrooms, **145**
Sikandar (Locke), 541–542, **542**
Sikander, Shahzia, 543–544
Sikander, Shahzia: *Perilous Order*, **543**
Silk Road, 542
Silk Route (Gupta), 543
Silvetti, Juror Jorge, 530
Singh, Arpita: *Munna Appa's Kitchen*, 127, **127**
Sino-Japanese war, 496
Sioux nation, 455
Sistine Chapel (Michelangelo), 193, 370, 371, **372**, 373, 399
site-specific art, 193–203; defined, 193–194; ephemeral art, 197; land art, 194–195
sketch, artist's, 108
Skoglund, Sandy: *Radioactive Cats*, 160, **160**

Slemmons, Kiff: *Transport*, 222, **222**
Sloan, John, 47, 55
Smith, David, 221
Smith, Jaune Quick-to-See, 522; *Trade (Gifts for Trading Land with White People)*, 522, **522–523**
Smith, Kiki, 191; *Untitled*, 191, **191**
Smithson, Robert, 193; *Spiral Jetty*, 194, **194**
Snefuru, Red Pyramid, 28
social commentary, in cinematography, 170–171
Soft Toilet (Oldenburg), 191, **191**, 505
Solomon R. Guggenheim museum, 556
Solo V (Albers), 141, **141**
Song Dynasty, 345, 384
SONY Building, New York City (Burgee Architects with Philip Johnson), **527**, 527–528
South America, ancient art in, 311
space, 11, 63–76; atmospheric perspective and, 69; linear perspective and, 70–71, 73–76; location, 67, 68; relative size and, 66; sculpture and, 72
Spain: Great Mosque of Córdoba, 337, **337**
Spain, Baroque period in, 399–401; Diego Velázquez, 400–401
special effects, in cinematography, 163
Spielberg, Steven: Film still from *Schindler's List*, **44**, 44–45
spiral, 104–105, **105**
Spiral: An Ordinary Evening in New Haven (Bartlett), **523**, 523–524
spiral brooch, **105**
Spiral Jetty (Smithson), 194, **194**
Splashed-ink (haboku) landscape (Sesshu Toyo), 387, **387**
spray paint, 130
Spring Fresco, 266–267
springing, **327**
squeegee, 142
stadium design, 296–297
Stage (as seen on Afghan Star) (Pica), 558, **559**
stained glass, 215
stainless steel, 221
stamped, 189
Stanze della Segnatura (Raphael), 370
Starck, Philippe: *Juicy Salif*, 203, **203**
Starry Night (van Gogh), 437, **437**
Statue of Khafre (Gizeh), 259, **259**
Statues from Abu Temple, Tell Asmar, Iraq, 253
Stebbins, Emma: *Angel of the Waters*, 198, **198**
steel, 234
steel-cable architecture, 238–239
steel-cage architecture, 234–236, **235**
The Steerage (Stieglitz), 152, **153**
Steichen, Edward, 150; *The Flatiron Building-Evening*, **159**, 159–160
Steiner, Wendy, 15
Steinert, Otto: *Ein-Fuß-Gänger (One-Foot Walker)*, 97, **97**
Stele of Hammurabi, 254, **254**
Stella, Frank, 500; *Mas o Manos (More or Less)*, 501; *Raft of the Medusa, Part I*, 60, **60**
St. Étienne, 323, **323**–324
Stevens, Frederick W.: Victoria Terminus (Chhatrapati Shivaji Terminus), 450, **450**
Stevens, Wallace, 217
Stiegel glass, 215
Stieglitz, Alfred, 152, 156, 159; *The Steerage*, 152, **153**
Still Life with Basket of Apples (Cézanne), 436, **436**
Still Life with Bottle of Olives (Chardin), **67**
Still Life with Musical Instruments (Lipchitz), 469, **469**

stippling, 25–26
St. Matthew, folio 15 recto of the Coronation Gospels (Gospel Book of Charlemagne), **321**
stoicism, 302
Stone Age, 247–248
stone architecture, 226–230; arches, 229, **229**; domes, **227**, 230; post-and-lintel construction, **227**, 227–228; vaults, **227**, 229–230
The Stone-Breakers (Courbet), **426**, 426–427
Stonehenge, Salisbury Plain, 228, **250**, 250–251
stone sculptures, 187
Stonewall Inn, 506
Storm King Art Center, 189, 190
Stowe, Harriet Beecher, 445
St. Paul's Cathedral, London (Wren), 407–408, **408**
St. Peter's Basilica, Rome. *See* Basilica of St. Peter's, Rome
Street, Dresden (Kirchner), **462**, 463
The Street Enters the House (Boccioni), 76, **76**
Street Light (Balla), 76, 470, **471**
St. Sernin, **322**, 322–323
Stuart, Gilbert: *George Washington,* 125, **125**
Studies for *The Cow* (van Doesburg), 8, 8–9
Study for a Portrait (Popova), 17, **17**
Study for Loïe Fuller at the Folies Bergére (Toulouse-Lautrec), **62–63**
A study of a woman's hands (Leonardo da Vinci), **106–107**
Stumpf, Bill: *Aeron Chair,* 204, **205**
Stupa of Sanchi, 230
stupas, 230, 307
style, 10, 12, 14–15
stylobate, 279
styropor, 192
subjective color, 52
subtractive color, 46, **46**
subtractive process, 180
subversive texture, 58
Subway (Furedi), 89, **89**
Sudden Shower over Shin-Ohashi Bridge and Atake (Hiroshige), 452, **452**
Suh, Do Ho, 548; *Fallen Star,* **548**
Sullivan, Louis, 204; Wainwright Building, 235, **235**
Sumer, 251–253
A Sunday Afternoon on the Island of La Grande Jatte (Seurat), 435, **435**
Sunnah, 334
Suprematist Composition (Malevich), 93, **93**
Surrealism, 478–480
Suspended (Kadishman), **190**
Susskind, Leonard, 63
Sutton Hoo, England, 318–319, **319**
Swing 64 (Gilliam), **22**, 23
symbol, color as, 52–53
symbolism: in art, generally, 5; in cinematography, 171
Syndics of the Drapers' Guild (Rembrandt), 403, **403**
Synthetic Cubist compositions, 468
Synthetism, 439

T

Taaffe, Philip: *Four Quad Cinema,* 96, 97
Taber, Isaiah West: *Loïe Fuller Dancing,* 78
Table with drawers, **385**
Taisho period, 484
Taj Mahal, 383, **383**
Talbot, William Henry Fox: *Botanical Specimen,* 155, **155**
Tamaris, France (Renoir), **12**
Tanaka, Atsuko: *Electric Dress,* 536

Tang Dynasty, 343
Tan Tan Bo (Murakami), **540**
Tapuae (Ryan), 454, **454**
Tarantino, Quentin: *Reservoir Dogs,* 164, **164**
Tar Beach (Ringgold), 519, **519**
Tassel House, Interior of (Brussels) (Horta), 447, **447**
Te Arii Vahine (The Noble Woman) (Gauguin), 429, **429**
"Technical Manual of Futurist Painting" (Boccioni), 76
techniques, 12
Ted (Macfarlane), **167**
telephoto lenses, 152
tempera painting, 124–125
Temple of Amen-Re, Karnak, 228, **228**
temples: Etruscan, **291**; Sumerian, 252
tenebrism, 43, 396
tensile strength, 188
Teotihuacán, 311, **311**, 389
terra-cotta, 207, 212–213
terra cotta army, 308–309, **309**
Testa, Peter: Carbon Tower, 242, **242**
textile arts, 218–220; basket weaving, 220; defined, 218; weaving, 218–220
texture, 10, 11, 55–58; actual, 57; defined, 56; pattern and, 58–59; subversive, 58; visual, 58
Theatre Characters (Botero), **102**
Theotokopoulos, Domeniko. *See* El Grego
The Third-Class Carriage (Daumier), **426**, 426
The Third of May, 1808 (Goya), 423, **423**, 425, 486
Thomas, Alma Woodsey: *Light Blue Nursery,* 22, 23
Thomas, Cheryl Ann: *Relic 130,* 209, 209–210
Thomas, Hank Willis: *White Imitates Black,* 41–42, **42**
Thousand Flowers vase, **414**
3D (Pfaff), **18–19**, 34, **34**, 193
Three Exact Rules (Mangold), 20, **21**
Three Figures and Four Benches (Segal), 184, **184**
Three Flags (Johns), 504, **504**
Three Goddesses (Parthenon), **286**, 286–287
Three Screens for Looking at Abstraction (McElheny), 85, **85**
thrown pottery, 210
tie-dyeing, 220
Tiffany Studios (Louis Comfort Tiffany): *Magnolia and Irises,* 68, **68**, 215, **215**
Tiger, Lionel, 324
time, 11, 76–81; actual motion and, 77; illusion of motion and, 79–80; implied, 81; manipulating in film, 164–165
Tinguely, Jean, 510; *Homage to New York,* 510, **511**
Tintoretto, 377–378; *The Last Supper,* 378; *Susannah and the Elders,* 396
tints of color, 48
Titian, 376–377; *Venus of Urbino,* 174, **376**, 376–377, 428, **428**
Titled (Art as Idea as Idea) (Kosuth), **3–4**
tonality of a work of art, 48
Toulouse-Lautrec, Henri de, 439–440; *Le Divan Japonais,* 147, **147**; *At the Moulin Rouge,* 440, **440**; *Study for Loïe Fuller at the Folies Bergére,* **62–63**
Tourists (Hanson), 506–508, **507**
Tournachon, Gaspard Felix. *See* Nadar
Tower of Babel, 252
Trade (Gifts for Trading Land with White People) (Smith), 522, 522–523
Training Crawl, Lewiston, ME (Pope.L.), 70, **70**
transept, 316

Transformation mask representing the sun, 457, **457**
Transient Rainbow (Cai Guo Qiang), 197, **197**
transversals, 70–71
transverse ribs, 323, **327**
Travelers among Mountains and Streams (Fan K'uan), 345, **345**
Treasury of Atreus (Mycenae), 268
Tribute in Light, **240**, 240–241
triforium, **327**, 328
triglyphs, 279
Triumph of the Sacred Name of Jesus (Baciccio), **398**, 399
Triumph of the Will (Riefenstahl), 169–170, **170**
Trockel, Rosemary: *Untitled,* **113**
trompe l'oeil, 58, 292, 399, 421, 468
trusses, **232**
tubular steel chair (Breuer), 484, **484**
Tutankhamen (king of Egypt), 263–264, **264**; coffin of, 263, **263**
twentieth-century art, 459–489; abstraction, 470–474; in Africa, 487–488; Bauhaus, 482–484; in China, 486–487; Cubism, 464–469; Dada, 476–478; Expressionism, 462–464; Fantastic art, 475–476; Fauvism, 460–462; figurative art, 480–481; Futurism, 470; Harlem renaissance, 482; in Japan, 484–486; in Mexico, 488–489; Surrealism, 478–480
twentieth-century art, postwar to postmodern, 491–537; abstraction, 500–501; architecture, 526–531; China, 531–532, 534–535; conceptual art, 512–513; feminist art, 514–517; figure, 499–500; India, 532–533; Japan, 531, 535–537; minimalism, 508–509; neo-expressionism, 524–525; new image painting, 523–524; New York School, 492–498; Pakistan, 532–533; performance art, 509–512; Pop art, 502–506; racial and ethnic identity, 518–523; realism and photorealism, 506–508; sexual identity, 517
twill weave, 218
twisted perspective, 75
Twittering Machine (Klee), 475, **475**
Two Children Are Threatened by a Nightingale (Ernst), 478, **478**
The Two Fridas (Kahlo), 489, **489**
Two Heads (Jain), 98, **99**
291 gallery, 471–472
two-point perspective, 73, **73**
tympanum, 324, **324**
typography in graphic design, 145

U

Uli statue, 455, **455**
Umayyad Caliphate, 335–337
Umayyad Mosque, 335–336, **336**
umber, 111
Un Chien Andalou (Dalí and Buñuell), 171, **171**
Under the Wave off Kanagawa (The Great Wave) (Hokusai), **451**, 451–452
Unique Forms of Continuity in Space (Boccioni), 76, 470, **470**
United States: twentieth-century art in, 470–473, 480–484
United States Pavilion (Buckminster Fuller), 230
United States Supreme Court Building, 5
unity, in design, 11, 84–91
Untitled (Adolphus), 35, **35**
Untitled (Berard), 159, **159**
Untitled (Brandenburg), 40–41, **41**
Untitled (Firmager), **222**, 222–223

Untitled (Flavin), 99, **186**, 186–187
Untitled (Hung Liu), 139, **139**
Untitled (Nes), 550, **550**
Untitled (Sherman), 160–161, **161**
Untitled (Shimomura), 129, **129**, 522
Untitled (Shiraga), 537, **537**
Untitled (Smith), 191, **191**
Untitled (We Don't Need Another Hero) (Kruger), 512, **513**
Untitled II (van Elk), 28, **29**
urban design, 243–245; Alexandria, Egypt, 244–245; Paris, 244; Washington, D.C., 244
Utamaro, Kitagawa: *Midnight: The Hours of the Rat; Mother and Sleepy Child*, 415, **415**; *Woman Wiping Face*, 132–133

V

Valadon, Suzanne: *The Blue Room*, 429, **429**
value, 9, 10, 48–49, **49**; chiaroscuro and, 42–43; contrast, 41–42; descriptive and expressive properties of, 44–45; light and, 40–44; tenebrism and, 43; as unifying factor, 85
value contrast, **41**, 41–42
value pattern, 42–44
van Doesburg, Theo, 8–9; *Counter-Composition of Dissonances*, **26**, 27; *Model Maison d'Artiste*, 27, **27**; *Studies for The Cow*, 8
Van Eesteren, Cornelius: *Model Maison d'Artiste*, 27, **27**
van Elk, Ger: *Lunch II*, 93, **93**; *Untitled II*, 28, **29**
van Eyck, Jan, 357–358; *Giovanni Arnolfini and His Bride*, **10**, 10–11, **357**, 357–358
van Gogh, Vincent, 55, 113, 122, 437, 438; *Bridge in the Rain*, 452, **452**; *Café Terrace, Place du Forum, Arles*, 115; *Café Terrace at Night, September 1888*, **113**; *Mulberry Tree*, 55, **56**; *Orchard in Blossom (Plum Trees)*, 55, **56**; *Self-Portrait with Bandaged Ear*, 438, **438**; *Starry Night*, 437, **437**
vanishing point, 70
vantage point, 70
variety, in design, 11, 87–91
Vasari, Giorgio, 123
Vase, Qing Dynasty, **414**
Vase (1368–1644 ce), Ming Dynasty, **385**
vase painting: Archaic period, 280–282
vaults, **227**, 229–230, **327**
vehicle, 123
Velázquez, Diego, 400–401; *Las Meninas*, **400**, 400–401
veneers, 230
Venezia #27 Revisited (Zago), 50, **50**
Venturi, Robert, 295
Venus, Cupid, Folly, and Time (The Exposure of Luxury) (Bronzino), **7**, 7–8
Venus de Milo, 290, **290**
Venuses, 249–250
Venus of Urbino (Titian), 174, **376**, 376–377, 426, **426**
Venus of Willendorf, **249**, 249–250
Venus pudica, 366, 377
Veracruz, 16, **16**
Vermeer, Jan: *Young Woman with a Water Jug*, 404, **405**
Veronese, Paolo: *The Wedding Feast at Cana*, 91, **91**
Verrocchio, Andrea del, 364; *David*, 64, 65, 374, **374**
Versailles, 407
vertical balance, 98

vertical positioning, 68
Vespucci, Simonetta, 366
Vessel (Ellsworth), 223, **223**
Victorian Couple (Shonibare), 52–53, **53**
Victory Stele of Naram Sin, **253**, 253–254, 255
video, 171–173
Vietnam Veterans Memorial, Washington, D.C. (Lin), 201, **202**, 202–203
View Towards the Rialto Bridge (Quill), 65
Vigée-Lebrun, Élisabeth, 409–410
Viola, Bill: *The Crossing*, **148–149**, 172, 173
Virgin Mary, 331, 332–333
Vishvanatha Temple, **342**
visible spectrum, 39, **40**
"Vision of God's Plan for the Seasons" (Hildegard of Bingen), 312–313, 326, **326**
A Visit To/A Visit From/The Island (Fischl), 525, **525**
visual elements of art, 8–11; texture, 55–58
Voltaire, 410
volume, shape and, 26–28
von Rydingsvard, Ursula: *Droga*, 188, **188**
Votive Tablet of a Horse (Yamaguchi), 547, **547**
voussoirs, 229

W

Wachowski, Andy and Lana: *The Matrix*, 165, **165**
Wainwright Building (Sullivan), 234–235, **235**
Walker, Kara, 520–521; *Insurrection! (Our Tools Were Rudimentary, Yet We Pressed On)*, 520, **520**, 522
Walking Woman (Archipenko), **469**, 469–470
Wall with Two Ridges, Lower Antelope Canyon (Barnbaum), 98, **98**
Wang Gongxin: *Our Sky Is Falling*, **544**, 544–545
Wang Lu, 546
Wang Zhen: *Crane and Plum Blossoms*, 486, **486**
Warhol, Andy, 12, 142–143, 504; *Ethel Scull Thirty-Six Times*, 88, **88**; *Four Marilyns*, 142–143, **143**; *Green Coca-Cola Bottles*, 504, **504**
warm color, 47, **48**
warp, 218
wash, 115–116
Washington, D.C.: architecture, symbolism of, 5; plan for (L'Enfant), 244, 421
watercolor painting, 127
Wave UFO (Mori), 547, **547**
Wearing, Gillian: *Family History* series, 173, **173**
webbing, 230
web design, 176–177
The Wedding Feast at Cana (Veronese), 91, **91**
Wedgwood, Thomas, 154
weft, 218
Wegman, William: *Blue Period*, 160, **160**; *Ethiopia*, 97, **97**
Weimar School of Arts and Crafts, 482
Weiser, Devyn: *Carbon Tower*, 242, **242**
Welcome to the World Famous Brand (Luo Brothers), 545, **545**
Weston, Edward, 149; *Dunes, Oceano*, 25, **25**
Whistler, James Abbott McNeill, 442–443; *Arrangement in Black and Gray: The Artist's Mother*, 442–443, **443**
White Imitates Black (Thomas), 41–42, **42**
White Iris (O'Keeffe), 471, **471**
White Temple at Uruk, Iraq, 252, **252**
wide-angle lenses, 152
Wiene, Robert: *The Cabinet of Dr. Caligari*, 171, **171**

Wiley Kehinde: *Napoleon Leading the Army Over the Alps*, 521, **521**
The Winding Road (Cézanne), 128, **128**
Wiremu Kingi Te Rangitake, Chief of the Te Ati Awa: *Tauihu*, 454, **454**
With a Heart of Gold (Cole), **82–83**, 92, **92**
Womanhouse, 514–515
Woman Wiping Face (Utamaro), **133**
Woman with a Hat (Matisse), 16, **17**
"Women hold up half of heaven, and, cutting through mountains and rivers, change to a new attitude," **534**
Wonderland (Schapiro), **208**, 208–209
Wood, Grant, 480; *American Gothic*, 480, 481
wood architecture, 230–233; balloon framing, **231**, 231–232; post-and-beam construction, 231, **231**; trusses, 231, **231**
wood craft, 222–223
wood engraving, 135–136
Woodman, Betty: *Aztec Vase #06-1*, 213, **213**
wood sculptures, 188–189
woof, 218
World War II, 485
World War II (Vanitas) (Flack), 506, **507**
Wren, Sir Christopher, 407–408; New St. Paul's Cathedral, London, 407–408, **408**
Wright, Frank Lloyd, 225, 236, 237, 482; Kaufmann House ("Fallingwater"), **237**, 237–238
Wudi (Han emperor), 310
Wu Guanzhong: *Pine Spirit*, 535, **535**

X

Xiaomo, Zhao: *Family by the Lotus Pond*, 134–135
Xuhai, Chen: *Golden Autumn*, 21, 135

Y

Yakshi sculpture, Great Stupa of Sanchi, 308, **308**
Yamaguchi, Akira, 547; *Votive Tablet of a Horse*, 547, **547**
Yombe mother and child (pfemba), 449, **449**
Yosemite IV (Bhavsar), 533, **533**
Yoshihara, Hideki: *Baseball Catcher*, 80, 80
Yoshikune, Hirose: *"In the Battle of the Sha River, a Company of Our Forces Drives a Strong Enemy Force to the Left Bank of the Taizi River,"* 485, **485**
Young Girl by the Window (Morisot), **416–417**, 433, **433**
Young Lady with an Umbrella (Lumiére), 155, **155**
Young Man with Red Hair (Modigliani), 103, **103**
Young Woman with a Water Jug (Vermeer), 404
Yuan Dynasty, 384
Yuichi, Takahashi: *Oiran (Grand Courtesan)*, 452, **453**

Z

Zaatari, Akram, 550; *Letter to a Refusing Pilot*, 550, **550**
Zago, Tino: *Venezia #27 Revisited*, 50, **50**
Zakanich, Robert: *By the Sea II*, 128, **128**
Zen Buddhism, 386–387, 492
Zeus (Greek god), 277
Zhang Xiaogang: *Big Family*, **544**, 545
ziggurat, 252
Zimbabwe, 350
Zoopraxiscope, 163